A HISTORY OF AMERICAN FOREIGN POLICY

SECOND EDITION

A HISTORY OF
American Foreign Policy

SECOND EDITION

by ALEXANDER DE CONDE

Maps from first edition by Edward A. Schmitz
New Maps by Robert Sugar

Charles Scribner's Sons

NEW YORK

The eight lines from "*The White Man's Burden*" by Rudyard Kipling on p. 352 are from The Five Nations and are reprinted with the permission of Mrs. George Bambridge, the Macmillan Company of Canada Ltd., and Messrs. Methuen & Co. Ltd.

The eight lines quoted from "*An Ode in Time of Hesitation*" on p. 354 and the two lines from "*The Quarry*" on p. 365 are from Selected Poems of William Vaughn Moody edited by Robert M. Lovett and are reprinted with the permission of Houghton Mifflin Company.

The four lines on page 511 from "*Hymn for the Pact of Peace*" by Robert Underwood Johnson appeared in The New York Times on August 26, 1928. Copyright by The New York Times. Reprinted by permission.

Preface

IN WRITING this book I have tried to present a coherent introduction to the history of American foreign policy, one that accurately embodies the latest scholarship. I have striven to be analytical without divorcing analysis from fact and historical development. Where possible, I have included pertinent references to political, social, and economic developments which influenced the shaping of policy. In particular, I have attempted to show and explain how and why American foreign policy developed as it did and how it arrived where it is. I have also tried to analyze the main forces and ideas that shaped that policy and the courses those forces followed. My primary emphasis, therefore, is on broad policy. I have not hesitated to advance interpretations in the light of my own ideas. I hope I have done so judiciously.

Max Beloff, the British historian, in the conclusion of his book *Foreign Policy and the Democratic Process*, said that "an historian of foreign policy who merely writes down what everyone knows and is agreed upon, and differentiates himself from the ordinary practical man only by the number and complexity of his footnotes, performs quite inadequately the function for which society supports him." Since I agree with Mr. Beloff's sentiments, words of explanation for my use of footnotes are in order. I have used footnotes to acknowledge the sources of most quotations and for bibliographical purposes, that is, to serve as guides to the periodical and other pertinent literature.

Like others who have attempted works of historical synthesis, I am indebted to the writings and help of many scholars. To them, I offer my gratitude and thanks.

ALEXANDER DECONDE

University of California
Santa Barbara

v

Contents

Maps and Charts

Illustrations

Chapter One

THEORY AND PRACTICE

A<small>LTHOUGH</small> statesmen and scholars differ as to the implications of national self-interest, almost all agree that in theory and practice the United States maintains relations with other nations to serve its own interests. The means it uses to advance those interests constitute its foreign policy.[1] Since national self-interest motivates the foreign policies of all nations, American foreign policy in its general objectives does not differ markedly from those of other countries. Various national interests, we know, are often in conflict. We cannot, therefore, consider American foreign policy apart from the foreign policies of other nations.

The interaction of those foreign policies of sovereign, or independent, states comprises the realm of international relations. To regulate international relations, to lessen conflicts between competing foreign policies, and to limit the actions of individual states, most nations recognize a body of rules, frequently ineffective, called international law. Despite the weakness of international law, without its rules, diplomacy, meaning simply negotiations between states, would be virtually impossible.[2]

As a young nation the United States accepted international law in the conduct of its foreign relations, but on its own could do little to attain goals it had set for itself in world politics. In time, as it grew in size and strength, it acquired not only the capability of attaining the specific objectives of its foreign policy but also the power to influence the foreign policies of other nations, particularly the weaker ones. This pattern of American growth illustrates a reality of international relations —that the policies of the great powers take precedence over those of the lesser nations.[3]

All strong nations have been conscious of their power and have, at times, dominated weaker countries. Although it has differed from other great powers, from Russia for example, in the use of its power, the United States has not been an exception to that general rule.

The use the United States has made of its power and the motives behind that use have in recent years led to speculation by scholars as to what the philosophy of American foreign policy has been and should be. Most of them recognize that isolationism, essentially abstention from the international politics of Europe, even during the nineteenth century when it had general acceptance as a basic philosophy of American foreign policy, was never absolute.[4] They recognize that it is not a suitable guide for policy in the twentieth century. Their speculation, therefore, has expressed itself cogently in the two opposing theories of idealism and realism.

Supporters of both theories agree that in comparison with that of most other nations, the diplomacy of the United States has been marked distinctively by streaks of moralism. Beyond this there is disagreement.

The idealist philosophy deprecates power politics as evil and barbaric. It holds that international struggles have centered in the clash between incompatible ideals and principles, not in rivalries for power and influence. Its adherents seek lofty goals such as enduring peace, justice among nations, the advancement of the welfare of all mankind, and cooperation in international organizations that they hope will eliminate war and power politics.

The philosophy of realism, on the other hand, accepts power politics, basically some form of strife between nations, as normal in international relations. Its supporters point out that in all social groups, whether in nations or small intimate communities, the struggle for power goes on without end. Since rivalries among nations, unlike those in the smaller communities, are not controlled by effective law, the task of diplomacy, they argue, is to limit the struggles for power, and the aim of foreign policy is to pursue new balances of power and rough equilibriums between the rival nations. This may be done through compromise and adjustment based on a mutual recognition that an equilibrium exists.[5]

Theorists realize, however, that those who formulate foreign policy cannot do so solely in terms of power, as if they were playing a game.[6] Domestic affairs and in- tangibles, such as national character and the passions of nationalism, sometimes carry greater weight in the making of foreign policy than does the strategy of power politics. No other great nation, in fact, has been more influenced by popular ideas, moods, issues in domestic politics, and sectional sentiments in the conduct of its foreign policy than has the United States. The most important reason for this appears to be that the United States is a democracy where in theory, and at times in practice, broad foreign policy, like sovereignty, comes from the people. This factor and the theorists' almost consuming concern for power may also account for the fact that no one has yet advanced a satisfactory theory that offers a key to the understanding of foreign policy, one that has found general acceptance among historians.[7]

The Constitutional Basis

The men who drafted our Constitution were steeped in political theory and knowledge of international politics, but they were also practical men who understood the realities of foreign policy. They sought to build a secure and prosperous nation, to establish a national government with full authority over foreign affairs. They wanted that government to speak for the whole nation, to use the united strength of all the people in dealing with other nations.

Among the powers the Constitution specifically assigns to the federal government, therefore, are the negotiation of treaties, the right to declare war, the authority to appoint and receive ambassadors, and to regulate foreign commerce. It expressly prohibits the states from entering "any treaty, alliance, or confederation" or from making "any agreement or compact" with a foreign power.

On many other questions concerning foreign relations the Constitution is vague.[8] It does not, for example, say that the national government has broader authority over foreign relations than over domestic affairs. The courts, however, have ruled that the federal government does in fact have a greater control over foreign affairs. Their decisions, on this point and others concerning foreign affairs, have become part of the constitutional foundation that supports the conduct of foreign policy.

Under the Constitution the President has assumed primacy in the conduct of foreign policy. Indeed, he has attained greater power over foreign relations than over domestic affairs, making the conduct and formulation of foreign policy probably the most important part of his job. The Constitution, however, is mute as to the extent of the President's power over foreign relations. Nonetheless, despite the fact that the authority granted the President has not been modified since the framing of the Constitution in 1787, his power over foreign policy, as the nation has grown, has steadily increased.

More than one hundred and twenty-five years ago the perceptive French writer Alexis de Tocqueville in his classic study *Democracy in America* foresaw the growth of presidential power based on its original constitutional source. "It is chiefly in its foreign relations," he said, "that the executive power finds occasion to exert its skill and its strength." In foreign affairs, de Tocqueville wrote, the President "possesses almost royal prerogatives."

At times, when the President attempted to extend those prerogatives into uncharted areas, the Supreme Court reviewed his actions. Generally, the Court has upheld the doctrine of the strong executive in foreign affairs.

In the final analysis, the effectiveness with which the President employs his constitutional powers in foreign affairs depends on many factors, particularly on his own interpretation of his prerogatives. Frequently, the power he exerts through

politics and public opinion has a greater influence on the course of foreign policy
than do his constitutionally derived powers. Practice, precedent, and court decisions, more than the Constitution, have given the President predominance in the
conduct of foreign policy.[9]

Congress

Despite his predominance, the President shares some of his power over foreign
affairs with Congress. This division of control, which is neither equal nor clear,
has produced a rivalry in the conduct of foreign relations between the executive
and legislative branches of government, a rivalry inherent in the American
governmental system of checks and balances. Thus, the separation of powers tends
in foreign affairs to emphasize competition and has at times, as in the case of
Woodrow Wilson's fight with the Senate over the League of Nations in 1919,
been a barrier to cooperation.

Congress, notably the Senate, has never fully accepted the role of subordinate
partner to the President in the conduct of foreign policy, though that is what it has
in fact been most of the time. Even so, its part in the making of foreign policy
has not been insignificant. The Senate's role in particular has often been decisive.
It can reject a treaty or refuse to approve a diplomatic appointment, but Congress
as a whole does not possess the authority to initiate and carry through foreign
policy. Most of Congress' authority in foreign affairs, except for its power to
declare war, is negative. And even that power to declare war may be severely
restricted by the President's actions.

Since Wilson's time, Presidents have become increasingly sensitive to the power
of Congress over foreign relations and its desire to participate in the making of
policy. They have tried, wherever possible, to include it in the formulating of major
policies. In seeking the cooperation of Congress, the President, or his Secretary of
State, has usually had to work through committees, for the committee system
forms the core of congressional procedure. The standing committees responsible
for matters pertaining to foreign affairs are among the most important in both
houses and normally determine congressional reaction to foreign policy.

Until the end of the Second World War, when foreign economic aid became a
vital part of foreign policy, the Foreign Affairs Committee of the House of
Representatives had been relatively unimportant. Since that time its influence has
expanded. The House Committee, however, is overshadowed by the Senate
Committee on Foreign Relations, one of the most powerful committees in our
government. This committee has generally regarded itself as a virtually independent
guardian of foreign policy. Its senior members, ordinarily men of considerable
political stature who have served in Congress much longer than the President has
held office, concede little to the President or his Secretary of State in matters of

foreign affairs. They seldom merely approve the President's foreign policies. They usually assess each policy, each problem, independently from their own point of view. If their viewpoint differs from that of the President, as in the case of the neutrality legislation of the 1930's, they believe that they and the President, as equals, should compromise.

Chairmanship of the Senate Committee probably carries more prestige than any other position in Congress. Under the tradition of seniority, men attain that coveted post only after long years of service. The President, therefore, seldom directly influences the selection of committee chairmen. So powerful have some chairmen been, such as Henry Cabot Lodge of Massachusetts and William E. Borah of Idaho, that they have considered themselves *de facto* Secretaries of State. Some Presidents, therefore, have been handicapped in having to deal with intractable chairmen they detested and could not remove. This power of the chairman, in addition to the general independence of the committee as a whole, has been the source of considerable friction between the executive branch and the committee, even when the same political party has controlled both the Congress and the Presidency.[10]

The Department of State

Even though Congress and its committees influence the making of foreign policy, the executive branch controls the machinery that carries it out. That branch is responsible to the people for the conduct of foreign policy. It decides on the methods to use in attaining objectives, ordinarily through negotiation and reasonable compromise, through the art of diplomacy.

Although some Presidents, such as Franklin D. Roosevelt, distrusted the Department of State, carried on an independent high-level diplomacy, and often bypassed it in making major decisions, that department, under the President, is the main agency charged by law with the formation and conduct of foreign policy. It normally advises the President on matters of policy and directs official relations with other countries. When George Washington persuaded Thomas Jefferson to become the nation's first Secretary of State, he said that the Department of State "involves many of the most interesting objects of the Executive Authority."[11] That observation is still true.

At the head of the State Department stands the nation's highest appointive official, the Secretary of State. Appointed by the President with the Senate's approval, the Secretary of State is the ranking member of the cabinet and customarily serves as the President's chief adviser in matters of foreign policy. Under the President, the Secretary is responsible for the work, the policies, and the administration of the Department of State.

All of the Secretary's important powers, and hence those of his department, derive from the President. The power and importance of the Secretary of State, therefore, depend on his relations with the President. Strong Presidents tend to dominate the conduct of foreign policy, and some of them have treated their Secretaries of State virtually as figureheads. In the case of James K. Polk and Secretary of State James Buchanan, one contemporary observer remarked that "Buchanan is treated as no gentleman would treat a sensible hireling." Other Presidents, such as Warren G. Harding and Dwight D. Eisenhower, have relied heavily on their Secretaries of State for the conduct of foreign policy and delegated vast powers to them.

Some Secretaries, on the other hand, have considered themselves almost prime ministers. William H. Seward, for instance, told friends that Abraham Lincoln wanted him for his "prime minister." When he accepted the post, Seward told his wife, "It is inevitable. I will try to save freedom and my country."

Most Secretaries of State have come from the higher ranks of professional and political life. More often than not, they have had little knowledge of world affairs or diplomacy before taking office. Many have been political appointees—men who held high status in the political party controlling the executive branch of the government, or who had lost out in the scramble for the Presidency and received the Secretaryship as a consolation prize. This was true of Seward, and also of James G. Blaine and William Jennings Bryan.

In recent years, as the office of Secretary of State has grown in stature, the men who have held it have been experienced in world affairs, though not professional diplomats. As the world-wide eulogies that poured into Washington on the death of former Secretary John Foster Dulles in May, 1959, have shown, peoples throughout the world now look upon the Secretary of State as a symbol of America, as the official spokesman of American foreign policy.[12]

To aid the Secretary of State in carrying out foreign policy, the United States maintains diplomatic and consular establishments abroad. At the head of its diplomatic posts, known collectively by the terms "diplomatic mission" or "foreign mission," it has ministers and ambassadors, diplomats who are appointed by the President, with the approval of the Senate, to serve at his pleasure. Ministers rank below ambassadors, but both, as chiefs of mission, are stationed in the capitals of foreign countries. The offices, residences, and staffs of ministers are called legations, and those of ambassadors are known as embassies. Unless a country is under American military government, the chief of mission assigned to it is responsible for all American officials within its borders. The United States exchanges ministers or ambassadors with all independent foreign countries with whom it maintains diplomatic relations and normally deals with foreign governments through them. Until 1893 the highest ranking American diplomatic official was the minister, but now most chiefs of mission are ambassadors.

In most important cities throughout the world, primarily seaports, commercial and communication centers, the United States maintains consulates general, consulates, and lesser consular offices, all of them known collectively under the term "consular station." Sometimes consular officers have to protect national dignity from aggressive foreign merchants, as in the case of a junior vice-consul in Prague who protested to a Czech dress manufacturer about his commercial use of the American flag. "But I only use the Stars and Stripes on our top-grade brassieres," the merchant replied.[13]

Among other important duties, the officers at the head of the consular posts have the responsibility for the commercial and travel interests of the United States and for American citizens, particularly seamen, in their areas. Those officers usually perform no diplomatic tasks. Although consular officers come under the general jurisdiction of the chief of mission in the country in which they serve, the United States normally maintains a supervising consul general in each major foreign country to coordinate the functions of consular officers stationed there.

At present, the diplomatic missions and consular stations are staffed by members of a professional corps called the Foreign Service. Formerly, the diplomatic and consular services were separate and most of their posts went to inexperienced political appointees. Not until the demands of the First World War had exposed a pressing need for trained and experienced diplomats did the United States give serious consideration to the idea of a professional diplomatic service.

By means of the Rogers Act of 1924 Congress created a career corps, the Foreign Service, and united all our official representatives abroad under it. The career idea did not, however, extend to the chiefs of mission, who, notably in places like London, Paris, and Rome, continued to be political appointees, usually men of wealth who could afford the costly entertaining and the various extra expenditures required by the positions. The ordinary Foreign Service officer who lived on his salary could not meet the expenses of those posts. Until recently, he usually could expect to go no higher than counselor of embassy, the second ranking post at an embassy, or consul general.

Until 1954, moreover, the Foreign Service was an independent unit of government under the Secretary of State, an elite corps with its own staff, distinct and separate from the civil service personnel of the Department of State. Now its officers are integrated with the State Department officials in a single Foreign Service Officer Corps. Although it has undergone change and lost its autonomy, the Foreign Service remains essentially what it has always been, the agency that carries out American foreign policy overseas.[14]

The Military Influence

Other agencies within the executive branch, some fifty of them, also carry out foreign policy or have a hand in shaping it. Of the major ones, none is more important than the military establishment consisting of the Department of Defense and its three service departments controlling the Army, Navy, and Air Force. All of the armed forces have intelligence staffs that send agents abroad to gain information on potential enemies, and many of the embassies have military, naval, and air *attachés* who gather foreign military and other technical data. Their duties reflect the fact that in a world where war has been a legitimate and ultimate test of a nation's ability to attain its international objectives, military power is an essential element in foreign policy.[15]

Whenever a decision in foreign policy involves the possibility of war, or almost any kind of military operation, American military leaders and their civilian superiors have a direct share in reaching that decision. They weigh the proposed action for its effect on America's military position throughout the world, as in the case of Secretary of State Cordell Hull's negotiations with the Japanese in 1941 when the military men said they were unprepared for war. Since they needed time, they asked President Franklin D. Roosevelt to prolong the talks and to soften the nation's policy toward Japan so as to postpone the impending war.

This almost inseparable partnership of foreign and military policy is rational, for both have the same basic objective, the maintenance of national security. Foreign policy, in fact, usually determines the nation's military needs. Our statesmen, moreover, often gear foreign policy to military calculations, meaning that they take into account the military capacity to carry out a policy if force is necessary. Thus, military power is usually taken as a main index of a nation's strength and prestige in international affairs.

Logically, therefore, national defense, like the control of foreign relations, belongs exclusively to the Federal government. Through Congress it maintains the Army, Navy, and Air Force and can declare war. The President, under the Constitution, is Commander-in-Chief of the Armed Forces and has the main responsibility for military policy. During the Second World War Franklin D. Roosevelt mixed foreign and military policy and emphasized his military powers. His meshing of foreign and military affairs, even though the two had always been close, was a departure from American tradition. In the past Americans had usually thought of them as functioning in two separate worlds. Not until after the Second World War did Americans fully appreciate the intimate relationship between the two. In creating the National Security Council in 1947, an agency in which the President, the Secretary of State, and the Secretary of Defense have the most important roles but which at first was predominantly military in character, Congress reflected the new awareness of military policy.

As established by law, the National Security Council has two basic tasks: to assess foreign policy in the light of the nation's military power, and to advise the President on the integration of domestic, military, and foreign policies as they pertain to national defense. Through it, the President attempts to deal with one of the perplexing problems of our time, how to make proper use of the vast military power our foreign policy has come to involve. Most students of foreign policy would perhaps agree that the performance of the National Security Council, particularly in helping to resolve that problem, has been disappointing and that the council is still mainly a monument to an aspiration.[16]

Nonetheless, the enormous presence of that problem has given the military a greater influence in the shaping of foreign policy than it has ever had. The Secretary of Defense is second only to the Secretary of State in helping to formulate foreign policy; and, as the President's principal military advisers, the Joint Chiefs of Staff of the three armed forces, who represent the views of professional military men, have frequent and direct access to him on matters of policy.

The planning and executing of military policy, as has been indicated, has ordinarily required information about potential enemies, what the military call intelligence and what others might describe as espionage and undercover intrigue. The enhanced influence of the military in the planning of foreign policy has therefore led to the growth of intelligence organizations within the executive branch devoted to obtaining, analyzing, and preserving the secrecy of intelligence from all over the world. This has led, in turn, to a conflict between the theory of democratic control over foreign policy and the reality of maintaining national security, for by definition intelligence is secret and available only to statesmen on the highest level who, more often than in the past, have to make decisions in foreign policy on the basis of information they cannot disclose to the public.

Of all the intelligence organizations the most important in the shaping of foreign policy is the Central Intelligence Agency, created in 1947 as an adjunct of the National Security Council and sometimes called the council's right arm. It coordinates all federal and foreign intelligence activities, or the work of what is known as the intelligence community, and advises the National Security Council on intelligence affecting military and foreign policy. The recent prominence of the Central Intelligence Agency in matters of national policy, some students have observed, may even represent the growth of a third force within the executive branch in the planning of foreign and military policy.[17]

Public Opinion, Politics, and Pressure Groups

Ironically, while military and intelligence activities have brought greater secrecy to the making of foreign policy, military policy has been exposed to greater publicity than in the past. One reason for this is historic. American foreign policy has usually been the subject of public debate and the give and take of the political process, and, because of the partnership of military and foreign policy, part of this political tradition has rubbed off on the making of military policy.

In practically no other country, furthermore, have statesmen and students of foreign affairs placed so much emphasis on public opinion, an emphasis seemingly incompatible with secrecy in the making of policy. Yet scholars disagree in defining public opinion and in evaluating its influence on foreign policy. On large issues, such as hostility to the Communist regimes of Russia and China, there has not been much disagreement, for in those instances public opinion seems to speak with a clear voice.[18]

Often the influence of public opinion has been great. For example, in 1898 William McKinley and his advisers did not want war with Spain, but the people and their representatives in Congress apparently did. The President, therefore, bowed to what he considered the mandate of public opinion and took the country to war.

Few Presidents have been as sensitive to the power of public opinion as was Franklin D. Roosevelt. In October, 1937, he gave a speech in Chicago suggesting a "quarantine" of "aggressor" nations. As soon as he found that some of the public, and leaders in Congress, were hostile to the suggestion, he backed away from it. Yet he had no way of knowing precisely what the true sentiments of the people were. Some of his contemporaries have maintained that he misjudged the strength of the public reaction.

Public opinion polls, although valuable in indicating the trend of public sentiment on many issues, have not always been reliable on the complex issues of foreign policy. Logically, the truest barometer of public opinion should be the ballot box, but seldom, if ever, has the American voter been confronted with a specific issue of foreign policy. Ordinarily, voters have to consider questions of foreign policy within a pattern of domestic issues. Both congressional and presidential elections have usually turned on domestic issues, but there have been some notable exceptions. In the election of 1916, for example, Woodrow Wilson and Charles E. Hughes made foreign policy a noteworthy issue.[19]

Political parties and their campaign platforms, moreover, sometimes influence public opinion on matters of foreign policy, as was the case with the Republican platform in the election of 1952 that attacked the foreign policy of Harry S. Truman and his conduct of the Korean War. In an effort to keep politics out of foreign policy, we have had periods of bipartisan support for foreign policy, but those instances have been unique and except for certain issues have not been entirely successful.[20] All this merely confirms the old principle that political considerations have always influenced the conduct of foreign policy.

Political parties try to manipulate issues of foreign policy for political profit, but pressure groups, usually organizations with definite objectives, attempt to do so to further the interests of a particular segment of the population or sometimes of a foreign power. Even though their goals may differ, political parties and pressure groups may find reciprocal advantages in pooling forces to influence public opinion. Economic groups interested in tariff protection, for instance, have traditionally leaned toward the Republican party, believing that party would give their views a friendly reception.

The influence of pressure groups is almost impossible to measure, yet we know that at times their activities, such as those of missionary organizations, commercial associations, or labor unions, have definitely affected foreign policy. Although pressure groups can be found at work in many countries, they have been particularly potent in the United States.[21]

The Economic Factor

Some writers, noting that economic interests have been among the most powerful of all pressure groups, have evolved what has been dubbed the "scandal theory" of foreign policy. War, they say, results from the schemes and pressures of capitalists who, in anticipation of profit from carnage, insidiously manipulate foreign policy. Certain historians and economists have even argued that the primary motivation behind foreign policy is economic.

Probably the best-known economic explanation of the cause of war and hence of motivation in foreign policy is the Communist or Marxist theory, according to which mature capitalist economies spawn surpluses of commodities, population, and capital. In the international struggle to export those surpluses, war results. For the historian, neither the scandal nor the surplus theory adequately explains the cause of war or the basic motivation behind foreign policy. All agree, nonetheless, that the economic factor has consistently been one of the most important in the history of American foreign policy.

Throughout its history the United States has been one of the world's major trading nations. From the beginning, therefore, notable principles in American foreign policy have been the promotion and protection of trade, and later, of investment and industry abroad. Many of the memorable phrases that stud the vocabulary of our diplomatic history, such as freedom of the seas, the Open Door, and Dollar Diplomacy, reflect the pervasive impact of those economic concerns.

The Secretary of the Treasury, therefore, has usually had a significant part in the shaping of foreign policy. Indeed, our first Secretary of the Treasury, Alexander Hamilton, had a greater influence in formulating and controlling foreign policy than did Secretary of State Thomas Jefferson. At present, foreign affairs, particularly economic and military aid programs, consume so great a share of our annual budget that the Secretary of the Treasury and his financial experts almost automatically become key figures in decisions of foreign policy.

Usually the Treasury Department concerns itself primarily with economic foreign policy, meaning simply the pattern formed by economic objectives in foreign policy and the means used to attain them. The difficulty in discerning whether a given policy is political or economic in intent has led to jurisdictional conflicts within the government, as between Hamilton and Jefferson. Our early interest in China, for example, was almost wholly economic, but as our traders expanded their activities, they sought government protection. Such protection involved political action, a function of the State Department. To eliminate some of the friction between the State and Treasury Departments, in December, 1954, President Dwight D. Eisenhower created a special interdepartmental agency called the Council on Foreign Economic Policy.

At times, as in the administration of William H. Taft, the State Department has taken the initiative in promoting economic penetration of foreign markets. Whatever the reason for economic penetration, it has led to some of the most striking criticisms of the United States. "Economic imperialism," critics have cried whenever the government supported American traders or investors abroad. Communists, in disparaging American policy, still use the phrase effectively in places like Southeast Asia and the Middle East.

There is, however, truth to the charge that Americans have tried to use economic pressure as a diplomatic weapon. Thomas Jefferson made the attempt against Great Britain with the Embargo Act of 1807, Franklin D. Roosevelt against Japan in 1941 by freezing trade with her, and John Foster Dulles against Egypt in 1956 by abruptly withdrawing the offer of a loan to help build a dam on the Nile River. The United States has even used economic pressure to try to force its allies and friends to support a special part of its foreign policy. In the Battle Act of 1951, Congress threatened to cut off military and economic aid to any country trading with Communist nations.

America's great internal economic strength has made such pressure possible. The fact that the United States has grown from a debtor nation to the world's greatest economic power with the largest customer market in the world has had a continuing impact on international politics. Shifts in American economic policy can cause riots in Latin America, misery in the Middle East, or depression in Europe. American economic power, as was the case with the Marshall Plan in 1948, can save whole nations from ruin and bring hope and dignity to millions of people.[22]

Whether one stresses economic interpretation, public opinion, idealism, realism, or any other theory of motivation, we can see that foreign policy is complex. Yet neither its theory nor its practice is wrapped in mystery, for it has left us a pattern of changing ideas, decisions, and deeds. We can understand that pattern through history, primarily through the study of our national policies toward other nations. We shall see that the history of American foreign policy is the record of a search for solutions to problems, solutions which usually seek more security and prosperity in peace, and victory in war. What follows is a history of that search.

NOTES

1. For an extended definition of foreign policy, see Kurt London, *How Foreign Policy Is Made* (New York, 1949), pp. 12–16.

2. For a definition of international law and perceptive comments on the instability of international relations and the role of power in those relations, see Charles de Visscher, *Theory and Reality in Public International Law*, trans. from the French by P. E. Corbett (Princeton, 1957), pp. 133–140. For an analysis of the weakness of international law, see Julius Stone, *Quest for Survival : The Role of Law and Foreign Policy* (Cambridge, Mass., 1961). For a definition of diplomacy, see Harold G. Nicolson, *Diplomacy*, 2nd ed. (London, 1950), pp. 13–16, and for techniques, see his *The Evolution of Diplomatic Method* (New York, 1955).

3. For the nature of power in international relations, see Georg Schwarzenberger, *Power Politics: A Study of International Society*, rev. ed. (New York, 1956), pp. 203–207 and Hans J. Morgenthau, *Politics Among Nations*, 2nd ed. (New York, 1959), pp. 26–28.

4. For theoretical analyses of isolationism, see Alexander DeConde, ed., *Isolation and Security: Ideas and Interests in Twentieth-Century American Foreign Policy* (Durham, N.C., 1957), pp. 3–32, 159–183.

5. For a discussion of self-interest, idealism, and realism, see Robert E. Osgood, *Ideals and Self-Interest in America's Foreign Relations: The Great Transformation of the Twentieth Century* (Chicago, 1953), pp. 4–10 and Kenneth W. Thompson, *Political Realism and the Crisis of World Politics: An American Approach to Foreign Policy* (Princeton, 1960). The idealist approach is presented in Dexter Perkins, *The American Approach to Foreign Policy*, rev. ed. (Cambridge, Mass., 1962), especially pp. 63–82 and Frank Tannenbaum, *The American Tradition in Foreign Policy* (Norman, Okla., 1955). That of the realist is in Hans J. Morgenthau, *In Defense of the National Interest: A Critical Examination of American Foreign Policy* (New York, 1951) and George F. Kennan, *Realities of American Foreign Policy* (Princeton, 1954).

6. Oskar Morgenstern, in *The Question of National Defense* (New York, 1959), pleads for diplomats and statesmen to become acquainted with the mathematical theory of the games of strategy to aid them in making foreign policy, and calls for a science of politics. See pp. 228, 261–291.

7. The place of theory in international relations is discussed in William T. R. Fox, ed., *Theoretical Aspects of International Relations* (Notre Dame, Ind., 1959) and Stanley Hoffman, ed., *Contemporary Theory in International Relations* (Englewood Cliffs, N.J., 1960).

8. Philip W. Buck and Martin B. Travis, eds., *Control of Foreign Relations in Modern Nations* (New York, 1957), p. 65.

9. Details are given in Edward S. Corwin, *The President: Office and Powers, 1787–1957: History and Analysis of Practice and Opinion*, 4th ed. (New York, 1957), pp. 170–226 and his older study, *The President's Control of Foreign Relations* (Princeton, 1917).

10. For details see Daniel S. Cheever and H. Field Haviland, Jr., *American Foreign Policy and the Separation of Powers* (Cambridge, Mass., 1952); Robert A. Dahl, *Congress and Foreign Policy* (New York, 1950); Holbert N. Carroll, *The House of Representatives and Foreign Affairs* (Pittsburgh, 1958); Albert C. F. Westphal, *The House Committee on Foreign Affairs* (New York, 1942); Eleanor E. Dennison, *The Senate Foreign Relations Committee* (Stanford, Calif., 1942); and David N. Farnsworth, *The Senate Committee on Foreign Relations* (Urbana, Ill., 1961).

11. New York, Oct. 13, 1789, in John C. Fitzpatrick, ed., *The Writings of George Washington* (39 vols., Washington, 1931–44), XXX, 446.

12. For an historical analysis of the Secretaryship of State, see Alexander DeConde, *The American Secretary of State: An Interpretation* (New York, 1962).

13. Charles W. Thayer, *Diplomat* (New York, 1959), p. 132. This book offers a witty informal study of an American diplomat's functions. See also, E. Wilder Spaulding, *Ambassadors Ordinary and Extraordinary* (Washington, 1961).

14. Zara S. Steiner, *The State Department and the Foreign Service: The Wriston Report— Four Years Later* (Princeton, 1958), pp. 14–16, 45–57. For details see J. Rives Childs, *American Foreign Service* (New York, 1948) and William Barnes and John H. Heath, *The Foreign Service of the United States: Origins, Development, and Functions* (Washington, 1961).

15. For a view that the military had come to dominate foreign policy, see C. Wright Mills, *The Power Elite* (New York, 1956), pp. 202–211. The following explore the military's place in foreign policy: Burton M. Sapin and Richard C. Snyder, *The Role of the Military in American Foreign Policy* (New York, 1954); William W. Kaufmann, ed., *Military Policy and National Security* (Princeton, 1956); Samuel P. Huntington, *The Soldier and the State: The Theory and Politics of Civil-Military Relations* (Cambridge, Mass., 1957); and Walter Millis and others, *Arms and the State: Civil-Military Elements in National Policy* (New York, 1958).

16. Hans J. Morgenthau, "Can We Entrust Defense to a Committee?" *The New York Times Magazine* (June 7, 1959), pp. 9, 62, 64, 66 and Millis, *Arms and the State*, pp. 181–182. For details on the National Security Council, see Robert Cutler, "The Development of the National Security Council," *Foreign Affairs*, XXIV (April 1956), 441–458 and Timothy W. Stanley, *American Defense and National Security* (Washington, 1956), especially pp. 28–37.

17. Harry H. Ransom, *Central Intelligence and National Security* (Cambridge, Mass.,

1958), pp. 203–204. This book describes the growth and function of central intelligence since the Second World War. Two other useful studies are Sherman Kent, *Strategic Intelligence for American World Policy* (Princeton, 1949) and Roger Hilsman, *Strategic Intelligence and National Defense* (Glencoe, Ill., 1956).

18. Walter Lippmann, in his *Essays in the Public Philosophy* (Boston, 1955), offers a striking criticism of the influence of public opinion in matters of foreign policy. That opinion, he says, is "a dangerous master of decisions when the stakes are life and death" (p. 20). For a defense of public opinion as "the strongest foundation for diplomacy," see Henry M. Wriston, *Diplomacy in a Democracy* (New York, 1956), particularly pp. 61–115.

19. For a discussion of politics, foreign policy, and public opinion, especially in the election of 1956, from the point of view of the pollsters, see Angus Campbell and others, *The American Voter* (New York, 1960), pp. 198–201. For a critical analysis, see Lindsay Rogers, *The Pollsters: Public Opinion, Politics and Democratic Leadership* (New York, 1949).

20. See Cecil V. Crabb, *Bipartisan Foreign Policy: Myth or Reality?* (Evanston, Ill., 1957).

21. See V. O. Key, Jr., *Politics, Parties, and Pressure Groups*, 4th ed. (New York, 1958), pp. 124–130. For a detailed study of the influence of a particular pressure group on recent foreign policy, see Ross Y. Koen, *The China Lobby in American Politics* (New York, 1960).

22. For the economic influence see Raymond F. Mickesell, *United States Economic Policy and International Relations* (New York, 1952) and Benjamin H. Williams, *Economic Foreign Policy of the United States* (New York, 1929). For a recent critical economic interpretation of American diplomatic history, see William A. Williams, *The Tragedy of American Diplomacy* (Cleveland, 1959).

Chapter Two

FROM COLONY TO NATION

AMERICAN diplomatic history, like the United States itself, has European roots. Originally, Spain and Portugal, by right of discovery, the authority of four Papal Bulls in 1493, and their Treaty of Tordesillas of 1494, claimed exclusive dominion over the New World. They tried to retain that dominion by controlling the seas and by keeping other nations from gaining a foothold in the Americas. France, England, and then Holland soon challenged their control by claiming that the seas were open to all. "The sun shines for me as for the others," Francis I of France said in 1541. "I should like to see the clause of Adam's will which excludes me from a share of the world." [1]

Since Portugal did not have the strength to fight off the French and British and in 1580 was conquered by Spain who controlled her empire for sixty years, Spain assumed the main task of guarding the Iberian monopoly in the New World. After England defeated the Great Armada in 1588, Spain's power also declined. She became too weak to keep the other countries out of the Western Hemisphere. France, England, and Holland, all hungry for Spanish loot, built up their holdings in the Americas at her expense. Then they themselves clashed.

After the three powers had forced Spain to recognize their American colonies in the seventeenth century, England fought two naval wars with Holland. By 1667, she had succeeded in forcing the Dutch out of North America. Then, between 1688 and 1763, England and France fought four great wars, each one of them at least in part a contest for North America. [2]

In the first three wars France and England followed different strategies. France turned her main efforts toward expansion in Europe, making the gain of colonial lands a secondary goal. England, with the help of one ally or another, met France's challenge in Europe and with her powerful navy acquired new colonies, generally at the expense of France and declining Spain.

In the duel for empire all the maritime powers, but England most successfully, followed the economic and political principles of mercantilism. According to mercantilist theory, the way to power lay in acquiring colonies. Through a monopoly of her colonists' trade, a country would try to sell more than she bought and thus would achieve a favorable balance of trade and grow wealthy. Colonial trade, moreover, would nurture sea power, for with both wealth and sea power a nation had two keys to greatness. At the same time, the powers accepted the principle that no one colonial empire should be allowed to become so great as to upset the balance of power in Europe. In practice, therefore, mercantilist theory and the principle of the colonial balance of power were bound to lead to conflict.[3]

Yet for two centuries European statesmen had tried to isolate America from Europe's quarrels and Europe from America's under the doctrine of two spheres. America, according to that doctrine, was a separate sphere "beyond the line" of European laws and treaties. In the Treaty of Whitehall of 1686, for example, France and England agreed that even though they should go to war in Europe a "true and firm peace and neutrality shall continue in America" between their colonies. The doctrine never really worked, mainly because the rivalries among the colonists were often as intense as they were in Europe. The foreign policies of the European powers, therefore, ultimately decided whether the colonists would be at peace or war.[4]

Colonial Rivalries

Those colonists, transplanted Europeans who had carried their Old World hates with them, lived on the frontiers of their new lands in fear and insecurity. Englishmen, Frenchmen, and Spaniards in America detested each other and fought when their mother countries fought, and sometimes when the homelands were at peace. Europe's diplomacy was their diplomacy.

Usually the English colonists in America accepted the bloodshed of the European wars as a matter of course and fought loyally for the mother country, even though they might not have grasped the reasons for those wars. They did, however, understand their own parts in the conflicts and sometimes identified their local interests and welfare with the waging of the wars. Many colonists realized that they were fighting the battles of Europe on American soil.

Even before England and France fought the first of their great imperial wars, the English colonists in North America gave evidence of a special fear in relations with other neighboring European colonists. Four of the northern English colonies, Massachusetts, New Haven, New Plymouth, and Connecticut, in 1643 organized the Confederation of New England, "a firm and perpetual league of friendship and amity for offense and defense, mutual advice and succor upon all just occasions."[5] Concerning itself with local diplomacy and relations with its foreign neighbors, this first federation of colonies in North America assumed the right to make war and treaties and sought security against the French and Dutch settlers and the Indians. It even made a treaty with the French of Nova Scotia at Boston in 1644 and another with the Dutch of New York at Hartford in 1650. After 1665, for internal reasons, the influence of the Confederation declined.

The next effort at colonial union, the Dominion of New England of 1686 that brought New York and the New England colonies under one head, originated in England. Although James II and his advisers created the Dominion for reasons of administrative control, they also had in mind the growing power of France in North America and defense of their colonies through firmer control.[6] Unpopular with the colonists, the experiment collapsed within three years.

As the Dominion expired, what was to be the first imperial conflict between England and France, known as the War of the League of Augsburg, broke out in Europe in 1688. Within a year it spread to America where the colonists called it King William's War. The French and their Indian allies invaded Maine, New Hampshire, and New York and in February, 1690, destroyed Schenectady, scalping and slaughtering the inhabitants. To meet the French threat, Jacob Leisler, temporarily at the head of New York's government, in April called all the colonies to a congress. Four of the colonies—Massachusetts, Plymouth, Connecticut, and New York—sent commissioners, who planned a land and sea attack upon Canada. Three other colonies—Rhode Island, Maryland, and Virginia—were not present at the New York congress, but apparently pledged cooperation. Although an expedition of New Englanders in May captured Port Royal in French Acadia, the larger plan of conquest failed.[7] The Treaty of Ryswick in 1697 restored all conquests, so that the first Anglo-French war ended indecisively in America.

The colonists did their own fighting. Neither England nor France contributed much to the American campaigns. By their limited joint action, moreover, the English colonists showed that they were, to a considerable extent, capable of defending themselves and of handling their own relations with hostile foreign neighbors.[8]

Four years later, when Louis XIV of France tried to place his grandson on the Spanish throne, England and France renewed their fighting in the War of the Spanish Succession. Again, within a year, English settlers in North America, who named their part of the conflict Queen Anne's War, were fighting Frenchmen and Spaniards. Again, French and Indian allies swooped across New England's frontier and in 1704 massacred or enslaved the villagers of Deerfield, Massachusetts. Again, to eliminate the French menace, to protect their homes from fire and tomahawk, the northern colonies wanted to conquer Canada and asked for British help. The southern colonies, particularly South Carolina, urged an advance against French and Spanish lands west to the Mississippi River. The English colonists, in other words, had objectives of their own and tried to influence Britain's policy in attaining them.[9]

In the Peace of Utrecht of 1713, victorious England forced France to surrender the region around Hudson Bay, as well as Acadia, or Nova Scotia, captured mainly by colonial troops, and Newfoundland. English control of that strategic region later contributed to France's complete defeat in North America. After Utrecht, because of England's overseas expansion, France and Spain drew together in defense of the colonial balance of power then established.

True peace, however, did not prevail in North America. The English and French built fortifications against each other, raided each other's frontier settlements, and negotiated alliances with Indian tribes. That skirmishing led England's advisory body on colonial policy, the Board of Trade, to frame a report, called the "State of British Plantations in America, in 1721," on how to provide better government and security for the colonies. It suggested that by unifying its colonies the British government would be "taking the necessary precautions to prevent the encroachment of the French, or any other European Nation" on English possessions. Although the plan never went into effect, it emphasized the old idea that union was the best way to protect the American colonies against foreign danger.[10]

English expansionists were not satisfied with mere defense; some apparently became entranced with the idea that destiny had marked their American colonies for expansion beyond the Allegheny Mountains. Seeking more Spanish territory and concessions in the Americas, the British touched off the War of Jenkins' Ear in 1739. The alleged cause was the hysteria created by the tales of a certain Captain Robert Jenkins who claimed that the Spaniards had lopped off one of his ears and had inflicted other cruelties, but agitation in the English colonies over the boundaries of Florida and Georgia was also a cause.[11]

A year later another general conflict, the War of the Austrian Succession, 1740–1748, broke out in Europe. When France allied herself with Spain in 1743, England declared war on her in the following year. The two wars merged and the result was another world-wide struggle, with an American phase known as King George's War, 1744–1748.

Again the colonists in America attacked each other. A large British and colonial expedition in June, 1745, captured the French fortress of Louisbourg on Cape Breton Island, but the general war ended in stalemate. By the Treaty of Aix-la-Chapelle in 1748, Britain, to the disgust of the New Englanders, exchanged Louisbourg for French evacuation of captured territory in the Netherlands.

British
French
Spanish
Dutch

Hudson
Bay

NEWFOUNDLAND

St.
Johns

CAPE BRETON
Louisbourg

L. Superior
Sault Ste.
Marie
Quebec
Montreal
Ft.
Frontenac

C A N A D A
St. Lawrence R.

NOVA
SCOTIA
(ACADIA)

Mississippi
L. Michigan
Huron
Detroit
L. Ont.
L. Erie
Albany
Boston

Ft. St. Louis
Philadelphia
New York

Cahokia
Kaskaskia
Ohio
R.
R.

Atlantic

BERMUDAS (Br.)

L O U I S I A N A
Charles Town

New
Orleans
Mobile
Biloxi
Pensacola
FLORIDA
St. Augustine

Ocean

Rio Grande

M E X I C O

Gulf of Mexico

BAHAMAS (Br.)

GUIANA

YUCATAN
CUBA
HISPANIOLA
PUERTO
RICO
St. Eustatius
(Dutch)
Nevis (Br.)
St. Christopher (Br.)
Montserrat (Br.)
Antigua
(Br.)
Guadeloupe (Fr.)

HONDURAS
MOSQUITO
COAST
Martinique (Fr.)
Curaçao (Dutch)
Barbados
(Br.)

Pacific
Ocean
Puerto
Bello
Cartagena
NEW
GRANADA
V E N E Z U E L A
GUIANA

NORTH AMERICA AFTER THE PEACE OF UTRECHT, 1713

England thus used her colonists' victory to stabilize the political balance in Europe. America's concerns, it was clear, were secondary to the European interests of the mother country.[12]

Peace was a mere interlude, for British and French rivalry in North America never slackened. Each appeared determined to destroy the power of the other. English advances into the Ohio Valley threatened France's control of the continent's interior. The French retaliated by sending military expeditions against English posts in the Ohio country and by building a chain of log forts across the frontier to close off the interior. When a force of Virginia militia under a young lieutenant colonel, George Washington, clashed with the French at the forks of the Ohio River in the summer of 1754, the French and Indian War began.

To unify the English colonies in the military effort against the French, basically "for their mutual security and Defense against the encroachment of their foreign neighbours," and to win Indian allies, the Board of Trade meanwhile called a general colonial congress to meet in Albany, New York, in June, 1754.[13] Seven colonies sent representatives who adopted a plan for a federal union of the colonies drafted by Benjamin Franklin. This Albany Plan of Union would have given the colonies the power to make peace or war, the most important power in foreign relations. Jealous of their individual powers, none of the colonies accepted either the plan or the general recommendations of the congress.

The Albany plan was important as a forerunner of later congresses and, for our purposes, because it dealt with foreign relations. As in the earlier plans, the fear of foreign danger spurred the movement toward union. Once the fighting began, however, the British, who had put aside their own plans for colonial union, sent troops to America. After the French and English had fought for two years in America, the conflict spread to Europe where it became the Seven Years' War, 1756–1763.

The Significance of the Seven Years' War

Unlike the other imperial struggles, the Seven Years' War originated in the colonial rivalries of America. To England, France, and Spain it was a colonial war fought to solve imperial problems, mainly to determine whether Britain or France would become master of North America. To the English colonists, however, it was a national war in which the whole Anglo-American nation was "directly and fundamentally concerned."[14]

In that war, because of the importance of the colonial stakes, France reversed her traditional policy of seeking dominance in Europe and instead tried to surpass England in America. Nonetheless, France still wasted her armies in Europe fighting England's Prussian ally while England herself threw her main strength against

French possessions overseas. In the war at sea and in America, England crushed France.

By the Treaty of Paris of 1763, France ceded Canada and all of her territory on the North American continent east of the Mississippi River except for New Orleans, to England. She kept only a few small islands in the Gulf of St. Lawrence and in the Caribbean. Spain surrendered Florida and all her possessions east of the Mississippi to England. A few hours after signing the Treaty of Paris, France gave New Orleans and all her territory west of the Mississippi, the land called Louisiana, to Spain. France parted with Louisiana ostensibly to compensate Spain for her losses, but in fact to keep it out of England's hands.

Since the Seven Years' War destroyed French power in North America and hence cleared the way to making it mainly an English-speaking continent and contributed to the later independence of the United States, it was one of the world's decisive conflicts. France's defeat freed the English colonists from the constant fear of invasion by a powerful enemy camped on their borders. With Spain on the decline, no one in the Western Hemisphere was now capable of challenging the expanding English colonies. It was this new security which fed a growing spirit of independence that finally led to the American Revolution.

The colonial experience thus shows that there never was a golden age of complete freedom from Europe's quarrels, that America was never truly isolated from Europe. Yet that experience, some historians have claimed, gave birth to certain of the nation's foreign policies that were at one time considered basic, such as nonentanglement and isolationism. It convinced later leaders that the United States should avoid European entanglements, that America's destiny lay in carving a nation from a virgin continent.

In the decade preceding the American Revolution, for example, writers in America urged their fellow colonists "to keep clear of the quarrels among other states." In 1770, Benjamin Franklin while in England said that the colonies paid more than their share for imperial defense, "for the sake of continental connections in which they were separately unconcerned." [15]

Six years later, Thomas Paine in his pamphlet *Common Sense* apparently convinced many colonists that the issues of foreign policy vital across the sea were of no immediate concern to them. ". . . any submission to, or dependence on, Great Britain," he wrote, "tends directly to involve this Continent in European wars and quarrels, and set us at variance with nations who would otherwise seek our friendship, and against whom we have neither anger nor complaint. . . . It is the true interest of America to steer clear of European contentions." [16] Thus it was, with the removal of the French menace, that the English colonists, who were soon to become Americans, lost their sense of identity with the European policies of English kings.

NORTH AMERICA AFTER THE PEACE OF PARIS, 1763

France Seeks Revenge

Having emerged from the Seven Years' War as the world's foremost colonial and maritime power, Great Britain no longer had to offer political concessions to her colonists, as she had previously done, to assure their support against foreign foes. She attempted, instead, to consolidate her enlarged empire and to strengthen the colonial system she had neglected during the imperial wars. To give relief to her own taxpayers, whose national debt had been doubled by the war, she required her American colonies to share not only the cost of the French war but also the expense of administering and defending newly acquired Canada and the eastern Mississippi Valley. This assertion of imperial authority, coupled with new taxes, provoked the colonists to unrest and resistance.

Humiliated, anxious for revenge against England, and eager to recover her former greatness, France saw in the colonial unrest the flaw in Britain's empire. Étienne François Duc de Choiseul, the Foreign Minister under Louis XV, told his king that England "is, and will ever be, the declared enemy of our power and your state," and made the separation of the American colonies from Britain a part of French policy. From 1764 until his retirement six years later, Choiseul sent secret agents to America to foment trouble and to report on dissatisfactions there. His successor in 1774, the resourceful Charles Gravier Comte de Vergennes who also declared that "England is the natural enemy of France," continued the policy of revenge. As the American crisis approached, William Pitt, one of England's greatest sons, warned that France was like a "vulture hovering over the British empire, and hungrily watching the prey that she is only waiting for the right moment to pounce upon." [17]

When an angry Parliament, beginning in March, 1774, passed a series of laws known as the Coercive Acts, the crisis came. Those five acts (among them the Boston Port Bill that closed the port to all shipping until the townspeople paid for the English tea they had destroyed a few months earlier, and the Massachusetts Government Act which practically nullified Massachusetts' charter) in one way or another denied the colonists rights they had been demanding for over ten years. Those acts led to the bloodshed a year later at Lexington and Concord, where Massachusetts farmers fired on British troops and started the American Revolution.

Although delighted by the trouble in America, Vergennes moved cautiously, unwilling to intervene until he knew the colonists were determined to fight for independence. For the colonists, despite the bloodletting, insisted that they were defending their rights as Englishmen and sought merely to settle their grievances within the empire. Vergennes wanted to destroy the British empire, not mend it.

By spurning compromise and resorting to force, Britain destroyed the colonial desire for reconciliation, forcing the colonists to seek French help. Inferior to the

British in wealth, manpower, and arms, the American colonists desperately needed outside assistance. For example, they had virtually no gunpowder and no powder mills for its manufacture. "We have no arms, we have no powder, we have no blankets," the New York Committee of Safety wrote the Continental Congress in July, 1775. "For God's sake, send us money, send us arms, send us ammunition." France could fill those needs.

Beaumarchais and Secret Aid

That same summer a daring and persuasive Frenchman, Pierre Augustin Caron de Beaumarchais, learned from Americans in London that the trouble in America had burst into a serious insurrection. In September he returned to Paris and urged Vergennes to assist the colonists. Known to posterity primarily as the author of the comedies, *The Barber of Seville* and the *Marriage of Figaro*, the handsome and talented Beaumarchais was an incredible man. In addition to being a poet, playwright, skilled musician, inventor, and politician, he was a wizard at intrigue who took up the American cause virtually as his own, pointing out in one of his memorials to Louis XVI that aid to the Americans "will diminish the power of England and proportionally raise that of France."

Following Beaumarchais' urging, Vergennes that September sent a secret agent, posing as a merchant from Antwerp, to America to sound out the colonists and to tell them that France favored their independence and would aid them in achieving it with no strings attached to her help, but he made no commitments. After talking to the Americans, the "merchant" sent home a glowing report that the colonists were determined to assert their independence.

Vergennes received the report in February, 1776, but still did not dare aid the Americans openly and risk war with England. At that point Beaumarchais stepped in. "If it be replied that we cannot assist the Americans without wounding England, and without drawing upon us the storm which I wish to keep off," he told the king and Vergennes, "I reply in my turn that this danger will not be incurred if the plan I have so many times proposed be followed, that of secretly assisting the Americans without compromising ourselves."[18] Despite the objections of the Minister of Finance, Anne Robert Jacques Baron Turgot, who argued that aid to the American colonies and the resulting war with England would bankrupt France, Vergennes persuaded the king to adopt a policy of limited secret assistance.

When Louis XVI, on May 2, set aside one million *livres* (about $200,000) worth of munitions from the royal arsenals for American use, secret aid became official. Spain, also thirsting for revenge against England, contributed a like amount. Those French and Spanish guns, powder, and other supplies were sent to America in a steady stream through Roderique Hortalez and Company, a dummy firm set up by Beaumarchais. Some ninety per cent of the gunpowder used by the American rebels in the first two years of the war, in fact, came from European arsenals.[19] In effect, two months before the colonists declared themselves free of England and before any American agent went to France to solicit aid, France had committed herself to a limited undercover support of the rebellion. She also rushed preparations for a possible war with England and urged Spain to do the same.

The Second Continental Congress

The Second Continental Congress, meanwhile, had begun a foreign policy of independence. In November, 1775, it had created one of its most important standing committees, the Committee of Secret Correspondence, to maintain contact with friends abroad. Consisting of five members, with Benjamin Franklin as its first chairman, this State Department in embryo had little real power. Congress, either through other special committees or the Committee of the Whole, controlled foreign policy even in its minute details.

To ascertain the attitudes of foreign powers toward the revolting colonies, Congress at first corresponded with several agents abroad, among them Arthur Lee, a turbulent young Virginian then in London as a commercial agent for Massachusetts, who was in close touch with Beaumarchais. After conferring with Vergennes' secret "merchant," Congress decided on March 3, 1776, to send a secret agent of its own to France to purchase arms and to sound out the French about an alliance. For the dual commercial and diplomatic mission it chose Silas Deane, a scheming politician from Connecticut.

Overplaying his role, Deane arrived in Paris in July ostensibly disguised as a rich Bermuda merchant. Lacking discretion and integrity, he betrayed his country by delivering himself into the hands of Edward Bancroft, an old friend who had become a paid British spy. Although Vergennes did his utmost to maintain the secrecy of his commitments to Deane, the American was like a sieve. Information on French actions poured through him directly to the British. Bancroft, for instance, acted as an interpreter between Deane and Beaumarchais when those two agreed on executing the Frenchman's plan for furnishing supplies to the American forces. George III, in fact, even complained of the sheer bulk of the information his spies were reporting from sources such as Deane.[20]

Congress, meanwhile, went ahead to make the final break with Britain. To attract foreign trade and aid, it opened American ports on April 6, 1776, to all countries, on July 2 voted independence, and two days later adopted the Declaration of Independence, making possible the establishment of formal diplomatic relations and the negotiation of treaties. That Declaration, in fact, was issued mainly to assure potential allies that the war was real and not a mere family quarrel that could be easily patched by parental leniency.

At the same time Congress appointed a committee to bring together guiding principles for the use of American diplomats in making treaties. Two weeks later that committee offered its report, adopted on September 17, embodying a model set of articles for commercial treaties that came to be known as the Treaty Plan of 1776. It included specific articles for a treaty with France and such principles as free ships make free goods, meaning that enemy materials of a peaceful nature should be immune from capture when transported on neutral ships. This, the basic document in American maritime practice, marked the beginning of the policy of freedom of the seas.

"Poor Richard" in Paris

Slightly more than a week later, on September 26, Congress appointed an official diplomatic mission, consisting of Deane, Arthur Lee, and Benjamin Franklin, to secure French recognition of independence. Deane and Lee might well be called the first of the "militia diplomats," men who were as innocent of diplomatic experience as were the militia men of military training. Yet Congress, without knowing whether or not they would be received, hastily pressed the militia diplomats into service and sent them abroad seeking recognition, a policy disliked by Franklin. ". . . a virgin state," he said, "should preserve the virgin character, and should not go about suitoring for alliances, but wait with decent dignity for the application of others." 21

Unlike his colleagues who were abroad gaining experience under fire, Franklin himself was not a militia diplomat. Having spent sixteen years in England as the agent of Pennsylvania, New Jersey, Georgia, and Massachusetts, he had come to know the European diplomats accredited to the court of St. James'. His inventions had won him a world-wide reputation, his *Poor Richard's Almanac* had run through several French editions, and his investigations in natural philosophy had brought him membership in the French Academy. Now in his seventieth year, Franklin was the American the French knew best and admired most and the man the British called the "chief of the American rebels."

When Franklin in plain dress and wearing a comfortable fur cap, arrived in Paris in December, 1776, he set off a wave of public excitement. In his charm and pleasant manner the French saw the natural man that their Rousseau had taught them to admire. He became the embodiment of the American cause, the symbol of a new and unspoiled land.

The shrewd Franklin took full advantage of his popularity. "It is my intention while I stay here," he said, "to procure what advantages I can for our country by endeavoring to please the court."

Franklin quickly played his trump, telling Vergennes of a possible *rapprochement* with England "unless some powerful aid is given us or some strong diversion be made in our favor."[22] Although he won increased support, Franklin was unable to gain French recognition of independence until the Americans gave concrete evidence that they could wage war successfully. America's arms showed the desired strength in October, 1777, at the Battle of Saratoga, where they forced General John Burgoyne to surrender his army of more than five thousand men. When news of the victory reached Paris in December, it assured French recognition, a recognition Vergennes already favored. The Battle of Saratoga, therefore, ranks as one of the decisive battles of American history.

The disaster at Saratoga had forced the British to reconsider their position. Early in December they rushed Paul Wentworth, a secret service agent, to Paris to forestall French recognition by offering Franklin and Deane liberal terms if only the colonies would lay down their arms and return to the empire. Since French police shadowed Wentworth from the moment of his arrival and Franklin made no effort to conceal his supposedly secret conversations with him, Vergennes knew of the British feelers and became uneasy lest they might lead to an Anglo-American reconciliation. In a bold move on December 17, therefore, he promised the United States formal recognition only if it insisted on maintaining independence from England.[23]

Wentworth continued his conversations, and on January 6, 1778, told the American commissioners that Britain would fight for another ten years rather than grant the independence the Americans sought. "America," Franklin answered, "is ready to fight fifty years to win it."[24] Two days later an agent from Vergennes asked Franklin and Deane what they wanted for terminating their talks with Wentworth. A treaty and an alliance, they said. Vergennes agreed.

The French Alliance

Bound to Spain by a defensive dynastic alliance of 1761, called the Family Compact, France had to consult the Spanish court before making a treaty with the Americans. Although Spain disliked England, she was opposed to American independence. She had secretly aided the colonists in the hope that they and the English would exhaust themselves, but she would not openly sanction the rebellion of colonies, for that would set a terrifying precedent for her own possessions in the New World. Despite the urgings of Vergennes, Spain refused to enter a triple alliance with the United States. France and the United States alone, therefore, on February 6, 1778, signed two treaties.

By the terms of the first, the Treaty of Amity and Commerce, both nations granted each other most-favored-nation treatment, meaning that any commercial favors one party gave to another country would automatically accrue to the other signatory, and other liberal trading privileges. More important, with that treaty France recognized the United States as an independent nation.

The second, the Treaty of Alliance, provided that if war broke out between France and Britain as a result of the first treaty, France and the United States would fight together until American independence was assured. Neither party was to "conclude either Truce or Peace with Great Britain, without the formal consent of the other first obtain'd." France guaranteed American independence and territory "forever" and renounced designs on any portion of the North American mainland held by Britain in 1763. The United States guaranteed French possessions in America against all powers "forever." At Valley Forge, General George Washington later greeted the news of the alliance with heartfelt joy, saying it must "chalk out a plain and easy road to independence."

Within two days after the French treaties were signed, the American commissioners' confidential secretary, Edward Bancroft, sent copies to London. At first the British took no hostile action against the French, though in March, 1778, after France announced the alliance, they broke off diplomatic relations. At the same time, through the offer of concessions, they continued to try to bring the colonies back into the empire. In March, Parliament passed laws offering the Americans virtual home rule. In April, hoping to prevent ratification of the French alliance, it sent a formal commission under Lord Carlisle, armed with money to bribe members of Congress, to America to propose the new terms, but Britain had acted too late. Since the French treaties offered everything that England did and independence as well, the Americans refused what once they might have accepted. Without even conferring with the Carlisle commission, Congress ratified the treaties on May 4, 1778.

A month later English and French warships clashed and the War of the American Revolution spread to Europe. In July, a French naval squadron, sent to "destroy the English forces upon the shores of North America," arrived at Philadelphia. With it came a minister plenipotentiary, Conrad Alexandre Gérard, the first accredited diplomatic official in the United States. Next, Vergennes tried to bring Spain into the war.

The Spanish Connection

Both France and the United States wanted Spain as an active ally and their own alliance had secretly provided for her adherence. For Spain, next to France, had what the United States needed most: money, arms, and sea power. "If the Spaniards," General Washington said, "would but join their Fleets to those of France, and commence hostilities, my doubts would all subside. Without it, I fear the British Navy has too much in its power to counteract the Schemes of France."[25] Spain, however, resented the Franco-American alliance and would not go to war against England unless she could gain objectives of her own, the most coveted of those being Gibraltar, taken from her in 1704 by Britain.

After France and the United States had concluded their alliance, Don José Moniño, Count Florida Blanca, Spain's Foreign Minister, attempted to force England to give up Gibraltar as the price for Spanish neutrality and even suggested mediation of the American rebellion on terms that would probably have killed independence, but England would not surrender Gibraltar or anything else to the Spaniards. Florida Blanca then bargained with Vergennes who offered the concessions necessary to lure Spain into the war. Using the pretense that England had slighted her in rejecting an unacceptable offer of mediation, Spain, on April 12, 1779, signed a secret treaty of alliance with France, the Convention of Aranjuez.

That treaty, ostensibly in execution of the Family Compact, pledged France and Spain not to lay down their arms until Spain recovered Gibraltar. Without becoming an ally of the United States and without recognizing its independence, Spain thus committed France to fight for her European objectives. Two months later, Spain declared war on England. Since by treaty the United States could not make peace without France and France could not do so without recovering Gibraltar, American independence, if all the treaties were observed, might now come to depend on the fate of "that pile of stones" at the entrance to the Mediterranean.

Encouraged by Spain's entry into the war but unaware of the secret commitment of Aranjuez, Congress in October, 1779, sent John Jay, recently its president, to Spain as minister plenipotentiary to seek recognition, Spanish adherence to the Franco-American alliance, and a loan of five million dollars. Jay's instructions also directed him to obtain the right of navigation down the Mississippi River through Spanish territory to the Gulf of Mexico. Arriving in Spain in January, 1780, he met constant evasion. At one point he became so exasperated by the refusal of Spanish officials to see him that he blurted out to the French Ambassador "that the object of my coming to Spain was to make *propositions*, not *supplications*, and that I should forbear troubling the minister with further letters till he should be more disposed to attend to them. That I consider America as being, and to continue, independent in *fact*." [26]

Nonetheless, the Spaniards refused to receive Jay officially and would not yield the right of navigation. Even when, as directed by Congress, he offered to waive American pretensions to navigation of the Mississippi, Spain would not recognize the new republic. Although Jay stayed in Spain for over two years, he won no concessions of any consequence, only a small loan of some $150,000.

The Armed Neutrality of 1780

England's naval practices, meanwhile, had aroused the ire of neutral nations such as Denmark and Russia, who in 1778 had considered an alliance to protect their shipping. Nothing came of it, but Catherine II of Russia in February, 1780, proclaimed a code of maritime principles for the protection of neutral shipping against all belligerents and invited the other maritime neutrals to join her in what came to be known as the Armed Neutrality of 1780. Those principles, most of them already included in the Treaty Plan of 1776 and the Franco-American commercial treaty, stated that neutral ships had the right to enter belligerent ports, that free ships make free goods, and that to be binding, a blockade had to be effective.

France and Spain accepted the Russian code, making it part of their maritime practice, but England would not, since she was the dominant naval power and those principles threatened that dominance. Ultimately, Denmark-Norway, Sweden, the Holy Roman Empire, Prussia, Portugal, and The Two Sicilies joined the league of armed neutrality, and for a while members succeeded in closing the Baltic Sea to all belligerent operations.

Although Catherine had not invited the United States to join the league, Congress quickly adopted its principles and tried to gain admittance as a means of winning recognition of American independence from the member nations, particularly from Russia. To obtain that recognition and a commercial treaty with Russia as well, Congress in the spring of 1781 sent one of its former members from Massachusetts, Francis Dana, to St. Petersburg as minister plenipotentiary. But Russia, like the other nations of Europe except France, had little interest in the American Revolution and would not recognize American independence. Since Catherine refused to receive Dana, his mission, like Jay's, ended in failure. As for the Armed Neutrality, even though Catherine at one time called it an armed nullity, it proved fairly effective in protecting neutral rights and did what Vergennes hoped it would. It served French policy by helping to isolate Britain from possible allies on the continent.

Holland's adherence to the Armed Neutrality, moreover, had the effect of spreading the war. The Dutch had two treaties with the British, a commercial treaty of 1674 and an alliance of 1678, later renewed. Three times the British demanded that the Dutch honor their alliance and aid them in the war, but the Dutch refused, arguing speciously that the war had originated in America and hence the alliance did not obligate them to act because it applied only to a European war involving England. What the Dutch really wanted was to remain neutral to profit from trade with France and other belligerents. Rather than have Holland join the Armed Neutrality and make her ships and goods available to France and Spain, the British preferred war, which would give them freedom to capture Dutch ships. Unwilling, however, to declare war on that basis, the British found another pretext.

In the autumn of 1778 William Lee, a militia diplomat from Virginia, and a minor Dutch official drew up the draft of an unauthorized commercial treaty for their two countries based on the Treaty Plan of 1776. Lee sent the draft treaty to

Congress. Later, Congress appointed Henry Laurens of South Carolina, another of its former presidents, as Minister to Holland. Members of the Lee family gave him William's draft treaty to use as a guide. While Laurens was on his way to Europe a British frigate captured his ship and he hastily dumped a bag of documents overboard, but without sufficient weights. The British captain had the bag fished from the sea. In it was the draft treaty.

The British then accused the Dutch of making a secret treaty with the American rebels and declared war on Holland in December, 1780. The true cause for war was Holland's decision to join the Armed Neutrality, but the armed neutrals, taking the view that Holland had gotten herself into trouble by meddling in British colonial affairs, did nothing to aid her. Britain quickly swooped down on Dutch shipping and cut off an important source of supplies for France and indirectly for the United States.

For Americans, the most stunning blow was Britain's capture of St. Eustatius, a Dutch island six miles long and three miles wide in the Caribbean, which had been the center of a huge trade between Europeans and Americans, much of it in contraband, or forbidden implements of war. Early in February, 1781, before the Dutch inhabitants had heard their country was at war, Admiral George B. Rodney, in command of fifteen ships of the line, fell on the island, plundering it and capturing some 2000 American merchants and seamen. Rodney lingered in the Dutch free port for three fateful months garnering his loot. While he did so, a French fleet under Admiral François J. P. de Grasse slipped by him to join other French ships which later gained a decisive control of the sea in the siege of Yorktown, Virginia.

Probing for Peace

Even though the Dutch were now in fact allies of the United States, they still refused to recognize American independence. Finally, in April, 1782, with French assistance, John Adams, who had succeeded Laurens as Minister to Holland, was received. Later he secured a loan from the Dutch and on October 8 signed a treaty of commerce with them. Thus, a second European state recognized the United States and placed its relations with Americans on a treaty basis.[27]

England, although engaged in what had become almost a world-wide war with most of Europe against her, meanwhile had refused two opportunities to end the war on terms short of American independence. The first came through the secret negotiations, from November, 1779 to March, 1781, between Thomas Hussey, an Irish priest working for the Spanish intelligence service, and Richard Cumberland, an English agent, who attempted to arrange a truce that would have brought Spain out of the war and would have left Britain in control of large parts of her rebelling colonies. The other involved an offer of mediation from Austria and

Russia in 1780–1781 that included a generally similar fate for the United States. One reason for the failure of the efforts at mediation was the fact that France in July, 1780, had sent an army to the United States and the British insisted that in any truce or mediation the French must withdraw their forces from North America.[28]

The war in America, however, went badly for the British. Even Spanish forces, who fought mainly for their own ends, contributed to Britain's defeat there. They launched a successful offensive against the British in West Florida and by February, 1781, were in control of that territory. Eight months later, at Yorktown on October 19, 1781, General Charles Cornwallis, hemmed in by de Grasse's fleet and by French and American armies, surrendered a British army of some seven thousand men. That surrender virtually ended hostilities in America.

"It is all over!" Lord North, Britain's Prime Minister, said after the defeat at Yorktown. Popular opinion in England, never happy with the war in America, clamored for peace, the House of Commons passed a motion demanding an end to the war, and George III talked of abdicating. In March, 1782, Lord North resigned and a Whig, Lord Rockingham, before replacing him as Prime Minister demanded and received the king's assurance that he would agree to recognize the United States as independent. Rockingham's Whig government, however, was divided into two rival factions, the liberals headed by Charles James Fox, the Foreign Secretary, who had always opposed the war in America and favored independence, and the conservatives led by Lord Shelburne, the minister responsible for colonial affairs, called by his foes "The Jesuit of Berkeley Square," who hoped he could patch up some kind of a peace without losing the American colonies.

Unable to agree over their respective functions and powers, particularly over peace negotiations with England's enemies, where Fox was responsible for peace with France and Shelburne for negotiations with the Americans, the two men quarreled. The split in the British cabinet became known to the French and Americans who used their knowledge to advantage, but in July, 1782, Rockingham died. Shelburne succeeded him as Prime Minister and Fox resigned. Shelburne, an unusually resourceful and capable man, therefore had responsibility for making peace with the Americans and with all of Britain's enemies.

The Terms of Negotiation

Informal peace talks began before Shelburne had become Prime Minister. In April, 1782, he had sent Richard Oswald, a philosophical old Scot who had been an army contractor and slave trader and had lived in Virginia, to Paris to talk with Franklin. Although Franklin accepted Oswald's advances, he and Vergennes made it clear that Britain could not expect an independent peace from either France or the United States. In July, while Shelburne was forming his new government, Franklin unofficially told Oswald what the United States expected in the peace.

Franklin divided American aims into "necessary" and "advisable" terms, fore-most among the necessary ones being recognition of complete independence and the evacuation of all British troops from the United States. They also included generous boundaries for the new nation and fishing privileges for Americans in Newfoundland and Canadian waters.

Among the advisable terms Franklin listed a large indemnity, free trade for American ships in British ports, acknowledgment by Britain that she had erred in warring on Americans, and her withdrawal from "every part of Canada." If she gave up Canada and withdrew from North America, Franklin said, Britain and the United States would never again have reason to fight. Impressed by Franklin's arguments, Oswald reported the terms to his government, urging acceptance of most of them. In any event, Oswald's report that the United States and France were willing to make peace led to the opening of formal negotiations.

Shelburne accepted Franklin's necessary terms as a basis of discussion, but would not recognize American independence before negotiating a treaty. Since Oswald's formal commission allowed him to treat only with representatives of England's "colonies," Franklin said Oswald's powers were inadequate and stopped the negotiations. At this point, John Jay, who had arrived in Paris in June to help with the peace negotiations and who, along with Franklin, John Adams, and Henry Laurens, had been designated a member of the peace commission by Congress, took a decisive part in the peacemaking.

When Franklin and Jay discussed Oswald's commission with Vergennes in August, 1782, the French Minister suggested continuing the negotiations, arguing that the form of the commission was unimportant as long as England recognized American independence in the final peace treaty. Franklin accepted Vergennes' advice, but Jay would not. With good reason as subsequent revelations were to show, Jay suspected that Vergennes wanted to delay American independence until he achieved his goals in Europe, such as Gibraltar. Since Vergennes could not deliver Gibraltar to Spain, he supported Spain's claim to the western territory in America between the Appalachian Mountains and the Mississippi, land desired by the Americans. Besides, American territorial aspirations struck Vergennes as exaggerated. France wanted an independent United States but also a weak one that would still need her.

Then on September 6, Joseph Rayneval, Vergennes' secretary, gave Jay a proposal that Franklin said looked as if Spain wanted "to coop us up within the Allegheny Mountains." Three days later, Jay learned that Rayneval had left for a secret trip to London, apparently to advance Spain's desires. Jay, therefore, became willing to violate Congress' instructions that the peace commissioners follow French guidance and do nothing without French "knowledge and concurrence."

THE PEACE NEGOTIATORS OF 1783

Seated from left to right are John Adams, Benjamin Franklin, and William Temple Franklin; standing are John Jay at the left and Henry Laurens at the right. These men, who took part in the preliminary negotiations, are pictured here in an unfinished painting by Benjamin West.

Furthermore, Jay believed correctly that Congress was under the thumb of French agents and that its instructions did not represent the nation's true interests.

Earlier Jay had told Franklin, "Let us be grateful to the French for what they have done for us, but let us think for ourselves. And, if need be, let us act for ourselves!" [29] Jay did just that. Without consulting the French or Franklin, he told Shelburne he was now willing to forego prior recognition of American independence if it came in the first article of a peace treaty and that he would discuss terms independently of France if the British agreed to prompt negotiations.

Seeing Jay's overture as an opportunity to break up the Franco-American alliance, Shelburne was delighted. He revised Oswald's commission, and Oswald and Jay proceeded in covert negotiations to draw up a draft treaty. When informed of these negotiations, Franklin at first protested mildly and then agreed with Jay, but sickness kept him from participating in the discussions at this time. British demands stiffened after news reached London late in September that their forces at Gibraltar, under siege by Spain and France for three years, had won a great victory. A month later John Adams arrived in Paris from Holland and joined the negotiations. He enthusiastically approved what Jay had done. Finally, on November 30, 1782, the American commissioners signed a preliminary peace treaty with England that was not to go into effect until France also made peace.

After the negotiations had been completed, Franklin immediately told Vergennes of the preliminary treaty. Vergennes, who had originally consented to concurrent American negotiations with the British but not to the secret ones and who probably knew all along of Jay's clandestine actions, expressed no surprise. The Americans, he said, had "managed well." Two weeks later he reproved Franklin, who admitted some "impropriety" in the American action, but, the alert Dr. Franklin quickly added, he hoped that the slight indiscretion would not destroy the alliance with France. "*The English, I just now learn,*" he said, "*flatter themselves they have already divided us.* I hope this little misunderstanding will therefore be kept secret, and that they will find themselves totally mistaken."[30]

Although the Americans had violated their own instructions and the spirit if not the precise letter of the French alliance, their treaty in fact served French interest as well as their own. Vergennes desperately wanted peace but was hamstrung by obligations to Spain he could not fulfill. By telling the Spaniards that with the American peace, continuation of the war would be useless, he could persuade them to settle for less and extricate himself from his impossible commitment to deliver Gibraltar to Spain. Therefore, he accepted the American treaty without undue protest.

The Treaty of Paris

Great Britain made peace with France and Spain at Versailles on September 3, 1783, and the United States signed the definitive Treaty of Paris on the same day. Except for a contingent secret article dealing with West Florida, an article no longer applicable and hence dropped because Britain gave the Floridas to Spain, the terms of the final treaty were those of the preliminary agreement. Those terms, by confirming independence, allowing Americans the "liberty" to fish off the coasts of Newfoundland and Canada, ceding them extensive boundaries, gave the United States its three primary objectives. Since Britain gave up her territory between the Appalachian Mountains and the Mississippi River south of the Great Lakes to the Floridas at the thirty-first parallel, the terms were generous.

The Treaty of Paris also appeared to meet Britain's two main objectives in the peace: the United States promised British creditors that they would "meet no lawful impediment" in trying to recover their prewar debts and agreed to

THE UNITED STATES IN 1783

"recommend" to state legislatures that they restore or pay for property confiscated from Loyalists, or American colonists who had retained their allegiance to England. Those provisions, plus the vague definition of boundary lines, were to cause trouble later.

When the war ended, the trans-Appalachian West was not in American hands, so that Americans could not claim it by right of conquest. George Rogers Clark, the Revolution's hero of the West, had taken and held only a small part of it. Why, then, did the British give it up? The answer lies in the fact that for England the American treaty was only part of a general peace settlement she made with the powers. Surrender of the Northwest seemed a negligible sacrifice if it could help in splitting the Franco-American alliance. British statesmen and merchants, furthermore, wanted to buy American good will and lay the basis for a profitable future trade with the United States.[31]

The United States, therefore, began its history as an independent nation with a vast domain, but jealous European neighbors still surrounded it. To the north, England held Canada; to the south and west, Spain controlled the Floridas and Louisiana. Yet those problems and the treaty's troublesome clauses were concerns for the future and minor in comparison to what the peace of Paris bestowed upon the United States.

In summary, through independent negotiations designed to advance her own objective of driving a wedge between France and the United States, Great Britain consented to a liberal peace out of proportion to American military achievements. With her generous grant of western territory, she conceded to the new nation room for future expansion and a good chance for survival as an independent state.

NOTES

1. Quoted in Charles de La Roncière, *Histoire de la marine française* (5 vols., Paris, 1899–1920), III, 300. In this statement can be seen the basic idea in the later doctrine of freedom of the seas. For the origins of that doctrine, see Alexander P. Higgins and C. John Colombos, *The International Law of the Sea* (London, 1943), pp. 39–41.

2. Richard W. Van Alstyne, *The Rising American Empire* (New York, 1960), p. 22. Van Alstyne points out that in all the wars American territorial questions had been major issues.

3. There has been academic controversy over the aims and character of mercantilism; see Jacob Viner, "Power versus Plenty as Objectives of Foreign Policy in the Seventeenth and Eighteenth Centuries," *World Politics*, I (Oct. 1948), 1–29 and Charles Wilson, "'Mercantilism:' Some Vicissitudes of an Idea," *Economic History Review*, 2nd ser., X (Dec. 1957), 181–188. The idea of a balance of colonial power comes from Max

H. Savelle, "The American Balance of Power and European Diplomacy, 1713–78," in Richard B. Morris, ed., *The Era of the American Revolution* (New York, 1939), p. 140.

4. The doctrine of two spheres is discussed in Max H. Savelle, "Colonial Origins of American Diplomatic Principles," *Pacific Historical Review*, III (Sept. 1934), 338–340 and in Felix Gilbert, *To the Farewell Address: Ideas of Early American Foreign Policy* (Princeton, 1961), pp. 104–106.

5. Albert B. Hart and Edward Channing, eds., "The Articles of the Confederation of the United Colonies of New England, 1643–1684," *American History Leaflets*, No. 7 (New York, Jan. 1893), p. 4. Harry M. Ward, in *The United Colonies of New England —1643–90* (New York, 1961), pp. 29–30, suggests that the vital force in the movement toward union was fear of the French and Dutch in the New World.

6. For details, see Viola F. Barnes, *The Dominion of New England: A Study in British Colonial Policy* (New Haven, 1923), especially pp. 31-32, 38.

7. Leisler's plan is discussed in Charles M. Andrews, *The Colonial Period of American History* (4 vols., New Haven, 1934-38), III, 130-132.

8. "In America," Daniel J. Boorstin points out, "war had become an institution for the citizenry as well as the warriors. The colonials were in the habit of defending themselves on neighboring ground instead of employing professionals on a distant battlefield." *The Americans: The Colonial Experience* (New York, 1958), p. 351.

9. Details on southern desires in Queen Anne's War are in Verner W. Crane, *The Southern Frontier, 1670-1732* (Ann Arbor, 1929, 1956).

10. For details see Andrews, *Colonial Period*, IV, 389-390.

11. The idea of destined colonial expansion is in Max H. Savelle, "Diplomatic Preliminaries of the Seven Years' War in America," *The Canadian Historical Review*, II (March 1939), 19. The boundary agitation as a cause for war is discussed in Trevor D. Reese, "Georgia in Anglo-Spanish Diplomacy, 1736-1739," *William and Mary Quarterly*, 3rd ser., XV (April 1958), 168, 190. On the question of union to gain colonial assistance against Spain at this time, see Jack P. Greene, "Martin Bladen's Blueprint for a Colonial Union," *ibid.*, XVII (Oct. 1960), 516-530.

12. Jack M. Sosin, "Louisburg and the Peace of Aix-la-Chappelle, 1748," *William and Mary Quarterly*, 3rd ser., XIV (Oct. 1957), 516-535. See also John A. Schutz, "Imperialism in Massachusetts during the Governorship of William Shirley, 1741-1756," *The Huntington Library Quarterly*, XXIII (May 1960), 217-236.

13. The quotation is from Alison G. Olson, "The British Government and Colonial Union, 1754," *William and Mary Quarterly*, 3rd ser., XVII (Jan. 1960), 26. For further details, see Robert Newbold, *The Albany Congress and Plan of Union of 1754* (New York, 1955).

14. Max Savelle, "The Appearance of An American Attitude toward External Affairs, 1750-1755," *The American Historical Review*, LII (July 1947), 662. Howard H. Peckham, in "Speculations on the Colonial Wars," *William and Mary Quarterly*, 3rd ser., XVII (Oct. 1960), 467, points out that the English colonists fought first for their homes and children and then for their king. Lawrence H. Gipson, in "The American Revolution as an Aftermath of the Great War for the Empire, 1754-1763," *Political Science Quarterly*, LXV (March 1950), 86-104, argues that the Seven Years' War was fought for the security of British North America.

15. Quoted in Gerald Stourzh, *Benjamin Franklin and American Foreign Policy* (Chicago, 1954), p. 120.

16. Moncure D. Conway, ed., *The Writings of Thomas Paine* (4 vols., New York, 1906), I, 88-89. For details on this theme, see Felix Gilbert, "The English Background of American Isolationism in the Eighteenth Century," *William and Mary Quarterly*, 3rd ser., I (April 1944), 138-160.

17. Quoted in Curtis P. Nettels, *The Roots of American Civilization: A History of American Colonial Life* (New York, 1938), p. 704.

18. Memorial of Feb. 29, 1776, in Louis L. Loménie, *Beaumarchais and His Times*, trans. by Henry S. Edwards (New York, 1857), p. 270. For a short popular biography, see Georges E. Lemaitre, *Beaumarchais* (New York, 1949).

19. Claude H. Van Tyne, "French Aid before the Alliance of 1778," *The American Historical Review*, XXXI (Oct. 1925), 20. For the objectives of the policy of secret aid, see John J. Meng, "A Footnote to Secret Aid in the American Revolution," *ibid.*, XLIII (July 1938), 795.

20. Julian P. Boyd, "Silas Deane: Death by a Kindly Teacher of Treason?" *William and Mary Quarterly*, 3rd ser., XVI (April, July, and Oct. 1959), 185–187, 319–322, 324. For Deane as a war profiteer, see Thomas P. Abernethy, "Commercial Activities of Silas Deane in France," *The American Historical Review*, XXXIX (April 1934), 477–485.

21. To Arthur Lee, March 21, 1777, in Francis Wharton, ed., *The Revolutionary Diplomatic Correspondence of the United States* (6 vols., Washington, 1889), II, 298.

22. Jan. 5, 1777, *ibid.*, p. 246.

23. Claude H. Van Tyne, "Influences which Determined the French Government to Make the Treaty with America, 1778," *The American Historical Review*, XXI (April 1916), 528–541, points out that Vergennes entered the alliance because France was convinced that war with England was inevitable with or without it. The various theories concerning France's decision in favor of an alliance are discussed in Stourzh, *Franklin and American Foreign Policy*, pp. 291–292, n. 104. Van Alstyne, *The Rising American Empire*, pp. 34–35, indicates that Americans wanted an alliance from France before independence.

24. Quoted in Helen Augur, *The Secret War of Independence* (New York, 1956), p. 259. For other details, see Carl Van Doren, *Benjamin Franklin* (New York, 1956), pp. 588–593; Samuel F. Bemis, "British Secret Service and the French-American Alliance," *The American Historical Review*, XXIX (April 1924), 474–495; and John J. Meng, *Despatches and Instructions of Conrad Alexandre Gérard, 1778–1780* (Baltimore, 1939), pp. 76–82.

25. To Gouverneur Morris, Oct. 4, 1778, in John C. Fitzpatrick, ed., *The Writings of George Washington* (39 vols., Washington, 1931–44), XIII, 22.

26. Nov. 6, 1780, in Wharton, *Revolutionary Diplomatic Correspondence*, IV, 131.

27. For details see James B. Scott, ed., *The Armed Neutralities of 1780 and 1800* (New York, 1918); J. Franklin Jameson, "St. Eustatius in the American Revolution," *The American Historical Review*, VIII (July 1903), 683–708; and Friedrich Edler, *The Dutch Republic and the American Revolution* (Baltimore, 1911).

28. For details, see Samuel F. Bemis, *The Hussey-Cumberland Mission and American Independence: An Essay in the Diplomacy of the American Revolution* (Princeton, 1931).

29. Quoted in Frank Monaghan, *John Jay* (New York, 1935), p. 196.

30. Dec. 17, 1782, in Wharton, *Revolutionary Diplomatic Correspondence*, VI, 144.

31. For details, see Paul C. Phillips, *The West in the Diplomacy of the American Revolution* (Urbana, Ill., 1913) and Thomas P. Abernethy, *Western Lands and the American Revolution* (New York, 1937). For a treatment favorable to British statesmanship, see Clarence W. Alvord, *Lord Shelburne and the Founding of British American Goodwill*, published for the British Academy (London, 1926).

Chapter Three

FEDERALIST POLICIES

"AMERICAN glory begins to dawn at a favourable period, and under flattering circumstances," the publicist Noah Webster wrote in the preface of his speller in 1783. "We have the experience of the whole world before our eyes." [1] On the surface, what Webster said was true enough. The new nation had inherent strength. It was big, sprawling over a million square miles of land and water and stretching from the Atlantic Ocean on the east to the Mississippi River on the west. Beyond the frontiers lay room for expansion, the Old Northwest, containing some 220,000,000 acres of wilderness, more than a third of the national domain, and unoccupied except for Indians. Over 3,000,000 people, strung out along the coast between the sea and the mountains, were homogeneous, except for about a half million Negro slaves. The majority were descendants of English stock.

America also had weaknesses. Even though the Revolution had produced interests transcending state boundaries and had in fact created a central government for a new nation, the bond uniting the thirteen states, the Articles of Confederation and Perpetual Union, was tenuous. That constitution expressly limited and circumscribed the powers of the national government, placing the power of levying taxes, for example, in the hands of the states. The Continental Congress, the central organ of government, had declared independence, raised armies, and made an alliance with France through what were later called "implied war powers." After the war those powers collapsed, and for a while so did Congress, a logical result of the long exhausting conflict.

Despite its feeble authority, the new government had entered the world of independent nations and, to take part in international politics and trade, had created a Department of Foreign Affairs. Congress had the basic powers to carry on foreign relations, but not much more. It had the sole right, under the first constitution, of making peace or war, of sending and receiving ambassadors, of entering into treaties and alliances and of adjudicating all disputes between states, but could not make commercial treaties with the assurance that all the states would comply with them.[2]

Europeans were aware of the weakness of the American Union. Many of them, even friendly sovereigns, had believed that the end of the war would remove the pressure for national cooperation and would surely bring the collapse of the Union itself. After all, they pointed out, no republic had ever before existed on so large a scale. "As to the future grandeur of America, and its being a rising empire under one head, whether republican or monarchical," a well-known Englishman, Josiah Tucker, Dean of Gloucester, said, "it is one of the idlest and most visionary notions that ever was conceived even by writers of romance. The mutual antipathies and clashing interests of the Americans, their difference of governments, habitudes, and manners, indicate that they will have no centre of union and no common interest."[3]

Nonetheless, the new nation immediately after independence sought a place in world trade and enlisted some of its ablest leaders, men like John Adams, John Jay, and Thomas Jefferson, in its diplomatic service. They attempted, without great success at first, to show the skeptics of Europe that America merited respect. When John Jay returned from Europe in 1784, for instance, and Congress appointed him to succeed Robert R. Livingston as Secretary for Foreign Affairs, the Secretary of the Congress offered the advice "that it is not only time but highly necessary for us to think and act like a sovereign as well as a free people."[4]

Commerce with Britain

Jay's most serious diplomatic problems were with Great Britain, and of those one of the most pressing was that of trade. Americans, ironically, wanted both the advantages of independence and all the commercial benefits they had enjoyed as members of the British Empire. For a time, during the peace negotiations, it had seemed as if those twin desires would be met. Lord Shelburne and the merchants whose chief business before the war had been trade with America favored the idea of allowing Americans to resume their commerce within the British Empire free of the restrictions of mercantilist laws, but the preliminary peace treaty, because of its generosity to Americans, was unpopular in England. Shelburne's government therefore fell in February, 1783, before the signing of the definitive treaty, and with it the policy he had fostered of trying to win American good will with trade concessions.

Various opposition groups in Parliament, among them shipowners and certain merchants who saw in the United States a future commercial rival, demanded rigorous treatment of the former colonies. "By asserting their independence, the Americans have at once renounced the privileges, as well as the duties of British subjects," the Earl of Sheffield wrote in a widely circulated book; "they are become foreign States." 5 In July, Shelburne's successors issued an Order in Council shutting Americans out of the lucrative carrying trade in the British West Indies, and then in the definitive peace treaty all commercial articles were dropped.

Later, the British placed other restrictions on American traders, causing bitter outcries in the shipbuilding and trading communities of New England. British discriminations had the effect of making trade with the United States one-sided. England would buy only raw materials, such as tobacco, furs, and lumber from the United States, but no manufactured goods. She admitted American ships carrying American products to her home ports on fairly liberal terms, but excluded them, as she did other foreign ships, from trade in her colonies. Legally, American goods that went to England's colonies went in English ships. Resourceful New Englanders partially overcame the British restrictions through smuggling, particularly in the British West Indies where they built up a large illicit trade.

Despite England's arbitrary restrictions, commerce between the United States and Britain flourished. At the end of the Confederation period about seventy-five per cent of all American exports went to England and about ninety per cent of America's imports, mostly manufactured goods, came from there. Many Americans, nonetheless, felt that England was levying commercial war against them. One of them expressed the view of many when he complained that Britain was apparently "aiming to bring about a general bankruptcy in America after finding our trade had returned to its former channel, and that our importations were as great as formerly." 6

In spite of their grievances, Americans persisted in trading with England because they needed manufactures, such as textiles and household items, and England offered them an established market for their products, such as naval stores and cotton, and was the only country where they could obtain long term credits. They preferred English goods, moreover, and were familiar with British business methods. Besides, even traders would not ignore the ties of language, blood, and culture to the mother country. Economic dependence on England in the era of the Confederation, therefore, was almost as great as it had been before the Revolution.

Protesting Britain's discriminations, Americans threatened retaliation. In 1785 New York, for instance, laid a double tax on all goods imported from England. But the United States could force no change in British policy, mainly because the various states would not act in concert against England and even discriminated against each other. Having nothing to fear in reprisal, England saw no reason to extend generous trading privileges to Americans. "It will not be an easy matter to bring the American states to act as a nation," Lord Sheffield said; "they are not to be feared as such by us." [7]

The American government hoped that it might be able to overcome some of the British restrictions, particularly in the West Indies, through negotiation of a commercial treaty. To seek such a treaty, Congress sent John Adams in May, 1785, as its first Minister to Great Britain. When Adams announced himself as the Minister from the United States, the British asked, according to legend, where were the other twelve? Although the British received him with glacial courtesy, they would make no treaty.

In despair, Adams wrote to Jefferson urging retaliation. "If we cannot obtain reciprocal liberality," he said, "we must adopt reciprocal prohibitions, exclusions, monopolies, and imposts." [8] Such "means of preserving ourselves," he later admitted, however, "can never be secured until Congress shall be made supreme in foreign commerce."

After spending three fruitless years in London, Adams saw that reconciliation and cooperation with the British were impossible. England, still believing that the new republic would break apart, treated it with contempt. Even though, for commercial reasons, she sent consuls to the United States, she refused to send a minister. At his own request, therefore, Adams came home in April, 1788.

When he left London the British were cold. "Mr. Adams," the king told him on his departure, "you may, with great truth, assure the United States that, whenever they shall fulfill the treaty on their part, I, on my part will fulfill it in all its particulars." [9] So, in 1789, at the end of the Confederation, an understanding with Great Britain seemed as remote as it had been in 1783.

Slaves, Debts, and Loyalists

Adams also had instructions to obtain redress for British violations of the peace treaty. That treaty said that in evacuating American soil, British troops should not carry away Negro slaves or other American property, but the soldiers had taken hundreds of—perhaps several thousand—Negroes, apparently allowing some to gain freedom and selling others to planters in the West Indies. Americans, mainly Southerners, demanded compensation for the lost slaves, but the British refused. The Americans, therefore, used this violation to justify their own infractions of the treaty.

Before the war, British merchants in Glasgow and elsewhere had loaned Americans, primarily southern planters, millions of dollars in goods. American lawyers argued that the Revolution had dissolved all laws under which the debts had been contracted. The British creditors insisted that the debts had been incurred in time of peace and were justly due. Their pressure on Shelburne had resulted in a provision in the peace treaty saying that creditors should meet no lawful impediment in recovering their debts.

Southerners, however, defied the terms of the treaty. Maryland, Virginia, and other states passed laws prohibiting the use of state courts for the collection of the prewar British debts. Virginia's House of Delegates, by a unanimous vote, even demanded that Congress should make no treaty that might conflict with any of the state laws. In some cities there were riots against attempts to recover the debts and threats to assassinate the collectors. Although Congress insisted that the peace treaty had become the law of the land binding on the states and that their legislatures did not have the right to pass laws in conflict with it, Congress could not open the state courts or force payment of the debts.

Congress was equally helpless in trying to carry out the two treaty articles pertaining to Loyalists. The treaty said that Congress should recommend to the states the restitution of Loyalist property and that there should be no further persecution of Loyalists or confiscation of their property. Americans greeted those recommendations with a storm of protest, for feeling between Loyalists and Patriots during the Revolution had been deep and bitter.

About a third of the colonists had been Loyalists. Some had fled to Britain, some to Canada and Florida, and others had stayed behind the British lines. After the peace, many wanted to return to their old homes, but every state had persecuted Loyalists and had passed laws that either confiscated their property or heavily taxed it. Returning Loyalists were often tarred and feathered, mobbed, and even hanged. Those "leeches," angry Americans said, should not be allowed to remain among a free people. "It is the command of God that in cursing we curse them," a leading preacher of Salem, Massachusetts, advised.[10] Finally, by the end of the Confederation era, many of the Loyalists had regained their estates, but the confiscation laws were not repealed.

The Northern Posts

The unpaid debts and the persecuted Loyalists, meanwhile, had given the British an excuse for retaining a chain of military and trading posts in the Northwest strung out along the southern shores of the Great Lakes, in territory that belonged to the United States. In the peace treaty England had promised to evacuate those Northwest posts with all convenient speed, but as soon as powerful Canadian fur traders and merchants in Britain heard of the terms, they protested and demanded retention of the posts. The fur traders who had built up a lucrative business in the region said they needed time to sell their holdings and wind up their business south of the Great Lakes and appealed to the British government to support them.

MAIN BRITISH POSTS IN UNITED
STATES TERRITORY AFTER 1783

Some Englishmen, moreover, believed that Lord Shelburne had made a mistake in ceding the Old Northwest to the United States. Others argued that he had violated obligations to Britain's Indian allies who lived there. British commanders in the region, fearing an uprising if the Indians were turned over to the United States, wanted to keep the posts and to retain the good will of the Indians.

The day before George III had proclaimed the peace treaty, therefore, the British government had instructed the Governor General of Canada not to deliver the posts to the Americans, who had expected a quick transfer, and thus had decided to retain the posts before the United States itself had clearly violated the treaty. New instructions in 1786 directed the Governor General not only to hold the posts but also to recapture those that Americans might seize. The presence of British troops on American soil angered many Americans, especially Westerners who wanted to open up the Northwest to settlement. They were convinced, moreover, that British agents from the posts were supplying the Indians with rifles, ball and powder, knives, and other goods, and were encouraging the raids on frontier settlements.

At the same time, the British, who had retained two posts on Lake Champlain and one on the south shore of the St. Lawrence River, in American territory, dabbled in the troubles of Vermont. Plagued by vicious boundary disputes with New Hampshire and New York, Vermont had not been granted statehood. The Vermonters, therefore, had a weak attachment to the Union and maintained themselves as almost an autonomous entity. The fact that their natural trade outlet, via the St. Lawrence to the sea, went through Canada made union with Canada seem attractive, and the British appeared to encourage a separatist movement in Vermont. The brothers Ethan, Ira, and Levi Allen talked to the British officials about a commercial treaty and a new connection with England, and in 1789 Ira went to London to advance the secessionist scheme. At the end of the Confederation period, therefore, the fate of Vermont was uncertain.

Relations with France

From France, ally of the Revolution, the United States expected and received better treatment than from England. "Commercial privileges granted to us by France, at this season of British ill-humour," John Jay wrote to the Marquis de Lafayette, "would be particularly grateful."[11] In August, 1784, France had relaxed some of her mercantilist restrictions and had granted American ships a limited right to trade in certain of her Caribbean ports, but Americans were disappointed in these French concessions. They had expected more, such as freedom to trade in France's home ports.

Thomas Jefferson, who became Minister to France in 1785, was a fitting successor to Dr. Franklin, winning a considerable influence there. Although, as the representative of a republic in the day of monarchy, he found his post "an excellent school of humility," he tried to cultivate French friendship and to strengthen it through commerce. He believed that commerce between France and the United States should thrive because for the most part it was supplementary, not competitive. The United States could exchange primary products such as cotton, for French manufactures such as textiles. That commerce would, moreover, cement the political bond between the two countries. While recognizing that French policy was based on self-interest, he considered France's friendship essential to American foreign policy. "I cannot," he wrote, "pretend to affirm that this country will stand by us on every just occasion, but I am sure, if this will not, there is no other that will."[12]

Jefferson's hope for a bustling trade with France was not illusory, for the French already had a commercial treaty with the United States, and a foremost aim of their aid during the Revolution had been to break America's economic dependence on England. Yet the policy of the French government in cutting away certain mercantilist restrictions to attract American trade was an audacious one, a policy unpopular with its merchants, who resented American competition and who vehemently objected to having former British subjects trading freely in French Caribbean ports. Their protests caused minor readjustments in their favor, but the basic commercial policy toward the United States continued and the French government sent special consuls to America to drum up trade.

American commerce did well under liberal French decrees, but the concessions were gratuitous, were subject to local exceptions, and could be withdrawn at any time. The thirteen states vied with each other for French trade, violated parts of the commercial treaty of 1778, and manipulated tariff and tonnage duties to the annoyance of French merchants. Congress could do little to enforce uniform treatment of French commerce. The French commercial treaty, moreover, while providing for consuls, said nothing about their privileges and immunities. In the summer of 1784, therefore, Franklin and Vergennes had agreed to a consular convention that called for French consuls to deliver their credentials to state authorities rather than to Congress and thus stressed the sovereignty of the thirteen separate states.

When the convention reached the United States, Jay urged Congress not to ratify and recommended negotiation of a new agreement that recognized the sovereignty of "The United States of America." Jefferson renegotiated and in November, 1788, signed a revised convention. The new agreement appeared technically reciprocal but in fact was not. It permitted consular courts to exercise civil jurisdiction over their own nationals and thus impinged on American sovereignty. Although the United States was allowed the same privileges in France, the agreement favored France because of the weakness of the United States, which lacked uniform laws. Under the convention, French consuls could and did meddle in American politics.

Despite the efforts of the French consuls and Jefferson to stimulate commerce, American trade, as Jefferson pointed out, did not find its way to France. Americans profited from the newly opened channels of trade by selling more to France than they bought. They preferred British manufactures. French commercial policy, therefore, failed.

America also defaulted on repayment of the money France had loaned her during the Revolution. Congress was powerless to pay installments on the principal or even keep up interest payments. It tried to pay, but could raise money only by requisitioning the states. No longer faced with an immediate foreign danger, the states were deaf to congressional demands. Yet the French government applied no great pressure for payment, even when faced with bankruptcy, taking the view that the debt was a bad one and must be written off as such.

French statesmen were not entirely displeased with the state of American affairs. A nation unable to raise enough money to maintain a strong government, they realized, would be more amenable to their control than would a financially stable one. They wished to keep the United States dependent. When, for example, after the peace treaty, the United States tried to wriggle out of the French alliance, the French insisted that it remained in effect. "Those who have once been the allies of France," Vergennes said, "are her allies always." [13]

Although relations between the two governments had cooled since the ardent courtship of the Revolution, difficulties with France during the Confederation were minor in comparison with America's other foreign troubles. A warm bond, moreover, still existed between the people of France and Americans. "I am egregiously deceived if the people of this Country are not in general extremely well affected to France . . . ," Washington told the French Minister; "no prejudice has been revived, no jealousy excited, no interest adduced, and, in short, no cause has existed (to my knowledge) which could have wrought a revolution unfriendly to your nation." [14]

Friction with Spain

No lesser term than unfriendly, however, could describe relations with Spain, who had refused to recognize the United States until after the peace of 1783. That recognition did not allay the bitterness between the two countries, a bitterness stemming from three main issues: the navigation of the Mississippi, the new nation's southwestern boundary, and commercial affairs.

The question of the Mississippi grew out of the peace treaty at the end of the Seven Years' War. In that treaty France had given the British the right to navigate the river to the sea, and Spain, who gained control of both banks of its lower reaches, had accepted that obligation when she took over Louisiana from France. In the final Treaty of Paris of 1783, to which Spain was not a party, England said she would share the right with the United States. Arguing that the British privilege had ended in 1779 when she and England had gone to war, Spain adamantly refused to recognize any American right to navigate the Mississippi through Spanish territory. England, she said, had no authority to transfer her navigation privilege, particularly since it no longer existed, to a third party. During the war, as a favor, the Spaniards had allowed Americans free use of the river, but suddenly in 1784 a royal order closed it to the Americans, touching off a crisis in the Southwest.

Friction over the southwestern boundary arose from the final treaty of peace of 1783. It had fixed the boundary between Spain's West Florida and the United States at the thirty-first parallel, but in the preliminary treaty of 1782, England had inserted a secret article saying that if West Florida remained in British hands, its boundary would be over a hundred miles farther north to the latitude of the mouth of the Yazoo River, about 32° 25', the line that had formed the boundary of West Florida in the twenty years the British had held it.

When the Spaniards heard of the secret article, they were furious. In the War of the American Revolution, the Spaniards had conquered the Floridas and territory to the north of the thirty-first parallel, and England in her treaty of peace with them in 1783 had ceded the Floridas with indefinite boundaries. They contended rightly, therefore, that they were not bound by the terms of the final Anglo-American treaty. Their extreme claim went far beyond the thirty-first parallel, as far north, in fact, as the Tennessee and Ohio Rivers, covering parts of Georgia, Tennessee, and Kentucky, and most of Alabama and Mississippi.

Spain attempted to enforce her claims to the Old Southwest through occupation, by holding military posts in Alabama, Mississippi, and Tennessee, and through intrigue with the Indians there, by supplying them with weapons and encouraging them to use the arms against American settlers, some 50,000 of whom had swarmed into lower Ohio. Spain also signed treaties with several of the tribes, offering them protectorates in the hope they would serve as a shield against advancing American frontiersmen. At the same time, American agents roamed the region, pledging the Indians to alliances with the United States. In 1785, therefore, when the Spanish order closing the Mississippi became known in the Southwest, part of that region, like the Northwest, lay under a foreign flag and seethed with international intrigue and murderous Indian warfare.

Insisting that their economic livelihood depended on unrestricted navigation of the Mississippi, the rugged men of the western waters cried out in angry protest against the Spanish closure. They found it far easier and less expensive to get their produce, such as tobacco and wheat, to eastern markets via the river and the sea than to attempt to haul it over the backbreaking trails of the mountains. Those impatient frontiersmen, supported by the southern states, demanded that Congress force Spain to reopen the river.

Delegates from the Northeast, representing merchant and shipowning interests, however, were not greatly concerned about the problems of the western settlers. What they wanted most from Spain was a commercial treaty that would allow them to trade in her ports, particularly in the New World, a trade they had enjoyed briefly during the war but that Spain had stopped after the peace.

Fearing that the frontiersmen might try to settle by force what Congress could not solve by diplomacy, the Spaniards appeared more concerned about the angry Westerners than did the American government. There was always the danger that they might try to sweep aside Spain's lamentable frontier defenses, occupy the disputed borderlands, force open the Mississippi, gain control of New Orleans, and impose an illicit commerce on Spain's wealthier domains to the south. To forestall that, Spain attempted to foster a separatist movement in the Southwest, particularly in the Kentucky area. With the bait of special trading privileges on the Mississippi she hoped to wean the settlers from their American ties and perhaps win them to Spanish allegiance.

Unlike England, moreover, Spain was willing to negotiate with the new republic over its grievances and make limited concessions, but not without some equivalent. In return for recognition of her exclusive right to control the lower reaches of the Mississippi, she was willing to modify her most extensive boundary claims and agree to a commercial treaty granting trading privileges in certain of her homeland ports to Americans. In its essentials, this was the position taken by Don Diego de Gardoqui, the envoy Spain sent to the United States in 1785 to negotiate over the unsettled issues.

The Jay-Gardoqui Treaty

Gardoqui, who knew Jay and spoke English well, was a clever diplomat and something of a gay blade who was prepared to suffer for his country in the drawing rooms of America. Jay, he reported, was "a very self-centered man, which passion his wife augments, because, in addition to considering herself meritoriously and being rather vain, she likes to be catered to and even more to receive presents." [15] Through Mrs. Jay, he believed, he would gain her and her husband's friendship. Gardoqui apparently did not find it a hardship paying special attention to the attractive Mrs. Jay, giving her presents and escorting her to dances and other festivities.

Jay's original instructions bound him to insist on free navigation of the Mississippi and a boundary settlement at the thirty-first parallel, but Gardoqui could not yield on both points. When he offered commercial concessions, eagerly desired by the American seaboard merchants, for a temporary closing of the Mississippi, Jay, a New Yorker, considered the terms good. After extended discussions, Jay and Gardoqui in 1786 agreed to a commercial treaty in which the United States, in return for Spanish trading concessions, would "forbear" use of the Spanish portion of the Mississippi for thirty years, but would not yield on the "right" of navigation.

In August, Jay asked Congress for a change of instructions so that he could complete the negotiation on the proposed terms, arguing that the immediate navigation of the Mississippi could be obtained only by a war for which the United States was unprepared. "Why, therefore," he asked, "should we not (for a valuable consideration, too) consent to forbear to use what we know is not in our power to use?" By a simple majority of seven to five Jay won a change of instructions, but had split Congress along sectional lines. All the southern states voted against him.

To the Southerner it appeared that Jay was willing to sacrifice the Southwest to the interests of the Northeast. The Virginian James Monroe, for example, condemned the proposal as one "of the most extraordinary transactions I have ever known, a minister negotiating expressly for the purpose of defeating the object of his instructions, and by a long train of intrigue & management seducing the representatives of the states to concur in it." [16] Furious Westerners talked of rebelling, even of seeking British protection if the treaty were ratified. "To sell us and make us vassals to the merciless Spaniards is a grievance not to be borne," one of them said. "Should we tamely submit to such manacles we should be unworthy of the name of Americans."

Since the approval of nine states was necessary for ratification and the southern states would not yield, Jay and Gardoqui never completed their treaty. Southern distrust of the North, nonetheless, lingered on, almost blocked ratification of the new federal Constitution in Virginia, and was largely responsible for the constitutional rule requiring a two-thirds vote of the Senate for approval of treaties.

Seeking to take advantage of the Southwest's suspicions of the Northeast and the central government, Gardoqui, after the failure of his treaty, turned to intrigue with the idea of creating an independent state in the Southwest amenable to Spanish policy. A murky figure in Spain's plans to detach the Southwest from the Union was General James Wilkinson, an American veteran of the Revolution. While holding a commission from his own government, Wilkinson accepted bribes and swore a secret oath of allegiance to Spain. To facilitate their plans of winning over the frontiersmen, the Spaniards in December, 1788, opened the Mississippi to American use under a special licensing system and even allowed Westerners to land their cargoes at New Orleans. Despite this toll use of the river, the basic difficulties between Spain and the United States, as the Confederation expired, remained unsettled.

The Nootka Sound Crisis

Under the Articles of Confederation American diplomacy lacked effectiveness. Keenly aware of their country's impotence, some of America's leading statesmen argued that a respected foreign policy could be based only on a stronger national government. John Jay, for instance, had summed up the problems of foreign relations by saying that "to be respectable abroad, it is necessary to be so at home: and that will not be the case until our public faith acquires more strength." [17] The new nation gained that confidence in 1789, when the federal Constitution gave the central government power over trade and commerce and exclusive control over foreign affairs.

George Washington, therefore, became President in April, 1789, with a government capable of acting decisively in foreign affairs for the whole nation. Since the Constitution did not provide for a foreign office, Congress created the Department of Foreign Affairs in July, but six weeks later changed the name to the Department of State. Although Washington appointed Thomas Jefferson the first Secretary of State, he did not wait for Jefferson's return from France before attempting to improve relations with England, the most pressing of the problems in foreign relations that he had inherited from the Confederation government.

In this, his first diplomatic venture, Washington made use of an old friend, Gouverneur Morris, then on private business in Paris, as a special executive agent. He asked Morris to go to London to try to open formal diplomatic relations with England, seek a commercial treaty, and begin negotiations for a settlement of American grievances. Morris went, but attained none of his objectives. Not until a crisis with Spain in North America threatened war did the British even consider exchanging ministers with the United States.

The crisis originated on remote Nootka Sound, on the west coast of Vancouver Island in what is now British Columbia. Spain claimed that territory and declared it closed to all foreigners. When some British traders attempted to establish a post on the Sound in 1789, Spanish authorities attacked them, seized several of their ships, and drove them out. Both England and Spain then alerted their allies and prepared for war.

During the crisis, Washington turned to his department heads for advice in shaping a policy in case England should try to strike at the Spaniards in Louisiana, Florida, and New Orleans by cutting across the United States from Canada and thus make American soil a battleground. Alexander Hamilton, the Secretary of the Treasury, favored granting England permission to move troops across American territory, but Jefferson, who feared British encirclement, opposed this view. Fortunately no war came, and the President did not have to act on the conflicting advice he received.

Spain had counted on France for help, but since France was in the throes of revolution, she turned down her ally's plea. Realizing that alone she could not cope with England, Spain bowed before an ultimatum. In the Nootka Sound Convention of 1790, she agreed to restore English property and recognized the right of Englishmen to trade and settle in territory she had formerly claimed as exclusively Spanish.[18]

Of special significance for the United States was the fact that the crisis had caused concern in London over the American reaction. British officials feared that if war had broken out with Spain, the United States might have attempted to settle some of its grievances by force, mainly by taking the Northwest posts. As a result, British policy toward the United States changed. American friendship now acquired a new importance and for the first time since independence the British government was ready to make limited concessions.

Commerce, Politics, and British Policy

More important than the Nootka Sound crisis in stimulating a change in British policy was the threat of commercial discrimination. The new federal government, the British realized, was strong enough to carry out discriminatory commercial legislation against them. Arguing that Englishmen were "mounting their navigation on the ruin of ours," Secretary Jefferson, for instance, urged a policy of retaliation against British trade and shipping. It might, he explained to the President, induce England to agree to a commercial treaty, end her violations of the peace treaty, and establish formal, or full, diplomatic relations. With his support, friends in Congress early in 1791 proposed several bills that would have imposed discriminatory duties on British goods and threatened, therefore, to destroy Britain's most valued commerce.

Since Hamilton had anchored his financial system on revenues from British trade, commercial foreign policy now became a political issue in the United States. If the anti-British bills became law, they would ruin Hamilton's system, and, as Hamilton himself saw it, the strong government he desired for the United States. Through his followers in Congress, therefore, he managed to block the Jeffersonian legislation. Nonetheless, the threat of retaliatory tariffs and tonnage duties had alarmed British traders, who feared the growing strength of the anti-British or Jeffersonian coalition in the American government.

All of these factors contributed to the change in British policy, a change reflected in Britain's decision to open normal diplomatic relations with her offspring. The first British Minister to the United States, George Hammond, a young man of twenty-seven years, arrived in Philadelphia in October, 1791, with instructions to combat anti-British trade legislation, but otherwise with severely limited powers. As a result of those limitations, Hammond's discussions with Jefferson of differences between their countries solved nothing. England, in effect, had not yet become sufficiently interested in a settlement to offer Americans the important concessions they desired.

Hamilton also contributed to Jefferson's failure to make headway. Opposed to anything which might injure relations with England, Hamilton secretly informed British officials that the Secretary of State's views did not represent administration policy and hence implied that they could be disregarded with impunity.

Such meddling in foreign affairs was possible because, next to Washington, Hamilton was the most powerful man in government. Although in theory the Secretary of State and not the Secretary of the Treasury should have the major role in shaping foreign policy, Hamilton had more influence over that policy than did Jefferson. Hamilton's power came from his ability to influence the President. His ideas were congenial to Washington's own views and hence usually became the basis for the administration's foreign policy.

So angry did Jefferson become over Hamilton's interference in his department that on the last day of 1793 the Virginian resigned his post to share the leadership with James Madison of an opposition movement against the administration. That movement crystallized into the Republican party.

Hamilton, on the other hand, ruled as leader of the administration forces and of those men who supported the policies of the administration. His followers became the core of the Federalist party.

The formation of these first national political parties reflected practical and philosophical differences over foreign policy, over the best means to advance the national interest. Hamilton based his thinking on the conviction that America's welfare was tied closely to England and that the French alliance should be destroyed. Jefferson, who called the French alliance the "sheet anchor" of American foreign policy, distrusted England and believed that a policy favorable to France would serve America best.

Before resigning, Jefferson had also tried to resolve the differences with Spain, but his Spanish policy, like his English policy, made no progress. Yet foreign policy made headway in one direction. Under Hamilton's skillful guidance the government from 1790 to 1795 paid off its war debts to Spain and France.[19] Events in France, meanwhile, had created new tensions in world affairs and new problems for American foreign policy.

Revolutionary France and Nonentanglement

Shortly after Washington's inauguration the French Revolution began. Its expansion so divided emerging political parties that foreign policy in the United States became perhaps the foremost political issue. The international wars stemming from that Revolution occupied the European powers so completely that the United States finally settled its frontier problems advantageously and peacefully with both Britain and Spain. The European wars of the French Revolution also gave a hothouse growth to a number of long-lasting principles, such as neutrality and nonentanglement, in the history of American foreign policy.

American statesmen realized they would have to shape new principles when they received news that on February 1, 1793, France had declared war on England, Holland, and Spain. What had been a war confined to continental Europe now spread to American shores as a result of bitter maritime controversies. By the terms of the French alliance, the United States in time of war, if called upon, was committed to defend France's West Indies. Washington, therefore, turned to his advisers and asked if the United States had to go to war to honor its treaty obligations to France. In effect, the President had to decide on principles that would guide the nation's official attitude toward the belligerents.

All of the advisers agreed that the government should adopt a policy of neutrality, but disagreed on its definition. Hamilton and his supporters urged a policy of "impartial" neutrality favorable to England because it called for a narrow interpretation of American obligations under the French treaties of 1778. In contrast, Jefferson desired a "benevolent" neutrality beneficial to France, one based on a broad interpretation of obligations under the French treaties.

Both sides were able to cite authorities in support of their own views, mainly because the idea of neutrality in international relations was changing. By definition, neutrality implies impartiality, meaning that a nonbelligerent should not favor one belligerent over another. In the past, however, most "neutral" powers had not been officially impartial. Without taking part in hostilities, they had usually favored one belligerent over another and had aided that favorite with special concessions. Hugo Grotius, the seventeenth-century Dutch jurist and "father of international law," had supported such a theory of neutrality. He expected neutrals to take sides.

In the eighteenth century, Emmerich de Vattel, a Swiss diplomat and publicist, propounded a new theory. Unless obligated by treaty to a belligerent, he said, a neutral could not give to one belligerent what it refused to another. A neutral nation, in other words, must be impartial.

In contrast to Jefferson, Hamilton urged the newer theory, and Washington accepted it. Most nations in the nineteenth century, in fact, came to adopt the idea of impartial neutrality in theory, but rarely in practice. Even in Hamilton's case, the new theory did not mean impartiality. It favored England, mainly because England had no special treaty rights with the United States.[20]

Washington made the new idea official policy in a proclamation of neutrality issued on April 22, 1793. It declared the United States at peace with both England and France and warned Americans against committing hostile acts against either belligerent. Disappointed, Jefferson maintained that only the "ardent spirit" of the political opposition could prevent the new policy from becoming a "mere English neutrality."

Next, Washington turned to his department heads for advice on general treaty obligations. Now that France had overthrown the monarchy, he wondered if the treaties of 1778 were still in effect and if he should receive a minister from France's republican government. Hamilton and Jefferson again differed. The Secretary of the Treasury argued that the President should suspend the treaties until the French Revolution clarified itself and should receive the new Minister with a carefully worded reservation on recognition of the republican regime. Hamilton, in other words, wished to use the French Revolution as an excuse for cutting loose from the French treaties and steering the United States closer to England.

Jefferson contended that the treaties were in force, for they were not between particular governments but between nations and hence the United States could not unilaterally abrogate them because the contracting government, the French monarchy, no longer existed. He also urged that Washington receive the new Minister without qualification. In this instance the President followed the Secretary of State's advice. He recognized the French Republic, accepted the treaties as continuing in force, and decided to receive the republican Minister.

Dilemmas of Neutrality

The French alliance, as some feared it might, did not drag the United States into the war. Since Americans had no navy and could contribute little in direct aid to the winning of the war, France did not invoke the alliance by asking them to defend her West Indies. The French, in fact, believed that American neutrality, if interpreted in their favor, would be more useful to them than would belligerency.

As provided in the treaties of 1778, France expected the United States to give her naval vessels and privateers special privileges, not available to the British, in American ports. With her shipping virtually swept from the seas by the British fleet, France also planned to use American merchantmen to bring urgently needed supplies to her home and colonial ports. To stimulate this trade previously closed to foreigners, she opened it to neutral, meaning American, shipping.

Eager for profit, Americans flocked into French Caribbean ports and immediately built up a flourishing commerce. Since it aided her enemy and strengthened a maritime rival, Britain resented this bloated trade and beginning in June, 1793, took steps to throttle it. By three Orders in Council, essentially executive decrees, of June and November, 1793, and January, 1794, the British government enforced the dictum that commerce prohibited in time of peace would not be allowed during war. Known as the Rule of 1756, from its application by England in the Seven Years' War, it was destroying American commerce with and between the French colonies.

Enforcing the Orders in Council, British warships in the Caribbean swooped down on American merchantmen, and their officers stripped Americans of property and dignity. They confiscated ships and cargoes and impressed seamen. In seizing ships running between American and French colonial ports, a trade France had permitted in time of peace, moreover, the British went beyond the Rule of 1756.

American newspapers played up the Caribbean indignities, whipping up anti-British sentiment. Demands for action against England became so insistent as to endanger Washington's policy of neutrality. Washington, as a result, now found himself in a dilemma. In the commercial treaty of 1778 with France, the United States had committed itself to the practice of maritime principles which Britain had not recognized and consistently violated, but without a navy the United States could not insist that the British respect those principles.

It seemed that to attempt enforcement of the "small navy" principles, such as free ships make free goods, in the French treaty against British naval power would mean war, a war with England that Federalists wished at almost all costs to avoid. Not to try to enforce them, in the view of the Republicans, would violate the French treaty and might lead to war with France.

News of the Caribbean captures had reached Philadelphia, the capital, together with evidence of renewed British hostility in the Northwest. The troubles in the Northwest had grown out of Washington's efforts to subdue Indians there with federal arms in 1790 and 1791. Although those two expeditions had failed, they had appeared to threaten British control over the Indians south of the treaty line of 1783. The British, therefore, had offered to mediate the conflict between the Americans and the Indians, hoping to profit from the mediation. They urged Americans to accept a "neutral, Indian barrier state" in the Northwest, one that would protect Canada against American advances and at the same time save the fur trade. Not even Hamiltonians, however, could accept the idea of carving a buffer state out of American soil.

Washington then tried for the third time to crush Indian resistance by placing General "Mad Anthony" Wayne in command of frontier forces on the Ohio. In the winter of 1793 Wayne moved his army into the Indian country of the Northwest, a move that British frontier officials saw as a threat to Canada, for they believed his true objectives were the posts they occupied.

In February, 1794, Lord Dorchester, Sir Guy Carleton, the Governor General of Canada, told a delegation of Indians, among them representatives of the ones Wayne was preparing to punish, that American settlements in the Northwest were unauthorized. Soon, he said, the Indians would be able to recover the settled lands because Britain and the United States would be at war within the year.

Dorchester's intemperate words, seemingly spoken to stiffen Indian resistance, as well as an order given to his troops at about the same time to occupy Fort Miami, sixty miles southwest of Detroit in territory clearly American, enraged Americans. Talk of war became common. Thus, early in 1794 the grievances of the peace treaty, the failure of Americans to obtain a commercial treaty, the Caribbean spoliations, and the frontier troubles all combined with anti-British propaganda to produce an Anglo-American crisis.

Responding to the public anger, Congress pressed anti-British legislation. In March it laid a one-month embargo against foreign shipping, an act directed against Britain, and later extended it another month. It also passed various defense measures, among them a bill to fortify harbors, another calling out eighty thousand militia, and one for obtaining additional military stores. In the Senate a non-intercourse bill against England met defeat only by the vote of Vice-President John Adams.

Catching the war spirit, Americans rushed their preparations for defense and even began drilling in volunteer companies. Mobs attacked British sailors and in such places as Norfolk and Baltimore tarred and feathered Americans alleged to sympathize with the British. "Even the Monocrat [Federalist] papers," Jefferson reported, "are obliged to publish the most furious Philippics against England."[21]

Several factors, however, prevented the country from immediately plunging into war. The French, for instance, believed that Americans were obligated to resist British seizure of goods on their ships bound for French ports. Angered by the American failure to attempt to enforce the treaty principle that free ships make free goods, they retaliated by seizing American ships carrying goods to England. They thus violated their treaty obligations to the United States and alienated American shipping interests.

England, moreover, relaxed her Orders in Council and allowed a temporary resumption of American trade in the Caribbean, and even paid for many of the cargoes her navy seized, whereas France did not. Furthermore, wartime trade with England was more lucrative than that with France. In England, too, there were those who sought to avert war, particularly the statesmen who realized that Washington's administration was basically friendly. At the height of the war hysteria, Hammond was even instructed to encourage the American government to maintain its congenial policy. Most important of all as a deterrent to immediate war was the fact that Federalists friendly to England controlled the Senate and the executive branch of the government.

Jay's Treaty

Federalist control of the government made it possible for the President to send a special mission to London to seek an agreement with the British and thus avert war. At first the Federalists agreed upon Hamilton to undertake the task, but he was too unpopular. At Hamilton's suggestion, therefore, Washington chose John Jay, then Chief Justice.

On the basis of diplomatic experience, Jay was admirably qualified for the mission, but politically he was not. As a staunch Federalist and an Anglophile, he was resented by Republicans. From the outset, therefore, his mission became a party issue. Federalists supported it and Republicans did not.

Jay's instructions, drawn up by Hamilton, gave him wide discretion, but told him to do nothing contrary to treaty obligations to France. He was to adjust the grievances arising from the peace treaty of 1783, gain recognition of American principles of neutrality, obtain compensation for seizures of American ships and property, and, if possible, negotiate a commercial treaty. Edmund Randolph, a lukewarm Republican who had succeeded Jefferson as Secretary of State, had managed to add that Jay should consult with Danish and Swedish Ministers in London on the possibility of joining a new armed neutrality then being formed to resist British maritime practices, if the British should prove intractable. Concern that such a league of neutrals might form, in fact, had been a factor in inducing the British to negotiate at this time.

Fearing any action that might endanger relations with the British, Hamilton blunted the only coercive weapon Jay possessed. He told the British Minister in Philadelphia that American policy was predicated on the principle of avoiding entanglement in European affairs and hence the United States would not join the new armed neutrality. Hamilton thus weakened Jay's already shaky bargaining position.

By ignoring most of his confusing instructions, Jay obtained a commercial treaty signed on November 19, 1794. The treaty itself was Britain's most important concession. Others were promises to evacuate the Northwest posts and to pay for the Caribbean spoliations. Britain did not, however, repudiate the spoliations.

Trading privileges were limited. Jay obtained few commercial concessions the United States had not enjoyed before the treaty. A privilege allowing trade with the British West Indies was so restrictive that later not even a Federalist senate would accept it. The treaty said nothing about the impressment of American seamen, nothing about abducted slaves, nothing about Britain's tampering with the Indians. Furthermore, contrary to the spirit of the French commercial treaty of 1778, Jay acquiesced in the Rule of 1756 and agreed that the British could seize enemy property and food on American ships if they paid for them. Other problems, namely definition of a disputed boundary between Maine and Canada and to the west of Lake Superior, payment of prewar debts to the British, and the amount of British compensation for maritime spoliations, were to be referred to mixed arbitral commissions.

When news of the treaty reached America the public reaction was hostile. Republicans condemned it as a sellout to England. One of them said, "YES, Sir, you have bitched it; you have indeed put your foot in it, Mr. Jay—for shame, Sir." Another expressed his resentment in rhyme:

> Is it again the patriot's fate,
> To mourn his country's fallen state,
> To weep her honour lost;
> To see her bend at Britain's throne,
> No wrongs redress'd, her freedom gone,
> Her independence an empty boast?[22]

Although crowds burned Jay in effigy and even stoned Hamilton when he spoke in defense of Jay's Treaty, Federalists gave it solid support. In the Senate they blocked Republican efforts to defeat the treaty by approving it 20 to 10 on June 24, 1795, with not a single vote to spare. After some hesitation President Washington ratified it. Ratifications were exchanged in London on October 28, and on February 29, 1796, Washington proclaimed the treaty as law. Still the Republicans refused to give up the struggle, carrying it to the House of Representatives where they tried to withhold funds necessary to carry out the treaty. Again, this time by the narrow margin of three votes, they failed. It was Washington's support that saved the treaty and hence probably averted war with England.

In spite of its obvious flaws and the harsh controversy it had aroused, Jay's Treaty served American foreign policy well. At a time when the country was unprepared for war and partisan feeling over foreign policy was so strong that a war with England might have split the Union, it kept the peace. It also finally brought Britain's full execution of the peace treaty of 1783 and stripped the Indians of the Northwest of British support. Thus those Indians, a year after General Wayne's victory in the Battle of Fallen Timbers, came to terms in the Treaty of Fort Greenville on August 3, 1795, when they ceded most of the Ohio country. The United States had finally won full control of the Northwest.

By easing old grievances, Jay's Treaty became the first major step since the American Revolution toward an Anglo-American *rapprochement*. This *rapprochement*, however, brought trouble elsewhere. The treaty's concessions to England on

THE BOUNDARY DISPUTE
WITH SPAIN, 1783–1795

neutral trade, particularly its acceptance of the seizure of noncontraband goods if payment were made for them, gave France grounds for claiming violation of her treaties of 1778. Many Americans, moreover, agreed with the view that Jay's Treaty was incompatible with obligations to France.

Pinckney's Treaty

While Jay had been negotiating in England, events in Europe had caused a change in Spanish diplomacy favorable to the United States. Spain had been ready for peace with France and even an alliance, but in withdrawing from the war as England's ally and thus reversing her foreign policy, she feared English reprisals. The fact that Spain had decided to break relations with England just as the American government was drawing closer to England influenced Spain's policy toward the United States. Spain feared an attack, perhaps by American frontiersmen, perhaps by Anglo-American forces, on her North American colonies while she was still involved in the European war and helpless to protect them. Her ministers, therefore, decided to forestall such an attack by buying American friendship.

In the summer of 1794 Spain asked the United States to renew disrupted negotiations by assigning a new envoy to Madrid. Washington complied by sending Thomas Pinckney, the Minister to Britain. Pinckney's instructions required that Americans be given the right to navigate the Mississippi River "in its whole length and breadth, from its source to the sea."[23]

For her good will and willingness to make concessions, Spain at first tried to induce the United States to join her and France in a triple alliance for the common preservation of Spanish and American territory in North America. When that plan failed she offered a boundary settlement and free navigation of the Mississippi for an alliance between herself and the United States. Pinckney refused both offers. Finally, in August, 1795, he wrote home that the Spanish king was ready "to sacrifice something of what he considered as his right, to testify to his good will to us."

A few months later, on October 27, the Spaniards signed the Treaty of San Lorenzo, usually called Pinckney's Treaty, which gave virtually all that Pinckney's instructions asked. In addition to unrestricted navigation of the Mississippi, the United States secured a three-year right, subject to renewal, to deposit goods at New Orleans for transshipment, a boundary settlement in the Southwest at the thirty-first parallel, and a promise that Spain would not incite the Indians on her frontier to attack Americans. The United States, in turn, said it would prevent Indians in its territory from striking at Spanish lands. Both countries also agreed on the following: that free ships make free goods, a liberal noncontraband list, and a plan for settlement of claims.

Pinckney's Treaty, a diplomatic victory for the United States, was as welcome to most Americans as Jay's Treaty was unwelcome. One senator remarked, "the Spanish treaty was so favorable, that if the Spanish Government had asked the American Minister to dictate his own terms, he could scarcely have asked for better." Yet it apparently was Jay's Treaty, which the Spaniards feared as the beginning of an Anglo-American alliance, as well as American frontier pressure, that spurred them into negotiating Pinckney's Treaty.[24] The Senate approved Pinckney's Treaty unanimously in March, 1796.

Federalist diplomacy thus achieved noteworthy objectives, but, it should be remembered, if England had not been at war with France, she might have conceded nothing, not even Jay's Treaty. If Spain had not faced war with England, she might not have yielded Pinckney's Treaty. Both countries made concessions because they were more concerned with their European policies than with those in America. Nonetheless, with the Jay and Pinckney Treaties, the United States for the first time since achieving independence reached agreements that would in fact free its soil of foreign troops and extend its sovereignty to the limits of its boundaries as established in the peace of 1783.

Citizen Genêt

Federalist policy toward France, however, did not lead to similarly fortunate results. Jay's Treaty, looked upon by the French as a betrayal of their alliance of 1778, brought France and the United States to a state of undeclared war between 1797 and 1800. Yet it was not Jay's Treaty alone that touched off hostilities, for relations with France had begun to deteriorate even before Washington had ratified it. It was the mission of "Citizen" Edmond C. Genêt, the French Republic's first emissary to the United States, that brought underlying differences with France to the surface.

Young Genêt was not instructed to invoke the alliance of 1778, but was directed to obtain a liberal interpretation favorable to France of certain articles in the commercial treaty of that year. He also had plans for French conquest, with American assistance, of Spanish America and Canada, for it should be remembered that at this time England and Spain were allied against France. To carry out that part of his mission, Genêt brought blank military commissions to be given to Americans willing to fight France's enemies. In addition, he was secretly instructed to shower Americans with pro-French propaganda.

Genêt's mission could not succeed without American aid, aid which would probably have led to British countermeasures and might have drawn the United States into the war. Genêt's objectives, moreover, conflicted with Washington's policy of impartial neutrality.

Landing in Charleston in April, 1793, amid wild cheers reflecting a French frenzy then sweeping the land, Genêt immediately began challenging American neutrality. Aided by South Carolina's governor, he set up prize courts and outfitted privateers to cruise against British shipping. He also commissioned George Rogers Clark to lead an army of frontiersmen against New Orleans.

The Girondin emissary then proceeded overland to Philadelphia, besieged on the way by welcoming crowds. At Richmond, Virginia, in the midst of this flattering acclaim, he received his first jolt when he heard of the proclamation of neutrality. The next one came in Philadelphia where Washington, who was already upset by his antics, greeted him coolly.

Then Genêt and the Hamiltonians clashed over differing interpretations of the commercial treaty of 1778. Seeking to use American ports and seamen for French privateers, Genêt argued that the treaty "expressly" authorized France to use those ports for equipping privateers and for condemning and selling prizes. Actually, as the Hamiltonians insisted, the treaty obligated the United States merely to close its ports to the outfitting of British privateers and to their prizes. While the United States could allow the French privateers and their prizes to use its ports, the treaty did not, as Genêt contended, automatically give France what was denied to Britain.

As a gesture of friendship, Jeffersonians at first believed that the government should grant France the privileges denied Britain, but the Hamiltonians did not. Such a gesture, they argued, would violate the policy of impartial neutrality and might lead to war with England. Despite his French sympathies, even Jefferson finally agreed that to remain neutral the United States had to prevent the French from using American ports as bases for hostile forays.

The Hamiltonians and Genêt also clashed over money. To finance his military expeditions and to pay for food he purchased and sent to France, Genêt requested advance payment on America's debt to France. Hamilton opposed such payment, and Washington then refused to make it. Furthermore, Washington asked the French Minister to order French privateers that offended neutrality from American ports.

Bitterly disappointed by the lack of sympathy within the government for France's cause, Genêt defied Washington, flagrantly so, when he outfitted a captured British ship, *The Little Sarah*, in Philadelphia and sent her to sea as a French privateer. Popular sympathy for the French Revolution had led him to believe that Washington and his policies lacked public support and that he himself could obtain the support he needed from the people. Allegedly, he threatened to appeal over the head of the President directly to the people, an accusation that Genêt insisted was false. Whether or not he uttered such a threat, Washington decided to get rid of him, a decision endorsed by Hamilton.[25]

Even Jefferson, who had at first praised Genêt, expressed disgust. "Never in my opinion," he said, "was so calamitous an appointment made, as that of the present Minister of F[rance] here. Hot headed, all imagination, no judgment, passionate, disrespectful & even indecent towards the P[resident] in his written as well as verbal communications, talking of appeals from him to Congress, from them to the people, urging the most unreasonable & groundless propositions. . . ."[26]

When Washington demanded Genêt's recall, a new revolutionary government in France obliged. It ordered the new Minister, Joseph Fauchet, to arrest Genêt and send him back for trial and probable execution, an order Washington would not allow Fauchet to carry out. Genêt later married an American and remained in the United States for the rest of his life.

Although headstrong and intemperate, Genêt was not a wild-eyed revolutionary. He was an intelligent, though rash, young man of thirty who tried to carry out an almost impossible mission. Any French minister with his instructions would probably have run into difficulties.

British complaints against Genêt's activities, meanwhile, had led Washington to define neutral obligations. On June 5, 1794, Congress passed a Neutrality Act that made Washington's principles of impartial neutrality the law of the land by prohibiting foreign recruiting in the United States and belligerent activity in coastal waters and ports.

Morris and Monroe in Paris

In Paris, at this time, Gouverneur Morris, the American Minister, was alienating the French government as effectively as Genêt had outraged Washington. As a confirmed aristocrat, a counterrevolutionary, and a dabbler in Royalist intrigue,

Morris had irked French governments from the beginning of his mission. Favoring a constitutional monarchy over a republic, he did his best to save Louis XVI from the guillotine, going so far as to draft a plan for Louis' rescue from virtual imprisonment in the Tuileries. During the height of the French Revolution, he even used the American legation and his own home as asylums for French nobles fleeing the clutches of Republican authorities. Such activity, while in some instances humanitarian to a laudable degree, violated French laws and provided cause for official resentment.

Morris' hostility to the French Revolution showed in the reports he sent home. Since he was a close friend of the President, he often went over the Secretary of State's head to correspond directly with Washington. Morris' reports, in fact, increased Washington's fears of happenings in France. Jefferson, for instance, had complained that Morris "kept the President's mind constantly poisoned with his forebodings." [27]

The French Foreign Office believed that Morris' reports were gradually destroying Franco-American friendship. One of the objectives of Genêt's mission, in fact, had been to offset Morris' "malevolent" influence on Franco-American relations. Finally, when Washington asked for Genêt's recall, the Jacobin government insisted that in return he must recall Morris and send an envoy who sympathized with their revolution. Washington reluctantly complied.

Since at this time Jay was headed for England and the French suspected that his mission might endanger the alliance of 1778, the French request fell in with Federalist plans, for Federalist statesmen wanted to calm French distrust of the Jay mission and assure France of American friendship. In the spring of 1794, therefore, Washington appointed James Monroe, an ardent Jeffersonian, to succeed Morris. Monroe was instructed to assure the French that Jay could do nothing that would weaken America's attachment to France.

Ironically, Monroe overplayed his part, at least from the Federalist point of view, and from the beginning incurred Federalist displeasure. In a florid speech before the National Convention, the French governing body that received him, a speech marked by anti-British overtones, Monroe stressed the bond between France and America and voiced sympathy for France in her war. Washington and other Federalists were agreed that Monroe had "stepped over the true line" of neutrality.

After Jay's Treaty was signed, Monroe found himself in an impossible position. When the French asked him if it were an alliance, he denied that it was. "I cannot believe," he said, "that an American minister would ever forget the connections between the United States and France, which every day's experience demonstrate to be in the interest of both Republics still further to cement." [28]

Later, when Monroe learned the contents of Jay's Treaty, he feared it would destroy Franco-American amity. Yet the new Secretary of State, Timothy Pickering, an uncompromising Federalist, sent him instructions to defend the treaty. "In our new engagements," Pickering said, "we violate no prior obligations."[29]

Nonetheless, the French threatened to abrogate the alliance of 1778 and other reprisals because of Jay's Treaty, and even talked of war. In March, 1796, when the French presented him with a list of their grievances against the American government, Monroe, it seemed to the Federalists, made merely a tepid defense of Federalist policy. Washington, therefore, recalled him in disgrace.

The Directory, France's new executive body, meanwhile, had begun reprisals short of war. In October, for example, it recalled its Minister to the United States without appointing a successor. At the same time it announced a decree that authorized French warships to deal with American vessels "as these suffer the English to treat them."

Before Monroe left Paris, the Directory said that it would "no longer recognize nor receive a minister plenipotentiary from the United States, until a reparation of the grievances demanded of the American government."[30] In an effort to overcome the French crisis, Washington, however, had already appointed Charles Cotesworth Pinckney, a Federalist, to succeed Monroe. The Directory not only refused to receive Pinckney, but also forced him to leave France under humiliating circumstances.

In the United States, meanwhile, Genêt's successors tried to defeat Jay's Treaty by tampering with Congress and meddling in domestic politics. This meddling infuriated Washington who threw his immense prestige behind the treaty and against the French. It also prompted him to carry out a decision he had made earlier.

Washington's Farewell Address

Tired by the strain and abuse of politics and upset by the tensions of foreign policy, Washington decided to announce his retirement. French intrigues "in the internal concerns of our country" convinced him, moreover, that a warning to the nation was needed. Following Hamilton's advice, he withheld the farewell warning until three months before the electors gathered to vote for a President. Then, on September 19, 1796, he offered it to the people through the newspapers.

Washington had planned a valedictory to the nation in 1792 and James Madison had drafted one, but Hamilton wrote most of the new version and made it a campaign document designed to assure a Federalist victory in the nation's first contested presidential election. Washington told Hamilton that were it not for the status of "party disputes" and foreign affairs he would not have considered it necessary to revise his valedictory. Yet the bulk of the message, one of the most influential statements on American foreign policy ever made, dealt with domestic affairs.

Washington opened the Farewell Address by announcing he would not be a candidate for a third term. Then he stressed the evils of party spirit which "opens the door to foreign influence and corruption." Through party passions, he said, "the policy and the will of one country, are subjected to the policy and will of another." Having in mind, undoubtedly, the French Republic, he advised against "a passionate attachment of one Nation for another." Such "sympathy for the favourite nation," he said, leads to wars and quarrels "without adequate inducement and justification."

A free people, Washington continued, ought to be "constantly awake" to "the insidious wiles of foreign influence." Then in the oft-quoted "Great rule of conduct" he advised that with Europe we should have "as little *political* connection as possible." While stressing fidelity to "existing engagements," he said, "'tis our true policy to steer clear of permanent alliances with any portion of the foreign world." But, he added, "we may safely trust to temporary alliances for extraordinary emergencies."

In summary, the President defended his policies, particularly his heavily criticized policy of neutrality, struck at French meddling in American politics, and denounced the dangerous implications of the French alliance.

Federalists praised the address, Republicans denounced it as political propaganda, the French disliked it, and a few days later Pierre A. Adet, the French Minister who had not yet been recalled, threw himself openly into the presidential campaign to see to it that Washington's words would not have their intended effect. By electioneering against John Adams, the Federalist candidate, and in favor of Thomas Jefferson, the Republican standard bearer, Adet made himself one of the main issues in the election. Only Jefferson's victory he warned, would eliminate the possibility of war with France.

Adet's interference actually did Jefferson more harm than good. Federalists campaigned successfully as representing the party of patriotism, pitting Washington and Adams against Adet and the Republicans, who appeared to be in league with a foreign power. Beware of foreign influence, Federalists told the voters, "decide between the address of the President and the [French]."[31] Adet's activities, in fact, seemed to confirm the warnings in Washington's Farewell Address. Adams won the Presidency.

Then in the last weeks of Washington's administration, relations with France deteriorated so badly that war seemed imminent. In the Caribbean, French decrees struck at American shipping. On March 2, 1797, two days before Washington left office, the Directory published a decree announcing renewed seizures of American ships and that Americans found serving the British would be treated as pirates. Charging that Jay's Treaty vitiated the commercial treaty of 1778, France again said she would no longer recognize the principle that free ships make free goods. In effect, she announced a limited maritime war against American commerce.

The XYZ Affair

When John Adams took over the Presidency, therefore, his most pressing problem was the crisis with France. To deal with it, he immediately called a special session of Congress. He asked Congress to enact defense measures and to appropriate funds for them so that the country would be prepared in case of war. Contrary to the desires of the war hawks within his own party, he also asked approval for a special mission to France to resolve the crisis. Congress did not enact all the legislation he requested, but did approve the mission.

Adams' mission consisted of Pinckney, then in Holland, John Marshall, a prominent Virginia Federalist, and Elbridge Gerry, a personal friend and lukewarm Federalist soon to become a Republican. Those commissioners were to offer concessions on neutral rights similar to those in Jay's Treaty. In return, France was expected to restore normal diplomatic relations, respect American rights at sea, consent to release the United States from its obligations under the treaties of 1778 and the later consular convention, particularly from the guarantee of the French West Indies.

The commissioners met in Paris in October, 1797, but Charles Maurice de Talleyrand-Périgord, the Directory's Minister of Foreign Affairs, refused to receive them officially. Through intermediaries, including a seductive woman, he demanded a bribe of $250,000, a "loan," but in fact a gift, of several million dollars, and an apology for unfriendly remarks about France that Adams had made in his message to Congress.

Bribery itself did not shock the Americans, but they had no money for a bribe and no instructions to negotiate a loan. Besides, the so-called loan would have violated American neutrality. Nor did they have assurances they could obtain what they desired if they paid. The bribe would pay only for the privilege of presenting their case, not for negotiation. Declaring that they would not make such an "absolute surrender of the independence of the United States," the commissioners rejected Talleyrand's proposals.

Nonetheless, the urbane Talleyrand, though never directly, persisted in his demands, for the French mistakenly believed that most Americans were still pro-French and would not tolerate failure of the mission and a complete rupture. Adams would not, they were convinced, risk war with France and civil war in the United States.

Thus, when one of Talleyrand's excitable agents threatened war, Marshall answered that America would then protect herself. "You do not speak to the point," the agent cried out, "it is expected that you will offer money. . . . What is your answer?"

"It is no; no;" Pinckney blurted out, "not a sixpence!" Legend later transformed this into the slogan, "Millions for defense, but not one cent for tribute."[32]

Finally, after months of waiting to be received, Marshall and Pinckney left Paris. Believing that he could prevent war, Gerry stayed a while longer. A few months later, in July, 1798, he sailed for home empty-handed, except for a message from Talleyrand saying that France desired a reconciliation, peace not war.

The first of the commissioners' dispatches telling of their shameful treatment, meanwhile, had arrived in Philadelphia. That story convinced Adams that he could not appease the Directory. On March 19, 1798, he went before Congress, explained that France had refused to receive his peace mission, and asked for power to arm merchant ships and take other defensive measures.

Republicans would not believe the President's charges. They accused him of sabre-rattling and on April 2 rammed a demand for the dispatches through the House of Representatives. Adams then sent the dispatches to the House and

NOT ONE CENT FOR TRIBUTE

This Federalist cartoon of 1799 shows the five-headed French Directory demanding money from the three American commissioners.

Senate, but substituted the letters X, Y, and Z for the names of Talleyrand's agents. Astounded by what they read, Republicans in the House voted solidly against a measure calling for publication, but in the Senate the Federalists had the upper hand and voted for publication.

The published dispatches sent a tremor through the country. Sea spoliations and other indignities had enraged Americans. Now the humiliation of Pinckney, Marshall, and Gerry appalled them. France's stock, even among Republicans, fell to unparalleled depths. Federalists now talked openly of war, and Adams, for the first time, became genuinely popular. He was publicly toasted as the nation's foremost patriot and his name was praised in song and poetry.

Reflecting the popular excitement, Adams sent a trenchant message to Congress on June 21, announcing that he would "never send another minister to France without assurances that he will be received, respected, and honored as the representative of a great, free, powerful, and independent nation."[33] Congress responded by authorizing naval retaliation against French sea marauders and other defensive measures previously refused. It created a Navy Department, voted appropriations for new warships, authorized increases in the regular Army, and in July abrogated the French treaties and consular convention. Washington agreed to come out of retirement to lead the new army, an army to be organized by Hamilton, the second in command. Americans, in other words, readied themselves for a war that appeared already upon them.

The Quasi-War and the Convention of 1800

Actually, the United States found itself in a state of quasi- or half-war with France. Neither country declared war and neither authorized offensive hostilities or the capture of private property by warships. The American Navy, whose ships, such as the frigate *Constellation*, won some notable victories, attacked only French warships and privateers and fought primarily to protect commerce.

Limited war suited Adams, but not all Federalists. The extremist, or high Federalists, wished to adopt a bellicose program as a matter of party principle. They wanted a full-scale war as an excuse for crushing the opposition party, expanding the nation's frontiers, and collaborating with England. They supported the alien and sedition acts, which were directed against French and Irish aliens in the United States, and helped muzzle Republican editors and politicians. They supported Hamilton's scheme to send his army into Louisiana and Mexico and expand at the expense of France's weak ally, Spain. They wished to extend naval cooperation with England, such as the exchange of naval recognition signals and the use of British convoys, into an alliance.

Yet, despite the fact that the war fever made the Federalists popular and even gave them majorities in the congressional elections of 1798–1799, most Americans did not want a full-scale conflict. The Federalists who desired war, moreover, were unable to command a majority even within their own party.

Nonetheless, the stepped-up tempo of the naval hostilities and news of the aroused anti-French nationalism in the United States alarmed Frenchmen such as Talleyrand. They were shocked to find that they had overestimated America's pro-French sentiment. An enlarged war offered France no advantage, and hence they wanted none of it. Furthermore, such a war might ruin their plans to reacquire Louisiana, details of which were nearly completed.

These considerations and the fact that France no longer had direct diplomatic relations with the United States led Talleyrand to make peaceful overtures to William Vans Murray, the American Minister at The Hague. Finally, at the insistence of Murray, Talleyrand agreed to meet Adams' conditions for the resumption of diplomatic negotiations. In a letter of September, 1798, he said that any envoy the United States would send to France to reconcile the differences between the two countries "would be undoubtedly received with the respect due to the representative of a free, independent, and powerful nation." [34] At the same time the French repealed decrees against American shipping, restrained their privateers in the West Indies, and respected America's neutral rights as they had not done previously. They had also told various Americans, such as George Logan, a Pennsylvania Quaker who had gone to Paris on his own to try to end the quasi-war, that they wanted peace. [35]

These overtures all had an influence on Adams, who had no sympathy for the high Federalists. With Talleyrand's letter he now felt that he had the necessary assurances for a peace with honor. Without the support of his cabinet, which was disloyal to him, he sent a message to Congress in February, 1799, proposing another attempt at negotiation with the French. He nominated Murray to carry out the mission. That nomination caused a decisive split in the Federalist party, since the extremists, men like Hamilton and Pickering, insisted that the French overtures were meaningless and urged their rejection.

Although the extreme Federalists were unable to defeat Murray's nomination, they forced Adams to expand the peace mission to a commission of three. The new commissioners were reliable Federalists, Chief Justice Oliver Ellsworth and William R. Davie, a former Governor of North Carolina.

The three envoys met in Paris in March, 1800, where Talleyrand, who had become Minister of Foreign Affairs for the Consulate, France's new government led by Napoleon Bonaparte, received them promptly. Negotiations began immediately with a French commission of three headed by Napoleon's brother, Joseph.

As directed by their instructions, the Americans asked the French to pay nearly twenty million dollars in reparations for spoliations against American shipping going back to 1793 and to accept as legal Congress' unilateral abrogation of the treaties of 1778 and 1788. The French argued that the Americans could not have both an indemnity and an annulment of the treaties. The treaties, they said, were either in effect or they were not. If they were dead, then the abrogation was an act that recognized a state of war. The spoliations, therefore, were acts of war and gave no grounds for claims against France. If the treaties were still in force, then France and the United States were still allies, and France could claim American support against her enemies.

Since the French had the better of the argument, when Talleyrand offered a compromise treaty, the American commissioners went beyond their instructions to accept it. That treaty, called the Treaty of Mortefontaine but better known as the Convention of 1800, was signed on September 30, 1800. As finally ratified, it suspended the treaties of 1778 and 1788 and dropped the spoliation claims.[36]

In effect, the American government, which eventually had to assume the claims of its own citizens, paid a bargain price for getting rid of the French treaties, for the Convention of 1800 marked a turning point in American diplomatic history. It paved the way for Napoleon to carry out grandiose schemes for the acquisition of Louisiana and the building of a French empire in North America and by securing his good will laid the groundwork for ceding that province to the United States. The convention also freed the United States from its first "entangling" alliance, an entanglement that contributed to a wariness toward all alliances for a hundred and fifty years.

In negotiating the convention and in thus keeping the peace, moreover, John Adams helped wreck his own party and may have contributed to his own defeat in the election of 1800, for the extreme Federalists deserted him. Yet Adams never regretted his peace missions. "They were," he wrote in later years, "the most disinterested and meritorious actions of my life."[37]

Although Adams bowed out of office in defeat and his administration marked the end of the Federalist era, Federalist statesmen in retrospect could take satisfaction in a proud record in foreign policy. They had successfully guided the young nation through a period of international turmoil and great danger. They left the center of the national stage with the nation's major grievances in foreign affairs settled, its flag flying over all its lands, and most important, its people at peace and not threatened by a major enemy.

NOTES

1. Quoted in Harry R. Warfel, *Noah Webster: Schoolmaster to America* (New York, 1936), p. 60.

2. For an extended analysis see Andrew C. McLaughlin, *The Confederation and the Constitution, 1783–1789* (New York, 1905), pp. 47–52.

3. Quoted in John Fiske, *The Critical Period of American History, 1783–1789* (Boston, 1893), pp. 57–58. Frederick the Great of Prussia also thought American independence would not amount to much. See Henry M. Adams, *Prussian-American Relations, 1775–1871* (Cleveland, 1960), p. 22.

4. Quoted in Frank Monaghan, *John Jay* (New York, 1935), p. 229.

5. John B. Sheffield, *Observations on the Commerce of the American States*, 6th ed. (London, 1784), p. 2.

6. "A Friend to Commerce" in the *Connecticut Gazette and the Universal Intelligencer* (New London, Conn.), Aug. 13, 1794.

7. Sheffield, *Observations on American Commerce*, p. 245.

8. Quoted in Gilbert Chinard, *Honest John Adams* (Boston, 1933), p. 199.

9. *Ibid.*, p. 217.

10. Quoted in George M. Wrong, *Canada and the American Revolution* (New York, 1935), p. 390.

11. Jan. 19, 1785, in Henry P. Johnston, ed., *The Correspondence and Public Papers of John Jay* (4 vols., New York, 1890–93), III, 138.

12. To Dr. Ramsay, Oct. 27, 1786, in Henry A. Washington, ed., *The Writings of Thomas Jefferson* (9 vols., Washington, 1853–54), II, 49.

13. Quoted in George H. Guttridge, *David Hartley, M.P.: An Advocate of Conciliation, 1774–1783* (Berkeley, Calif., 1926), p. 319.

14. To the Comte de Moustier, March 26, 1788, in John C. Fitzpatrick, ed., *The Writings of George Washington* (39 vols., Washington, 1931–44), XXIX, 447–448.

15. Quoted in Monaghan, *John Jay*, p. 257.

16. For the Monroe and Jay quotations, see *ibid.*, pp. 258–259.

17. To Thomas Jefferson, July 14, 1786, in Johnston, *Correspondence of John Jay*, III, 206.

18. For details, see William K. Manning, "The Nootka Sound Controversy" in *Annual Report of the American Historical Association for the Year 1904* (Washington, 1905), pp. 279–478, and Frederick J. Turner, "English Policy toward America in 1790–1791," *The American Historical Review*, VII (July 1902), 706–735 and VIII (Oct. 1902), 78–86.

19. For discussion of the debts, see Samuel F. Bemis, "Payment of the French Loans to the United States, 1777–1795," *Current History*, XXIII (March 1926), 824–831, and Alphonse Aulard, "La Dette américaine envers la France, sous Louis XVI et sous la révolution," *La Revue de Paris*, XXXII (Mai–Juin 1925), 319–338.

20. For details on the obligations of a neutral in the light of existing international law, see Charles S. Hyneman, *The First American Neutrality: A Study of the American Understanding of Neutral Obligations during the Years 1792 to 1815* (Urbana, Ill., 1934). See also *Neutrality: Its History, Economics and Law* (4 vols., 1935–36), II; W. Alison Phillips and Arthur H. Reede, *The Napoleonic Period* (New York, 1936); and Charles G. Fenwick, *The Neutrality Laws of the United States* (Baltimore, 1912), pp. 3–11.

21. To James Monroe, May 5, 1793, in Paul L. Ford, ed., *The Writings of Thomas Jefferson* (10 vols., New York, 1892–99), VI, 238.

22. The quotation on Jay and the poem are printed in the *Virginia Herald and Fredericksburg Advertiser,* July 3 and Aug. 11, 1795.

23. Quoted in Dice R. Anderson, "Edmund Randolph" in Samuel F. Bemis, ed., *The American Secretaries of State and Their Diplomacy* (10 vols., New York, 1927–29), II, 124.

24. For the quotation, see James Iredell to Mrs. Iredell, March 3, 1796, in J. Griffith McRee, *Life and Correspondence of James Iredell* (2 vols., New York, 1858), II, 462–463. It must be pointed out that historians disagree as to the influence of Jay's Treaty on Pinckney's negotiations. For details, see Samuel F. Bemis, *Pinckney's Treaty: A Study of America's Advantage from Europe's Distress, 1783–1800* (Baltimore, 1926), pp. 249–331; Arthur P. Whitaker, *The Spanish-American Frontier, 1783–1795* (Boston, 1927), pp. 201–222; also, Whitaker's, "New Light on the Treaty of San Lorenzo," *Mississippi Valley Historical Review,* XV (March 1929), 435–454 and his "Godoy's Knowledge of the Terms of Jay's Treaty," *The American Historical Review,* XXXV (July 1930), 804–810.

25. The early difficulties with Genêt and the political disputes over neutrality had led Hamilton, under the pseudonym "Pacificus," to defend and to outline the foreign policy philosophy of the Federalist party as well as it has ever been done. His seven newspaper articles published in the summer of 1793 have been hailed as an embodiment of the "realist" position in foreign affairs. For analyses of the "Pacificus Papers," see Alexander DeConde, *Entangling Alliance: Politics and Diplomacy under George Washington* (Durham, N.C., 1958), pp. 227–230 and John C. Miller, *Alexander Hamilton: Portrait in Paradox* (New York, 1959), pp. 369–372.

26. To James Madison, July 7, 1793, in Ford, *Writings of Jefferson,* VI, 338–339.

27. "The Anas," March 12, 1792, *ibid.,* I, 188.

28. To the Committee of Public Safety, Dec. 27, 1794, in Stanislaus M. Hamilton, ed.,

The Writings of James Monroe (7 vols., New York, 1898–1903), II, 162–163.

29. Sept. 12, 1795, in *American State Papers, Foreign Relations* (6 vols., Washington, 1832), I, 596–598.

30. Dec. 11, 1796, *ibid.,* I, 746–747.

31. Printed in *The Herald: A Gazette for the Country* (New York), Dec. 3, 1796.

32. Quoted in Albert J. Beveridge, *The Life of John Marshall* (4 vols., Boston, 1916–19), II, 273.

33. James D. Richardson, ed., *A Compilation of the Messages and Papers of the Presidents, 1789–1897* (10 vols., Washington, 1896–99), I, 266.

34. Quoted in Alexander DeConde, "William Vans Murray and the Diplomacy of Peace: 1797–1800," *The Maryland Historical Magazine,* XLVIII (March 1953), 14.

35. For details on Logan, whose private diplomacy led to the passage of the Logan Act of 1799 that prohibits unauthorized negotiations by private individuals with foreign governments on matters in dispute with the United States, see Frederick B. Tolles, "Unofficial Ambassador: George Logan's Mission to France, 1798," *William and Mary Quarterly,* 3rd ser., VII (Jan. 1950), 1–25.

36. For details, see E. Wilson Lyon, "The Franco-American Convention of 1800," *Journal of Modern History,* XII (Sept. 1940), 305–333.

37. To James Lloyd, Jan. 1815, in Charles F. Adams, ed., *The Works of John Adams* (10 vols., Boston, 1850–56), X, 113. It must be pointed out that the idea of full-scale war was unpopular and that Adams believed the machinations of Federalists like Hamilton led to his defeat. See Zoltán Haraszti, *John Adams and the Prophets of Progress* (Cambridge, Mass., 1952), pp. 346–347 and Stephen G. Kurtz, *The Presidency of John Adams* (Philadelphia, 1957), p. 253.

Chapter Four

JEFFERSONIAN DIPLOMACY

FROM THE moment of independence, the future of Louisiana, the vast domain west of the Mississippi River, had been a prime topic of speculation among Americans. Ceded to Spain by France at the close of the Seven Years' War, Louisiana touched the interests of four nations: Spain, the United States, France, and Great Britain. Never having reconciled themselves to permanent loss of Louisiana, Frenchmen looked forward to the day when they would reverse the decision of 1763 and once again control the heart of the American continent. Although convulsed by revolution and involved in great international conflicts, successive French governments in the 1790's cast covetous eyes on Louisiana, and French statesmen prepared various plans for repossession.

Bringing Spain to her knees, France, in the Treaty of Basel of July, 1795, tried to persuade Spain to cede Louisiana, but failed. She did succeed, however, in acquiring the Spanish half of the island of Santo Domingo.

Rumors of French efforts to regain Louisiana in peace negotiations with Spain at Basel in 1795 reached the United States during the election campaign of 1796, when party animosities were at high pitch. Federalists seized upon the rumors, along with known French border intrigues, as evidence of French efforts in collusion with Republicans, not only to take Louisiana but also to dismember the Union by incorporating the trans-Appalachian states into a Louisiana controlled by France. Such reasoning, while not unjustified, stemmed from partisan political thinking and from Federalist distrust of France.

Secretary of State Pickering expressed well the Federalist viewpoint. "We have often heard," he said, "that the French Government contemplated repossession of Louisiana; and it has been conjectured that in their negotiations with Spain the cession of Louisiana & the Floridas may have been agreed on. You will see all the mischief to be apprehended from such an event. The Spaniards will certainly be more safe, quiet and useful neighbors." [1]

Napoleon's Plans

Three years later Pickering's fears became fact. On October 1, 1800, the day after Joseph Bonaparte signed the Treaty of Mortefontaine, another of Napoleon's ministers signed a secret agreement with Spain, the second Treaty of San Ildefonso. For the promise of a kingdom in Italy, Spain gave France six warships and Louisiana, but would not, as Napoleon desired, include the Floridas, territory the British had called East and West Florida, in the cession.

Napoleon wanted Louisiana, the "Granary of America," as a base and source of raw materials and food for a new French empire in North America. The commercial foundation of that empire would be France's "sugar islands" in the Caribbean, particularly rich Santo Domingo. After Negro slaves had rebelled and destroyed white rule in 1795, Santo Domingo had been virtually independent of France. Before Napoleon could build his balanced empire in the New World, therefore, he had to reconquer that island.

If Napoleon succeeded and occupied Louisiana, the United States would lose the advantage of rapid growth of its western settlements, a growth which had alarmed the Spaniards. "Their method of spreading themselves," the Spanish governor of Louisiana had written as early as 1794 of Americans, "and their policy are so much to be feared by Spain as are their arms. Every new settlement, when it reaches thirty thousand [sic] souls, forms a state, which is united to the United States, so far as regards mutual protection, but which governs itself and imposes its own laws."

While it was true that England might intervene if France became too powerful in North America, her intervention would not help the United States. The British, who would then encircle the United States, would be as powerful and as unpalatable as neighbors as the French. Besides, Britain's attitude after preliminary peace negotiations with the French in October, 1801, appeared to offer encouragement to Napoleon's dreams of a New World empire. She seemed willing to allow Napoleon to occupy himself with North American colonies so as to divert his attention from projects nearer home, as in the Mediterranean and on the continent.

Spain's attitude toward Louisiana also made Napoleon's task easier. After Pinckney's Treaty, Spain no longer considered Louisiana worth its annual cost. Expensive to govern and difficult to defend, especially against aggressive American frontiersmen, the province had never been profitable. "Frankly," Spain's Chief Minister confessed to his Ambassador in France in June, 1800, "it [Louisiana] costs us more than it is worth." [2]

Talleyrand persuaded Spain that France could check the Americans. "The

French Republic," he said, "will be a wall of brass forever impenetrable to the combined efforts of England and America." Spain's statesmen liked the idea of placing France between their American lands and the United States.

When Napoleon finally offered the Spanish king the newly created Kingdom of Etruria, comprising Tuscany and Piombino, for his son-in-law, Spain gave up Louisiana. Since the Treaty of San Ildefonso had not defined the Italian kingdom, France, on March 21, 1801, signed a second treaty which did, the Convention of Aranjuez. Still, Napoleon experienced difficulty in obtaining physical possession of Louisiana.

Insisting that Napoleon had not installed the Spanish sovereign in Etruria as he had promised, Spain refused to make delivery of Louisiana. Finally, she offered to surrender the province with conditions. France would have to gain international recognition for the King of Etruria, agree to restore Louisiana to Spain if the new king should lose his Italian throne, and promise "not to sell or alienate" any part of Louisiana. "In the name of the First Consul," France agreed.[3]

Jefferson's Attitude

In the United States, meanwhile, the Republicans had won control of the government. When Thomas Jefferson became President in March, 1801, he did not know that France had regained Louisiana. Within six months of the Treaty of San Ildefonso he heard rumors of it, and all during the year more undercover information of Louisiana's transfer drifted into the United States, but Jefferson did not appear as alarmed as the Federalists had been.

Nonetheless, the transfer of coveted Louisiana from weak Spain to strong France could not fail to disturb any government in the United States, even an ostensibly pro-French Republican government. Despite his French predilections and initial appearance of calmness over the rumors of retrocession, Jefferson became alarmed over the fate of the Mississippi Valley. "There is considerable reason to apprehend that Spain cedes Louisiana and the Floridas to France," he wrote. "It is a policy very unwise to both, and very ominous to us."[4]

Without England's help it appeared that Jefferson could do little to prevent the French from regaining Louisiana, for the position of the United States as a relatively weak neutral between two powerful rivals was not one to be envied. He seemed at first able to do little more than temporize, particularly since he did not know the details of Spain's agreement with France. He was not idle, however, for he quietly began a program of military preparation along the Mississippi to prepare the country for whatever might happen to Louisiana.[5]

First, Jefferson worked through influential Frenchmen who sympathized with the position of the United States, and through one of them, Pierre Samuel du

Pont de Nemours, an old friend who had spent three years in the United States, he made his initial effort to oppose Napoleon. He gave Du Pont two letters to take with him when he returned to France in April, 1802. In one of them, an open letter to the American Minister in France, Robert R. Livingston, he wrote an often quoted passage. "There is on the globe one single spot," he said, "the possessor of which is our natural and habitual enemy. It is New Orleans, through which the produce of three-eighths of our territory must pass to market. . . . France, placing herself in that door, assumes to us the attitude of defiance. Spain might have retained it quietly for years. . . . The day that France takes possession of New Orleans, fixes the sentence which is to restrain her forever within her low water mark. It seals the union of two countries, who, in conjunction, can maintain exclusive possession of the ocean. From that moment, we must marry ourselves to the British fleet and nation." [6]

Du Pont advised against using threats with Napoleon, who would be more "offended than moved." He tried to demonstrate that a British alliance would bring greater dangers than would France in Louisiana. If the United States would not be satisfied with assurance of free navigation of the Mississippi, he suggested, then the most logical course would be to try to buy what it desired. This suggestion fell in with the ideas of the Secretary of State, James Madison, who had instructed Livingston on May 1, 1802, to find out how much France would take for Louisiana and the Floridas.[7] Americans assumed that Spain had surrendered the Floridas as well as Louisiana to France.

As time passed, Jefferson's fears of early 1802 increased. That summer he said publicly, according to a British diplomat, that if the United States could not expel the French from Louisiana "they must have recourse to the assistance of other powers, meaning unquestionably Great Britain."

Then in the fall the Spaniards delivered an alarming blow. On October 16, the day after the Spanish king gave the final order transferring Louisiana to France, his Acting Intendant of Louisiana at New Orleans, in apparent violation of Pinckney's Treaty, withdrew the American "right of deposit"—that is, the privilege of leaving goods in New Orleans to await shipment in seagoing vessels.

Although the order did not affect freedom of navigation, it caused inconvenience and aroused talk of war in the West. "Scarcely any Thing has happened since the Revolution," a British observer wrote in January, 1803, "which has so much agitated the minds of all Descriptions of People in the United States as this Decree."[8] Assuming that the order came from Napoleon and that he would close the Mississippi once he took over, Westerners demanded that Jefferson do something about this blow to their economic well-being.

The Spaniards, in fact, had suspended the right of deposit on their own initiative, and later, when the United States protested, they revoked the suspension, but not until April, 1803. Not knowing of Spain's independent action and thinking that

France had the Floridas as well as Louisiana, Westerners feared that when Napoleon took possession he would exclude them from the entire gulf coast.

Jefferson was confronted with a dilemma. Strong measures against France and Spain would lead to a war he did not want, but to do nothing would play into the hands of his political opponents and perhaps lead to his overthrow or even to a disruption of the Union. For political reasons Federalists backed western demands for forcible seizure of New Orleans. These fears finally induced Jefferson to go beyond indirect threats in the crisis. "The measures we have been pursuing being invisible, do not satisfy" Westerners and Federalist war hawks, he told Monroe. "Something sensible, therefore, has become necessary."[9]

So, while Livingston in Paris argued that France could not gain from driving America into Britain's arms and that she did not need all of Louisiana, meaning essentially New Orleans, and the Floridas, Jefferson had to act. In spite of Federalist support of the western demands for strong measures, most Westerners still trusted Jefferson and the Republicans more than they did the Federalists.

At this juncture Du Pont extricated Jefferson from his predicament. In a letter from Paris, which arrived in Washington on December 31, 1802, he made his earlier suggestion more specific. He advised Jefferson to offer to buy New Orleans and the Floridas for six million dollars. He too thought France had gained the Floridas.[10]

Less than two weeks later Congress appropriated two million dollars for the use of a special mission to France, and Jefferson authorized Livingston to purchase New Orleans and the Floridas. At the same time, to aid Livingston in the negotiations and to placate western fears, he appointed James Monroe a special envoy to France. Monroe, the ardent Republican, owned land in the West and for twenty years had championed free navigation of the Mississippi. Understandably, he was popular in the West. Since the French still considered him a friend, his selection was wise from more than one viewpoint.

Although Monroe's appointment removed the threat of an immediate explosion in the West, it did not end all danger of war. Shortly before he sailed, the Republican members of Congress gave him a public dinner, where among the many toasts one revealed the temper of Americans. It went, "peace if peace is honorable, war if war is necessary." Yet, Westerners calmed down while awaiting news from France.

Jefferson, moreover, did not abandon plans for a British alliance. "According to all I can gather," the French Minister in Washington wrote, "I see that Mr. Monroe has *carte blanche* and that he will go to London if he is badly received at Paris." The Minister was partially correct. Only as a last resort, if France refused all overtures and the Americans learned that she planned to seal the Mississippi against American commerce or planned hostilities against the United States, were the envoys to go to England and seek an alliance. Basic in Jefferson's policy toward

Louisiana was the idea that negotiations and purchase were cheaper than fighting for New Orleans and far less dangerous than an alliance with England.

When Monroe sailed for France early in March, 1803, American statesmen had little reason to believe his mission would be easy or even successful, but when he arrived in Paris on April 13 the whole situation concerning Louisiana had changed. Napoleon had already offered to sell not merely New Orleans, but all of Louisiana.

Jefferson and Secretary of State Madison had not even considered acquiring all of Louisiana at this time. Their immediate objective had been New Orleans and the Floridas. For that territory, all of it east of the Mississippi, they had been willing to pay as much as ten million dollars and guarantee France free navigation of the river and special commercial privileges in the surrendered ports. If Livingston and Monroe made a good bargain, the President and his Secretary of State had even been willing to guarantee France's possession of Louisiana, meaning all of the land stretching west from the Mississippi to the Rocky Mountains.

Acquisition of Louisiana

Obviously, Napoleon could have retained all of Louisiana as well as American good will merely by making only minor concessions to the United States. His reasons for offering to sell the entire province, therefore, are important.

Napoleon's colonial venture in the New World had turned out badly, particularly on Santo Domingo, the key to his plans of empire. Pouring men and money into the island, he had made a determined effort to conquer it. An army of veterans under the command of his brother-in-law, General Charles Leclerc, had slashed at the rebels, but behind the leadership of a brilliant Negro, Toussaint L'Ouverture, the blacks had fought back savagely. Even though the French captured Toussaint within three months, the fierce resistance and the ravages of yellow fever proved too much even for Napoleon's veterans.

When Leclerc himself, as well as thousands of French soldiers, died of yellow fever in 1802, Napoleon's dreams of empire received a blow from which they never recovered. In one year Santo Domingo had swallowed fifty thousand French troops he could not spare. Fighting there had also delayed occupation of Louisiana.

During the fall and winter of 1802–1803, Napoleon had assembled an expedition in Helvoët Sluys, a small port near Rotterdam, to reinforce Santo Domingo and to occupy New Orleans. He gave General Claude Victor, in command of the expedition, secret orders to take and hold a strong position in Louisiana. "The intention of the First Consul," the instructions read, "is to give Louisiana a degree of strength which will permit him to abandon it without fear in time of war, so that its enemies may be forced to the greatest sacrifices merely in attempting an attack on it." [11]

THE TRANSFER OF LOUISIANA
TO THE UNITED STATES

THE LOUISIANA PURCHASE

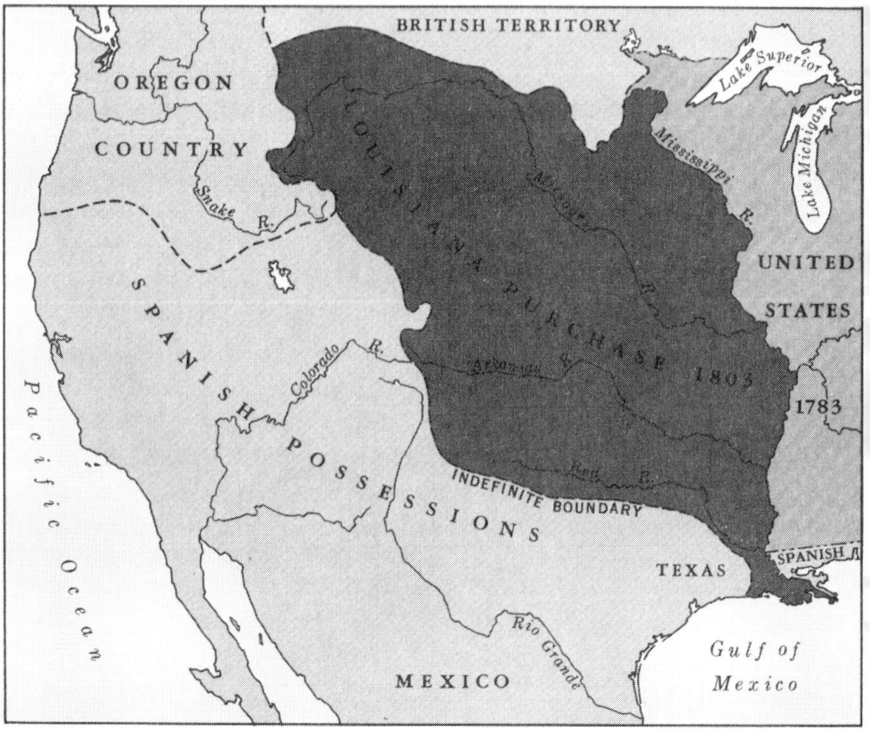

Again Napoleon's plans failed. Various impediments held up provisioning, and in January and February a severe cold gripped the French ships fast in a vise of ice. When spring came, storms and events in Europe kept the transports from sailing.

By the spring of 1803, in fact, Napoleon was ready to admit that the Peace of Amiens of March, 1802, that had ended the war between France and England, was merely a truce. Relations with England were now so bad that a new war appeared certain. Even if he wanted to try to defend Louisiana against England, he believed he could not hold it without the Floridas. Since Spain would not give up the Floridas, he felt that without them Louisiana lost much of its value. With England in control of the seas and with no troops in Louisiana, he knew that English forces would probably seize New Orleans as soon as war started. Great Britain might even make a firm alliance with the United States as the price for ousting France. Thus, the failure to acquire the Floridas, conquer Santo Domingo, and occupy Louisiana combined with events in Europe, apparently led the Corsican to abandon his New World empire.

To keep Louisiana out of British hands and to prevent an Anglo-American combination against him, Napoleon offered the whole province to the United States. He could, moreover, use the money in his military preparations, though money was not a prime consideration in his action. He had to work quickly, however, while the nominal peace with England continued. He authorized Talleyrand, his Foreign Minister, to act. What, Talleyrand had asked Livingston the day before Monroe reached Paris, would the United States give for the whole of Louisiana? In the ensuing negotiations Livingston and Monroe overcame their jealousy of each other and were wise enough to recognize a bargain and to go beyond their instructions to clinch it.

As France originally wanted about twenty-five million dollars, the Americans haggled with François Barbé-Marbois, the French Minister of Finance, over the price. "We shall do all we can to cheapen the purchase," Livingston wrote to Madison on April 13, "but my present sentiment is that we shall buy." They did buy, signing a treaty and two conventions which provided for the cession of and payment for Louisiana. These agreements, all dated April 30, 1803, bound the United States to pay fifteen million dollars in cash and claims. For some 828,000 square miles of land this amounted roughly to three cents an acre. Livingston and Monroe had bought an empire to get a city. "We have lived long," Livingston said, "but this is the noblest work of our whole lives." [12]

France had acted just in time. On May 9 the American envoys heard that if war broke out, England would send an expedition to Louisiana. Within a week England and France ended their truce and went to war. This did not, however, stand in the way of completing the Louisiana transactions. Since Napoleon wanted cash, not American securities, and French banks would not float a loan, the United States turned to English and Dutch bankers for the money. The firm of Baring

Brothers & Company of London loaned the United States over ten million dollars. Alexander Baring, the future Lord Ashburton, even traveled to Paris and the United States to finance the purchase. With the approval of the British government, the money finally reached Napoleon, England's enemy.[13]

Constitutional Problems

Seemingly, the purchase extricated Jefferson from his delicate fix. Yet, acquisition of the vast territory posed serious problems of conscience, principle, and politics. Being a strict constructionist, Jefferson believed he did not have the constitutional power to buy Louisiana and to incorporate its inhabitants into the Union. He thought he could take advantage of the bargain only through a constitutional amendment. By overcoming conscience and overturning principle, Jefferson made the purchase. He did not allow what he called "metaphysical subtleties" to stand in his way.

Federalists, too, did violence to alleged principles. Reversing their previous demands for forcible acquisition and challenging the legality of title and constitutionality of the transaction, they now opposed the purchase. Yet Federalist chieftain Alexander Hamilton favored it, but gave Jefferson no credit for consummating it.[14] Although not responsible for planning the purchase, Jefferson deserved credit for quickly taking advantage of a propitious moment.

In addition to raising grave constitutional questions, the circumstances of Napoleon's sale created other problems. One was the legality of the transfer. Napoleon had never fulfilled his obligations to Spain under the Convention of Aranjuez. He had not secured adequate international recognition of Etruria, and French troops had never left the kingdom.

Napoleon also broke his promise to the Spanish king. "The King, my master," the Spanish Ambassador in Paris, protested, "decided to deliver the aforesaid Colony only on condition that it should at no time, under no pretext, and in no manner be alienated or ceded to any other power." Using the same argument, Spain protested many times to the United States that France lacked "the power to alienate the said province without the approbation of Spain." Nonetheless, Spain was powerless to block the transfer. She did not have the force to prevent American occupation of Louisiana, and only force could now keep Americans out.

If Napoleon had acted constitutionally, France probably would have rejected the Louisiana treaties. According to France's constitution of December, 1799, he could not legally alienate the national domain without consent of the legislative chambers. In addition, he antagonized a substantial body of French public opinion. His brothers, Joseph and Lucien, protested the sale but were unable to stop the negotiations. These were, however, matters of French domestic politics and did not affect the American title.

In giving up Louisiana, the French framed the boundaries so ambiguously that they were bound to lead to trouble between the United States and its neighbors. Napoleon wanted it that way. "If an obscurity did not already exist, it would perhaps be good policy to put one there," he told one of his ministers.[15] When Livingston questioned the vague boundaries, Talleyrand said, "I can give you no direction; you have made a noble bargain for yourselves, and I suppose you will make the most of it."[16] Americans did make the most of it. They assumed, on dubious evidence, that they had purchased West Florida also.

Livingston and Monroe, and then Jefferson, insofar as they knew of them, did not let a questionable title and vague boundaries keep them from making a "noble bargain." Neither did Congress let ethical obstacles stand in the way of the purchase. The Senate, by a substantial majority, on October 20, 1803, approved the three treaties covering the transfer of Louisiana. Delighted Westerners greeted the news of the purchase with wild celebrations.

After taking possession of Louisiana for only twenty days, France turned the province over to the United States on December 20. Some Frenchmen considered the transfer a tragedy. The prefect in New Orleans spoke for them when he said, "What a magnificent New France have we lost."

Through fortuitous developments in Europe and Santo Domingo, Jefferson had avoided possible war with France and an unwanted alliance with England. That same good fortune gave him a province which more than doubled the national domain. By placating the West, moreover, the purchase of Louisiana averted the danger of disunion. It also set a precedent for acquiring territory and people by treaty. All of this did not stem from planned policy; but a foreign policy intelligently conceived is one flexible enough to take quick advantage of unexpected opportunities. Jefferson understood that principle, for he was a shrewd statesman.

Commerce and the Tripolitan War

After the acquisition of Louisiana, Jefferson's main problem in foreign relations was the protection of American commerce in a hostile world, for during the remainder of his Presidency Europe was at war. This obligation, when the use of force appeared necessary to defend maritime rights, placed him in another predicament, for he had made peace, though not at any price, the cornerstone of his foreign policy. Peace, he once explained, is "the most important of all things for us, except the preserving [of] an erect and independent attitude."[17]

Besides having a "passion for peace," Jefferson was economy-minded, and as President combined his hatred of war with money-saving measures. Believing that large armies were the hotbeds of dictatorship, he cut down the Army by one third. "We keep in service no more than enough men to garrison the small posts dispersed at great distances on our frontiers," he said.

Although Jefferson believed that navies were less to be feared than armies, because they could "never endanger our liberties," he disliked them also. "I am . . . for such a naval force as may protect our coasts and harbors from such depredations as we have experienced," he wrote, not "for a navy, which by its own expenses and the eternal wars in which it will implicate us, will grind us with public burthens, and sink us under them." [18] As soon as he took office, therefore, he reduced the active Navy to six ships with small crews.

Practical statecraft forced Jefferson to reverse his stand on war, peace, and navies. He was not, however, necessarily inconsistent. He was willing to fight when the cost of peace was high and victory appeared cheap. In war, he believed, American commitments and objectives should be limited, the chances of success good, and the cost relatively low. His war with Tripoli, from 1801 to 1805, met those conditions.

Almost from the day the United States had become independent, American shipping in the Mediterranean had suffered blackmail, plunder, capture, and enslavement of crews by the pirates of North Africa's Barbary shore. Spread over two thousand miles of coastline from the Atlantic to the Mediterranean, the four Barbary states of Morocco, Algiers, Tunis, and Tripoli preyed on shipping going to and from the Mediterranean. Their rulers styled themselves the "sovereigns of the Mediterranean" and relied on piracy, their main industry, as a primary source of revenue.

Morocco was virtually independent. The other states owed a nominal allegiance to Turkey. None respected the usual amenities of international law. European governments escaped the depredations of the pirate states only by paying tribute.

Since the sea and military power of the Barbary states even by contemporary standards was contemptible, the great powers of Europe, such as Britain or France, could easily have destroyed the pirate nests. They preferred not to, for they were, an American poet wrote,

> Great fall'n powers, whose gems and golden bribes
> Buy paltry passports from these savage tribes— [19]

The European states bought protection because it was cheaper than war and offered them a convenient means of gaining political and commercial advantages over less powerful rivals, such as the United States. "Bribery and corruption," an American consul in Algiers explained, "answers their purpose better, and is attended with less expense, than a noble retaliation."

Before the Revolution, American colonists had profited from the protection England bought, and had developed a lucrative Mediterranean trade. After they gained independence, Americans lost their immunity to capture and robbery. At first, the newly independent United States sought help from England and France against the corsairs. France gave only promises, and Britain would do nothing. Therefore, the American government had to make its own terms with the Barbary states. Since the pirates exacted higher tributes from weak states, such as the United States, than from the strong, the terms were never satisfactory.

The United States purchased its first treaty, a fairly liberal one, in 1786 from the ruler of Morocco. Although the initial cost seemed high, the treaty did not call for continuing payments of tribute, but Morocco did exact tribute in other ways, such as in bribes and ransoms.

Algiers, the most formidable of the Barbary states, in the late 1780's and early 1790's captured more than a dozen American ships and held well over a hundred Americans as slaves. Those humiliating conditions led Congress in March, 1794, to authorize construction of six frigates, the nucleus of the Navy, to protect American commerce and lives.[20] In September, 1795, before the frigates were launched, the Dey of Algiers made a treaty with the United States. For peace, the United States paid a heavy price, ransom money, presents, and large commissions. In addition, it promised to furnish an annual tribute in naval stores amounting to $21,600.

In the following year, the United States paid for a treaty with Tripoli and in 1797 for a more expensive one with Tunis. Although neither treaty called for additional tribute, Americans paid it in one form or another. This was the Mediterranean policy of the Federalist government which gloried in the slogan "millions for defense but not one cent for tribute."

The treaties with the Barbary states were, in fact, worthless. All the rulers, when the opportunity arose, were anxious to break them and to prey on American commerce. The first state to repudiate its treaty and to launch large-scale hostilities against the United States was Tripoli. In May, 1801, less than three weeks after Jefferson had taken office, its Pasha declared war.

That declaration forced Jefferson, lover of peace and foe of armaments, to meet force with force. First he authorized only defensive measures against the corsairs, then offensive action, and finally he increased the Navy. The Navy fought for four years, but because Jefferson insisted on a war without expense, it fought with true energy for only one year. In June, 1805, after winning a limited victory, the United States signed a peace treaty that forced some valuable concessions from the Pasha but was still humiliating. It recognized the right of the pirates to obtain ransom for imprisoned Americans, and did not end the plundering. Jefferson withdrew his naval squadron in 1807, and for the next eight years American shipping in the Mediterranean was virtually defenseless.

Finally, in March, 1815, Congress authorized hostilities against the Dey of Algiers, who had declared war against the United States. That summer Commodore Stephen Decatur, commander of the naval squadron sent to the Mediterranean, dictated peace to Algiers, and then to Tunis and Tripoli. His guns ended the Barbary blackmail. Within the year, after European warships had joined in destroying the pirate nests, the payment of tribute ended and with it America's troubles with the Barbary states.

Trade and the European War

Jefferson had bought peace with Tripoli in 1805 and had withdrawn the war-ships from the Mediterranean in 1807 because he faced greater dangers than those posed by the petty tyrants of North Africa. The war between Britain and France threatened to stifle American trade.

Since the President could not chastise those powerful states as he might the pirates of North Africa, he followed a policy of "peaceable coercion" in dealing with them, meaning that he would threaten them with the loss of trade if they persisted in violating American rights. "Our commerce," he once explained, "is so valuable to them that they will be glad to purchase it when the only price we ask is to do us justice. I believe we have in our own hands the means of peaceable coercion; and that the moment they see our government so united as that they can make use of it, they will for their own interest be disposed to do us justice."[21]

In keeping with this policy and his other ideas, Jefferson relied for defense mainly on small gunboats, used with some success in Tripoli. They would patrol the American coastline. "I believe," he had written years earlier, "that gunboats are the only *water* defence which can be useful to us, and protect us from the ruinous folly of a navy." Despite Federalist jeers, he built large numbers of those small one-gun ships.

When trouble with Britain and France mounted, Jefferson's policy of practicing economy with national defense seemingly backfired as the whole swarm of gunboats was useless against warships. Actually, even the frigates would not have been able to challenge British, or French, sea power in distant waters. The United States in those years was not yet strong enough to fight overseas against any major power.

Yet when Jefferson ended his first term he was satisfied with his foreign policy. He told his friends that "peace is smoothing our path at home and abroad . . . with England we are in a cordial friendship; with France in most perfect understanding; with Spain we shall always be bickering, but never at war till we seek it. Other nations view our course with respect and friendly anxiety." Those words were true enough for the years 1803 and 1804.

Even after May, 1803, when England and France ended the Peace of Amiens and renewed their long war, American peace and prosperity continued. For two years, in fact, American traders enjoyed a rich commerce and war-swollen profits, as in the earlier years of the Anglo-French conflict. All this led to a phenomenal growth of the American merchant marine. Indeed, the United States had become the world's foremost neutral trader.

American shippers enjoyed a particularly lucrative trade, denied them in time of peace, in carrying goods between French and Spanish ports and between them and French and Spanish colonies in the Caribbean. Since such direct trade violated

Britain's Rule of 1756, the Americans took their cargoes from French or Spanish Caribbean ports to an American port where they would go through certain formalities, such as payment of duties which might later be refunded, and thus would convert the cargoes to American property, making them "free goods." Then the ships with their "neutralized" cargoes might proceed to France or Spain.

England herself recognized the legality of that commerce in 1800 in a decision handed down by the High Court of Admiralty in the case of the American ship *Polly*. That kind of trade, which circumvented the Rule of 1756, was known as "broken voyage."

In 1805 that trade and America's good fortune ended. After long protest by British shippers and others against the leniency shown to neutral trade, particularly to Americans, the Lords Commissioners of Appeals in London, in the case of the American brig *Essex*, upheld a reversal of the *Polly* decision. The *Essex* verdict destroyed the principle of broken voyage. Goods could not be neutralized merely by bringing them into a neutral country, it said. The shipper had to pay a *bona fide* import duty. To refund the duty upon re-exporting the goods was a subterfuge and constituted a "continuous voyage" from enemy homeland to enemy colony. Broken voyage, the British decreed, violated the Rule of 1756 and under the doctrine of continuous voyage they would no longer allow such trade.[22]

Without advance warning and before the *Essex* decision was publicized, British cruisers seized scores of American ships carrying French or Spanish goods, especially in the Caribbean. British cruisers hovered off American harbors in such numbers that they practically blockaded the ports. Few American ships going to sea escaped "visit and search" by vigilant British cruisers. The seizures and "the sudden and peremptory manner of enforcing" the *Essex* decision, actually a new principle, infuriated Americans.

Several months later, at the Battle of Trafalgar of October 21, 1805, Admiral Horatio Nelson, at the cost of his own life, smashed the combined French and Spanish fleets, thereby reinforcing England's maritime supremacy and making possible an even tighter control of neutral shipping. On the same day there appeared in London a pamphlet entitled *War in Disguise; Or, the Frauds of the Neutral Flags*. Written by an Admiralty lawyer named James Stephen, it expanded the principles of the *Essex* decision.

Neutral shipping, Stephen said, should be regulated and taxed for the benefit of Britain's war effort. Allowing neutrals, particularly Americans, to trade unhampered with the enemy, he maintained, "sustains the ambition of France, and prolongs the miseries of Europe." At the same time, he argued, England denies herself the advantage of her command of the seas. Since she controlled the seas, he said in effect, neutrals had no rights. Nelson's victory at Trafalgar made it possible for England to carry out Stephen's plan, for his cogent arguments had considerable appeal. His pamphlet went through three editions in three months in

England. Later, through a series of Orders in Council, English naval practice toward American shipping practically followed the pattern he had outlined.

Then, in little more than a month after Trafalgar, Napoleon won a tremendous victory at the Battle of Austerlitz which crushed the armies of Russia and Austria, destroyed the third coalition against France, and strengthened his mastery of Europe. Now the efforts of Napoleon and England to get at each other resembled a fight between the tiger and the shark. Each ruled its own sphere but could not directly injure the other. In this desperate battle neutral rights virtually disappeared and the United States suffered whenever it would not submit to the will of either belligerent, lord in its own domain.

England blockaded territory under French control and Napoleon retaliated by throwing a "paper" blockade, a blockade by proclamation, around the British Isles. Caught in the middle of the sweeping blockades, the United States insisted that the blockades of both belligerents were illegal. It held that a blockade was legal only when applied to "ports which may be actually invested."

Orders in Council and Napoleonic Decrees

An Order in Council of May 16, 1806, known as "Fox's blockade," touched off the battle of paper blockades. It established a partial blockade of Europe's coast. Under it the Royal Navy would seize American ships carrying contraband, or enemy goods, anywhere outside the three-mile limit of the United States. Americans could trade with Europe, therefore, only as England allowed.

In November, Napoleon retaliated with his Berlin Decree, declaring the British Isles under blockade. He would seize and condemn any ship coming under his control that had previously touched a British port, but made an exception for American ships. This decree launched his "Continental System," a scheme designed to exclude British shipping from Europe and, if possible, from ports throughout the world. With it he hoped to destroy England's commerce. If that commerce died, he reasoned, England's finances would collapse and then she would not have the power to support a navy and make war.

England struck back at the Continental System with new Orders in Council in January and November, 1807, prohibiting all trade with ports under France's control except that going through her own system of controls. England designed her plan to push goods through Napoleon's self-imposed blockade and, when neutral shipping carried those goods, to profit from that trade by imposing a tax on it. All trade with Europe, in other words, had to pay tribute to Britain in one way or another.

Napoleon countered the British system with his Milan Decree of December, 1807. Any ship that submitted to visit and search by Britain, that visited a British port, or paid taxes to the British, he would treat as a British ship. If it came to a

French port or fell into French hands, he would seize it. Since Napoleon could not enforce his decrees as effectively as the British, his Continental System cut off American trade with Europe but not with England.

If American traders tried to follow the French system, they were almost certain to be stopped by British cruisers and lose ship and cargo. If they conformed to the British decrees and avoided ports under French control, however, they were usually safe because France's navy had been driven from the seas. Under the British licensing system, therefore, though Americans hated it, their commerce continued to prosper because of the wartime demand for American products in England. Yet, some Americans suspected England of playing the familiar game of using the war to crush commercial rivals, the foremost of which was now the United States.

The Impressment Issue

The licensing system and ship seizures were not the only grievances Americans had against England. The rock-ribbed issue that embittered Anglo-American relations for many years was impressment, or naval recruiting by force.

One reason why impressment was a bitter issue was that England and the United States held conflicting views on neutral rights. Except for military personnel, Secretary of State James Madison said, "we consider a neutral flag on the high seas as a safeguard to those sailing under it. Great Britain on the contrary asserts a right to search for and seize her own subjects." Lord Harrowby, Britain's Foreign Secretary, expressed his country's view quite clearly. "The pretension advanced by Mr. Madison that the American Flag should protect every Individual sailing under it on board of a Merchant Ship," he said, "is too extravagant to require any serious Refutation."

Another reason for difficulties was that England and the United States followed differing theories of citizenship. England insisted that once an Englishman always an Englishman. This was the doctrine of "inalienable allegiance." The United States, a nation of immigrants, upheld the right of "expatriation," that a person could of his own choice renounce allegiance to one country and become the citizen of another. "I hold the right of expatriation," Jefferson said, "to be inherent in every man by the laws of nature."

A more important reason for the bitterness of the impressment issue was England's desperate need for seamen. For centuries England had recruited her seamen through press gangs. Her statesmen held that impressment was "a prerogative inherent in the crown, founded upon common law and recognized by many acts of Parliament."

Conditions aboard English warships during the Napoleonic wars were so harsh that few British subjects would enlist, and when impressed, often deserted. So the

Royal Navy stepped up recruiting by force. By using press gangs in British sea-ports, or by boarding its own merchantmen on the high seas and impressing seamen, it filled crews, but it never claimed the right to impress other than British subjects. To escape impressment thousands of Englishmen, particularly seamen, took service in the rapidly expanding American merchant marine. There the berths were safer, the pay higher, and the treatment more humane.

To secure immunity from the press gangs, many Englishmen became American citizens, or secured naturalization papers illegally or forged them. Some fled merchant berths; others deserted naval service. According to one estimate made by an American in 1807, English ships of all kinds in the war years lost about twenty-five hundred men a year to American ships. Since England's major weapon against Napoleon was sea power, this loss appeared to her statesmen a matter of life and death.

To keep its ships staffed, the Royal Navy insisted on, and enforced, its right to examine neutral ships in British ports and at sea for deserters and other British subjects fleeing naval service. Since the United States was the most important neutral carrier and many Americans had been born in England, this practice led to trouble with the American government. English searching parties would not recognize the right of Englishmen to become American citizens, though they never insisted on the right to impress natural-born Americans.

Yet the press gangs often impressed even native Americans. They made frequent and convenient mistakes, usually in ratio to their captain's immediate need for seamen. Besides, the British officers argued, it was often almost impossible to distinguish Americans from Englishmen.

In theory, England made a concession to American objections. If the impressed seamen could prove that they were natural-born Americans, the Royal Navy would release them. This placed the burden of proof on the Americans. Getting the proof often took months, even years. Then, after long service, the Admiralty would release them without redressing the suffering it had caused. Too often, however, impressed Americans were killed or died in service, leaving their friends and relatives with a deep hatred of England.

In a partial effort to meet the impressment problem, the American government furnished seamen with official statements of citizenship, but would concede nothing on the right of expatriation. The statements did not distinguish between natural-born and naturalized Americans. In addition, sailors often sold the "protections" to British subjects. The British, therefore, would not recognize those "protections" as evidence of citizenship.

The basic issue of impressment was that in time of war it provided Britain with essential manpower. Englishmen defended it as a matter of national survival. For the United States it was a standing insult and a threat to national sovereignty. Americans believed that their flag flying at the mast of a ship should protect the crew. More important than any violation of a theoretical right, however, was the fact that impressment struck Americans as a vicious waste of lives.

From the beginning of the Anglo-French wars, the United States had tried many times to settle the impressment question, but had always failed. After suffering under the impact of the *Essex* decision, Jefferson decided on retaliatory legislation. In April, 1806, Congress passed a Non-Importation Act, which would exclude certain British manufactures from the United States after November 1 unless England settled American grievances.

At the same time, as it had in past crises, the American government decided to send a special mission to London to negotiate the grievances. This time Jefferson chose William Pinkney, a Baltimore lawyer, to assist James Monroe, who was then the regular Minister to England. Monroe and Pinkney were "to settle all matters of difference" with Great Britain. They had the power to make a new treaty defining neutral rights, such as on matters of contraband and blockade, and to resolve the impressment controversy. They were, moreover, to replace the parts of Jay's Treaty that were due to expire in October, 1807.

On the issue of impressment, Monroe and Pinkney's instructions were firm. Any agreement had to forbid impressments from American ships at sea. Meanwhile, Jefferson postponed execution of the Non-Importation Act.

The British were willing to make only an informal written pledge that naval officers would exercise "the greatest caution" in impressing British seamen, but refused to incorporate even this limited concession into a treaty. Since Monroe and Pinkney could do no better and were reasonably satisfied with other concessions, on December 31, 1806, they signed an agreement similar to Jay's Treaty.

In the Monroe-Pinkney Treaty the United States gave up the principle that free ships make free goods, as it had done in Jay's Treaty, and England modified its Rule of 1756. This was not enough to please Jefferson. Since he had taken a strong stand on impressment, he withheld the treaty from the Senate. Secretary Madison, meanwhile, instructed Monroe and Pinkney to reopen negotiations on the basis of their original instructions, but the British would not again negotiate on those terms.

Even though Jefferson considered retaliation and even talked of war, he did not invoke the Non-Importation Act.[23] As long as England acted in the spirit of the informal understanding on neutral trade and impressment, he said, he would recommend that Congress continue the suspension.

The CHESAPEAKE Affair

Then the *Chesapeake* affair made impressment a burning issue. On June 22, 1807, the forty-gun American naval frigate *Chesapeake*, Commodore James Barron senior officer aboard, left Norfolk for African waters. On board were four seamen who had escaped from British warships in Hampton Roads and had enlisted in the United States Navy. Since the *Chesapeake* did not anticipate hostilities, her gun deck was cluttered with lumber, sails, and cables to be stowed away while at sea. Her guns were virtually unworkable.

In this condition, not far beyond the three-mile limit, she met the fifty-gun British frigate *Leopard*. The *Leopard* hailed her and demanded that she submit to search for the deserters. When Barron refused, the *Leopard* poured several broadsides into the *Chesapeake*, killing three and wounding eighteen men. Within thirty minutes, after firing only one shot, the *Chesapeake* struck colors. Then a British search party climbed aboard, lined up the crew, and took off the four alleged deserters. Thoroughly humiliated, Barron brought the wrecked and bloody ship back to port.

Only one of the four seamen was a real British deserter. The British hanged him from the yardarm of his own ship. The other three were natural-born Americans, two of them Negroes. After recapturing these seamen, the British imprisoned them and did not surrender two of them until 1812. The third died in prison.

Nothing the British had done before aroused the public to such fury as did the *Chesapeake* impressment. In Norfolk a mob ran wild, attacked British sailors, and clamored for war. Jefferson himself told friends that the British had "their foot on the threshold of war" and that the United States "has never been in such a state of excitement since the battle of Lexington."

This time the British had fired on a warship and killed sailors of the United States Navy, something they had not done previously. Although her naval officers

THE "LEOPARD" AND THE "CHESAPEAKE"

had done it more than once, Britain had never claimed the right to seize men from a foreign naval vessel. Such conduct insulted the American flag and trampled national honor. The United States, the British Minister in Washington reported, "will engage in war rather than submit to their national armed ships being forcibly searched on the high seas."

If Jefferson had wanted it, he apparently could have had war. The country, according to contemporary evidence, would have supported him, but to go to war against England virtually without a navy and with an exposed seacoast seemed foolhardy. Instead, he tried to use the *Chesapeake* affair as a weapon of peaceable coercion. With it and with economic pressure, he thought, he could force the British to give up impressment.

Under a provision in Jay's Treaty, British warships had been using American territorial waters and ports for provisioning. After calling an emergency session of the cabinet, Jefferson issued a proclamation on July 2, 1807, forbidding such usage. A few days later he asked the state governors for one hundred thousand militia, made plans for war, readied coastal defenses, and called Congress to meet in special session late in October. This was the extent of Jefferson's warlike measures.

In the subsequent negotiations over the *Chesapeake* affair, the British admitted that in this instance they had been wrong, disavowed the *Leopard*'s violence, and offered amends, but would not abandon impressment. The war spirit of 1807 melted away in the extended negotiations. Yet the bitterness of the *Chesapeake* affair rankled for five years. To Americans it, and continued impressments, marked the depth of national disgrace.

The Embargo

In spite of the failure of his efforts to use the *Chesapeake* incident to force a settlement of grievances with Britain, Jefferson did not lose faith in the idea that economic coercion was enough to force respect for American rights. On December 14, 1807, the Non-Importation Act, which had been suspended several times, finally went into effect. Although it reflected Jefferson's idea, it was not strong enough. Basically, the President wanted to shut off all trade with England and France. If the United States completely cut off exports of raw materials and food-stuffs the belligerents needed, he reasoned, they would come to terms.

Therefore, on December 21, at Jefferson's urging, the Congress he had called into special session passed the Embargo Act. That law forbade all American ships to leave for foreign countries and required shipowners engaged in coastal trade to post heavy bonds assuring compliance. Later, Congress tried to remedy defects in the Embargo law with supplementary legislation and by giving government agents almost inquisitorial powers in enforcing it. This was indeed a rigorous self-blockade.

In theory, the Embargo was impartial. Madison, for instance, said that Britain would "feel it in her manufactures, in the loss of naval stores, and above all in the supplies essential to her colonies." France would feel it in the loss of colonial luxuries. Since England controlled the seas, however, it had the effect of shutting off trade with her only. In practice, therefore, it complemented Napoleon's Continental System. "Mr. Jefferson," a Bostonian Federalist exclaimed, "has imposed an embargo to please France and to beggar us!"

Although the Embargo inflicted considerable injury on Britain, and even more on her West Indies, Jefferson's plan misfired. The Embargo hit the United States harder than it did England. Depression fell on the seaports and elsewhere. A British traveler described New York in this period. "The port indeed was full of shipping, but they were dismantled and laid up; their decks were cleared, their hatches fastened down, and scarcely a sailor was to be found on board." Then he added, "The coffee-houses were almost empty; the streets, near the water-side, were almost deserted; the grass had begun to grow upon the wharves."

Federalists denounced the Embargo, and many Republicans joined them. Smuggling, often in open defiance of federal officers, flourished along the Canadian border and traders abused the privilege of coastal shipping. New Englanders revolted against the law and talked of separation from the Union. More than one New Englander damned the Embargo in doggerel similar to this:

> O Jefferson! with deep amaze,
> Thou'st overset our cargo;
> We've nought to do but stand and gaze
> At thy own curst embargo.[24]

New England's resistance to the Embargo, in fact, drove Jefferson to enforce it by federal action. In so using the Federal government, he overturned his own political creed of states' rights and the principles of his own party. Again foreign policy had forced Jefferson, the strict constructionist, to reverse himself. He had interpreted the Constitution under its authority to "regulate" commerce so loosely that he stopped all foreign trade. His inquisitors even endangered the personal liberties he held dear. The Embargo and supporting laws clamped controls, restrictions, and regulations on Americans and their property in time of peace, which the Constitution could hardly justify.

Napoleon shrewdly took advantage of the Embargo to serve his own ends. Since American ships could not legally leave port, he said, those in European harbors must be English ships. Under his Bayonne Decree of April, 1808, therefore, he seized them. After all, he said, he was merely helping the American government enforce its own Embargo law.

In spite of the pressure against it, Jefferson strove to the last to preserve the Embargo. He consoled himself for its diplomatic failure by stressing its protective effects. It has, he wrote to a friend, "produced one very happy & permanent effect. It has set us all on domestic manufacture, & will I verily believe reduce our future demands on England fully one half." [25]

Finally, the political pressure became too great for Congress to withstand. Federalist victories in state elections showed the tide of opinion running against Republicans. Fear of war, threats of secession from New England, and election losses, drove Congress on March 1, 1809, just three days before Jefferson left office, to repeal the Embargo for all countries except England and France. It did not, however, repeal the principle of peaceable coercion. In place of the Embargo, Congress substituted the Non-Intercourse Act.

Jefferson's peaceable coercion had failed. Yet historians have differed as to the effectiveness of the Embargo. Even though it caused England considerable hardship, it alone apparently was not a weapon capable of forcing her to capitulate to American demands, such as giving up impressment. Smuggling, internal resistance, and the opening of Spanish America to British trade after the outbreak of the war in Spain in August, 1808—as a compensation for lost American trade—all worked against the Embargo's effectiveness. Perhaps the most important factor in the failure of the Embargo lay in the very existence of the American merchant fleet. Jefferson underestimated the determination of the shippers and merchants to fight for wartime wealth. So great was the chance for profit, even under the British and French restrictions, that they would not submit to any law which prevented it. [26]

The Non-Intercourse Act of March 1 excluded American ships from French and British ports and closed American ports to both countries after May 20, 1809. If either France or England relaxed maritime restrictions against the United States, the President was empowered to reopen trade with the cooperative nation while continuing Non-Intercourse against the other. In effect, the law did three things: it invited concessions from England and France while continuing pressure against them, permitted trade with the few remaining neutral countries, and thus gave Americans a backdoor access to belligerent markets.

Although supposedly impartial, Non-Intercourse, unlike the Embargo, favored Britain. She could gain more from concessions than could blockaded France. Non-Intercourse ended Jefferson's efforts to uphold American neutral rights through peaceable coercion. The next steps came under his successor, James Madison.

NOTES

1. To Rufus King, Feb. 15, 1797, Timothy Pickering Papers, Massachusetts Historical Society, Boston (Microfilm copy).

2. Quoted in E. Wilson Lyon, *Louisiana in French Diplomacy 1759–1804* (Norman, Okla., 1934), p. 104.

3. Henry Adams, *History of the United States of America during the Administration of Jefferson and Madison* (9 vols., New York, 1889–1909), I, 400.

4. To James Monroe, May 26, 1801, in Paul L. Ford, ed., *The Writings of Thomas Jefferson* (10 vols., New York, 1892–99), VIII, 58.

5. Mary P. Adams, "Jefferson's Reaction to the Treaty of San Ildefonso," *Journal of Southern History*, XXI (May 1955), 173–188.

6. April 18, 1802, in Ford, *Writings of Jefferson*, VIII, 144–145. Ironically, this was basically the same policy Federalists had suggested five years earlier. If France should regain Louisiana, Timothy Pickering had said, "the United States could not fail to associate themselves with Great Britain, and make common cause against France." To C. C. Pinckney, Feb. 25, 1797, National Archives, Dept. of State, Diplomatic and Consular Instructions.

7. Gilbert Chinard, ed., *The Correspondence of Jefferson and Du Pont de Nemours* (Baltimore, 1931), pp. xxxiv–xxxvi.

8. Quoted in Bradford Perkins, *The First Rapprochement: England and the United States, 1795–1805* (Philadelphia, 1955), p. 163.

9. Jan. 13, 1803, Ford, *Writings of Jefferson*, VIII, 190.

10. Oct. 4, 1802, Chinard, *Jefferson and Du Pont*, pp. 63–65.

11. Quoted in Lyon, *Louisiana in French Diplomacy*, p. 135.

12. Quoted in François Barbé-Marbois, *The History of Louisiana* (Philadelphia, 1830), p. 310.

13. For financial details, see Ralph W. Hidy, *The House of Baring in American Trade and Finance: English Merchant Bankers at Work, 1763–1861* (Cambridge, Mass., 1949), pp. 33–34.

14. See [Douglas Adair], "Hamilton on the Louisiana Purchase: A Newly Identified Editorial from *The New York Evening Post*," *William and Mary Quarterly*, 3rd ser., XII (April 1955), 268–281.

15. Quoted in Barbé-Marbois, *Louisiana*, p. 286.

16. Quoted in Charles E. Hill, "James Madison," *The American Secretaries of State and Their Diplomacy*, ed. by Samuel F. Bemis (10 vols., New York, 1927–29), III, 42–43.

17. To R. R. Livingston, Oct. 10, 1802, Ford, *Writings of Jefferson*, VIII, 173.

18. To Elbridge Gerry, Jan. 26, 1799, *ibid.*, VII, 328.

19. Extract from a poem by David Humphreys, quoted in Ray W. Irwin, *The Diplomatic Relations of the United States with the Barbary Powers, 1776–1816* (Chapel Hill, N.C., 1931), p. 15.

20. Marshall Smelser, *The Congress Founds the Navy, 1787–1798* (Notre Dame, Ind., 1959), pp. 52–58.

21. To George Logan, March 21, 1801, Ford, *Writings of Jefferson*, IX, 220.

22. Bradford Perkins, "Sir William Scott and the *Essex*," *William and Mary Quarterly*, 3rd ser., XIII (April 1956), 169–183, and his *Prologue to War: England and the United States, 1805–1812* (Berkeley, Calif., 1961), pp. 77–82.

23. Lawrence S. Kaplan, "Jefferson, the Napoleonic Wars, and the Balance of Power," *William and Mary Quarterly*, 3rd ser., XIV (April 1957), 199. Anthony Steel, in "Impressment in the Monroe-Pinkney Negotiation, 1806–1807," *The American Historical Review*, LVII (Jan. 1952), 352–369, plays down the impressment issue as the decisive factor in Anglo-American relations at this time. He maintains that Jefferson merely used it as an instrument of policy. An analysis of the Monroe-Pinkney negotiations is in Perkins, *Prologue to War*, pp. 101–139.

24. Quoted in Louis M. Sears, *Jefferson and the Embargo* (Durham, N.C., 1927), p. 178.

25. Jefferson to Lafayette, Feb. 24, 1809, *ibid.*, p. 137. There is, however, reason to believe that the Embargo restrained rather than encouraged American industrial growth. See Perkins, *Prologue to War*, p. 172.

26. Reginald Horsman, in *The Causes of the War of 1812* (Philadelphia, 1962), pp. 142–143, suggests that the Embargo had injured American policy abroad as well as at home.

Chapter Five

THE WAR OF 1812

As Secretary of State, James Madison had believed in, and had carried out, Jefferson's policy of economic pressure, but even before he became President he knew it had failed. Several months before entering the White House, therefore, he explained what his own policy would be in dealing with the maritime crisis. As President, he said, he would quickly call a special session of Congress "with an understanding that War will then be the proper course, if no immediate change abroad shall render it unnecessary."[1] Thus, in March, 1809, when he took his inaugural oath and told the people that "the present situation of the world is indeed without parallel and that of our own country full of difficulties," he apparently believed that war with England would come.

Yet for several years Madison made Jefferson's basic idea of economic coercion the heart of his own policy and sought to obtain redress for grievances without resorting to war. This course appeared logical in view of the actions of David M. Erskine, the British Minister in Washington.

The Erskine Agreement

Believing war imminent, Erskine had talked to Madison and his friends following the presidential election about the crisis in Anglo-American relations and had concluded that if Britain were conciliatory, a settlement could be worked out. He even believed that the focus of American foreign policy might shift and become favorable to England, and hence suggested to Foreign Minister George Canning that he sacrifice the Orders in Council in order to win American good will.

Canning accepted the suggestion and in April, 1809, instructed Erskine to negotiate a settlement and explore the possibility of a new commercial treaty with the United States. Seemingly, the Non-Intercourse Act had been successful in forcing the British to come to some kind of terms.

Erskine's instructions, however, had serious limitations. They said that if the United States accepted the Rule of 1756, again opened its waters to British warships, and immediately placed the Non-Intercourse Act into effect against France, England would not apply her Orders in Council against American shipping. Canning also expressed willingness to settle the *Chesapeake* affair with an "honorable reparation for the aggression." The stickler, as far as Americans were concerned, was Canning's insistence that England must enforce the Non-Intercourse Act against France, meaning that the Royal Navy would be allowed to seize American ships caught violating it.

Anxious for a settlement and realizing he could not obtain America's formal agreement to all of Canning's conditions, Erskine departed from his instructions. On April 19, 1809, he and Secretary of State Robert Smith exchanged notes for what has come to be known as the Erskine Agreement, in which nothing was said about the Royal Navy enforcing American law and American acceptance of the Rule of 1756.

On that same day, Madison issued a proclamation saying that on June 10, when the Orders in Council would cease to apply to the United States as agreed to by Erskine, the Non-Intercourse Act would no longer be in effect against Britain. Joyous traders praised Madison's statemanship and when the proper day in June arrived some six hundred ships swarmed out of American ports loaded with cargoes for England. Madison's new popularity lasted only a few months, for he had acted prematurely.

Canning not only repudiated the Erskine Agreement almost as soon as he had glanced at it, but also immediately recalled that "damned Scotch flunkey" who had signed it. Since Englishmen hungered for the raw materials the American ships were carrying, Canning magnanimously allowed those ships already at sea to proceed to English ports.

On August 9, a humiliated Madison again placed Non-Intercourse into effect against England. The collapse of the Erskine Agreement thus ended the efforts to settle the *Chesapeake* incident and added new bitterness to Anglo-American relations. In fact, it proved to be the beginning of a fatal rupture between England and the United States.[2]

Macon's Bill No. 2

Early in September, Francis J. Jackson, Erskine's successor, arrived in the United States. Called "Copenhagen" Jackson for browbeating the Danes two years earlier when a British fleet had smashed Copenhagen, he soon showed himself as arrogant and tactless as his nickname suggested. He quickly charged Madison with knowing beforehand that Erskine was violating his instructions and in effect called the President a liar. Madison, therefore, refused to have anything to do with him. Jackson then left Washington but lingered in the United States until the following September consorting with Federalists and denouncing Madison's government. Madison demanded his recall and the British finally summoned him home, but with honor, and sent no replacement for two years. Diplomatic relations with England thus became partially suspended.

Meanwhile, Napoleon, who had been pleased with the Embargo, protested the Non-Intercourse Act, saying it favored England. In ostensible retaliation, he issued two decrees, one from Vienna in August, 1809, and another from Rambouillet the following March, which gave him the excuse to seize scores of American ships in French ports. Under the Rambouillet decree alone he seized about ten million dollars in American property, but even worse, he imprisoned hundreds of crewmen from captured ships.

Since Non-Intercourse now obviously had failed to bring the expected results from either Napoleon or England, and, like the Embargo, placed an almost unbearable strain on American commerce, it was dropped. Congress replaced it on May 1, 1810, with Macon's Bill No. 2, a law that reopened American trade to all the world but excluded British and French warships from American waters. The critical feature of that law said that if either England or France agreed to respect American maritime rights before March 3, 1811, the President could again apply Non-Intercourse against the recalcitrant nation, but only after an interval of three months had elapsed that gave that nation an opportunity to follow its rival's example.

Regardless of its theoretical impartiality, Macon's Bill No. 2 from Napoleon's point of view was virtually a surrender to British maritime policy. Since the Royal Navy dominated the seas, whatever trade the new law permitted would in fact be subject to British control. He tried, therefore, to persuade Madison that he had withdrawn his own decrees against American shipping.

In an ambiguous letter of August 5, 1810, Napoleon's Foreign Minister, the Duc de Cadore, told the American Minister in Paris "that the decrees of Berlin and Milan are revoked, and that after the 1st of November they will cease to have effect." [3] This was followed, however, by a nullifying qualification which said that the revocation would apply only if the English rescinded their Orders in Council or if the United States under its new law forced the English to respect its rights.

Even though Napoleon had not truly lifted his decrees, Madison, who was aware of the equivocal nature of the Corsican's act, accepted his conditional repeal as meeting the terms of Macon's Bill No. 2. Therefore, on November 2, after the British logically refused to repeal their Orders in Council because of the Cadore letter, the President issued a proclamation saying he would apply Non-Intercourse against Britain, which the American government did on February 11, 1811.

Madison and his advisers were now apparently convinced that war with England was only a matter of time. The Secretary of State even told the French Minister in Washington that the measures the President would take to protect American maritime rights against England "will necessarily lead to war." [4]

The LITTLE BELT Incident

A cluster of other developments now also contributed to the war crisis. In late February of 1811 William Pinkney, who had become the American Minister in London, withdrew from the legation and left it in the hands of only a *chargé d'affaires*. Pinkney's announcement of his departure jarred the British government and prompted it to make a belated effort to improve the rapidly deteriorating relations with the United States. It finally decided to send another minister to Washington. Before that minister arrived, a chance encounter between an American and a British warship revealed the raw temper of the American public over the question of neutral rights and underscored the critical need for conciliatory measures.

On May 16 a forty-four-gun American frigate, the *President*, caught the twenty-gun British sloop-of-war *Little Belt* off the Virginia capes. American and British versions differ as to who fired the first shot, but in the battle that followed the frigate almost blasted the sloop out of the water, killing nine and wounding three of her crew. The *President* suffered little damage and only one crew member was injured. Disregarding the heavy odds the *Little Belt* had faced, the American public greeted the news of the encounter with joy, believing that the Navy had at last avenged the five-year-old disgrace of the *Chesapeake*.

Many Englishmen considered the attack on their ship unprovoked. "The blood of our murdered countrymen," one London newspaper said, "must be revenged, and war must ensue."

Thus, when the new British Minister, Augustus John Foster, arrived in Washington at the end of June, the American people were in an ugly mood, bitterly anti-British, and seemingly ready for war. Since he was himself hostile to the United States and had only limited powers, Foster faced an almost impossible task in trying to reach a settlement on the maritime issues that might prevent war. [5] The harsh realities of his difficulties became even clearer when the Twelfth Congress convened in special session early in November.

THE WAR HAWKS OF 1812

Left to right: William H. Crawford, Henry Clay, John C. Calhoun,
General Peter B. Porter, Richard M. Johnson, and Felix Grundy.

The War Hawks

The leadership of that Congress was made up of a new generation of statesmen who had replaced the old Revolutionary leaders who had guided the government since its founding. In the elections of the previous year, in fact, almost half of the former Congress had failed to win re-election. The leaders of the new Congress, such as Henry Clay of Kentucky, John C. Calhoun of South Carolina, and William H. Crawford of Georgia, were young men from the West and lower South, most of them between thirty and forty years old.

These men were ardent nationalists who considered impressment and British maritime restrictions a national humiliation. They were also politicians who brought with them anti-British grievances from their own parts of the country. Some of their constituents, as in South Carolina, for instance, were suffering from an economic distress they blamed on the British. They resented the Orders in Council which they believed ruined their overseas markets.[6] Some of these new congressmen also represented agrarian expansionists who had steadily pushed the Indian westward and had taken over his lands.[7] The new Congress, therefore, represented a cross section of anti-British grievances and was weighted with vigorous nationalists who saw advantages in war with Britain.

Although the young nationalists did not comprise a majority in Congress, or even of the Republican membership, they controlled most of the important committees and were in a position to make their will felt. One of the first things they did to insure their control was to elect Henry Clay, then thirty-four years old, Speaker of the House. Then they demanded war with Britain. These were the men who led the war party—the war hawks of 1812.

The Frontier Problem

One of the most striking of the non-maritime grievances was the Indian problem. As they had done in the 1790's Westerners of the following decade acquired Indian lands for settlement piecemeal in treaties with individual tribes. Unlike the earlier period, however, the British were no longer occupying American soil in the Northwest and did not openly support Indian resistance to the advancing frontiersmen. Nonetheless, after 1807, when Anglo-American relations grew tense, Westerners began to give credence to rumors saying that the British in Canada were inciting the Indians against settlers.

Actually, Indian hostility stemmed from the land policies of the Westerners themselves. In September, 1809, William Henry Harrison, Governor of the Indiana Territory, had made treaties at Fort Wayne with several tribes, opening three million acres of splendid farm land to settlement. As a result the Indians were forced back to the Wabash River. Many Indians resented the surrender of their lands and two of them, a far-sighted Shawnee chieftain named Tecumseh and his brother, the Prophet, organized a movement to unite all the tribes against further white encroachments. They proposed no additional surrender of land to the whites, questioned the legality of the Fort Wayne treaties, and threatened to resist white occupation.

Westerners believed that the British were behind Tecumseh's confederation and his resistance to their advance. They were convinced that the British were supplying the Indians with arms from settlements near Detroit. The British officials, in fact, did not want Indian hostilities with the United States at this time, but they did try to win Indian friendship with presents and arms so that they could use those Indians as allies when war came.[8]

On November 7, 1811, three days after the Twelfth Congress had convened, Westerners uncovered what they considered decisive evidence of British intrigue with the Indians. On that day Tecumseh's warriors clashed with about a thousand troops under the command of General Harrison at an Indian village on Tippecanoe Creek, a tributary of the Wabash in present-day Indiana, inflicting nearly two hundred casualties before Harrison defeated them. Among the weapons the Indians left behind, Harrison found some made in Britain. The Battle of Tippecanoe, but especially the evidence of British aid to the Indians, aroused the West to an anti-British frenzy and helped crystallize war sentiment in Congress. Although some believed that Harrison's blundering had caused the high loss of life at Tippecanoe, most Westerners blamed the British.

In the following months those Westerners who wanted war argued that the only sure way to end the Indian troubles on the northwest frontier was to conquer Canada. This argument appealed to other war hawks who pointed out that the United States lacked a strong navy and that an attack on Canada offered the only effective way of striking at the British.

Southern war hawks, too, combined the desire to strike at Britain with sectional expansion. They wanted to invade Spanish Florida. When war came, they feared, the British would occupy Florida and use it as a base against them. Since Spain was once again Britain's ally, moreover, the Southerners had a good excuse for attacking Florida if war should break out with Britain.

A war to acquire Canada and Florida, according to this war hawk interpretation, seemingly had other virtues. The sectional balance between North and South was already a problem in American politics. Neither section, it seemed, wished to promote an increase in territory, population, or influence for the other. The acquisition of both Canada and Florida would retain that balance and would rid the country of dangerous neighbors.[9]

The Decision for War

Both the President and his new Secretary of State, James Monroe, sided with the war hawks. Monroe had come into office after the Battle of Tippecanoe as an advocate of peace with England, but in a month he became an advocate of war. "Gentlemen," he told the war hawks, "*we must fight.* We are forever disgraced if we do not."[10]

Yet the war party was unable to bring about an immediate declaration of hostilities against the British. Federalists and moderate Republicans resisted the pressure of the administration and the war hawks, and they were sufficiently strong in Congress to prevent immediate action. New England Federalists in particular believed that war against England would be a national tragedy, seeing in Napoleon, whom they considered a tyrant, the real foe. Timothy Pickering summed up their views in a toast, "The world's last hope—Britain's fast-anchored Isle."

Nonetheless, anti-British sentiment continued to gain strength, particularly from such incidents as the President's publication of the letters of John Henry, a British secret agent, in March, 1812. Those letters, bought by Madison for the exorbitant price of fifty thousand dollars, hinted at but did not prove British dealings with allegedly treasonable New England Federalists.[11]

Thus, by the spring of 1812, the various demands of the West and South for war and the anger of the other sections over maritime grievances brought the nation to the razor edge of decision. Then on April 1 Madison took decisive action. He confidentially recommended that "a general embargo be laid on all vessels now in port or hereafter arriving for the period of sixty days." Instead, Congress voted a ninety-day embargo to save American shipping from wholesale seizure when war came.

In England, meanwhile, merchants and manufacturers had been urging the government to seek an accommodation with the United States. The Jeffersonian policy of economic coercion, especially when coupled with Napoleon's Continental System, had hit them hard. Despite the fact that the opening of new markets in Latin America had given them some relief from the Embargo and Non-Intercourse, they suffered from economic depression and desperately needed American markets and raw materials. For some time, moreover, English public opinion had been turning against the Orders in Council and pressing for their repeal against the United States.

Information from the United States, furthermore, indicated that Americans were at last seriously preparing for war. Although the British considered American military power trifling, the acquisition of another enemy would be a serious blow to a public that had long been carrying the crushing burden of the French wars. In April, 1812, therefore, the British government, fearing a permanent loss of the American market, said it was willing to repeal the Orders in Council. Before it could do so, however, it needed a pretext, an authentic act by the French, such as the repeal of the Berlin and Milan decrees, that would make its own repeal appear a graceful countermeasure. In the following month the French, by coincidence, provided the necessary pretext.

Late in 1811, Joel Barlow, the American Minister in France, had complained to the Foreign Minister, at that time the Duc de Bassano, of France's continuing seizures of American ships. Finally, in May, 1812, Barlow asked for evidence of Napoleon's repeal of the Berlin and Milan decrees as they applied to the United States. A few days later, Bassano showed him a decree dated St. Cloud, April 28, 1811, which met the American desires by stating that the Berlin and Milan decrees had not existed for American ships for over a year and a half. Apparently the French had hastily drafted the heretofore unknown paper to meet the American request and had moved the date back a year.

Barlow, who considered the French decree a forgery but potentially useful to his government, immediately sent a copy to the American *chargé* in London, who showed it to the British Foreign Minister, now Lord Castlereagh, and asked for a repeal of the Orders in Council. Castlereagh then took advantage of the dubious St. Cloud decree to meet the pressures of domestic politics by announcing to Parliament on June 16 that the government would suspend the Orders in Council as they applied to the United States. The government did so on June 23.

That repeal was five days too late. On June 18, 1812, Madison had signed a declaration of war against England. If, as most Americans apparently believed at the time, the major cause for war was maritime rights, "its principal Cause and Justification was removed precisely at the moment when it occurred."[12]

In his war message Madison had stressed that the United States must defend itself against England's flagrant violation of its neutral rights. He placed impressment at the head of his list of British injustices and devoted only a few sentences to the Indian troubles. British cruisers, he said, were "in the continued practice of violating the American flag on the great highway of nations, and of seizing and carrying off persons sailing under it."

Yet, in spite of Madison's message and the depth of public feeling over violated neutral rights, many of the representatives of the maritime states, those states most injured by impressments and ship seizures, voted against war. Even though they suffered most from British maritime restrictions, the New England and Middle Atlantic states also profited most from the wartime trade. That trade, even with the humiliation of impressment, seemed to some too valuable to be destroyed by war.[13] Those states were also the strongholds of French-hating Federalists. Staunch Federalists could not approve a war against England, a war that made the United States a virtual ally of Napoleon.

In the House of Representatives the vote on June 4 on the declaration of war was seventy-nine to forty-nine. The large dissenting minority represented mainly the northern maritime states. The West, according to one interpretation, voted most solidly for war. The deep South followed a similar pattern, while the upper South showed some division.

In the Senate, where the war hawks were not as strong as in the House, Federalists debated the declaration for two weeks. Finally, on June 17, the Senate, seemingly also along sectional lines, voted nineteen to thirteen for war. Since the United States had good cause for war against France also, the Senate debated for days on whether or not to include France in the declaration. A proposal to that effect lost by only four votes.[14]

On the basis of the vote in Congress, some scholars have concluded that neutral rights and impressment served as righteous pretexts for those who desired war for other reasons. Others have pointed out that if Congress had known that England would repeal the Orders in Council, there would have been no war, despite the influence of the war hawks. Despite these theories of scholars, what seems clear is that the causes of the war were not only complex but also rooted in years of controversy, and that the major source of controversy was the question of neutral rights.[15]

Ironically, on the day that Madison proclaimed the war, New Englanders, those most concerned with maritime rights, lamented the government's action in fast and prayer. William Cullen Bryant, then seventeen years old, expressed New England's feeling in these words:

> The same ennobling spirit
> That kindles valor's flame,
> That nerves us to a war of right,
> Forbids a war of *shame*.[16]

As if bothered by inner feelings of guilt, for allowing themselves to drift into an unnecessary war, both sides made efforts to stop it as soon as it began. On June 26, in the same message that carried the news of the war declaration, Secretary of State Monroe asked the American *chargé* in London to arrange an immediate armistice if England would give up impressment. On that question,

Lord Castlereagh would not yield. That was "a right upon which the naval strength of the empire mainly depends," he said.[17]

In America, the new British Minister several times urged an armistice, and in September an English admiral under direct instructions from London did the same. The United States rejected those efforts to stop the war before it was truly launched because Britain refused to yield on the question of impressments.

An Unpopular War

Dwarfed by the conflict in Europe, the War of 1812 was a minor war fought on the fringes of Britain's empire. It was also a peculiar war. Usually a nation at war seeks allies and tries to injure the enemy in any way it can, but the United States, having deep grievances against Napoleon as well as England, made no effort to form an alliance with France or in any way to cooperate with Napoleon against England. The United States, for reasons of its own, entered the war alone, fought alone, and made peace alone. Yet when Napoleon invaded Russia in the summer of 1812, President Madison believed that he carried the fortunes of the United States with him.

Napoleon failed in Russia, and Americans realized none of their objectives in their own war. Their war ended in a stalemate, almost in a defeat. Militarily and politically, they were unprepared for war. Party feeling over the war was bitter, and sectional loyalties seriously divided the people.

New England Federalists offered the greatest opposition to the war. They considered it the Republican party's struggle, and derisively called it "Mr. Madison's War." Some talked of secession and were even disloyal. One New England clergyman, for instance, explained to his congregation that Moses had dissolved the union with Egypt. Then he called on "a resolute, a pious people" to follow the Biblical example. During the war New Englanders supplied invading British troops with food and other provisions, and some did not hesitate to take an oath of allegiance to King George. So strong was Federalist and antiwar opposition that in his bid for re-election in 1812, Madison lost all but two of the states north of the Potomac River. The South and West re-elected him.

England realized that the northern maritime states opposed the war, so she cultivated secessionist sentiment in those states. England's commander-in-chief in Canada made it his policy, he said, "to avoid committing any act which may even by a strained construction tend to unite the eastern and southern states." From the beginning, Britain's most powerful weapon was her blockade of the American coast, but she exempted northern New England from its rigors until the spring of 1814. New Englanders, therefore, traded with Canada and England during almost the entire war and even withheld money from the Federal government and invested it in British treasury notes.

Other sections of the country also lagged in support of the government. Some Republicans, even in Madison's Virginia, disliked the war, but usually Federalists outside New England suffered at the hands of aroused pro-war Republicans. In Baltimore in July, 1812, a pro-administration mob killed and mutilated Federalists and other prominent citizens who had publicly opposed the war. The opposition claimed that "Mr. Madison's Mobs" crushed honest criticism and free speech.

The Military Struggle

Aware of the deep divisions within the country and of the nation's unpreparedness, Madison and his advisers wanted an early peace and tried to get one, but the war hawks clamored for a swift victory in Canada first. Therefore, even though it had only an inadequate army, the United States launched a three-pronged attack against Canada in the summer of 1812. Under the leadership of an able British general, Isaac Brock, the Canadians repelled the attack and later invaded American territory. This was during the period when Britain was so involved in the European war that she could give scant attention to the defense of Canada.

The entire nation did not support the expedition against Canada. The South, for instance, had refused full support. Angry Northerners argued that Madison and Monroe as Southerners were unenthusiastic about conquering Canada. The North, however, did not support southern efforts to take Florida. In July, 1812, and in February, 1813, northern opposition in Congress killed legislation which would have empowered the President to take and occupy Florida.

Poor preparations and incompetent leadership, more than sectional friction, accounted for the specific American failures in 1812 and 1813. The notable victory of this period belonged to Lieutenant Oliver Hazard Perry of the Navy. In September, 1813, with an improvised fleet made of green timbers, he defeated the British forces on Lake Erie.

In 1814 the war took a new turn because of events in Europe. The United States had gone to war, by "coincidence" according to Madison, just as Napoleon invaded Russia. By the end of the year that invasion turned to disaster, and by April, 1814, the defeated Napoleon was on his way to exile on Elba. The fall of Napoleon left the United States alone to face the full might of Britain. In the summer of 1814 Britain tightened her blockade and sent thousands of veteran troops released from European service to Canada.

Then British forces invaded the area of Chesapeake Bay, captured Washington, and burned the White House and the Capitol, but failed to take Baltimore. They also attempted an invasion of New England and New York by way of Lake Champlain, but Lieutenant Thomas Macdonough saved that part of the country, and the nation from possible disunion, by winning a decisive naval victory near Plattsburgh in September.

The only decisive American land victory won independent of naval power was the Battle of New Orleans of January 8, 1815. Andrew Jackson gained this victory after the peace treaty was signed. It did not, therefore, affect the outcome of the war.

Since the United States went to war with a pitifully small navy, it could do little to challenge Britain's maritime supremacy. American sloops-of-war and super-frigates, such as the *Constitution*, won a number of individual naval duels. "Our little naval triumphs" Madison called them, but before the end of the war the Royal Navy swept the American Navy and merchant fleet from the seas.

American privateers inflicted greater damage on the British than did the regular Navy. They roamed the seas and preyed on shipping, even in the English Channel itself. Altogether they captured or destroyed almost 1,350 British merchant ships, but Britain strangled even privateering with a convoy system and with an ever-tightening blockade.

Thus, when the war ended, the United States had no navy, its coast was tightly blockaded, and the British held considerable American territory. They occupied part of Maine, and in the Northwest they, or their Indian allies, controlled the upper Mississippi Valley and even portions of northern Illinois and northern Iowa.

The Diplomatic Problems

The diplomacy that brought peace was another of the unusual features of the War of 1812. Since the United States and Britain maintained diplomatic relations while they fought, peace negotiations began almost as soon as hostilities started. Throughout the negotiations, the results of the fighting and developments in Europe influenced the demands of both sides. The first efforts, English and American, to make an armistice failed, as we have seen, because neither side would retreat on the issue of impressment.

After those failures, Russia offered to mediate between her British ally and the United States. The Tsar, Alexander I, was anxious to relieve England of the responsibilities of the American war which diverted energy from the European conflict. Moreover, Russia wanted the American trade England now kept from her ports.

Although the Tsar made his offer in September, 1812, it did not reach Madison until March, nine months after the war began. With the war unpopular, the fighting going badly, the British blockade growing increasingly severe, and with Napoleon's defeat in Russia now a fact, Madison knew he had to grasp the offer. So anxious was he to quiet the clamor of the peace party and to end the embarrassing war that he even acted without finding out how Britain would respond to the Tsar's offer.

Madison immediately appointed two special envoys, Albert Gallatin, his Secretary of the Treasury and one of his most trusted advisers, and James A. Bayard, a Federalist Senator from Delaware, to join John Quincy Adams, the American Minister in St. Petersburg, to negotiate peace with British envoys under the Tsar's mediation. With polite expressions of regret, Castlereagh, however, refused the Tsar's offer, but did say that England was willing to negotiate directly with the United States. For reasons of his own, the Tsar ignored Castlereagh's counter-offer and continued to press his own mediation offer on the British.

Finally, in November, 1813, Castlereagh wrote directly to Secretary of State Monroe offering to negotiate a peace without intermediaries. Madison jumped at the offer and appointed a peace commission of five men to meet with the British in Ghent. It included Adams, Gallatin, and Bayard, and two new envoys, Henry Clay and Jonathan Russell, formerly the American *chargé* in London. Gallatin was the outstanding figure, but the commission as a whole was exceedingly able. Since it took many weeks for the exchange of dispatches and instructions between Washington and the negotiators, the commission had wide discretionary powers.

The British commission, composed of three men, was undistinguished. Since it had no power of initiative, it referred almost everything to superiors in London. Its members were, according to Gallatin, little more than puppets of Castlereagh. One reason for this was that the American negotiations were a mere sideshow in comparison to the more important negotiations at the Congress of Vienna.[18] England sent her finest statesmen there.

The contrast between Vienna and Ghent, the Flemish town garrisoned by British troops where the American envoys met the British peacemakers, was striking. In Vienna the diplomats could enjoy the rhythm of dancing, but in Ghent the American commissioners had to negotiate to the rhythm of marching boots. After keeping the American envoys waiting over a month, the British commissioners arrived on August 6, 1814. Negotiations began two days later.

Originally the American instructions had called for an end to "illegal blockades," a recognition of American neutral rights, and a settlement of other controversial matters. The one indispensable condition dealt with impressment. If Britain will not abolish impressment, Secretary of State Monroe wrote, "the United States will have appealed to arms in vain." If you fail on the question of impressment, he said, "all further negotiations will cease, and you will return home without delay."[19]

Those instructions would have placed the American commissioners in a weak negotiating position. The status of their government did not help them either. It was almost bankrupt, without friends, and its military future appeared bleak. With England's armed forces no longer tied down in Europe, they could not expect her to make any concessions, particularly on the issue of impressment. Even though impressment now became an academic question, because the Royal Navy stopped the practice with the end of the European war, England would not give up her right to impress.

In June, therefore, Madison had asked his cabinet, "Shall a treaty of peace, silent on the subject of impressment, be authorized?" In effect, the advisers answered "Aye."[20] Then Monroe instructed the envoys to put aside the impressment question. This abandonment of the one indispensable condition reached the commissioners on the evening of August 8 and placed them in a stronger bargaining position than they had anticipated. It allowed them to insist, as they did throughout the negotiations, that the settlement must be based on the *status quo ante bellum*, meaning a mutual restoration of territory. This, of course, was far different from the objectives Americans had held when they started the war, but it reflected a realistic appraisal of America's position in the negotiations. The fate of Canada or Florida was not mentioned.

The British demands were sweeping. "Their terms," Bayard complained, "were those of a Conqueror to a conquered People." Yet those terms appeared to reflect important opinion in Britain. When the negotiators had prepared to leave for Ghent, for example, *The Times* of London offered its instructions. "Our demands may be couched in a single word," it said, "Submission!"[21]

From the first the British said they would make no concessions on impressment or neutral rights. They demanded initially that Americans place no forts or armed ships on the Great Lakes and cede territory in Maine, northern New York, and between Lake Superior and navigable water on the Mississippi River. The British commissioners also advanced as an indispensable condition the twenty-year-old idea of a nominally independent Indian buffer state between Canada and the aggressive Americans, seeking to carve that state out of American territory in the Northwest.

The Americans flatly rejected the British terms. They would not, they said, "surrender both the rights of sovereignty and of soil over nearly one-third of the territorial dominions of the United States to Indians." The British demands, they felt, "were above all dishonorable." Bayard warned the British that their terms would prolong the war.

At this point so hopeless did the Americans consider their position that they prepared to break off the negotiations. Fortunately, Castlereagh himself did not insist upon the Indian buffer state as an indispensable condition to peace. "The substance of the question is," he wrote to the Prime Minister, "are we prepared to continue the war for territorial arrangements?"[22] The British cabinet was unwilling to do so and the two commissions, therefore, continued their negotiations.

In the place of the Indian buffer state and exclusive control of the Great Lakes, the British were willing to accept a general amnesty for the Indians which would restore them to the lands they held before the war. In place of the boundary revisions they had demanded originally, they now proposed peace on the basis of *uti possidetis*, meaning that each nation would retain the territory it had won.

The Americans were discouraged. Early in October they heard news of the capture and burning of Washington. "Let them feast on Washington," Britain's Prime Minister said. The British terms appeared now as demands for American territory, demands which might be enforced by arms. Later in the month, however, the Americans received the pleasant news of Macdonough's victory on Lake Champlain. Therefore, they again refused the British terms and prepared to leave Ghent. The only acceptable principle, they insisted, now as before, was the *status quo ante bellum*.

After Macdonough's victory the British proposal for territorial settlement was not as sweeping as it could have been. The British did not demand the upper Mississippi Valley still held by their troops and Indian allies. Under the principle of *uti possidetis*, as they advanced it, their main acquisition would have been northern Maine.

After the Americans had rejected their revised demands, the British sought some means of breaking the deadlock. First they asked the American commissioners to present a draft of a treaty acceptable to the United States. Then they tried to find a means of ending the American war through force, for the negotiations at Vienna were going badly and the strain of the war was weakening Britain's foreign policy in Europe.

The government, and the public, wanted the Duke of Wellington to take command of British forces in America. He was willing, but warned that "you could not spare me out of Europe" this year, and that his going would give Europe an exaggerated notion of British defeats in America. He also said his trip might be futile, for "that which appears to me to be wanting in America is not a General, or a General officer and troops, but a Naval superiority on the Lakes." In regard to negotiations at Ghent, he added, "I confess that I think you have no right, from the state of war to demand any concession of territory from America . . . why stipulate for the *uti possidetis?*" [23]

Wellington's advice settled the outcome of the negotiations. Although the British cabinet had at first intended to use the treaty the American commissioners had drafted on November 10 merely as a basis for further negotiation, it now accepted that draft as the foundation for a peace settlement.

The Treaty of Ghent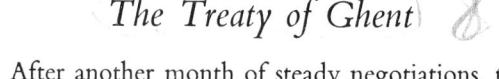

After another month of steady negotiations, the American and British envoys signed the Treaty of Ghent on Christmas Eve, 1814. "I hoped," John Quincy Adams said, "it would be the last treaty of peace between Great Britain and the United States." [24]

The President accepted the treaty without question the day it arrived. "Peace, at all times a blessing," he told the Senate, "is peculiarly welcome. . . ."[25] The Senate approved it two days later, that is on February 16, 1815, by a unanimous vote. Within two more days Madison exchanged ratifications, proclaimed the treaty, and published it.

By restoring all territory occupied by the forces of both nations, the treaty embodied the American principle of the *status quo ante bellum*. It assured an amnesty for the Indians who had fought on either side and provided for several joint commissions to settle boundary controversies, but did not mention impressment, neutral rights, Canada or Florida, or any of the issues that had led to war. The United States, in fact, was fortunate in not losing any of its own territory. Moreover, that treaty was followed by a lasting peace, and unlike many peace treaties, it did nothing that had to be undone.

The reasons for Britain's leniency in her second peace with the United States were the pressures of foreign policy in Europe and politics at home. After twenty years of war, the English government wisely preferred a satisfactory peace in Europe to a complete victory in America.

British nationalists, nonetheless, were disappointed with the treaty. The negotiators, one London newspaper said, "had humbled themselves in the dust and thereby brought discredit on the country." The masses and others who were sick of war, on the other hand, welcomed the return of peace. They were unwilling to fight except in a war of self-defense, and the war in America in 1814 was not that. Manufacturers, shippers, and merchants were also pleased. They wanted to end an unpopular property tax the government had long levied to finance the war in Europe. More important, perhaps, they desired and needed renewed access to American markets. The news of Jackson's victory at New Orleans and of Napoleon's return to Paris from his exile on Elba reached London simultaneously in March. After that, even the nationalists and other critics of the peace accepted it without further grumbling.

Americans were delighted with the treaty. Most of them, even Westerners, recognized that under the circumstances the terms were good, as good as they had any reason to expect. Even though the Federalist press criticized it, the treaty was one of the most popular Americans have ever negotiated. Terms of the settlement reached Washington in February, about a week after the people had learned that Jackson had saved New Orleans. In New York, where the news arrived first, church bells rang in every spire and people filled the streets shouting joyfully, "A peace! A peace!" As the news traveled, other cities responded with similar demonstrations.

The unthinking, while rejoicing in Jackson's victory, assumed as a result that the United States had beaten Britain into submission. "In the fulness of our glory," one naïve American wrote, "we grant peace to a worsted enemy." How else, some Americans reasoned, could the United States with large portions of its territory still occupied, have won such a favorable peace?

Canadians, who had fought hard and well in defense of their homes, were disappointed. The treaty, they felt, left them exposed to future American aggression.

Since the Treaty of Ghent gave the United States none of its original war objectives, some writers, with considerable justification, have called the War of 1812 a useless war. It was not entirely that. Although Westerners had failed to conquer Canada, they realized one objective: the war ended the Indian menace on the northwest frontier.[26] Since the British surrendered the regions of the American Northwest that they had occupied, they lost prestige and influence with the Indians there. Tecumseh had died in 1813 fighting for the British, and with the peace his plan for an Indian confederation collapsed.

In the South, even though Americans did not obtain all of Florida as quickly as they had desired, they had removed a powerful Indian barrier to expansion and settlement. Andrew Jackson, in the Battle of Horseshoe Bend of March 27, 1814, in present-day Alabama, defeated the most powerful group of southern Indians, the Creek confederacy. In the peace treaty that followed, Jackson compelled the Creeks to surrender half their lands, comprising southern Georgia and two-thirds of Alabama.

More important in the long run than the indirect advantages previously cited were the larger results. The war strengthened nationalism by ultimately uniting the country, and the Treaty of Ghent marked the beginning of what would ultimately be a new Anglo-American friendship, but these developments might have come later without a costly war.

Other Anglo-American Settlements

The peace at Ghent was only the beginning of a larger Anglo-American settlement. The American commissioners had been instructed to make a commercial treaty that would replace the commercial provisions of the expired Jay's Treaty. Three of them, John Quincy Adams, who became the Minister in London, Clay, and Gallatin, tried to win acceptance of the maritime principles that England had rejected at Ghent. Finally, on July 3, 1815, they signed a convention that freed American and British trade from discriminatory duties and in other essentials renewed commercial relations as they had been before the war. Britain, however, refused to renew certain fishing privileges and to admit American ships to her West Indies. The commercial convention, considered a stopgap at the time, was limited to four years. The next agreement, dealing with disarmament, proved more satisfactory.

After failing to exclude Americans from the Great Lakes and Lake Champlain,

England, according to John Quincy Adams, had decided "not only to maintain, but to increase the British naval armament upon the lakes." As control of the lakes had been critically important in the war, the United States would not allow England to gain naval ascendancy there. To prevent that ascendancy, the United States had either to embark on a costly naval race or work out an agreement for mutual disarmament on the lakes. Therefore, the American government instructed John Quincy Adams in November, 1815, to propose mutual disarmament to the British government.

When Adams first advanced the idea in January, 1816, Castlereagh agreed that "everything beyond what is necessary to guard against smuggling is calculated only to produce mischief." [27] The British Foreign Minister, however, did not fully accept the suggestion until April.

Since Adams did not have full powers to conclude a definite agreement, Castlereagh transferred the conversations to Washington. There, Secretary of State Monroe and the British Minister, Charles Bagot, discussed the disarmament problem and reached an agreement. Final consent from London did not arrive until Monroe became President. Then, Acting Secretary of State Richard Rush exchanged notes with Bagot on April 28 and 29, 1817. Thus, the agreement that naval forces on the Great Lakes and Lake Champlain should be limited to a few light naval vessels, a force sufficient only for police and customs service, became the Rush-Bagot Agreement.

Wanting the arrangement to be permanently binding, Bagot suggested that the President send it to the Senate for approval. After considerable delay, Monroe did so. The Senate approved it on April 16, 1818. Monroe then ratified and proclaimed it, thus giving it the status of a treaty.

That agreement, which either government could terminate after giving a notice of six months, applied only to naval armaments on the lakes. It did not extend to the land frontier. [28] The Rush-Bagot Agreement, the first example of reciprocal reduction of naval armaments, though modified, is still in force.

The Rush-Bagot Agreement settled only one of the lesser problems in Anglo-American relations. American statesmen had long wanted to bring all of them together in one general negotiation. Since the commercial convention of 1815 would expire in July, 1819, President Monroe appointed Rush, Adams' successor, as Minister to England, and Albert Gallatin, then Minister to France, special commissioners in 1818 to negotiate a new commercial treaty and to settle all issues with Great Britain.

One of the most important of those issues was that of the northwest boundary between Canada and the United States. The controversy over that boundary stemmed from the geographical ignorance of the peace negotiators of 1783. The treaty of that year read that the boundary ran from the northwest corner of the Lake of the Woods, located in present-day Minnesota, on "a due west course to the River Mississippi," but the source of the Mississippi was far south of such a line. Beyond the Lake of the Woods, therefore, the boundary between Canada and the United States was undetermined.

After the United States had acquired Louisiana, Secretary of State Madison had tried to settle the controversy by fixing the boundary at the forty-ninth parallel. Britain had agreed to that line in the abortive Monroe-Pinkney Treaty of 1806, but that solution died with the treaty. During the negotiations at Ghent the Americans again suggested a boundary settlement at the forty-ninth parallel, only to drop the proposal when the British insisted on access to the source of the Mississippi with the right of free navigation.

When Rush and Gallatin took up the question in 1818, they also proposed a boundary that ran westward from the Lake of the Woods on the forty-ninth parallel to the Pacific Ocean. They refused any change which would give the British a claim to the headwaters of the Mississippi. The British negotiators then gave up their efforts to reach the Mississippi and agreed to a compromise boundary that ran west from the Lake of the Woods on the forty-ninth parallel, but only to the Rocky Mountains.

The Convention of 1818, which was signed on October 20, provided that territory west of the Rockies claimed by either side would be free and open for ten years to Englishmen and Americans without injury to the claims of either country. This clause was the basis for what has been commonly called the "joint occupation" of the Oregon country.

Besides the boundary issue, the negotiators settled a controversy over slaves that the British had carried away after the War of 1812, renewed the stopgap commercial convention for ten years, and resolved a dispute over the fisheries off the coast of British North America.

At Ghent the American commissioners had been unable to secure a renewal of the "liberty" to fish along the coast of British North America as allowed in the

THE BOUNDARY AGREEMENT OF 1818 WITH GREAT BRITAIN

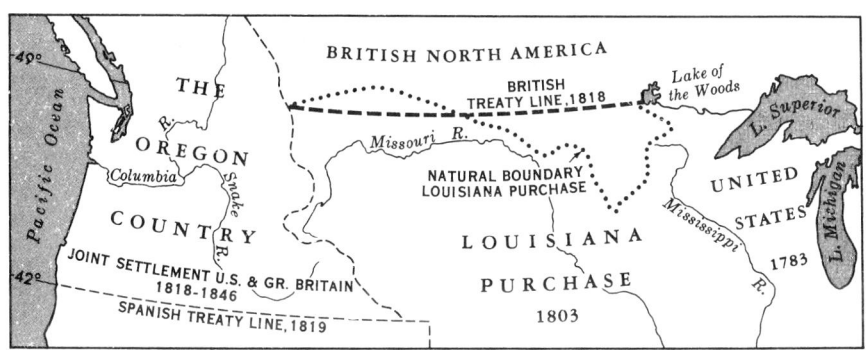

peace treaty of 1783. American statesmen had always contended that the "liberty" to fish in those waters was an inalienable "natural" right, but the British argued that Americans had lost their fishing rights under the rule that mutual declarations of war abrogate existing treaties between the warring powers. They refused, therefore, to renew the old fishing "liberty" and insisted that the whole fisheries question had to be considered anew.

Without a renewal of their right to navigate the length of the Mississippi, which also stemmed from the treaty of 1783 and which the war had also nullified, the British said, they would not give Americans the "liberty" to fish in their waters. Finally both sides compromised. The British gave up their demand for free navigation of the Mississippi, and the Americans accepted restricted fishing "liberties." Nonetheless, the Convention of 1818 granted enough privileges to make fishing off Newfoundland and Labrador profitable for Americans and made those privileges perpetual.

"It settles at best but a few of the many disputed points between the two nations," Rush said of the convention.[29] Yet with it the United States resolved most of the major conflicts of 1812. It, along with the other settlements, constituted another important step toward a lasting peace with Great Britain.

NOTES

1. To William Pinkney, Jan. 3, 1809, quoted in Abbot Smith, "Mr. Madison's War: An Unsuccessful Experiment in the Conduct of National Policy," *Political Science Quarterly*, XVII (June 1942), 229–246.

2. In "George Canning, Great Britain, and the United States, 1807–1809," *The American Historical Review*, LXIII (Oct. 1957), 20–21, Bradford Perkins suggests that even if Canning had accepted the Erskine Agreement, Anglo-American discord probably would not have ended. See also his *Prologue to War: England and the United States, 1805–1812* (Berkeley, Calif., 1961), pp. 217–218.

3. *American State Papers, Foreign Relations* (6 vols., Washington, 1832), III, 386–387.

4. Quoted in Charles C. Tansill, "Robert Smith," in Samuel F. Bemis, ed., *The American Secretaries of State and Their Diplomacy* (10 vols., New York, 1927–29), III, 179.

5. The quotation is from the *Courier*, July 17, 1811, in Reginald Horsman, *The Causes of the War of 1812* (Philadelphia,

1962), p. 220. For appraisals of Foster, see pp. 202–203, 220–221, and 259–260.

6. The idea of agrarian discontent and distress is advanced in George R. Taylor, "Prices in the Mississippi Valley Preceding the War of 1812," *Journal of Economic and Business History*, III (Nov. 1930), 148–163; Taylor, "Agrarian Discontent in the Mississippi Valley Preceding the War of 1812," *The Journal of Political Economy*, XXXIX (Aug. 1931), 471–505; and Margaret K. Latimer, "South Carolina—A Protagonist of the War of 1812," *The American Historical Review*, LXI (July 1956), 914–929.

7. For the land hunger thesis, see Louis M. Hacker, "Western Land Hunger and the War of 1812: A Conjecture," *Mississippi Valley Historical Review*, X (March 1924), 365–395, and its rejection by Julius W. Pratt in "Western War Aims in the War of 1812," *ibid.*, XII (June 1925), 36–50.

8. Reginald Horsman, in "British Indian Policy in the Northwest, 1807–1812," *ibid.*,

XLV (June 1958), 51–66, points out that through their aid the British, in effect, helped organize Indian resistance to the Americans. See also his "American Indian Policy in the Old Northwest, 1783–1812," *William and Mary Quarterly*, 3rd ser., XVIII (Jan. 1961), 35–53.

9. Irving Brant, in *James Madison: Commander-in-Chief, 1812–1936* (Indianapolis, 1961), pp. 17–18, suggests that there was no balanced Canada-Florida objective and that Canada was desired as bargaining material at the peace talks. See also Perkins, *Prologue to War*, p. 289 and Horsman, *The Causes of the War of 1812*, pp. 168–175 and 183.

10. Quoted in Julius W. Pratt, "James Monroe," in Bemis, *Secretaries of State*, III, 223.

11. For details, see Samuel E. Morison, "The Henry-Crillon Affair of 1812" in *By Land and By Sea* (New York, 1953), pp. 265–286.

12. John Quincy Adams to Thomas Boylston Adams, Sept. 29, 1812, in Charles Francis Adams, ed., "Correspondence of John Quincy Adams, 1811–1814," *Proceedings of the American Antiquarian Society*, New Series, XXXIII (April 1913), 120.

13. John H. Reinoehl, however, in "Post-Embargo Trade and Merchant Prosperity: Experiences of the Crowninshield Family, 1809–1812," *Mississippi Valley Historical Review*, XLII (Sept. 1955), 229–249, suggests that profitable trade was already on the decline before war was declared. Reginald Horsman, in "Western War Aims, 1811–1812," *Indiana Magazine of History*, LII (March 1957), 1–16, concludes that British maritime policy was the fundamental cause for war. See also Horsman, *The Causes of the War of 1812*, pp. 263–267, where he emphasizes that the basic cause for war lay in Europe.

14. Perkins, *Prologue to War*, p. 410, rejects the sectional pattern as a cause for war and suggests that party regularity was more important.

15. Norman K. Risjord, in "1812: Conservatives, War Hawks, and the Nation's Honor," *William and Mary Quarterly*, 3rd ser., XVIII (April 1961), 196–210, argues that concern for national honor and integrity was the main cause, an interpretation shared by Perkins, *Prologue to War*. John S. Pancake, in "The 'Invisibles': A Chapter in the Opposition to President Madison," *Journal of Southern History*, XXI (Feb. 1955), 17–37, stresses the influence of the war party in the Senate, which based its actions on maritime grievances, as a cause. For an analysis of various theories on the causes of the war, see Warren H. Goodman, "The Origins of the War of 1812: A Survey of Changing Interpretations," *Mississippi Valley Historical Review*, XXVIII (Sept. 1941), 171–186.

16. "A Fourth of July Ode" in Parke Godwin, *A Biography of William Cullen Bryant* (2 vols., New York, 1883), I, 106.

17. *American State Papers, Foreign Relations*, III, 590.

18. This is strikingly emphasized in the memoir of Henry Goulburn, one of the British negotiators. See Wilbur D. Jones, ed., "A British View of the War of 1812 and the Peace Negotiations," *Mississippi Valley Historical Review*, XLV (Dec. 1958), 481–487. The British government did, however, give serious, though intermittent thought to the American negotiations. See Fred L. Engleman, *The Peace of Christmas Eve* (New York, 1962), pp. 120–121

19. Quoted in Pratt, "Monroe," in Bemis, *Secretaries of State*, III, 270.

20. June 23 and 24, 1814, in James Madison, *Letters and Other Writings of James Madison*, published by order of Congress (4 vols., New York, 1884), III, 408.

21. Bayard to Robert G. Harper, Aug. 19, 1814, in Elizabeth Donnan, ed., "Papers of James A. Bayard, 1796–1815," *Annual Report of the American Historical Association, 1913* (2 vols., Washington), II, 318. *The Times* quotation is in Engleman, *Peace of Christmas Eve*, p. 123.

22. Quoted in Samuel F. Bemis, *John Quincy Adams and the Foundations of American Foreign Policy* (New York, 1949), p. 205.

23. The quotations are from Dudley Mills, "The Duke of Wellington and the Peace Negotiations at Ghent in 1814," *The Canadian Historical Review*, II (March 1921), 25, 27–28.

24. Entry of Dec. 24, 1814, in Charles F. Adams, ed., *Memoirs of John Quincy Adams, Comprising Portions of His Diary from 1795 to 1848* (12 vols., Philadelphia, 1874–77), III, 126.

25. Quoted in Brant, *Madison: Commander-in-Chief*, p. 369.

26. Charles M. Gates, in "The West in American Diplomacy, 1812–1815," *Mississippi Valley Historical Review*, XXVI (March 1940), 510, points out that in this sense the American expansionists had won a victory.

27. Quoted in Alfred L. Burt, *The United States, Great Britain, and British North America* (New Haven, 1940), p. 389.

28. The building of land fortifications on the border by both sides did not end until 1872. See C. P. Stacey, "The Myth of the Unguarded Frontier, 1815–1871," *The American Historical Review*, LVI (October 1950), 2.

29. Quoted in John H. Powell, *Richard Rush: Republican Diplomat, 1780–1859* (Philadelphia, 1942), p. 119.

Chapter Six

THE EVOLUTION OF THE MONROE DOCTRINE

Expansionists had long been as eager to acquire West and East Florida from Spain as they had been to conquer Canada. Those provinces, Americans said, were like a pistol held by an alien hand pointed at the heart of the nation. The analogy of the pistol, according to the geography of the provinces, was true enough, but fundamentally Americans wanted land, particularly the plantation land with its rivers flowing into the Gulf of Mexico. The United States eventually got the land of the Floridas, but not all at one time.

The United States began nibbling at the Floridas immediately after it had achieved independence. When Spain reacquired the Floridas in 1783, she had claimed all the territory formerly known as British East and West Florida. Under the British, West Florida ran north from the Gulf of Mexico to the line of thirty-two degrees and twenty-eight minutes between the Mississippi and Apalachicola Rivers. East Florida extended east and south of the Apalachicola. The United States contested Spain's claim to all of West Florida by setting its southern boundary at the thirty-first parallel. Faced with the growing power of the United States and with war in Europe, Spain finally yielded in Pinckney's Treaty of 1795 and accepted the thirty-first parallel as the northern boundary of West Florida. This was America's first step toward acquiring all of the Floridas.

After Spain ceded Louisiana to France in 1800, the United States mistakenly believed that the Louisiana grant included the Floridas. Jefferson, therefore, tried to buy them along with New Orleans, but when he purchased all of Louisiana in 1803 he did not get the Floridas. This disappointed both the expansionists and the two negotiators, James Monroe and Robert R. Livingston, who were at first convinced that the United States had no claim to West Florida. Less than two weeks after signing the Louisiana treaties, however, Livingston interpreted the vague eastern boundary of the Louisiana territory to include West Florida to the Perdido River. Monroe supported that claim, thinking it "too clear to admit of a doubt." Both men urged Jefferson and his Secretary of State to claim West Florida as part of the Louisiana territory. The President did that, but did not occupy the territory to the Perdido. Instead, he made the American claim a "subject of negotiation with Spain"—a subject to be brought up while Spain was at war and helpless to resist American advances. "We shall certainly obtain the Floridas," he said, "and all in good time."

The Mobile Act

Congress supported Jefferson's efforts to acquire West Florida by passing the Mobile Act of February 24, 1804, which gave him authority to annex and to establish a new customs district at Mobile Bay, clearly Spanish territory. When Spain protested, Jefferson did not push the annexation. Instead he proclaimed the revenue district to include territory lying within the boundaries of the United States and placed the port of entry on the Mobile River a few miles above the thirty-first parallel in American territory.[1] Although that plan of "aggression" failed, Jefferson did not give up.

In Madrid, meanwhile, Charles Pinckney, the American Minister, urged Spain to surrender the Floridas, but the Spaniards would not yield. Therefore, in April, 1804, Jefferson ordered Monroe to Madrid to assist Pinckney. Spain was now Napoleon's ally in the war against England. This, thought Jefferson, was a good time to take advantage of Spain's weakness in America.

Monroe and Pinckney's instructions directed them to insist upon Spain's recognizing that Louisiana included West Florida to the Perdido and to offer to buy East Florida. The United States offered cash, withdrawal of certain financial claims against Spain, and concessions on the southwestern boundary of the Louisiana territory. Spain, supported by France, still refused to make any concessions or to sell. When the Madrid negotiations collapsed in May, 1805, Monroe and Pinckney wrote to Secretary of State James Madison recommending seizure of West and East Florida. Then, they said, the United States could bargain on retaining the provinces as payment for the claims against Spain.

Although he had previously refused to support American efforts to acquire the Floridas, Napoleon, who needed money, now changed his mind. In 1805, he offered indirectly to force Spain to yield those provinces for seven million dollars. While paid to Spain, most of the money would really go to Napoleon, and Jefferson knew it. Even though John Randolph, chairman of the House Ways and Means Committee, considered it "a base prostration of the national character to excite one nation by money to bully another nation out of its property," Jefferson persuaded Congress in February, 1806, to appropriate secretly two million dollars to start the negotiation.[2] When revealed, this maneuver became notorious as the "Two Million Act."

Before the negotiations started, Napoleon's situation in Europe changed to his advantage, so that he reversed his stand on aiding the United States in its bid for the Floridas. Jefferson's devious plans then collapsed, but later might have revived. Napoleon wanted American support for his Continental System, and in January, 1808, tried in vain to induce Jefferson to enter the war against England by offering him the Floridas.

Later that same year, Napoleon took over Spain and then decided against giving the Floridas to the United States. He deposed the king and placed his brother Joseph on the throne. Civil war in Spain and revolution in Spain's colonies in America followed. The United States, meanwhile, suspended diplomatic relations with any Spanish government. When Jefferson left office in March, 1809, therefore, his expansionist plans had failed. The United States had no official relations with Spain and had failed to acquire the Floridas.

Nonetheless the American desire for the Floridas did not slacken. President Madison shared Jefferson's views and was himself eager to obtain those provinces. "The acquisition of the Floridas," a French minister in Washington had noted, "is the object of all of Mr. Madison's prayers."

Madison believed that Americans living in West Florida would help bring that territory into the United States. His views were sound. Unlike Spain's other colonies, West Florida had a population that was largely American, in part because Spanish authorities had unwisely encouraged Americans to settle there. In 1810, Spain's authority in the populated districts declined to almost nothing. Secretary of State Robert Smith sent agents into West Florida who spread the word among the settlers "that in the event of a political separation from the parent country, their incorporation into our Union would coincide with the sentiments and policy of the United States." In September, while revolution rocked Spain's other colonies, American settlers encouraged by Madison's agents captured Baton Rouge, declared West Florida "free and independent," adopted a blue flag with a lone star, and asked the United States to annex them.

Needing no urging, Madison acted two days after the declaration of independence reached him. Claiming that West Florida to the Perdido River belonged to the United States by right of the Louisiana Purchase, Madison proclaimed American control over that territory on October 27, 1810, and authorized the governor of the Louisiana Territory to occupy the land, or as much of it as he could without using force against Spanish troops. American troops took possession in December, but only as far east as the Pearl River. They avoided Spanish soldiers at Mobile. Shortly after, while still skirting the Mobile area,

American forces took control to the Perdido. This was the second step in acquiring the Floridas. "One keeps on growing bit by bit in this world," the Tsar of Russia smilingly told the American Minister there on hearing of the Florida acquisition.[3]

Other foreign powers, particularly France and England, protested the American occupation. Secretary of State Smith said the United States acted to forestall English seizure of the territory, but the British *chargé d'affaires* in Washington asked an embarrassing question. "Would it not have been more worthy of the generosity of a free nation like this" and more in keeping with existing ties of friendship between the United States and Spain, he said, "to have simply offered its assistance to crush the common enemy of both, rather than to have made such interference the pretext for wresting a province from a friendly power, and that at the time of her adversity?"[4]

Although embarrassing, the foreign protests did not decrease Madison's appetite for the Floridas. Already, war with England seemed probable and expansionists wanted the rest of the Floridas. If the nation went to war against England, Florida might become an English base. The Spanish governor at Pensacola, moreover, had indicated that he would be willing to surrender the Floridas to the United States. Madison, therefore, threw the influence of his administration behind an effort to obtain congressional approval for the occupation of West Florida beyond the Perdido, and of East Florida.

Congress gave that approval on January 15, 1811, in a secret resolution and an act. The resolution said that the United States "cannot, without serious inquietude, see any part of the said territory [Florida] pass into the hands of any foreign power."[5] This "no-transfer resolution" expressed an idea that was to become a fundamental principle in American foreign policy in the Western Hemisphere. From this time on United States policy clearly opposed the transfer of territory in the Americas to outside nations.

The act empowered Madison to take Florida east of the Perdido if local authorities gave it up, or if necessary to prevent seizure by a foreign power. It also gave him the authority to spend up to one hundred thousand dollars and to use the Army and Navy in seizing the territory.

Revolution in East Florida

Now strengthened by the support of Congress, Madison employed General George Mathews, a Revolutionary soldier and a former Governor of Georgia, now in his seventies, as a special agent to acquire the Floridas and gave orders to the Army and Navy to support Mathews. The general thought he would have no trouble in taking what Spain still held of West Florida. "But East Florida," he told the President, "will be a harder nut to crack than West."

Madison then said that "English occupation of East Florida must be prevented,

General Mathews, whatever the cost. For a weak and decadent power such as Spain to control so lengthy an area on our southern border is embarrassing; to have Great Britain in possession would be impossible. The United States must have the Floridas."

"I'll do my best, sar," Mathews answered.

"A revolution," Madison went on, "would create possibilities. As my special agent our army and navy will be at your command. But hide your hand and mine, general."

"Sar," Mathews said, "you can count on my discreetness."

"Remember that this is not West Florida," Madison warned. "There the revolution gave excuse for intervention, but our reiterated claim to the province was justification for the occupation. Except for geography and the indebtedness of bankrupt Spain to our citizens, we have no claim on East Florida."[6]

Mathews found that the Spanish governors of West and East Florida would not deliver their provinces peacefully to the United States. He decided, therefore, to employ the same tactics the lone-star rebels had used at Baton Rouge, of which Madison had approved. He would foment rebellion, supported by Georgia volunteers and American troops, and establish a new government in East Florida. Then he would accept the territory, as the President desired, from the new "local authority."

With an army of "patriots" Mathews launched his revolution in March, 1812. Supported by American gunboats, he captured Fernandina on Amelia Island. Then he attacked the fortress of San Marcos near St. Augustine, but failed to take it. Yet the "patriots" organized a government, chose a governor, and ceded East Florida to the United States.

The first reports of the "patriot" revolution in East Florida reached Secretary of State James Monroe and the President when they were exploiting the letters of John Henry for war propaganda against Britain. The British, through Henry, had merely sought information among New England Federalists, but Mathews had incited revolution and had used American naval forces against a peaceful Spanish colony. Since Madison had denounced the British for meddling in New England, he knew he could not logically defend Mathews' armed intervention in East Florida. He therefore disavowed Mathews and the "patriot" revolution.

"I am sorry to have to state," Monroe wrote to Mathews, on April 4, 1813, "that the measures which you appear to have adopted for obtaining possession of Amelia Island and other parts of East Florida, are not authorized by the law of the United States, or the instructions founded on it, under which you have acted." A few weeks later he told Jefferson that Mathews' "extravagances place us in a most distressing dilemma."

At first Madison promised to return the occupied half of East Florida, but since war with England now seemed certain, he retained the territory ceded by the revolutionists. When war came, he used American military forces to support the "patriots," even against the will of Congress.

"The East Florida Revolution has been extremely embarrassing," the Secretary of State later told Mathews' secretary. "In all my years of service, the government has never before been placed in such a distressing dilemma." Then he added, "But the province of East Florida must never go back to Spain." [7]

While some Americans occupied a part of East Florida during the War of 1812, others completed the conquest of West Florida. General Andrew Jackson left Nashville, Tennessee, in January, 1813, with frontier troops who hated the Spaniards and were eager to raise the American flag over Mobile and Pensacola, still held by Spanish soldiers, but they did not achieve their goal. The government ordered Jackson to dismiss his troops before they could launch their attack. General James Wilkinson then occupied the Mobile area bloodlessly in April, 1813, and completed the third step in acquiring the Floridas.

Jackson returned to Mobile in 1814 and defended it against the British, who used the neutral Spanish port at Pensacola as a base for their attack. After throwing back the invaders, Jackson, on his own authority, marched on Pensacola, stormed it, destroyed its protecting fort, and withdrew his forces to Mobile. From there he went to New Orleans to win his greatest victory.

Since Spain had not joined England in the war against the United States, she had no part in the peace treaty, though she tried in vain to have her interests considered in the negotiations. The War of 1812 thus ended with the United States in full possession of West Florida to the Perdido River, and with Spain, after the United States had returned the occupied regions, still in control of East Florida.

During and after the peacemaking following the Napoleonic wars, Spain tried to save Florida from the aggressive Americans, but knew she could not do so alone. She turned to the European powers at the Congress of Vienna for help and repeatedly sought England's assistance against the United States. "If all Europe or its principal governments," the Spanish Minister in Washington warned, for instance, "do not take steps in time against the scandalous ambition of this Republic when they perceive the need of doing so and of obstructing the well-established scheme of conquest which she has set for herself it may well be too late; and she may be master of Cuba and of the New Kingdom of Mexico or whatever other region suits her." [8]

Finally Spain realized she had to settle her difficulties with the United States alone. Since her colonies in the Western Hemisphere were still in revolt, she reconciled herself to losing Florida in exchange for a settlement of other disputes with the United States.

Americans knew that Spain would have to cede East Florida, for she could not control or adequately govern the colony. Escaped slaves found refuge there, and British agents operated there freely, selling arms and encouraging Indians to resist

American encroachments. By not controlling the Indians, the United States said, Spain violated Pinckney's Treaty. Spain in turn complained that Americans were transgressing neutrality by aiding the rebelling Spanish colonies in the Americas.

The Adams–Onís Negotiations

The fact that Spain's empire was disintegrating, in other words, offered the United States the opportunity of realizing long-held expansionist desires without war. The Spanish Minister in Washington, Don Luis de Onís, was supposed to help in keeping the empire intact by preventing the United States from recognizing the rebelling colonies. He had come to the United States in 1809, but because Napoleon had overthrown the Spanish monarchy, years passed before the government received him. Madison's government finally accepted his credentials in December, 1815, after the restoration of the monarchy. Then he began conversations with Secretary of State Monroe on the question of East Florida. He also had powers to discuss the undetermined boundaries of the Louisiana Purchase, particularly the western frontier and the ownership of Texas. He launched his talks with Monroe by stating that Spain would recognize American title to portions of West Florida already taken, if the United States would accept the Mississippi River as its western boundary and thus give up Louisiana.

By the time John Quincy Adams became Secretary of State and took up the negotiations in December, 1817, however, Onís was prepared to modify his demands. He suggested a western boundary for the United States at about the middle of the Louisiana Territory. Adams countered with a proposal that placed that boundary in Texas, gave the United States both the Floridas, and relieved Spain from payment of damages claimed by Americans. Before Adams and Onís could reconcile their differences, two incidents in East Florida disrupted the negotiations.

In the summer of 1817 some military adventurers, who claimed authority from various revolutionary governments in Latin America, had captured Amelia Island. One of them, who said he represented the revolutionary regime in Mexico, claimed East Florida for that government in the fall of that year. This was all that President Monroe needed to move into East Florida himself, for the "no-transfer resolution" of January, 1811, under which Mathews had acted, gave him authority to take Florida if a foreign power should try to seize it. Since Mexico was a foreign nation, Monroe sent troops to Amelia Island and took possession in December while Adams and Onís were negotiating.

The United States then followed that violation of Spanish sovereignty with another. Creek Indians and their Seminole cousins from Florida had frequently attacked Americans in American territory and then fled into Spanish Florida. After those Indians had massacred a party of Americans on the Apalachicola River late in 1817, Monroe ordered Andrew Jackson to punish them and if necessary to pursue them into Spanish Florida. If they took refuge behind Spanish forces, however, he was to withhold his attack and notify the War Department.

Pinckney's Treaty obligated Spain to restrain the Indians within the borders of her possessions. Since she was incapable of doing so, the United States was justified in allowing Jackson to pursue them into Florida, but Jackson hoped to do more. In January, 1818, he wrote to the President saying he wanted to seize all of Florida in the same way the United States had taken Amelia Island. "This can be done," he said, "without implicating the Government; let it be signified to me . . . that the possession of the Floridas would be desirable to the United States, and in sixty days it will be accomplished." [9]

Jackson made good his boast. In March, 1818, he invaded Florida with 3,000 men, pushing the Indians before him. He seized the fort and town of St. Marks, captured and executed two British subjects on charges that they had aided enemies of the United States, and then captured Pensacola. Since the powers under which he executed the two British subjects were ill-defined, their deaths caused trouble with England and might have touched off a serious crisis if England had not then faced more pressing diplomatic problems in Europe.

England's Foreign Minister, Castlereagh, told the American Minister in London, that "such was the temper of Parliament, and such the feeling of the country, that he believed WAR MIGHT HAVE BEEN PRODUCED BY HOLDING UP A FINGER." [10] England however, never held the finger up, and Spain realized again that England would not support her against the United States, either in boundary disputes or in keeping the United States from recognizing the independence of her rebelling colonies.

Jackson finished his campaign in May, 1818, and returned to Nashville. He had done far more than win an Indian war. He had conquered a province, a Spanish province that Monroe had coveted since he had helped acquire Louisiana in 1803, but Jackson's intemperate actions embarrassed the President. Monroe could not now grasp what he wanted to take because he feared the international repercussions.

Monroe then denied that he had given Jackson authority to take East Florida. Jackson believed that he had, and insisted, years later, that a congressman from Tennessee, Mr. John Rhea, an old friend, had written him stating that the President approved his plan for conquest. Jackson said he had burned the letter according to Monroe's instructions. Most of the evidence, though controversial, supports Monroe in the argument, but there is little doubt that Jackson did what Monroe wanted in conquering Florida. [11]

The public applauded Jackson's invasion, but political enemies did not. Congress investigated his deeds, but ultimately four resolutions of condemnation went down to defeat by substantial majorities. All of the cabinet except John Quincy Adams wanted to disavow Jackson, or to discipline him. Adams argued that the government must sustain him, and it did. For political reasons, Monroe went along with Adams and then attempted to mollify the furious Jackson.

Onís, too, was furious. He demanded an indemnity, and said he would sign no treaty until the United States punished Jackson, disavowed his "outrage," and restored East Florida to Spain. Adams defended Jackson, justifying the invasion as self-defense. He insisted that Spain must either control Florida or cede it. Florida, he said, is "a derelict, open to the occupancy of every enemy, civilized or savage, of the United States, and serving no other earthly purpose than as a post of annoyance to them." [12]

Actually, Spain had already decided to offer more concessions for an understanding with the United States, though the pressure of Jackson's invasion forced her to do now what she knew she must do eventually. She could not keep Florida from as hostile a country as the United States. The alternative to cession appeared to be a war Spain did not want, for she had no European allies to help her and her own hands were full with the revolutions in South America. In January, 1818, Britain had offered to mediate the difficulties between the United States and Spain, but the United States had refused. Under the circumstances Spain appeared to have no choice but cession.

Therefore, when Monroe appeased Spanish honor by agreeing to restore the territory Jackson had overrun, Spain proceeded with the disrupted negotiations. Spain was ready as she had been earlier to cede the Floridas if the United States would agree to a satisfactory western boundary, but now, in October, 1818, Onís was willing to concede a boundary farther west than he had previously proposed. Adams then suggested that the boundary between American and Spanish territory in North America be drawn all the way to the Pacific Ocean. Onís said he would accept Adams' proposal for the western boundary of the United States at the Sabine River, the eastern edge of Texas, but added that he had no authority to extend the line to the Pacific.

In January, Onís received new instructions, sent in October and prompted by Jackson's invasion, to concede the United States a boundary to the Pacific. Then the negotiations went rapidly until February 22, 1819, when Adams and Onís signed the completed treaty.

The Florida or Transcontinental Treaty

By that agreement, sometimes called the Adams-Onís Treaty, sometimes the Florida Treaty, and sometimes the Transcontinental Treaty, Spain ceded East and West Florida without payment, though the United States agreed to assume the claims of its own citizens against Spain to the extent of five million dollars. The treaty defined the western boundary of the Louisiana Territory, and by it Spain surrendered her claims to the Oregon country to the United States and agreed to a northern boundary at the forty-second parallel to the Pacific Ocean. The United States reluctantly gave up its shadowy claim to Texas. That was about all Spain got out of the treaty, except for the settlement of claims and peace.

The Senate approved the treaty unanimously two days after Adams signed it, and Monroe ratified it the next day. Americans liked the treaty. "The fact has long been evident," an influential journal commented, "that a sovereignty over these countries was needful to our peace and quietness, and that we would possess them by fair or foul means—by treaty or by force. We have preferred the former, and Spain has happily agreed to do that which her own interest prompted—for the Floridas, though so valuable to us, have always been a real incumbrance on her." [13]

Spain, however, did not seal the bargain immediately; she delayed her ratification for almost two years, fearing that the United States would recognize the independence of her rebelling colonies in the Americas. Before ratifying, she demanded a pledge that the United States would not aid them or recognize their independence. The United States refused. "As a necessary consequence of the neutrality between Spain and the South American provinces," Adams told the new Spanish Minister in Washington, "the United States can contract no engagement not to form any relations with those provinces."

Irked at the delay, Andrew Jackson wanted to enforce the treaty "at the mouth of the cannon." Adams thought the use of force would be justified. Wanting to avoid war, the Spanish king finally ratified the treaty in October, 1820.

Since a limitation within the treaty said it had to be ratified within six months, Monroe sent it to the Senate for a second time. Before the Senate could act, opposition to the treaty arose in the West. With Henry Clay as their spokesman, Westerners demanded that the cession of Texas be included in its provisions. The government, however, refused to hold out for Texas, though not because it was unwilling to buck Spanish resistance. It already feared that the issue of Texas would arouse an internal controversy over the territorial limits of slavery.

The opposition, though vocal, was not strong. The Senate gave the treaty its second approval by a big majority on February 19, 1821. Three days later, exactly two years from the date of signature, ratifications were exchanged. That completed the fourth step. All the Floridas, and more, now belonged to the United States.

John Quincy Adams was proud of the treaty he had negotiated. "It was, perhaps, the most important day of my life," he said when he signed it. His was in fact a transcontinental treaty, stretching American claims from the Atlantic to the Pacific Oceans. "The acknowledgment of a definite boundary to the South Sea," he wrote, "forms a great epocha in our history." [14]

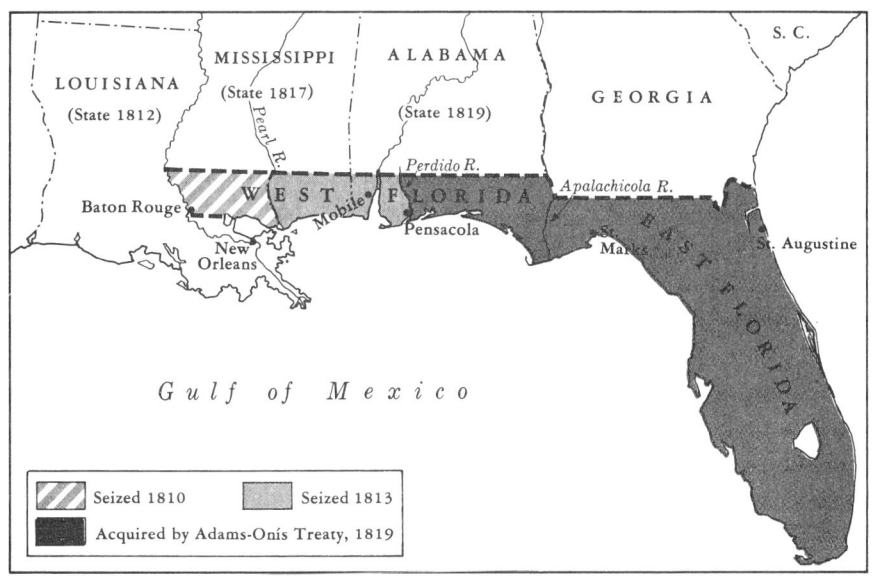

EXPANSION INTO THE FLORIDAS, 1810–1819

THE TRANSCONTINENTAL LINE OF THE ADAMS-ONÍS TREATY

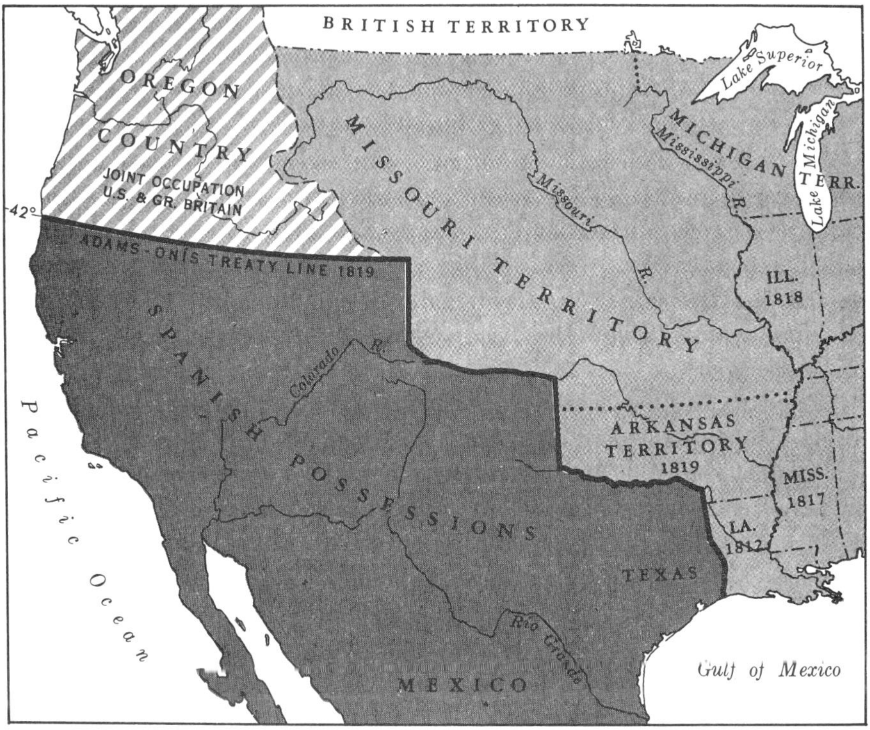

The Holy Alliance
and the Spanish-American Colonies

Adams also helped shape the diplomacy that led to the enunciation of the
Monroe Doctrine, a development connected in principle with his treaty and one
that would come to be considered another epochal event in the history of American
foreign policy. Since that doctrine evolved as a response to European diplomacy, it
is necessary to follow a few developments in the international politics of Europe
after the fall of Napoleon in 1815 to understand how the United States formulated
this most famous of its doctrines.

At the Congress of Vienna, the major powers tried to reconstruct Europe as it
had been before Napoleon by restoring the old balance of power and maintaining it through the Quadruple or Grand Alliance. Great Britain, Russia,
Prussia, and Austria had formed that alliance in March, 1814, and renewed it in
November of the following year to preserve the territorial arrangements made at
Vienna and to prevent Napoleon from returning to France. Three years later,
when a reconstructed France was admitted, the agreement also became known as
the Quintuple Alliance.

Under that arrangement the five powers met at fixed intervals to discuss the
peace and politics of Europe. Altogether they sponsored four congresses, the last
of which met in Verona in 1822 and broke up with the Grand Alliance in virtual
dissolution. Yet that alliance launched the stabilizing Concert of Europe, and its
congresses began the modern system of conference diplomacy.

In addition to this broad arrangement, Alexander I of Russia induced the
sovereigns of Austria and Prussia in September, 1815, to join him in the Holy
Alliance, a vague treaty designed apparently to buttress the political alliance and
uphold autocracy. Those three sovereigns invited other rulers to come in, and most
of them did. The Prince Regent of England would have done so, but as a constitutional ruler without independent power could not. The members of the Holy
Alliance even invited the United States to join, but it politely refused.

Thus, both England and the United States were outside the Holy Alliance. Yet
England belonged to the Grand Alliance and supported the balance of power it
had created. Since Europe's statesmen at first did not take the Holy Alliance
seriously, that coalition meant little to nonmembers such as England and the
United States. Prince Clemens Metternich of Austria dismissed it as a "loud-
sounding nothing," but later changed his mind, and Castlereagh considered it
mystical nonsense. Nonetheless, the public confused the Holy Alliance with the
Grand Alliance and acquired the habit of calling the combination of powers
the Holy Allies. Regardless of precise title, the European Allies functioned as
enemies of liberal government.

One of the persistent problems that confronted the European Allies was what should be done about Spain's rebelling colonies in the New World. The Grand Alliance in 1814 had restored Ferdinand VII to the Spanish throne, but he failed to regain the allegiance of his colonies which continued their fight for independence. Disturbed by this challenge to a legitimate monarchy, the European sovereigns wanted to see a strong effort made to reestablish Ferdinand's old authority in the Americas, but England did not.[15]

The motive behind England's policy was simple enough. Before Napoleon's invasion Spain had monopolized the trade of her colonies, but during the war those colonies had opened their ports to British and other foreign trade. England's trade with them, and to a lesser extent that of the United States, too, had prospered. Thus England, and the United States also, wished to continue that Latin-American trade and did not want Spain to reestablish her commercial monopoly.[16] Both countries, therefore, had a stake, primarily commercial, in the independence of the Spanish-American colonies. The sympathy of the European monarchs for Ferdinand's plight appeared to endanger that stake.

At the first congress of the Concert of Europe, held at Aix-la-Chapelle in 1818, Britain said she would not assist, except through peaceful mediation, in restoring the Latin-American colonies to Ferdinand. At the second congress, held at Troppau in 1820, Prince Metternich suggested that the Allies had a sacred duty to crush revolution wherever it appeared. The British government would not accept Metternich's reactionary doctrine, but Russia, Prussia, and Austria did.

In that same year four liberal revolutions, in Naples, Piedmont, Spain, and Portugal, appeared to convert the Holy Alliance into a real compact. The Tsar, with a million men under arms, was eager to send some of them to smother the uprisings in Italy. At this time the Grand Allies dissuaded him, but at their congress in Laibach in 1821 they sent an Austrian army to crush the revolutionaries in Piedmont and Naples. If the Allies, Holy or otherwise, could smash revolution in Europe, it seemed logical that they could do the same in the Americas.

Even before the meeting of the first European congress, President Monroe and Secretary of State Adams fearfully anticipated just such a development. They knew that the United States alone could do little to stop the Allies if they should try to defeat the revolutions in Spanish America. Monroe's government, more-over, was not even ready to offer the Spanish colonies the support of recognizing their independence, especially not before it had completed the Adams-Onís Treaty.

Yet from the beginning of the long struggle the United States had watched the Spanish-American movements for independence with growing compassion. The American people sympathized with the revolutionaries because they saw a resemblance between their own revolution against George III and the wars against Ferdinand VII. American publicists gave the struggles of the Spanish-American liberators, Simón Bolívar, José San Martín, and others, wide circulation. The drama and continental sweep of the Latin-American battles, swirling among snow-clad mountains and fought in steaming jungles, gripped the imagination.

Reflecting, in part at least, the sympathy of its people, the government of the United States received agents from the revolutionary governments cordially, but always unofficially, and sent its own agents to care for its interests in Spanish America. It did not, however, intervene in the revolutionary wars. Instead, it assumed a position of official neutrality in 1815 between Ferdinand and the rebels and in so doing recognized the belligerency of the Spanish-American states. Toward the more important question of recognition of independence, it adopted a policy of watchful waiting.

At the same time, the United States permitted the revolutionaries to buy supplies and war materials within its borders and allowed their ships to use its ports. So widespread was public sympathy for the colonials and so defective the neutrality laws, that violations of neutrality were common. The Spanish Americans outfitted and equipped privateers in American ports and then sailed them against Spain, a power friendly to the United States.[17] These infractions of neutrality were so embarrassing to the government while Adams was negotiating with Onís that in March, 1817, and April, 1818, it passed new and stronger neutrality laws.

Many Americans, moved by the epic struggle to the south, demanded that the government recognize the independence of the Latin states. Speaker of the House, Henry Clay, their foremost spokesman, urged such recognition and attacked Monroe and Adams for hesitating. In a moving speech on March 25, 1818, he pleaded with Congress for recognition of the United Provinces of the Rio de la Plata (Argentina) and gave American sympathies their fullest expression.

"We behold the most sublime and interesting objects of creation; the loftiest mountains, the most majestic rivers in the world . . . and the choicest productions of the earth," he said. "We behold there a spectacle still more interesting and sublime—the glorious spectacle of eighteen millions of people, struggling to burst their chains and to be free."[18]

Clay's speech thrilled Congress, but for practical reasons it would not act. At the time Congress was interested mainly in Florida and the other Spanish border-lands that Secretary Adams was trying to obtain peacefully.

Later, but before the Monroe administration was ready, Congress did act. In May, 1820, the House of Representatives, under Clay's leadership, passed a resolution calling for the appropriation of funds for the expenses of diplomatic agents in the Spanish-American states which had already declared independence, but the administration ignored the resolution.

Monroe and Adams had good reasons for hesitating. Premature recognition would offer Spain a cause for war they did not want, particularly over the question of recognition. What they had to decide was under what conditions they could recognize the independence of the Latin-American republics without grievously offending Spain and endangering the acquisition of East Florida. International law offered them no clear precedent.

Adams, therefore, derived his own formula. The United States, he said, should recognize the Spanish-American states "when independence is established as a matter of fact so as to leave the chance of the opposite party to recover their dominion utterly desperate." Under this formula Monroe and Adams had to determine when the Latin-American governments were ready, but they were not relieved from speculating if Spain and the European Allies would so strongly resent recognition that they would go to war against the United States.

In the following year, 1821, before Monroe and his advisers could make a decision, a Greek revolution against Turkey broke out and complicated the question of recognition. The statesmen of Europe thought that the Tsar would use the Greek war of independence to gain a foothold in the Mediterranean. This problem, along with another dealing with French intervention in Spain to crush the liberal revolution there, led to arrangements for another congress for the fall of 1822.

John Quincy Adams, meanwhile, had observed Britain's reluctant drift away from the Grand Alliance and her cautious resistance to the principles of the Holy Alliance. With Europe divided into two camps, one constitutional and the other autocratic, Adams believed that the position of the United States had grown more secure. He realized that the British government would now do almost anything reasonable to avoid a break with the United States. It was with this understanding and with the European situation in mind that in January, 1821, he bluntly explained his position to the British Minister in Washington.

At that time the Minister questioned Adams about American claims to the area of the Columbia River. Great Britain, he said, had a prior claim there. Adams insisted that she did not. "And how far would you consider," the Minister said, "this exclusion of the right to extend?" "To all the shores of the South Sea," Adams replied. "And in this," the English diplomat asked, "you include our northern provinces on this continent?" "No," Adams, answered, "there the boundary is marked, and we have no disposition to encroach upon it. Keep what is yours, but leave the rest of this continent to us."[19]

This was a clear statement of the noncolonization principle that Adams was to place in the Monroe Doctrine. Six months later, in a violently anti-British July Fourth address, he restated the principle.

A few months later Russia gave Adams another opportunity to expound his noncolonization principle. Russia had long claimed a stretch of America's northwest coast, but did not try to enforce her claim until 1799 when she chartered the Russian-American Company and gave it exclusive trading rights and jurisdiction along the coast as far south as fifty-five degrees north latitude. The company planted settlements north of that line and in 1812 moved south into Spanish

California. It set up a trading post, called Fort Ross, on Bodega Bay just north of San Francisco.

The American government, while apprehensive, never showed much concern about Fort Ross, but was alarmed by an imperial ukase the Tsar issued on September 14, 1821. With that decree the Russian government, on behalf of the Russian-American Company, extended its exclusive claim to Russian America down the Pacific Coast to the fifty-first parallel and forbade all foreign ships, on penalty of confiscation, to come within one hundred Italian miles of the coast north of that parallel. Therefore Russia's claim extended into the Oregon country, territory claimed by both the United States and Britain. Luckily, Russia never enforced the ukase, and when the United States and Britain protested, she invited them separately to negotiate a settlement in St. Petersburg.

Adams used his protest against Russia's new claim to reiterate the noncolonization principle. He told the Russian Minister in Washington on July 17, 1823, that "we should contest the right of Russia to *any* territorial establishment on this continent, and that we should assume distinctly the principle that the American continents are no longer subjects for any new European colonial establishments."[20] A few days later he embodied the same idea in instructions to the American Ministers in Russia and Britain.

Although the ukase gave Adams the opportunity of again stressing noncolonization, Russia apparently was not his primary target. He appeared to aim his announcement primarily at Britain, whom he considered a more menacing territorial rival than Russia.

A Cautious Recognition

Meanwhile, with the Adams-Onís Treaty ratified, the time for watchful waiting toward the Latin-American wars had ended. Impressive military victories of the Spanish-American patriots had made it clear that Spain's plight in the colonies was "utterly desperate," according to the Adams formula. Events in Europe, moreover, made war over recognition unlikely. News of Bolívar's victory at the Battle of Carabobo in June, 1821, which destroyed Spanish power in Colombia and Venezuela, had prodded the American government into bringing recognition to a decision.

Even though he himself favored recognition, Monroe still hesitated. Congress had to prompt him before he wrote the special message recommending recognition of the independence of the United Provinces of the Rio de la Plata (Argentina), Colombia, Chile, Peru, and Mexico which he sent to Congress on March 8, 1822. Since Spaniards and patriots were still fighting in parts of South America, he said the United States should observe "the most perfect neutrality" between Spain and the patriot governments. Congress responded by appropriating one hundred thousand dollars to maintain the expense of "such Missions to the independent nations on the American continent" as the President might deem proper.[21] The President signed an act establishing those missions on May 4.

Monroe was so cautious that he waited almost a year before appointing ministers to the United Provinces of the Rio de la Plata and to Colombia. His caution stemmed from his desire to measure Europe's reactions to recognition before taking the last step. American policy toward the new governments, as given in the instructions to those two ministers, called for support of republicanism against monarchy, for complete separation from Europe, for trade with the United States on the most-favored-nation terms, and for acceptance of the doctrine of freedom of the seas.

Like so many decisions in foreign policy, Monroe's actions were a mixture of caution and boldness. They were bold because the United States became the first nation outside of Latin America to recognize the Spanish-American republics. They were cautious because the United States did not give the Spanish-American patriots tangible assistance such as arms, men, or money. "We do not see the probability of any particular benefit to the [patriots] or to the United States from the act," the *National Gazette* said on March 11. With recognition, the United States simply announced officially that it believed Spain had lost her colonies. American recognition did not deter Spain or the European Allies. Only force could do that. Those Allies still hoped, through peaceful accommodation, or perhaps through force, to save the colonies for Ferdinand.

Spain protested, but the Spanish Americans were pleased with the recognition. It marked a turning point in their long struggle. Even though not backed by tangible aid, it gave moral support and offered official evidence of the sympathy of American people.

In their recognition of Spanish-American independence, Monroe and Adams had also taken advantage of the fact that the leaders of Europe were divided as to how they should deal with the Greek war of independence. As the Grand Alliance prepared for the Congress of Verona in the fall of 1822, that division had a marked effect on both American and European diplomacy. Meanwhile, Castlereagh committed suicide and the clever George Canning became Britain's Foreign Minister on September 9.

When the congress assembled in October at Verona, a French army stood on the Spanish border ready to rescue Ferdinand VII, whose reactionary rule had sparked a revolution, from the rebels who held him prisoner. Canning warned the Allies that England would not take part in any collective intervention in Spain. The Allies, despite England's objections, authorized France to intervene. On April 6, 1823, a French army plunged into Spain and in a few months occupied most of the country.

Americans were alarmed, fearing that the Holy Allies might next attempt to smother revolution in Spanish America. That fear haunted American statesmen in the summer and fall of 1823. It also bothered Canning. He had hoped that England's prestige would keep the French out of Spain and that his warning would stop the Allies from meddling in Spanish America. Like his predecessor, he followed a policy of neutrality between Spain and her colonies to preserve the Spanish-American market for English traders. In the summer of 1823 that policy appeared to have failed.

John Quincy Adams, like Canning himself, did not believe that the Allies would in fact invade the Spanish-American republics. He was more concerned about Cuba, fearing that as the Spanish crisis mounted England might rush to the defense of Spain's revolutionary regime and then demand Cuba as a reward. Adams had ideas of his own about the future of that island. He told the American Minister to Spain that if Cuba separated itself from the mother country it "can gravitate only towards the North American Union." Then he wrote, "you will not conceal from the Spanish government the repugnance of the United States to the transfer of the island of Cuba by Spain to any other power." This time Adams had applied the no-transfer principle directly to a Spanish possession.

Canning's Overtures

The United States had several times suggested a joint Anglo-American policy on the Spanish colonies. The British had never responded favorably, but in the fall of 1823 Canning himself took the lead. On August 16, he began conversations with Richard Rush, the American Minister in London. These conversations furnished the impulse for the Monroe Doctrine.

First, Rush raised the question of possible French intervention in Spanish America. He was pleased, he said, that England would not allow France to snuff out the freedom of the Spanish republics. Then Canning asked if the United States would cooperate with England in upholding that anti-intervention policy. Co-operative "*action*," he said, would not be necessary. If France knew that England and the United States supported the same policy, that knowledge would be enough to check any of her designs on Spanish America.

Several days later, on August 20, Canning explained in "unofficial and confidential" terms what he considered the basis for a common understanding. He said that Britain believed "the recovery of the Colonies by Spain to be hopeless," but recognition was a matter of "time and circumstances." England, however, was "by no means disposed to throw any impediment in the way of an arrangement between them and the mother country by amicable negotiations." England did not desire to acquire any part of them, but "could not see any portion of them transferred to any other Power with indifference."

"If these opinions and feelings are," Canning added, "as I firmly believe them to be, common to your government with ours, why should we hesitate mutually to confide them with each other, and to declare them in the face of the world?" Then he asked, are you "authorised to enter into negotiation and to sign any convention upon this subject?"

Rush replied three days later that the American government agreed with Canning's sentiments, but that his instructions did not permit him to commit his government without advance approval. If Canning would promise immediate instead of future recognition, however, Rush was willing "to make a declaration, in the name of my Government, that it will not remain inactive under an attack upon the independence of those States by the Holy Alliance."[22] He knew such a commitment would exceed his instructions and that his own government might disavow him, but was prepared to take full responsibility. Canning answered that his government was not yet ready for recognition. Rush, therefore, forwarded Canning's proposal to Washington without further action.

Meanwhile, Canning received word that as soon as the French completed their campaign in Spain the European Allies planned to call a new congress to deal with the problem of Spanish America. He then renewed his overtures. The United States, he said, was the leading power on the American continent. "Were the great political and commercial interests which hung upon the destinies of the new continent," he asked, "to be canvassed and adjusted in this hemisphere, without the co-operation or even knowledge of the United States?" Rush stubbornly insisted that he would sign a joint declaration only if Canning would pledge England to an immediate recognition of the South American states. Since the British government was not yet willing to break openly with the powers of Europe, and time was running out, the discussion ended.

The Polignac Memorandum

France took Cádiz, the last liberal stronghold in Spain, on September 30, 1823, and thus completed the destruction of the constitutional revolution. That alarming news did not reach London until October 10, but Canning, unwilling to wait for the uncertain official American response to his overtures, had already acted alone to soften its impact. Although he believed that the French could not intervene successfully in Spanish America against the opposition of British sea power, he now thought they planned to try. Early in October, therefore, he had begun talks with Prince Jules de Polignac, the French Ambassador in London, warning him against any French interference in Spanish America.

The prince explained that France disclaimed any intention of appropriating any part of the Spanish possessions in America. She asked for nothing more than the right to trade there on the same terms as Britain. "She abjured, in any case," he said, "any design of acting against the Colonies by force of arms."[23] Polignac's assurances, embodied in a memorandum concluded on October 12, removed the threat of European interference in Spanish America.

While Canning and Polignac were talking, Rush's first dispatches carrying Canning's overtures arrived in the United States. Monroe and Adams looked them over, and then Monroe turned to his Virginia friends, former Presidents Jefferson and Madison, for advice. He disliked the idea of deserting the principle of non-entanglement, yet he asked Jefferson, "If a case can exist in which a sound maxim may, and ought to be departed from, is not the present instance precisely that case?" Then he added, "My own impression is that we ought to meet the proposal of the British government."[24]

Jefferson agreed with the President. "Great Britain," he said, "is the nation which can do us the most harm of any one, or all on earth; and with her on our side we need not fear the whole world." He, as did Madison, urged Monroe to "join in the declaration proposed."[25] With that advice, Monroe was prepared to link American policy with that of Britain.

Meanwhile, on October 16, Russia's Minister in Washington told Adams that Russia would not recognize the rebel governments and that she was pleased with America's neutral policy toward the Spanish-American wars. To the Secretary of State that note seemed to imply that if the United States championed Spanish-American freedom, the Tsar would support Spain and France in South America.

The cabinet met on November 7 to discuss Canning's overtures and the Russian "crisis." Secretary of War John C. Calhoun suggested giving Rush discretionary authority to make a joint declaration with Canning, even if it pledged the United States never to acquire Cuba or Texas. Even though the suggestion agreed with Monroe's own ideas, Adams disagreed. Although the United States had no designs on Cuba or Texas, he said, one day those provinces might want to join the Union. The government, he thought, should not therefore tie itself with a joint declaration. Deeply impressed, Monroe said he did not wish to take an action which might subordinate the United States to Britain.

Adams still believed, and rightly so, that the European Allies would not invade South America, but he wanted the United States to take the lead from Britain as the protector of Spanish-American independence so that the United States could win special commercial advantages in South America. He thought Monroe should, therefore, take a stand against Russia, France, and the Holy Alliance, and at the same time refuse Britain's overtures. "It would be more candid," he said, "as well as more dignified, to avow our principles explicitly to Russia and France, than to come in as a cock-boat in the wake of the British man-of-war."[26] The cabinet then agreed with him, and his ideas governed the writing of a reply to Canning and to the Russian Minister.

Adams then instructed Rush to decline Canning's proposal for a joint declaration, but assured the British Minister that the United States accepted his stated principles except the one concerning recognition. He insisted that the Spanish colonies "were of *right* independent of all other nations, and that it was our duty so to acknowledge them." Then he added that the United States "could not see with indifference, any attempt by one or more powers of Europe to restore those new states to the crown of Spain, or to deprive them, in any manner whatever of the freedom and independence which they have acquired." He did not, however, rule out the idea of a joint declaration. Emergency conditions, he said, might make such an announcement necessary.[27]

Monroe and his advisers did not know of the Polignac Memorandum. When the news reached the United States in mid-November that France had crushed the constitutional revolution in Spain, Monroe himself feared that the Allies would next attack Spanish America. Therefore, he again talked of a joint declaration with Britain.

In a cabinet meeting a few days later, Calhoun shared the President's alarm. The Holy Allies with ten thousand men, he said, could restore Mexico and all South America to Spain. Adams, however, was still not alarmed and still opposed linking American action with Britain. "I no more believe that the Holy Allies will restore the Spanish dominion upon the American continent," he declared, "than that the Chimborazo will sink beneath the ocean."[28]

Two days later, on November 17, the Russian Minister gave Adams another note. The Tsar's policy, the note said, was "to guarantee the tranquillity of all the states of which the civilized world is composed." That policy, he indicated, included support of Spain's supremacy in Latin America.

Adams now connected the Russian problem with Canning's overtures, and wished to answer both Russia and Britain in diplomatic notes that clearly asserted his country's policy in the Western Hemisphere. Later, he felt, the notes could be published. The President had different ideas. He wanted to announce that policy in his annual message to Congress on the State of the Union. His word was final. On November 21, therefore, Monroe read a draft of his message to the cabinet.

That draft outlined foreign affairs as Adams had sketched them for the President the week before, but went beyond the Secretary's draft. The message, Adams said, now "alluded to the recent events in Spain and Portugal, speaking in terms of the most pointed reprobation of the late invasion of Spain by France, and of the principles upon which it was undertaken by the open avowal of the King of France. It also contained a broad acknowledgment of the Greeks as an independent nation, and a recommendation to Congress to make an appropriation for sending a Minister to them."

Adams urged the President not to take so strong a stand. It would, he explained, be a grave departure from the principles of George Washington. It would be "a summons to arms—to arms against all Europe, and for objects of policy exclusively European—Greece and Spain."

On the next day, when alone with the President, the Secretary pressed his case with greater urgency. "The ground that I wish to take," he advised, "is that of earnest remonstrance against the interference of the European powers by force with South America, but to disclaim all interference on our part in Europe; to make an American cause, and adhere inflexibly to that." [29] Monroe then changed his message to meet Adams' suggestions.

The Monroe Doctrine

The President delivered his views to the world on December 2, 1823, in two widely separated passages in his message to Congress. He announced as a principle "that the American Continents, by the free and independent condition which they have assumed and maintain, are henceforth not to be considered as subjects for future colonization by a European power." This, the noncolonization principle, was the work of Adams.

Then in his own words Monroe referred to the Holy Allies and declared "that we should consider any attempt on their part to extend their system to any portions of this Hemisphere, as dangerous to our peace and safety. With the existing Colonies or dependencies of any European power, we have not interfered, and shall not interfere. But with the Governments who have declared their Independence, and maintained it, and whose Independence we have, on great consideration, and on just principles, acknowledged, we could not view any interposition for the purpose of oppressing them, or controlling in any other manner, their destiny, by any European power, in any other light than as the manifestation of an unfriendly disposition towards the United States."

The Monroe Doctrine stated nothing new. It summed up old principles and applied them to immediate circumstances. It was a theoretical justification of a policy of self-interest and was concerned basically with three principles: noncolonization, meaning that no European power could in the future form colonies in either North or South America; nonintervention, which warned Europe against meddling in American affairs and said "hands off"; and noninterference in European affairs, which implied that Europe's political system was distinct from that of the Western Hemisphere.

The Monroe Doctrine also had a fourth principle not stated in the message but expressed in supporting documents. It was the no-transfer principle that had been American policy since 1811.

Monroe's words had no real threat of force behind them, but the President and Secretary Adams both knew that British policy opposed European intervention in

Spanish America. They could, therefore, make their bold pronouncement without fear and without force of their own. To be effective, the Monroe Doctrine needed the support of the British fleet, which indirectly it had. Yet Monroe, not knowing of the Polignac Memorandum, believed he was addressing himself to an immediate crisis. It was the French memorandum, agreed upon two months before the President's message, and not the Monroe Doctrine, that had removed the danger of intervention by the Holy Allies, a danger that probably never truly existed.

Unaware that the Allies had decided against intervention and that hence the Monroe warning was directed against a nonexistent danger, most Americans accepted it at face value and greeted it warmly. They did not, however, refer to the principles of 1823 as the Monroe Doctrine until more than a quarter of a century later. Congress, furthermore, despite efforts to gain its express endorsement, refused to make the doctrine anything more than merely a unilateral presidential statement of policy. As such, through the years, it grew into one of the nation's most enduring foreign policies.

European statesmen, however, did not take Monroe's message seriously. They considered it merely an empty threat meant to influence domestic politics. The Russian government said the doctrine "merits only the most profound contempt." Metternich condemned Monroe's words as mere "indecent declarations" which cast blame and scorn on the institutions of Europe most worthy of respect. Although the message made most of them angry, none of the European powers protested. Their statesmen, who were aware of the substance of the Polignac Memorandum before learning of Monroe's message, rightly regarded that memorandum as the decisive document in Spanish-American affairs.

Britain's reaction to the American doctrine differed from that of the European statesmen. Since his overtures to Rush had been largely responsible for its announcement, Canning at first considered it a reflection of his own diplomacy. As he examined it closely, however, the noncolonization clause came to irk him. In March, 1824, therefore, he published the Polignac Memorandum, giving it wide circulation in Latin America, to show that Britain and not the United States was the first and real protector of Spanish-American freedom.

Even in Latin America, as a result, the reaction to Monroe's doctrine was not generally enthusiastic. The liberal thinkers there received it cordially, and the governments of Colombia and Brazil endorsed it, but conservative leaders, and even some of the liberals, on second thought, were cool to it. They knew that if any outside force had saved their independence, it was the British fleet, not Monroe's blast on the republican trumpet. When several of the new states, among them Colombia, Brazil, and Mexico, approached the United States for an alliance or assistance based on Monroe's ideas, the immediate practical emptiness of the doctrine became clear. The United States coolly and evasively turned them down.[30]

The Panama Congress of 1826

Within a few years of Monroe's message, the United States again showed its reluctance to carry out the doctrine's broad principles and even admitted its inability to do so. In December, 1824, Símon Bolívar, hoping to form an inter-American organization to protect the newly independent states of Latin America against possible attack from Europe, called those states to a congress to be held in Panama in October of the following year. Although Bolívar himself, who considered Britain a better source of protection, had not included the United States, several of the Latin governments invited it to participate. They wished to draw the United States into an agreement supporting the principles of the Monroe Doctrine.

John Quincy Adams had now become President, and Henry Clay, a former champion of Latin-American independence, his Secretary of State. They accepted the invitations, and Adams nominated two delegates to attend the conference. The nominations immediately ran into trouble. For domestic reasons stemming from the bitterness engendered by the presidential election of 1824, Adams' enemies were willing to do almost anything to oppose and injure him. In Congress they tried to block participation in the Panama Conference, but cloaked their opposition with a mantle of principle, saying that participation would violate Washington's and Jefferson's advice against foreign entanglements. Southerners, for instance, were hostile to participation because they feared that the conference would call for the establishment of relations with the Negro republic in Haiti and the abolition of the slave trade by the nations of the Americas.[31]

Finally, the opposition was overcome. The Senate confirmed the delegates in March, 1826, and the House then appropriated funds for the mission, but Congress had debated so long on the issue of participation that the delegates never reached Panama. One of them died on the way, and the other, upon learning that the meeting had adjourned, never went to Panama.

Even if the commissioners had been able to participate in the Panama Congress, it is clear that they could have done nothing to uphold the principles of the Monroe Doctrine. In nominating them, for instance, Adams had assured the Senate that the mission was "neither to contract alliances, nor to engage in any undertaking or project importing hostility to any other nation." It would only be permitted to accept an agreement reaffirming the noncolonization principle, but without any commitment from the United States. Even that limited gesture was too much for the Senate, which tacked an amendment to its approval expressing opposition to any commitment. There must be, the Senate said, no "departure from the settled policy of this government, that, in extending our commercial relations with foreign nations, we should have with them as little political connexion as possible."

The Panama Conference itself accomplished little. All that can be said for it is that it was a forerunner of the Pan-American movement and hence had launched an idea that did not die.

British statesmen, meanwhile, had concluded that the Monroe Doctrine had been designed in a spirit unfriendly to their country, but approved of the non-intervention principle because it fitted their own objectives. Despite the weakness of the American claim, Canning felt, moreover, that he could not allow the United States to pose as the protector of Spanish-American freedom without further action by his government on behalf of the Latin Americans. He persuaded his government to recognize the independence of the Spanish-American republics, which it did in December, 1824. More than a year and a half later, Canning claimed credit for preserving the freedom of those republics. "I called the New World into existence," he boastfully told Parliament, "to redress the balance of the Old."[32]

The Monroe Doctrine had also stimulated another reaction in Canning. He and other British statesmen had been so upset by the noncolonization principle, that he abandoned a plan for joint negotiations with the United States at St. Petersburg concerning Russia's claims on the northwest coast of North America. Therefore, the United States engaged itself in separate negotiations with the Russians and concluded a convention with them in April, 1824, that resolved the conflicting claims. Britain signed a similar treaty in February, 1825.

In these treaties Russia agreed to make no settlements south of the line fifty-four degrees forty minutes north latitude on the west coast of North America, and the United States and Britain promised to establish none north of that line. Those treaties thus left the United States and Britain as the only claimants to the Oregon country. Although the Monroe Doctrine was in part, at least, directed against Russia, she did not limit her claims in North America or make a treaty with the United States because of it. Other reasons, mainly more important stakes in the Balkans, motivated her statesmen.[33]

NOTES

1. Isaac J. Cox, *The West Florida Controversy, 1798–1813: A Study in American Diplomacy* (Baltimore, 1918), p. 97.

2. The quotation is in Henry Adams, *History of the United States of America during the Administrations of Jefferson and Madison* (9 vols., New York, 1889–1909), III, 134.

3. Entry of May 6, 1811, in Charles Francis Adams, ed., *Memoirs of John Quincy Adams* (12 vols., Philadelphia, 1874–77), II, 261.

4. Quoted in Henry Adams, *History of the United States*, V, 315.

5. See Rufus Kay Wyllys, "The East Florida Revolution of 1812–1814," *Hispanic American Historical Review*, IX (Nov. 1929), 420. The no-transfer principle antedated this resolution. For the history of the principle, see John A. Logan, Jr., *No Transfer: An American Security Principle* (New Haven, 1961). The resolution and act are quoted on pp. 119–120.

6. The quotations are in Rembert W. Patrick, *Florida Fiasco: Rampant Rebels on the Georgia-Florida Border, 1812–1815* (Athens, Ga., 1954), pp. 13–14.

7. For Monroe's comments, see *ibid.*, pp. 121, 130. Like others who have written on the Florida revolution, Patrick is harsh toward Madison and Monroe and sympathetic toward Mathews. See, for instance, Isaac J. Cox, "The Border Missions of George Mathews," *Mississippi Valley Historical Review*, XII (Dec. 1925), 309–333 and Paul Kruse, "A Secret Agent in East Florida: General George Mathews and the Patriot War," *Journal of Southern History*, XVIII (May 1952), 193–217.

8. Notes of June 18, 1818, to the Spanish Ambassadors in London and Paris, quoted in Philip C. Brooks, *Diplomacy and the Borderlands: The Adams-Onís Treaty of 1819* (Berkeley, Calif., 1939), p. 105.

9. Jan. 6, 1818, in John S. Bassett, ed., *Correspondence of Andrew Jackson* (7 vols., Washington, 1926–35), II, 345.

10. Quoted in John H. Powell, *Richard Rush: Republican Diplomat, 1780–1859* (Philadelphia, 1942), p. 129.

11. For details, see Richard R. Stenberg, "Jackson's 'Rhea Letter' Hoax," *Journal of Southern History*, II (Nov. 1936), 480–496.

12. The full text of the note of Nov. 28, 1818, is in the *American State Papers, Foreign Relations* (6 vols., Washington, 1832), IV, 539–543. Samuel F. Bemis calls this the greatest state paper in Adams' diplomatic career. See *John Quincy Adams and the Foundations of American Foreign Policy* (New York, 1947), p. 326.

13. *Niles' Weekly Register*, XVI (Baltimore, Feb. 27, 1819), 3.

14. Entry of Feb. 22, 1819, Adams, *Memoirs*, IV, 274–275.

15. Dexter Perkins, "Russia and the Spanish Colonies, 1817–1818," *The American*

Historical Review, XXVIII (July 1923), 672, insists that any notion that the Holy Alliance intended to subjugate South America is a myth.

16. See Dorothy B. Goebel, "British Trade to the Spanish Colonies, 1796–1823," *ibid.*, XLIII (Jan. 1938), 288–320.

17. See, for instance, John J. Johnson, "Early Relations of the United States with Chile," *Pacific Historical Review*, XIII (Sept. 1944), 260–270 and William L. Neumann, "United States Aid to the Chilean Wars of Independence," *Hispanic American Historical Review*, XXVII (May 1947), 204–219.

18. *Annals of Congress*, 15th Congress, 1st sess., II, 1476.

19. Entry of Jan. 27, 1821, Adams, *Memoirs*, V, 252–253.

20. *Ibid.*, VI, 163.

21. William S. Robertson, "Recognition of the Hispanic American Nations by the United States," *Hispanic American Historical Review*, I (Aug. 1918), 257.

22. The Canning and Rush quotations are in Powell, *Richard Rush*, pp. 158–160.

23. Quoted in Dexter Perkins, *The Monroe Doctrine, 1823–1826* (Cambridge, Mass., 1927), p. 118. For details on British diplomacy, see William W. Kaufmann, *British Policy and the Independence of Latin America, 1802–1828* (New Haven, 1951), pp. 156–159.

24. Oct. 17, 1823, in Stanislaus M. Hamilton, ed., *The Writings of James Monroe* (7 vols., New York, 1898–1903), VI, 324.

25. Oct. 24, 1823, in Paul L. Ford, ed., *The Writings of Thomas Jefferson* (12 vols., New York, 1904–05), XII, 319–320.

26. Entry of Nov. 7, 1823, Adams, *Memoirs*, VI, 179.

27. Gale W. McGee, in "The Monroe Doctrine—A Stopgap Measure," *Mississippi Valley Historical Review*, XXXVIII (Sept.

1951), 233–250, stresses the disposition of the American government to work in concert with Britain and suggests that Adams' rejection was merely temporary, a stopgap measure.

28. Entry of Nov. 15, 1823, Adams, *Memoirs*, VI, 185–186.

29. For the quotations, see *ibid.*, entries of Nov. 21 and 22, 1823, VI, 194–198.

30. For details see William S. Robertson, "South America and the Monroe Doctrine, 1824–28" *Political Science Quarterly*, XXX (March 1915), 82–105.

31. Arthur P. Whitaker, *The United States and the Independence of Latin America, 1800–1830* (Baltimore, 1941), p. 577. For details on the conference, see Joseph B. Lockey, *Pan-Americanism: Its Beginnings* (New York, 1920), pp. 312–324.

32. Quoted in Harold W. V. Temperley, *The Foreign Policy of Canning, 1822–1827* (London, 1925), p. 154.

33. Anatole G. Mazour, "The Russian-American and Anglo-Russian Conventions, 1824–1825: An Interpretation," *Pacific Historical Review*, XIV (Sept. 1945), 303–310.

Chapter Seven

THE SPUR OF DESTINY

For about twenty years, from the middle of the 1820's to the early 1840's, the United States was not entangled in any major diplomatic crisis. Europe's rivalries did not threaten it and its people were not themselves looking for foreign adventures. Instead, Americans devoted themselves to populating a continent and to domestic politics. Nonetheless, a number of frustrating foreign problems demanded the attention of their government. One of them concerned trade with Britain's colonies in the West Indies. Although minor in itself, that problem became important because John Quincy Adams and Andrew Jackson made an issue of it in domestic politics.

The West Indian Trade

From the moment of its independence, the United States had tried to break into Britain's exclusive mercantilist system so as to secure an equality and freedom of trade, and by 1815 had largely succeeded. The commercial convention of that year with Britain and Jay's Treaty had placed trade between the United States and the British Isles on a reciprocal most-favored-nation basis and had admitted American ships to the ports of the British East Indies, but had not allowed Americans to trade with Britain's West Indies.[1]

Resenting the exclusion, the United States enacted retaliatory trade legislation against the British in 1817, 1818, and 1820. By 1820, in fact, it had ended direct trade with the British West Indies and had blocked the importation of West Indian products through Canada, New Brunswick, Nova Scotia, and even England.

At first the legislation had no effect. The actions of the American Congress, a London newspaper explained, "affect, in truth, so small and so inconsiderable a portion of our general trade, as to be worthy of no other notice than as indicating the spirit in which they originate." True enough, the West Indian trade with the United States was small, but to the planters of those islands, who suffered from its loss, it was not unimportant.

With the support of those who advocated a broad program of free trade, the planters petitioned Parliament to resume direct commerce with the United States. Yielding finally to the pressure, Parliament opened certain of its ports in the West Indies to American merchants in July, 1822. Its terms and privileges, however, were restrictive and also contingent on the American government granting similar treatment to British ships in its ports.

Delighted with these concessions, Secretary of State John Quincy Adams wanted even more. Congress, therefore, enacted legislation on March 1, 1823, that opened American ports to British ships carrying goods directly from the West Indies and from other recently unlocked ports and gave the President authority to meet British restrictions on that trade with a discriminatory tariff of his own on certain of the colonial products imported in British ships. Accordingly, President Monroe imposed a tariff that would remain in effect until Britain should give up her inter-colonial preferences. The United States, in other words, wanted its ships admitted into the West Indies on the same terms as British ships and cargoes.

Since legislation obviously offered no solution to the West Indian problem, the two governments tried unsuccessfully to reach a settlement in 1824 through diplomatic negotiation. Believing that colonial preference within the empire was a domestic matter, the British still would not allow Americans completely free trade in the Indies, though they were willing to make other concessions. Colonial preference, they held, was essential in maintaining English sea power.

Despite the failure of the negotiations, Parliament made certain limited concessions in the West Indian trade in 1825 after Adams became President. They would apply, however, only if the United States removed its discriminations against British shipping.

Assuming wrongly that the pressure in Parliament from the West Indian planters would force the British government to make further concessions, Adams refused to compromise. As a result, Britain, in July, 1826, excluded all American ships from the West Indies until the United States should repeal its discriminatory duties.

Adams, meanwhile, had decided to soften his demands. Early in July Albert Gallatin was sent to London to negotiate an agreement on the West Indian question and other problems. Although Gallatin had conciliatory instructions which gave him the power to agree to a reciprocal suspension of discriminatory legislation, he arrived too late. The British had again closed the West Indies to American shipping.

When Gallatin tried to reopen the question he got nowhere. Canning, the Foreign Minister, would not even discuss it.

Although Adams himself now felt that "there should be an act of Congress totally interdicting the trade with all the colonies, both in the West Indies and North America," he decided that if Congress would accept trade in the West Indies without complete reciprocity, he would also. Congress offered no support. Instead, political enemies attacked his West Indian diplomacy. He was, one of them pointed out, "very unfortunate in this affair & [he] will find it difficult to resist the imputation of having trifled with a very valuable portion of commerce." And, he added, "*You may rest assured that the re-election of Mr. Adams is out of the question.*"

Nonetheless, as required by law, Adams issued a proclamation on March 17, 1827, closing the nation's ports to ships coming from any of Britain's colonies in the Americas. A month later he tried once more to negotiate, this time on the basis of accepting the West Indian trade virtually on Britain's terms, but the British were still unwilling to reopen their ports in the West Indies. One critic pointed out that Adams and his advisers, "after huckstering for an unattainable shadow till they lost the substance," then became "willing and anxious to do what they grossly neglected to do when they had the power."

Finally, the West Indian controversy helped ruin Adams politically. His loss of that trade in 1826 and his failure to regain it in 1827 became an important issue in the election of 1828 that swept Andrew Jackson into power.

When Jackson took over the government in March, 1829, the British West Indies were still closed to American ships, but political conditions in both England and the United States had changed enough to make a settlement of that question appear possible. Early in 1827, Canning, who Adams considered "an implacable, rancorous enemy of the United States," had died. Canning's successor, Lord Aberdeen, held a friendlier view of the United States and wanted to settle the controversy.

Although in the past Jackson had often expressed hatred of the British, his attitude toward the old enemy had softened. He, too, wanted a settlement. His Secretary of State, Martin Van Buren, even went so far as to inform the British that the American people had repudiated the views of the Adams administration.

After some delay in preliminary negotiations, Jackson, with the support of Congress, gave up the demand that Britain abandon her policy of colonial preference before the United States would remove its discriminatory duties. Through a proclamation of October 5, 1830, he declared the retaliatory duties repealed and opened American ports to British ships on the same terms as American ships. Two days after receiving Jackson's proclamation, the British government issued an Order in Council opening its West Indies to direct trade with the United States, but subject to duties it might choose to impose. This was called the "reciprocity of

1830." Although a compromise settlement that allowed only a limited trade, it resolved another Anglo-American controversy without serious loss to the United States.

Claims Against France

A problem that had defied Adams and that Jackson also finally settled was that of the claims of American citizens against France, claims based on France's destruction of American property in the Napoleonic wars between 1803 and 1815. Americans had tried unsuccessfully to settle their claims since 1815, although Europeans had similar claims, and France had paid them. Understandably, Americans felt the sting of discrimination.

Soon after becoming President, Jackson took up the cause of the American claimants and after involved negotiations arrived at a settlement. In a treaty of July 4, 1831, France agreed to pay twenty-five million francs in six annual installments, but her government could make no payments until the legislative chambers approved the treaty and voted the money. Since many Frenchmen considered the amount to be paid as unnecessarily high, the chambers would not execute the treaty.

Therefore, when Jackson's Secretary of the Treasury drew a draft on the French government for the first installment in February, 1833, France's Minister of Finance refused payment because the chambers had not ratified the treaty, and no money had been appropriated. When Jackson pressed the French to execute the treaty, the king explained to the American Minister in Paris that "unavoidable circumstances" alone had prevented it, but added that "it will be faithfully performed."

Despite those assurances, in April, 1834, the French Chamber of Deputies defeated a bill appropriating the money. Jackson bristled, ordered the Navy ready for sea duty, and in his annual message of December asked Congress to support strong measures against France. The United States, he said, would not permit solemn treaties "to be abrogated or set aside." He recommended "that a law be passed authorizing reprisals upon French property in case provisions shall not be made for the payment of the debt at the approaching session of the French Chambers."[2]

Even though the Senate, under Whig leadership, refused to back the President in a policy of reprisals, his words angered and hurt the French. They recalled their Minister in Washington and suggested that the American Minister leave Paris. He sailed, shortly after, for the United States, leaving the Paris legation to a *chargé d'affaires*.

The French chambers finally voted the money, but said it could not be paid until the American government satisfactorily explained the harsh language in the

President's annual message. Jackson refused. "We would not permit any foreign nation to discuss such a subject," he said. "Nor would we permit any or all foreign nations to interfere with our domestic concerns, or to arrogate to themselves the right to take offense at the mode, or manner, or phraseology of the President's message or any official communication between the different co-ordinate or other branches of our government." [3]

Since neither France nor the United States would now retreat, they broke off diplomatic relations. Jackson was convinced that he had a popular issue and that the people stood behind him. They shouted as one, from Maine to Florida, he said, "No apology, no explanation—my heart cordially responds to that voice." His advisers finally overcame his stubborn pride and persuaded him to soften his attitude.

In his annual message of December, 1835, therefore, Jackson denied he had intended "to menace or insult the Government of France." Yet he also said that "the honor of my country shall never be stained by an apology from me for the statement of truth and the performance of duty." Since neither country wanted to prolong this minor tempest and neither wanted to back down first publicly, they both accepted a British offer to mediate in January, 1836. Then the British mediator announced that France accepted the explanation in Jackson's recent message as satisfactory. That settled the matter. France paid her installments, Jackson sent France a gracious message, and the two countries resumed cordial relations.

Although both Frenchmen and Americans had talked of war and made warlike preparations, the claims dispute never reached the stage of a real war crisis. This episode illustrated the tremendous influence that the personality of a strong President, such as Jackson, had on foreign policy. His attitude could magnify an unimportant issue into a minor crisis and even arouse the American people into thinking about war with a friendly nation. [4]

The CAROLINE *Incident*

About a year and a half after Jackson's blunt diplomacy had disposed of the claims question, his successor, Martin Van Buren, had to deal with a crisis in relations with Great Britain that the United States did not settle until the signing of the Webster-Ashburton Treaty in 1842. The immediate difficulties began with two rebellions in Canada in 1837.

Even though the British authorities quickly suppressed the rebellions, the rebel cause aroused widespread sympathy among Americans who mistakenly identified the uprisings with their own revolution against England. One New York newspaper reflected American sentiment when it reported that "99 out of 100 people here wished success to the Canadians." [5] Many Americans hoped that Canada would declare herself independent and were willing to help in driving the British from North America.

Concerned over the violent feelings on both sides of the Canadian border, President Van Buren issued a proclamation on November 21, 1837, calling on Americans to remain neutral. Since the proclamation had no force behind it, Van Buren sent no troops to the frontier to guard American neutrality. Less than a month later, William Lyon Mackenzie, a defeated leader of the rebellion in Upper Canada, fled across the border and established headquarters in Buffalo. He rapidly raised funds and recruited volunteers for a "patriot" army to fight the British in Canada.

With a small band of his "patriots" Mackenzie then moved to Navy Island on the Canadian side of the Niagara River. There he ran up the rebel flag, set up a provisional government, and attracted other recruits, many of them Americans. Soon his "army" numbered almost a thousand. To carry supplies from the New York shore, the "patriots" engaged an American-owned steamboat of forty-six tons, the *Caroline*. The Canadian authorities decided to prevent its use as a supply ship and on the night of December 29 sent a force of fifty men under the command of a naval officer to destroy the *Caroline*.

Since the *Caroline* was not at Navy Island, the raiders continued across the river to the New York side where the ship was tied to a dock. While overcoming the crew and some passengers, they killed one American and wounded several others. Then they set fire to the ship and towed it out into the river where it sank.

On the American side of the frontier the attack aroused new and more violent anti-British feeling. Extremists demanded retaliation. Some, like those in Richford, Vermont, resolved it was the right of every American "*who can*, to cross the line into Canada, and volunteer to help the *patriots* to obtain their liberties, and execute justice on their oppressors, and those who have shed innocent blood in the United States." [6] Fearing that the flaming sentiment along the border might lead to war, the more moderate Americans urged mutual forbearance.

As soon as Van Buren himself learned of the *Caroline* attack, he summoned Major General Winfield Scott to take command of the border area. "Blood has been shed," he told Scott; "you must go with all speed to the Niagara frontier." [7] On the following day, January 5, 1838, he issued another proclamation, this time warning that all those "who shall compromit the neutrality of this Government by interfering in an unlawful manner with the affairs of the neighboring British provinces will render themselves liable to arrest and punishment under the laws of the United States, which will be rigidly enforced."

At the same time, Secretary of State John Forsyth protested "the destruction of the property and assassination of citizens of the United States on the soil of New York" to the British Minister in Washington. The United States, he said, would demand redress. The Englishman did not argue the matter, but referred it to his superiors with his own point of view. "If the Americans either cannot or will not guard the integrity of their own soil or prevent it from becoming an arsenal of outlaws and assassins," he wrote, "they have no right to expect that the soil of the United States will be respected by the victims of such unheard of violence."

Taking the position that the *Caroline* raiders had acted in self-defense and legally under the rules of international law, the British government would not accept responsibility for the act or meet the American demands for redress. It took the whole affair coolly and did as little about it as had the United States about Jackson's execution of two British subjects in his Florida raid twenty years earlier. The diplomatic problem raised by the *Caroline* incident, therefore, remained unsettled.

Border Strife and Secret Societies

Strife and tension along the frontier did not end either. Extremists and Canadian refugees in the United States kept alive the threat of armed invasion into Canada. After the failure of the "patriots" to foment revolution in Canada they resorted to secret societies, organizing five of them in 1838 and 1839. The first of these, the Canadian Refugee Relief Association formed in New York in March, 1838, sought to embroil the United States in a war with Britain. Since the United States was suffering from the effects of the Panic of 1837, recruits for the societies were not difficult to find among the unemployed who sympathized with the rebel cause, particularly when the organizations offered the lure of a cash bounty and free land.

The Refugee Association's first act sought to avenge the *Caroline*. Shouting "Remember the *Caroline*," some twenty-two of its followers, disguised as Indians, in the early morning hours of May 29, 1838, captured the British steamboat *Sir Robert Peel* in American waters of the St. Lawrence, routed the passengers and burned the ship. The Association followed this with two blundering attacks on Canada along the Niagara frontier. Then its activities ended. Most of the secret societies, in fact, were short-lived. They died after the fiascoes of their first attacks.

The largest and most feared of those societies, the Hunters and Chasers of the Eastern Frontier, however, lasted longer than most, and at its height had about fifty thousand members. Originating in Vermont, it spread its "Hunters Lodges" across the northern part of the United States, into Canada, and even into some of the southern states. Its avowed purpose was to eliminate British monarchial rule from North America and each member had to take an elaborate secret oath pledging him "never to rest till all tyrants of Britain cease to have any dominion or footing whatever in North America."[8]

Like those of the other secret societies, the raids of the "Hunters," organized by

Americans and launched from American soil, all ended ingloriously. Understandably, the attacks enraged Canadians, invited reprisals, and kept alive the threat of war. The moderate elements in the United States were disgusted and alarmed. "The game of pirating upon our neighbors has been carried far enough," one American newspaper said early in 1839. "Neither Canada nor Great Britain can stand it much longer. The United States would not."

Although Van Buren, anxious to avoid war, acted vigorously to prevent Americans from attacking Canada, his powers were inadequate. Congress, moreover, offered little assistance. In March, 1838, it amended the Neutrality Act of 1818 in order to provide punishment for those engaging in the illegal raids, but the amendments added little to the President's existing powers. Even Winfield Scott, though successful in curbing certain minor activities, proved unable to check the more dangerous sorties, such as those of the "Hunters."

Finally, by the end of 1839, the activities of the secret societies died down and the frontier tension eased, but Van Buren's efforts, which included a visit to the border in June, were not the only reason the attacks stopped. The raiders in time grew disgusted with their leaders, realized the futility of the invasions, and took fright at the severe treatment Canadian authorities meted out to prisoners.

The Controversy over Alexander McLeod

The relative calm on the frontier did not last long. In the following year, the case of Alexander McLeod revived the tension and the threat of war. New York authorities arrested McLeod, a deputy sheriff from Niagara, Upper Canada, on November 12, 1840, charging him with arson and the "murder" of Amos Durfee, the American killed during the *Caroline* raid. The authorities might have freed him on the bail offered by the Canadian government, but a mob prevented the release by training a cannon on McLeod's cell.

Brushing aside the question of guilt or innocence, the British government made it a matter of policy and of national honor to secure McLeod's release without trial. The attack on the *Caroline*, the British Minister in Washington insisted, was "the publick act of persons obeying the constituted authorities of Her Majesty's Province." Even if McLeod had participated in the raid, the British government argued, he himself could not be held responsible for what had occurred since he had acted under the official orders of his superiors. In taking this position, the British government did what it previously had refused to do. It now assumed responsibility for the *Caroline* attack.[9]

Secretary of State John Forsyth would not accept the British argument. Neither he nor the President, he said, was "aware of any principle of international law, or indeed of reason or justice" giving legal immunity to offenders even though they "acted in obedience to their superior authorities."

The dispute dragged on, but when Daniel Webster became Secretary of State in March, 1841, under the Whig President William Henry Harrison, and a month later under John Tyler, he reversed the position Forsyth had taken. He agreed with the British that international law did not justify punishing as criminals those who acted under military orders, but pointed out that the Federal government had no power to interfere with the jurisdiction of the New York courts.

Supported by a ruling of the Supreme Court of New York, the state authorities said the trial must go on. Justice must take its course regardless of the international repercussions. Even though he insisted on upholding the rights of his state, New York's governor, William H. Seward, assured Webster confidentially that he would pardon McLeod if found guilty.

Webster needed that support because McLeod's case had aroused angry nationalistic outbursts on both sides of the Atlantic. Earlier the American Minister in London, at the urging of Lord Palmerston, Britain's Foreign Secretary, had written to the President that "the excitement is indeed violent among all Parties & the case is treated as one of the most monstrous character. Some . . . talk of seizing and retaliating upon Americans here. One thing is certain, if McLeod is executed, there will be *immediate war*! Of this you may rest assured." This threat of war was probably an exaggeration, but feelings were violent.

In the United States, members of Congress debated angrily and the opposition attacked Webster for his subservience toward Britain. Americans demanded redress for the *Caroline*. That, from their point of view, was the essence of the McLeod case. "Sir—the waves of Niagara have extinguished the fires of that vessel," one congressman from Tennessee said—"they have silenced forever the agonizing shrieks of her remaining crew—but the cry for vengeance still comes up from her deep and agitated bosom, in tones louder than the thunder of her own mighty cataract." [10]

A change of ministry in England in September, 1841, then helped to ease the crisis. Lord Aberdeen, as conciliatory as Webster toward the case, replaced the truculent Palmerston as Foreign Secretary. Finally, on October 12, a New York court in Utica acquitted McLeod. After his release, the troubles arising from the Canadian rebellions died down.

Since the British had admitted responsibility for the *Caroline* attack, the questions of its legality, or reparation, and of apology, remained. Webster and a special emissary from Britain, Lord Ashburton, took them up in their negotiations in 1842. Although Ashburton insisted that the *Caroline* raiders had invaded American territory in self-defense, he admitted that "what is perhaps most to be regretted is that some explanation and apology for this occurrence was not immediately made." Webster took this as a satisfactory apology. Since the United States accepted the destruction of the *Caroline* as an act of self-defense and admitted that the ship had engaged in illegal activity, it demanded no indemnity.

To prevent similar conflicts between Federal and state jurisdiction in the future, Webster, with President Tyler's support, drafted a bill to cover such cases. Congress passed it on August 29. That act gave the Federal courts jurisdiction in all cases where aliens were charged with crimes committed under the authority of a foreign government.

Again, aroused passions and questions of prestige and national honor had magnified minor issues into a prolonged crisis between two friendly peoples. Fortunately, sane statesmanship and good will on both sides finally kept the crisis within the bounds of a peaceful settlement.

The Maine Boundary Dispute

Before the McLeod controversy had waned, difficulties over the northeastern boundary led to another minor Anglo-American crisis. The United States and Britain both claimed some twelve thousand square miles of land between Maine and New Brunswick. No one had ever been able to run the boundary in that area because for nearly sixty years the United States and Britain had been unable to

THE SETTLEMENT OF
THE MAINE BOUNDARY
CONTROVERSY, 1842

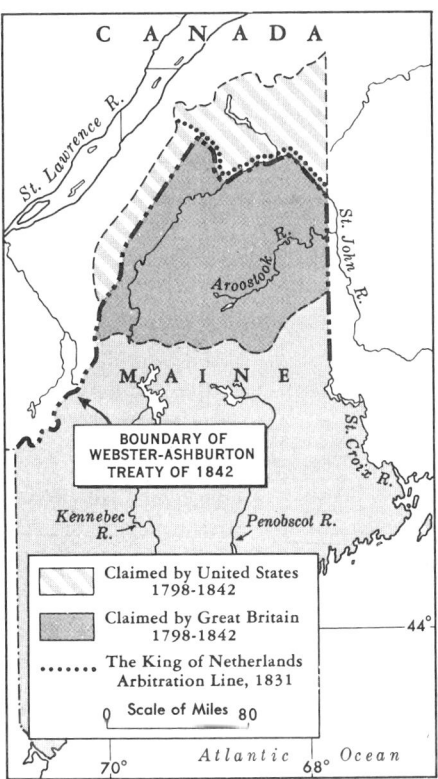

agree on the location of the line, defined vaguely in the treaty of peace at the end of the American Revolution. After trying a number of times to agree on a boundary through direct diplomacy, the two countries submitted the dispute in 1827 to the arbitration of the king of the Netherlands, who could not reach a judicial decision on the evidence available to him and hence decided on a compromise line in January, 1831.

Technically, as arbitrator, the king should have decided between the opposing claims on the basis of the evidence. Since he had not, and had essentially split the difference, Britain and the United States agreed that he had exceeded his authority, but Britain was willing to accept the compromise if the United States would. Maine, however, protested against what it considered a loss of territory rightfully its own, and thus when President Jackson asked the Senate's advice, it voted in June, 1832, not to accept the king's recommendations.

In the next decade population in Maine and New Brunswick increased, and railroads became an important means of travel. Rail traffic between Canada proper and the maritime provinces would be most direct if it passed through the border area.[11] The rebellions of 1837, moreover, had shown the need for an all-weather route, for military purposes, from Halifax, on the Atlantic shore, to Quebec, located inland. The best route ran from St. John, on the mainland, through the disputed territory.

Toward the end of the decade a new crisis flared up in that very area, now considered strategically important. Late in 1838 lumberjacks from New Brunswick began cutting timber there, in the fertile valley of the Aroostook River. In February, 1839, a land agent from Maine with a party of two hundred men attempted to expel the lumberjacks. In a night clash the New Brunswick men captured fifty of the Americans and threw them into jail. Both Maine and New Brunswick mustered their militia and Congress appropriated ten million dollars for the protection of Maine and authorized the President to call for fifty thousand volunteers.

For awhile it looked as if the trivial and bloodless "Aroostook War" of 1838–1839, might erupt into a real conflict, but neither side wanted that.[12] President Van Buren, therefore, again called on Winfield Scott who went to the Aroostook country and in March, 1839, arranged a truce. Since the truce gave each side possession of the territory it actually occupied without endangering its claim to the disputed land, it left Maine in nominal control of the Aroostook Valley.

Since Britain and the United States now recognized that the unsettled boundary might at any time produce another crisis, the time appeared ripe for a negotiated settlement. Before they could proceed toward a negotiation, however, another controversy, this time primarily involving the South, created new tensions stemming from the old problems of the slave trade and freedom of the seas in time of peace.

The CREOLE Incident

Early in November, 1841, a cargo of one hundred and thirty-five slaves aboard the *Creole*, an American ship sailing from Virginia for slave markets in New Orleans, revolted, killed one of the white men, overpowered the ship's officers and crew, and forced the mate to put into Nassau in the Bahamas, a British port. The authorities there hanged the murderers but allowed the other Negroes to retain the freedom they had won when they reached free British soil. When the United States demanded the surrender of the Negroes, the British authorities refused to give them up. That refusal, coupled with Britain's efforts to stop the African slave trade, infuriated Southerners.

The United States had outlawed that trade in 1808 but had not adequately enforced its own laws. Britain had abolished the slave trade a year earlier, freed all slaves under her flag in 1833, and thereafter carried on a vigorous international crusade against slavery. Through treaties with other nations, her cruisers stopped suspected slave ships on the seas, but the United States would not allow those cruisers to stop and search ships flying the American flag. John Quincy Adams when he was Secretary of State clearly expressed the American view. The British Minister in Washington once asked him if he could conceive of a more atrocious evil than the slave trade. "Yes," Adams said, "admitting the right of search by foreign officers of our vessels upon the seas in time of peace; for that would be making slaves of ourselves." [13] To Americans the right of visit and search brought back bitter memories of impressment during the Napoleonic wars.

After 1839 the United States became the only major maritime power not obligated by treaty to allow the British to crush the slave trade wherever they found it, even if carried on by foreigners using the American flag. After that date, in fact, more and more of the slave ships used the American flag to protect their trade. "The chief obstacle to the success of the very active measures pursued by the British government for the suppression of the slave trade on the [African] coast," a governor of Liberia wrote in 1839, "is the *American flag*. Never was the proud banner of freedom so extensively used by those pirates upon liberty and humanity as at this season." [14]

As the British increased their activities, the guns of their cruisers stopped many slave ships flying the American flag that were not American. They also mistakenly detained legitimate American ships, thus creating exacerbating incidents. Americans, particularly Southerners, became more determined than ever to resist any interference with legitimate commerce and with freedom of the seas.

Then the British framed a doctrine allowing them to stop ships in time of peace. They called it the "right of visit." Under this principle, while disclaiming the right of search in time of peace, the British said they would board only ships "strongly suspected of being those of other nations unwarrantably assuming the American flag." The United States argued that the new doctrine was the old "right of search" in disguise, and that it violated the freedom of the seas. That doctrine, in effect, merely increased American determination to prevent the British from stopping any American ships. In 1841 along with the *Creole* case and the border tension, it added to the martial fever in the United States.

Lord Ashburton's Mission

War sentiment and hatred of Britain in the winter of 1841–1842, therefore, were strongest on the frontier, in the South, and among Democrats. Whigs and businessmen in the seaport cities were neither martial nor anti-British. They profited from their trade with England and most of them believed that their prosperity depended on continued peace with her.

Secretary of State Daniel Webster was himself a Whig who shared the sentiments of his party's primary supporters. In his policies he catered to American business and worked to uphold his announced principle that "no difference shall be permitted seriously to endanger the maintenance of peace with England." Not long after he took office, therefore, he let the British know that his government was willing to settle the most serious controversy, that of the Maine boundary, through negotiation and a treaty.

England's Foreign Secretary, Lord Aberdeen, also wanted peace and realized that something had to be done to clear away the difficulties. He took advantage of Webster's offer and, as we have seen, sent a friend as a special envoy to the United States, "one who would be peculiarly acceptable to the United States as well as eminently qualified for the trust," and empowered him to make a treaty on the boundary question and to settle the other problems.[15]

Lord Ashburton, Alexander Baring, was well suited for his mission. His wife was an American, he had many social and business connections in the United States, and earlier in his life had even lived there. Also, Webster knew him. The Secretary had met Ashburton, and many of Britain's leading statesmen and businessmen, when he visited England in 1839 for some American concerns. Therefore, when Ashburton arrived in Washington in the spring of 1842, he could meet informally with Webster to settle Anglo-American problems through cordial diplomacy. In the words of a contemporary observer, they dispensed with the "mere etiquette, the unnecessary mystery and mummeries of negotiations."[16]

At the outset, on the question of the Maine boundary, the two men decided to put aside the documentary evidence and the arguments of almost sixty years and to work out an agreement on a new line. To reach a compromise they had to over-come two main obstacles. On the British side, the snag was the proposed military road from Halifax and St. John to Quebec. Ashburton's instructions insisted that any settlement must assure it to Britain.

On the American side, the impediment was the claim of Maine and Massachusetts to the whole of the disputed land. Before 1820 Maine had been a part of Massachu-setts, and after the separation Massachusetts had retained ownership of half of the public lands in the disputed area. Both states were politically important, both insisted that the Federal government could make no settlement without their consent, and both opposed a compromise boundary. Before Webster could make a settlement, therefore, Maine and Massachusetts had to agree to accept a surrender of lands they considered rightfully theirs. Webster won them over in a carefully worked out campaign of propaganda, persuasion, and coercion.[17]

First, the Secretary of State launched a newspaper campaign in Maine designed to win the people's consent to a compromise boundary. To finance Webster's propaganda, President Tyler placed seventeen thousand dollars in State Depart-ment "secret service" funds at his disposal. Next, the Secretary persuaded Maine and Massachusetts to send commissioners to Washington to participate in working out a settlement.

Then, as Webster said later, he delivered his "grand stroke."[18] He knew that at the peace negotiations in Paris in 1785 Benjamin Franklin had marked a map "with a strong red line" to indicate the boundary, but neither he nor anyone else had been able to find a copy of the marked map in the American archives. An authentic copy of that map would have proved which side had the stronger claim.

Webster did not really care who had the better legal title. What he wanted was a successful negotiation. He picked up an old map from a second-hand dealer with markings on it that supported Britain's claims and then backed it with evidence supplied by his friend Jared Sparks, a professor at Harvard College. Sparks had seen a map in the French archives he thought was Franklin's red-line map. From memory and his notes he marked a map of Maine and sent it to Webster. It, too, conceded almost half of the disputed land to Britain. Those maps fitted the objectives of the Secretary's diplomacy.

Webster showed the old map, marked according to Sparks' memory, to the Maine and Massachusetts commissioners and forced them to agree to the com-promise he wanted. They realized that the map, if authentic, destroyed their case. Then the Federal treasury paid Maine and Massachusetts one hundred and fifty thousand dollars each and expense money to compensate them for the lands they surrendered. Having overcome the "states' rights" opposition, Webster then concluded a treaty with Ashburton. In addition, they exchanged notes covering the various other questions in dispute.

The Webster-Ashburton Treaty

The treaty, signed on August 9, 1842, divided the disputed territory, giving Britain some five thousand square miles including the site of the proposed military route. The United States received some seven thousand square miles, including the Aroostook Valley and the right to navigate the St. John River through New Brunswick. Since he obtained the coveted military and railroad route, Ashburton was willing to make concessions elsewhere.

Ashburton conceded most of the American claim to some one hundred and fifty square miles of disputed territory at the head of the Connecticut River in New Hampshire. He also surrendered a narrow strip of land on the forty-fifth parallel along the northern borders of New York and Vermont that rightfully belonged to Britain. This land was important because the original surveyors of the line had made a mistake. At the northern end of Lake Champlain, at Rouse's Point, New York, the United States had built a fort that cost about one million dollars. That structure, named Fort Montgomery but commonly called "Fort Blunder," was, as a new survey showed, in Canadian territory, about a half mile north of the true line. Ashburton agreed to keep the boundary at the old line and the United States retained its costly fort.

Ashburton's most important boundary concession lay in the West, in a disputed area between Lake Superior and the Lake of the Woods. There, he gave up some sixty-five hundred square miles of "wild country" that he considered of "little importance to either party." The important thing, he believed, was "that some line should be fixed and determined." That region contained the iron ore fields of Minnesota, including the eastern part of the rich Mesabi Range.

A second treaty, signed on the same day but later consolidated with the other to form one agreement, provided for the extradition, or mutual surrender, of fugitive criminals between the United States and Canada and for the cooperation of the British and American navies in suppressing the slave trade. The Canadians and the British hoped the extradition agreement would help to end the border troubles. "If you can succeed," the Governor General of Canada wrote Ashburton in July, "in making some arrangement by which we may be able reciprocally to give up our own respective delinquents you will have done more for the peace and quiet of These Provinces than I perhaps shall ever be able to do."

As to the slave trade, Britain suggested that each nation allow the naval vessels of the other a limited "right of visit" on suspected slave ships flying their flags. So strong was American sentiment against the right of search in any form that Webster would not even discuss it, but did agree to commit the United States to take stronger measures against its own nationals engaged in the slave trade. The treaty also obligated the United States to keep a naval force of eighty guns in

African waters under an independent command that would cooperate with the British in suppressing the slave traffic. Until the Civil War the United States never fully kept its part of the bargain and the slave trade continued to flourish under the illegal protection of the American flag.[19]

The treaty did not mention the *Caroline* and *Creole* cases. Webster and Ashburton included them in the notes they exchanged, which did not have the binding qualities of the treaty itself.

Since the treaty was a compromise and did not give Americans all that they wanted, Webster expected strong opposition to it in the Senate. With the Senate, and with the country as a whole, he employed the same tactics he had used with Maine and Massachusetts. Even before he signed the treaty, he had enlarged his propaganda campaign on its behalf. By the time the treaty reached the Senate, therefore, he had built up considerable public support for it.

Webster's propaganda stressed two main themes, one positive and one negative. He pointed out that the treaty would end all the difficulties with Britain to the advantage of the United States and warned that even if the terms were not fully satisfactory, the United States had no choice but to accept them as the alternative was war. His propaganda was successful. Most newspapers, Whig and Democratic, accepted the treaty as an instrument of peace.

Still, some senators, particularly Democrats, were not satisfied. Behind the closed doors of a secret session, Senator Thomas Hart Benton, a Democrat from Missouri, denounced the treaty as merely a sectional victory. He said it sacrificed the interests of the West and South to those of the Northeast.[20] Some other Democrats supported his views, but Webster and President Tyler had sent the red-line map to the Senate along with the treaty, and it overcame most of that body's resistance. The Senate approved the treaty on August 20, 1842, by a vote of thirty-nine to nine, the largest majority it had ever given a treaty. All but one of the opposing votes were Democratic.

While astute propaganda made the Webster-Ashburton Treaty popular in the United States, Canadians, and some Englishmen, attacked it. In Parliament, Lord Palmerston denounced it as the "Ashburton Capitulation" and said later that it was "one of the worst and most disgraceful treaties that England ever concluded."[21] When Englishmen learned of Webster's red-line map, they assumed that Ashburton could have forced better terms from the Americans, so they condemned him in even harsher terms than before for allegedly selling out his country.

Later, after both the United States and England had ratified the Webster-Ashburton Treaty, debates in Parliament revealed that England all along had possessed a copy of the original map authentically marked. Since that map confirmed the full American claim, as did two other copies that turned up in later years, it silenced the treaty's opponents.[22] Although the United States had in fact surrendered land it rightfully owned, the sacrifice had not been entirely one-sided. England and the United States had both adjusted to political and economic realities. Britain had certainly made important concessions elsewhere, and to the United States the minerals of Minnesota were more important in the long run than the timber of New Brunswick.

Since both countries had strong economic and business ties with the other, war probably would not have occurred even if the agreement had not been concluded. Nonetheless, the Webster-Ashburton Treaty did clear up long festering difficulties and closed incidents that had led men on both sides of the water to talk of war.

The Oregon Question

There was one important problem that Webster and Ashburton had discussed but failed to settle, that of dividing the Oregon country, a vast wilderness on the Pacific Coast north of California and forty times the size of the disputed land between Maine and New Brunswick. Agreement on that division proved difficult because, in part, Ashburton's instructions were uncompromising. Since insistence on an agreement over Oregon appeared likely to endanger the Maine settlement, the Webster-Ashburton Treaty contained nothing on the West Coast problem. "It must," Ashburton wrote to his superior, "therefore, I fear, sleep for the present."

At that time, neither Ashburton nor Webster considered the Oregon question urgent or a threat to peace. "I much doubt," Ashburton said, "whether the Americans will for many years to come make any considerable lodgment on the Pacific."[23] He believed, as did Webster, that an independent republic would rise on the Pacific and would remove the Oregon question as a source of Anglo-American friction.

Webster considered the whole Northwest as poor country and virtually value-less to the United States, and certainly not worth serious trouble with Britain. Like most Whigs, moreover, he feared the results of national expansion. He accepted the doctrine that antedated the Republic and that had long been held by Jeffersonians; namely, that a democracy in annexing distant territories did so at its own peril. "In seeking acquisitions, to be governed as Territories, & lying at a great distance from the United States," he wrote to an expansionist, "we ought to be governed by our prudence & caution; & a still higher degree of these qualities should be exercised when large Territorial acquisitions are looked for, with a view to annexation."[24] With these ideas running through their heads, Webster and Ashburton found it relatively easy to let the Oregon problem sleep for awhile.

A few years later, however, political developments in the United States and a great migration to Oregon created such tension with England that again war appeared probable if the problem were not settled by negotiation. The basic source of difficulty was that neither the United States nor Britain had clear title to the whole Oregon country.

The conflicting claims of both countries went back many years.[25] Americans held that Captain Robert Gray's discovery of the Columbia River in 1792, the official expedition of Lewis and Clark that descended the Columbia in 1805, and John Jacob Astor's Pacific Fur Company post (the first American settlement in Oregon, planted in Astoria near the mouth of the Columbia in 1811) gave them possession of the river's entire valley to the fifty-first parallel. The British had seized Astor's post in 1813, but had restored it to the United States in 1818. By the Adams-Onís Treaty, the United States had also succeeded to all of Spain's claims, based on early voyages and explorations, north of the forty-second parallel. Up to the time of the Webster-Ashburton negotiations, however, the United States had been willing to compromise by limiting its claim to the forty-ninth parallel.

The Louisiana Purchase had given the United States still another, though not legal, claim stating that the Oregon country was a natural extension of Louisiana. In the words of Albert Gallatin, "the United States claimed a natural extension of their territory to the Pacific Ocean, on the grounds of contiguity and population, which gave them a better right to the adjacent unoccupied land than could be set up by any other nation."

With sound reasoning the British dismissed all of the American claims, except those based on Gray's and Lewis and Clark's explorations, as inconsequential. They acknowledged American rights of first discovery of the Columbia, particularly from Gray's voyage, but said that the discoveries of their own explorers in the region, going back to Sir Francis Drake's voyage in 1579, Captain James Cook's in 1778, and Captain George Vancouver's in 1792 gave them a stronger claim since they had followed up exploration with occupation. As for the Spanish claims in the Oregon country, Britain said that Spain had surrendered them in the Nootka Sound Convention of 1790. The American claims based on Spain's rights, therefore, had no standing.

Since the claims stemming from discovery and exploration were confused, the British suggested that the Oregon country be divided on the basis of possession. Britain offered this solution for many years, but the United States would never accept it.

When the United States had negotiated the Convention of 1818 with Britain, it had refused to divide Oregon, as Britain had suggested, on a boundary that followed the Columbia River to the sea. Nor had Britain been willing to extend the boundary of forty-nine degrees from the Rocky Mountains to the Pacific Coast. Therefore, in that treaty, as we have seen, the two countries had compromised their rival claims by agreeing to leave the region open to both Americans and Englishmen for ten years without prejudicing the claims of either country.

In the following year the Adams-Onís Treaty had established the southern boundary of the Oregon country at the forty-second parallel. Then the American and British treaties with Russia in 1824 and 1825 had set the northern boundary at fifty-four degrees forty minutes. By 1827 the United States and Britain were the only rivals for that land and its boundaries were clear. They ran westward from the Rocky Mountains to the sea and north from the forty-second parallel to the parallel of fifty-four degrees forty minutes.

In that year, on August 6, since Britain and America could not decide on a division of the country and since open or "joint" occupation had produced no serious friction, they agreed by treaty to extend the open occupation indefinitely.[26] Each country could end the arrangement by giving a one-year notice of intention to do so.

To obtain a settlement on the line of the Columbia River, the British were willing, however, as they had been in 1818, to make a concession on the Pacific Coast north of the Columbia. George Canning, the British Foreign Minister, offered Albert Gallatin, the American negotiator, the Olympic Peninsula adjoining the Strait of Juan de Fuca. He made the offer to meet the American demand for harbors inside the strait, particularly for a harbor that could be used as a naval base. Since the area the British offered was an enclave with no overland connection with the United States and surrounded on every side by British territory or by waters the British navy could dominate, Gallatin rejected the offer. With shrewd foresight he favored postponing a settlement "until the citizens of the United States shall have acquired a respectable footing in the country."

The Hudson's Bay Company and the Columbia River

Americans were slow in settling in the Oregon country. Until 1842 Britain had profited far more from the open occupation than had the United States. Since 1807 British trading companies had continuously controlled the whole region north of the Columbia. After 1821, except for a few American trappers, the Hudson's Bay Company, exercising exclusive trading and administrative privileges granted it by the British government, alone occupied most of the disputed land. It controlled a series of posts located on the banks of rivers that cut through the region.

Its main post in Oregon was Fort Vancouver, located on the north bank of the Columbia River opposite the Willamette River. The Columbia, Hudson's Bay contended, was the central transportation system of the Oregon country. It insisted that Britain's continued possession of that river was essential for preserving its fur trade in Oregon. That trade, until the mid-1840's, shaped the objectives of British diplomacy in Oregon.

Even though the Hudson's Bay Company held scattered posts south of the

Columbia, the fur trade there was less important than in the north, and the British government had long given up its claims there. The United States held unchallenged claims to the land between the forty-second parallel and the Columbia River. Yet Americans would not, as the British had long insisted they should, accept a division of the Oregon country at the Columbia, partly because they sought a good harbor on the Pacific Coast. From the Columbia south, the Oregon coast, rugged, rocky, and wild, contained no port accessible even to the smallest seagoing ships.

The problem of a harbor for American shipping, despite the personal indifference of Webster and Ashburton to the fate of Oregon, had proved to be one of the main obstacles to a compromise boundary. "What they are principally looking to is to have a harbour of their own on the Pacific," Ashburton wrote. "The mouth of the Columbia is a barred and indifferent harbour, but they say that the estuary to the North of it, entered, I believe, by the Strait of Juan de Fuca is the only good harbour on this part of the coast, and hence the obstinacy with which they have hitherto persisted in carrying the boundary line further north." [27]

Since Ashburton's instructions had insisted on the Columbia River as a boundary, and the United States had demanded a harbor on the Pacific Coast, Webster had concluded that the best way to settle the Oregon question would be to take a new approach. With President Tyler's support, Webster told Ashburton that the United States might make a settlement if Britain would persuade Mexico to cede to the United States part of her province of California, including the magnificent harbor of San Francisco. Then the American need for a port on the Pacific Coast would be met; the United States would no longer have to insist on a harbor in the Strait of Juan de Fuca; and they themselves could make a treaty dividing the Oregon country at the Columbia River. All this could be done without loss to either Britain or the United States. Only Mexico would lose.

This tripartite plan had fascinated Ashburton, who reported it to his government. The British government, however, would not act on it, and nothing came of it.

Although some Americans wanted a harbor on the Pacific primarily for strategic reasons (in particular, for a naval base) Webster's plan also reflected the determination of some Americans who desired such a port for commercial reasons—to build a trade with Asia. The mouth of the Columbia did not offer such a harbor.

In June, 1842, a few weeks after Ashburton had forwarded the tripartite plan to London, Lieutenant Charles Wilkes, U.S. Navy, who had been away from the United States for four years exploring the Pacific area, returned and reported on his explorations of the Oregon coast. He aroused a new public interest in Oregon and shattered any possibility that the United States might surrender its claims north of the Columbia as proposed in the tripartite plan. Wilkes told of the perilous bar at the mouth of the Columbia. "Mere description," he reported, "can give little idea of the terrors of the bar of the Columbia; all who have seen it have spoken of the wildness of the scene, and the incessant roar of the waters, representing it as one of the most fearful sights that can possibly meet the eye of the sailor."

Of the Strait of Juan de Fuca and its sea arms to the east, Wilkes told a different story. "Nothing can exceed the beauty of these waters, and their safety: not a shoal exists within the Strait of Juan de Fuca, Admiralty Inlet, Puget Sound, or Hood's Canal, that can in any way interrupt their navigation by a seventy-four gun ship," he wrote. "I venture nothing in saying, there is no country in the world that possesses waters equal to these." [28] Since those were the only harbors in the Oregon country that ships could enter or leave in any season of the year, he suggested that the United States demand a boundary north of forty-nine degrees so as to include Vancouver Island and the harbors of the strait. Such a boundary became a primary objective in America's Oregon diplomacy.

The Great Migrations of 1843 and 1844

Until the Webster-Ashburton Treaty and Wilkes' return, most Americans, except in the West, had shown little concern over the Oregon question or over the region itself. American settlers had not challenged the Hudson's Bay Company for possession, but some Americans, particularly in the Old Northwest, had always been interested in Oregon. In the 1830's a few bold men had pioneered the way to Oregon overland via the Oregon Trail and laid the basis for later great migrations. Still, the efforts of early Oregon promoters such as those of the Boston school teacher Hall J. Kelley and the Cambridge businessman Nathaniel J. Wyeth, and of missionaries such as the Protestant, Marcus Whitman, and the Catholic, Father Pierre de Smet, brought only a few American pioneers to Oregon. In 1840 there were only sixty families, consisting of missionaries, trappers, and Canadians who had been employed by the Hudson's Bay Company, settled in the Willamette Valley that ran south from Fort Vancouver on the Columbia.

Although the earlier promoters, even with enthusiastic letters, speeches, and pamphlets on Oregon, had brought few settlers, they had publicized the region widely. After 1835 government writers and travelers, who had visited Oregon, had advertised the rich agricultural possibilities of the land, particularly of the Willamette Valley. That valley, the writers said, was the most desirable part of Oregon, and it lay outside territory claimed by the Hudson's Bay Company. Americans could settle there under their own flag.

The publicity of a decade lured the first large party of pioneers, more than a hundred, over the Oregon Trail in 1842. In the next two years almost two thousand restless pioneers, fleeing years of depression following the Panic of 1837, and seeking virgin land, took to the Oregon Trail. These settlers demanded that the United States annex Oregon.

In the United States, meanwhile, Westerners and other Oregon enthusiasts expressed disappointment over Webster's failure to settle the Oregon question in his negotiations with Ashburton. When Westerners heard rumors of the tripartite plan, moreover, they voiced angry disapproval. "Oregon Conventions" then sprang up throughout the West demanding immediate occupation of all of Oregon. One such convention meeting in Cincinnati in April, 1843, concluded that "the rumored negotiation for a surrender of any part of Oregon for an equivalent in California was dangerous to peace and a repudiation of Monroe's doctrine." Western expansionists wanted all of Oregon, and California. Those expansionists met in a national convention in Cincinnati in July and "resolved that the right of the United States to the Oregon territory, from 42° to 54° 40' north latitude, is unquestionable, and that it is the imperative duty of the General Government forthwith to extend the laws of the United States over said territory."

The Oregon question had now captured the minds of Democratic expansionists. The migrations of 1843 and 1844 and the rapidly increasing strength of the American position in Oregon led them to challenge Britain's claim to any of that country. Members of Congress took up the cry for the whole of Oregon. They proposed various warlike measures, such as fortifying the Oregon Trail, immediately abrogating the joint occupation treaty of 1827, and setting up a territorial government in Oregon.

Even President John Tyler, a Southern expansionist, responded to the fresh demand for all of Oregon. "After the most rigid and, as far as practicable, unbiased examination of the subject," he said in his annual message of December, 1843, "the United States have always contended that their rights appertain to the entire region of country lying on the Pacific and embraced within 42° and 54° 40' of north latitude." In July, 1844, as the "Oregon fever" in the United States mounted, the British suggested another attempt to settle the Oregon question. Finally, Tyler's last Secretary of State, John C. Calhoun, turned down a British offer to arbitrate. He preferred a policy of "masterly inactivity" whereby American pioneers would clinch the claim to Oregon. Yet, as late as 1845 the Hudson's Bay Company still exercised almost unchallenged dominion north of the Columbia. American settlements were still concentrated primarily in the Willamette Valley.

Polk's Oregon Policy

The popular cry for the "whole of Oregon," in the presidential campaign of 1844, made the diplomacy of the Oregon question a domestic issue. Western Democrats and other expansionists exploited it, and the nationalist sentiment it aroused, to nominate their candidate, James K. Polk of Tennessee. At its convention in Baltimore, the Democratic party accepted the demands of its expansionists by resolving in its platform "that our title to the whole of the territory of Oregon is clear and unquestionable; that no portion of the same ought to be ceded to England or any other power; and that the re-occupation of Oregon and the re-annexation of Texas at the earliest practicable period are great American measures."[29] That resolution implied what was not so—that all of Oregon rightfully belonged to the United States.

Since that resolution linked the Oregon question with that of Texas and hence balanced the objectives of southern and western expansionists, it has been referred to as the "Bargain of 1844." While it may not have resulted from a formal bargain, it certainly expressed the sentiments of expansionists from those regions. Texas and Oregon became foremost issues in the campaign, but Texas more than Oregon, helped bring Polk into office.[30]

Although Polk had won only a narrow victory, he took it as a mandate to press for as much of Oregon beyond the Columbia River as he could get.[31] He had identified himself fully with the platform demanding the whole of Oregon and was prepared to carry out his party's expansionist demands. In his inaugural address, he delivered a bellicose warning to Britain. "Our title to the country of the Oregon is 'clear and unquestionable,'" he said, "and already are our people preparing to perfect that title by occupying it with their wives and children."[32]

More than the words, the tone and official character of Polk's inaugural speech aroused angry talk of war in England. He had now spoken not as a politician seeking election, but as President. As an answer to Polk the London *Times* declared that Englishmen were "prepared to defend the claims of this country to the utmost, wherever they are seriously challenged." Yet Lord Aberdeen, Britain's Foreign Secretary, as in the Maine crisis, sought a means to preserve peace through compromise.

While committed politically to demanding all of Oregon, Polk privately preferred a compromise settlement to war. Even in his belligerent speech he had not insisted on the "whole" of Oregon. All of Oregon, he told Richard Pakenham, the British Minister in Washington, on July 12, 1845, really belonged to the United States, but since preceding administrations had several times offered to settle on the forty-ninth parallel he was willing to concede the same boundary. Influenced, no doubt, by nationalistic outbursts in England calling for the defense of British claims, Pakenham made the mistake of rejecting the offer without referring it to his government. Secretary of State James Buchanan, according to Polk's instructions, then withdrew the offer and the administration again took up the claim to all of Oregon.

Britain's rejection of his offer, Polk asserted in his first annual message to Congress in December, "afforded satisfactory evidence that no compromise which the United States ought to accept, can be effected." The American title "to the whole Oregon territory," he maintained, was supported by the "irrefragable facts and arguments," and hence asked for authority to give the one year's notice abrogating the treaty of joint occupation and for power to extend the protection of American laws over settlers in Oregon. Apparently with California, as well as Oregon, in mind, he restated the noncolonization principle of the Monroe Doctrine. Polk's stand now appeared uncompromising, but he had not said he *must* have all of Oregon and that he would settle for nothing less.

Aberdeen, who was himself willing to negotiate a settlement on a boundary at the forty-ninth parallel, meanwhile reproved Pakenham for rejecting Polk's offer on his own responsibility and directed the Minister to offer arbitration. Pakenham did so twice, but the President turned him down. Polk now held that Britain had to make concessions and that the people were behind a bold policy toward Oregon. When a South Carolina congressman expressed fear that the bold policy might lead to war, Polk told him "that the only way to treat John Bull was to look him straight in the eye; that I considered a bold and firm course on our part the pacific one." [33] In fact, he wanted the power to end the treaty of joint occupation as a means of putting pressure on Britain, not as a preliminary to war.

Manifest Destiny

While Congress debated Polk's proposals, the "Oregon fever" reached its peak. The "true title" to Oregon, wrote John L. O'Sullivan, editor of the New York *Morning News*, lay in "our manifest destiny to overspread and to possess the whole of the continent which Providence has given us. . . ." A week later a member of Congress picked up O'Sullivan's newly coined phrase of Manifest Destiny. Our title to Oregon, he told the House of Representatives, now appeared founded on "*the right of manifest destiny to spread over the whole continent.*" [34]

A congressman from Illinois said he had little regard for "musty records and the voyages of old sea captains, or the Spanish treaties," since the United States had a better title to Oregon "under the law of nature and of nations." God, Americans said, preferred to be on the side of morality than law.

Others advanced the right of "geographical predestination" in claiming all of Oregon. Vast distances separated it from England; it was contiguous to the United States. Obviously, they pointed out, nature meant that land for Americans. The *Democratic Review* summed up that theory in two lines of verse:

> The right depends on the propinquity,
> The absolute sympathy of soil and place. [35]

Agrarian nationalists of the Midwest now talked more and more of fighting for "the whole of Oregon."

Many Americans, particularly Whigs, did not want to fight for Oregon to the line of fifty-four degrees forty minutes. They ridiculed those who did by calling them "fifty-four forties." In derision they coined the phrase "fifty-four forty or fight," though it probably started as the pun referring to "Political Principles of President Polk," "P.P.P.P. Phifty-Phour Phorty or Phight." This, for example, appeared in an opposition paper in Cleveland:

> Don't you phurious phifty phour phorties pheel phleasantly phlat and phoolish at the phunny phizzle out of your phearless phile leader, who phortiphied his claim to the whole of Oregon by repeated official declarations that 'our title is clear and unquestionable?' Phoor phellows! [36]

Expansionist Democrats of the Old Northwest then adopted the slogan of "fifty-four forty or fight" as their own.

Even though Polk appeared the spokesman of the northwestern agrarian nationalists, their demands alone did not finally shape American policy toward Oregon. Men of commerce, many of them Whigs with their eyes on the trade of Asia, still wanted Oregon, but were willing to compromise for a line below fifty-four forty. "It is the key to the Pacific," a New York congressman said of Oregon. "It will command the trade of the isles of the Pacific, of the East, and of China." In the same month a New Englander told Congress what merchants wanted. "We need ports on the Pacific," he asserted. "As to land, we have millions of acres of better land still unoccupied on this side of the mountains." Business groups and merchants still wanted the Strait of Juan de Fuca and its harbors, but did not want to fight for more.

Spokesmen for the merchants and Whigs, who viewed with alarm the possibility of war with England, pointed out that the United States could get the harbors and still compromise. A boundary at the forty-ninth parallel would give the United States access to the strait. With Texas safely in the Union, as of December, 1845, Southerners now joined the merchants of the Northeast in favoring a compromise. They, too, were unwilling to risk war with England by demanding more than forty-nine degrees. "Possessed, as by this line we should be, of the agricultural portion of the country, of the Straits of Fuca, and Admiralty Inlet," Jefferson Davis of Mississippi said, "to American enterprise and American institutions we can, without a fear, intrust the future." [37] Democratic expansionists of the Northwest considered the willingness of southern Democrats to compromise a breach of faith and treachery to the party.

In 1845, especially following the annexation of Texas, concern for the future of California, held by a weak Mexico but being overrun by American pioneers, convinced many of the men of commerce who wanted a harbor that America's true Manifest Destiny lay in California. Many Americans who coveted San Francisco Bay now urged a compromise on Oregon. Fearing incorrectly that England had designs on California, they believed that a compromise on Oregon would ease alleged English pressure on Mexico to obtain California. "We must surrender a slice of Oregon," the New York *Herald* maintained, "if we would secure a slice of California."

By early 1846 those who desired a compromise settlement had blunted demands for all of Oregon. They stressed the maritime and agricultural advantages of California as compared to those of Oregon. "Oregon is but a bleak, barren waste," the Nashville *Union* explained, "compared with California." Many disciples of Manifest Destiny who preferred California now denounced those in Congress who still insisted on all of Oregon, even at the cost of war with England. The California expansionists, too, were willing to settle for a boundary at forty-nine degrees.

Congress reflected the growing sentiment for peace and compromise on Oregon. After debating more than four months, it finally passed a joint resolution in April, authorizing the President to terminate the agreement of joint occupation, but with a preamble stressing it was a resolution intended to bring peace, not war. Referring to opinion in Congress, the New York *Herald* captured what was probably the prevailing sentiment of most Americans in these words:

> This is the line that we define,
>   The line for Oregon;
> And if this basis you decline,
>   We go the "whole or none,"
> We go the "whole or none," Lord John,
>   Up to the Russian line;
> Then, if you're wise, you'll "compromise"
>   On number forty nine.[38]

Aberdeen's Domestic Problems

Within a week, in accord with the congressional resolution, Polk gave England the required year's notice abrogating the joint occupation treaty of 1827, but with it expressed the hope that a friendly settlement would be promoted. Realizing that the Senate would now probably back a compromise settlement, Polk also hoped that his action would induce England to renew negotiations on Oregon on the basis of a compromise. The notice had the desired effect.

Lord Aberdeen welcomed Polk's friendly suggestion and immediately prepared an offer acceptable to most Americans. Since he held a low estimate of Oregon's worth—a "pine swamp," he called it—and had long favored a settlement at forty-nine degrees, the Foreign Secretary did not want to fight for that wilderness. Yet Britain's claims to the region between the Columbia River and forty-nine degrees were superior to those of the United States. To give the region to the Americans meant, to most Englishmen, an unwarranted surrender. Aberdeen's problem, therefore, was a domestic one of persuading the British people, his own government, and the opposition party, to accept a retreat to the forty-ninth parallel.

Aberdeen finally won support for his Oregon policy through convincing argument, a careful propaganda campaign, and unexpected developments in Oregon and England. Throughout 1845 American pioneers had continued flocking to Oregon. By the end of that year about five thousand had settled there. Yet all but a handful lived in the Willamette Valley. The Hudson's Bay Company, which still exercised almost unchallenged dominion north of the Columbia, nonetheless, viewed their presence with alarm. Some of the settlers were frontiersmen who made their own law with pistol and rifle, hating the company for standing in the way of American control of the region. More than once they had threatened to storm Fort Vancouver and put its well-dried pine timbers to the torch. In defense, the company posted guards and mounted cannon, for inside the fort in that year were goods valued at £100,000.

Earlier, because of the decline of the fur trade in the Columbia area, the company had decided to shift its center of operations in Oregon north to Vancouver Island. It began moving in 1845, and fear of an American attack probably hastened the move.[39] It was obvious now that the Columbia River was no longer vital to the company's fur trade. That move destroyed one of the main arguments for retaining the region between the Columbia and the forty-ninth parallel. Investigators from the Royal Engineers and the Royal Navy who had surveyed the Oregon situation agreed, moreover, in their reports submitted at this time, that England could not hold the region against attack and that inevitably American pioneers would overrun it.

All this strengthened Aberdeen's view that Britain would lose nothing vital in settling at forty-nine degrees. After those developments, Sir Robert Peel, the Prime Minister, and the cabinet were willing to support Aberdeen's policy.

At the same time, in England the movement for free trade and repeal of the corn laws, special tariffs on grain, helped overcome the resistance of the opposition party. Lord John Russell, the Whig opposition leader, supported Peel's Tory government in its efforts to repeal the corn laws and wanted no war that would interfere with that trade reform.[40] Lord Palmerston, the former Whig Foreign Secretary and a belligerent nationalist, however, had often denounced Aberdeen's foreign policies as cowardly and as "truckling" to American pressure. He would allow no retreat in Oregon.

In 1845, Palmerston's warlike utterances did not fit the times. Most Englishmen wanted peace. In December, when Peel's Tory government fell from power, a war scare followed the news that Palmerston would again become Foreign Secretary. Lord John Russell could not form a government to take over as other Whig leaders refused to serve in the cabinet with Palmerston. Peel, therefore, headed the government again. Russell then spoke boldly in favor of a compromise on Oregon, and in February, 1846, secretly told Aberdeen and the Tories that he would, in effect, accept any Oregon treaty they drafted.

Aberdeen and Peel had also launched a propaganda campaign to win public opinion to their Oregon policy. The Tory press, and even some Whig journals, took up Aberdeen's arguments that England could get all that was worth fighting for by retreating to Vancouver Island and forty-nine degrees. With that boundary and with the island she could still have fine ports, access to the Strait of Juan de Fuca, and keep the peace.

Through press propaganda, Aberdeen apparently convinced his countrymen that Britain's claims to Oregon had flaws, that Oregon was not worth a war, that the fur trade there was dying, that the Columbia River was not necessary for commerce, and that American claims to good harbors on the Pacific Coast were reasonable. The London *Examiner*, a leading Whig newspaper, published an article in April, 1845, describing the valley of the Columbia as a barren wasteland and urging a settlement at forty-nine degrees. "The value of the whole territory in fee simple would not be worth the expense of one year's war," another London journal announced later that year. Then in January when the ostensibly independent London *Times* took up Aberdeen's arguments, most of the press did also, and the Tory government won its propaganda campaign.[41] When Polk's notice terminating joint occupation reached him, therefore, Aberdeen could respond with the knowledge that he had the people's support for a compromise settlement.

The Oregon Treaty

Aberdeen then sent Polk a draft treaty offering a boundary at forty-nine degrees to the middle of the channel between the mainland and Vancouver Island and thence south through the Strait of Juan de Fuca to the Pacific Ocean. This left all of Vancouver Island to the British. The treaty also provided for free navigation of the Columbia for the Hudson's Bay Company and for protection of certain of its property rights in the disputed area.

That draft treaty reached Polk on June 6, a few weeks after Congress had declared war on Mexico. Even so, the President objected to it at first, but his cabinet persuaded him to follow the unusual procedure of submitting it to the Senate for its advice before deciding either to accept or reject it. There, some of the "fifty-four forty" Westerners shouted their dismay at the "surrender" of American land, but they were now an impotent minority. By a vote of 38 to 12 the Senate on June 10, 1846, advised the President to accept the proposed treaty. Five days later Secretary of State Buchanan and the British Minister in Washington signed it. Then, on June 18, the Senate by a vote of 41 to 14 gave its formal consent to the treaty without adding a single change. The President ratified it on the next day.

Polk had retreated from the line of fifty-four forty and accepted a compromise on forty-nine degrees for several reasons. He was convinced, apparently, that the British would not give up more than forty-nine degrees without war, and neither

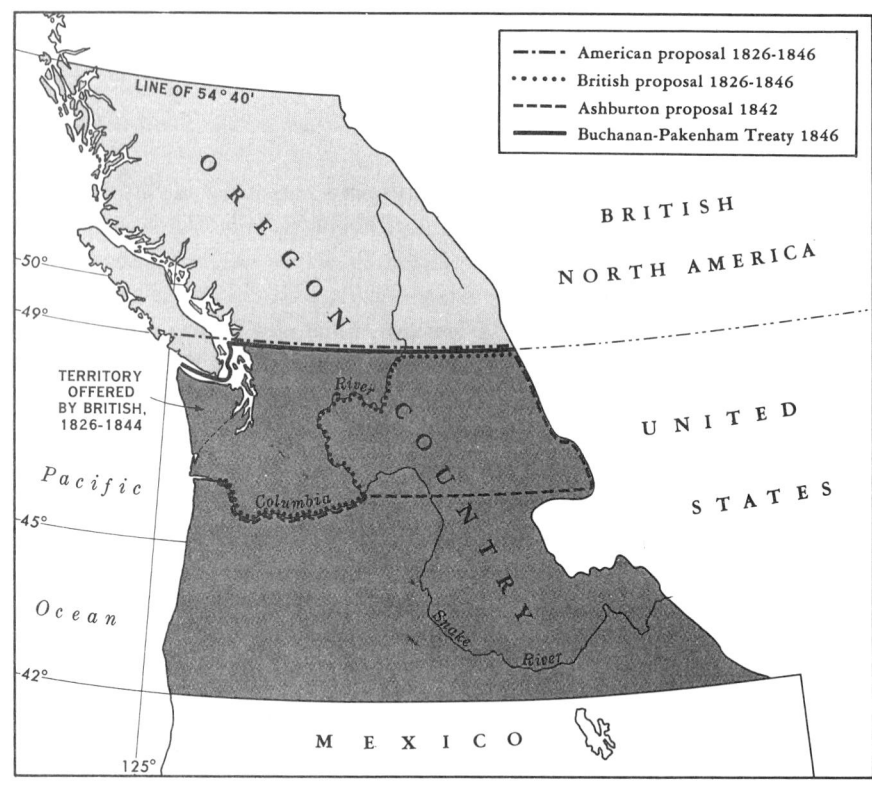

DISPUTED OREGON, 1846

he nor the people as a whole wanted a war with England. In fact, he had hoped to clear up the Oregon question before going to war with Mexico. Since taking office, Polk had been willing to settle on the forty-ninth parallel, including ports in the Strait of Juan de Fuca, and had several times said so, but had not dared admit that publicly as he feared public opinion, aroused by the expansionist cries for all of Oregon, would not support him. He could not publicly abandon the Democratic platform of 1844, yet he could not risk breaking up his party over the issue of 54° 40'. When public opinion appeared to shift in favor of peace, he safely retreated to forty-nine degrees.[42]

To the "fifty-four forties" the Oregon treaty appeared a surrender. To nationalistic Englishmen, who had long expected more, it also smacked of capitulation. On the basis of claims and possession, the English made the real sacrifice. Yet both countries obtained what they really wanted—good ports and land for future populations. Most important, the English-speaking peoples had again settled a bitter quarrel peacefully.

NOTES

1. For the details in this account of the West Indian trade, see Frank L. Benns, *The American Struggle for the British West India Carrying-Trade, 1815–1830* (Bloomington, Indiana, 1923).

2. Message of Dec. 1, 1834, James D. Richardson, ed., *A Compilation of the Messages and Papers of the Presidents, 1789–1897* (10 vols., Washington, 1896–97), III, 106.

3. Quoted in John S. Bassett, *The Life of Andrew Jackson* (2 vols. in one, New York, 1928), p. 669.

4. For a summary of the claims episode, see Richard A. McLemore, "The French Spoliation Claims, 1816–1836: A Study in Jacksonian Diplomacy," *Tennessee Historical Magazine*, ser. 2, II (July 1932), 234–254.

5. Quoted in Albert B. Corey, *The Crisis of 1830–1842 in Canadian-American Relations* (New Haven, 1941), p. 28.

6. *Ibid.*, p. 38.

7. Quoted in Winfield Scott, *Memoirs of Lieut.-General Scott, LL.D.* (2 vols., New York, 1864), I, 307.

8. The full text of the oath is in Corey, *The Crisis of 1830–1842*, p. 76. For other details, see Wilson P. Shortridge, "The Canadian-American Frontier during the Rebellion of 1837–1838," *Canadian Historical Review*, VII (March 1926), 13–26.

9. Alastair Watt, "The Case of Alexander McLeod," *Canadian Historical Review*, XII (June 1931), 145–167.

10. The two quotations are from Corey, *The Crisis of 1830–1842*, pp. 135, 137.

11. For details, see Thomas Le Duc, "The Maine Frontier and the Northeastern Boundary Controversy," *The American Historical Review*, LIII (Oct. 1947), 30–41.

12. David Lowenthal, "The Maine Press and the Aroostook War," *Canadian Historical*

Review, XXXII (Dec. 1951), 336, points out that the newspapers were more belligerent than the people.

13. Entry of June 29, 1822, in Charles Francis Adams, ed., *Memoirs of John Quincy Adams* (12 vols., Philadelphia, 1874–77), VI, 37.

14. Quoted in Hugh G. Soulsby, *The Right of Search and the Slave Trade in Anglo-American Relations, 1814–1862* (Baltimore, 1933), p. 46.

15. Ashburton's instructions are summarized in Ephraim D. Adams, "Lord Ashburton and the Treaty of Washington," *The American Historical Review*, XVII (July 1912), 766–770. See also Wilbur D. Jones, "Lord Aberdeen and the Maine Boundary Negotiations," *Mississippi Valley Historical Review*, XL (Dec. 1953), 477–490.

16. Quoted in Oliver P. Chitwood, *John Tyler: Champion of the Old South* (New York, 1939), p. 310.

17. Richard N. Current, "Webster's Propaganda and the Ashburton Treaty," *Mississippi Valley Historical Review*, XXXIV (Sept. 1947), 187–200.

18. To Jared Sparks, March 11, 1843, in Claude H. Van Tyne, ed., *The Letters of Daniel Webster* (New York, 1902), p. 286.

19. For details on these minor issues, see Wilbur D. Jones, "The Influence of Slavery on the Webster-Ashburton Negotiations," *Journal of Southern History*, XXII (Feb. 1956), 48–58. See also Harral E. Landry, "Slavery and the Slave Trade in Atlantic Diplomacy, 1850–1861," *ibid.*, XXVII (May 1961), 184–207.

20. See Thomas H. Benton, *Thirty Years' View* (2 vols., New York, 1854–56), II, 425.

21. Quoted in Frederick Merk, "British Politics and the Oregon Treaty," *The American Historical Review*, XXXVII (July 1932), 665.

22. For details, see Laurence Martin and Samuel F. Bemis, "Franklin's Red-Line Map Was a Mitchell," *The New England Quarterly*, X (March 1937), 105–111.

23. Ashburton's quotations, dated June 29 and April 25, 1842, are from dispatches to Aberdeen and are in Frederick Merk, "The Oregon Question in the Webster-Ashburton Negotiations," *Mississippi Valley Historical Review*, XLIII (Dec. 1956), 395, 401.

24. To Waddy Thompson, June 27, 1742, in Van Tyne, *Letters of Webster*, p. 269.

25. For details, see Frederick Merk, "The Genesis of the Oregon Question," *Mississippi Valley Historical Review*, XXXVI (March 1950), 583–612 and "The Ghost River Caledonia in the Oregon Negotiation of 1818," *The American Historical Review*, LV (April 1950), 530–551.

26. For a discussion as to the difference between joint and open occupancy, see Samuel F. Bemis, *John Quincy Adams and the Foundations of American Foreign Policy* (New York, 1949), p. 482.

27. To Aberdeen, April 25, 1842, quoted in Merk, "The Oregon Question in the Webster-Ashburton Negotiations," *Mississippi Valley Historical Review*, XLIII (Dec. 1956), 395.

28. Wilkes is quoted in Norman A. Graebner, "Maritime Factors in the Oregon Compromise," *Pacific Historical Review*, XX (Nov. 1951), 333. For a similar stress on the theme of continental expansion that "looked seaward as well as landward," see Richard W. Van Alstyne, "The Significance of the Mississippi Valley in American Diplomatic History, 1686–1890," *Mississippi Valley Historical Review*, XXXVI (Sept. 1949), 230.

29. *Niles' National Register*, LXVI (Baltimore, June 8, 1844), 227.

30. Edwin A. Miles, "'Fifty-four Forty or Fight'—An American Political Legend," *Mississippi Valley Historical Review*, XLIV (Sept. 1957), 301, maintains that Oregon was not an important factor in the campaign.

31. The popular, not the electoral, vote was narrow. See Frederick Merk, "Presidential Fevers," *ibid.*, XLVII (June 1960), 10.

32. March 4, 1845, in Richardson, *Messages of the Presidents*, IV, 381.

33. Entry of Jan. 4, 1846, Milo M. Quaife, ed., *The Diary of James K. Polk: During His Presidency, 1845–1849* (4 vols., Chicago, 1910), I, 155.

34. Sullivan, Dec. 27, 1845, and Robert C. Winthrop, Jan. 3, 1846, are quoted in Julius W. Pratt, "The Origin of 'Manifest Destiny,'" *The American Historical Review*, XXXII (July 1927), 795, 796.

35. Quoted in Albert K. Weinberg, *Manifest Destiny: A Study of Nationalist Expansionism in American History* (Baltimore, 1935), p. 148.

36. July, 1846, quoted in Hans Sperber, "'Fifty-four Forty or Fight': Facts and Fictions," *American Speech*, XXXII (Feb. 1957), 9.

37. Quoted in Norman A. Graebner, *Empire on the Pacific: A Study of American Continental Expansion* (New York, 1955), pp. 130–131.

38. New York *Herald*, April 6, 1846, quoted in Norman A. Graebner, "Polk, Politics, and Oregon," East Tennessee Historical Society's *Publications*, No. 24 (1952), p. 17.

39. Frederick Merk, "The Oregon Pioneers and the Boundary," *The American Historical Review*, XXIX (July 1924), 691, and John S. Galbraith, *The Hudson's Bay Company as an Imperial Factor, 1821–1869* (Berkeley, Calif., 1957), pp. 218–250.

40. For details see Frederick Merk, "The British Corn Crisis of 1845–46 and the Oregon Treaty," *Agricultural History*, VIII (July 1934), 95–123; Thomas P. Martin, "Free Trade and the Oregon Question, 1842–1846," *Facts and Factors in Economic History: Articles by Former Students of Edwin Francis Gay* (Cambridge, Mass., 1932), pp. 470–491; and John S. Galbraith, "France

as a Factor in the Oregon Negotiations," *Pacific Northwest Quarterly*, XLIV (April 1953), 69–73. Galbraith points out that the British government feared that war with the United States might bring on war with France also and that this fear led the British to seek a settlement short of surrender.

41. For the connection between Aberdeen and *The Times*, see Frederick Merk, "British Government Propaganda and the Oregon Treaty," *The American Historical Review*, XL (Oct. 1934), 51–56.

42. See Merk, "Presidential Fevers," *Mississippi Valley Historical Review*, XLVII (June 1960), 30; Wilbur D. Jones and John C. Vinson, "British Propaganda and the Oregon Settlement," *Pacific Historical Review*, XXII (Nov. 1953), 353–364; Julius W. Pratt, "James K. Polk and John Bull," *Canadian Historical Review*, XXIV (Dec. 1943), 341–349—all of which offer reasons why Polk backed down from "fifty-four forty"—and Norman A. Graebner, "Politics and the Oregon Compromise," *Pacific Northwest Quarterly*, LII (Jan. 1961), 7–14.

Chapter Eight

THE ACQUISITION OF TEXAS AND CALIFORNIA

THAT SAME expansionist fervor, expressed in the phrase Manifest Destiny, that had sent pioneers swarming over the Oregon Trail, had driven others into Texas. Between 1800 and 1820, while Texas still belonged to Spain, the first American frontiersmen had drifted across the Sabine River. Some were armed invaders intent on destroying Spanish control, others were settlers who squatted on the land illegally, appropriating farms near Nacogdoches in east Texas or to the north on the south bank of the Red River. Whether filibusters or settlers, most of them were tough and unruly, and all paid little attention to international boundaries.

Spain did not want those or any other Americans in Texas. In those years, in fact, she had expected Texas to serve as a buffer against such intruders, a barrier protecting her other lands to the west and south. Yet she did not force those squatters from Texas, for in those years that vast province was virtually unguarded and almost without people. In 1820 only three small Spanish outposts guarded the entire province, and cattle far outnumbered its four thousand people. If it were to prosper and form a screen against the American pioneers, Texas needed people.

As early as 1801 Spanish authorities had talked of attracting immigrants to Texas, but fearing that most of them would come from the United States, did nothing. Inaction prevailed until December, 1820, when Moses Austin, a Connecticut-born Yankee who had settled in the West, asked permission to bring three hundred settlers into Texas. The authorities there, now serving a liberal Spanish government, reversed previous policy and approved in January, 1821.

Later that year, Mexico won her independence from Spain, and Texas became a Mexican province. Mexico's relations with the United States in that year of independence were unusually cordial. Mexicans were grateful for aid Americans had given them in their revolution and believed that friendship with the United States was firmly rooted. Their statesmen realized, moreover, that the growing strength of the United States stemmed, in part at least, from a steady flow of immigrants. They decided to follow a similar pattern in populating Texas and hence inaugurated a policy of encouraging American settlers to come into the province.

Mexican Policies in Texas

Meanwhile, on his way to Missouri to recruit colonists, Moses Austin died. His twenty-seven-year-old son, Stephen, then took over the task of building a colony, and since many Americans wanted Texas land, he had no difficulty. After settling his colonists in Texas, however, he encountered difficulty over his land grant which he finally overcame after making a special trip to Mexico City. There, the new Mexican government, in April, 1823, confirmed his grant under terms which set a pattern for future grants. Those terms allowed young Austin to bring into Texas three hundred families who would agree to become Mexican subjects and accept the Catholic religion. Each family, without cost, could have one square league, or 4,428 acres, of land. In addition to receiving a bonus in land proportionate to the number of settlers he brought, Austin, for his services, could collect 12½ cents an acre from the settlers.

Under those terms Austin's colony grew and prospered and others, therefore, tried to imitate his success. They were encouraged, furthermore, by the Mexican government which enacted a liberal national colonization law in August, 1824, that in effect gave the states of the Mexican nation the unoccupied land within their borders to dispose of as they wished. The law's main restrictions were minor. It said foreigners, without official permission, could not settle within twenty leagues of an international boundary or ten leagues from the coast, and that no one could obtain more than eleven square leagues of land.

Under that law the state of Coahuila-Texas, of which Texas was a district, adopted its own land law in the following March. It opened Texas to those of "Christian and good moral character" who would swear allegiance to Mexico, offered them special tax exemptions, and gave responsibility for handling immigration to land agents, or *empresarios*. The law promised handsome rewards in land to the successful *empresario*, and in general followed the pattern of Austin's grant.

News of that law sent American speculators flocking into Coahuila-Texas for land grants. Most of them wanted only a quick profit by selling their rights to others. Only a few lived up to the contracts they received. The sincere *empresario* found colonists easily, for the Mississippi Valley teemed with prospective settlers who wished to escape the still deadening effect of the depression following the Panic of 1819. Since most pioneers did not have cash in a lump sum, land prices in the United States for them were high. The Land Act of 1820, for instance, required a cash payment of $1.25 an acre. Across the United States border, an easy journey by land or sea, Mexico now offered rich land for a few cents an acre.

Even the speculators and those responsible *empresarios* who failed as colonizers lured hundreds of pioneers into Texas through their newspaper advertisements and personal recruiting. By 1830 American settlers numbered about eight thousand. Mexico's policy of populating Texas through the bait of cheap land was succeeding, but that very success now caused alarm. The "Texas fever" that swept the lower Mississippi Valley would not stop. Yet Mexico, already experiencing difficulty with some Americans in Texas, now wanted to halt the immigration.

Although most of the settlers were loyal to the Mexican government, some conflict between them and the Mexican authorities was bound to arise. All but a few of the Americans in Texas were Southerners who either had brought Negro slaves with them or who expected to acquire some later to work their lands. The Americans, therefore, were shocked when the state of Coahuila-Texas in 1827 obtained a constitution calling for the gradual freeing of all bond servants, and two years later when Mexico's president decreed slavery abolished everywhere. They were able, however, to exert enough pressure to force the Mexican authorities to exempt Texas from the anti-slavery laws. Although the Americans had won a concession, the slavery question created a lasting ill will.[1]

Religious differences, in time, also brought on difficulties. To own land, the Protestant Americans had to become Catholics. Since their desire for land was stronger than religious scruples, the early settlers outwardly at least accepted Mexico's official religion. Since the Mexican authorities did not force them to attend Catholic churches, they did not have to become practicing Catholics, and few did. Later settlers, particularly illegal squatters who had taken no oath of allegiance to Mexico, ignored the law allowing none but Catholics to worship publicly. They wanted their own Protestant churches, which they went ahead and built in defiance of law. The authorities did nothing to prevent them from worshipping as they pleased and even conceded a limited religious toleration. Yet most Americans resented the religious restrictions, and the Mexican officials were angered by the resistance to their laws.

Armed clashes between American settlers and Mexican authorities added to the mutual distrust. One of the most serious of those early conflicts broke out in the autumn of 1826 when Haden Edwards, an *empresario*, tried to remove American and Mexican squatters from his land grant in east Texas. Taking the side of the squatters, the Mexican authorities annulled Edwards' contract and ordered him from the country. His brother, Benjamin W. Edwards, then gathered a handful of men, rode into Nacogdoches, and under a red and white flag, inscribed "Independence, Liberty, and Justice," on December 16 proclaimed the Republic of Fredonia, stretching "from the Sabine to the Rio Grande." The Edwards brothers had counted, mistakenly, on outside help. "Our friends in the United States," Benjamin said, "are already in arms, and only waiting for the word." Stephen F. Austin, at the head of a small army acting for the Mexican authorities, quickly snuffed out the Fredonian Rebellion.

That revolt did irreparable harm to relations between Americans and the Mexicans. To some Americans in Texas, Haden Edwards, a speculator contemptuous of Mexicans and Mexican law, in time appeared as something of a martyr who suffered at the hands of a tyrannical government. Mexicans probably remembered the shape of conquest in Florida and saw in the Fredonian Rebellion evidence that aggressive Americans intended to take Texas by force, even though Austin and other Americans loyal to Mexico had helped to suppress it. Fear and distrust, nevertheless, continued to cloud relations between Americans and Mexicans.

Mexican Laws and American Immigration

The diplomacy of the American government, at the time, added to Mexican distrust and led Mexican officials to suspect the United States of encouraging Americans to colonize Texas as part of a plot to annex the province. Ever since John Quincy Adams in his treaty with Luis de Onís in 1819 had given up the vague American claims to Texas, Americans, mostly Westerners, had demanded that the government recover that province. When Adams became President in 1825, he tried unsuccessfully to obtain as much of Texas as he could by instructing his Minister to Mexico, Joel R. Poinsett, to negotiate a new boundary. Then in 1827 Poinsett offered one million dollars for all of Texas, but Mexico would not sell.

Adams' successor, Andrew Jackson, also tried to acquire Texas through diplomacy and purchase. He instructed Poinsett to try again for Texas and increased the offer to five million dollars, but still Mexico refused to sell. Jackson replaced Poinsett with Anthony Butler, an unprincipled Minister who for six years resorted to various shady devices to get Texas. He attempted to bribe Mexican officials into selling, tried to force an unpayable loan on them with Texas as security, and urged the President to seize eastern Texas by force. Mexico's rulers did not know the details of Butler's unsavory schemes, but were aware that he had orders to secure Texas at any cost.[2]

Butler's mission, moreover, began right after the pro-Jackson press had launched a campaign urging and predicting the acquisition of Texas. A Mexican officer at Nacogdoches reported in December, 1829, that Americans were recruiting "colonists" to revolutionize Texas. There is, he said, "no other subject of conversation on the frontier but the views of President Jackson to take possession of Texas."

Since the blundering Jacksonian diplomacy, the ominous press campaign, and the threatening frontier rumors followed on the heels of the alarming Edwards revolt, the Mexican government reviewed its immigration policy in Texas. A Mexican official who had investigated the situation made a report in January, 1830, and sounded the alarm against losing Texas to the United States. "Either the government occupies Texas *now*," he warned, "or it is lost forever." [3] He suggested that the government encourage Mexican and European immigrants to come to Texas, that it create an economic bond between Texas and the rest of Mexico by stimulating trade, and that it strengthen old garrisons and establish new ones in the province.

In April the Mexican congress incorporated those suggestions into a law. Although never fully enforced, that law, in addition, prohibited further American immigration into Texas. Nonetheless, Americans kept coming, most of them illegally. The Texas border was too long for Mexico to police adequately. The new law thus had the effect of barring serious immigrants selected by responsible *empresarios* and of encouraging lawless adventurers who respected no authority, Mexican or American, to take their chances in Texas.

Serious trouble began in 1831 when the Mexican government planted garrisons at strategic points among the Texans to prevent the spread of American colonies. The settlers hated them, particularly some of the renegade American commanders who showed less regard for them than did the Mexicans. In 1832 Mexican soldiers clashed several times with settlers and blood flowed. In that year Texans demanded settlement of various grievances, namely that Mexico repeal its anti-immigration law, and that it grant them some privileges of self-government, especially that it give Texas the status of a state separate from Coahuila. Then they organized "committees of safety" to build up public support for their program.

Late in 1833 the Mexican congress offered substantial concessions and repealed the anti-immigration law, but would not grant separate statehood. The state of Coahuila-Texas also granted some concessions. In 1834, as a result, peace reigned in Texas and seemed destined to continue. With the borders open once more, a new "Texas fever" swept the Mississippi Valley and land-hungry Americans again rushed into Texas. By the end of 1835, Americans, about thirty thousand of them, greatly outnumbered the three thousand Mexicans in Texas. Culturally and ethnically, Texas was becoming an American province. In some of the prosperous American settlements one listened in vain for the soft sounds of the Spanish tongue. In others, it seemed an alien and strange sound. The political allegiance to Mexico City of the Americanized province by 1835 was tenuous.

The Texas Revolution

Mexico's pitifully weak control over its province became unmistakably clear after April, 1834, when Antonio López de Santa Anna, an unprincipled adventurer, made himself dictator of Mexico. He repudiated existing reforms and attempted to establish a highly centralized government. In Texas he tried to enforce measures that appeared repressive. Fearing that Santa Anna would abolish all their rights, some forty Texans, members of a minority war faction, on June 30, 1835, captured a Mexican fort and garrison at Anahuac on Galveston Bay. When Santa Anna moved to punish the attackers, "committees of safety and correspondence" sprang up in the American communities and armed resistance became a revolution.

On November 3, while still professing loyalty to Mexico, the Texans met at San Felipe de Austin, drafted a "Declaration of Causes" that compelled them to take up arms, set up a provisional government, and appointed Andrew Jackson's friend, the frontier fighter Sam Houston, commander of their army. A few months later, on March 2, 1836, the government adopted a declaration of independence and the Republic of Texas was born.

Santa Anna, meanwhile, marched into Texas. At San Antonio his army of some four thousand besieged less than two hundred Americans who stood off his forces for thirteen days behind the adobe walls of an abandoned mission, the Alamo. Finally, with the dawn of March 6, the massed Mexicans swarmed over the walls. Fighting back with rifle butts and knives, the Americans inflicted a heavy toll, but by noon the last man was dead. From that day "Remember the Alamo" became a cry of revenge for Americans in Texas and a barrier to reconciliation.

A few weeks later the Texans suffered another blow that fanned their desire for revenge. A force of three hundred and fifty men under the command of James W. Fannin, Jr., surrendered to a superior Mexican army near Goliad. In violation of the surrender terms, the Mexicans roused the prisoners from their sleep, marched them a short distance from the town, and shot them in cold blood on Sunday morning, March 27. Like the slaughter at the Alamo, the massacre at Goliad sent aroused volunteers flocking to join Houston's army.

At first, seemingly with little hope for victory, Houston retreated steadily eastward before Santa Anna's forces. Then suddenly, on April 21, just west of the San Jacinto River near Galveston Bay, Houston, with his army swollen to almost eight hundred men, turned. Shouting "Remember the Alamo," the Texans charged the unprepared Mexicans during the siesta hour and within thirty minutes slaughtered more than six hundred and captured over seven hundred, including Santa Anna. The Texan losses were negligible, nine killed, thirty-four wounded.

Despite the protests of his officers and men, Houston later set Santa Anna free, but before he did, the Mexican leader signed two treaties. One declared hostilities ended and called for Mexican forces to evacuate Texas. The other, a secret treaty, pledged his support for an independent Texas with a boundary at the Rio Grande River. Those agreements meant nothing, for the Mexican congress repudiated them as soon as it learned of Santa Anna's capture. Nonetheless, since the Mexican forces remaining in Texas after the Battle of San Jacinto had already retreated into Mexico, that battle had won Texas a *de facto* independence.

American Aid and Neutrality

The Texans had not won their independence unaided. When they started the revolution, they had sought and expected help from the American people, and Americans as individuals or in groups, wholly sympathetic to them, had responded liberally. As early as October, 1835, the people of New Orleans, for instance, had organized a Texas committee to recruit volunteers and raise money. It helped raise three "volunteer" companies which within two months were fighting in Texas. Before the end of November, cities in most western and southern states, and even in northern states such as New York and Pennsylvania, were holding mass meetings in support of the fighting Texans. Those cities organized "Texas committees" that solicited money and brought together bands of "emigrants" to fight in Texas. "Emigrate to Texas!" urged a speaker at a Philadelphia meeting. "It abounds in game of all kinds. You will find plenty of employment for as many rifles and muskets as you can get there."

The revolutionary authorities in Texas had sent special commissioners into the United States to take advantage of popular enthusiasm and to lure emigrants to Texas with promises of handsome land grants. Those commissioners obtained money through donations and loans. Some capitalists, eager to speculate in Texas lands, even made contracts with the Texans under the guise of "loans" whereby they would take bargain-price land in repayment. The loans tied powerful American financiers to the Texan cause, for repayment would come only with victory. With the money they raised, the commissioners bought arms, medicines, and other supplies and shipped them to Texas. Without such support the Texans probably could not have defeated Mexico.

Mexico realized the importance of the American aid and protested. The American government answered that it tried to enforce its neutrality laws prohibiting the raising of hostile forces against a friendly state. When the Texas revolution began, in fact, President Jackson ordered the district attorneys, "when indications warranted," to prosecute violators of neutrality, but they and other government officials generally disregarded their instructions. Some of them so openly sympathized with the Texans that they connived at violations of the laws. Public opinion favoring the Texans, particularly in the South and West, was so strong that even if the government had made strenuous efforts to stop the Texas volunteers, which it did not, it would have had difficulty doing so. In contrast to Jackson, Martin Van Buren made strong efforts to enforce American neutrality, during the Canadian rebellion of 1837, but Britain was powerful and could retaliate. Mexico was weak.

An Independent Texas

In addition to expecting American aid, the Texans had hoped to join the United States. As soon as they began fighting, in fact, they appealed to Jackson to recognize their independence or to annex them. Although he personally wanted Texas, the President reacted cautiously and did nothing immediately. If the United States annexed Texas, war with Mexico would follow. Equally ominous was the question of slavery. It made immediate annexation impossible. After the Battle of San Jacinto, Texas asked to be annexed on terms calling for recognition of property in slaves. Abolitionists feared that Texas might add four or five slave states to the Union and argued that the Texas revolution was part of a dark conspiracy by the slave power in the United States to gain more slave territory.

"*People of the North!*" the foremost anti-Texas abolitionist declared, "*Will you permit it?* Will you sanction the abominable outrage; involve yourselves in the deep criminality, and perhaps the horrors of war, *for the establishment of slavery in a land of freedom*; and thus put your necks and the necks of your posterity under the feet of the domineering tyrants of the South, for centuries to come?" [4] Despite this and similar charges, there is no convincing evidence to support the theory that a conspiracy of slaveholders had sparked the Texas uprising and annexation movement.

Northern Whigs opposed the annexation, charging that Jackson and Houston had plotted the Texas revolution to add one or more Democratic states to the Union. The President feared, with reason, that annexation would create so great a political upheaval that it might destroy the Union. The same fears did not, however, apply to recognition of independence. Yet Jackson hesitated in this, too, for in the approaching election of 1836 he did not want in any way to weaken the chances of his hand-picked candidate, Martin Van Buren. To recognize Texas would appear to align the administration with slavery, might split the Democrats, and would imperil Van Buren's chances for the Presidency. Jackson also delayed recognition for another reason. He hoped, apparently, to acquire Texas through direct negotiations with Mexico as represented by Santa Anna, but that plan failed.

Meanwhile, petitions calling for immediate recognition of an independent Texas poured into Congress from all over the Union, north and south. In response, both houses of Congress in July, 1836, passed resolutions favoring recognition. Texans, a few months later in a special plebiscite, overwhelmingly favored annexation to the United States as soon as possible. Finally, on March 3, 1837, the day before he left office and after Van Buren had been elected, Jackson recognized the independence of Texas.

Many in Texas and in the United States regarded that recognition as merely a preliminary to annexation. The Texan Minister in Washington, Memucan Hunt, therefore, formally offered Texas for annexation on August 4. Van Buren rejected the offer. "If the overture of General Hunt were even to be reserved for future consideration," Secretary of State John Forsyth explained, "it would imply a disposition to espouse the quarrel of Texas with Mexico, something wholly at variance with the spirit of the treaty of amity with Mexico and contrary to the uniform policy and obvious welfare of the United States."[5]

Van Buren feared the political opposition of the Whigs and abolitionists. Already the American Antislavery Society had circulated anti-Texas petitions, securing thousands of signatures, and the legislatures of northern states were passing anti-Texas resolutions. Then, while occupied with the trials of the Panic of 1837 and the difficulties on the Canadian border, he made it clear that he wanted no additional troubles from Texas. In October, 1838, therefore, Texas formally withdrew her offer of annexation and followed a course of independence.

Mexico refused to recognize Texan independence and continually threatened invasion. The government of Texas, therefore, sent agents to Europe to gain recognition from the major powers. With their support, it hoped to force Mexico to recognize its independence, an only partially successful plan. France granted official recognition in October, 1839; Britain in November, 1840; and lesser European countries did the same later, but repeated efforts to gain Mexican recognition failed. Mirabeau B. Lamar, an expansionist and the second president of Texas, therefore, tried unsuccessfully to extend the borders of Texas to the Pacific Ocean and thereby create a republic that could stand on its own among the powers of the world.

When Sam Houston became president of Texas for the second time late in 1841, he found an empty treasury, a heavy debt, and war with Mexico. In 1842, as a consequence, he approached the American government with two offers on the possibility of annexation. President John Tyler, a pro-slavery Virginian, favored annexation as did a majority of his cabinet. He might have accepted one of the offers if he had been certain of getting a treaty of annexation through the Senate. He had even told his Secretary of State, Daniel Webster, that "could the North be reconciled to it, could anything throw so bright a lustre around us?" Webster, a Northern Whig, however, was opposed to annexation. He would do nothing that would add more slave territory to the Union.

After Webster resigned, in the spring of 1842, Tyler went ahead with plans for annexation, motivated in part by the standard southern argument that the United States must acquire Texas before Britain succeeded in winning a dominant influence over the Texan government and in abolishing slavery there. There was some truth to that argument, for the British did not want the United States to acquire Texas. They desired an independent Texas that would act as a barrier to the expansion of the United States and would balance its power in North America. They also wished to relieve their mills from an uncomfortable dependence on southern cotton grown by slaves.

English abolitionists believed, furthermore, that Britain, through a guarantee of independence and financial aid, could persuade Texas to free her slaves and to remain independent. Texas could then sell her cotton grown by free men to England, and the English manufactured goods could go to Texas without climbing a tariff wall. To keep Texas independent and from rushing into the arms of the United States, Britain tried unsuccessfully, therefore, to persuade Mexico to recognize Texas as independent.

Houston's actions also gave the impression that the United States might lose Texas. When Mexico, in February, 1843, offered political autonomy and separate statehood if Texas would return to Mexican rule, Houston hinted that a return might be possible if Mexico granted a temporary armistice. Santa Anna, again president of Mexico, granted the armistice and late that year began negotiations with the Texans. Those negotiations, as Houston hoped they would, aroused stronger annexationist sentiment in the United States and alarmed Tyler. He now wanted annexation for two main reasons: as an extension of the area of slavery and as a popular issue to help elect him President in 1844.

The Upshur-Calhoun Treaty

In June, 1843, Tyler had appointed Abel P. Upshur, a pro-slavery fellow Virginian, Secretary of State. According to Tyler, there was no man "whose energies of body and mind were more unremittingly devoted to" annexing Texas than Upshur. To counter British policies, the new Secretary offered Texas a treaty of annexation in October. "Texas must not be permitted to throw herself into the arms of England under any impression that this government or this people is either hostile, or even cold, toward her," he had said.[6]

At first Houston refused the offer but later consented to negotiations. He imposed two conditions: protection from the United States in case Mexico attacked, and assurances that the treaty would gain approval from the Whig Senate. Upshur offered military and naval protection from the moment the treaty was signed and said a poll of the Senate assured a two-thirds approval. Since Tyler had hoped to prevent the annexation plan from stirring up the antislavery forces, Upshur negotiated secretly.

Before completing the negotiations, Upshur went on a presidential cruise aboard the warship U.S.S. *Princeton* on January 28, 1844. During the firing exercises, a twelve-inch cannon, called the "Peacemaker," exploded while the Secretary was watching it, killing him and leaving the Texas treaty unfinished. Tyler then appointed the South's foremost defender of slavery, John C. Calhoun, Secretary of State. Now sixty-two years old and approaching the twilight of a long and active career, Calhoun did not want the position, but accepted because his southern friends told him they needed his influence to secure Texas and thereby advance the cause of slavery. Thus, with the idea of winning a victory for slavery, Calhoun, on April 12, signed the treaty of annexation that Upshur had negotiated.

Then, a few days later, Calhoun took a step that linked the treaty publicly with the expansion of slavery. He had long resented the efforts of British abolitionists to end slavery in Texas. In answering a note from Lord Aberdeen explaining British policy on Texas and slavery, therefore, he defended the annexation treaty, but did not limit himself to an ordinary defense. He went out of his way to praise slavery as a positive good. The United States, he said, must annex Texas to prevent it from falling under the influence of the British who would wipe out slavery there and threaten the "peculiar institution" in the neighboring southern states of the Union.[7]

Calhoun's note, addressed to the British Minister in Washington, Richard Pakenham, when published with the treaty of annexation aroused immediate opposition in the North. There, the people urged their senators to vote against the Upshur-Calhoun Treaty and defeat the sinister plot to expand the empire of slavedom. Calhoun had aroused the very controversy that Tyler and Upshur had tried to avoid in their secret negotiations.

President Tyler submitted the agreement to the Senate on April 22, on the eve of the presidential campaign and before the parties held their conventions. The rising public opposition to the treaty fused itself with the politics of the campaign. Whigs and Democrats both passed over Tyler as a candidate. The leading Whig candidate was Henry Clay, and for the Democrats, Van Buren. Both men, while the Texas treaty was before the Senate, publicly opposed immediate annexation. The Whigs, as expected, nominated Clay and thus committed the party against immediate annexation. Unwilling to accept Van Buren's stand against annexation, the Democrats nominated the avowed expansionist James K. Polk. In their platform they demanded "the reannexation of Texas." With their candidate and platform, therefore, the Democrats became the party of expansion.

When the Senate, on June 8, voted on the treaty, the influence of the campaign and of Calhoun's note seemed clear. Whig Senators, since their standard-bearer was against it, as were their constituents, could not support the treaty. Offended by the defeat of their candidate, the Van Buren Democrats would not vote at this time for a treaty he had opposed. Therefore, with only southern support, the treaty failed by a vote of thirty-five to sixteen. Although Texans had expected the defeat, they resented it. The negotiations had cost them their temporary armistice, for Mexico resumed hostilities.

Two developments helped reverse the defeat. First, as has been seen, Americans, perhaps mistakenly, viewed Polk's election as a mandate for expansion. "It is the will of both the people and the States," Tyler told Congress in his annual message in December, "that Texas shall be annexed to the Union promptly and immediately."[8]

Secondly, Lord Aberdeen contrived, as soon as he had heard of the Upshur-Calhoun Treaty in May, to block American annexation. He approached the French government, proposing that Britain, France, Mexico, Texas, and perhaps the United States, join in a "diplomatick Act," or treaty, guaranteeing the boundaries of Texas and hence preventing her from joining the Union. If the United States persisted in trying to acquire Texas, Aberdeen told the Texans, England "would go to the last extremity . . . in support of her opposition to the annexation," if France were "perfectly agreed."[9]

Even though France agreed to join England in this bold proposal, in effect pledging both countries to guard Texan independence by war if necessary, they never adopted it. The British and French Ministers in the United States warned against the plan. European intervention, particularly before the presidential election, they said, would strengthen the expansionist forces in the United States. Polk's election then showed the depth of expansionist fervor, and Aberdeen lost interest in the plan. That expansionist sentiment so alarmed the French that they told the British the annexation of Texas hardly seemed "of sufficient importance to us to justify our having recourse to arms in order to prevent it."

The Anglo-French designs, particularly Lord Aberdeen's scheme, aided rather than hindered annexation, for when Americans heard of these plans, they took them as proof that England was willing to go to war to keep the United States from having Texas. Most Americans, apparently, then decided that Texas must be theirs, with or without slaves.

Annexation by Resolution

Tyler was aware of the shift of opinion in favor of annexation, particularly as shown in Polk's election, but also knew that he could not obtain a two-thirds majority in the Senate to approve a treaty. When Congress assembled in December, therefore, he suggested annexation by joint resolution, which required only a simple majority in both houses. A resolution calling for annexation passed in the House of Representatives on January 25, 1845, by a vote of 120 to 98, and in the Senate on February 27, by 27 to 25.

In both houses the vote followed party, rather than sectional, lines. All the

Democrats voted in favor of the resolution, and all but two Whigs opposed it. Tyler signed it on March 1, three days before leaving office. Two days later he sent word to his diplomatic agent for Texas, Andrew J. Donelson, to invite Texas to join the Union under the terms of the resolution.

Since the Constitution said "new states may be admitted by the Congress into this Union," the resolution invited Texas to come into the Union as a state, and not as a territory. Other terms allowed Texas, when she had enough population, to make as many as four states out of her territory. She could retain her own public lands, but had to pay her own public debt, and would come into the Union as a slave state.

The Mexican Minister in Washington protested the resolution, calling it an act of aggression that deprived his country of an integral part of her territory, demanded his passports, and quit his post. The British and French, meanwhile, made another effort to prevent annexation. In May they finally persuaded Mexico to agree to recognize the independence of Texas, if that province would agree "not to annex herself or become subject to any country whatever."

Texas now had to make her decision. Some Texans, particularly Sam Houston, did not like the American terms, but public opinion overwhelmingly favored annexation. President Anson Jones, who had assumed office in December, therefore submitted the American offer to his congress, along with the Mexican treaty, sponsored by the British and French, offering peace and recognition. That congress, on June 16, chose unanimously to join the United States. Three weeks later, on July 4, a popularly elected convention ratified that decision and accepted a constitution for the new state of Texas. On December 29 President Polk signed the final resolution that brought Texas, after waiting nine years, formally into the Union. "The final act in this great drama is now performed," Anson Jones said. "The Republic of Texas is no more." [10]

The Opening of California

Another Mexican province that lay in the path of Manifest Destiny was California, a land of majestic mountains, barren deserts, and rich valleys, stretching along the Pacific shore south of Oregon. Spain had used California as she had Texas, as a buffer protecting her provinces in Mexico from foreign encroachments, particularly from southward-moving Russians. Spain's control over California had never been firm. One reason for this was that fifteen hundred miles of desert, made doubly formidable by bands of Apaches, Yumas, and other fierce desert Indians, separated California from the seat of Spanish authority in Mexico City. Spain's officials had maintained infrequent communication with California only by sea.

The first Americans to reach California had also come by sea. A few of them came before 1800, mostly New England merchant adventurers seeking sea otter skins to use in their trade with China, but the sea otter trade did not become important until after the turn of the century. Since they were engaged in a clandestine commerce forbidden by Spanish authorities, those Yankee traders, as well as the men of the New England whaling ships who visited the province, built no lasting ties with California. Nevertheless, those men publicized it when they returned to New England.

After California became a Mexican province in 1821, it retained its semi-autonomous status. In the 1820's and 1830's, the Californians, mainly men of Spanish blood who had settled the province, rebelled about ten times against the incompetent governors Mexico sent north to rule them. Turmoil and revolution in Mexico added to their spirit of independence. Isolated and virtually autonomous, California had developed its own way of life. Few Californians had any strong sense of loyalty to their Mexican rulers.

It was in these decades of political ferment that Americans made their first firm foothold in California. Some of the first Americans to reach that province in the Mexican period sought furs, particularly beaver pelts. They broke California's isolation by piercing the mountain and desert barrier protecting its eastern side. The first of these path-finding "mountain men," Jedediah S. Smith, reached California late in 1826. Others followed. Then for about a decade the fur traders pushed into the rich valleys and coastal lands, blazing the major transcontinental trails into the territory. They opened California by land and advertised what they saw.

While certain fur traders were coming by land, other Americans, New Englanders, came by sea for the "hide and tallow trade." The Mexican government opened California's ports to foreign traders in hides and tallow, but until 1827 the British, through an agreement with the Mexican government, monopolized that trade. Then, after the agreement expired, American traders swarmed into the ports. The crews of the Boston hide ships, since they sometimes spent two or three years in acquiring a cargo, obtained an intimate knowledge of the California coast. In the early 1830's, American shippers planted agents in the ports to buy hides and to store them in warehouses until a company ship called for them.

Except for a few sailors who had remained from earlier visits, those agents became the first permanent American residents in California. They bought ranches, became Catholics, married Mexican wives, and adopted Mexican ways. They liked California. In letters they sent home they told of the good life they lived and praised the virtues of their adopted land. Others who visited California or who settled there, British and American, wrote books and articles, and also publicized the province, praising the climate, fertile soil, and the magnificent bay of San Francisco. Richard Henry Dana, Jr., for example, made the hide and tallow trade famous in his classic, *Two Years Before the Mast*. Appearing in 1840, this book, along with other accounts, aroused an intense American interest in California, a land now reputed to be a "pioneer's paradise."

To the restless pioneer, harried by depression, those accounts had magnetic appeal. Equally attractive were the political reports which pointed out that most of the land was thinly populated, the government inadequate, and Mexico's hold on the province "miserably weak and ineffective." In addition, military defenses were virtually nonexistent. Only a handful of pioneers, the accounts implied, could drive out the backward Mexicans and make the lush valleys American. In the wake of the "Oregon fever," as a result, a lesser fever for California began to rise in the Middle West in the 1840's.

The first landseekers from the Midwest arrived in 1841. Then, after the mass western migrations of 1843, trains of covered wagons rolled into California in increasing numbers. Those people did not settle among the Californians along the coast, but squatted illegally in the fertile Sacramento Valley and established their own way of life.

Although the Californians had been friendly to the small number of Americans who had earlier settled among them, they now became alarmed by the large-scale invasion, particularly since the Protestant newcomers, unlike the Americans already in the province, brought with them an unconcealed contempt for Mexicans, a hatred of Catholics, and a disregard for Mexican law. Friction between the alien American invaders and the Mexican authorities, therefore, developed almost immediately.

The Efforts to Purchase California

Before the covered wagons had started moving into California, American diplomacy had tried to acquire that province from Mexico and in effect contributed to the bitter state of Mexican-American relations. That "incompetent rascal" Anthony Butler suggested buying the province in 1835. Through him Andrew Jackson tried to purchase San Francisco Bay and northern California for a half million dollars, but Butler's negotiations failed. Mexico would no more part with California than she would with Texas.

After Mexico got rid of Butler, Jackson nonetheless persisted in trying to obtain San Francisco Bay, the portion of California he considered most desirable. In 1836 he sent William A. Slacum, a naval officer, to investigate the Pacific Coast. Slacum too insisted that the United States must have the bay of San Francisco.

Early in the following year, while discussing a possible mediation between Mexico and Texas with Santa Anna, Jackson said he was willing to offer three and a half million dollars for California lying north of thirty-eight degrees of latitude, assuming mistakenly that such a boundary included all of San Francisco Bay. At the same time, he urged Texas to extend her boundaries to include California. If

Texas acquired control of San Francisco Bay, the main harbor on the Pacific Coast, he thought, New England and other commercial sections of the North would accept Texas. "He is very earnest and anxious on this point of claiming the Californias," the Texan Minister in Washington wrote, "and says we must not consent to less."[11]

After Jackson left the White House in 1837, direct efforts to acquire California ceased. Van Buren did nothing diplomatically, but did send Lieutenant Charles Wilkes of the Navy to the Pacific. In the fall of 1841 Wilkes visited San Francisco Bay, traveled through the surrounding country, and gathered detailed information on the life of the province. Most of all he was impressed by San Francisco Bay, "one of the finest, if not the very best harbor in the world." Wilkes' activities aroused the suspicions of Californians, who believed his expedition was part of an American program of annexation.

John Tyler revived the question of acquiring California. His Minister to Mexico, Waddy Thompson, urged annexation. "I would like to be instrumental in securing California," he explained. His dispatches described it as "the richest, the most beautiful, the healthiest country in the world." The harbor of San Francisco, he said, was "capacious enough to receive the navies of all the world," and was destined to control the trade of the entire Pacific. "I am profoundly satisfied," he wrote in one letter, "that in its bearing upon all the interests of our country, agricultural, political, manufacturing, commercial, and fishing, the importance of the acquisition of California cannot be overestimated."[12]

Tyler and Secretary of State Webster supported Thompson's plans and authorized him to negotiate a treaty for the acquisition of the province. Webster considered San Francisco Bay more valuable than all of Texas. In his "tripartite plan," as we have seen, he was even willing to sacrifice Oregon north of the Columbia River for that bay and northern California.

Thompson's ideas for acquiring California probably would not have succeeded anyway, but the rash act of Commodore Thomas Ap Catesby Jones, the commander of an American naval force in the Pacific, gave Mexico new cause to fear the United States and hence removed *any* chance of success for Thompson's plans. While in Peru, Jones received news that led him to believe that the United States was at war with Mexico, and that Mexico intended to cede California to Britain. He quickly sailed for Monterey, California's provincial capital, reaching it on October 18, 1842. Although he found no sign of war, everything was "normally dilapidated," he said; he captured the town and raised the American flag. Two days later, finding that he had been mistaken, he restored Monterey to the Mexican authorities and apologized.

Although Jones' behavior created little ill will in California, it aroused a violent reaction in Mexico City. It forced Thompson to admit that it was now "wholly out of the question to do anything as to California." Still, the American desire for

California persisted and, after Calhoun became Secretary of State, that desire grew more intense for the following reasons: the accelerating rate of American immigration, fear of English designs on the province, stemming from the activities of British agents there, and reports that California would separate from Mexico to become an independent republic.

The mounting interest in California led President Tyler to appoint Thomas O. Larkin, a New Englander who had become Monterey's wealthiest merchant, American consul in California. Larkin formally opened his consulate in April, 1844, and reported on all that happened there, particularly on political developments. He urged Calhoun to acquire California, and the Secretary tried to buy it, but his efforts, like the earlier ones, failed.

President Polk, like Calhoun and Tyler, wanted California and at practically any cost. Soon after his inauguration in 1845 he apparently told his Secretary of the Navy that he placed the acquisition of California on the same plane as the "Oregon question." It would be, he said, one of the "four great measures" of his administration. As in the acquisition of the Oregon Territory, Polk's desire to obtain California reflected the gospel of Manifest Destiny. Scarcely two weeks after his inaugural, newspapers were saying the Rio Grande would not stop the westward march of the Anglo-Saxons. "The process by which Texas was acquired," a Baltimore paper said, "may be repeated over and over again."

Mexico's reaction to the annexation of Texas, however, complicated Polk's efforts to acquire California peacefully. In taking over Texas, the United States inherited her smoldering state of war with Mexico, for ever since Tyler had made it clear that his plans to annex were serious, Mexico had said annexation would be cause for war. After Tyler signed the resolution of annexation, therefore, Mexico had broken off diplomatic relations. The Mexican press warned that American greed had marked all of Mexico for its prey. "Union and war" should be our answer, one paper declared. Although the Mexican government made some preparations for war, it was so rocked by revolutions that it could not at that time launch hostilities against the United States.

Grievances against Mexico

Mexico's periodic revolutions, on the other hand, had given the United States cause for grievance. Those disturbances had destroyed American lives and property in Mexico. In one uprising alone, in 1835, Mexican forces had executed twenty-two Americans without trial. In addition, Mexico owed Americans money for munitions and supplies they had sold to her during her revolt against Spain from 1810 to 1821. Beginning in the days of Andrew Jackson, the American government had taken up the claims of its citizens and had demanded payment.

A claims commission of Americans and Mexicans, established by treaty in 1839,

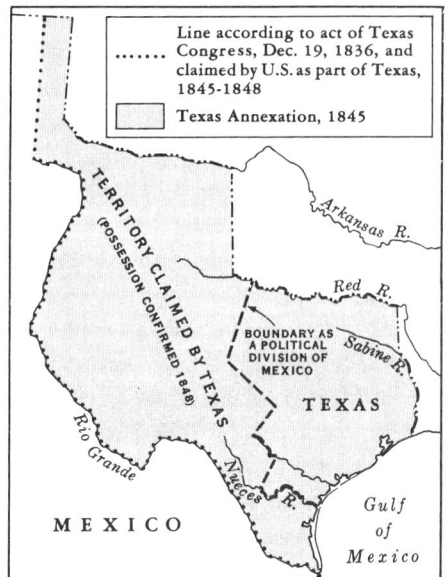

Line according to act of Texas
.... Congress, Dec. 19, 1836, and
claimed by U.S. as part of Texas,
1845-1848

☐ Texas Annexation, 1845

THE BOUNDARIES OF TEXAS,
1836–1848

TERRITORY CLAIMED BY TEXAS
(POSSESSION CONFIRMED 1848)

Arkansas R.

Red R.

BOUNDARY AS
A POLITICAL
DIVISION OF
MEXICO

Sabine R.

TEXAS

Rio Grande

Nueces R.

MEXICO

Gulf
of
Mexico

had finally worked out a partial settlement whereby Mexico agreed to pay slightly over two million dollars in twenty installments over five years. She made only three payments before defaulting at the end of April, 1843. Mexico was not unwilling to pay the debts, but with an empty treasury was unable to do so. When Polk became President, expansionists had taken up the claims question, denouncing Mexico for alleged perfidy. In pressing the claims Polk did not, however, demand cash. If Mexico would recognize the annexation of Texas with a boundary at the Rio Grande River, he would accept that recognition in place of cash payment for the claims.

Polk was willing to make that offer because the Texan, and hence the American, claim to the Rio Grande boundary was dubious. Texas had claimed the Rio Grande as her western and southern boundary when she gained independence and had forced Santa Anna to recognize that boundary by treaty, but the Mexican government had repudiated that treaty and refused to recognize any boundary with Texas. Since Texas' southern boundary, under both Spanish and Mexican rule, had never extended beyond the Nueces River, her claim to the Rio Grande was weak. Yet when Texas voted to join the Union, Polk accepted her claim to the line of the Rio Grande as legitimate and was determined to uphold it.

Before annexation, neither Mexico nor Texas had occupied the area between the Nueces and the Rio Grande, an almost unsettled no man's land between two states technically at war. As far as Mexico was concerned, there was no dispute over that land between the rivers. All of Texas was Mexican. She denied the existence of Texas as an independent state and claimed that Texas did not have the power to annex herself to the United States.

In July, 1845, immediately after Texas voted to join the Union, Polk ordered Brigadier General Zachary Taylor to take several thousand troops from the Louisiana border into Texas to occupy the debatable region south of the Nueces. He was, however, instructed not to disturb Mexican settlements or attack Mexican troops, "unless an actual state of war should exist." By the end of the month, Taylor had camped his army near the town of Corpus Christi at the mouth of the Nueces River. By October that force had increased to four thousand men, half of the entire American army and the largest concentration of troops since the end of the War of 1812, thirty years earlier. Taylor's troops remained in the heat of Corpus Christi for eight months.

Polk, meanwhile, sought ways to acquire California and at the same time settle the claims and boundary questions. This required bargaining with Mexico, which he could not do without reopening diplomatic relations. In April, therefore, he had sent William S. Parrott, a confidential agent, to Mexico to see if the government there would agree to resume those relations and reopen negotiations for settling the difficulties between the two countries.

In August, Parrott wrote several times that the Mexican government would accept an American minister. Polk decided, as a result, to send John Slidell of New Orleans on a secret mission to Mexico with full diplomatic powers. Before sending him, the President wanted official assurance from the Mexican government that it would resume diplomatic relations. The Mexicans obliged on October 15, saying they would receive any "commissioner" sent to Mexico City "with full powers to settle the present dispute in a peaceable, reasonable, and honorable manner." Polk received the assurance on November 9 and immediately dispatched Slidell on his mission.

Slidell's instructions allowed him to offer a choice of four settlements. Since Mexico could not pay the claims, they said, the United States would assume them if Mexico would accept the Rio Grande boundary. If the boundary included New Mexico, the United States would pay five million dollars in addition. If Mexico would also sell California, the United States would pay twenty-five million more, or if she would sell only part of California north of Monterey, the United States would give five million more. Slidell could conclude a treaty if Mexico accepted any one of the proposals, but could make no settlement that excluded the Rio Grande boundary.

When Slidell arrived in Mexico City on December 6, the government of President José Joaquín Herrera was in danger of collapse. Since news of Slidell's mission had leaked and had aroused a violent opposition to the negotiation, the Herrera government did not dare recognize him, let alone negotiate. "You know," the Mexican Foreign Minister told Slidell, "the opposition are calling us traitors for entering into this arrangement with you." [13]

The Herrera government had to reject Slidell or fall. It announced, therefore, that it could not accept a minister with full powers, but only a special "commissioner" empowered to settle the Texas question alone. Slidell's rejection did not save the Herrera regime. It fell on the last day of December. Although Polk would not change Slidell's commission, he instructed him to approach the new Mexican government, which Slidell did and was again rejected. In March, 1846, therefore, he left Mexico, convinced that only force would win American objectives.

Many Americans shared Slidell's feelings. All during the summer and autumn months of 1845, tension with Mexico had mounted. Some impetuous Americans had demanded war. In August one politician reported from Philadelphia that he had heard "nothing else talked of but war with Mexico." [14] News of Slidell's rejection stimulated an even more violent reaction. The United States, a New Orleans paper said, "are now left no alternative but to extort by arms the respect and justice which Mexico refuses to any treatment less harsh." [15]

Behind Mexican stubbornness, many Americans believed, stood the power of Britain and France, but particularly of Britain. Polk, too, found this possibility easy to believe. During the summer and fall of 1845, he had heard disturbing reports from American officials in Britain, Mexico, and California, of British designs on California. "England must never have California," the consul at Liverpool said. [16] Parrott reported from Mexico City that British intrigue had blocked him. The British, he warned, wanted California. Thomas O. Larkin wrote from Monterey that the British and French had designs on California.

Even though the British government itself had no such designs, rumors had reached Polk that England and France would recognize the Californians as independent if they would agree never to annex themselves to the United States. [17] Since the Californians, in February, 1845, had defeated the forces of a Mexican governor, demonstrating the ineffectiveness of Mexican rule, such tales appeared to have substance. Regardless of the rumors, California, it seemed, was becoming an international derelict.

As in the case of Texas, fear of English intervention aroused a wide enthusiasm for expansion into California. Newspaper editors, Democratic and Whig, warned against British designs, saying that the province must become American, if only to limit Britain's power.

To counter alleged British influence, Polk appointed Larkin his secret agent in California. "The future destiny of that country," Secretary of State James Buchanan wrote to Larkin, "is a subject of anxious solicitude for the Government and people of the United States." The President, therefore, "could not view with indifference the transfer of California to Great Britain or any other European Power." If, on the other hand, he added, the Californians "should desire to unite their destiny with ours," we would receive them as "brethren."[18]

Larkin's instructions told him, in effect, to persuade the native Californians to part voluntarily from Mexico and place themselves under American protection. Polk had also sent additional warships to join the Pacific squadron with orders to take San Francisco if war broke out with Mexico.

Then, in his first annual message to Congress in December, Polk revived the Monroe Doctrine, directing it against Britain and France. With California in mind, he said "that the people of this continent alone have the right to decide their own destiny. Should any portion of them, constituting an independent state, propose to unite themselves with our Confederacy, this will be a question for them and us to determine without any foreign interposition."[19] In warning against European diplomatic interference in North America, Polk thus expanded the Monroe Doctrine.

A month later, on January 12, 1846, Polk learned that Herrera's government had refused to receive Slidell and hence realized that his plans for purchasing California and the Southwest were failing. Although he preferred a peaceful settlement, he now became convinced that only a policy of force would impress Mexico. On that same day, he ordered General Taylor to march his forces across the no man's land to the north bank of the Rio Grande.

The War with Mexico

On February 13 Polk received some dubious assurance that a show of force would bring Mexico to terms. A friend of Santa Anna, who had just returned from a visit to the former dictator, then in exile in Havana, told him that Santa Anna intended to return to Mexico soon to resume power. If Polk aided Santa Anna financially, the friend said, the exiled general, once he assumed power, would be willing to sell part of the Southwest and part of California. "The U.S. would never be able to treat with Mexico," however, he added, "without the presence of an imposing force by land and sea."[20]

Impressed by the suggestions of Santa Anna's agent, Polk wanted to send Mexico an ultimatum. If it were rejected, then he would be ready for "aggressive measures." Since the Oregon crisis was smoldering, Secretary of State Buchanan persuaded him not to start a war with Mexico until he was sure there would be none with England. General Taylor's forces, meanwhile, had brought the nation to the verge of war.

Taylor's army began the move to the Rio Grande on March 8, 1846, and twenty days later four thousand American soldiers stood on the banks of the river. In April, Mexican troops began arriving in large numbers across the river and gathering in the town of Matamoros until they numbered well over five thousand.

Tension built up. On April 23 Mexico's president proclaimed a "defensive war" against the United States. Then, in the morning two days later, American dragoons clashed with Mexican cavalry on the north side of the Rio Grande. The Americans counted sixteen killed or wounded.

Before that blood had been shed, Polk had decided on war. He had received word of Mexico's final refusal to accept Slidell on April 7, but had waited until Slidell could report to him in person before asking for a declaration of war. Slidell arrived in Washington on May 8, still convinced that only force would bring Mexico to terms. On the next day, a Saturday, Polk told his cabinet that on Tuesday he wanted to send a message to Congress recommending a declaration of war because Mexico had rejected Slidell and had not paid the claims. All of the President's advisers agreed except George Bancroft, the Secretary of the Navy, who said if Mexican forces committed an "act of hostility" then he would favor immediate war. That night news arrived telling of the clash on the Rio Grande. Polk now had an "act of hostility."

The President immediately called another meeting of his cabinet and that Sunday prepared the war message he sent to Congress on Monday, May 11. That message recited the accumulated grievances of twenty years against Mexico and stressed her "breach of faith" in refusing to receive Slidell. Those offenses, he said, had already exhausted the "cup of forbearance." "But now," he added, "after reiterated menaces, Mexico has passed the boundary of the United States, has invaded our territory, and shed American blood upon American soil." Despite "all our efforts to avoid it," he insisted, war now "exists by the act of Mexico herself."[21] Neither side had truly tried to avoid war. It came because neither Mexico nor the United States had the will to keep the peace.

Polk's policy toward Mexico had been a combination of sabre-rattling, intrigue, and unpalatable, but not fundamentally unreasonable, peace offers. If he had not been an expansionist, determined to have California and the Southwest, he might have worked harder to keep peace, but peace would not have given him California and the other western lands. To obtain them he did not flinch at the prospect of war, even on the flimsy pretext of unpaid claims and a rebuffed diplomat.

On the day after Polk's message, a resolution authorizing the President to declare war against Mexico passed the House of Representatives by a vote of 174 to 14 and the Senate by 40 to 2. All the Democrats voted for war, joined by forty-seven Whigs in the House and sixteen in the Senate.

"Mr. Polk's War," as critics called it, soon became unpopular. Whigs and some Democrats opposed it. Northern Whigs and abolitionists viewed the war as a conspiracy hatched by slaveholders and Southerners in the Polk administration. A Whig convention in New Hampshire declared that it was being waged "for the dismemberment of a sister republic upon pretexts that are false, and for a purpose that is abhorrent to all feelings of humanity and justice." Abraham Lincoln, then a young Whig congressman from Illinois, asked repeatedly in his "spot resolutions" that the President name the "spot" on American soil where American blood had been spilled. The New England poet, James Russell Lowell, even recommended northern secession:

> Ef I'd *my* way I hed ruther
> We should go to work an' part,—
> They take one way, we take t'other,—
> Guess it wouldn't break my heart.[22]

The opposition to the war upset Polk. He had expected a short easy conflict that, as Santa Anna's friend had said, would quickly force Mexico to sell him the territory he wanted. In his memoirs Thomas Hart Benton, the Democratic Senator from Missouri, wrote that the administration "wanted a small war, just large enough to require a treaty of peace, and not large enough to make military reputations, dangerous for the presidency."[23] The two leading generals were Whigs.

On May 13 the Secretary of the Navy told the commander of the American naval squadron off Vera Cruz, "If Santa Anna endeavors to enter the Mexican ports, you will allow him to pass freely." Polk hoped to make an immediate peace with Santa Anna on the terms Santa Anna's agent had proposed in February. Santa Anna returned to Mexico, but did not keep his bargain with Polk. Instead, he took command of the Mexican army and directed the war against the United States. Polk then decided "to prosecute the war with vigor," and it became long, costly, and bloody.

Mexico's leaders had counted on the opposition to the war within the United States to help them. With an exaggerated estimate of their military prowess and unfounded expectations of European aid, primarily from England and France, they had wanted war and had expected victory. Mexico, however, found herself on the defensive from the beginning and met nothing but defeat. Polk launched a triple thrust against her. General Taylor's army struck across the Rio Grande into northern Mexico. Another smaller force under General Stephen W. Kearny moved West to conquer New Mexico and to occupy California. The third army, under General Winfield Scott, in March, 1847, went by sea to Vera Cruz and then fought inland to Mexico City to dictate terms of peace.

Developments in California, meanwhile, looked as if they might make that province a second Texas. The activities of the pioneers, who had continued to arrive in large numbers, and of a young American Army officer, John Charles Frémont, upset Larkin's plans to win California through peaceful persuasion. In the summer of 1845, the War Department had sent Frémont deep into Mexican territory with a well-armed party of sixty-two men. Ostensibly his task was to find a shorter land route to California, and "in arranging this expedition," Frémont wrote later, "the eventualities of war were taken into consideration."

Frémont's "exploring" expedition reached California in December, 1845, and after spending two months there retreated into Oregon when the California authorities threatened to fight. In May, 1846, a special messenger from Polk overtook Frémont. What secret or verbal orders that messenger brought are unknown, but Frémont marched his men back into California and made camp "to await positive orders in regard to the war" with Mexico.[24]

Then, within a few weeks, some of the newer American emigrants in the Sacramento Valley revolted against the Mexican rulers and in June set up the "California Republic" with a flag depicting a bear as their emblem. Frémont supported this "Bear Flag Revolt," and took over its leadership. Thus, when he learned that war had broken out, northern California, partly through his efforts, was already in American hands. In July, when Commodore Robert F. Stockton took command of American naval and military forces in California, he and Frémont conquered the rest of the province. General Kearny arrived in December, in time to help crush a revolt against American authority in southern California. By January 13, 1847, all resistance had ceased, and California was an American province.

With the conquest of California, Polk had placed the American flag over all the territory he had included in his war objectives. He wrote in his diary repeatedly after the war started that he would agree to no peace treaty that did not give the United States New Mexico and California, but Mexico, despite her defeats would make no peace on Polk's terms.

The Mission of Nicholas P. Trist

Polk needed an early treaty because the political tensions over slavery and expansion threatened to disrupt the Union.[25] Whig opposition to the war had become so fierce early in 1847 that the President did not dare to declare openly his war aims of annexing New Mexico and California. In mid-April he decided to send an inconspicuous executive agent, Nicholas P. Trist, to join Winfield Scott's army in Mexico.[26] Moving toward Mexico City with the army, Trist could take advantage of Scott's victories and of any sudden opportunity Mexico offered to make a treaty that would cede California and the Southwest.

Polk used Trist, the chief clerk in the Department of State, and not a more prominent person because Trist was a loyal Democrat who held a position of no political importance and therefore could begin negotiating with the Mexicans without arousing factional resentment in Polk's own party. With Trist merely an executive agent, moreover, Polk kept all power in his own hands. Trist was not important enough to deprive the administration of full credit for any successful negotiation. Yet he had ability, intelligence, and previous diplomatic experience with Latin Americans, and spoke Spanish fluently.

Trist's instructions, dated April 15, were like Slidell's and told him to secure the Rio Grande boundary, California, and New Mexico. In addition, he was to acquire what the Mexicans called Baja, or Lower, California and the right of transit across the Isthmus of Tehuantepec. The territorial acquisitions were to serve as the war indemnity in place of cash, but Trist could offer Mexico as much as thirty million dollars beyond assumption of claims for all that he demanded. Since Polk had not yet disclosed his territorial aims publicly, the instructions demanded absolute secrecy.

Trist reached Vera Cruz early in May and immediately quarrelled with General Scott, a Whig who distrusted Polk. Scott believed that the administration was trying to degrade him by placing a mere "clerk" over him. At first Scott and Trist argued so bitterly that they gave up speaking to each other. For days, thereafter, they bombarded each other and Washington with angry letters.

In his early efforts to negotiate, Trist came to realize that he needed Scott's cooperation to succeed and hence made overtures to him. The General responded cordially so that overnight the two men cast aside their enmity and became friends. Scott now called Trist "able, discreet, courteous, and amiable," and said, "I am perfectly willing that all I have heretofore written to the Department [of War] about Mr. Trist, should be suppressed." Scott, Trist told his wife, was "the soul of honour and probity, and full of the most sterling qualities of heart and head." [27]

As the American army paused before the gates of Mexico City in August, Santa Anna, through the British legation, asked for an armistice. Believing the chance of concluding a peace treaty justified an armistice, Scott and Trist granted one. Before Trist could forward the results of his preliminary negotiations to Polk, negotiations in which he appeared willing to accept something less than the Rio Grande boundary, the armistice broke down. Therefore, Scott advanced, and on September 15 his Marines patrolled the Halls of Montezuma.

Before the end of September, Polk heard of the August armistice. Trist, it appeared, was ignoring his instructions and must be recalled. "Mr. Trist is recalled," Polk explained in his diary, "because his remaining longer with the army could not, probably, accomplish the objects of his mission, and because his remaining longer might, & probably would, impress the Mexican Government with the belief that the U.S. were so anxious for peace that they would ultimate[ly] conclude one upon the Mexican terms. Mexico must now first sue for peace, & when she does we will hear her propositions." [28] The President was now convinced that Mexico would make peace only if the United States increased the tempo of the war, and urged Congress to do that.

For the first time since the beginning of the war, moreover, Polk announced his aim of territorial gain, stressing the need to acquire New Mexico and California. He told Congress on December 7, 1847, that "the doctrine of no territory is the doctrine of no indemnity; and, if sanctioned, would be a public acknowledgment

GENERAL WINFIELD SCOTT'S ENTRANCE INTO MEXICO CITY

that our country was wrong, and that the war declared by Congress with extraordinary unanimity was unjust, and should be abandoned." The Whigs did not
agree, and on January 3, 1848, the House of Representatives declared, by a vote of
85 to 81, that the war had been "unnecessarily and unconstitutionally begun by
the President of the United States."

At the same time, the long war and the refusal of Mexico to make a peace
treaty aroused some Democratic expansionists to demand all of Mexico. "Schemes
of ambition, vast enough to have tasked even a Roman imagination to conceive,"
a Virginia Senator told Congress on January 3, "present themselves suddenly as
practical suggestions." The "all-Mexico movement" did not sway Polk from his
own more limited, but still vast, objectives. He had never wanted, he had said in
his December message, "to make a permanent conquest of the Republic of Mexico,
or to annihilate her separate existence as an independent nation."[29] Polk, in effect,
desired a peace treaty before the election of 1848 because he wanted to take the
war out of politics.

Trist, meanwhile, on November 16, 1847, had received Polk's letters ordering
him home. He was ready to obey even though Santa Anna had fled and a new
Mexican government that appeared ready to negotiate a satisfactory peace had
assumed power. Mexican officials, the British legation, and General Scott, however, all asked him to negotiate a treaty before leaving. Trist, therefore, disregarded
the President's instructions and remained.

Trist wrote to Polk and Secretary of State Buchanan explaining his decision. It still left the administration, he said, at "perfect liberty to disavow his proceeding, should it be deemed disadvantageous to our country." Then, after some delay, he sat down with the Mexican commissioners.

The Treaty of Guadalupe Hidalgo

Night and day, all through January, 1848, Trist negotiated. Finally, on February 2, in the little town of Guadalupe Hidalgo near Mexico City, he signed a treaty in which Mexico recognized the American conquests. The United States paid fifteen million dollars and assumed the claims of its own citizens up to three and a quarter million dollars. The Treaty of Guadalupe Hidalgo gave the United States the Rio Grande boundary, California, and an area comprising Nevada, Utah, New Mexico, Arizona, and parts of Wyoming and Colorado. This was the minimum Polk had authorized Trist to accept in April. Yet, including Texas, Mexico had lost half of her national territory.[30]

When Polk first heard of his clerk's insubordination, he concluded that Trist and Scott had conspired to embarrass him. "Mr. Trist has acted very badly," the

ACQUISITIONS FROM MEXICO, 1848

President said when he received the treaty. Then as he went through it, he recorded in his diary "if on further examination the Treaty is one that can be accepted, it should not be rejected on account of his bad conduct."[31] Polk did not reject it. He accepted his repudiated emissary's treaty because the state of politics made peace necessary and because it gave him his territorial objectives.

In the Senate, Democrats who clamored for the whole of Mexico, and Whigs who wanted none of Mexico's territory, opposed the treaty. Extremes, as Polk remarked, "sometimes meet and act effectively for negative purposes." They could not, nevertheless, block the treaty. The Senate, on March 10, gave its consent by a vote of thirty-eight to fourteen. A few days later, a disgruntled Whig wrote that the peace treaty "negotiated by an unauthorized agent, with an unacknowledged government, submitted by an accidental President to a dissatisfied Senate, has, notwithstanding these objections in form, been confirmed."[32]

After Mexico ratified the treaty, Polk told Congress that "the results of the war with Mexico have given the United States a national character which our country never before enjoyed." New Mexico and California, he said, "constitute of themselves a country large enough for a great empire, and their acquisition is second only in importance to that of Louisiana in 1803."[33] The future would prove whether or not he was right.

NOTES

1. Eugene C. Barker, "The Influence of Slavery in the Colonization of Texas," *Mississippi Valley Historical Review*, XI (June 1924), 3–36, concludes that slavery was not an important factor in bringing on the Texas revolution.

2. For details, see Eugene C. Barker, "President Jackson and the Texas Revolution," *The American Historical Review*, XII (July 1907), 788–809 and Richard R. Stenberg, ed., "President Jackson and Anthony Butler," *Southwest Review*, XXII (July 1937), 391–404, a collection of some of Butler's letters.

3. Quoted in Ray A. Billington, *The Far Western Frontier, 1830–1860* (New York, 1956), p. 118.

4. Benjamin Lundy quoted in Samuel F. Bemis, *John Quincy Adams and the Union* (New York, 1956), p. 356.

5. *Ibid.*, p. 359.

6. Quoted in Randolph G. Adams, "Abel Parker Upshur," in Samuel F. Bemis, ed., *The American Secretaries of State and Their Diplomacy* (10 vols., New York, 1927–29), V, 96. As Secretary of the Navy, Upshur had been active in foreign policy; see Claude H. Hall, "Abel P. Upshur and the Navy as an Instrument of Foreign Policy," *Virginia Magazine of History and Biography*, LXIX (July 1961), 290–299.

7. For details, see St. George L. Sioussat, "John Caldwell Calhoun," in Bemis, *Secretaries of State*, V, 148–155 and Charles M. Wiltse, *John C. Calhoun: Sectionalist, 1840–1850* (Indianapolis, 1951), pp. 167–171.

8. James D. Richardson, ed., *A Compilation of the Messages and Papers of the Presidents, 1789–1897* (10 vols., Washington, 1896–99), IV, 344.

9. Quoted in Ephraim D. Adams, *British Interests and Activities in Texas, 1838–1846* (Baltimore, 1910), pp. 168–169.

10. Quoted in Herbert P. Gambrell, *Anson Jones: The Last President of Texas* (Garden City, N.Y., 1948), p. 419.

11. Quoted in Robert G. Cleland, *Early Sentiment for the Annexation of California, 1835–1846* (Austin, Tex., 1915), p. 17.

12. *Ibid.*, pp. 27–28.

13. Quoted in Norman A. Graebner, *Empire on the Pacific* (New York, 1955), p. 120.

14. *Ibid.*, p. 151.

15. New Orleans *Commercial Bulletin*, March 16, 1846, quoted in Justin H. Smith, *The War with Mexico* (2 vols., New York, 1919), I, 121.

16. Quoted in Graebner, *Empire on the Pacific*, p. 108.

17. For evidence that the British had no official designs on California, see Ephraim D. Adams, "English Interest in the Annexation of California," *The American Historical Review*, XIV (July 1909), 744–763.

18. Oct. 17, 1845, John Bassett Moore, ed., *The Works of James Buchanan* (12 vols., Philadelphia, 1908–11), VI, 275–277.

19. Dec. 2, 1845, in Richardson, *Messages of the Presidents*, IV, 398. See also Dexter Perkins, *A History of the Monroe Doctrine*, rev. ed. (Boston, 1955), pp. 77–81.

20. Milo M. Quaife, ed., *The Diary of James K. Polk: During His Presidency, 1845–1849* (4 vols., Chicago, 1910), I, 224–225.

21. The full text is in Richardson, *Messages of the Presidents*, IV, 437–443.

22. Homer Wilbur, ed., *The Biglow Papers*, ser. 1, 4th ed. (Boston, 1889), p. 59.

23. Thomas H. Benton, *Thirty Years' View* (2 vols., New York, 1854–56), II, 680.

24. For details, see Richard R. Stenberg, "Polk and Frémont, 1845–1846," *Pacific Historical Review*, VII (Sept. 1938), 211–227; George Tays, "Frémont Had No Secret Instructions," *ibid.*, IX (June 1940), 157–171;

and Werner H. Marti, *Messenger of Destiny: The California Adventures, 1846–1847, of Archibald H. Gillespie, U.S. Marine Corps* (San Francisco, 1960), pp. 37–42, which gives a full analysis of the Frémont-Gillespie episode.

25. Church sentiment, too, was split; see Clayton S. Ellsworth, "The American Churches and the Mexican War," *The American Historical Review*, XLV (Jan. 1940), 301–326.

26. For favorable appraisals of Trist, see Louis M. Sears, "Nicholas P. Trist, a Diplomat with Ideals," *Mississippi Valley Historical Review*, XI (June 1924), 85–98 and Norman A. Graebner, "Party Politics and the Trist Mission," *Journal of Southern History*, XIX (May 1953), 137–156.

27. Quoted in Graebner, *Empire on the Pacific*, pp. 198–199.

28. Entry of Oct. 5, 1847, Quaife, *Polk Diary*, III, 186.

29. Polk is quoted in Norman A. Graebner, "James K. Polk's Wartime Expansionist Policy," *East Tennessee Historical Society's Publications*, No. 23 (1951), pp. 43–44. See also Richard R. Stenberg, "The Failure of Polk's Mexican War Intrigue of 1845," *Pacific Historical Review*, IV (March 1935), 39–68 and John D. P. Fuller, "The Slavery Question and the Movement to Acquire Mexico, 1846–48," *Mississippi Valley Historical Review*, XXI (June 1934), 31–48, which points out that slaveholders did not want all of Mexico.

30. For details, see Jesse S. Reeves, "The Treaty of Guadalupe Hidalgo," *The American Historical Review*, X (Jan. 1905), 309–324.

31. Entry of Feb. 19, 1848, Quaife, *Polk Diary*, III, 345.

32. Bayard Tuckerman, ed., *The Diary of Philip Hone, 1828–1851* (2 vols., New York, 1889), II, 347.

33. Message of July 6, 1848, Richardson, *Messages of the Presidents*, IV, 587–588.

Chapter Nine

YOUNG AMERICA

In the decade following the peace with Mexico, internal affairs, primarily the sectional conflict over slavery, dominated politics. Yet American diplomacy had to deal with a number of scattered problems, a few of which might have burst into serious crises. One of them concerned the control of transit routes across Central America for a possible interoceanic canal.

The new empire in the West had made the United States a major power in the Pacific and pointed to the need for a canal linking California and Oregon with the Atlantic coast. The discovery of gold on California's American River in January, 1848, and the ensuing rush that quickly expanded the population in the state, dramatized this need.

Bidlack's Treaty

As if by coincidence, during the Mexican War the United States had acquired transit rights across the Isthmus of Panama. New Granada, which became the state of Colombia, had been nervously watching Britain expand her control over the Mosquito Coast of nearby Nicaragua and then move threateningly toward the isthmus, at that time a province of New Granada. To forestall any lunge toward Panama, Granadan officials turned to the United States for help, offering it transit rights on the same terms enjoyed by their own people if the United States would guarantee the "perfect neutrality" of the isthmus in time of war, guarantee Granadan sovereignty over it, and maintain a free transit. On December 12, 1846, Benjamin A. Bidlack, the American *chargé d'affaires* in Bogotá, on his own initiative signed a treaty with New Granada that included those terms. President Polk accepted it and the Senate, which feared the entangling commitment but desired the transit more, finally approved in June, 1848.[1]

In urging ratification, the Granadans had called attention to the non-intervention principle of the Monroe Doctrine. In that case, Polk did not act in the name of that doctrine; but in regard to the Yucatán peninsula (presently a part of Mexico), he expanded the doctrine with what has been called the "Polk Corollary." In March, 1848, the local authorities of Yucatán had offered their land to the United States, to Britain, and to Spain. Fearing that one of the other powers might accept the offer, Polk sent a special message to Congress on April 19 that cited the Monroe Doctrine, indirectly suggested American occupation of the peninsula, and in effect expressed opposition to the transfer of territory in the New World to a foreign power even with the consent of the inhabitants. Nothing came of the Yucatán proposal as the new government there withdrew the March offer.

Nonetheless, Polk's concern over Central America reflected a growing rivalry with Britain, at that time the dominant power in the Caribbean. The British, in fact, noted this new extension of American power with increasing uneasiness. Since Bidlack's Treaty gave the United States special rights over one of the two best routes for a possible interoceanic canal, they sought control over the other. That second route, long considered the better of the two, went through Nicaragua, beginning on the east coast at San Juan, at the mouth of the San Juan River. In January, 1848, the British, who controlled the east coast of Nicaragua through a protectorate over the Mosquito Indians, a savage tribe that lived there, had seized San Juan from the Nicaraguans and had renamed it Greytown.

When Nicaragua appealed to the United States for help, Polk sent a diplomatic agent, Elijah Hise, to Central America. He vied with Britain for control of the Nicaraguan route. On June 21, 1849, Hise made an unauthorized treaty with Nicaragua, giving the United States exclusive rights over the Nicaraguan route and committing it to a guarantee of Nicaragua's sovereignty.

On the west coast of Central America the Gulf of Fonseca dominated one of the possible Pacific Ocean approaches to the Nicaraguan route. In the gulf lay Tigre Island, belonging to Honduras. Hise's successor, Ephraim G. Squier, signed a treaty with Honduras on September 28, 1849, temporarily giving the United States that island for a naval base. Squier also negotiated another treaty with Nicaragua, modifying the Hise treaty.

To block American control over the Nicaraguan route, the British agent in Central America signed a treaty with Costa Rica, protecting that country's claim to the northern bank of the San Juan River. Then in October a British naval officer seized Tigre Island. Although this act aroused resentment in the United States, the Whig President, Zachary Taylor, did not retaliate and did not ratify the Hise and Squier treaties. The British government, too, was more peacefully inclined than its agents. It disavowed the seizure of Tigre Island and did not accept the treaty with Costa Rica.

Neither Britain nor the United States wanted the other to have exclusive control over canal routes in Central America; yet, if they persisted in their rivalry, it seemed as if one of the minor crises might lead to a larger conflict. "We are deeply anxious to avoid any collision with the British Government in relation to this matter," Taylor's Secretary of State, John M. Clayton, wrote, "but that collision will become inevitable if great prudence be not exercised on both sides." Both countries, therefore, agreed to try to settle their differences in Central America through diplomacy.

The Clayton-Bulwer Treaty

In December, 1849, the British government had sent a new Minister to the United States, Sir Henry Lytton Bulwer, who promptly began negotiations with Clayton to adjust the Central-American difficulties. Finally, on April 19, 1850, they signed a treaty which denied either country exclusive control over the canal routes. Both parties also agreed not to build fortifications along a canal route, not to exercise dominion over any part of Central America, and to guarantee the neutrality of any canal when built.

Since the treaty was a compromise with purposely ambiguous wording, both countries could accept it without appearing to surrender to the other. After the Senate had approved the treaty on May 22, Clayton and Bulwer tried to clarify some of the ambiguities through an exchange of notes interpreting the commitments of their respective countries. Bulwer said Britain did not regard the treaty as applying "to Her Majesty's Settlement at Honduras or to its dependencies."[2] Clayton accepted that interpretation with qualifications and went ahead with the exchange of ratifications. Nonetheless, disputes arose.

Americans believed that under the terms of the treaty the British had agreed to give up their protectorate over the Mosquito Indians. Claiming that the treaty's provisions applied only to any extension of dominion in Central America, Britain rejected the American view and retained her protectorate. Then in March, 1852, she converted some islands in the Bay of Honduras into the "Colony of the Bay Islands." That act again aroused American indignation. Americans claimed that it violated both the Clayton-Bulwer Treaty and the Monroe Doctrine, and Democrats in Congress attacked the treaty itself as ineffectual.

Thus, like many compromises, the Clayton-Bulwer Treaty was unpopular, but was not, as many Americans believed, a surrender to British imperialism. In the 1850's the United States was not strong enough to defy Britain's naval power in upholding its claim to an exclusive control over a canal route through Central America. Yet with the Clayton-Bulwer Treaty the United States attained a legal equality with Britain in an area vital to its security, and in that sense, therefore, the treaty was a gain for American diplomacy.[3]

Despite the treaty, the Anglo-American rivalry continued all through the

1850's. In 1854 it sparked a minor crisis when, during disorders in Greytown, the American Minister there suffered insult and a small injury. In July, an American naval officer demanded reparation and an apology. When they did not come, he bombarded the town and destroyed it. The British government considered the bombardment an outrage, one "without parallel in the annals of modern times," it said, and sought a disavowal. The United States not only refused to disclaim it but President Franklin Pierce went so far as to defend the deed in his annual message to Congress in December.

Britain meanwhile became so deeply involved in the Crimean War, that she did not press the issue. Sharp division in American opinion also helped to ease the crisis. In particular, the British found some consolation in the denunciations of the brutal bombardment printed in the American press. Then the activities of American filibusters and capitalists in Central America led the British to believe that the United States intended to flout the Clayton-Bulwer Treaty.

As the California gold fields attracted travelers over the Central-American transit routes, American capitalists tried to profit from the heavy traffic. A group of them hauled passengers across Panama and financed a railroad there that began construction in 1850 and finished in 1855. To the north, the capitalist Cornelius Vanderbilt and some associates developed a rival route through Nicaragua. With a monopoly over the Nicaraguan route, the Vanderbilt company became a formidable competitor to the Panama line.

Violence and disorder in both Nicaragua and Panama, meanwhile, had threatened to interrupt and at times did disrupt traffic, leading to demands that the United States police the routes. Nothing came of that idea, but in 1854, William Walker, a Southern filibuster, or adventurer, often called the "grey-eyed man of destiny," added to the turmoil. He landed in Nicaragua with fifty-eight followers, called "the American Phalanx," and in time, with the aid of officials of the Vanderbilt company, made himself dictator of Nicaragua.

England feared that Walker was playing the "Texas game" in Central America in violation of the Clayton-Bulwer Treaty. President Pierce recognized Walker's government in May, 1856, saying he did so to make satisfactory arrangements for keeping the Nicaraguan transit route open. In June, however, Secretary of State William L. Marcy explained that Pierce had recognized Walker's government because Britain had aided that adventurer's enemies. The United States, Marcy asserted, "could not remain entirely inactive and see Great Britain obtain complete ascendancy in all the states of Central America." Yet Walker denied that he intended to annex Nicaragua to the United States. He dreamed, instead, of a federal government, with himself at its head, embracing all of Central America and Cuba, but his followers thought they were fighting to bring Nicaragua into the Union. At a celebration in August, 1856, for instance, they drank to such toasts as, "The American Eagle. May she drop her feathers in Nicaragua."[4]

Anti-slavery Northerners believed, as did the British, that Walker was trying to add more slave territory to the Union, an assumption based on impressive evidence. In September, 1856, Walker decreed the re-establishment of slavery in Nicaragua and planned to revive the slave trade. The object of the decree, he said, was "to bind the Southern States to Nicaragua as if she were one of themselves." Southern expansionists were pleased and expressed approval of Walker's exploits. They had even written into the Democratic platform of June of that year that "the people of the United States cannot but sympathize with the efforts which are being made by the people of Central America to regenerate that portion of the continent which covers the passage across the interoceanic isthmus."

Walker's artificial government could not, however, last without outside support. He had made enemies of the neighboring Central-American states, which had joined in an alliance against him, and had antagonized Vanderbilt by siding with that entrepreneur's enemies in his own transit company. A vengeful Vanderbilt switched his ships to the Panama crossing and cut off Walker's supplies and flow of recruits from the United States. In addition, he threw his support to the Central-American alliance which drove the filibuster from Nicaragua in May, 1857.

Walker contributed nothing but more disorder to the jungle of Central-American diplomacy in the 1850's. The expansionist Democrat, James Buchanan, several times wanted to take advantage of that chaos by sending American troops into Central America to keep the transit routes open, but Congress would not support him. Walker tried again to take over Central America but finally died before a Honduran firing squad in September, 1860, after a British officer had surrendered him to his enemies.

After Walker's downfall, Britain and the United States adjusted most of their differences in Latin America. By means of treaties with Honduras and Nicaragua in 1859 and 1860, Britain gave up her Mosquito protectorate and returned the Bay Islands to Honduras. "Our relations with Great Britain are of the most friendly character," Buchanan could therefore say in his annual message of December, 1860. "The discordant constructions of the Clayton and Bulwer treaty between the two Governments," he pointed out, have been settled "entirely satisfactory to this government." [5]

The Tehuantepec Question

The transit routes across Central America were not the only ones that interested the United States in the 1850's. At the beginning of that decade many Americans considered the route across the Isthmus of Tehuantepec in Mexico the most practicable for a railroad connection between the East coast and California. Interest in that route grew out of the Mexican War. Polk had authorized Trist to pay as much as fifteen million dollars for transit rights across that isthmus, but Mexico would not include those rights in the Treaty of Guadalupe Hidalgo.

After the war, the same reasons that impelled Americans to acquire transit concessions in Central America led them to seek similar rights across Tehuantepec. In January and in June, 1850, the United States signed two transit treaties with Mexico. The opposition of Mexican public opinion to any transit treaty with the United States destroyed the first agreement, and the American Senate's insistence on amendments which were unacceptable to Mexico killed the second. When the American Minister in Mexico threatened to use force if a treaty were not agreed to, the Mexican Minister of Foreign Relations said, "Your government is strong; ours is weak. You have the power to take the whole or any portion of our territory. . . . We have not the *faculty* to resist. We have done all we could to satisfy your country. . . . We can do no more." [6] If the Mexican government had surrendered to the American demands, it would have fallen immediately, so strong were anti-American passions in Mexico.

When the United States slightly modified some of its demands, the Mexican government finally signed a new treaty on January 25, 1851, and the American Senate approved it, but no Mexican congress dared accept it. Then in December Millard Fillmore's Secretary of State, Daniel Webster, heard that the Mexican senate planned to give Britain the concession across Tehuantepec. He warned against it, saying that the United States "could not see with indifference that isthmus . . . under the sway of any European state." [7]

The situation in Mexico changed when Santa Anna again became president in April, 1853. By that time the Tehuantepec project had become enmeshed in other Mexican-American problems. Franklin Pierce, an expansionist who had become President a month before Santa Anna had returned to power, wanted to settle all outstanding issues with Mexico. Those problems included a dispute over New Mexico's southern boundary, destructive Indian raids into Mexico from the United States—raids the United States was obligated to prevent under the terms of the Treaty of Guadalupe Hidalgo—and the Tehuantepec question. Pierce also wanted more Mexican land. He planned, therefore, to merge all those issues into a negotiation for Mexican territory. Since Santa Anna needed money to finance his despotic regime, Pierce thought that he would be willing to sell his country's land and settle the other problems for money.

The Gadsden Purchase

To handle the negotiations, Pierce appointed James Gadsden, a South Carolina politician and railroad promoter, Minister to Mexico in May, 1853. Along with Jefferson Davis, the Secretary of War and perhaps the most powerful man in the Pierce administration, Gadsden wanted some of the Mexican land for a proposed southern railroad to the Pacific Ocean. He arrived in Mexico City in August and immediately began negotiations with Santa Anna.

Using threats of force, Gadsden urged the Mexicans to cede a large part of northern Mexico and Baja California.[8] American absorption of that territory, he said, was inevitable; Mexico had better sell to avoid future troubles. The Mexicans, however, would part with no more than the minimum necessary for the proposed railroad. On December 30, Gadsden signed a treaty whereby Mexico sold the southern parts of Arizona and New Mexico, including a disputed region near El Paso called Mesilla Valley, for twenty million dollars, fifteen million to be paid to Mexico and five million to American citizens to satisfy claims against Mexico.

The Senate added amendments that reduced the money to ten million, all to go to Mexico, annulled the provision of the Treaty of Guadalupe Hidalgo which made the United States responsible for Indian depredations, and settled the Tehuantepec question. The amended treaty gave Americans the right to use any means of transit across the Isthmus of Tehuantepec, and the American government the right to protect the transit by force. Santa Anna accepted the amended treaty and exchanged ratifications on June 30, 1854. Even he, however, could not get away with such a treaty. That sale forced his removal in August of the following year.

The Gadsden Purchase was the last acquisition from powerless Mexico, but Mexicans never forgot the land hunger of their northern neighbor. A later dictator of Mexico coined an aphorism covering his country's plight. "Poor Mexico," he said, "so far from God and so near the United States."

Annexationist Sentiment in Canada

Mexico was not the only neighbor who seemed destined for annexation during the 1850's. Canada appeared willing to join the United States of her own free will. Annexationist sentiment in Canada had its roots in two related problems, one political and the other economic.

Political unrest, stemming from the two rebellions of 1837 against Canada's government, had combined with an economic depression in 1846–1847 to give strength to the movement for annexation. After the rebellions, Britain through various political reforms had given Canada a limited measure of responsible government. In Canada's general election of 1848 those reforms led to the over-whelming defeat of the Tory Loyalists, the party of merchants and professional men who had long controlled government affairs. These men took their defeat with a bitterness that expressed itself in a special hatred for the French-Canadians who had in effect voted them out.

The economic problem was related to the political one. Under Britain's mercan-tilist laws, Canada's products, mainly raw materials such as wheat, timber, and fish, had had a favored market in England, one protected from foreign competition. In 1846, England had repealed her Corn Laws and had opened her markets to the world without favored treatment for Canadians or anyone else. Loss of that protected market had caused serious economic distress in Canada. "Three-fourths of the commercial men are bankrupt, owing to Free-trade," Lord Elgin, who became Canada's Governor General in 1847, wrote; "a large proportion of the exportable produce of Canada is obliged to seek a market in the States. It pays a duty of twenty per cent on the frontier. How long can such a state of things be expected to endure?"[9]

Some conservative Tory Loyalists, with their center of activity in Montreal, believed that annexation to the United States would solve their problem. It would, they thought, open the vast American market to their produce and bring a "new day" in their political life by making the French-Canadians an impotent minority in the population of a greater United States. The annexationists, however, were themselves a minority among Canadians. Nonetheless, they expressed their views in a manifesto "to the people of Canada" issued from Montreal early in October, 1849. It called for a "friendly and peaceful separation from British connexion, and a union upon equitable terms with the great North American confederacy of sovereign states." Within a few days it gained more than a thousand signatures from Montreal's financial and political leaders.

Americans, mainly those in the North and East, followed Canada's annexation movement with approval. In 1849, for example, the Vermont legislature passed a resolution saying that the annexation of Canada "is an object in the highest degree desirable to the people of the United States." Yet these apostles of Manifest Destiny did not stir up a widespread annexationist sentiment in the United States, and the Whig administration of Zachary Taylor did nothing to encourage the Canadian annexationists. Taylor followed a cautious policy because the South did not want Canada. If Canada entered the Union she would add more free-soil states, making the slaveholding South a smaller sectional minority than it was. The administration, therefore, wished to avoid any action which might have caused the South to secede and thus split the Union.

Even Northerners who wanted Canada did not attempt to arouse popular emotions, for they saw no need to rush. They believed annexation was inevitable. The Toledo *Blade* expressed their attitude when it said that "when the fruit is fully ripe it will fall into our lap without any exertion on our part."[10]

The British government, however, opposed the annexation movement and instructed its administrators in Canada to discourage it. Those officials, such as Lord Elgin, saw in reciprocal free trade with the United States the best means of allaying the annexationist sentiment. To obtain that reciprocity they had to persuade the United States to lower its tariffs against Canadian products, but Americans would not consider doing so without gaining something in return.

Specifically, they desired increased fishing privileges off the coast of Britain's maritime provinces and free navigation of the St. Lawrence River and Canada's canals.

Canada tried to work out some kind of legislative agreement that would meet the American terms and permit free trade, but her efforts failed because the American Congress would not reciprocate. At this time the United States was more concerned with other problems, particularly with slavery. Finally, the British decided to exert pressure to bring about a trade agreement, mainly by enforcing the restrictions on American fishermen imposed by the Convention of 1818. Before 1852 the British authorities in the maritime provinces had been lenient in interpreting that convention, but in that year several of the provinces demanded equivalent privileges from the United States in reciprocal free trade. They would not open their fisheries to Americans, beyond narrow treaty requirements, without those concessions.

In June the British ordered naval protection for their fisheries in North America to force observance of the convention and to prevent encroachments by Americans. That order, as well as the seizure of fishing vessels which violated treaty restrictions, angered Americans, particularly New Englanders. Secretary of State Daniel Webster said the British action would disrupt the "extensive fishing business of New England," and warned that it would be "attended by constant collisions of the most unpleasant and exciting character, which may end in the destruction of human life, in the involvement of the Government in questions of a very serious nature, threatening the peace of the two countries." [11] President Millard Fillmore then announced that he was willing to settle the questions of reciprocal trade, the fisheries, and the navigation of the St. Lawrence River and the canals.

That suited the British, who had been willing to exchange navigation of the St. Lawrence and the fisheries for the privilege of bringing the products of their North American colonies into the United States without paying duties, but Britain and the United States could reach no agreement in 1852 and 1853. As the fishing season of 1854 approached, therefore, conflict in the northern waters appeared likely, for the United States had also sent warships to those waters to protect American interests, but with orders to avoid trouble if possible.

The Marcy-Elgin Treaty

Finally, after Secretary of State Marcy made an overture, the British sent Lord Elgin, accompanied by a commission, to the United States in May, 1854, to negotiate a treaty. Elgin and his staff approached their task as accomplished diplomats. His snobbish young secretary said that the treaty they negotiated "floated through on champagne," though "a lot of senators" preferred brandy-and-water and cigars.

"Lord Elgin pretends to drink immensely," his secretary disclosed, "but I watched him [at a party], and I don't believe he drank a glass between two and twelve. He is the most thorough *diplomat* possible,—never loses sight for a moment of his object, and while he is chaffing Yankees and slapping them on the back, he is systematically pursuing that object." [12]

In the Marcy-Elgin Treaty, signed on June 5, 1854, the United States obtained almost all that it had desired in the fisheries. That agreement allowed Americans to fish the inshore waters of all the maritime provinces except Newfoundland, and in return, offered British subjects the privilege of fishing along the Atlantic shore as far south as Albemarle Sound, North Carolina, at the thirty-sixth parallel. Americans, the treaty said, could use the St. Lawrence and the Canadian canals between the Great Lakes and the sea on the same terms as British subjects, while those subjects obtained free navigation of Lake Michigan.

The reciprocity provisions, of most importance to the Canadians, admitted a large number of agricultural products, seafoods, and raw materials into both the United States and the British North American provinces duty free. This reciprocity treaty, the first the United States ever negotiated, was to run for ten years. After that, either party could terminate it with a year's notice. The Senate, won over by Lord Elgin's diplomacy, approved the treaty on August 4.

Northerners still believed that Canada would someday join the United States and that the treaty would not injure annexation. They were wrong. Reciprocity brought increased trade between Canada and the United States, ended the waning talk of annexation, helped to relieve Canada's economic distress, and immediately eased the tension in the fishing grounds.

John F. Crampton and Neutrality

The next minor quarrel with Britain involved a violation of American neutrality growing out of the Crimean War. Heavy losses in fighting the Russians led Parliament in December, 1854, to authorize the enlisting of foreigners for the British army. The British Minister in the United States, John F. Crampton, and consuls in various cities worked out a scheme for obtaining soldiers in the United States by paying their expenses to Halifax in Nova Scotia where the recruits enlisted. Acting cautiously, Crampton followed American legal advice and tried not to violate the neutrality laws that prohibited recruiting in the United States for, and by, foreign countries at war. Some of his agents were not as careful. They openly advertised for recruits and violated the laws. [13]

At first the American authorities were indulgent, but when public opinion, aroused by anti-British elements, denounced the recruiting, Secretary of State Marcy complained to Crampton and then formally protested to the British government. Alarmed by the protests and also by the arrest of several private adventurers, the British government ordered the recruiting stopped. Meanwhile, in September, 1855, the American government had arrested and convicted a British agent whose confession and trial brought out evidence implicating Crampton and British consuls in New York, Philadelphia, and Cincinnati in violations of American neutrality.

The Attorney General and the government took the position that the violation of domestic laws was not the basic issue. "The main consideration," he said, "is the sovereign right of the United States to exercise complete and exclusive jurisdiction within their own territory; to remain strictly neutral, if they please."[14] President Pierce asked the British government to recall Crampton and the three consuls, but it refused. On May 28, 1856, therefore, the day before the opening of the Democratic presidential convention at which he sought the nomination, Pierce dramatically expelled Crampton and revoked the exequaturs, or written orders, of the consuls.

Pierce's action caused hard feelings in England, but the British did not retaliate by dismissing the American Minister in London. They did, however, delay naming a new minister to the United States for ten months, until after Pierce went out of office. When Crampton went home, moreover, he was knighted.

Sympathy for Europe's Liberals

While Americans resented Britain's interference in their internal politics, they had not hesitated to meddle in European affairs. In 1848, Germans, Italians, Frenchmen, and Hungarians, motivated by liberal and nationalistic sentiments, revolted unsuccessfully against their conservative monarchial rulers. Many of the revolutionists wanted republican governments. The Hungarians, under the leadership of Lajos Kossuth, declared themselves independent of Austria's Hapsburg rulers in April, 1849, and set up a republic. With the aid of Russian troops, Austria crushed the new republic by August. In fact, all the liberal revolutions had failed by the following year.

Americans sympathized with all the liberal revolutionary movements, but the Hungarian struggle particularly appealed to them. One reason may have been that the Hungarian republic was supposedly modeled on their own. In any event, Secretary of State Clayton secretly instructed Ambrose Dudley Mann, a diplomatic agent in Paris, to go to Hungary. If Hungary appeared "able to maintain the independence she had declared," Mann had the authority to recognize Kossuth's government.

Before Mann reached Hungary the republic fell. Although he did nothing, the Austrian government learned of his instructions and protested through its *chargé* in Washington, Chevalier J. G. Hülsemann, at first informally and in September, 1850, formally, against American interference in its domestic affairs. Daniel

Webster, again Secretary of State, this time under Millard Fillmore, took Hülse-mann's protest as an opportunity to win the plaudits of American nationalists and to boost his own candidacy for President. "I wished to write a paper which should touch the national pride," he said, and he did.

In his note to Hülsemann, Webster defended Mann's mission, upheld republican principles, and bombastically exalted the status of the United States. "The power of this republic at the present moment," he boasted, "is spread over a region one of the richest and most fertile on the globe, and of an extent in comparison with which the possessions of the house of Hapsburg are but as a patch on the earth's surface."[15] Webster pleased Americans but infuriated the Austrians. Indeed, a New York newspaper announced, "if the Austrian minister does not like our interference in the affairs of Hungary, he may go home as soon as he pleases."

The American government next turned its attention to Kossuth himself, "the general representative of liberty in Europe," who had escaped from Hungary into Turkey where he was held prisoner for two years. America helped secure his release and sent a naval vessel to bring him to the United States. Arriving in New York on December 5, 1851, he met a tumultuous welcome. One paper described the scene in verse:

> When Kossuth came that splendid day
> Ah! who shall e'er forget
> When first upon our city's soil
> His wandering feet were set
> The scene transcending e'en the scene
> To welcome Lafayette.[16]

When Kossuth, an impressive and eloquent figure who had said he looked upon Americans "as the natural supporters of freedom and civilization," visited Washington, he dined with President Fillmore and received a special banquet from Congress. There Webster said that Americans would rejoice in seeing a model of the United States on the lower Danube and that Hungary ought to be "independent of all foreign powers."

Kossuth's official and popular welcome, as well as Webster's speech, deeply offended the Austrian government, which demanded Webster's dismissal. Fillmore refused to remove his Secretary of State. The Austrian government, therefore, would have nothing more to do with the Secretary, and American relations with Austria remained strained until Webster died in October, 1852.[17]

The only other serious friction with Austria in the nineteenth century came the following year in the case of Martin Koszta, a Hungarian refugee who had taken out his first papers declaring his intention of becoming an American citizen. While on a visit to Turkey, Koszta was abducted by Austrian authorities and thrown into chains aboard an Austrian brig in the harbor at Smyrna. On July 2, 1853, the commander of an American sloop of war in the harbor delivered an ultimatum to the Austrians and forced Koszta's release, an act that led to a harsh diplomatic exchange between the Austrian and American governments. Americans were delighted with Secretary of State Marcy's nationalistic, if not legally correct, defense of Koszta. Americans should, one journal declared, "rally as one man around the Government . . . in the defense of weakness against violence, right against despotism, humanity against oppression." [18]

This cocky nationalism in the Koszta case had grown out of the Kossuth excitement and the liberal and nationalistic movements in Europe, such as "Young Italy," "Young Germany," and "Young Ireland," which had stimulated a movement in 1852 within the Democratic party called "Young America." European immigrants, particularly from Germany and Ireland, imbued with republican ideals had flocked into the Democratic party, supported the movement, and urged cooperation with the republican movements in Europe. John Crampton's description of the movement is as good as any. He said "the 'Young America' or 'Manifest Destiny' Party" was composed of "those who possess extreme democratic doctrines in the usual sense of the word . . .; and also those who urge it to be a duty, as well as the true policy of the United States to intervene in the affairs of Foreign Nations in support of Democratic & Republican Principles."

The Young America group urged a vigorous foreign policy, and Franklin Pierce had stressed such a policy in his inaugural address in order to please that wing of his party. Marcy had reflected the bumptious nationalism of Young America when in a "Dress Circular" he had asked American diplomats not to wear uniforms, but to appear in the courts of Europe "in the simple dress of an American citizen." [19] He had also told them not to employ foreigners in their legations and to use only "the American language." The aggressive foreign policy urged by the "Young America" Democrats, however, can best be seen in the efforts to acquire Cuba.

The Quest for Cuba

Long before the era of Manifest Destiny and of Young America, some American statesmen were convinced that Cuba was destined to belong to the United States. Spain appeared unable to hold very long the meager remnants of her once magnificent empire in the New World. The United States, fearing British and French designs on Cuba, opposed its transfer to any power stronger than Spain. It wanted Cuba, and Puerto Rico also, to remain in Spain's feeble hands until those islands drifted under American control.

Henry Clay had explained in 1825 what became established policy. The United States, he said, "could not see with indifference" Cuba passing into the hands of any European power other than Spain. In June, 1837, when the government had heard various rumors about the future of Cuba, particularly that Britain was negotiating with Spain for the island in exchange for a loan, the American Minister in London had protested and reiterated American policy. He told the British Foreign Secretary that "*it was impossible that the United States could acquiesce in the transfer of Cuba from the dominion of Spain to any of the great maritime powers of Europe.*" [20]

During the war with Mexico some expansionists had included Cuba among their objectives. "Cuba must be ours!" a New York newspaper had said. "We want its harbors for our ships to touch at to and from Mexico—for the accommodations of American and English transatlantic steamers—for its products and trade, and as the Grand key to the Gulf of Mexico. Give us Cuba, and our possessions are complete." [21]

After the war, Cuba, which lay athwart the Central-American transit routes to newly acquired California, became more than ever an object of American foreign policy. Responding to the demands of pro-slavery Democratic expansionists, Polk had decided to try to buy Cuba and in June, 1848, instructed his Minister in Madrid to open negotiations for the purchase and to offer Spain, if necessary, as much as a hundred million dollars. News of the project leaked and Spanish newspapers chorused a loud protest. The Spanish Minister of State then refused to negotiate. "Sooner than see the Island transferred to *any power*," he had said, the people of Spain "would prefer seeing it sunk in the Ocean."

During the succeeding Whig administrations of Presidents Taylor and Fillmore, the pro-slavery expansionists could not obtain official support for annexing Cuba. Some of them, therefore, turned to filibustering expeditions against the island with the idea of detaching it from Spain and ultimately bringing it into the Union. The leading filibuster was a Cuban exile who had been born in Venezuela, General Narciso López. At one time he had held high office under Spain in Cuba, but in the summer of 1848, after Spanish authorities had found him involved in a plot to overthrow their rule on the island, he had fled to the United States.

López planned to invade Cuba with a force of Americans, Cuban exiles, and various adventurers, and to arouse the people there to revolution against Spain. Most of his support came from Southerners who wanted to bring Cuba into the Union as a slave state to balance the political preponderance of the North. López organized his first expedition in New York in 1849. It was composed of the "most desperate creatures as ever were seen," a government agent said, toughs who "would murder a man for ten dollars." [22] Federal authorities broke up the expedition in September before it left the city.

Undaunted, López shifted his headquarters to New Orleans where the climate was more congenial to his plotting. Since some of the lower South's most important political leaders supported him, he had little trouble in recruiting more than five hundred men. Slipping through a cordon of American and Spanish warships, López and his band landed in Cuba on May 18, 1850, and captured the

Spanish garrison at Cárdenas, but the Cubans did not rally to his banner as he had expected. The expedition then retreated before Spanish lancers and fled to Key West, Florida. Although he had failed again, the South greeted López as a conquering hero.

President Fillmore, however, was determined to stop the filibustering. "We instigate no revolutions," he announced, "nor suffer any hostile military expeditions to be fitted out in the United States to invade territory or provinces of a friendly nation."[23] Nevertheless, López organized a third expedition, again composed mostly of Southerners, and the federal authorities failed to stop him. He landed near Havana on August 11, 1851, with over four hundred men and fell into a Spanish trap. The Spaniards captured or killed all the invaders, including López whom they garroted publicly in Havana. Before dying he shouted defiantly: "My death will not change the destiny of Cuba!"

The Spaniards also executed some of the American prisoners, including the son of the Attorney General of the United States, while ultimately letting others go. The executions infuriated Southerners. Mobs in New Orleans wrecked the Spanish consulate, and in Mobile they assaulted shipwrecked Spanish sailors. Already deeply embittered by the filibustering expeditions, the Spanish government demanded redress for the attacks and for the destruction of Spanish property. Finally, in 1852, the Spanish and American governments worked out a settlement whereby the United States apologized and paid for some of the damage.

Meanwhile, Spain had sought European help in defending Cuba against the filibusters. After the first expeditions, she had asked Britain and France several times for support, and to guarantee her possession of Cuba. Although concerned about the fate of Cuba, Britain and France would not intervene directly in Spain's quarrel. After López's death, however, Britain became interested in a plan whereby she, the United States, and France would join in making a treaty declaring that none of them would try to acquire Cuba. In April, 1852, the British and French formally asked the United States to agree to such a three-power treaty.

Before preparing an answer, Secretary of State Webster told the British and French Ministers in Washington of "his own entire concurrence in their views with regard to Cuba," but he died without delivering a formal reply. In November, the presidential elections brought victory to Franklin Pierce and the Young America expansionists. Fillmore and his new Secretary of State, Edward Everett, therefore, agreed finally to reject the proposed treaty.

In his nationalistic reply to the British and French Ministers, Everett stressed the strategic significance of Cuba to the United States and said that the President would not enter the treaty because "he considers the condition of Cuba as mainly an American question."[24] Everett's note ended the Whig effort to deal with the Cuban question. Pierce and his Young America and Southern supporters next took up the question.

Pierce frankly wanted Cuba. "The policy of my Administration," he said in his inaugural, "will not be controlled by any timid forebodings of evil from expansion." Referring to Cuba, though not by name, he explained that "the acquisition of certain possessions" was "eminently important for our protection."[25] In trying to carry out a vigorous foreign policy, Pierce appointed avowed expansionists to important cabinet and diplomatic posts. Secretary of State Marcy believed that an expansionist record would help him in obtaining the next Democratic presidential nomination. Pierre Soulé, Pierce's Minister to Spain, was a French-born radical from Louisiana who aspired to the leadership of Young America, and who was an outspoken advocate of taking Cuba for the expansion of slave territory. He had defended and supported López and his filibusters. Soulé believed that the main objective of his mission was to acquire Cuba.

In its very first year the Pierce administration appeared to expect a filibustering expedition to free Cuba from Spain. John A. Quitman, an extreme pro-slavery Southerner who had been Governor of Mississippi, began organizing just such an expedition in 1853. He had grandiose plans and dreamed of a southern empire of slavery that would include Cuba and Mexico. He and other Southerners feared that Spain, encouraged by England, would free slaves in Cuba and "Africanize" the island in the manner of Haiti. His filibuster would prevent that.[26]

According to a Whig newspaper, Quitman had gathered a war chest of one million dollars, an army of some fifty thousand men, and equipment that included twelve ships, eighty-five thousand arms, and ninety field pieces by the summer of 1854. At first the Pierce administration supported his undertaking. The plan was, apparently, to make Cuba independent and then to bring it into the Union as a slave state like Texas, but Quitman and his formidable force never sailed. The politics of the slavery controversy forced the administration to withdraw its support. Still, Quitman would not abandon his project.

The events that finally led to its abandonment began on February 28, 1854, when Spanish authorities in Cuba confiscated the cargo of the American steamship *Black Warrior* for a technical violation of port regulations she had ignored with impunity on at least seventeen previous voyages. This appeared to be the needed "incident" that could serve as an excuse for war and the taking of Cuba by direct force. American excitement ran high, and on March 15 Pierce asked Congress for authority "to obtain redress for injuries received, and to vindicate the honor of our flag."[27] The time appeared ripe for strong action against Spain, for Britain and France were preparing to go to war against Russia, and did so on March 28. With their military forces committed to the Crimea, they probably would not interfere with any American effort to take Cuba.

Marcy instructed Soulé in Madrid to demand an apology and three hundred thousand dollars as indemnity for the injuries sustained by the *Black Warrior*. The impetuous Soulé then went beyond his instructions. On April 8 he delivered the demand for an indemnity as a forty-eight-hour ultimatum. Suspecting that he had exceeded his instructions, the Spanish Foreign Minister ignored the ultimatum and finally settled the *Black Warrior* affair directly with the ship's owners. The Pierce administration went along with the settlement because of domestic developments.[28]

A month earlier, on March 3, the Senate had approved the Kansas-Nebraska Bill and Pierce's party then tried to force it through the House of Representatives. Since that bill favored the South and aroused intense opposition in the North, Pierce did not now dare launch a war to grab Cuba as additional slave territory. Congress, moreover, would not support him. The Kansas-Nebraska Bill passed the House late in May and Pierce signed it on May 30. On the following day he issued a proclamation warning that the government would prosecute those who violated the neutrality laws. It appeared to crush what remained of Quitman's filibustering plans.

Pierce next tried to acquire Cuba through purchase and vigorous diplomacy. On April 3 Marcy authorized Soulé to offer as much as one hundred and thirty million dollars for Cuba. If Spain refused to sell, he told Soulé, "you will then direct your efforts to the next most desirable object, which is to detach that island from the Spanish dominion and from all dependence on any European power."[29] The administration apparently desired a revolution in Spain that would make Cuba independent. Despite Soulé's tampering with rebellion, that plan also failed. The administration then tried other methods. In August Marcy instructed Soulé to confer with James Buchanan, the Minister to Great Britain, and with John Y. Mason, the Minister to France, to make plans that would advance the efforts to acquire Cuba.

The three Ministers met supposedly in secrecy from October 9 to 18, first in Ostend, Belgium, and then in Aix-la-Chapelle, Rhenish Prussia. They signed their report, later known as the Ostend Manifesto, on the last day and sent it to Marcy by confidential messenger. That dispatch, drafted by Buchanan from Soulé's notes, restated old arguments as to why Spain should sell Cuba and why the United States should buy it.[30] It compared the alleged "Africanization" of Cuba to a neighbor's burning house, a fire that justified tearing down the building if there were no other means of preventing the flames from destroying one's own house. Under the circumstances, "by every law, human and Divine," it said, "we shall be justified in wresting it [Cuba] from Spain, if we possess the power."

Since the report was not a public statement of policy but a secret dispatch to the Secretary of State, it was not in any sense a "manifesto." News of the meeting and of the report leaked and stimulated unsavory publicity that shocked Europeans and Americans. The Ostend Manifesto proved to be the high point of American efforts to acquire Cuba in the 1850's. The dispatch reached Washington on November 4, 1854, just as the administration suffered defeats in the mid-term congressional elections. Since the blatant efforts of the Young America diplomats

THE PRINCIPLES OF THE OSTEND MANIFESTO IN ACTION

Here four thugs explain to President Buchanan why he must hand over his wallet, watch, coat, and hat immediately.

to acquire Cuba contributed to those defeats, the administration retreated from its aggressive Cuban policy.

On November 13 Marcy wrote to Soulé, that "damned little Frenchman," repudiating the Ostend Manifesto and told him to cease his efforts to buy Cuba. Since this was a repudiation of Soulé himself, the Minister resigned a month later. Then the administration finally convinced Quitman to give up the filibustering plan he had never fully abandoned.[31] Hostile congressmen forced publication of a trimmed version of the Ostend Manifesto in the following March, a publication that aroused new criticism at home and in Europe of American efforts to "steal" Cuba.

"Cuba at any cost," one newspaper headline shouted in referring to the Ostend Manifesto. Horace Greeley's New York *Tribune* called it "The Manifesto of the Brigands." "What could have got into able and intelligent men," a Democratic senator, asked, "to write such a letter?" Although the criticism, blundering diplomacy, and the obvious pro-slavery character of the Pierce Cuban policy killed any chance of obtaining Cuba, the Democrats did not stop trying.

Pierce's successor, James Buchanan, won election on a platform that called for annexation of Cuba. He was an expansionist who tried several times to interest Congress in proposals to buy the island, but with no success. He had hoped to carry out an expansionist foreign policy to divert the nation from its preoccupation with slavery. "The great desire to acquire Cuba and to throw before the country a new and exciting topic, one which will override all others, and cover up the errors of this administration," a Southern diplomat wrote, "is the policy of the Democratic Party." Buchanan's foreign policy, particularly his Cuban policy, like that of Pierce, failed because it appeared to advance the interests of slavery.

The China Trade

During the decades in which the diplomacy of Manifest Destiny and Young America was capturing public imagination, dramatic events unfolded in the Far East that were ultimately to have a profound influence on American foreign policy. American diplomacy, while not usually at the center of those events, had a part in them. Actually, American interest in the Far East did not erupt suddenly in those decades. It had begun quietly a half century earlier.

After losing the markets in the British Empire, the newly independent American traders sought new outlets, one of which appeared to be China. The *Empress of China*, a ship of 360 tons owned by a group of New York merchants, slipped out of New York's harbor on February 22, 1784, with a cargo of ginseng, raw cotton, and furs, and sailed directly for China. She returned in May of the following year with a cargo of silk, tea, and porcelain. Since the voyage brought a profit of some twenty-five per cent of the original investment, other ships, primarily from New England, entered the China trade.[32] By 1800, American merchants had built a modest, but profitable, commerce with China.

Since those who went to China bought more than they sold, the American trade with China, like that of other Western nations, was not a balanced one. A main reason for that was China's economic self-sufficiency. The Chinese considered their civilization superior to that of the West and had far less desire for Western products than the Westerners had for their goods. The Chinese would buy a few luxury items such as the ginseng root, clocks, watches, and furs, but little else. Westerners made up the balance in their purchase of Chinese goods, such as tea and silks, by bringing great quantities of silver.

American ships usually did not sail directly for China. They would leave New England with batches of the ginseng root and cargoes of rum, kettles, hatchets, and arms. Then they would sail around Cape Horn and up the Pacific Coast as far north as the Columbia River. There, and along the way, they would barter their rum and hardware with the Indians for valuable furs, usually for the glossy pelt of the sea otter or the seal. With their furs and ginseng the Americans sailed for China, taking with them also kegs of silver dollars they obtained on Mexico's Pacific coast.

The Chinese, who considered all Westerners barbarian inferiors and were not anxious to trade with them, restricted the Western traders to the port of Canton in South China. Within the port the Chinese government regulated commerce through a monopoly it granted to a group of merchants called the "Co-hong." Americans and other foreigners could trade only with the merchants of the "Co-hong" and only in factories, or trading posts, located outside the walls of Canton. They could not go into the interior or even spend the night in Canton.

Despite those restrictions, American trade with China increased rapidly during the first half of the nineteenth century and reached its peak during the era of the swift clipper ship, between 1850 and 1855. America's trade with China was second only to that of Britain, but it was only a small fraction of the United States' total foreign commerce. For those who participated in it, however, the profits were good, particularly after British merchants found a market for opium in China. That narcotic reversed the balance of trade. The Chinese smoked so much opium that American ships and those of other Western nations soon sailed away from China with quantities of silver as well as with silks and porcelains.

Alarmed at the loss of silver and the evils of opium, which officials said "flows and poisons the land," the Chinese government tried to enforce regulations prohibiting the traffic in the drug. But certain British merchants, interested in maintaining their established market, urged their government to force the Chinese to continue accepting the import of opium, whether or not their own government approved. Some other British interests, representing a new manufacturing class seeking enlarged markets for its goods, especially textiles, demanded that their government force the Chinese government to accept the principle of free and equal opportunity in trade for all merchants dealing in any commodities. Since the British manufacturers framed their demands in terms of free and equal trade opportunity, they won the support of manufacturers and traders in other countries, and in effect spearheaded a new international development in China.

This drive of Western commercial interests for unhampered trade, backed by the British government, came to a crisis in 1839 when a zealous Chinese official seized and destroyed a large stock of British opium. The ensuing controversy developed into the Opium War of 1839–1842, in which the British government supported its merchants with arms. Victory in this one-sided struggle enabled the British to force the Treaty of Nanking of August 29, 1842, on the Chinese. The terms of that treaty, and of other negotiations which immediately followed, changed the international status of China and of American trade and diplomacy there.

The British compelled the Chinese to recognize them as equals and to pay not only for the destroyed opium but also for Britain's costs in fighting the war. The indemnity for the Opium War, as well as other indemnities imposed later, burdened the Chinese government with an international debt it could not pay under its existing system of taxation. In order to raise the money for payment, China, with the aid of Europeans, later created a special customs service. The customs officials collected dues at the flat rate of five per cent of the value of all goods which penetrated the country. This rate, imposed by treaty, deprived China of control over her own trade.

Beginning with the Treaty of Nanking, the British, and then other foreigners, secured the right to trade freely in four ports in addition to Canton. Since China opened them under treaties forced upon her, these became known as the "treaty ports." In most of the ports foreigners lived in "international settlements" or national concessions under local self-government. As the Europeans considered Chinese law barbarous, they forced the Chinese to give their consuls in the European settlements jurisdiction over their own people and even over Chinese who brought civil suits against Europeans. Since those legal rights, known as "extra-territoriality," impinged on China's sovereignty, the treaties upholding them came to be known as the "unequal treaties."

Under a separate treaty signed in October, 1843, the British established the most-favored-nation principle in China's foreign relations. That principle subjected the Chinese to the practice, of particular value to Americans, that said that any privilege any foreign country won from the Chinese would accrue automatically to the other foreign countries having treaties with them.

Unable to withstand the military power of the Western nations, China, by the 1860's, became something of an international colony of those powers who had merchant ships trading on her coasts and the naval power to support them. Britain's victory in 1842, therefore, had inaugurated a new international system for the control of that vast country. That pattern of "unequal treaties" limited China's sovereignty and gave the treaty powers special rights there that laid the basis for American commercial and diplomatic policy in China. The United States, as one of the treaty powers, profited from the system.

Trade Negotiations with China

Before the new developments had transformed China's international status, American interest in China had been almost wholly commercial. Major Samuel Shaw, the American government's first representative in China, appointed Consul in Canton in 1786, had no diplomatic status. Like all Consuls serving in China before 1854, he did so without salary and his interests were commercial. The Chinese government did not officially recognize the American Consuls, but considered them as head merchants. Those Consuls had no authority over American traders in China. Unlike the British government, the American government in the first half of the nineteenth century did little to help its traders in China.

Since the American merchants at Canton did not expect support from the government and were satisfied with the status of their trade there, the first American diplomatic mission to Asia did not even attempt to open diplomatic relations with China. In January, 1832, Andrew Jackson commissioned Edmund Roberts, a merchant from New Hampshire who had traded in the area of the Indian Ocean and had served in the consular service, as a special agent to make commercial treaties with Cochin-China, Siam, Muscat, and Japan. When Roberts arrived in Canton, the Chinese refused to recognize his official status. They ordered the American warships accompanying him to "unfurl their sails and return home; they will not be permitted to delay and loiter about, and the day of their departure must be made known. Hasten, hasten!"[33]

Roberts failed in Cochin-China but succeeded in negotiating treaties with Siam and Muscat in 1833 that opened those countries to American trade on terms of the most-favored-nation principle and with fixed tariff charges. Believing himself and his mission inadequately prepared for negotiations with the Japanese, he did not go on to Japan as planned. Instead, he returned to the United States with his two treaties. In 1835, Jackson sent him back to Asia to exchange ratifications and to negotiate a treaty with Japan. At Macao, on his way to Japan, Roberts died of the plague in June, 1836. Although the results of his diplomacy were meager, he had for the first time placed American trade with an Asian nation on a treaty basis.

The first American treaty with China stemmed from the Opium War and the Treaty of Nanking. During the hostilities, the United States had remained neutral and had watched developments with sympathy for the Chinese, and American merchants at Canton had carried on their trade with greater profit than usual. Yet they asked for protection and the American government sent a naval squadron, under the command of Commodore Lawrence Kearny, to Chinese waters. Six weeks after the Treaty of Nanking, Kearny asked the Chinese authorities to place Americans "upon the same footing as the merchants of the nation most favored."[34] A Chinese official assured him that American interests would be safeguarded since foreign trade would "be regulated uniformly by one rule, without the least partiality to be manifested toward any one." Although the Chinese acted on their own initiative in insisting on the most-favored-nation clause in their later Treaty of the Bogue with Britain, some writers have believed that Kearny's suggestion may have had some influence on their action.[35]

Realizing that the Treaty of Nanking had changed China's international status and the conditions of trade, American merchants in China feared that they might not be able to enjoy fully the commercial privileges the British had extorted from the Chinese. Although Americans were building their own industrial system behind tariff walls, they embraced the principle of world-wide trade. They did not want any nation to exclude them from trading with China on the same basis as others. Therefore, they pressed their government to open diplomatic relations with China to protect their commercial interests there. "How much of our tobacco," one congressman said in hopes of gaining more trade in China, "might be there chewed, in place of opium!"

President Tyler responded favorably to the merchants and others, and in May, 1843, appointed Caleb Cushing, a Whig lawyer of Newbury, Massachusetts, and a member of the Committee on Foreign Affairs of the House of Representatives, the first commissioner to the Chinese empire. Cushing, who arrived at Macao in February of the following year, had instructions to obtain the same commercial privileges by treaty, without using force, that Britain had obtained through war. He was to "signify, in decided terms and a positive manner, that the Government of the United States would find it impossible to remain on terms of friendship and regard with the emperor, if greater privileges or commercial facilities should be allowed to the subjects of any other Government than should be granted to the citizens of the United States." [36]

Even though the Chinese had already granted most-favored-nation privileges to foreign countries, they did not wish to negotiate another treaty. Why make a treaty, they said, "when the Americans have already been given all the advantages in trade which have been conceded to the English?" Backed by four warships and using indirect threats, Cushing nonetheless persuaded the Chinese to sign an agreement on July 3, 1844, at Wanghia, a village near Macao.

The Treaty of Wanghia gave Americans the same privileges the British had forced from China, including fixed tariff duties and most-favored-nation guarantees. Cushing also gained some privileges that went further than those of the British, particularly in the matter of extraterritoriality. The British had won extraterritorial rights only in civil matters; the American treaty extended those rights to criminal cases as well. So superior was Cushing's treaty to that of the British that through the operation of the most-favored-nation principle, it became the basic treaty for Western nations in their relations with China for the next fourteen years. [37]

The Treaty of Wanghia, approved unanimously by the Senate, placed policy toward China on a firm foundation. It marked the end of an era of economic relations without benefit of diplomatic protection for Americans in China and the beginning of American participation in the international politics of the Far East.

After the Treaty of Wanghia, American interest in China, stimulated by the new official relations, grew rapidly. Possibilities of increased trade helped draw the attention of merchants and others to the Pacific Coast. From the Pacific shores, they said, the United States would be able to tap the riches of Asia as would no other nation, and China would provide a vast market for American products.

Then, with the acquisition of the Oregon territory and California, Americans turned even more intently toward the Pacific and Asia. Traders, and particularly missionaries, flocked to China. They found a land racked by turmoil and controlled by an officialdom that had nothing but contempt for foreigners such as themselves. In 1849, the smoldering discontent of the masses with the rule of the Manchu dynasty burst into a long and bloody civil war called the Taiping Rebellion. Although the Taiping rebels, under a visionary leader who gave his cause a pseudo-Christian character, failed to destroy the dynasty at Peking, they conquered large parts of China and in 1853 established themselves at Nanking where they ruled for a decade. Before the Taipings collapsed in 1864, the rebellion took a toll estimated at twenty million lives.

Many Americans, particularly the missionaries, at first mistakenly considered the Taiping uprising a truly Christian movement which might strengthen China and give it a new regime that would break down Chinese hostility to the West. Secretary of State Marcy, for instance, spoke of "the wonderful events in China, events which threaten the overthrow of the Tartar rule, and the establishment in its stead of a government more in accordance with the tenets of Christianity."

In time, however, American officials concluded that the overthrow of the Manchus would be inimical to American interests, meaning commerce, their main concern. It appeared logical, therefore, for the American government to abandon its initial sympathy for the Taipings and to support the authority of the imperial government that had offered most-favored-nation treatment in trade.

Yet, even while imperilled by the Taipings, the imperial government's contempt for foreigners led it to evade its treaty obligations. The Treaty of Wanghia, for example, had called for direct diplomatic relations between the signatories, but Chinese officials rebuffed all advances from the United States. Although Americans lacked the military power in Asia necessary to force their diplomats upon the Chinese, the British and the French did not. In 1857, they went to war to compel the Manchu government to carry out its agreements and give them further privileges. In the conflict, called the "*Arrow* War," they easily defeated China.

Britain had asked the United States to join the alliance against China, but the American government refused, preferring a policy of neutrality. It did, however, send a naval squadron to Chinese waters that on one occasion met Chinese belligerence with force. Some Americans felt that the United States, like Britain and France, should have resorted to a policy of military coercion. "Diplomatic intercourse can only be had with this government," the American diplomatic official in China said, "at the cannon's mouth."[38] He recommended cooperation with Britain and France.

Although the United States had remained neutral in the fighting, it, along with

Russia, sent diplomatic representatives to cooperate with the British and French in negotiating new treaties with China. The Treaties of Tientsin, signed by the four powers with China in 1858, opened eleven more ports to foreign trade and residence, enlarged the principles of the treaty settlement of 1842–1844, and conceded foreigners the right of diplomatic representation at Peking, the capital. Later negotiations legalized the traffic in opium, and established the five per cent tariff limit on imports into China. Britain's Treaty of Tientsin now became the basic document in China's international relations.

Through the most-favored-nation principle, the United States in its Treaty of Tientsin, signed on June 18, 1858, gained the privileges Britain and France had had to fight to obtain. It thus followed a policy that has been called "hitch-hiking" imperialism, one that took the benefits of British and French imperialism while incurring none of the risks. When further friction led Britain and France to renew the war with China in 1859 and their troops occupied Peking, the United States again profited from the concessions they forced the Chinese to make. "The English barbarians," the Chinese imperial commissioner wrote to the emperor, "are . . . full of insidious schemes, uncontrollably fierce and imperious. The American nation does no more than follow in their direction."

Although Americans did not use force in China and did not stake out their own concessions in the treaty ports, they accepted the fruits of battle. American merchants lived in the concessions held by other countries and claimed the privileges of the "unequal treaties."

Another group of Americans who claimed those privileges as zealously as the merchants were the missionaries. Those missionaries, mostly Protestant, began arriving in China in the 1830's. Since they could not go inland, and seldom, at first, learned to speak Chinese, they worked primarily among the Co-hong merchants and Chinese servants of the Western traders. Later, they learned Chinese, acted as interpreters for diplomatic officials, and held minor diplomatic posts. Few missionaries at that time saw virtue in China's social system. To them the Chinese were "benighted heathen," who somehow they had to save.

The missionaries converted few Chinese, but did transmit, in a limited way, Western culture to China. Through the treaty provisions forced on the Chinese, they won the right to build churches and hospitals in China, but the protection they demanded and their aggressive tactics antagonized the Chinese. Even if they had been more circumspect, they would probably have caused trouble since their Christian religion was in effect a revolutionary force that required converts to turn against the traditional Chinese way of living and thinking.[39]

More important than the missionaries' influence on the Chinese was their role in interpreting China to America. Through their official reports, books, and magazines they gave Americans, who were hungry for information, a special view of China, and helped to create a philanthropic concern in her that was perhaps as important as the economic interest. Despite their fault-finding, they aroused a sympathy for China that influenced foreign policy and has long remained with Americans.

Anson Burlingame and the "Cooperative" Policy

After the Treaties of Tientsin, Abraham Lincoln's Secretary of State, William H. Seward, followed a policy of cooperating with the other treaty powers in China. The main principles of that "cooperative" policy were that the United States would not seek Chinese territory, would not interfere in China's political struggles "further than to maintain our treaty rights," and would act diplomatically with the other powers in upholding those rights. The man who inaugurated and carried out that policy was Anson Burlingame, the first American Minister to reside in Peking. Burlingame, a former congressman from Massachusetts who obtained his post as a political reward, arrived in China in October, 1861.

Soon after his arrival, Burlingame realized that China's weakness would encourage the other Western nations to partition her. He tried, therefore, to preserve China's territory, and hence equal commercial opportunity, by working closely with the British, French, and Russian Ministers in Peking. That cooperative policy, designed to safeguard American commercial interests, and which held China to a strict observance of the treaties, helped keep foreign powers from taking full advantage of her weakness. Since it was based on personalities and did not appeal equally to the self-interest of all the powers, it lasted only a few years.

Burlingame's charm and efforts to help China understand the ways of the West won the confidence of the Chinese, whom he had long urged to send diplomatic representatives abroad. When he retired in 1867, therefore, they asked him, in his private capacity as an American citizen, to serve as a special minister abroad "for the Management of China's Diplomatic Relations"[40] with the treaty powers. Associated with him and having equal status were a Chinese and a Manchu envoy. Burlingame's own objective in this mission was to revive the cooperative policy by securing direct support from the treaty powers. He also wanted to win sympathy in the West for China.

Acting for China, Burlingame signed a treaty with Secretary of State Seward on July 28, 1868, that added eight articles to the American Treaty of Tientsin. The Burlingame Treaty reaffirmed American privileges in China, disavowed any desire to intervene there, and gave the Chinese the most-favored-nation privileges of travel, visit, and residence in the United States. That was its most significant feature, the opening of the United States to unrestricted Chinese immigration. Burlingame continued his mission to the capitals of Europe, but died of pneumonia in St. Petersburg in February, 1870, before completing it.

The Burlingame mission and relations with China up to that point left Americans with the impression that China was particularly friendly to the United States. "Of all the great powers who have had treaties with them," the *Nation* wrote of the Chinese, "America stands alone as their constant friend and adviser, without territorial aspirations, without schemes of self-aggrandizement—the unpretending but firm advocate of peace and justice." [41] Burlingame's successor at Peking wisely pointed out that such was not the case. The dominant attitude of the Chinese, he said, was one of "antipathy and distrust" toward all foreigners. The Chinese considered Americans, who profited from the concessions gained by British and French arms, the "accomplices in the acts of hostility committed by those powers."

Early Trade with Japan

While the United States was developing its policy in China in the wake of British policy there, it took the lead in opening relations with Japan. Until the discovery of gold in California and the rapid populating of that territory, American interest in Japan had been incidental to the commercial concern in China. When Americans did turn their attention to Japan, they found a people insulated from the outside world.

Japan had not always tried to shut herself off from foreigners. In the sixteenth century she had traded with Western merchants from Spain, Portugal, Holland, and England, and had allowed Christian missionaries, primarily Catholic, to work among her people. At the beginning of the seventeenth century, however, a warrior clan, the Tokugawa, seized power and clamped an iron-fisted dictatorship on the country. The Tokugawa succeeded for two and a half centuries in isolating Japan from outside influences which might have threatened their rule.

The military power of the Western nations was only one outside influence the Japanese feared. They considered Christianity a symbol of that power, a subversive force which they believed menaced their rule. The Tokugawa, therefore, expelled Westerners and persecuted Christians and by 1638 had rooted out Western influence, and with blood and fire had eliminated Christianity. They left one "window" open looking out on the outside world, the port of Nagasaki. They allowed the Dutch, on the tiny island of Deshima in Nagasaki's harbor, a strictly limited trade. After 1790, the Dutch had the privilege of bringing only one ship a year to Nagasaki.

The first American ships to enter Japanese waters did so in the early 1790's. Between 1797 and 1809, during the period of the Napoleonic wars, the Dutch were cut off from their Japanese trade and therefore hired American ships to make their annual voyages to Nagasaki. Then, as the China trade increased, ships sailing the great circle route from San Francisco frequently passed Japan's shores, and in the 1820's American whalers began cruising in Japanese waters. The captains of those ships wanted to use Japanese ports to take on fresh water and supplies, but the Japanese would not allow them to enter. Storms frequently wrecked American ships on Japan's rocky coasts. Since Japanese law decreed death for foreigners entering the country, officials, while not always enforcing the death penalty, imprisoned shipwrecked sailors as criminals and treated them cruelly.

In the 1830's and 1840's American traders in China tried unsuccessfully a number of times to extend their commerce to Japan. During this period the United States made several official efforts, the first being that of Edmund Roberts, to open relations with Japan, but these had failed. The American government wanted the right to use a Japanese port of call for supplies for the China ships and also wanted to obtain humane treatment for shipwrecked sailors. It therefore instructed Commodore James Biddle, who exchanged ratifications of the Treaty of Wanghia, to proceed to Japan and open negotiations for a treaty of commerce. Biddle sailed for Japan and in July, 1846, anchored his two ships at Edo Bay, later called Tokyo, and immediately found himself surrounded by hostile ships. The Japanese rudely rejected his overtures for a treaty and warned him "to depart immediately, and to consult your own safety by not appearing again upon our coast." Biddle withdrew, his mission a failure.

Within a few years as Americans populated the Pacific Coast their interest in Japan, as in China, increased rapidly. The steamships, then beginning to push the sleek clipper ships from the China trade, needed coaling stations in Japan, and the traders, more than ever, wanted a foothold in Japan.

The time was ripe for forcing Japan to open her doors. Russian and British warships were appearing in Japanese harbors, and through the Dutch at Deshima the Japanese knew of what was happening in China and elsewhere in the world. They were aware that the United States had conquered Mexico and had become a Pacific Ocean power. As the ships of the Western nations converged on Japan, she appeared ready for a decided change in her foreign relations and for a remarkable internal revolution. The action of the American government triggered the change.

A naval officer, who returned to the United States in 1851 after visiting Nagasaki, reported that Japan was ready for a commercial treaty. We should try to make one, he recommended, "if not peaceably, then by force."[42] In March, 1852, therefore, Millard Fillmore placed Commodore Matthew C. Perry in command of a naval expedition to Japan, and appointed him special envoy to that country. Perry spent almost a year studying Japan from books and navigation charts he purchased from the Dutch, and in acquiring sample goods from American merchants to show to the Japanese.[43] Then, on July 8, 1853, he led his squadron of four "black ships," two of them steamers, to the entrance of Edo Bay, his gun decks cleared for action. Although Perry's visit was no surprise to the Japanese, his steamers, belching black smoke and sailing against the wind, caused an uproar in Edo.

Perry's instructions told him to obtain a treaty that would protect shipwrecked sailors and open ports to traders and to American ships needing coal and other supplies. He also had orders to survey Japanese coastal waters, if possible, to be firm, and to display "some imposing manifestations of power," but not to use force except in self-defense. When he got in touch with Japanese officials at Uraga, only twenty-seven miles from Edo, they urged him to withdraw to Nagasaki. He refused, threatened to advance directly to Edo, gave them a letter from the President addressed to the emperor, which they accepted because of his threat, and said he would return in the spring with a "larger force" for an answer. He then spent a few days surveying the waters of the bay and sailed south to pass the winter in China.

On his way south Perry took possession of the Bonin Islands. At Okinawa, in the Ryukyus, he established a coaling station, and a year later, on July 11, 1854, made a treaty with the ruler of those islands, giving the United States other privileges there. Perry was an overseas expansionist who wanted the United States to take and hold the Bonins, the Ryukyus, and the island of Formosa. "I assume," he said, "the responsibility of urging the expediency of establishing a foothold in this quarter of the globe, as a measure of positive necessity to the sustainment of our maritime rights in the east." [44] Pierce's expansionist administration, ironically, rejected his proposals.

First Treaties with Japan

While Perry was in China the Tokugawa Shogun, who was the real ruler of Japan, died, and power fell to a less able successor. Perry's demand that the Shogunate open the country to foreign trade had thrown the Japanese officials into consternation. The Shogunate had taken the unprecedented step of submitting the American proposals to the emperor at Kyoto, a mere figurehead, and his anti-Shogun lords. They insisted on continuing the policy of seclusion and rejecting the demands, but the new Shogun's advisers, fearing the power of Perry's ships, decided to receive the Americans amicably.

Thus, when Perry sailed into Edo Bay on February 12, 1854, with seven warships, several months earlier than he had planned because he feared Russian maneuvers in Japanese waters, he met a cordial reception. At the town of Kanagawa, on March 31, Perry signed a simple treaty of friendship, Japan's first with a Western nation. It fell far short of establishing full diplomatic and trade relations, allowing Americans only a restricted trade, under the immediate control of Japanese officials, at two isolated ports. Japan also agreed to treat shipwrecked sailors humanely and to allow an American consul to reside at Shimoda, one of the ports.

This Treaty of Kanagawa said nothing about extraterritorial rights or a coaling station, but it allowed the United States most-favored-nation treatment and hence laid the foundation for future demands. The most significant feature of that treaty was that it ended Japan's long policy of seclusion.

Perry had not really opened Japan's doors; he merely unlocked them. Yet he set in motion forces in and out of Japan that transformed that country. His Treaty of Kanagawa served as a signal for Britain, Russia, and Holland to make similar treaties with Japan within a few months. Through the working of the most-favored-nation principle, the United States automatically obtained all the additional concessions Japan had given them.

As the Treaty of Kanagawa allowed, President Pierce in August, 1854, appointed Townsend Harris Consul General to reside at Shimoda. Harris was a New York merchant of ability who had had considerable experience in China and the Far East, and was, moreover, "a sound, reliable and influential Democrat." With full diplomatic powers, he had the authority to negotiate a commercial treaty, and was aware of the historic importance of his mission. "I shall be the first recognized agent from a civilized power to reside in Japan," he said as he approached the Japanese shore. "This forms an epoch in my life, and may be the beginning of a new order of things in Japan. I hope I may so conduct myself that I may have honorable mention in the histories which will be written on Japan and its future destiny."[45] He arrived at Shimoda aboard a warship in August, 1856.

From the outset Harris encountered a hostility that would have discouraged a man with less fortitude. Fearing difficulties with the people if a foreigner were stationed among them, the Japanese officials asked him to return to the United States. Harris refused. Then they tried to force him to leave, using a campaign of harassment. They stationed guards around the temple he used as his home and obstructed his servants when they shopped. Harris, however, stayed on and through patience and tact gradually won the confidence of the Japanese.

Harris' main objective was to secure a comprehensive commercial treaty that would open the doors Perry had unlocked. Ten months after his arrival, he finally took a first step by persuading the Japanese to sign a convention on June 17, 1857. Basically, it clarified disputed points in the Treaty of Kanagawa and reinforced and expanded privileges, as in matters of trade and extraterritoriality, that Americans were already enjoying through the most-favored-nation principle.[46]

While an improvement on Perry's treaty, the Convention of Shimoda still did not give the United States the commercial treaty it desired. Harris then launched negotiations for such a comprehensive agreement. He played on the Japanese fears of Britain, France, and Russia, warning that as soon as Britain and France ended the "*Arrow* War" with China, they would send fleets to Japan and demand concessions by force. The United States, he said, did not want possessions in Asia. "If you accept the treaty I now offer you, no other country will demand more," he told the Shogun's prime minister in January, 1858. "If I display the treaty to the Europeans, they will desire to conclude identical treaties, and the matter will be settled by the mere sending over of a minister."

Therefore, the Japanese signed a full commercial treaty with the United States on July 29, aboard an American warship in Edo Bay, the first such treaty they made with any Western nation. "The pleasure I feel in having made the treaty," Harris wrote, "is enhanced by the reflection that there has been no show of coercion, nor was menace in the least used by me to obtain it."[47] The agreement opened several more ports to American trade and residence, recognized extraterritoriality for Americans in civil as well as criminal matters, established a fixed tariff, and called for diplomatic representation at the capitals of both countries by each signatory. Other Western nations quickly signed similar treaties a few months later, but Harris' carefully drawn document became the basic one in Japan's foreign relations until 1894.

Since Harris' treaty called for the exchange of ratifications in Washington, Japan sent a mission of seventy-one to the United States in February, 1860, aboard an American warship with the ratified treaty.[48] Following the exchange, Abraham Lincoln appointed Harris Minister to Japan, a post he held until he resigned two years later.

Meanwhile, the Shogunate's efforts to enforce the American treaty, and those made by other foreign nations in 1858, brought to the surface long-smoldering resentment against the Tokugawa clan. Feudal lords hostile to the Tokugawa directed some of the discontent against the government for opening the country to foreign trade and residence, and part of it against the foreigners. Resentment against the Tokugawa and against the foreigners now became synonymous. "Honor the emperor—expel the barbarians" became a popular slogan, taken up especially by the emperor's court at Kyoto and the feudal clans of the west. The antiforeignism was strongest after the signing of the treaties to about 1865.

During this period the Shogunate appeared to act in good faith in attempting to comply with the treaties. Understanding the difficulties confronting the Shogunate, which was losing its power to the lords from the feudal clans in western Japan, Harris himself did not hold it responsible for the lawless acts of its opponents. While the Japanese considered all the treaties as "necessary evils," Harris told Secretary of State Seward, "there is no doubt that the Japanese regard us in a more friendly light than any of the other powers with whom they have come in contact." Not sharing Harris' views of the Japanese, the other foreign diplomats favored a tough policy.

Secretary Seward urged a similar policy, believing that the Japanese might otherwise expel foreigners from the treaty ports. He told Harris that "very large interests, not of our own country only, but of the civilized world, are involved in retaining the foothold of foreign nations already acquired in the Empire of

Japan." [49] On his own responsibility, however, Harris softened the tough policy Seward wanted.

Meanwhile, the nobles at the emperor's court in Kyoto disregarded the treaties. They decided, with the Shogun as a virtual prisoner, that on June 25, 1863, they would begin once again to close the country and expel the foreigners. When the Shogun attempted to carry out an imperial decree to that effect, the foreign diplomats warned him that their governments would resist. Harris' able successor, Robert H. Pruyn, sided with those diplomats and told the Shogunate that the closing of the ports would lead to war with the United States, as well as with the other powers.

"You will represent to the minister of foreign affairs," Seward told Pruyn, "that it is not at all to be expected that any of the maritime powers will consent to the suspension of their treaties, and that the United States will cooperate with them in all necessary means to maintain and secure the fulfillment of the treaties on the part of the Japanese government."

Serious attacks against foreigners took place in June and July when the lord of the Choshu clan, whose holdings overlooked the narrow Straits of Shimonoseki, took upon himself the enforcement of the expulsion decree by firing on American, French, and Dutch ships in the strait. An American warship, the *Wyoming*, at the time in Yokohama, then sailed to Shimonoseki and sank an armed steamer and a brig belonging to the Choshu. Pruyn believed that the prompt retaliation strengthened the hand of the Shogunate and discouraged other antiforeign lords from launching similar attacks.

Nevertheless, the haughty Choshu lord remained defiant until September when an allied fleet of warships, nine British, four Dutch, three French, and one American, heavily bombarded Shimonoseki. The American ship, a rented steamer with a few guns, merely went along in a gesture of cooperation. The Shimonoseki expedition broke the back of the antiforeign movement and gave fresh courage to the vacillating Shogun, who told the foreign diplomats that Japan would respect the treaties. The Shogunate then accepted full responsibility for the Choshu incident, and in October, 1864, concluded a convention with the injured nations, agreeing to pay an indemnity of three million dollars, of which the American share was seven hundred and fifty thousand. Since its share was in excess of the loss sustained, the United States refunded the money in 1883 in a gesture of friendship.

In November, 1865, the Shogunate informed the foreign powers that the emperor had at last fully sanctioned the treaties of 1858 and would revise the tariffs downward. That weakened the antiforeign elements. In 1868, the western clans overthrew the Tokugawa Shogunate and restored the emperor to nominal power. The imperial government then switched from its support of antiforeignism to a policy of encouraging increased foreign intercourse, and Japan was on her way to becoming a great power.

The Principles of American Policy

American policy in the Far East as it developed in the first half of the nineteenth century was based on two related principles: equal commercial opportunity and most-favored-nation treatment. In Japan, those principles helped transform the country and in China they later developed into the Open Door policy. Since the United States did not have a powerful navy available for duty in Asia and no property or leased holdings there, it followed a policy of "hitch-hiking" imperialism in China. It favored peace, free trade, and a reliance on treaties, because such a policy benefited American commerce. Yet in Japan it had not hesitated to use threats of force.

The United States cooperated with the European powers and accepted the results of their imperialism because such a policy brought profits to its commerce and aided American missionary enterprise. Although many Americans have believed that the peaceful policy of abstention won friends in both China and Japan, it seems doubtful.

The policies of free trade and cooperation with European powers in the Far East were the opposites of American policies in other parts of the world. At home Americans, behind a protective tariff wall, denied other countries the right of free trade. In Latin America they upheld the principles of "hands off" as embodied in the Monroe Doctrine, and toward Europe followed the principles of isolation and nonentanglement. Yet they were consistent: everywhere they followed a policy of self-interest.

NOTES

1. For background material on the negotiation, see Joseph B. Lockey, "A Neglected Aspect of Isthmian Diplomacy," *The American Historical Review*, XLI (Jan. 1936), 295–305. See also Rob R. MacGregor, "Treaty of 1846," *Clark University Thesis Abstracts, 1929* (Worcester, Mass., 1939), I, 35–39.

2. Mary W. Williams, "John Middleton Clayton," in Samuel F. Bemis, ed., *The American Secretaries of State and Their Diplomacy* (10 vols., New York, 1927–29), VI, 66. See also David Waddell, "British Honduras and Anglo-American Relations," *Caribbean Quarterly*, V (1957), 50–59.

3. Richard W. Van Alstyne, in "British Diplomacy and the Clayton-Bulwer Treaty, 1850–1860," *Journal of Modern History*, XI (June 1939), 168, says the treaty "made the United States an American power, equal in every respect to the only other first-class American power, Great Britain." For other details, see David Waddell, "Great Britain and the Bay Islands, 1821–61," *The Historical Journal*, II (1959), 59–77.

4. Quoted in William O. Scroggs, *Filibusters and Financiers: The Story of William Walker and His Associates* (New York, 1916), p. 226.

5. James D. Richardson, ed., *A Compilation of the Messages and Papers of the Presidents, 1789–1899* (10 vols., Washington, 1896–99), V, 639. For British policy, see Kenneth

Bourne "The Clayton-Bulwer Treaty and the Decline of British Opposition to the Territorial Expansion of the United States, 1857-60," *Journal of Modern History*, XXXIII (Sept. 1961), 287-291.

6. Quoted in J. Fred Rippy, *The United States and Mexico* (New York, 1926), p. 55.

7. Quoted in James M. Callahan, *American Foreign Policy in Mexican Relations* (New York, 1932), p. 200.

8. Santa Anna claimed that he had no choice. He had to sell because of American threats. See Wilfrid H. Callcott, *Santa Anna: The Story of An Enigma Who Once Was Mexico* (Norman, Okla., 1936), p. 296.

9. Quoted in Lester B. Shippee, *Canadian-American Relations, 1849-1874* (New Haven, 1939), p. 6.

10. Quoted in Cephas D. Allin and George M. Jones, *Annexation, Preferential Trade, and Reciprocity: An Outline of the Canadian Annexation Movement of 1849-50* (Toronto, 1911), p. 384.

11. Quoted in Shippee, *Canadian-American Relations*, p. 44.

12. Quoted in Margaret O. W. Oliphant, *Memoir of the Life of Lawrence Oliphant and of Alice Oliphant, His Wife*, 2nd ed. (2 vols., Edinburgh, 1891), I, 120.

13. For details, see Sister M. Michael Catherine, *Caleb Cushing: Attorney General of the United States, 1853-1857* (Washington, 1955), pp. 181-211 and Richard W. Van Alstyne, "John F. Crampton, Conspirator or Dupe?" *The American Historical Review*, XLI (April 1936), 492-502.

14. Quoted in Claude M. Fuess, *The Life of Caleb Cushing* (2 vols., New York, 1923), II, 167-168.

15. For the full text of the note, dated Dec. 21, 1850, see Daniel Webster, *The Writings and Speeches of Daniel Webster* (18 vols., Boston, 1903), XII, 165-178.

16. New York *Herald*, Jan. 1, 1852, quoted in Arthur J. May, *Contemporary American Opinion of the Mid-Century Revolutions in Central Europe* (Philadelphia, 1927), p. 93.

17. For details, see Merle E. Curti, "Austria and the United States, 1848-1852," *Smith College Studies in History*, XI, No. 3 (April 1926).

18. New York Weekly *Tribune*, Oct. 8, 1853, quoted in Andor Klay, *Daring Diplomacy: The Case of the First American Ultimatum* (Minneapolis, 1957), p. 132.

19. The circular was dated June 1, 1853; see Merle E. Curti, "Young America," *The American Historical Review*, XXXII (Oct. 1926), 54.

20. Quoted in Basil Rauch, *American Interest in Cuba, 1848-1855* (New York, 1948), p. 33.

21. New York *Sun*, July 23, 1847, quoted in Rauch, *American Interest*, p. 59.

22. *Ibid.*, p. 114.

23. First annual message of Dec. 2, 1850, Richardson, *Messages of the Presidents*, V, 78.

24. Note of Dec. 1, 1852, quoted in Foster Stearns, "Edward Everett," in Bemis, *Secretaries of State*, VI, 130.

25. Richardson, *Messages of the Presidents*, V, 198.

26. For an analysis of Southern filibustering in the 1850's based on the assumptions of social psychology, see C. Stanley Urban, "The Ideology of Southern Imperialism: New Orleans and the Caribbean, 1845-1860," *Louisiana Historical Quarterly*, XXXIX (Jan. 1956), 48-73. Cuba held a key position in the ideology of slavery expansionists. See Robert F. Durden, "J. D. B. De Bow: Convolutions of a Slavery Expansionist," *Journal of Southern History*, XVII (Nov. 1951), 452-454.

27. Quoted in Roy F. Nichols, *Franklin Pierce: Young Hickory of the Granite Hills*, 2nd ed. (Philadelphia, 1958), p. 328.

28. For details, see Henry L. Janes, "The Black Warrior Affair," *The American Historical Review*, XII (Jan. 1907), 280–298.

29. Quoted in Ivor D. Spencer, *The Victor and the Spoils: A Life of William L. Marcy* (Providence, R.I., 1959), p. 321.

30. Nichols, *Pierce*, p. 596. Amos A. Ettinger, in *The Mission to Spain of Pierre Soulé, 1853–1855* (New Haven, 1932), p. 368, holds that Soulé had the primary responsibility for the note.

31. For details, see C. Stanley Urban, "The Abortive Quitman Filibustering Expedition, 1853–1855," *Journal of Mississippi History*, XVIII (July 1956), 175–196.

32. Kenneth S. Latourette, *The History of Early Relations between the United States and China, 1784–1844* (New Haven, 1917), p. 15.

33. Quoted in Foster Rhea Dulles, *China and America: The Story of Their Relations since 1784* (Princeton, 1946), p. 17.

34. Quoted in Tyler Dennett, *Americans in Eastern Asia* (New York, 1922), p. 108.

35. John K. Fairbank, in *Trade and Diplomacy on the China Coast: The Opening of the Treaty Ports, 1842–1854* (Cambridge, Mass., 1953), pp. 195–196, points out that the idea of equal treatment of barbarians is an old one in Chinese history and that Kearny's claim that he inaugurated the policy of equal treatment for the United States is weak.

36. Quoted in Dennett, *Americans in Eastern Asia*, p. 141.

37. Ping Chia Kuo, in "Caleb Cushing and the Treaty of Wanghia, 1844," *Journal of Modern History*, V (March 1933), 54, points out that Chinese inexperience in diplomacy made possible Cushing's favorable treaty.

38. Quoted in Dulles, *China and America*, p. 48.

39. For a summary of the early missionary movement, see Paul A. Varg, *Missionaries, Chinese, and Diplomats: The American Protestant Missionary Movement in China, 1890–1952* (Princeton, 1958), pp. 3–30.

40. Knight Biggerstaff, "The Official Chinese Attitude toward the Burlingame Mission," *The American Historical Review*, XLI (July 1936), 684.

41. Quoted in Dulles, *China and America*, p. 68.

42. Commander James Glynn quoted in Dennett, *Americans in Eastern Asia*, p. 257.

43. William L. Neumann, in "Religion, Morality, and Freedom: The Ideological Background of the Perry Expedition," *Pacific Historical Review*, XXII (Aug. 1954), 247–257, points out that Perry's objective was basically commercial.

44. Quoted in Dennett, *Americans in Eastern Asia*, p. 272.

45. Quoted in Carl Crow, *He Opened the Door of Japan* (New York, 1939), p. 90.

46. For details, see Payson J. Treat, *Diplomatic Relations between the United States and Japan, 1853–1895* (2 vols., Stanford, Calif., 1932), I, 44.

47. *Ibid.*, p. 58.

48. For details, see E. Taylor Parks, "The First Japanese Diplomatic Mission to the United States—1860," *Department of State Bulletin*, XLII (May 9, 1960), 1–10 and Chitoshi Yanaga, "The First Japanese Embassy to the United States," *Pacific Historical Review*, IX (June 1940), 113–138.

49. Dec. 19, 1861, quoted in Dennett, *Americans in Eastern Asia*, p. 412.

Chapter Ten

THE CIVIL WAR

W<small>HILE</small> diplomats were establishing Far Eastern policy, internal politics brought the United States to its greatest crisis. Abraham Lincoln's election in November, 1860, led South Carolina to secede from the Union on December 20. By February 1, 1861, Mississippi, Florida, Alabama, and Louisiana had followed her. When Lincoln became President on March 4, therefore, his main problem was the secession crisis. He made his position clear in his inaugural address. "I have no purpose, directly, to interfere with the institution of slavery in the States where it exists," he said, but added that "no State, upon its own mere motion, can lawfully get out of the Union." [1]

Lincoln's Secretary of State, William H. Seward of New York, had his own ideas on how to meet the crisis. He had been Lincoln's main rival for the Republican nomination and believed that he instead of Lincoln should rightfully have been President. Convinced that he had the most ability in the administration, he considered himself a prime minister who would make policy while the untried Lincoln accepted the role of a figurehead. On April 1, therefore, a mere three weeks after inauguration, Seward sent Lincoln a memorandum headed "Some Thoughts for the President's Consideration."

"We are at the end of a month's administration," Seward said, "and yet without a policy either domestic or foreign." [2] He suggested filling the gap with a policy of hostility or war against Spain, France, Britain, and Russia—one that would win back the loyalty of the seceded states and avoid a civil war. Lincoln put aside his Secretary's desperate proposal and did nothing to create foreign enemies for his government. He told Seward that he himself would conduct the government with "the advice of all the Cabinet."

Less than two weeks later, with the dawn of April 12, Southern cannon opened fire on Fort Sumter in Charleston's harbor. Two days later the tired smoke-stained garrison surrendered. On the following day, Lincoln called for seventy-five thousand militia for three months' service and for a special session of Congress. Four years of civil war had begun.

Belligerent Status for the South

Other Southern states, eleven in all, joined the secession movement. On April 19 Jefferson Davis, president of the Confederacy, offered to commission privateers to prey on Union shipping. Two days later Lincoln proclaimed a blockade of Southern ports and announced that the Union would treat privateers as pirates. Lincoln wanted to regard the war as a mere domestic quarrel, one that would not involve foreign nations and would thus avoid questions of neutral rights. Lincoln's proclamation of blockade, however, violated his own theory. The Union, according to international law, could not impose a blockade without a state of war and without placing restrictions on neutral shipping that would give the Confederacy belligerent rights.

News of Lincoln's blockade proclamation reached London on May 4, and England immediately recognized the flaw in the Union's theory. "The Northern party in fact," an English writer said, "demanded that we should recognize a state of war by admitting their blockade, and at the same time deny a state of war by treating Southern vessels as pirates." The British cabinet decided quickly to treat the civil conflict as a full-fledged war. On May 13 Queen Victoria issued a proclamation of neutrality recognizing the belligerency of the Confederacy, meaning that England recognized the South as having a responsible government capable of conducting war.

Lincoln, Seward, and the people of the North objected to Britain's neutrality proclamation first as unfriendly and then as "premature." Charles Francis Adams, Lincoln's Minister to Great Britain, arrived in London just as the Queen issued the proclamation. He considered it the first step toward foreign recognition of the Confederacy as an independent nation, which it was not. It was merely a customary proclamation of impartial neutrality, similar in principle to the position the United States had taken during the Canadian rebellion of 1837. Other European governments considered Britain's action proper. They followed her example and also accorded the South belligerent rights. From the beginning, therefore, the Civil War raised the old questions of maritime rights between belligerents and neutrals.

Although the maritime questions were old ones, the Civil War reversed the traditional positions of the United States and Britain.[3] For the first time, the United States held the position of the big navy power and its opponent that of the small navy belligerent. For the first time England was the major neutral, and for the first time also the United States insisted on the rights of the belligerent rather than on the privileges of the neutral.

Another unique feature of the diplomacy of the Civil War was that the European nations for the first time could apply a body of international law covering maritime rights that had been adopted at the end of the Crimean War. The principles adopted in the Declaration of Paris of April, 1856, abolished privateering, stated that a neutral flag covered all enemy goods except contraband, that neutral goods, except contraband, were free from capture under an enemy flag, and that a blockade was binding only if strong enough to prevent ships from entering enemy ports.

The Declaration of Paris embodied most of the neutral principles the United States had upheld since achieving independence. Yet when the European powers had asked the United States to adhere to the declaration, it had refused because it would not give up the right of privateering. At the time the United States believed that in a war with a stronger naval power it would need privateers to supplement the striking power of its small navy.

In the Civil War, however, privateering gave an advantage to the South, which had no navy. A week after Jefferson Davis said he would commission privateers, therefore, Secretary Seward offered to adhere unconditionally to the Declaration of Paris which would now benefit the Union. Speaking for the other powers as well as for herself, Britain would accept only a conditional adherence, saying that the ban on privateering would not apply during the Civil War. One reason for this statement was that the South, when approached informally about accepting the declaration, had said it would adhere to the principles of Paris except for the article on privateering.

In practice privateering did not help the South. The European nations closed their ports to both Northern and Southern ships of war and their prizes. The Confederacy, with its own ports blockaded, as a result, had no ports where it could send prizes. It tried privateering in 1861, but after that year it gave up the effort; blockade-running proved more lucrative.

Seward had refused the offer of the European powers for a conditional adherence to the principles of the Declaration of Paris, but told the British that the United States would follow them in practice. After the South's unsuccessful efforts at privateering, it also followed those principles during the course of the war.[4]

The Question of Recognition

Agreement on maritime principles did not, however, solve the major diplomatic problem of the Civil War: would Europe, primarily England and France, the two most powerful countries in Europe, recognize the Confederacy as an independent nation? The North's primary objective was to prevent such recognition. The

South's aim was to win it, mainly through European political intervention. Although recognition depended more on the success of Confederate arms than on diplomacy, the material advantages to be derived from it were considered important enough to help bring victory to the South. Northern diplomacy and intelligence activities, as well as victories in battle, helped prevent such recognition.

Europe's recognition of the South's belligerency had given the Confederacy the status of a nation for purposes of fighting the war. Southern statesmen hoped from the beginning that England and France would take the next step and aid them in the same way France had helped the fighting colonies in the American Revolution. "England will recognize us," Jefferson Davis had said on the way to his inaugural, "and a glorious future is before us." With hopes high the South tried immediately to aid its armies through diplomacy. It sent agents, without official status, to Europe to work for recognition, to float loans, to spread propaganda, and to buy ships and supplies. European statesmen would not receive the Confederates officially. "I shall see the Southerners when they come," the British Foreign Secretary, Lord John Russell, wrote to his Minister in Washington, "but not officially, and keep them at a proper distance."[5]

To add new strength to the South's diplomatic offensive Jefferson Davis, in August, 1861, appointed James M. Mason of Virginia a special commissioner to England and John Slidell of Louisiana a commissioner to France to replace Confederate agents already there. Those veteran diplomats ran the blockade from Charleston to Havana, where they took passage on the British mail steamer *Trent* for the neutral port of St. Thomas in the Danish West Indies. From St. Thomas they expected to sail for England.

Capture of the TRENT

Meanwhile, in the West Indies Captain Charles Wilkes, commanding the Union sloop of war *San Jacinto* recently returned from an African cruise, heard that the Confederate commissioners were on the *Trent*. On his own responsibility, as the *Trent* steamed through the Bahama channel on November 8, he overhauled her, fired two shots across her bow, and over the protests of the British captain, plucked Mason and Slidell from her decks. He then took the two agents to Boston where they were imprisoned.

Wilkes' bold deed created great excitement in both England and the United States. Northerners, hungrily seeking some kind of a victory, rejoiced over the capture of two important Confederates and the insult Wilkes had given England. Cheering crowds in Washington serenaded Wilkes at his home as "the hero of the *Trent*"; the House of Representatives voted him a gold medal; and the Secretary of the Navy commended him for his "brave, adroit and patriotic conduct." The Northern press almost unanimously praised him. "As for Commodore

Wilkes and his command," *The New York Times* said, "let the handsome thing be done. Consecrate another *Fourth* of July to him."[6]

Resenting the insult to their flag, Englishmen shook with anger. They suspected Seward, whom they distrusted, of wanting to provoke an international war and believed that Wilkes had acted under orders. Ships of the Royal Navy cleared their decks for action and eight thousand troops boarded transports for Canada. Henry Adams, a son of the American Minister to Britain, wrote to his brother from London: "This nation means to make war. Do not doubt it."[7]

A Northern politician working in England to counter Southern propaganda was alarmed by London's grim excitement. "If it be not too late," he wrote to Lincoln, "let me beseech you to forbear—to turn if need be the other cheek, rather than smite back at present."

European statesmen—French, Italian, Prussian, Danish, and Russian—all agreed that the United States had done the wrong thing. Wilkes, according to international law, could stop and search the *Trent*, and if he discovered contraband, he could take the ship into port for judgment by a prize court. He compounded his blunder by taking only Mason and Slidell while allowing the *Trent*, which carried Southern diplomatic dispatches which might be considered contraband, to proceed. His act, moreover, smacked of impressment, a practice the United States had always denounced.[8]

Although knowing little of the fine points of international law, President Lincoln grasped the difficulties of the case. At first he had been pleased by the capture, but soon realized that his country held a weak position. He did nothing to encourage the public rejoicing. "One war at a time," he told Seward. Yet the President did not like to retreat before British threats and hence sought a solution that would not appear a surrender. That was difficult. The British cabinet insisted that a "gross outrage and violation of international law has been committed." "The danger of a collision," Lord Russell told an American politician, "might be averted by the surrender of the rebel commissioners."

Prime Minister Palmerston and Russell drew up an ultimatum threatening war. When Prince Albert, Queen Victoria's dying consort, read the dispatch, he cautioned restraint and toned it down. The revised instructions sent to the British Minister in Washington, dated November 30, 1861, and approved by Queen Victoria, demanded release of the two prisoners and a suitable apology. If the United States did not indicate compliance within seven days, the Minister had orders to break off diplomatic relations and return to London, but he also had private instructions not to threaten war.

Lincoln's cabinet met on Christmas day to consider the British demands. Finally, after long discussion, all eight members agreed that the government must release Mason and Slidell. It was a wise decision. Failure to meet the English demands probably would have meant war, and victory for the South. Although

Lincoln feared the political consequences arising from public anger over the surrender, the public reaction, except for the anti-British press, was less violent than he and his advisers had expected.

One reason for the relatively calm reaction was the tone of Secretary Seward's reply of December 26 to Lord Russell, which he immediately released to the newspapers. He admitted that Captain Wilkes had made a mistake and promised to release Mason and Slidell. But, the Secretary said, Wilkes had been correct in seizing the Confederates since "persons, as well as property, may become contraband."[9] This was a novel and untenable interpretation of contraband. Wilkes erred, Seward himself wrongly pointed out, in not sending the ship to an American port as a prize. In forcibly removing men from the decks of a neutral ship, Seward added, Wilkes had been guilty of doing what Britain had long practiced despite American protests.

"We are asked to do to the British nation," Seward said, "just what we have always insisted all nations ought to do to us."[10] Great Britain, according to his note, at last appeared to accept the principles of neutrality concerning impressment that the United States had defended in 1812.

Lord Russell accepted Seward's note as satisfactory, despite its masterly confusion of legal concepts, though he said he did not assent to all of the Secretary's reasoning. Despite the furor the *Trent* affair had created, neither the British government nor the people really wanted a war with the United States. Such a war would have opened Canada to invasion, would have placed the British merchant marine at the mercy of American privateers, and would have aligned Britain, the leader of the world crusade to stamp out slavery, on the side of the slaveholding South. To the satisfaction of both England and the United States, Lincoln's government thus peacefully overcame its first major diplomatic crisis of the war.[11]

That crisis brought no benefit to the South. When the Confederate commissioners arrived in England at the end of January, 1862, public interest in them had almost disappeared. In referring to them the London *Times* had said, "We should have done just as much to rescue two of their own Negroes."[12]

King Cotton

The South's main diplomatic weapon, other than the power of its armies, was the coercive economic power of cotton, on which English and French textile industries were critically dependent. In England alone some five million people, about a fifth of the population, in one way or another relied on the textile industries for a living. The South supplied about eighty per cent of England's raw cotton. The London *Times* said that "so nearly are our interests intertwined with America that civil war in the States means destitution in Lancashire."[13] Southerners believed that England and France's dependence on their cotton would force those countries to recognize the Confederacy as independent and to end any long war by intervening on their side.

Without the South's cotton, a South Carolina senator had claimed, "England would topple headlong and carry the whole civilized world with her, save the South. No, you dare not make war on cotton. No power on earth dares to make war upon it. Cotton is king!" [14] These were the principles of the "King Cotton" theory, a Southern article of faith comparable to the states' rights doctrine.

So much an article of faith was the theory that the South could not wait for the North's blockade to take effect. It tried to produce an immediate cotton famine with an embargo. "Let the blockade be effectual," a Southern spokesman said in the summer of 1861, "the stricter the better; the sooner will it be over; the sooner will rescue from Europe reach us; the sooner will the strong hand of the 'old country' remove our difficulties." [15] So the South at first actually welcomed the Union blockade.

In the first year of the war state and local officials in the South, and the people themselves, prevented the export of cotton. Southerners refused to plant a new crop and before the end of the war as a matter of patriotic duty had burned some two and a half million bales of cotton. Later, as its forces blockaded and occupied Southern ports, the North helped to strangle the export of cotton. During the entire war only a trickle of Southern cotton reached Europe. Yet neither England nor France, nor any other European nation, recognized the Confederacy. They did not for many reasons, but one reason stemmed from a fatal flaw in the King Cotton theory.

In normal times English and French brokers stored a one-year supply of cotton, but when the Civil War began their warehouses bulged with bales good for two and a half years. Bumper crops in the years immediately preceding the war and the fact that the South had already shipped its 1860 crop had built up the surplus. Thus the war itself, the South's self-blockade, and the North's blockade, came as a boon to British and French cotton brokers. They profited from the high wartime prices cotton brought. The war, in fact, saved England's cotton industry from a severe panic and turned impending ruin, in some instances, into glowing prosperity. A long war, therefore, worked to the advantage of the cotton industrialists.

As the British and French textile manufacturers exhausted their stored cotton supplies, Europeans had found, by late 1862, substitutes in cotton from India and Egypt, and in linen and woolen goods. The Union, as its armies captured cotton, moreover, made strenuous efforts to ship it to England to help alleviate the shortage.

Nevertheless, the working class suffered as thousands of English and French cotton spindles stopped. Tens of thousands of British textile operators had no work because of the "paralysis of the cotton trade." In Lancashire the mills ran half time

KING COTTON BOUND; OR,
THE MODERN PROMETHEUS

for a while, then two days a week, and finally they stopped. At times hundreds of hungry unemployed cotton operatives, with pinched faces, stood around the newspaper offices staring at bulletin boards, searching for news of Northern victories and the end of the war. In France the textile industry in fifteen Departments was prostrate; three hundred thousand people were destitute. In Rouen alone, some thirty thousand operatives out of fifty thousand were unemployed.[16]

The starving British workers, however, did not agitate for intervention at any time during the war, mainly because they believed in the Union cause, and because poor relief, public and private, and some supplied by Northern philanthropists, helped ease their suffering. They saw the war as a struggle of free against slave labor. By 1863, moreover, the war began definitely to favor the North, and other pressures for English and French intervention eased.

Some students of Civil War diplomacy have maintained that Britain did not intervene to break the cotton shortage because "King Corn," or wheat from the North, was more vital than cotton. If Britain had intervened, that would have meant war with the United States and the consequent cessation of the flow of wheat during bad harvests. Since the British needed Northern wheat more than Southern cotton, this theory holds; they did not dare intervene.[17] Critics of the theory have pointed out that England was able to obtain wheat from the interior of Russia and elsewhere without real difficulty. She bought it from the United States in large quantities because it was cheaper and because she could use wheat as a medium of international exchange when she sold war supplies to the Union.

Another theory, also based on economic motivation, has held that England's swollen war profits weakened the coercive power of King Cotton. Both North and South bought most of their war supplies from England, giving handsome profits to her munitions makers. Soaring textile prices also offered huge profits to cotton brokers and industrialists, and to linen and woolen manufacturers. Britain's shipowners profited from the South's destruction of the Union's merchant marine, their main prewar rival. Some English shipowners even rejoiced over the war. According to the "war profiteer" theory, therefore, England profited from the Civil War to such an extent that she did not want to intervene and thereby kill prosperity.[18]

Still another reason why Britain and France did not intervene was that of divided opinion among their people. Their upper classes had long believed that the American democratic experiment would collapse. "Democratic institutions," the London *Times* said after Lincoln's election, "are now on their trial in America." The impending collapse of American democracy did not displease Europe's aristocracy. England's governing aristocracy, for instance, had much in common with the South's planter class and little sympathy for the more democratic society of the North. "You know," an upper-class character in Disraeli's novel *Lothair* said, this Southern Colonel "is a gentleman; he is not a Yankee. People make the greatest mistakes about these things." Most of Britain's leaders, men like Prime Minister Palmerston and Foreign Secretary Russell, favored the South. They were convinced at first that the South's independence was inevitable.[19]

Britain's liberal humanitarians from first to last favored the Union. Yet even some of them wavered when Lincoln made it clear that he did not intend to declare war on slavery. British liberals, men like John Bright and Richard Cobden, saw the Civil War as the test of democracy and shared the desire of the working classes for a Northern victory. Even though without the right to vote, the working people made their influence on government felt through mass meetings and other demonstrations in favor of the North. "It is the duty of the working-men," one mass meeting resolved in January, 1862, "to express their sympathy with the United States in their gigantic struggle for the preservation of the Union."

One old rhyme even had the workingmen sing:

> Our mules and looms have now ceased work, the Yankees are the cause.
> But we will let them fight it out and stand by English laws;
> No recognizing shall take place, until the war is o'er;
> Our wants are now attended to, we cannot ask for more.[20]

Mediation Offers

The attitude of Britain's upper classes toward the Civil War contributed to another crisis for the North in the fall of 1862. Secretary Seward had insisted from the beginning that foreign intervention would mean enlarging the war and that the Union would reject all offers of mediation. If Europe intervenes, he said in

July, 1862, "this civil war will, without our fault, become a war of continents—a war of the world." Yet after the crushing Northern defeat in the Second Battle of Bull Run, August 29–30, England's rulers were more convinced than ever that the Union cause was hopeless. On September 14, therefore, Palmerston suggested to Russell that the time had come for Britain and France to propose a joint mediation to the Union government "on the basis of a separation."

Three days later, Lord Russell replied that he agreed and suggested that "in the case of failure, we ought ourselves to recognize the Southern States as an independent State."[21] Meanwhile, General Robert E. Lee followed the Confederate victory at Bull Run with an invasion of Maryland. Union forces under General George B. McClellan stopped the Confederates on September 17, in the Battle of Antietam.

Palmerston learned of the results at Antietam at the end of September and on October 22 told Russell "that we must continue merely to be lookers-on till the war shall have taken a more decided turn." The British cabinet, therefore, voted against Russell's mediation scheme, which, if carried out, would probably have meant war with the Union.

A Southern victory at Antietam might have changed the course of the war. Instead, that battle delivered a mortal wound to Confederate chances for diplomatic recognition. Possible English intervention depended fundamentally on the success of Southern arms. Antietam, because of its diplomatic significance, was thus one of the decisive battles of the war.

Lord Russell's scheme was not the only effort at mediation. Emperor Napoleon

BROTHER JONATHAN PUTS ENGLAND AND FRANCE IN THEIR PLACES

This cartoon reflects Northern resentment against those countries for their supposed sympathy for the Confederacy.

III of France and the French upper classes also favored the Confederacy and believed that the North could not defeat the South. Napoleon had talked of mediation soon after the Civil War began. In October, 1861, he had approached the British with a proposal for a joint intervention to break the Northern blockade. Lord Russell would not consider it. "But we must wait," he told Palmerston on October 17. "I am persuaded that, if we do anything, it must be on a grand scale. It will not do for England and France to break a blockade for the sake of getting cotton."[22]

Napoleon was always ready to recognize the Confederacy and intervene if England would support him. He dared not risk a lone intervention because of divided opinion at home.[23] Basically, then, the South's hopes for direct foreign intervention rested with England.

Shortly after the collapse of the British mediation scheme, Napoleon made his most determined bid to intervene. Would Britain and Russia act jointly with France, he asked, in proposing a six-months armistice and a suspension of the blockade? The plan would have assured independence for the South. The North was certain to reject it. Britain and Russia would have nothing to do with it.[24]

Later, in February, 1863, Napoleon offered a friendly mediation, suggesting that Northern and Southern representatives meet on neutral ground to discuss peace terms. Seward promptly rejected the offer and both houses of Congress supported him with a joint resolution of March 3, denouncing mediation as "foreign interference." The emperor, deeply involved in Mexico, then gave up the idea of interfering directly in the Civil War.

One of the reasons Lord Russell had given for not joining Napoleon's armistice proposal, as advanced formally in November, 1862, was Russia's refusal to join.[25] Whether or not Russia participated would probably have made little difference, yet all during the war Northerners had gratefully received expressions of Russian good will. Russia would do nothing that would weaken the United States as a counterweight to Britain. She wanted to remain on good terms with the Union so she could use its ice-free ports as bases for cruisers in case of war with England.

This was Russia's motive when she sent her Baltic fleet to New York in September, 1863, and her Pacific squadron to San Francisco in the following month. The threat of a European war over troubles in Poland which would pit Russian ships against the British fleet prompted the visits which ended in April, 1864. Northerners viewed the naval visits as a demonstration of Russian support for the Union cause and greeted the Russians enthusiastically as friends who had come to help in time of need. The fleet visits did boost Northern morale, and even Union prestige abroad. They also contributed to the legend of long-standing Russian friendship for the United States. "God bless the Russians," the Secretary of the Navy had written.[26]

The Slavery Question

The issue of slavery profoundly affected diplomatic moves during the Civil War. Lincoln knew that Europe's liberals and humanitarians were disappointed because he had not converted the war into a crusade to end slavery. Southern statesmen, too, realized that a main obstacle to obtaining foreign support was slavery. As early as May, 1861, the first Southern commissioners in England had reported that "the public mind here is entirely opposed to the Government of the Confederate States of America on the question of slavery, and that the sincerity and universality of this feeling embarrass the Government in dealing with the question of our recognition." Antislavery sentiment in France, a Confederate agent disclosed, was a "deep-rooted antipathy, rather than active hostility, against us." [27]

Lincoln's stand on slavery was directed towards winning the support of the Republicans, War Democrats, and loyal border slave states. The effect of those policies on foreign policy was at first of secondary concern. Finally, however, he had to take European opinion into account. Since his armies had failed and the fear of foreign intervention haunted him, the President believed in the summer of 1862 that he had to take some drastic action to save the Union. Charles Francis Adams reported from London in July that a definite stand against slavery would greatly strengthen the Union position in Europe.

On July 22 Lincoln called his cabinet members together. "I have got you together to hear what I have written down," he said. Then he read a proclamation he had prepared as a war measure freeing slaves in the rebelling states. Seward suggested that the time was not right for the proclamation because of military reverses. It should, he said, be "borne on the bayonets of an advancing army, not dragged in the dust behind a retreating one." [28] Recognizing the logic of the argument, the President put the paper in his pocket and waited for the right time.

All through the summer Lincoln waited anxiously for a victory so that he could issue his preliminary Emancipation Proclamation. Although the Battle of Antietam was more a draw than a victory, he used it to herald emancipation. On September 23 newspapers carried Lincoln's announcement that on January 1, 1863, all slaves in any state in rebellion would be free. The proclamation did not apply to slaves in the border and loyal slave states.

The immediate reactions, at home and abroad, to the emancipation policy were disappointing to the Union government. Northern critics and British liberals said it did not go far enough; Southerners and their sympathizers denounced it as a desperate effort to achieve victory through the incitement of the slaves to rebellion; and European skeptics pointed out that it was not a broad humanitarian gesture, but a limited war measure. A few of Britain's liberals, however, were pleased. "I wish the 1st of January to be here, and the freedom of the Slaves declared from Washington," John Bright told an audience at Rochdale. "This will make it impossible for England to interfere for the South, for we are not, I hope, degraded enough to undertake to restore three and one half millions of Negroes to slavery."

Although disappointed in the criticism of his new slavery policy, Lincoln remained firm, and on January 1, 1863, issued the final proclamation. Immediate public reaction to it was mixed, but ultimately its effect abroad, particularly in England, proved decisive in winning public opinion to the North. In France liberals hailed it, and in England Charles Francis Adams reported it had created a wide sympathetic influence. "It has rallied all the sympathies of the working classes," he said, "and has produced meetings the like of which I am told, have not been seen since the days of the corn laws." Another American in London reported that "the President's Emancipation policy is working here" and more than anything else has helped prevent war with England.[29]

From many of those meetings came resolutions commending Lincoln's action. Reports from Spain, Switzerland, and elsewhere told of popular approval of his policy. Yet the Emancipation Proclamation had little immediate effect on the slaves themselves. It applied only to areas the Union government did not control and left slavery undisturbed where the government could control it.

Finally, with defeat appearing certain, the South itself offered to abolish slavery if England and France would offer recognition. In December, 1864, at the suggestion of Judah P. Benjamin, the Confederate secretary of state, Jefferson Davis sent Duncan F. Kenner, a Louisiana planter, to Europe with the offer of abolition. Napoleon was willing to accept it, but not alone. "He is willing and anxious to act with England," Slidell wrote, "but will not move without her."[30] For England the offer came too late, even in the opinion of pro-Confederate Englishmen.

All during the war Southerners had been aware of Europe's hostility to slavery. This last futile diplomatic effort was an official recognition that slavery had been a serious handicap in their quest for foreign support.

The Union Blockade

Another vital factor that contributed to the South's ultimate defeat was the Union blockade. Lincoln tried to strangle the South with the greatest commercial blockade yet undertaken, stretching the Union navy over thirty-five hundred miles of coast from Alexandria on the Potomac River to the Mexican border at the mouth of the Rio Grande River. In past maritime wars, the United States had complained of Britain's wide-ranging blockades as being ineffective, as being mere "paper blockades," for under international law a blockade, to be binding on third parties, had to be effective. In other words, the blockading nation had to station

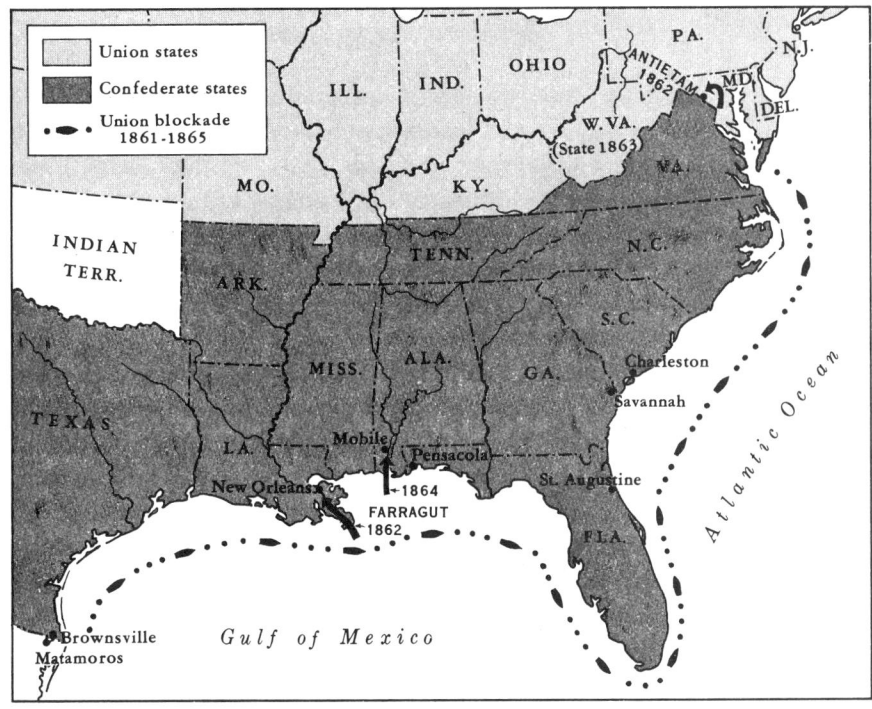

THE CIVIL WAR BLOCKADE OF THE SOUTH

enough ships outside blockaded ports to make their use clearly dangerous. The South argued, as had the United States against England, that the Union blockade was never effective enough to be binding under international law.

When the Civil War started, the blockade was in fact a blockade in name only. The Union navy had only about ninety ships on its register. Some were not seaworthy and others were old wooden sailing ships. Only twenty-four of its steamers were fit for service. Almost all the seaworthy ships were widely dispersed, but the South began the war without a navy. Thus, the North could, and did, use anything that would float and could mount a few guns as blockade ships.[31] Later, the Union government bought and built ships for purposes of blockade and used them to cover the entire Confederate coast, with its many rivers, bays, and inlets.

Since Napoleon would not act without British support, the main problem in maintaining the blockade was whether or not Britain would respect it. "You will not insist that our blockade is to be respected, if it be not maintained by a competent force," Secretary Seward told Charles Francis Adams. But, he added, "the blockade is now, and it will continue to be, so maintained, and therefore we expect it to be respected by Great Britain."[32] Despite Southern protests and the fact that at first the blockade was ineffective, Britain accepted it as binding because her statesmen realized it was to her long-term interest to encourage the United States in upholding the principle of a loose, but legal, blockade.[33]

As early as November, 1861, the British Minister in Washington said the blockade was "very far from being a mere Paper Blockade. A great many vessels are captured; it is a most serious interruption to Trade." [34] The London *Times* pointed out that "England is too great to be often neutral, and should not forget that the arguments she might now employ against her neighbour might, we know not how soon, be retorted against herself with all the force of admissions." England, therefore, accepted Seward's reasoning that "the true test of the efficiency of the blockade will be found in its results."

Since the North could not legally blockade the ports of a neutral country, it resorted to another practice acceptable to the British, one designed to stop blockade leaks through neutral ports. It restricted neutral rights through the doctrine of "continuous voyage" first used by the British in 1805. As in the blockade itself, the United States went beyond the British practice in applying that doctrine.

Taking advantage of its immense coastline with its many shallows and indentations, the South pierced the blockade with specially constructed blockade-runners that ran all during the war and supplied Southerners with at least minimum necessities. British ships from London and Liverpool, for example, sailed for Havana, Nassau, or other neutral ports in the West Indies with blankets, arms, and ammunition. From the West Indies the small, swift blockade-runners would carry the goods to Confederate ports.

The Union navy tried to stop that trade by seizing neutral ships for breach of blockade before they reached the West Indies on the ground that the "ultimate destination" of their cargoes was a blockaded port. The United States Supreme Court in two notable opinions at the end of the war, that of the *Bermuda* in December, 1865, and the *Springbok* in December, 1866—both British ships— upheld the doctrine that goods sent from one neutral port to another but destined ultimately for a blockaded port, were in fact making a "continuous voyage" to the belligerent port and hence were legally subject to seizure.

In a third opinion in December, 1866, that of the British merchant ship the *Peterhoff*, the Supreme Court sanctioned an enlarged interpretation of the doctrine of continuous voyage. When captured, the *Peterhoff* was on her way to Matamoros, Mexico, with a cargo destined for the Confederacy. Since the goods would not go through a blockaded port and would complete the last lap of their journey over-land, no breach of blockade was involved. Nevertheless, as the cargo was destined for the Confederacy, the court said the voyage was continuous and ruled that the contraband goods in the cargo were liable to seizure.

European jurists attacked the American practice of expanding the doctrine of continuous voyage, but the British, even though they suffered most of the property losses through Union captures, did not protest. They were pleased with the American reversal on neutral rights, being again concerned with their own long-term interests.

The Confederate Navy

Although British maritime policy generally favored the Union, Northerners believed that in one important area Britain failed to fulfill the obligations of a neutral: the building of warships, and of their equipment, for the Confederacy in her shipyards and factories. One reason for the diplomatic difficulties that arose over this serious problem was that international law had not yet clearly defined a belligerent's right to build or buy warships in a neutral nation. Another reason was that Northerners resented Britain's loose interpretation of her own neutrality laws.

When the Civil War began, the South, without a navy and without its own means of building one, had planned to build one in neutral ports, primarily British. The United States had at the time one of the world's largest merchant fleets and wanted to prevent the South from creating a navy which might destroy its merchant fleet and break the blockade. Britain's neutrality law, the Foreign Enlistment Act of 1819, modeled after the American neutrality law of 1818, forbade the equipping and arming of ships in British ports for a belligerent's use. Britain's interpretation of her own law, however, allowed her shipbuilders to construct ships for belligerents if the builders did not themselves arm and equip them.

Taking advantage of England's loose neutrality laws, Captain James D. Bulloch, a Confederate agent with naval experience and a knowledge of maritime and international law, made arrangements with English firms for the building of unarmed warships for his government. During his first month in England, he made a contract for the steamer *Oreto*, supposedly a merchant ship destined for a firm in Palermo. That ship left Liverpool in March, 1862, and at Nassau several months later took on British armament and equipment to become the Confederate cruiser *Florida*. On July 29, another of Bulloch's powerful ships, the *Enrica* or "No. 290," steamed out of Liverpool. Off the Azores she took on English guns and supplies, and even an English crew, and became the Confederate commerce destroyer *Alabama*.

The *Florida*, the *Alabama*, and other Confederate raiders, such as the *Shenandoah*, burned and sank over two hundred and fifty Union merchant ships. By forcing shipowners to sell their ships or transfer them to foreign registry, the Confederates practically drove the Northern merchant fleet from the seas. The career of the *Alabama*, the most successful raider, in particular angered Northerners. It was, they said, a British ship, built in Britain, armed with British guns, manned by a British crew, and allowed purposely to escape from Liverpool by an unfriendly British government. Could anyone call this neutral conduct?

Charles Francis Adams, the son of John Quincy Adams and, like his father, one of America's outstanding diplomats, had tried to prevent the *Florida* and *Alabama* from leaving England. He and the American Consul at Liverpool had given evidence to British officials that the *Florida* was intended for Confederate service, but the Crown's law officers said that the American Minister had not presented "sufficient proof," so the ship sailed unmolested.

The case of the *Alabama*, however, was different. Adams had gathered a mass of affidavits as the ship neared completion, exposing her true character, and had given them to the proper British officials. The evidence convinced the Queen's Counsel, who advised "detaining the vessel." "It appears difficult," he said, "to make out a stronger case of infringement of the Foreign Enlistment Act." Then, on July 31, 1862, after a critical delay caused by the derangement of the Queen's Advocate, Lord Russell sent telegrams to Liverpool and nearby ports to stop the *Alabama*. He had, however, acted too late. The ship was gone.[35]

Although Northerners believed that British officials had connived at the *Alabama*'s escape and hence had violated neutrality, there was no convincing evidence to support that view. Later, Charles Francis Adams himself said that he believed Lord Russell had sincerely tried to prevent the ship's escape.

Before the *Alabama*'s escape, Captain Bulloch had contracted with her builders, Laird Brothers of Birkenhead, for two armored steamers, each to mount four nine-inch rifled guns in turrets and an iron ram, or "piercer," at the bow. Those armored ships, known as the Laird rams, would have been a greater menace to the Union than the *Alabama*.

The raiders destroyed commerce but in themselves could not determine the course of the war. Potentially more powerful than any ship in the Union navy, the Laird rams practically alone could, when completed, crush the wooden block-ade ships, smash the blockade, and perhaps win the war.[36] The Secretary of the Navy said the departure of the rams must be stopped at all hazards. "We have no defense against them," he warned. "It is a matter of life and death." As the rams became ready for delivery to the Confederates in 1863 they touched off the last major diplomatic crisis of the Civil War.

The watchful Charles Francis Adams presented Lord Russell with persuasive evidence of the true character of the Laird rams and urged him to seize them im-mediately. Finally, on September 5, he warned that if the rams escaped, he would regard it "as practically opening to the insurgents full liberty in this kingdom" to build a navy. "It would be superfluous in me," he said, "to point out to your Lordship that this is war."[37]

The threat was unnecessary. Russell had already ordered the rams held. He told Adams on September 8 that "instructions have been issued which will prevent the departure of the two ironclad vessels from Liverpool." Later, the British govern-ment bought the rams for the Royal Navy. It had never intended allowing the rams to depart. Lord Russell had merely waited for decisive evidence before seizing them.

One reason why the British seized the rams on their own initiative was the fear of retaliation. In July, 1862, at the time of the *Alabama*'s escape, Congress considered a bill empowering the President to commission privateers. The administration revived the privateering bill in January, 1863, as the Laird rams crisis became serious. The bill became law on March 3. Since the South had no merchant marine that privateers could attack, it appeared that the Union intended to use a "flood of privateers" against neutral shipping, primarily British, if the blockade were broken. Lord Russell saw in this the danger of clashes with the Union that would lead ultimately to war. Then, if war came, the entire British merchant fleet would be prey to the privateers. This, in essence, was the threat used to offset that of the Laird rams.

The British government, therefore, tried a new and tighter neutrality policy. On April 5, 1863, it seized the *Alexandra*, another commerce raider intended for the Confederacy, on the ground she was about to violate the neutrality law. "The orders given to watch, and stop when evidence can be procured, vessels apparently intended for the Confederate service will, it is hoped," Russell wrote on April 7, "allay the strong feelings which have been raised in Northern America by the escape from justice of the *Oreto* and *Alabama*." [38]

By June, moreover, alarm over what future *Alabamas* might do to British commerce in a war replaced Britain's earlier satisfaction over the destruction of the rival Northern merchant fleet. In September the London *Times* demanded that the government make the sale of warships to belligerents clearly illegal. If England were at war, it said, then "any power with a little money or credit, however otherwise insignificant, might purchase in the ports of any maritime State a squadron sufficient to occupy a large portion of our navy." For these and other reasons, including the victories of Union armies, the British enforced a more rigid neutrality policy, seized the Laird rams, and ended their last diplomatic crisis with the North.

The Laird rams crisis, however, did not end Confederate efforts to build a navy. When Britain began tightening her neutrality policy, Confederate agents, with the approval of Napoleon III, tried to build ships in France. In April, 1863, Captain Bulloch and John Slidell drew up contracts for four cruisers to be built at Nantes and Bordeaux. In June, Bulloch signed a contract with a French firm for two formidable double-screw ironclad rams. If the rams had gone to sea under the Confederate flag, the American Consul-General in Paris said later, "they would not only have opened every Confederate port to the commerce of the world, but they might have laid every important city on our seaboard under contribution."

Those ships never sailed for the Confederate navy. Through the activities of secret agents who bribed French clerks in the employ of business firms with whom the Confederates dealt, Union diplomats in France gathered documents showing that the ironclads were being built for the South. [39] The Northern Minister in

Paris then protested and showed the emperor the indisputable evidence. Since the emperor would not now allow the ironclads to be delivered, the shipbuilders sold them to Denmark and Prussia who were at war with each other. When Denmark refused one of the rams, it finally reached the Confederates, who named it *Stonewall*, but the war ended before they could make use of it. Thus, although the French government itself had encouraged the South more than had the British government, France contributed far less to the Confederate navy.

When General Robert E. Lee met General Ulysses S. Grant in the village of Appomattox Courthouse on April 9, 1865, to discuss terms of surrender, the Union had already won the diplomatic war. The United States was fortunate in its foreign relations. The Union lost only its large merchant fleet that had already begun a decline as ships of steam and iron were replacing those of wood and sail.[40] Union diplomacy, moreover, had proved itself competent and effective.

NOTES

1. Roy P. Basler, ed., *The Collected Works of Abraham Lincoln* (9 vols., New Brunswick, N.J., 1935–55), IV, 263, 265.

2. *Ibid.*, IV, 317.

3. For details, see James P. Baxter, III, "The British Government and Neutral Rights, 1861–1865," *The American Historical Review*, XXXIV (Oct. 1928), 9.

4. Details are in Charles Francis Adams, "The Negotiation of 1861 Relating to the Declaration of Paris of 1856," *Massachusetts Historical Society Proceedings*, XLVI (Oct. 1912), 23–84.

5. Quoted in Ephraim D. Adams, *Great Britain and the American Civil War* (2 vols., London, 1925), I, 67.

6. *Ibid.*, I, 220n.

7. The secretary of the American legation in London felt the same way. "The excitement among the English people," he said on Dec. 6, 1861, "is strengthened daily and unless checked will drive the nation to war." Sarah A. Wallace and Frances B. Gillespie, eds., *The Journal of Benjamin Moran, 1857–1865* (2 vols., Chicago, 1949), II, 918.

8. For a discussion of the legal issues involved, see John Bassett Moore, *A Digest of International Law* (8 vols., Washington, 1906), VII, 768–779. For the attitude of France and her influence on the outcome, see Lynn M. Case, "La France et l'affaire du 'Trent,'" *Revue historique*, fasc. CDLIX (Juillet–Septembre 1961), 57–86.

9. Quoted in Frederic Bancroft, *The Life of William H. Seward* (2 vols., New York, 1900), II, 238.

10. *Ibid.*, II, 241.

11. For details, see Charles Francis Adams, "The Trent Affair, 1861–1862," *Massachusetts Historical Society Proceedings*, XLV (Nov. 1911), 35–148; his "The Trent Affair," *The American Historical Review*, XVII (April 1912), 540–562; and Arnold Whitridge, "The Trent Affair, 1861: An Anglo-American Crisis that Almost Led to War," *History Today*, IV (June 1954), 394–402.

12. Jan. 11, 1862, quoted in E. D. Adams, *Britain and the Civil War*, I, 238.

13. April 13, 1861, quoted in Frank L. Owsley, *King Cotton Diplomacy: Foreign*

Relations of the Confederate States of America, 2nd ed., rev. by Harriet C. Owsley (Chicago, 1959), p. 11.

14. M. B. Hammond, March 4, 1858, *ibid.*, p. 16. A senator from Georgia told his Northern colleagues that "Cotton is king and it will find means to raise your blockade and disperse your ships." James M. Callahan, *The Diplomatic History of the Southern Confederacy* (Baltimore, 1901), p. 80.

15. Quoted in Owsley, *King Cotton Diplomacy*, p. 24.

16. For a summary of the French cotton famine, see Henry Blumenthal, *A Reappraisal of Franco-American Relations, 1830–1871* (Chapel Hill, N.C., 1959), pp. 153–156.

17. The theory is stated in Louis B. Schmidt, "The Influence of Wheat and Cotton on Anglo-American Relations during the Civil War," *Iowa Journal of History and Politics*, XVI (July 1918), 400–439, and refuted in Eli Ginsberg, "The Economics of British Neutrality during the American Civil War," *Agricultural History*, X (Oct. 1936), 147–156.

18. Martin P. Claussen, in "Peace Factors in Anglo-American Relations, 1861–1865," *Mississippi Valley Historical Review*, XXVI (March 1940), 511–522, points out that British commercial interests wished to avoid conflict with the United States.

19. See, for instance, Henry Adams, *The Education of Henry Adams* (Boston, 1918), pp. 114–115. Wilbur D. Jones, in "The British Conservatives and the American Civil War," *The American Historical Review*, LVIII (April 1953), 527–543, shows, however, that the Conservative party was neutral in attitude and that it even favored the North.

20. Quoted in Joseph H. Park, "The English Workingmen and the American Civil War," *Political Science Quarterly*, XXXIX (Sept. 1924), 452.

21. Quoted in Henry Adams, *Education*, p. 153.

22. Quoted in Spencer Walpole, *The Life of Lord John Russell* (2 vols., London, 1889), II, 344.

23. See Louis M. Sears, "A Confederate Diplomat at the Court of Napoleon III," *The American Historical Review*, XXVI (Jan. 1921), 255–281.

24. For details, see Charles Francis Adams, "A Crisis in Downing Street," *Massachusetts Historical Society Proceedings*, XLVII (May 1914), 372–424.

25. Albert A. Woldman, in *Lincoln and the Russians* (Cleveland, 1952), p. 133, has concluded that the Russian government's attitude, in effect, determined the issue of intervention. In May, 1863, Seward, in turn, refused to consider intervention in a Polish rebellion against Russia. See Harold E. Blinn, "Seward and the Polish Revolution of 1863," *The American Historical Review*, XLV (July 1940), 828–833.

26. Entry of Sept. 25, 1863, Howard K. Beale, ed., *Diary of Gideon Welles* (3 vols., New York, 1960), I, 443. On Dec. 12 Welles wrote that "Our Russian friends are rendering us a great service," p. 484.

27. The quotations are in Owsley, *King Cotton Diplomacy*, pp. 530, 531.

28. Quoted in Henry W. Temple, "William H. Seward," in Samuel F. Bemis, ed., *The American Secretaries of State and Their Diplomacy* (10 vols., New York, 1927–29), VII, 76.

29. John M. Forbes, April 29, 1863, quoted in Douglas H. Maynard, "The Forbes-Aspinwall Mission," *Mississippi Valley Historical Review*, XLV (June 1958), 80.

30. March 6, 1865, quoted in Owsley, *King Cotton Diplomacy*, p. 538.

31. For the initial blockade effort, see Richard S. West, *Mr. Lincoln's Navy* (New York, 1957), pp. 57–72.

32. May 21, 1861, quoted in Bancroft, *Seward*, II, 170.

33. On Feb. 10, 1862, the London *Times* explained, for instance, that "a blockade is by far the most formidable weapon of offence we possess. Surely we ought not to be over-ready to blunt its edge or injure its temper?" Quoted in Baxter, "British Government and Neutral Rights, 1861–1865," *The American Historical Review*, XXXIV (Oct. 1928), 12.

34. Nov. 29, 1861, quoted in E. D. Adams, *Britain and the Civil War*, I, 255.

35. For details, see Douglas H. Maynard, "Plotting the Escape of the *Alabama*," *Journal of Southern History*, XX (May 1954), 197–209 and his "Union Efforts to Prevent the Escape of the *Alabama*," *Mississippi Valley Historical Review*, XLI (June 1954), 41–60.

36. The Confederate Secretary of the Navy believed that a seagoing ironclad could "traverse the entire coast of the United States, prevent all blockades, and en-counter, with a fair prospect of success, their entire Navy." Quoted in Theodore Ropp, *War in the Modern World* (Durham, N.C., 1959), p. 169.

37. Quoted in Brooks Adams, "The Seizure of the Laird Rams," *Massachusetts Historical Society Proceedings*, XLV (Dec. 1911), 297. For additional details, see Martin B. Duberman, *Charles Francis Adams, 1807–1886* (Boston, 1961), pp. 310–313 and Wilbur D. Jones, *The Confederate Rams at Birkenhead: A Chapter in Anglo-American Relations* (Tuscaloosa, Alabama, 1961), which is based on British documents.

38. Quoted in E. D. Adams, *Britain and the Civil War*, II, 136.

39. Harriet C. Owsley, "Henry Shelton Sanford and Federal Surveillance Abroad, 1861–1865," *Mississippi Valley Historical Review*, XLVIII (Sept. 1961), 211–228. Shelton, the American Minister to Belgium, was in charge of the Union secret service in Europe during the Civil War.

40. For details, see George W. Dalzell, *The Flight from the Flag: The Continuing Effect of the Civil War upon the American Carrying Trade* (Chapel Hill, N.C., 1940).

Chapter Eleven

POSTWAR EXPANSION AND ARBITRATION

D$_{URING}$ the Civil War, Spain and France took advantage of American distress and attempted to regain lost influence in North America. Spain temporarily re-annexed the Dominican Republic, which had won a precarious independence in 1844 after revolting against Haiti's control. Fearing that without help from a strong power independence from Haiti's Negro rulers could not last, the republic's whites had sought protection, and even annexation, at different times from Britain, France, the United States, and Spain.

Although the Spanish government itself at first did not actively seek to regain the island republic's territory, in 1860 some of its officials acting on their own made arrangements to take it over. James Buchanan was so deeply involved in the slavery problem that he could do nothing to stop the Spaniards. On March 18, 1861, therefore, the Dominican Republic's president, acting primarily on his own responsibility, proclaimed his country annexed to Spain. On April 2, Secretary of State William H. Seward sent a note to Spain invoking the principles of the Monroe Doctrine, threatening reprisals, and asking her to get out of the Dominican Republic.

Seward's words had no effect. Spain's queen, supported by a revived nationalism at home, proclaimed the Dominican Republic once again Spanish territory on May 19. Spain said she would defend her hold on the island republic with all means at her disposal. Occupied with the problems of the Civil War, Seward, therefore, could do nothing to stop her, but on June 19, through the American *chargé* in Madrid, he formally protested the annexation as violating the Monroe Doctrine. Spain replied that she had occupied the country at the request of the Dominicans themselves and refused to recognize the validity of the Doctrine.

Within two years, when Spain's rule proved disappointing, the Dominicans revolted and asked the United States to assist them and to recognize their independence from Spain. Seward, who would not heed the insurgent pleas, followed a policy of strict neutrality toward the revolution. Since the Union was trying to prevent European nations from recognizing and helping the Confederacy, he could not afford to recognize Dominican independence or aid the insurgents there. In reprisal, Spain might recognize the Confederacy.

Finally, the guerilla resistance, the heavy costs of the enterprise, and the scourge of yellow fever among her troops contributed to Spain's decision to leave. Her last troops left Dominican soil in July, 1865. Neither American threats nor fear of the Monroe Doctrine had forced Spain to end her rule; it was primarily the resistance of the Dominican people themselves.

In another intervention, however, Spain voluntarily accepted the Monroe Doctrine. In a quarrel with Peru, a Spanish naval squadron seized the Chincha Islands off Peru's coast in April, 1864. Seward protested the seizure in May and spoke of the danger to "the general peace of nations." Spain had no designs on those islands. As soon as she heard of the seizure she disavowed it. In August her Minister of State said Spain would not question the Monroe Doctrine "in or against Peru." "If President Monroe were alive and on the spot," he added, "he should see nothing running counter to his famous declaration." [1]

The Triple Intervention in Mexico

While Spain intervened in the Dominican Republic, France attempted to create a puppet empire in Mexico. That effort was a far more menacing challenge to the Monroe Doctrine than anything Spain could do. The French intervention had its roots in the civil strife that had disrupted Mexico since she had achieved independence from Spain.

From 1858 to 1861, in what is known as the War of the Reform, two factions struggled for control of Mexico. One side, headed by the Zapotec Indian, Benito Juárez, was liberal, republican, anticlerical, and friendly to the United States. This faction had agreed, in the McLane-Ocampo Treaty of December 14, 1859, to make Mexico a virtual protectorate of the United States by giving it the right to intervene and exercise a police power in Mexico. The United States Senate, divided by the slavery issue, had, however, rejected the treaty in May, 1860.[2] The other Mexican faction, supported by the landed aristocracy and the church hierarchy, was conservative, fearful of the United States, and friendly to Europe. It wanted a monarchy, with some European prince on the throne.

During the Mexican civil war, guerilla bands destroyed property owned by Englishmen, Spaniards, Frenchmen, and Americans, and even killed some foreigners. Foreign governments expected Mexico to pay for those losses and also the debts various Mexican governments had owed them, threatening to force payment.

Finally, the liberals emerged victorious. Juárez, in a plain black coach and in simple black clothes, entered Mexico City as constitutional president on January 11, 1861. For the first time, a civilian ruled Mexico. Since his administration was without money, on July 17 it declared a suspension of two years on payments to foreign creditors, though Juárez was willing to pay for damages that could be proved genuine. Therefore, on October 31, Britain, France, and Spain signed a convention in London calling for a joint expedition against Mexico to force her to pay her debts. They said they would not take Mexican territory, tamper with her independence, or interfere with the right of Mexicans to choose their own government.[3]

The European nations asked the United States, also one of Mexico's creditors, to join them. Secretary Seward tactfully refused. The United States, he said, preferred to avoid foreign alliances and wished to retain the good will of its Mexican neighbor, but, he added, the President did not question their right to use force to redress their grievances.

Spanish troops landed in Mexico in December, and in January, 1862, English and French detachments joined them. After some disagreements, the three powers dissolved their alliance, and England and Spain withdrew from Mexico in May. Napoleon III, however, had plans of his own. Conservative Mexican exiles in France had convinced him that the Mexican people would welcome French troops, a monarchy, and the stability they would bring. He therefore kept his soldiers in Mexico and made impossible demands on Juárez' government. He demanded an indemnity, payment of debts' to France, and redemption at face value of certain bonds a Swiss banker and owner of Mexican mines had obtained from the conservative government at about one-twentieth of their worth. Napoleon then sent some thirty thousand fresh troops to Mexico, who drove Juárez' guerilla forces before them and occupied Mexico City in June, 1863.

Maximilian in Mexico

Napoleon planned to create a Catholic monarchy in Mexico, linked to France. It would, he thought, counterbalance the United States in North America and be "an insuperable barrier" to further American expansion southward at Mexico's expense. France would benefit, he believed, through special financial privileges. He himself might at the same time win back some of the Catholic good will in France that he had lost in supporting Italian unification against the Pope.

As Napoleon desired, an assembly of notables, composed of Mexican conservatives, invited Archduke Maximilian, thirty-one-year-old brother of Austria's Hapsburg emperor, to become emperor of Mexico. Maximilian had insisted as a condition of acceptance that the people should vote their approval of the offer. The French occupation forces, terrorizing the liberal opposition, organized favorable plebiscites. On April 10, 1864, therefore, Maximilian, gentle-hearted but naïve, signed an agreement known as the Convention of Miramar. Napoleon had made the terms. He promised to support Maximilian with French troops until 1867. In return, Maximilian pledged himself to pay for the intervention and debts Mexico owed France.

With his beautiful young wife, Carlota, a Belgian princess, Maximilian arrived in Mexico City in June. Maximilian had grand ideas. He wanted to be a benevolent ruler who would regenerate strife-torn Mexico, but from the beginning his empire was a disappointment. Only French bayonets kept it from falling apart. Juárez' guerilla forces still fought and controlled large areas of the countryside.

Americans, North and South, had been watching developments in Mexico with special concern. Lincoln's government disliked the French intervention but at first did nothing. It did not even register a formal protest, not daring to alienate France and thereby drive her to recognize the Confederacy. Seward himself moved cautiously. He told the American Consul in Paris that "we are too intent on putting down our own insurrection, and avoiding complications which might embarrass us, to seek for occasion of dispute with any foreign power." [4]

Yet when the French asked Seward at the end of 1863 to recognize the monarchial regime that had been proclaimed in July, he refused to do so, saying that the United States would maintain a strict neutrality in the war between France and Mexico. The Union continued to recognize Juárez as the head of Mexico's legitimate government, whereas most European governments recognized the empire. In his correspondence with the French, Seward did not mention the Monroe Doctrine, but its principles were implicit in many of the statements he made expressing opposition to foreign intervention.

Confederate statesmen offered to jettison the Doctrine and support Maximilian in exchange for French recognition of the Confederacy's independence. Maximilian himself sympathized with the South. In January, 1864, Jefferson Davis even appointed a minister to "His Imperial Majesty, Maximilian," but the emperor, when he arrived in Mexico, hoping to avoid difficulties with the Union, would not receive the Confederate agent. Then the Confederates threatened an "offensive and defensive alliance" with the North after the war to force Maximilian from Mexico if he and France did not recognize the Confederacy. Still, the French and Maximilian would not deal officially with the South. [5]

In the North, meanwhile, as Union armies smashed their way to decisive victories, the people, the government itself, and Seward became bolder in denouncing the French intervention. "Only the influence of executive moderation holds the popular action under restraint now," Seward told the American Minister in France on February 8. Reflecting popular sentiment, the House of Representatives resolved unanimously on April 6 that the United States considered the French action in Mexico as "deplorable" and would not "acknowledge any monarchical Government erected on the ruins of any republican Government in America under the auspices of any European Power."[6]

"I think," the American Minister in Paris told Seward two weeks later, that "the European press generally looks upon those resolutions as implying that the United States Government will not rest satisfied with the condition of things established by the French in Mexico." The French Minister of Foreign Affairs, aware of the resolution, when he next saw the American Minister greeted him with this question. "Do you bring us peace, or bring us war?" Seward assured the French that the congressional opinions were "not in harmony with the policy of neutrality, forbearance, and consideration which the President has so faithfully pursued."[7]

Maximilian and Napoleon both realized that the fate of their Mexican empire probably hinged on the outcome of the Civil War. Maximilian tried on his own, therefore, to win Union recognition through diplomacy and propaganda, hoping that Lincoln would appreciate his efforts to bring stability to Mexico.[8] With the end of the Civil War and Lincoln's death, Maximilian's hope for an accommodation died. He could expect no consideration, though he tried to obtain it, from Lincoln's successor, Andrew Johnson. On accepting the nomination for Vice-President, Johnson had threatened to "attend to this Mexican affair" after the war by using Union soldiers to wipe out the French. Other Americans shared his views. The Chicago *Tribune* even boasted that "California alone would drive Maximilian from Mexico if our government would give her permission."

The United States could now afford to state its policy in stronger terms. United and powerful, it had a formidable navy and a battle-hardened army. Generals Grant, Sherman, and others wanted to lead their veterans against the French in Mexico. American troops massed on the Mexican border, and veterans enlisted as volunteers in Juárez' forces. Seward believed, however, that he could get the French out of Mexico peacefully, through diplomacy. His tone toward France became increasingly firm.[9]

When the French suggested recognition of Maximilian in exchange for their withdrawal, Seward refused. French authority in Mexico, he said on November 6, is in direct antagonism to the policy and basic principles of the American government. That language upset the French Minister of Foreign Affairs. "If you mean war," he asked, "why not say so frankly?"

Seward persisted. In polite terms, a month later, he asked the French to withdraw from Mexico, and on February 12, 1866, requested "definitive information of the time when French military operations may be expected to cease in Mexico." He still did not mention the Monroe Doctrine.

Napoleon, who had grown tired of the Mexican venture, announced on

February 22 that he would withdraw his troops. "What I really want," he told the American Minister in France, "is to get out of Mexico altogether." The intervention there was a costly failure, but he wanted to retreat as gracefully as possible and not appear openly to violate the terms of the Convention of Miramar. He had written to Maximilian a month earlier that "though the departure of our troops may prove a momentary cause of weakness, it will have the advantage of removing all pretext for intervention on the part of the United States."[10] On April 5, therefore, he announced that he would pull out his troops in three detachments, one in November, another in March, 1867, and the last in the following November. He withdrew, in fact, sooner than he had promised. The last French soldiers left Mexico on March 12.

Maximilian, the victim of bad advice, would not leave. Despite the entreaties of Napoleon and of friends to flee to the safety of Europe, he chose to fight to the end. Finally, Juárez captured him at Queretaro. Seward and the kings of Europe begged Juárez to spare the fallen Hapsburg, but the Indian leader insisted that Maximilian must die and serve as a warning to other would-be conquerors of Mexico. As decreed by a courtmartial, Maximilian fell before a Mexican firing squad on June 19, 1867.

There are many puzzling questions in this tragedy, but one is of particular concern to American diplomacy. Did fear of the United States force Napoleon to give up the Mexican adventure? A number of circumstances apparently contributed to his decision. Since the expedition was costly and had never been popular in France, Napoleon probably tried to regain some public support by withdrawing his troops, which were needed in France anyhow since war with Prussia threatened. Finally, and probably most important, he could not ignore the increasing hostility of the United States and its formidable military position in North America. Whatever the precise reason for the French withdrawal, it marked an impressive victory for the Monroe Doctrine.[11]

Even though the American government had not invoked the doctrine by name, that victory won respect for the Monroe Doctrine in Europe. What had done so was not the doctrine's principles but America's increased power and knowledge that the United States could, and probably would, prevent European nations from intervening in the affairs of its neighbors. The French withdrawal also elevated the status of the Monroe Doctrine at home. From that time on the American people regarded it as a fundamental principle of national policy.

Seward in the Caribbean

While Seward had striven to ease France out of Mexico, he had also tried to carry out a program of expansion. The Civil War had, for some, buried the expansionist fervor of Manifest Destiny and Young America of the 1850's, but had not destroyed Seward's own unlimited visions.[12] He was a prewar expansionist who had written in 1846 that "our population is destined to roll its resistless waves to the icy barriers of the north, and to encounter oriental civilization on the shores of the Pacific."[13] He held similar and larger views in the 1860's, after the war. As Secretary of State under Andrew Johnson he made a number of attempts to annex new territory.

Since the Union navy had encountered difficulties in controlling Confederate blockade-runners and cruisers in the Caribbean during the Civil War, Seward and American naval officers believed that the United States should acquire a naval base on one of the Caribbean islands. In January, 1866, Seward took a month's cruise to the West Indies, ostensibly for his own health and for that of his son. While there, he visited islands suitable for naval bases. One that impressed him was St. Thomas in the Danish West Indies, or Virgin Islands. The fine harbor there was, in fact, his first stop.

Seward had first expressed interest in buying the three islands of that group to the Danish Minister in Washington, General Waldemar R. Raasloff, about a year before the cruise.[14] Having just lost two provinces in a war with Prussia, the Danes did not want to sell at that time. Before Seward's cruise, however, a new Danish ministry had come to power and had authorized Raasloff to negotiate a sale. The Secretary returned from his cruise on January 28, and the next day began discussions with Raasloff, who suggested twenty million dollars "as the absolute minimum price" for the islands. The negotiations dragged on and then shifted to Copenhagen. By July, 1867, the United States and Denmark agreed on seven and a half million dollars as the price for two of the islands.

Before signing a treaty ceding them, Denmark insisted on allowing the people there to vote on the annexation. Seward at first objected, saying the vote would cause unnecessary delay, but finally yielded and a treaty of transfer was signed at Copenhagen on October 24.

The treaty was unpopular in the United States. Congress considered the purchase extravagant and unnecessary. On November 25 a congressman from Wisconsin offered a resolution denouncing "any further purchases of territory." The House of Representatives immediately passed it. "I intend to serve notice upon the kingdom of Denmark" the congressman said, "that this House will not pay for that purchase."[15] In the same month an earthquake and a hurricane devastated the Danish Islands, leading many Americans to question more than before the alleged advantages of acquiring them.

Despite popular opposition, President Johnson and Seward went ahead with the treaty. In two plebiscites in January, 1868, the people of both islands voted overwhelming approval of the annexation. At the end of that month the Danish government ratified the treaty, but in the United States the treaty could not get by the Senate, where Johnson had sent it in December.

General Raasloff, who had become Denmark's Minister of War, returned to the United States in December, 1868, to use his "personal influence" with the Senate. He appeared before the Senate Committee on Foreign Relations, gave dinners for its members, and hired American propagandists to explain the alleged advantages of the treaty to the people. He wasted his efforts. The Senate committee opposed the treaty unanimously, but out of consideration for Raasloff, tabled it instead of recommending rejection.

Raasloff even sought the help of Ulysses S. Grant, when Grant became President, but failed to get it. "That is entirely Seward's plan," Grant said, "with which I desire absolutely nothing to do." Later, in March, 1870, the Senate Committee on Foreign Relations gave the Danish treaty an adverse report and that ended the matter.

While trying to buy the Danish islands, Seward also attempted to acquire a naval base in the Dominican Republic, on spacious Samaná Bay on the east coast of the island. Since it could command the Mona Passage into the Caribbean, American expansionists called it the "Key of the West Indies."

Expansionists, in fact, had long desired that bay. President Pierce had sent a special agent, William L. Cazneau, to the Dominican Republic in July, 1854, to negotiate a commercial treaty and to buy or lease the bay. "Such a place in the occupancy of the United States, constantly resorted to by our steamers and other vessels," his instructions said, "could not fail to give stability to the Dominican Republic."[16] Cazneau obtained the treaty on October 5, but Britain and France persuaded the Dominican government to omit the cession of Samaná Bay and to make other changes. The United States would not accept the mutilated treaty and recalled Cazneau in December.

After the Spanish intervention, the republic's rulers, chronically in need of money, offered to sell the bay and then the entire country to the United States. Seward, with Johnson's support, was eager to buy. He visited the island, stopping at Haiti as well as at the Dominican Republic, on his "health cruise," and induced the President to say in his annual message of December, 1868, that the people "of the two Republics of the island of St. Domingo" wanted to annex themselves to the United States. Haiti had not offered itself, but its ruler was willing to cede the harbor of Môle St. Nicolas and adjacent land if the United States would assume that country's debt to France.

As in the case of the Danish islands, Congress opposed the annexations. "We cannot have colonies, dependencies, subjects," the New York *Tribune* had declared in denouncing Seward's projects, "without renouncing the essential conception of democratic institutions."[17] Supporting those sentiments, the House of Representatives defeated a resolution authorizing a protectorate over Haiti and the Dominican Republic on January 13, and on February 1, voted decisively against another calling for annexation of the Dominican Republic.

Seward's plans to obtain naval bases in the Caribbean failed because the people, absorbed in recovery from the Civil War and in industrial growth at home, would not support his expansionist program.[18] "The true interests of the American people," the Philadelphia *Press* had said appropriately, "will be better served at this important period of our national history by a thorough and complete development of the immense resources of our existing territory than by any rash attempts to increase it."

Despite the lack of popular support, not all of Seward's schemes failed. He also wanted to expand into the Pacific, and tried unsuccessfully to buy the Hawaiian Islands. In 1867 he did succeed in annexing the atoll-enclosed Midway Islands, located about a thousand miles northwest of Hawaii. Seward's other annexation, Alaska, far more impressive than the tiny Midways, also took the American flag to the Pacific.

The Annexation of Alaska

When Russia offered to sell Alaska, or Russian America, antiexpansionist sentiment was so strong that the American people did not really want to buy it. The Tsarist government, however, wished to sell because Alaska was an economic liability and virtually indefensible against a strong naval power such as Britain.

During the Crimean War, Britain and Russia had agreed to neutralize Alaska, but that conflict had convinced Russian statesmen they could not hold it in a future war. The Russian Minister to the United States, Baron Edouard de Stoeckl, had recommended selling Alaska to the United States in December, 1856. Other Russian statesmen did the same. The government, therefore, had instructed Stoeckl to forward any offer the United States might make for the province. He reported in January, 1860, that the Assistant Secretary of State and a senator from California had asked him if Russia would sell Alaska. They said President Buchanan favored purchasing the province and was willing to pay as much as five million dollars. Since the Russian government was not yet prepared to make a final commitment, and the Civil War intervened, nothing came of the informal negotiations.

In December, 1866, a council of ministers in St. Petersburg discussed the future of Alaska. Russia had administered Alaska through the Russian-American Company, a trading company whose charter had expired in 1862 and which now faced bankruptcy. If Russia wanted to retain Alaska, she either had to subsidize the company or take over direct administration of the unprofitable territory. The government decided to sell.[19]

Since Russia wanted to strengthen America as a counterbalance to Britain, the United States was the logical customer. The Russian government, therefore, commissioned Stoeckl, who was in Russia at the time, to return to Washington to sell Alaska for no less than five million dollars, a moderate price when one considers that the Russians knew of the existence of gold there. Stoeckl was convinced that Americans would some day take over Alaska as they had Oregon and California. When they learned of the gold, he thought, they would probably swarm into the province in great numbers, and Russia would not be able to stop them.[20] Fortunately for Russian policy, Stoeckl returned to the United States at a time when Seward eagerly sought new territories.

Few Americans shared Seward's expansionist views and, except for some on the Pacific Coast, few even knew of Alaska's existence. Yet in January, 1866, the legislature of the Washington Territory (which had been carved out of the Oregon Territory thirteen years before) sent President Johnson a statement urging an agreement with Russia which would give American fishing vessels, whose crews wanted to buy fuel, water, and provisions, visiting privileges in Alaskan ports. Not knowing of Russia's decision to sell, Seward tried to use the petition as the means of persuading her to give up Alaska. Stoeckl arrived in New York in February, 1867, and soon after dropped a hint through a friend of Seward's that Russia, if persuaded, might sell Alaska. That was all that Seward needed to move quickly.

On his arrival in Washington, about March 8, Stoeckl went immediately to the State Department. Seward brought up the fishing petition and Stoeckl assured him that Russia would not grant the desired privileges. Seward then asked if Russia would sell Alaska and Stoeckl said yes. After Seward obtained the President's approval, the two men began swift negotiations.

Seward offered five million dollars; Stoeckl asked for seven million. Realizing that the Secretary had set his heart on the purchase, Stoeckl refused to lower the price. Seward finally agreed to seven million and later offered an additional two hundred thousand dollars to obtain Alaska free of all claims by the Russian-American Company. The two men then sealed the bargain, and Stoeckl used the new transatlantic cable to obtain the Tsar's approval.

On Friday night, March 29, Stoeckl called the Secretary of State at his home. "I have a dispatch, Mr. Seward, from my Government by cable," he said. "The Emperor gives his consent to the cession. Tomorrow, if you like, I will come to the department, and we can enter upon the treaty."

Seward, with a satisfied smile, said, "Why wait till to-morrow, Mr. Stoeckl? Let us make the treaty to-night."[21]

Then, in the middle of the night after they had aroused startled secretaries, Seward and Stoeckl went to the State Department. Lights burned steadily until four o'clock in the morning of March 30, when they signed the treaty. Later that day the President sent a special message to a surprised Senate asking approval for "a treaty for the cession of Russian America."

Seward and Stoeckl had kept their negotiations so secret that no one, except a handful of people in Washington, had suspected that the United States was seriously considering the purchase. The news of Seward's treaty, therefore, surprised everyone and shocked some. Newspaper editors tried hastily to discover what available information there was on Alaska and to comment on the treaty.

Antiadministration papers explained to an ignorant public that Alaska's only products were icebergs and polar bears. They called it "Seward's Folly," "Frigidia," "Walrussia," and "Johnson's Polar Bear Garden." "Will the newly acquired coast be erected into a territory?" the New York *Evening Post* asked. "Or are we to invent and add to our present system a colonial policy . . .?" The New York *Tribune* said disparagingly, "We have more territory than we want."

The Senate was hostile. Charles Sumner, chairman of its Committee on Foreign Relations, even advised Stoeckl to withdraw the treaty rather than risk rejection. Stoeckl refused. Despite the antagonism, Seward believed that he could win enough popular support to force the treaty through the Senate. He launched a nation-wide campaign to convince the people that Alaska was worth its price. It had, his propaganda said, known resources in fish, furs, and lumber, and its commercial and strategic importance in the Pacific Ocean area justified the purchase. Seward used another effective argument, that of Russian friendship. Since Russia wanted to sell and the administration had already agreed to buy, the argument went, America's debt of gratitude to her for support during the Civil War called for completion of the treaty.

Sumner, who did not share Seward's dream of expansion in the Pacific and even considered the Alaska treaty of dubious advantage, now became the Secretary's most powerful ally in obtaining Senate support, apparently because he wanted to retain Russia's friendship. "It is difficult to see," he said in a memorable three-hour speech in defense of the treaty, "how we can refuse to complete the purchase without putting to hazard the friendly relations which happily subsist between the United States and Russia."

Seward also advanced four other main reasons for approving the treaty: special commercial advantages that possession of Alaska would bring to the Pacific Coast, extension of American dominion, spread of republican institutions, and Britain's exclusion from this part of the American continent.[22] The Senate approved the treaty on the same day, April 9, 1867, by a majority of 27 to 12. So far, Seward's policy of secret diplomacy, swift action, and propaganda, had worked admirably.

One hurdle still remained. The House of Representatives had to appropriate the money. Impeachment proceedings against Johnson so delayed consideration of the appropriation that it appeared the House would not take favorable action. One reason for opposition to the appropriation arose from an alleged contract an American had made with a Russian agent to provide military supplies during the Crimean War. Since the conditions of the contract were not clear the Russian government would not pay the American. Therefore, he had advanced his claim

for payment through the State Department. Certain congressmen took up the inflated claim and insisted on holding up the Alaska appropriation until the Russian
government agreed to pay it.[23]

Some anti-Johnson congressmen opposed the treaty for other reasons. "Alaska,
with the Aleutian Islands," a representative from New York said, "is an in-
hospitable, wretched, and God-forsaken region, worth nothing, but a positive
injury and incumbrance as a colony of the United States." There was, however,
considerable open support for it from the West Coast where men appreciated the
value of the Alaskan fisheries with their abundant codfish, halibut, and salmon. A
number of West Coast representatives also stressed that possession of Alaska would
aid trade in the Pacific.

While trying to win support for the treaty, Stoeckl spent large sums on publicists,
lobbyists, and on propaganda, and even bribed congressmen. He reported to his
own government that he had spent most of the $200,000 that had been added to
the purchase price for "secret expenses."

The American government, meanwhile, had already taken formal possession of
Alaska and raised the flag over Sitka on October 18, 1867. When the House of
Representatives was ready to take final action in the summer of 1868, it was thus
confronted with an accomplished fact. "Shall the flag which waves so proudly
there now be taken down?" a congressman asked. "Palsied be the hand that
should dare to remove it! Our flag is there, and there it will remain." This proved
a decisive argument. On July 23 the House approved the appropriation.

Unlike other continental annexations, there was never any popular demand for
Alaska, yet Seward's "educational campaign" had undoubtedly convinced a
number of Americans that Alaska would be an economic asset and had created some
public support for the purchase, particularly among those who believed it was a
bargain the government should not pass up.[24] In a few decades the returns to the
American people from gold production, from the fisheries, and from furs alone
far surpassed the purchase price. Later, Alaska and its adjacent islands, stretching far
into the Pacific, were recognized as being invaluable strategic assets. "Seward's
Folly," a majestic domain of nearly 600,000 square miles, more than twice the
size of Texas and almost equal to one-fifth of the rest of the United States, has
proved a bargain second only to the Louisiana Purchase.

Agitation for Canada

In urging the acquisition of Alaska, Seward and other Republican expansionists
had argued that it would bring the annexation of Canada one step closer.[25] This
argument was nothing more than the renewal of an old but apparently still
popular demand. On July 2, 1866, for instance, an expansionist had gone so far as
to introduce a bill in the House of Representatives making provision for Britain's

North American provinces to come into the Union.[26] "I know that Nature designs that this whole continent, not merely these thirty-six states," Seward himself claimed in a speech in Boston in June, 1867, "shall be, sooner or later, within the magic circle of the American Union."

Although related to the annexationist agitation of the 1840's and 1850's, this renewed demand for Canada stemmed in part at least from Union resentment against Britain during the Civil War. "Let them [the British] remember, however, that when the termination of our civil conflicts shall have arrived," the New York *Herald* had warned six years earlier, ". . . Four hundred thousand thoroughly disciplined troops will ask no better occupation than to destroy the last vestiges of British rule on the American continent, and annex Canada to the United States."[27]

Northerners channeled some of the hostility they felt for Britain against Canada, even though Canada and Britain's other North American provinces at first sympathized with the Union. One reason for this ill feeling was that the Civil War had created some special problems in relations with Canada and had even reopened some old grievances. Canadians resented the fact that Northerners openly recruited or forced their young men into the Union army.[28] When Union military police invaded Canada to take back deserters, Canadian authorities protested and resisted, but those resentments appeared minor in comparison with Northern anger against Canada.

Most Northerners believed that Canada, like England, had sympathized with the Confederacy. They resented this, but what angered them more was the use Confederate agents had made of Canadian soil. Early in the Civil War Canada became a refuge for Confederate soldiers who escaped from Northern military prisons. Later in the war Confederate agents raided Union border towns, using the British provinces as their bases. They made their biggest raid near the end of the war. Under orders of the Confederate War Department, some twenty Confederates fell upon the tiny village of St. Albans, Vermont, on October 19, 1864. They set fires, robbed banks, wounded two people, killed one, and fled back across the border.[29]

This raid inflamed Northern public opinion as nothing had since the *Trent* affair. Lincoln's government had talked earlier of giving Britain the required six months' notice terminating the Rush-Bagot Agreement. Now the government decided to act. Confederate activities on the Great Lakes and the "insufficiency of the British Neutrality Act," Seward said, compelled the United States to take that step, which, however, was never completed, since the Civil War was drawing to a close and the Union had not placed any armaments on the lakes. In March, 1865, therefore, Seward told the British that his government was willing to allow the Rush-Bagot Agreement to remain in effect, and the British agreed.

The Marcy-Elgin Treaty of 1854 did not survive the accumulated grievances of the war. Reflecting public sentiment, the New York *Herald* had said "it becomes

one of the first duties of the new Congress to manifest its resentment at the unfriendly and dishonest treatment by doing away with the treaty under which
Canada derives such advantage from us." [30] Congress passed a joint resolution in
January, 1865, calling for repeal of the reciprocity treaty, and the President then
gave Britain the necessary twelve-month notice of termination.

With this notice, expansionist newspapers, such as the Philadelphia *Press* and
Philadelphia *Inquirer*, reported "a growing feeling in Canada in favor of annexation to the United States." The Toronto *Globe*, two years later, charged Seward
with abrogating the treaty to facilitate the annexation of Canada.

Even though many Americans believed that the inevitable destiny of the
British in provinces of North America was union with the United States, most
Canadians did not want to become Americans. True, some Canadians still saw in
annexation a solution to their economic and social problems, but theirs was a
minority view, for sentiment for annexation was generally localized and sporadic. [31]
Annexationist agitation in the United States, in fact, strengthened Canadian
nationalism and the movement toward confederation in Britain's North American
provinces.

Some Canadians believed that American expansionists were so intent on
annexation that they encouraged a society of Irish-Americans, called the Fenian
Brotherhood, to invade Canada. Although the organization began in 1858 in
New York, with the aim of forcing Ireland's independence from Britain, its
activities did not reach threatening proportions until 1866. In that year the Fenians
launched a series of raids into Canada with the idea of annoying England and involving the United States in a war with her that might lead to Irish independence.
Some Fenians even talked of conquering Canada.

The Fenians held conventions in the United States, organized a government for
their future republic, raised uniformed "armies," and even had an anthem, the
"Fenian Marseillaise." It went:

> Away with speech, and brother, reach me down that rifle gun
> By her sweet voice, and hers alone, the rights of man are won
> Fling down the pen; when heroic men, pine sad in dungeons lone,
> 'Tis bayonets bright, with good red blood, should plead before the throne. [32]

Radical Republicans encouraged the Fenians in order to embarrass Andrew
Johnson, Democrats courted the Irish vote, and some Americans considered the
Fenian assaults just reprisal for the Confederate raids of the Civil War. The
American government allowed the Fenians to demonstrate and did not prevent
their raids. "In fact this Fenian demonstration is probably winked at by the U.S.
Government," the Montreal *Gazette* remarked, "in the hope that it may produce
terrorism in these colonies, which may favour their annexation projects; but in
this they again commit an error, which will put further off the desired object." [33]

The Fenians made their first large incursion in May, 1866, when eight hundred of them, mostly Civil War veterans, crossed the Niagara River from Buffalo and occupied the Canadian village of Fort Erie. They defeated a force of inexperienced Canadian volunteers but then retreated before organized military forces. The Canadians suffered twelve dead and the Fenians eight, plus other casualties. President Johnson did not issue a proclamation forbidding violation of the neutrality act until five days after the raid.

Four years later the Fenians staged their last raid from St. Albans. "Fenians," their leader said, "the eyes of Ireland are upon you." Seventy-five Canadians drove back two hundred of them at the border with one volley of rifle fire. Before the smoke had cleared, the United States marshal from Vermont dashed among the Fenians and arrested their "general" for violating the neutrality law.

Since the United States had tolerated the Fenians for years, Canadians believed there would have been no raids if the government had tried seriously to prevent them instead of acting after the invasions began. In comparison to the vigilant action of their own government against Confederate raiders, the American enforcement of neutrality laws seemed amazingly lax. The Canadian government had paid promptly for the damage of the St. Albans raid, but the United States had ignored Canada's bills for the damages inflicted by the Fenians. Some Americans, like Charles Sumner, took the view that the British flag in Canada had caused the Fenian troubles. If England would withdraw and allow the United States to annex Canada, they said, the threat of Fenian incursions would end.

Fenian activity and annexationist agitation in the United States in 1866 had been sufficiently menacing to solidify the movement for confederation in the British provinces, a movement expansionists did not like.[34] The House of Representatives objected in a resolution in May, 1867, but the Canadians went right ahead. Under the British North America Act of 1867, which went into effect on July 1, they formed a nation, the Dominion of Canada. Ironically, fear of the United States, mainly the truculent ambition of expansionists and their support of Fenian threats, had given Canadians the final impulse to form the national union.[35]

The Johnson-Clarendon Convention

While Canada was demanding payment for the Fenian damages, the United States insisted on compensation for losses it had suffered in the Civil War because Britain had been lax in enforcing her neutral obligations. As early as October, 1863, Charles Francis Adams had asked Lord Russell to arbitrate claims arising from the depredations of the *Alabama* and other Confederate cruisers. Russell refused. In 1865, when the United States wanted to discuss the *Alabama* claims, covering losses from all Confederate raiders, Russell, who was then Prime Minister, again refused. "England," he said, "would be disgraced forever if a foreign government were left to arbitrate whether an English secretary of state had been diligent or negligent in his duties."

Russell resigned in June, 1866, and a more conciliatory government came to power. It reflected the view of many Englishmen who felt that previous governments had been short-sighted in ignoring the American claims. They realized the danger when the House of Representatives voted unanimously in July to modify the neutrality laws so as to permit Americans to sell ships to belligerents. If the Americans changed their neutrality laws and if Britain went to war, say with Russia, cruisers built in America flying the flag of the Tsars might destroy the British merchant fleet.

Aware of those ominous possibilities, the new British Foreign Secretary offered to arbitrate the *Alabama* claims. Since Seward insisted on including Britain's alleged "premature" recognition of the Confederacy as a grievance and the British would not consider debating whether or not that recognition was justifiable, the negotiations collapsed.

In 1868 a new British ministry under William E. Gladstone came to power, and Reverdy Johnson, a former senator from Maryland, succeeded Adams as Minister to Britain. Johnson arrived in London in August and immediately tried to conciliate the British, but his impolitic speeches infuriated radical Republicans in the Senate.

"I like some things that Mr. Reverdy Johnson says," a friend wrote to Senator Sumner, "but he made a terrible mistake in calling Mr. Roebuck his friend, and shaking hands with him and Mr. Laird—Roebuck had done everything in his power to break up the American Union." Roebuck had been Parliament's chief advocate for recognition of the Confederacy, and Laird was the unrepentant builder of the *Alabama*.

Under precise instructions from Seward, Johnson worked out an agreement with the British known as the Johnson–Clarendon Convention. Signed on January 14, 1869, it covered all claims held by both sides since 1853, but offered settlement for individual claims only, without recognizing the indirect losses Americans had suffered from the Confederate raiders. It contained no apology for the *Alabama*'s escape. For those reasons and others essentially political, the Senate rejected it on April 13 by a vote of fifty-four to one.

On that same day, before the Senate had voted, Charles Sumner denounced the agreement and attacked England in a long speech. The convention, he said, included only a small part of England's wartime debt to the United States. He presented three bills. The first, for direct damage wrought by Confederate sea raiders, he estimated at fifteen million dollars. The second, for indirect damage to the merchant fleet from increased insurance rates and loss of revenue from commerce driven from American ships, amounted to one hundred ten million dollars. And the third, for England's "premature" recognition of belligerency and aid to the South which allegedly had doubled the duration of the war, he estimated at half the cost of the Civil War, or two billion dollars. His total bill amounted to a staggering two billion one hundred twenty-five million dollars. Although Sumner did not say it, what he sought in payment was Canada.[36]

Sumner's speech, published in newspapers and in pamphlet form, received wide circulation and stimulated excitement on both sides of the Atlantic. Rather than cede Canada to pay for the bloated claims, the British were willing to fight.[37] Sumner's swaggering speech and the rejection of the Johnson–Clarendon Convention aroused widespread resentment in Britain, blocking further negotiation over American claims. The most serious obstacle was the British conviction that Sumner's ideas represented the policy of Ulysses S. Grant's new administration.

Even though President Grant in May, 1869, appointed a close friend of Sumner's, the historian John Lothrop Motley, Minister to Britain, Sumner's ideas did not, as he himself thought they would, dominate the administration's foreign policy. Grant's capable Secretary of State, Hamilton Fish of New York, like Sumner, desired Canada, but took firm control of foreign policy and followed a discreet course.

When Motley, contrary to Fish's instructions, presented the views of Sumner's speech to the British as the basis of administration policy, Grant decided quickly that "Motley must be dismissed at once." Fish agreed that Motley deserved dismissal but persuaded the President to retain him. By keeping Motley, the Secretary tried to avoid further discredit to the Grant administration in England and an immediate rupture with Sumner. Therefore, he merely reprimanded Motley and told him to inform the British that whenever they wished to renew discussion of the *Alabama* claims, they should take the negotiations to Washington. In this way Fish bypassed Motley.

Hamilton Fish obtained his opportunity to renew negotiations on July 8, 1869, when Sir John Rose, a distinguished Scotsman and Canada's Minister of Finance, visited him. Rose had come to Washington to discuss a number of Canada's problems, particularly trade reciprocity. "At dinner," Fish told his diary next day, "Mr. Rose and I conversed on the subject of the *Alabama* Claims, etc."[38] Rose wanted to settle those claims as well and suggested that Britain might send a special mission to Washington to negotiate an agreement.

Upon his return to England, Rose discussed the *Alabama* claims and other American questions with leading statesmen there, who were now prepared to adopt a more conciliatory policy. In July, 1870, the Franco-Prussian War erupted, and in October, Russia took advantage of it by repudiating the provisions of the Treaty of Paris of 1856 which limited her fleet on the Black Sea. War between Russia and Britain appeared probable. In such a conflict, British statesmen feared, *Alabamas* built in America might swarm over the seas against their shipping. For those and other reasons the British were now willing to negotiate.

As Fish suggested, Grant's annual message announced that when Britain wanted a settlement of the claims controversy, the United States would consider it "with an earnest desire for a conclusion consistent with the honor and dignity of both nations."[39] Grant also referred to disputes with Canada. When the British decided to negotiate, therefore, they agreed beforehand to lay the basis for a general arbitration covering Canadian-American differences as well as the *Alabama* claims. The London *Times* expressed a widespread sentiment, saying that "this constant speculation, this supposition that war may come is half as bad as war itself. What we want is settled peace and the conviction that peace will remain until there is just and sensible cause for war."

In rejecting the Johnson–Clarendon Convention, the United States had injured British pride, and Britain could not with dignity reopen negotiations directly. She first sent Rose to Washington unofficially on a confidential mission. He arrived in January, 1871. The British government, he told Fish, was willing to place all matters in dispute before a joint commission empowered to make a settlement by treaty. The United States agreed.[40]

A month later, on February 27, a Joint High Commission held its first meeting in Washington. On the commission were five Americans, headed by Secretary Fish, and four British and one Canadian statesmen. After meeting formally thirty-seven times, the commissioners signed a treaty on May 8.

The Treaty of Washington

The Treaty of Washington contained four main problems to be settled by arbitration. Its foremost agreement covered the *Alabama* claims. In it the British expressed regret "for the escape, under whatever circumstances, of the *Alabama* and other vessels from British ports, and for the depredations committed by those vessels."[41] The treaty called for an international Tribunal of Arbitration consisting of five men that would meet in Geneva to settle the *Alabama* claims.

To facilitate the settlement, the British agreed to three rules defining neutral obligations that were to guide the arbitrators. The first said that a neutral government had to use "due diligence" to prevent ships, which it believed intended to make war on another nation, from arming and leaving its ports. Secondly, it had to prevent any belligerent from using its ports as bases for naval operations or sources of supplies, arms, or recruits. Thirdly, it had to exercise "due diligence" over all persons in its jurisdiction to prevent violation of those obligations.[42]

Those rules were not a part of international law at the time of the Civil War. Since they were retroactive, Britain in effect made an advance surrender of her case. She did that to establish a precedent for the future. The treaty said nothing

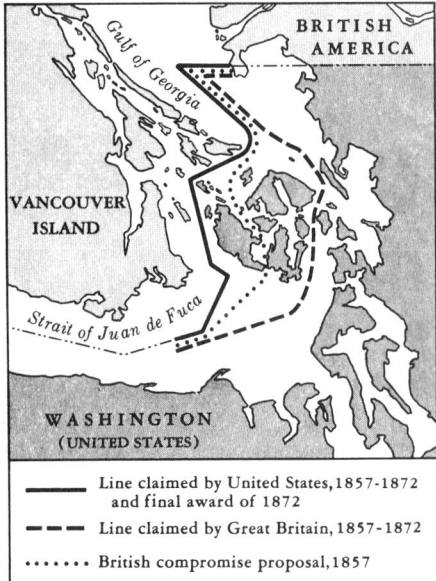

THE SAN JUAN ISLANDS
CONTROVERSY, 1872

about "indirect claims," but the British commissioners were convinced the United States had abandoned them.

The second major provision, which the Canadians considered the most important of all, covered American fishing rights in Canadian waters. The fisheries dispute stemmed from the American abrogation of the Marcy-Elgin Treaty in 1866. Canada had wanted to renew the treaty, but the United States, committed to a policy of high protective tariffs, had rebuffed overtures for any kind of trade reciprocity. Canadians, therefore, retaliated with tariffs of their own on American coal, lumber, bread, and other items. Their most serious reprisal excluded Americans from the rich inshore fisheries and denied them the right to buy bait and provisions in Canadian ports. In January, 1870, Canada's government had abolished previously generous privileges for American fishermen and had returned to the restricted privileges of the Convention of 1818, enforcing them to the letter.

Under the Treaty of Washington Americans secured the right to use the Canadian fisheries for at least ten years, and Canadian fishermen obtained similar rights along the American coast to the thirty-ninth degree of north latitude. Since the United States obtained the larger advantages, the treaty provided for an international arbitration commission to decide on how much it should give Canada in additional compensation.

The third main question the treaty embraced was a controversy in the Northwest over a group of islands, the largest of which was San Juan, in the channel separating Vancouver Island from the mainland. Since the terms of the Oregon treaty defining the boundary were vague, the United States and Britain had long argued over who rightfully owned the islands.[43] The Washington Treaty turned the San Juan controversy over to the German emperor for arbitration.

Less significant than the other three, the fourth agreement called for a mixed commission to settle other British and American claims distinct from the *Alabama* claims, particularly those arising from American seizure of British property during the Civil War. Since the British agreed to compensate Canada separately for damages arising from the Fenian raids, the Canadians did not press those claims during the negotiations, and the treaty said nothing about them.

Americans were pleased with the treaty. The New York *Tribune* called it a "triumph of American principles and American diplomacy." It received Senate approval without much trouble in May, 1871, by a vote of fifty to twelve. Canadians called it a "betrayal" of their interests and one of their newspapers said it was a "wanton sacrifice of honour" and a "disgraceful capitulation."[44] Yet, after long debate, their parliament approved it.

As the Treaty of Washington provided, the five men comprising the international Tribunal of Arbitration selected to settle the *Alabama* claims met in Geneva on December 15 to hear the arguments. Boldly and unexpectedly the

THE APPLE OF DISCORD AT THE GENEVA TRIBUNAL

The rulers of Europe watch while John Bull disposes of the
"Alabama" claims by consenting to arbitration.

American case revived the claim for "indirect damages," demanding payment of the full cost of the Civil War after the Battle of Gettysburg with seven per cent interest.

The British reacted angrily to the "enormous and intolerable" demands. Since they had assumed that the claims for "indirect damages" were dead by mutual agreement, they accused the United States of trickery and refused to allow the arbitrators to consider them. Prime Minister Gladstone told Queen Victoria on January 30 that the American case presented claims and pretensions "such as it is wholly incompatible with national honour to admit or to plead to before a Tribunal of Arbitration." If the United States did not give up its swollen claims, the British press urged, the government must abandon the arbitration.

Secretary Fish had included the indirect claims because he feared the Senate and public opinion, which, he thought, would cry out in protest against any case that did not include them. Merely by presenting the inflated demands he could satisfy them, forestall criticism, and allow the tribunal to reject them once and for all.

Despite the British protests, therefore, Fish would not withdraw the exaggerated claims. "We are content to let the Tribunal pass upon the indirect claims," he told the British Minister in Washington, "and if it rejects them we shall make no complaint; but we will never allow Great Britain or any other Power to dictate what form our Case shall take or what claims we shall advance." [45] Since Fish insisted on the indirect claims as a matter of political necessity and the British government, as a matter of national honor and political necessity, refused to consider them, the arbitration appeared doomed.

"It is all over. This is the end of the Treaty," the American Minister in London said after a sleepless night. "Very well, sir," his ardent young secretary answered. "We shall fight Great Britain: and, thank God, we are ready for it!" [46]

Finally, five months later, as panic hit the stock markets and Americans and Englishmen again muttered words of war, statesmen groping for peace found a solution. Charles Francis Adams, the American member of the Tribunal of Arbitration, persuaded the other arbitrators to consider the indirect demands, even though those claims were not within their jurisdiction. In an extrajudicial or "advisory" opinion in June, 1872, the tribunal declared the indirect claims invalid under recognized rules of international law and thus ended the controversy. Fish accepted the declaration, the British agreed to present their case, and the arbitration continued.

The tribunal held its final session on the afternoon of September 14, and announced its decision. Britain, it said, according to the rules of "due diligence" was responsible for the damage the *Alabama*, the *Florida*, and the *Shenandoah* had wrought and awarded the United States an indemnity of $15,500,000. Sir Alexander Cockburn, the British arbitrator scowled, refused to sign the award, and filed a dissent. After the Tribunal finished its work, applause filled the crowded hall, but Cockburn did not listen. He snatched his hat and rushed to the door. The British government itself did not protest the award. A year later it gave the United States a check for the full amount.

None of the other arbitrations under the Treaty of Washington created a major diplomatic crisis. In the case of the San Juan Islands, the German emperor in October, 1872, decided on a boundary that gave the disputed islands to the United States.

After meeting in Washington and Newport, Rhode Island, over a period of two years, the general claims commission in September, 1873, dismissed all American claims and awarded the British $1,929,819, primarily for illegal seizures of British property, imprisonment, and other losses during the Civil War.

After long delay, the Fisheries Commission, composed of three arbitrators, met in Halifax in June, 1877, to hear American and Canadian arguments. In November it awarded Canada $5,500,000 to compensate for fishing privileges conceded to the United States. Americans considered the sum excessive, and their commissioner, like Cockburn, refused to sign the award, and filed a dissent, but the United States paid.

"While nearly every other nation of the world settles its difficulties with other powers by the dreadful arbitrament of the sword," the Halifax commissioners said in final judgment of the Treaty of Washington, "England and America, two of the most powerful nations upon the earth, referred their differences to peaceful negotiation and made an epoch in the history of civilization." The commissioners exaggerated somewhat. Yet the Treaty of Washington, with its arbitrations, was a noteworthy victory for diplomatic negotiation. Although it did not dispel all frictions, it ended an era of ill will in relations with Britain and Canada and ushered in a decade of peace undisturbed by claims, recurring border clashes, and boundary disputes.[47]

Grant and the Dominican Republic

The Treaty of Washington, the outstanding accomplishment in the Grant administrations, was not typical of Grant's own approach to foreign affairs. Usually he left matters of foreign policy to Secretary of State Fish, but in the case of the Dominican Republic he himself took an active interest. Soon after assuming office, Grant fell under the influence of speculators who wanted to annex the Dominican Republic for their own gain. So interested did the President become, that he set his heart on the annexation.

To take up where Seward had left off and to lay the basis for another annexation agreement, Grant sent his military secretary, General Orville E. Babcock, to the island in July, 1869, as a special executive agent. Even though Babcock possessed no diplomatic powers, he signed an informal agreement on September 4 committing the United States to annex the Dominican Republic and to pay $1,500,000 to cover its public debt, or to buy Samaná Bay for $2,000,000. He also pledged the President "privately to use all his influence" with Congress in winning acceptance for the idea of annexation. The agreement, made according to Fish's instructions, was little more than a memorandum embodying the terms of annexation, but Grant and the Dominican president considered it virtually a treaty.

Although not as enthusiastic about Babcock's agreement as Grant was, Fish sent Babcock back to the Dominican Republic with two draft treaties. The first provided for annexation of the republic as a territory with the promise of ultimate statehood. The Dominicans had to agree to annexation by a plebiscite, which they did. As an alternative, the second treaty gave the United States a ninety-nine-year lease of Samaná Bay with an annual rental fee and with the right of purchase at any time for $2,000,000. Since Babcock still had no diplomatic powers, a consular agent signed the two treaties for the United States on November 29.[48]

Grant was so anxious to gain the Senate's approval of the treaty that on Sunday evening, January 2, 1870, he called on Sumner at his home. "Now, I am told that you are chairman of the Judiciary Committee, before whom such matters come," Grant said, "and that if you will aid it the thing can be accomplished." Sumner corrected the President several times, informing him that he was Chairman of the Foreign Relations Committee. Before Grant left, he erroneously thought he had won Sumner's support for the acquisition. On January 10, therefore, the President sent the two Dominican treaties to the Senate.

Using whatever influence he could exert, Grant lobbied in person for the annexation treaty. He would summon senators and ask their support. "I hear you are a member of the Senate Committee that has the San Domingo treaty under consideration," he told one, "and I wish you would support that treaty. Won't you do that?"[49] Despite the President's pressure, most senators disliked the treaty. After long debate, the Senate killed it on June 30. The Senate did not vote on the second treaty.

Sumner's opposition infuriated Grant. Since he regarded Sumner as chiefly and treacherously responsible for the treaty's defeat, he retaliated by immediately removing Sumner's friend, Motley, from his post in London. Later, in March, 1871, Grant used his influence to depose Sumner as Chairman of the Foreign Relations Committee.

Grant did not give up easily. He tried in several ways to revive the annexation scheme, but could or would not by-pass Congress. In October, 1871, the Dominican Minister of Foreign Relations suggested a lease of Samaná Bay through an executive agreement that would not require Senate approval. "I will not be a party," Grant said, "to any such arrangement." He was now resigned to the fact that the Dominican question was unpopular. "We will drop the matter," he added, "and leave the whole question for Congress and the people." "Thus," a pleased Hamilton Fish told his diary, "a troublesome, vexatious, and unnecessary question is, as I trust, finally got rid of."

Forestalling Intervention in Cuba

Even more vexing than the Dominican question were problems raised by a rebellion in Cuba, called the Ten Years' War, that began in the fall of 1868. The rebels declared their independence from Spain in October and formed a shadowy provisional government for a republic. When Grant took office, no one knew how well organized the rebel government was or how effective its fighting forces. Soon, however, it became clear that the rebels had no organized army, but fought the Spaniards in savage hit-and-run guerilla warfare.

Cuban exiles and refugees in the United States stimulated sympathy for the rebel cause. Those Cubans, their American friends, and many newspapers urged intervention to aid the rebels. Since the Cuban government was little more than a shadow, Secretary of State Fish opposed intervention. He could not, under international law, justify recognizing it as a belligerent and much less as the government of an independent nation. He had, moreover, criticized England's "premature" recognition of Confederate belligerency and could hardly, with far less justification, recognize Cuban belligerency.

To forestall the interventionists, Fish offered to mediate the "civil war" in July, 1869. He urged Spain to give Cuba independence for payment by the Cubans of an indemnity of about $150,000,000 guaranteed by the United States. Spain delayed acceptance and finally the mediation plan died. Grant, anxious to recognize Cuban belligerency partly because he considered it proper revenge for Spanish recognition of Confederate belligerency during the Civil War, decided to take matters into his own hands.

One of the staunchest advocates of intervention was General John H. Rawlins, Secretary of War, and a close friend of Grant. He apparently persuaded the President to recognize Cuban belligerency, for on August 14, 1869, Grant asked Fish to proclaim neutrality and hence recognition, but the Secretary put aside Grant's signed proclamation. Rawlins died on September 6, thus easing the pressure on Grant and Fish for recognition.[50] Occupied with the problem of the Dominican Republic and other matters, the President forgot about his proclamation. Fish even persuaded him, in his annual message in December, to say that the rebellion in Cuba "has at no time assumed the conditions which amounted to a war in the sense of international law, or which would show the existence of a *de facto* political organization of the insurgents sufficient to justify a recognition of belligerency."

Most Republicans in Congress did not like the President's words; they preferred intervention. In February, 1870, they began massing support for a joint resolution calling for recognition of Cuban belligerency. Public opinion, particularly as shown by the New York press, appeared to favor the congressional interventionists.

Fish was alarmed. Recognition probably would mean war with Spain. He asked the unpredictable President, therefore, to fight the interventionist offensive by sending a special message, which Fish wrote, to Congress denouncing the folly of recognition. If Grant would not go ahead with the declaration, he said, he would resign. Grant yielded and on June 13 sent the message, one of his ablest, to Congress. "The question of belligerency," he said, "is one of fact, not to be decided by sympathies for or prejudices against either party. The relations between the parent state and the insurgents must amount in fact to war in the sense of international law."

When a resolution calling for recognition came to a vote in the House of Representatives three days later, it failed. Fish's policy had won a victory, and for three years the interventionist tide receded.

The VIRGINIUS Affair

From the beginning of the war in Cuba the United States had been embarrassed by filibustering expeditions that rebels and their American sympathizers had launched from American soil. More than once those expeditions had touched off nasty "incidents." The most serious occurred in October, 1873, when a Spanish gunboat captured the *Virginius,* a rebel steamer flying the American flag, on the open sea between Cuba and Jamaica. The Spanish captain brought the ship into Santiago and there, after hasty court-martial trials, the authorities shot fifty-three of the passengers and crew, some of them Americans and Englishmen, as "pirates." More executions would probably have followed if the commander of a British warship, the *Niobe,* had not hurried to Santiago from Jamaica and threatened to bombard the city if the killings did not stop.

Some Americans clamored for war. Even those who had cared nothing for the Cuban rebels now resented the insult to their flag. The government strengthened coastal fortifications and prepared the Navy for hostilities. Yet most Americans appeared to demand redress, not war. On November 14, Fish telegraphed a virtual ultimatum to the Spanish government, demanding a salute to the American flag, release of the *Virginius* and her survivors, payment for the killings, and punishment of the guilty officials. If Spain did not meet those demands, he said, the United States would sever diplomatic relations. The next step would be war. "If Spain cannot redress the outrages perpetrated in her name in Cuba," Fish said later, "the United States will."[51]

Fish soon learned that the *Virginius* belonged to Cubans, was fraudulently flying the American flag, and was carrying arms and filibusters contrary to American law. Therefore, he dropped the demand for a salute to the flag. Nonetheless, since no recognized state of war existed and the Cuban rebels did not have belligerent rights, Spain had no authority under international law to seize the ship on the seas.

Spain released the *Virginius* and the surviving prisoners, admitted that the seizure had been illegal, and in May, 1875, paid an indemnity of $80,000 to go to the relatives of the executed Americans. The American people apparently accepted the *Virginius* settlement as fair.

The continuing butchery in Cuba led the United States to make one more effort to intervene. In November Fish asked the Spanish government to end the war by giving Cuba self-government. If Spain did not, he said, "the time is at hand when it may be the duty of other governments to intervene." [52] He sent copies of his proposal to England and the other principal nations in Europe asking that they too exert pressure on Spain to make peace.

Spain then made necessary concessions and promised specific reforms, but not self-government. The European governments, meanwhile, would not support Fish's proposal. At home, critics said Fish's approaches to the European nations violated the spirit of the Monroe Doctrine. Thus, the plan for cooperative intervention failed.

In 1878, Spain forced a peace in Cuba and promised further reforms, such as colonial autonomy. Yet there was no true peace, merely a long truce. The reforms proved inadequate, and the Cubans were still determined ultimately to win their independence.

NOTES

1. Quoted in Dexter Perkins, *A History of the Monroe Doctrine*, rev. ed. (Boston, 1955), p. 146. For a detailed study, see William C. Davis, *The Last Conquistadores: The Spanish Intervention in Peru and Chile, 1863–1866* (Athens, Ga., 1950).

2. For details, see Howard L. Wilson, "President Buchanan's Proposed Intervention in Mexico," *The American Historical Review*, V (July 1900), 687–701 and Agustín Cue Cánovas, *El Tratado McLane-Ocampo: Juárez, los Estados Unidos y Europa*, 2nd ed. (Mexico City, 1959).

3. See William S. Robertson, "The Tripartite Treaty of London," *Hispanic American Historical Review*, XX (May 1940), 167–189.

4. To John Bigelow, Sept. 9, 1863, in Frederic Bancroft, *The Life of William H. Seward* (2 vols., New York, 1900), II, 426.

5. For details, see Frank L. Owsley, *King Cotton Diplomacy*, 2nd ed. (Chicago, 1959), pp. 507–529. For an account of Confederate activity in the French intervention during and after the Civil War, see Kathryn A. Hanna, "The Roles of the South in the French Intervention in Mexico," *Journal of Southern History*, XX (Feb. 1954), 3–21.

6. *Congressional Globe*, 38th Congress, 1st sess., p. 1408.

7. The quotations are in Bancroft, *Seward*, II, 429.

8. See Robert W. Frazer, "Maximilian's Propaganda Activities in the United States,

1865–1866," *Hispanic American Historical Review*, XXIV (Feb. 1944), 4–29.

9. He told one emissary he sent to France, for instance, "I want you to get your legs under Napoleon's mahogany, and tell him he must get out of Mexico." John M. Schofield, *Forty-six Years in the Army* (New York, 1897), p. 385.

10. Quoted in Egon C. Corti, *Maximilian and Charlotte of Mexico*, trans. from the German (2 vols., New York, 1928), II, 580.

11. For various analyses of the reasons for Napoleon's withdrawal, see Henry Blumenthal, *A Reappraisal of Franco-American Relations, 1830–1871* (Chapel Hill, N.C., 1959), pp. 175–180; Perkins, *History of the Monroe Doctrine*, pp. 135–138; Richard B. McCornack, "James Watson Webb and the French Withdrawal from Mexico," *The American Historical Review*, XXXI (May 1951), 274–286; Lynn M. Case, ed., *French Opinion on the United States and Mexico, 1860–1867* (New York, 1936), pp. 402–435; Frank E. Lally, *French Opposition to the Mexican Policy of the Second Empire* (Baltimore, 1931), pp. 147–150; and Clyde E. Duniway, "Reasons for the Withdrawal of the French from Mexico," *American Historical Association Annual Report, 1902* (2 vols., Washington, 1903), I, 315–328. Nathan L. Ferris, in "The Relations of the United States with South America during the Civil War," *Hispanic American Historical Review*, XXI (Feb. 1941), 65, points out that the Spanish and French interventions increased the feeling of reliance on the United States in Latin America.

12. *The Nation*, Nov. 29, 1866, for instance, said that "every interest of our society calls for more condensation of our people and less expansion of our territory," William M. Armstrong, *E. L. Godkin and American Foreign Policy, 1865–1900* (New York, 1957), p. 103. Joe Patterson Smith, in *The Republican Expansionists of the Early Reconstruction Era* (Chicago, 1933), maintains that the radical Republican minority kept expansionism alive mainly to further its

political fortunes. See also Brainerd Dyer, "Robert J. Walker on Acquiring Greenland and Iceland," *The Mississippi Valley Historical Review*, XXVII (Sept. 1940), 263–266.

13. March 31, 1846, George E. Baker, ed., *The Works of William H. Seward* (5 vols., New York, 1853–84), III, 409.

14. For Seward's earlier interest in the islands, see Halvdan Koht, "The Origin of Seward's Plan to Purchase the Danish West Indies," *The American Historical Review*, L (July 1945), 762–767.

15. Quoted in Theodore C. Smith, "Expansion after the Civil War, 1865–1871," *Political Science Quarterly*, XVI (Sept. 1901), 412–436.

16. Quoted in Charles C. Tansill, *The United States and Santo Domingo, 1798–1873: A Chapter in Caribbean History* (Baltimore, 1938), p. 178.

17. Quoted in Smith, "Expansion after the Civil War," *Political Science Quarterly*, XVI (Sept. 1901), 434.

18. Donald M. Dozer, in "Anti-Expansionism during the Johnson Administration," *Pacific Historical Review*, XII (Sept. 1943), 253–275, sees the antiexpansionist sentiment of this period as the beginning of the later anti-imperialist movement.

19. For documents on Russia's desire to sell Alaska, see Hunter Miller, "Russian Opinion on the Cession of Alaska," *The American Historical Review*, XLVII (April 1943), 521–531.

20. Anatole G. Mazour, in "The Prelude to Russia's Departure from America," *Pacific Historical Review*, X (Sept. 1941), 311–319, brings out the point that the Russians knew of the gold in Alaska.

21. The conversation is recorded in Frederick W. Seward, comp., *William Henry Seward: An Autobiography and Memoir of His Life, with Selections from His Letters* (3 vols., New York, 1891), III, 348.

22. The text of the speech is in Charles Sumner, *The Works of Charles Sumner* (15 vols., Boston, 1875–83), XI, 186–349.

23. For details, see William A. Dunning, "Paying for Alaska," *Political Science Quarterly*, XXVII (Sept. 1912), 385–398; Frank A. Golder, "The Purchase of Alaska," *The American Historical Review*, XXV (April 1920), 411–425; and Reinhard H. Luthin, "The Sale of Alaska," *Slavonic Review*, XVI (July 1937), 168–182.

24. Thomas A. Bailey, in "Why the United States Purchased Alaska," *Pacific Historical Review*, III (March 1934), 39–49, stresses that Americans considered the purchase a bargain. The information supplied by a scientific expedition sent to Alaska by a subsidiary of Western Union also helped bolster the argument that Alaska was a good buy. Charles Vevier, "The Collins Overland Line and American Continentalism," *ibid.*, XXVIII (Aug. 1959), 252–253.

25. See F. W. Seward, *Seward's Autobiography*, II, 535, and Charles Vevier, "American Continentalism: An Idea of Expansion, 1845–1910," *The American Historical Review*, LXV (Jan. 1960), 332.

26. Fred H. Harrington, *Fighting Politician: Major General N. P. Banks* (Philadelphia, 1948), p. 178. See also Goldwin Smith, "The Gospel of Annexation on the Eve of the Treaty of Washington," *Transactions of the Royal Society of Canada*, 3rd ser., sec. II, XXXI (Ottawa, 1937), 79–86.

27. Sept. 12, 1861, quoted in Lester B. Shippee, *Canadian-American Relations, 1849–1874* (New Haven, 1939), p. 158.

28. For an analysis of Canadian opinion toward the Union, see Robin W. Winks, *Canada and the United States: The Civil War Years* (Baltimore, 1960), pp. 208–210. For details on crimping, see pp. 192–200, and Marguerite B. Hamer, "Luring Canadian Soldiers into Union Lines during the War between the States," *Canadian Historical Review*, XXVII (June 1946), 150–162.

29. For details, see Winks, *Canada and the U.S.*, pp. 295–302.

30. Nov. 9, 1864, quoted in Shippee, *Canadian-American Relations*, p. 178. Winks, in *Canada and the U.S.*, pp. 341–347, points out that abrogation of the reciprocity treaty was not in direct retaliation for the St. Albans raid.

31. For details, see Donald F. Warner, *The Idea of Continental Union: Agitation for the Annexation of Canada to the United States, 1849–1893* (Lexington, Ky., 1960), pp. 42–45.

32. Quoted in William D'Arcy, *The Fenian Movement in the United States: 1858–1886* (Washington, 1947), p. 99.

33. Feb. 12, 1866, in Shippee, *Canadian-American Relations*, p. 220.

34. C. P. Stacey, "Fenianism and the Rise of National Feeling in Canada at the Time of Confederation," *Canadian Historical Review*, XII (Sept. 1931), 238–261. See also D. G. Creighton, "The United States and Canadian Confederation," *ibid.*, XXXIX (Sept. 1958), 209–222.

35. Ironically, too, the Fenian raids had also stimulated annexationist sentiment, for some Canadians felt that their country had been exposed as defenseless and hence should join the Union. Warner, *Continental Union*, p. 54n.

36. The text of the speech is in *Sumner's Works*, XIII, 53–93. There was still strong sentiment for annexation in the United States, particularly of Canada's northwest. Zachariah Chandler, a senator from Michigan, on April 19, 1870, even offered a resolution calling for "negotiations with the people of Winnipeg, with a view to the annexation of that district to the United States as a Territory or a State" in Alvin C. Gluck, Jr., "The Riel Rebellion and Canadian-American Relations," *Canadian Historical Review*, XXXVI (Sept. 1955), 209. See also Donald F. Warner, "*Drang Nach Norden*: The United States and the Riel Rebellion,"

Mississippi Valley Historical Review, XXXIX (March 1953), 693–712.

37. When news of Sumner's speech and rejection of the convention reached London, Lord Clarendon, the Foreign Minister, said grimly: "I believe that Grant and Sumner mean war; or rather that amount of insult and humiliation that must lead to it." C. P. Stacey, "Britain's Withdrawal from North America, 1864–1871," *Canadian Historical Review*, XXXVI (Sept. 1955), 185–198.

38. Quoted in Allan Nevins, *Hamilton Fish: The Inner History of the Grant Administration*, rev. ed. (2 vols., New York, 1957), I, 213.

39. Dec. 5, 1870, in James D. Richardson, ed., *A Compilation of the Messages and Papers of the Presidents, 1789–1899* (10 vols., Washington, 1896–99), VII, 102.

40. For details, see Robert C. Clark, "The Diplomatic Mission of Sir John Rose, 1891," *Pacific Northwest Quarterly*, XXVII (July 1936), 227–242.

41. The expression of regret had the advantage of satisfying the United States without committing Britain to payment for damages. See Maureen M. Robson, "The *Alabama* Claims and the Anglo-American Reconciliation, 1865–1871," *Canadian Historical Review*, XLIII (March 1961), 11.

42. The rules are given in James P. Baxter, III, "The British High Commissioners at Washington in 1871," *Massachusetts Historical Society Proceedings*, LXV (June 1940), 356.

43. For details, see John W. Long, Jr., "The Origin of the San Juan Island Boundary Controversy," *Pacific Northwest Quarterly*, XLIII (July 1952), 187–213.

44. The Canadian reaction is summarized in Goldwin Smith, *The Treaty of Washington, 1871: A Study in Imperial History* (Ithaca, N.Y., 1941), pp. 91–113.

45. The Gladstone and Fish quotations are in Nevins, *Hamilton Fish*, II, 524–526.

46. Quoted in Frank W. Hackett, *Reminiscences of the Geneva Tribunal of Arbitration, 1872: The Alabama Claims* (Boston, 1911), p. 202n.

47. C. P. Stacey, in "Britain's Withdrawal from North America," *Canadian Historical Review*, XXXVI (Sept. 1955), 192, points out that Britain's concern with affairs on the European continent influenced her concessions in the Treaty of Washington and its arbitrations.

48. The most reliable account of this affair is in Charles C. Tansill, *United States and Santo Domingo*, pp. 338–379.

49. Carl Schurz, *The Reminiscences of Carl Schurz* (3 vols., New York, 1908), III, 307.

50. William B. Hesseltine, *Ulysses S. Grant: Politician* (New York, 1935), p. 173.

51. Quoted in Joseph V. Fuller, "Hamilton Fish," in Samuel F. Bemis, ed., *The American Secretaries of State and Their Diplomacy* (10 vols., New York, 1927–29), VII, 183.

52. Nov. 5, 1875, *ibid.*, p. 194. This instruction to the American Minister in Madrid is usually known as "No. 266."

Chapter Twelve

PUGNACIOUS DIPLOMACY

DURING the 1880's and 90's the Department of State had to deal with a number of problems which in themselves may be considered minor, but when lumped together reveal a new pattern of behavior in international affairs. This pattern shows that in those years foreign affairs were assuming an increasingly complicated role in the conduct of national policy. It suggests that despite the varied nature of most of those problems, they *either* stemmed from or were involved in issues of domestic politics, *or* the policymakers, and even the people, exhibited a new brashness, a pugnacious and at times a scarcely restrained nationalism, a kind of chip-on-the-shoulder attitude toward even minor issues of foreign policy. In some instances, both of these characteristics, prominent in the diplomacy of the 80's and 90's, can be seen in the American approach to a single problem.

Evolution of Policy toward an Interoceanic Canal

This new sense of national concern for America's status in the world, while evident in some of Seward's and even Grant's expansionist projects, can be discerned in the government's changed attitude toward the building of a canal across Central America. In the decades following the Civil War the government had shown a quickening interest in such a canal. In June, 1867, Seward had concluded a treaty with Nicaragua which gave the United States transit rights across that country, but rights that were not exclusive. Two years later, in January, 1869, he negotiated the first canal treaty with Colombia. Since the concessions were restricted, the Senate refused consent to ratification.

Then with the opening of the Suez Canal in the following November, which transformed communications and trade between Europe and Asia, public interest in a Central-American waterway mushroomed. Grant himself took an interest in the project. "The subject of an interoceanic canal to connect the Atlantic and Pacific oceans through the Isthmus of Darien," he announced in his first annual message, "is one in which commerce is greatly interested." [1] Other Presidents had favored a canal under international control, but he was the first to declare his support for a waterway owned and controlled exclusively by the United States.

Hamilton Fish now took up where Seward had left off and in January, 1870, made another treaty with Colombia, one that gave the United States the sole right to construct a canal across Panama. Since the Colombian senate added unacceptable amendments, that treaty, too, collapsed.

After United States naval survey expeditions had explored possible canal routes, as called for by a Senate resolution of March, 1872, Grant appointed an Interoceanic Canal Commission to evaluate the work of the individual survey parties and recommend the best route for a waterway. Four years later it reported a unanimous decision in favor of a route through Nicaragua.

American interest in a canal now lagged for a few years. In 1879 when Ferdinand de Lesseps, the enterprising French builder of the Suez Canal, organized a private stock company with a concession from the Colombian government to build a sea-level canal across the Isthmus of Panama, interest suddenly picked up. Americans now became alarmed. They did not like the idea of a canal owned and operated by Europeans in their own back yard. In Congress, and in the press too, angry citizens denounced the project as a violation of the Monroe Doctrine.

Aware of the public hostility and shocked by the extent of the official disapproval of his enterprise, de Lesseps visited the United States in February, 1880, to promote support for his canal and to allay government fears. He talked with President Rutherford B. Hayes and Secretary of State William M. Evarts, hoping to gain consent for his undertaking, but they did nothing to encourage him.

On March 8, three days after his conversation with de Lesseps, who was still in the United States, Hayes delivered a special message to Congress, written by Evarts, in which he announced that "the policy of this country is a canal under American control. The United States cannot consent to the surrender of this control to any European power or to any combination of European powers." A canal across the isthmus, he added, "would be the great ocean thoroughfare between our Atlantic and our Pacific shores, and virtually a part of the coast line of the United States." [2]

That attitude, reflecting Grant's views, now became national policy. A month later, the House of Representatives asked the President to take steps to abrogate the Clayton-Bulwer Treaty, the main obstacle to carrying out that policy.

Concerned over American hostility the French government, meanwhile, had assured the United States that the de Lesseps project was a private one and that it did not intend to support the undertaking in any way. De Lesseps' engineers began work on the canal in February, 1881, and the United States did nothing to interfere. Two years earlier, however, a group of American promoters had organized a company to build a competitive canal through Nicaragua. This company tried to gain government support but failed.

Since the Clayton-Bulwer Treaty stood in the way of a canal controlled exclusively by the United States, Secretaries of State Evarts, James G. Blaine, and Frederick J. Frelinghuysen, all tried to amend or abrogate it. Blaine's arguments were particularly vigorous. That treaty, he said, injures the spirit of the Monroe Doctrine and "impeaches our rightful and long established claims to priority on the American continent."[3] Since Britain would not surrender any of her rights under the treaty, Frelinghuysen disregarded it and on December 1, 1884, signed a treaty with General Joaquín Zavala of Nicaragua to supersede Seward's inadequate treaty of 1867.

That new treaty gave the United States the exclusive right to build a canal across Nicaragua, to be owned jointly. In return, the United States guaranteed Nicaragua's territorial integrity and agreed to a permanent alliance. For the first time the United States included the principle of a canal constructed and owned by the government in a treaty, and for the first time it deliberately took a step that violated the Clayton-Bulwer Treaty.

The Senate rejected the Frelinghuysen-Zavala Treaty by a close vote in January, 1885, and then proceeded to reconsider it. Two months later Grover Cleveland became President. On March 13, following the advice of his Secretary of State, Thomas F. Bayard, he withdrew the treaty from the Senate. If the Senate had approved it, a serious quarrel with England would probably have followed.

Cleveland did not adopt the policy of his immediate predecessors for a waterway controlled exclusively by the United States. The canal, he said in his first annual message, "must be for the world's benefit—a trust for mankind, to be removed from the chance of domination by any single power, nor become a point of invitation for hostilities or a prize for warlike ambition."[4]

Despite the failure of the Frelinghuysen-Zavala Treaty and the lack of government assistance, the American promoters went ahead in 1887 with their own plans for a Nicaraguan canal. With a concession from Nicaragua's government and under an act of Congress, they incorporated the Maritime Canal Company of Nicaragua. They no longer feared the rival French canal at Panama, for de Lesseps' company went bankrupt in February, 1889, and in May, with about two-fifths of the digging completed, stopped construction.

The Maritime Canal Company began work in October, 1889, using some of the equipment from Panama. That company soon ran out of money and asked the American government to finance its project. Since such aid would make the canal almost a government project and would violate the Clayton-Bulwer Treaty, Congress again refused to offer support. Work stopped and in August, 1893, the subsidiary construction company went bankrupt. The Maritime Canal Company, though it tried, never resumed work.

The failure of the private companies in Panama and Nicaragua convinced many Americans that only the government had the resources necessary to build a canal. The main obstacle to a canal built and owned by the American government was still the Clayton-Bulwer Treaty, which remained in effect until the beginning of the twentieth century.

Blaine's Latin-American Policy

American concern over a canal in the 1880's reflected a new governmental interest in all of Latin America. By that time the larger countries of South America, although plagued by wars, had achieved a higher level of political stability than in the past and had become more important commercially. In the United States the stepped-up industrial revolution following the Civil War had reached the point where manufacturers sought new markets and new sources of raw materials for their factories. One of the Americans who came to acquire an intense interest in promoting an increased trade with Latin America was James G. Blaine, who became James A. Garfield's Secretary of State in March, 1881.

Since Blaine had been the outstanding Republican leader and Garfield merely a fortunate dark-horse candidate, Blaine believed that he, not Garfield, deserved to be President. Blaine had spent a quarter of a century in public life, but in that time had had no experience in foreign affairs. Yet he became Secretary of State with the intention of functioning as the administration's prime minister. Since Garfield gave him a free hand in foreign affairs, he was able, during that short tenure, to put his own "spirited foreign policy" into practice.[5]

Blaine's policy toward Latin America had two main objectives: promotion of peace and increased trade. Both were in a sense anti-European. Peace, he believed, could be maintained by eliminating opportunities for European intervention in the Americas, an objective that called for effort on his part to try to end the turbulence and wars then sweeping over parts of Latin America. As for trade, even though the Latin-American states sold raw materials to the United States, they bought most of their manufactured goods from Europe. Blaine wanted to redress that unfavorable balance.

Blaine made his first effort to advance both trade and peace in his relations with Mexico. He assumed that the government there had now acquired a stability hitherto unknown. He wanted Mexico's prosperity to grow, he said, aided by Americans who wish to "take an active share in the prosecution of those industrial enterprises for which the magnificent resources of Mexico offer so broad and promising a field."[6] Later in that same month, however, an old boundary quarrel between Mexico and Guatemala injured his Mexican policy before it really began.

On June 15 Guatemala appealed to the United States for aid. Blaine then offered the good offices of the United States for an arbitration. Mexico, believing rightly that he sided with Guatemala, flatly refused his offer. Blaine's attempted peacemaking not only failed but also angered Mexico, and contributed nothing to closer trade relations.

Another territorial quarrel, this one in South America, seemingly presented the Secretary with another opportunity to advance his peace policy. In 1879 Chile had gone to war against Bolivia and Peru over rival claims to a desert region rich in guano, a valuable fertilizer, and nitrates. In this conflict, called the War of the Pacific, Chile was overwhelmingly victorious by January, 1881. She took over the nitrate territories and refused to give them up, but despite the defeat no Peruvian government would make a peace treaty.

When Blaine took office he immediately tried to work out a peace treaty between the belligerents. As in the Mexican dispute, he hoped to prevent or restrict any large cession of territory. Since Chile was determined to keep Peru's nitrate beds as an indemnity for her victory, he found himself in the position of partisan peacemaker. The American Ministers in Chile and Peru, moreover, complicated Blaine's diplomacy; each became a partisan of his host country. Blaine tried, therefore, to arrange a settlement by sending a special envoy to the belligerent countries. Since Chile would agree to no settlement unless the nitrate lands were ceded to her, and Blaine opposed such terms, his peacemaking again failed. All that he accomplished was to earn Chile's ill will.

In the peace treaties of 1883 and 1884 with Peru and Bolivia that finally ended the War of the Pacific, Chile obtained, with some minor restrictions, the territories she demanded. Although many Americans regretted the fate of Peru and Bolivia, apparently the only way that Blaine or anyone else could have saved them from Chile was with force, which the United States had never intended to use.

The Pan-American Idea

Ironically, Blaine's outstanding accomplishment in Latin-American relations, the launching of the Pan-American movement, grew out of his effort to exert moral pressure on Chile in favor of Peru through cooperation with other Latin-American nations. Before an assassin's bullet had struck down Garfield in July, 1881, Blaine had persuaded him to call a meeting of those states in Washington, ostensibly to discuss the general problem of preventing war in the Americas. The basic idea of a conference, however, did not originate with Blaine. In the United States it went back to Henry Clay who had suggested a league of American states in 1820. In Latin America, Simón Bolívar had made the first effort to bring those states together in his futile Panama Congress of 1826.

Blaine's Pan-Americanism contained two basic ideas: that the American states, mainly because they vaguely supported principles of republican government, should discuss common problems, and that they should seek cooperation in matters of peace and trade. It also included the hope that the conference, as a dramatic stroke of statesmanship, would save his Latin-American policy and enhance his stature as a candidate for the Presidency.[7]

Garfield's successor, Chester A. Arthur, reluctantly consented to go ahead with the gathering, and on November 28 Blaine sent invitations to all the independent Latin-American countries except Haiti. He announced the conference for November of the following year. Three weeks later Arthur replaced him with Frederick J. Frelinghuysen, a man whose politics were more congenial to Arthur's.

Secretary Frelinghuysen said the conference would "create jealousy and ill will" among those nations not invited, and "peace, the object sought by such consultation, would not be promoted." He was in fact, more disturbed by Blaine's bungling intervention, touched by rumors of scandal, in the hostilities between Chile and Peru. Therefore, he abruptly withdrew the invitations.[8]

The Pan-American idea did not die. Seven years later, in May, 1888, Congress asked President Cleveland to call a conference of American states to promote trade and preserve peace. Its scope was wider than that of Blaine's original conference. Congress' resolution called for an American customs union and uniform trade regulations to promote free trade in the Western Hemisphere. Cleveland's Secretary of State, Thomas F. Bayard, sent out the invitations in July.

Several months later Benjamin Harrison defeated Cleveland for the Presidency and appointed Blaine his Secretary of State. Thus Blaine, who eight years earlier had revived the Pan-American idea, welcomed the delegates from seventeen Latin-American states to the first Inter-American Conference that opened in Washington on October 2, 1889. He was chosen president of the conference.

With the idea of showing off the size and immense resources of the United States and hence help the promotion of trade, the government sponsored a railroad tour of some 5,400 miles for the Latins. At the end of forty-two days the exhausted delegates returned to Washington, duly impressed with the nation's wealth.

The work of the conference itself was disappointing. It rejected the proposal for a customs union and instead recommended that the countries desiring to do so negotiate separate reciprocal trade treaties. It adopted a plan for the arbitration of all disputes and various resolutions. Few of the Latin-American countries had enough interest in the agreements to ratify them.

Before the conference closed on April 19, 1890, it became entangled in domestic politics, and Blaine's critics had attacked it. Calling it "Mr. Blaine's Congress," one paper for instance, had said it would "accomplish nothing as long as the Republican party remains in power and continues to be the champion of high protection."

Realizing that Blaine wanted to take their Latin-American trade from them, Europeans also viewed the conference skeptically. A French paper pointed out that it had accomplished nothing practical. "Wholly platonic recommendations, which even so encountered a good deal of dissent, all the main proposals aborted— there is the balance sheet of the Pan-American Congress," it concluded.[9]

The critics were too harsh. The conference had not failed in everything. In establishing the International Bureau of the American Republics, later called the Pan-American Union, for the exchange of economic, scientific, and cultural information, it made a lasting contribution to the Pan-American movement. Even more important was the precedent of the gathering itself. It was the first of many conferences wherein matters of common interest to the American republics were discussed. Blaine left his own imprint on these early conferences. They avoided political matters and devoted themselves to the primary objective of promoting trade.

Blaine himself tried immediately to promote the trade objective. He opposed the protective McKinley tariff bill of 1890, calling certain of its provisions a "slap in the face to South Americans with whom we are trying to enlarge our trade." When the tariff became law on October 1, it contained a limited reciprocity clause his efforts had helped secure. Under it, Blaine negotiated a number of reciprocity agreements with Latin-American governments, but before the limited reciprocity had a fair trial a hostile Congress repealed it in 1894.

The ITATA Incident

Within a year of the conference Blaine encountered new difficulties in his Latin-American policy, again in relations with Chile. Since his failure to mediate the War of the Pacific to the benefit of Peru, Blaine and the United States had been unpopular in Chile. In January, 1891, a civil war broke out in Chile between her president on one side and the supporters of her congress on the other, who revolted against the president's efforts to increase executive power at the expense of the legislature.

The rebels, who controlled the Chilean navy, sent a steamer to San Diego, California, to obtain arms. Charging that the ship, the *Itata*, had violated neutrality laws, Federal authorities detained it on May 5. The next day the crew overpowered the American deputy marshal on board and sailed for Chile. Aware of the precedent of the *Alabama*'s escape and indignant over this affront to American authority, President Harrison sent a cruiser after the *Itata* to bring it back by force if necessary. Even though the cruiser failed to overtake the *Itata*, there was some danger it might clash with a Chilean cruiser designated to convoy the transport.

When the *Itata* reached Chile, the rebel authorities surrendered her to the United States. American courts later released the ship, saying it had not violated the neutrality laws, but the damage to relations with Chile had already been done. The revolutionists won the war with arms from Germany, despite the fact that the United States had denied them guns when desperately needed. "Since the unfortunate incident of the *Itata*," the American Minister in Chile wrote, "the young and unthinking element of those who were in opposition to the Government have had a bitter feeling against the United States."[10] The former rebels resented the hostility the American government had shown to their cause and in particular the threat of force it had used in recovering the *Itata*.

The BALTIMORE *Affair*

While this anti-American feeling was still running high, the captain of the U.S.S. *Baltimore*, one of three warships sent to Chile to protect American interests there during the civil war, gave shore leave in Valparaiso to 117 of his crew. That evening, October 16, 1891, Chilean hostility against the United States exploded in a street fight in the "Maintop," the city's tenderloin district, where a mob beat, stoned, and knifed the American sailors, killing two and wounding others. The skipper of the *Baltimore* placed full blame on the Chileans. The Chilean authorities argued that neither country was responsible since the affair was a drunken brawl between American and Chilean sailors.

When the news of the fight reached the United States, it aroused demands for retaliation. Accepting the interpretation of his naval officer, President Harrison took the view that it was not a mere sailors' brawl but a premeditated assault sparked by hatred of Americans that demanded "prompt and full reparation."

Concerned lest his Pan-American and reciprocity programs be damaged, Blaine wanted to play down the incident. He wished to "make a friend of Chile—if that is possible," but Harrison, a former soldier intensely proud of the flag and the uniform, regarded the attack as so serious that it required vigorous action. When Blaine offered his views in a cabinet meeting, the President, gesturing emphatically, said, "Mr. Secretary, that insult was to the uniform of the United States sailors."[11]

Chile was slow in making amends. In his annual message of December 9, therefore, Harrison threatened strong action. That threat angered Chile's Foreign Minister who publicly insulted Harrison and his government. Both countries now prepared for war and the *Baltimore* affair spawned the most serious crisis in Latin-American affairs since the French invasion of Mexico.

Since Blaine and the United States had proposed arbitration of disputes at the

Inter-American Conference, Chile suggested that kind of settlement for the *Baltimore* crisis, but Americans would not think of it. "When the United States is willing to submit the question of the murder of her sailors in uniform to arbitration," an American naval officer in Valparaiso wrote in his journal, "I must look for other employment—the navy won't any longer suit me." [12] Harrison's private secretary recorded in his diary that "the President stated that all members of the Cabinet are for war."

In trying to find a diplomatic solution for the crisis, Blaine had to overcome the opposition of the Navy Department, which was anxious for war. At its head stood Benjamin F. Tracy, one of the ablest Secretaries of the Navy and one of Harrison's two or three most trusted advisers. He was an expansionist who was carrying out a "big Navy" program and replacing old wooden ships with fast modern ones, armored with steel. He was a precursor of a new imperialism. [13]

The President backed Tracy against Blaine, often substituting his own notes to Chile, which were stronger in tone and fitted Navy policy, for those of Blaine and the State Department. During the crisis with Chile the Navy practically made foreign policy. An English diplomat in Washington wrote, for instance, that the United States was on the verge of war and that Blaine "has prevented war with Chile so far, and may do so still; but the President and the Navy are bent on it." [14]

Ignoring the views of his Secretary of State, Harrison sent Chile an ultimatum on January 21, 1892, demanding suitable apologies or he would terminate diplomatic relations. He waited four days and no reply came. On Sunday, January 24, he worked all day on a "war" message, which he sent to Congress the next day.

Without allies and fearing destruction by the more powerful United States, Chile had already wisely decided to give in to the American demands. Her note of surrender and apology arrived in the United States on Tuesday, January 26. That ended the crisis. Later, Chile paid $75,000 to the injured men and to the relatives of the dead sailors.

Although satisfactory to the United States, the settlement humiliated Chileans who resented the threat of naked force used against them. The *Baltimore* affair long embittered relations with Chile, and throughout Latin America reawakened suspicions of American imperialism. It wiped out whatever friendly feeling for the United States Blaine's Inter-American Conference may have stimulated. Latin Americans believed that the United States had interfered in Chile's domestic politics and had hectored her into paying an unjust indemnity.

Other nations, too, had observed the new bellicose tone of American foreign policy. A British student of American affairs wrote that "the moral for us is: what will the U.S. be like when their fleet is more powerful, if the administration acts in a similar manner?" [15] The British had reason to be concerned, for the next important problem in the Latin-American policy of the United States, over a disputed boundary between Venezuela and British Guiana, directly involved them, and the United States again displayed a jingoistic vigor.

Chinese Immigration

Meanwhile another problem, that of restricting Chinese immigration, had grown out of a domestic situation on the Pacific Coast. Before 1848 there were probably no more than fifty Chinese in the entire United States. After the discovery of gold in California thousands of laborers from densely populated southern China flocked to California to escape poverty at home and perhaps acquire wealth in a strange land. At first Californians welcomed the Chinese, who worked long hours in the mines or as cooks and launderers in the miners' camps. Yet from the beginning the Chinese suffered discrimination from racial prejudice written into local laws.[16]

After employment in the mining areas became slack, the Chinese filled the demand for cheap labor in the building of the Central Pacific Railroad, the western link of the transcontinental line. From 1860 to 1870 that railroad's construction company employed over ten thousand men, nine-tenths of them Chinese. When railroad construction ended, the Chinese laborers sought work wherever they could in a flooded labor market, becoming competitors for jobs with native Americans and with the increasing number of European workers who were coming to the United States. Californians, and others on the Pacific Coast, now added an economic argument to that of prejudice, saying that the Chinese were depriving whites of their livelihood and were lowering the white standard of living.

After 1870 Caucasian hostility led to demands for the exclusion of Chinese laborers from the United States, and a social and economic problem became a political and diplomatic one. Since the Chinese were concentrated in the Pacific Coast states, mostly in California, the problem was also essentially sectional. The panic of 1873 caused increasing unemployment on the Pacific Coast and intensified the hostility against the Chinese, leading to mob violence. Striking out blindly against economic forces they did not understand and seeing in the Chinese helpless scapegoats, the workingmen attacked them.

Since the slogan "The Chinese Must Go" became popular on the Pacific Coast and would bring votes, both Republicans and Democrats included demands for action against Chinese immigration in their national platforms of 1876. In that year, aware of the political possibilities of the issue, Congress appointed a special committee to investigate Chinese immigration.

At the same time California's laborers sought economic relief through politics. In 1877 they organized their own party, the Workingmen's Party of California. That summer, leaders of the new party held mass meetings in San Francisco's sand-lots and denounced the allegedly twin evils of capitalism and Chinese laborers. The most colorful of those sand-lot orators, an Irish-born agitator named Denis Kearney, preached an anti-Chinese doctrine of violence. After one meeting of some six thousand workingmen, hoodlums among them invaded San Francisco's Chinatown, burned buildings, sacked fifteen laundries, and broke windows in the Methodist Mission there. Usually, however, the Chinese suffered more from economic boycotts and job discrimination than from mob violence.

Californians were more interested in trade with China than were the people of any other section of the country; yet they were willing to sacrifice benefits that trade would bring rather than continue to accept the Chinese. They demanded that Congress ban Chinese immigration.

The main obstacle to exclusion was the Burlingame Treaty that allowed the Chinese to migrate freely to the United States. That obligation did not appear to bother Congress. In February, 1879, it passed the "Fifteen Passenger Bill," which said no ship could bring more than fifteen Chinese to an American port at any one time.

People of the Pacific Coast deluged President Rutherford B. Hayes with petitions urging him to sign the bill. Other sections, particularly the East, demanded that he veto it. The New York Chamber of Commerce, for example, denounced the bill as "establishing a bad precedent; as an unworthy political concession to the lawless spirit of a single State, under whose laws the subjects of China have enjoyed neither peace nor safety; as tending to degrade the national character in the sight of all other nations." [17]

"Our treaty with China forbids me to give it my approval," Hayes wrote in his diary. "The treaty was of our asking." [18] On March 1, therefore, he vetoed the bill. Even so, the "Fifteen Passenger Bill" was a turning point in immigration policy. It was only a matter of time before Chinese restriction would become national law. Hayes and Secretary of State Evarts realized that. Therefore, they sent a special mission to China to revise the Burlingame Treaty and obtain the legal right to restrict Chinese immigration.

The Coming of Chinese Exclusion

James B. Angell, president of the University of Michigan, who headed the commission, had discussed Chinese immigration with Secretary Evarts. Restriction, he had told Evarts, would probably win popular support. Any absolute prohibition, he warned, however, would be "diametrically opposed to all our national traditions and would call down the censure of a very large portion if not a majority of our most intelligent and high-minded citizens." [19]

Angry over the mistreatment of their people in California, the officials of the Chinese Foreign Office would not consider prohibition, but finally agreed to some limitations on the immigration of laborers. On November 17, 1880, the commission signed two treaties with China. The first, a commercial agreement, contained a noteworthy clause prohibiting Americans from trading in opium in China.

The other, the immigration treaty which modified the Burlingame Treaty, was itself China's major concession. It gave the United States the right to "regulate, limit, or suspend," but not to prohibit, entry of Chinese laborers into the United States. The "limitation or suspension," the treaty said, should be "reasonable," and should apply only to Chinese who "may go to the United States as laborers, other classes not being included in the limitation." Congress approved both treaties. Then it passed an act suspending Chinese immigration for twenty years.[20] President Chester A. Arthur believed that under the terms of the Angell Treaty twenty years was not "reasonable," and vetoed the bill in April, 1882.

Since Congress did not succeed in overriding the veto, it hurriedly passed another bill suspending the flow of Chinese laborers for ten years and declaring that "hereafter no state court or court of the United States shall admit Chinese to citizenship." The President signed it on May 6. Two years later Congress amended and strengthened the law. The act of 1882, usually called the Chinese Exclusion Law, marked a radical departure from the nation's policy of offering a haven to the peoples of all nations. It also violated the spirit of treaties with China and created ill will in China, which grew as anti-Chinese violence spread throughout the American West. One of the most serious outbreaks was the massacre in Rock Springs, Wyoming, in September, 1885. A white mob attacked the Chinese quarter there, burning and destroying property, murdering twenty-eight Chinese, and seriously wounding fifteen others. The Chinese Minister in Washington complained. Secretary Bayard expressed regret and promised an investigation.

While the government investigated the Rock Springs massacre, the people of Seattle, Washington Territory, took the law into their own hands and expelled the Chinese from their homes, chanting "The Chinese Must Go." "The Civilization of the Pacific Coast," one newspaper declared, "cannot be half-Caucasian and half-Mongolian." Even soldiers sent to protect the Chinese beat them up and cut off their queues. "The chances are," another paper remarked, "that the people will be called on to protect the Chinese."[21]

After almost six weeks of continuous anti-Chinese agitation, mass meetings, and newspaper propaganda, the people of Tacoma, Washington Territory, also resorted to mob violence against the Chinese. Abetted by local authorities, they expelled two hundred Chinese on November 3 and burned their property. President Cleveland warned the people of the Washington Territory by proclamation against mob violence and ordered Federal troops there to "preserve order."

The Chinese government demanded redress for the injuries its people had suffered. When Secretary of State Bayard explained that the Federal government could not interfere with the administration of local and state laws unless allowed by the Constitution, the Chinese could not understand. Why, they asked, should dual government protect wrongdoing in the United States and not offer the same immunities to Chinese authorities when Chinese mobs injured Americans and other foreigners? Chinese provincial and local authorities had several times indemnified Americans for losses incurred through riots.

Bayard answered some of the complaints in February, saying that he was himself outraged by the attacks on the Chinese. Since private individuals, not Federal officials, had made them, the government denied responsibility or obligation for redress. Out of "generosity and pity," he added, however, the President might ask Congress to offer assistance to those Chinese who had suffered losses from mob violence.

Those Chinese who returned home reported on the humiliations they had suffered in the United States, and their stories contributed to the stirring up of anti-American mobs in China. So worried did the American Minister in Peking become over possible retaliatory attacks against Americans that he asked the government to send warships to Canton and other ports "to give what protection and asylum they can to American citizens who may become the objects of mob-assault in that region." [22]

China was then weak. She had no warships to send to San Francisco and Seattle to protect her citizens there. [23] She therefore expressed willingness to make a treaty prohibiting Chinese laborers from emigrating to the United States if the government would guarantee the safety of Chinese already there and would pay for past injuries and losses. In February, 1887, Congress offered payment for the losses at Rock Springs, but said nothing about responsibility.

Finally, on March 12, 1888, Bayard and the Chinese Minister in Washington signed a treaty excluding Chinese laborers from the United States for twenty years. The United States agreed, as a gesture of friendship, to pay the Chinese government an indemnity of $276,619 for losses through mob violence, but without admitting the Federal government's responsibility. In essence, with the treaty, China agreed to recognize the principle of exclusion that Americans had enacted into law six years earlier. The Senate amended the treaty, approved it, and enacted legislation to carry it into effect, but China did not ratify it. For the first time in the history of a treaty, the Chinese Foreign Office said, the people protested. A mob in Canton demonstrated against the treaty.

Without waiting for China to indicate her reaction to the treaty, but assuming rejection, William L. Scott, Cleveland's friend and campaign manager, introduced a bill into the House of Representatives excluding Chinese laborers. It passed quickly, and Cleveland, anxious to win votes in California in the presidential campaign of that year, signed it on October 1.

The Scott Act prohibited Chinese who had gone home for a visit from returning, and abrogated the Angell Treaty without the courtesy of notifying the Chinese government beforehand. In the past China's own foreign relations had been motivated by prejudice and antiforeignism. Now, ironically, the United States had permitted racial prejudice and political opportunism to take the place of statesmanship in the policy toward the Chinese.

China protested but that made little difference. Since President Harrison, who succeeded Cleveland, and Secretary of State Blaine favored exclusion, they ignored the protests and virtually broke off diplomatic relations with China. In the spring of 1889, the Supreme Court declared the Scott Act constitutional but said it violated the Angell Treaty. In July the Chinese Minister in the United States said he was shocked by the fact that American law allowed the government to "release itself from treaty obligations without consultation with, or the consent of, the other party to what we had been accustomed to regard as a sacred instrument."

With the Geary Act of May 5, 1892, Congress extended the provisions of the Scott Act for another ten years and strengthened Chinese exclusion. The Supreme Court a year later declared that law, the most stringent of the anti-Chinese legislation, constitutional. The Chinese government protested against the injustice of the law, but the American government ignored the protests. It continued, however, to demand special rights through unequal treaties for American merchants and missionaries in China.

Finally, on March 17, 1894, in exchange for a more lenient enforcement of the exclusion laws, China signed a treaty that "absolutely prohibited" Chinese laborers from emigrating to the United States for ten years. It was almost identical to the unratified treaty of 1888, and either country could renew it for another ten years unless either gave formal notice of termination.

Since Congress again renewed the exclusion laws in April, 1902, without consulting China, this time indefinitely, the Chinese government gave formal notice in January, 1904, of intention to terminate the treaty of 1894 the following December. On April 27, therefore, Congress amended the act of 1902 by omitting previous reference to treaty obligations. Chinese exclusion, based on an unfounded theory of Chinese inferiority, remained national policy. "Congress had done its work so well," Secretary of State John Hay wrote, "that even Confucius could not become an American—though he should seek it with prayers and tears."[24]

In parts of China, hatred of Americans, sparked by a rising nationalism, burned deeply. In 1904 and 1905 people boycotted American goods, and anti-American feeling swept through the treaty ports and several provinces. Even though the United States was the only great power which had not used force against China, it was, because of its exclusion policy and mistreatment of Chinese, the first country whose goods and people were boycotted.[25]

"The Chinese people are in earnest," the Chinese Ambassador said. "Your exclusion act is humiliating. They would prefer to pay a huge indemnity or surrender a slice of territory rather than be insulted and menaced as they are by the attitude of the United States."[26] The prejudices of one section of the country, catered to by politicians, had sown ill will among the Chinese. Although no one knew how much, it seems clear that those domestic actions had also injured American foreign policy in China.

The Northeast Fisheries

While the people of the West Coast were fighting for Chinese exclusion, those of New England found the old problem of the Canadian fisheries as irritating as ever. They had always resented the large award Canada had received under the Treaty of Washington and had disliked some of its other fisheries provisions. On March 3, 1883, by joint resolution, therefore, Congress abolished the special privileges of that treaty as of July 1, 1885. American fishing rights in Canadian waters would then rest on the obsolete Convention of 1818. Since July fell in the middle of the fishing season, and sudden termination might create friction and misunderstandings between Canadians and American fishermen, Secretary of State Bayard worked out a "temporary diplomatic agreement" in June, 1885, that allowed Americans to continue fishing in Canadian waters under the terms of the Treaty of Washington.

The agreement obligated President Cleveland to ask Congress for authority to appoint Americans to a joint commission with the British to settle the whole question. Cleveland requested the authority in December. Since he was a Democrat, and Republicans controlled Congress, he was refused. During the next fishing season Canadian and Newfoundland officials strictly enforced and even went beyond the rules of the Convention of 1818, seizing American fishing craft and arresting their crews for true and alleged violation of regulations.

At the end of that season, therefore, Bayard offered to negotiate a permanent understanding on the issue through a joint commission that would study the problem. Congress, meanwhile, had passed a bill, which the President approved in March, 1887, authorizing him at his discretion to retaliate against Canadians by suspending their trading privileges in the United States. Even though Cleveland signed the bill, he had no intention of using it as anything but a lever to force concessions from Britain and Canada.

Perhaps Cleveland's lever worked, because the British immediately agreed to a negotiation in Washington by a joint commission. Bayard headed the American commissioners, and Joseph Chamberlain led the British representatives who met in November. After long negotiation, they signed a compromise treaty in February, 1888. Although this agreement promised the end of this old problem, it encountered strong opposition in the Senate.

Cleveland signed the treaty on February 20 and transmitted it to the Senate the same day, urging approval, but 1888 was an election year and New Englanders and other Republicans, who narrowly controlled the Senate, would not allow a Democratic President to win credit for settling the long-festering dispute. "The better the treaty," one of the commissioners wrote, "the worse it is likely to fare at the hands of the extreme men who do not mean that the Administration shall get any help from it." [27] In criticizing the agreement, opponents tried to make it appear a surrender to the British and thus place the President in a weak position with the Irish-American voters and other Anglophobes. In a strictly party vote on August 21 the Republican senators killed the treaty.

In a political countermove two days later, Cleveland sent a strong message to Congress, ostensibly aimed at Canada but designed to embarrass the Senate, urging Congress to grant him power to strike against Canadian trade. "And above all things," he said, "the plan of retaliation, if entered upon, should be thorough and vigorous." [28] Fearing business losses and injury in the presidential election, the Republicans would not grant him the retaliatory power he requested.

Even though the death of the Bayard-Chamberlain Treaty embittered Canadians, it did not lead to conflict over the fisheries because the commissioners had also agreed to a two-year working arrangement, or *modus vivendi*. Although never fully satisfactory, the arrangement continued, with renewals, for several years. Yet partisan politics and sectional interests had destroyed the opportunity for a permanent settlement of a long smoldering dispute.

Sackville-West

In Pomona, California, a Republican fruit grower named George Osgoodby read Cleveland's retaliatory message on the fisheries question and suspected it of being an electioneering device designed to catch votes among Irish-Americans and New Englanders. He therefore sent the British Minister in Washington, Sir Lionel Sackville-West, a letter saying he was a naturalized American who had been born an Englishman and signed it Charles F. Murchison. He asked "privately and confidentially" if Cleveland's foreign policy would in the long run "favor England's interests" and if he should vote for Cleveland.

Lord Sackville blundered into Osgoodby's trap. He replied in September, 1888, that he favored Cleveland. Republican campaign managers obtained Sackville's letter and shortly before the election published it. In the furor that followed, Democrats and Republicans both denounced the diplomat for interfering in America's domestic politics. Republicans said his letter proved that Cleveland was a tool of Britain. Democrats demanded that Cleveland dismiss Sackville. "Now kick out Lord Sackville with your biggest boot of best leather, and you've got 'em," a Democratic editor advised Cleveland. "*Hesitation is death.*" [29]

The President in effect followed that advice. First he demanded Sackville's recall. "The President feels deeply this conduct of the British Minister," Bayard told the British Foreign Secretary, "and the sentiment of both political parties is in concurrence that his usefulness in this country has ended."[30]

The Foreign Secretary refused to recall Sackville without having the opportunity to examine the complaint against him. Cleveland then dismissed the unfortunate diplomat to show that he and the Democratic party were in no way subservient to Britain. Nonetheless, Republican campaign orators insisted that the administration had always been pro-English. "They have given Sir Sackville the shake, and now all that remains for you to do," a prominent Republican told campaign audiences, "is to give Mr. Cleveland the sack."[31]

The British were angry because they believed that the President had sacrificed Sackville-West for political reasons and not for any wrongdoing. They refused to send another minister to the United States until after Cleveland left the White House.[32]

The German Pork Dispute

Another question stemming from domestic developments, but more economic than political, was that of pork exports to Europe. By 1881 Britain, France, Austria, Italy, Turkey, Greece, and Germany restricted, or prohibited, imports of American pork and pork products such as ham, bacon, and lard, alleging that those meats were infected with trichinosis, a parasitic disease harmful to man and hence dangerous to the health of their peoples.[33] The German ban was the one most offensive to the United States and touched off a dispute that spread over a decade.

One reason for the bitterness between Germany and the United States over the pork products was that both countries had adopted a protective tariff as national policy at about the same time, the United States after the Civil War and Germany in 1879 in the decade after her unification. Germany's protective policy was essentially agrarian, while that of the United States was industrial. Both Germany and the United States in this period became industrial nations, but Germany also changed from a food exporting to a food importing nation. The United States soon became the world's greatest exporter of pork products.

The restrictions on pork struck hard at American farmers and the great meat packing industry of the Midwest. The hog raisers and meat packers exerted considerable pressure on the Department of State and Congress to persuade the Europeans to lift their restrictions. Some believed that the Germans used the "dreadful parasites" as an excuse to enable their hog raisers to maintain high prices for native pork. When the German government planned total exclusion of American pork products, the American Minister in Berlin advised in January, 1883, that "the only argument that would be effective against the measure would be fear of reprisals." In March, Germany went beyond restriction and excluded all American pork products.

Hog raisers, among them German-Americans who had settled in the pork centers of the Midwest, cried for relief and denounced the German government. What particularly irked Americans was that Germany banned only American pork—"and that," one paper said, "on a pretext which, being officially set up by a responsible government, tends to injure the reputation of American hog products in all other countries." [34]

Since Chancellor Otto von Bismarck considered the large landowners, who produced pork and resented low-priced American competition, pillars of the German monarchy, he wanted to protect them. "It is absolutely necessary for us people of Europe," he told an American journalist in July, 1884, "to protect ourselves in time against your competition, for whenever the point arrives that the United States is not checked in its inroads on our agriculture, complete ruin will overtake our landholding classes."

Americans demanded retaliation against Bismarck's policy, but that did not prove necessary. Beginning in 1886, Congress met most of the German complaints by passing laws subjecting meats to rigid inspection before export. Those laws gave Germany the excuse to remove the ban on American pork without appearing to surrender to threats of retaliation. Yet such a threat, particularly as embodied in a new tariff, was more effective than the inspection laws.

In this period, Germany profited from the export of beet sugar to the United States. Republican protectionists came to power when Benjamin Harrison became President in 1889. On October 1, 1890, Congress passed the McKinley tariff empowering the President to impose a duty on German sugar. Germany suggested that it would accept the meat inspection laws as satisfactory and remove the ban on pork if the United States would not impose a duty on German sugar under the new tariff. The United States accepted this compromise in an exchange of declarations with a German diplomat at Saratoga, New York, on August 22, 1891. The "Saratoga Agreement" ended the pork dispute.

The New Orleans Affair

Shortly before the settlement of the pork controversy, the United States ran into a quarrel with Italy, another newly unified European power. A large number of Italians had settled in New Orleans where unknown assassins killed the popular superintendent of police in March, 1891. Most people believed that the murderers had come from the local Sicilian population. The authorities rounded up suspects, all of them Italians or of Italian origin, and brought them to trial. The jury failed to make any convictions. To aroused onlookers the accused appeared guilty and the verdict unjust. A roaring mob of six to eight thousand, led by prominent citizens, rushed to the jail. Within twenty minutes, without restraint from state or local law officers, the mob systematically lynched eleven of the suspects. Three were Italian subjects, and the others were naturalized Americans or had declared their intentions of becoming citizens.

Baron Francesco Saverio Fava, the Italian Minister in Washington, immediately protested to Secretary of State Blaine, denouncing the inaction of the New Orleans authorities and asking him to take "precautions" against further violence to the Italian colony there. Blaine expressed regret and sent a telegram to the governor of Louisiana asking him to protect Italian subjects from further mob violence and to investigate the lynchings.

That action did not satisfy the Italian government. It wanted official assurance that the guilty parties would be brought to trial, and an indemnity for the families of the mob victims. The Italian demands placed the Federal government in a dilemma similar to those in the cases of mob violence against the Chinese. "The recent outbreak in New Orleans against the Italians," William Howard Taft, then solicitor general, wrote, "has raised some rather embarrassing international questions, and emphasizes the somewhat anomalous character of our Government, which makes the National Government responsible for the action of the State authorities without giving it any power to control that action."[35]

After a few weeks of fruitless negotiation, the Italian government recalled Baron Fava and the United States called home its Minister from Rome. The Italian press attacked the United States, and mass meetings in Italy demanded satisfaction for the New Orleans violence. In the United States, Baron Fava's recall turned the affair into a front-page sensation. While most newspapers advised moderation, some spoke of war, reflecting the new and rising militancy and pugnacious nationalism in this period.[36]

Although serious, the situation did not create any real danger of war. Italy's Premier, Marquis Antonio Starabba di Rudini, had to deal with aroused public emotions. Since his coalition government was unstable, he had recalled Fava to impress his own people with a show of energy and not particularly with the intention of exerting unreasonable pressure on the United States. The fact that a grand jury sat for two months in New Orleans and failed to indict any of the leaders of the lynch mob made his domestic position even more difficult.

After public tempers had cooled, both governments attempted to find a peaceful settlement. President Harrison and Secretary Blaine sought a constitutional means of enabling the Federal government to prosecute the leaders of the mob, but uncovered no law giving the Federal courts jurisdiction. They did, however, find an indirect way of meeting Italian demands for an indemnity.

In his annual message in December, Harrison in effect offered an apology, and in April, 1892, after extended negotiations, Blaine said the "lamentable massacre at New Orleans" obligated the United States to pay a satisfactory indemnity. The President, he added, had instructed him to offer $25,000 to the families of the victims and hoped that the indemnity would compensate for the tragedy and that Italy and the United States might resume friendly relations. The Italian government accepted the indemnity and immediately restored full diplomatic relations.

In paying the indemnity Harrison circumvented the usual procedure of asking Congress for an appropriation. He took the money from the contingent fund of the Department of State for "expenses." Since Congress on previous occasions had been reluctant to pay indemnities, the St. Paul *Pioneer-Press* said the action was "proper and wise." If the question of an appropriation had gone to Congress, it pointed out, it "would have been fought and delayed and haggled over until all the graciousness was taken out of the act." [37] Some members of Congress were dissatisfied. They believed that Harrison had usurped their prerogatives and had violated precedent.

Despite the passions it aroused, the brief New Orleans affair was a minor diplomatic incident, but it exposed the struggle between Congress and the President for control of foreign policy and emphasized the constitutional gap in cases of mob violence against aliens. According to international law, the Federal government is obligated to protect aliens, but under the Constitution the states have the main responsibility for maintaining public order, including the protection of aliens and their property from mob violence.

The Bering Sea Controversy

In contrast to its inadequate powers to protect aliens from mob violence, the Federal government in the 1880's tried to stretch its domestic laws beyond the traditional three-mile limit of national jurisdiction in order to protect fur seals in the North Pacific. One of three surviving seal herds would spend each summer on two of the Pribilof Islands in the Bering Sea that the United States had acquired from Russia with the purchase of Alaska. Almost from the beginning the United States took the position that since the seals had their breeding grounds on American territory, they were American property wherever they went, even beyond the three-mile limit. In 1870 it gave the Alaska Commercial Company, a private concern, the sole right to hunt male seals on the Pribilof Islands for twenty years.

In 1881 and 1882 American and Canadian hunters, attracted by the high prices the seal skins were bringing, defied the monopoly and began hunting the seals as they swam or floated beyond the three-mile limit, a practice called pelagic sealing. That practice, on a commercial scale, threatened to exterminate the herd. Since the seals were polygamous, and only about one male for each hundred females was necessary to propagate the herd, hunters could slaughter the males with profit and without endangering the species. While the seals swam, however, hunters

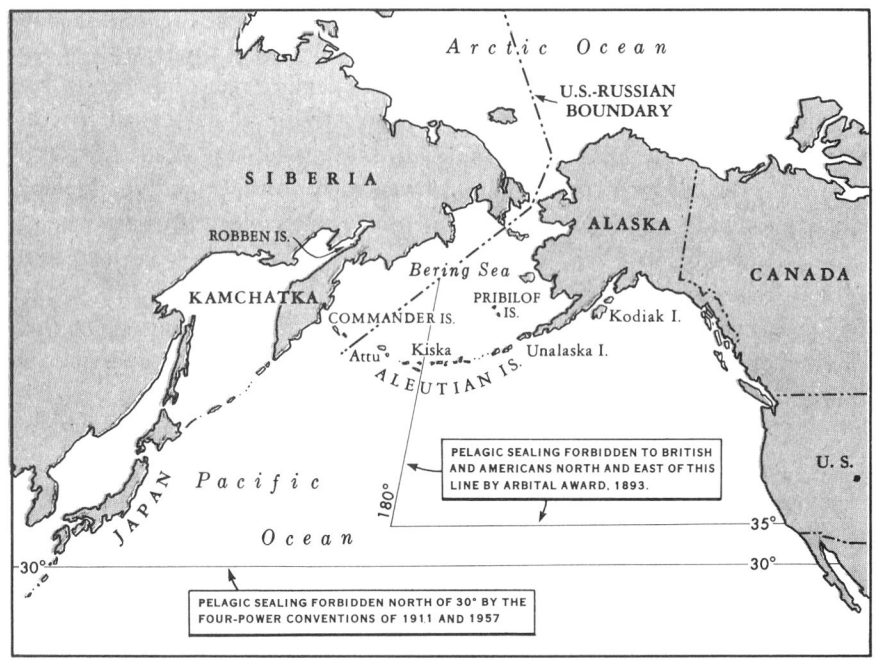

THE BERING SEA SEAL CONTROVERSY

could not easily distinguish male from female. Since the cow-mother roamed the sea searching for food while the bull remained on the beach, over eighty per cent of the seals the pelagic hunters killed were females. The hunters did not always recover mortally wounded animals and all the others they killed. Each female they killed, moreover, usually had an unborn pup within her and a nursing pup on land which would die if she did not return. For every seal the pelagic hunters killed and recovered, therefore, about four others died.

To stop the indiscriminate slaughter, American officials, in August, 1886, began seizing ships engaged in pelagic sealing. They arrested Canadians on the theory that the Bering Sea was a closed sea, a *mare clausum*, covered by American laws which Canadians had violated. Britain immediately protested, and a long diplomatic dispute ensued. The British insisted that the Bering Sea was not a closed area controlled by American law and that American revenue cutters had no right whatever to take their vessels on the high seas.

Americans became angry because the pelagic sealing did not stop, and Canadians fumed over the seizure of their ships. Newspapers in both countries demanded drastic action. In 1887 Secretary of State Bayard tried unsuccessfully to settle the controversy through international agreement.

When Blaine became Secretary of State for the second time in 1889, he took up the dispute. Instead of claiming that the Bering Sea was a closed sea, he maintained that pelagic sealing threatened to destroy the Pribilof herd and hence violated good morals and involved a permanent injury to the United States. He then argued that through long-continued acquiescence of all nations, Russia had acquired a pre-eminent right over the seals in that sea beyond the three-mile limit, and that the United States had succeeded to that prescriptive right.[38]

Britain rejected Blaine's arguments of prescriptive right. She insisted, as before, that pelagic sealing did not justify the taking of foreign vessels on the high seas. International law allowed such seizures in time of peace only by mutual agreement, or if the ships were pirate craft. The British said that if the United States continued to interfere with their flag on the seas they would take strong action, but also offered to submit the whole sealing question to an impartial arbitration.[39]

After arguing for over a year, the United States and Britain signed a treaty on February 29, 1892, which submitted the dispute to seven arbitrators. The Senate approved the treaty in March, and a year later the arbitral tribunal met in Paris. In August, 1893, it announced that every one of the major points was decided against the United States. It denied any right of American jurisdiction over the Bering Sea, upheld the freedom of the seas in time of peace, and destroyed the theory that the United States had a "property right" in the seals of the Bering Sea. Later, in June, 1898, the United States paid $473,151 to Britain for claims concerning her ships that had been seized by American revenue cutters.

Pelagic sealing continued, and after 1900 the Japanese took an even greater toll of the herd than did the Canadians. Some of the Japanese sealers even poached within the three-mile limit. In July, 1906, for instance, Japanese hunters landed on one of the Pribilofs and began slaughtering seals. American authorities fired on the poachers, killing five and wounding two, and took five prisoners.

To avoid more dangerous international incidents and to save the seals, the United States offered important concessions to Japan and Canada if they would agree to stop their nationals from pelagic sealing. Since Russia was losing seals from a herd she controlled, she was ready to join any international agreement to save the seals. The four Pacific powers, Russia, Japan, Britain, and the United States, signed the North Pacific Sealing Convention on July 7, 1911. Each of them promised to prohibit their own nationals from pelagic sealing, and the United States agreed to give Japan fifteen per cent of the seal skins it took each year from the Pribilof herd and a similar amount to Canada.[40]

In the years following the convention, the herd increased rapidly and Japan, Canada, and the United States profited from the regulated killing of the males. Japan, however, was not satisfied. She claimed that the seals were injuring im-portant fisheries and in October, 1940, denounced the convention by giving the one-year notice. Canada and the United States continued to forbid pelagic sealing to their own citizens. On February 9, 1957, after negotiating for two years, Russia, Japan, Canada, and the United States signed another North Pacific Sealing Convention. This one prohibited pelagic sealing, allowed visit and search, gave Japan and Canada fifteen per cent of the Russian and American annual kill, and provided for a cooperative research program under a four-power Fur Seal Commission.[41]

NOTES

1. Dec. 6, 1869, in James D. Richardson, ed., *A Compilation of the Messages and Papers of the Presidents, 1789–1899* (10 vols., Washington, 1896–99), VII, 33.

2. *Ibid.*, VII, 585–586. Evarts' biographer calls this his greatest state paper. Chester L. Barrows, *William M. Evarts: Lawyer, Diplomat, Statesman* (Chapel Hill, N.C., 1941), p. 364.

3. Quoted in Philip M. Brown, "Frederick Theodore Frelinghuysen," in Samuel F. Bemis, ed., *The American Secretaries of State and Their Diplomacy* (10 vols., New York, 1927–29), VIII, 28.

4. Dec. 8, 1885, in Richardson, *Messages of the Presidents*, VIII, 327–328.

5. Russell H. Bastert, "A New Approach to the Origins of Blaine's Pan-American Policy," *Hispanic American Historical Review*, XXXIX (Aug. 1959), 379–380, points out that Blaine did not develop his Latin-American policy until after he became Secretary of State.

6. To P. H. Morgan, June 1, 1881, *Foreign Relations of the United States, 1881*, p. 761.

7. For details, see Bastert, "A New Approach to Blaine's Pan-American Policy," *Hispanic American Historical Review*, XXXIX (Aug. 1959), 403–405.

8. For details, see Russell H. Bastert, "Diplomatic Reversal: Frelinghuysen's Opposition to Blaine's Pan-American Policy in 1882," *Mississippi Valley Historical Review*, XLII (March 1956), 653–671.

9. The quoted newspapers are the New York *Herald*, April 16, 1890, and the *Revue Sud-Américaine*, May 18, 1890, in A. Curtis

Wilgus, "James G. Blaine and the Pan-American Movement," *Hispanic American Historical Review*, V (Nov. 1922), 702, 705. See Thomas F. McGann, *Argentina, the United States, and the Inter-American System, 1880–1914* (Cambridge, Mass., 1957), pp. 130–164, for a detailed analysis of the first Pan-American Conference.

10. Quoted in Osgood Hardy, "The *Itata* Incident," *Hispanic American Historical Review*, V (May 1922), 198. Chileans also thought that the American Minister, Patrick Egan, had aided the presidential party. For details, see Hardy, "Was Patrick Egan a 'Blundering Minister'?" *ibid.*, VIII (Feb. 1928), 65–81.

11. Quoted in Albert T. Volwiler, "Harrison, Blaine, and American Foreign Policy, 1889–1893," *Proceedings of the American Philosophical Society*, LXXIX (Nov. 15, 1938), 640.

12. Dec. 31, 1891, in Robley D. Evans, *A Sailor's Log: Recollections of Forty Years of Naval Life* (London, 1901), p. 279.

13. For details, see John K. Mahon, "Benjamin Franklin Tracy: Secretary of the Navy, 1889–1893," *New York Historical Society Quarterly*, XLIV (April 1960), 179–201.

14. Cecil Spring-Rice, Jan. 19, 1892, quoted in Volwiler, "Harrison, Blaine, and American Foreign Policy," *Proceedings of the American Philosophical Society*, LXXIX (Nov. 15, 1938), 645.

15. Spring-Rice, *ibid.*, p. 647.

16. See Rodman W. Paul, "The Origin of the Chinese Issue in California," *Mississippi*

Valley Historical Review, XXV (Sept. 1938), 181–196.

17. Feb. 27, 1879, quoted in Charles C. Tansill, The Foreign Policy of Thomas F. Bayard, 1885–1897 (New York, 1940), p. 129.

18. Quoted in Claude G. Bowers and Helen D. Reid, "William M. Evarts," in Bemis, Secretaries of State, VII, 253.

19. March 11, 1880, quoted in Tansill, Bayard, p. 132.

20. The text of the treaties is in Shirley W. Smith, James Burrill Angell: An American Influence (Ann Arbor, Mich., 1954), pp. 136–139. For additional details, see James B. Angell, "The Diplomatic Relations between the United States and China," Journal of Social Science, XVII (Sept. 1882), 27–36. He denies that the Chinese conceded the immigration treaty in exchange for the prohibition of the opium trade. For a summary of anti-Chinese legislation, see Li Tien-lu, Congressional Policy of Chinese Immigration (Nashville, Tenn., 1916).

21. The Seattle Post-Intelligencer of Sept. 11, 1885 and the Seattle Call of Nov. 9 quoted in Jules A. Karlin, "Anti-Chinese Outbreaks in Seattle, 1885–1886," Pacific Northwest Quarterly, XXXIX (April 1948), 114. See also, Karlin, "The Anti-Chinese Outbreak in Tacoma, 1885," Pacific Historical Review, XXII (Aug. 1954), 271–283.

22. Charles Denby to Bayard, Feb. 27, 1886, quoted in Tansill, Bayard, p. 143n.

23. A few years later when China acquired two battleships, each larger than any in the American Navy, one uneasy congressman suggested that it would be wise to "build ships equal in power to the ships of the nation we treat with such contumely." Quoted in Robert Seager, III, "Ten Years Before Mahan: The Unofficial Case for the New Navy, 1880–1890," Mississippi Valley Historical Review, XL (Dec. 1953), 492.

24. To Theodore Roosevelt, March 2, 1904, quoted in Howard K. Beale, Theodore Roosevelt and the Rise of America to World Power (Baltimore, 1956), p. 214.

25. For details, see Mary R. Coolidge, Chinese Immigration (New York, 1909), pp. 468–485.

26. May 21, 1905, quoted in Beale, Theodore Roosevelt, p. 218.

27. James B. Angell to Bayard, Feb. 24, 1888, quoted in Tansill, Bayard, p. 301.

28. Richardson, Messages of the President, VIII, 621.

29. Quoted in Allan Nevins, Grover Cleveland: A Study in Courage (New York, 1932), p. 430.

30. To Edward J. Phelps, Oct. 26, 1888, in Tansill, Bayard, p. 334.

31. John Sherman quoted in Nevins, Cleveland, p. 431.

32. For a critical analysis of the episode, see Charles S. Campbell, Jr., "The Dismissal of Lord Sackville," Mississippi Valley Historical Review, XLIV (March 1958), 635–648.

33. See John L. Gignilliat, "Pigs, Politics, and Protection: The European Boycott of American Pork, 1871–1891," Agricultural History, XXXV (Jan. 1961), 3–12, which points out that fear of trichinosis was a godsend to European protectionists.

34. New York Herald, March 17, 1883, quoted in Louis L. Snyder, "The American-German Pork Dispute, 1879–1891," Journal of Modern History, XVII (March 1945), 24.

35. March 18, 1891, quoted in Jules A. Karlin, "The Indemnification of Aliens Injured by Mob Violence," Southwestern Social Science Quarterly, XXV (March 1945), 35.

36. For a convenient, balanced summary of the antiforeignism this episode aroused, see John Higham, Strangers in the Land: Patterns of American Nativism, 1860–1925 (New Brunswick, N.J., 1955), pp. 90–92. For other details, see John E. Coxe, "The

New Orleans Mafia Incident," *Louisiana Historical Society*, XX (Oct. 1937), 1067–1110.

37. April 16, 1892, quoted in Karlin, "Indemnification of Aliens," *Southwestern Social Science Quarterly*, XXV (March 1945), 242. Karlin also suggests that the incident produced a war scare that contributed to a new sense of national unity. See his "The Italo-American Incident of 1891 and the Road to Reunion," *Journal of Southern History*, VIII (May 1942), 242–246.

38. For details, see Joseph B. Lockey, "James Gillespie Blaine," in Bemis, *Secretaries of State*, VIII, 132–135.

39. In "The Anglo-American Crisis in the Bering Sea, 1890–1891," *Mississippi Valley Historical Review*, XLVIII (Dec. 1961), 393–414, Charles S. Campbell, Jr., points out that land sealing was just as blameworthy as pelagic sealing for the decline in the Pribilof herd and that this influenced a *modus vivendi* with Britain in June, 1891.

40. See Thomas A. Bailey, "The North Pacific Sealing Convention of 1911," *Pacific Historical Review*, IV (1935), 1–14.

41. Details are in Henry Reiff, *The United States and the Treaty Law of the Sea* (Minneapolis, 1950), pp. 182–184, 285–288. So successful did this four-power program become that it was "regarded as one of the most felicitous ventures in international cooperation," and was renewed in February, 1962. See *The New York Times*, Feb. 10, 1962, 3.5.

Chapter Thirteen

DAWN OF A NEW DESTINY

THE LAST two decades of the nineteenth century also witnessed the burgeoning of another distinctive pattern of ideas in foreign relations, an intensified spirit of expansion usually called the New Manifest Destiny. It, too, was based on a belligerent nationalism, but also on recently acquired industrial wealth and notions of racial superiority. In some ways the new imperialism was not new. Some of its ideas, or at least similar ones, were implicit in the Manifest Destiny preceding the Civil War.

What made the New Manifest Destiny different from the old expansionism was its unvarnished racism, its claim to scientific foundations, and its popularity. Its claim to scientific respectability rested on the work of the English naturalist, Charles R. Darwin, mainly on two of his books published twelve years apart, *On the Origin of Species* (1859) and *Descent of Man* (1871). The central idea in his theory of evolution was that of "natural selection," or that the struggle for life favored those who possessed the characteristics enabling them to survive in their environment at the expense of their fellows.

Other men, particularly the self-made English philosopher and sociologist, Herbert Spencer, took Darwin's ideas and applied them to man in social, economic, and political situations. This became Social Darwinism, which popularized such terms as the "survival of the fittest" in the "struggle for existence." If the "fittest" survived among men and animals, the same might hold true for peoples and nations. This was an attractive doctrine for a young, vigorous, and expansive people such as Americans were at the end of the nineteenth century.

American writers and thinkers quickly took up the gospel of Social Darwinism and made it a part of their expansionist philosophy. The bumptious nationalism of the New Manifest Destiny, with or without the racism of Social Darwinism, was evident, for instance, in the *Baltimore* affair with Chile and in the reaction to Italian protests over the New Orleans lynchings. Among the Americans most prominent in preaching the new expansionist doctrine and in working its ideas into thinking on foreign policy were the historian John Fiske, the Congregational clergyman Josiah Strong, the political scientist John W. Burgess, and the naval officer Alfred Thayer Mahan.

Basic to the New Manifest Destiny was the dogma of Anglo-Saxon superiority. Since the Anglo-Saxons were superior, the racial theory went, they must expand to show their fitness. John Fiske advanced that idea and made it popular, particularly in his essay "Manifest Destiny," published in *Harper's Magazine* of March, 1885. He presented the same idea in a book that year, and he repeated it over twenty times in lectures in cities throughout the nation.

In that same year Josiah Strong published his book, *Our Country: Its Possible Future and Its Present Crisis*. It soon sold over 175,000 copes. America's progress and greatness, he wrote, "are the results of natural selection," and he went on, "this powerful race will move down upon Mexico, down upon Central and South America, out upon the islands of the sea, over upon Africa and beyond. And can anyone doubt that the result of this competition of races will be the 'survival of the fittest'?" In his *Descent of Man*, Darwin himself had written that probably the backward races would disappear before the advance of higher civilizations. "We must not forget," a prominent journalist wrote, "that the Anglo-Saxon race is expansive."

Members of the Anglo-Saxon cult recognized a powerful bond of race and culture with England and preached a *rapprochement* that became an unwritten alliance in the beginning of the twentieth century. "There is," a former Secretary of State wrote in 1898, "a patriotism of race as well as of country." [1] The unwritten alliance with England was perhaps the most important and enduring feature of the New Manifest Destiny.

Mahan also desired close ties with England. After he published his book, *The Influence of Sea Power upon History, 1660–1783*, in 1890, he became the nation's foremost exponent of expansion and naval power. Since America's industrial growth demanded new markets and sources of raw materials, he announced in books and articles, the United States needed a large merchant marine protected by a great navy to compete in the world-wide struggle for commerce. To support that expanded sea power, he said, the United States also required overseas bases and colonies. Other nations, mainly the great powers of Europe, were scrambling for colonies in Asia, Africa, and among the islands of the Pacific Ocean. [2] The United States must not be left behind in the march toward greatness.

Some were not impressed by the ideas of the new imperialists and the arguments of the Social Darwinists. Critics exposed the flaws in their theories. Social Darwinism, critics said, was like a circle. It led nowhere. It defined power in terms of survival and explained survival in terms of power and strength. "You might infer, to hear them buzz," a critical historian wrote a few years later, "that only the fittest survive, or, to put it conversely, the fact that you survive is proof that you are the 'fittest.'" [3]

The critics were right in arguing that the Social Darwinists were mistaken in ignoring the struggle of man with his environment and in emphasizing the battle of man with man. They and the apostles of the New Manifest Destiny were also mistaken in interpreting "fittest" in terms of force, implying that the strongest and most brutal survive. Darwin himself defined the fittest as those who adapted themselves best to existing conditions. Natural selection seldom operates among men. Since there is nothing "natural" about nations, and nations are made of men, the theory can not logically apply to international relations.

Yet, as Mahan said, "whether they will or not Americans must now begin to look outward." He and others foresaw the possibilities of naval and commercial greatness in the Pacific Ocean. Beginning in 1883 Congress made successive appropriations for a modern battle fleet, but, even before, the United States had started its overseas expansion in the Pacific. There, among the islands of Samoa and Hawaii, Americans saw the first bloom of the New Manifest Destiny. [4]

Early Interest in Samoa

American interest in Samoa, an archipelago of fourteen islands located south of the equator in the central Pacific, about halfway between Honolulu and Sydney, Australia, went back beyond the era of the new expansionism. Yankee traders, American whalers, and even warships stopped there.

The United States, however, did not investigate the islands until Lieutenant Charles Wilkes of the Navy led an official exploring expedition there in October, 1839. Wilkes was especially impressed by the harbor of Pago Pago on Tutuila, one of the larger islands. Before leaving, he appointed an Englishman as American Consul in Samoa and made an agreement with native chiefs covering trade and the protection of foreigners on the islands.

During the next thirty years English missionaries and traders and German merchants established themselves on the islands, mainly on Upolu, the second largest island. By 1870 the Germans owned most of the land and controlled most of the commerce, principally in copra.

Although the American government did nothing to establish a foothold in Samoa, a group of land speculators from Honolulu and San Francisco had moved in and in 1868 organized the Polynesian Land Company. Through dubious methods, they acquired large tracts of land from the natives on Upolu and Tutuila. Those speculators tried unsuccessfully to persuade the United States to take over the islands so they could strengthen their claims to the land.

In 1870 a New York shipbuilder, who had organized a steamship line to run from San Francisco to Australia, tried unsuccessfully to obtain a subsidy from the government. Nonetheless, in the following year he sent an agent to Samoa to see if Pago Pago could be used as a coaling station for his ships. That agent called Upolu the "garden spot of the Pacific" and reported Pago Pago to be "the most perfectly landlocked harbor that exists in the Pacific Ocean."

The agent's report, stating that New Zealand and Germany were scheming to annex the islands, aroused the Navy Department. The rear admiral in command of the Pacific fleet, therefore, sent Commander Richard W. Meade to survey the harbor of Pago Pago. "I think some kind of treaty with the native chiefs will be necessary to frustrate foreign influence," Meade wrote, "which is at present very active in this matter, seeking to secure the harbor."[5]

On his own authority, Meade made a treaty with the chief of Pago Pago on February 17, 1872, which gave the United States exclusive control of the harbor for a naval station. Three months later President Grant submitted the unauthorized agreement to the Senate. Opposed to overseas expansion at this time, the Senate would not approve. Yet Meade's unratified treaty marked the beginning of new and closer relations between Samoa and the United States, and aroused German and British suspicions.

A group of Samoan chiefs, probably guided by American expansionists, next petitioned the United States to annex their islands or establish a protectorate over them. Now curious about Samoa, Grant sent a friend, Colonel Albert B. Steinberger, as a confidential agent to investigate in June, 1873.

Steinberger returned to the United States in December with letters from native chiefs that again asked the President to extend a protectorate over Samoa. He then went back to the islands as Grant's special agent, but soon gave up that post to make himself premier of the kingdom of Samoa, an office he held until deposed in 1876.

Following Steinberger's departure, native warfare and international rivalry rocked the islands and rumors circulated that either Germany or England would annex them. Preferring American control and encouraged in this sentiment by the American Consul in the islands, the Samoan chiefs sent an envoy, M. K. Le Mamea, to the United States to offer their country for annexation. The Senate, Le Mamea was told, would not approve a treaty of annexation, so he and Secretary of State Evarts signed a treaty of peace and friendship on January 17, 1878, the first such agreement Samoa made with any major power. It gave the United States the right to establish a naval station at Pago Pago in return for a promise that the American government would use its good offices in disputes between Samoa and third powers. Since the treaty committed the government to very little, the Senate gave its consent.

Not to be outdone, Germany in January and Britain in August, 1879, signed treaties with Samoa giving them naval stations. The native chiefs then asked the three treaty powers to exercise a joint protectorate over the islands, which the powers did informally as the result of a convention their consuls signed at Apia on Upolu on September 2. Although the convention never went to the Senate for approval, the American government accepted it as an executive agreement and abided by its terms.

The tripartite control of Samoa's government' did not bring peace. The islands seethed with the intrigues of the three rival consuls and the turmoil of native wars. In November, 1884, the German Consul forced a treaty on Samoa's king calling for German control of his government. Disregarding the treaty, the king appealed to England and the United States for protection. Since Germany now appeared determined to seize the archipelago, Cleveland's Secretary of State, Thomas F. Bayard, announced American opposition to German or any other foreign control of the islands.

Samoa's Fate

By the summer of 1886, Germany and the United States both recognized that their rivalry in Samoa threatened their peaceful relations. When Bayard suggested a three-power conference to deal with the Samoan problem, Britain and Germany accepted. At the conference, which met in Washington in June and July, 1887, the United States suggested equal control by the three powers under a plan that would assure Samoa's independence. On the strength of the fact that her commercial interests in the islands outweighed those of the other powers, Germany demanded preponderant political influence, and Britain supported her position in exchange for concessions elsewhere in the South Pacific. Since the United States opposed the German demand and insisted on Samoan autonomy, the conference adjourned without accomplishing a thing.

In Apia, meanwhile, international rivalry grew more intense. The Germans had sent four warships, declared war on the Samoan king, deported him, and entrenched their own puppet king. A native chief, encouraged by British and Americans, revolted against the puppet government. In December, 1888, the rebels ambushed a detachment of German sailors, killing twenty and wounding thirty. Swearing vengeance, the Germans shelled and burned rebel areas, including American property.

Americans who had never before heard of Samoa now became aroused by reports of German violence there. A wave of anti-German feeling swept over the United States, and leading newspapers demanded a vigorous defense of American interests in Samoa. Some spoke of war. One of them was convinced that "Germany in this affair has simply played the highwayman." [6] In the midst of this excitement President Cleveland placed the Samoan situation in the hands of Congress. "I have insisted," he said in expressing his suspicions of Germany, "that the autonomy and independence of Samoa should be scrupulously preserved. ..."[7] Congress then voted $500,000 for the protection of American life and property and $100,000 for developing the harbor at Pago Pago.

The debates on the appropriations brought up the whole question of policy in Samoa. Expansionist senators made it clear that they would not abandon the foothold there. The United States, they insisted, needed naval bases and overseas possessions to strengthen and maintain its position in the Pacific. The "sound and fury" over the distant islands alarmed some liberals who opposed deep involvement.

The Nation suggested abandoning Samoa to Germany. "The more the matter is looked into," it said, "the more plainly does it seem, on our part, an outbreak of sheer Jingoism and meddlesomeness in other people's affairs." True enough, the United States had no vital interest in the islands, but the New Manifest Destiny, espoused by expansionist Republican senators, demanded a more aggressive policy.[8]

Believing that the existing tension was dangerous and Samoa not worth a possible clash with the United States, Chancellor Bismarck of Germany suggested that the United States, Britain, and Germany resume the disrupted negotiations of 1887 in Berlin. Cleveland and Bayard agreed but left the conference details to Benjamin Harrison's incoming administration.

In Apia, meanwhile, one British, three German, and three American warships crowded the harbor, and their sailors glowered at each other over ready guns. Then, on March 16, 1889, before any of the ships could get out to sea, a hurricane struck the harbor, sinking or beaching the six German and American warships with a tragic loss of life. Only the British *Calliope*, by forcing steam on her boilers, battled her way through mountainous waves to open sea and safety. The hurricane blew away the immediate crisis between Germany and the United States. "Both paused aghast," Robert Louis Stevenson wrote in his classic account of Samoan affairs; "both had time to recognise that not the whole Samoan Archipelago was worth the loss in men and costly ships already suffered."[9]

When the delegates of the three powers met in Berlin in April they were apparently sobered by the effects of the hurricane. After negotiating for six weeks, they signed a treaty on June 14 that established condominium, or three-power control of Samoa, though the fiction of Samoan independence was still maintained.[10] "We see but one serious fault in the treaty," the New York *Herald* said. "It is that it involves us in agreements with European Governments which are contrary to the fixed policy of this country."

That was true enough, but the United States accepted this departure from its traditional policy of nonentanglement because the apparent alternative—German control of Samoa—was unacceptable to expansionists and others. Despite the opposition of a strong minority, therefore, the Senate approved the treaty.

As the rivalry and intrigue of the three powers continued and the natives resented their rule, the protectorate never worked well. "Who asked the Great Powers to make laws for us," a native orator asked; "to bring strangers here to rule us? We want no white officials to bind us in the bondage of taxation."

Cleveland, who had returned to power in 1893, deplored the entangling condominium. "Our participation in its establishment against the wishes of the natives," he said in his annual message of the following year, "was in plain defiance of the conservative teachings and warnings of the wise and patriotic men who laid the foundations of our free institutions."[11] He suggested a withdrawal, but Congress would not follow his recommendations.

Early in 1899 civil war broke out in Samoa. The Germans supported one side, and the British and Americans the other. This time British and American warships fired on rebel villages, destroyed German property, and suffered the loss of sailors in a Samoan ambush.

Anti-German feeling had now become so strong that many Americans blamed only Germany for the difficulty in Samoa. "Does she want to fight?" a senator from Nevada asked. "If so, she may be accommodated." Anti-imperialists, however, denounced American policy and demanded a withdrawal. "The Americans have one more evidence of what empire-building means," an editor explained. "It means shelling defenseless native villages, making our flag the symbol of high-handed interference."[12] Since British and American sailors stood shoulder to shoulder in the Samoan conflict, some Americans and Englishmen saw in this more evidence of a growing intimacy between their two countries.

With Republican expansionists now in power under William McKinley, the United States abandoned the theory it once held that Samoan independence was the object of its policy. When Germany suggested a partition of the islands, therefore, McKinley and Secretary of State John Hay agreed. "Our interests in the Archipelago were very meagre," Hay wrote to a friend, "always excepting our interest in Pago Pago, which was of the most vital importance. It is the finest harbor in the Pacific and absolutely indispensable to us."[13]

Germany, Britain, and the United States settled the Samoan question in a convention they signed on December 2 in Washington. The United States acquired Tutuila and some lesser islands. Germany obtained the other islands. To compensate the British for surrender of their claims, Germany gave them the Tonga Islands, also part of the Solomon chain, and concessions in West Africa.

THE PARTITION OF SAMOA, 1899

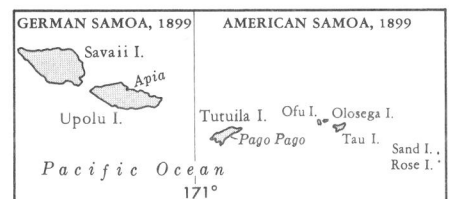

The Senate approved the treaty. The Navy Department was pleased with Pago Pago and some newspaper editors rejoiced "that the United States is now finally divorced from all political entanglements with either Germany or England." Anti-imperialists protested. "We blot out, then," a Democratic Senator said, "a sovereign nation, a people with whom we have treaty relations, and divide the spoils." [14]

In February, 1900, President McKinley placed the islands under the Navy Department, and in April the chiefs of Tutuila ceded their island to the United States. Other chiefs did the same in 1904. During the First World War, New Zealand seized the German islands and retained them. The United States did not formally accept its islands as full-fledged possessions until February, 1929, when Congress confirmed the Samoan cessions by joint resolution.

Early Interest in Hawaii

It was American policy in Hawaii, much more than that in Samoa, which focused public attention on expansion in the Pacific. An archipelago of seven major islands in the eastern half of the North Pacific, about two thousand nautical miles from San Francisco, Hawaii was closer to the United States than to any other major power.

American interest in Hawaii, or the Sandwich Islands, also grew out of the early days of the China trade. Those islands offered a delightful halfway resting place for sailors weary of the sea, a source of fresh supplies, and a trade in sandalwood, a product that brought large profits in China.

Even before Americans had started visiting the islands, English, French, Spanish, and Russian ships stopped there. Some of the sailors from those and from American ships liked the islands so well that they stayed permanently, forming the nucleus of a foreign colony. Early in the nineteenth century, Honolulu, on the island of Oahu, became an important trading center, often called the "Crossroads of the Pacific."

In 1819, American whalers came to the islands and soon gave Hawaii a commercial importance that aroused the interest of the American government. At about the same time, in April, 1820, the first band of New England missionaries landed in the islands. Those "Pilgrims of Hawaii" soon converted the natives to Protestant Christianity, and even more than traders, whalers, and planters, they and their children made Hawaii, in effect, a Pacific frontier of the United States. Those missionaries also came to dominate the political life of the islands, becoming self-appointed advisers to the native government.

Americans, however, did not threaten Hawaii's independence, as did agents of other countries. Under the influence of American missionaries, the Hawaiian government passed a law in April, 1831, banning Catholic priests from the islands and also persecuted native Catholics. Considering herself the protector of Catholic missions in the Pacific, France took the anti-Catholic laws in Hawaii as serious affronts and sent a frigate to Honolulu in 1839. The captain forced two treaties on the Hawaiian government, allowing Catholics freedom of worship and giving special trade concessions to France.

This successful use of force impressed the Hawaiian government with the need of gaining guarantees of its independence, especially from Britain, France, and the United States. American policy became clear when Hawaiian commissioners presented their plea to Secretary of State Daniel Webster in December, 1842.

Although Webster would make no treaty guaranteeing independence, he stated that "the United States . . . are more interested in the fate of the islands, and of their Government, than any other nation can be." American policy, he added, opposed any kind of foreign control over the Hawaiian Islands.[15]

In the following year an unofficial and unsuccessful attempt of a British naval officer to take over Hawaii as a protectorate led the acting Secretary of State to protest and to declare that the United States might be justified in using force to keep the islands out of European hands. Six years later another French intervention led the United States to sign a commercial treaty with the Hawaiian kingdom in August, 1849, which formally recognized its independence. After that, some Americans, particularly on the newly acquired Pacific Coast, clamored for annexation.

Franklin Pierce was willing to oblige, and in 1854 his agent in Hawaii negotiated a treaty of annexation that Secretary of State Marcy never completed because it called for large annual annuities to the king and royal family and for Hawaii's entrance into the Union as a state. Many native Hawaiians, moreover, also opposed annexation because of American racial attitudes, citing the position of the Negro in the United States as representative of the contempt for colored peoples.[16]

Marcy next tried to draw Hawaii closer to the United States with a trade reciprocity treaty negotiated in July, 1855. Fearing the competition of Hawaiian sugar, the cane planters of Louisiana opposed it. The Senate, therefore, killed it.[17]

After the Civil War high tariffs threatened to deprive Hawaiian sugar of its main market in California. The Hawaiian government therefore sought another reciprocity treaty. Although Secretary of State Seward preferred annexation, he welcomed the overtures as a step toward annexation and negotiated such a treaty in May, 1867. It, too, failed in the Senate. Ironically, some senators voted against it because they feared that reciprocity might make the islands prosperous and thus prove a barrier to annexation.[18]

In 1872 depression struck Hawaii's sugar industry. So desperate were the planters that they were willing to offer Pearl Harbor to the United States in exchange for a reciprocity treaty. That proved unnecessary. In January, 1875, the

United States signed a reciprocity treaty that ran for seven years and allowed Hawaiian sugar to enter the country free of duty. The Senate, this time fearing that another refusal might drive Hawaii into the arms of Britain, approved, adding an article that pledged the kingdom not to lease or dispose of any of its territory to any other power. That treaty, by making the islands economically dependent on the United States, marked a turning point in relations with Hawaii.

Reciprocity triggered a vast expansion in sugar, creating a boom that brought far-reaching changes to the Hawaiian kingdom. To meet the ensuing labor shortage, planters imported cheap contract labor, mostly Chinese and Japanese. The Asian influx alarmed Americans who disliked the change in the racial composition of the islands. Native Hawaiians, on the other hand, resented the Americanization of the islands, a process strengthened by reciprocity. Hence they attacked reciprocity. In the United States powerful sugar refiners in the East and cane planters in Louisiana also opposed it.[19]

Even though the American government was sensitive to that opposition and realized that reciprocity brought its people no genuine economic benefits, it was friendly to the idea because through reciprocity Hawaii had in effect become its strategic outpost in the Pacific. In December, 1884, therefore, the United States signed a convention extending reciprocity for another seven years. After considerable delay, the Senate finally approved the new treaty in January, 1887, but added an amendment giving the United States the exclusive right to use Pearl Harbor as a naval station. Despite its dislike of the amendment, Hawaii accepted the treaty. Hawaiian independence, it now appeared, could not last.[20]

Although white Hawaiians, many of them the sons of American missionaries, in effect controlled the islands, the native Hawaiians resented their rule and were more alarmed than ever by the virtual protectorate the United States had come to exercise over them. Determined to retain independence, some of them started a movement calling for "Hawaii for the Hawaiians." When Secretary of State Blaine offered Hawaii a new treaty in 1889 which in fact would have converted it into an American protectorate, the native leaders protested so loudly that their government dropped the project.

In the following year an economic crisis added to the political unrest. The McKinley tariff that became law in October removed the duty on raw sugar imported into the United States and gave American producers a bounty of two cents a pound, thus wiping out the advantage the Hawaiian product had enjoyed over other foreign sugar. The effect in Hawaii was disastrous. Sugar production dropped precipitously, property values fell, and workers lost their jobs or took wage cuts.

During this period of tension, actually in January, 1891, a politically experienced and strong-willed princess, Liliuokalani, became queen. She disliked the dominant influence of the whites in the government and the constitutional safeguards they had imposed. In particular, she sympathized with the native movement of "Hawaii for the Hawaiians." By royal decree on January 14, 1893, she unsuccessfully attempted to replace the existing constitution with an autocratic new one that would return greater political power to the natives.

Previously the sugar planters and industrialists, most of them Americans, had opposed annexation because they feared that American laws would cut off their supply of Asian labor and hence bite into their profits. The McKinley tariff and "Queen Lil" changed their views. Annexation now seemed the only safeguard for their property and profits.[21] A small group of American Hawaiians in Honolulu, therefore, had organized an Annexation Club. News of the queen's arbitrary decree drove the annexationists to action. They decided to overthrow the monarchy, establish a provisional government, and ask for American annexation. The American Minister in Honolulu, John L. Stevens, a close friend of Secretary Blaine and an ardent annexationist himself, agreed to support the revolutionists.

Revolution, Independence, and Annexation

On January 16 the revolutionists asked Stevens to land troops when necessary. "We are unable," they said, "to protect ourselves without aid, and therefore pray for the protection of the United States forces."[22] The queen and her advisers became alarmed and on that same day declared they would make no changes in the constitution, except through legal means, but the queen's retreat came too late. That afternoon Stevens ordered over one hundred and fifty armed men from the cruiser *Boston*, then in Honolulu's harbor, to land and protect American lives and property. Instead, they took up positions that intimidated the queen's forces.

On the next day, the revolutionary Committee of Safety proclaimed the monarchy abolished and established a provisional government "to exist until terms of union with the United States of America have been negotiated and agreed upon." Stevens immediately recognized this regime, which thirty hours before had considered itself so weak that it needed American protection. Under protest, the queen then surrendered her authority, saying she yielded "to the superior force of the United States" which Stevens had used against her.[23] Within three days the bloodless revolution was over.

Five white commissioners from the new government immediately left for Washington to negotiate a treaty of annexation. As soon as they arrived in San Francisco the American press spread the story of the Hawaiian revolution over the nation. Expansionists welcomed it. "The popular verdict is clear, unequivocal, and practically unanimous," the New York *Tribune* announced. "Hawaii is welcome."

Less than two weeks after the revolution, Stevens himself wrote that "the Hawaiian pear is now fully ripe, and this is the golden hour for the United States to pluck it."[24] On that same day he hoisted the American flag and proclaimed

Hawaii a protectorate. Secretary of State John W. Foster later disavowed that act, but the American flag continued to fly over government buildings in Honolulu.

Himself an imperialist, Foster quickly signed a treaty with the commissioners on February 14 which would incorporate Hawaii into the Union as a territory. The next day President Harrison submitted it to the Senate, saying that the United States had no hand in the revolution, that the Hawaiian government offered annexation voluntarily, and that, therefore, his government had no alternative but to accept the treaty. Aware of Democratic opposition, the Senate would not act in the two weeks remaining in Harrison's administration.

Five days after he became President for the second time, Grover Cleveland, on the advice of Secretary of State Walter Q. Gresham, withdrew the treaty from the Senate. Two days later he appointed a special commissioner, James H. Blount, a retired congressman from Georgia, to investigate the overthrow of the monarchy and to seek a guide for administration policy. Immediately after arriving in Hawaii, Blount repudiated the protectorate Stevens had proclaimed, hauled down the flag, and launched a thorough investigation.[25]

In his report, Blount condemned Stevens' role in the revolution, saying that "the undoubted sentiment of the people is for the Queen against the Provisional Government, and against annexation." Gresham now wanted to reverse Stevens' policy. "Should not the great wrong done to a feeble but independent State by an abuse of the authority of the United States," he asked the President, "be undone by restoring the legitimate government? Anything short of that will not, I respectfully submit, satisfy the demands of justice."[26]

Accepting Blount's findings and Gresham's advice, Cleveland condemned the American role in the revolution as morally wrong. He replaced Stevens with a new minister who had secret instructions to restore Liliuokalani to her throne if she would grant amnesty to the revolutionists. Although the former queen at first was unwilling, saying angrily that "my decision would be, as the law directs, that such persons should be beheaded and their property confiscated," she ultimately agreed to Cleveland's terms.[27]

Sanford B. Dole, the son of a missionary and president of the provisional republic, refused to restore the monarchy. The President of the United States, he said ironically, had no right to interfere in the domestic affairs of Hawaii. Many Americans, even Democrats, sided with Dole. "The Democratic party," the Atlanta *Constitution* announced, "has not been in the habit of restoring monarchies anywhere."[28]

The question of annexing Hawaii, meanwhile, had set off a strident debate on imperialism in Congress and in the press. Expansionists lauded imperialism and urged annexation for strategic reasons, but anti-imperialists, including Cleveland himself, attacked the wisdom of acquiring alien peoples and territory outside the continent.

Since Cleveland could restore Liliuokalani only through force, and Congress would not support him in a policy of bloodshed, he did nothing more after Dole's rebuff and allowed the provisional government to continue without American interference. That government established the Republic of Hawaii on July 4, 1894, under a constitution authorizing its president, whenever possible, to make a treaty of union with the United States. Cleveland promptly recognized the new republic.

The Republic of Hawaii never intended independence to be permanent, nor did expansionists in the United States. In 1896, for instance, the Republican campaign platform announced that "the Hawaiian Islands should be controlled by the United States."[29] When the Republicans returned to power in March, 1897, even though William McKinley himself was not at first an expansionist, they were prepared to carry out their commitment on Hawaii.

Those imperialists, moreover, were alarmed by possible Japanese control of the islands through immigration. Between 1883 and 1896 so many Japanese had crowded themselves into Hawaii that by 1897 they comprised about one-fourth of the population and were steadily increasing. The Japanese government disliked the discriminatory laws directed against its people in Hawaii, and, as early as March, 1893, had asked the government there to give them voting rights along with the whites and native Hawaiians.

Hawaii's relations with Japan blossomed into a crisis in March, 1897, when Hawaiian authorities arbitrarily refused to admit about twelve hundred Japanese immigrants who had already reached the islands. Japan protested and in May sent a warship to Honolulu. Rumors of war in Honolulu, an observer said, were as "thick as creditors around the Government building on pay day." Many in Hawaii now looked upon annexation as a necessary shield against Japan. The government, therefore, appealed to the United States for protection and urged annexation. Then, on June 16, a little over three months after taking office, McKinley sent another treaty of annexation to the Senate.

While the Senate had the treaty under consideration, Japan protested, saying annexation would upset the *status quo* in the Pacific and endanger Japanese rights in Hawaii. That protest played into the hands of the administration which used fear of Japanese action to gain Senate approval. "We cannot let those Islands go to Japan," the President told a senator. "Japan has her eye on them."[30] If something were not done, he added, there would soon be another revolution, and Japan would gain control. Secretary of State John Sherman went so far as to instruct the American Minister in Honolulu to announce a provisional protectorate pending annexation if Japan used force.

"The annexation of Hawaii is for the benefit of the Hawaiian, the Latin, and the Anglo-Saxon races of these Islands," the *Hawaiian Star* announced. "It is not and does not pretend to be for the benefit of the Asiatics. It is meant as a bar to the Asiatics."[31] Japan ultimately withdrew her protest and accepted an indemnity of $75,000 as a settlement of her claims against the Hawaiian government.

Opposition from anti-imperialist Democrats and producers of beet sugar, meanwhile, had blocked the treaty in the Senate. Champ Clark, a Democratic congressman from Missouri, said "manifest destiny" was "the specious plea of every robber and freebooter since the world began, and will continue to be until the elements shall melt with fervent heat." Nonetheless, the expansionist fervor that marked the Spanish-American War drew Hawaii into the Union.

In this war the Hawaiian government made no pretense of being neutral. It did all it could to aid the United States. Despite this, Republican expansionists argued that they needed Hawaii as a base under American control for ships and troops going to the Philippines. At one time McKinley appeared ready to annex Hawaii by executive decree as a war measure. "We need Hawaii just as much and a good deal more than we did California," he told his secretary. "It is manifest destiny."[32]

Spurred on by Manifest Destiny and war fever, Congress hastily drew up a joint resolution of annexation. It passed both Houses by July 6, 1898, and the President signed it the next day. A month later, on August 12, the Hawaiian Islands became American territory.

In acquiring Hawaii, the United States completed a process it had started many years before. Yet it also broke the pattern of past foreign policy since Hawaii, later the fiftieth state, was the first important overseas acquisition.

The Venezuelan Boundary Dispute

While dealing with the results of the Hawaiian revolution, Cleveland had become embroiled in a dispute over a boundary in South America that at first had nothing to do with the United States. It had begun merely as a quarrel between Britain and Venezuela over ownership of a sparsely settled jungle of 50,000 square miles, an area slightly larger than the state of New York, claimed by both Venezuela and British Guiana. That land had been in dispute long before Venezuela had become an independent nation. No one had ever drawn a satisfactory boundary. In 1841, Sir Robert Schomburgk, a distinguished British geographer, surveyed the territory for the British government and drew a boundary that favored his employer. Venezuela protested and refused to make a settlement along the Schomburgk line. Both countries then agreed not to encroach on the disputed territory.

After 1875 a few settlers, gold miners and others, filtered into the area and friction between Venezuelan authorities and those of British Guiana developed. Both countries advanced inflated claims to the land. Since Venezuela was the weaker party, she repeatedly asked the British to arbitrate the whole area in dispute, but they were willing to do so only for the territory west of, or beyond, the Schomburgk line. The Venezuelans, therefore, appealed to the United States for help and attempted to invoke the principles of the Monroe Doctrine.

Beginning in 1887, after a rupture in relations between Venezuela and Britain, the United States more than once offered to assist in arbitrating the boundary. The British refused the American good offices, persisting in their stand that the territory inside the Schomburgk line was not open to arbitration. This was the situation when Cleveland became President for the second time in March, 1893.[33]

The change in administrations left Harrison's Minister to Venezuela, William L. Scruggs, without a diplomatic job. In August, 1894, the Venezuelan government hired him as a legal adviser and propagandist to work in Washington. He immediately wrote a pamphlet entitled *British Aggressions in Venezuela, or the Monroe Doctrine on Trial*. It presented only the Venezuelan side of the dispute and linked it with the Monroe Doctrine, now a revered American policy. He published the booklet in October, selling it on newsstands and distributing it free to newspaper editors, members of Congress, governors, and other leaders of opinion. Before December it ran through four editions.

Scruggs did not rely solely on his pamphlet to arouse American opinion in support of Venezuela and the Monroe Doctrine. In January, 1895, he persuaded his congressman to introduce a resolution urging Britain and Venezuela to arbitrate. It passed both Houses unanimously, and Cleveland signed it on February 20. Then the press took up the cause of the Monroe Doctrine. To the New York *Tribune* the problem was "perfectly simple." Venezuela owned the land and Britain was trying to take it.[34]

At this time a seemingly unrelated episode, the Corinto affair, intruded on relations with Britain. In April about four hundred British marines occupied the port of Corinto in Nicaragua in an effort to collect compensation for harsh action Nicaragua had taken in 1894 against several British subjects and a vice consul. Nicaragua appealed to Cleveland, asking him to intervene against an alleged violation of the Monroe Doctrine. Secretary of State Gresham replied that since Britain did not intend to occupy Corinto permanently, the Monroe Doctrine was not in danger.

Newspapers kept the Corinto affair in the headlines by denouncing England's strong-arm tactics in dealing with Nicaragua, and criticizing the Cleveland administration for permitting the British to act as they pleased. "What is the most amazing and embittering," one complained, "is that this act of British aggression is consummated with the assent and sanction of the American Administration."[35]

Nicaragua finally made arrangements for payment of the indemnity, and so the British left Corinto on May 2. That did not end the matter for Cleveland. Political opponents, and even some Democrats, attacked his foreign policy for being weak and pro-British. The Corinto affair and the political criticism, as well as fear of foreign political and economic encroachments in Latin America, now influenced Cleveland's policy toward Venezuela.[36] To aid the Democratic party and enhance his own political stature, friends urged him to meet the attacks of his critics by taking a strong stand in support of Venezuela.

Olney's "Twenty-Inch Gun"

Shortly before the British left Nicaragua, therefore, Cleveland asked Gresham to prepare a note on the Venezuelan question, but the Secretary died before completing it. Richard Olney, a strong-willed, brusque, and vigorous lawyer from Boston, who had been Attorney General, took over as Secretary of State on June 10 and in a few weeks finished the Venezuelan document. While Olney prepared his note, an article by Henry Cabot Lodge, a young Republican senator from his own state, appeared in a national magazine. Lodge declared that "the supremacy of the Monroe Doctrine should be established and at once—peaceably if we can, forcibly if we must."[37] He wanted the United States to halt British "imperialism" in Venezuela.

Olney's note, his first important state paper, was similar in spirit to Lodge's article. Cleveland, who later dubbed it a "twenty-inch gun," liked the note and said it was "the best thing of the kind" he had ever read. He "softened" it a bit, but still it remained forceful and essentially as Olney had written it. The Secretary sent it to the American Ambassador in London on July 20.

Olney asked Britain to submit the disputed territory to arbitration and to accept his own extreme interpretation of the Monroe Doctrine which he called a "doctrine of American public law." By holding territory claimed by Venezuela, he said, Britain violated that doctrine and justified American intervention in the dispute. "Today the United States is practically sovereign on this continent, and its fiat is law upon the subjects to which it confines its interposition," he emphasized. That is so, he went on, because "in addition to all other grounds, its infinite resources combined with its isolated position render it master of the situation and practically invulnerable as against all other powers." He asked the British to reply before the President addressed Congress in the session that would open in December.[38]

With its time limit and belligerent tone the note had the characteristics of an ultimatum. In referring to rumors of a ninety-day ultimatum, one English journal said mockingly, "Isn't it awful? But it might be still more awful if we only knew what the blessed Monroe Doctrine was, or what on earth the United States government has got to do with a quarrel between Great Britain and another independent state."[39]

The impatient Olney received no reply for four months. On December 2, Congress convened without an answer to Olney's note. For various reasons, the

British had delayed their response, but had intended to send it before Congress met. Because they miscalculated the date set for Congress to convene, the reply, dated November 26, did not reach Olney until December 7.

Lord Salisbury, Britain's Foreign Secretary, was an experienced diplomat and a blunt aristocrat as self-righteous about British honor as Olney was about American policy. He said the Monroe Doctrine had no validity under international law, could not bind Britain, and did not apply to the Venezuela boundary dispute. Britain, he added, was willing to arbitrate only the land beyond the Schomburgk line. He made not a single concession.

Salisbury's reasoning was clear and logical, more so than Olney's. The imperious tone of his two notes, with their cutting sentences, however, infuriated Cleveland and Olney. After Olney drafted a special message, Cleveland sat up all night re-writing it and sent it to Congress on December 17. He said that Britain had refused to arbitrate, and in truculent passages written by Olney, recommended strong action. He requested authority to appoint an independent commission to investigate and decide where the boundary should be and for power to enforce its decision. "In making these recommendations," the President declared, "I am fully alive to the responsibility incurred, and keenly realize all the consequences that may follow." [40]

That was the language of war, which neither Cleveland nor Olney truly wanted. Cleveland's menacing use of the investigating commission was, in fact, probably less a threat of war than a means of forcing the British to arbitrate the entire disputed region.

Congress instantly applauded the message and gave Cleveland the authority he requested. The House of Representatives voted unanimously for the boundary commission and appropriated $100,000 for its expenses. A wave of warlike enthusiasm swept over the country. "It is the call to arms," the Washington *Post* cried out; "the jingoes were right after all, and it is not to be the fashion hence-forth to sneer at patriots and soldiers." The Springfield *Union* joined in with, "Good for Mr. Cleveland!"

Yet some Americans and a few of their newspapers denounced the message. Moderates, fearful of war, urged peace. The governor of Massachusetts wrote the President, for instance, that "public opinion here is extremely strong and earnest in favor of a peaceful and honorable solution of the difficulty." [41]

English politicians, moreover, did not respond to Cleveland's message with nationalistic explosions of their own. Nor did the British people. Few of them knew or cared anything about Venezuela. Lord Salisbury and his supporters did not want war. He realized that he had underestimated Cleveland's determination to force a solution. Backed by a favorable public opinion and anxious to allay the unexpectedly violent American sentiment, the British government reopened the subject of arbitration.

Britain's reasons for backing down are complex, but two stand out: she wanted to retain American friendship and feared the power of a united Germany who was challenging her industrially and on the seas. In Europe she had no friends, so she did not want to make another enemy in the American people. Her own people considered a war with the United States virtually unthinkable.[42]

At this time, furthermore, Britain's troubles with the Boers, or Dutch settlers in South Africa, came to a head. An Englishman, Dr. Leander Starr Jameson, led an armed raiding party into the Boer republic of the Transvaal. The Boers repulsed the raiders, on January 3, 1896, and Germany's Kaiser sent an open telegram to Paul Kruger, president of the Transvaal, congratulating him on thwarting the "Jameson raid." The Kaiser implied ominously that Germany supported the Boers in their quarrel with England.

That telegram aroused British anger. Englishmen shouted defiance of Germany and prepared for war. The German war scare, although it followed Britain's decision to back down on the Venezuelan matter, diverted attention from that crisis and made easier a retreat on Venezuela and hence a reconciliation with the United States.[43] "War between the two nations, England and the United States," the British Colonial Secretary announced "would be an absurdity as well as a crime."

After long negotiation with the United States, Britain agreed to submit the entire disputed territory to an arbitration tribunal of five men under a formula excluding areas that settlers had held for fifty years. Britain and Venezuela signed a treaty of arbitration in February, 1897, which embodied the fifty-year formula. The American boundary commission then disbanded and turned its work over to the new tribunal.

In October, 1899, the arbitration tribunal handed down a unanimous award that gave Britain about ninety per cent of the territory in dispute. The settlement followed the Schomburgk line, but with two important exceptions. Venezuela received some five thousand square miles in the interior on the headwaters of the Orinoco River, but more important strategically, she gained the mouth of the Orinoco and hence control of that great river. The award, nonetheless, was a diplomatic compromise that favored Britain and embittered Venezuela.[44]

Even though the award failed to recognize the wide claims of Venezuela that American editors and jingoes had championed, American opinion seemed generally satisfied with it. Cleveland and Olney had successfully challenged England and had persuaded her to recognize the predominant position of the United States in the Western Hemisphere. Americans were more interested in this diplomatic victory over Britain than in the merits of the boundary settlement itself.

Britain's satisfaction is also understandable. Even though the British had retreated on the principle of arbitration, they had won most of what they desired in the settlement. They had, after all, wanted to fix the boundary at the Schomburgk line

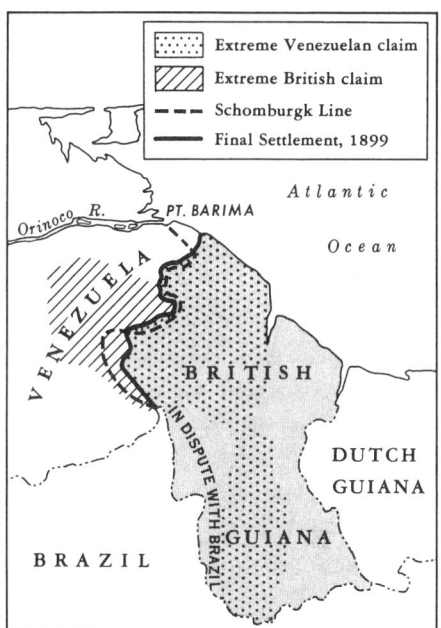

THE DISPUTED BOUNDARY
BETWEEN VENEZUELA AND
BRITISH GUIANA, 1893–1899

for many years. They had at the same time retained American friendship without great sacrifice. Even though the United States and Britain had appeared close to war, the Venezuelan crisis marked the beginning of a new Anglo-American *rapprochement* that heralded the birth of a strong but unofficial alliance.

For the United States alone, the Venezuelan crisis marked the hardening of a militant and belligerent nationalism. Americans accelerated their efforts to build a large and powerful navy. They took a new interest in foreign policy and in affairs abroad. They were ready to back their now expanded view of the Monroe Doctrine with force. Although the United States had long had the potential for being a world power, the Venezuelan crisis showed that it was willing and capable of acting as one. The powers of Europe would now have to take the possible reaction of the United States into consideration when they planned major moves in foreign policy.

The Olney-Pauncefote Convention

During the Venezuelan crisis some Americans and some Englishmen believed that their countries might not have come so close to war if they had been committed to a general arbitration treaty. They were shocked by the irresponsible talk of war that had spread over the United States. American and British efforts to negotiate an arbitration treaty were not new. They had begun in 1873 and Cleveland himself had a great interest in arbitration. Nothing definite happened, however, until after the Venezuelan crisis.

Secretary Olney and Sir Julian Pauncefote, the British Ambassador in Washington, signed a general arbitration convention on January 11, 1897. It committed their countries, for five years, to submit to arbitration, within certain limitations, all disputes they failed to settle through diplomacy. American public opinion appeared to support the treaty, and Cleveland and Olney tried to mobilize that opinion to impress the Senate, but the opposition was strong. Referring to Canada and the West Indies, the Chicago *Tribune* claimed that Americans wanted "to get rid of foreign influence on the North and South American continents. . . . We don't want to be tied up with any general arbitration treaty." Disturbed by the Senate opposition to the treaty, the English *Saturday Review*, on the other hand, lamented that America was "misrepresented by its stupid and mischievous Congress."[45]

William McKinley, Cleveland's Republican successor, supported the treaty and in his inaugural address said he hoped the Senate would approve it. The Senate, reflecting a popular distrust of Britain and unwilling to surrender any of its control over foreign policy through an advance commitment to arbitration, defeated the treaty in May. Despite disappointment in the ruling elites of both England and the United States, the defeat of the convention did not impair the newly strengthened friendship with Britain.

NOTES

1. Richard Olney, "International Isolation of the United States," *Atlantic Monthly*, LXXXI (May 1898), 588. The journalist is A. Lawrence Lowell and is quoted in Richard Hofstadter, *Social Darwinism in American Thought*, rev. ed. (Philadelphia, 1955), p. 81.

2. For the contemporary and related European imperialism, see Parker T. Moon, *Imperialism and World Politics* (New York, 1926), which stresses ideas and interests; and the more detailed and scholarly, William L. Langer, *The Diplomacy of Imperialism, 1890–1902* (2 vols., New York, 1935).

3. William R. Thayer, quoted in Hofstadter, *Social Darwinism*, p. 198. Hofstadter's entire chapter, "Racism and Imperialism," pp. 170–200, is basic reading for the ideas of the New Manifest Destiny.

4. Mahan's views on expansion in the Pacific are synthesized in William E. Livezey, *Mahan on Sea Power* (Norman, Okla., 1947). Another fine analysis of the ideas of the New

Manifest Destiny is in the first chapter of Julius W. Pratt, *Expansionists of 1898: The Acquisition of Hawaii and the Spanish Islands* (Baltimore, 1936). See also the discussions in Ralph H. Gabriel, *The Course of American Democratic Thought* (New York, 1940) and Edward M. Burns, *The American Idea of Mission: Concepts of National Purpose and Destiny* (New Brunswick, N.J., 1957).

5. To the Secretary of the Navy, Jan. 21, 1872, quoted in George H. Ryden, *The Foreign Policy of the United States in Relation to Samoa* (New Haven, 1933), p. 57.

6. San Francisco *Examiner*, Nov. 27, 1888, quoted in Charles C. Tansill, *The Foreign Policy of Thomas F. Bayard, 1885–1897* (New York, 1940), pp. 99–100.

7. Message of Jan. 15, 1889, in James D. Richardson, ed., *A Compilation of the Messages and Papers of the Presidents, 1789–1899* (10 vols., Washington, 1896–99), VIII, 805.

8. For an analysis of a possible German war with the United States, see Alfred Vagts, "Hopes and Fears of an American-German War, 1870–1915," *Political Science Quarterly*, XIV (Dec. 1939), 516–520.

9. *A Footnote to History: Eight Years of Trouble in Samoa* (London, 1892), p. 276 and J. A. C. Gray, "The Apia Hurricane of 1889," *United States Naval Institute Proceedings*, LXXXVI (June 1960), 35–40.

10. See Edward Younger, *John A. Kasson: Politics and Diplomacy from Lincoln to McKinley* (Iowa City, 1955), pp. 344–360.

11. Dec. 3, 1894, in Richardson, *Messages of the Presidents*, IX, 532.

12. New York *Evening Post*, April 6, 1899, quoted in Joseph W. Ellison, "The Partition of Samoa: A Study in Imperialism and Diplomacy," *Pacific Historical Review*, VIII (Sept. 1939), 268.

13. To Joseph H. Choate, Nov. 13, 1899, in William R. Thayer, *The Life and Letters of John Hay* (2 vols., Boston, 1915), II, 282.

14. Quoted in Foster Rhea Dulles, *The Imperial Years* (New York, 1956), p. 196.

15. Quoted in Sylvester K. Stevens, *American Expansion in Hawaii, 1842–1898* (Harrisburg, Pa., 1945), p. 3.

16. For details, see Richard W. Van Alstyne, "Great Britain, the United States, and Hawaiian Independence, 1850–1855," *Pacific Historical Review*, IV (1935), 15–24, and Merze Tate, "Slavery and Racism as Deterrents to the Annexation of Hawaii, 1854–1855," *Journal of Negro History*, XLVII (Jan. 1962), 1–18.

17. Details in Osborne E. Hooley, "Hawaiian Negotiations for Reciprocity, 1855–1857," *Pacific Historical Review*, VII (June 1938), 128–146.

18. John Patterson, "The United States and Hawaiian Reciprocity, 1867–1870," *ibid.*, VII (March 1938), 14–26.

19. Donald M. Dozer, "The Opposition to Hawaiian Reciprocity, 1876–1888," *ibid.*, XIV (June 1945), 157–183.

20. For Britain's concern, see Merze Tate, "British Opposition to the Cession of Pearl Harbor," *ibid.*, XXIX (Nov. 1960), 381–394.

21. William A. Russ, Jr., "The Role of Sugar in Hawaiian Annexation," *ibid.*, XII (Dec. 1943), 339–350, maintains that white concern for sugar and Oriental immigration led to revolution and annexation. Richard D. Weigle, in "Sugar and the Hawaiian Revolution," *ibid.*, XVI (Feb. 1947), 41–58, points out that even though the revolution was not an uprising of sugar planters, sugar contributed heavily to its consummation.

22. *Foreign Relations, 1894*; App. II, 1056.

23. The capitulation is printed in William A. Russ, Jr., *The Hawaiian Revolution (1893–94)*, (Selingsgrove, Pa., 1959), pp. 95–96. Russ stresses that the queen surrendered to the U.S., not to the insurgents, pp. 349–350.

24. Feb. 1, 1893, quoted in Montgomery Schuyler, "Walter Gresham," in Samuel F. Bemis, ed., *The American Secretaries of State and Their Diplomacy* (10 vols., New York, 1927–29), VIII, 244.

25. The young imperialist, Theodore Roosevelt, felt strongly about Hawaii. "I am a bit of a believer in the manifest destiny doctrine," he wrote on April 22, 1893. "I don't want to see our flag hauled down where it has been hauled up," in Howard K. Beale, *Theodore Roosevelt and the Rise of America to World Power* (Baltimore, 1956), p. 47.

26. The report, dated July 17, 1893, is in *Foreign Relations, 1894*, App. II, 567–605. Gresham's plan, Oct. 18, 1893, is on p. 463.

27. Nov. 13, 1893, quoted in Schuyler, "Walter Gresham," in Bemis, *Secretaries of State*, VIII, p. 248.

28. Quoted in Allan Nevins, *Grover Cleveland* (New York, 1932), p. 558.

29. Kirk H. Porter, *National Party Platforms* (New York, 1924), p. 204.

30. Quoted in William A. Russ, Jr., *The Hawaiian Republic (1894–98): And Its Struggle to Win Annexation* (Selingsgrove, Pa., 1961), p. 320.

31. Sept. 9, 1897, in Stevens, *American Expansion in Hawaii*, p. 288. For details, see Thomas A. Bailey, "Japan's Protest against the Annexation of Hawaii," *Journal of Modern History*, III (March 1931), 46–61.

32. Quoted in Margaret Leech, *In the Days of McKinley* (New York, 1959), p. 213. For an analysis of the annexation in the larger context of expansion, see Julius W. Pratt, "The 'Large Policy' of 1898," *Mississippi Valley Historical Review*, XIX (Sept. 1932), 219–242. For an exposure of the flaws in the argument that annexation was necessary for the war effort, see Thomas A. Bailey, "The United States and Hawaii during the Spanish-American War," *The American Historical Review*, XXXVI (April 1931), 550–560. Annexation also brought the American labor movement to grips, for the first time, with the ideology of imperialism. See John C. Appel, "American Labor and the Annexation of Hawaii: A Study in Logic and Economic Interest," *Pacific Historical Review*, XXIII (Feb. 1954), 1–18.

33. For background details, see Paul R. Fossum, "The Anglo-Venezuelan Boundary Controversy," *Hispanic American Historical Review*, VIII (Aug. 1928), 299–329.

34. Nelson M. Blake, "Background of Cleveland's Venezuelan Policy," *The American Historical Review*, XLVII (Jan. 1942), 263.

35. Philadelphia *Press*, April 30, 1895, *ibid.*, p. 264.

36. For an analysis that stresses the economic factor and fear of European encroachment, see Walter La Feber, "The Background of Cleveland's Venezuelan Policy: A Reinterpretation," *The American Historical Review*, LXVI (July 1961), 947–967. In "American Depression Diplomacy and the Brazilian Revolution, 1893–1894," *Hispanic American Historical Review*, XL (Feb. 1960), 107–118, La Feber suggests that the Panic of 1893 led to Cleveland's puffing up of the Monroe Doctrine.

37. *American Review*, CLX (June 1895), 658.

38. Olney to Bayard, June 20, 1895, *Foreign Relations, 1895*, I, 545–562.

39. *St. James Gazette*, quoted in Blake, "Background of Cleveland's Venezuelan Policy," *The American Historical Review*, XLVII (Jan. 1942), 270.

40. Quoted in Nevins, *Cleveland*, p. 640.

41. For the quotations, see *ibid.*, pp. 641–642. Walter La Feber, in "The American Business Community and Cleveland's Venezuela Message," *Business History Review*, XXXIV (Winter 1960), 393–402, stresses businessmen's support of Cleveland.

42. Ernest R. May, in *Imperial Democracy: The Emergence of America as a Great Power* (New York, 1961), pp. 45–47, points out that British statesmen did not consider the Venezuelan issue important primarily because they had not thought of the U.S. as a potential factor in the balance of power.

43. The extent of British anger against Germany and its influence on American policy is weighed in Jennie A. Sloan, "Anglo-American Relations and the Venezuela Boundary Dispute," *Hispanic American Historical Review*, XVIII (Nov. 1938), 499–501.

44. Theodore C. Smith, in "Secretary Olney's Real Credit in the Venezuela Affair," *Massachusetts Historical Society Proceedings*, LXV (May 1933), p. 145, questions the view that the award favored Britain. Otto Schoenrich, in "The Venezuela-British Guiana Boundary Dispute," *American Journal of International Law*, XLIII (July 1949), 523–530, reveals inside pressures that brought about an award favorable to Britain; see also Clifton J. Child, "The Venezuela-British Guiana Boundary Arbitration of 1899" and William C. Dennis, "The Venezuela-British Guiana Boundary Arbitration of 1899," *ibid.*, XLIV (Oct. 1950), 682–693 and 720–727.

45. The papers, dated Jan. 12 and Feb. 15, 1897, are quoted in Nelson M. Blake, "The Olney-Pauncefote Treaty of 1897," *The American Historical Review*, L (Jan. 1945), 234–236. See also William Stull Holt, *Treaties Defeated by the Senate* (Baltimore, 1933), pp. 154–156.

Chapter Fourteen

THAT SPLENDID
LITTLE WAR

A<small>NOTHER</small> crisis in nearby Cuba brought the New Manifest Destiny much more dramatically to the attention of the American people than had Samoa or Hawaii. The crisis began with a world-wide depression in 1893, followed by an American tariff law of 1894 that raised the duties on raw sugar, the backbone of Cuba's already depressed economy, to a level forty per cent higher than under the previous tariff. The new tariff wrecked Cuba's sugar market and brought crushing poverty and more misery to the island. Economic exhaustion, added to smoldering discontent with Spain's misrule since the end of the Ten Years' War—a discontent fanned by Cuban exiles in the United States—led the Cubans to revolt against their Spanish rulers in February, 1895.

Since the United States had long been interested in Cuba, the insurrectionists found it relatively easy to arouse American feelings against Spain. The American people showed their temper a few weeks after the revolt began when they learned that on March 8 a Spanish gunboat had fired on an American steamer, the *Alliance*, about six miles off Cuba's coast. That attack made the Cuban revolution headline news in practically every newspaper in the country and set off a wave of jingoism. A senator from Alabama wanted to "despatch a fleet of warships to Havana" to avenge the insult to the flag.[1] Other Americans clamored for similar action. After that, incident after incident embittered relations with Spain and built up sympathy for the Cuban rebels.

Capitalizing on American sympathy, Cubans established revolutionary committees, or *juntas*, in the United States, with general headquarters in New York, in order to spread propaganda, raise funds, and to recruit and outfit filibustering expeditions.[2] Joseph Pulitzer's New York *World* and William Randolph Hearst's New York *Journal*, which were locked in a circulation war that fed on sensationalism, dramatized the rebellion as a struggle between good and evil. Seldom, if ever, reporting Spanish actions in a favorable light, Hearst and Pulitzer's "yellow" journals used stories of Spanish atrocities to increase circulation. When there were no suitable incidents, their reporters sometimes dressed up the latest rumors as dispatches. At the same time, both journals preached intervention and urged a foreign policy of imperialism. Throughout the country other newspapers, though their influence was not exercised through sensational journalism, demanded the same policy, calling on Americans to take up their Manifest Destiny by accepting their obvious responsibilities in Cuba.[3]

The religious press, mostly Protestant, joined the crusade against alleged Spanish barbarism. Most of the business press, trade journals and others, however, opposed the general clamor for war. Whether the yellow press created a mood of imperialism or merely expressed the existing sentiment of the people, it is clear that it preached what many Americans wanted to hear. The revolution in Cuba offered Americans an excuse for an imperialism based on humanitarian principles.

Precarious Neutrality

Given the attitude of the American people and the nature of the struggle in Cuba, the United States found it difficult to hold to a policy of neutrality. The American government patrolled its own coasts at considerable expense to prevent smugglers, filibusters, and gunrunners from reaching Cuba's shores, but some always got through.

In Cuba the revolutionists, ignoring the usual rules of warfare, inaugurated a scorched earth policy, plundering and destroying loyalist property, and burning sugar plantations, many of them owned by Americans. Cubans aimed to drive the Spaniards from the island by exhausting Spain's resources. At the same time they charged the Spaniards with following a policy of calculated brutality, and Americans, seeing only one side of the conflict, believed them.

Some recently naturalized Americans, formerly Cubans, fought the Spaniards. When captured, they demanded the protection of the American flag. In almost every case when the American government intervened officially in their behalf the Spanish government cooperated. But Spain, understandably bitter, accused the American government of failing to uphold its neutrality since most of the money and munitions that kept the rebellion aflame came from the United States. Without American assistance, she said, the rebellion would die.

In the first year of the rebellion Spain made little headway against Cuban forces. In February, 1896, therefore, she sent an energetic and ruthless general, Valeriano Weyler, to Cuba with orders to crush the rebels. To fight fire with fire he instituted a harsh concentration camp policy designed to control rebels who appeared peaceful farmers in the day and fought as guerrillas at night. Although no more drastic than similar measures used by other commanders at other times in fighting guerrilla armies and no more brutal than the tactics of the rebels themselves, Weyler's policy outraged Americans. Since sanitation was primitive and Spanish administration notoriously bad, many men, women, and children herded into the concentration camps died from malnutrition and disease.

The yellow press played up the misery of the Cubans in the camps, denounced Weyler's brutal methods, and labelled him "Butcher." Most Americans knew him by no other name; even statesmen referred to him as "Butcher" Weyler.

Grover Cleveland opposed the clamor for intervention. In June, 1895, he had issued a proclamation of neutrality recognizing the existence of an insurrection in Cuba, but not the belligerency of the rebels. That policy, he believed, was the best way of enforcing the neutrality laws and protecting American interests, but it did not satisfy Congress. In the following April both houses, motivated by partisan political considerations, overwhelmingly passed a concurrent resolution favoring recognition of Cuban belligerency and calling on the President to offer the nation's friendly offices "to the Spanish Government for the recognition of the independence of Cuba."[4] Since such action was an executive function, Cleveland ignored the resolution. He was more concerned, however, over talk that Congress might try to force him to recognize Cuba, which might have brought on war with Spain. At one time he was heard to say that even if Congress declared war there would be no hostilities. "I will not mobilize the Army," he allegedly told a group of congressmen.[5]

Two days before the final passage of the resolution, Secretary of State Olney offered to mediate the quarrel between Spain and her rebelling colony. Fearing that the United States wanted Cuba for itself, Spain refused the offer, and that summer her statesmen drew up a plan for joint action by Europe's major powers to prevent the United States from intervening. "This question is a Spanish one," the Spaniards pointed out, "but the interests it touches are not Spain's alone, but all Europe's." The plan fell through, and American demands for intervention increased.

There were jingoes and imperialists in both political camps, but in the Republican party the jingoes shaped the platform of 1896. "We believe," that platform stated, "that the government of the United States should actively use its influence and good offices to restore peace and give independence to the Island," meaning Cuba.[6] Foreign policy was by no means the main issue of the campaign, but imperialists believed that the Cuban revolution offered a rare opportunity to drive Spain from the Western Hemisphere. A highly articulate coterie of publicists, naval strategists, and nationalist politicians, mostly in the Republican party, did not want to lose that opportunity and urged intervention.

The Republican who won the Presidency, William McKinley, was no imperialist. He was a small town Ohio politician who had advanced far in politics under the wing of the Cleveland capitalist, Mark Hanna. An affable, handsome man who made friends easily and won the affection of those close to him, McKinley paid little attention to foreign affairs. He wanted peace. There will be "no jingo nonsense under my administration," he said. In his inaugural address he virtually ignored foreign policy. "We want no wars of conquest," he announced; "we must avoid the temptation of territorial aggression." McKinley was not one to inspire men, yet, as someone remarked, if men would not die for him they were happy to vote for him. He was not a man to resist the pressures of public opinion and politics.

In September, 1897, through the American Minister in Madrid, McKinley offered his good offices to Spain to restore peace in Cuba. The United States, the Minister said, "had no intention of annexing the Island of Cuba, nor did it aspire to the responsibilities of a protectorate." [7] Yet, the offer carried the threat of intervention if Spain did not reverse her policy in Cuba.

Even though a new and liberal Spanish government had come to power in October, it turned down the President's offer. It did, however, inaugurate reforms in Cuba: it recalled Weyler, granted Cubans political rights similar to those held by Spaniards, and promised eventual home rule.

The rebels spurned Spain's concessions. Home rule no longer satisfied them; they wanted complete independence. Yet Spain's conciliatory attitude softened the sentiment of the American government, if not of the yellow press and the people. "No War with Spain—All Indications Point to Peace," the Washington *Post* announced in its headline of November 6. In his first annual message in December, McKinley recognized Spain's new efforts and urged his people to give her a "reasonable chance" to effect satisfactory changes. He seemingly repudiated intervention. "I speak not of forcible annexation," he said, "for that cannot be thought of. That, by our code of morality, would be criminal aggression." [8]

The MAINE Goes Down

Spanish loyalists in Cuba, who violently opposed the thought of being ruled by native Cubans, also attacked the new liberal policy. On January 12, 1898, some of them rioted in Havana's streets shouting "Viva Weyler." Fearing attacks on Americans, Fitzhugh Lee, the interventionist American Consul-General in Havana, suggested sending several warships to Key West, Florida. From there they could easily sail to Havana if needed. Even though the tension in Havana eased and Lee advised against sending warships to the city, the second-class battleship *Maine,* which was in fact a sleek armored cruiser, entered Havana's harbor on the morning of January 25. The President, American officials insisted, had sent the *Maine* not as a threat but as "an act of friendly courtesy." The visit, nonetheless, displeased the Spaniards in Havana and added new tensions to an already taut situation there.

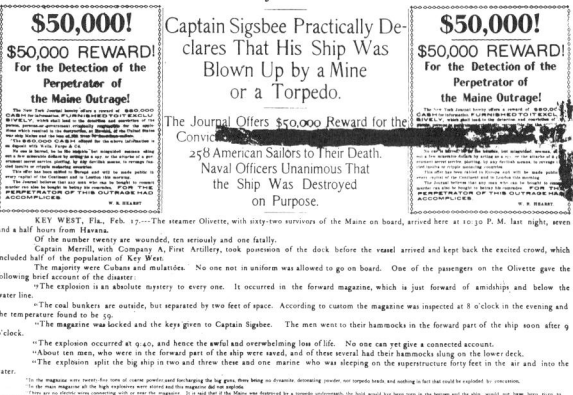

Then, as the *Maine* lay at anchor, what might have been a trifling incident became an outrage. On February 9 Hearst's *Journal* published a private letter written by Enrique Dupuy de Lôme, the Spanish Minister in the United States, to a friend in Cuba. That document, filched by an insurgent spy and placed into the hands of a Hearst reporter, proved a sensation. President McKinley, Dupuy de Lôme wrote, is weak, "a would-be politician who tries to leave a door open behind himself while keeping on good terms with the jingoes of his party." 9

The fact that a Spaniard dared criticize an American President, particularly in contemptuous terms, whipped the jingoes and the yellow press to fury. Within twelve hours, before the United States demanded Dupuy de Lôme's recall, he resigned. The Spanish government accepted the resignation, but his unwittingly indiscreet comments had already irreparably harmed Spanish-American relations.

Less than a week later, news from Havana gave the nation another shock. On the night of February 15, something or somebody blew up the *Maine*, killing 260 men. The interventionist journals flooded the country with "war extras," even though the captain of the *Maine* himself had suggested that "public opinion should be suspended until further report." "THE MAINE WAS DESTROYED BY TREACHERY," the New York *Journal* announced in a massive headline, and offered diagrams to prove its conclusion.[10] "The slightest spark," the Secretary of the

Navy noted in his diary, "is liable to result in war." On March 9 Congress rushed through a unanimous vote for an appropriation of fifty million dollars for war preparations.

On March 17, in the midst of the *Maine* hysteria, a conservative and respected Republican senator from Vermont and a former Secretary of War, Redfield Proctor, made a speech reporting on the death and misery he had seen in concentration camps in Cuba. Weyler's cruelties and the loss of the *Maine*, he said, did not move him as did "the spectacle of a million and a half people, the entire native population of Cuba, struggling for freedom and deliverance from the worst misgovernment of which I ever had knowledge." [11]

Those who were not impressed by the exaggerations of the yellow sheets believed Proctor and concluded that something had to be done about Cuba. "Senator Proctor's speech," the *Wall Street Journal* observed two days later, "converted a great many people in Wall Street, who have heretofore taken the ground that the United States had no business to interfere in a revolution on Spanish soil." There was no question, it said, about the accuracy of Proctor's statements: "they made the blood boil."

Eleven days after Proctor's speech a naval court of inquiry published its findings that a submarine mine had blown up the *Maine*. The people, already believing Spain guilty, were now convinced. War fever spread from coast to coast. The yellow journals called for war and even the religious press joined the chorus. "And if it be the will of Almighty God, that by war the last trace of this inhumanity of man to man shall be swept away from this Western Hemisphere," the *Evangelist*, a Presbyterian journal, announced, "let it come!" [12]

On March 28, the same day in which the President announced the court's findings, the American Minister in Madrid presented the Spanish government with a virtual ultimatum. It suggested an immediate armistice until October 1, with an end to the concentration camp policy and American mediation of the revolution. The Minister asked for a reply in a few days. What the United States wanted, Assistant Secretary of State William R. Day made clear in a subsequent telegram, was an independent Cuba.

Spain Attempts Negotiation

Anxious to avoid war, the Spanish government met most of the American demands in its reply three days later. It ordered the end of the concentration camp policy and said it would grant an armistice if the rebels asked for one. The issue of the armistice, which the rebels, confident of ultimate American intervention, would not ask for, made the reply unsatisfactory. [13] The United States wanted an unconditional armistice, that is, actual independence. If the Spanish government did not accept McKinley's demands in full, a disastrous war appeared certain; if it conceded all, an angry public would probably overthrow the government and perhaps the monarchy itself.

In her dilemma Spain appealed to the major European powers for help, but none offered direct assistance. Although anxious to prevent war between Spain and the United States, the German Foreign Minister was blunt. "You are isolated," he told the Spanish Ambassador, "because everybody wants to be pleasant to the United States, or, at any rate, nobody wants to arouse America's anger; the United States is a rich country, against which you simply cannot sustain a war." [14] The Pope, however, offered to mediate the Cuban conflict and Spain, desperately looking for a way out, was willing to grant an armistice if he asked for it. An armistice sponsored by the Vatican would not appear to the Spanish people an ignominious surrender to an American ultimatum.

The American Minister in Madrid cabled the President on April 5 that Spain had agreed to stop hostilities under the Pope's terms. "I believe this means peace;" and he added, "I believe that you will approve this last conscientious offer for peace." [15] For a moment the people of Europe seemed convinced that the threat of war between Spain and the United States had subsided, and all breathed more easily. McKinley, however, sent a noncommittal reply, indicating that all now depended on Congress.

Despite their previous reluctance to interfere, the great powers of Europe—Britain, Germany, France, Austria-Hungary, Russia, and Italy—at the urging of Austria backed by Germany, tried to avert war through an amicable intervention. The ambassadors of the European powers in Washington, acting in a body, presented McKinley with a joint note on April 7 appealing "to the feelings of humanity and moderation of the President and of the American people" to preserve peace with Spain.[16] The American government knew beforehand that the collective act of the European powers was not a serious one. It knew definitely that England would not interfere with American plans. In his reply McKinley spoke of fulfilling "a duty to humanity" and would concede nothing.

Two days later the European powers exerted greater pressure on Spain than they had on the United States. On the same day Spain, on her own initiative, ordered an end to hostilities in Cuba, thus meeting virtually all of McKinley's demands except American mediation. "I hope that nothing will now be done to humiliate Spain," the American Minister in Madrid wired the next day, "as I am satisfied that the present government is going, and is loyally ready to go, as fast and as far as it can. With your power of action sufficiently free you will win the fight on your own lines." [17]

McKinley, despite his personal desire to avert war, did not feel he had freedom of action. He would not buck the popular outcry for war and the jingoes of his own party. War, the Richmond *Times* said, "would undoubtedly have a wholesome effect in knitting the bonds of the Union closer together, and in allaying

Handwritten margin notes:
- *U.S.S. Alliance*
- *propaganda + yellow press*
- *Weyler, Proctor*
- *desire to get Spain out of West Hem.*
- *De Lome Letter*
- *U.S.S. Maine*
- *underlying causes*
- *if Spain had given in — why go to war?*

sectional and class strife." Consciously, or unconsciously, many Americans agreed with that idea, and they swelled the sentiment for intervention in Cuba. If they did not give the people the war they wanted, Republican politicians believed, then the people in the approaching fall elections would turn them out of office. The President himself feared that if he did not act, Congress would pass a war resolution over his head and humiliate him and his party.[18] Thus McKinley, even though most of his cabinet and certain leading Republican senators favored peace, yielded to the war hawks.

The Onset of War

On April 11, two days after Spain's final capitulation, McKinley sent Congress his message recommending forcible intervention. He had prepared this six days earlier but had delayed delivering it until Americans in Cuba were evacuated. He spoke "in the name of humanity, in the name of civilization;" said he had exhausted every effort to relieve the intolerable conditions in Cuba; and asked Congress for authority to use the Army and Navy to end hostilities there, in effect, a request for war. In two brief paragraphs, added to the end of a speech covering nine printed pages, he mentioned Spain's surrender on the points that ostensibly were the causes for war.[19]

On that same day Spain made one more desperate try for European assistance. Her plea brought forth another effort from the Austrian government which urged the powers to take diplomatic action on behalf of Spain. Three days later the ambassadors of the great powers met in the British Embassy in Washington where they prepared a joint note with the idea of placing pressure on the United States. Spain's concessions, they held, made armed intervention unjustifiable.

This was as close as Spain could come to achieving the European intervention on her behalf that she desired. The powers never delivered the note, mainly because Britain, who sought American friendship, and the German Kaiser, who considered the move pointless, opposed this last-minute diplomatic intervention. "It seems very doubtful whether we ought to commit ourselves to a judgment adverse to the United States," the British Foreign Office said, "and whether in the interests of peace such a step would be desirable."[20]

That episode reflected the attitude of the foreign powers. None of the countries of continental Europe were friendly to the United States. Most of them disliked America's badgering of impotent Spain. England, the American Ambassador in London wrote, "is the only European country whose sympathies are not openly against us."[21] There is, however, no basis to the story that the powers had created a new concert of Europe to intervene in the New World and that only British friendship thwarted it.

Although there were many reasons for Britain's friendliness, one was especially significant as it also formed the basis of the entire Anglo-American *rapprochement* at the turn of the century. Since Britain's delicate international position left her without friends, she could not afford to alienate the United States. So conspicuously friendly were the British, that many Americans suspected a secret Anglo-American alliance. Irishmen in New York were so concerned that they organized an Anti-British Alliance Association of the United States.[22]

In Congress, meanwhile, the fate of Spain's empire was being debated and the President's influence over his party being shattered. McKinley's reasons for leading the country to war had a hollow ring, but a Congress eager for a fight not only gave them its full support but wished to go beyond them. On April 19, after a long harsh wrangle over a Senate amendment recognizing the insurgent republic, one that would have infringed the President's constitutional prerogatives of recognizing a foreign state, Congress passed a joint resolution without that recognition that declared Cuba independent and authorized intervention. It added, without dissent, an amendment proposed by Senator Henry M. Teller of Colorado pledging the United States not to annex Cuba. The Teller amendment, more than McKinley's high-sounding phrases, reflected some of the humanitarian impulse behind the drive to war. The President signed the resolution of intervention on the following day. Spain, in desperation, after receiving a three-day ultimatum, declared war on April 24, and Congress, the next day, declared war to have existed since April 21, when McKinley had established a blockade.

Why did this unnecessary war come when the leading statesmen on both sides did not want it? At one time it was fashionable to place the blame on vested and expansionist business interests, but American investors in Cuba desired peace. They wanted to save their property from the destruction of war, and business interests in the United States, with a few exceptions, opposed war until it came.[23] Even the *Maine*'s destruction did not change their desire for peace.

"We here in Washington," war-bent Theodore Roosevelt had written to a friend in disgust, "have grown to feel that almost every man connected with the big business interests of the country is anxious to court any infamy if only peace can be obtained and the business situation be not disturbed."[24] American businessmen were far more concerned with recovery from an industrial depression that had gripped the country from 1893 to early 1897 and with the opportunities of economic expansion at home than they were with expansion abroad.

American public opinion and political leaders, as much as any other forces, apparently brought on the war, particularly after the destruction of the *Maine*. The newspapers, the people, and the politicians demanded it. McKinley headed a businessmen's administration that did not want war. "I did all that in honor could be done to avert the war," he said three years later, "but without avail." He probably sincerely believed that, but he cannot be absolved from blame. He chose war rather than risk the breakup of his party. No President, regardless of political and popular pressures, can evade responsibilities that are his in leading his people into war. If McKinley, who had shown courage in bucking political pressure up to a point, had had the sterner qualities of leadership in time of crisis, he could have tried, at least, to hold Congress in check and to overcome the popular hysteria.[25]

Ten Weeks of Warfare

As to the war capabilities of Spain and the United States, they were vastly unequal. Spain's main asset was a misguided concept of national honor. On paper her military power appeared formidable. She had almost two hundred thousand troops in Cuba and a navy that contained more armored cruisers and torpedo boats than did the American Navy, but the United States had more battleships and its Navy was newer and better disciplined. Spain's ships were hardly sea-worthy, were based thousands of miles from the scene of fighting, and her leaders were haunted by the anticipation of defeat.

Even before the war started, Admiral Pascual Cervera, commander of Spain's main naval squadron, recorded privately: "We may and must expect a disaster. But . . . I hold my tongue and go forth resignedly to face the trials which God may be pleased to send me."[26]

With most Americans, apparently, the war was popular. They entered it light-heartedly, their young men marching off to the strains of "The Stars and Stripes Forever." Despite this gay martial spirit of its people, the United States was militarily unprepared. The Army totalled only 28,183 officers and men, scattered in small detachments from coast to coast. It had enough rifles of a new type for the regulars, but the two hundred thousand volunteers the President had called into service received outmoded rifles that fired a black-powder cartridge. The Army lacked the necessary equipment for a field campaign—shoes, blankets, tents—and could get no light khaki cloth. So the soldiers fought a hot summer campaign in Cuba in heavy blue winter uniforms.

The casualty lists softened the war spirit, but Spain proved a feeble opponent and the fighting was mercifully short. She appeared to have placed her trust almost wholly on outside help, on European intervention that never came.

The first blows of the war, which proved to be the most important ones, did not fall on Cuba but in the Far East, on Spain's Philippine Islands. One day, two months before the outbreak of war, Theodore Roosevelt, then Assistant Secretary of the Navy, became Acting Secretary for three or four hours while the Secretary was away. At this time, the traditional story goes, he took a grave responsibility upon himself and may have influenced the course of history. He cabled Commodore George Dewey, in command of the Asiatic Squadron, orders to prepare for "offensive operations in the Philippine Islands."

Since Roosevelt's deed reflected standard naval policy, it did not, in fact, shape events. Dewey would have prepared his ships with or without Roosevelt's orders.[27] Nonetheless, those instructions stood, and after war began the White House ordered Dewey to proceed to the Philippines from Hong Kong, which a British proclamation of neutrality forced him to leave, to destroy or capture the Spanish fleet there. "While we remained at war with Spain," Dewey explained later, "our purpose [was] to strike at the power of Spain wherever possible."[28] And strike he did. As soon as he received the President's orders, he set out full steam for the Philippines. On the night of April 30 his ships entered Manila Bay, and at dawn destroyed the Spanish fleet there. "The guns of Dewey at Manila have changed the destiny of the United States," the Washington *Post* announced prophetically. "We are face to face with a strange destiny and must accept its responsibilities. An imperial policy!"[29]

Two days before Dewey's victory, Admiral Cervera, in a state of despair, had steamed out of the Cape Verde Islands with four armored cruisers and three destroyers for Cuban waters. His officers sensed impending doom. "I think it un-doubted," one of them wrote to the Prime Minister, "that the sacrifice of these naval forces will be as certain as it will be fruitless and useless for the termination of the war."[30] Since no one knew the destination of Cervera's ships, panic gripped the cities along the Atlantic coast. Fear followed the joy of Dewey's victory. "Telegrams, letters, and statesmen representing the imperilled localities poured into the War Department," the harassed Secretary of War wrote. "They wanted guns everywhere; mines in all the rivers and harbors on the map."

The brooding Cervera had not planned offensive operations. On May 19 he led his ships into narrow landlocked Santiago Bay, and an American fleet promptly bottled him up. After two hard-fought engagements, an American army began closing in on the city of Santiago on July 1. Cervera was now caught between American land and sea forces. Two days later, on orders from his superiors, he led his ships from the harbor to meet senseless death and destruction to preserve Spanish "honor." The American naval forces suffered only two casualties, one man killed and another wounded. The news of the Santiago victory reached the United States on July 4. Independence day commemorations expanded into victory celebrations throughout the nation. Santiago surrendered on July 16, and later American troops took over Puerto Rico. After ten weeks of fighting, the war was over.

In the Philippines, meanwhile, Dewey waited for reinforcements. He did not have the troops to take Manila. After stopping to take Guam in the Spanish Marianas, an American expeditionary force on June 30 reached the Philippines. While Dewey had been waiting, several countries, including Germany and Britain, had sent warships to the Philippines. Germany had sent a squadron more powerful than Dewey's. Friction over blockade measures and other issues broke out between Dewey and the German commander. Since Dewey's relations with the British were unusually friendly, a legend emerged from Manila that the British had saved Dewey from attack by the German forces by threatening to support him in any battle. Although the Germans were anxious to take the Philippines for themselves, they had not intended to provoke war or to threaten Dewey. He did not, therefore, have to be saved by the British.[31]

Peace Terms

With her fleets destroyed and her forces stranded in Cuba and the Philippines, Spain finally conceded that further resistance was useless and sued for peace. McKinley dictated terms on July 30, 1898, demanding complete surrender of Cuba, cession of Puerto Rico, one island in the Marianas, and occupation of the city and harbor of Manila pending the final disposition of the Philippines.[32]

Even though the terms seemed severe to Spain, she accepted them and signed the preliminary peace protocol on August 12, protesting sadly that "this demand strips us of the very last memory of a glorious past and expels us . . . from the Western Hemisphere, which became peopled and civilized through the proud deeds of our ancestors." John Hay, soon to become Secretary of State, commented in a far different mood. "It has been a splendid little war," he wrote; "begun with the highest motives, carried on with magnificent intelligence and spirit, favored by that Fortune which loves the brave."[33]

The formal peace negotiations began in Paris on October 1. Secretary of State William R. Day headed the American commission of five. Two facts stand out in the composition of that commission. Four of the five commissioners were expansionists committed to a "large policy" of imperialism and the fifth eventually came around to the view of the others.[34] Three were ranking members of the Senate Foreign Relations Committee. Realizing that he might run into difficulty obtaining Senate approval for the treaty, McKinley set something of a precedent by including senators in the peace commission.

The Spanish commissioners accepted the demands for Cuban independence, cession of Puerto Rico, and after strong protests even agreed to assume the Cuban debt of some four hundred million dollars, but balked at demands for the Philippines. Since the United States had not conquered them, Spain said, it could not rightfully claim them in the peace settlement. Manila did not surrender to American and Filipino forces until August 13, the day after the signing of the peace protocol.

Internal problems also complicated the status of the Philippines. Before the war Spain had crushed a revolt of Filipino patriots. After the battle of Manila Bay, an American warship brought General Emilio Aguinaldo, exiled leader of the Filipino insurgents, to Manila where Dewey had encouraged him to lead a new revolt against the Spaniards. Aguinaldo had organized rebel forces under the impression that the United States would liberate the Philippines from Spanish rule, as it had pledged itself to a free Cuba. On August 6, he had announced the independence of the Philippine Republic and sought foreign recognition.

Dewey, however, had cabled that the "republic" represented only a faction and could not keep order in the area it allegedly controlled. Expansionists, moreover, had already mounted a campaign demanding that the United States keep the Philippines. They were unwilling to surrender them to allegedly uncivilized natives when those islands could serve as a portal to the rich trade of the Orient. Naval interests, too, emphasized the commercial and strategic importance of the Philippines, suggesting that Germany or Japan would take them if the United States did not.

Big business, the industrial and commercial interests important within the Republican party, now swung behind an expansionist policy it had formerly opposed. The religious press also threw its support behind an "imperialism of righteousness." Commercial expansion, a prominent Presbyterian leader explained, was "a necessary part of the great outward impulse of civilization, the missionary movement welcomes it as an ally." The Chicago *Times-Herald*, a paper close to the administration, said, "We find that we want the Philippines" and added that "the people now believe that the United States owes it to civilization to accept the responsibilities imposed upon it by the fortunes of war." [35]

McKinley, once again, went along with the tide of public opinion. After returning from a speechmaking trip during the congressional campaigns to Chicago, Omaha, and other points in the Middle West, where he carefully measured the response to his remarks on assuming colonial burdens, he concluded that the American people wanted to annex the Philippines. He told the peace commissioners, therefore, that the Philippines stood on a "different basis than did Cuba." The war, he explained, "has brought us new duties and responsibilities which we must meet and discharge as becomes a great nation," and incidental to our tenure in the Philippines is "the commercial opportunity to which American statesmanship cannot be indifferent." [36]

McKinley decided to surrender to Manifest Destiny by taking all of the Philippines, but only after praying for divine guidance. "And one night late it came to me this way . . .," he told a visiting group of Methodist clergymen, "(1) That we could not give them back to Spain—that would be cowardly and dishonorable; (2) that we could not turn them over to France or Germany—our commercial rivals in the Orient—that would be bad business and discreditable; (3) that we could not leave them to themselves—they were unfit for self-government—and they would soon have anarchy and misrule over there worse than Spain's was; and (4) that there was nothing left for us to do but take them all, and to educate the Filipinos, and uplift and Christianize them." And then, he added, "I went to bed . . . and slept soundly." [37]

Not strong enough to resist, but protesting the American demands as violations of the protocol, Spain, therefore, reluctantly parted with the Philippines for twenty million dollars. Technically she gave up the islands as a war indemnity. With the signing of the Treaty of Paris on December 19, the United States took in the fruits of its "splendid little war." For the first time it brought under its flag a distant land and alien masses without offering the hope of future statehood. Not all Americans, not all senators, and certainly not all Filipinos, were pleased.

Many Americans considered the annexation of the Filipinos without their consent unconstitutional and a perversion of the idealistic crusade to free Cuba. Even before McKinley had submitted the Treaty of Paris to the Senate, the foes of expansion opened a great debate on the future of American foreign policy. A group of them in Boston had grasped the initiative by launching an Anti-Imperialist League. Other cities formed similar leagues. The leaders of the anti-imperialist cause were distinguished, including industrialist Andrew Carnegie, labor leader Samuel Gompers, university presidents, Charles W. Eliot of Harvard and David Starr Jordan of Stanford, numerous other intellectuals, and writers such as Hamlin Garland and Mark Twain.[38]

The Republican president of one of the Anti-Imperialist Leagues argued that territorial expansion into the Pacific would lead ultimately to war. "For us, independence in policy, peace, and self-assertion will be impossible," he said, "if we enter into the islands of the east." Whether or not such views were sound, the movement had a fatal weakness. It failed to attract a large popular following.[39]

There could be no stopping the march of the flag, a Republican imperialist had argued in a campaign speech. "It is God's great purpose made manifest in the instincts of our race, whose present phase is our personal profit, but whose far-off end is the redemption of the world and the Christianization of mankind."[40]

Expansionist Americans were supported by the British prophet of the new imperialism, Rudyard Kipling, who urged in February, 1899, the acceptance of the task of civilizing the lesser colored peoples, especially the Filipinos:

> Take up the White Man's burden—
> Send forth the best ye breed—
> Go bind your sons to exile
>   To serve your captives' need;
> To wait in heavy harness,
>   On fluttered folk and wild—
> Your new-caught, sullen peoples,
>   Half-devil and half-child.[41]

"Rather poor poetry, but good sense from the expansionist standpoint," Theodore Roosevelt wrote to his friend Henry Cabot Lodge.[42]

Lodge, the junior senator from Massachusetts, led the Senate fight for the

Treaty of Paris. "I confess," he wrote, "I cannot think calmly of the rejection of that Treaty by a little more than one-third of the Senate. It would be a repudiation of the President and humiliation of the whole country in the eyes of the world, and would show we are unfit as a nation to enter into great questions of foreign policy." [43]

Faced with a determined opposition in the Senate, the administration made support of the treaty a party issue and used its patronage power freely. That was not enough, for the senior senator from Massachusetts, George F. Hoar, was a Republican, and also an anti-imperialist, who led the fight against the treaty. To annex the Philippines, he insisted, would be a dangerous break with the past, a violation of American ideals, and a departure from the principles of the Declaration of Independence. The country's greatest asset, he and other anti-imperialists pointed out, was its heritage of freedom. To take the Philippines would deny that heritage. They agreed with the Democrat William Jennings Bryan that no nation could endure half-republic and half-colony. They reminded the people that the United States had gone to war as a liberator, not as a conqueror.

Ironically, at the critical moment the treaty received unexpected aid from Bryan, then the leader of the Democratic party. Although himself opposed to imperialism and the acquisition of the Philippines, he took the position that the Senate should accept the treaty to make peace official. Later, after the election of 1900, if the Democrats won, the United States could give the Philippines their

GOT HIS LESSON BY HEART NOW

As a smart little boy Uncle Sam shows what he learned from his war with Spain.

freedom. He urged the Democratic senators, therefore, to vote for the treaty. Whether or not Bryan's aid was decisive is questionable, but by the narrow margin of 57 to 27, one more vote than the necessary two-thirds, the Senate approved the treaty on February 6, 1899. Lodge called it the closest, "hardest fight I have ever known."[44]

Carnegie was among those who overstressed Bryan's influence. "One word from Mr. Bryan," he wrote later with lasting bitterness, "would have saved the country from disaster. I could not be cordial to him for years afterwards. He had seemed to me a man who was willing to sacrifice his country and his personal convictions for party advantage."[45]

The Filipinos and Destiny

Two days before the Senate had approved the treaty, Aguinaldo's forces revolted against American rule. The Filipinos, the most Christian people in Asia, did not want to be "uplifted and Christianized" by Americans. The Army, therefore, began civilizing them with rifle and bayonet. "These Filipinos must be taught obedience," the Washington *Star* said, "and must be forced to observe, even if they cannot comprehend, the practice of civilization."[46] Before the United States succeeded in stamping out the revolt, which lasted four years, it used more troops than in the Spanish war, expended six hundred million dollars, and sacrificed over four thousand lives.[47] Americans found their soldiers resorting to brutal repressive measures, just as the Spaniards had done in Cuba. They too used forms of torture and concentration camps to break the fighting spirit of the insurrectionists.

Already skeptical of the Philippine venture, many Americans showed their anger in a renewed outburst of anti-imperialism. From the beginning, in fact, opinion on the Philippines was so divided that a week after approving the peace treaty the Senate defeated a resolution calling for independence only by the casting vote of the Vice-President. Mark Twain, seared by the Philippine conquest, suggested changing the flag with "the white stripes painted black and the stars replaced by the skull and cross bones." A more powerful denunciation of imperialism came from the pen of the young poet William Vaughn Moody:

> Lies! Lies! It cannot be! The wars we wage
> Are noble, and our battles still are won
> By justice for us, ere we lift the gage.
> We have not sold our loftiest heritage.
> The proud republic hath not stopped to cheat
> And scramble in the market-place of war. . . .
> Ah no!
> We have not fallen so.[48]

Bryan, the Democratic candidate, tried to make imperialism the paramount issue in the presidential campaign of 1900. His party's platform announced "that any government not based upon the consent of the governed is a tyranny; and that to impose upon any people a government of force is to substitute the methods of imperialism for those of a republic." [49] McKinley had an answer. "Do we need their consent," he asked, "to perform a great act for humanity?"

With McKinley again their standard bearer, the Republicans went to the people with the slogan, "Don't haul down the flag." "Who," Senator Hoar asked, "shall haul down the President?" Nonetheless, imperialism made no headway as a primary issue, for the Republicans insisted that free silver, or currency was the main issue. The country was prosperous and apparently did not want to repudiate the results of the war. McKinley won the Presidency with a more impressive vote than in 1896.[50]

THE WHITE MAN'S BURDEN IN THE PHILIPPINES

This drawing shows the Twentieth Kansas Volunteers marching through the village of Caloocan after having set fire to its flimsy huts. Their commander, Colonel Frederick Funston, wanted to "rawhide these bullet-headed Asians until they yell for mercy" and later to teach them not "to get in the way of the bandwagon of Anglo-Saxon progress and decency." Drawn from life by G. W. Peters.

With the Spanish-American War and the Treaty of Paris the United States took its place among the great powers of the world. "Our war in aid of Cuba has assumed undreamed of dimensions," the Philadelphia *Record* said, and then added, ". . . willy nilly we have entered upon our career as a world power."[51] Actually, the Spanish-American War did not itself make the United States a world power; the nation already had the potential for such status. The war and the treaty offered foreigners, and more important, Americans themselves, the occasion to recognize that status. "We are face to face with a strange destiny," the Washington *Post* had remarked in a perceptive editorial. "The taste of empire is in the mouth of the people even as the taste of blood in the jungle. It means an imperial policy, the Republic renascent, taking her place with the armed nations."[52]

The war was a turning point in the history of American foreign policy. From that time on Americans could no longer look merely inward. The United States had established undisputed dominance of the Caribbean and had extended its influence to the shores of Asia. It had become a recognized world power through its own inherent strength, and that strength affected the international politics of all the great powers of the world. Even if it wanted to, the United States in the new century could no longer remain aloof from the politics of the rest of the world.

NOTES

1. John T. Morgan, quoted in Walter Millis, *The Martial Spirit* (Boston, 1931), p. 29.

2. For details, see George W. Auxier, "The Propaganda Activities of the Cuban *Junta* in Precipitating the Spanish-American War, 1895–1898," *Hispanic American Historical Review*, XIX (Aug. 1939), 286–305 and John C. Appel, "The Unionization of Florida Cigarmakers and the Coming of the War with Spain," *ibid.*, XXXVI (Feb. 1956), 38–49, which shows how Cuban nationalism affected a part of the labor movement.

3. The sensational yellow journals represented only a minority of the press, but in other parts of the country, in the Middle West for instance, the more conservative papers were anti-Spanish and urged intervention to preserve American interests in the Caribbean. See George W. Auxier, "Middle Western Newspapers and the Spanish-American War, 1895–1898," *Mississippi Valley Historical Review*, XXVI (March

1940), 523–534. See also William E. Leuchtenburg, "The Needless War with Spain," *American Heritage*, VIII (Feb. 1957), 34, which stresses the same point and offers an excellent summary of the causes of the war and Ernest R. May, *Imperial Democracy: The Emergence of America as a Great Power* (New York, 1961), p. 71. William J. Schellings, in "Florida and the Cuban Revolution, 1895–1898," *Florida Historical Quarterly*, XXXIX (Oct. 1960), 175, points out that the important papers in Florida did not echo the Hearst-Pulitzer demands for intervention.

4. Quoted in French E. Chadwick, *The Relations of the United States with Spain: Diplomacy* (New York, 1909), p. 438.

5. Quoted in Millis, *Martial Spirit*, p. 65. See also Allan Nevins, *Grover Cleveland* (New York, 1932), p. 719.

6. Kirk H. Porter, *National Party Platforms* (New York, 1924), p. 205.

7. The full text of the note, dated Sept. 23, 1897, is in *Foreign Relations, 1898*, pp. 568–573.

8. James D. Richardson, ed., *A Compilation of the Messages and Papers of the Presidents, 1789–1897* (10 vols., Washington, 1896–99), X, 131.

9. *Foreign Relations, 1898*, p. 1007.

10. The captain and the *Journal* are quoted in Jacob E. Wisan, *The Cuban Crisis as Reflected in the New York Press, 1895–1898* (New York, 1934), pp. 389, 392. May, in *Imperial Democracy*, p. 139, points out, however, that few advocated immediate war.

11. The Secretary of the Navy and Proctor are quoted in Millis, *Martial Spirit*, pp. 111, 124.

12. *The Wall Street Journal* and the *Evangelist*, March 31, 1898, are quoted in Julius W. Pratt, *Expansionists of 1898* (Baltimore, 1936), pp. 246, 285.

13. This point is stressed in Margaret Leech, *In the Days of McKinley* (New York, 1959), p. 180. See also Ernest R. May, ed., *The Ultimate Decision: The President as Commander-in-Chief* (New York, 1960), p. 95 and May, *Imperial Democracy*, pp. 153–159. May, who has carefully studied the cause of the war, says the *casus belli* lay in Spain's refusal to grant independence.

14. April 5, 1898, von Bülow quoted in Orestes Ferrara, *The Last Spanish War: Revelations in "Diplomacy"* (New York, 1937), p. 127. See also Alfred Vagts, *Deutschland und die Vereinigten Staaten in der Weltpolitik* (2 vols., New York, 1935), II, p. 1300.

15. Quoted in Chadwick, *Relations with Spain: Diplomacy*, p. 571.

16. *Ibid.*, p. 573.

17. *Ibid.*, p. 575. May, in *Imperial Democracy*, p. 168, points out that the American Minister in Madrid, Stewart L. Woodford, should have realized that all Spain sought was time.

18. An influential Republican senator, for instance, angrily told the Secretary of State, "Day, by——, don't your President know where the war-declaring powers is lodged? Tell him by——, that if he doesn't do something Congress will exercise the power." Quoted in Leech, *McKinley*, p. 184. For a careful, sympathetic analysis of McKinley's dilemma, see May, *Imperial Democracy*, pp. 129–130.

· 19. The full text is in Richardson, *Messages of the Presidents*, X, 139–150.

20. Arthur Balfour to Julian Pauncefote, April 15, 1898, quoted in Charles S. Campbell, Jr., *Anglo-American Understanding, 1898–1903* (Baltimore, 1957), p. 35. See also Lester B. Shippee, "Germany and the Spanish-American War," *The American Historical Review*, XXX (July 1925), 761–762. May, in *Imperial Democracy*, p. 218, says the British did not impose a veto and that it was the Kaiser's opposition which was decisive.

21. John Hay to Henry Cabot Lodge, April 5, 1898, in William R. Thayer, *The Life and Letters of John Hay* (2 vols., Boston, 1915), II, 165.

22. Campbell, *Anglo-American Understanding*, p. 48.

23. For details, see Julius W. Pratt, "American Business and the Spanish-American War," *Hispanic American Historical Review*, XIV (May 1934), 163–201.

24. To Robert Bacon, April 5, 1898, quoted in Howard K. Beale, *Theodore Roosevelt and the Rise of America to World Power* (Baltimore, 1956), p. 60.

25. Margaret Leech, in *McKinley*, pp. 180–185, points out that McKinley did not fail in the conduct of his diplomacy, "but in restraining the belligerence of Congress and the American people," and believes that even if he had courageously defied Congress, he would not have prevented war. In "Manifest Destiny and the Philippines," *America in Crisis*, Daniel Aaron, ed. (New York, 1952),

p. 182, Richard Hofstadter suggests that the war "served as an outlet for aggressive impulses while presenting itself, quite truthfully, as an idealistic and humanitarian crusade." He rejects the idea that it was a newspaper war. See also May, *Imperial Democracy*, pp. 147, 268–269, which explains McKinley's moral concern for Cuba as well as his succumbing to public hysteria.

26. Quoted in Millis, *Martial Spirit*, p. 119.

27. Roosevelt's cable of Feb. 25, 1898, is reproduced in facsimile in Frank Freidel, *The Splendid Little War* (Boston, 1958), p. 14, an excellent, brief, illustrated account of the war. Details on the episode are in Beale, *Theodore Roosevelt*, pp. 61, 63, who maintains that Roosevelt's act was carefully planned and important history made by chance authority. Margaret Leech, in *McKinley*, p. 168, holds that Roosevelt's cable had no bearing on subsequent events. Louis Halle, *Dream and Reality: Aspects of American Foreign Policy* (New York, 1958), pp. 183–185, stresses that Dewey acted according to presidential orders and standard naval procedure; hence Halle agrees with Leech. J. A. S. Grenville, in "Diplomacy and War Plans in the United States, 1890-1917," *Transactions of the Royal Historical Society*, 5th ser., XI (London, 1961), 1-12, traces the origin of the idea of attacking the Philippines.

28. Quoted in Halle, *Dream and Reality*, p. 184. See also William R. Braisted, "The Philippine Naval Base Problem, 1898–1909," *Mississippi Valley Historical Review*, XLI (June 1954), 21-33.

29. June 3, 1898, quoted in Foster Rhea Dulles, *America's Rise to World Power, 1898–1954* (New York, 1954), p. 43.

30. Quoted in Millis, *Martial Spirit*, p. 170.

31. For details, see Thomas A. Bailey, "Dewey and the Germans at Manila Bay," *The American Historical Review*, XLV (Oct. 1939), 59–81; also Vagts, *Deutschland und die Vereinigten Staaten*, II, pp. 1326 ff.

32. The island chosen in the Marianas was Guam, captured in June, 1898; see Leslie W. Walker, "Guam's Seizure by the United States in 1898," *Pacific Historical Review*, XIV (March 1945), 1–12.

33. To Theodore Roosevelt, July 27, 1898, Thayer, *Hay*, II, 337.

34. According to May, *Imperial Democracy*, p. 251, only three commissioners were outright annexationists.

35. Quoted in Millis, *Martial Spirit*, p. 317.

36. Quoted in Pratt, *Expansionists of 1898*, pp. 335–336. Earlier, McKinley is reported to have said, "If old Dewey had just sailed away when he smashed that Spanish fleet, what a lot of trouble he would have saved us." In Herman H. Kohlsaat, *From McKinley to Harding: Personal Recollections of Our Presidents* (New York, 1923), p. 68. In *Dream and Reality*, Halle, who has carefully investigated why the United States came to take the Philippines, concludes that their acquisition was unplanned, that it had not occurred to the imperialists such as Roosevelt and Mahan, but that it would have been virtually impossible for the McKinley administration to have avoided the acquisition. See pp. 176–201. See also Seward W. Livermore, "American Naval-Base Policy in the Far East, 1850–1914," *Pacific Historical Review*, XIII (June 1944), 116–117, and Braisted, "Philippine Naval Base Problem," *Mississippi Valley Historical Review*, XLI (June 1954), 21–23. Some historians have maintained that the rivalries of the great powers over the Philippines, rivalries that might have led to war, influenced the decision to keep them. See, for instance, James K. Eyre, Jr., "Russia and the American Acquisition of the Philippines," *ibid.*, XXVIII (March 1942), 539-562 and his "Japan and the American Annexation of the Philippines," *Pacific Historical Review*, XI (March 1942), 55-71.

37. Charles S. Olcott, *The Life of William McKinley* (2 vols., Boston, 1916), II, 110–111. Finley Peter Dunne, or "Mr. Dooley,"

pointed out, "An' yet, tis not more thin two months since ye larned whether they were islands or canned goods." Finley Peter Dunne, *Mr. Dooley in Peace and in War* (Boston, 1899), p. 43.

38. Republicans who joined the anti-imperialists were older conservatives; the progressives supported imperialism. See William E. Leuchtenburg, "Progressivism and Imperialism: The Progressive Movement and American Foreign Policy, 1898–1916," *Mississippi Valley Historical Review*, XXXIX (Dec. 1952), 486.

39. For details, see Fred H. Harrington, "The Anti-Imperialist Movement• in the United States, 1898–1900," *Mississippi Valley Historical Review*, XXII (Sept. 1935), 211–230 and his "Literary Aspects of American Anti-Imperialism, 1898–1902," *New England Quarterly*, X (Dec. 1937), 650–667.

40. Albert Beveridge quoted in Claude G. Bowers, *Beveridge and the Progressive Era* (Boston, 1932), p. 76.

41. *Collected Verse of Rudyard Kipling* (London, 1912), p. 321. The poem, intended primarily for Americans, was written in December, 1898 and first published the following February in the New York papers.

42. Jan. 12, 1899, in Henry Cabot Lodge, ed., *Selections from the Correspondence of Theodore Roosevelt and Henry Cabot Lodge, 1884–1918* (2 vols., New York, 1925), I, 384.

43. Quoted in John A. Garraty, *Henry Cabot Lodge: A Biography* (New York, 1953), p. 200.

44. Paolo E. Coletta, in "Bryan, McKinley, and the Treaty of Paris," *Pacific Historical Review*, XXVI (May 1957), 131–146, points out that Bryan was not the decisive factor in the treaty's passage. For the earlier contrasting view, see William Stull Holt, *Treaties*

Defeated by the Senate (Baltimore, 1933), pp. 165–177; see also Merle E. Curti, "Bryan and World Peace," *Smith College Studies in History*, XVI, nos. 3–4 (April, July 1931), 131–132.

45. *Autobiography of Andrew Carnegie* (Boston, 1920), p. 364.

46. Quoted in Foster Rhea Dulles, *The Imperial Years* (New York, 1956), p. 177.

47. Filipino casualties were much higher. The figures on casualties and costs are in Leon Wolff, *Little Brown Brother: How the United States Purchased and Pacified the Philippine Islands at the Century's Turn* (New York, 1961), p. 360.

48. "An Ode in Time of Hesitation," in Robert Morss Lovett, ed., *Selected Poems of William Vaughn Moody* (Boston, 1931), pp. 18, 24.

49. Porter, *National Party Platforms*, pp. 210–211.

50. Details are in Thomas A. Bailey, "Was the Election of 1900 a Mandate on Imperialism?" *Mississippi Valley Historical Review*, XXIV (June 1937), 43–52. Hoar is quoted in Robert L. Beisner, *Twelve Against Empire: The Anti-Imperialists, 1898–1900* (New York, 1968), p. 155.

51. Quoted in Dulles, *America's Rise to World Power*, p. 43.

52. Quoted in Robert E. Osgood, *Ideals and Self-Interest in America's Foreign Relations: The Great Transformation of the Twentieth Century* (Chicago, 1953), p. 48. For a stimulating analysis that stresses America's earlier emergence as a great power, see Thomas A. Bailey, "America's Emergence as a World Power: The Myth and the Verity," *Pacific Historical Review*, XXX (Feb. 1961), 1–16.

Chapter Fifteen

OPEN DOOR
AND BIG STICK

During the years of the New Manifest Destiny, events of far-reaching significance in Asia formed a new framework for America's Far Eastern policy. In 1895 Japan defeated China in a war over Korea that exposed China as a helpless giant unable to defend itself and saw Japan rise virtually to the status of a great power. Before Japan could gather the fruits of her victory, however, Russia, Germany, and France intervened. In April they forced her to give up the territory on the mainland that she had taken from China. This triple intervention marked a new era in China's relations with Japan and the West.

In the next three years China became a market for Western investment, principally railroad and mining capital, as well as for trade. The great powers scrambled for economic concessions and spheres of political interest. "The various powers," China's Dowager Empress said, "cast upon us looks of tiger-like voracity, hustling each other in their endeavors to be the first to seize upon our innermost territories." The hungry imperialists threatened to dismember China. By 1899, with the Manchu government helpless to resist, the West had reduced parts of the country to semi-colonial status.

Since the war between China and Japan and its results seemed remote, those developments did not at first alarm Americans. "The deplorable war between China and Japan," Secretary of State Walter Q. Gresham had told the Japanese, "endangers no policy of the United States in Asia." [1] Later, however, the threatened partitioning of China did alarm the American government, and particularly some businessmen.

Trade with China had never amounted to much; it never exceeded three per cent of America's total foreign commerce. Yet businessmen and others believed that the Chinese market offered the opportunity for a vast future trade. That was one reason why commercial American interests had approved of keeping the Philippines. In China there were four hundred million people, more than five times as many as in the United States, a Massachusetts business journal explained. Their wants were increasing every year. "What a market!"

Future trade in that market would depend on equal commercial opportunity for all nations, including such things as equal customs duties and harbor dues, or what was commonly called the Open Door, a privilege Americans had enjoyed since the Treaty of Wanghia. Partitioning of China into spheres of influence, and eventually colonies with their exclusive privileges, would mean the end of the Open Door and of American hopes for a growing portion of China's trade.

Great Britain's Position

Russian, German, and French expansion in China alarmed the British more than it did the Americans. The British had controlled most of China's foreign trade, some eighty per cent of it, and had always supported the Open Door. As the European powers began to stake out their spheres of influence, however, British opinion divided. Some British officials feared that European expansion would close the door in their own spheres and that British trade would suffer. Others believed that the European powers would bring order in the interior, and that British trade might even prosper within these spheres. Other Englishmen, for strategic and political reasons, did not like the spheres and naval leaseholds.

In the spring of 1898 the British reacted to the new international situation in China with a threefold strategy. They stressed the importance of retaining the Open Door, secretly sought an agreement with some other power to block Russia's penetration, and worked out plans for their own sphere of influence in the Yangtze Valley, or as one of their statesmen said, they prepared themselves "to pounce the moment anyone else pounces." They realized that the old doctrine of the Open Door was not really appropriate to the new situation in China where the powers sought mining and railway concessions and other opportunities for capital investment, and not merely to trade. Yet the British continued to support the Open Door because they still profited from trade more than any other nation and did not want their traders excluded anywhere.

On March 8, therefore, about a month before the beginning of the Spanish-American War, the British government confidentially invited the United States to cooperate in maintaining the Open Door, asking in effect: "Will you stand with us in our China policy?" It said nothing about the spheres of influence and the special investment privileges within them.

McKinley rejected the British overture. He was at the time concerned primarily with the Cuban crisis, did not wish to espouse, for political reasons, what appeared to be a British policy, did not think the new developments in China seriously threatened American interests there, and did not wish to depart from the "traditional policy" of avoiding foreign entanglements.

John Hay, the American Ambassador to England and a thorough Anglophile, did not like the administration's rebuff. He was not at the time concerned with China or American policy there, but with relations in England. He wanted to cooperate closely with England whenever an opportunity arose. Late in September Hay became Secretary of State.

That summer, though still professing to support the principle of the Open Door, the British went into the concession business in a big way by carving out the largest sphere of influence yet in the Yangtze Valley, and by obtaining several strategic leaseholds. During that winter, especially after the Treaty of Paris had confirmed the United States as an imperialist power in Asia, American opinion on the Open Door changed. Lord Charles Beresford, a Member of Parliament and a representative of the Associated Chambers of Commerce of Great Britain, visited the United States after a tour of China and Japan and urged American and British cooperation in preserving the Open Door. He wanted to have "free and equal commercial relations for all time in the Orient," and to save China from partition. His speeches, and a book he wrote at the time, *The Break-Up of China*, popularized the idea of the Open Door among Americans.

The American Position

That idea, an old one in America's Far Eastern policy, now appealed more strongly than ever to businessmen with their expanded visions of trade in China. That trade, through the recently acquired Philippines, they argued, depended on preserving China as a free market. American missionaries, rejoicing over the annexation of the Philippines and fearing the antiforeignism stirred up by the concession hunters, also urged a stronger policy in China. The McKinley administration, sensitive to business views, began reacting to the new pressures. Secretary of State Hay, for instance, told Congress that the sale of American products in China should not be endangered by exclusive privileges for other powers, meaning that the door should remain open to Americans.

As his adviser on Far Eastern affairs Hay had chosen a friend, William W. Rockhill, who had served in China and Korea. Rockhill took up his new duties in the spring of 1899. That June an old friend from Peking, an Englishman named Alfred E. Hippisley, who worked for the Chinese government in the Imperial Maritime Customs Service, visited the United States and discussed China's situation with him.

Hippisley urged that the American government "do what it can to maintain the Open Door for ordinary commerce in China."[2] He accepted the spheres of influence as existing facts, but wanted the United States to approach the powers and obtain assurances that they would adhere to the principle of the Open Door within their own spheres. Since England was no longer greatly disturbed about the Open Door, Hippisley did not speak for the British government. His primary concern was the probable breakup of the Customs Service and the financial ruin and threatened partitioning of China.

Rockhill listened to Hippisley's ideas with sympathy. He preferred, in fact, to go further than Hippisley proposed. "You know what my views are about the position the United States should take in China," he said; "I would like to see it make a declaration in some form or other, which would be understood by China as a pledge on our part to assist in maintaining the integrity of the Empire."[3] Both men realized that such a broad policy was unrealistic. The American government, for political and traditional reasons, could not support it. Therefore, they restricted their plan to maintaining the Open Door for trade within the spheres.

Hippisley shrewdly suggested that the McKinley administration could deliver a diplomatic stroke that would win popular support and bring it political advantage. "The public need know nothing of the steps taken by the Sec. of State," he wrote, "till the negotiations have been consummated, and the announcement then that the U.S. had secured China's independence and so served the cause of peace & civilization would be a trump card for the Admin. and crush all the life out of the anti-imperialism agitation. . . ."[4]

The Open Door Notes

Hay, probably remembering Britain's earlier overture and himself already favorable to the Open Door idea, liked the Hippisley-Rockhill plan.[5] In August, therefore, he authorized Rockhill to go ahead with Hippisley's suggestion and to draft notes for the great powers in the Orient. Rockhill drew up instructions for the American Ambassadors to the powers based on a memorandum drafted by Hippisley a week before. The instructions went to Hay and McKinley, who approved them virtually without change. Hay sent those, the first Open Door notes to Britain, Germany, and Russia on September 6, and in November to Japan, France, and Italy.

In the notes Hay said nothing about special preference and monopoly in mining, railroad, and other capital investments in the spheres of influence. He asked the powers merely to allow equal commercial opportunity within them, not to interfere with the treaty ports in them, not to impede collection of Chinese customs duties, not to charge discriminatory railroad rates or harbor dues, and to cooperate with the United States in securing the support of the other powers for the principle of the Open Door. Even though the notes were moderate and limited in scope, the United States merely by sending them put aside its traditional policy of noninterference in the affairs of the major powers.

Only Italy, who did not have a sphere, fully accepted Hay's suggestions. All the other countries answered evasively with faint gestures of approval, and Russia virtually rejected the whole idea of the Open Door.[6] Yet six months later, in May, 1900, Hay announced that the powers had given him satisfactory assurances and that he regarded them as "final and definitive." He thus placed the powers publicly on record as supporting the Open Door and left the American people with the impression that he had achieved a diplomatic triumph, one that had prevented the breakup of China by predatory powers. The press supported his policy and praised him warmly. Some newspapers called it a "diplomatic victory" and others a "victory for civilization."

Hay had not won a victory of any kind. He had merely announced his country's support of the Open Door, a principle the powers had refused to accept without qualification. Even if they had accepted it on Hay's terms, there could have been no real equality of commercial opportunity in China so long as the spheres of influence, meaning special financial and investment privileges, continued to exist. Only force could destroy the spheres, and the American people would not support the use of arms and thereby become more directly entangled in the international politics of Asia. Nonetheless, the Open Door and the traditional policy of isolation were incompatible. Without force, furthermore, Hay's policy represented a pious hope rather than a realistic appraisal of conditions in Asia.

Just as Hay announced his satisfaction with the replies to the Open Door notes, a violent antiforeign, anti-imperialist uprising, fomented by a secret society that Westerners called Boxers and encouraged by the imperial government, broke out in China. The Boxer Rebellion offered an opportunity for the first real test of Hay's Open Door policy.

In June, 1900, powerful bands of Boxers, armed with swords and spears, overran Peking, rioting and pillaging throughout the city. Joined by imperial troops, they laid siege to the foreign legations in the city. The siege lasted until August 14, when an international rescue expedition of some twenty thousand soldiers lifted it. Ignoring the traditional nonentanglement principle, the United States contributed some twenty-five hundred men to the rescue force. The need "to secure for our merchants, farmers, and wage-workers the benefits of the open market," Theodore Roosevelt argued, made the sending of troops into China legitimate.

While concerned over the fate of the Americans in Peking, Hay did not overlook the broader implications of the Boxer uprising. He realized that some of the powers, Russia and Germany in particular, would use the troubles as an excuse to expand their spheres of influence. When the Boxers attacked Russians in Manchuria, for example, the Russian Minister of War was pleased. "This will give us an excuse for seizing Manchuria," he said. Hay decided, therefore, on another announcement.

Hay's Attempt to Retain the Open Door

In his earlier notes Hay had merely implied the desirability of maintaining China's integrity. In the middle of the Boxer crisis he sent a circular note to the powers informing them that the United States wanted to "bring about permanent safety and peace to China, preserve Chinese territorial and administrative entity, protect all rights guaranteed to friendly powers by treaty and international law, and safeguard for the world the principle of equal and impartial trade with all parts of the Chinese Empire." [7]

Unlike the earlier notes, this July circular did not ask for replies. Hay's new policy, actually an addition to the earlier position, was merely an American policy announced to the other powers without asking them formally to join in upholding it. The complete Open Door policy thus comprised the notes of 1899 and circular of 1900. It included the two principles of equal commercial opportunity and respect for China's independence.

The circular, announced one day before the meeting of the Democratic National Convention, won public approval. In the election year of 1900 it struck an idealistic note in foreign policy that contrasted sharply with the harsh campaign in the Philippines and the shrill charges of the anti-imperialists. "Nothing so meteoric," according to Henry Adams, "had ever been done in American diplomacy." [8]

On the great powers, however, Hay's notes had practically no effect. Those powers used the Boxer troubles to increase their influence in China. By the end of October Russia, for instance, had won military control over Manchuria and appeared ready to convert her sphere there into a protectorate. That posture threatened both principles of the Open Door. Nonetheless the general threat to China's independence seemed less formidable than before.

Although the powers did not completely ignore the Open Door policy, it in itself did not prevent partition. At first, as William Vaughn Moody described the situation in his poem "The Quarry,"

> Came many brutes of prey, their several hates
> Laid by until the sharing of the spoil. [9]

Finally, however, the mutual jealousies and rivalries of the powers became so strong that they could not agree as to how the quarry should be dismembered. Each of the potential partitioners feared a first move that might set off a chain reaction and then a world war. So each hesitated to strike decisively.

Hay himself realized that he had made no true converts to China's territorial integrity. "There is . . . not a single power we can rely upon," he complained later, "for our policy of abstention from plunder and the Open Door." There was

something sanctimonious and even false in that lament. The United States in its
own Asian possession, the Philippines, did not allow the Open Door it asked
others to permit in their spheres. Furthermore, in December, 1900, only five
months after announcing his concern for China's territorial entity, Hay too joined
the concession hunters. He secretly instructed the American Minister in Peking to
try to obtain a naval coaling station at Samsah Bay on China's coast opposite the
northern tip of Formosa. Since Japan regarded Fukien, opposite Formosa, as her
own sphere of influence, she blocked the move, reminding Hay of his concern
for China's territorial integrity.[10]

Meanwhile, Rockhill had gone to China as a special commissioner and then
became Minister in Peking. He too became disillusioned with the Open Door
policy. "England has her agreement with Germany," he wrote, "Russia has her
alliance with France, the Triple Alliance comes in here, and every other combination you know of is working here just as it is in Europe. I trust it may be a long
time before the United States gets into another muddle of this description."[11]

What Hay and Rockhill had begun to realize was that the United States, with
the acquisition of the Philippines and its expanded Open Door policy, had entered
the entanglements of world politics through the back door of Asia. This was a
logical outcome of the New Manifest Destiny and overseas expansion. The irony of
it all was that the American people believed that the Open Door policy was a
triumph of idealism over power politics, an American policy that saved China.

While the powers negotiated a settlement of the Boxer Rebellion, Russia
pressed China secretly for a separate agreement on Manchuria that would increase
her control over that province. The Russian moves alarmed Britain and the
United States, but especially Japan, who asked the American government what
steps it would take to uphold the Open Door in Manchuria. Hay replied that the
United States was "not prepared to attempt singly, or in concert with other
Powers, to enforce these views in the east by any demonstration which could
present a character of hostility to any other Power."[12] That showed Japan, who
considered Manchuria worth fighting for, that the United States would not go
beyond words.

Hay continued to use words. In April he asked Russia for assurances that she
would not discriminate against American enterprise in Manchuria. For awhile
the diplomatic pressure appeared to work. Russia eased her own pressure on
Manchuria, but renewed it in November. Not satisfied with a diplomacy of words,
Britain and Japan signed their first alliance in January, 1902, a five-year treaty
aimed directly at Russia. That alliance readjusted the balance of power in the Far
East and also caused a shift in the European balance.

Meanwhile, after McKinley's death, Theodore Roosevelt retained Hay as
Secretary of State and accepted the Open Door as the basis of American Far
Eastern policy. Not adequately informed by the diplomatic service, Hay received

the news of the Anglo-Japanese alliance as a surprise. When Russia, under pressure from the alliance, agreed in April to evacuate her troops from Manchuria, he seemed satisfied. He had not, apparently, grasped the warlike significance of that alliance.

Russia did not keep her word. Instead of removing her troops, she pressed new demands on China. If China had met them, they would have ended all pretense of an Open Door in Manchuria. Russia's actions also threatened negotiations Hay had begun with China for a commercial treaty. After Russia vaguely assured Hay that she "had never opposed the development of foreign commerce in Manchuria," he went ahead with the Chinese treaty embodying the Open Door principles, concluding it on October 8, 1903. Yet, when China appealed for America's good offices in her difficulties with Russia, he refused to be drawn directly into the complicated international politics of Manchuria. He had already told President Roosevelt that he believed American "public opinion" would not support cooperative action "which would seem openly hostile to Russia."

Japan's Emergence as a World Power

At this point, Japan opened direct negotiations with Russia in an effort to reach an understanding on Manchuria and Korea. She wanted a free hand in Korea where she feared Russian encroachments even more than in Manchuria. Russia would not agree. Japan broke off negotiations and on February 8, 1904, launched a surprise attack on the Russian fleet at Port Arthur, declaring war two days later. All the fighting took place on Chinese soil, and the Russo-Japanese War clearly endangered what remained of the Open Door policy.

As soon as hostilities began, Roosevelt reaffirmed that policy. He asked Japan and Russia to respect "the neutrality of China and in all practical ways her administrative entity," but said nothing about Korea. The Russian Ambassador in Washington wanted to know later why the United States should wish to deprive Russia of Manchuria and not Japan of Korea. Since neither the Russian nor the Japanese reply was satisfactory, Roosevelt's request was useless, but Hay, again bluffing, announced that the belligerents had given proper assurances. A year later Roosevelt, through Hay, circularized the neutral powers asking them to respect "the integrity of China and the 'Open Door' in the Orient." All responded favorably, but the most dangerous threats to the Open Door would come from Russia and Japan.

Roosevelt's sympathy in the war, and that of the American people, was with the Japanese. "Public opinion in this country," a contemporary survey announced, "... supports the position assumed by Japan—that Russia shall give her a free hand in Korea and guarantee Chinese sovereignty in Manchuria." [13] Roosevelt said later, in an assertion historians have considered dubious, that on the outbreak of hostilities he had notified Germany and France that he would "promptly side with Japan and proceed to whatever length was necessary on her behalf" if the European powers intervened against her.[14] "I like the Japanese," he explained more than once.[15] They had, he maintained, the kind of fighting stock he admired.

Yet as the war went on, with one Japanese victory following another, Roosevelt began to change his views. He decided that the best situation for the Open Door and America's interest in the Far East would be a balance of power between Russia and Japan, not a triumph that would make Japan supreme in eastern Asia. He tried, therefore, to mediate a peace that would not drive Russia completely out of eastern Asia.

Roosevelt's opportunity came through the Japanese. Despite their victories, they desperately needed peace. They had failed to break the Russian armies, and their government was on the verge of bankruptcy. Even though Roosevelt had been trying for several months to bring the war to an end, he imposed one condition when the Japanese indicated they wanted him to arbitrate—that they support the Open Door. In April, 1905, the Japanese government assured him "that Japan adheres to the position of maintaining Open Door in Manchuria and of restoring that province to China."[16] That statement was the closest to what might be called a pledge that he received on the Open Door.

A month later the Japanese asked Roosevelt on his own "initiative to invite the two belligerents to come together for the purpose of direct negotiation."[17] He then approached the Tsar who also needed peace.[18] The Tsar's funds were exhausted, he could obtain no more credit from French bankers, and revolutionary movements at home, where the war was never popular, threatened the entire war effort and his regime as well. He therefore accepted the peace proposal.

Roosevelt then immediately offered his good offices to both countries. In August the belligerents met at Portsmouth, New Hampshire. As a basis for peace, Russia withdrew from Korea and surrendered her special interests in Southern Manchuria. The most serious obstacles to a treaty were Japan's demands for all of the island of Sakhalin and a large monetary indemnity. Russia refused to consent to either and threatened to break up the conference and renew hostilities. Roosevelt, even though he remained strongly pro-Japanese, then persuaded Japan to give up her demand for an indemnity and arranged a compromise that gave half of Sakhalin to Japan.[19]

"Peace Arranged; Japan Gives In," *The New York Times* headline announced the next day. Russia and Japan signed the Treaty of Portsmouth on September 5. Almost everybody praised Roosevelt's diplomacy. "The President's prestige throughout the world is beyond anything that he can imagine," a friend wrote. "Without regard to party or section," *Public Opinion* said, "the papers praise him for his skill and tact in holding the conference together till an agreement could be reached." He had become, it added, "the most popular man in the

THE PEACEMAKERS, 1905

Theodore Roosevelt (center) at Portsmouth with the Russian and Japanese representatives.

world." [20] In the following year Roosevelt received the Nobel Peace Prize for his role at the Portsmouth conference.

Ominously, the Japanese people did not join the popular acclaim for Roosevelt's peacemaking. They had counted heavily on an indemnity and believed that he had robbed them of their compensation for victory. Since the Japanese government knew that it had made an unpopular peace, it used Roosevelt as the scapegoat. It did not dare tell the people it could not continue the war. The people, therefore, turned against the United States. Anti-American riots swept over Japan.

Shortly after, Americans began to lose their sympathy for Japan. Her demands at the peace conference, the stiffness of her diplomats, and the limited success of Russian statesmen in trying to win American public opinion through careful handling of public relations, helped make the Portsmouth conference, in the long run, a turning point in Japanese-American relations. [21] Thus, for the second time in Asia, the United States had played an important role in the international politics of the great powers, and for the second time the results were unsatisfactory.

It was fitting, nonetheless, that the increasingly powerful United States should have had a hand in the Treaty of Portsmouth, one of the most important treaties of the modern Far East and a landmark in the history of the modern world. It recognized that for the first time an Asian nation had defeated a major European power. That victory aroused, in time, a latent nationalism in many parts of Asia, and in a sense marked the beginning of the end of European predominance in Asia. It established Japan undisputably as a world power, the first time an Asian nation had reached that status. It also confirmed Japan as the dominant power in Southern Manchuria and Korea, a fact of considerable significance for the United States.

The Taft-Katsura Agreed Memorandum

In Korea, Japan made no pretense of upholding the Open Door. Her influence in this country had been gradually increasing since 1895, despite Russia's opposition. With the Treaty of Portsmouth it became an exclusive control. When the Russo-Japanese War had broken out, Korea had proclaimed her independence, but had taken no measures to defend it. She believed apparently that the United States and the other great powers of the West would guarantee her independence. When Japan went ahead and converted Korea into a protectorate, Britain and the United States, however, acquiesced and hence abandoned the idea of the Open Door for Korea. "We can not possibly interfere for the Koreans against Japan," Roosevelt told Hay. "They couldn't strike one blow in their own defence." [22] Since Roosevelt knew that he could not prevent Japan's action, he realistically accepted the inevitable.

Japan's victories over Russia had caused some uneasiness in the United States over the safety of the Philippines. While on a trip to the Philippines, Secretary of War William Howard Taft, under Roosevelt's instructions, stopped off at Tokyo. In conversations there with Count Taro Katsura, Japan's Prime Minister, he brought up the concern over the Philippines and also said that he believed Japanese suzerainty over Korea would contribute to lasting peace in the Far East. Katsura, in turn, disavowed any aggressive Japanese designs against the Philippines. Following this exchange of views on July 27, 1905, an "agreed memorandum" of the discussion was drawn up, which some have called the "Taft-Katsura Agreement." Although the memorandum was not a formal agreement of any kind, it did embody the President's ideas. He cabled Taft that the conversation was absolutely correct and that "I confirm every word you have said." [23]

When England renewed her alliance with Japan in August, she too recognized Japan's "paramount political, military, and economic" interests in Korea. A few months later, actually on November 24, the United States instructed its Minister in Seoul to close the legation there, thus becoming the first nation to recognize Japan's complete control. Japan had now sealed the door in Korea with the approval of the United States. [24] Actually, since Hay had first announced the Open Door policy, Korea's door had never been opened very much.

Anti-Japanese Prejudice

Despite the Taft-Katsura memorandum, developments within the United States added to the Japanese-American antagonisms engendered by the Portsmouth treaty. In October, 1906, San Francisco's school board segregated some ninety-three Japanese children in a special school. That move climaxed a series of discriminations against the Japanese in California where the people wanted to exclude them as they had the Chinese. The Japanese already there suffered from racial prejudice, restrictive legislation, boycotts, and riots. Their mistreatment fed a bitter anti-Americanism in Japan just as the Chinese discrimination a year earlier had sparked an anti-American boycott in China.

Japan protested "the condition of the affairs in San Francisco," saying that the segregation of Japanese children because of race was "an act of discrimination carrying with it a stigma and odium which it is impossible to overlook." Roosevelt realized that relations with the proud and sensitive Japanese had now become the major problem in American foreign relations. He saw the contradiction in America's position. On the one hand the United States sought equal commercial treatment in Asia and, on the other, closed its door to Asian immigrants and discriminated against them. At the same time, even though Japan had assured him she would uphold the Open Door in Manchuria, her statesmen saw American support of the Open Door there as an obstacle to their own plans for exploiting Manchuria and actually closing the door there.

War between Japan and the United States, it seemed to foreign observers, was not improbable. Roosevelt recognized the danger. "The infernal fools in California, and especially in San Francisco," he told his son, "insult the Japanese recklessly, and in the event of war it will be the Nation as a whole which will pay the consequences." [25] So he pursued a firm but conciliatory policy toward the Japanese, making every effort to adjust differences peacefully. His policy can be summed up in the words of the old West African proverb he was fond of quoting, "Speak softly and carry a big stick." For awhile he negotiated patiently with the Japanese but always held in reserve the power of the Navy, his big stick.

First, Roosevelt told the Japanese that he opposed the discriminatory action of the San Franciscans and assured them he would deal with the matter. He investigated the segregation and in his annual message in December told Congress that the school board's action was a "wicked absurdity," and suggested legislation conferring the right of naturalization on the Japanese. Roosevelt's attitude pleased the Japanese but enraged West Coast Japanophobes.

Since the action of the school board was local and beyond the jurisdiction of the Federal government, unless the courts held that it violated a commercial treaty of 1894 with Japan, Roosevelt could not use his office to effect an immediate easing of the crisis. He therefore exerted his personal influence with the Californians and at the same time tried to reach a diplomatic settlement with the Japanese. He invited San Francisco's mayor and the entire school board to Washington where he persuaded them to rescind the segregation order in exchange for a promise to stop the immigration of Japanese laborers.

With the Japanese, the President tried more than once to obtain a treaty whereby they and the United States would mutually exclude each other's laborers, but

Japan would not agree. Finally, in return for an understanding that the United States would not stigmatize the Japanese as inferiors by barring them by law, Japan agreed voluntarily to withhold passports from her laborers seeking to enter the American mainland. This executive arrangement, worked out with Japan's Ambassador in Washington through an exchange of notes in 1907 and 1908, became known as the Gentlemen's Agreement. Through it Roosevelt recognized the justice of Japan's case and at the same time upheld the right of the United States to determine its own immigration policy.

Yet, anti-Japanese agitation on the Pacific Coast did not end. Rumors of war circulated in foreign capitals The best information in France, England, and Germany, Roosevelt wrote, "is that we shall have war with Japan and we shall be beaten." [26] He went so far as to send orders to General Leonard Wood, commanding American troops in the Philippines, to prepare to meet a Japanese attack. In October he again sent Taft to Tokyo. The Secretary of War reported on the eighteenth that "the Japanese Government is most anxious to avoid war."

Then, to overcome the continuing crisis, Roosevelt prepared a demonstration of naval power and made concessions to Japan, seemingly at China's expense, in Manchuria. He decided to send the battleship fleet, the second largest in the world, on a world cruise to impress Japan with the futility of war with the United States. Many Americans, particularly those on the East Coast, protested. They considered the cruise dangerous. It might, instead of easing the crisis, actually provoke war. The fleet, they said, should remain in home waters, to protect the country. Roosevelt persisted, personally reviewing the fleet on the eve of its departure in December, 1907, and handing the commanding officer sealed orders.

After the fleet had arrived in the Pacific, the emperor invited it to visit Japan. When the ships dropped anchors in Tokyo's waters, the people gave them a tumultuous welcome, the high point of the entire cruise. "The fleet made a vivid and far-reaching impression," a correspondent of the Chicago *Tribune* reported. "It caused the Japanese to realize the formidable power of the United States, as nothing else could possibly have done." Roosevelt himself believed the same thing. "Every particle of trouble with the Japanese Government and the Japanese press," he wrote later, "stopped like magic as soon as they found that our fleet had actually sailed, and was obviously in good trim." [27]

The Root-Takahira Agreement

While the fleet was on its cruise Roosevelt took other steps to dispel the crisis. On May 5, 1908, he concluded a five-year treaty of arbitration with Japan. Although a limited agreement, excluding all questions of "vital interest," it was a peaceful gesture. More important were the notes Secretary of State Elihu Root exchanged with the Japanese Ambassador in Washington, Baron Kogoro Takahira, after the fleet left Yokohama.

In the Root-Takahira Agreement, signed November 30, the United States and Japan said they would respect each other's possessions in the Pacific area, would support the "existing *status quo*" and would uphold "by all pacific means at their disposal the independence and integrity of China and the principle of equal commercial opportunity for commerce and industry of all nations in that Empire."[28] In case of a threat to those principles the two countries agreed to communicate with each other in search of an understanding on the action they would take.

On the surface, the ambiguous executive agreement appeared to be a victory for the Open Door. Actually, it was a self-contradictory declaration designed to ease mutual antagonisms. The existing *status quo*, in effect, recognized Japan's special position in South Manchuria. There is no evidence to support the thesis that the agreement was a bargain in which the United States surrendered the Open Door in Manchuria in exchange for Japanese support of its principles in China proper, and another renunciation of aggressive tendencies toward the Philippines.[29] Some Americans, however, recognized it as essentially a concession to the realities of Japan's position in Asia.

Roosevelt's policy closed another chapter in the history of the Open Door with a realistic appraisal of America's position. Manchuria and Korea were of secondary concern to American foreign policy. Trade there was negligible, and Americans would not support an Asian war at this time merely for idealistic reasons. To Japan, on the other hand, the closed door in Korea and Southern Manchuria was vital. She had gone to war twice to advance and hold her interests in those areas and presumably would do so a third time if necessary.

Roosevelt felt that a limited retreat on the Open Door was a small price to pay for a general agreement with Japan and for peace in an area where the United States had no essential interests. He made this clear in a long letter to his successor explaining his view on Far Eastern policy.

"The Open Door policy in China was an excellent thing," Roosevelt said, "and I hope it will be a good thing in the future, so far as it can be maintained by general diplomatic agreement; but, as has been proved by the whole history of Manchuria, alike under Russia and under Japan, the 'Open Door' policy, as a matter of fact, completely disappears as soon as a powerful nation determines to disregard it, and is willing to run the risk of war rather than forego its intention."[30] That was the heart of the matter. It was not to the interest of the United States to risk war over principles not vital to its foreign policy.

Cuba's Status

In addition to thrusting the United States into the morass of Far Eastern politics, the Spanish-American War left it in control of Cuba and dominant in the Caribbean. Expansionists wanted to insure that dominance by annexing Cuba and thereby brush aside the embarrassing Teller amendment. "I cannot believe it an evil for any people," the Assistant Secretary of State announced, "that the Stars and Stripes, the symbol of liberty and law, should float over them." Europeans believed the United States would take Cuba as it had the Philippines.

The occupation of Cuba and the behavior of the McKinley administration appeared to give substance to European fears. The United States never recognized the government of the Cuban rebels and ignored the claims of rebel leaders that Cuba was an independent nation. The Philippine insurrection, however, weakened imperialist demands for Cuba, and hence McKinley went ahead with plans for an independent Cuba, but one tied firmly to American Caribbean policy. Cuba, he told Congress, "must needs be bound to us by ties of singular intimacy and strength."[31]

General Leonard Wood, an expansionist who wanted to annex Cuba, took over as American military governor in December, 1899. With an iron hand he introduced needed reforms in education, sanitation, public works, and government, hoping to bind the island to the United States. "Clean government, quick, decisive action and absolute control in the hands of trustworthy men, establishment of needed legal and educational reforms," he told his friend Theodore Roosevelt, "and I do not believe you could shake Cuba loose if you wanted to."[32]

Despite the benefits which Wood's rule conferred, most Cubans resented it, preferring the freedom they thought should be theirs. Weary Cubans expressed their feeling in doggerel:

> Don't eat, don't spit;
> Don't scratch, don't smoke;
> Arrive very early;
> Depart almost by night.
> There is no time for lunch
> Nor anything other than writing;
> He who wishes to work here
> Is he who wishes to die.[33]

Cuban demands for freedom and the pressure of anti-imperialists at home led Wood to call Cuban leaders together in Havana in November, 1900, to frame and adopt a constitution. They drew up a constitution based in part on that of the United States, but did not, as Wood had asked them to do, provide for special future relations with the United States. Jealous of the independence that appeared within their grasp, Cubans feared that the United States desired a protectorate over their country.

Since the McKinley administration was unwilling to accept a truly independent Cuba, Secretary of War Elihu Root brought together administration ideas on what Cuba's connection to the United States should be, and Orville H. Platt of Connecticut, chairman of the Senate Committee on Foreign Relations, attached them as a "rider" to the Army appropriation bill of March 2, 1901. They became law as the Platt Amendment.

That amendment authorized the President to end the military occupation as soon as a Cuban government established itself under a constitution that defined future relations with the United States. Its main provisions prevented Cuba from making financial or diplomatic agreements with foreign powers which would impair independence, gave the United States the legal right to intervene in Cuban affairs, forced Cuba to ratify all the acts of the American military government, allowed the United States to buy or lease coaling or naval stations in Cuba, and required Cuba to embody those terms into a permanent treaty with the United States.

At first the Cuban constitution makers rejected the Platt Amendment, but the United States made it clear that its troops would continue to occupy the island until the Cubans accepted the Platt terms. Root tried to mollify the Cubans. "The Platt Amendment," he maintained, "is not synonymous with intermeddling or interference with the affairs of the Cuban Government."[34] The United States would intervene only to maintain proper government and to preserve Cuba's independence. Under pressure, the Cubans reconsidered, and then reluctantly accepted the Platt Amendment, making it an appendix to their constitution. Later, on May 22, 1903, they also accepted it as part of a treaty they signed with the United States.

Since that agreement was one-sided, forcing obligations only on Cuba and giving rights only to the United States, it impaired Cuba's sovereignty and made the island a virtual protectorate of the United States. Europeans, as did Latin Americans, considered the Platt Amendment a decisive step toward annexation. "Of the independence of Cuba nothing remains," a Paris newspaper said; "of the promises of the United States equally little." A Berlin paper said the amendment was "the beginning of absolute control by the Americans," a view shared by General Wood and other expansionists.[35] To the surprise of the world, however, Roosevelt withdrew the American troops in May, 1902, and ended the first Cuban intervention.

That withdrawal did not dispel sentiment for annexation. Several senators, for instance, introduced legislation calling for direct admission of Cuba into the Union as a state. In Cuba itself, the next few years saw bitter strife leading to open rebellion. In September, 1906, at the request of Cuba's president, Roosevelt reluctantly exercised the right of intervention under the Platt Amendment, and American troops again patrolled Havana's streets.

The United States sent another governor to the island, one the Cubans grew to hate, comparing his extensive powers to those of "the Czar of Russia added to the Shah of Persia and the Grand Turk."[36] In April, 1909, after bringing forced peace and stability, the United States, again to the surprise of foreigners,

withdrew its troops and ostensibly left Cuba to the Cubans. In its second intervention the United States had shown that it intended to maintain its strategic security
in the Caribbean and would not hesitate to use force in doing so.

The Interoceanic Canal

More important than control of Cuba was command of the possible canal
routes across Central America. Protection of the approaches to a future canal, the
heart of America's Caribbean policy, had in fact prompted insistence on the Platt
Amendment.

During the Spanish-American War, the voyage of the battleship *Oregon* from
Puget Sound around Cape Horn to Cuban waters had captured public imagination
and dramatized the need for a canal that would cut sailing time from one coast to
another by at least a third. The new island possessions in the Pacific and the Caribbean, moreover, made the construction of such a waterway appear more important than ever to national security. McKinley had pointed out that need for a
canal in his annual message of December, 1898, and had added that "our national
policy now more imperatively than ever calls for its control by this Government."[37]

The failure of the French and American companies to build waterways at
Panama and Nicaragua had convinced the United States that the construction of
an interoceanic canal was beyond the resources of private capital. If one were to
be built, the government would have to do it. As McKinley had pointed out,
however, the government wanted to control any canal it would build. The main
obstacle to such control was still the Clayton-Bulwer Treaty of 1850.

Congress appeared ready to disregard the Clayton-Bulwer commitment and
to authorize the building of an exclusively American canal through Nicaragua.
Such action would have damaged increasingly friendly relations with Britain, a
possibility that alarmed Secretary of State John Hay. He urged the British government, therefore, to negotiate a revision of the treaty. Since Britain's Caribbean
interests no longer appeared as vital as they once were, it was willing, but for a
price.

In return for a more liberal treaty, the British wished the United States to make
concessions in a controversy over the boundary between the Alaskan panhandle
and British Columbia. Finally, after holding up canal negotiations for a year, and
after a temporary settlement of the boundary controversy in the fall of 1899, the
British Foreign Secretary suggested taking up the canal treaty on America's terms.
He yielded because he knew the United States was so determined to have its canal
that it would go ahead in defiance of the Clayton-Bulwer Treaty and because the
Boer War had exposed the weakness of Britain's international position. "America
seems to be our only friend just now," the British Ambassador in Washington
reported, " & it would be unfortunate to quarrel with her."[38]

As a result, Hay and Sir Julian Pauncefote, the British Ambassador, signed a treaty on February 5, 1900, amending the Clayton-Bulwer agreement by permitting the American government to construct and control an interoceanic canal. The treaty also called for a neutralized waterway and barred the United States from fortifying it.

When the text of the Hay-Pauncefote Treaty became public, influential newspapers and politicians attacked it. Theodore Roosevelt, at the time governor of New York, expressed a major objection. "I do not see why," he wrote, "we should dig the canal if we are not to fortify it so as to insure its being used for ourselves and against our foes in time of war." [39] The Detroit *News* commented that "another of the administration's 'great diplomatic victories' has been won—by the British government." [40]

In approving the treaty, almost a year later, the Senate wrote the major objections into three amendments which the British refused to accept. Still anxious to strengthen the American friendship and not truly caring if the United States fortified its canal, the British finally negotiated another treaty, which Hay and Pauncefote signed on November 18, 1901. This second Hay-Pauncefote Treaty gave the United States what it desired by expressly superseding the Clayton-Bulwer Treaty and by saying nothing about fortifications. By tacit agreement the British expected the United States to fortify any canal it built. Since the second treaty cleared the way for an exclusively American canal, the Senate, on December 16, overwhelmingly approved it.

Britain surrendered to American demands without exacting equivalent concessions because she could no longer maintain supremacy in the Caribbean in the face of American naval construction and because she sought to retain American friendship. In the next few years, in fact, Britain reduced her garrisons in the West Indies and withdrew her naval squadron from the Caribbean, leaving the United States supreme in that strategic sea. [41]

The United States now had to decide where it would build the canal. That proved a thorny problem. A French corporation, the New Panama Canal Company, had taken over the rights and assets of the bankrupt de Lesseps organization. It hoped to sell those rights and its costly equipment, rotting and rusting in the jungle, to the United States if Colombia would give her consent.

The Nicaraguan government had canceled the concession of the Maritime Canal Company and was eager to negotiate with the American government for canal rights through its land. Thus, the United States had a choice of two routes, each of which ultimately gained powerful supporters in Congress.

Most congressmen had long preferred the Nicaraguan route. Two official commissions, one in 1895 and another in 1899, had investigated that route and reported in its favor. Even before the second commission had made its report, the Senate had passed a bill calling for a canal through Nicaragua. If that bill passed in the House of Representatives, a Panama canal appeared doomed, and the stock-holders of the New Panama Canal Company would get nothing.

To advance its interests, the New Panama Canal Company had employed a prominent New York lawyer and lobbyist, William Nelson Cromwell, as general counsel. Wise in the ways of politics, Cromwell made friends with important politicians, particularly with powerful Mark Hanna who had become a senator from Ohio. Cromwell even contributed $60,000 to the Republican campaign fund of 1900. As a result, the Republican platform called for an isthmian canal, but the Democratic platform favored one through Nicaragua.

In part through Cromwell's influence, it appears, the House defeated the Nicaraguan canal bill. In its stead, the House called for a new investigation of both routes, giving Panama equal status with Nicaragua. President McKinley then appointed a new commission to determine the best route for a canal.

That commission found many advantages in the Panama route. It was shorter than the Nicaraguan route, ships would be able to travel over it in slightly more than one third the time it would take to go through a Nicaraguan canal, and construction and maintenance costs would be less. But the New Panama Canal Company wanted $109,000,000 for its assets whereas the commission said $40,000,000 would be a fair price. In November, 1901, therefore, the commission recommended the Nicaraguan route.

The Hepburn Bill and Spooner Amendment

Acting on the commission's report, on the following January 9 the House passed the Hepburn bill authorizing the President to secure the necessary rights for a Nicaraguan canal and appropriating funds for construction. Fearing complete loss, the New Panama Canal Company quickly lowered the price for its assets to $40,000,000. President Roosevelt, who at first had favored the Nicaraguan route, now preferred Panama. He reconvened the canal commission and ordered it to reconsider its recommendation. It submitted a supplementary report on January 18 favoring the Panama route if Colombia would agree to suitable arrangements.

Ten days later Senator John C. Spooner of Wisconsin, acting for the administration, offered an amendment to the Hepburn bill. The Spooner amendment authorized the President to pay not more than $40,000,000 for the holdings of the New Panama Canal Company and to begin construction of a canal through Panama. If he could not arrive at satisfactory terms with either the French company or Colombia within a "reasonable time," he was to proceed with the Nicaraguan canal.

Supporters of the Panama route had also launched a careful propaganda campaign. Philippe Bunau-Varilla, formerly chief engineer of the de Lesseps company and at the time a speculator and large stockholder in the New Panama Canal

Company, had come to the United States a year earlier to work for the Panama route. A dynamic man, skillful in the use of propaganda, he was fired with the idea that the canal had to go through Panama to vindicate the judgment of his countryman, de Lesseps. Through lectures, pamphlet writing, and newspaper publicity he advanced his idea. Even though he and Cromwell disliked each other, they managed between them to persuade important politicians to support the Panama route.

Still, the advocates of the Panama route might have lost out if they had not been able to take advantage of an act of nature. On May 2, 1902, while Congress was considering the rival routes, volcanic Mont Pelée on the Caribbean island of Martinique erupted, spewing tons of lava and ash, destroying a city, and killing some 30,000 of its people. Twelve days later a report reached the United States that Mt. Momotombo, an old volcano in Nicaragua about one hundred miles from the proposed canal line, had become active and that an accompanying earthquake had wrought destruction in a nearby town.

When Nicaragua's president denied that the old volcano was active, Bunau-Varilla obtained Nicaraguan postage stamps showing Momotombo "belching forth in magnificent eruption," and presented each senator with a stamp and this comment: "An official witness of the volcanic activity on the Isthmus of Nicaragua."[42] The Senate then adopted the Spooner amendment, the House concurred, and the amended Isthmian Canal Act became law on June 28.

The Hay-Herrán Treaty

In attempting to obtain other rights it considered essential for the control of a Panama canal, the United States ran into difficulties. The President of Colombia, José Manuel Marroquín, an eighty-year-old intellectual of limited political experience, had a weak grip on his office. Colombian political conditions were such that if he granted the United States the privileges it sought, some of his enemies would accuse him of surrendering his country's sovereignty to "imperialists." If he did not meet American demands, he might lose the canal to Nicaragua, and some of his enemies would damn him for not bringing it and expected economic benefits to Colombia. Even worse, if he did not yield, it appeared that the United States might take Panama by force.

Finally, Marroquín instructed Dr. Tomás Herrán, his *chargé* in Washington, to make a treaty on the best terms he could get. After Secretary of State Hay delivered an ultimatum threatening to deal with Nicaragua unless Colombia accepted the American terms, Herrán signed a treaty on January 22, 1903. It gave the United States a lease of one hundred years on a strip six miles wide across the isthmus for $10,000,000 gold and an annual rent of $250,000 beginning in nine years. The Senate approved the treaty on March 17, but Colombians in Bogotá objected to the terms. Marroquín, nevertheless, submitted the treaty to the Colombian senate which had the right to accept or reject it. Despite a threat of retaliation by Secretary Hay if Colombia did not ratify, that senate unanimously rejected the Hay-Herrán Treaty on August 12.

Colombians maintained rightly that the treaty infringed on their country's sovereignty, but the real obstacle to ratification was money. Colombians wanted to modify the treaty so that the New Panama Canal Company would pay them $10,000,000 and the United States would increase its payment to $15,000,000. The American government refused to consider any amendments. The Colombian senate, moreover, argued that the New Panama Canal Company's franchise, which ran to 1910, was illegal and would by law expire the following year. After it expired, Colombia could take over the company's assets and herself sell them to the United States, for $40,000,000. Since Panama was a part of the national domain, Colombia had acted within her rights.

Yet Colombia's tactics infuriated Roosevelt, who had decided that he must have the Panama route. "I do not think that the Bogotá lot of jack rabbits," he told Hay, "should be allowed permanently to bar one of the future highways of civilization."[43] He was prepared to recommend to Congress that the United States buy the French rights, occupy the isthmus in defiance of Colombia, and "proceed to dig the canal," but such extreme action was not necessary.

Before Colombia had rejected the Hay-Herrán Treaty, her maneuvering had alarmed Cromwell, Bunau-Varilla, and officials of the New Panama Canal Company. Moreover, the people of Panama, who had expected great benefits from the canal, feared that if it should go to Nicaragua, the isthmus would sink into insignificance. Since they had long been discontented with rule from isolated Bogotá and had often revolted against it, they were prepared to take drastic action to insure the canal for their area. A small group of them, linked closely with officials of the New Panama Canal Company, had even made plans for seceding from Colombia if she rejected the Hay-Herrán Treaty. The conspirators had approached Cromwell in New York, and he had assured them of support.

The plans did not go well until Bunau-Varilla returned to New York from Paris in September, 1903. He met with some of the conspirators in the Waldorf-Astoria Hotel and promised $100,000 to support a revolution. In October he talked with Secretary Hay and President Roosevelt. Even though they made no promises, he assured himself from Roosevelt's sentiments that "as certain as if a solemn contract had been signed between us" the President would take advantage of a revolution to win his canal rights.[44] Bunau-Varilla, therefore, sent word to the schemers in Panama that the United States would not allow their revolution to fail.

Hay had told the President that if a revolt broke out in Panama the United States must act "to keep the transit clear." "Our intervention," he added, "should not be at haphazard, nor, this time, should it be to the profit, as heretofore, of Bogotá."[45] He had in mind a twisted interpretation of Bidlack's Treaty of 1846.

The original purpose of that treaty had been to block some outside power, primarily Britain, from seizing Panama, and not to protect a secessionist movement. During numerous uprisings in Panama prior to 1903 the United States had, at least six different times, landed troops there to protect the free transit, but only with the consent of Colombian authorities. Hay now intended to use the treaty against Colombia herself.

The Panama Revolution and Canal Settlement

Late in October, 1903, the United States ordered several warships to Central-American waters, and on November 2 orders went to their commanders to seize the Panama railroad, keep the free transit, and prevent Colombia from landing troops within fifty miles of the isthmus if a revolution broke out. On the following day, according to plan, the revolution began. It was sparked by a motley army of less than a thousand composed of section hands from the Panama Railroad, a subsidiary of the French canal company, the fire brigade of the city of Panama, and bribed deserters from Colombia's garrison in Panama. The governor of Panama submitted to arrest, a key Colombian naval commander accepted a bribe to sail away, and troops from the u.s.s. *Nashville* prevented loyal Colombian forces from suppressing the uprising. In thus maintaining the free transit, Americans insured the success of the virtually bloodless revolution.

The next day, November 4, Panama declared herself independent. The government at Bogotá then asked the United States to help it recover its estranged province, promising to ratify the Hay-Herrán Treaty as signed. The American government rejected the offer, and on the same day, November 6, Hay instructed the Consul-General in Panama to extend *de facto* recognition to the new Republic of Panama. *De jure* recognition followed a week later when Roosevelt officially received Bunau-Varilla as Panama's first Minister to the United States, a post the Frenchman had forced from Panama as part of the bargain he had made in financing the revolution. On November 18, only fifteen days after the revolution, Hay signed a treaty with Bunau-Varilla on terms similar to those of the Hay-Herran Treaty, only more favorable to the United States.

Under the Hay-Bunau-Varilla Treaty the United States guaranteed Panama's independence and obtained a grant in perpetuity of a canal zone ten miles wide instead of six. That treaty made Panama the second United States protectorate in the Caribbean. Panama accepted the treaty and the Senate, even though the President had acted contrary to the Spooner amendment in dealing with Panama instead of Colombia, approved it on February 23, 1904.

Roosevelt's big stick diplomacy had gained him the right to build the vital canal on bargain terms, but it also incurred the hatred of Colombians, ultimately increased resentment throughout Latin America against Yankee imperialism, and caused a split in opinion at home. Liberals reacted with shame and shock to Roosevelt's action, calling it "disgraceful" and "piracy," but expansionists, particularly Republicans, were pleased and praised his policy. The Detroit *News* spoke candidly. "Let us not be mealy-mouthed about this," it said. "We want Panama."[46]

Sensitive to criticism, the President was quick to defend his policy, saying that "the recognition of the Republic of Panama was an act justified by the interests of collective civilization" and that he had received a mandate from civilization to take Panama. There is a story that in a cabinet meeting, while justifying his policy, he turned to Secretary Elihu Root. "Well," he demanded, "have I answered the

PANAMA AND THE CANAL ZONE, 1903

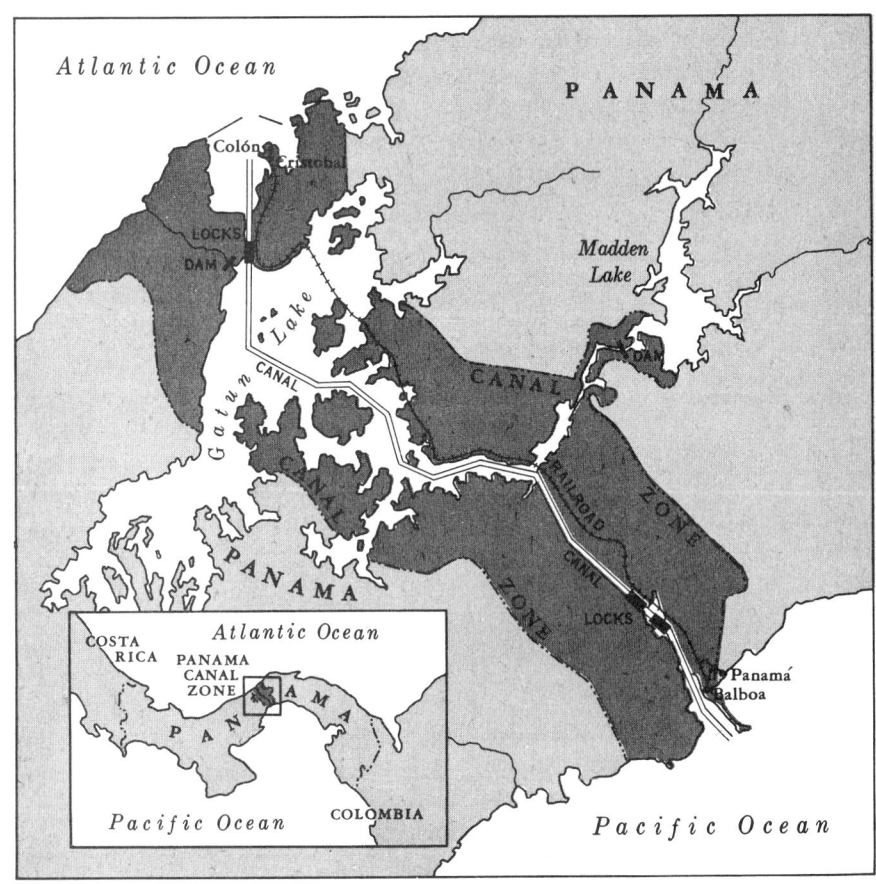

charges? Have I defended myself?" "You certainly have, Mr. President," Root replied. "You have shown that you were accused of seduction and you have conclusively proved that you were guilty of rape."[47]

Later Roosevelt boasted, "I took the Isthmus, started the canal and then left Congress not to debate the canal, but to debate me."[48] The most logical explanations for his ruthless policy appear to be his impatient desire to "make the dirt fly" before the election of 1904, his contempt for Latin Americans, and his view that the end justified the means. If he had been more considerate of the political dilemma of a weak neighbor and less impatient, he probably could have obtained the necessary treaty rights from Colombia without compounding ill will in Latin America.

The United States began construction on the canal in May, 1904, and ten years later opened it to the ships of the world. Roosevelt's Republican successor, William H. Taft, tried to placate Colombia and to obtain her recognition of Panama's independence, but she refused. She asked repeatedly for arbitration of the legality, according to treaty and international law, of American action in the Panama revolution. The American government persistently refused, saying it would not arbitrate a matter of national honor.

Woodrow Wilson's administration tried more effectively to mollify Colombia and hence improve Latin-American relations. In April, 1914, it negotiated a treaty with Colombia expressing regret for the American role in the Panama revolution and offering $25,000,000 in compensation. Roosevelt denounced the treaty as blackmail, and his friends in the Senate, notably Henry Cabot Lodge, blocked it. In 1921, two years after Roosevelt's death, the Senate revived that treaty, but without the expression of regret. Lodge now insisted that compensating Colombia would improve commercial relations. The real reason for the Republican change appeared to be the extensive oil fields discovered in Colombia. Payment of the indemnity, it seemed, would ease the way to oil concessions that resentful Colombians had denied American companies while granting them to foreign rivals.

The Senate approved the treaty on April 21, and the United States paid Colombia $25,000,000, the same amount she had appeared willing to accept in 1903 in exchange for canal concessions. The belated payment at least showed that the United States, despite the materialistic concern in the Senate, was willing to admit doing Colombia an injustice and willing to compensate her for it.[49]

The Virgin Islands

In its Caribbean policy the United States would not allow any political disturbance to threaten control of the approaches to its planned canal, and was especially sensitive to possible European encroachments. Control of the Caribbean required suitable naval bases that it did not have at the end of the Spanish-American War. The base acquired in Puerto Rico appeared inadequate for large naval forces, and the government had not yet made arrangements with Cuba for one at Guantanamo. The United States, therefore, desired additional bases, particularly in the port of St. Thomas in the Danish West Indies.

Prompted by rumors that Germany sought bases in the Caribbean and that she might acquire the Virgin Islands, the United States signed a treaty with Denmark in 1902 for the sale of those islands for $5,000,000. The Senate approved the treaty but the upper house of Denmark's parliament rejected it by one vote. Some Americans believed that German influence had spoiled the sale.

European Intervention in Venezuela

At the same time, while Congress was considering the rival canal routes, a dispute in Venezuela created new tension between Germany and the United States. Venezuela's unscrupulous dictator, Cipriano Castro, had defaulted on some foreign debts. After futile negotiations, Germany and Britain, whose nationals appear to have suffered most abuse, completed plans by November, 1902, to use force to bring Castro to terms.

Both countries were careful not to offend the United States. Germany had informed the American government first of her decision to punish Castro, giving assurances she did not intend to seize Venezuelan territory. Britain advised the United States of her plans in November, and the American government raised no objections.

At first Roosevelt himself saw nothing wrong in the Europeans using force. "If any South American State misbehaves towards any European country," he had written while still Vice-President, "let the European country spank it."[50] The Monroe Doctrine, he said later, did not protect rulers like Castro from deserved punishment. "We do not guarantee any state against punishment if it misconducts itself," he announced in his first annual message to Congress, "provided that punishment does not take the form of the acquisition of territory by any non-American power."[51]

On December 7 Britain and Germany served ultimatums on Venezuela. Within the next few days their naval forces captured four Venezuelan gunboats; the Germans destroyed two because they were unseaworthy. The British landed troops at La Guayra, both countries blockaded Venezuela's main ports, and the British bombarded forts at Puerto Cabello. Italy joined the blockade on December 16.

Since Castro knew he could expect no sympathy from Secretary Hay, he immediately appealed to the American people for help and tried to associate American interests, especially the Monroe Doctrine, with those of Venezuela. Then he

Public opi—
x

appealed for arbitration through the American government. Hay merely forwarded the appeal to Britain and Germany "without comment."

American public opinion, meanwhile, began to turn against Germany. It grated sensibilities, the New York *American* said, "to see an American republic kicked and cuffed by a brace of European monarchies."[52] Hay, therefore, abandoned his passive attitude and urged the European powers to arbitrate. Desiring to remain on good terms with the United States, both Germany and Britain had already decided to arbitrate, but with reservations as to certain of the claims against Castro.

Roosevelt asserted later that he had compelled a reluctant Germany to arbitrate by delivering an informal ultimatum to her Ambassador in Washington threatening to send Admiral Dewey and the fleet to Venezuela. There is doubt as to whether or not he did. In any case, it is clear that Americans suspected German motives. Roosevelt may well have exerted pressure, for Dewey, in command of fleet maneuvers in the Caribbean in December, 1902, did prepare to defend American interests there. A few months later Dewey himself told newspaper reporters that he saw in the maneuvers "an object lesson to the Kaiser, more than to any other person."[53]

Once the European powers had agreed to the principle of arbitration, a peaceful solution to the intervention appeared certain. Hay, to the President's delight, persuaded the powers to submit their grievances to the International Court of Arbitration at The Hague. "It seems to me," Roosevelt wrote to former President Cleveland, "that you have special cause for satisfaction in what we have succeeded in accomplishing this time in connection with getting England and Germany explicitly to recognize the Monroe Doctrine in reference to their controversy with Venezuela and in getting all of the parties in interest to accept arbitration by the Hague Court."[54]

Nonetheless, the principle behind the intervention alarmed some of the Latin-American countries, who considered it a dangerous precedent. Argentina's Minister for Foreign Affairs, Luis M. Drago, sent a note to the United States suggesting as something of a corollary to the Monroe Doctrine that the use of armed forces by a European nation to collect public debts from an American nation was wrong.[55] Although the American government did not at the time accept the Drago Doctrine, later when the Second Hague Conference in 1907 embodied it in modified form in a convention, the United States supported it.

Meanwhile in January, 1903, before the Venezuela arbitration began, the guns of Fort San Carlos at Maracaibo fired on one of the blockading German ships. A few days later several German ships bombarded and destroyed the fort. "Are people in Berlin crazy?" an angry Roosevelt asked. "Don't they know that they are inflaming public opinion more and more here?"[56] He was right. Anti-German sentiment swept the country.

Reluctant to arouse more American resentment, the Germans reduced their cash demands and hastened the arbitration negotiations. The powers lifted their blockade on February 14.

Several features stood out in the Venezuela intervention. Most Americans, showing a widespread distrust of Germany, apparently considered that country the villain of the entire affair. Secondly, the episode gave the Monroe Doctrine new dignity at home and in Europe.

England's Prime Minister, in an effort to dispel the American resentment created by the intervention, paid public homage to the Monroe Doctrine. "We welcome any increase of the great influence of the United States of America upon the great Western Hemisphere," he said. Then he added, "I believe it would be a great gain to civilization if the United States of America were more actively to interest themselves in making arrangements by which these constantly recurring difficulties between European Powers and certain States in South America could be avoided." [57] This advice was not lost on Roosevelt, for out of the Venezuela experience grew his determination to formulate a corollary to the Monroe Doctrine that he subsequently applied to the Dominican Republic.

The Roosevelt Corollary

The Dominican Republic, like Venezuela, had borrowed heavily from foreigners. Torn by frequent civil strife, it was unable to pay its public debt of some $32,000,000. Europeans claimed about $22,000,000. The Dominican government recognized the claims of foreigners in agreements that pledged the income from some of its customs houses to the payment of those debts, but civil wars continued. Late in 1903 American, French, and Italian forces stepped in briefly to protect the interests of their nationals. A few months later it was clear that the Dominican Republic was bankrupt and that European powers might intervene as they had in Venezuela to force some kind of debt settlement. [58]

Roosevelt no longer held to the view that Latin-American misbehavior justified European intervention. The award of the tribunal in the Venezuela debt case had shown that those who used force could expect preferred payment of their claims, for, as one State Department official said, it "put a premium on violence." [59] The United States, therefore, sought an alternative to European naval demonstrations in the Caribbean.

The President then decided to intervene himself to prevent European use of force and possible control of territory in the Caribbean, an idea implicit in the Platt Amendment and various British suggestions. He expressed his idea publicly in May, 1904. Any nation which paid its debts and kept itself in order, he wrote, need not fear interference from the United States, but brutal wrongdoing would require intervention "by some civilized nation, and in the Western Hemisphere the United States cannot ignore this duty."

TEDDY'S BIG STICK

This cartoon was published in 1905 under the title "The World's Constable."
Note the enlarging of the principle of the Roosevelt Corollary, "The New
Diplomacy," to the Monroe Doctrine.

Republicans and nationalists approved Roosevelt's theory as a necessary extension of the Monroe Doctrine, but Democrats and anti-imperialists denounced it as "a flagrant exhibition of jingoism," and as a policy of trying to boss the world. Roosevelt insisted that he spoke only the simplest common sense. "If we are willing to let Germany or England act as the policemen of the Caribbean, then we can afford not to interfere when gross wrongdoing occurs," he told Root. "But if we intend to say 'Hands off' to the powers of Europe, sooner or later we must keep order ourselves."[60] That was the essence of what came to be known as the Roosevelt Corollary to the Monroe Doctrine.

Under pressure from the United States, meanwhile, the Dominican government had made arrangements to pay its debt to an American concern, the Santo Domingo Improvement Company, in monthly installments guaranteed by customs collected at certain ports. When the Dominicans failed to meet the first payment, one of the Improvement Company's agents took over collection of customs at Puerto Plata in October. European nations protested and appeared ready to use force to collect the debts of their own nationals. In his annual message in December Roosevelt then reaffirmed his Corollary, adding that "in the Western Hemisphere the adherence of the United States to the Monroe Doctrine may force the United States, however reluctantly, in flagrant cases of such wrongdoing or impotence, to the exercise of an international police power." [61]

A few weeks later Hay pointed out the danger of European intervention to the Dominican government and asked if it wished the United States to take charge of the collection of duties. The Dominicans agreed and in January, 1905, the two countries signed an agreement giving the United States control of the customs. The United States said it would give forty-five per cent of the revenues to the Dominican government and allot the balance to the foreign creditors. It also guaranteed that republic's territorial integrity. Fearing that the executive agreement would invade the Senate's treaty prerogative, Congress protested. Roosevelt's Minister in the republic, therefore, embodied most of the terms of the arrangement in a protocol, but omitted the territorial guarantee.

The President submitted the protocol, with a special message urging approval, to the Senate in February, pointing out that "those who profit by the Monroe Doctrine must accept certain responsibilities along with the rights which it confers; and that the same statement applies to those who uphold the doctrine." Democrats objected to the prôtocol and blocked consideration, so the Senate closed its session in March without approving it. Roosevelt was furious. The Senate's power over treaties should be like the President's veto, he said, "it should be rarely used." [62]

Undaunted, Roosevelt reverted to his original plan of an executive agreement, and in April completed a *modus vivendi* with the Dominicans placing their country in American hands. For more than two years Americans collected Dominican customs, made payments on the republic's debts, and gave it an unaccustomed financial stability. The protecting guns of American warships discouraged revolutions, so that the Dominicans also enjoyed an unusual political stability.

Democrats and others opposed making the Dominican Republic another Caribbean protectorate and denounced Roosevelt's arrangement as unconstitutional. Republicans, and apparently most Americans who thought about it, approved the Roosevelt Corollary. The Senate, therefore, after bitter debate, finally consented to the essential terms of the executive agreement in another treaty of February, 1907, and the Dominican receivership continued. Most foreign creditors were willing to see it continue since it paid them a reasonable return on their debts. [63]

Elihu Root and Latin America

Even though Latin Americans showed no widespread opposition to the Roosevelt Corollary, they resented Roosevelt's highhanded actions, his contemptuous statements about them, and his assumption of superiority. [64] Elihu Root, who had succeeded Hay as Secretary of State in July, 1905, wanted to counteract the adverse effect of Roosevelt's policies upon Latin America. He suggested a good will trip, and the President, who had become concerned about the resentment, because it appeared to affect the expansion of investment and trade in Latin America, endorsed the idea. Root, therefore, attended the Third Inter-American Conference which opened at Rio de Janeiro late in July, 1906, and on the way visited seven Latin-American countries.

In his address to the conference, Root assured Latin Americans that the United States had no aggressive designs against them and sought only their cooperation. "We wish for no victories but those of peace," he said; "for no territory except our own; for no sovereignty except over ourselves." [65] Even though the Secretary's words in Rio de Janeiro and elsewhere in Latin America were reassuring, neither he, nor any other American statesman, could soften the distrust of the United States. The crowds which cheered him and the champagne toasts in his honor were demonstrations of hospitality and esteem for him, not signs of good will toward the United States.

Latin Americans could not forget Panama, the Platt Amendment, and the Roosevelt Corollary. Many of them were economically and otherwise dependent on the United States, and they lived under the shadow of the big stick. What universal power, some asked themselves, gave the United States "the mission to put in order those who live in disorder?" A few expressed a view that "lesser" peoples of later years were to voice again and again. "If we live in disorder," they said, "we live in our own house, and nobody has the right to meddle in it."

United States policy in the Caribbean clearly worked for the advancement of its own interests there, and in the long run for the protection of the Latin Americans. Few could deny, however, that it was an arrogant policy, insensitive to the rights of the Latin Americans. The United States in the beginning of the twentieth century was young as a great power and overused its strength.

NOTES

1. Nov. 6, 1894, quoted in Alfred L. P. Dennis, *Adventures in American Diplomacy, 1896–1906* (New York, 1928), p. 175.

2. To Rockhill, July 25, 1899, quoted in Alfred Whitney Griswold, *The Far Eastern Policy of the United States* (New York, 1938), p. 65.

3. To Hippisley, Aug. 3, 1899, *ibid.*, p. 67.

4. To Rockhill, Aug. 21, 1899, *ibid.*, p. 71.

5. In "Brooks Adams and American Expansion," *New England Quarterly*, XXV (June 1952), 217–232, William A. Williams stresses the influence of Adams' ideas on Hay and the Open Door policy.

6. The notes and the replies are in *Foreign Relations, 1899*, pp. 128–143.

7. July 3, 1900, *ibid., 1900*, p. 299.

8. *The Education of Henry Adams* (Boston, 1918), p. 392.

9. Robert Morss Lovett, ed., *Selected Poems of William Vaughn Moody* (Boston, 1931), p. 28.

10. See Seward W. Livermore, "American Naval-Base Policy in the Far East, 1850–1914," *Pacific Historical Review*, XIII (June 1944), 123–124.

11. To Hippisley, July 6, 1901, quoted in Griswold, *Far Eastern Policy*, p. 83.

12. Feb. 1, 1901, quoted in Dennis, *Adventures in American Diplomacy*, p. 242.

13. Quoted in Foster Rhea Dulles, *The Imperial Years* (New York, 1956), pp. 270–271.

14. To Cecil Spring-Rice, July 24, 1905, quoted in Tyler Dennett, *Roosevelt and the Russo-Japanese War* (Garden City, N.Y., 1925), p. 2.

15. See, for instance, letters to Meyer, Feb. 6, and Kennan, May 6, 1905, in Elting E. Morison, *The Letters of Theodore Roosevelt* (8 vols., Cambridge, Mass., 1951–54), IV, 1115, 1169.

16. Quoted in Dennett, *Roosevelt and the Russo-Japanese War*, p. 180.

17. Komura to Roosevelt, March 31, 1905, quoted in Howard K. Beale, *Theodore Roosevelt and the Rise of America to World Power* (Baltimore, 1956), p. 285.

18. Roosevelt already knew of the Russian terms for peace before receiving Japan's request for good offices. See Ernest R. May, "The Far Eastern Policy of the United States in the Period of the Russo-Japanese War: A Russian View," *The American Historical Review*, LXII (Jan. 1957), 349.

19. For details, see Robert K. Godwin, "Russia and the Portsmouth Peace Conference," *American Slavic and East European Review*, IX (Dec. 1950), 279–291.

20. Quoted in Dulles, *Imperial Years*, p. 276.

21. Winston B. Thorson, in "American Public Opinion and the Portsmouth Peace Conference," *The American Historical Review*, LIII (April 1948), 439–464, points out that the conference produced no "overnight" change in opinion toward Japan. Eleanor Tupper and George E. McReynolds, *Japan in American Public Opinion* (New York, 1936), p. 17, makes the same point. See also Thorson, "Pacific Northwest Opinion on the Russo-Japanese War of 1904–1905," *Pacific Northwest Quarterly*, XXXV (Oct. 1944), 305–322, and for the reaction in California, Raymond L. Buell, "The Development of Anti-Japanese Agitation in the United States," *Political Science Quarterly*, XXXVII (Dec. 1922), 614–615.

22. Jan. 28, 1903, Morison, *Roosevelt Letters*, IV, 1112.

23. July 31, 1905, *ibid.*, IV, 1293. For details on this episode, see Raymond A. Esthus, "The Taft-Katsura Agreement—Reality or Myth?" *Journal of Modern History*, XXXI (March 1959), 46–51, which points out that there was no agreement, secret pact, or *quid pro quo* in the nature of a guarantee for the Philippines, and Ralph E. Minger, "Taft's Missions to Japan: A Study in Personal Diplomacy," *Pacific Historical Review*, XXX (Aug. 1961), 279–294.

24. Fred H. Harrington, *God, Mammon, and the Japanese: Dr. Horace N. Allen and Korean-American Relations, 1884–1905* (Madison, Wis., 1944), pp. 332–333.

25. To Kermit Roosevelt, Oct. 27, 1906, in Morison, *Roosevelt Letters*, V, 475.

26. To Elihu Root, July 23, 1907, *ibid.*, V, 725. Raymond A. Esthus, in "The Changing Concept of the Open Door, 1899–1910," *Mississippi Valley Historical Review*, XLVI (Dec. 1959), 439, points out that Roosevelt and Root believed that the threat of war was the product of sensational journalism.

27. Quoted in Dulles, *Imperial Years*, p. 284.

28. *Foreign Relations, 1908*, p. 511.

29. This point is in Esthus, "Changing Concept of the Open Door," *Mississippi Valley Historical Review*, XLVI (Dec. 1959), 448–450, who stresses that there was no bargain giving Japan a free hand in Manchuria. This view is similar to Thomas A. Bailey's in "The Root-Takahira Agreement of 1908," *Pacific Historical Review*, IX (March 1940), 19–35. The "free hand" interpretation is in Griswold, *Far Eastern Policy*, p. 129.

30. To William H. Taft, Dec. 22, 1910, quoted in Griswold, *Far Eastern Policy*, p. 132.

31. Annual message, Dec. 5, 1899, *Foreign Relations, 1899*, p. xxix.

32. Quoted in Carleton Beals, *The Crime of Cuba* (Philadelphia, 1933), p. 173.

33. Quoted in Russell H. Fitzgibbon, *Cuba and the United States, 1900–1935* (Menasha, Wis., 1935), p. 31n.

34. To Leonard Wood, April 3, 1901, quoted in Dennis, *Adventures in American Diplomacy*, p. 265.

35. The Paris *Temps* and *Kreuz-Zeitung* are quoted in Dulles, *Imperial Years*, p. 190.

36. The governor was Charles E. Magoon. The quotation is from Fitzgibbon, *Cuba and the United States*, p. 142n. See also Ralph E. Minger, "William H. Taft and the United States Intervention in Cuba in 1906," *Hispanic American Historical Review*, XLI (Feb. 1961), 75–89.

37. *Foreign Relations, 1898*, p. lxxii.

38. Pauncefote to Salisbury, Jan. 19, 1900, quoted in Charles S. Campbell, Jr., *Anglo-American Understanding, 1898–1903* (Baltimore, 1957), p. 190.

39. To Alfred T. Mahan, Feb. 4, 1900, in Morison, *Roosevelt Letters*, II, 1185.

40. Quoted in Dwight C. Miner, *The Fight for the Panama Route: The Story of the Spooner Act and the Hay-Herrán Treaty* (New York, 1940), p. 97.

41. J. A. S. Grenville, in "Great Britain and the Isthmian Canal, 1898–1901," *The American Historical Review*, LXI (Oct. 1955), 48–69, stresses that the British made this crucial decision because their naval power could no longer hold the Caribbean while meeting the demands in the other vital areas of the empire.

42. Quoted in Miles P. Du Val, Jr., *Cadiz to Cathay: The Story of the Long Diplomatic Struggle for the Panama Canal*, 2nd ed. (Stanford, Calif., 1947), p. 165.

43. Aug. 19, 1903, quoted in Miner, *Panama Route*, p. 345.

44. Philippe Bunau-Varilla, *Panama: The Creation, Destruction, and Resurrection* (London, 1913), p. 312.

45. Sept. 13, 1903, quoted in Miner, *Panama Route*, p. 351.

46. Quoted in Dulles, *Imperial Years*, p. 251. John Patterson, in "Latin American Reactions to the Panama Revolution of 1903," *Hispanic American Historical Review*, XXIV (May 1944), 342–351, suggests that indignation against the United States in Latin America was neither immediate nor widespread.

47. Quoted in Philip C. Jessup, *Elihu Root* (2 vols., New York, 1938), I, 404–405.

48. Speech of March 24, 1911, quoted in Du Val, *Cadiz to Cathay*, p. 438.

49. For details, see Watt Stewart, "The Ratification of the Thomson-Urrutia Treaty," *Southwestern Political and Social Science Quarterly*, X (March 1930), 416–431.

50. To Speck von Sternberg, July 12, 1901, in Morison, *Roosevelt Letters*, III, 116.

51. Dec. 3, 1901, in *Foreign Relations, 1901*, pp. xxxvi–xxxvii.

52. Quoted in Dulles, *Imperial Years*, p. 255.

53. Dewey is quoted in Beale, *Roosevelt and the Rise to World Power*, p. 418. The fullest treatment of the historiography of the Venezuela question and Roosevelt's

diplomacy toward Germany is in pp. 395–431. See also Seward W. Livermore, "Theodore Roosevelt, the American Navy, and the Venezuela Crisis of 1902–1903," *The American Historical Review*, LI (April 1946), 452–471.

54. Dec. 26, 1902, in Morison, *Roosevelt Letters*, III, 398.

55. Dec. 29, 1902, *Foreign Relations, 1903*, pp. 1–5; also Dennis, *Adventures in American Diplomacy*, pp. 292–293.

56. Quoted by Albert W. von Quadt, Jan. 25, 1903, in Alfred Vagts, *Deutschland und die Vereinigten Staaten in der Weltpolitik* (2 vols., New York, 1935), II, 1595.

57. Lord Balfour, Feb. 14, 1903, quoted in Campbell, *Anglo-American Understanding*, p. 299. See also, J. Fred Rippy, "Antecedents of the Roosevelt Corollary of the Monroe Doctrine," *Pacific Historical Review*, IX (Sept. 1940), 267–279.

58. J. Fred Rippy, "The Initiation of the Customs Receivership in the Dominican Republic," *Hispanic American Historical Review*, XVII (Nov. 1937), 419–457.

59. Quoted in Dexter Perkins, *A History of the Monroe Doctrine*, 2nd ed. (Boston, 1955), p. 238.

60. The quotations are from letters to Elihu Root, May 20 and June 7, 1904, in Henry F. Pringle, *Theodore Roosevelt: A Biography* (New York, 1931), pp. 294–295.

61. Dec. 6, 1904, *Foreign Relations, 1904*, p. xli.

62. For the message, Feb. 15, 1905, see *ibid., 1905*, p. 334 and Roosevelt's comment is in Pringle, *Roosevelt*, p. 296.

63. There was some dissatisfaction among British bondholders, however. See J. Fred Rippy, "The British Bondholders and the Roosevelt Corollary of the Monroe Doctrine," *Political Science Quarterly*, XLIX (June 1934), 195–206.

64. *La Prensa* of Rio de Janeiro, for example, called the Roosevelt Corollary "the most serious and menacing declaration against South American integrity which has come out of Washington." Dec. 8, 1904, quoted in Thomas F. McGann, *Argentina, the United States, and the Inter-American System, 1880–1914* (Cambridge, Mass., 1957), p. 223.

65. Quoted in James B. Scott, "Elihu Root," in Samuel F. Bemis, ed., *The American Secretaries of State and Their Diplomacy* (10 vols., New York, 1927–29), V, 217.

Chapter Sixteen

BRITAIN'S RAPPROCHEMENT AND DOLLAR DIPLOMACY

W$_{\text{ITH}}$ the Open Door policy the United States had become involved in the international rivalries of Europe in Asia. Acting in support of similar principles—the Open Door, the balance of power, and peace—Theodore Roosevelt also intervened in the international politics of North Africa.

International Rivalries in Morocco

The United States had no direct interest in North Africa, particularly in Morocco, a center of European rivalry. American trade there was small and strategic interest negligible. Yet in 1880 the United States had participated in a conference in Madrid dealing with the abuse of extraterritoriality that threatened to extinguish Morocco's independence. At that time Britain and Spain wished to uphold Morocco's integrity whereas France did not. Since Germany was not yet interested in colonies and anxious to divert French attention from the provinces of Alsace and Lorraine, lost in the Franco-Prussian War, she supported France at the conference. The treaty that grew out of the conference, therefore, merely defined extraterritorial protection without providing means to correct the abuses, and thus allowed France to tighten her grip on Morocco. Although the United States had no part in the rivalry, it signed the Madrid treaty because it required no binding political commitment.

In the quarter of a century that followed, France and Britain dissolved their colonial rivalry. By agreements reached in 1904 Britain accepted the French plans to take over Morocco, and France acquiesced in British control of Egypt. This marked the beginning of an *entente cordiale* designed to withstand the rising might of Germany. In the years since 1880, German foreign policy had changed. Germany, too, had become a competitor for African colonies and had built up a considerable trade in Morocco.

Concerned over French efforts to take complete control of Morocco and over the *entente*, Germany decided early in 1905 to oppose the extension of France's power. She insisted on an international conference to decide the fate of Morocco. Since the United States had treaty rights there, the German Chancellor, Bernhard von Bülow, sought Roosevelt's support for the Open Door in Morocco and a conference. Roosevelt gave a noncommital answer, but von Bülow interpreted it as meaning that the President had "drawn a parallel between maintaining the Open Door in China and in Morocco."[1]

Taking advantage of the fact that Russia, France's ally, was absorbed in war with Japan, von Bülow decided to test the *entente* and persuaded the reluctant Kaiser, William II, to visit the Sultan at Tangier. The Kaiser arrived in March and delivered a belligerent speech which in effect told France that Germany intended to take part in any Moroccan settlement. This speech infuriated the French Foreign Minister, Théophile Delcassé, who was willing to risk war by taking over Morocco anyway, and England supported him. Delcassé's policy created apprehension in Paris. Since his country was poorly prepared, the French Premier, Pierre-Maurice Rouvier, was unwilling to gamble on war without Russian aid. The cabinet, therefore, voted unanimously against Delcassé, forcing him to resign in June. To avert war, Rouvier conciliated Germany, but still hoped to avoid a conference. Germany's show of strength, however, had humiliated France and won a limited diplomatic victory.

In an effort to seal her triumph, Germany then urged Roosevelt to intervene and to do so by persuading France and England to agree to a conference. Roosevelt promised his help and asked the Germans to be moderate in their demands. "I know your government will consider that I am meddling in its affairs," he told the French Ambassador in Washington, "but since the Moroccan question threatens war between Germany and France that would destroy world peace, I feel justified." He asked the French to accept a conference. In a war with Germany, he said, France could only lose. "It would cause me anguish," he confessed, "if any misfortune overtook France."[2] He convinced the French that he wanted to prevent war and not to serve the interests of Germany.

The Kaiser, meanwhile, promised Roosevelt that in any differences of opinion at the conference between Germany and France, he would support any decision the President considered fair. When Roosevelt told the French of the Kaiser's promise they agreed to the conference which met in January, 1906, in Algeciras, a small seaport in southern Spain.

At home, critics attacked the President for joining the Moroccan negotiations. One senator introduced a resolution saying the intervention violated the "settled policy" of not taking part in political controversies between European nations. Even Secretary of State Elihu Root believed that American interests in Morocco were insufficient to warrant participation. Nevertheless, Roosevelt went ahead.

At the conference France insisted on a control that would make Morocco a virtual protectorate. Germany wanted several powers, including herself, placed in control and ultimately a partition with a share for herself. Although officially neutral, Roosevelt sympathized with the French and told them so. Germany therefore found herself practically alone in her demands for a place in the control of Morocco. Only Austria-Hungary supported her. It became clear that Germany had blundered in insisting upon a conference. Instead of driving a wedge between France and England, she had strengthened the *entente*. Even the United States seemed to believe that Germany was trying to drive France to war.

When Germany refused to come to terms, Roosevelt offered a compromise that preserved the principle of international control but gave the substance of power in Morocco to France. He persuaded Germany to accept the compromise by recalling the Kaiser's promise to support any fair decision he proposed. Although on the surface both countries seemed satisfied with the General Act of Algeciras, signed in April, 1906, it proved ultimately to be a diplomatic defeat for Germany.

Roosevelt was pleased with his role in the negotiations and was convinced that the conference had prevented a war that had seemed imminent. His friend Henry Cabot Lodge was also happy about the results. "We are the strongest moral force —also physical—now extant," he wrote, "and the peace of the world rests largely with us. So far you have saved the situation." [3]

In adhering to the Act of Algeciras, Secretary of State Root insisted that the United States had no political interest in Morocco and assumed no obligation to enforce the settlement. Yet when the treaty reached the Senate later in the year, critics again attacked Roosevelt and demanded more reservations. When the Senate finally consented to the treaty in December, it reiterated in a formal reservation that adherence did not mean a departure from the traditional non-entanglement policy.

How significant Roosevelt's role was in keeping the peace is not clear. One point, however, is evident: on the theory that a threat to world peace justified American intervention, he had openly broken the tradition of avoiding problems of European politics, something none of his predecessors had dared do. He realized, as did some of his contemporaries, that the United States, now a recognized great power, could not entirely avoid the tensions of Europe. His intervention in Morocco foreshadowed a significant shift in American foreign policy toward closer ties with the Anglo-French *entente*.

Yet, Roosevelt's venture into Europe's diplomacy for awhile seemed nothing more than a temporary aberration. When Germany and France again appeared on the verge of war in another Moroccan crisis in 1911, President William H. Taft remained aloof.[4]

The Hague Peace Conferences

In the first decade of the twentieth century many Americans believed that the United States had an obligation to help maintain world peace. The government, therefore, evinced an interest in peace projects, disarmament, international organization, and arbitration. Yet, when the Tsar of Russia, Nicholas II, called an international conference of twenty-six nations to meet at The Hague in 1899 to discuss disarmament and the prevention of war, the American government did not at first show much interest. It finally yielded to the pressures of a peace movement, emphasizing disarmament and arbitration, that had already gathered considerable strength among the reformers of the period, and sent a delegation to The Hague Peace Conference.

Sitting from the middle of May through July, the conference failed to achieve its major objective of disarmament. The advocates of peace, moreover, were disappointed with the attitude of the American delegation, which regarded the reduction of armaments as purely a European problem.

The conference did adopt conventions and declarations designed to "humanize" war. Its most noteworthy achievement was a Permanent Court of Arbitration, a panel of slightly over a hundred individuals upon whom nations could call to act as arbitrators. The countries who signed the convention did not pledge themselves to use the court, and none were willing to accept arbitration as a means of settling those disputes that usually led to war. Another point worthy of note was the fact that the American delegates consistently supported Great Britain.

The United States was particularly reluctant to surrender any of its control over vital national issues to the court. When the Senate approved the various agreements signed at the conference, such as those dealing with the outlawing of inhumane weapons, it insisted again that those commitments could not require the United States to depart from its nonentanglement policy. The Senate attempted to do what was virtually impossible—to draw a line between political and non-political international obligations.

After the First Hague Conference a widespread discussion of international organization gave new hope to the leaders of the peace movement. Some talked of holding periodic peace conferences and others suggested improvements in the Permanent Court of Arbitration. In September, 1904, President Roosevelt promised members of a private peace society that he would ask the nations of the world to participate in a second conference at The Hague. The United States appeared ready to take the lead in the movement for world peace, but the Russians wanted to sponsor the conference, so Roosevelt stepped aside. The Tsar called the Second Hague Conference which met in 1907. This time, at the insistence of the United States, the conference included representatives from the Latin-American nations, making a total of forty-four participating states.

The second conference, too, failed to achieve either a reduction or limitation of armaments. Secretary of State Root wanted to replace the old ineffective Permanent Court with a true court that would sit in regular session with a small staff of genuine jurists, but the conference would not accept the American proposal.

The disappointing conference did adopt a number of minor conventions dealing with such matters as restrictions on the right of capture at sea. The cynical but perceptive Mr. Dooley, remarked that the conference also discussed "th' larger question iv how future wars shud be conducted in th' best inthrests iv peace."[5]

Arbitration Treaties

In setting up the Permanent Court of Arbitration the First Hague Conference had reflected a broad international interest in the settlement of disputes through arbitration. A few years after the conference, in 1904 in fact, Secretary of State John Hay negotiated ten bilateral arbitration treaties that obligated the United States in advance to arbitrate through The Hague Court certain kinds of disputes not settled by diplomacy. Even though the treaties were broad, excluding issues that touched "vital interests" and "national honor" and hence would not deal with disputes that actually brought on wars, the Senate would not approve them without drastic change.

Jealously guarding its prerogative in foreign relations, the Senate insisted that it had to approve every special agreement defining the questions at issue in each arbitration. In other words, it regarded each arbitration agreement as a treaty and would not surrender the power of defining the arbitration to the President, as called for in the original Hay treaties. Since Hay believed that the Senate amendments made the treaties meaningless and the President agreed with him, Roosevelt withdrew the treaties from the Senate. Since we already have the power to make special arbitration treaties, Roosevelt said, to pass "these amended treaties does not in the smallest degree facilitate settlements by arbitration, to make them would in no way further the cause of international peace."[6]

Hay's successor, Elihu Root, took a different view of the Senate's position. He believed that weak arbitration treaties were better than none and converted Roosevelt to his thinking. In the year following the Second Hague Conference Root negotiated twenty-four bilateral treaties with all of the leading nations of the world except Germany. All were similar to Hay's treaties except that the special agreement defining the scope of each arbitration needed the approval by the usual two-thirds vote of the Senate. Most of the pacts had a limit of five years, and most were renewed at the end of the five years.

Perhaps, as some critics pointed out, the Root treaties were so narrow in scope that they contributed little to settling significant international disputes. Yet, the Senate would not go beyond the Root formula.

William H. Taft believed in and supported the peace movement. In the interests of peace he wanted to go beyond the Root treaties. "I do not see," he said, "why questions of honor may not be submitted to a tribunal supposed to be composed of men of honor who understand questions of national honor."[7] He instructed Secretary of State Philander C. Knox, therefore, to negotiate general arbitration treaties with Britain and France that included even questions of "national honor" as subjects for arbitration. Those two treaties, signed in August, 1911, and designed to serve as models, said all "justiciable" questions—meaning in Taft's view infringements of legal rights under the principles of international law—not settled by diplomacy should go to The Hague Court or some other suitable tribunal. In any dispute a joint high commission would decide whether or not a question at issue was "justiciable" and whether it could be submitted for arbitration.

The advocates of peace organized a nation-wide campaign to win the Senate's approval, and Taft himself appealed directly to the people and thus made the approval of the pacts almost a personal issue. The Senate, as jealous as ever of any infringement of its treaty power, drastically amended the treaties, reserving to itself the right to determine whether or not an issue was "justiciable." Since Taft would not ask Britain and France to accept the emasculated amendments that excluded virtually every issue of importance from arbitration, he did not ratify the treaties. He recalled a few years later that the Senate "had truncated them and amended them in such a way that their own father could not recognize them."[8]

The "Cooling Off" Treaties

Despite the crushing effect of the defeat of the Taft treaties, the friends of peace gained renewed hope when Woodrow Wilson became President—hope that international disputes might be settled without resort to war. Both Wilson and his Secretary of State, William Jennings Bryan, approached the problem with an evangelical zeal. Although the idea was not original with him, Bryan had long advocated the use of joint commissions to determine disputed facts in international controversies. When he accepted the Secretaryship, in fact, one of the conditions he insisted upon was that the President must give him a free hand to negotiate treaties for the maintenance of peace.

Soon after taking office, Bryan began negotiating a series of conciliation pacts entitled "Treaties for the Advancement of Peace," but popularly called "cooling off" treaties. They supplemented the Root treaties by committing signatory nations to submit all disputes not capable of settlement through diplomacy, even those touching questions of "national honor," to permanent international commissions for investigation. During the period of investigation, usually one year, neither party would begin hostilities. The disputants could either accept or reject the commission's recommendation. The basic idea behind the pacts was that of delay in time of acute tension.

Bryan's first "cooling off" treaty, with El Salvador, was signed in August, 1913. By October of the following year he had concluded twenty-nine others, among them treaties with Britain, France, and Italy. Germany refused to negotiate a treaty. Since the recommendations of the investigating commissions were not binding and the pacts committed the United States to little more than a period of delay, the Senate approved most of them. Critics and cynics condemned the treaties as unrealistic but Bryan considered them the outstanding achievements of his long career.[9]

The Anglo-American Rapprochement

During the era of the peace movement the new Anglo-American *rapprochement* grew stronger. There were, nonetheless, a number of lesser conflicts that Britain and the United States had to resolve before they could cement their new friendship. One of these arose out of the Boer War.

When war broke out in October, 1899, between Britain and the Boer republics of South Africa, the British found themselves almost universally disliked. The peoples and governments of Europe appeared solidly pro-Boer. The attitude of the United States, therefore, was especially important to Britain, and as expressed in the Republican Congress and in government policy, was friendly. On the eve of the war, for instance, Secretary Hay said that as long as he headed the Department of State it would take no action "contrary to my conviction that the one indispensable feature of our foreign policy should be a friendly understanding with England."[10]

Most Americans, but particularly those of Dutch, German, and Irish blood, in contrast to government policy, sympathized with the Boers. "There is no disguising the fact," Henry Cabot Lodge wrote, "that sympathy here is overwhelmingly with the Boers."[11] Since Britain was the dominant sea power and the United States a leading neutral, incidents over British seizures of American ships aroused strong feelings. So strong was sentiment against Britain that in the election of 1900 the Democrats tried to make an issue of government sympathy for Britain. Their platform condemned "the ill-concealed Republican alliance with England" extended "sympathy to the heroic burghers in their unequal struggle to maintain their liberty and independence."[12]

When Roosevelt became President the Boers hoped that this young man with a Dutch name might show more understanding of their cause than had McKinley and Hay, but they were disappointed. "The downfall of the British Empire," he had written before becoming President when the English were faring badly in the war, "I should regard as a calamity to the race, and especially to this country."[13] Roosevelt, too, turned his back on the Boers and favored a British victory.

One reason for America's friendly policy toward Britain, despite the sentiment of the people, was Britain's own friendliness during the Spanish-American War. "England stood by us," *The New York Times* reminded the people. "Let us stand by her. We had the great help of her moral support. Let us give her our sympathy and good wishes."[14] At the time, moreover, imperialism was fashionable, and the American government could not justifiably condemn the British when it had rebels of its own to crush in the Philippines. The fact that official American friendship for Britain stood firm under pressure strengthened the Anglo-American *rapprochement*.

Some Englishmen had feared that the United States might take advantage of their trouble in Africa by forcing a settlement of disputes over the Clayton-Bulwer Treaty and the Alaskan boundary, and were gratified when no such move was made. Yet, even though Britain defeated the Boers, her distresses ultimately forced her to resume the stalemated negotiations over the Clayton-Bulwer Treaty and to express a willingness to compromise on the issue of the Alaskan boundary. Thus in the American disputes with Canada she was more willing to make concessions than was Canada.

The Alaskan Frontier

The most serious controversy with Canada, and hence with Britain, since the British government was responsible for the Dominion's external affairs, grew out of differing interpretations of the vague boundary between Alaska's panhandle and Canada. According to the Anglo-Russian Treaty of 1825, part of which was incorporated into the Russo-American Treaty of 1867 giving Alaska to the United States, the boundary ran inland thirty miles from the Pacific Ocean. For over seventy years the United States, Russia, and Britain had assumed that the boundary followed the irregularities of the coastline.

After the discovery of gold in the region of Canada's Klondike River, near Alaska, Canada challenged the old interpretation. She insisted that the boundary did not follow the windings of the coast but instead ran in a relatively straight line from the outer limits of the coast cutting across the tips of land projections and the mouths of inlets. What made Canada's interpretation especially significant was the fact that the best route to her interior region and to the gold fields lay through the Alaskan panhandle, mainly through the Lynn Canal, a fjord about two or three miles wide that penetrated about a hundred miles through frozen mountains into the interior. The canal was the artery that gave Canada access to the sea and controlled the trade of the interior into the gold fields.

Under the Canadian interpretation the ports at the head of the canal would have fallen on the Canadian side of a boundary cutting across the canal. This would have broken American control of the trade of the interior. Americans considered the Canadian claim preposterous, believing it had been trumped up because of the gold discoveries. Canadians insisted that theirs was not a manufactured case. They said they had long neglected their claim because it was in a remote region that was virtually inaccessible prior to the gold discoveries. Still, it seemed clear that Canada and Britain sought a generous settlement over the boundary in exchange for concessions elsewhere.

Since thousands of rough and lawless goldseekers from all over the world, but mainly from the United States, had stampeded to the Klondike, a settlement of the boundary dispute appeared urgent. Those men might get out of hand and touch off a conflict between American and Canadian authorities. The United States and Britain agreed to submit the dispute, along with other Canadian problems, to a Joint High Commission which met in Quebec in August, 1898. For political reasons the Canadian commissioners demanded an American retreat at the Lynn Canal. Also for political reasons, primarily pressures from the Pacific Coast, the Americans could not retreat, and the commission failed to settle the boundary problem.

The British offered to arbitrate but the United States refused. In October, 1899, therefore, Secretary Hay negotiated a temporary agreement, or *modus vivendi*, with Britain that pleased no one but brought some stability to the Alaskan frontier. Later when Britain tried to obtain concessions for Canada on the Alaskan boundary in return for her own canal concessions in Central America, the United States refused.

That refusal reflected Roosevelt's view that "the Canadian contention is an outrage pure and simple," although at first he had been willing to let the *modus vivendi* continue.[15] In March, 1902, he ordered troops to southern Alaska to prevent disturbances among the mining population.

Since the Canadians, too, dreaded outbreaks among the miners and the British feared that the festering dispute might endanger the new *rapprochement*, they sought some kind of a settlement. John Hay negotiated and on January 23, 1903, signed a treaty with Sir Michael Herbert, the British Ambassador in Washington, calling for a panel of six "impartial jurists of repute," three to be chosen by the President and three by Britain's king, to define the boundary by majority vote.

The shipping and trading interests of the state of Washington denounced the Hay-Herbert Treaty as endangering American control of the Lynn Canal, and opposition in the Senate appeared so strong that for awhile it looked as if the agreement would die there. Senator Lodge, who supported the treaty, overcame opposition by obtaining the names of the commissioners the President intended to appoint and confidentially revealing them to his colleagues.

The three "jurists" Roosevelt appointed were: Secretary of War Elihu Root;

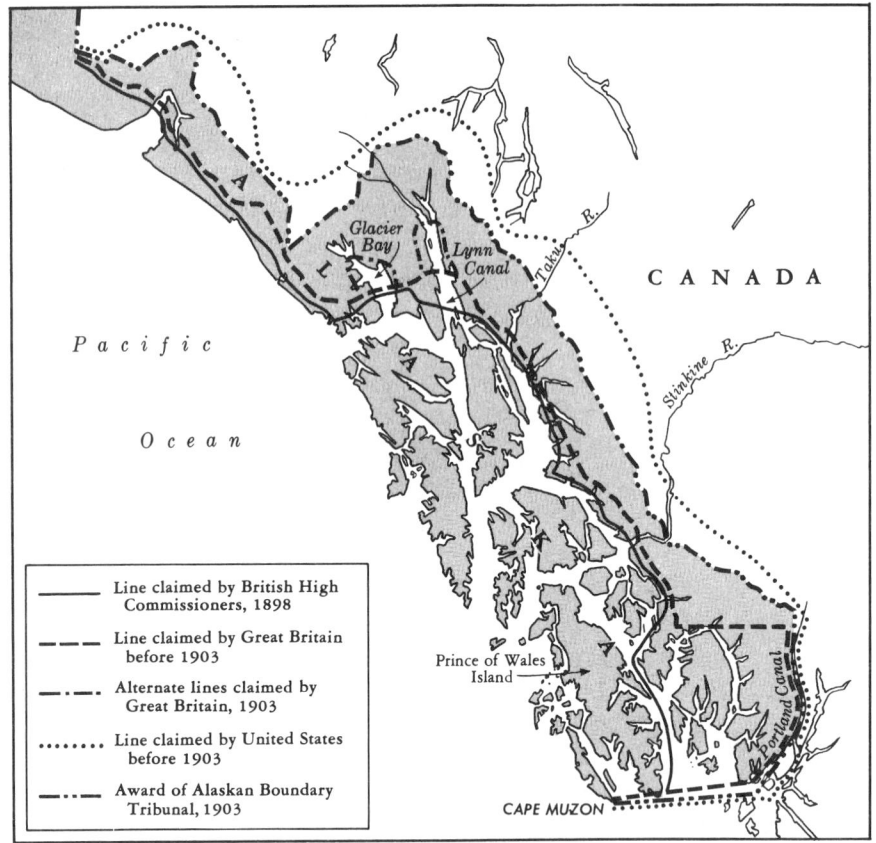

Line claimed by British High
Commissioners, 1898

Line claimed by Great Britain
before 1903

Alternate lines claimed by
Great Britain, 1903

Line claimed by United States
before 1903

Award of Alaskan Boundary
Tribunal, 1903

ALASKA'S DISPUTED BOUNDARY, 1903

a former senator from the state of Washington, George Turner; and Lodge.
Since all three were known to be firmly committed to the American case, and only
Root enjoyed a reputation as a jurist, the partisan selections infuriated the
Canadians. Sir Michael was "disgusted and disheartened." "Everything in this
country," he said, "is subservient to politics, and really an ambassador in Washing-
ton needs more than an ordinary stock of patience."[16]

Roosevelt had not desired unbiased jurists, though he had asked two justices of
the Supreme Court to serve who had refused. He said he had consented to the
commission only out of friendship to England, wishing her to be able to retreat
gracefully from the untenable position "in which she has been placed by Canada."
Perhaps the Louisville *Courier-Journal* summarized the American view: "It is not
likely that England will get anything she is not entitled to from that trio," it
predicted.[17]

England appointed her most eminent jurist, Lord Chief Justice Richard E. W.
Alverstone, and two prominent Canadian jurists. After some preliminary haggling,
the Alaska Boundary Tribunal convened in London in September. Since the
American commissioners adamantly upheld the claim of their government and the

Canadians were as committed to their own position, the decision rested with Lord Alverstone who in effect assumed the role of an arbitrator rather than that of a jurist.[18]

Even before the tribunal met, but particularly during its deliberations, Roosevelt let the British know indirectly that if the commissioners did not decide in favor of the United States he would run the boundary by force. "The plain fact is that the British have no case whatever," he told Lodge, "and when this is so Alverstone ought to be satisfied, and indeed must be satisfied with the very minimum—simply enough to save his face and bring an adjustment."[19] British officials passed on Roosevelt's threats to use the "big stick" to Alverstone.

Aware of the dangers of a deadlock, Alverstone apparently took the hint and voted with the Americans. Although the United States was given a narrower coastal area than its commissioners had demanded, the award, announced on October 2, was almost wholly favorable to it. Canada received only two of four disputed islands. The United States retained an unbroken coastal strip and control of the strategic Lynn Canal. The decision was obviously diplomatic rather than judicial. The Canadians were so bitter that they refused to sign the award. The *Montreal Gazette* hit the mark when it charged that the decision was "merely one of those concessions due to a desire to have the good will of Washington, which many English public men seem to think are always in order."[20] Yet Lord Alverstone always insisted that he had been strictly "judicial."

Americans were delighted with what they considered a just decision. The New York *Tribune* said it "removes from the field of controversy the one point of serious difference that might possibly disturb the harmony of the two great Anglo-Saxon nations."[21] The British could agree with those sentiments, for they were sick of the whole dispute and pleased to have it out of the way. Seven years later Roosevelt maintained that "the settlement of the Alaskan boundary settled the last serious trouble between the British Empire and ourselves, as everything else could be arbitrated."[22]

The North Atlantic Fisheries Settlement

What Roosevelt said was essentially true. Yet the oldest dispute with Britain, over the great fishing grounds of the North Atlantic, remained unsettled while he was in the White House and jeopardized the stability of the new *rapprochement*.

Since Britain had several times renewed the *modus vivendi* of 1888, allowing American fishing vessels to buy bait and other supplies in the harbors of Canada and Newfoundland under a licensing system, the dispute lay quiet for ten years. Canada and Newfoundland resented the *modus vivendi* because it offered privileges to the United States without giving them equivalent concessions. In 1898, they suggested a permanent settlement of the old controversy. If the United States would repeal its tariff on their fish, the British dominions said, they would agree to remove the restrictions on American fishermen imposed by the Anglo-American Convention of 1818.

Finally, on November 8, 1902, John Hay and the Prime Minister of Newfoundland signed a treaty giving Americans free fishing privileges in the waters of Newfoundland and allowing fish and some other products of that province free access to the American market. The New England fishing interests opposed the treaty. Why, they reasoned, open the American market to competitors for privileges already enjoyed? Influenced by that opposition, led by Henry Cabot Lodge, the Senate killed the treaty in 1905. In June of that year, Newfoundland's parliament retaliated with a law terminating the *modus vivendi* and placing punitive restrictions on American fishing vessels in its waters. In May of the following year Newfoundland enacted additional discriminatory legislation against American fishing ships.

Anxious to keep the fisheries controversy from becoming a serious problem, Secretary of State Elihu Root visited Newfoundland and Canada. In September, 1907, he arranged another temporary agreement with Britain that allowed Americans to continue fishing in the waters of Newfoundland but under restricted conditions. Then, in the following April, he signed a general arbitration treaty with Britain under whose terms both countries formally agreed in January, 1909, to submit the fisheries problem to a panel of five judges from the Permanent Court of Arbitration at The Hague, including one American and one Canadian judge. The tribunal assembled in June, 1910, and delivered its award on September 7 of that year.[23] Root regarded the decision as a "great and substantial victory" for the American case, although it was essentially a compromise that gave something to both sides.

The most important feature of the award sustained Britain's right to make and enforce local fishing regulations, but the regulations had to be reasonable. If the United States contested their reasonableness, then the objections would go to a permanent mixed fishery commission that would determine who was right. The British had long claimed the right, challenged by Americans, to exclude American fishermen from all bays regardless of size. The tribunal ruled that bays less than ten miles wide at the mouth were inshore waters and hence closed to American fishermen. When the mouth exceeded ten miles, the area of local jurisdiction was three miles along the shore of the bay and Americans could fish in the bay beyond the three-mile limit.

An Anglo-American commission signed a convention in July, 1912, modifying The Hague award, but confirming its essential points. This resolved the most vexatious problems of the longest dispute in the history of American foreign policy. Later in the twentieth century other controversies over fisheries caused friction with Canada, but they never truly endangered American friendship with that Dominion.

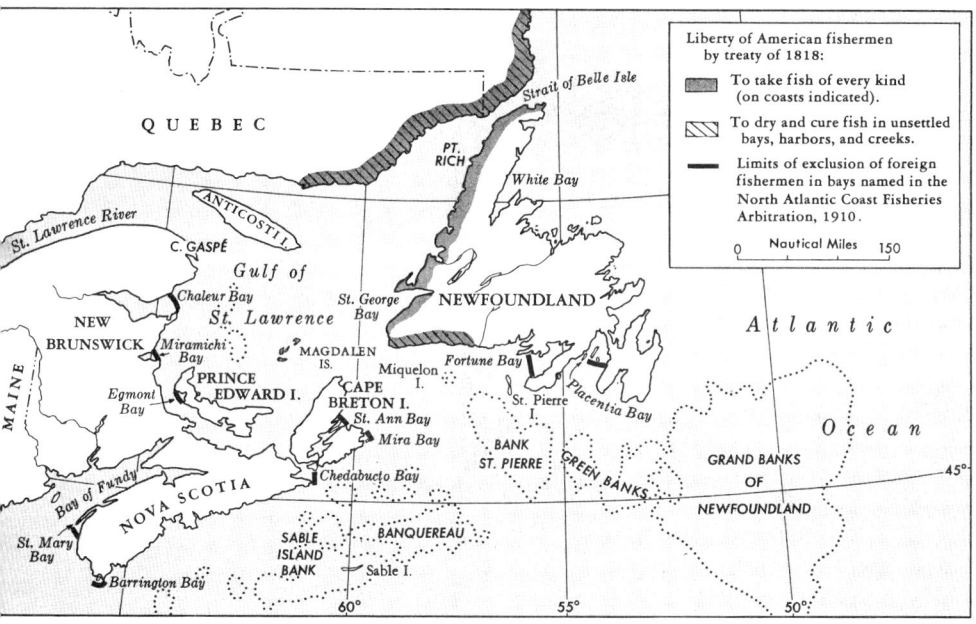

THE NORTHEAST FISHERIES CONTROVERSY

The Reciprocity of 1911

Another problem, related to that of the fisheries, that had long endangered relations with Canada was that of trade reciprocity. Since the abrogation of the Marcy-Elgin Treaty in 1866, Canada had sought some kind of reciprocal trade agreement with her southern neighbor, but the United States had refused all proposals. Republicans, who had controlled the government most of the time in the years since the Civil War, upheld the principle of a protective tariff almost as a matter of party faith. In 1909 they passed the Payne-Aldrich tariff, a protectionist measure that struck at Canada with special severity. Canadians threatened retaliation.

To avoid a seemingly inevitable tariff war if nothing more were done, President Taft and Prime Minister Sir Wilfrid Laurier, the head of Canada's Liberal government, signed an agreement on January 26, 1911, for commercial reciprocity. It allowed most of Canada's main products, primarily agricultural, to enter the United States subject to no duties or to low ones, and American manufactures could go into Canada on the same terms. Since the agreement was not a treaty, it was to go into effect by concurrent legislation, meaning that a simple majority in both houses of Congress could make it law.

The reciprocity bill won approval in the House of Representatives without delay, but the Senate, sensitive to the opposition of lumber, fish, and agriculture interests, adjourned in March without acting on it.[24] Regarding the bill as one of the most important measures of his administration, Taft called a special session of Congress in April. Despite the continued opposition of certain protected economic interests and of a significant portion of his own Republican party, he got the bill through the Senate in July with the aid of Democratic votes, the Hearst press, and Washington's stifling heat.

In urging passage, Taft and other supporters of the bill gave the impression that free trade would lead to the annexation of Canada. "The amount of Canadian products we take," the President said privately, "would make Canada only an adjunct of the United States."[25] He repeated similar ideas publicly, and a number of congressmen and the Hearst papers used the same argument. One prominent senator announced that he favored reciprocity because he hoped to see the day "when the American flag will float over every square foot of the British North American possessions clear to the North Pole."[26]

In Canada public sentiment had changed and reciprocity became a party issue. Liberals supported it and Conservatives, backed by manufacturers, the railroads, and other financial interests, opposed it. This forced the Prime Minister to dissolve parliament and to call a general election. The main issue was reciprocity, but propaganda, feeding on a latent distrust of the United States and on an aroused nationalism, reduced it to the issue of choosing between the United States or the empire. A builder of the Canadian Pacific Railroad, for instance, announced that he was out to do all that he could "to bust the damned thing."[27] Other Conservatives followed the same principle.

The inept statements of Taft and American congressmen proved to be valuable campaign material for the Conservatives. One editor said that "the answer from the Canadian people is that Canada is, and intends to remain, British."[28] So it was. The Canadians rallied round the flag and in September marched to the polls to give the Conservatives a decisive victory. Later, the Conservative party defeated the reciprocity bill in parliament.

The defeat of reciprocity did not precipitate a tariff war with Canada or harm the Anglo-American *rapprochement*, but it embarrassed the Taft administration and smothered trade reciprocity for a quarter of a century. Especially significant was the fact that after the election of 1911 American relations with Canada became distinct from those with England.

The Panama Tolls Controversy

Another controversy with England arose from differing interpretations of the Hay-Pauncefote Treaty over the matter of toll payments for the use of the Panama Canal as it approached completion. The canal should be open to the ships of all nations "on terms of entire equality," the treaty read, so that there would be no discriminatory charges against any nation. In August, 1912, Congress exempted

American ships engaged only in the coastwise trade, as from California to New York, from payment of tolls. Viewing the exemption as a violation of the Hay-Pauncefote Treaty and a breach of faith that would lead to higher tolls for foreign ships, the British protested. They asked for adjudication of the dispute under the arbitration treaty of 1908.

President Taft refused, saying that "when the treaties are properly construed, owning the canal and paying for it as we do, we have the right and power, if we choose, to discriminate in favor of our own ships."[29] Other Americans believed the United States was bound by honor not to discriminate.

In the presidential campaign of 1912 the platforms of both the Democratic and Progressive parties supported the exemption. Those who favored its repeal, critics argued, were Anglophiles and tools of the transcontinental railroads. Yet President Wilson, even though he had approved the exemption during the campaign, soon became convinced that the British had a good case and that the nation's honor was at stake. He also realized that arbitration would require a treaty and that the mood of the Senate was such that it probably would not give the necessary two-thirds approval. Fortunately, he obtained the support of Henry Cabot Lodge, who suggested repeal of the clause which made the trouble.[30]

Wilson followed that procedure. He met with the Senate Foreign Relations Committee in January, 1914, and pointed out that he needed British support for his policy in Mexico and could probably get it with a friendly understanding over the tolls controversy. When he went before a joint session of Congress in March to ask for repeal of the exemption, he referred to the difficulties in Mexico, but not specifically. "I ask this of you in support of the foreign policy of the administration," he said. "I shall not know how to deal with other matters of even great delicacy and nearer consequence if you do not grant it to me in ungrudging measure."[31]

The House of Representatives repealed the exemption a few weeks later, but the Senate debated two months and did not do so until June 11. That repeal was more than just a victory for Wilson's foreign policy. It settled the last important controversy with Britain before the *rapprochement* met the test of the First World War.

Dollar Diplomacy in Asia

These years preceding the First World War also saw a change in the concept of the Open Door. Priding itself on close relations with business, the Taft administration wanted American capital to expand into foreign fields. The President and his Secretary of State, Philander C. Knox, were particularly eager to have dollars penetrate China for profitable investment, an area where they had refused to go of their own accord.

This policy of seeking to open China for investment became known as Dollar

Diplomacy. It was, Taft claimed, a policy of substituting dollars for bullets, "an effort frankly directed to the increase of American trade upon the axiomatic principle that the Government of the United States shall extend all proper support to every legitimate and beneficial American enterprise abroad." [32] The man who helped inaugurate Dollar Diplomacy in China, the diplomat Willard Straight, called it "the financial expression of John Hay's 'Open Door' policy" and saw it as "the alliance of diplomacy, with industry, commerce and finance." [33]

Although it was the policy of Taft and Knox, Dollar Diplomacy had its roots in the Roosevelt period. In the summer of 1905 the railroad financier, Edward H. Harriman, who controlled a large part of American shipping in the Pacific, visited Japan. There he made arrangements to purchase a controlling interest in the South Manchuria Railway, which Japan hoped to acquire at the end of the Russo-Japanese War.

Harriman explained his plan to the American Minister in Tokyo. "There's no doubt about it," he said. "If I can secure control of the South Manchuria Railroad from Japan, I'll buy the Chinese Eastern from Russia, acquire trackage over the Trans-Siberian to the Baltic, and establish a line of steamers to the United States. Then I can connect with the American transcontinental lines, and join up with the Pacific Mail and the Japanese transpacific steamers. It'll be the most marvelous transportation system in the world. We'll girdle the earth." [34]

After the peace with Russia, Japan backed out of her arrangement with Harriman, which she had never signed. She decided to exploit her railroad properties in Manchuria herself, basically with Japanese and Chinese capital. Harriman did not abandon his idea, but it might have died if Straight, then Consul-General at Mukden, Manchuria, had not kept it alive.

Harriman had met Straight, a restless young man in his mid-twenties, while in the Orient and was impressed by his "character and force." Straight distrusted the Japanese and believed that their control of southern Manchuria threatened American economic interests there. He was convinced that meager investments accounted for the lack of power of the United States in that part of the world. Believing that investments in Manchuria would lead to American political influence there, he wrote to Harriman in 1906, stressing the profitable opportunities there. He even devised a plan for a railroad to compete with Japan's South Manchuria Railway. [35]

Straight told Harriman of his plan, pointing out that the railroad builder could play a "principal part in the development of Manchuria" and at the same time advance American influence in China proper. [36] The financial panic of 1907 in the United States made investment capital scarce, so Harriman rejected Straight's idea.

Meanwhile, in July, 1907, Japan and Russia signed two conventions, one of them secret, that recognized northern Manchuria and Outer Mongolia as Russian spheres of influence and southern Manchuria and Inner Mongolia as Japanese

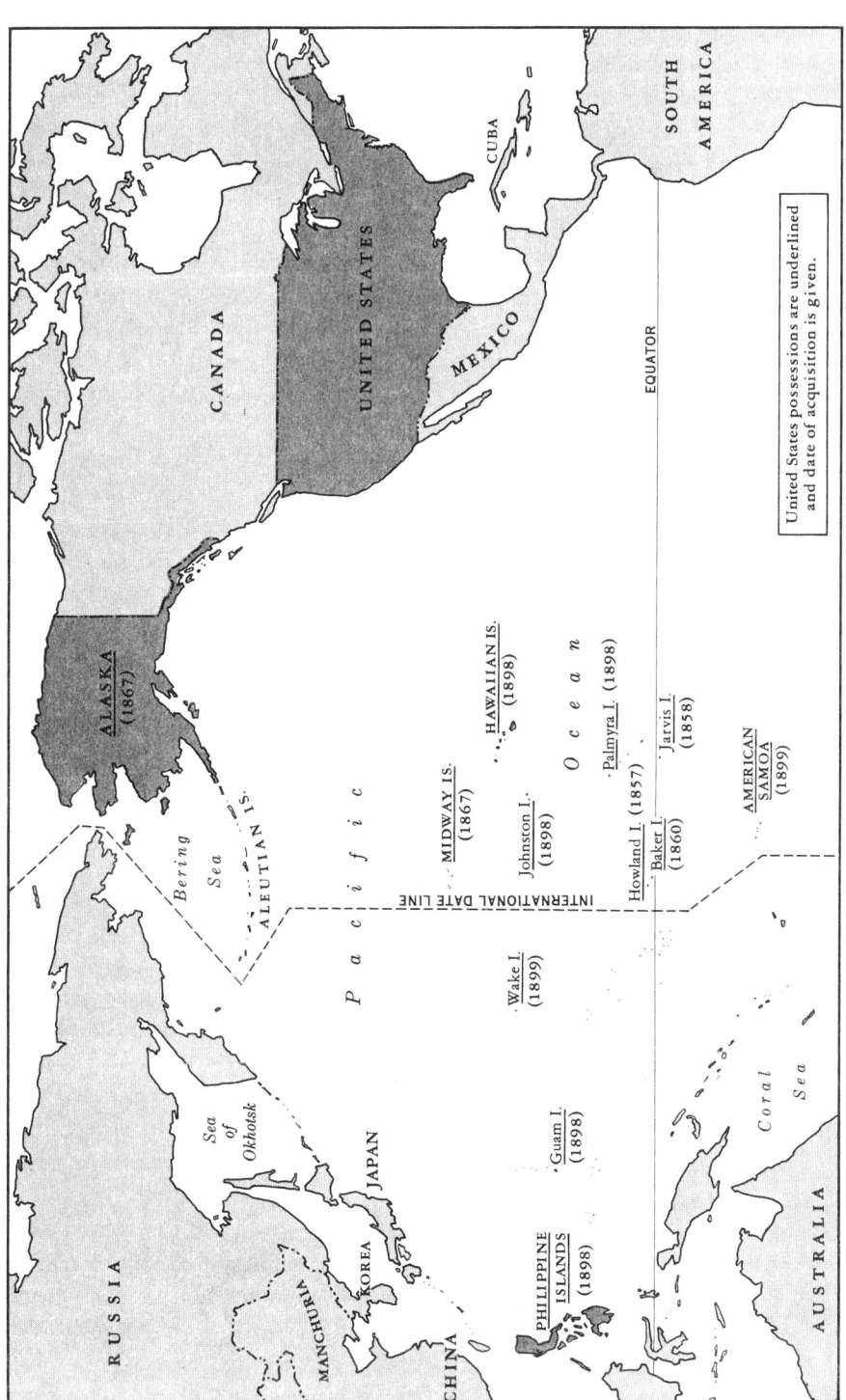

THE AMERICAN EMPIRE IN THE PACIFIC, 1910

United States possessions are underlined and date of acquisition is given.

RUSSIA

CANADA

ALASKA
(1867)

UNITED STATES

CUBA

MEXICO

SOUTH
AMERICA

EQUATOR

Bering
Sea

ALEUTIAN IS.

MIDWAY IS.
(1867)

HAWAIIAN IS.
(1898)

Johnston I.
(1898)

Pacific   Ocean

Palmyra I. (1898)

INTERNATIONAL DATE LINE

Howland I. (1857)

Baker I.
(1860)

Jarvis I.
(1858)

Wake I.
(1899)

AMERICAN
SAMOA
(1899)

Sea
of
Okhotsk

MANCHURIA

JAPAN

KOREA

Guam I.
(1898)

Coral
Sea

CHINA

PHILIPPINE
ISLANDS
(1898)

AUSTRALIA

spheres. These agreements, though not entirely clear at the time, threatened the Open Door and opportunities for foreign investment in Manchuria. President Roosevelt, realizing that he could do nothing to stop the Russians and the Japanese without using force he did not have, did not challenge their predominance in Manchuria.

Straight, however, wanted to block the Japanese. He kept in touch with Harriman, urging him to invest in China. Nothing happened until the end of the panic when Harriman asked Secretary of State Root to recall Straight for consultation on opportunities for investment in Manchuria. "'Wall Street' is feeling confident again and is looking for the investment of capital in foreign lands," the Chief of the State Department's Far Eastern Division said. "It has turned to Manchuria and wants the latest advice on the situation up there. . . ." [37]

Straight returned to the United States in September, 1908, with ideas that were to dovetail with the broad objectives of Dollar Diplomacy, and in November became Acting Chief of the Division of Far Eastern Affairs. While in Washington, he worked to maintain Harriman's interest in Manchuria's railroads and tried to gain (for his own schemes) the support of New York bankers, who sought investment abroad.

Serving as a link between the Department of State and Harriman, Straight aided in arrangements for a loan to China, through Harriman's banking associates, Kuhn, Loeb and Company, to finance a program of economic reform. He also tried to pave the way for Harriman and the bankers to buy the South Manchuria Railway and Russia's Chinese Eastern Railway in nothern Manchuria. As long as Roosevelt was in the White House, however, Straight's ideas received scant attention from the government.

When Taft became President, the ideas of Straight and Harriman gained official support. Taft and Knox believed that the government should aid private enterprise in seeking markets and investment opportunities abroad. They also felt that in pumping capital into China they would block Japan's menacing policy there, help preserve China's administrative integrity, and extend the principles of the Open Door.

Straight himself tried to stimulate interest in railroad finance by pointing out that China was trying to centralize her railroads and thus offered rich opportunities for investment. Once developed, he said, the railroads would also open up large untapped markets for manufactured goods.

When China signed an agreement with English, French, and German bankers in June, 1909, known as the Hukuang Railway loan, to finance the construction of railroads in southern and central China, the Taft administration sought a share of the loan for American bankers. Straight, who resigned from the Department of State that same month, immediately went to work for the banking group that became "the official agent of American railway financing in China."

Since the Taft policy obviously threatened what appeared to be a lucrative financial monopoly, the Europeans resisted the American attempt to intervene. Therefore, Taft himself sent a telegram to the Chinese Prince Regent demanding a share of the railroad loan for the American bankers. China and the powers finally admitted the American bankers in May, 1910, and what had been a three-power consortium became the first four-power consortium. "I think that quite a diplomatic victory," Taft said.[38]

Willard Straight, meantime, while working to obtain the Chinese loan, also kept alive his earlier plan for the purchase of the railroads in Manchuria. He and Harriman tried to buy the Chinese Eastern Railway from Russia so they could expand the line southward, threaten Japan with competition, and force her to sell the South Manchuria Railway that Harriman really wanted. But Harriman, the one American financier intensely interested in Manchuria, died in September, 1909.

Without Harriman the American bankers hesitated to support the financing of railroads in Manchuria. The full burden of luring capital and the government into activity in Manchuria, therefore, fell on Straight's shoulders. He managed to transfer the interest of the bankers to Manchuria, and since the Taft administration feared that Japan's control of trade, railroads, and mineral deposits in southern Manchuria would freeze out American economic rights, he also succeeded in involving the government in Manchurian affairs.

Knox's Neutralization Scheme

Late in October, 1909, Secretary of State Knox, aware of Harriman's and Straight's activities, told the American banking group of a plan to "neutralize" Manchuria's railroads. He wanted an international syndicate to lend money to China to purchase all the Manchurian railroads, with the syndicate supervising them during the term of the loan. If Britain found the plan impracticable, then he would ask her to support an alternative idea of building a line to compete with Japan's South Manchuria Railway.

This neutralization scheme, Knox thought, would preserve the Open Door in Manchuria and help China gain control there. It would, he said privately, "smoke Japan out" of her dominant position in southern Manchuria. Knox's plan and Straight's ideas fitted together so well that they appeared to be part of a grand design.

In November the Secretary of State approached England first with the idea of having her present his plan to her Japanese ally. If Japan refused to cooperate, she would then find herself stigmatized as an enemy of the Open Door in Manchuria. Since Britain's main concern was the rising power of Germany in Europe, she relied on her alliance with Japan for support in Asia and, since concluding an *entente* with Russia in 1907, looked to Russia and France for aid in Europe. She would do nothing to alienate either Japan or Russia, for those two countries resented Knox's transparent scheme to deprive them of their spheres of influence in Manchuria. When, in fact, he asked them to join his plan, Japan and Russia bluntly rejected it in January, 1910, with notes that were so similar as to indicate collaboration. Since France supported the British position, all the powers but Germany opposed the neutralization scheme.

Knox's blundering scheme had in fact driven Russia and Japan together to tighten their grip on Manchuria. In July, they announced, as they had three years earlier, that they had signed a treaty promising mutual consultation to preserve the *status quo* in Manchuria and cooperation in developing its railroads. They had also concluded a secret convention reaffirming their spheres of influence and promising "common action" to defend them. Their announcement just about crushed China's hopes in Manchuria.

Thus, American policy had antagonized Japan and Russia and had lost the confidence of China. Moreover, since Roosevelt had, in effect, acquiesced in a closed door there, Taft and Knox had reversed his Far Eastern policy. Their failure also aroused the ire of the American banking group. Since the opposition of the other powers precluded financial success, it threatened to withdraw from the whole of China. Instead of opening the door to American investment in Manchuria and China, Dollar Diplomacy had virtually closed it.[39]

Still, the Taft administration did not abandon its policy. China had, meanwhile, revived an old scheme for currency reform as part of a larger program of general reform. Since American bankers were at the time still interested in making loans, the State Department decided to use the currency reform as a means of restoring shattered prestige in China. Taft invited England, France, and Germany to participate, and a second four-power consortium drew up a Chinese Currency Reform and Industrial Development Loan in April, 1911. That loan was never floated.

A month later the first four-power consortium finally reached an agreement on the Hukuang Railway loan. Although accepted by the Chinese government, the Hukuang loan, for thirty million dollars, was unpopular with the people who resented foreign economic exploitation of their country. Instead of being used immediately to build railroads, it helped touch off a revolution that overthrew the Manchu dynasty.

The Six-Power Consortium

After their revolution of 1911, the Chinese set up a republic in February, 1912. Desperately in need of money, the new government turned to the members of the four-power consortium for aid. The bankers were willing to make a loan for the reorganization of China's government, but Britain and France wanted their Japanese and Russian allies to share in it. Japan and Russia, therefore, became members of a six-power consortium in June. In enlarging the consortium the powers recognized the Japanese and Russian spheres in Manchuria and Mongolia. The Taft administration, as a result, in fact accepted Japan's dominant position in southern Manchuria and abandoned the Open Door in that region.

Before the six-power consortium could complete its agreement with China, the American banking group lost its desire to participate. Agents of the bankers reported that the international market could not handle a large amount of Chinese bonds. That news, coupled with Chinese opposition to several features of the proposed loan and fear of the incoming Wilson administration, finally led the banking group to decide that it must have full government support or it would give up its share of the loan.

Five days after Wilson took office, representatives of the American bankers, Straight among them, interviewed Secretary of State Bryan. They said their group would not go through with its share of the reorganization loan unless the administration asked it to do so and indicated it would use force, if necessary, to make China live up to the contract.

Wilson and Bryan discussed the loan problem in two cabinet meetings. Then the President issued a statement directly to the press. His administration, he said, would not ask the bankers to participate in the loan "because it did not approve the conditions of the loan or the implications of responsibility on its own part," and he added, "the conditions of the loan seem to us to touch very nearly the administrative independence of China itself." [40]

Wilson thus repudiated Dollar Diplomacy, and the bankers withdrew from the first four-power consortium and from the six-power consortium. The other members of the six-power consortium went ahead without the American bankers and concluded a loan for the reorganization of the Chinese government in April, 1913.

Wilson's decision on the loan led foreign statesmen to wonder if he would adopt a similarly independent policy in recognizing the new Chinese Republic. Secretary Knox had followed a policy of cooperating with the other powers who individually wanted specific concessions from the Chinese government as the price of recognition. American public opinion, distrustful of the powers and sympathetic to China's republican form of government, had demanded recognition. Reflecting that sentiment, Congress had passed resolutions in February and April of 1912 praising China for adopting a republican form of government and urging President Taft to extend early recognition. Knox had resisted those pressures, believing that his cooperative policy served the national interest better than would individual action. Taft's government, therefore, had retired with the United States maintaining only *de facto* relations with the Chinese Republic.

When Wilson took office, he was anxious to extend *de jure* recognition and did not want that recognition to depend on the other powers. Before acting, however, he invited the powers to cooperate by extending recognition with the United States. Since only four Latin-American states accepted Wilson's offer, the United States on May 2, 1913, became the first of the great powers to recognize the Chinese Republic. In acting alone, Wilson repudiated another of the Taft-Knox policies.[41]

The California Land Laws

When a new crisis arose over the status of Japanese aliens in California, Wilson did not show the same benevolent attitude toward Japan as he had toward China. The prejudice of the Californians was an old problem. Every California legislature from 1907 to 1913 had considered discriminatory measures against the Japanese. In March, 1913, the anti-Japanese agitation erupted with particular force when both Democrats and Republicans catered to the racial feeling of voters by introducing legislation designed to bar Japanese from owning land.

Many governments prohibited foreigners from owning land. The Japanese government's main objection was not to the legislation itself, but to the injustice of its discriminatory features. Japan demanded treatment for her nationals equal to that accorded other aliens in the United States and resented the laws that stigmatized Asians as inferiors.

Since he himself favored the exclusion of allegedly unassimilable foreigners, Wilson did not attempt to stop the Californians from enacting their discriminatory laws. He merely asked them to act so "as to offend the susceptibilities of a friendly nation as little as possible."[42] He even suggested a means of keeping the Japanese from owning land in California without violating a Japanese-American commercial treaty of 1911.

At first the California legislators followed Wilson's suggestion by drawing up an alien land bill indirectly prohibiting the Japanese from owning land in the state. Later, they substituted another bill directed specifically against the Japanese. The Japanese protested against the proposed law and newspapers carried reports of a mass meeting in Tokyo demanding war rather than have the nation submit to humiliation by California.

Alarmed by the developments in the West and by the mounting war fever in Japan, Wilson appealed publicly to the California legislators in April not to embarrass the Federal government with a law that openly discriminated against the proud Japanese. He also sent Bryan to California to plead for moderation with the lawmakers and the governor. Since Wilson took a narrow view of the Federal government's authority over the police powers of a state, he would go no further. He would not use Federal power to coerce a state. Therefore, even though Bryan begged the Californians to modify their proposed legislation, they would not.

As the tension with Japan increased, the California legislature on May 3, 1913,

passed its Alien Land Bill depriving aliens "ineligible to citizenship" of the right
to own land except as guaranteed by treaty. What rankled the Japanese was the
humiliating phrase "ineligible to citizenship" and the fact that other aliens were
still allowed to own land. "We have prevented the Japanese from driving the root
of their civilization deep into California soil," California's governor announced
after passage of the law, emphasizing its specific racial discrimination.[43]

Considering the law a vicious affront to national honor, the Japanese government on May 9 lodged a strong protest with the Department of State.[44] So violent
was the reaction in Japan, that the Joint Board of the Army and Navy, the highest
defense agency in the United States, began preparations for war and wanted to
order several warships to the Philippines to protect them against any surprise
attack from Japan. Bryan and Wilson wished to avoid any move that might
arouse more excitement in Japan; hence the President refused to send the warships.[45]

Bryan tried to persuade California's governor to veto the Alien Land Bill, but
the governor signed it and it became law on May 19. The President, at the same
time, assured newspaper reporters that talk of war was foolish and that the crisis
would be overcome amicably. He and Bryan tried to conciliate the angry Japanese
as best they could. The Secretary told them that what California had done did not
represent national policy.

Since Wilson and Bryan seemed sincere in their efforts to arrive at a just solution
to the problem and did not deny the justice of the Japanese complaints against
the discriminatory features of the land law, they helped to ease the wound in
Japan's pride. Bryan told the Japanese "that nothing is final between friends" and
that "a satisfactory solution can be found for all questions if the parties approach
the subject with patience and in the right spirit."[46] Gradually the tension in both
Japan and the United States eased.

The Twenty-One Demands

When the First World War spread to Asia, it brought new menaces to the Open
Door in China and new tensions to relations between Japan and the United States.
Japan entered the war on the Allied side in August, 1914. Her navy seized the Ger-
man islands in the Pacific north of the equator, the Marianas (except Guam), the
Carolines, and the Marshalls. Her army invaded the Shantung Peninsula and
swiftly expelled the Germans from their leasehold there.

In the fighting on Shantung the two main belligerents, Japan and Germany,
violated China's neutrality, but the Japanese violations were the most flagrant.
Helpless to protect herself, China appealed to the United States, as a champion of
the Open Door, to intervene on her behalf. While expressing friendship for China,

Acting Secretary of State Robert Lansing replied that "it would be quixotic in the extreme to allow the question of China's territorial integrity to entangle the United States in international difficulties."[47] Yet some Americans shared Chinese fears that Japan intended not only to remain in the Shantung province but also to use it as a base for taking over other portions of China.

In January, 1915, within a month after completing her conquests, Japan showed that the Chinese and American fears were sound ones. Taking advantage of the fact that all the other great powers except the United States were mired in the European war, she presented the Chinese government with the Twenty-One Demands, a document that would virtually have transformed China into a vassal state. Although the Japanese had warned China to keep them secret, Chinese authorities let the substance of the demands leak to the United States.[48]

In March Bryan sent a note to Japan that reflected both Wilson's concern that the Japanese were going too far and his own effort to be conciliatory. Bryan objected to several of the demands, but added, in Shantung, southern Manchuria, and eastern Inner Mongolia, "the United States frankly recognizes that territorial contiguity creates special relations between Japan and these districts."[49] At this time the President neither approved nor disapproved of the demands. To the Chinese and Japanese it appeared that the United States, the only great power in a position to block the Japanese if it so desired, no longer championed the Open Door policy. As Japan's pressure on China increased, however, Wilson changed his position. "I feel," he explained, "that we should be as active as the circumstances permit in showing ourselves to be champions of the sovereign rights of China. . . ."[50]

Japan gave in to the American protests by abandoning or modifying some of her more obnoxious demands. The Chinese, nevertheless, still balked at accepting all of the remaining terms, so on May 7 the Japanese resorted to an ultimatum. Concerned over American rights in China, Bryan, two days after China had accepted the ultimatum, sent identic notes to Japan and China saying the United States could not recognize any agreement between them "impairing the treaty rights of the United States and its citizens in China, the political or territorial integrity of the Republic of China, or the international policy relative to China commonly known as the Open Door policy."[51] Although the note had little effect on the Japanese, other than to increase anti-American sentiment among them, it announced a nonrecognition principle that the United States would use again in its troubled relations with Japan. Meanwhile, in two treaties signed on May 25, China formally agreed to most of the Twenty-One Demands.

Significantly, although American protests had helped in preventing Japan from reducing China to a protectorate, Japan had won a commanding position in China. Wilson, like Roosevelt before him, realized that the American people would not go to war to defend distant China and the principle of the Open Door.

The Lansing-Ishii Agreement

While the war in Europe continued to sap the energies of the Allied powers, Japan exploited her victory with a program of loans designed to insure her economic dominance over China. Since the nations fighting in Europe had no surplus capital to invest, they were forced to abandon their active interest in China's finances and hence could not prevent Japan's economic penetration. As early as December, 1916, therefore, the Europeans turned to the United States, urging it to return to the consortium Wilson had abandoned. The United States, the British and French pointed out, was the only country with available investment capital that could stop the Japanese.

Since American bankers did not consider China a good place for investment, Wilson found that he could not counter Japan's financial expansion in China through private investment. In the fall of 1917, after the United States and China had both entered the war, Wilson yielded to the urgings of the British and French, and decided to use a new consortium to offset Japan's gains in China. He had, therefore, to convert American bankers once more into agents of diplomacy.

Noting this change in policy, the Japanese decided to ask for a definite statement of the American attitude toward their policy of expansion in China. In September they sent one of their ablest diplomats, Viscount Kikujiro Ishii, to the United States as the head of a special mission, ostensibly to discuss cooperation in the war against Germany. Actually, Secretary of State Robert Lansing and Viscount Ishii debated the conflicting Japanese and American objectives in China.

Ishii wanted Lansing's public recognition of Japan's "special interests" in China as "paramount interests." Lansing would not agree. He defined "special interests" as growing out of geographical propinquity but not as giving Japan title to rights beyond those belonging to any other nation.

Lansing and Ishii finally compromised by putting the Secretary's restrictive interpretation of "special interests" into a secret protocol of October 31, 1917. "The Governments of Japan and the United States," that protocol said, "will not take advantage of the present conditions to seek special rights or privileges in China which would abridge the rights of the subjects or citizens of other friendly states."[52] That protocol was kept secret for eighteen years.

Two days later, Lansing and Ishii signed the protocol and in an exchange of notes publicly reaffirmed that their countries respected the Open Door and the territorial integrity of China. The heart of their agreement, however, was the statement recognizing that "territorial propinquity creates special relations between countries, and consequently the Government of the United States recognizes that Japan has special interests in China, particularly in the part to which her possessions are contiguous."[53]

The ambiguity of the Lansing-Ishii Agreement allowed each signatory to con-
strue it to suit its own purposes. Acting as though the secret protocol did not
exist, Japan interpreted the agreement as a recognition of her "paramount"
position in China and hailed Viscount Ishii for winning a "great diplomatic
victory." The United States interpreted the agreement as Japan's pledge to respect
the Open Door and China's independence. Since the agreement without the
protocol appeared to nullify the Open Door and to surrender more to Japan than
she really got, Americans who considered their country a friend and defender of
China viewed it as a diplomatic blunder. Believing the United States had betrayed
them, the Chinese protested the agreement. What the agreement actually did was
to make a temporary public concession to Japan that helped alleviate Japanese-
American tension during the war.[54]

Wilson's Four-Power Consortium

Wilson had not, in fact, given up the principle of the Open Door or the diplomatic defense of China's sovereignty. He still hoped to restrict Japan's capital
investment in China through international means. A week after exchanging notes
with Ishii, Secretary Lansing cabled the American Minister in China that the
government was considering a new consortium to aid China in a program of
broad economic reconstruction. On July 8, 1918, the American bankers he had
invited to join the consortium agreed to consider loans to China on two conditions.
The aid, they said, must be broadly international, including British, French, and
Japanese bankers, and the American government must announce that the loans
were being made at its suggestion.

Wilson's government immediately accepted the banker's conditions and two
days later sent the plan to Britain, France, and Japan with an invitation to join the
new consortium. All ultimately agreed to participate, but Japan, resenting the
American challenge to her program of gaining a financial monopoly in China, did
so only after obtaining recognition of her "special position" in southern Manchuria
and Mongolia. Discussions between the powers on the consortium plan went on
during the peace conference in Paris at the end of the First World War and continued until October, 1920, when the final compromise agreement was signed.

Wilson had viewed the new four-power consortium as a means of weakening
Japan's planned hegemony over China by strengthening the principle of the Open
Door. Ironically, China refused salvation through the new consortium, preferring
to seek loans in the world market where she could borrow on the best terms
available. Nonetheless, the new four-power consortium was significant in marking
a reversal of Wilson's stand of 1913 on Dollar Diplomacy.

NOTES

1. Quoted in Howard K. Beale, *Theodore Roosevelt and the Rise of America to World Power* (Baltimore, 1956), p. 359. In the preceding year the United States had shown some interest in Morocco by intervening in the case of Jon Perdicaris, allegedly an American citizen who had been kidnapped and held for ransom by a native chieftain. For details, see Alfred L. P. Dennis, *Adventures in American Diplomacy, 1896–1906* (New York, 1928), pp. 443–445 and Harold E. Davis, "The Citizenship of Jon Perdicaris," *Journal of Modern History*, XIII (Dec. 1941), 517–526.

2. The quotations are from Beale, *Theodore Roosevelt*, p. 366.

3. To Roosevelt, July 25, 1906, in Henry Cabot Lodge, ed., *Selections from the Correspondence of Theodore Roosevelt and Henry Cabot Lodge, 1884–1918* (2 vols., New York, 1925), II, 171. See also Alfred Vagts, *Deutschland und die Vereinigten Staaten in der Weltpolitik* (2 vols., New York, 1935), II, 1905–1913.

4. For details, see William C. Askew and J. Fred Rippy, "The United States and Europe's Strife, 1908–1913," *Journal of Politics*, IV (Feb. 1942), 70–71.

5. Finley P. Dunne, *Mr. Dooley at His Best*, Elmer Ellis, ed. (New York, 1938), p. 142.

6. To Shelby M. Cullom, Feb. 10, 1905, in Elting E. Morison, ed., *The Letters of Theodore Roosevelt* (8 vols., Cambridge, Mass., 1951–1954), IV, 1119.

7. Quoted in Henry F. Pringle, *The Life and Times of William Howard Taft* (2 vols., New York, 1939), II, 739.

8. Quoted in William Stull Holt, *Treaties Defeated by the Senate* (Baltimore, 1933), p. 235.

9. Wilson himself took great pride in the wide acceptance the treaties had gained. See Herbert C. F. Bell, "The Genesis of Wilson's Foreign Policy," *Thought*, XXIII (Dec. 1948), 661 and Harley Notter, *The Origins of the Foreign Policy of Woodrow Wilson* (Baltimore, 1937), p. 240. For details on the treaties, see Merle E. Curti, "Bryan and World Peace," *Smith College Studies in History*, XVI, nos. 3–4 (April, July 1931), 143–164.

10. To Henry White, Sept. 24, 1899, in William R. Thayer, *The Life and Letters of John Hay* (2 vols., Boston, 1915), II, 221.

11. To Henry White, Jan. 27, 1900, quoted in Beale, *Theodore Roosevelt*, p. 95.

12. Kirk H. Porter, *National Party Platforms* (New York, 1924), p. 216.

13. To A. C. Cowles, Dec. 17, 1899, quoted in Beale, *Theodore Roosevelt*, p. 95.

14. Dec. 13, 1899, quoted in Charles S. Campbell, Jr., *Anglo-American Understanding, 1898–1903* (Baltimore, 1957), p. 179.

15. To Hay, July 10, 1902, in Morison, *Roosevelt Letters*, III, 287.

16. Quoted in Henry F. Pringle, *Theodore Roosevelt: A Biography* (New York, 1931), p. 291.

17. Quoted in Campbell, *Anglo-American Understanding*, p. 313.

18. "He regards himself as the arbitrator really," Lodge wrote, " & knows that everything really turns on his decision." To his daughter, Sept., 19, 1903, in John A. Garraty, "Henry Cabot Lodge and the Alaskan Boundary Tribunal," *New England Quarterly*, XXIV (Dec. 1951), 484.

19. Oct. 5, 1903, in Morison, *Roosevelt Letters*, III, 616.

20. Oct. 21, 1903, quoted in Charles C. Tansill, *Canadian-American Relations, 1875–1911* (New Haven, 1943), p. 265.

21. Quoted in Campbell, *Anglo-American Understanding*, p. 344.

22. To A. T. Mahan, June 8, 1911, in Morison, *Roosevelt Letters*, VII, 280. In

"Theodore Roosevelt and the Alaska Boundary Settlement," *Canadian Historical Review*, XVIII (June 1937), 123–130, Thomas A. Bailey questions Roosevelt's use of big stick tactics in this affair and his callous disregard for Canadian feelings.

23. For details, see Robert Lansing, "The North Atlantic Coast Fisheries Arbitration," *American Journal of International Law*, V (Jan. 1911), 1–31.

24. For details on agricultural opposition, see L. Ethan Ellis, "The Northwest and the Reciprocity Agreement of 1911," *Mississippi Valley Historical Review*, XXVI (June 1939), 55–66. For the economic factors, see Willis G. Swartz, "The Proposed Canadian-American Reciprocity Agreement of 1911," *Journal of Economic and Business History*, III (Nov. 1930), 118–147.

25. Quoted in Hugh L. Keenleyside and Gerald S. Brown, *Canada and the United States*, rev. ed. (New York, 1952), p. 267.

26. Champ Clark, Feb. 14, 1911, quoted in Tansill, *Canadian-American Relations*, p. 463.

27. Sir William Van Horne, quoted in L. Ethan Ellis, *Reciprocity, 1911: A Study in Canadian-American Relations* (New Haven, 1939), p. 153.

28. Quoted in Keenleyside and Brown, *Canada and the U.S.*, p. 271.

29. To H. S. Drinker, July 27, 1911, quoted in Pringle, *Taft*, II, 649.

30. For details, see John A. Garraty, *Henry Cabot Lodge* (New York, 1953), p. 299. Elihu Root also helped. See Philip C. Jessup, *Elihu Root* (2 vols., New York, 1938), II, 262–269.

31. Ray S. Baker and William E. Dodd, eds., *The Public Papers of Woodrow Wilson* (6 vols., New York, 1925–27), *The New Democracy*, I, 93.

32. Annual message of Dec. 3, 1912, quoted in Alfred W. Griswold, *The Far Eastern Policy of the United States* (New York, 1938), p. 134.

33. Quoted in Pringle, *Taft*, II, 682–683. Dollar Diplomacy was also practiced in other parts of the world, often with different emphasis on details. In Turkey, for instance, it did not seek to sustain existing American investments there or to preserve that country's integrity. Taft merely wanted a greater share of the commerce of the Near East for American businessmen. See Naomi W. Cohen, "Ambassador Straus in Turkey, 1909–1910: A Note on Dollar Diplomacy," *Mississippi Valley Historical Review*, XLV (March 1959), 632–642.

34. Lloyd C. Griscom, *Diplomatically Speaking* (Boston, 1940), p. 263. Some of the details on the Harriman plan are based on Richard T. Chang, "The Failure of the Katsura-Harriman Agreement," *The Journal of Asian Studies*, XXI (Nov. 1961), 65–76, an analysis that has made careful use of important Japanese sources.

35. See Raymond A. Esthus, "The Changing Concept of the Open Door, 1899–1910," *Mississippi Valley Historical Review*, XLVI (Dec. 1959), 440–441.

36. Quoted in Charles Vevier, *The United States and China, 1906–1913: A Study of Finance and Diplomacy* (New Brunswick, N.J., 1955), p. 49.

37. Phillips to Rockhill, July 16, 1908, *ibid.*, p. 72.

38. *Ibid.*, p. 115.

39. Esthus, in "Changing Concept of the Open Door," *Mississippi Valley Historical Review*, XLVI (Dec. 1959), 453, points out that Dollar Diplomacy was actually an expansion of the Open Door policy in that it "demanded equal investment as well as commercial opportunity." For a convenient summary, see Charles Vevier, "The Open Door: An Idea in Action, 1906–1913," *Pacific Historical Review*, XXIV (Feb. 1955), 49–62.

40. March 18, 1913, *Foreign Relations, 1913*, p. 170.

41. For details, see Meribeth E. Cameron, "American Recognition Policy Toward the Republic of China, 1912–1913," *Pacific Historical Review*, II (June 1933), 214–230.

42. To James D. Phelan, April 9, 1913, quoted in Arthur S. Link, *Woodrow Wilson and the Progressive Era, 1910–1917* (New York, 1954), p. 85.

43. Hiram Johnson, May 5, 1913, quoted in Arthur S. Link, *Wilson: The New Freedom* (Princeton, 1956), p. 296.

44. Sutemi Chinda to the Secretary of State, in *Foreign Relations, 1913*, pp. 629–631.

45. See Thomas A. Bailey, "California, Japan, and the Alien Land Legislation of 1913," *Pacific Historical Review*, I (1932), 55.

46. May 18, 1913, quoted in Link, *Wilson: The New Freedom*, pp. 299–300.

47. To Paul S. Reinsch, Nov. 4, 1914, in *Foreign Relations*, Supplement, *The World War*, p. 190. For an analysis of American concern over Japan's objectives in going to war, see Ernest R. May, "American Policy and Japan's Entrance into World War I," *Mississippi Valley Historical Review*, XL (Sept. 1953), 279–290.

48. The demands were embodied in the draft of a treaty proposed by Japan, the text of which is in *Foreign Relations, 1915*, pp. 93–95.

49. March 13, 1915, *ibid.*, p. 108. At this time Lansing was willing to make a bargain in which the United States would recognize Japan's special claims in return for concessions on the matter of the California land legislation. See Burton F. Beers, "Robert Lansing's Proposed Bargain with Japan," *Pacific Historical Review*, XXVI (Nov. 1957), 391–400.

50. To Bryan, April 14, 1915, quoted in Tien-yi Li, *Woodrow Wilson's China Policy, 1913–1917* (New York, 1952), p. 122.

51. May 11, 1915, in *Foreign Relations, 1915*, p. 146.

52. *Foreign Relations, The Lansing Papers, 1914–1920*, II, 450.

53. *Ibid.*, II, 446.

54. See Burton F. Beers, *Vain Endeavor: Robert Lansing's Attempts to End the American-Japanese Rivalry* (Durham, N.C., 1962), pp. 115–118.

Chapter Seventeen

MISSIONARY DIPLOMACY

As THEY had done in China, President Taft and Secretary of State Knox encouraged American bankers to invest in Latin America, particularly in the republics of the Caribbean area.[1] The objectives of their Dollar Diplomacy in the Caribbean differed from those in China, but had the same characteristics. In addition to advancing their own foreign policy, they wanted to help the people of the Caribbean by bringing them economic and political stability.

The republics of Central America and the Caribbean had always been turbulent, but their unrest had not threatened the strategic interest of the United States. As the Panama Canal neared completion, however, the United States became increasingly sensitive to any disturbances that might invite European nations to intervene to protect their investments in the canal area. So Taft and Knox, like Theodore Roosevelt, refused to tolerate disorders in the Caribbean.

Actually, the Taft administration went further in its interventions than had Roosevelt under his Corollary to the Monroe Doctrine. Taft tried to preserve order and prevent European intervention by placing pressure on the governments of the Caribbean countries to keep new European capital out and to force capital already there to leave. American dollars, with assurances of protection from the government, could then go into the republics. In theory, those countries would gain peace and stability, the United States government would forestall outside intervention in the sensitive canal area, and American investors would earn profits from their dollars.

Intervention in Nicaragua

Taft's intervention in Nicaragua offered the clearest example of his Dollar Diplomacy in action.[2] American investment in Nicaragua was small in comparison to that in some other Caribbean republics, but because of Nicaragua's proximity to the canal, the United States was particularly sensitive to any disturbance there. Yet, Nicaragua's ironfisted dictator, José Santos Zelaya, who had ruled since 1893, turned his country into the most turbulent of Central America. His ambition had been to dominate the five republics of Central America. From 1894 to 1908 he had led his country into a number of petty wars with its neighbors. In 1907 he invaded Honduras and removed her president; later, he endangered El Salvador and Guatemala. He also threatened American business investments in his country.

In May, 1909, Zelaya financed Nicaragua's entire debt through an international syndicate of European investors formed in London, and pledged the nation's customs income and other properties to the payment of the loan. This loan and Zelaya's general anti-Americanism suggested a willingness to turn Nicaragua's economy over to Europeans. If he failed to pay the debt, the Europeans had the right to take over the country's major source of revenue.

Several months later a revolution, apparently partly stimulated and financed by American firms, broke out against Zelaya. During the battles of the following month, Zelaya's forces captured and executed two Americans fighting with the insurgents. On December 1 Knox sent the Nicaraguan *chargé* in Washington a scorching note condemning Zelaya as a tyrant and his regime a "blot upon the history of Nicaragua."[3] Knox then dismissed the *chargé* and broke off relations with Zelaya's government. Since Zelaya realized he could not withstand the hostility of the United States, particularly the open aid it gave to the insurgents, he resigned a few weeks later and fled to Mexico.

The fighting continued, but by August, 1910, the insurgents had the country under control. The new president, Adolfo Díaz (a former bookkeeper of an American mining company in his country), who had the support of Americans in Nicaragua and of the Taft administration, turned to the United States for aid in stabilizing the republic's precarious finances. His Minister in Washington, Salvador Castrillo, signed a convention in June, 1911, with Knox that would have turned Nicaragua into an American protectorate if the agreement had been accepted by the United States Senate.[4]

The Knox-Castrillo Convention sought to create a stable currency by refunding the Nicaraguan debt with American loans and by pledging Nicaragua's customs revenues to the payment of the debt. Nicaragua agreed to place the administration of her customs houses during the life of the loan in the hands of an official approved by the President of the United States. This plan, it was hoped, would remove an incentive to revolution since the customs houses would no longer be one of the prizes of victory. Since American bankers would float the loan, it would also eliminate a main cause for intervention in behalf of European creditors.

So desperate was Nicaragua's plight that in less than a month after the signing of the convention, she defaulted her foreign debt contracted in 1909. American bankers encouraged by the Department of State, "unofficially" took over control of Nicaragua's finances. In September the bankers made a short-term loan to the Nicaraguan government, promised to negotiate some kind of a settlement with the European creditors, and set up a receivership for the customs. In December an American Army officer, approved by President Taft, took over as Nicaragua's collector of customs.

Since the Senate, in May, 1912, refused to approve the Knox-Castrillo Convention, the bankers continued their private customs receivership. In June they made an agreement with Nicaragua's European creditors, mostly British, whereby they would pay off the debt with part of the customs revenues. Taft and Knox thus maintained what was virtually a protectorate through private sources.

When a formidable revolt against Díaz broke out in July, imperilling the American investments, he asked for armed assistance. Maintaining that intervention was necessary to protect the lives and property of foreigners, the Taft administration landed over twenty-five hundred Marines and Bluejackets from eight warships in Nicaragua, crushed the revolt, and saved Díaz. The United States then stationed a warship and a legation guard of a hundred Marines in Nicaragua to discourage future revolutions.

Realizing that his Dollar Diplomacy was unpopular in Latin America, Knox had made a good will tour through most of the Caribbean republics in March. "I beg to assure you," he said in one speech, "and I am sure what I say meets with the approval of the people and President of the United States, that my Government does not covet an inch of territory south of the Rio Grande."[5] In view of his interventionist policy, Knox's words did little to win the trust of Latin Americans.

By the beginning of 1913 American control over Nicaragua was firm, but the republic's treasury remained shaky. Nicaragua, therefore, sought an alternative to the Knox-Castrillo Convention that might bolster her finances. In February she signed a treaty with the United States ceding potential naval bases and the exclusive right to build, control, and operate a canal through her territory in exchange for the small sum of three million dollars to pay her debts, but the United States Senate refused to approve the agreement.[6]

Honduras

Meanwhile, the same motives had led Taft to intervene in the affairs of other Central-American countries, all of whom, except El Salvador, had defaulted on their foreign debts. Since Knox feared that the European creditors might seize customs houses, he wanted to establish some form of control over the revenues of the Central-American republics.

While drawing up his unsuccessful convention with Nicaragua, Knox also tried to promote a reorganization of Honduras' finances. By 1909 Honduras' defaulted foreign debt, with accumulated interest, had become so large that it probably could never be repaid. After long negotiations the foreign creditors, mostly British, agreed to accept a few cents on the dollar from money Honduras would obtain from an American loan guaranteed by a customs collectorship. In January, 1911, Knox signed a treaty with Honduras establishing the collectorship, but both the Honduran congress and the American Senate rejected it. In Honduras, therefore, Knox's Dollar Diplomacy failed.

At that time Knox also expressed willingness to aid in financial reforms in all the Central-American countries, but the republics did not welcome his offer. In 1911, Costa Rica forestalled possible American intervention by making a new loan agreement with her European creditors. Guatemala's dictator, who had been particularly notorious in his treatment of foreign creditors, negotiated with a group of American bankers for a loan to refund his foreign debt. Despite the efforts of the Department of State in support of the agreement, it was never completed.

The Lodge Corollary

Another problem grew out of a commercial development in Mexico's isolated Baja California. On that province's west coast lay the large natural harbor of Magdalena Bay in which the United States had long been interested as a potential naval base, but had not exploited because the area around the bay lacked an adequate water supply. Nonetheless, a strong foreign naval power in possession of the bay would pose a threat to the security of California and to the Panama Canal.

In 1911 a group of Japanese in San Francisco offered to buy a large tract of land on the shores of Magdalena Bay, and a fishing concession, from an American company that owned them. Since it seemed that a Japanese colony at the bay, for whatever purpose, would endanger American security, particularly the canal, the Department of State ordered the American company to stop the negotiations because they violated the Monroe Doctrine.

In February, 1912, Henry Cabot Lodge, chairman of the Senate Committee on Foreign Relations, revived the issue of the alleged Japanese threat against Magdalena Bay. In a speech against Taft's arbitration treaties, he warned of "some great Eastern power" taking either direct or indirect possession of a harbor on Mexico's west coast for naval or military purposes. The Los Angeles *Examiner*, a Hearst newspaper, took up the theme of the Japanese threat by printing a "Tokio dispatch" revealing "practical completion of plans for establishment of a big Japanese colony at Magdalena Bay."[7] The Mexican government, on the following day, denied all rumors of Japan gaining a foothold in Baja California, and the Japanese government on April 6 firmly denied it had any interest in a settlement at the bay.

William Randolph Hearst, nonetheless, would not give up his concern over the "yellow peril." His Los Angeles newspaper chartered a steamer and sent three reporters and a photographer to Magdalena Bay to get "facts, and nothing but the facts." The reporters found two Japanese living near a fish cannery on an island off the bay.

Secretary Knox told Lodge that the charges in the press concerning Japanese intrigue were groundless and would likely injure relations with Japan. Yet Lodge insisted upon clarifying American policy toward colonization by foreign states where the "thin veil of a corporation does not alter the character of the act."[8] Though convinced that the Japanese government was not directly involved in the negotiations over Magdalena Bay, he and his committee decided that the Senate should declare its attitude on such negotiations.

On August 2, 1912, by a vote of fifty-one to four, the Senate adopted a resolution submitted by Lodge disapproving the transfer of harbors or other strategic sites in the Americas to any private company connected with a government outside the American continents.[9] That resolution, though it mentioned neither Japan nor the Monroe Doctrine, was significant because it extended the principles of the doctrine to an Asian power, specifically Japan, and to private companies having connections outside the Western Hemisphere.

Missionary Zeal

Since Woodrow Wilson and William Jennings Bryan had been critical of intervention in the Caribbean, Latin Americans had expected them to reverse Republican policy. Only a week after taking office Wilson denounced Dollar Diplomacy in the Caribbean. He went even further in the promise of a new Latin-American policy in a speech at Mobile, Alabama, in October, 1913. Speaking of a "spiritual union" between the American continents, he foresaw the day when foreign creditors would lose their grip on the Latin republics, and announced that "the United States will never again seek one additional foot of territory by conquest."[10]

The record of the Wilson administration in Latin-American affairs did not fit the pattern of the President's fine words. In the Caribbean and Mexico the commitments of the past and the inconsistencies of its own policies so entangled the administration's program that it carried out a series of interventions more extensive than any under Theodore Roosevelt and Taft.[11] Those interventions also grew out of an attitude of moral superiority and a missionary zeal to do good. Eager to help the peoples of the Caribbean republics and Mexico establish sound and stable governments, Wilson and Bryan thought of their interventions as actions in behalf of helpless friends they were trying to save from internal anarchy and foreign dangers.

If any country needed salvation according to the Wilson formula, it was Nicaragua. As soon as Wilson had taken office, the government of Adolfo Díaz tried to renegotiate the unsuccessful canal treaty it had made with Knox. The treaty that emerged from the new negotiations contained provisions similar to those of the Knox convention, but went further, giving the United States the right to intervene in Nicaragua in the same manner that the Platt Amendment had in Cuba. "If all goes well," a prominent newspaper commented, "we shall soon see the dawn of a new era in our Latin-American relations, but it will be due to a cheerful acceptance and an amplification by President Wilson's administration of the much-condemned Dollar Diplomacy of his predecessors." [12]

Since the Platt Amendment clause had aroused opposition in the Senate, the treaty that Bryan finally signed in August, 1914, with Emiliano Chamorro, Nicaragua's Minister in Washington, and that the Senate approved two years later, omitted the provision allowing American intervention. The removal did not in fact change American policy; the United States intervened virtually at will in Nicaragua's affairs. [13]

When Costa Rica, El Salvador, and Honduras all protested the Bryan-Chamorro Treaty as infringing on their rights, the United States ignored their objections. Under Wilson, as under Taft, therefore, the United States continued to control Nicaragua's finances, a control supported by a small occupation force of Marines.

The Dominican Republic

Conditions in the Dominican Republic, where for a number of years there had been relative stability under the United States customs receivership established in 1907, also offered the Wilson administration an opportunity to advance its Latin-American policy. In September, 1913, another revolution broke out. Even though the United States supported the government in power, the rebels triumphed almost everywhere.

By the summer of 1914 conditions became so bad that Wilson intervened. He arranged an armistice and sent a commission to the republic to investigate. The commission suggested certain reforms, and Secretary Bryan urged the Dominicans to grant the United States control over all finances and the armed forces, a greater power over their country than the treaty of 1907 allowed.

Meanwhile, the commission worked out a plan whereby elections under American supervision were held in November. One of the revolutionary leaders was elected president, but his rule proved unsatisfactory, and revolution erupted again in May, 1916. After repeated warnings that the United States would not stand for the continued state of armed anarchy, American Marines landed and occupied the capital city.

The United States then insisted on a treaty giving it control of the republic's finances and armed forces, but the Dominicans refused. The Marines, therefore, took over the entire country by November and established a military government.

In authorizing military rule, Wilson said he did it "with the deepest reluctance," but had to do it because he was "convinced that it is the least of the evils in sight in this very perplexing situation." [14] The customs receivership remained in effect, but it now turned over its revenues to the American military governor who exercised all the functions of government, as though he were president. At one time he even exchanged diplomatic correspondence with the United States.

Although there was some armed resistance to the occupation, on the whole it brought stability to the country. Yet, it was a peace based on naked force that fostered among Dominicans a deep-seated distrust of the United States.

The Haitian Protectorate

Violence, revolution, and Wilson's missionary zeal also brought American bayonets to Haiti. Various foreign governments had several times landed troops there to protect their nationals during disturbances. Hoping to stabilize finances and forestall further European intervention, the Department of State asked the Haitians to sign a treaty in July, 1914, giving the United States control of the customs. In December continued disturbances led Marines to take a half million dollars from a Haitian bank controlled by Americans to a United States warship to keep it from falling into the hands of Haiti's latest dictator.

In January, 1915, another revolution brought more chaos. Agreeing that they could not long postpone intervention, Wilson and Bryan sent a commission to negotiate a treaty giving them a naval base and control of the customs. Before the commission arrived in Haiti, a new government under General Vilbrun Guillaume Sam came to power. Sam refused to negotiate. In fact, it soon became clear that no Haitian government would willingly agree to the extensive control of the republic the United States desired. Force appeared the only way to gain such control, a policy Bryan was reluctant to follow.

After Bryan had resigned, a new revolution presented the United States with an excuse for intervention. President Sam brutally executed some 167 political prisoners. In furious retaliation, the people of Port-au-Prince dragged him from the French legation, where he had fled for sanctuary, and tore his body to pieces in the streets.

That bloody violence temporarily ended Haiti's independence. That afternoon, July 28, 1915, Marines and Bluejackets swarmed ashore and occupied Port-au-Prince. More troops came later and occupied the entire country. Since the *cacos*, professional fighters, retreated to the mountains and fought the occupation, the pacification became a war of extermination. Before the war ended, American troops had slaughtered over two thousand of the resisting Haitians.

Meanwhile, an American admiral took over control of Haiti's government, and the State Department forced a treaty on the Haitians that established a tighter control over them than the United States had imposed on any other Caribbean country, including Cuba. That treaty, signed on September 16, was to run for twenty years, gave the United States command of Haiti's finances, armed forces, public works, foreign affairs, and the right to intervene in other ways to preserve Haiti's independence. The Senate approved it in February, 1916, without a dissenting vote.

Two years later, through a controversial new constitution, the United States tried to perpetuate the reforms it had introduced. The Haitians approved the new constitution in a plebiscite conducted by American Marines, but it failed to bring true stability and democratic government to Haiti.[15]

Wilson's Pan-American League

The Wilson administration's missionary diplomacy in the Caribbean differed from the Dollar Diplomacy of Taft and Knox primarily in its motivation. Bryan was willing to use dollars to advance foreign policy, but mainly as a substitute for his predecessor's direct Dollar Diplomacy. In August, 1913, he had suggested lending money from the federal treasury to Nicaragua and to other Latin-American countries at a low rate of interest to help in freeing them from the control of European creditors. Bryan's plan seemed too bold to the President, and he turned it down. Even though the United States may have feared it, there was actually no real danger of serious European intervention in the Caribbean during the Wilson years.

Wilson and Bryan, despite their reliance on force, hoped that their policies would lead to peace and unity in all the Americas. Wilson himself took the lead in trying to bind the countries of the Western Hemisphere together in a Pan-American league in which they would agree to settle all their disputes by peaceful means and would guarantee each other's territorial integrity and political independence "under republican forms of government."

A leader in the peace movement had proposed such a treaty in 1910, as had the Colombian government in 1912, but the Taft administration had paid no attention to the proposal. Wilson, however, liked the idea. In December, 1914, therefore, the Department of State drafted a treaty and circulated it among Latin-American governments.[16] Colonel Edward M. House, Wilson's personal adviser, saw the treaty as a model for the warring nations of Europe to copy when peace came. Brazil, Argentina, and at least six of the smaller Latin republics supported the pact, but Chile, fearing that under it she might lose lands she had conquered from Peru, opposed it, and the treaty failed.

Some students of Latin-American relations have seen Wilson's Latin-American policy, particularly his proposed Pan-American pact, as marking a new day in relations with the southern republics. There is, however, little evidence to support the view that Wilson was willing to change national policy in the Caribbean or to renounce the so-called right of intervention, despite his support of the idealistic Pan-American treaty.[17]

The Danish West Indies

Although it did not directly involve the Latin republics, Wilson's purchase of the Danish West Indies, now called the Virgin Islands, was another facet of his Caribbean policy. Some Americans had long feared that Denmark would sell her Caribbean islands to some other more powerful European power, particularly Germany, and that fear increased after the outbreak of the First World War. Secretary of State Robert Lansing told Denmark in the summer of 1916 that the United States would seize the islands if German control appeared imminent. Therefore, in a treaty signed on August 4, Denmark agreed to sell her possessions for twenty-five million dollars.

The United States willingly paid five times more than it had offered for the three small impoverished islands in 1902 to keep them from falling into German hands, even though, because of other American holdings in the Caribbean, they were now of no real value as a naval base. As Lansing pointed out, their purchase was a kind of strategic insurance for the security of the Panama Canal.

The Mexican Revolution

More perplexing than the problems of the Caribbean, were developments in Mexico. In fact, they constituted Wilson's main concern in foreign affairs until the war in Europe came to absorb most of his attention by the summer of 1915. Wilson's missionary diplomacy launched its most drastic intervention against Mexico, again with the idea of establishing a democratic government that would help an oppressed people meet pressing economic and social needs.

The Mexican problem began in 1911 when a revolution led by Francisco I. Madero, a young reformer educated in France and briefly at the University of California, overthrew the entrenched dictatorship of Porfirio Díaz. Madero planned to destroy the old order of privileges for the few, including foreign investors, and to reconstitute Mexican society on a new democratic base. Madero's leading general, Victoriano Huerta, betrayed him and led a successful counter-

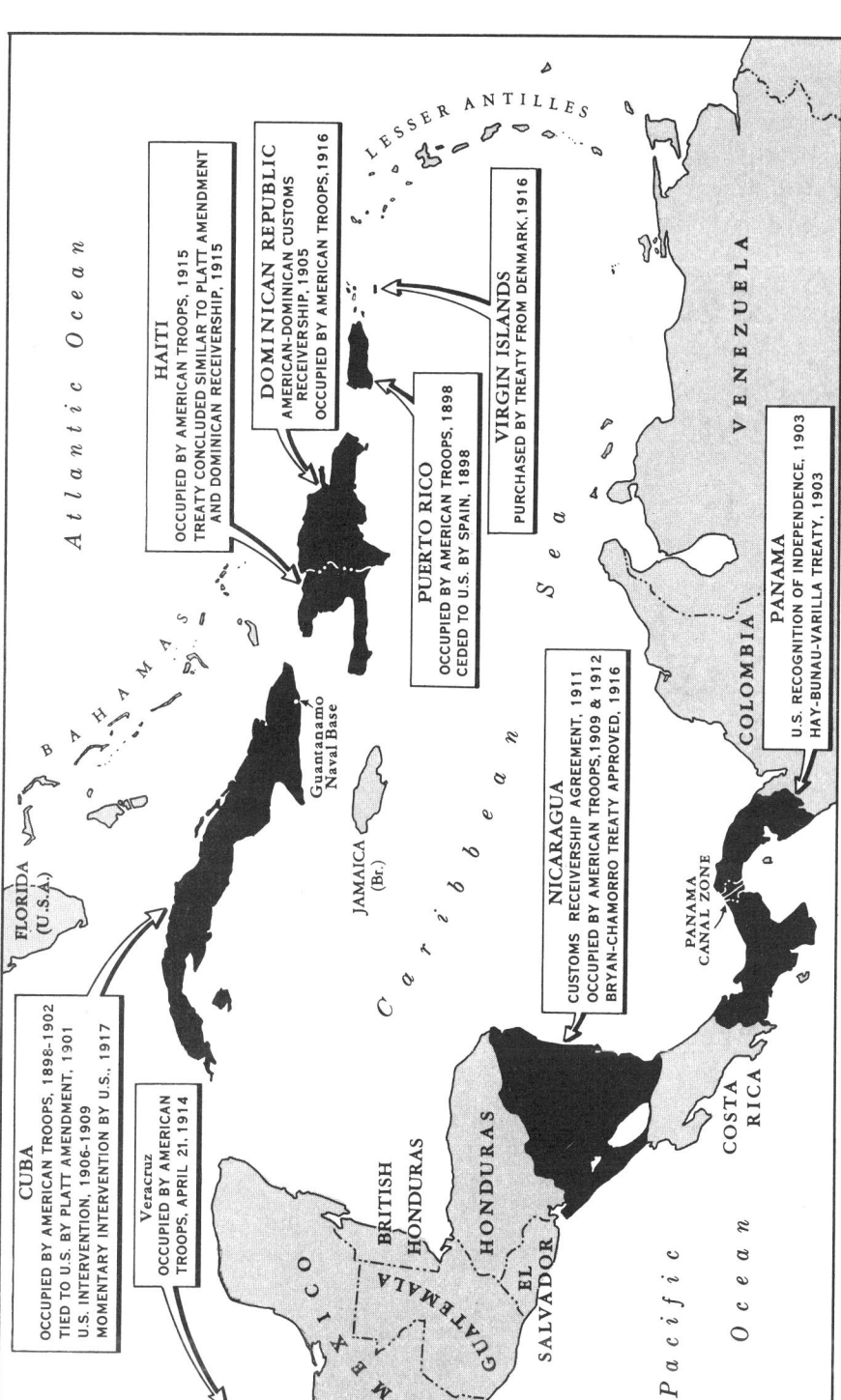

CUBA
OCCUPIED BY AMERICAN TROOPS, 1898-1902
TIED TO U.S. BY PLATT AMENDMENT, 1901
U.S. INTERVENTION, 1906-1909
MOMENTARY INTERVENTION BY U.S., 1917

Veracruz
OCCUPIED BY AMERICAN
TROOPS, APRIL 21, 1914

HAITI
OCCUPIED BY AMERICAN TROOPS, 1915
TREATY CONCLUDED SIMILAR TO PLATT AMENDMENT
AND DOMINICAN RECEIVERSHIP, 1915

DOMINICAN REPUBLIC
AMERICAN-DOMINICAN CUSTOMS
RECEIVERSHIP, 1905
OCCUPIED BY AMERICAN TROOPS, 1916

PUERTO RICO
OCCUPIED BY AMERICAN TROOPS, 1898
CEDED TO U.S. BY SPAIN, 1898

VIRGIN ISLANDS
PURCHASED BY TREATY FROM DENMARK, 1916

NICARAGUA
CUSTOMS RECEIVERSHIP AGREEMENT, 1911
OCCUPIED BY AMERICAN TROOPS, 1909 & 1912
BRYAN-CHAMORRO TREATY APPROVED, 1916

PANAMA
U.S. RECOGNITION OF INDEPENDENCE, 1903
HAY-BUNAU-VARILLA TREATY, 1903

Guantanamo
Naval Base

PANAMA
CANAL ZONE

FLORIDA
(U.S.A.)

B A H A M A S

JAMAICA
(Br.)

MEXICO

BRITISH
HONDURAS

GUATEMALA

HONDURAS

EL
SALVADOR

COSTA
RICA

COLOMBIA

VENEZUELA

LESSER ANTILLES

Atlantic Ocean

Caribbean Sea

Pacific Ocean

THE AMERICAN EMPIRE IN THE CARIBBEAN, 1898–1917

revolution against him. Although he denied it, Huerta apparently ordered Madero murdered in February, 1913, an act that shocked Americans.

Henry Lane Wilson, the American Ambassador in Mexico City, urged President Taft to recognize Huerta's government, but Taft would not until Huerta promised concessions in several American disputes with Mexico. Other countries, among them Britain, France, and Germany, recognized Huerta's government.[18]

As soon as Woodrow Wilson became President, Ambassador Wilson and others within the Department of State advised him to recognize Huerta's regime, pointing out correctly that the United States had usually extended *de facto* recognition to revolutionary governments. Believing that if he recognized Huerta he would be encouraging assassination throughout Latin America, the President departed from the traditional recognition policy. He advanced the doctrine that the United States would not recognize governments that came to power by force against the peoples' will and in violation of their country's constitution. "I will not recognize a government of butchers," he said privately of Huerta's regime.[19]

Huerta, moreover, did not control all of Mexico. On the day after he proclaimed himself provisional president, General Venustiano Carranza, a follower of Madero, began a new revolt in northern Mexico. Carranza and his followers, calling themselves Constitutionalists, swore to depose Huerta and to re-establish constitutional government.

President Wilson decided that Huerta must go, and offered to "mediate" the war in such a way as to eliminate Huerta. In August, 1913, he sent John Lind, a former Democratic governor of Minnesota acting as his personal agent, to Huerta to ask him to hold a fair election in which he would not be a candidate so that a constitutional government the United States could recognize would come to power. Wilson also sent a circular note to the powers asking them to urge Huerta to accept American mediation of the civil war. Huerta refused Wilson's demands. "I will resist with arms," he said, "any attempt by the United States to interfere in the affairs of Mexico."[20]

Although not a serious threat, Huerta's outburst did represent the views of many Mexicans. Their country was not Nicaragua or the Dominican Republic; Wilson could not rule it through a puppet government supported by a few hundred Marines. Yet Huerta gave Lind the impression that he would before long give up the presidency of Mexico, which was essentially what Wilson desired.

On August 27 Wilson went before a joint session of Congress and explained his policy toward Mexico. It was up to Huerta, he pointed out, to accept American mediation, and hence to resign. He would, Wilson said, pursue a patient policy of nonintervention and watchful waiting while "forbidding the exportation of arms or munitions of war of any kind" to either side in the Mexican civil war.[21]

Huerta soon showed he had no intention of abdicating. In October his troops dispersed the congress and clamped a military dictatorship on Mexico. That new act of violence shocked Wilson. He sent a circular note to governments with representatives in Mexico asking them to withhold recognition from Huerta. Two weeks later he warned those governments that he would use whatever means were necessary to force Huerta from office. For six months Wilson now did all he could, short of war, to depose Huerta. His plan was simple and direct. He tried to isolate the dictator diplomatically and encouraged the Constitutionalists in their war against him.

Wilson exerted his greatest pressure against the British, forcing them, in effect, to choose between American friendship and the Mexican oil they needed for their fleet. Since war in Europe seemed imminent and Wilson's good will would be worth more than Mexico's oil, the British government withdrew its support from Huerta.

To hasten Huerta's fall, Wilson at one time even considered joint action between American forces and those of Carranza, but Carranza did not want American support. All he sought was recognition of his belligerent status and the privilege that went with it of buying arms from the United States.

Since Wilson found that he had either to allow the Constitutionalists to obtain arms or carry out his threats to depose Huerta with American troops, he recognized the belligerency of the Constitutionalists and in February, 1914, revoked the arms embargo against them. His action actually strengthened Huerta. Many Mexicans who were formerly apathetic now rallied behind the dictator as the symbol of resistance to American domination. Force, which Wilson had been reluctant to use, now seemed to offer the only way of toppling Huerta.

Bloodshed at Veracruz

An incident at Tampico on April 9 gave Wilson the excuse. A whaleboat with seven sailors and one officer from the u.s.s. *Dolphin*, a warship, went ashore without permission behind Huerta's Federalist lines to buy gasoline. A Federalist colonel arrested the Americans. When the Federalist commander in the area learned of the arrest, he immediately released the Americans and sent a personal apology to Admiral Henry T. Mayo, commander of the American Squadron off Tampico, explaining that his subordinate had made a mistake.

The apology might have ended any further difficulty if Wilson had not decided to use it as a means of overthrowing Huerta. Admiral Mayo, on his own initiative, immediately demanded a twenty-one gun salute to the American flag, and the President supported the ultimatum. They thus converted a petty incident to an affront against national honor. Ironically, Wilson demanded the discharge of an international obligation from a government he would not recognize. Huerta resisted, saying he would salute only if the United States returned volley for volley.

Meanwhile, Wilson had ordered the North Atlantic battleship fleet to Tampico and on the afternoon of April 20 asked Congress for authority to use the armed forces. If war should come, he said, it would be only against "General Huerta and those who adhere to him and give him their support," not against the Mexican people.[22]

While Congress debated the President's request, news reached Washington that the German steamer *Ypiranga* was headed for Veracruz with a cargo of guns and ammunition for Huerta. Wilson decided to substitute the seizure of Veracruz for naval action at Tampico and immediately ordered the Navy to seize the customs house at Veracruz to prevent the entry of the munitions. Mexican naval cadets and soldiers offered a determined resistance. The dead and wounded, mostly Mexican, totaled over four hundred. The Americans took control of the entire city on April 22, and on the next day Congress authorized the use of armed forces.

Since Wilson insisted that he had invaded Veracruz to avenge a personal insult, but really had done it to hasten Huerta's downfall, few people understood why he had acted as he did. On the surface he appeared willing to start a war over a dubious point of honor. A London journal expressed the point well. "If war is to be made on points of punctilio raised by admirals and generals," it said, "and if the Government of the United States is to set the example for this return to mediaeval conditions it will be a bad day for civilization."[23]

Throughout Latin America, newspapers generally condemned the occupation of Veracruz as more evidence of imperialism, and mobs demonstrated against it. Even Carranza, a proud nationalist who hated Huerta, denounced it as foreign aggression. Most North Americans, apparently, did not approve the seizure and deplored the possibility of war. The thought of war also appalled Wilson, so he halted further offensive operations. "We have been in a blind alley so long," he wrote to a friend, "that I am longing for an exit."[24]

Argentina, Brazil, and Chile then stepped in with a timely offer to mediate the conflict. When Wilson and Huerta accepted their offer, most Americans were relieved. In agreeing to negotiate with a government he would not recognize, however, Wilson again acted inconsistently. That made little difference to the delegates of the ABC powers and the United States who met with representatives from Huerta's government at Niagara Falls, Canada, from May 18 to July 2. Since Carranza refused to send a delegation, permit Wilson to mediate the civil war, or allow the Niagara delegates to determine the fate of Mexico's revolution, the conference accomplished nothing except to extricate Wilson from a difficult position.[25]

Two weeks later, with his regime crumbling under pressure from Wilson and the blows of his internal foes, Huerta resigned. A month later Carranza's forces entered Mexico City, but the Constitutionalist coalition fell apart almost immediately, and Mexico plunged into three more years of civil war. One of the leading Constitutionalist generals, an illiterate former bandit named Francisco Villa, drove Carranza from Mexico City and took over the government. In

August the Wilson administration shifted its support to Villa, but Carranza fought back and in February, 1915, returned to Mexico City. Meanwhile, Wilson switched to a policy of neutrality, insisting that the Mexicans should settle their own problems in their own way.

Yet within the United States, pressure for intervention mounted rapidly. The Hearst papers, the hierarchy of the Catholic Church, Theodore Roosevelt, and others, all clamored for intervention to stop the loss of American life and property and attacks against the church. In June, therefore, Wilson again interfered by asking the Mexican leaders to compose their differences and stop their fighting. Carranza denied his right to meddle.

At the same time growing friction with Germany over the use of the submarine led administration leaders to try to avoid any overt action that would lead to war with Mexico. The new Secretary of State, Robert Lansing, turned to several Latin-American states for help in settling the Mexican civil war. In August, he began a series of conferences with the six ranking Latin-American envoys in Washington, representing Argentina, Brazil, Chile, Bolivia, Guatemala, and Uruguay, who appealed to the various Mexican leaders to compose their differences, but Carranza refused. Since he controlled most of Mexico and was growing stronger, Wilson and Lansing decided to recognize him. The United States and the six states of the Pan-American Conference formally recognized Carranza's regime as the *de facto* government of Mexico in October.[26]

Relations with Carranza's government went relatively smoothly for several months, but Villa, who resented the recognition of Carranza, soon turned on his former friends and tried to embroil the United States in a war with Mexico. He hoped to return to power as a national hero fighting to prevent American conquest. On January 10, 1916, he stopped a train at Santa Ysabel in northern Mexico, removed seventeen young American engineers, and shot sixteen of them on the spot. Two months later he sent some four hundred raiders into Columbus, New Mexico. They shot everybody in sight, killing nineteen Americans, and burned the town.

The Pershing Expedition

The demand for military intervention then became so strong that Wilson could not resist it. Since Carranza's government was incapable of preventing Villa's outrages, orders went out to military commanders in Texas to prepare an expedition to pursue Villa into Mexico. Lansing negotiated a protocol with Mexico's representative in Washington on March 13 allowing the United States and Mexico in the future to pursue bandits across the international boundary. Two days later a punitive expedition, under the command of Brigadier General John J. Pershing, crossed the border, but with explicit orders not to attack Carranza's forces.

Pershing's force grew to more than six thousand men and penetrated more than

INTERVENTION IN MEXICO, 1914–1917

three hundred miles into Mexico in pursuit of the elusive Villa. Since Carranza had thought only in terms of small forces with limited striking power, he expressed alarm at the size and strength of Pershing's expedition and began diplomatic action almost immediately to force Pershing to withdraw.

In April an incident almost touched off war and prevented Pershing from retreating quietly. At the town of Parral, some 180 miles inside Mexico, American and Mexican soldiers exchanged fire, leaving forty Mexicans and two Americans dead. Mexican opinion now became so hostile to the American expedition that Carranza could not remain in power without taking steps to compel its withdrawal. Wilson would not retreat, but fortunately the generals in the field worked out a temporary compromise that prevented war.

In May, Villistas raided the little town of Glen Springs, Texas, killing three soldiers and a boy. When Wilson sent a new detachment into Mexico in pursuit of the raiders, Carranza concluded that a showdown must come and demanded the withdrawal of Pershing's forces under the threat of war. He then instructed his generals to prevent any new expeditions from entering Mexico and to resist Pershing's force if it moved in any direction but north toward the border. On June 18 Wilson called out the entire National Guard and incorporated it into the Army, and made other preparations for war. Two days later Secretary Lansing told the Mexican government that the United States would not recall its troops and warned that any attack on them would "lead to the gravest consequences."[27]

The next day, only a few hours after Lansing's message reached Mexico City, Mexican and American troops clashed again, at a place called Carrizal. Both sides suffered casualties. This appeared to be the final incident that would precipitate war. Wilson accused the Mexicans of deliberately attacking the Americans, which was not so, and even prepared a war message, but never delivered it. Neither he nor Carranza wanted war. The Mexican leader released the twenty-three American prisoners his troops had captured at Carrizal.

Realizing that the approaching crisis with Germany was more serious, Wilson pleaded for peace. "Do you think the glory of America would be enhanced by a war of conquest in Mexico?" he asked on July 1.[28] Three days later Carranza asked either for direct negotiations or Latin-American mediation to end the tension. Since Lansing and Wilson preferred the direct negotiations, a joint high commission met in New London, Connecticut, in September and broke up in acrimony in January, 1917. Although it failed to settle the controversy, it helped preserve the peace.[29]

Since no issue vital to the security of the United States was at stake in Mexico, and since involvement in the European war seemed probable in the near future, Wilson decided to withdraw Pershing's troops to Texas. By the first week of February the last of the punitive expedition had left Mexico and the danger of a possibly tragic war was over.

Mexico, meantime, had drawn up a new constitution and in March had elected Carranza president. The United States extended immediate *de jure* recognition by sending an ambassador. Mexico's revolution finally established a broad new social order and in time firm constitutional government. Historians still debate whether Wilson's meddling helped or hindered that revolution in achieving its objectives.

NOTES

1. In "Battleship Diplomacy in South America, 1905–1925," *Journal of Modern History*, XVI (March 1944), 31–48, Seward W. Livermore points out that Taft and Knox also used the Navy Department to advance their Dollar Diplomacy, essentially for the benefit of armament-makers and shipbuilders who wished to sell their wares in South America.

2. The best account is Dana G. Munro, "Dollar Diplomacy in Nicaragua, 1909–1913," *Hispanic American Historical Review*, XXXVIII (Feb. 1958), 209–238.

3. The text is in *Foreign Relations, 1909*, pp. 455–457.

4. For the Convention, see *ibid., 1912*, pp. 1074–1075.

5. Quoted in Herbert F. Wright, "Philander Chase Knox," in Samuel F. Bemis, ed., *The American Secretaries of State and Their Diplomacy* (10 vols., New York, 1927–29), IX, 339.

6. For background details, see Roscoe R. Hill, "The Nicaraguan Canal Idea to 1913," *Hispanic American Historical Review*, XXVIII (May 1948), 197–211.

7. April 1, 1912, quoted in Eugene K. Chamberlin, "The Japanese Scare at Magdalena Bay," *Pacific Historical Review*, XXIV (November 1955), 354.

8. *Ibid.*, p. 358.

9. The resolution is printed in Thomas A. Bailey, "The Lodge Corollary to the Monroe Doctrine," *Political Science Quarterly*, XLVIII (June 1933), 223–224. Daniel Cosío Villegas, Montgomery Lecturer at the University of Nebraska, 1960, has summarized American-Mexican diplomacy concerning Magdalena Bay in a scholarly paper, "Magdalena Bay: An Historical Lesson" (mimeographed).

10. The text, dated Oct. 27, 1913, is in Ray S. Baker and William E. Dodd, eds., *The Public Papers of Woodrow Wilson* (6 vols., New York, 1925–27), *The New Democracy*, I, 64–69.

11. Intervention in the Caribbean, in fact, reached its apogee under Wilson, who has been called "the greatest interventionist in the history of the United States." See Samuel F. Bemis, "Woodrow Wilson and Latin America," in Edward H. Buehrig, ed., *Wilson's Foreign Policy in Perspective* (Bloomington, Ind., 1957), pp. 129, 137.

12. *The New York Times*, July 21, 1913, quoted in Arthur S. Link, *Wilson: The New Freedom* (Princeton, 1956), p. 336.

13. See Selig Adler, "Bryan and Wilsonian Caribbean Penetration," *Hispanic American Historical Review*, XX (May 1940), 216–217. Adler also points out that Wilsonian Caribbean policy originated mainly with Bryan.

For additional details on the Bryan-Chamorro treaty, see Thomas A. Bailey, "Interest in a Nicaragua Canal, 1903–1931," *Hispanic American Historical Review*, XVI (Feb. 1936), 3–13.

14. To Secretary of State, Nov. 26, 1916, in *Foreign Relations, 1916*, p. 242.

15. At one time Franklin D. Roosevelt, then Assistant Secretary of the Navy, claimed that he had drafted that constitution, but he was not in fact its father. See Frank Freidel, *Franklin D. Roosevelt: The Apprenticeship* (Boston, 1952), pp. 283–284.

16. The draft articles of the treaty are printed in Bemis, "Woodrow Wilson and Latin America" in Buehrig, ed., *Wilson's Foreign Policy*, pp. 132–134.

17. For details, see Charles H. Carlisle, "Woodrow Wilson's Pan-American Pact," *South Carolina Historical Association Proceedings*, XIX (1949), 3–15.

18. For details, see Stanley R. Ross, *Francisco I. Madero: Apostle of Mexican Democracy* (New York, 1955), 293–340. Ross details the extent of Ambassador Wilson's dabbling in Mexican politics and his part in Madero's overthrow.

19. Quoted in Howard F. Cline, *The United States and Mexico* (Cambridge, Mass., 1953), p. 144.

20. Aug. 9, 1913, quoted in Arthur S. Link, *Woodrow Wilson and the Progressive Era, 1910–1917* (New York, 1954), p. 113.

21. The message is in Baker and Dodd, *Wilson Papers, New Democracy*, I, 45–51.

22. *Ibid.*, I, 101.

23. *Economist*, April 18, 1914, quoted in Link, *Woodrow Wilson and the Progressive Era*, p. 124.

24. To Dr. Jacobus, April 29, 1914, quoted in Ray S. Baker, *Woodrow Wilson: Life and Letters* (8 vols., Garden City, N.Y., 1927–39), IV, 335.

25. For details, see Robert E. Quirk, *The Mexican Revolution, 1914–1915* (Blooming-

ton, Ind., 1960), p. 46, and especially his *An Affair of Honor: Woodrow Wilson and the Occupation of Veracruz* (Lexington, Kentucky, 1962).

26. Louis G. Kahle, in "Robert Lansing and the Recognition of Venustiano Carranza," *Hispanic American Historical Review*, XXXVIII (Aug. 1958), 353–372, stresses that the United States recognized Carranza because the pressures of the war in Europe compelled Wilson to seek some kind of a solution for the Mexican problem.

27. To Secretary of Foreign Relations, June 20, 1916, in *Foreign Relations, 1916*, p. 591.

28. Quoted in Link, *Woodrow Wilson and the Progressive Era*, p. 143.

29. Since the conference averted what appeared to be an inevitable war, Clarence C. Clendenen calls it a success. See his *The United States and Pancho Villa: A Study in Unconventional Diplomacy* (Ithaca, N.Y., 1961), p. 285.

Chapter Eighteen

PITFALLS OF NEUTRALITY

On June 28, 1914, while Wilson sought to avoid war with Mexico in the Niagara Falls Conference, a Serbian nationalist, at Sarajevo in the province of Bosnia (now a part of Yugoslavia), assassinated Archduke Franz Ferdinand, heir to the throne of Austria-Hungary. Few Americans realized that the revolver shots in that distant Balkan province would lead to a world war. Since Austria was determined to crush Serbian nationalism. she served an ultimatum on Serbia that started the war. By August 12 the major *Entente* powers, France, Great Britain, and Russia, later joined by Japan and Italy, were at war with the principal Central Powers, Germany and Austria-Hungary, joined later by Bulgaria and Turkey.

Sympathy for the Allies

The actual outbreak of war stunned most Americans. Numbed by previous European crises, they could hardly believe that war had truly come. They were, however, grateful that the fighting was remote and apparently not vital to their interests. The United States, they believed, could remain aloof. It was, Wilson said, "a war with which we have nothing to do, whose causes cannot touch us. ..." [1] He promptly issued formal declarations of neutrality and also offered to mediate the conflict, but the belligerents refused. [2] Two weeks later he appealed to Americans not to take sides. "We must," he said, "be impartial in thought as well as in action. ..." [3]

Although most Americans did not want to become involved in the fighting they and their government soon found it impossible to be impartial. As Britain and Germany, the major maritime belligerents, fought desperately to destroy each other, the United States saw that any action it took against one of them in defense of its rights would benefit the other. If it acquiesced in the maritime restrictions of one belligerent, it would injure the other. As the war went on, it became clear that whatever the United States did or perhaps did not do, because of its power and resources, could mean the difference between victory or defeat for either side. American neutrality, therefore, had a deep significance not only for the American people but also for the peoples of the world.

The United States hoped to trade with all the warring powers, subject to the usual rules of war, and relied on traditional international law to safeguard its rights. It generally observed its technical obligations as a neutral but encountered trouble in enforcing its neutral rights as it understood them.

One reason for American difficulties was that not since the Declaration of Paris of 1856 had the powers recodified international maritime law. In 1914, therefore, maritime law contained rules of conduct that were outmoded. Its rules defining contraband of war and blockade, for example, were based on a relationship between neutrals and belligerents that had prevailed before the industrial era. Powerful sovereign states, recognizing no authority higher than their own and fighting for survival, refused to be bound by those old rules when they ran contrary to their own interests. Neutrality ceased to have the same meaning as in the past.

At the expense of traditional neutral rights, belligerents expanded their own rights in technical violation of international law of the nineteenth century. Fighting in an era when a nation needed to mobilize its total resources to survive, they destroyed the old idea that war could be limited to combatants. Ironically, the United States found itself forced to rely on traditional neutral rights precisely when they were undergoing radical change.

Another reason why the United States found neutrality a burden was the attitude of the American people toward the belligerents. Americans were never impartial; most of them favored the Allied powers. Ties of blood, language, and culture bound many of them to England, and England's careful cultivation of American friendship since the end of the nineteenth century had made the bond stronger than ever. Sentimental ties of friendship dating back to the Revolutionary War drew many Americans to France. One popular poem, for instance, reminded them of their sympathy for France.

> Give us a name to fill the mind
> With stirring thoughts that lead mankind,
>   *   *   *   *
> A name like a star, a name of light.
> I give you *France*![4]

Although Americans of Irish and German ancestry generally favored the Central Powers, Germany had been unpopular with Americans since the 1880's. They distrusted the German government, considering it unprincipled and militaristic.

Germany, a Salt Lake City newspaper said, will have to "bear the responsibility for opening another era of carnage." [5] This, apparently, was a common attitude. Later, Germany's crushing of Belgian neutrality, her deportation of Belgian civilians for labor in Germany, and her other violations of traditionally accepted standards of international conduct, all added to popular resentment against the Central Powers and hence increased American sympathy for their enemies.

Since immigrants in the United States and first generation descendants of immigrant parents still had close ties with friends and relatives in the belligerent countries, the war divided their loyalties. Yet, the pattern of opinion toward the belligerents among these "new" Americans was about the same as among the older elements of the population. According to the census figures of 1910, the "new" Americans accounted for about 35 per cent of the total population, or approximately 32 million out of a total population of 92 million. Only 9 per cent of them were German and only 3 per cent were Austrian. Few others, except some of the Irish, sympathized with the Central Powers. Sentiment for the Allies among the foreign-born, however, did not preponderate until after Italy joined the Allies in 1915. Like those of English ancestry, those Americans of continental European ancestry felt the pull of blood and culture but were unable to influence policy directly because they had meager political power.

Those who made and influenced foreign policy within the Wilson administration reflected the popular support for the Allies, except that they were generally more strongly pro-Ally and anti-German in their sentiments than were other Americans. Wilson's cabinet, except for Secretary of State Bryan, favored the

PRO-ALLIED SENTIMENT

This cartoon, with the caption, "What Will you Give For Her," reflected American hostility toward Germany and sympathy for Belgium.

Allies. Robert Lansing, the Counselor for the Department of State, and Colonel Edward M. House, Wilson's personal adviser, were pro-British, as were most of the ambassadors at important posts. Walter Hines Page, the Ambassador to England, believed so intensely that nothing was as important as friendship with England, that the President in time had to discount his dispatches as being little more than British propaganda.

Wilson himself favored the British, but struggled within himself to think and act impartially. Although there is no evidence to support the view that Wilson's personal sympathy for the British controlled the development of his foreign policy, Sir Cecil Spring-Rice, the British Ambassador in the United States, could write that "all the State Department are on our side except Bryan who is incapable of forming a settled judgment on anything outside party politics. The President will be with us by birth and upbringing. . . ."[6]

Neither the President nor the American people were so devoted to the Allied cause that they were willing to fight by the side of the Allies. Most Americans wanted a policy of neutrality that would keep their country at peace.

Neutral Rights

Controversies with the belligerents over neutral rights, mainly those of trade and travel by sea, began shortly after the war started. Britain and Germany tried to throttle all maritime trade with their enemies. Each violated international law and American rights, but each, until 1917, tried to keep her violations from injuring the United States so seriously that it would intervene.

Almost all of the early troubles over neutral rights were with the British. Although the Germans had entered the war better prepared, hoping for a quick victory, Britain had the advantage in the maritime war. Her superior navy gave her control of the seas and access to the strategic materials of the world outside of Europe.

As soon as the war broke out, the United States anticipated difficulties in trying to carry on its export trade. Seeking to avoid misunderstandings, Bryan asked the belligerents to govern their conduct by the rules of the Declaration of London that had grown out of an international naval conference held in 1909.[7] Although the declaration represented a codification of the law of the sea as generally accepted at the time, the British felt that on certain controversial points, on contraband and blockade for example, it favored neutrals and small navy powers over belligerents with a large navy. Hence the House of Lords had rejected it, and the other powers therefore had refused to adhere to it. When the war broke out, as a result, the declaration was not in force and traditional international law prevailed.

In response to Bryan, the Central Powers said they would abide by the rules of the declaration if the Allies would. Since the British believed that unrestricted adherence would nullify their naval superiority, Sir Edward Grey, Britain's Foreign Minister, so qualified his country's acceptance as virtually to reject Bryan's request.

Through a series of Orders in Council, starting on August 20, Britain expanded her contraband lists so that she could intercept most goods headed for Germany, whether directly or through neutral countries. Ultimately she stopped almost all maritime trade with Germany through a broad interpretation of the doctrine of continuous voyage and by wiping out practically all distinction between contraband and non-contraband.

Since the British began almost immediately to interfere with American shipments to Germany and neighboring neutral countries, Counselor Lansing in the Department of State prepared a note in September for Wilson's signature specifying the legal rights of neutrals and listing Britain's violations of those rights in her modifications of the Declaration of London. The President consulted Colonel House, who objected to the note as being severe and "exceedingly undiplomatic." House talked the matter over with Spring-Rice, who also considered the note too strong. So House and the British Ambassador drafted a version of their own, deleting some of the strong words, in objection to the British violations of neutral rights, but it was Lansing who drafted and Wilson who edited the final version that was sent on September 28. That version was briefer and less blunt than the original and warned that British behavior would have an adverse effect on American public opinion.[8]

Ambassador Page in London softened the note when he communicated its contents verbally to Sir Edward Grey. Finally, late in October, the United States gave up its effort to gain British adherence to the Declaration of London but reserved all of its rights under existing international law.[9]

The Allied Blockade and American Loans

Britain also modified other parts of prevailing international law. The size of modern steamships and the complex nature of their cargoes as well as the danger from submarine attack to her cruisers stopped at sea, she said, made the traditional method of visit and search at sea impractical. Instead, British cruisers brought all neutral ships whose papers or cargoes appeared suspicious into port for a minute search. This practice violated existing maritime law.

In November, after the Germans had sowed mines in the North Sea, the British announced that the "whole of the North Sea must be considered a military area" and planted mines there in retaliation. Thereafter neutral ships could navigate there at their own risk or could go to Allied ports for pilots or charts that would

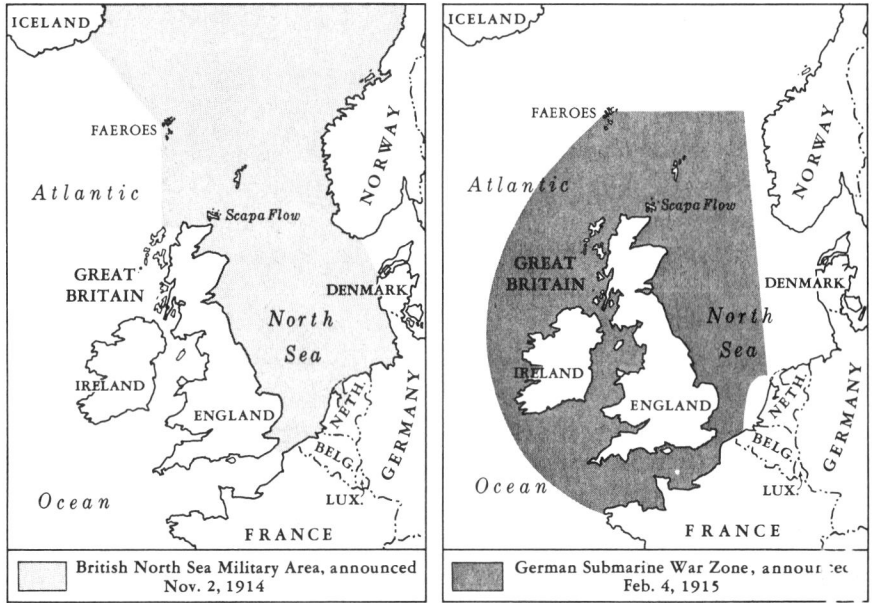

	British North Sea Military Area, announced Nov. 2, 1914
	German Submarine War Zone, announced Feb. 4, 1915

BRITISH AND GERMAN WAR ZONES, 1914–1915

assure them safe passage. Once the neutral ships were in port the Allies could easily search them for contraband.

Although the British effort to strangle trade with Germany has generally been called a blockade, the Allies never formally declared a blockade, but beginning in March, 1915, they tried openly to stop all trade with Germany whether or not it was in contraband.[10] By applying what was a blockade in all but name to neutral ports as well as to Germany, the British enlarged the concepts of blockade and continuous voyage beyond existing legal standards. They forced neutral states bordering Germany—Denmark, Holland, and Sweden—who imported supplies by sea, to agree that they would not re-export the goods to Germany and would not substitute similar goods of their own for export to Germany. The British gradually compelled American shippers, who traded with the neutrals of western Europe, to do so through special corporations they organized.

The British maritime system, by the summer of 1915, choked off virtually all American trade with the Central Powers and the neutral states of Europe. The United States protested. "This Government," Secretary Bryan wrote, "cannot but regard the detention of cargoes of non-contraband goods as without legal justification. . . ."[11] Sometimes the British heeded American complaints. Fearing the wrath of the American cotton interests, for example, they did not immediately put cotton on the list of absolute contraband even though it was an ingredient of gunpowder.[12] Occasionally they paid for cargoes they held, sometimes they ignored American complaints, and at other times they evaded or delayed replies to American protests.

In answering some protests, Sir Edward Grey pointed out that in her blockade Britain was following the practice of the United States in the Civil War. He also argued that new methods of trade called for modifications of international law. The British people spoke in blunter terms. "If the American shipper grumbles," a London newspaper commented, "our reply is that this war is not being conducted for his pleasure or profit. The violation of the laws of war by German soldiers and sailors has conferred upon us a clear moral right to put pressure upon the German people by intercepting the whole of their sea-borne commerce." [13]

The United States never accepted the British arguments as valid, yet it never went beyond protests in attempting to enforce its interpretation of neutral rights. One reason for the American attitude was that the British followed the policy of placing as much restraint on neutral rights as was compatible with retaining American friendship. "Blockade of Germany was essential to the victory of the Allies, but the ill-will of the United States meant their certain defeat," Grey wrote. "The object of diplomacy, therefore, was to secure the maximum of blockade that could be enforced without a rupture with the United States." [14]

While the Allies were strangling American trade with the Central Powers, they were also strengthening their own economic ties to the United States. When the war broke out, the United States was suffering from a business depression. Within six months, Allied purchases of munitions and other supplies transformed the depression into a modest war boom. Germany lamented bitterly that the sale of munitions was making the United States an arsenal of the Allies. [15] For, as the German Ambassador in Washington, Count Johann H. Bernstorff, pointed out, American industry was "actually delivering goods only to the enemies of Germany." [16]

Technically, the one-sided munitions trade did not grow out of American partiality for the Allies. It was, under international law, a legal trade for a neutral. The United States made its goods available exclusively to the Allies primarily because Britain controlled the seas.

At first the Allies paid cash for American goods, but France, as soon as the war began, tried to obtain a loan from the New York banking firm of J. P. Morgan & Company. Early in August, 1914, the bank asked the Secretary of State what the attitude of the government would be toward private loans to certain belligerents. With the support of Wilson, Bryan replied that loans, although legal, were "inconsistent with the true spirit of neutrality." Five days earlier he had written that "money is the worst of contrabands because it commands all other things." [17] The bankers did not make the loan.

This policy of opposing loans to belligerents worked to the disadvantage of the Allies and hence lasted barely two months. In the middle of October the Department of State, backed by Wilson, changed its position. One spokesman explained that there was a distinction between loans made by the government of the United States to belligerent governments and loans made by individual citizens. Loans by individuals were legal; loans by neutral governments violated neutrality. Before the month was over New York bankers began extending short-term commercial credits to Allied governments. Even Bryan reversed himself. He announced that the government still disapproved of loans but had no objection to "credit arrangements." [18] There was virtually no difference between credit arrangements and loans.

As the Allies increased their purchases in the United States and depleted their gold balances, they found that they needed more credits and even large outright loans to continue buying. In September, 1915, Secretary of State Lansing, who had replaced Bryan, and the Secretary of the Treasury persuaded the President to allow the Allies to float large loans on the American market. The Secretaries argued that without such loans the Allies could not continue to buy American goods and without Allied purchases the United States would slip into another depression.

The House of Morgan, acting as the purchasing agent for the Allied governments, then assisted in floating an issue of a half-billion dollars in Allied war bonds in the United States. Although the loans linked American prosperity to the Allied cause and operated to the disadvantage of Germany, there is no evidence that Wilson himself showed an unneutral preference for the Allies for economic reasons. [19]

Germany and the Submarine

While not cordial, American relations with the Central Powers during the first six months of the war, unlike those with the Allies, were relatively tranquil. German leaders had counted on a lightning victory by land, so they had avoided direct controversy with the United States. By the end of 1914, Germany's attempt to deliver a knockout blow had failed, and both sides settled down to monotonous trench warfare.

Now that the war had become one of attrition, the Germans lost their initial advantage of better preparation. Unless they could regain access to raw materials overseas, their war machine might break down. Since their navy could not destroy England's surface fleet, German military commanders decided to retaliate against the Allied blockade with the only weapon at their disposal—the untried submarine.

"England wants to starve us!" the head of the German admiralty announced in a public interview. "We can play the same game. We can bottle her up and torpedo every English or Allied ship which nears any harbor in Great Britain thereby cutting off large food supplies." [20]

Ordinarily, belligerent warships had the right to stop and search merchantmen on the high seas and to sink those who resisted search, but international law also required the warship to provide for the safety of the passengers and crew. Small, cramped, thin-shelled, and lightly armed for surface warfare, the submarine could not comply with these rules of traditional cruiser warfare. If it surfaced to search a merchantman, it ran the risk of destruction by ramming or by deck guns, since many merchant vessels were armed. Therefore, the submarine usually had to deliver its torpedo without warning, sink its prey, and flee. This would lead to the indiscriminate destruction of neutral passengers and property, a particular concern of Americans because they traveled and shipped goods on Allied ships.

At the beginning of 1915, Germany had only about seven submarines able to operate in Allied waters. She could not strike decisively without more, so she adopted a policy of cutting the flow of American goods to the Allies without provoking war with the United States. In effect, she adjusted her early sea warfare to the demands of the United States and to the capabilities of her limited submarine fleet.

Germany launched her submarine policy on February 4 by proclaiming a war zone around the British Isles. After the eighteenth of the month, she said, her submarines would destroy enemy ships within the zone on sight. Since the British were disguising their ships with neutral flags, she warned neutrals that they entered the area at their own peril. Germany justified her new policy as a reprisal against British violations of international law, particularly the food blockade, and argued that new weapons and conditions of war called for a revision of traditional international law.

The submarine policy abruptly changed the character of Germany's relations with the United States. Although Wilson had not protested Britain's illegal blockade of the North Sea, he immediately sent a stern warning to Germany. The United States, he said, would hold the German government to a "strict accountability" for attacks on American ships and lives. It would, moreover, take any steps necessary "to secure to American citizens the full enjoyment of their acknowledged rights on the high seas."[21]

Less than a week later, the United States tried to effect a compromise between the blockade policies of the belligerents. It asked Germany to restrict her use of mines and employ submarines only for visit and search, and Britain to relax her food blockade and abandon the use of neutral flags. Both belligerents opposed the plan. Germany demanded access to raw materials as well as food.

Soon, Germany's submarines began taking a heavy toll of Allied shipping. Without allowing sufficient time for the passengers and crew to escape, a U-boat on March 28, 1915, torpedoed the British liner *Falaba* off the Irish sea and took one American life. The sinking shocked the American people. It also stimulated a debate within the Department of State on national policy.

Headed by Secretary Bryan, one group argued that if Americans traveled on belligerent ships they should do so at their own risk. True neutrality, it held, required the United States to condone the German violations of international law as it had done the British violations. Speaking for the other group, Counselor Lansing insisted that the government must defend the right of Americans to travel on Allied ships. He denounced the sinking of the *Falaba* as a "flagrant violation of international law and international morality," and so inhumane that the United States in defense of its honor must protest strongly.

Even though Lansing had not been entirely accurate in his interpretation of the rights of neutrals on belligerent ships, the President in theory sided with him, but was finally so moved by Bryan's pleas that he decided to make no protest. According to international law, those who traveled on belligerent ships, since a ship was a part of a nation's territory for jurisdictional purposes, could properly look to the belligerent government for protection. Yet, the United States came to adopt the policy that its citizens had the lawful right to travel in safety on British ships and could turn to their own government for protection of that right.[22]

While the President was considering the implications of the *Falaba* case, he received news that on May 1 an American oil tanker, the *Gulflight*, suffered several casualties when hit by a torpedo in a fight between a British naval patrol and a submarine. The German attacks were violent, dramatic, and ruthless. The average American who could not understand the grievances against the Allies rooted in the intricacies of international law could feel the resentment the submarine sinkings aroused. Contemporary opinion held Germany responsible for a barbaric innovation in warfare.

The LUSITANIA Crisis

Aware of American resentment, German officials in the United States, on the very day of the *Gulflight* incident, placed in some fifty newspapers an unusual advertisement which warned Americans not to take passage on British ships carrying munitions. That afternoon almost two hundred Americans left for Europe on the British Cunard liner *Lusitania*. Besides her passengers and other cargo, the *Lusitania* carried 4200 cases of rifle cartridges. Off the Irish coast, in a chance encounter on May 7, 1915, a U-boat torpedoed the great ship. The liner sank in eighteen minutes, with the loss of 1198 lives, 128 of them American, including women and children.[23]

Americans were horrified by what they construed to be mass murder by order of the German government. Some of them screamed for war. "The nation which remembered the sailors of the *Maine* will not forget the civilians of the *Lusitania*!" the New York *Tribune* announced with some truth. The British were able to take advantage of the heated anti-German feelings through publication, six days later, of the Bryce *Report* on German atrocities in Belgium. In view of the ruthless submarine campaign, the *Report*'s thesis, based on dubious evidence, that the German army had used cruelty as a deliberate policy in Belgium, seemed plausible to many Americans.[24] "Proof," *The New York Times* explained, "now comes to hand."

Despite the uproar, the majority of Americans did not want war. The President immediately placed himself at the head of the moderate forces. "There is such a thing as a man being too proud to fight," he told a Philadelphia audience three days after the *Lusitania* tragedy. "There is such a thing as a nation being so right that it does not need to convince others by force that it is right."[25]

Wilson now put his policy of strict accountability to its first real test. In a stiff protest he demanded that Germany disavow the sinking. There was, the Baltimore *Sun* said, "all the red blood in the message that a red-blooded nation can ask."[26] Germany answered two weeks later, but regarding the reply as unsatisfactory, Wilson drafted a second *Lusitania* note that was so vigorous that Bryan objected. He believed it might lead to war. The only way to keep peace, he insisted, was to curtail American travel on belligerent ships.

Unable to persuade the President to accept his reasoning, Bryan resigned rather than sign the second note. Sent on June 9, under the signature of Robert Lansing, Bryan's successor, that note again demanded that the German government disavow the sinking of the *Lusitania*, pay a reparation for injuries, and abandon its campaign against passenger liners. The United States, Wilson said, was concerned with more than rights of property; it was "contending for nothing less high and sacred than the rights of humanity."[27]

Already inflamed against the United States for its sale of munitions to the Allies, the German public now believed that Wilson was trying to force its government to sheath its most potent naval weapon without compelling the British to adhere to international law. The German government itself was unwilling to surrender publicly on the issue of the *Lusitania*, but it also did not want to risk a break with the United States. While the diplomats argued, therefore, it had already issued secret orders to submarine commanders to spare large passenger liners. The new instructions failed to prevent a U-boat from sinking the British liner *Arabic* on August 19 with a loss of two American lives.

Under pressure from Wilson, who considered breaking off relations with Germany, Count von Bernstorff, expressed regret for the sinking of the *Arabic* and offered an indemnity. In a note of September 1, sometimes known as the *Arabic* pledge, he went beyond his instructions and promised that German submarines would not attack unarmed passenger ships without warning unless the ships resisted or tried to escape.

Even though Wilson had won a significant diplomatic victory and tension with Germany eased, the sinkings did not stop. When a German submarine flying Austrian colors sank the Italian liner *Ancona* on November 7 with loss to American life, Wilson sent Austria a virtual ultimatum. Austria-Hungary disavowed the sinking and promised indemnity payments. Finally, on February 4, 1916, Germany apologized for the destruction of the *Lusitania* and offered an indemnity, but would not admit that the sinking was illegal. "I cannot," the German Chancellor Theobald von Bethmann-Hollweg said, "concede a humiliation of Germany and the German people, or the wrenching of the submarine weapon from our hands." [28]

The SUSSEX *Crisis*

A week later Germany again expanded her submarine warfare by announcing that after March 1 her U-boats would sink armed merchant ships without warning. Although it made some Americans indignant, the new policy tended to confirm the views of others that the President's insistence on upholding the rights of his people to travel as they pleased would lead to war. Sentiment in Congress then crystallized behind two resolutions, introduced by Representative Jeff McLemore of Texas and Senator Thomas P. Gore of Oklahoma, warning Americans against travel on armed belligerent ships. Congress appeared ready to approve the Gore-McLemore resolutions with large majorities.

Wilson met this threat to his control of foreign policy from members of his own party with an open letter to the chairman of the Senate Foreign Relations Committee. He could not, the President said, "consent to any abridgement of the rights of American citizens in any respect." After he conferred with congressional leaders on the following morning, Congress shelved the resolutions. [29]

Americans continued to take passage on belligerent ships without restraint, and on March 24 several of them were injured in the torpedoing of the French passenger steamer *Sussex* in the English channel. At the time, the sinking appeared to be a deliberate violation of the *Arabic* pledge and hence touched off one of the most serious crises yet with Germany.

Secretary Lansing urged breaking off relations. Wilson proceeded slowly but finally acted on the views of his advisers. In a virtual ultimatum he warned that "unless the Imperial Government should now immediately declare and effect an abandonment of its present methods of submarine warfare against passenger and freight-carrying vessels, the Government of the United States can have no choice but to sever diplomatic relations with the German Empire altogether." [30]

Faced with the possibility of war with the United States, Germany's military and civilian leaders debated whether or not to leash the submarine. Over the protests of the military, who wanted unrestricted submarine warfare, the civilians yielded to American pressure for the last time. On May 4 the German government promised that its submarines would not sink merchant ships without warning and without saving lives. This so-called *Sussex* pledge also contained the contingency that the United States must compel England to stop her illegal practices, particularly the food blockade. Wilson accepted the promise, but not the reservation.

During the *Sussex* crisis, and even before, the British took certain actions that provoked American antagonism against them. In January, 1916, in seeking another solution to the submarine question, Secretary Lansing had asked the Allies to disarm their merchant ships and the Germans to observe the usual rules of visit and search. The British answered that the proposal would so handicap their side that if the United States persisted, Allied ships would no longer visit American ports and prosperity would suffer. Germany's renewal of submarine warfare against merchantmen kept the issue from arousing bitter controversy with Britain.

In April, when British authorities in Ireland ruthlessly crushed the Easter Rebellion there and later executed its leaders, even American Anglophiles were shocked.[31] "The Dublin executions have done more to drive America back to isolation than any other event since the war began," the *New Republic* declared. Americans also resented and protested the seizure and examination of their mail, but what angered them most was Britain's publication in July of a "blacklist" for the United States. The Allies forbade their subjects to trade with eighty-five American firms and individuals on the list.

Although the Allies had the legal right to boycott those suspected of trading with their enemies, the blacklist infuriated Wilson. "I am, I must admit," he wrote, "about at the end of my patience with Great Britain and the Allies. This blacklist business is the last straw."[32] After he had protested and the British refused to withdraw their blacklist, the President asked Congress for retaliatory powers. Before adjourning in September, Congress voted him the authority he requested, but Wilson never used it since the British eased their boycott of American firms.

Propaganda, Sabotage, and Preparedness

Even though Americans resented the British maritime and economic policies, there was never any real danger that they would turn decisively against the Allies. In the first week of the war the British had cut the transatlantic cable connection between Germany and the United States. Americans were still able to obtain war news from Germany by other means, but the Allies did have the advantage of direct and uninterrupted communication with Americans. British propaganda, skillful though it was, basically had an easier task than had the German. German propagandists faced the almost impossible assignment of making most Americans change their minds about Germany and her war aims. The British disseminated stories of German atrocities to turn Americans against the Central Powers and relied on other sentimental ties to win Americans to their version of the war. Allied propaganda would have had little impact on Americans, however, if German actions, particularly the violation of Belgium's neutrality and the submarine sinkings, had not seemingly confirmed their views that Germany was responsible for a return to barbarism.

The Germans' propaganda, some of it skilled, some of it inept, failed to persuade Americans that their cause was just because most Americans had long distrusted Germany. As early as October, 1914, Elihu Root had written that "the Germans have had some very skillful men at work trying to change the opinion, but so far as I can see they have not accomplished anything." [33] In some ways German and Allied propaganda efforts canceled out each other, and in all it seems fair to conclude that propaganda did not decisively shape basic American policy or attitudes toward the war.

In defying international law the British violated only property rights whereas the German use of the submarine destroyed lives as well and hence aroused greater resentment. Wilson made the distinction clear in one of his speeches. When American rights were violated, he said, "this was our guiding principle: that property rights can be vindicated by claims for damages when the war is over, and no modern nation can decline to arbitrate such claims; but the fundamental rights of humanity cannot be. The loss of life is irreparable." [34]

Antagonism toward the Central Powers increased when their agents in the United States tried to sabotage supplies destined for the Allies. He was convinced, Wilson once admitted, that the country was "honeycombed with German intrigue and infested with German spies." Documents captured by the British revealed that Dr. Constantin Dumba, the Austrian Ambassador in the United States, had tried to incite strikes in munitions factories. In September, 1915, Secretary Lansing immediately asked for his recall. In December, Lansing demanded the recall of the German naval and military *attachés*, Franz von Papen and Karl von Boy-Ed, for violating American laws and neutrality.

The German effort to promote sabotage in a neutral country was not only foolish but also futile. German agents never had the resources to block the flow of munitions to the Allies. They had, ironically, aroused a spy-hunting mania that spread over the country like an epidemic, goaded Americans into a harsher view of the submarine campaign, and helped in whipping up sentiment for a "preparedness" campaign that was in progress in 1915 and 1916.

Agitation for preparedness had begun in October, 1914, with a small but articulate group headed by Theodore Roosevelt. Fearing and distrusting Germany, the men in this group, Elihu Root, Henry Cabot Lodge, and others, believed that the United States should intervene in the war on the side of the Allies. "I am entirely convinced," one of the preparedness advocates explained, "that the German cause is unholy and, moreover, a menace to the principles of democracy." Since public opinion overwhelmingly favored neutrality, the interventionists cloaked their objectives with patriotic pleas for enlarging the armed forces. [35]

At first the preparedness propaganda had little effect, for many Americans saw no danger to their country from the European war and hence little justification for building up a powerful navy and army. Opponents of the preparedness movement saw in it the seeds of war. The President apparently spoke for most Americans when he announced that "no one who speaks counsel based on fact or drawn from a just and candid interpretation of realities can say that there is reason to fear that from any quarters our independence or the integrity of our territory is threatened."[36]

Since the early preparedness movement had an anti-administration bias and most of its leaders were Republicans, Wilson opposed it, but the German submarine campaign in 1915 changed his mind. On the day he sent the third *Lusitania* note, July 21, 1915, he instructed his Secretaries of War and Navy to make plans for a wise and adequate national defense.[37] In November, he presented his preparedness program to the country, calling for naval expansion and an increase of the Army.

Pacifists, progressives, and peace groups immediately began a nation-wide campaign opposing Wilson's program, which, they said, was merely disguised militarism and imperialism. Since nothing threatened American security, they pointed out, the United States should not prepare for war but should try to bring peace to the world. The opposition, particularly in Congress, was so strong that Wilson decided to take the issue to the people.

In January, 1916, the President began a speaking tour of the East and Middle West to sell the voters military preparedness. At St. Louis he said the United States should have "incomparably the most adequate navy in the world."[38] He also gave the impression that he opposed militarism and would do all in his power to keep the nation out of war. Wilson apparently made few converts to preparedness and gained little support from the interventionists, who denounced him for not arming directly against the Germans.

The House-Grey Memorandum

While involved in the preparedness controversy, Wilson made one of his major efforts to end the war. At the end of January, 1915, he had sent Colonel House to London, Paris, and Berlin to explore the possibilities of mediation. After months of negotiation, nothing came of House's efforts. "Everybody seems to want peace," he wrote, "but nobody is willing to concede enough to get it."[39] House returned to the United States in June believing his country would be drawn into the war.

Convinced that the only sure way of keeping the United States out of the war was to end it, Wilson sent the Colonel on another peace mission to Europe in January, 1916. The President had already come to believe that intervention was preferable to a German victory, but at this time he considered the war a stalemate. Hence the military situation provided the United States with an opportunity to promote a peace without a crushing victory for either side. Wilson was prepared, if necessary, to use American power to bring the reluctant side into line.

House talked with British, French, and German leaders. He assured the French that the United States would intervene before allowing Germany to defeat them. In London he and Sir Edward Grey signed an agreement on February 22 known as the House-Grey Memorandum, saying that whenever England and France considered the time "opportune," Wilson would call a peace conference. If the Allies accepted the invitation and Germany refused it, the United States would probably enter the war against Germany. If the Germans accepted, Wilson would help the Allies secure a favorable peace. If the Germans refused reasonable terms at the conference, the United States would join the war on the Allied side.

Before accepting the agreement, the President inserted the word "probably" before the second clause promising American intervention. He did not change the essential meaning of the commitment. Since only Congress could declare, he merely made the memorandum conform to his constitutional power.[40]

As the Allied military position improved in the spring and summer of 1916 and Grey doubted that the President could bring the United States into the war if the projected conference failed, nothing came of the memorandum. Both sides, more-over, at this time were opposed to mediation because each was still confident of ultimate victory.

The Re-Election Campaign

After the failure of his peace plan, Wilson devoted himself to his re-election campaign which began during the controversy over preparedness. His leadership of this cause virtually killed it as a campaign issue. To strengthen the Army, Congress passed the National Defense Act on June 3, followed by a huge Naval Appropriations Bill of August 15 that prompted a congressional leader of the anti-preparedness forces to exclaim that "the United States today becomes the most militaristic naval nation on earth."[41] Despite angry opposition, the President signed the bill.

Yet neither preparedness nor the horror excited by German sabotage and sub-marine warfare had aroused a broad sentiment for war. At the presidential nominating conventions politicians of both major parties realized that the voters passionately desired peace. The Democrats renominated Wilson, this time by acclamation, and endorsed his foreign policy. The Republicans passed over Theodore Roosevelt and other interventionists and nominated Charles Evans Hughes, an associate justice of the Supreme Court.

From the outset the Democrats advertised Wilson as the champion of peace, covering the country with the cry, "he kept us out of war." At times the President felt the slogan raised false hopes. "I can't keep the country out of war," he confided to a cabinet member. "They talk of me as though I were a god. Any little German lieutenant can put us into the war at any time by some calculated outrage." Yet he could also say that "I am not expecting this country to get into war." [42]

On the eve of the election some of Wilson's supporters summed up the issue in an advertisement that read in part:

> You Are Working—*Not Fighting!*
> Alive and Happy;—*Not Cannon Fodder!*
> Wilson and Peace with Honor?
> or
> Hughes with Roosevelt and War? [43]

Republican politicians tried to convince the electorate that Hughes opposed intervention more than Wilson did. "A vote for me is not a vote for war," Hughes declared. "It is a vote for lasting peace." [44] He could not, however, control Roosevelt's fiery demands for intervention. Since he accepted Roosevelt's support and stood behind his bellicose speeches, many voters gained the impression that the Republican party stood for war. The German Ambassador was probably close to the truth when he reported that "if Hughes is defeated he has Roosevelt to thank for it." [45]

Other issues perhaps were equally important, but the distribution of votes indicated that where the peace issue was decisive, Wilson led. He had, in effect, fused the peace issue with the ideals of progressivism. Wilson narrowly won the election, but his party did not do as well as he, retaining only a precarious control in Congress.

During the election campaign, in September and October, the Germans indicated that they were anxious to make peace. They told Wilson they would be receptive if he were to offer his good offices, hinting that otherwise they might resume unrestricted submarine warfare. Even though he feared that American involvement might become inevitable unless the war ended, Wilson would not move until after the election. As soon as he had won, he decided to try to bring the belligerents together in a peace conference, hoping that it would result in a compromise settlement and an international organization to keep the peace.

When November passed and Wilson did not act, the Germans grew impatient. Before the President could reveal his plan, they took the initiative. Anxious to exploit a military situation that had turned in their favor on both the western and eastern fronts, they announced on December 12 that they were willing to discuss peace with their enemies.

That announcement forced Wilson to modify his own plan but not to abandon it. Six days later he sent identical notes to the belligerents asking them simply to state their war objectives. Publicly, the Allies said they would consider neither the

German nor the American proposal, but privately the British told the President they were willing to talk peace if the Germans would do so on reasonable terms. The Germans informed Wilson they preferred the direct negotiations they had suggested. Actually, neither side was willing to discuss peace on Wilson's terms. Their objectives were so sweeping that only a victor's peace could justify them.

Wilson, meanwhile, had decided to explain his concept of what kind of a peace there should be to the peoples of the world. For months he had considered the idea of trying to ensure peace at the end of the war with a league of nations. In January, 1917, he went before the Senate and outlined the kind of peace he thought the United States would support. There must be, he said, "a peace without victory" since a conqueror's peace would not last. It must be a peace based on the equality of all nations, upon freedom of the seas, upon a general reduction of armaments, and other general principles, "a peace made secure by the organized major force of mankind." [46]

Unrestricted Submarine Warfare

The President's unprecedented offer to use the power of the United States for world peace brought no results. Three days earlier, Ambassador Bernstorff had received word that his government would resume unrestricted submarine warfare beginning February 1. Germany's decision, made firm at a memorable "Crown Council" at Pless on January 9, constituted a victory for the military authorities and a defeat for the civilian government.

The civilian leaders believed that the submarine campaign would fail and would assure Germany's defeat by bringing the United States into the war. The military leaders knew that unrestricted submarine warfare would push the United States into the war but calculated that it would make no difference. The German generals had decided that the army could not break the stalemate on land and that only the submarine could bring victory. They counted on the underwater fleet, now enlarged to more than a hundred U-boats, to knock out the Allies before the military power and resources of the United States could become effective. "We are counting on the possibility of war with the United States," one of them explained, "and have made all preparations to meet it. Things can not be worse than they are now." [47]

Bernstorff tried to persuade his superiors to reconsider, but was unsuccessful. On January 31, at the same time he delivered Germany's answer to Wilson's request for peace terms, he announced the decision to resume unrestricted submarine warfare. Three days later Wilson broke off diplomatic relations. Still hoping to avoid war, he told a joint session of Congress that only "actual overt acts" would make him believe that Germany would carry out her threat. [48]

Germany had not been bluffing; her submarines began their campaign of terror on schedule. Frightened by the undersea warfare, many American shippers kept their ships and cargoes in port. Wilson's advisers and others demanded armament and protection for American ships. The President at first refused to ask Congress for authority to arm merchant vessels, but the Zimmermann Telegram, received in the State Department on the evening of February 24, convinced him of Germany's hostile intentions and changed his mind.

Sent originally by the German Foreign Minister, Alfred Zimmermann, to Bernstorff for relay to the German Minister in Mexico, the telegram had been intercepted and decoded by British naval intelligence and turned over to the Department of State. If the United States went to war against Germany, it said, the German Minister in Mexico should ask Mexico to join an alliance with Germany and Japan, Britain's ally. Mexico's reward, if Germany won, would be her "lost territory" of Arizona, New Mexico, and Texas.[49]

Two days later Wilson asked a joint session of Congress for authority to arm merchant ships and to "employ any other instrumentalities and methods" to protect American ships and lives. What he wanted, he explained, was an "armed Neutrality" that need not lead to war.[50] On the following day, black newspaper headlines shouted that a German submarine sank the Cunard passenger liner *Laconia*. Two American women and an American seaman lost their lives in the icy waters of the Atlantic. Many Americans considered this the "overt act" the President awaited.

Three days later the government published the Zimmermann Telegram. Americans were stunned; here was another overt act of German hostility. Strong anti-German feeling swelled up throughout the country, particularly in the Southwest where it previously had been mild. Even though Germany had an undeniable right to seek allies against a possible enemy, the Zimmermann proposal was a blunder, compounded when Zimmermann admitted its authenticity. As an ally to Germany, Mexico was virtually useless. Her nuisance value hardly justified the risk of precipitating more American anger against Germany. The Washington *Post* called the proposal "sheer lunacy" and the *Literary Digest* aptly described it as "elephantine diplomacy."

Publication of the Zimmermann Telegram prompted the House to give quick approval to Wilson's request to arm merchant ships, but a dozen senators under the leadership of Robert La Follette and George W. Norris filibustered it to death. The President denounced them as "a little group of willful men, representing no opinion but their own," and then armed the ships on his own authority.[51] American merchantmen, with guns ready to shoot, were moving through the war zones before the end of March. More Americans lost their lives on March 18 when three American ships went down in torpedo attacks. "Now Germany has committed an indisputable overt act," the Chicago *Daily Tribune* pointed out. "If the United States is going to make good its word, it must go to war."[52]

In the face of the German attacks on American lives and property, neutrality seemed no longer possible. Germany's several overt acts, Wilson believed, left no alternative but war. The policy of strict accountability had run its course. The decision for war tormented the President. "Once lead this people into war," he told a newspaper friend, "and they'll forget there ever was such a thing as tolerance. To fight you must be brutal and ruthless, and the spirit of ruthless brutality will enter into the very fibre of our national life. . . ."[53] On the following evening, April 2, 1917, Wilson read his war message to the Congress he had called into joint session.

Since a March revolution in Russia held promise of a democratic regime in place of the autocratic tsars, Wilson could say in his message that the major Allied governments were democratic. "The world must be made safe for democracy. Its peace must be planted upon the tested foundations of political liberty," he declared. He also denounced the submarine as waging "a warfare against mankind" and "against all nations."[54]

Four days later Congress passed a formal declaration of war. In the House the vote was 373 to 50 and in the Senate, 82 to 6.

Since the President had consistently condemned the unbridled use of the submarine and only retreat or war seemed possible when Germany persisted in using it, war came over the immediate issue of the submarine.[55] Wilson and his advisers, however, also believed that the welfare of their country would be served better with a victory for the Allies than for Germany.[56] In addition, Wilson apparently feared that Germany, if victorious, would destroy the balance of power necessary for the new order based on democracy and international law he wanted to see in the postwar world.

Most Americans, on the other hand, apparently went to war with reluctance or indifference, envisaging nothing beyond the defeat of Germany. Senator William E. Borah of Idaho spoke for others besides himself when he said, "I join no crusade; I seek or accept no alliances; I obligate this Government to no other power. I make war alone for my countrymen and their rights, for my country and its honor."[57] This fundamental difference between the President's objectives and those of some of his own people was to influence the peace.

NOTES

1. From the second annual message, Dec. 7, 1914, in *Foreign Relations, 1914*, p. xviii. The most comprehensive scholarly analysis of the causes of the war is in Luigi Albertini, *The Origins of the War of 1914*, trans. from the Italian (3 vols., London, 1952–57).

2. There were ten official proclamations, virtually identical in text, issued between Aug. 4 and Nov. 6, 1914. See *Foreign Relations, 1914, Supplement*, pp. 547–551.

3. *The New York Times*, Aug. 19, 1914, quoted in Arthur S. Link, *Wilson: The Struggle for Neutrality, 1914–1915* (Princeton, 1960), p. 66.

4. Excerpt from "The Name of France," Henry Van Dyke, *Red Flower* (New York: Charles Scribner's Sons, 1916), pp. 26-27.

5. *Deseret News*, Aug. 3, 1914, quoted in Charles C. Tansill, *America Goes to War* (Boston, 1938), p. 23.

6. To Sir Edward Grey, Aug. 25, 1914, in Stephen L. Gwynn, ed., *The Letters and Friendship of Sir Cecil Spring-Rice: A Record* (2 vols., Boston, 1929), II, 220.

7. The text of the declaration is in *Foreign Relations, 1909*, pp. 318-333.

8. For differing interpretations as to the significance of the note, see Link, *Wilson: Neutrality*, pp. 109-114 and Tansill, *America Goes to War*, pp. 141-146. From a careful use of State Department files, Link has established the identity of the true authors of the note.

9. For details, see Richard W. Van Alstyne, "The Policy of the United States Regarding the Declaration of London, at the Outbreak of the Great War," *Journal of Modern History*, VII (Dec. 1933), 434-447.

10. This point on the legality of the blockade is discussed in Marion C. Siney, *The Allied Blockade of Germany, 1914-1916* (Ann Arbor, Mich., 1957), pp. 67-70.

11. To W. H. Page, June 8, 1915, in *Foreign Relations, 1915, Supplement*, pp. 434-435.

12. See Arthur S. Link, "The Cotton Crisis, the South, and Anglo-American Diplomacy, 1914-1915," in J. Carlyle Sitterson, ed., *Studies in Southern History in Memory of Albert Ray Newsome* (*James Sprunt Studies in History and Political Science*, XXXIX: Chapel Hill, N.C., 1957), 122-138.

13. *Daily Graphic*, March 20, 1915, quoted in Tansill, *America Goes to War*, p. 195.

14. Sir Edward Grey, *Twenty-Five Years, 1892-1916* (2 vols., New York, 1925), II, 107.

15. German-Americans raised the same complaint and tried to prevent the export of munitions through the application of political pressure. See Clifton J. Childs, "German-American Attempts to Prevent the Exportation of Munitions of War, 1914-1915," *Mississippi Valley Historical Review*, XXV (Dec. 1938), 351-368.

16. April 4, 1915, to Secretary of State, in *Foreign Relations, 1915, Supplement*, p. 158. See also Johann H. Bernstorff, *My Three Years in America* (New York, 1920), pp. 76-79.

17. The quotations, dated Aug. 10 and 15, 1914, are in Link, *Wilson: Neutrality*, pp. 63-64.

18. The quotation, March 31, 1915, is in *Foreign Relations, 1915, Supplement*, p. 820. For background details, see Lansing to Wilson, Oct. 23, 1914, and two memoranda of the same date in *Foreign Relations, Lansing Papers, 1914-1920*, I, 138-140; Richard W. Van Alstyne, "Private American Loans to the Allies, 1914-1916," *Pacific Historical Review*, II (June 1933), 180-193; and Paul Birdsall, "Neutrality and Economic Pressure," *Science and Society*, III (Spring 1939), 217-228.

19. Nor does available evidence suggest that American businessmen wanted war any more than did the majority of Americans. See Harold C. Syrett, "The Business Press and American Neutrality, 1914-1917," *Mississippi Valley Historical Review*, XXXII (Sept. 1945), 215-230.

20. Grand Admiral Alfred von Tirpitz, New York *Sun*, Dec. 23, 1914, quoted in Tansill, *America Goes to War*, p. 227.

21. Bryan to Gerard, Feb. 10, 1915, *Foreign Relations, 1915, Supplement*, p. 99.

22. Detailed discussions, with differing interpretations, of the *Falaba* case are in Link, *Wilson: Neutrality*, pp. 358-367; Tansill, *America Goes to War*, pp. 251-262; Ernest R. May, *The World War and American Isolationism, 1914-1917* (Cambridge, Mass., 1958), pp. 146-148; and Edwin Borchard and William P. Lage, *Neutrality for the United*

States, 2nd ed. (New Haven, 1940), pp. 135–136.

23. For statistics on passengers and losses, see Charles E. Lauriat, Jr., *The Lusitania's Last Voyage* (Boston, 1915), pp. 130–132, but this account uses the figures in Thomas A. Bailey, "The Sinking of the Lusitania," *The American Historical Review*, XLI (Oct. 1935), 57n. For other details, see Adolph A. and Mary Hoehling, *The Last Voyage of the Lusitania* (New York, 1956) and Thomas A. Bailey, "German Documents Relating to the 'Lusitania'," *Journal of Modern History*, VIII (Sept. 1936), 320–337.

24. For details, see James M. Read, *Atrocity Propaganda, 1914–1917* (New Haven, 1941), pp. 200–208.

25. May 10, 1915, in Ray S. Baker and William E. Dodd, eds., *The Public Papers of Woodrow Wilson*, (6 vols., New York, 1925–27), *The New Democracy* I, 321.

26. May 14, 1915, quoted in Tansill, *America Goes to War*, p. 305. The note, dated May 13, Bryan to Gerard, is in *Foreign Relations, 1915, Supplement*, pp. 393–396.

27. Lansing to Gerard, June 9, 1915, *ibid.*, p. 437. For Bryan's point of view, see William J. and Mary B. Bryan, *The Memoirs of William Jennings Bryan* (Philadelphia, 1925), pp. 395–428.

28. In the New York *World*, Feb. 9, 1916, quoted in Tansill, *America Goes to War*, p. 403.

29. For the quotation, see Wilson to Sen. William J. Stone, Feb. 24, 1916, in Baker and Dodd, *Wilson Papers, New Democracy*, II, 123. For details and proper chronology on the resolutions and the conference, see Monroe Billington, "The Sunrise Conference: Myth or Fact?" *The Southwestern Social Science Quarterly*, XXXVII (March 1957), 330–340.

30. Lansing to Gerard, April 18, 1916, in *Foreign Relations, 1916, Supplement*, p. 234.

31. For details, see Charles C. Tansill, *America and the Fight for Irish Freedom, 1866–1922* (New York, 1957), pp. 169–214.

32. To Colonel House, July 23, 1916, quoted in Ray S. Baker, *Woodrow Wilson: Life and Letters* (8 vols., Garden City, N.Y., 1927–39), VI, 312. For additional details, see Thomas A. Bailey, "The United States and the Blacklist during the Great War," *Journal of Modern History*, VI (March 1934), 14–35.

33. To Chandler P. Anderson, Sept. 23, 1914, quoted in Tansill, *America Goes to War*, p. 599.

34. Sept. 2, 1916, in Baker and Dodd, *Wilson Papers, New Democracy*, II, 282.

35. See, for instance, Robert D. Ward, "The Origin and Activities of the National Security League, 1914–1919," *Mississippi Valley Historical Review*, XLVII (June 1960), 51–65.

36. Second annual message, Dec. 8, 1914, in Baker and Dodd, *Wilson Papers, New Democracy*, I, 224.

37. Link, *Wilson: Neutrality*, p. 591.

38. Feb. 3, 1916, in Baker and Dodd, *Wilson Papers, New Democracy*, II, 114.

39. To Bryan, April 15, 1915, in Charles Seymour, ed., *The Intimate Papers of Colonel House* (4 vols., Boston, 1926–28), I, 417.

40. Ernest R. May, one of the latest students of this problem, points out that House's plan will be misunderstood if it is not realized that he regarded war with Germany as inevitable; see *World War and Isolationism*, p. 350.

41. Claude Kitchin quoted in Arthur S. Link, *Woodrow Wilson and the Progressive Era, 1910–1917* (New York, 1954), p. 190.

42. Oct. 21, 1916, in Baker and Dodd, *Wilson Papers, New Democracy*, II, 371.

43. Quoted in Link, *Woodrow Wilson and the Progressive Era*, p. 244.

44. *The New York Times*, Nov. 1, 1916, quoted in Robert E. Osgood, *Ideals and Self-Interest in America's Foreign Relations* (Chicago, 1953), p. 235.

45. Oct. 19, 1916, quoted in Link, *Woodrow Wilson and the Progressive Era*, p. 244. Hughes sought Roosevelt's support; see Russell Buchanan, "Theodore Roosevelt and American Neutrality, 1914–1917," *The American Historical Review*, XLIII (July 1938), 775–790.

46. Jan. 22, 1914; the text is in Baker and Dodd, *Wilson Papers, New Democracy*, II, 407–414.

47. Field Marshal Paul von Hindenburg, Jan. 8, 1917, quoted in May, *World War and Isolationism*, p. 414. For additional details, see Karl E. Birnbaum, *Peace Moves and U-Boat Warfare: A Study of Imperial Germany's Policy towards the United States, April 18, 1916–Jan. 9, 1917* (Stockholm, 1958), pp. 315–327.

48. Feb. 3, 1917, in Baker and Dodd, *Wilson Papers, New Democracy*, II, 425.

49. The note is in Page to Secretary of State, Feb. 24, 1917, *Foreign Relations, 1917, Supplement*, I, 149.

50. The text, Feb. 26, 1917, is in Baker and Dodd, *Wilson Papers, New Democracy*, II, 428–432.

51. March 5, 1917, *ibid.*, 435.

52. The newspaper and periodical quotations are from Samuel R. Spencer, Jr., *Decision for War, 1917: The Laconia and the Zimmermann Telegram as Key Factors in the Public Reaction against Germany* (Rindge, N.H., 1953), p. 75n, 80. For additional details, see Barbara W. Tuchman, *The Zimmermann Telegram* (New York, 1958).

53. Frank Cobb, editor of the New York *World*, quoted in Baker, *Wilson: Life and Letters*, VI, 506–507.

54. The text is in Baker and Dodd, *Wilson Papers, War and Peace*, I, 6–16.

55. This appeared to be the general view of newspaper editors, see Russell Buchanan, "American Editors Examine American War Aims and Plans in April 1917," *Pacific Historical Review*, IX (Sept. 1940), 253–265.

56. Daniel M. Smith, in "Robert Lansing and the Formulation of American Neutrality Policies, 1914–1915," *Mississippi Valley Historical Review*, XLIII (June 1956), 59–81, argues that Lansing exerted considerable influence in shaping policy according to this view. For emphasis on the idea of national interest being at stake in the crisis, see Edward H. Buehrig, "Wilson's Neutrality Re-Examined," *World Politics*, III (Oct. 1950), 1–19.

57. April 4, 1917, *Congressional Record*, LV, 65th Congress, 1st sess., p. 253.

Chapter Nineteen

WAR AND PEACEMAKING

Since Germany's main allies, Austria-Hungary and Turkey, had not killed Americans through submarine warfare, the United States did not declare war against them, but both countries, immediately after the declaration against Germany, broke off relations with the United States.[1] At first, Wilson had hoped to divide Austria-Hungary from Germany through separate peace negotiations that offered a guarantee against dismemberment of her lands. When that pressure failed, the United States declared war on Austria-Hungary in December, 1917.

Clinging to its isolationist tradition, the United States did not become one of the "Allies." It became, instead, an "associated power." "It will not do," the New York *Evening Post* explained, "to say that because Americans as a whole sympathize with the Allies, therefore they must lose their identity in a European alliance."[2]

The technical distinction between "the Allied and Associated Powers" meant little since the United States cooperated in the war as fully as any other member of the Allied coalition. Yet Wilson and other American leaders insisted that the United States was fighting for reasons of its own, not for the fruits of conquest.

The Secret Treaties

American war objectives, other than the defeat of Germany, appeared vague. The Allies had spelled out their own war aims in five formal agreements between March, 1915, and March, 1917. There was nothing innately evil in these arrangements. The belligerents in seeking to gain and hold allies had acted normally, but because the agreements were not published they came to be known as the "secret treaties."

These treaties and supplementary agreements offered territorial rewards to the Allied nations through dismemberment of the enemy empires. Germany's colonial possessions were to go to Japan, Great Britain, and France. All of the major European Allies, Russia, France, Britain, Italy, and Greece also, were to profit from the complete destruction of Turkey's Ottoman Empire. And Italy, Russia, Rumania, and Serbia, were to share in the breakup of Austria-Hungary. There were inconsistencies between these war aims and others the Allies had publicly espoused. Some of the secret commitments conflicted with each other, but all shared the objective of advancing the self-interest of the Allied countries involved. The only country that did not have territorial aspirations was the United States. Its remote geographical position made possible an aloofness toward territorial gains that the other belligerents could not attain.[3]

When the United States entered the war, Allied leaders wondered if Wilson would participate fully without asking them to give up some of their territorial objectives. To gain complete American cooperation, and probably also to discuss war objectives with their new ally, the British and French sent special delegations to the United States at the end of April, 1917. Italian and Belgian missions followed.

Foreign Secretary Arthur J. Balfour, head of the British mission in the United States, discussed the "secret treaties" with Wilson and Colonel House. The Americans agreed that to study the treaties and peace terms at that time would produce uncontrollable friction among the Allies. "It seems to me," House told the President, "that the only thing to be considered at present is how to beat Germany in the quickest way."

Later, Balfour sent Wilson copies of some of the "secret treaties," but American officials offered no criticism and made no demands of their own. The Allied leaders concluded that the United States was more concerned with winning the war than with making its war objectives specific.[4]

The American Contribution

At first the Allies were not anxious to involve raw American soldiers directly in the fighting. Their urgent needs were credit to finance the purchase of supplies and naval assistance to fight the submarine so that the supplies could cross the Atlantic safely.

Congress immediately passed an emergency loan act, authorizing an addition to the national debt of five billion dollars. Wilson advocated two billion for expenditure in the United States but made the remaining three available to the Allies. As the demands of the Allies increased Congress repeatedly authorized new loans, amounting to a total of some seven billion dollars by the end of the war.

In April, 1917, German submarines were sinking ships twice as fast as the Allies could replace them. The American Navy, therefore, immediately contributed a flotilla of destroyers to the anti-submarine campaign. Later, it helped the British in laying a barrage of some sixty to seventy thousand mines across the narrows of the North Sea, from Scotland to Norway, to close it to the U-boats. The Navy also cooperated with the British in tightening the blockade against Germany, but its most impressive achievement in overcoming the challenge of the submarine was in convoying merchantmen and troop transports across the Atlantic.

As the winter of 1917–18 approached and Allied military fortunes suffered a number of reverses, Allied leaders asked for American troops to bolster sagging morale and to fill gaps in French and British regiments. That request led to the first serious friction with the Allies. General John J. Pershing, commander of the American Expeditionary Force that went to France, would not let American units lose their identity through consolidation with the British and French armies. The President supported that position.[5]

When the Germans launched a great offensive in March, 1918, Pershing met the emergency by temporarily placing all American troops and resources at the disposal of French and British commanders. Later, the American Army acted as a unit under its own officers with its own sector on the battle front. Before the war was over, the United States had succeeded in placing four million men under arms. Over two million of them reached France.

The desperate need for fresh American troops had first become evident in October, 1917, when German and Austrian forces launched an offensive at Caporetto that almost crushed the Italian army. With the aid of hasty French and British reinforcements, the Italians averted disaster. In November, when the Bolsheviks took control of the Russian government and offered the Germans an armistice and peace, Russian resistance on the eastern front collapsed.

The Bolshevik Challenge

On November 8, the day after seizing power, Nikolai Lenin and the Congress of Soviets issued a "Decree on Peace." It appealed to the belligerent governments, and over the heads of the governments to the people, "for a just and democratic peace," which the Bolsheviks defined as excluding seizure of foreign territory and indemnities.[6] Since the Bolsheviks made their plea to the world without warning the Allied governments, and hence violated Russia's wartime obligations to the *Entente* governments, the Allies viewed it as a betrayal.

Two weeks later Leon Trotsky, the Soviet Commissar for Foreign Affairs, began publishing the texts of the "secret treaties," which the Bolsheviks had found in the official Russian files. When the British, French, and Italians protested, Trotsky denounced the treaties as rapacious and imperialistic and published other appeals, one of which closed with these words:

> Down with the old secret treaties and diplomatic intrigue
> Hail the honest and open struggle for universal peace![7]

The Central Powers responded cautiously but seemingly with favor to the Bolshevik peace proposals, and on December 3 began negotiations for an armistice. Three days later Trotsky sent the terms of the proposed armistice to the Allied governments and the United States, inviting them to join the negotiations and asking them to announce their war aims. The Allies did not reply, and on December 15 the Bolsheviks signed an armistice with the Germans, to be followed later by a treaty of peace.

On Christmas day the Austrian Foreign Minister, apparently agreeing with the Bolshevik plea for a general peace on the basis of "no annexations or indemnities," said the Central Powers wanted no forcible annexations. The Allies, on the other hand, were unable to agree on any bold stroke of their own to counter the Bolshevik challenge. Since the Bolshevik propaganda seemingly had a profound effect on liberal opinion in neutral countries as well as among Allied peoples, who demanded a reply to the Soviet and German overtures, President Wilson and Colonel House decided to formulate an independent American answer.

The Fourteen Points

In September Wilson had asked Colonel House to assemble a group of experts to study the war aims of the belligerents. The committee of five that House brought together came to be known as "The Inquiry," a group to which Wilson turned for information and recommendations that he could incorporate into his statement. The President personally presented his program to Congress on January 8, 1918. Wilson's plan sought to remove from the Allied cause the "imperialist" label that Trotsky had placed on it, discuss war aims, bring Russia back into the Allied fold, and capture the imagination of the world.

The heart of the program was the Fourteen Points, of which the first five dealt with general principles of world-wide significance. In summary, they called for:

1. The end of secret diplomacy.
2. Freedom of navigation on the seas in peace and in war.
3. Removal of barriers to international free trade.
4. Reduction of armaments.
5. Impartial adjustment of colonial claims, taking into account the welfare of colonial populations.

The next eight covered specific territorial adjustments in Europe and the Near East. They asked for:

6. German evacuation of Russian territory and a welcome to Russia "into the society of free nations under institutions of her own choosing."
7. German evacuation of Belgium and restoration of her sovereignty.
8. Return of Alsace-Lorraine, taken by Prussia in 1871, to France.

9. Readjustment of Italy's frontiers according to nationality.

10. Autonomy for the diverse peoples of Austria-Hungary.

11. Rearrangement of the boundaries of the Balkan countries according to nationality, with free access to the sea for Serbia (Yugoslavia).

12. Autonomous development for nationalities under Turkish rule and free passage through the Dardanelles for ships of all nations.

13. An independent Poland with free access to the sea.

The last point was Wilson's key to future peace. It offered:

14. "A general association of nations." [8]

Later Wilson elaborated on some of the points and added others calling essentially for an open peace based on justice and for the right of minority peoples to determine their own governments, better known as the right of national self-determination. In all, twenty-seven points and principles ultimately were referred to under the general title of the Fourteen Points.

Since those points were broad enough to include something for almost everyone, enemies as well as allies, they seemingly proved potent propaganda among liberals everywhere, but their greatest impact seems to have been made in the United States. Even the Republican New York *Tribune* praised them, saying that "the President's words are the words of a hundred million. . . . Today, as never before, the whole nation marches with the President." Some statesmen of the Central Powers appeared willing to accept some of the points, but the German Chancellor rejected most of them. [9]

Ten days after the United States had gone to war, President Wilson, under authority of Congress, had established a Committee of Public Information to mobilize public opinion behind the war effort. George Creel, the head of the committee, printed copies of the Fourteen Points and some of Wilson's other phrases in vast numbers and shot them behind the German lines with cannon, dropped tons of leaflets by plane on German soldiers, and publicized them in other spectacular ways. The result was that peoples everywhere apparently accepted Wilson's phrases as the Allied peace program.

The Allies were delighted with the Fourteen Points as counterpropaganda, but French, British, and Italian statesmen were disturbed by Wilson's effort to solve specifically European problems and hence tamper with their war aims. The Fourteen Points did not impress the Bolsheviks. "There is not a single Marxist," Lenin said, "who, while adhering to the foundations of Marxism and socialism, would not say that the interests of socialism are above the right of nations to self-determination." [10]

The true answer of the German government to the Fourteen Points came in the peace negotiations at Brest-Litovsk. The negotiations broke down when the Germans demanded more territory than the Bolsheviks were willing to give up.

The Germans then launched a new attack and on March 3, 1918, the Bolsheviks signed the harsh Treaty of Brest-Litovsk. Germany demanded no reparations but deprived Russia of about one-third of her population and gained control of a vast slice of eastern Europe stretching from the Baltic to the Black Sea. Wilson's Fourteen Points had not brought the Russians back to the Allied cause nor had they converted the Germans to the principles of no annexations and self-determination.

There was no convincing evidence, moreover, that the Fourteen Points had made any decisive impression on the morale of German soldiers.[11] After the Russian collapse, the Germans shifted about five hundred thousand troops to the western front and achieved a numerical superiority there. In March, May, and July, they launched mighty offensives designed to defeat France before American troops arrived in large numbers. Those assaults brought the Germans within forty miles of Paris and nearly broke the Allied armies. In desperation the Allies decided on a unified command under Marshal Ferdinand Foch of France and pleaded for American reinforcements.

By mid-July enough fresh American troops were fighting by the side of the French and British to turn the tide of battle. Marshal Foch then mounted a counter-offensive, and the Germans began a steady retreat. In September, as Allied and American armies fought toward the Belgian and German borders, the German generals, hoping to prevent a military disaster, decided they must have peace.

The Armistice

Facing certain defeat, the German military leaders sought a way out through the Fourteen Points.[12] The German government and the Austrians, therefore, appealed directly to Wilson for peace on the basis of the Fourteen Points and their supplements. The Germans had turned to him rather than to the Allies because he possessed greater prestige and appeared to be more moderate than the Allied leaders.

Without consulting the Allies, Wilson answered the Germans, insisting that they must accept the Fourteen Points before he would consider negotiations. On October 12 the Germans fully accepted those points as the basis for peace and asked assurance that the Allied governments would also agree to them. Wilson then added other conditions and told the Germans he would not deal with their existing government. A few days later he transmitted his correspondence with the Germans to the Allied leaders in Paris and commissioned Colonel House to secure their approval of his terms.

Britain, France, and Italy, all had objections to the Fourteen Points but finally accepted them as the basis for an armistice with only two reservations. One related to freedom of the seas and the other to reparations for damage the Germans had done to civilians.

During the armistice negotiations the Allied armies maintained their pressure against the enemy, and Austria's Hapsburg empire disintegrated. Desperately anxious to stop the fighting and unable to wait for Wilson's slow diplomacy, Austria-Hungary opened negotiations directly with Italy, who represented the Allied powers, and signed an armistice on November 3. The Austrian peace, as a result, was not based on the Fourteen Points.[13]

On November 9 Kaiser William II abdicated, and the Germans organized a republican government. At five o'clock on the morning of November 11, 1918, in Marshal Foch's private railway car in the forest of Compiègne, Germany and the Allies signed the armistice. Fighting stopped at eleven o'clock that morning and the war ended before a single Allied soldier had set foot on German soil.

During the armistice negotiations, Republican critics, led by Theodore Roosevelt, had attacked the Fourteen Points and what they considered soft peace terms. Senator Henry Cabot Lodge demanded unconditional surrender. "Let us dictate peace by the hammering guns," Roosevelt insisted, "and not chat about peace to the accompaniment of the clicking of typewriters."[14] Those critics denounced Wilson's war aims and called for the election of a Republican congress in November to safeguard the national interest.

Alarmed by the attacks, Wilson consulted the leaders of his party and on October 25 appealed to the voters for Democratic majorities in both houses of Congress. If they chose a Republican congress, he said, the Allies would interpret the election as a repudiation of his leadership. No one knows how the appeal itself affected the November elections, but the voters, by narrow margins, returned a Republican congress. What seemed clear was that Wilson had tried to make the election a test of national confidence in his conduct of foreign affairs and had failed.[15]

The Peace Conference

Most Americans apparently assumed that with the defeat of Germany their country would revert to its traditional aloofness from Europe's politics, for they had not asked for territories or indemnities that would chain them to Europe. By saying in his Armistice Day announcement that "everything for which America fought has been accomplished," Wilson seemingly expressed the popular mood. But he went on. "It will now be our fortunate duty," he disclosed, "to assist by example, by sober, friendly counsel, and by material aid in the establishment of a just democracy throughout the world."[16]

To secure the kind of peace he wanted and to make his "association of Nations" a part of it, Wilson decided to attend the peace conference in Paris. That decision, announced on November 18, provoked considerable criticism. No President had hitherto gone to Europe during his term of office, and at that time many believed that the President could not rightfully leave the country.

Wilson's announcement aroused particularly angry outbursts from leading Republicans. "Our allies and our enemies and Mr. Wilson himself," Theodore Roosevelt asserted, "should all understand that Mr. Wilson has no authority whatever to speak for the American people at this time. His leadership has just been emphatically repudiated by them." [17]

A few days later, when Wilson announced the personnel of the peace commission, he again shocked Republicans. In addition to Wilson himself, the delegation included Colonel House, the President's most trusted adviser, Secretary of State Lansing, General Tasker H. Bliss, a member of the Supreme War Council in Paris, and Henry White, an experienced diplomat and the sole Republican member. By failing to include a single senator or an important Republican, the President had again defied precedent. He had chosen men he thought would be loyal to him, but in so doing had injected another partisan issue into the peacemaking. White was not active in the councils of the Republican party and none of the other delegates possessed independent political influence that would help get a peace treaty through the Senate. For technical advice and information Wilson brought "The Inquiry" and other experts with him, but he himself dominated the peace commission and made the basic decisions.

Wilson arrived in Europe on December 13 and spent a month visiting Allied cities. His appearances produced great ovations reflecting his popularity with the Allied peoples.

While Wilson was at sea someone had asked him about his plans for a league of nations. "I am going to insist that the league be brought out as part and parcel of the treaty itself," he answered. "A league I believe will of necessity become an integral part of such a treaty as I trust we shall work out." The popular demonstrations convinced the President that the peoples of Europe looked to him to help them achieve a permanent peace and build a better world. They confirmed his belief that his league of nations must precede, not follow, the peace.

The peace conference, composed of representatives from thirty-two "allied and associated powers," held its first plenary session on January 18, 1919. Since the plenary meeting was too cumbersome for the efficient conduct of business, the major responsibility went into the hands of the five big powers. At first the Supreme Council, or the Council of Ten, consisted of Wilson; David Lloyd George, England's Prime Minister; Georges Clemenceau, France's Premier; Vittorio E. Orlando, Italy's Prime Minister; Marquis Kimmochi Saionji, Japan's chief delegate; and their ranking assistants. This group handled the main problems.

Later the Council of Ten also proved too large to be efficient. When Japan dropped out, therefore, it became the Council of Four: Wilson, Lloyd George, Clemenceau, and Orlando. After Orlando left Paris, it became the "Big Three." These men, often sitting alone in a room without even secretaries present, made the basic decisions of the conference. Since Wilson represented the wealthiest and freshest power and was the only chief of state, he stood out as the chief figure among them.

Wilson's League of Nations

Wilson's efforts to win immediate consideration for his league of nations dominated the first phase of the conference. As soon as the conference opened, the French offered a plan of procedure placing the treaty of peace first and the league last. Although most delegates supported the league idea, they agreed with the French. Internal unrest in Europe and the pressing need for economic reconstruction, they believed, gave the peace treaty first claim to attention. In Wilson's mind the League of Nations took precedence over all else, and he introduced a plan placing the league first on the agenda. His prestige, plus some diplomatic bargaining, were enough to give him his way.

The second plenary session of January 25 adopted a resolution to establish a league of nations "as an integral part of the general Treaty of Peace." It also appointed a committee, the League of Nations Commission, composed of representatives of fourteen governments, "to work out the details of the constitution and functions of the League." Wilson became chairman of the commission and chose an American plan for the League, modified and supported mainly with ideas from British drafts. The commission completed the draft of the constitution, henceforth known as the Covenant of the League of Nations, in ten days. The President's triumph came on February 14 when he read a draft of the completed covenant to a plenary session of the conference. "A living thing is born," he said, "and we must see to it that the clothes we put upon it do not hamper it." [18]

As Wilson walked out into the cold rain of Paris to take a train for Brest, he smiled warmly, probably thinking of the magnitude of his accomplishment. The next day he left for the United States to sign bills Congress had passed before it adjourned on March 4 and to explain the covenant to the people and Congress.

The League of Nations, as Wilson's covenant had created it, had several unique features. In theory it was universal. It would admit all states as members and would consider all disputes between two or more members. It was the first international organization of its kind to have a permanent constitution. In the Assembly, or international parliament, every member had one vote, but the more powerful organ was the Council, an executive body where each of the "Big Five" had a permanent seat and several smaller states held temporary membership through election.

The "heart of the Covenant," as Wilson insisted, was Article Ten. It pledged all members of the League to respect and preserve the independence of all members against "external aggression." "In case of any such aggression or in case of any threat or danger of such aggression," it read, "the Council shall advise upon the means by which this obligation shall be fulfilled." This article embodied the idea of collective security, meaning that the League would regard an attack on any one as an attack on all states and that all would cooperate to enforce peace. Opponents of Wilson and of the League later focused considerable criticism on this article.[19]

The Senate and the Round Robin

Before leaving Paris, Wilson, at the suggestion of Colonel House, had cabled the members of the congressional committees dealing with foreign affairs inviting them to dine with him and to discuss the covenant informally. He also asked them not to debate the covenant until he had had a chance to explain it. Then he spoiled the effect of his gracious gesture by announcing that he would land at Boston and would make a speech there.

The senators thought Wilson had acted unfairly in asking them to remain silent while he spoke. "Mr. Wilson has asked me to dinner," Henry Cabot Lodge told a friend. "[He] also asked me to say nothing. He then goes to my own home town and makes a speech—very characteristic."[20] Other senators, ignoring the President's request, attacked the covenant. The great debate over the League of Nations had begun.

Wilson held his White House dinner for the senators on February 16, and discussed the covenant with them until after midnight. To his enemies he appeared befuddled; to his friends he seemed human and attractive. In any case, he won no new supporters for the League.

Just after midnight on March 4, Lodge arose in the Senate and asked unanimous consent for a resolution, known as the "Round Robin," rejecting the League as proposed and opposing any league until after the peace settlement. When the Democrats objected, as Lodge had anticipated, he read into the record the names of thirty-seven Republican senators and two senators-elect who had signed the document. Since the signers comprised more than the one-third of the Senate plus one necessary to defeat any treaty, they had told the world that the Senate would subject the League to harsh treatment. Later that day the Republicans filibustered several vital appropriation bills to death so that the President would have to call Congress into special session before July 1, thus hastening the day when they could take control of the Senate.

That evening, tired and angry, Wilson struck back defiantly. ". . . when that treaty comes back," he told an audience in New York's Metropolitan Opera House, "gentlemen on this side will find the Covenant not only in it, but so many threads of the treaty tied to the Covenant that you cannot dissect the Covenant from the treaty without destroying the whole vital structure. The structure of peace will not be vital without the League of Nations, and no man is going to bring back a cadaver with him."[21] He then left for Paris.

While Wilson was gone, the statesmen in Paris had become indifferent toward the covenant. They had worked on the peace treaty and had pushed the League aside for later consideration. Annoyed by this development, Wilson acted decisively. On the day he returned to Paris, he announced through the press that the conference's decision to make the League an integral part of the treaty "is of final force and that there is no basis whatever for the reports that a change in this decision was contemplated."[22]

Although Wilson was satisfied with the covenant as drawn, even friends of the League pointed out that it had defects and hence should be modified. The President reluctantly agreed to seek changes to meet some of the criticism. "I am yielding to the judgment of men who have little knowledge or appreciation of the world situation," he complained, "but who, alas! control votes."[23]

The League of Nations Commission reconvened, and the President finally obtained approval of several amendments. They exempted domestic questions such as immigration and tariffs from the jurisdiction of the League, allowed members to refuse a mandate over former enemy colonies, permitted members to withdraw after giving due notice, and gave formal recognition to the Monroe Doctrine.

Since Wilson considered the League indispensable, the other statesmen at Paris used the League, in making the peace treaty, to force concessions from him on matters vital to themselves. In pursuing their national self-interests, they all clashed, at one time or another, with Wilson.

British and French Reactions

Of all the major powers, Britain offered Wilson the least opposition at the conference. Her aims were precise and limited: she wanted to expand her colonial holdings and those of her dominions at the expense of Germany, eliminate German naval power, and obtain reparations. The British had no problems of minorities and national boundaries involving the debatable question of self-determination. They were usually able, therefore, to avoid bitter quarrels with Wilson and at the same time to achieve most of their objectives.

The sharpest clash with Britain came in the opening days of the conference when Lloyd George, supported by France, Italy, and Japan, suggested disposing of Germany's colonies before completing work on the League. Wilson said that if they parceled out the helpless parts of the world first a league would be impossible, but he agreed with the Allied leaders that the colonies should not be restored to Germany. At first he wished to make the colonies the common property of the League administered by small nations which would act as trustees for the League, but the British dominions, Australia, New Zealand, and the Union of South Africa demanded outright annexation. Lloyd George, therefore, accepted the mandate system, except for the German colonies in the Pacific and in South Africa. He sought to obtain what the dominions desired before the League was completed and could place restrictions on their claims.

Wilson finally gave up his idea of mandates under small nations and conceded that the powers with claims to the German colonies, those who had conquered them, must be permitted to administer them. The result was a compromise. Wilson won adoption of his principle that the colonies must come under the League as mandates, and the British dominions, Japan, and other nations obtained control of the territories they wanted under a loose mandate from the League. Since the distribution of the former German colonies followed closely the division of spoils outlined in the secret treaties, Wilson appeared to have abandoned the fourth of his Fourteen Points.[24]

The main problem in making the peace was how to assure France of security against an intrinsically more powerful Germany who had invaded her twice within a half century. The French desired firm military guarantees against Germany and were willing to dismember her if necessary to weaken her. They had little faith in Wilson's Fourteen Points and in the League as protection against Germany. "There is an old system of alliances," Clemenceau had told the French Chamber of Deputies, "called the Balance of Power—this system of alliances, which I do not renounce, will be my guiding thought at the Peace Conference."[25]

France wanted to separate the land west of the Rhine River, containing about five million people, from Germany and to create one or more autonomous republics out of it that she could control. In tense debates with Clemenceau, Wilson opposed the plan, saying it violated his principle of self-determination. Seeing no necessarily vital connection between self-determination and peace-making, Clemenceau replied that he would not sign a treaty "which fails to give France the guarantees to which she has a right." Since Wilson would not budge and even threatened to walk out, the conference appeared ready to break up in failure.

The French finally agreed to a compromise in which they made the vital concessions. They allowed Germany to keep the Rhineland, but it had to be permanently demilitarized to a depth of about thirty-one miles east of the Rhine. Allied troops would occupy it for fifteen years.

To compensate for Germany's deliberate destruction of coal mines in northern France, and to assure security, the French had also desired the Saar Basin. They gave up that claim and received ownership of the Saarland's mines for fifteen years while a League of Nations Commission governed the region. At the end of that time, the people of the Saarland would decide their own future through a plebiscite.

In return for the French concessions, Wilson and Lloyd George, who supported Wilson on the Rhineland issue, offered two treaties promising British and American military aid if Germany attacked France. If either Britain or the United States failed to ratify its treaty, the other would automatically be released from its commitment. France and Britain ratified their alliance, but the American Senate never acted on the Treaty of Guarantee of 1919. Since France obtained neither the Rhineland nor the Treaty of Guarantee, she felt deceived.[26]

On France's second major demand, the question of reparations for the destruction Germany had wrought in areas she had occupied, Wilson made the important concessions. There would be no "punitive damages," Wilson had said. When Germany accepted the armistice terms, moreover, she had understood that the victors would assess payment only for damages to civilians and their property. Clemenceau and Lloyd George, pushed by aroused publics who held Germany responsible for the war, demanded that she pay the full cost of the war to the Allied peoples. Yielding to their pressure, Wilson agreed that Germany should pay for pensions to disabled Allied soldiers and their relatives, thus expanding the category of "civilian damages," agreed upon in the armistice, and virtually doubling Germany's reparations.

Wilson also wanted to assess Germany a fixed sum for reparations and to include the amount in the peace treaty. The Allies opposed establishing a definite figure, and the Treaty of Versailles, therefore, did not fix the amount of the reparation and did not set a time limit on the payments. It left the total amount to be assessed by a Reparation Commission.

The Germans, and others, later objected, saying that the enlarged reparations violated Wilson's expanded Fourteen Points and would be beyond their capacity to pay. Later events were to show that Germany had the capacity to pay the reparations bill but for political reasons considered it impractical to do so.[27]

Italian and Japanese Demands

Wilson's friction with Italy also stemmed from his determination to adhere to the principle of self-determination, and from Italy's desire to advance her own interests. After bargaining with both sides, Italy had signed the "secret" Treaty of London of April, 1915, which promised her the South Tyrol, or Trentino, also some land at the head and on the eastern shore of the Adriatic, and other territories.

Early in the conference Wilson readily conceded Italy's claim to the South Tyrol up to the Brenner Pass to give her a strategically defensible northern frontier, even though the new boundary violated the principle of self-determination by placing about two hundred thousand Austrian Germans under Italian rule. Later, he also accepted Italy's claim to Trieste on the Adriatic, but objected strenuously when Italy expanded her demands to include the city of Fiume that had been promised to Croatia, now a part of Yugoslavia.

Fiume itself contained an Italian majority, but the suburbs and the countryside were distinctly Slav. It was, moreover, Yugoslavia's most important outlet to the sea. When Orlando and his Foreign Minister, Sidney Sonnino, persisted in demand-ing Fiume, Wilson appealed in vain over their heads directly to the Italian people. Orlando and Sonnino walked out of the conference and received a vote of con-fidence from the Italian legislature.

While the Italians were gone, the Big Three distributed the first set of mandates. As punishment for leaving the conference, they disregarded Italy's claims to enemy colonies under the Treaty of London. With the question of Fiume still unsettled, the Italians returned to Paris just before the peace treaty was presented to the Germans. Later, Italy worked out a temporary solution directly with Yugoslavia and ultimately obtained Fiume.

The Japanese took advantage of the Italian crisis to press one of their major demands. They had come to Paris with three. They wanted to annex the German islands in the Pacific north of the equator, to obtain formal recognition of the principle of racial equality, and to acquire German rights—such as railroad and coal-mining concessions—in Shantung province on the mainland of China.

Japan obtained control of the German islands in the north Pacific without much difficulty through a League of Nations mandate, but Wilson had made a reserva-tion concerning the island of Yap in the Carolines. Since it served as a cable center to China, the Netherlands East Indies (now Indonesia), the Philippines, and Guam, he thought it should be internationalized.[28]

The seemingly innocent question of racial equality caused trouble for Wilson. The proud Japanese felt strongly about the prejudice their people had to endure in other countries. Yet attempts to place a statement in the covenant committing the League to the principle of racial equality failed because of the opposition of the British dominions, mainly that of Australia whose domestic laws discriminated against Asians. Since Wilson was chairman of the League of Nations Commission and was forced to rule against racial equality when the issue came to a crucial vote, the Japanese public held the United States responsible for the decision.

Japan had taken Shantung from Germany and through her Twenty-One Demands had forced China to agree in advance to a cession of German rights there at the close of the war. Secret treaties with Britain and France in 1917 and another with China in the following year sanctioned Japan's claim to those rights. At the conference the Chinese protested, saying they had signed their treaties with Japan under duress, and asked that Shantung be restored to them. Although Wilson sympathized with the Chinese and feared that Japan would jeopardize the principle of self-determination by staying in the province, he surrendered to the Japanese in order to save the League. "If Italy remains away and Japan goes home," he asked an adviser, "what becomes of the League of Nations?"

The Treaty of Versailles gave Japan the former German rights in Shantung. Japan promised to return the province "in full sovereignty to China retaining only the economic privileges granted to Germany." This compromise did not satisfy the Chinese who refused to sign the treaty.

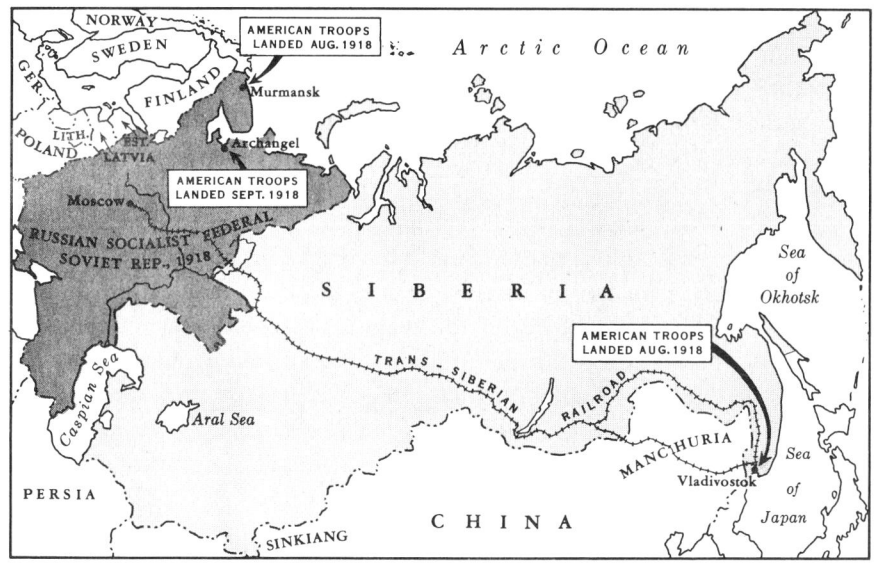

AMERICAN INTERVENTION IN RUSSIA, 1918

Central Europe and the Russian Revolution

Wilson acquiesced in the greatest deviation from the principle of self-determination when he supported the peace settlement for central Europe. The problems of national unity, economic viability, and defensible frontiers were so involved that boundaries in that region defied demarcation according to nationality.

The new state of Czechoslovakia, comprising the most valuable part of the fallen Austrian empire, included the Sudetenland with over three million Germans. A reborn Poland, created from German, Austrian, and Russian territory, gained control over millions of Germans and other minorities. Poland also obtained a "corridor" that separated East Prussia from Germany proper so she could have access to the sea. While the "corridor" was essentially Polish, the city of Danzig within it, which Poland controlled in partnership with the League as a free city, was wholly German.

Although the peace conference defined Poland's western boundaries, it was unable to delineate her eastern frontiers. That required agreement with Russia, who was not represented at Paris.

While the peacemakers were meeting in Paris, civil war was disrupting Russia. In 1918 the Allies had intervened in Russia to prevent military supplies they had sent there from falling into German hands, and also with the hope of drawing the

Russians back into the war. Wilson had reluctantly participated in the intervention by sending limited numbers of American troops to Murmansk and Archangel in northern Russia where they joined British and French forces in offensive operations against Bolshevik troops. He also sent some eight thousand soldiers to Vladivostok in Siberia where they cooperated with other Allied forces, principally Japanese.[29]

When the Allies, primarily the French and British, wanted to launch a large-scale anti-Bolshevik intervention, Wilson had resisted. "In my opinion," he said, "trying to stop a revolutionary movement with armies in the field is like using a broom to hold back a great ocean."[30] He insisted that the Russian people must be permitted to settle their internal problems without outside interference. Yet the Allies, primarily the French, supported anti-Bolshevik armies in the civil war.

Since Russia covered half of Europe and no peace settlement could be truly complete without her, Wilson, Lloyd George, and others, had wanted to include the Russians in some of the peace discussions. Clemenceau protested, saying that French public opinion was so strongly anti-Bolshevik that he could not tolerate dealing with the Bolshevik leaders. Since British and American public opinion was also violently anti-Bolshevik, and it was still difficult to discern which of the warring groups truly represented the Russian people, Wilson had suggested a separate conference between the Bolsheviks and other Russian political groups to be held on the island of Prinkipo in the Sea of Marmora. The Soviet government belatedly agreed, but the leaders of the counterrevolution in Russia would not deal with the Bolsheviks.

Believing that the Bolsheviks were tools of the Germans, the Allies had refused to withdraw their troops from Russia. During the peace conference, therefore, the Allies were virtually at war with the Soviet government. The Bolsheviks had forced Allied diplomats out of Russia and had denounced the United States for cooperating in the military operations against them.

A number of independent states, supported by the Allies, had sprung up along Russia's frontiers out of former Russian territory. The fate of any of the new states, Lithuania, Latvia, and Estonia, could not be definitely settled until the end of the civil war in Russia. With Russia diplomatically isolated, the peace settlements, therefore, did not embrace eastern Europe.

A Compromise Peace

The German delegates came before the conference in the Trianon Palace at Versailles on May 7, 1919, to receive the completed treaty. "You have asked for peace," Clemenceau told them. "We are ready to give you peace."[31] After studying the treaty, the Germans protested, saying essentially that they had been tricked into disarming by the Fourteen Points, for this was not the peace of justice they had been promised.

Actually, Germany had lost the war on the field of battle and had sought peace because she had no other choice. The Allies replied that they were offering "fundamentally a peace of justice." Under the threat of an Allied march on Berlin, the Germans finally accepted the Treaty of Versailles on June 23, and signed it in the Hall of Mirrors five days later. Each of the other Central Powers later signed separate treaties with the Allies.

Some critics have denounced the Treaty of Versailles as a "Carthaginian Peace" of vengeance. Others have condemned it as too mild. It was what it had to be when one considers the diverse aims of those who made the peace. It was a compromise between a conqueror's peace and a peace freely negotiated by all concerned on the basis of accommodation.

Wilson failed at Paris, some writers have said, and returned home a fallen Messiah because he had compromised his principles, particularly that of self-determination. Self-determination was not *the* key to a stable peace, as later years were to show, and too often it meant different things to different people. Germany remained whole and intrinsically strong, and the peoples of Europe were closer to being ruled by men of their own nationality after Versailles than ever before.

Compromise, moreover, was no crime. All of the Allied statesmen had to compromise. None of them attained all of their objectives. Clemenceau's own countrymen turned on him as the man "who had won the war and lost the peace" and who compromised the security of his country. Wilson, after all, got what he wanted most—the League of Nations. He recognized that the treaty settlement had flaws, but looked to the League to review the decisions of Paris and to iron out the imperfections.

The Battle for the League

While Wilson was in Paris, influential Republicans, led by Henry Cabot Lodge, made plans to oppose the League of Nations. They saw an advance copy of the revised covenant with Wilson's amendments, and most of them considered it still unsatisfactory. William E. Borah of Idaho, an old Progressive and an isolationist, headed a small but powerful group of senators, numbering about fourteen, that was uncompromisingly opposed to the League in any form. This group was later known as the "irreconcilables," and sometimes as the "bitter-enders" or the "Battalion of Death."

"I said to Senator Borah," Lodge wrote, "it seemed perfectly obvious to me that any attempt to defeat the treaty of Versailles with the League by a straight vote in the Senate, if taken immediately, would be hopeless, even if it were desirable." [32]

The Senator from Idaho reluctantly agreed with Lodge's estimate and said that he and his group would join the other Republicans in supporting any amendments and reservations that Lodge might offer. After supporting the changes, Borah insisted, he would still vote against final approval of the treaty.[33]

Lodge's strategy, as worked out at this time and accepted by other Republican leaders, assured him of strong opposition to the League and also of unity within his own party. Unity was important because the Republican majority was thin. The new Senate would have 49 Republicans and 47 Democrats. "If we should fail to organize the Senate," Lodge told a newspaper editor, ". . . all hope of intelligent resistance to the League will vanish and the Republican party will be shattered."[34]

Since opponents of the League agreed that sentiment in the Senate as well as among the people, favored the League, they organized their own League for the Preservation of American Independence and used it in a campaign of opposition to Wilson. To finance their anti-League of Nations campaign, they obtained money from two of America's wealthiest men, Henry C. Frick and Andrew W. Mellon of Pennsylvania.

Wilson had tried to postpone the day when the Republicans could use the Senate as a forum for attacks on the League, but finally called Congress into special session on May 19, 1919. The Republicans quickly organized the Senate, choosing Lodge as majority leader and Chairman of the Committee on Foreign Relations.

Some historians have said Lodge was an "irreconcilable" who opposed any league. Others have concluded that he favored the League of Nations with strong reservations. Although he had doubts about the practicability of the League of Nations idea, Lodge himself maintained that he favored a league but not Wilson's league.

Several things about Lodge are clear. He was not an isolationist; he was an ardent nationalist, a believer in the balance of power, and a party partisan. Wilson detested him and he hated Wilson. "I never expected to hate any one in politics," Lodge had once confessed, "with the hatred I feel towards Wilson."[35] Rather than accept Wilson's league, Lodge worked closely with the "irreconcilables" to destroy the peace settlement.

The Committee on Foreign Relations would have a decisive voice in consideration of the Treaty of Versailles, and Lodge packed it with opponents of the League. Six out of ten Republicans, a number sufficient to dominate the majority, were "irreconcilables." When Democrats and pro-League Republicans objected, an "irreconcilable" retorted that Wilson had "stacked the Peace Conference with Democrats."

On the floor of the Senate, Republicans demanded an official copy of the treaty that was at the time being circulated unofficially in Europe. Wilson refused because he had promised the Allies he would not reveal the treaty's terms until they were final. Borah then took the unprecedented step of obtaining an unofficial version and placing it in the *Congressional Record* on June 9.

The next day another Republican "irreconcilable," Senator Philander C. Knox of Pennsylvania, introduced a resolution asking for separation of the treaty from the League. Since many Republicans would not support the drastic Knox resolution, Lodge and other Republican members of the Committee on Foreign Relations decided on a change of tactics. Instead of amendments, they would in the future usually advise reservations to the treaty. Amendments would require the President to reopen negotiations with the other powers for their acceptance, but reservations would go into effect unless the other signatories specifically objected to them.

Angered by the Republican tactics, Wilson was determined on his return home "to take a most militant and aggressive course" against his opponents. On July 10, shortly after returning to America, he revealed his fighting mood. A reporter asked if he thought the treaty could be ratified if the Senate were to add certain reservations. "I do not think hypothetical questions are concerned," the President replied. "*The Senate is going to ratify the treaty.*" [36]

That afternoon Wilson told the Senate of the peace settlement and then asked for prompt and unqualified approval of the treaty. "Shall we or any other free people hesitate to accept this great duty?" he asked. "Dare we reject it and break the heart of the world?" He was confident that the people would support his plans for world peace. "America," he concluded, "shall in truth show the way." [37]

Wilson's belief that the people would support his plans appeared justified by the evidence available on the state of public opinion in the spring of 1919. The Senate, moreover, had never before rejected a peace treaty, and Wilson had made it impossible to separate the treaty from the League. The opposition senators, who objected mainly to the covenant, therefore, could not kill the League while accepting the treaty.

If public sentiment had remained strongly behind the League, Wilson's strategy might have worked, but as the debate dragged on, dissatisfaction with the treaty increased. Many liberals were disillusioned with it, considering it unnecessarily harsh. It was, one of them said, "purple with revenge." [38] These idealists opposed the League because they saw it as an instrument designed to freeze an unjust *status quo*.

Non-English ethnic groups, some of them forced into silence or conformity during the war, now expressed their resentment toward the peace settlement. German-Americans, Italian-Americans, Jews, and Americans of Irish descent, among others, all found fault with it.

Isolationism versus Collective Security

The strongest and most widespread opposition to the League came from an isolationism that seemed to grow from a spreading disillusion with the peace settlement. American soldiers seemingly had lost faith in Wilson's great crusade. Even one of their popular songs expressed an isolationist mood that the folks back home could appreciate.

> We drove the Boche across the Rhine,
> The Kaiser from his throne.
> Oh, Lafayette, we've paid our debt,
> For Christ's sake, send us home.[39]

When they returned, the doughboys made it clear that all they wanted was to keep out of another war overseas.

Instead of promoting international understanding, the war, followed by the quarrels at Paris and the upheavals in Russia and Central Europe, added to an intensified nationalism and antiforeignism. Many Americans were indifferent to the League and were more concerned with the domestic problems of inflation, strikes, race riots, and the fear of Bolshevism. Late in June a group of twenty-six legislators in Massachusetts, for instance, had sent Wilson a telegram saying, "The citizens of the United States want you home to help reduce the high cost of living which we consider far more important than the League of Nations."

Other opponents included staunch Republicans who could never forget that Wilson was a Democrat and that the League represented his ideas. Many of them would have opposed any international organization he sponsored, and they, therefore, supplied money and leadership to the isolationist cause.

There were also many distinguished leaders of American society who were not isolationists but who opposed the League as Wilson presented it. These men believed that the United States should be cooperative and active in world affairs but would not accept the system of collective security embodied in the covenant, particularly in Article Ten. They were willing to accept the League only with modifications. Opponents insisted that Wilson's idea of collective security would not work. "If perpetual," Elihu Root said, "it would be an attempt to preserve for all time unchanged the distribution of power and territory made in accordance with the views and exigencies of the Allies in this present juncture of affairs."[40]

Wilson and his supporters insisted that collective security would work and was the best means of safeguarding peace. Under Article Ten, Wilson said in defense, "we all stand together in a common pledge, and that pledge is essential to the peace of the world."[41]

When separated from deep emotions and bitter partisanship, the great debate of 1919–1920 was between the theories of isolationism and collective security. There was also a third alternative of limited international cooperation that most Americans seemed to prefer, but neither Wilson nor the isolationists were willing to adopt it.

After the treaty had been referred to the Committee on Foreign Relations, Lodge used his strategy of delay, believing correctly that public opposition would grow. About halfway through its deliberations the committee asked Wilson for a public conference. He agreed, and on August 19 invited the entire committee to lunch at the White House. For over three and one-half hours the President answered questions and talked about the treaty and the covenant. Many of the questions dealt with Article Ten. Wilson stressed that the obligation under it was moral not legal. Some senators attacked the Shantung settlement. The President came out well in the interrogation but did commit a number of blunders. He denied, for instance, that he had known of the secret treaties before going to Paris.[42]

Wilson's Western Tour

Since this conference had not won any new support among the Republican senators, and other signs showed that public interest in the League was sagging, Wilson decided to stump the country, particularly the West and Midwest, seeking support for the treaty. If he explained his case to the people, he thought, they would support him and an aroused public opinion would force the Senate to act favorably on the treaty without loading it with amendments.

Wilson was now sixty-three years old. His doctor and friends warned him that a strenuous speaking tour might damage his health beyond repair. Ignoring their advice, he visited twenty-nine cities, traveled 8000 miles, and delivered thirty-two major addresses and eight minor ones, all in twenty-two days.

The President drew sympathetic crowds and his words often carried emotional appeal. What impact he made on public sentiment is difficult to assess because "bitter-enders," notably Borah and Senator Hiram W. Johnson of California, trailed him and in many cities also drew enthusiastic audiences. Johnson, who denounced the League in one city as an "infamous nostrum" and in another as "a gigantic war trust," seemed particularly successful in arousing anti-League emotions.

Wilson's tour ended in tragedy. Late in the evening, after his speech at Pueblo, Colorado, on September 25, he collapsed from exhaustion. His physician canceled the remaining speeches and the presidential train, with shades drawn in the President's car, roared through the night directly for Washington.[43]

A few days after his return, Wilson suffered a stroke which paralyzed his left side and almost took his life. The President, incapacitated for six months, recovered slowly. He did not meet his cabinet for seven and a half months. Fortunately his mind remained clear. Yet his wrecked body had an effect on his thinking and on his emotions. He could no longer offer the leadership necessary to bring victory to his cause. Since there was no leader of comparable stature available to fight for him, the League lost whatever small chance it might have had to move through the Senate unscathed.

Even if Wilson had not broken down, his troubles with the Senate Republicans probably would not have eased. His tour had not converted his opponents to the support of the treaty and in some instances his biting words had antagonized previously mild critics. "The only people who have votes on the treaty are here in the Senate," Lodge told a friend before Wilson started his trip.[44] That was the situation when the President returned.

The Lodge Reservations

On September 10, a week before Wilson began his western trip, Lodge reported his committee's recommendations on the Treaty of Versailles to the Senate. Five days later the report became the regular order of business. The Republican majority recommended forty-five amendments and four reservations, most of them designed to eliminate objectionable parts of the treaty and to protect America's freedom to act independently of the League.

Loyal Democrats and Republicans who did not want such strong reservations defeated all of the amendments. Lodge then reported a resolution of approval accompanied by fourteen reservations, the so-called "Lodge reservations." They covered the major objections of opponents to the treaty. The most significant one, which virtually rejected Wilson's idea of collective security, was the second reservation, which stated that only Congress had the right to decide on the United States' obligation to protect another country's independence. Although this reservation struck at Wilson's cherished Article Ten, none of the Lodge reservations seemed strong enough to impair the covenant itself.

On the following day Senator Gilbert M. Hitchcock of Nebraska, the Democratic minority leader, visited the sick President. He told Wilson that the Democrats could not gain approval of the treaty without reservations and urged him to compromise.

"Let Lodge compromise!" Wilson snapped.

"Well, of course, he must compromise also," the senator said, "but we might well hold out the olive branch."

"Let Lodge hold out the olive branch," the President answered. That closed the subject.[45]

Wilson believed that revision of the covenant should be left for later consideration, after the United States had ratified the treaty. Yet, before he had gone West, he had worked for four reservations of his own that he had given to Hitchcock to use when necessary. His reservations did not differ markedly from the more important Lodge reservations. He opposed the Lodge changes because he distrusted the senator and believed that Lodge intended to use his reservations to kill the treaty.

Hitchcock introduced Wilson's reservations plus others, the five so-called "Hitchcock reservations," to the Senate. Republicans prevented their consideration, but adopted the Lodge reservations. The President now had a choice of accepting the Senate's approval of the treaty with the Lodge reservations or of risking its defeat.

Wilson revealed his choice to the Democratic senators by announcing that the Lodge resolution "does not provide for ratification, but rather for nullification of the treaty. I sincerely hope that the friends and supporters of the treaty will vote against the Lodge resolution of ratification.

"I understand that the door will then probably be open for a genuine resolution of ratification." [46]

The President hoped that the defeat of the Lodge resolution would produce a deadlock and out of it would come an acceptable compromise. Lodge thought differently. If the Democrats rejected the treaty with reservations, he had told a friend, "it will stay defeated." Although Wilson was successful in securing the defeat of the Lodge resolution, no mutually satisfactory compromise settlement could later be worked out.

Most thoughtful Americans, who wanted the treaty approved with some kind of reservations, were shocked by what had happened. Public pressure demanded some way out of the deadlock that ultimately would mean death for the treaty in the United States. Wilson wanted to carry the issue to the people. He told fellow Democrats that the voters should "give the next election the form of a great and solemn referendum" on the League. [47]

In the middle of January, 1920, a bipartisan group of senators, including Lodge, began meeting to devise reservations acceptable to both Democrats and "reservationist" Republicans. They made some progress, but the "bitter-enders," by threatening Lodge with a bolt from the Republican party in an election year, blocked the compromise effort.

Alarmed by the Senate's rejection of the treaty, spokesmen for the British government also tried to find ways of breaking the deadlock. They made it clear that England, preferring limited participation to none at all, would accept American membership in the League even with reservations. Clemenceau, who thought as did other Frenchmen, that France would accept the Senate's reservations, said Wilson and Lodge were two "stubborn old mules kicking each other around." The European willingness to accept modifications strengthened the reservationists.

Responding to the public pressure, the Senate voted to reconsider the treaty and again referred it to the Committee on Foreign Relations. That committee promptly reported it back to the Senate with the Lodge reservations, now increased to fifteen. Wilson still opposed them. "If I accept them," he told a friend, "these senators will merely offer new ones, even more humiliating." After a pause, he added, "These evil men intend to destroy the League." When the treaty came to a vote on March 20, it was defeated for the last time by a vote of 49 for to 35 against, only seven short of the necessary two-thirds majority.

Party politics had helped kill the treaty and so had the feud between Wilson and Lodge. By stubbornly refusing to allow loyal Democrats to vote for it with the Lodge reservations, Wilson had contributed to the defeat of the League he had himself created.

The Referendum of 1920

Yet the President would not admit that the League was lost. He placed his hopes for the covenant in the election of November, 1920, looking upon it as a national referendum on the League. He even considered running for a third term with the League as the great issue. "I suggest," he said a week before the election, "that the candidacy of every candidate for whatever office be tested by this question: 'Shall we, or shall we not, redeem the great moral obligation of the United States?'"[48]

Wilson's hopes were not justified by events or by the mood of the American people, who appeared to be tired of the wrangle over the League. The Democratic convention, meeting in San Francisco, had passed over Wilson to choose James M. Cox, the colorless governor of Ohio, who was not closely identified with Wilson.[49] The party platform was fairly explicit on the League, calling for immediate approval of the treaty without crippling reservations but without opposition to clarifying reservations. In his campaign Cox supported the League but did not make it the central issue.

The Republicans had met in Chicago with Lodge as chairman of the convention. They equivocated on the League. "The Republican Party," their platform said, "stands for agreement among the nations to preserve the peace of the world."[50] They would seek to achieve that objective through an "international association" that would not compromise national independence. They denounced Wilson's League and praised the senators who had opposed him. For their presidential standard bearer they chose Warren G. Harding, an amiable and unsophisticated senator from Ohio.

In the campaign the Republicans straddled the issue of the League and relied on their ambiguous platform and on the people's resentment against the administration, for various irritations that had piled up in eight years of Democratic rule, to bring them victory. Prominent Republicans who had supported the League assured the voters that Harding's election would bring the United States into the League because he would eliminate the objectionable features of Article Ten and would persuade the powers to accept the change. Other Republicans, particularly the "irreconcilables," insisted that a vote for Harding was a vote against the League. Harding himself was vague. In some of his speeches he said he favored "an association of nations for the promotion of peace."[51] At other times he opposed the League. All prominent Republicans at least agreed that they were opposed to Wilson's League.

Harding won by a landslide, capturing every part of the country but the solid South. Lodge interpreted the election as the solemn referendum Wilson had desired. "I was satisfied by the result that the people at large were much more decided about not having anything to do with the League of Nations," he wrote later, "than were the men in public life."[52]

Actually, all kinds of issues clouded the results. Foreign policy, as has happened often in American elections, was so entangled with domestic questions that the election probably offered no clear mandate for any policy toward the League. Yet Harding and his advisers saw the election as a rejection of the international organization. After his inauguration he said his administration would not enter the League. "It doesn't propose to enter now," he announced, "by the side door, back door, or cellar door."[53]

The new Republican Congress, by joint resolution finally declared the war ended on July 2, 1921. Although the United States never ratified any of the peace treaties, Congress reserved to the United States all rights secured by the war and the peace settlements. Late in August, Harding negotiated separate peace treaties with Germany, Austria, and Hungary.

The American people were apparently satisfied and seemingly had accepted the election of Harding as the final verdict against the League. In 1920 they were not ready to assume the responsibilities that Wilson's system of collective security offered. They chose, instead, to retreat into another era of isolationism.

NOTES

1. Relations with Turkey during the war are discussed in Robert L. Daniel, "The Armenian Question and American-Turkish Relations, 1914–1927," *Mississippi Valley Historical Review*, XLVI (Sept. 1959), 252–275.

2. Quoted in Robert E. Osgood, *Ideals and Self-Interest in America's Foreign Relations* (Chicago, 1953), p. 265.

3. The terms of the principal secret treaties are in Ray S. Baker, *Woodrow Wilson and World Settlement* (3 vols., Garden City, N.Y., 1923–27), I, 47–63.

4. For the quotation, see April 22, 1917, Charles Seymour, ed., *The Intimate Papers of Colonel House* (4 vols., Boston, 1926–28), III, 37. Arthur S. Link, in *Wilson the Diplomatist* (Baltimore, 1957), p. 98, points out that Wilson jealously guarded his freedom of action by refusing to discuss the Allied war aims.

5. For details on this dispute, see David F. Trask, *The United States in the Supreme War Council: American War Aims and Inter-Allied Strategy, 1917–1918* (Middletown, Conn., 1961), pp. 70–99.

6. Quoted in Arno J. Mayer, *Political Origins of the New Diplomacy, 1917–1918* (New Haven, Conn., 1959), pp. 262–263.

7. Trotsky to the army, Nov. 24, 1917, quoted in George F. Kennan, *Russia Leaves the War* (Princeton, 1956), p. 106.

8. The text of the speech is in Ray S. Baker and William E. Dodd, eds., *The Public Papers of Woodrow Wilson* (6 vols., New York, 1925–27), *War and Peace*, I, 155–162. For Wilson's own commentary on the Fourteen Points as recorded by Sir William Wiseman, see John L. Snell, "Wilson on Germany and the Fourteen Points," *Journal of Modern History*, XXVI (Dec. 1954), 364–369.

9. In "Wilson's Peace Program and German Socialism, January–March, 1918," *Mississippi Valley Historical Review*, XXXVIII (Sept. 1951), 208, John L. Snell maintains that as a result of the Fourteen Points Wilson, not Lenin, was hailed by Europe's liberals as the apostle of peace.

10. Jan. 20, 1918, quoted in Kennan, *Russia Leaves the War*, p. 261. This account follows Kennan's interpretation. For the view that Lenin was pleased with the Fourteen Points, privately at least, see Robert D. Warth, *The Allies and the Russian Revolution from the Fall of the Monarchy to the Peace of Brest-Litovsk* (Durham, N.C., 1954), p. 213 and Mayer, *New Diplomacy*, p. 367.

11. This interpretation is based on that in Étienne Mantoux, *The Carthaginian Peace, or the Economic Consequences of Mr. Keynes* (London, 1946), pp. 52–53. For the view that the Fourteen Points had a decisive effect on the morale of German soldiers, see George G. Bruntz, *Allied Propaganda and the Collapse of the German Empire in 1918* (Stanford, Calif., 1938), p. 212.

12. This point is stressed in Harry R. Rudin, *Armistice, 1918* (New Haven, 1944), which demolishes the theory that civilians betrayed the German army, in effect, with a "stab in the back."

13. By recognizing the independence of the Czechoslovaks and Yugoslavs, Wilson himself modified the Fourteen Points. For details, see Victor S. Mamatey, *The United States and East Central Europe, 1914–1918: A Study in Wilsonian Diplomacy and Propaganda* (Princeton, 1957), pp. 334–345.

14. Quoted in Thomas A. Bailey, *Woodrow Wilson and the Lost Peace* (New York, 1944), p. 40.

15. Seward W. Livermore, in "The Sectional Issue in the 1918 Congressional Elections," *Mississippi Valley Historical Review*, XXXV (June 1948), 29–60. See also Selig Adler's perceptive article, "The Congressional Election of 1918," *South Atlantic Quarterly*, XXVI (Oct. 1937), 447–465.

16. Nov. 11, 1918, Baker and Dodd, *Wilson Papers, War and Peace*, I, 293.

17. Quoted in Bailey, *Wilson and the Lost Peace*, p. 72.

18. Baker and Dodd, *Wilson Papers, War and Peace*, I, 426. Wilson's support and sponsorship of the League owes much to the ideas of Jan Smuts. See George Curry, "Woodrow Wilson, Jan Smuts, and the Versailles Settlement," *The American Historical Review*, LXVI (July 1961), 968–986.

19. The text of the covenant and pertinent documents are in David Miller, *The Drafting of the Covenant* (2 vols., New York, 1928). For the long term influence of Wilson on the idea of collective security, see Robert E. Osgood, "Woodrow Wilson, Collective Security, and the Lessons of History," *Confluence*, V (Winter 1957), 341–354; Richard N. Current, "The United States and 'Collective Security' Notes on the History of an Idea," in Alexander DeConde, ed., *Isolation and Security* (Durham, N.C., 1957), pp. 33–55; Roland N. Stromberg, "The Riddle of Collective Security, 1916–1920," in George L. Anderson, ed., *Issues and Conflicts* (Lawrence, Kans., 1959), pp. 147–170; and Edward H. Buehrig, "Woodrow Wilson and Collective Security," in *Wilson's Foreign Policy in Perspective* (Bloomington, Ind., 1957), pp. 34–60.

20. To W. R. Thayer, Feb. 21, 1919, quoted in John A. Garraty, *Henry Cabot Lodge* (New York, 1953), p. 351.

21. March 4, 1919, Baker and Dodd, *Wilson Papers, War and Peace*, I, 451.

22. March 15, 1919, *ibid.*, I, 457.

23. Quoted in Thomas A. Bailey, *Woodrow Wilson and the Great Betrayal* (New York, 1945), p. 11.

24. For the mandate system's development at Paris and in the League, see Hessel D. Hall, *Mandates, Dependencies and Trusteeships* (Washington, 1948). For details on relations with Britain, see Seth P. Tillman, *Anglo-American Relations at the Paris Peace Conference of 1919* (Princeton, 1961).

25. Quoted in Osgood, *Ideals and Self-Interest*, p. 288.

26. For a detailed summary of negotiation of the treaties, see Louis A. R. Yates, *United States and French Security, 1917–1921* (New York, 1957).

27. The most influential indictment of the reparation provisions and hence of the treaty was John Maynard Keynes, *The Economic Consequence of the Peace* (New York, 1920), a bitter attack which was not effectively discredited until more than a quarter of a century later by Étienne Mantoux's *Carthaginian Peace*. Various writers, most of them influenced by Keynes, have called the reparations section the major failure of the Versailles treaty, mainly because it sought to achieve the unattainable. See, for instance, René Albrecht-Carrié, "Versailles Twenty Years After," *Political Science Quarterly*, LV (March 1940), 1–24. For an account of the reparations settlement with supporting documents, see Philip M. Burnett, *Reparation at the Paris Peace Conference from the Standpoint of the American Delegation* (2 vols., New York, 1940). The question of reparations also brought Britain and the United States into fundamental conflict. See Tillman, *Anglo-*

American Relations at the Paris Peace Conference, pp. 229–259.

28. Further details are in Russell H. Fifield, "Disposal of the Carolines, Marshalls, and Marianas at the Paris Peace Conference," *The American Historical Review*, LI (April 1946), 472–479; Earl S. Pomeroy, "American Policy Respecting the Marshalls, Carolines, and Marianas, 1898–1941," *Pacific Historical Review*, XVII (Feb. 1948), 43–53; and Werner Levi, "American Attitudes toward the Pacific Islands, 1914–1919," *ibid.*, pp. 55–64.

29. The most detailed, scholarly analysis of this intervention is George F. Kennan, *The Decision to Intervene* (Princeton, 1958). See also his *Russia and the West under Lenin and Stalin* (Boston, 1961), pp. 120–150, for Russia and the peace conference.

30. Paul J. Mantoux, *Les délibérations des Conseil des quatre (24 mars-28 Juin 1919)* (2 vols., Paris, 1955), I, 55.

31. Quoted in Allan Nevins, *Henry White: Thirty Years of American Diplomacy* (New York, 1930), p. 444.

32. Henry Cabot Lodge, *The Senate and the League of Nations* (New York, 1925), p. 147.

33. For details, see Marian C. McKenna, *Borah* (Ann Arbor, Mich., 1961), p. 157.

34. To J. T. Williams, May 13, 1919, quoted in Garraty, *Lodge*, pp. 361–362.

35. To Theodore Roosevelt, March 1, 1915, *ibid.*, p. 312.

36. Quoted in Bailey, *Wilson and the Great Betrayal*, p. 9.

37. July 10, 1919, Baker and Dodd, *Wilson Papers, War and Peace*, I, 548, 552.

38. William Allen White, quoted in Selig Adler, *The Isolationist Impulse: Its Twentieth Century Reaction* (New York, 1957), p. 57.

39. *Ibid.*, p. 99.

40. Quoted in Philip C. Jessup, *Elihu Root* (2 vols., New York, 1938), II, 392. For an analysis of the opposition to collective security see John C. Vinson, *Referendum for Isolation: Defeat of Article Ten of the League of Nations Covenant* (Athens, Ga., 1961).

41. Sept. 22, 1919, Baker and Dodd, *Wilson Papers, War and Peace*, II, 333.

42. For details, see Mary R. Frear, "Did President Wilson Contradict Himself on the Secret Treaties?" *Current History*, XXX (June 1929), 435–443 and Robert H. Ferrell, "Woodrow Wilson and Open Diplomacy," in Anderson, *Issues and Conflicts*, pp. 200–204.

43. For details, see Dexter Perkins, "Woodrow Wilson's Tour," in Daniel Aaron, ed., *America in Crisis* (New York, 1952), pp. 245–265 and Gregg Phifer, "Woodrow Wilson's Swing around the Circle in Defense of His League," *Florida State University Studies*, No. 23, *Woodrow Wilson Centennial Issue*, Victor S. Mamatey, ed. (Tallahassee, Fla. 1956), pp. 65–102.

44. To L. A. Coolidge, Aug. 7, 1919, quoted in Garraty, *Lodge*, p. 371.

45. Quoted in Bailey, *Wilson and the Great Betrayal*, p. 178.

46. Quoted in Denna F. Fleming, *The United States and the League of Nations, 1918–1920* (New York, 1932), p. 395.

47. Jan. 8, 1920, Baker and Dodd, *Wilson Papers, War and Peace*, II, 455.

48. To pro-League Republicans, Oct. 28, 1920, *ibid.*, II, 510. Wilson had even considered the idea of a separate election on the League issue. See Kurt Wimer, "Woodrow Wilson's Plan for a Vote of Confidence," *Pennsylvania History*, XXVIII (July 1961), 282.

49. Wesley M. Bagby, in "Woodrow Wilson, a Third Term, and the Solemn Referendum," *The American Historical Review*, LX (April 1955), 575, suggests that Wilson's illness and his desire for a third nomination frustrated compromise on the Treaty of Versailles.

50. Kirk H. Porter, ed., *National Party Platforms* (New York, 1924), p. 451.

51. *The New York Times*, Oct. 8, 1920, p. 1. On the same page Senator Borah was quoted as saying that Harding would "refuse to enter any League that impairs the sovereignty of the United States."

52. To James L. Barton, June 8, 1921, quoted in Garraty, *Lodge*, p. 400.

53. Quoted in Fleming, *U.S. and the League*, p. 472. For interpretations of the election, see Wesley M. Bagby, *The Road to Normalcy: The Presidential Campaign and Election of 1920* (Baltimore, 1962), pp. 160–161.

Chapter Twenty

ARMAMENTS AND
THE PEACE CRUSADE

WHEN the war in Europe ended, relations with Japan were badly strained. Many Americans believed that the Japanese had made no important contribution to the defeat of Germany and had used the war primarily to expand their own interests in China and other parts of East Asia, even at the expense of their allies. Distrust of Japan at the Paris Peace Conference and Wilson's opposition to her objectives there and elsewhere added to the tension between the two countries. The most serious of the wartime problems that contributed to the mounting postwar bitterness was the Siberian intervention, carried out in 1918 mainly by Japanese and American troops assisted by small British and French contingents, ostensibly to rescue a Czech legion of some 50,000 men fighting its way across Siberia to join French armies on the western front.

Japan's true objective, supported primarily by her military leaders, had been to gain control of eastern Siberia and of the Chinese Eastern Railway in northern Manchuria. Although never stated publicly, President Wilson's motives in intervening had been to aid the Czechs, to watch the Japanese and prevent them from seizing Russian territory, and to preserve the principle of the Open Door in eastern Siberia and northern Manchuria.[1] Throughout the occupation, however, the American people believed that their government had intervened to combat Bolshevism.

Friction with Japan

Almost from the beginning distrust between Americans and Japanese had marked the joint intervention, particularly over control of the Chinese Eastern Railway. When the Japanese expanded their forces in Siberia from an expected

7000 to over 72,000 troops, the suspicions of the American government appeared justified. After the war ended, Wilson would not withdraw American troops, over eight thousand of them, and leave Japan in full control of eastern Siberia, even though he himself found the intervention distasteful.

Congressmen and the public, meantime, demanded withdrawal of the soldiers. Yielding to the domestic pressure, and also to the fear of serious armed conflict with the Bolsheviks, Wilson withdrew all American troops by April 1, 1920. The small British, French, and Canadian forces soon pulled out, and Japan remained in sole control of eastern Siberia.

The Japanese explained that their geographic proximity to Siberia made their position there unique. Their troops remained, they said, because chaotic conditions in eastern Siberia threatened their interests in Korea and Manchuria and endangered the lives and property of Japanese living in those areas. To Americans, the firmly entrenched Japanese appeared bent on holding eastern Siberia permanently.

In another attempt to preserve the Open Door on the Asian mainland against Japan's efforts to close it, Wilson had revived the idea of a consortium in November, 1917. The long economic and diplomatic contest over the consortium, culminating in 1920, did nothing but add to Japanese bitterness toward the United States.

Another rankling sore in relations with Japan was the Shantung question. During the battle for the Treaty of Versailles, Republicans had attacked the Shantung articles, calling them a main flaw in the peace settlement. Reflecting the Republican resentment, much of it politically inspired, the sixth Lodge reservation to the treaty, for instance, had called for withholding American assent to the Shantung settlement. Since Wilson believed that the Japanese intended to stay in Shantung permanently, he confessed that the Shantung articles were the most difficult part of the treaty to defend. Yet he had defended them as necessary and had pointed out that the League would bring China security and justice. The American attacks, moreover, did not budge the Japanese from their policy of trying to extract extensive privileges from China before relinquishing Shantung.[2]

About a year earlier, Japan had obtained a mandate over the former German islands, situated in the Pacific north of the equator, from the League of Nations. Now the United States revived the objections, that Wilson had made in Paris, to Japanese control of the island of Yap in the Carolines. When the European Allies supported Japan's right to Yap, the American government protested the entire Japanese mandate, saying that the United States had not ratified the Treaty of Versailles and hence could not be bound by its award and insisted that as one of the conquerors of Germany it had rights on Yap that could not be ignored. Americans wanted to prevent a possible monopoly control over the cable network running through Yap, particularly over their communications with the Philippines. In

1921 the issue of Yap was another small piece of unfinished business with Japan that the Harding administration took over from Wilson.

More ominous than the Yap controversy was the postwar revival of agitation for discriminatory laws against Japanese and for their exclusion by statute. In September, 1919, Californians reorganized an old Oriental Exclusion League. Supported by the newly organized American Legion, the State Federation of Labor, the Hearst newspapers, and other groups, the Exclusion League adopted a program demanding cancellation of the Gentlemen's Agreement and exclusion of Japanese immigrants.

The platforms of the two major parties in the 1920 presidential campaign reflected the growth of anti-Japanese sentiment. Both contained Oriental exclusion planks. In that November, moreover, California's voters, by a majority of three to one, passed a new alien land law that forbade the Japanese even to rent land. In the next year other western states, Arizona, Washington, and Texas, passed similar discriminatory laws of their own against the Japanese.

When news of the exclusion agitation and the land laws reached Japan, the people demonstrated in angry anti-American outbursts and the newspapers denounced Americans. To ease the developing crisis, Japanese and American statesmen negotiated a revision of the Gentlemen's Agreement in 1921 that would tighten restrictions against Japanese immigration and would assure the Japanese already in the United States most civil rights except citizenship through naturalization. Opposition from the Pacific Coast was so great that the treaty never reached the Senate.

In April of that year the California legislature passed a resolution urging Congress to enact an Oriental exclusion law. Not even one legislator dared vote against it. Although not directed solely against the Japanese, the Emergency Quota Act of May, 1921, based on the national origins of aliens in the United States in 1910, did not give the Japanese a quota. All of these factors aroused bitter antagonism between Japan and the United States and stimulated talk of war on both sides, leading to a race in naval armaments.

Naval Rivalry

The American program of naval expansion had begun with the Naval Appropriations Act of 1916 that called for a navy second to none. Wilson had seen it as a part of his wartime preparedness program, not necessarily as a weapon of coercion against Japan. Some Americans had viewed it as that and others as mainly a threat to Britain's traditional mastery of the seas.[3]

After the United States entered the war it slowed down or suspended construction on big ships—battleships and battle cruisers   to concentrate on anti-submarine vessels and other types. Yet when the war ended, the United States had a navy second only to that of Britain. If it went ahead and completed its scheduled expansion, as Congress authorized in July, 1918, its navy would have surpassed the British navy within five or six years.

Japan's plans for naval expansion had begun in 1911, but the war and limited resources had held expansion back. Nonetheless, with the destruction of Germany's fleet and the decline of French and Italian naval forces at the end of the war, Japan had emerged with the third largest navy in the world. Viewing the American naval building program and American policy toward her as a threat to her ambitions on the Asian mainland and in the Pacific, Japan then took up her plans for naval expansion and accelerated them. In 1919, her parliament approved a building program that would give Japan the largest navy in her history. The Japanese appeared willing, moreover, to expand their navy even more, depending on the extent of American construction.

The Japanese naval program, rumors that Japan was fortifying the former German islands in the Pacific in violation of her mandate, and the increasing tension over other matters, in turn caused a shift in American strategy. Americans began to shape their program in the naval race as preparation for a possible war in the Pacific.

In 1919, Wilson had broken with the past by establishing a separate battle fleet in the Pacific, apparently as a means of exerting pressure on Japan. By the end of that year the United States had assembled a fighting fleet in the Pacific almost as formidable as Japan's entire navy then afloat. Early in 1921 the combined Atlantic and Pacific fleets held maneuvers in the Pacific, and in the following June the new Harding administration announced that it would station most of the Navy's fighting ships permanently in the Pacific.

American rivalry with Britain added a third force to the naval armaments race in the Pacific. The British had opposed Wilson's demand for "freedom of the seas" and had viewed the American naval program as unnecessary for defense and as a threat to the security of their empire which depended upon their continued control of the seas. "Great Britain would spend her last guinea," Lloyd George told Colonel House, "to keep a navy superior to that of the United States or any other Power. . . ."[4] At the Paris Peace Conference Wilson had agreed to postpone naval construction in return for Lloyd George's support of the covenant and the amendment on the Monroe Doctrine, but American rejection of the League and the resumption of the naval building program wrecked the truce.

American naval experts, at the same time, resented Britain's attempt to gain control of most of the world's known oil resources, particularly in the Middle East where she had obtained League mandates. They believed that in pursuing her alleged efforts to gain an oil monopoly Britain was discriminating against American firms which were attempting to force their way into the oil fields of the Middle East in 1918 and 1920. Naval strategists feared that as American oil resources diminished, the fleet would in the near future become critically dependent on oil supplies controlled by the British.[5]

In March, 1921, when Britain announced plans for resuming naval construction to maintain her fleet as the largest in the world, some Americans became apprehensive over the future of relations with her. Even though the friendship between the two countries remained basically strong, tension over naval armaments and oil had, in some instances, replaced good will.

A greater menace to friendly relations with Britain was the Anglo-Japanese Alliance. When Britain had renewed it for ten years in 1911, she had tried to strip it of any threat to the United States by inserting a clause excluding any third nation who had a treaty of general arbitration with either herself or Japan from joint attack under the treaty. Since the Taft administration did not at that time ratify its arbitration treaty with England, the alliance technically still bound England to go to war against the United States if Japan did so.

After the European war, with the collapse of Russia and the defeat of Germany, many Americans felt that there was no longer any sound reason for continuing the alliance. It appeared to them mainly as a threat to American security and policy in the Far East. Some of them said it implied that England gave some measure of support to Japan's policy of expansion in Asia. Naval strategists argued therefore that the United States needed a navy equal to the combined British and Japanese fleets to preserve the Open Door in Asia as well as for American security.

Popular feeling in the United States against the alliance was so strong that in the spring of 1920, when rumors reached the Department of State that Britain had started negotiations for renewal of the alliance, due to expire in July of the following year, the American government suggested several basic changes. It asked for assurances that the alliance would safeguard China's independence and that it would not be aimed against the United States.

Even though the British assured Americans that they would not allow the alliance to thrust them into a war against the United States, the Hearst press and others demanded its abrogation. Senator James A. Reed of Missouri, an irreconcilable, even charged that the alliance contained a "secret clause directed against the United States."

Disarmament and Economy

At the same time, other Americans had launched two movements that conflicted with the program of naval expansion: a drive for economy in the government and another for reduction in armaments. Although the United States had come out of the war as the strongest economic power in the world and could afford to bear the costs of naval competition better than could its rivals, politicians shuddered at the thought of adding to an already heavy tax burden when the country was slipping into a postwar depression. Heeding the clamor of the tax-payers for relief, many members of Congress favored a reduction in armaments.

Numerous Americans also thought that the United States should take the lead in promoting universal disarmament. "War may be banished from the earth," Senator Hiram Johnson said, "more nearly by disarmament than by any other agency or in any other manner." General Tasker H. Bliss suggested to a Philadel-phia audience that the United States should take the lead in a "definite proposal and demand for a reasonable limitation of armaments."[6]

Acting as if limitation of armaments offered a substitute for the League of Nations, Senator Borah placed himself at the head of the congressional dis-armament movement. He offered a resolution in December, 1920, asking the President to invite Britain and Japan to a conference to negotiate an agreement for the limitation of armaments. If the conference succeeded, the resolution said, then Congress could cut its appropriations for armaments. Since the Borah resolution served the causes of both peace and economy, it aroused wide popular support.

In his inaugural address Warren G. Harding endorsed the idea of peace and economy through reduction of armaments, saying he sought "a way to approxi-mate disarmament and relieve the crushing burdens of military and naval establish-ments."[7] Yet he opposed the Borah resolution·and supported naval expansion. Despite the efforts of Britain and Japan to match the American naval program, Harding believed that the United States would attain naval supremacy in a few years. Hence, he wished to postpone a reduction of armaments until that time.

Demands for curtailing naval armaments in Britain coincided with the dis-armament movement in the United States. British finances, drained by the war, could not support an unrestrained naval race. For this and other reasons the British sought an agreement on naval limitation. Early in 1921 they even indicated a willingness to give up their traditional primacy on the seas by accepting naval parity with the United States in any agreement that would end the competition.

Japan could not afford to keep up with the United States in the naval race either. Her armed forces were eating up nearly one-half of the government's revenues. Business groups and others stimulated a popular movement for limitation of armaments, and Japanese statesmen responded by saying repeatedly that they were willing to cooperate in any reasonable project for limitation. They insisted, how-ever, that Japan's control of the western Pacific was essential to her security and policy in Asia.

Since Japan refused to limit naval construction unless the United States curtailed its expansion, and since the United States was unwilling to do so while the Anglo-Japanese Alliance continued, that alliance became a key to naval limitation. While not yet ready to abandon the alliance, the British were willing to modify it to meet American objections.

At an imperial conference in London in July, 1921, consisting of representatives

STATESMEN OF THE BIG FOUR AT THE WASHINGTON CONFERENCE, 1921

Left to right: Prince Tokugawa of Japan, Arthur James Balfour of Great Britain, Charles Evans Hughes of the United States, and Aristide Briand of France.

from Britain, the dominions, and India, the Anglo-Japanese Alliance became the main subject of debate. Canada, for instance, fearing that she might sometime in the future under the alliance be compelled to fight the United States, helped persuade England to terminate the commitment.[8]

Since Japan favored renewal of the alliance, Prime Minister Lloyd George faced the dilemma of finding a substitute for it that would not offend Japan and that the United States would accept. He decided, finally, to try to bring the United States, Japan, and other interested powers, together in a conference to discuss Far Eastern affairs and naval limitation. The British presented their idea to the United States and Japan in the first week of July, 1921.

Congress, meantime, at the end of June, had overwhelmingly adopted the Borah resolution, the Senate by a vote of 74 to 0 and the House by a majority of 332 to 4. Responding, apparently, to public and congressional demand, Harding decided to call a conference on naval limitation. Secretary of State, Charles E. Hughes, a few hours before receiving the British request, sent notes to Britain, Japan, France, and Italy, asking them if they would be willing to attend an armaments conference in Washington. The next day, July 9, he amplified his proposal to include discussion of Far Eastern problems as the British had suggested.

Only Japan delayed accepting the Hughes proposal. She was willing enough to confer on limitation of naval armaments but wanted to limit discussion of Far Eastern questions, fearing an Anglo-American attack on her policies in Asia and the Pacific. In finally agreeing to participate, she won Hughes' pledge to take an impartial stand between Japan and China and said certain Far Eastern problems should be avoided.[9]

The agenda of the nine-power conference, which opened on November 12, limited negotiations on disarmament to the United States, Britain, Japan, France, and Italy, but included China, Belgium, the Netherlands, and Portugal in the discussion of Far Eastern issues. Since the powers did not recognize the Soviet regime, Russia did not receive an invitation. The Russians protested their exclusion, citing their undeniable interest in Far Eastern affairs and saying beforehand that they would not recognize the decisions taken at the conference.

The fact that the conference met in Washington and that the United States, Britain, and Japan, comprised its "Big Three" reflected a significant shift in the balance of power away from Europe. Secretary of State Hughes, who headed the American delegation, won election as permanent chairman of the conference. In selecting the other delegates, Harding, unlike Wilson, had taken into account the Senate's role in foreign policy, choosing Elihu Root, a former senator and now elder statesman of the Republican party, Henry Cabot Lodge, and Oscar W. Underwood of Alabama, minority leader in the Senate, a member of the Committee on Foreign Relations, and one of the leading Democrats in Congress. To the surprise of many, Harding conspicuously omitted Borah.

Catering to the public demand for disarmament, Hughes in his introductory address placed limitation of armaments first on the agenda. He startled the assembled delegates by proposing an immediate halt in major naval construction "for a period of not less than ten years."[10] The United States, he said, was ready to destroy thirty of its battleships. He asked Britain and Japan to cooperate by scrapping thirty-six of theirs and even named specific ships. One British observer remarked that the delegates sat in stunned silence while Hughes in thirty-five minutes destroyed more ships "than all the admirals of the world have sunk in a cycle of centuries."[11]

The Washington Treaties

The public overwhelmingly embraced the Hughes proposal and concentrated its attention on the "open diplomacy" of naval limitation. While it did so, representatives of the "Big Three" worked quietly, secretly, and swiftly to frame a substitute for the Anglo-Japanese Alliance. All the other problems of the Far East and disarmament, Britain and Japan agreed, depended on getting the alliance out of the way. The United States, it appeared, would not go through with a reduction in naval armaments until the alliance was nullified.

The British and the Japanese suggested a three-power substitute. Hughes expanded it to include France, who resented her secondary role at the conference. With France, moreover, he added balance to the arrangement by giving it the support of the only other important naval power in the Far East.

The Four-Power Treaty, signed December 13, 1921, committed the United States, Britain, Japan, and France to respect each other's rights in their island possessions in the Pacific. If any dispute arose among them concerning their rights in the Pacific, they agreed to refer it to a conference of all four powers. They also promised to consult with each other in case of an outside attack against them. The treaty contained no pledge of military assistance or other coercive obligation and was to remain in force for ten years, after which time any of the contracting powers could withdraw upon a year's notice. Most important, the treaty specifically abrogated the Anglo-Japanese Alliance.[12]

This vague international agreement permitted the British to extricate themselves gracefully from the alliance without badly offending the Japanese and yet saved face for the Japanese by allowing them to give up the alliance without suffering political isolation. The United States paid practically nothing and received Japan's formal pledge for the security of the Philippines, but it would pay Japan's price in the next agreement, the treaty on naval limitation.

Hughes wanted Japan to accept a ratio of three ships to every five for the United States and Britain. Determined to maintain naval supremacy in the western Pacific, the Japanese insisted on a ratio of $10:10:7$. Since they refused to sign any naval agreement with the lower ratio that did not give them greater security than the consultative features of the Four-Power Treaty, the conference appeared to be stalemated.

Japan finally accepted the smaller ratio when the United States agreed not to fortify its islands in the Pacific except Hawaii, and Britain pledged that she would not erect fortifications in the western Pacific except on islands adjacent to Canada, Australia, and New Zealand. These concessions met Japan's price for agreeing to the $5:5:3$ ratio and the Four-Power Treaty, the price of supremacy in her home waters.

The Hughes formula also called for a ratio of $1.67:1.67$ for France and Italy. Since Italy's main interest was the Mediterranean and she could not afford to build up to her allotment, that ratio satisfied her, but France possessed two coastlines, one in the Mediterranean and one on the Atlantic, and had overseas colonies to defend. Before the war she had been a naval power of first rank but since had allowed her navy to deteriorate while she concentrated on land armaments in a quest for security against Germany. Her national pride, moreover, would not allow her to accept a fixed status of naval inferiority; she demanded a ratio as high as Japan's.

When France's unexpected demands threatened to wreck the conference, Hughes appealed over the heads of the French delegation directly to Premier

Aristide Briand. France then accepted the 1.67 ratio, but only in battleships and battle cruisers.

As signed on February 6, 1922, the Five-Power Treaty froze the *status quo* in fortifications in the western Pacific, set a holiday of ten years in the construction of capital ships, provided for the scrapping of certain battleships and battle cruisers in the United States, Britain, and Japan, set limits on the sizes of capital ships, cruisers, and aircraft carriers and on the caliber of their guns, and established the ratio of 5 : 5 : 3 : 1.67 : 1.67 on capital ships and aircraft carriers. The treaty was to remain in force until December 31, 1936. After that time any signatory could terminate it with two years' notice.

American naval leaders criticized Hughes for giving more than he received, particularly for conceding Japan's mastery of the western Pacific and hence leaving the Philippines a hostage to her fleet. Since Hughes knew that Congress would not vote funds for fortifications west of Hawaii, he had not surrendered anything but potential naval supremacy in those waters. Geography, not Hughes, therefore, had allowed the Japanese to become masters of the western Pacific.

Hughes did not, as it appeared that he had done in the Five-Power Treaty, abandon established policy toward China. In return for his concessions, he won a diplomatic victory for the traditional principles of American policy in the Far East in the third major treaty of the Washington Conference.

The British brought the idea of an international pledge in support of China's independence to the conference, but Hughes made it his own. He believed that in the past the Open Door had been ineffective because the powers concerned had never legally bound themselves to uphold its principles. In seeking support for those principles he encountered the greatest resistance from the Japanese, who insisted that they had a special position on the Asian mainland. Hughes' persistance, aided by his naval concessions, succeeded in winning Japan's agreement.

In the Nine-Power Treaty, also signed on February 6, all the nations represented at the conference agreed to respect China's independence and to uphold the principle of equal commercial and industrial opportunity in China, basically the Open Door. That treaty thus made American principles binding under international law upon all of the major powers in the Far East except Russia. It constituted the most solemn international pledge in support of American Far Eastern policy yet achieved.

It was, nevertheless, a limited victory. Since the treaty required none of the powers to defend the principles of the Open Door, merely to respect them, its only sanction was the good faith of the signatories. Since it was not retroactive, the treaty did nothing about existing violations of the Open Door.[13] It merely limited future action. Yet the treaty was as far as any nation, particularly the United States, was willing to go at the time. None was willing to pledge force to defend China, or the abstract principles of the Open Door.

During the negotiation of the major treaties, delegates at the conference also attempted to adjust a number of other issues that aggravated relations between Japan and the United States. Japan helped clear the air by announcing to the conference on January 23 that she had no designs on Russian territory. She promised to withdraw her troops from Siberia and later from the Russian half of Sakhalin Island. Under steady pressure from the United States, she finally withdrew her troops from Siberia in October, 1922, and from northern Sakhalin in January, 1925.

In an effort to break the stalemate over Shantung, the United States and Britain brought the Chinese and Japanese delegates together to discuss the status of the province. After thirty-six meetings they agreed to a compromise settlement that was acceptable to the United States, if not to China. In a treaty with China, signed on February 4, 1922, Japan restored Shantung in full sovereignty to China but retained considerable economic control in the province as well as the political influence that went with that control.[14]

The United States also carried on separate negotiations with Japan over its claims on Yap. A few days after the close of the conference, on February 11, the two countries signed a treaty giving the Americans cable and other rights on the island equal to those of the Japanese. In return the United States recognized Japan's mandate over the former German islands in the Pacific north of the equator.

One of Hughes' objectives in trying to strengthen Far Eastern policy had been cancellation of the controversial Lansing-Ishii Agreement that had appeared to give recognition to Japan's special position in China. Americans believed that Japan's pledge of self-denial in the Nine-Power Treaty had annulled the agreement and its secret protocol, but the Japanese did not. Hughes, therefore, threatened to publish the secret protocol if Japan did not agree to an annulment. After complicated negotiations, the Japanese consented to a formal cancellation on January 2, 1923. The final notes were not exchanged until April 14, more than a year after the close of the Washington Conference.[15]

President Harding had, meanwhile, submitted the Washington treaties to the Senate. "I can bring you assurance," he said, "that nothing in any of these treaties commits the United States, or any other power, to any kind of an alliance, entanglement, or involvement."[16] This did not satisfy the Senate, particularly a group of irreconcilables led by Borah, which concentrated its attack on the Four-Power Treaty, contending that it was an alliance in disguise which would, like the League, entangle the United States in an alien balance of power.

The President gave repeated assurances that the treaties contained no secret clauses. Senator Lodge, who had the responsibility of guiding the treaties through the Senate, told his colleagues that the Four-Power Treaty carried not even a moral commitment to use force. It would help bring peace to the world, he said, "without alliances or penalties or the sanction of force lurking in the background."[17] "Who would have thought it," one senator had remarked earlier, "Senator Lodge is the father of a baby League of Nations."[18]

Despite some vigorous opposition, the administration had the votes. By the end of March, 1922, the Senate had approved the Nine-Power Treaty unanimously, the Five-Power Treaty with only one dissenting vote, and the Four-Power Treaty with a margin of only four votes and with a reservation saying "there is no commitment to armed force, no alliance, no obligation to join in any defense."[19] In this isolationist era, one observer commented, the Senate would not have consented to the Ten Commandments without reservations.[20]

Most Americans hailed the Washington Conference, resulting in the first international agreement for naval limitation, as beginning a new era of disarmament and peace. Naval leaders regarded its treaties with dismay, arguing that the United States sacrificed too much for what it gained. Liberals regretted the fact that the treaties limited only capital ships and did not effectively curb Japanese expansion.

Japanese military men and nationalists attacked the treaties as constituting a diplomatic loss for Japan. The British, in general, supported the treaties but recognized them as marking a shift in the world balance of power that ended Britain's long reign as the supreme naval power. With the treaties, one English editor remarked, "the trident of Neptune passes into the joint guardianship of the English-speaking peoples. . . ."[21]

No nation, except in theory, gained a special advantage from the Washington treaties. They did not end naval competition; they regulated it. They did not settle the issues of the Far East; they recorded a political accommodation. Essentially, the treaties tried to stabilize existing conditions by recognizing the superior power of the United States, Britain, and Japan in the areas they already controlled. The Washington settlement offered a weak peace formula in place of Wilson's idea of collective security without departing from the traditional principles of isolationism.

The Peace Movement

Whatever its weakness, the Washington Conference reflected one of the prominent themes in American foreign policy in the two decades following the First World War, a passion for peace which grew out of a revulsion against participation in the European war. Never before had Americans discussed peace as much as they did in the 1920's. In that decade the organized peace movement grew stronger than ever before.[22]

New peace organizations multiplied and old ones gained new vigor. Foremost among them was the Carnegie Endowment for International Peace, organized in 1910 by Andrew Carnegie, the immigrant Scotsman who made his millions in the manufacture of steel. He wanted his organization, he said, "to hasten the abolition of war, the foulest blot upon our civilization."[23] His words, as well as any, expressed the main idea behind the peace crusade.

Another millionaire, the Dutch immigrant Edward W. Bok, who had made his fortune in publishing, believed the world could not achieve the goal of abolishing war without the participation of the United States. In 1922, he sponsored a great national peace contest, offering $100,000 to the person who submitted a workable peace plan. Newspapers gave the contest wide publicity, ninety-seven influential national organizations supported it, over a quarter of a million Americans wrote to Bok's agents for contest details, and more than twenty-two thousand of them submitted peace plans. William Jennings Bryan offered a peace formula and Franklin D. Roosevelt, the Democratic candidate for the vice-presidency in 1920, drafted a plan but did not submit it, apparently because his wife became one of the judges.

Americans flocked to the peace movement with the hope that it might prevent another world war. Peace, many of them believed, depended more on avoiding war than on diplomatic accommodations. *The Nation* expressed the mood of many. "Words for peace are very well," the magazine said. "But what we must have in addition is a burning, an unconquerable, an undeviating hatred of war, any war for whatever reason. When war becomes unthinkable, then and then only is peace assured."[24]

Avoidance of war rather than the advancement of national self-interest, the peace advocates believed, should be the essence of foreign policy. They and other Americans also thought that the peoples of the world could achieve lasting peace through disarmament. Believing that armaments were evil and bred wars, they wanted to eliminate force as a legitimate instrument of national policy. They regarded the Washington Conference as opening a new era of international peace through the limitation of armaments. They wanted more pledges for further disarmament and also international declarations in favor of peace, particularly agreements that required no departure from what they considered the traditions of isolation.

The advocates of disarmament, in fact, could appeal to the traditions of isolation because disarmament, in their view, would bring a stable peace and would make foreign entanglements unnecessary. Through disarmament the United States could isolate itself from war, the utopian goal of most isolationists.

The United States in the 1920's and 1930's, therefore, was willing to cooperate with other nations in disarmament conferences and in agreements in favor of peace, but outside the jurisdiction of the League of Nations. In this way America could demonstrate that it was not truly isolated from world affairs.

Whether or not Americans favored membership in the League, many of them thought that wars stemmed from "old fashioned" power politics and that some form of international parliament could make peace permanent. The "internationalists" among them maintained their faith in the League as an instrument for peace. Gradually the government itself had to recognize that the League was of some importance to American foreign policy.

Toward Cooperation with the League

In January, 1920, two months before its final rejection by the Senate, the League came officially into existence with twenty-four countries as members. By the end of the year its membership had grown to forty-eight. Since the League had won wide support and was functioning in a number of important areas in international affairs, Harding had to decide how the United States would deal with it.

Republican irreconcilables, who had the President's ear, opposed cooperation with the League or its agencies. So Harding ignored it. "In the existing League of Nations, world-governing with its super powers," he told Congress in his first message, "this Republic will have no part." [25]

Secretary of State Hughes had favored joining the League with reservations and at first apparently was willing to work with its agencies, but when the irreconcilables of his own party objected to any dealings with the world organization, he followed a policy of nonrecognition toward it. During the period of nonrecognition, lasting about six months, the Harding administration refused to answer letters from officials in Geneva, seat of the League's Secretariat.

When League officials sent registered mail, forcing a receipt from the Department of State, the American government explained that it would not reply because it did not recognize the existence of the League. In July, 1921, a correspondent of The New York Times began a series of articles from Europe that charged the American government with gross discourtesy. Public pressure, therefore, forced Hughes to adopt a policy of tolerance toward the League. A subordinate in the Department of State, he said, had placed League mail in the dead letter file without informing him. By September the department began answering letters from the League with perfunctory acknowledgments.

Before the war the United States had worked with other nations in the international control of the opium traffic, in an international health agency, and in other nonpolitical international organizations. When the League attempted to bring the opium and health agencies under its jurisdiction, Hughes objected. In 1921, the Secretary General of the League reported that the United States "was not willing that any international organizations, on which it was represented, should in any way be attached to the League." [26]

As in the case of the correspondence, the American attitude of hostility toward League agencies slowly changed. In 1923, the Republican National Chairman told an audience in Illinois that "simply because the United States did not enter the League of Nations it does not mean that the United States is going to withhold its support of the good that the League will accomplish."[27] This statement was merely a public recognition of the change to a policy of unofficial cooperation with the League that had already begun.

The United States began its cooperation cautiously in 1922 by sending silent "unofficial observers" to conferences sponsored by League agencies. Soon, these observers began talking and participating in the work of League committees and agencies, as in conferences dealing with the opium traffic, and in other ways looking after the interests of the United States. The American government, however, always insisted that the sending of observers implied no official recognition of the League. They were, Hughes said, "official representatives acting in an unofficial capacity."[28]

Succeeding administrations continued and expanded Harding's cooperative policy. They recognized the League as a necessary part of American foreign relations, even to the extent of abandoning the fiction of "unofficial" cooperation.

The World Court

At about the time that Harding began his cooperative policy toward the League, his administration touched off the biggest, though certainly not the most important, political battle over foreign policy since the defeat of the Treaty of Versailles and the longest such struggle of the 1920's and 1930's. That fight involved the effort to bring the United States into the Permanent Court of International Justice, the juridical organ of the League known as the World Court.

Leading Republicans, such as John Hay in 1899 and Elihu Root in 1907, had long advocated the idea of creating a court capable of settling international disputes by law in place of force. The League to Enforce Peace, a wartime organization whose leaders were predominantly Republicans, had made the creation of such a court a major part of its program. As the Republican presidential candidate in 1916, Charles Evans Hughes had supported the court idea, and in 1920, Root had gone to Europe to help write the statute for the World Court.

Unlike a court of arbitration, such as The Hague Court, the World Court was to apply legal principles, as derived principally from international law, in its decisions. Since it could take jurisdiction only when all parties to a dispute asked it to do so, its powers were in effect limited to minor international incidents. Even the "optional clause" to the Court's protocol, whereby members could agree in advance to refer certain categories of disputes to the Court, was so restrictive as to add little to the peaceful settlement of major international disputes.

Yet the peace crusaders, convinced that law must supersede force in international affairs, saw the Court as an important instrument for peace. In May, 1922, when the League announced that the Court was open to all nations, there was considerable support in the United States for joining the Court. Since the Court functioned through a protocol separate from the Treaty of Versailles, states which did not belong to the League could join. Some "internationalists," nevertheless hoped that adherence to the Court would be a first step toward joining the League.

Secretary of State Hughes wanted to bring the United States into the World Court and, to overcome the Senate's fear of any entanglement with the League, formulated four reservations to accompany adherence. The first reservation stressed that America's adherence would bring no legal connection to the League. The others dealt with the election of judges, the sharing of expenses, and the amending of the Court's statute. All were ostensibly designed to safeguard the nation's vital interests.

Harding approved Hughes' plan and in February, 1923, sent the treaty of adherence to the Senate, saying the four reservations would leave the United States "wholly free from any legal relation to the League." Still dominated by irreconcilables, the Senate Committee on Foreign Relations attacked the Court, calling it a bait leading to the League of Nations trap. Harding died soon afterward.

One of the first decisions the new President, Calvin Coolidge, had to make was whether or not to seek entrance into the World Court. Since he retained Hughes as his Secretary of State, he supported his Secretary's plan and in his first annual message to Congress urged favorable consideration of the Court. The Senate's Committee on Foreign Relations then tried to defeat adherence by stalling. Despite considerable evidence showing that the majority of the people approved of the court, the committee delayed action for over two years.

In January, 1924, shortly after Coolidge had prodded the Senate, Bok announced the winner of his Peace Award, Charles E. Levermore, an elderly secretary of the New York Peace Society who had been associated with pressure groups working in favor of the League and the World Court. Levermore's peace plan urged full cooperation with the League and immediate entry into the World Court with the Hughes reservations.

The irreconcilables were furious. Bok, they said, was ready to squander his last dollar to entice America into the League. Bok's widely publicized award and the activity of his organization, The American Foundation, in favor of the World Court, apparently stiffened rather than softened the Senate's opposition to the Court. So widespread was popular approval of the court that in the presidential campaign of 1924 the platforms of both major parties endorsed entrance, but Borah, who had succeeded Lodge as chairman of the Senate's Foreign Relations Committee, and other isolationists still opposed it.

The forces favoring the Court held mass meetings in dozens of cities and virtually smothered Congress with petitions from all over the country urging the Senate to approve adherence to the Court. Opponents appealed to the traditions of nonentanglement and to antiforeignism. Senators called out the names of foreign judges, such as Didrik Galtrup, Gjedde Nayholm, Dionisco Anzilotti Yorozu Oda, and Wang Ch'ung-hui. The Chicago *Tribune* defied its readers to pronounce such names, and asked: "HOW MANY FRIENDS CAN UNCLE SAM COUNT ON IF HE SUBMITS HIS AFFAIRS TO THE WORLD COURT?" [29]

Even though the House of Representatives had overwhelmingly approved a resolution urging membership, in March, 1925, a small group in the Senate threatened to filibuster against the Court. Before the proposal came to a vote in the Senate, moreover, the Foreign Relations Committee had added a fifth reservation saying the Court should not entertain "any request" for an advisory opinion without American consent on any dispute in which the United States had an interest. An advisory opinion dealt with the right or wrong of a dispute before it came up for litigation. The committee also expanded the reservations to give the United States special treatment and the Senate a virtual veto over certain Court activities.

The Senate finally resorted to cloture, a limiting of debate to prevent a filibuster, and voted on January 27, 1926. It approved adherence to the Court, 76 to 17, but with the expanded reservations recommended by the committee.

Coolidge was unwilling to ask the Senate to modify its position, saying that "unless the requirements of the Senate resolution are met by the other interested nations I can see no prospect of this country adhering to the Court." [30] The members of the World Court were willing to accept all the reservations except the fifth. This impasse ended the first prolonged effort to bring the United States into the World Court.

The second attempt began a few months after Herbert Hoover won election to the Presidency. In February, 1929, Elihu Root, then eighty-four years old, went to Geneva and sat with a commission of jurists to work out a compromise known as the "Root Formula," that would bring the United States into the World Court but would allow it to withdraw if its objections to an advisory opinion were overruled by other members. Since Hoover's Secretary of State, Henry L. Stimson, was a close friend and admirer of Root and wanted to bring the United States into the Court, Hoover reluctantly agreed to present the matter to the Senate once more. [31]

Beset by problems of the great depression, Hoover did not submit the proposal for adherence to the Court, with the "Root Formula," to the Senate until December, 1930. Available evidence indicated that the public still favored entrance into the Court, but the isolationists in the Senate were stronger than ever and delayed consideration for four more years.

Public pressure finally induced the Foreign Relations Committee, in March, 1934, to hold hearings on the question of entering the Court. In a special message, President Franklin D. Roosevelt urged that "the Senate's consent be given in such form as not to defeat or delay the objective of adherence." [32] For awhile it appeared that the administration, with a Senate that was preponderantly Democratic, had enough votes to take the country into the Court.

Old irreconcilables, Borah and Hiram Johnson, with new allies such as Huey P. Long of Louisiana, resisted more fiercely than ever. Outside the Senate, William Randolph Hearst begged the readers of his newspapers to deluge their senators with demands to vote against the Court. In Detroit a popular radio priest, Father Charles E. Coughlin, pleaded with millions of his listeners to fight the Court, saying "whether you can afford it or not, send your senator a telegram telling him to vote no on our entrance into the World Court with or without reservations."[33]

By a vote of 52 for and 36 against, seven votes shy of the necessary two-thirds, the Senate defeated the resolution of adherence to the World Court on January 29, 1935. Few could doubt that the issue of the Court was at last dead.

Naval Disarmament at Geneva—1927

Many Americans, meanwhile, had retained their faith in disarmament as the means of achieving lasting peace. "The conviction that competitive armaments constitute a powerful factor in the promotion of war," President Coolidge told Congress, in January, 1926, "is more widely and justifiably held than ever before, and the necessity for lifting the burden of taxation from the peoples of the world by limiting armaments is becoming daily more imperative."[34] Yet the Five-Power Treaty had not halted the naval race. The competition had merely shifted from capital ships to the unrestricted construction of cruisers, destroyers, and submarines.

Coolidge soon found, therefore, that he would probably have to agree to naval expansion in cruisers and other smaller vessels to keep pace with Britain and Japan if the armaments race did not stop. Since he was committed to a program of economy in government and also felt the need for a positive achievement in foreign policy, he decided to call another conference on naval limitation.

The other signatories of the Five-Power Treaty, Britain, Japan, France, and Italy, were sending delegates to a session of the League's Preparatory Commission on Disarmament at Geneva. In June, 1927, therefore, Coolidge asked those countries to allow their delegates to confer separately with the United States in hopes of reaching an agreement "for limitation in the classes of naval vessels not covered by the Washington Treaty."[35]

Britain and Japan accepted the invitation, but France and Italy, concerned with security and viewing naval armaments primarily as a part of the larger problem of disarmament, refused to participate in a separate naval conference. The Geneva gathering, which opened on June 20, therefore, became a three-power conference that avoided the general problem of security and concentrated on technical naval problems. Naval technicians, rather than statesmen, were pre-eminent.

The main controversy, between Britain and the United States, centered on cruisers. The Americans wanted to extend the ratio of 5 : 5 : 3 to cruisers and other smaller craft and to reduce the total tonnage of each class of ships. Since they did not have a world-wide network of bases, as the British did, they wished to concentrate their cruiser strength in ships of fairly long cruising radius displacing ten thousand tons and carrying eight-inch guns. The British were willing to extend the ratio to that extent but not immediately to the smaller warships they considered essential in guarding their trade routes and empire. They wanted a large number of lighter cruisers, above the limits set by the American naval experts, displacing seventy-five hundred tons and carrying six-inch guns that could operate effectively from their overseas bases.

Japan's delegates, who had gone to Geneva with instructions to take a strong stand in favor of existing cruiser strength, had a minor part in the conference. At times they unsuccessfully attempted to act as mediators in the Anglo-American dispute. Since the British and American experts could find no way of reconciling their views on cruiser strength so as to assure parity, or naval equality, the conference broke up on August 4 without an agreement.

The failure of the three-power conference showed the futility of attempting to settle technical problems of naval disarmament without prior diplomatic agreement. Only a political arrangement could adjust the differing requirements of the American and British fleets. The breakdown at Geneva embittered Anglo-American relations, contributed to a loss of public confidence in disarmament as a means of achieving a lasting peace, and paved the way for the largest American naval bill since the European war, calling for the construction of fifteen large cruisers.[36]

The Kellogg-Briand Pact

Before the failure of the Geneva conference, the American peace forces had made a strong effort to abolish war by outlawing it. The mass enthusiasm for peace seemed to sweep the statesmen into the outlawry movement. "Humanity is not helpless," one of its leaders wrote. "This is God's world! We can outlaw this war system just as we outlawed slavery and the saloon."

Salmon O. Levinson, a wealthy lawyer from Chicago who had the idea of making war illegal by treating a warring nation as an international outlaw, started the outlawry movement. In December, 1921, he organized the American Committee for the Outlawry of War and drew up "A Plan to Outlaw War" which he distributed widely, particularly among politicians and crusading organizations. Senator Borah, who opposed any peace scheme based ultimately on the use of force, became a convert to the outlawry idea and its spokesman in Congress. In February, 1923, at the urging of Levinson, he introduced a resolution in the Senate calling for a universal treaty that would make war "a public crime under the law of nations." It attracted little attention.

Other peace leaders, notably Dr. Nicholas Murray Butler, president of Columbia University and of the Carnegie Endowment for International Peace, and James T.

Shotwell, a professor of history at Columbia and a director in the Carnegie organization, had adopted a similar idea. They believed that nations should abolish war as a means of policy. Since Butler and Shotwell hoped their plan would draw the United States closer to the League, and Levinson and Borah wanted to have nothing to do with the League, the two groups were rivals. Both, nonetheless, supported and worked for the outlawry idea.

In March, 1927, Shotwell, while visiting in Paris, seemingly converted France's Foreign Minister, Aristide Briand, to the antiwar idea. In April, Briand sent a message drafted by Shotwell directly to the American people, proposing an agreement that would renounce and outlaw war between France and the United States. More than he wanted to outlaw war, Briand yearned to enhance France's security with a treaty that would link the United States indirectly with her own system of alliances. At that time France had alliances, or similar agreements, with Belgium, Poland, Czechoslovakia, Rumania, and Yugoslavia.

President Coolidge and his second Secretary of State, Frank B. Kellogg, were irritated by Briand's appeal over their heads and ignored the proposal. Briand, nonetheless, persisted and in June sent a draft treaty, through proper diplomatic channels, renouncing war between France and the United States, titling it a "Pact of Perpetual Friendship." "Isolationists" and "internationalists," particularly the Levinson and Shotwell groups, now became united to place pressure on the government to accept the antiwar treaty with France.

Since Kellogg and his advisers believed that Briand's pact would be in effect a kind of perpetual alliance making American neutrality difficult during any European war that France might fight, the Secretary of State stalled. If he rejected Briand's treaty, he would offend public opinion; if he accepted, he would commit his country to a foreign entanglement.

Borah pointed a way out. In November he suggested the idea of a multilateral treaty. "M. Briand has suggested the first step," he announced to a peace group in New York. "Let us suggest the second and include Great Britain, Japan, Germany, and Italy. That would furnish a real foundation for Outlawing War sincerely." [37] In the following month, therefore, Kellogg proposed that he and Briand expand the projected treaty into a multinational pact outlawing war.

The French did not like the counterproposal. France's commitments to the League and her allies provided for the contingency of defensive war, but Briand, holder of the Nobel Peace Prize, could not publicly spurn an offer to outlaw war in the world. Now Kellogg became persistent. Although he had at first made his multilateral proposal to appease American public opinion, his skepticism soon turned to enthusiasm. He began to believe that a multilateral antiwar treaty would be a boon to the world.

After delaying for three months, Briand finally accepted the principles of a multilateral treaty, but with reservations that would not impair France's right of "legitimate self-defense." On August 27, 1928, the most distinguished gathering of diplomats since the days of the Peace Conference met in Paris to sign the Kellogg-Briand Pact, also known as the Pact of Paris. Fifteen nations, all the great powers except Russia, were represented.

The treaty itself was simple, containing only two major articles that pledged the signatories to renounce war "as an instrument of national policy" and to seek to solve their disputes "by pacific means."[38]

The poet Robert Underwood Johnson, who witnessed the ceremony at Paris, probably caught the spirit of the peace movement with these lines:

> Lift up your heads, ye peoples,
> The miracle has come.
> No longer are ye helpless,
> No longer are ye dumb.[39]

Most Americans read only the treaty's two articles, believing what they said, and doubtless lost sight of the important interpretative notes, really reservations, many powers had added. Kellogg himself had insisted that the pact contain no sanctions, no commitment for the United States to go to war, and nothing that would draw it into European affairs. "Every nation is free at all times and regardless of treaty provisions," he said officially, "to defend its territory from attack and it alone is competent to decide whether circumstances require war in self-defense."[40]

Right after the signing, the peace crusaders began a great popular campaign for ratification of the Kellogg-Briand Pact. In December, for instance, representatives of the Federal Council of Churches brought a monster petition of more than 180,000 signatures to the White House asking for prompt ratification. That same month Coolidge announced that he was receiving 200 letters a day and the State Department approximately 600 a day on the treaty. "I haven't seen one that is in opposition," the President told a press conference.[41]

The Senate offered no important opposition, though some senators said the treaty was worthless because it had no provision for its own enforcement and that it would lull the United States into a state of unpreparedness. One of them scoffed that it would be "as effective to keep down war as a carpet would be to smother an earthquake."[42] On January 15, 1929, the Senate approved the treaty 85 to 1.

Although the Senate had added no formal reservations, it had adopted the Foreign Relations Committee's interpretations, which in effect were reservations. They said the treaty did not impair the right of self-defense, interfere with the Monroe Doctrine, commit the nation to the use of force, or alter its position under its other treaties. The Senate then turned to the next order of business, a bill for the appropriation of $274 million for fifteen heavy cruisers that the House had approved ten months earlier. The Senate passed it, and the President signed it in less than a month after ratifying the Kellogg-Briand Pact.

After all fifteen signatories and thirty-one adhering nations had ratified the pact,

President Herbert Hoover declared it in force, on July 24, 1929. "I dare predict," he said, "that the influence of the Treaty for the Renunciation of War will be felt in a large proportion of all future international acts."[43]

Hoover's prediction was not fulfilled. The antiwar treaty, the crowning achievement of the peace movement of the 1920's, brought only disillusionment. Borah and the isolationists saw the pact as an end in itself. Others, such as Shotwell, envisaged it as a link to the League of Nations or some form of collective security. It was, at least, a grand gesture toward international peace. The United States in this period was willing to go no further in any international commitment.[44]

The Kellogg Arbitration Treaties

The negotiation of the Kellogg-Briand Pact also led to a series of bilateral arbitration and conciliation treaties concluded during the Coolidge and Hoover administrations. The Kellogg arbitration treaties, as they came to be known, began with the "model treaty" with France in February, 1928, that renewed the expiring Root arbitration treaty of 1908. The preamble, like those of the other Kellogg pacts, renounced war as an instrument of national policy.[45]

Another distinctive feature of the Kellogg treaties was that they changed the formula of the Root treaties they replaced. The new agreements excluded from arbitration all disputes within the domestic jurisdiction of the signatories and those that involved the Monroe Doctrine or the League Covenant, whereas the Root treaties had excepted questions of "vital interests" and "national honor." The exclusion of matters of "domestic jurisdiction" meant that the Kellogg treaties were virtually no advance over the Root agreements, for the United States and the other nations still retained a loophole allowing them to refuse to arbitrate the very questions that most often led to war. Kellogg himself thought the new formula had little "practical importance."

In approving the treaties the Senate weakened them even more by adding its usual reservation requiring each arbitration to receive its specific approval. This made little difference as the United States never resorted to adjudication under the arbitration treaties and never invoked the conciliation treaties. These pacts of the Coolidge and Hoover era at least mollified the peace advocates who had faith in them and showed that the United States desired international friendship.

The London Naval Conferences

In his inaugural address Herbert Hoover had said that the Kellogg-Briand Pact "should pave the way to greater limitation of armament, the offer of which we sincerely extend to the world."[46] He was convinced that disarmament offered "the only effective way to bring militarism under control." In the summer of

1929, therefore, he made a preliminary agreement on naval armaments with Britain's Labour government headed by Ramsay MacDonald. In October, Prime Minister MacDonald visited the United States and talked informally with Hoover at the President's fishing camp on the banks of the Rapidan River in Virginia. "What is all this bother about parity?" MacDonald told the Senate. "Parity? Take it, without reserve, heaped up and flowing over." [47]

The Rapidan Conference settled no particular problems, but it helped restore a spirit of friendliness to Anglo-American relations and produced final assurance that Britain and the United States would cooperate in a forthcoming five-power naval conference in London. During MacDonald's visit, the British government formally invited Japan, France, and Italy. All accepted and the London Conference opened on January 21, 1930.

This time politicians and diplomats rather than naval technicians were in control. The United States sent a strong delegation, including two important senators, and headed by Secretary of State Henry L. Stimson.

Although Britain had agreed to American parity in all categories of ships, the main technical question was how to arrive at a formula that measured the fighting qualities of ships, which depended on variables such as age, speed, armor, and caliber of guns carried. Before the conference British and American negotiators accepted a complicated technical "yardstick" equating small cruisers with heavy cruisers, but were unable to find a scientific yardstick acceptable to naval men on both sides. Hence the statesmen had to work outside the framework of any formula. [48]

The central political question of the conference was French security, the main problem of Europe's international politics after the First World War. Without an agreement assuring her additional security against Germany and against an increasingly hostile Italy in the Mediterranean, France said she would not adhere to any new plan for naval limitation. Italy insisted on a parity that France would not allow. Since Italy would accept no naval limitation that did not include France, the main work fell to the United States, Britain, and Japan.

Before the conference opened, Japan had asked for a higher ratio in smaller warships than she had achieved in battleships at Washington and had sent her delegates to London with instructions to insist on a ratio of 10 : 10 : 7 in heavy cruisers and smaller ships. Japan obtained her higher ratio only in smaller ships. [49]

The London Naval Treaty, signed on April 22, extended the "holiday" in the construction of capital ships agreed to at Washington for another five years, limited the tonnage of cruisers, destroyers, and submarines, and established rules prohibiting unrestricted submarine warfare. It also contained an "escalator clause" allowing each signatory to exceed the established limits if it believed the naval program of an outside power endangered its security. [50]

France and Italy did not accept Part III, the vital section containing the naval ratios, but signed the other parts. Although weakened by such abstention, the treaty was the first on naval limitation in all categories of ships in the history of the modern world.

The London Naval Treaty encountered delay in the Senate, but it was finally approved on July 21 by a vote of 58 to 9. France and Italy were dissatisfied and did not ratify. Japanese admirals resented their country's "position of inferiority" and denounced their government for agreeing to the treaty over their opposition. Ratification precipitated a wave of domestic violence that led to the assassination of Japan's premier and the fall of his government. Since Japan kept building ships and France and Italy entered a naval race, the London Naval Treaty did not bring a true limitation of armaments and failed to shape a sound political accord essential to such limitation.

The important naval powers, with the exception of the United States, in fact, built up to their treaty quotas and hence the American Navy fell behind in the power and efficiency of its ships. In 1933, therefore, Franklin D. Roosevelt diverted $250 million from funds under the National Recovery Act, a piece of legislation designed to aid the domestic economy during the great depression, for a new shipbuilding program. In March, 1934, Congress gave its support to rearmament by passing the Vinson-Trammel Bill authorizing naval construction up to the limits allowed by existing treaties. Appropriations for the construction were to come later.

In June and July, American, British, and Japanese naval experts began preliminary discussions for another conference to be held in 1935, as called for by the London Naval Treaty. Maintaining that her cruiser allotment of 1930 was inadequate to her needs, Britain insisted on an increase. In Japan naval equality had become a national shibboleth, and the Japanese demanded parity with the United States and Britain. France and Italy objected to a continuation of the ratio system.

On December 29 Japan gave the required two-year notice of her intention of withdrawing from the Five-Power Treaty of Washington. That agreement, together with the London Naval Treaty, would thus expire on December 31, 1936. A main problem of the new conference, therefore, would be to frame a new agreement replacing the Washington and London treaties. In view of the Japanese demands and the enlarged armament programs of the great powers, the delegates of the five nations who assembled in London in December, 1935, had little hope of agreeing on any new system of naval limitation.

When the other delegations would not even negotiate over Japan's demand for a "common upper limit," which would have insured her supremacy in the Far East and the waters of the western Pacific, her delegates walked out of the conference. The United States, Britain, and France nonetheless agreed among themselves to preserve the principle of naval limitation and signed a three-power treaty on March 25, 1936, calling for "qualitative" rather than "quantitative" limitation and restricting the size of different classes of warships and the caliber of their guns.

It also contained an escape clause releasing each signatory from its limitations if other nations exceeded them.

The United States and Britain agreed on the principle of naval equality between themselves, and the United States retained the right to maintain naval superiority over Japan. At least the treaty freed Americans from any concern over naval rivalry with Britain and France and allowed them to concentrate on Japanese naval construction. Yet the London Naval Treaty of 1936, since Japan and Italy would not adhere, marked the collapse of the structure of naval limitation built since 1922.

In 1937, after the expiration of the Washington and London treaties, Japan's naval budgets soared to new highs. In March, 1938, therefore, the United States, Britain, and France invoked the escape clause of the London Treaty of 1936. Naval limitation was now unmistakably dead. Congress voted the largest peacetime naval appropriations in its history, and the Roosevelt administration began building a two-ocean fleet, designed to be superior to the total navies of Japan, Germany, and Italy.

The World Disarmament Conference

All through the 1920's the League of Nations had sought some means of achieving general disarmament and in particular had been preparing for a world-wide disarmament conference, one that was blocked by various obstacles. Probably the most important of a number of attempts to strengthen the League and hence international security as the basis for disarmament was the Geneva Protocol of 1924. This treaty, open to members and nonmembers of the League, such as the United States, attempted to fill two gaps in the covenant and thereby broaden the League's power to prevent war. It called for compulsory arbitration of disputes not settled by the League's Council, extension of the World Court's compulsory jurisdiction by requiring allegedly domestic disputes to be submitted to it, joint military action against an aggressor, and it attempted to define the aggressor as the power unwilling to accept arbitration.

Taking the position that the Geneva Protocol represented the shaping of an unfriendly European concert, one which could threaten the Monroe Doctrine and the Roosevelt Corollary, the United States opposed it. Under the Protocol, for instance, the United States could not act unilaterally against a Latin-American country. France, supported by various small countries, championed the Protocol with its binding guarantees of security and believed that its failure would lead to an arms race.

Despite his previous concern for disarmament, Secretary of State Hughes did not want it under League auspices and went so far as to say that if the Protocol were approved without change, "America could hardly help regarding the League of Nations as a potential enemy."[51] Britain's dominions, in part because of American absence from the League and the Protocol, also opposed adherence to the Geneva Protocol. Britain, as a result, went along with its dominions and refused to sign the treaty. American opposition, therefore, helped kill the Protocol.

In place of the Protocol the European powers signed a number of treaties at the Swiss town of Locarno in 1925. These agreements guaranteed peace along Germany's western borders. Kellogg and Coolidge encouraged this regional arrangement as an alternative to the defunct Protocol. "These recent Locarno agreements," Coolidge said, "represent the success of this policy which we have been insisting ought to be adopted, of having the European countries settle their own political problems without involving this country."[52]

In 1925, people spoke of the "spirit of Locarno" as marking a high point in international good will, a spirit that saw the end of Germany's diplomatic isolation. Yet the attitude of the American government seemed to strengthen the isolation of the United States, for Locarno had guaranteed only regional security. As one critic pointed out, this meant that disarmament was to be considered essentially a European question, an attitude that seemingly left no room for general disarmament.

The Geneva Protocol had contained a provision for a disarmament conference after ratification, but the Protocol's failure prevented such a conference from being held in 1925. It was not until February, 1932, in fact, that a Conference for the Reduction and Limitation of Armaments, known also as the World Disarmament Conference, opened at Geneva. Representatives from fifty-nine nations attended, making it the largest international gathering up to that time. Although President Hoover sent a delegation, he regarded the conference as essentially a European affair. Its main problem was land disarmament whereas the United States considered naval limitation to be the essence of disarmament.

Shortly after the conference opened the American delegation presented a program for the limitation of armaments that virtually ignored the requirements of European security. France insisted, as she had done continuously, that disarmament could come only after guarantees of security. Her plan called for an international armed force and for close international supervision of any agreement made. Germany, disarmed by the Treaty of Versailles, added to French anxiety by demanding equality of armaments.

To break the resulting deadlock, Hoover unexpectedly proposed a reduction of all armaments by one-third. Since most of the concessions would have to come from France, who possessed the strongest army in Europe, Germany, Italy, and Russia, who were dissatisfied with the *status quo*, greeted the plan enthusiastically, but nothing came of it.

Franklin D. Roosevelt reversed Hoover's position toward French security. In May, 1933, he urged the conference to adopt a plan for the gradual reduction of armaments and offered all nations a nonaggression pact that would have pledged them to keep their armed forces within their own frontiers. Six days later the head of the American delegation added that "we are willing to consult the other states in case of a threat to peace, with a view to averting the conflict."[53]

Roosevelt's gesture toward a form of collective security came too late. It could not, moreover, be more than a gesture unless an isolationist Congress supported it. Germany, now in the grip of Chancellor Adolf Hitler, who had come to power in January, was already planning rearmament. In October, Hitler's government withdrew from the conference and from the League.

The World Disarmament Conference itself had adjourned in June, but met again in May and June, 1934, and then broke up in failure. Rearmament, instead of disarmament, soon became the main concern of the great powers. Thus the peace and disarmament movements of the 1920's and early 1930's, after sixteen years of agitation and conferences, ended with the United States itself rearming and engaging in a great naval race. The disarmament dream of the peace crusaders remained a dream.

NOTES

1. This point is stressed by Betty M. Unterberger in "President Wilson and the Decision to Send American Troops to Siberia," *Pacific Historical Review*, XXIV (Feb. 1955), 63–74; "The Russian Revolution and Wilson's Far-Eastern Policy," *Russian Review*, XVI (April 1957), 35–46; and *America's Siberian Expedition, 1918–1920* (Durham, N.C., 1956), pp. 231–232. George F. Kennan, in *The Decision to Intervene* (Princeton, 1958), pp. 388–404, emphasizes the anti-Bolshevik overtones of the intervention, and in *Russia and the West under Lenin and Stalin* (Boston, 1961), pp. 103–104, stresses aid to the Czechs and insists that there was no intention to overthrow the Soviet regime.

2. See Robert E. Hosack, "The Shantung Question and the Senate," *South Atlantic Quarterly*, XLIII (April 1944), 181–193, which analyzes the opposition to the Shantung clauses as a tactical political maneuver within the Senate.

3. Outten J. Clinard, *Japan's Influence on American Naval Power, 1897–1917* (Berkeley, Calif., 1947), p. 171, for instance, states that the legislation was directed against Japan.

4. Harold and Margaret Sprout, *Toward a New Order of Sea Power: American Naval Policy and the World Scene, 1918–1922* (Princeton, 1940), p. 59.

5. For details, see John A. DeNovo, "The Movement for an Aggressive American Oil Policy Abroad, 1918–1920," *The American Historical Review*, LXI (July 1956), 854–876.

6. *The New York Times*, Dec. 11, 1920, 10.

7. *Ibid.*, March 5, 1921, 4:2.

8. For details, see John B. Brebner, "Canada, the Anglo-Japanese Alliance and the Washington Conference," *Political Science Quarterly*, L (March 1935), 45–58 and John C. Vinson, "The Imperial Conference of 1921 and the Anglo-Japanese Alliance," *Pacific Historical Review*, XXXI (Aug. 1962), 257–266, which modifies Brebner's interpretation.

9. Sadao Asada, "Japan's 'Special Interests' and the Washington Conference, 1921–22," *The American Historical Review*, LXVII (Oct. 1961), 64.

10. In Merlo J. Pusey, *Charles Evans Hughes* (2 vols., New York, 1951), II, 469.

11. Colonel Repington, correspondent for the London *Daily Telegraph*, quoted in Mark Sullivan, *The Great Adventure at Washington: The Story of the Conference* (Garden City, N.Y., 1922), p. 28.

12. Charles N. Spinks, "The Termination of the Anglo-Japanese Alliance," *Pacific Historical Review*, VI (Dec. 1937), 336, and Fred Greene, "The Military View of American National Policy, 1904–1940," *The American Historical Review*, LXVI (Jan. 1961), 360, stress that pressure from the American Navy contributed to forcing the termination of the alliance.

13. Japan, for instance, did not feel bound to observe the treaty relative to Manchuria and Inner Mongolia. See Asada, "Japan's 'Special Interests' and the Washington Conference," *The American Historical Review*, LXVII (Oct. 1961), 69.

14. Russell H. Fifield, in "Secretary Hughes and the Shantung Question," *Pacific Historical Review*, XXIII (Nov. 1954), 373–385, suggests that Hughes was "the driving force, the catalytic agent, in the settlement of the Shantung question."

15. For details, see John C. Vinson, "The Annulment of the Lansing-Ishii Agreement," *Pacific Historical Review*, XXVII (Feb. 1958), 57–69.

16. Quoted in John C. Vinson, "The Parchment Peace: The Senate Defense of the Four Power Treaty of the Washington Conference," *Mississippi Valley Historical Review*, XXXIX (Sept. 1952), 309n.

17. Quoted in John C. Vinson, *The Parchment Peace: The United States Senate and the Washington Conference, 1921–1922* (Athens, Ga., 1955), p. 198.

18. O. A. Stanley, Dec. 12, 1921, *ibid.*, p. 162.

19. *Foreign Relations, 1922*, I, 379. William A. Williams in "China and Japan: A Challenge and a Choice of the Nineteen Twenties," *Pacific Historical Review*, XXVI (Aug. 1957), 265, dissents from the usual view that this lack of provision for enforcement was a fatal weakness in the Four- and Nine-Power Treaties.

20. Cited in Selig Adler, *The Isolationist*

Impulse: Its Twentieth Century Reaction (New York, 1957), p. 152.

21. *Brassey's Naval Annual*, quoted in Sprout, *Toward a New Order of Sea Power*, p. 260.

22. For a brief analysis of the movement, see Robert H. Ferrell, "The Peace Movement," in Alexander DeConde, ed., *Isolation and Security* (Durham, N.C., 1957), pp. 82–106.

23. Quoted in Robert H. Ferrell, *Peace in Their Time: The Origins of the Kellogg-Briand Pact* (New Haven, 1952), p. 7.

24. July 22, 1931, quoted in Robert E. Osgood, *Ideals and Self-Interest in America's Foreign Relations* (Chicago, 1953), p. 324.

25. April 12, 1921, *Foreign Relations, 1921*, I, xvii–xviii.

26. Quoted in Clarence A. Berdahl, *The Policy of the United States with Respect to the League of Nations* (Geneva, 1932), p. 102.

27. Simeon D. Fess, *The New York Times*, Dec. 16, 1922, *ibid.*, pp. 104–105.

28. Quoted in Berdahl, *The Policy of the United States*, p. 106. For additional details, see Clarence A. Berdahl, "The Relations of the United States with the Assembly of the League of Nations," *American Political Science Review*, XXVI (Feb. 1932), 99–112.

29. Quoted in Adler, *Isolationist Impulse*, p. 206.

30. Quoted in Denna F. Fleming, *The United States and the World Court* (Garden City, N.Y., 1945), p. 81.

31. Elting E. Morison, in *Turmoil and Tradition: A Study of the Life and Times of Henry L. Stimson* (Boston, 1960), p. 313, points out that Hoover and Stimson held conflicting views on the Court issue and argued over policy toward it.

32. Jan. 16, 1935, Samuel I. Rosenman, comp., *The Public Papers and Addresses of Franklin D. Roosevelt* (13 vols., New York, 1938–50), IV, 41.

33. Quoted in Fleming, *U.S. and the World Court*, p. 130.

34. Quoted in Merze Tate, *The United States and Armaments* (Cambridge, Mass., 1948), p. 75.

35. *Ibid.*, p. 141.

36. John W. Davis, Ambassador to Britain, 1918–1921, analyzed Anglo-American bitterness in "Anglo-American Relations and Sea Power," *Foreign Affairs*, VII (April 1929), 345–355.

37. *The New York Times*, Nov. 11, 1927, quoted in Ferrell, *Peace in Their Time*, p. 130.

38. The text and list of signatories are in *Foreign Relations, 1928*, I, 153–157.

39. Quoted in Ferrell, *Peace in Their Time*, p. 201.

40. *Ibid.*, p. 174.

41. *Ibid.*, p. 239n.

42. William Bruce of Maryland quoted in John C. Vinson, *William E. Borah and the Outlawry of War* (Athens, Ga., 1957), p. 171.

43. William S. Myers, ed., *The State Papers and Other Public Writings of Herbert Hoover* (2 vols., Garden City, N.Y., 1934), I, 79–80.

44. For an analysis of later developments, interpreted as shaping the Kellogg Pact idea into one of collective security, see Richard N. Current, "Consequences of the Kellogg Pact," George L. Anderson, ed., *Issues and Conflicts* (Lawrence, Kans., 1959), pp. 210–229.

45. To nations who had no conciliation agreements with the United States, Kellogg offered two draft treaties, one of arbitration and one of conciliation based on Bryan's "cooling-off" pacts. See L. Ethan Ellis, *Frank B. Kellogg and American Foreign Relations, 1925–1929* (New Brunswick, N. J., 1961), pp. 222–223.

46. Myers, *Hoover State Papers*, I, 9.

47. Quoted in Robert H. Ferrell, *American Diplomacy in the Great Depression: Hoover-Stimson Foreign Policy, 1929–1933* (New Haven, 1957), p. 85.

48. Raymond G. O'Connor's article, "The 'Yardstick' and Naval Disarmament in the 1920's," *Mississippi Valley Historical Review*, XLV (Dec. 1958), 441–463, shows that the real significance of the yardstick idea in American policy was psychological. See also O'Connor's broader scholarly study, *Perilous Equilibrium: The United States and the London Naval Conference of 1930* (Lawrence, Kans., 1962).

49. In the preceding year the American and British governments had secretly agreed to deny Japan's demand for an increase in ratio. See Gerald E. Wheeler, "Isolated Japan: Anglo-American Diplomatic Co-operation, 1927–1936," *Pacific Historical Review*, XXX (May 1961), 169.

50. For a summary of the Anglo-American issue, see James L. Godfrey, "Anglo-American Naval Considerations Preliminary to the London Naval Conference of 1930," *South Atlantic Quarterly*, XLIX (July 1950), 303–316.

51. Quoted in David D. Burks, "The United States and the Geneva Protocol of 1924: 'A New Holy Alliance?'" *The American Historical Review*, LXIV (July 1959), 897, the best treatment of American policy toward the Protocol. The subject is also covered in Denna F. Fleming, *The United States and World Organization, 1920–1933* (New York, 1938), pp. 196–205. The full title of the Protocol is Protocol for the Pacific Settlement of International Disputes.

52. Dec. 8, 1925, *Foreign Relations, 1925*, I, xii–xiii.

53. Norman H. Davis, May 22, 1933, quoted in Robert A. Divine, *The Illusion of Neutrality* (Chicago, 1962), pp. 50–51. The consultation idea originated with the British, p. 48.

Chapter Twenty-One

ASIA AND THE AMERICAS BETWEEN WARS

T HE Washington Conference of 1921–22 had temporarily resolved some of the major political problems of the Far East but had not eased tension between Japan and the United States over the sensitive issue of discrimination against Asians. The Supreme Court, in two cases in 1922 and 1923, ruled that the Japanese and other Asians were ineligible for citizenship through naturalization and that the anti-Japanese land laws of California and the state of Washington were legal.

In December, 1923, Congress began considering permanent immigration legislation to replace the Emergency Quota Act of 1921. In the following February, Albert Johnson of the state of Washington, chairman of the House Committee on Immigration, introduced a bill denying entry into the United States to aliens "ineligible to citizenship," meaning all Asians but directed mainly against the Japanese. Secretary of State Hughes protested that such statutory discrimination would needlessly insult the Japanese. Why not, he suggested, amend the bill by recognizing the Gentlemen's Agreement and placing the Japanese on the same quota system as the Europeans? A quota for the Japanese would not have allowed more than 250 of them to enter each year, a mere trickle.

A month later, Johnson's committee, composed mainly of Southerners and representatives from the Pacific Coast who favored racial discrimination, issued a report condemning the Gentlemen's Agreement and calling for Oriental exclusion. The Gentlemen's Agreement, it said, infringed on Congress' prerogative of regulating immigration. Congress, it seemed clear, wanted to end the executive agreement with Japan.

A senator from Tennessee apparently expressed the mood of Congress when he said, "the wishes and desires of the white race of California should be respected. It is far more important to respect their views than to uphold the so-called 'gentlemen's agreement.'" [1]

At the suggestion of Hughes, the Japanese Ambassador in Washington, Masanao Hanihara, sent the Department of State a note on April 10, 1924, politely pointing out that Japan had scrupulously adhered to the policy of self-regulation of immigrants in the Gentlemen's Agreement so as to avoid statutory discrimination. Exclusion, he warned, would bring "grave consequences" and mar "the otherwise happy and mutually advantageous relations between our two countries." [2]

Instead of being persuaded to place the Japanese on a quota, Congress took offense at the two indiscreet words "grave consequences" and converted Hanihara's note from a normal protest to an international incident. Several senators insisted that the note carried a "veiled threat" of war if exclusion were enacted. A number of newspapers called the note a "bristling protest," and the *Atlanta Constitution* said "Japan has thrown down a serious challenge to the American Congress." [3] Within a week of Hanihara's protest, both houses of Congress voted for the Johnson immigration bill with the exclusion clause intact.

Eleven days after Congress had approved the final version of the bill, President Coolidge reluctantly signed it. "If the exclusion provision stood alone," he said, "I should disapprove it without hesitation. . . ." [4] The *Cincinnati Enquirer* apparently summed up public sentiment by saying that "the crux of this matter is that the United States, like Canada and Australia, must be kept a white man's country."

The Japanese, who had never questioned the right of the United States to exclude immigrants, resented the immigration law of 1924 because it abrogated the Gentlemen's Agreement and singled out Asians as inferiors, an unwarranted stigma that any proud and sensitive people would resent. Fifteen Tokyo newspapers published a joint declaration condemning that law as "inequitable and unjust," and for weeks the press throughout Japan denounced the United States for "persecution" of the Japanese and for enacting a "deliberate insult." [5] In various Japanese cities outraged citizens organized anti-American demonstrations and boycotts of American goods. On July 1, when exclusion went into effect, both houses of Japan's Diet passed resolutions of protest.

The Chinese Nationalist Revolution

Beginning in 1925, China's second revolution of the twentieth century became for the next few years the dominant issue in the politics of Asia and the main concern of American Far Eastern policy. After the First World War the peoples of Asia, particularly the Chinese, had demanded equality with those of the West.

This produced no immediate results, for the great powers did not apply Wilson's principles of national self-determination to Asia and, except for Japan, Asian countries did not have strong enough governments to deliver effective protests.

When China asked the powers at the Washington Conference to give up their privileges, such as special tariff concessions and extraterritoriality guaranteed by the "unequal" treaties, they replied that she must put her house in order and develop a capacity to govern herself according to Western standards before they would do so. The United States, along with the other powers, offered China only a modest program of treaty revision for the future.

Dissatisfied with the Western promises and increasingly resentful of the unequal treaties, the Chinese embraced a violent nationalism. "Whose semi-colony is China?" asked Sun Yat-sen, the leader of nationalist revolutionary forces. "China is the colony of every nation that has made treaties with her," he pointed out to his people, "and the treaty-making nations are her masters. China is not the colony of one nation but of all, and we are not the slaves of one country but of all."[6]

Under the leadership of Sun's Kuomintang, or Nationalist Party, with headquarters in Canton, the insurgent Nationalist movement slowly gained strength. What passed for the Republic of China's government in Peking was a coterie of corrupt and quarreling war lords. More and more Chinese looked to Sun's movement to save the country. To mount a successful revolution that would crush the government at Peking and the various provincial war lords, Sun needed help. Since the Western powers, including the United States, offered none, he turned to Soviet Russia. Sun welcomed Chinese Communists into his Nationalist Party and with the aid of Russian advisers planned a great military campaign to conquer and unite China, but before completing his plans he died in March, 1925.

After Sun's death the revolution erupted unexpectedly in Shanghai with a skirmish in May between Chinese mobs and foreign police. Antiforeignism and anti-imperialism now became main features of the revolution. The Chinese believed that the treaty system stood in the way of their national development and hence attacked the privileges of the treaty powers.

Although he was to waver in adhering to it, Secretary of State Kellogg soon made the policy of the Coolidge administration clear. In instructions to the American delegation that was to represent the United States in a Special Conference on the Chinese Customs Tariff, scheduled to meet in Peking in October, 1925, he said that he believed the United States would have to release China from her conventional tariffs and give up extraterritoriality. "It is reasonable to suppose," he pointed out, "that a great nation like China will not long permit foreign control of its domestic affairs."[7]

Nothing came of the tariff conference, but before it closed in July, 1926, the Kuomintang had reorganized itself. Its armies, under the leadership of General

Chiang Kai-shek, had plunged northward in June, winning victory after victory. By the end of the year the Nationalists had conquered over half of China. The anti-imperialist tone of Nationalist propaganda and the insistent demands of the Nationalists for immediate revision of the unequal treaties now forced the United States and the other treaty powers to consider whether to come to terms with the Nationalists or attempt to maintain old privileges with force of arms.

Since the Chinese abused Americans and their property, the Coolidge administration sent troops and warships to protect American interests in the port areas, but otherwise followed a policy of nonintervention. Kellogg reiterated that China's internal struggle was her own affair and that the United States wished to maintain a strict neutrality between the warring factions.

Articulate opinion sympathized with the Chinese revolution, regarding it as comparable to the American struggle for independence and meriting support. Reflecting such sympathy, the chairman of the House Committee on Foreign Affairs introduced a resolution in January, 1927, calling for a new treaty with China that would end America's special privileges and grant China full equality, a resolution that won overwhelming approval.

Even some of those who opposed the resolution expressed good will toward the revolution. "I myself," one opponent said, "desire to express my sympathy for poor, struggling China in this hour of her great trial. I want my country to do her utmost to free China from the curse of unequal treaties and foreign misrule."[8] Many Americans, obviously, wanted the government to take the lead in aiding China to achieve full national independence.

A few days later Secretary of State Kellogg stated the administration's official policy. The United States, he said, had always desired the unity and independence of China. It was ready to give up extraterritoriality and to restore China to complete tariff autonomy and to do so alone, if necessary. "The only question," he explained, "is with whom it shall negotiate." He was willing to negotiate, and hence recognize, any government that represented "the people of the country."[9]

Yet the Coolidge administration moved slowly. The two most powerful American groups in China advocated conflicting policies. Most of the missionaries, and their governing boards in the United States, favored the abolition of extra-territoriality and urged the government to give up its privileges in China. The business groups did not wish to see the United States lose any privileges enjoyed by other powers.

American businessmen in China, disturbed by continuing antiforeign violence, demanded additional protection through military intervention. Some members of the government and many other Americans, moreover, opposed any concessions to the Nationalists, fearing the spread of Communist influence.

If it were not, The New York Times pointed out, "for the powerful influence of Soviet Russia in stimulating anti-foreign sentiment among the Cantonese, the sympathy of the American people would probably be largely in their behalf." [10] A few weeks later, on March 24, as Nationalist troops streamed into Nanking, a spectacular clash temporarily thrust aside the question of the unequal treaties and made intervention the primary concern of American policy.

Enraged mobs, including Nationalist soldiers, attacked foreigners and their property in Nanking, killing and wounding American, British, French, Italian, and Japanese nationals. "You are all alike," a Nationalist soldier told the American Consul in Nanking. "The British and Italians are killing our men at Shanghai and you Americans have drunk our blood for years and become rich." [11]

Fleeing before the antiforeign fury, some Americans and other foreigners took refuge on what was called Socony Hill, property of the Standard Oil Company. When Nationalist soldiers attacked them, an American and a British gunboat anchored in the Yangtze River laid down a barrage that drove off or killed the soldiers and allowed the foreigners to escape to the warships.

Acting jointly with Britain, France, Japan, and Italy, the United States vigorously protested the incident, demanding an apology, punishment for those responsible and adequate reparation for damages. The Chinese Minister for Foreign Affairs promised reparation only where the powers could prove that Nationalist troops had caused the damage.

Considering the replies "wholly unsatisfactory and unacceptable," the powers decided to take joint military action against the Nationalists to enforce their demands. The government was ready to protect the life and property of American citizens in China wherever such protection could be given, Kellogg said, but would not participate in any joint display of force. "The time has passed," he added, "when foreign countries can take over Chinese territory or maintain by force special spheres of influence in trade." [12] Since the United States broke their solid front and negotiated directly with the Nationalists for a peaceful settlement of the Nanking incident, the other powers abandoned their policy of force and followed the American example.

Growing tension between moderates and radicals within the Kuomintang, meanwhile, had split the party. Chiang Kai-shek turned against the Communists and radicals and established his own Nationalist government at Nanking, supported by the conservatives in the revolutionary movement. After forcing the Communists out of the party, Chiang broke off diplomatic relations with the Russians and fought a civil war with an unconquered remnant of the Chinese Communists. He continued his northern advance, and in June, 1928, Peking, which he renamed Peiping, fell to his Nationalists. His government now asserted a greater control over China than had any modern regime up to that time.

Purged of its Communists, the Nationalist government toned down its anti-imperialism and antiforeignism and sought to reach a peaceful understanding with the powers. Kellogg also wanted a settlement, partly because he wished to strengthen the conservative forces and partly because he wanted to help stabilize conditions within China and then contribute to making her truly independent of foreign control.

Any understanding first required a settlement of the Nanking incident. Accepting more moderate terms than those insisted upon by the other powers, the United States had reached an accord with the Nationalist government over that incident in March, 1928. After that, two more important questions remained: formal recognition of the Nationalist government and treaty revision.

Less than two months after Nationalist troops had reached Peiping, the United States, in a treaty of July 25, 1928, granted China complete autonomy over her tariff as of January 1, 1929. The United States thus became the first country to offer China such autonomy and hence shattered the old international bloc that had long opposed any concessions to the Chinese. The signing of the treaty, moreover, constituted recognition of the Nationalist government, and Kellogg so informed the Chinese. The Senate approved the tariff treaty on February 13, and a week later ratifications were exchanged in Washington.

The tariff treaty was not, as some Americans thought, the beginning of the end of the unequal treaties. The United States and the other powers would not change the extraterritorial provisions of their treaties with China. Kellogg was willing, however, to negotiate over extraterritoriality and to sign a treaty ending it, but not if the other treaty powers retained theirs. In spite of later attempts to negotiate, the United States did not conclude such a treaty until January, 1943.

Invasion of Manchuria

Chiang Kai-shek's relations with Russia had deteriorated steadily. When his Nationalists tried to extend their authority to Manchuria and attacked Russia's privileges there under two treaties of 1924, they clashed with the Soviets and put the Kellogg-Briand Pact to its first test.

In May and July, 1929, Nationalist police raided Soviet consulates in Manchuria, arrested Russian agents, and took over certain Russian facilities of the Chinese Eastern Railway. Russia broke off diplomatic relations and prepared to defend her interests in Manchuria. China and Russia, who had recently signed the Kellogg-Briand Pact, appeared ready to fight just as President Hoover was preparing to proclaim the Pact. Secretary of State Stimson, thinking war imminent, wishing to prevent a declaration on the very day the Pact went into effect, and taking the position that the United States was mainly responsible for the treaty, reminded China and Russia of their obligation to settle their differences peacefully.

Several months later Russian forces invaded Manchuria and defeated the Chinese. "The main question," Stimson's Assistant Secretary of State wrote at the time, "is what, if anything, to do about the Russian advance in Manchuria. It is making the Kellogg Pact look like 30 cents. . . ." [13]

On December 2, after appealing to the signatories of the Pact for support, Stimson invoked it against China and Russia. The Russians, who had imposed their terms on the Chinese and had begun evacuating Manchuria, rebuffed him. Maxim Litvinov, the Soviet Foreign Commissar, indignantly told the Secretary of State "that the Pact of Paris does not give any single State or group of States the function of protector of this pact." He concluded by "expressing amazement that the Government of the United States, which by its own will has no official relations with the Soviet Union, deems it possible to apply to it with advice and counsel." [14]

Stimson's diplomacy, as his Assistant Secretary pointed out, "did not enhance the value of the Pact, but tended to make it a little absurd." [15] The Russians regarded his admonitions as un-neutral interference, especially since the United States recognized China's government but not theirs. Japan's imperialists, who had a special stake in Manchuria, carefully noted Stimson's failure to convert the Kellogg Pact into a system of collective security.

By any tangible standard of measurement Japan had greater interests in Manchuria than any other foreign power except China. In 1931, Manchuria accounted for more than forty per cent of her foreign trade and investment. To most Japanese, Manchuria was a symbol of their country's status as an imperial power. They believed that the interests they had built up there, through treaties and investments, were essential to the welfare of their country. They had, therefore, watched the extension of Nationalist Chinese power into Manchuria with undisguised anxiety.

Despite their failure to dislodge the Russians from their control of the Chinese Eastern Railway, the Chinese Nationalists continued their efforts to gain full control of Manchuria, or what they called China's three northeastern provinces. They tried to destroy Japan's economic and political ascendancy in southern Manchuria by colonizing it with Chinese, by attacking Japan's special privileges, and by disseminating anti-Japanese propaganda.

Anti-Japanese feeling among Chinese in Manchuria became so bitter in 1931 that numerous incidents between them and the Japanese were common. Late in June, Chinese soldiers in Manchuria executed a Japanese army officer, Captain Shintaro Nakamura. A few weeks later fighting broke out there between Chinese farmers and police on one side and Korean farmers and Japanese consular police on the other. Widespread anti-Chinese riots in Korea and an anti-Japanese boycott in China followed. These incidents led certain of Japan's leaders to demand a settlement of the Manchurian question by force.

Aware of sentiment favoring a forcible settlement, headstrong Japanese officers of the Kwantung army stationed in Manchuria acted independently of the civilian government and engineered an explosion on the night of September 18, 1931, on a Japanese railroad track a few miles north of Mukden.[16] Blaming the Chinese for endangering the safety of the railway, the Kwantung army immediately drove Chinese troops out of Mukden and several other cities of southern Manchuria. Fanning out from the Mukden area, the Japanese forces moved so swiftly and efficiently in capturing strategic points that few doubted that they had moved according to a preconceived plan.

A few days after the attack began, the Chinese government appealed to the United States as sponsor of the Kellogg Pact and to the League of Nations under the Covenant to help in keeping the peace. Then both the Chinese and the League tried to draw the United States into some kind of joint action against the Japanese. Since Hoover was devoting most of his energy to the problems of the great depression, the immediate handling of the Manchurian crisis fell to Stimson. This time Stimson at first moved cautiously in framing policy.

The Secretary of State told the Japanese Ambassador in Washington that Japan's action had placed the Kellogg Pact and the Nine-Power Open Door Treaty at stake. Yet at this time the Hoover administration followed a policy of trying to avoid commitments that would antagonize the Japanese and allow the military to gain complete ascendancy in Japan. Toward League action Stimson adopted a policy of not participating but of lending the League itself "all moral support that we can."[17]

After the Council of the League passed a resolution urging China and Japan to restore "normal relations" in Manchuria, Stimson thought the two antagonists could meet that request through negotiations between themselves. "We have not attempted to go into the question of right or wrong . . . , we are not taking sides," he told the Chinese a week later, "we are 'playing no favorites.'"[18]

Most Americans, however, favored China. They believed, as newspaper and congressional sentiment revealed, that Japan was mocking the peace treaties and violating international law. "Even though Japan's reasons were ten times as truthful as it can be assumed they are," the chairman of the Senate Committee on Foreign Relations, Borah, said, "there is no justification for force in Manchuria."

When Stimson received news, in the second week in October, that the Japanese army was expanding its conquest in Manchuria, he began to change his attitude. "I am afraid," he told himself, "we have got to take a firm ground and aggressive stand toward Japan."[19]

The Secretary searched for "some way of formally expressing the moral disapproval of the world against the breach of peace in Manchuria, and if possible to put behind that expression a sanction." Hoover opposed economic or military sanctions, insisting that they "meant all the penalties of war except shooting," and would lead to war itself. The only sanction he would support was that of public opinion.[20]

Both men agreed, nonetheless, that an American official should meet with the Council of the League, but that he must confine himself to discussions on the possible application of the Kellogg Pact. Despite the resistance of the Japanese, who considered the move a hostile one, an American began sitting with the Council on October 16.

On the following day Britain, France, and Italy reminded Japan and China of their obligations under the Kellogg Pact. Three days later the United States also invoked the Kellogg Pact. Moving faster than Stimson was willing to go at this time, the Council passed a resolution on October 24, 1931, asking Japan and China to compose their differences and calling upon Japan to evacuate within a month the territory she had seized.

Since Japan did not stop her conquest, the League cautiously asked Stimson if the United States would support sanctions. He then declared that the Hoover administration would not do so because an embargo might lead to war. Up to this point the United States had followed League policy, but reluctantly and at a distance. Then, with Japan's approval, the League's Council appointed a neutral Commission of Enquiry on December 10 composed of five men, including one American, and headed by the Earl of Lytton, to go to the Far East to investigate the Manchurian crisis.

Still the Kwantung army pressed on and at the beginning of the new year had most of Manchuria in its grip. Stimson was furious. Three and one-half months of note-writing had proved futile. He and the President agreed, therefore, to adopt the nonrecognition doctrine William Jennings Bryan had used against Japan in 1915 as a means of protesting her Manchurian conquest.

The Hoover–Stimson Doctrine

On January 7, 1932, Stimson sent identical notes to Japan and China saying the United States would not recognize any agreement or situation impairing American rights, the Open Door policy, or any gains made in violation of the Kellogg Pact.[21] This idea, known either as the Stimson or the Hoover-Stimson Doctrine, now became the pivot of American policy.

The Secretary had hoped to gain support for the doctrine from the other signatories of the Nine-Power Treaty, but the British would not associate themselves with it. *The Times* of London insisted that England had no business defending the administrative integrity of China while it was no more than an ideal.[22] Japan's reaction was a stinging rebuff. At this time, therefore, the United States stood alone in its commitment to the nonrecognition principle. A few critics sneered. "The belated activity of Secretary Stimson," a Louisville paper said, "is suggestive of locking the stable door after the horse has been stolen."[23] Nonetheless, the Secretary's one consolation was that American opinion responded favorably to his doctrine.

Labels in cartoon:
JAPANESE GOV'T. PROMISES
WORLD COURT
L. OF N. COVENANT
KELLOGG PACT
NINE POWER TREATY
TR...
SHANGHAI PORT TREATY
JAPAN

THE CHALLENGE TO COLLECTIVE SECURITY

This cartoon implies that paper promises and treaties were valueless in the face of Japan's seizure of Manchuria in 1931.

Just three weeks later, in retaliation for a devastatingly effective Chinese boycott against Japanese goods, Japan's navy, acting independently of the army in Manchuria, attacked the Chinese sections of Shanghai. The Chinese forces there put up stiff resistance and the Japanese shelled and bombed the city. Since the indiscriminate slaughter of civilians was not yet commonplace in war, Americans were appalled and almost wholly hostile to Japan. "The bombing of residential sections, the murder of helpless men, women, and children," the *Philadelphia Inquirer* declared, "puts Japan beyond the pale of civilized warfare." 24

Hoover immediately sent ships and troops to Shanghai to protect lives and property, as did the British who protested the Japanese attack and now offered some cooperation with the United States. At this time the American battle fleet was holding annual maneuvers in Hawaiian waters. Stimson persuaded the President to keep it there for a while as a warning to Japan.

In his next move Stimson invited England to join him in invoking the Nine-Power Treaty, hoping such cooperation might lead to economic sanctions against Japan by the League. England refused. Undeterred by the nonrecognition doctrine, the Japanese proclaimed the state of Manchukuo on February 18, a state ostensibly independent but in fact a puppet.

Stimson's answer was another unilateral statement of principle. In a long public letter to Senator Borah he challenged Japan's action, extended the nonrecognition doctrine to cover violations of the Nine-Power Treaty as well as the Kellogg Pact, threatened Japan with possible fortification of Guam and the Philippines, and invited the rest of the world to join in applying the nonrecognition principle to the Manchurian conquest.[25]

The full effect of the letter is not clear, but the Assembly of the League adopted a resolution in March containing the nonrecognition principle.[26] Most League members refused to recognize Manchukuo.

Two months later peace came to Shanghai. After "saving face" by expelling the Chinese troops, the Japanese forces withdrew, but this presaged no important change in Japanese policy. On September 15, slightly less than two weeks after the Lytton Commission had completed its report, Japan signed a treaty formally recognizing Manchukuo.

The League published the Lytton report on October 2. It condemned Japan's invasion of Manchuria and the puppet regime there but did not absolve China from blame. It also recommended an autonomous Manchuria under the political control of China but with safeguards for Japanese interests there. After extensive debate, the League adopted the report in February, 1933. The Japanese delegates walked out, and later Japan announced her resignation from the League, effective in two years.

Some Americans considered the League's action a vindication of their government's Far Eastern policy, yet neither the efforts of the League nor of the United States had halted the Japanese. Stimson, sympathetic to China, had tried to persuade the President to cooperate with the League in punishing Japan through sanctions, but Hoover would not use any but peaceful means to support the nonrecognition principle.[27]

Perhaps one New York paper had aptly summarized the dilemma of American policy. "Now that the League has told Japan to get out of Manchuria, and Japan has said 'to hell with that noise in diplomatic language,' who," it asked, "is going to throw Japan out?"[28]

Roosevelt's Policies in the Far East

Having tested the principle of collective security and found it ineffective, Japan expanded her conquests. In January, 1933, her forces had driven beyond Manchuria's borders into China's province of Jehol, outside the Great Wall, and in March annexed it to Manchukuo. In May, after piercing the Great Wall and invading China proper, Japanese forces made a truce. They forced a broad demilitarized zone, south of the Great Wall, on China.

Some Americans talked of war. "We can allow Japan to go ahead in Jehol and keep silent," one writer said, "or we can protest all over the place and go to war."[29]

Despite their sympathy for China, the American people were in no mood for war. They wanted to work their way out of the great depression and to isolate themselves from distant foreign troubles.

Secretary Stimson, meantime, had conferred with President-elect Franklin D. Roosevelt and had received vague assurances that the new Democratic administration would continue his Far Eastern policy. "I have always had the deepest sympathy for the Chinese," Roosevelt told two of his protesting advisers. "How could you expect me not to go along with Stimson on Japan?"[30]

After taking office, Roosevelt, as he had said he would, continued the Far Eastern policy of his predecessor. He refused to recognize Manchukuo, cooperated with the League on Asian matters, kept the battleship fleet in the Pacific, and inaugurated a program of building the fleet up to its treaty limits. His Secretary of State, Cordell Hull, even took office with the idea of "preventing Japan from gaining overlordship of the entire Far East."[31]

Roosevelt was not as openly hostile to Japan as Stimson had been, and his tactics were different, but one of his early diplomatic moves that caused uneasiness in Japan was his *rapprochement* with Soviet Russia.

Recognition of Soviet Russia

For sixteen years four different administrations, from Wilson through Hoover, had refused to recognize the Soviet regime. They would not permit formal relations with a Communist government that had repudiated Russia's debts, confiscated private property without compensation, preached world revolution, and plotted the overthrow of capitalism and democracy. Other nations, Japan among them, had nonetheless recognized the Soviet Union.

In the first years of the great depression some Americans had urged the recognition of the Soviets in the interest of increased trade, hoping it would help bolster their sagging economy. To Russia and to other Americans, the threat of Japanese hegemony over Asia formed a more potent reason for a diplomatic *rapprochement*.

Fearing that her Asian provinces would be Japan's next target after the Manchurian conquest, Russia felt that the United States would be a valuable collaborator in any effort to curb the Japanese. In any event, the Communists thought they could use the growing antagonism between Japan and the United States to strengthen their own position in Asia.

Roosevelt took the initiative in approaching Russia, a move that aroused apprehension in Japan. To calm Japanese fears, his administration announced early in November, 1933, that it would soon move a large part of the battle fleet from the Pacific to the Atlantic for maneuvers.

After an exchange of notes dated November 16, the United States formally recognized the Soviet Union. In return, the Russians promised religious rights to Americans in Russia, pledged themselves to refrain from propaganda and subversive activity against the American government, and agreed to negotiate later over the Tsarist debts to the United States.

Roosevelt announced that the impelling motive behind recognition "was the desire of both countries for peace," but foreign observers believed that the United States had recognized Russia to counterbalance German militarism in Europe and especially Japanese power in Asia. Russia's labor newspaper, *Trud*, announced flatly that Japan's imperialism had produced recognition.[32] Whatever the true motive, recognition created concern in Japan and enhanced Soviet prestige.

The other results of recognition, however, were a disappointment to the United States. Trade with the Soviets never reached the expectations of those who desired it; Russia made no settlement of the debts question; Communist propaganda continued; and the Soviet Union did not cooperate in any policy of opposition to Japan.[33]

Japan's Monroe Doctrine

During the next few years neither the United States, Russia, nor any other power interfered with Japan's consolidation of control over Manchuria and her attempt to gain hegemony over northern China. From the time of the First World War, at least, many Japanese had spoken vaguely of their own Monroe Doctrine in Eastern Asia. Basically, they advanced the idea of Asia for Asians, but under Japanese hegemony.

A spokesman for the Foreign Office gave official sanction to the idea of a Japanese Monroe Doctrine. Japan, he claimed, had the "sole responsibility for the preservation of peace in the Far East" and would oppose the League or individual countries if they interfered in China.[34] Mildly but firmly, Secretary of State Hull replied two weeks later that the United States held to its treaty rights in China and would not acquiesce in Japan's "hands off" policy toward her.

At the same time the Kwantung army began moving westward from Manchuria by penetrating Inner Mongolia. In Manchuria Japanese officials set up an oil monopoly. In November, 1934, Hull protested the monopoly, and the consequent discrimination there against American trade and investment as a violation of the Open Door principle, but got nowhere. The Japanese said they did not consider "that the Nine-Power Treaty applies to 'Manchukuo.'"

Late in 1935, the Japanese attempted unsuccessfully to convert the two provinces of Inner Mongolia and three northeastern provinces of China proper into an autonomous area. By 1937, it became clear that Japan had to try other means to gain control over North China.

During this period of expansion the relations of the Roosevelt administration with Japan were relatively friendly. Although the administration made no retreat in principle, it followed a policy of nonintervention in Asia. Only when Japan coupled her expansion with a campaign for naval parity did Roosevelt take a firm stand against her. One reason for Roosevelt's cautious policy was his concern for the security of the Philippines and other American possessions in the Pacific.

Philippine Independence

From the time of the acquisition of the Philippines, Americans had looked at the position of those islands in their political economy from two differing points of view. There were those, primarily Republicans and certain business groups, who considered the islands a key to America's commercial and political interest in China. Others, mainly anti-imperialists and Democrats, wanted to give the Filipinos their freedom.

In keeping with the latter point of view, President Wilson had approved the Jones Act in August, 1916, promising the Filipinos independence as soon as they should establish a stable government.[35] After the First World War, as tension with Japan mounted, it became clear that the Philippines were the weakest part of America's Far Eastern policy. The islands had not fulfilled the hope of bringing a substantial trade with Asia, and increasingly Americans realized that they could not be defended against attack by a powerful foe such as Japan.

Domestic political expediency rather than strategic considerations, however, spurred the movement for granting the Philippines freedom. Agricultural and labor pressure groups, wishing to rid themselves of competition from Philippine tobacco, sugar, and coconut oil, and seeking to stop the flow of Filipino immigrants into the United States, agitated to give the islands independence. In December, 1932, Congress passed the Hare-Hawes-Cutting bill granting the Filipinos independence after a transition period of ten years, during which they were to enjoy autonomy under a commonwealth status with American supervision and protection.

President Hoover, while not opposed to the principle of ultimate independence, vetoed the bill. The Filipinos, he said, were not yet prepared for freedom and probably could not maintain it in the chaotic conditions of the international politics of the Far East. A few days later, reflecting what were probably the feelings of the American people, Congress overrode his veto.

Since they were dependent on a free market in the United States and economic disaster would probably follow if the ties were completely severed, most Filipino leaders opposed independence under the American terms. Objecting to certain features of the independence act, particularly its tariff and immigration restrictions and its provisions for American military and naval bases in the islands, the Philippine legislature rejected it in October, 1933.

The Filipinos obtained only slightly better terms from the Roosevelt administration. Except for the deletion of the provision giving the United States a permanent military base in the islands, the Tydings-McDuffie bill, which the President signed on March 24, 1934, did not differ much from the earlier law. "I do not believe," Roosevelt said, "that other provisions of the original law need to be changed at this time."[36] Convinced it could get no better terms, the Philippine legislature accepted the new independence proposal. The Commonwealth of the Philippines was inaugurated in November, 1935, with Manuel L. Quezon as President.

In assessing the foreign implications of the conditional grant of independence, some Americans considered it an attempt to get rid of a costly hostage. Many believed it signified the withdrawal of the United States from active participation in Far Eastern politics and a renunciation of its economic interest in China. The Japanese, apparently, also viewed it as evidence that the United States cared little for the affairs of the Far East. None of those interpretations were entirely sound. Since the Philippines were not yet free, they still remained a hostage in Japan's back yard.

Yankeephobia in Latin America

Another part of the world to whose problems the United States was especially sensitive was Latin America. Before and during the First World War there prevailed throughout most of Latin America, particularly among intellectuals, a hostility toward the United States that historians have called "Yankeephobia." In 1912, for instance, Manuel Ugarte, an Argentine writer, wrote a bitter letter to President-elect Wilson condemning intervention south of the Rio Grande. "We ask, in short," he said, "that the star-spangled banner cease to be a symbol of oppression in the New World."[37]

A few years later Rufino Blanco-Fambona, a Venezuelan author, ridiculed American culture and denounced "the Yankees, the Yankees," saying "these are the enemies of our soul, of our civilization, of our character, of our independence."[38] After the war Ugarte poured his resentments into a book, *Destiny of a Continent*, that became the classic indictment of "yankee imperialism" in Latin America.

Yet, after the United States had gone into the war, the republics to the south appeared to support their northern neighbor in this time of crisis. This apparent solidarity, however, reflected no genuine respect for the United States. Among the large and important Latin republics, only Brazil entered the war as a full belligerent. Argentina and Chile remained neutral, and Mexico and Colombia were hostile to the United States. Most of the other lesser republics who supported the United States, Cuba, Haiti, Santo Domingo, and the majority of the Central-American states, were virtual protectorates or were so closely tied to the United States that their actions hardly constituted an expression of true friendship.

After the war, Wilson's ideas on collective security as embodied in the League aroused warm response in Latin America, but again this support of the League did not reflect affection for the United States. Many Latin-American leaders saw in the League an alternative to the Pan-American movement dominated by the United States, but were alarmed when the United States insisted on writing its unilateral interpretation of the Monroe Doctrine into the covenant. They were no longer apprehensive of danger from Europe but feared that the United States wished to use the excuse of protecting them to dominate and exploit them. The failure of the United States to join the League, the rising postwar nationalism in the United States, its continued occupation of Nicaragua, Haiti, and the Dominican Republic, and its efforts to coerce Mexico, all tended to confirm Latin America's distrust.

Many Americans were aware of the antagonism toward them in the southern republics. In the campaign of 1920 Harding criticized Wilson's interventions in the Caribbean, but after taking office continued most of his predecessor's Latin-American policies, even the moralistic and unsuccessful recognition policy. Secretary of State Hughes, to whom Harding gave full responsibility for Latin-American affairs, tried in a limited way to inaugurate a new policy toward the republics to the south. "We covet no territory; we seek no conquest," Hughes told the Latins at a meeting in Rio de Janeiro; "the liberty we cherish for ourselves we desire for others; and we assert no rights for ourselves that we do not accord to others." [39]

Hughes tried to work out a plan in 1921 for evacuating American troops from the Dominican Republic. He admitted later that "no step taken by the government of the United States in Latin America in recent years has given rise to more criticism, and in this instance just criticism, than the military occupation of the Dominican Republic by the armed forces of the United States." [40]

An agreement was signed in June, 1922, and after various delays, such as Dominican elections supervised by Americans, the troops were finally removed in September, 1924, under the Coolidge administration. Yet the Dominicans and other Latin Americans were not satisfied, for the United States still retained control over finances through a receiver of customs and virtually exercised the power of a protectorate over the republic.

Although unusual at such conferences, the Latin Americans expressed their distrust of the United States at the Fifth Pan-American Conference in Santiago, Chile, in the spring of 1923. A delegate from Colombia, for example, openly attacked Yankee intervention and the Monroe Doctrine. Even though the North Americans defended their doctrine and policies, their defense did not reduce Latin suspicions, particularly since Hughes made it clear that the United States would not renounce the right of intervention, the main source of ill will.

As Coolidge's Secretary of State, Hughes sent Marines into Honduras in March,

1924, and at the request of the President of Panama also placed a small force of Marines in the isthmian republic in October, 1925, but they remained only a short time. According to a survey made in 1924 only six of the twenty Latin-American republics were free, in one way or another, including control of their financial policies, from North American domination, and in six of the twenty the United States had backed its interference with occupying troops.

Controversy with Mexico

Coolidge began his second term with a new Secretary of State, Frank B. Kellogg. For a short time in 1925, Coolidge and Kellogg withdrew troops from Nicaragua, but returned them as another revolution gripped the country. Complications had set in when Coolidge recognized one warring faction as legal and Mexico recognized another. The United States placed an embargo on arms going to the Liberal faction, headed by Dr. Juan B. Sacasa, but allowed them to flow freely to the Conservative regime of Adolfo Díaz, who paid for them with money from American loans.

Mexico continued to slip arms to the opposition forces of Sacasa, and critics at home and in Latin America denounced Coolidge's "private war" in Nicaragua. The criticisms so upset Coolidge and Kellogg that the usually taciturn President finally spoke out. "We are not making war on Nicaragua," he said, "any more than a policeman on the street is making war on passers-by."[41]

In defense of its intervention, the Coolidge administration accused Mexico of acting as Communist Russia's catspaw in Nicaragua. "The Bolshevist leaders," Kellogg told the Senate's Committee on Foreign Relations, "have had very definite ideas with respect to the role which Mexico and Latin America are to play in their general program of world revolution." In establishing an international revolutionary movement in the New World, they plan to use Mexico and Latin America, he said, "as a base for activity against the United States."[42] Since Kellogg offered no evidence to substantiate his accusation, the administration did not win public support for its policy.

Finally, in March, 1927, Coolidge sent his own trouble shooter, former Secretary of War Henry L. Stimson, to end the difficulties in Nicaragua. "I want you to go down there," Coolidge told Stimson, "and if you can see a way to clean up that mess, I want you to do it."[43] With full power to mediate, Stimson brought the hostile Nicaraguan factions to an uneasy truce in May known as the Tipitapa Agreement, but one of the rebel chieftains, Augusto Sandino, refused to be pacified.

The rivalry over Nicaragua touched only one phase of difficulties with Mexico that had not ceased since Wilson's interventions. During the First World War, Mexicans had remained hostile to the United States and friendly toward Germany. One of

Mexico's main controversies with the United States at that time grew out of Article 27 of her constitution of 1917, vesting subsoil rights in the nation. Under that article President Venustiano Carranza had threatened to nationalize all oil holdings in the country, many of them owned by Americans. Through a decree of February, 1918, he taxed the oil lands and the profits from their exploitation.

American oil companies protested, denouncing the law as confiscatory and put pressure on their government to intervene to protect their property rights in Mexico. When Alvaro Obregón succeeded Carranza as Mexico's president in 1920, Wilson's administration, and then Harding's, refused to recognize his government unless it agreed by treaty not to enforce Article 27 against American property owners. Obregón resisted the pressure, but in August, 1923, as the result of an executive agreement, a compromise known as the Bucareli Agreements, he partially satisfied the oil companies and received American recognition.[44]

Obregón's successor, strong man Plutarco Elias Calles, however, did not consider himself bound by the Bucareli Agreements, and in December, 1925, his congress passed two land and petroleum laws that narrowly restricted foreign ownership of Mexican land under the terms of Article 27. Those laws, which went into effect in January, 1927, during the rivalry over Nicaragua, plus drastic anticlerical legislation, antagonized American property owners in Mexico, Catholics, and the Coolidge administration. Many Americans again clamored for intervention.

In an effort to ease the strain in relations, President Coolidge appointed Dwight W. Morrow, a former classmate of his at Amherst College and a Wall Street lawyer, as Ambassador to Mexico in September. "My only instructions," Coolidge told Morrow, "are to keep us out of war with Mexico."[45] Morrow did. He studied the sources of difficulty and tactfully helped improve relations with the Mexicans. A timely decision by Mexico's supreme court in November aided his diplomacy by upholding some of the contentions of the oil companies.[46]

In December, 1929, Morrow's son-in-law, the international hero Charles A. Lindbergh, also dramatically aided the Ambassador's diplomacy by making a non-stop flight from Washington to Mexico City that pleased the Mexicans. Morrow, moreover, persuaded church officials to moderate their demands on the Mexican government and Calles to tone down some of his regime's anticlericalism, and thus helped placate Catholic opinion in the United States.[47] So effective was Morrow's diplomacy that it marked a turning point in relations with Mexico.

Meanwhile, in Rio de Janeiro at a meeting of the International Commission of American Jurists in April and May, 1927, Nicaragua and several other Latin republics urged the jurists to adopt a resolution condemning United States policy. The North American delegates succeeded in blocking that move but acquiesced, without giving approval, in a formula saying that "no state has a right to interfere in the internal affairs of another." They went along with that principle, to be presented for adoption at the forthcoming Sixth Pan-American Conference scheduled to meet in Havana in January, 1928, because they wished to avoid a harsher attack on United States policy at Havana.

To aid in forestalling the expected attack, Coolidge appointed an unusually strong delegation to the Havana conference headed by former Secretary of State Hughes, and at the urging of Kellogg reluctantly went to Havana to deliver the opening speech. Since this was only the second time a United States President had ever set foot on Latin-American soil, the visit ostensibly reflected a new concern for Latin-American affairs.

Despite Kellogg's precautions, Latin Americans bitterly attacked United States policy, particularly the Caribbean interventions. Hughes fought the adoption of the Rio formula and defended his country's past interventions, calling them "interposition of a temporary character."[48] He thus made what was to be the last public defense of the United States' right of intervention. He tried to substitute a milder resolution for the Rio formula, but all of the countries, except four who were especially dependent on North American good will, voted against it. This was a resounding diplomatic defeat, one reflecting the low state of relations with Latin America.

Hoover and the Good Neighbor Idea

Well aware of the "Yankeephobia" in the Latin-American countries, Herbert Hoover went farther than had Coolidge in efforts to decrease it. As President-elect, a few weeks after his victory at the polls in November, 1928, Hoover embarked on a good will tour of Central and South America. In ten weeks he visited half the American republics and in a number of speeches stressed that the United States wanted to be their good neighbor. "We have a desire," he told the Hondurans, "to maintain not only the cordial relations of governments with each other but also the relations of good neighbors."[49] He also announced that he disapproved of intervention.

In some places, particularly in Argentina, Hoover received chilly receptions. Some skeptics there feared that his words might not be "more than wind blowing across the Pampas." While true that his trip did not put to rest Latin fears of the United States, it nonetheless created some good will where previously there had been virtually none.

Soon after taking office, Hoover aided several Latin-American governments in settling some of their diplomatic disputes over boundaries, notably the long festering Tacna-Arica dispute between Peru and Chile and the Leticia incident between Peru and Colombia in 1932. In the summer and autumn of 1932, he, and in particular the Department of State, tried to prevent Paraguay and Bolivia from formally going to war over a jungle wilderness known as the Chaco Boreal, but failed.

To support the policy of nonintervention announced in his inaugural address, Hoover repudiated the Roosevelt Corollary to the Monroe Doctrine, which most Latin Americans detested. He did it by adopting as his own and issuing as a public document in 1930 a *Memorandum on the Monroe Doctrine*, prepared in the Department of State under the direction of Undersecretary of State J. Reuben Clark, near the end of the Coolidge administration. Although he did not renounce the "right" of intervention, Clark denounced the use of the Monroe Doctrine as a shield for intervention, as used under the Roosevelt Corollary.

Although some Latins were skeptical as to the true intent of the document, a survey of Latin-American press opinion at the time showed general approval of its principles. Secretary Stimson, a short time later, assured the American republics that his government's nonintervention policy even went beyond the Clark Memorandum, saying that "the Monroe Doctrine was a declaration of the United States versus Europe—not of the United States versus Latin America." [50]

During the great depression, revolutions rocked Latin America with a rapidity unusual even for that part of the world long accustomed to political violence. In dealing with the revolutionary changes, Hoover reversed Wilson's moralistic recognition policy and returned to the traditional one of recognizing a government as soon as it had gained effective control of the country and had expressed its willingness to carry out the nation's international obligations. When, for instance, a revolution in Brazil in 1930, headed by Getulio Vargas, overthrew the government that had been unusually friendly to the United States, Hoover promptly recognized the Vargas regime.

Many of the revolutions stemmed from the depression which struck the Latin-American countries, most of them debtors and producers of raw materials that could not find markets, with a shattering impact. Blaming it for some of their woes, the Latins bitterly resented the Hawley-Smoot Tariff of 1930. It, more than anything else in the Hoover period, injured relations with the southern republics. North Americans, on the other hand, who had invested millions of dollars in Latin America, resented it when the Latins defaulted on their debts.

Unlike his predecessors, Hoover did not use the defaults as an excuse for intervention. His administration, in fact, carried out no new interventions. In 1931, when revolutions broke out in Panama, Cuba, and Honduras, Hoover and Stimson did not exercise the treaty right of intervention in Panama and Cuba, and stayed out of Honduras even though the Hondurans attacked and looted American property. Hoover and Stimson also began the liquidation of existing interventions. Shortly after he took office Hoover said he would remove American troops from Nicaragua and Haiti. "I have no desire," he told a press conference, "for representation of the American Government abroad through our military forces." [51]

Yet in Nicaragua, Sandino attacked Americans and their property and defied the Marines who tried to capture him. Nonetheless, Hoover kept his pledge and in January, 1933, the last detachment of Marines left the republic. According to treaty, the United States did, however, retain supervision over Nicaraguan finances. A month after the Americans left, Sandino made peace, but a year later government forces assassinated him.

In dealing with Haiti, Hoover appointed a special commission to prepare for the withdrawal of troops. In September, 1932, after the commission had made its report, the United States signed a treaty with the Haitians calling for the occupation to end by December 31, 1934, two years earlier than required under a previous agreement. Since the new treaty still gave the United States some control over Haitian finances, Haiti's legislature rejected it. Yet Hoover went ahead with plans for withdrawal of the troops. Thus it was that the Good Neighbor idea took root in the Hoover years.[52]

Roosevelt's Good Neighbor Policy

Hoover's successor, Franklin D. Roosevelt, expanded the Good Neighbor idea, making it his own. Roosevelt's Good Neighbor policy, based on the principles of equality and partnership among the American republics, brought relations between the peoples of the Americas to the highest point of friendship yet achieved. One reason for Roosevelt's success was his personal attractiveness to Latin Americans. They liked his New Deal program of social and economic reform and his emphasis on anti-imperialism in foreign affairs, seeing in him a champion of the oppressed at home, and later, of those abroad.

Roosevelt's first opportunity to deal with an important Latin-American problem, a rebellion in Cuba, gave his Good Neighbor policy an inauspicious start. Conditions in Cuba in 1932 and 1933, under the iron-fisted dictator Gerardo Machado y Morales, were so bad that Machado could not cope with the civil strife that rocked the island. Hoover had followed a policy of nonintervention, but Roosevelt sent an experienced diplomat, Sumner Welles, to Havana as Ambassador to mediate the civil conflict. Before Welles could achieve any positive results, the army deposed Machado in August, 1933.

Since violence continued, Roosevelt sent warships to Cuban waters but landed no troops. When another revolution established a left-wing government in Cuba, under the leadership of Dr. Ramón Grau San Martín, Roosevelt refused to recognize the new regime, saying it lacked popular support. Since Grau San Martín's military supporters saw that they could not long defy the disapproval of the United States, they replaced him with a more conservative president, whom the United States speedily recognized. When Grau San Martín resigned, he said bitterly, "I fell because Washington willed it."

Many Cubans and other Latin Americans agreed with him. They believed that nonrecognition and warships were a form of intervention. Yet Roosevelt did not land troops and, as he himself said, this proved in a practical way that the United States "could apply the doctrine of the Good Neighbor."[53]

While dealing with the troubles in Cuba, the Roosevelt administration went ahead with plans for the Seventh Pan-American Conference, scheduled to meet in Montevideo in December, 1933. At a meeting of the governing board of the Pan-American Union in January, Hoover's representative had agreed to an Argentine proposal calling for a draft of an antiwar treaty prepared by Dr. Carlos Saavedra Lamas, Argentina's Foreign Minister, to be placed on the agenda at Montevideo. Since the Kellogg-Briand Pact already covered the antiwar objectives, the true purpose of the Argentine plan was to bring the subject of intervention out into the open at the conference.

At Montevideo, as expected, the Latins again attacked American policy. Intervention, a Cuban delegate said, was the "curse of America." [54] When the non-intervention proposal, saying that "no state has the right to intervene in the internal or external affairs of another," came to a vote, country after country supported it. To the surprise of the other delegates, Secretary of State Cordell Hull, the head of the United States delegation, also voted for it, but added a vague reservation retaining the "right" of intervention as sanctioned by international law.

Hull also offered to adhere to the Saavedra Lamas antiwar treaty, which the United States later signed. At Montevideo he also made the first public announcement of his plan to reduce tariffs through reciprocal trade agreements. This pleased the Latins, who adopted a resolution embodying the substance of Hull's proposal.

The Secretary of State considered the Montevideo Conference the beginning of a new era in the Western Hemisphere. At Montevideo, Roosevelt's vague Good Neighbor attitude became definite Latin-American policy.

After Montevideo, Roosevelt gave up all right of unilateral intervention. In a treaty of March 29, 1934, abolishing the Platt Amendment, the United States voluntarily relinquished its legal right to intervene in Cuban affairs, but retained its naval base at Guantanamo.

In dealing with Haiti, the Roosevelt administration took up Hoover's plan for withdrawing troops and embodied it in an executive agreement in August, 1933. A year later the last of the Marines left, and for the first time in two decades North American troops were not patrolling Latin-American streets, though United States financial control of Haiti did not terminate until 1941.

One of the striking evidences of Roosevelt's restraint was his treatment of tiny Panama. He voluntarily agreed to revise the Hay-Bunau-Varilla Treaty of 1903 that restricted Panama's sovereignty. In a new treaty, signed on March 3, 1936, the United States gave up its right to intervene in Panama's affairs and released the Panamanians from its legal control.

Concerned over the defense of the Panama Canal, the Senate withheld approval for several years. Finally, in an exchange of notes in February, 1939, Panama agreed to allow the United States to act unilaterally in defending the canal in emergencies. A few months later the Senate gave its consent to the Panama treaty. The delay did not injure the reputation of the Good Neighbor policy since the American concessions were substantial and helped to remove a grievance of thirty years.

In 1940, the United States also signed a treaty with the Dominican Republic relinquishing its legal right to intervene there. When ratified in 1941, that treaty did away with the last of the Latin-American agreements sanctioning the right of the United States to intervene on its own initiative.

Like Hoover, Roosevelt used diplomacy to help resolve a number of Latin-American disputes. With five other American nations, the United States aided in mediating the Chaco War, a mediation that led to a peace treaty between Bolivia and Paraguay in July, 1938.

In the meantime, increasingly belligerent actions by Germany, Italy, and Japan had alarmed Roosevelt more than any minor war between American states. Shrewdly emphasizing dangers to peace from within and without the Western Hemisphere, he sent personal letters to the presidents of the other American republics in January, 1936, suggesting a special Pan-American Conference for the Maintenance of Peace.

The Latin Americans accepted the idea, and Roosevelt, fresh from a sweeping triumph at the polls giving him a second term, traveled seven thousand miles by battleship to Buenos Aires in November, 1936. More than a half million Argentines jammed the sidewalks to welcome him. In his opening speech the President warned that "vast armaments are rising on every side," stressed the need for continental solidarity, and urged the American republics to consult with each other for the protection of the Western Hemisphere.[55]

Argentina resisted the United States plan for a permanent body, consisting of the foreign ministers of the republics, that would deal with emergencies as they arose, but the conference accepted a compromise, the Convention for the Maintenance, Preservation, and Re-establishment of Peace, that called for consultation among all the republics to deal with any threat to peace. This was an effort to broaden the Monroe Doctrine.

Once again the republics denounced intervention, adopting a nonintervention protocol stronger than the agreement at Montevideo three years earlier. The United States this time accepted nonintervention without reservation and thus convinced the Latin Americans it had abandoned intervention as a principle.

Mexico gave nonintervention, and hence the Good Neighbor policy, its most trying test. From 1933 to 1936, when Mexico's government feuded with the Catholics in the country, some American Catholics, notably the Knights of Columbus, demanded a strong policy toward Mexico, but Roosevelt refused to retreat from his nonintervention policy.[56]

In 1938, a renewed Mexican nationalism, exemplified by the slogan of "Mexico for the Mexicans," met opposition from American, British, and Dutch oil companies in Mexico which refused to meet the demands of their newly organized workers for wage increases and other "fringe benefits." Mexico's president, Lázaro Cárdenas, intervened, and in March after the oil companies turned down the terms his government offered, he expropriated most of them. This act precipitated a crisis with the United States that lasted nearly four years. The American oil companies involved in the dispute, claiming an investment of over one hundred million dollars, believed that Mexico would never be able to compensate them. They and the conservative press in the United States demanded intervention.

Dismayed by the seizures, Roosevelt and Hull nonetheless held to the principle of nonintervention. Britain, on the other hand, broke off relations with Mexico. Hull acknowledged Mexico's right to expropriate but insisted on fair and prompt compensation. Cárdenas promised to pay but denounced the claims of the oil companies as exorbitant.

Mere promises, Hull said, were not enough. The dispute dragged on until Manuel Ávila Camacho succeeded Cárdenas in December, 1940. Hull then renewed negotiations and in November, 1941, announced an agreement.

Two experts, one American and the other Mexican, appraised the oil properties and worked out what they considered "just compensation." The American oil companies said the valuations were much too low, but since they had no alternative, they accepted the settlement which ultimately gave them some twenty-four million dollars for their claims. Under the agreement Mexico also settled and paid for agrarian and other American claims, and the United States promised to help stabilize Mexico's peso, purchase newly mined Mexican silver, negotiate a trade agreement, and lend the Mexican government money for road construction.

Through his persistent protests, Hull had made good his principle that expropriation required compensation. The United States, the Mexican tangle made clear, placed such importance on the Good Neighbor policy that it was willing to sacrifice the economic claims of some of its citizens to maintain it, and in effect to furnish funds for Mexico to pay for property it had expropriated.[57]

The Lima Conference and Hemispheric Unity

During the years of the Mexican controversy, Italian Fascists, German Nazis, and Japanese militarists had all taken aggressive actions that bit by bit eroded peace in Europe and Asia. Concerned over Fascist and Nazi infiltration, Roosevelt wanted the nations of the Western Hemisphere to meet what he considered a common danger with a greater unity than they had shown previously.

The Eighth Pan-American Conference, which met in Lima in December, 1938, offered the opportunity to gain greater cooperation. Secretary of State Hull, who headed the American delegation, urged the Latin governments to pledge them-

THE NEUTRALITY ZONE OF THE WESTERN HEMISPHERE, 1939

selves to resist any threat, direct or indirect, to their peace from any non-American country. Some of the Latins, notably Argentines, who were usually suspicious of the United States, did not share Hull's apprehension and would not commit themselves to such a sweeping proposal.

Finally, the republics agreed to a compromise in the Declaration of Lima, based on the consultative pact adopted at Buenos Aires. That declaration said that in the case of any threat to the peace of the Americas from abroad, the foreign ministers of the republics, on the initiative of any one of them, would consult. Even though not the strong commitment the United States had wanted, it was a substantial moral agreement. For the first time the American republics had agreed to work as a unit in meeting certain international problems.

Eight months after the closing of the Lima Conference, war in Europe set the new consultative machinery in motion. Roosevelt, who had decided to request a conference of foreign ministers the moment war broke out, immediately called one to take measures to preserve peace and neutrality in the Americas. The republics responded promptly, and the First Meeting of American Foreign Ministers opened in Panama on September 21, 1939, and completed its work in eight days.

Since all the nations, including Argentina, wanted to maintain neutrality, there were no controversies. The most important action of the conference was the Declaration of Panama, decreeing a safety zone of about three hundred miles around the Western Hemisphere, except for Canada, already a belligerent. The zone was designed to keep war away from the New World as long as the American nations remained neutral. This grandiose scheme, a form of hemispheric isolationism, was Roosevelt's pet idea. Hull looked upon it with skepticism, saying that the safety zone was without precedent in international relations and that the belligerents would not respect it. Hull was right. The belligerents never accepted it.

In December, three British cruisers fought and seriously damaged the German pocket battleship *Graf Spee* within sight of the Uruguayan shoreline. In answer to the joint protest of the American republics against this violation of the Declaration of Panama, Britain, France, and Germany pointed out that it had no validity under international law, thus in effect nullifying the declaration. Yet the American nations refused to abandon their concept of a security zone.[58]

Within six months the war in Europe created new anxieties in the Americas. In May and June, 1940, the Germans overran the Netherlands and France. Stunned by the swiftness of the Nazi victories, many Americans feared that the Germans might gain control of French and Dutch possessions in the Western Hemisphere and use them as military bases. At that time leading military authorities rated the protection of the Western Hemisphere second in importance to the defense of the United States itself. Roosevelt and his advisers now considered the problem of defending the whole hemisphere against a possible German and Italian attack.

A few days before France capitulated, Congress expressed its concern over the fate of the French and Dutch colonies in the Americas. In a joint resolution, approved overwhelmingly on June 17 and 18, it said that the "United States would not recognize any transfer, and would not acquiesce in any attempt to transfer, any geographic region of this hemisphere from one non-American power to another non-American power."[59] If such appeared likely, it added, the United States would consult with the other American republics to determine what steps to take. Latin Americans generally praised the resolution and some of their newspapers even had a few good words for the Monroe Doctrine.

At the same time Secretary Hull sent out invitations for a second meeting of foreign ministers that was held in Havana in July. In line with the congressional resolution, the ministers adopted a Convention on the Provisional Administration of European Colonies and Possessions, saying that if a non-American state, meaning Germany, should attempt to gain control of the European colonies, one or more

American states could take them over and administer them until they could govern themselves or return to their former status.

The ministers also agreed to the Act of Havana, designed to place the convention into effect through a special committee in case of an emergency. In a grave emergency one or more nations, mainly the United States, could act immediately and consult later. Since the Germans never attempted to take over the French and Dutch possessions, the machinery evolved at Havana, ratified by the necessary two-thirds of the republics, never functioned.

The ministers also adopted a declaration saying that any outside attack on an American state "shall be considered as an act of aggression against the states which sign this declaration." [60] This resolution of general security went beyond the Lima Declaration and indicated a greater continental solidarity than actually existed, yet it served as a basis for later wartime cooperation in the Americas. As a whole, the meeting at Havana was one of the more important inter-American conferences, for it transformed the Monroe Doctrine into a defensive multilateral policy accepted by the Latin Americans themselves for the first time. "Never," a Brazilian journal declared, "has the sentiment of continental solidarity been so strong nor the links which bind us together so close as today." [61]

Roosevelt went beyond mere paper declarations in his efforts to bolster the defense of the hemisphere, trying to use the good will generated by his Good Neighbor policy to secure bilateral military agreements with some of the Latin-American republics. In view of the lingering memories of past interventions, this proved difficult. Yet several of the republics had sufficient confidence in Roosevelt to grant the use of sites on their soil for military purposes. In addition, the United States concluded executive agreements, before December, 1941, with eleven Latin-American countries allowing American military missions of various kinds to aid in their defense.

To counteract German and Italian propaganda in the Americas, the delegates at the Buenos Aires Conference of 1936 had sponsored a convention for the promotion of Inter-American Cultural Relations. The cultivating of cultural relations, the United States believed, offered a practical means of promoting continental solidarity. In 1938, it supported the Buenos Aires convention by creating within the Department of State a Division of Cultural Relations to advance cultural projects in Latin America.

Before 1940, the cultural program of the United States concentrated on the exchange of students and professors with the Latin Americans. In that year it established the Office for Coordination of Commercial and Cultural Relations between the American Republics and expanded its cultural program. By the end of 1941, Roosevelt's policy, despite some shortcomings, particularly in the field of economics, had fairly well demonstrated to many Latin Americans that the formerly hated colossus to the north had in fact become their good neighbor.

Canada's Special Status

Although Canada could have become part of the Pan-American system, she never did. The United States had at times taken the view that Canada could not be a member of the Pan-American family because her ties with the British Commonwealth kept her from being a truly American nation. As a result, Canada, although included within the scope of the Good Neighbor policy, held a special status in American foreign policy. She was, as Canadians themselves believed, the linchpin between Britain and the United States, even though in 1927 she sent her own Minister to Washington and in 1931, under the Statute of Westminster, became an independent dominion within the British Commonwealth in complete control of her own foreign relations. In dealing with her, because of her Commonwealth ties, the United States felt that she represented more than herself.

American relations with Canada, after the death of the reciprocity treaty of 1911, were relatively the smoothest and closest of those with any important power in the Western Hemisphere. There were, nonetheless, minor misunderstandings and grievances, due partly to isolationism and economic nationalism within both countries.

After the First World War the United States regained its position as the chief market for Canadian exports, and, as British investments in Canada began to decline, Canada looked increasingly to the United States for aid in her industrial expansion. In 1918, one estimate showed that American investors owned approximately thirty per cent of all Canadian industry.

The Fordney-McCumber Tariff of 1922 cut into the export of Canadian products to the United States, but a number of important staples continued to sell on the American market in increasing quantities. A much more serious blow was the Hawley-Smoot Tariff of 1930 that aggravated the impact of the depression on Canada. Resentment was so intense, that the Canadian government swiftly retaliated, touching off a tariff war that lasted until 1935 when the two countries signed a reciprocal trade agreement.

Political differences with Canada were few. One that led to considerable note writing arose in March, 1929, when an American Coast Guard cutter sank a rum-running sloop, *I'm Alone*, flying the Canadian flag, some 215 miles at sea southeast of New Orleans. One crew member of the *I'm Alone* lost his life. Six years later an arbitration settled the dispute with an apology and payment of indemnities by the United States.[62]

Americans and Canadians had long wanted to improve the navigation channels of the St. Lawrence waterway between Montreal and the Great Lakes by deepening them, and to exploit and share the electric power resources of the St. Lawrence River. In July, 1932, the two countries signed the St. Lawrence Seaway Treaty, designed to make the project a reality through a plan of shared costs, but strong sectional opposition in the United States led to the treaty's defeat in the Senate in March, 1934.[63]

After Italy's conquest of Ethiopia in 1936 had convinced Canada of the weakness of the League of Nations as an instrument for collective security, many Canadians wanted to build up their own defenses and draw closer to the United States. Two years later, while speaking at Queen's University at Kingston, Ontario, President Roosevelt made the first formal commitment to aid in the defense of Canada, in effect an extension of the Monroe Doctrine. "The Dominion of Canada," he said, "is part of the sisterhood of the British Empire. I give to you assurance that the people of the United States will not stand idly by if domination of Canadian soil is threatened by any other Empire."[64]

After the fall of France, Canada and the United States drew closer and even considered a defensive alliance. Prime Minister William Lyon Mackenzie King and Roosevelt met on August 17, 1940, at Ogdensburg, New York. The next day they announced the formation of a Permanent Joint Board on Defense, to be composed of an equal number of Americans and Canadians, for the defense of the northern half of the Western Hemisphere.[65] The Ogdensburg executive agreement was the first defense commitment Canada had ever made with a country outside the British Commonwealth.

Since Canada's war commitments and aid to Britain placed a great financial strain on her, the Ogdensburg agreement needed an economic counterpart to help keep Canada stable. After another meeting, this time at Hyde Park, Mackenzie King and Roosevelt issued the Hyde Park Declaration on April 21, 1941, in which each country agreed to provide the other with defense materials.[66] By the end of the year Canada was more than ever the linchpin between Britain and the United States. At the same time she enjoyed the protection of the enlarged Monroe Doctrine and the Good Neighbor policy without being a part of the Pan-American machinery.

NOTES

1. Kenneth D. McKellar, quoted in Rodman W. Paul, *The Abrogation of the Gentlemen's Agreement* (Cambridge, Mass., 1936), p. 53.

2. *Foreign Relations, 1924*, II, 373.

3. April 12, 1924, quoted in Paul, *Gentlemen's Agreement*, p. 69.

4. Quoted in Eleanor Tupper and George E. McReynolds, *Japan in American Public Opinion* (New York, 1937), p. 189.

5. The quoted material is in Raymond L. Buell, "Japanese Immigration," *World Peace Foundation Pamphlets*, VII (Boston, 1924), 314. For the long-term shock felt by Japanese, see Robert S. Schwantes, *Japanese and Americans: A Century of Cultural Relations* (New York, 1955), pp. 34–35.

6. Quoted in Dorothy Borg, *American Policy and the Chinese Revolution, 1925–1928* (New York, 1947), p. 18.

7. *Ibid.*, p. 65.

8. Carroll L. Budy of Maine. *Ibid.*, p. 254.

9. Kellogg to Mayer, Jan. 25, 1927, *Foreign Relations, 1927*, II, 352.

10. March 6, 1927, quoted in Eorg, *Chinese Revolution*, pp. 264–265.

11. Quoted in John K. Davis to Kellogg, in *Foreign Relations, 1927*, II, 153.

12. Kellogg to MacMurray, April 25, 1927, *ibid.*, II, 211.

13. William R. Castle Diary, Nov. 25, 1929, quoted in Robert H. Ferrell, *American Diplomacy in the Great Depression: Hoover-Stimson Foreign Policy, 1929–1933* (New Haven, 1957), p. 57.

14. *Foreign Relations, 1929*, II, 404–406.

15. William R. Castle quoted in Ferrell, *Depression Diplomacy*, p. 65.

16. For details, see Robert H. Ferrell, "The Mukden Incident: September 18–19, 1931," *Journal of Modern History*, XXVII (March 1955), 66–72, and Robert J. C. Butow, *Tojo and the Coming of the War* (Princeton, 1961), pp. 34–36.

17. Quoted in Elting E. Morison, *Turmoil and Tradition: A Study of the Life and Times of Henry L. Stimson* (Boston, 1960), p. 376.

18. Oct. 18, 1931, quoted in Paul L. Clyde, "The Diplomacy of 'Playing No Favorites': Secretary Stimson and Manchuria, 1931," *Mississippi Valley Historical Review*, XXV (Sept. 1948), 195.

19. Quoted in Richard N. Current, *Secretary Stimson: A Study in Statecraft* (New Brunswick, N.J., 1954), p. 76.

20. *The Memoirs of Herbert Hoover: The Cabinet and the Presidency, 1920–1933* (New York, 1952), p. 366.

21. The text is in *Foreign Relations, Japan, 1931–1941*, I, 76.

22. Cited in Morison, *Turmoil and Tradition*, p. 387.

23. Louisville *Courier-Journal*, Jan. 9, 1932, quoted in Tupper and McReynolds, *Japan in American Public Opinion*, p. 316.

24. Feb. 2, 1932, *ibid.*, p. 322. Payson J. Treat, "Shanghai: January 28, 1932," *Pacific Historical Review*, IX (Sept. 1946), 337–343, suggests lack of planning in the Shanghai attack.

25. Feb. 23, 1932; the text is in *Foreign Relations, Japan, 1931–1941*, I, 83–87.

26. The effect on the Japanese, however, was clear. It was negative. See Morison, *Turmoil and Tradition*, p. 397.

27. For an analysis of the conflicting views of Stimson and Hoover on sanctions, see *ibid.*, p. 383n. Richard N. Current in "The Stimson Doctrine and the Hoover Doctrine," *The American Historical Review*, LIX (April 1954), 513–542, suggests that there were two separate doctrines, one Hoover's and the other Stimson's, which reflected the difference over sanctions. Relying heavily on evidence in the *Foreign Relations* volumes, Ernest R. Perkins, in "The Non-Application of Sanctions against Japan, 1931–1932," in Dwight E. Lee and George E. McReynolds, eds., *Essays in History and International Relations in Honor of George Hubbard Blakeslee* (Worcester, Mass., 1949), pp. 215–232, points out that the United States was unwilling to support sanctions.

28. New York *Daily News*, Oct. 4, 1932, quoted in Tupper and McReynolds, *Japan in American Public Opinion*, p. 352.

29. M. Sommers, *ibid.*, p. 356.

30. Quoted in Raymond Moley, *After Seven Years* (New York, 1939), p. 95.

31. Cordell Hull, *The Memoirs of Cordell Hull* (2 vols., New York, 1948), I, 270. At this time, however, Roosevelt apparently had not yet become a confirmed believer in collective security. See Robert A. Divine, "Franklin D. Roosevelt and Collective Security, 1933," *Mississippi Valley Historical Review*, XLVIII (June 1961), 42–59.

32. Nov. 20, 1933, cited in Robert P. Browder, *The Origins of Soviet-American Diplomacy* (Princeton, 1953), pp. 154–155. This is the best monograph on its subject. Pauline Tompkins in *American-Russian Relations in the Far East* (New York, 1949), p. 263, says that Far Eastern policy had only an oblique influence on recognition. She holds that the depression was the important factor. William A. Williams, in *American-Russian Relations, 1781–1947* (New York, 1952), pp. 235–237, stresses economic pressures.

33. For a statement and refutation of the thesis that recognition was the result of a conspiracy by those who were soft on Communism, see Paul Boller, Jr., "The 'Great Conspiracy' of 1933: A Study in Short Memories," *Southwest Review*, XXXIX (Spring 1954), 97–112.

34. The statement of April 17, 1934, by Eiji Amau, is in *Foreign Relations, Japan, 1931–1941*, I, 224–225. See also Joseph C. Grew, *Ten Years in Japan* (New York, 1944), pp. 129–130.

35. For details, see Roy W. Curry, "Woodrow Wilson and the Philippine Policy," *Mississippi Valley Historical Review*, XLI (Dec. 1954), 435–452.

36. Quoted in Garel A. Grunder and William E. Livezey, *The Philippines and the United States* (Norman, Okla., 1951), p. 222.

37. Quoted in J. Fred Rippy, "Pan Hispanic Propaganda in Hispanic America," *Political Science Quarterly*, XXXVII (Sept. 1922), 366.

38. *Ibid.*, p. 364.

39. Sept., 1922, quoted in Samuel F. Bemis, *The Latin American Policy of the United States* (New York, 1943), p. 203.

40. *The New York Times*, June 19, 1924, quoted in Graham H. Stuart, *Latin America and the United States*, 5th ed. (New York, 1954), p. 276.

41. Quoted in Current, *Stimson*, p. 30.

42. *The New York Times*, Jan. 13, 1927, p. 2: 2.

43. Quoted in Claude M. Fuess, *Calvin Coolidge: The Man from Vermont* (Boston, 1940), p. 415.

44. The Bucareli Conferences are summarized in John W. F. Dulles, *Yesterday in Mexico: A Chronicle of the Revolution, 1919–1936* (Austin, Texas, 1961), pp. 158–172 and Aarón Sáenz, *La política internacional de la Revolución: Estudios y Documentos* (Mexico, D.F., 1961), pp. 50–72.

45. Quoted in Fuess, *Coolidge*, p. 413.

46. Stanley R. Ross, in "Dwight Morrow and the Mexican Revolution," *Hispanic American Historical Review*, XXXVIII (Nov. 1958), 514–515, points out that the settlement was a compromise.

47. For details, see L. Ethan Ellis, "Dwight Morrow and the Church-State Controversy in Mexico," *Hispanic American Historical Review*, XXXVIII (Nov. 1958), 482–505.

48. Quoted in Bemis, *Latin American Policy*, p. 252.

49. Quoted in Alexander DeConde, *Herbert Hoover's Latin-American Policy* (Stanford, Calif., 1951), p. 18.

50. Feb. 6, 1931, *ibid.*, p. 51.

51. *Ibid.*, p. 86.

52. For a detailed analysis of the origins of the Good Neighbor idea and policy, see Bryce Wood, *The Making of the Good Neighbor Policy* (New York, 1961), pp. 118–135.

53. Dec. 8, 1942, quoted in E. David Cronon, "Interpreting the New Good Neighbor Policy: Cuban Crisis of 1933," *Hispanic American Historical Review*, XXXIX (Nov. 1959), p. 567. Welles, in effect, deposed Machado. Welles also asked for troops to be landed in Cuba. See Wood, *Good Neighbor*, pp. 63–72, 95.

54. Portell Vilá, quoted in Edward O. Guerrant, *Roosevelt's Good Neighbor Policy* (Albuquerque, N.M., 1950), p. 6.

55. *Ibid.*, p. 74.

56. For details, see E. David Cronon, "American Catholics and Mexican Anticlericalism, 1933–1936," *Mississippi Valley Historical Review*, XLV (Sept. 1958), 201–230.

57. A detailed account is in Wood, *Good Neighbor*, pp. 203–259.

58. For details, see Donald M. Dozer, *Are We Good Neighbors? Three Decades of Inter-American Relations, 1930–1960* (Gainesville Fla., 1959), pp. 58–59.

59. This Pittman-Bloom resolution is quoted from John A. Logan, Jr., *No Transfer: An American Security Principle* (New Haven, 1961), p. 327.

60. Quoted in J. Lloyd Mecham, *The United States and Inter-American Security, 1889–1960* (Austin, Tex., 1961), p. 188.

61. *Correio de Manhã* of Rio de Janeiro, July 1940, quoted in Dozer, *Are We Good Neighbors?*, p. 69. The same point is stressed in W. Stull Holt, "The United States and the Defense of the Western Hemisphere, 1815–1940," *Pacific Historical Review*, X (March 1941), 29–38.

62. For details, see James M. Callahan, *American Foreign Policy in Canadian Relations* (New York, 1937), pp. 547–548. See also Richard N. Kottman, "Volstead Violated: Prohibition as a Factor in Canadian-American Relations," *Canadian Historical Review*, XLIII (June, 1962), 106–126.

63. This agreement, signed on July 18, 1932, is also known as the Hoover-Bennett Treaty. The best sources on this subject are Carleton Mabee, *The Seaway Story* (New York, 1961), pp. 96–115 and William R. Willoughby, *The St. Laurence Waterway: A Study in Politics and Diplomacy* (Madison, Wis., 1961), pp. 133–159.

64. Aug. 18, 1938, in Samuel I. Rosenman, comp., *The Public Papers and Addresses of Franklin D. Roosevelt* (13 vols., New York, 1938–50), VII, 493.

65. *Ibid.*, IX, 331.

66. *Ibid.*, X, 582n–583n.

Chapter Twenty-Two

ECONOMIC NATIONALISM AND ISOLATIONISM

Along with the utopian idealism of the peace movement, the two decades following the First World War witnessed the flowering of a vigorous nationalism and an intensified isolationism. Social and economic changes within and outside the United States, ideas of American institutional and racial superiority, as well as the nation's enhanced international status, contributed to the new growth. The war itself had accentuated a nationalism and an antiforeignism that went back to the end of the nineteenth century. During the war, impatiently eager for intervention on the side of England, Theodore Roosevelt had denounced those who opposed his views as being un-American and had criticized Americans of Irish and German blood as "hyphenates." [1] Soon the word "hyphenate" had cast odium on virtually all except those of British stock.

In seeking unified support for his war policies, Woodrow Wilson had also denounced some of his critics as "hyphenates." "We Americans," said his Ambassador to England, using more extreme language than Wilson himself, "have got to ... hang our Irish agitators and shoot our hyphenates and bring up our children with reverence for English history and in the awe of English literature." [2]

George Creel's wartime Committee on Public Information, which had tried to create a uniform standard of loyalty, had stressed a doctrinaire idea of Americanism. Using the earlier attacks on "hyphenated" Americans, it had questioned their loyalty and even their place in American society. To counteract an inherited Anglophobia, many "one hundred per cent" Americans had extolled English institutions and the bond of blood and culture with the mother country.

At the same time, ignoring Wilson's early distinction between the German government and the German people, those patrioteers had attacked the whole of German culture. The virus of hatred had soon spread to German-Americans and then to virtually every other non-British group in the United States. Americans of foreign background, as well as aliens, found themselves suspected of being untrustworthy and disloyal.

After the war the enmity against foreigners persisted. Prosperity receded. Foreign competition and the contraction of domestic markets lowered levels of production, bringing unemployment. A depression threatened the economy.

Strikes, particularly a great steel strike in 1919, raised the fear that radicals aimed to overthrow American institutions and ideals. Identifying the radical with the alien, many Americans feared that the nation itself was endangered, and this fear helped to generate the great Red scare of the next few years.[3] The Red scare, a movement to purge America of radicals, was rooted in the popular belief that the United States could be secure only with full conformity and the loyalty of one hundred per cent Americanism. It focused distrust on the immigrant, somehow making the foreigner in the land responsible for the alleged threat to the American way of life.

Racist assumptions again influenced American thinking. Various writers, some of them with scholarly reputations, argued that American culture had been deteriorating since the infusion of masses of new immigrants, "inferior" peoples from southern and eastern Europe. To purify the nation, they said, the government must shut the gates against the now unwanted foreigner and reverse America's traditionally liberal immigration policy.

The bitter sentiments of antiforeignism and other causes finally led to the passage of the Emergency Quota Act of 1921 and the superseding Immigration Act of 1924 that placed immigrants from most nations on highly restrictive quotas. Those laws went beyond restriction by making discrimination a basic policy of the nation. The Act of 1924, which became fully operative in 1929, ranked peoples according to desirability by placing northern and western Europeans at the top and southern and eastern Europeans at the bottom. It stigmatized Asians as completely undesirable by barring them.

Immigration from Europe, for diverse reasons, immediately dwindled to a trickle. Foreign peoples resented the assumptions of superiority in the American immigration laws. Antiforeignism and nationalism, as well as isolationism, thus contributed to the distrust of the United States that was evident in Europe in the 1920's.[4]

Economic Giant of the World

Europeans also resented American economic foreign policy and the enormous strength of the United States in the postwar decades. Of all the major belligerents in the First World War, only the United States emerged unscathed and stronger than at the start of the war. In urging support of the League covenant, Wilson had said: "The financial leadership will be ours. The industrial primacy will be ours. The commercial advantage will be ours. The other countries of the world are looking to us for leadership and direction." [5] His prediction proved accurate.

In four years the war had transformed America's industrial and financial relations abroad, making the United States the new international economic leader. New York instead of London ruled as the financial center of the world. Most other nations, in some form, became economically dependent on the United States.

The war had reduced Europe's industrial production to a low level, but American production had risen and continued to rise after the war. According to the estimates of economists, by 1929 American industrial production amounted to forty-six per cent of the world's total, and American national income equaled the combined incomes of twenty-three of the world's important countries, including Britain and France.

The war had accelerated American industrialization, resulting in an expansion in industrial output of fifteen per cent and an establishment of industries producing goods formerly imported from Europe. Before the war Europe had supplied about fifty per cent of America's imports; after the war she provided only about thirty per cent. The European countries never regained their prewar position as sources of finished goods for the United States.

Since the war had also hastened industrialization in other countries, as in Japan, Canada, and parts of Latin America, the older industrial nations of Europe could not easily compensate for the losses in the American market. This trend away from dependence on European manufactures continued all through the 1920's and 1930's.

In those years the United States also became the world's most important market for raw materials and semi-finished goods. This shift in the nature of American imports might not have caused immediate difficulty in Europe if the United States had remained in debt to European nations, but from a debtor owing 3.7 billion dollars in 1914, the United States in 1919 had become a creditor nation who was owed twelve and a half billion dollars. Some ten billion dollars of this money represented debts connected with the war that European nations had incurred. Since the Allied nations had liquidated their investments in the United

States to help finance the war, they found themselves suddenly faced with fewer opportunities to earn dollars and with new obligations to the United States to be paid in dollars.

The United States, moreover, had captured another source of Europe's income. It replaced Europe as a supplier of capital, particularly to "underdeveloped" countries, or those countries producing essentially raw materials.

As was the case with its enhanced political power, the United States did not use its strategic position in the world's economy with a sense of responsibility. In 1918, for example, Congress passed the Webb-Pomerene Act, which provided that the Sherman Antitrust Act would not apply to combinations of industrialists engaged solely in the export trade if those combinations did not restrain trade within the United States or injure domestic competitors. The Webb-Pomerene Act, endorsed by President Wilson and by business leaders, emphasized the drive of manufacturers for expanded exports and buttressed the economic nationalism that characterized American foreign relations in the 1920's and 1930's.

Internally, the United States followed an antimonopoly and antitrust policy. Yet its leaders saw nothing inconsistent in giving government support to combinations of manufacturers to engage in monopolistic marketing practices abroad. A number of trade associations became members of international combinations engaged in dividing up markets and fixing prices. In 1939, there were 179 international cartels, or organizations designed to control prices and production; 109 of them included American firms. Not until that year did the Department of Justice begin action against American firms participating in international cartels controlling such vital products as optical instruments, petroleum, explosives, and synthetic rubber. Throughout the 1920's and 1930's the American people, imbued with economic nationalism, also insisted on a high tariff and on payment of war debts by European nations.

The War Debts

During the First World War, when the United States had suddenly found itself transformed from a debtor to a creditor nation, it had loaned its allies 7.7 billion dollars. The American government had charged five per cent interest, a rate related to the cost of borrowing from its own people through the sale of "liberty bonds." Most of the money, since the Allies spent nine-tenths of their loans on American supplies and war materials, never left the United States.

After the war, until May, 1922, the American government had continued to loan money to its former Allies and to other European governments as well. Those loans were for relief and reconstruction in areas struck hard by the war. The United States also contributed billions of dollars in direct relief to the countries devastated by the war and its aftermath. Americans referred to all those loans, those made during the war and those made afterward for peaceful purposes, as the foreign war debts. All the loans amounted to 10.3 billion dollars, exclusive of interest.

In actual war debts at the end of 1918, Britain owed the American government 4.1 billion dollars, France 2.9 billion, Italy 1.6 billion, and the lesser European countries owed smaller amounts. The American people and their Congress assumed that the debtor countries would pay their obligations in full, though some congressmen had voted the wartime loans without expecting repayment. "I am perfectly willing to give to any of the allied nations the money which they need to carry on our war," one senator told his colleagues, "for it is now our war." [6]

Some of the European statesmen had believed that the United States would consider the debts as part of its general contribution to the defeat of Germany and hence would cancel them. Britain, France, and Italy were all creditors as well as debtors. Britain, for instance, had loaned her allies ten billion dollars. She offered to cancel her claims against her debtors if the United States would cancel its claims against her, but President Wilson and his advisers at the Paris Peace Conference had refused to discuss the debts. Later Wilson told Prime Minister Lloyd George that it was "highly improbable that either the Congress or popular opinion in this country will ever permit a cancellation of any part of the debt of the British government to the United States," or of the debts of any of the Allied governments, as a practical settlement of all claims. [7]

Several years later Secretary of the Treasury Andrew W. Mellon wrote that "these were loans and not contributions and though not in form in actual effect loans from individual American citizens rather than contributions from the Treasury of the United States." This was the view that prevailed in the United States throughout the 1920's and 1930's. "What we allowed our associates to do, in effect," Mellon explained, "was to borrow money in our investment market, but since their credit was not as good as ours, to borrow on the credit of the United States rather than on their own."

To facilitate collection of the war debts, President Harding asked Congress in June, 1921, to authorize negotiations with the debtor governments over terms of payment. In the following February, Congress created the World War Foreign Debt Commission with the Secretary of the Treasury as chairman. Under the terms of the act, the commission could not accept an interest rate lower than 4.25 per cent and a maturity date beyond 1947, or of twenty-five years. It could not cancel any of the principal or accept any transfer of Allied obligations to former enemy countries to be paid as reparations. The Act of 1922, therefore, recognized no connection between debts and reparations, ignored the capacity of the debtors to pay, and did not take into account the difficulty of what economists call the transfer problem, the means of transferring money across international boundaries.

To most Americans, repayment of the debts was a matter of integrity and of national honor. "Well," President Coolidge said in speaking for his countrymen, "they hired the money, didn't they?" The Europeans, regarding the war as a common cause in which they had borne the brunt of the fighting, insisted that the United States had benefited from the victory as much as had any belligerent. Moreover, since the United States had not claimed reparations from Germany, they thought that they could repay the American loans from the reparations they expected to receive from Germany.

When the Debt Commission attempted to negotiate settlements with the debtors, it found that none were willing to accept the terms imposed by Congress. The commission, therefore, went ahead and negotiated thirteen funding agreements on the best terms obtainable. It began its negotiations with Britain in January, 1923, and continued with the other debtors until 1926. During that time the United States gradually came to recognize the principle of capacity to pay.

Although the terms of the British debt settlement, as did the others, called for full repayment of the principal, the commission accepted a low interest rate averaging 3.3 per cent and extended the maturity date to sixty-two years. This amounted to a cancellation of 19.3 per cent of the British debt. In the other settlements the United States retained the payment period of sixty-two years and was more generous in reducing the interest rate, cancelling from 50 to 80 per cent of the debts, as in the case of Italy.

As the debt settlements did not adhere to the terms of the Act of 1922, the commission sought congressional approval for each case. In urging approval of the Italian agreement in January, 1926, Secretary of the Treasury Mellon told a congressional committee that "the settlements are made in the real interests of those American producers who must have a foreign market able to pay. The American producer needs these debt settlements. The entire foreign debt is not worth as much to the American people in dollars and cents as a prosperous Europe as a customer."[8] The settlements, considered fair and even generous by Americans, involved a large part of the income in dollars the rest of the world received from the goods and services it sold to the United States.

Meanwhile, the question of reparations became more entangled in power politics and added complications to the repayment of the war debts. In April, 1921, a special Allied Reparations Commission had set the amount Germany was to pay in reparations at about thirty-three billion dollars. This was a figure lower than most Frenchmen considered adequate but higher than some other financial experts, particularly the British, regarded as fair. Substantial annual payments were to begin at once. Later payments were to be adjusted according to capacity to pay and to an evaluation of payments in kind that the Germans had already made.

Within fifteen months, whether wilfully or through inability to pay, a resentful Germany defaulted. The Reparations Commission, as allowed under the Treaty of Versailles, therefore, voted for strong measures against Germany. In January, 1923, French and Belgian troops began marching into the industrial Ruhr Valley and occupied it until September, 1924. The British deducted twenty-six per cent from their payments for German imports and applied that money to their reparations account. The Germans attempted to defeat the occupation with a policy of inflation that reduced the value of their currency, the mark, by more than 99.9 per cent. Reparations payments stopped completely.

Two weeks before the occupation of the Ruhr began, Secretary of State Hughes had suggested that an independent commission of financial experts study Germany's capacity to pay and devise a plan to facilitate reparations deliveries. In autumn, 1923, Germany abandoned passive resistance, and all governments concerned accepted Hughes' suggestion. In November, the Reparations Commission appointed two committees to study the German problem. The United States did not participate in the investigations, but Charles G. Dawes, a banker from Chicago who acted solely as a private citizen, headed the committee that submitted the plan which the Reparations Commission adopted.

Accepted by all concerned as a temporary expedient, the Dawes Plan, as it came to be known, went into effect in September, 1924. Under it, Germany received an international loan of two hundred million dollars, most of it from American bankers, to replenish her working capital. She agreed to make reparations payments on a rising scale, ostensibly to be parallel with the growth of her economic life.

For five years, from 1924 to 1928, the Dawes Plan worked well. Germany's creditors, therefore, decided to attempt a final settlement. In September, 1928, a new committee of financial experts headed by Owen D. Young, a financier from New York also acting as a private citizen, proposed a plan that Germany and her creditors finally accepted in modified form in January, 1930. The Young Plan, calling for fifty-nine annual payments, reduced Germany's reparations debt by about nine billion dollars.

That plan also recognized a connection between reparations and the war debts owed to the United States. Through a "concurrent memorandum," the Europeans agreed that if the United States scaled down the war debts they would reduce the reparations. Instead of being linked to Germany's capacity to pay, the obligations under the Young Plan were fixed so as to cover the payment of Allied debts to the United States.

Germany had been able, in part, to meet her obligations under the Dawes Plan because inflation had wiped out her domestic debts, and because she did not need to divert huge sums to armaments that were forbidden her under the Treaty of Versailles. During the prosperous 1920's when Germany met her reparations obligations, the Allies paid their debts to the United States. The debtors might have continued to pay with funds obtained from Germany under the Young Plan if the great depression had not intervened.

Private American loans complicated the payment of reparations and war debts. In the 1920's Americans had invested in the bonds of German state governments, in German industries ranging from steel mills to chain stores, and had loaned money to other European nations. The heavy flow of American capital into Germany had helped make possible the payment of her reparations. The result was a chain of private and public international payments. "Reparations and Interallied Debts," John Maynard Keynes, the British economist, explained in 1926, "are being mainly settled in paper not in goods. The United States lends money to Germany, Germany transfers its equivalent to the Allies, the Allies pay it back to the United States Government."

From 1919 to 1930 total private American capital, in loans and investments abroad, amounted to 11.4 billion dollars, or a flow of long-range loans of about a billion dollars a year. By 1929, the rest of the world owed the American government and private investors some twenty billion dollars.

Many of the private loans to Germany and other countries did not meet the tests of sound international lending by providing adequate means of repayment. Most of them were for reconstruction, restocking, and for stabilizing currencies. They did not go into projects that could be expected to earn foreign funds necessary to repay the lenders. With the onset of the depression, moreover, private American international loans to Germany were suspended and the chain of payments broken. A large number of defaults, therefore, should have been expected.

THE RELATIONSHIP OF PRIVATE LOANS AND WAR DEBTS AFTER THE FIRST WORLD WAR

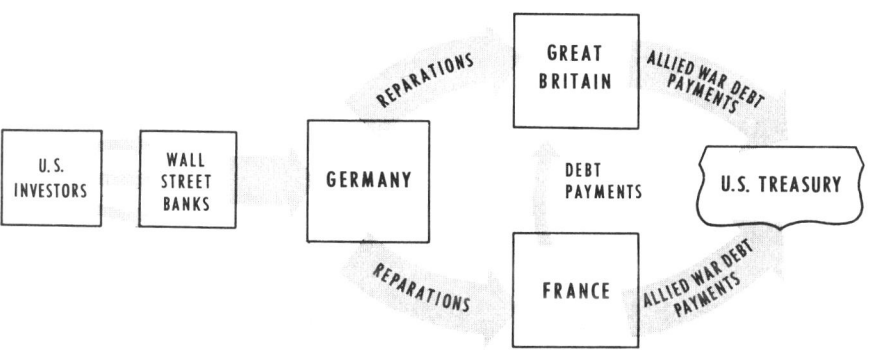

Tariff Policy

American tariff policy also made repayment of foreign loans, public and private, difficult. Foreigners said they could not pay their debts unless the United States allowed them to earn dollars by selling their goods and services in the American market, but a high protective tariff kept foreigners from obtaining the dollars they needed.

Since its birth the Republican party had been committed to the principle of a protective tariff and had supported that principle whenever it held power. In 1913, the Democrats had reversed the trend toward increasingly higher tariffs by passing the Underwood-Simmons Act, the lowest tariff since the Civil War.

After the First World War, Harding's victory and an economic slump seemed to give urgency to Republican demands for the restoration of higher tariff walls. Congress passed an emergency tariff act that Wilson vetoed the day before he left office. Congress re-enacted it and Harding signed it in May, 1921, thus placing higher duties on certain farm products and on industrial goods. A year later, in September, 1922, despite the protests of European financial leaders who warned that Europe could not pay her debts if the bill became law, Harding approved the Fordney-McCumber Tariff Act that established the highest average duties up to that time.

During the boom years of the 1920's, Americans thus insisted that the Europeans pay their debts, sought high returns from investments abroad, tried to expand their exports, and raised tariff barriers against imports. This was a paradoxical economic foreign policy. It lasted until the creditors caught up with the borrowers. When the stock market crashed in October, 1929, and world-wide depression followed, that policy collapsed.

When the flow of dollars for foreign investment stopped, foreigners were unable to buy American goods and to pay their American debts. A lower tariff might have helped in easing the plight of the debtors by allowing them to sell some of their products in the United States, but Herbert Hoover, before he became President, had warned against tampering with the tariff. "A general reduction of the tariff," he said, "would fill our streets with idle workers." When Congress passed the Hawley-Smoot Act in June, 1930, raising tariff rates to their highest point in history, Hoover signed it.

Over a thousand economists had pleaded with the President not to sign the bill, pointing out that higher rates would hamper foreign exports, block collection of the war debts, invite foreign retaliation, and embitter foreign relations. The predictions proved true. Other countries viewed the Hawley-Smoot Tariff as the unfriendly act of a powerful creditor country and as a symbol of American isolationism and economic nationalism. Since many countries raised their own tariffs against the United States and placed quotas on imports, international trade dwindled.

The Hoover Moratorium

As the great depression spread to Europe, it struck Austria with particular severity. In March, 1931, the Germans attempted to form a customs union with Austria. The French opposed the move, fearing it would lead to a permanent political union, or *Anschluss*, prohibited by Austria's peace treaty, and withdrew their funds from Austrian banks. In June, the *Kreditanstalt*, Austria's largest private bank and one of the most important in Europe, almost collapsed. The financial crisis also affected Germany, where bankruptcy seemed imminent.

Alarmed by the crisis, President Hoover thought that a temporary suspension of reparations and debt payments might help ease the strain on Germany by giving her time to strengthen her credit and thus avert world-wide economic chaos. On June 20, therefore, he announced that the United States would waive all inter-governmental payments for one year beginning on July 1 if other governments would do the same. "This is," Hoover told his press secretary, "perhaps the most daring statement I ever thought of issuing."⁹

Other countries, except France who hesitated for over two weeks before agreeing, promptly accepted the proposed moratorium. In December, Congress approved the moratorium but refused the President's request to revive the World War Foreign Debt Commission and give it authority to re-examine the problem of the war debts. Congress said it would not allow any of the debts to be "in any manner canceled or reduced."

Although the Hoover Moratorium brought temporary relief, it was no substitute for international discussion of the entire problem of intergovernmental debts. Germany and her creditors, therefore, met in Lausanne, Switzerland, in June and July, 1932, to discuss the status of reparations after the expiration of the Hoover Moratorium. Although invited, the United States refused to participate.

At Lausanne, Germany's creditors agreed to forgive her about ninety per cent of her reparations bill due under the Young Plan if, according to a "gentlemen's agreement" between them, they could obtain corresponding relief from their creditors. This meant that the debtors had shifted the burden of cancelling the reparations to the United States.

This shift appeared logical to the Europeans. When France's Premier, Pierre Laval, had visited Hoover in October, 1931, the two leaders had issued a vague statement saying that during the depression further adjustments of inter-governmental debts might be necessary. Europeans had assumed that the United

States had at last become ready to recognize the connection between reparations and war debts, but they were wrong. Americans regarded the Lausanne agreement as an anti-American conspiracy, and Hoover announced publicly that the United States would not cancel the war debts.

After his defeat in November, 1932, Hoover met twice with President-elect Franklin D. Roosevelt in vain efforts to try to reach some agreement on meeting the immediate crisis of war debt payments. Hoover wanted Roosevelt's support in urging Congress to reconstitute the old War Debts Commission with the purpose of renegotiating the debt settlements. Roosevelt refused to bind his administration to any policy on the debts before taking power.[10]

Some European debtors, notably Britain and Italy, paid the first installment after the end of the Hoover Moratorium. France, Poland, and others defaulted. On the next installment, due in June, 1933, Britain and Italy among the great powers made token payments acknowledging at least the validity of the debt. France and others continued to default. The token payments continued until December but ceased after the Attorney General ruled that they did not save debtor governments from being held in default. After that only Finland among the European debtors, who had a small postwar loan and a favorable balance in dollars, continued to meet her payments. Thus, payments on reparations and debts ceased. No formal settlement of the debts has ever been made.

The World Economic Conference

Before going out of office, Hoover had agreed to send a delegation to a monetary and economic conference, usually known as the World Economic Conference, in London to formulate means of overcoming the world-wide depression. The delegates at Lausanne had discussed plans for the conference, and all through the year of 1932 the powers had made preparations for it. When Roosevelt took office, he postponed it for several months but finally all agreed to open the conference in June, 1933. Before the opening, statesmen and delegations of statesmen had visited Washington and had discussed conference plans with Roosevelt. All apparently assumed that the stabilizing of currencies should receive foremost consideration at the conference.

Meanwhile, Roosevelt had announced in his inaugural address that "our international trade relations, though vastly important, are, in point of time and necessity secondary to the establishment of a sound national economy. I favor as a practical policy the putting of first things first."[11] In May, he had taken the United States off the gold standard, that is, removed the dollar from its fixed relationship to gold, so that he could manipulate the currency to force prices up.

At the conference, the "gold bloc" nations, led by France, Italy, Switzerland, and Belgium, insisted that economic recovery and the stabilization of currencies could come only if the countries who had abandoned the gold standard, among them Britain, the United States, and Japan, would return to it. The head of the American delegation, Secretary of State Cordell Hull, agreed to a temporary stabilization plan, but in a statement usually referred to as the "bombshell" message that destroyed the conference, Roosevelt rejected the idea of stabilized currencies and placed domestic economic recovery ahead of international financial cooperation.

The conference limped through a few more weeks, with the American delegation refusing to discuss war debts. In fact, the Democratic platform in 1932 had declared its opposition to cancelling the debts. Hull, who had hoped to reduce tariff barriers through a system of reciprocal trade agreements, accomplished nothing, primarily because he received no support from the President or Congress. The conference, therefore, adjourned on July 27 with no important accomplishment.

The Significance of Economic Policy

Within a year, on April 13, 1934, Congress passed the Johnson Debt Default Act, sponsored by the old "irreconcilable" Hiram Johnson of California, prohibiting American citizens from making loans to governments of nations in default to the United States. This act failed to stimulate payment of the debts and increased foreign ill will against the United States.

The great depression, the breakdown of the international currency system of the early 1930's, and other complex economic, political, and psychological factors, more than the Johnson Debt Default Act, caused a sharp decline of American investments abroad. The structure of international trade and indebtedness that characterized the 1920's and 1930's required a substantial volume of American foreign investment to help maintain the world's economic equilibrium. Having a surplus of savings over the demand of domestic investors for capital, when the rest of the world did not, the United States held a large part of the world's savings. It was, therefore, the logical market for most of the world's capital needs.

The large foreign investments of the 1920's, moreover, had stimulated the government's interest in world affairs. That period, despite Republican opposition to the League and the World Court, was not one of adamantine isolationism.[12] Nonetheless, the refusal of the United States to continue as an international investor and the defaults on the public and private debts had serious repercussions abroad and in the United States. The defaults stimulated a bitterness that led to a hardened isolationism in the 1930's, and American economic nationalism contributed to serious political upheavals abroad.

Yet economic nationalism was not an exclusively American phenomenon. It gripped other peoples and governments with equal tenacity. The attitude of the

American people and their governments in the 1920's and 1930's toward international investments and debts, moreover, was in keeping with the general foreign policy of the period. Governments who commit themselves to a policy of political isolation, however modified by conferences and vague international agreements, are unlikely to recognize responsibility for their economic policies beyond their own borders.

Reciprocal Trade Agreements

President Roosevelt did not give much encouragement to Secretary of State Hull and others who wanted to lower the nation's tariff walls. Yet in the presidential campaign of 1932 the Democrats had condemned the Hawley-Smoot Tariff and had committed themselves to a program of "reciprocal tariff agreements with other nations" to lower the barriers to international trade. At the same time, the Republicans had reaffirmed their faith in high protective tariffs.

Hull, who had devoted a quarter of a century in Congress to a crusade for lower tariffs, was disappointed when Roosevelt did not include a trade agreements bill in the mass of domestic economic legislation he pushed through Congress in the spring of 1933.[13] Powerful figures in the administration opposed Hull's ideas on foreign trade. Finally, Roosevelt took up the tariff issue. In March, 1934, Congress held hearings on the Reciprocal Trade Agreement Amendment to the Tariff Act of 1930, and in June the bill became law.

The Reciprocal Trade Agreements Act gave the President the power, through bilateral executive agreements, to reduce existing tariff rates up to fifty per cent. It also embodied the unconditional form of the most-favored-nation principle. This principle meant that a trade concession granted to one country would automatically be extended to all other countries producing the same product, if they did not discriminate against American goods.

Under the act, the administration could bargain with other governments for a reciprocal lowering of tariffs without the need of congressional approval for each agreement since Congress had given blanket approval beforehand. By making concessions on foreign imports, the government could persuade other countries to reduce their duties on American goods. Actually, the concessions the United States made, not the lower foreign duties, expanded American exports. For in a world short of dollars, the purchase of American exports depended largely on the number of dollars made available to foreigners. From the time the Reciprocal Trade Act was passed to January, 1940, the United States signed agreements with twenty-one countries who accounted for sixty per cent of American foreign trade.

Although the reciprocal trade program was an important step toward a liberal commercial policy, it is difficult to estimate how much it contributed to a genuine reduction of tariffs in the 1930's, but it is clear that in those years the government looked upon it as a means of combating the great depression. The program emphasized the expansion of foreign markets for American products, but at the same time limited, as far as possible, concessions on tariff rates to those items that did not compete with domestic products. The rates of the Hawley-Smoot Tariff, moreover, were so high that even the full reduction of fifty per cent permitted under law gave considerable protection to many commodities.

Strong political opposition to the trade agreements program and the need for congressional renewal every three years led the administration to act cautiously in reducing duties on goods that competed seriously with domestic products. Yet the act of 1934 was the most liberal that could have been expected in an era of economic nationalism, and certainly it represented a significant innovation in American tariff history. It also helped in overcoming some of the international ill will created by the Hawley-Smoot Tariff.

Until the great depression, the making of tariffs in the United States had been essentially a domestic issue, usually marked by conflict between those who desired protection for their domestic markets and those who wanted cheaper foreign goods. The reciprocal trade program, as the Hawley-Smoot Act had not done, finally recognized that tariffs against American goods were related to high tariffs against foreign goods.[14]

Despite this beginning in liberalizing tariff policy, a politically powerful isolationism was actually tightening its grip on foreign policy. Like his Republican predecessors, moreover, Roosevelt at first accepted the economic nationalism and isolationist mood of the country.

The Isolationist Mood

Only a few weeks before Roosevelt took office, Adolf Hitler had become Chancellor of Germany and, in a short while, swept away the constitutional foundations of the Weimar Republic and ruled the country as a dictator through his National Socialist Party, popularly called the Nazi party. The rise of the Nazis reflected the bitter nationalism of the German people, their hatred of the Treaty of Versailles, and their despair over the great depression.

In Italy, a less powerful dictator, Benito Mussolini, governed through his Fascist party. Like the Germans, the Italians were dissatisfied with the Treaty of Versailles, but Mussolini, who had come to power in 1922, did not challenge the international *status quo* for over two decades.

After withdrawing from the League, Hitler announced in March, 1935, that Germany was resuming compulsory military service and rearming in defiance of the prohibitions of the Treaty of Versailles. The failure of the other powers to disarm, he argued, had released Germany from her obligations. Britain, France, and Italy condemned Hitler's treaty violation but otherwise did nothing. The British, in fact, even agreed in June to a new German navy, thirty-five per cent as large as their own and far larger than allowed under the Treaty of Versailles.

Developments in Europe, as well as those in Asia, seemed to strengthen the isolationist convictions of most Americans, who were disillusioned with the precarious peace of 1919 and felt that only by avoiding entangling political connections with Europe could they keep out of war. Wilson's crusade to "make the world safe for democracy" appeared, in retrospect, a mockery.

Works by some of America's foremost writers in the 1920's and 30's gave expression to the disillusion and isolationist attitude of the American people. Novels and plays by Ernest Hemingway, Robert Sherwood, and John Dos Passos, and immensely popular motion pictures, like *The Big Parade* and Erich Maria Remarque's *All Quiet on the Western Front*, stressed the waste and futility of war, implying that the First World War had been a tragic mistake. A school of historians, called "revisionists," re-examined the causes of the war, placed considerable blame on the Allies, and implied or said that American intervention had been wrong. Walter Millis' *The Road to War*, published in 1935, carried the disturbing message that the United States had not gone to war in defense of high ideals but had stumbled into an unnecessary carnage.[15]

Others, meanwhile, attacked American participation in the European war for different reasons. In March, 1934, *Fortune* magazine published a sensational article, "Arms and the Men," on the armaments trade and how it incited war. That same year a popular book described the arms manufacturers as "merchants of death."

Two months after the appearance of the *Fortune* article, the Senate decided to investigate the trade in armaments and placed an isolationist Republican from North Dakota, Gerald P. Nye, in charge. Months of publicized hearings, beginning in September, disclosed that munitions-makers and bankers had made tremendous profits from the sale of arms to the Allies. Shocked by the revelations, many Americans came to believe that Wall Street bankers and arms manufacturers had sucked the nation into war to protect their profits. This conclusion came easily in a period of depression when bankers were unpopular. Many Americans, as public opinion polls were to show, came to consider intervention in the war a grave mistake.[16]

One of the nation's most widely read historians, Charles A. Beard, made effective use of the Nye disclosures. As perhaps the clearest spokesman of the isolationists, he advanced the idea that America could be safe in a hostile world only if she shunned collective action in international affairs, developed her own resources, and built up the defenses of the Western Hemisphere.

Another idea that flowed easily out of the findings of the Nye Committee was that the United States must not make the same mistake twice. Many Americans assumed that by taking the profits out of war and by limiting the wide discretion of the President in foreign affairs, involvement in future wars could be prevented.

The Neutrality Laws

Responding to the isolationist mood, Congress discussed legislation in the summer of 1935 which would place an embargo on all trade in armaments in time of war. President Roosevelt, who approved the idea of an embargo, wanted a broad law that would permit him to prohibit the sale of arms to the side he considered the aggressor, while permitting sale to the side he called the victim. The Department of State prepared a bill embodying the President's views.

Since the administration bill would have meant taking sides in a war and hence implied American involvement, Congress would not accept it. Instead, it passed a joint resolution, known as the First Neutrality Act, calling on the President, whenever he proclaimed a state of war to exist, to declare an arms embargo against all belligerents without distinction between them, and also authorizing him to warn Americans they could take passage on belligerent ships only at their own risk. Expressing the view that its "inflexible provisions might drag us into war instead of keeping us out," Roosevelt nonetheless signed the act into law on August 31, 1935.[17]

In October, Mussolini, seeking an African empire, sent his Blackshirt soldiers marching into Ethiopia without declaring war. Acting immediately, the President announced a state of war between Italy and Ethiopia and applied the neutrality law to both countries. A few days later the Council of the League of Nations declared that Italy had violated the covenant and had committed an act of "aggression." A month later, the League voted sanctions, an embargo on "arms, ammunition and implements of war," against her.

Italy's most vital import was oil, but Britain and France feared that tighter economic sanctions might provoke Mussolini into touching off a larger war or drive him into Hitler's arms. Therefore, the League did not class oil, coal, or steel as implements of war. Britain and France were more concerned with what Hitler might do than with Mussolini's conquest of an African province remote from the vital centers of their interests.

The Roosevelt administration refused outright cooperation with the League in imposing sanctions. "With the isolationist sentiment so strong," Secretary of State Cordell Hull explained later, "it was impossible to join any League body considering sanctions. I preferred that any action we took should be entirely independent and not even seem to be suggested by the League."[18] Yet the administration was concerned over the fact that the neutrality law worked to the disadvantage of Ethiopia, the victim of aggression. Before the League sanctions began to operate, therefore, Roosevelt and Hull had called on American exporters to impose a "moral embargo" or voluntary curtailment on shipments of oil, steel, and other commodities going to Italy.[19]

Neither the League's sanctions nor the American moral embargo effectively slowed down Mussolini's war machine. Some League members urged an oil embargo to stop the Italians, and in December, 1935, the British Ambassador asked Hull if the United States would cooperate with the League in imposing such an embargo. Hull said it could not.

After shunning cooperation against Italy, Congress passed the Second Neutrality Act, signed on February 29, 1936, that extended the original law for a year and hardened its embargo provisions. The first law had permitted the President to apply the embargo to any new nation entering the war; the second required him to do so.[20] In addition, by forbidding loans to belligerents, the new legislation accepted the thesis of the Nye findings that bankers had virtually pushed the United States into the First World War.

A week later, taking advantage of the international crisis, Hitler again defied the Treaty of Versailles and thereby shifted attention away from Ethiopia. He sent troops into the hitherto demilitarized Rhineland.

The League's sanctions failed, and Mussolini's Fascists swiftly conquered Ethiopia in defiance of world opinion. In May, the Italian government decreed the annexation of Ethiopia, and in July the League voted to end sanctions against Italy. Adhering to the Stimson Doctrine, the United States refused to recognize Mussolini's annexation. In December, 1937, Italy withdrew from the League.

Some advocates of collective security charged that the refusal of the United States to join in strong sanctions against Mussolini was the main reason for the ineffectiveness of the League. Actually, the policy of the United States toward sanctions was not the decisive factor, for the Ethiopian war demonstrated certain practical difficulties that stood in the way of using economic sanctions as a substitute for force. Mussolini had threatened to fight if the League embargoed oil. His threat, when coupled with Hitler's actions, appears to have been the determining factor in preventing the imposition of stronger sanctions.

Meanwhile, in July, 1936, civil war had broken out in Spain. Since Germany and Italy favored the insurgent forces led by General Francisco Franco, and Russia, Britain, and France sympathized with the Spanish Republican government, the civil war appeared likely to expand into an international conflict. The European governments therefore agreed in August on a policy of nonintervention in Spain. Under the leadership of Britain and France, they even set up a special committee in London to supervise nonintervention.

In the past, particularly in revolutions in Latin America, the United States had usually permitted the legitimate governments to purchase arms from American firms while denying them to the insurgents. In the Spanish conflict, however, it followed a policy of nonintervention similar to that of Britain and France. Under the existing neutrality law, the President had no authority to impose an arms embargo in a civil war, but Secretary of State Hull asked American exporters to conform to the spirit of the neutrality law by refusing to sell arms to either side in Spain.

Since the voluntary system did not work, the President asked Congress to extend the neutrality law to the Spanish civil war and thus make the moral embargo legal. Congress did so in a joint resolution of January 6, 1937, but liberal critics argued that in embargoing arms to both sides the United States was penalizing the recognized government of a friendly power by shutting it off from a needed source of arms. The plight of the Spanish Loyalists seemed especially difficult because they received only a limited assistance from Russia while Italy and Germany, in violation of their pledges of nonintervention, sent Franco arms and also troops.[21] Thus, the critics charged that American policy had the effect of aiding the spread of fascism.

Other developments made the charge appear plausible. Drawn together by their common goal in the Spanish civil war, Hitler and Mussolini had signed a treaty in October, 1936, usually known as the pact that established the Rome-Berlin Axis, in which they pledged collaboration in various political matters, particularly in Spain and against Communism. A month later they recognized Franco's fascist regime, and on November 25 Germany and Japan signed an Anti-Comintern Pact, promising each other to combat the Communist Third International. A secret addendum called for political and possibly military cooperation against the Soviet Union itself. A year later Mussolini joined this treaty, thus creating the Rome-Berlin-Tokyo Axis and uniting the three nations who had defied the League into a tenuous league of their own. As for Spain, Franco fought on to ultimate victory and clamped a fascist dictatorship on the country.

Meanwhile, Congress decided to make the neutrality legislation "permanent" by extending or replacing the law of 1936 that was to expire in May, 1937. It drew up a bill that sought to insure profit while aiming to avoid involvement in any future war, essentially a compromise between a complete embargo and the unrestricted sale of goods as in the period of the First World War. "We seek," Senator Borah said, "to avoid all risks, all dangers, but we make certain to get all the profits."[22]

The Third Neutrality Act, passed as a joint congressional resolution on April 30, 1937, and signed into law on the following day, extended the main features of the temporary law indefinitely and included two innovations: instead of merely discouraging the travel of Americans on belligerent ships, it made such travel unlawful, and permitted warring nations to buy arms and other supplies in the United States if they paid cash and carried away their purchases in their own ships. The law also allowed the President to decide on the list of commodities to which the "cash and carry" provision would apply, but "cash and carry," limited to a period of two years, was never used under this act.

So strong was the passion for peace among Americans that the neutrality program won overwhelming popular support. According to public opinion surveys, support for the neutrality law was broader than any political, sectional, or factional alignment in Congress or elsewhere.

From the isolationist point of view, a majority position in 1937, the neutrality law protected the country against being drawn into a foreign war on the issues of neutral rights and wartime trade and loans, as supposedly had been the case in 1917 according to general congressional theory. Those who believed in collective security pointed out that it abandoned America's traditional concept of freedom of the seas, and argued that it was a surrender to the totalitarian dictators who would destroy democracy. By condoning "aggression," they said, the neutrality law tended to make war probable and hence endangered American security. Expressing the sentiments of the collective security advocates, the New York *Herald Tribune* paraphrased the law's enacting clause to read: "An Act to Preserve the United States from Intervention in the War of 1917–1918." 23

Japan and the "China Incident"

While European tensions were still high over the Spanish civil war, Japanese troops on the night of July 7, 1937, while on maneuvers near the Marco Polo bridge ten miles west of Peiping, clashed with Chinese soldiers. Three weeks later, after fruitless negotiations, Japan's troops invaded China in force and a large-scale war began. To circumvent her embarrassing pledge in the Kellogg Pact, Japan did not declare war, but referred to the fighting as the "China incident."

President Roosevelt and most Americans favored China in the struggle. To invoke the neutrality act would hurt China and help Japan. Therefore, Roosevelt reversed the policy he had followed in the undeclared war between Italy and Ethiopia. On the technical ground that there had been no declaration of war, he refused to apply the neutrality law and thus made possible the shipment of munitions to China. "We have not put into effect the neutrality proclamation," he explained, "for the very simple reason that if we could find a way of not doing it, we would be more neutral than if we did." 24

In a speech on October 5 in Chicago, the President seemingly made a more dramatic departure from impartiality toward the "China incident." Referring most obviously to Japan, though not by name, he condemned the "present reign of terror and international lawlessness." The United States was not immune from attack, for no nation, he pointed out, could escape the consequences of international anarchy "through mere isolation or neutrality." Departing from the outline suggested by his State Department advisers, he warned that the epidemic of world lawlessness was spreading. "When an epidemic of physical disease starts to spread," he said, "the community approves and joins in a quarantine of the patients in order to protect the health of the community against the spread of the disease." And, he added, "there must be positive endeavors to preserve peace."[25]

Advocates of collective security rejoiced, greeting the President's words as a break with isolationism. The *Foreign Policy Bulletin* praised the speech under the caption: "Roosevelt Abandons Isolation."[26] But the isolationist mood of the country was still too strong to be overcome. Most Americans apparently interpreted the speech as a call for sanctions against Japan. The President, they feared, was willing to run the risk of drawing the country into war. Even some of the President's closest advisers felt that he had gone too far in challenging the isolationist temper of the people.

Roosevelt himself was surprised by the violent public reaction to his words and indignant that leaders of his own party, particularly in Congress, did not support him. "It's a terrible thing," he told one of his close advisers, "to look over your shoulder when you are trying to lead—and to find no one there."[27] He was thus forced to give up the "quarantine" idea.

On the day following Roosevelt's speech, the League, with whom the United States was now cooperating, condemned Japan for violating both the Nine-Power Treaty and the Kellogg Pact. That same day the Department of State announced American concurrence with the League's decision, thus openly siding with China against Japan.

The League, stimulated by Roosevelt's speech, suggested that the signatories of the Nine-Power Treaty should meet and try to offer a solution for the "China incident."[28] None of the great powers, awed by events in Europe, would sponsor the conference but they persuaded Belgium to issue invitations for a meeting in Brussels. Early in November the United States and eighteen other nations, including Soviet Russia, sent representatives. Germany and Japan refused to participate.

Other nations, particularly Britain, looked to the United States for a leadership against Japan that never came, in part because of the caution imposed by the unfavorable reaction to the quarantine speech. Before the conference began, Roosevelt himself had assured the American people that the purpose of the conference was peaceful negotiation, not the coercion of the belligerents. He had advised the American delegate to "observe closely the trend of public opinion in the United States and to take full account of it."[29]

From the beginning, therefore, the chances that the conference would take decisive measures to restrain Japan were negligible. It did not even consider sanctions. After aimless talk, it broke up on November 24, with a reaffirmation of the principles of the Nine-Power Treaty which Japan had insisted were obsolete. The failure of the Brussels Conference emphasized anew the futility of collective action without American cooperation, which the American government was unwilling to offer at that time because of isolationist sentiment at home.

To avoid incidents that might lead to war, the United States then began evacuating its nationals and forces, primarily legation guards and river gunboats, stationed in China. Before completing the evacuation Japanese aviators in clear daylight on December 12, 1937, bombed, strafed, and sank the plainly marked gunboat u.s.s. *Panay* while it was assisting in the evacuation of American officials and escorting American tankers up the Yangtze River. Several crew members died and other Americans suffered wounds. Before the United States had time to protest, the Japanese government apologized and later offered reparations for the injured and to the families of those killed, an offer accepted by the American government. The American people, after a brief burst of warlike anger, took the matter relatively calmly. The crisis passed within a few weeks. Nonetheless, it showed how precarious peace was, even for the United States.

Two days after the sinking of the *Panay*, largely due to fear that the crisis might precipitate war, the House of Representatives took up consideration of a constitutional amendment sponsored by Louis Ludlow, a Democrat from Indiana. The Ludlow amendment would have required a national referendum before a declaration of war except when American soil was attacked.

Available evidence showed a widespread popular support for the Ludlow referendum. Public opinion polls at the time revealed that eighty per cent of those questioned favored a referendum on war, and 218 congressmen had signed a petition approving it. Since the amendment would have deprived the President of a fundamental control over foreign policy, both Roosevelt and Hull exerted every possible pressure to defeat it. The vote to take the Ludlow amendment out of committee, where it had been bottled up, and place it before the House failed on January 10, 1938, by the narrow margin of twenty-one votes. The popularity of the Ludlow proposal reflected the national fear of war, the distrust of the Executive in foreign affairs, and marked the high point of isolationist sentiment.

Appeasement and Munich

At the same time fear of war paralyzed the British and French governments. Although the Nazis had failed in an earlier attempt to take over Austria, in February, 1938, Hitler increased his pressure on the Austrian Republic for union with Germany. In March, ostensibly at the invitation of the Austrian government, Nazi troops moved into the country, and later Hitler proclaimed Austria a state of the German Reich. France and Britain protested this new violation of the treaty structure of 1919, but neither they nor anyone else offered resistance.

Hitler next directed a campaign of threats and propaganda against Czechoslovakia, demanding the Sudetenland, a region at the western side of the republic inhabited by some three million Germans. Czechoslovakia, who had defensive alliances with France and Russia, refused to meet the German demands without a fight.[30] The Czechs began mobilizing; the German army held ominous maneuvers; and early in September, 1938, France began calling up army reservists. If Germany attacked Czechoslovakia, a general war seemed certain.

Desperately seeking a way of dealing peacefully with Germany, Prime Minister Neville Chamberlain of Britain visited Hitler twice in late September. With the support of France and the reluctant acquiescence of Czechoslovakia, he offered a plan that met most of Hitler's demands. The German dictator rejected it and said his troops would occupy the Sudetenland on October 1 regardless of what the Czechs did. Czechoslovakia spurned the new German demands and ordered full mobilization of her army. France followed with partial mobilization and began to confer with Russia who had been urging a strong stand in support of the Czechs.

At this point, with another world war seemingly imminent, Roosevelt intervened with a plea for peace. First he appealed to the German, Czech, British, and French leaders to negotiate a "peaceful, fair and constructive settlement," and on the following day urged Hitler to bring his dispute before an international conference. On the same day he also sent a plea to Mussolini urging him to use his influence to avoid war. Persuaded by *Il Duce* to yield slightly, Hitler agreed to a conference with Mussolini, Chamberlain, and France's Premier, Edouard Daladier, in Munich. There is no reason for assuming that Roosevelt's intervention decisively influenced the calling of the conference. Mussolini and Hitler acted for reasons of their own.[31]

At the meeting in Munich on September 29 and 30, 1938, Hitler insisted on the terms of his ultimatum, offering Czechoslovakia only a little more time to evacuate the Sudetenland. At the insistence of Britain and France, the Czechs capitulated.

The world assumed that the Munich agreement had averted war. As he returned home Chamberlain told his people that he had brought back "peace with honour." "I believe," he added, "it is peace in our time."[32] It was not that. What he had obtained was no more than a brief truce won by appeasement.

Although the American reaction was mixed, most Americans, according to public opinion polls, also thought that Munich meant peace. The sacrifices of the Czechs, the Washington *Post* said, "would seem a small price to pay for peace, particularly if the peace thereby obtained is stabilized." The Norfolk *Virginian-Pilot*, however, called Munich an "ill-smelling peace."[33]

Japan's "New Order"

In Asia, meantime, Japanese troops drove deeper into China, capturing most of her main railway lines and coastal cities. Since Chiang Kai-shek would not capitulate, Japan set up puppet regimes in the areas she occupied. At the same time, she squeezed foreign business firms out of those areas despite American protests.

In November, Japan proclaimed a "new order" in East Asia and spoke of a

Greater East Asia Co-Prosperity Sphere based on a league with Manchukuo and China under her leadership. In a reply to American protests she announced that the old principles of the Open Door no longer applied to the "new order" in East Asia.

Refusing to recognize the "new order" and having lost faith in protests, the United States explored the possibility of economic retaliation for violations of American rights. That December it loaned Chiang Kai-shek $25 million to aid him in resisting Japan. Previously Roosevelt and his advisers had feared that the fortification of Guam, lying only 1350 miles from Tokyo, might provoke Japan to retaliatory action. In February, 1939, however, the President asked for, and Congress appropriated, additional defense funds that included provisions for harbor improvements and fortifications in Guam, Samoa, and Alaska.

"Methods Short of War"

The chronic anti-Semitism of Hitler's government, meanwhile, had resulted in an unprecedented outbreak of organized violence against Jews in Germany in November, 1938. These persecutions alarmed Roosevelt. He expressed amazement that "such things could occur in twentieth century civilization" and abruptly called home the American Ambassador in Berlin for "consultation."[34]

In his annual message in January, the President offered the most distinct public sign of a change in policy by suggesting that "methods short of war" might curb the aggressor governments. What he sought was repeal of the neutrality law, particularly of its mandatory embargo, so that he could make American arms available to friendly nations. "We have learned that when we deliberately try to legislate neutrality," he said, "our neutrality laws may operate unevenly and unfairly—may actually give aid to the aggressor and deny it to the victim. The instinct of self-preservation should warn us that we ought not to let that happen any more."[35]

In his budget message on the next day and in a special message in the following week, Roosevelt asked Congress for huge defense appropriations, particularly for airplanes. Later that month a senator quoted the President as saying that the American frontier lies on the Rhine, a statement Roosevelt denied but one that probably revealed the extent of his alarm over the international developments.

Roosevelt's anxiety was not ill-founded. At Munich, Hitler had said that the Sudetenland was "the last territorial claim which I have to make in Europe," but on March 15, 1939, he destroyed what remained of the Czech nation. Taking advantage of the new crisis over Czechoslovakia, Mussolini carried out an old plan by sending troops into Albania on April 7. Several days later he added that state to the Italian empire. At the same time Hitler directed a "war of nerves" against Poland, demanding that she surrender the city of Danzig to Germany.

These last acts of violence forced Britain and France to reverse their policy of appeasing Hitler. Late in March they had guaranteed aid to Poland if Hitler attacked and two weeks later made a similar pledge to Greece and Rumania, periled by Mussolini's invasion of Albania. Applying the Stimson Doctrine, the United States refused to recognize Hitler's annexation of Czechoslovakia and Mussolini's acquisition of Albania. "Do we really have to assume," Roosevelt asked in a speech, "that nations can find no better methods of realizing their destinies than those which were used by the Huns and the Vandals fifteen hundred years ago?" [36]

Casting aside the principle of nonintervention, the President sent a special appeal on the following day, known as the "Saturday surprise" message, to Hitler and Mussolini, asking them to demonstrate their often-repeated desire for peace by giving thirty-one nations in Europe and the Near East guarantees against attack for at least ten years. If they agreed, he said, the United States would join international discussions to ease the burden of armaments, to reduce the barriers to international trade, and to consider necessary political questions.

Mussolini did not reply, but did comment that Roosevelt's suggestion was "absurd." Two weeks later, in a sarcastic speech before the Reichstag that the President took as a personal affront, Hitler denied any aggressive intentions. Then on May 28, Germany and Italy signed a military alliance, the "Pact of Steel."

Roosevelt's unconventional intervention had accomplished nothing tangible, but it had evoked tremendous popular response. It had, moreover, placed his opposition to the Axis on record and perhaps exerted some influence on American public opinion.

The Treaty of 1911 Abrogated

Japan's forces, meantime, were moving southward toward Indochina, the Philippines, and the Dutch East Indies. In February, 1939, the Japanese seized the island of Hainan off the coast of Indochina, and on March 30 they occupied the Spratly Islands, some 700 miles southwest of Manila and claimed by France. Japan now appeared to threaten French, Dutch, British, and American possessions. In April, Roosevelt ordered the fleet, which was in the Atlantic on maneuvers, back into the Pacific.

Many Americans, angered by Japanese bombings of civilians in China, demanded an embargo on war supplies going to Japan. Earlier, in the summer of 1938, the government had asked airplane manufacturers not to send equipment to Japan. Although this "moral embargo" worked, Congress threatened to take more decisive action. Before Congress took the initiative, the Department of State, on July 26, 1939, suddenly gave Japan the required six months' notice terminating her Treaty of Commerce and Navigation of 1911 with the United States. This stroke upset the Japanese and removed a major legal obstacle to placing pressure on Japan through economic sanctions.

Meanwhile, on May 1, the "cash and carry" provision of the neutrality law of 1937 had expired, and the President increased his pressure for repeal of the entire law. Secretary Hull told congressional leaders that the next war in Europe would not be just, "another goddam piddling dispute over a boundary line," but of vital concern to the United States. The neutrality law, he said, "substituted a wretched little bobtailed, sawed-off domestic statute for the established rules of international law" and aided probable aggressors, but leaders in Congress refused to support a repeal.[37]

On the evening of July 18, therefore, the President held a White House conference with Senate leaders of both parties. He asked them to repeal the arms embargo so that he could ship arms to Britain and France if needed. "I've fired my last shot," he said, referring to his efforts to preserve peace. "I think I ought to have another round in my belt."[38]

The Senators were not convinced. When Hull predicted war in Europe by the end of summer, Senator Borah contradicted him, either saying or implying he had sources of information on the subject that he had found more reliable than the State Department.

The Democratic leaders then informed the President that they could not overcome the strong isolationist sentiment in the Senate. "Well, Captain," Vice-President John N. Garner told Roosevelt, "we may as well face the facts. You haven't got the votes, and that's all there is to it."[39] So Congress adjourned on August 4 without acting on the neutrality legislation.

The Nazi-Soviet Pact and War

While Congress had been debating, Britain and France had been trying to bolster their guarantees to Poland with an alliance with the Soviet Union. Earlier, even though ignored at Munich, the Soviets had offered the European democracies a defensive treaty against Hitler. The British and French negotiations with the Russians proved indecisive because Poland, Rumania, and the Baltic states feared Russia as much as they did Germany. To them a Russian guarantee meant occupation by hated Communist troops. "With the Germans we risk losing our liberty," a prominent Pole said; "with the Russians we lose our soul."[40]

Distrusting the European democracies, the Russians had opened parallel negotiations with Hitler; on August 20 they announced the signing of a trade agreement with Germany. Four days later they shocked the world by concluding a non-aggression pact with Germany, thus assuring Hitler of their neutrality when he attacked Poland. A secret protocol partitioned Poland between the Nazis and the Soviets and also divided spheres of influence in the Baltic states between them.

The Nazi-Soviet Pact freed Russia from the fear of a simultaneous attack by Germany and Japan and strengthened her position in the Far East. No nation was more stunned by the treaty than Japan. Germany had violated the Anti-Comintern Pact, a deception that caused Japan to adopt a more conciliatory attitude, for a while at least, toward the United States.

Knowing of Hitler's tactics through intelligence reports, Roosevelt again decided to intervene personally in the international politics of Europe. Just as Hitler's negotiator and Russia's dictator, Josef Stalin, were completing their treaty, the President appealed to the King of Italy and on the following day to Hitler and the President of Poland to strive to avoid war, and offered himself as a conciliator. After receiving a favorable reply from Poland but hearing nothing from the *Führer*, Roosevelt sent a second special plea to Hitler, but there was no desire for peace in Berlin. Roosevelt had not expected positive results from his intervention, but he said as he sent his second message to Hitler, "This puts the bee on Germany, which no one did in 1914."[41]

After some hesitation, Hitler pressed his uncompromising territorial demands on Poland. On September 1, 1939, when the Poles refused to submit, his troops plunged across the Polish frontier without a declaration of war. Two days later Britain and France declared war on Germany. The Second World War, heralded by the awesome screech of Stuka dive bombers over Warsaw, had started.

NOTES

1. Speaking of German-Americans, Theodore Roosevelt said that "they represent that adherence to the politico-racial hyphen which is the badge and sign of moral treason to the Republic." To the Progressive National Committee, June 22, 1916, in Elting E. Morison, ed., *The Letters of Theodore Roosevelt* (8 vols., Cambridge, Mass., 1951–54), VIII, 1072. For an analysis of ethnic influences on foreign policy, see the pertinent chapters in John Higham, *Strangers in the Land: Patterns of American Nativism, 1860–1925* (New Brunswick, N.J., 1955); Selig Adler, *The Isolationist Impulse* (New York, 1957); and Louis L. Gerson, "Immigrant Groups and American Foreign Policy," in George L. Anderson, ed., *Issues and Conflicts: Studies in Twentieth Century American Diplomacy* (Lawrence, Kans., 1959), pp. 171–192. See also Horace C. Peterson and Gilbert C. Fite, *Opponents of War, 1917–1918* (Madison, Wis., 1957).

2. W. H. Page to Edwin A. Alderman, June 22, 1916, in Burton J. Hendrick, *The Life and Letters of Walter H. Page* (2 vols., New York, 1924), II, 144.

3. For details, see Robert K. Murray, *Red Scare: A Study in National Hysteria, 1919–1920* (Minneapolis, 1955).

4. For details, see Maldwyn A. Jones, *American Immigration* (Chicago, 1960), pp. 270–277 and Oscar Handlin, *The American People in the Twentieth Century* (Cambridge, Mass., 1954), pp. 136–162, a brief study containing keen insight.

5. Sept. 5, 1919, in Ray S. Baker and William E. Dodd, eds., *The Public Papers of Woodrow Wilson* (6 vols., New York, 1925–27), War and Peace, I, 640.

6. The quotation is in Benjamin H. Williams, *Economic Foreign Policy of the United States* (New York, 1929), p. 219.

7. Aug. 5, 1920, Denna F. Fleming, *The United States and World Organization, 1920–1933* (New York, 1938), p. 121n.

8. Jan. 4, 1926, in Harold G. Moulton and Leo Pasvolsky, *World War Debt Settlements* (Washington, 1926), p. 401.

9. Theodore G. Joslin, *Hoover Off the Record* (Garden City, N.Y., 1934), p. 91.

10. Robert H. Ferrell, *American Diplomacy in the Great Depression* (New Haven, 1957), p. 236.

11. March 4, 1933, in Samuel I. Rosenman, comp., *The Public Papers and Addresses of Franklin D. Roosevelt* (13 vols., New York, 1938–50), II, 14.

12. For an interpretation that suggests that the United States was not following a policy of isolationism in this period, see William A. Williams, "The Legend of Isolationism in the 1920's," *Science and Society*, XVIII (Winter 1954), 1–20. For a brief but broad analysis of isolationism in the twentieth century see the essays by Alexander DeConde and Kenneth Thompson, in DeConde, ed., *Isolation and Security* (Durham, N.C., 1957). For sectional analyses of isolationism, see Ray A. Billington, "The Origins of Middle Western Isolationism," *Political Science Quarterly*, LX (March 1945), 44–64 and Alexander DeConde, "The South and Isolationism," *Journal of Southern History*, XXIV (Aug. 1958), 332–346.

13. For the origins of Hull's ideas on the tariff, see William R. Allen, "International Trade Philosophy of Cordell Hull, 1907–1933," *American Economic Review*, XLIII (March 1953), 101–116.

14. For details, see William R. Allen, "Cordell Hull and the Defense of the Trade Agreements Program, 1934–1940," in DeConde, ed., *Isolation and Security*, pp. 107–132.

15. For a critical analysis of revisionist writings, see Selig Adler, "The War-Guilt Question and American Disillusionment, 1918–1928," *Journal of Modern History*, XXIII (March 1951), 1–28.

16. For the "merchants of death" thesis, see Helmuth C. Engelbrecht and F. C. Hanighen, *Merchants of Death: A Study of the International Armament Industry* (New York, 1934). For analyses of the Nye Committee and its work, see John E. Wiltz, "The Nye Committee Revisited," *The Historian*, XXIII (Feb. 1961), 211–233 and Robert A. Divine, *The Illusion of Neutrality* (Chicago, 1962), pp. 62–80.

17. Rosenman, comp., *Papers of Franklin D. Roosevelt*, IV, 346.

18. *The Memoirs of Cordell Hull* (2 vols., New York, 1948), I, 431.

19. The question of oil and sanctions is discussed in Herbert Feis, *Seen From E. A.: Three International Episodes* (New York, 1947), pp. 193–275 and in Henderson B. Braddick, "A New Look at American Policy during the Italo-Ethiopian Crisis, 1935–36," *Journal of Modern History*, XXXIV (March 1962), 64–73. For an analysis of Italian propaganda in the United States, see John Norman, "Influence of Pro-Fascist Propaganda on American Neutrality, 1935–1936," in Dwight E. Lee and George E. McReynolds, eds., *Essays in History and International Relations in Honor of George Hubbard Blakeslee* (Worcester, Mass., 1949), pp. 193–214.

20. Roosevelt had wanted a discretionary embargo but accepted a mandatory one rather than risk defeat in Congress. See Wayne S. Cole, "Senator Key Pittman and American Neutrality Policies, 1933–1940," *Mississippi Valley Historical Review*, XLVI (March 1960), 654.

21. George F. Kennan, in *Russia and the West under Lenin and Stalin* (Boston, 1961), p. 309, points out, however, that Russia intervened in a major way, taking over whole areas of governmental power in Spain. A similar view is in Hugh Thomas, *The Spanish Civil War* (New York, 1961). Foreign intervention is summarized on pp. 634–638.

22. Quoted in Divine, *Illusion of Neutrality*, p. 185.

23. Quoted in Adler, *Isolationist Impulse*, p. 265.

24. April 21, 1938, Rosenman, comp., *Papers of Franklin D. Roosevelt*, VII, 287.

25. *Ibid.*, VII, p. 287.

26. Cited in Charles A. Beard, *American Foreign Policy in the Making, 1932–1940* (New Haven, 1946), p. 199. There is no convincing evidence to support the view that the speech was a call for sanctions or other strong measures. In her scholarly analysis, "Notes on Roosevelt's Quarantine Speech," *Political Science Quarterly*, LXXII (Sept. 1957), pp. 405–453, Dorothy Borg suggests that the speech was not a landmark in Roosevelt's foreign policy, but was instead a groping effort to forestall war.

27. Quoted in Samuel I. Rosenman, *Working with Roosevelt* (New York, 1952), p. 167. John McV. Haight, Jr., in "Roosevelt and the Aftermath of the Quarantine Speech," *Review of Politics*, XXIV (April 1962), 233–259, suggests that Roosevelt did not retreat immediately from the quarantine idea.

28. Roosevelt's speech was the genesis of the conference. See Nancy H. Hooker, ed., *The Moffat Papers: Selections from the Diplomatic Journals of Jay Pierrepont Moffat* (Cambridge, Mass., 1956), p. 156.

29. To Norman Davis, quoted in Herbert Feis, *The Road to Pearl Harbor* (Princeton, 1950), p. 14. See also Roosevelt's memorandum in *Foreign Relations, 1937*, IV, 85. Haight, in "Roosevelt and the Aftermath of the Quarantine Speech," *Review of Politics*, XXIV (April 1962), 239, suggests that Roosevelt regarded the Brussels Conference as a means of implementing the quarantine idea.

30. For a detailed analysis of one aspect of this pressure against the Czechs, see Gerhard L. Weinberg, "The May Crisis, 1938," *Journal of Modern History*, XXIX (Sept. 1957), 213–225.

31. This is the view of William L. Langer and S. Everett Gleason, *The Challenge to Isolation, 1937–1940* (New York, 1952), p. 34. John M. Haight, in "France, the United States, and the Munich Crisis," *Journal of Modern History*, XXXII (Dec. 1960), 340–358, however, suggests that throughout the Munich crisis the United States, at least indirectly, had a part and that Roosevelt's failure to commit himself contributed to appeasement.

32. Neville Chamberlain, *In Search of Peace* (New York, 1939), p. 200.

33. The newspapers, dated Sept. 29 and 30, 1938, are quoted in Charles C. Tansill, *Back Door to War: The Roosevelt Foreign Policy, 1933–1941* (Chicago, 1952), pp. 428–429.

34. Quoted in Langer and Gleason, *Challenge to Isolation*, p. 36.

35. Jan. 4, 1939, in Rosenman, comp., *Papers of Franklin D. Roosevelt*, VIII, 3–4.

36. April 14, 1939, *ibid.*, p. 198.

37. Quoted in Langer and Gleason, *Challenge to Isolation*, p. 137

38. *Ibid.*, p. 143.

39. Quoted in Foster Rhea Dulles, *America's Rise to World Power, 1898–1954* (New York, 1954), p. 186, and in Marian C. McKenna, *Borah* (Ann Arbor, Mich., 1961), pp. 362–363 where the exchange between Hull and Borah is recorded.

40. Marshal Rydz-Smigly quoted in Langer and Gleason, *Challenge to Isolation*, p. 178.

41. Aug. 24, 1939, *ibid.*, p. 190.

Chapter Twenty-Three

NEUTRALITY AND NONBELLIGERENCY

A few hours after Great Britain and France had declared war, Roosevelt spoke to the American people by radio in what he called a fireside chat. "This nation will remain a neutral nation," he said, "but I cannot ask that every American remain neutral in thought as well." [1] He also promised to try to keep the United States out of the war.

That same evening radio bulletins announced the sinking without warning of the British passenger liner *Athenia*. Over one hundred passengers, including twenty-eight Americans, lost their lives in the U-boat attack. Two days later the President issued two proclamations. One announced traditional neutrality, and the other invoked the neutrality law of 1937. Since the British and French had practical control of the seas, the law had the effect of cutting them off from American arms.

Unlike the divided sentiment that marked the outbreak of the First World War, Americans this time overwhelmingly held Germany responsible for the war and wished to see her defeated. [2] They were also broadly united in their determination to stay out of the conflict. Roosevelt's main concern, however, was not to maintain an impartial neutrality but to find some way within the letter of the neutrality law of transmitting arms and other supplies to the Allies. He quickly supplemented that objective with efforts to repeal the arms embargo.

Two weeks after Hitler had invaded Poland, Roosevelt called Congress into special session to undertake a revision of the neutrality legislation. In the face of isolationist opposition, he proceeded cautiously, for congressional leaders made it clear that outright repeal was impossible. He realized that he would have to compromise.

In his message to the opening session of Congress, therefore, the President tried to avoid controversy by stressing that a repeal of the embargo on arms would protect neutrality and add to the nation's security. This statement did not candidly express the administration's position, for Roosevelt was not so much concerned about American neutrality as he was about preventing a German victory. He and his advisers did believe, however, that a revision of the neutrality legislation might help keep the United States out of the war, because, as Secretary Hull explained, "if Britain and France won the war, we could remain at peace, whereas if Germany won, there was every likelihood that we should soon have to fight." [3]

Six weeks of stormy debate, between those who supported collective security and those who upheld traditional isolationist ideas, swirled about the proposed revision of the neutrality law. In essence, the opposition argued that repeal of the arms embargo meant taking sides and would eventually lead to war as in 1917. Opponents and proponents of repeal agreed on one thing, however, and in this they apparently represented the views of most Americans. They all sought to keep the nation out of war.

The Fourth Neutrality Act

The debate ended when Congress passed the Fourth Neutrality Act. The voting followed party lines. Only six Republicans in the Senate and nineteen in the House favored the measure. The President signed the bill into law on November 4, 1939, and American neutrality entered a new phase.

The new legislation incorporated most of the measures of the previous neutrality laws, but now Congress itself might invoke the law if the President failed to "find" the war it thought he should. The law slightly relaxed the previous prohibition on loans to belligerents by allowing short-term credits of ninety days. A major new provision—a concession to isolationists—forbade American ships, regardless of cargo or destination, from entering combat zones along the coastlines of belligerent countries as designated by the President. More important, the new law repealed the arms embargo and allowed the Allies to buy on a "cash and carry" basis.

The old law had given Germany an advantage; the new one favored the British and French. This, as far as the administration was concerned, was its main purpose.[4]

So swift was the German *Blitzkrieg*, or lightning war, that the Polish state disappeared before the new neutrality act became law. On September 17, Russian troops had invaded Poland from the east, and two weeks later the Nazis and

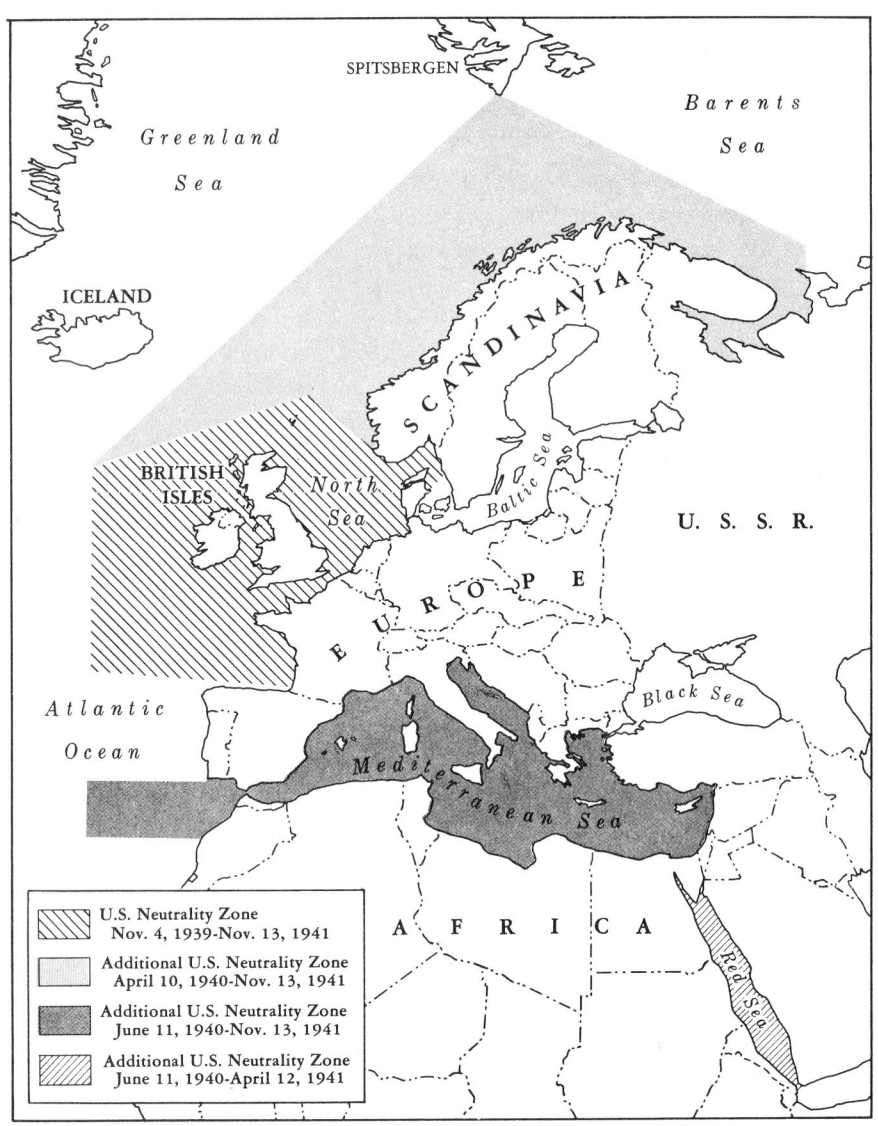

COMBAT ZONES CLOSED TO AMERICANS, 1939–1941

Soviets had divided that helpless country between them. Even though Poland had declared war against Russia, Roosevelt did not recognize the Polish-Russian hostilities as war and refused to invoke the neutrality law in this instance. He argued that this facet of the European war had little relation to the peace of the United States, but most of all he did not wish to do anything that might drive Russia into closer collaboration with Hitler.

After disposing of Poland, Hitler offered Britain and France peace if they would recognize his conquests and tried to interest Roosevelt in acting as mediator. The

Allies rejected the offer, and Roosevelt would not accept the role of peacemaker on Hitler's terms. After this, during the winter of 1939–1940, the western front settled down into what many called the "phony war" or *Sitzkrieg*.

Hitler's *Blitzkrieg* had stunned most Americans, but during the lull of the so-called "phony war," they believed that the superior economic and sea power of the British and French would strangle Germany and bring an Allied victory. As soon as the war began, the British had clamped a long-range blockade on Germany, though they did not formally declare one. They published a broad contraband list and blacklists, stopped neutral ships at sea, and brought some of them to control ports where they removed contraband cargo, including mail addressed to Germany. Since Britain could not live without imports, Hitler tried in turn to blockade her with submarines. At first he ordered strict observance of the rules of international law since he sought to avoid any maritime incident with the United States that would provoke retaliation.

From the beginning, the United States was determined to be indulgent toward the Allied blockade and to avoid the bitter arguments of the First World War. When the British violated American rights under the traditional rules of international law, the Roosevelt administration protested only for the record. In fact, it did everything it could to facilitate the carriage of American goods by Allied ships while denying German submarines any privileges in American ports.

After the rejection of his peace proposals, Hitler threw aside the restraints of maritime international law. In November he planted magnetic mines, a new weapon, at the entrances of British harbors and took a heavy toll of Allied shipping. Since this action violated traditional maritime law, the British took advantage of it by retaliating with a blockade of German exports, also an illegal act. Thus the Allied blockade sought to plug every line of trade in or out of Germany and even extended its restrictions to goods going from one neutral to another if they had in them anything of German origin.

In December, so as not to abandon its rights by default, the United States complained mildly against British practices. Later it protested the practice of the British navy of forcing American ships into control ports located in the combat zones the President had forbidden Americans to enter. The angriest protests stemmed from British seizure and censoring of American mail, but these frictions over technicalities blew over in the spring of 1940.

Finland's Winter War

To the American people the most frustrating development during the *Sitzkrieg* was the winter war between Russia and Finland. Distrusting Hitler, Russia's dictator, Josef Stalin, sought to secure his northern borders against Germany. Immediately after grabbing part of Poland, he forced the three Baltic republics of

Estonia, Latvia, and Lithuania, to submit to Russian control. Then he demanded that Finland cede strategic territory to him.

In resisting the Soviet demands, the Finns appealed to Roosevelt to intervene with Moscow in their behalf. Sympathetic to Finland's plight, the President sent a message to the president of the Soviet Union in October, 1939, expressing the hope that Russia would temper her demands and later offered his good offices for a peaceful solution, but his intervention had no effect on the Russians. In the early hours of November 30, without a declaration of war, the Red army invaded Finland.

The American people, who held the Finns in special favor because they had paid their debts, burned with indignation against what Roosevelt called "this dreadful rape of Finland."[5] Although he considered severing diplomatic relations with Russia, the President never did so; nor did he invoke the neutrality legislation. His strongest move was a moral embargo on the shipment of airplanes and other strategic equipment to Russia. In an action supported by Roosevelt, however, the League, in its last meeting, expelled Russia for her aggression against Finland.

The Finns persistently pleaded for American aid. They received wide sympathy but little tangible assistance.[6] The American government granted them a moratorium on their debt payments and loans totaling $30 million, but with a proviso that these funds could not be used to purchase munitions.

To the amazement of the world the doughty Finns held off poorly prepared Russian troops for several months, but the mass of numbers was too much for them, and on March 12, 1940, they made peace on Russia's terms. Although these terms were harsh, the Finns managed to retain their independence.

Despite American dislike of the Soviets, Roosevelt's policy was based on avoiding any action that might encourage the Russians to lean more heavily on the Germans. Nonetheless, American relations with the Soviet Union at the end of the winter war, relations which had never been cordial, were marked with a new bitterness.

The Italian Problem

With the coming of spring, Hitler launched a great offensive in the west and shattered American illusions about a deadlock in the phony war. On April 9, Nazi forces occupied Denmark, invaded Norway, and overcame Allied resistance there. A month later German armies plunged into Belgium, the Netherlands, and Luxembourg, and swept into France.

During these weeks of Nazi *Blitzkrieg*, Roosevelt tried to keep Mussolini from joining his German ally, attacking Yugoslavia and Greece, and endangering the Allied routes through the Mediterranean to the East. After the German offensive began, Roosevelt sent Mussolini four personal pleas to stay out of the war, but Hitler had already committed *Il Duce* to joining him.

On June 10, as French armies were crumbling before the blows of German armored columns in the north, Mussolini declared war on France and Britain and invaded France from the south. Before the Italians struck, Britain's new Prime Minister, Winston Churchill, and France's new Premier, Paul Reynaud, had implored Roosevelt by transatlantic telephone to send planes, guns, ships, and whatever aid the United States could offer. "Can you stretch your hand across the ocean to help us save civilization?" Reynaud asked.[7] Since the United States lacked supplies even for its own defense, Roosevelt could offer little, but on June 5 he did announce the sale of surplus arms and munitions from the First World War to France and Britain.

America Becomes a Nonbelligerent

Although Roosevelt's gesture offered meager consolation to the reeling Allies, it marked a significant turn in American policy. The President now took the position that traditional neutrality offered no safeguard against war. By sending arms from government supplies, he violated international law and adopted a position of "nonbelligerency," meaning that the United States would aid the Allies in every way it could, short of war.

In a speech at Charlottesville, Virginia, on the day Italy invaded France, he first denounced Mussolini's deed as a "stab in the back" and then announced his new policy to the world. "In our American unity," he said, "we will pursue two obvious and simultaneous courses: we will extend to the opponents of force the material resources of this nation, and at the same time we will harness and speed up the use of those resources in order that we ourselves in the Americas may have equipment and training equal to the task of any emergency and every defense."[8]

As a supporter of the administration explained it to a prominent isolationist critic, if the new policy offended Hitler he would have to make war on the United States because American forces would not attack him. If, on the other hand, it helped the Allies to stop Hitler, then it would prove itself the best policy for defending the country and keeping it out of war.

Several days later, as France was falling, Reynaud begged desperately for assurance that the United States would enter the war to keep France from going under "like a drowning man." Deeply touched, Roosevelt answered that he had gone as far as he could in promising increasing quantities of supplies. He could offer no military aid. "Only Congress," he said, "could make such commitments."[9]

On June 22, in the same railroad car where Marshal Foch had presented the Allied armistice terms to the beaten Germans in 1918, France surrendered to Hitler. An authoritarian government, under eighty-four-year-old Marshal Henri Philippe Pétain, governed unoccupied France.

Hitler's triumphs aroused a sense of peril in the minds of many Americans.

Surveys of public opinion from March through June revealed a marked change among those questioned in favor of increased aid to the Allies.[10] A powerful pressure group, the Committee to Defend America by Aiding the Allies, contributed to this shift in opinion. Headed by a Republican newspaper editor from Kansas, William Allen White, it spawned six hundred branches within six weeks of its founding in May. It sought to keep America out of the war by giving the Allies enough material aid to defeat Hitler. It rallied support behind the President when he discarded neutrality for nonbelligerency and, after the fall of France, developed an effective propaganda campaign calling for support of Britain as America's best defense.

Within the Committee to Defend America were certain influential Easterners who thought the Committee not sufficiently militant. They formed the Century Group which favored active intervention, war if necessary. At the very least, they wanted greater aid to the Allies than was possible under the existing legislation. Aware of the shift in public sentiment that had brought many of Roosevelt's former critics to support his foreign policy, William Allen White sent the President some friendly advice. "As an old friend," he said, "let me warn you that maybe you will not be able to lead the American people unless you catch up with them. They are going fast."[11] Nonetheless, isolationist sentiment was still strong and the majority of Americans shrank from the thought of direct intervention.

Roosevelt, meantime, had already taken steps to oppose the Axis powers. He froze all the economic assets in the United States of the countries seized by Germany and Russia. In addition to economic warfare against the totalitarians, he consistently refused to recognize their conquests and maintained diplomatic relations with governments in exile of the fallen countries.

Spain, too, felt the pressure of American displeasure. After the fall of France, she abandoned neutrality for nonbelligerency. For a while it looked as if Franco might bring Spain into the war on the Axis side, but he was too dependent on Britain and the United States for food, oil, and other supplies to do so. Roosevelt cooperated closely with the British in applying a constant economic pressure on Spain to keep Franco out of the war and help safeguard Britain's position at Gibraltar, the vital gate to the Mediterranean.

At the same time, the President stepped up demands for rearmament, telling Congress that "the American people must recast their thinking about national protection" and emphasizing a vast increase in the nation's air power.[12] Congress responded speedily, authorizing greater war production, more Army personnel and air strength.

If France and Britain were both defeated and the Axis powers acquired their fleets, Germany and Italy would have an overwhelming naval superiority over the United States. To meet such a contingency and to maintain a superiority over Japan, the President asked Congress in June to appropriate funds for a two-ocean navy. Less than one month later, Congress responded by agreeing to an un-precedented naval increase of 1,325,000 tons and the largest naval appropriation ever authorized up to that time. By the end of September, when the defense legislation was completed, Congress had broken all peacetime records by ap-propriating over five billion dollars. This was more than the President had requested.

In a uniquely farsighted move, the President had set up a National Defense Research Committee in June to work on new weapons, particularly to give government financial support to atomic research. It was a race against time because German scientists had succeeded in splitting the uranium atom in January, 1938, and were known to be working on an atomic bomb.[13]

A controversial issue that met with far more resistance than the defense ap-propriations was conscription. In June, as France fell, Senator Edward R. Burke, an anti-New Deal Democrat from Nebraska, and James W. Wadsworth, a New York Republican, presented a bill calling for compulsory military service. When the President finally admitted that he favored such a bill, isolationists set off a barrage of denunciation. Senator Gerald Nye attacked the bill, saying that "the only emergency in this country is the one conjured up by those who want to send our boys to Europe or Asia."[14] Nonetheless, by the middle of September, the Burke-Wadsworth Bill became law, and the nation had its first peacetime conscription.

Embargoes Against Japan

After the fall of France, Britain and China, although committed to separate wars, were the only two major opponents of the Axis powers still fighting. Roosevelt supported both, but his aid to China was much more limited than the assistance offered the British. Even though he had made clear his determined opposi-tion to Japan's "new order," he moved cautiously against her. During the first six months of the European war, in fact, relations with Japan were outwardly quiet. When the commercial treaty of 1911 expired in January, 1940, he did not impose sanctions against Japan, despite the insistence of many Americans for economic action against her. The Department of State merely informed the Japanese that trade relations would henceforth be on a day-to-day basis and would be contingent on future developments.

When Hitler overran western Europe, the Japanese took advantage of the crisis by increasing the tempo of their war against Chiang Kai-shek and by threatening British, French, and Dutch possessions in the Far East. In response to Japan's southward threats, particularly against French Indochina, American policy began to change. In May, as a warning of displeasure, Roosevelt moved the fleet's base from San Diego, California, to Pearl Harbor, two thousand miles into the Pacific.

On July 2, 1940, Congress passed a law placing certain strategic materials under a strict licensing system, and on July 26 the President signed an order to include aviation gasoline, lubricating oils, and high-grade iron and steel scrap under the licensing system. Japan protested, but in vain.

Roosevelt had imposed only a partial embargo on strategic exports to Japan because he feared that stringent economic sanctions might provoke her to a war he wanted to avoid. He was convinced that Germany presented a greater danger to the United States than did the Japanese, and he would do nothing that would detract from his efforts to stop Hitler. Yet the new policy, even though it proved ineffectual, was the beginning of economic sanctions that would eventually threaten to strangle Tokyo.[15]

In August, the Japanese began their southward expansion by forcing the French to surrender bases in northern Indochina. Although the United States did not give the French in Indochina the assistance they pleaded for, it did retaliate against the Japanese. On September 25, the government announced a huge new loan to Chiang Kai-shek and on the following day established a complete embargo on all types of iron and steel scrap. "This is a direct hit at Japan," Secretary of War Henry L. Stimson recorded in his diary, "a point which I have hoped we would hit for a long time."[16]

Two days later in Berlin, Japan signed a formal military alliance with Germany and Italy, the Tripartite Pact. Japan recognized Hitler's "new order" in Europe, and Germany and Italy accepted Japan's in Greater East Asia. The most significant part of the treaty, Article 3, was directed against the United States. If the United States went to war against any one of the signatories, the other two promised to assist the third party.

Hitler, who feared American intervention in the European war, hoped to deter it with the threat of a two-ocean war. Japan's Foreign Minister, in fact, explained the purpose of the alliance as meeting Germany's desire to prevent American entry into the war and Japan's wish to avoid war with the United States.[17] The Japanese insisted that Article 3 did not bind them automatically to attack the United States if it went to war against Germany. Even though the Tripartite Pact left Japan a certain freedom of action, Americans were convinced that the fighting in Asia and Europe had become one war.[18]

Destroyers for Bases

Hitler, meanwhile, had turned the fury of his air force against England. Americans watched the grim British resistance to the Nazi pummeling with admiration and horror, expecting daily that Hitler would add a new conquest to his earlier triumphs. Aware of the intensely pro-British sentiment of the American people, Prime Minister Winston Churchill hoped that the bombing of British cities would

DESTROYERS FOR BASES, 1940

The map labels: CANADA, NEWFOUNDLAND, Placentia (St. Johns), UNITED STATES, Atlantic, Bermuda, Ocean, BAHAMAS, Great Exuma I., CUBA, PUERTO RICO, Jamaica, Antigua, Caribbean Sea, St. Lucia, Trinidad, SOUTH AMERICA, Georgetown, BR. GUIANA, ★ Bases acquired by U.S. from Britain, 1940

rouse them to join the war against the Axis powers. Although Americans were unwilling to go that far, Roosevelt did make a spectacular gesture to aid the British.

Losses to submarines plus continuing destruction by the Nazi air force had cut the number of British destroyers to so few that the Royal Navy was unable to protect vital sea lanes and patrol Britain's coastlines. In July, 1940, therefore, Churchill appealed to Roosevelt for the loan or lease of forty or fifty old destroyers of the First World War vintage that were tied up in American shipyards. Since the British needed the ships immediately, the President was certain he could not overcome the opposition of the Republican minority in the Senate quickly enough to do any good. Lawyers from the Century Group and his own Attorney General finally persuaded him that he could legally make the transfer without a treaty. Wendell Willkie, the Republican presidential candidate, moreover, offered indirect assurance that he would not make a campaign issue of the proposed transfer.

Isolationists increasingly opposed the exchange. The Chicago *Tribune*, for instance, warned that "the sale of the Navy's ships to a nation at war would be an act of war. If we want to get into war, the destroyers offer as good a way as any of accomplishing the purpose."[19]

After some involved negotiations, the President nonetheless acted. In an executive agreement completed on September 2, he turned over fifty of the overage destroyers directly to the British. As outright gifts, Churchill gave the United States sites for air and naval bases on Bermuda and Newfoundland for ninety-nine years, and in return for the destroyers granted leases to bases on British possessions ranging from the Bahamas to Guiana. He also pledged never to scuttle or surrender the British fleet.

Roosevelt's deed made the United States a virtual ally of Britain, violated existing international law, and may have violated domestic law forbidding the sale of military property to a foreign government. The Attorney General justified the act on the principle of retaliation. Hitler's aggressions and repeated flouting of international law, he said, released the United States from the rules of neutrality.

Roosevelt presented the transfer to the people as a bargain in national defense. "It is," he told Congress, "an epochal and far-reaching act of preparation for continental defense in the face of grave danger."[20] Most Americans apparently also considered it a good bargain and generally approved. Even some isolationists, who for years had wanted to secure similar bases in exchange for a cancellation of the war debts, went along with the destroyer deal, and Congress later indirectly gave its consent when it voted money to develop the bases.

Some administration critics could not be won over. A headline in the St. Louis Post-Dispatch said that "Dictator Roosevelt Commits an Act of War."[21] Even Churchill admitted in his later writings that the destroyer deal was "a decidedly unneutral act."[22] The United States had now clearly entered a state of "limited war," another turning point in foreign policy.

Until the destroyer deal became public, isolationists had consistently opposed the administration's unneutral foreign policy, but only in various unconnected clusters. The day after the President had disclosed the destroyer trade, a group of them announced the formation of the America First Committee, destined to be the strongest of the isolationist organizations. It counted a number of colorful personalities among its leaders, including General Robert E. Wood, chairman of the board of Sears, Roebuck and Company, as its national chairman and Colonel Charles A. Lindbergh, the aviator, as its leading orator.

Most of the America First supporters were middlewestern Republicans who distrusted the President for various reasons, but it was not a purely sectional organization or a partisan political movement.[23] Thousands of sincere Americans of varied background and from both political parties joined and contributed to it. It also attracted support from a number of fringe hate organizations, from anti-Semites, and from Nazi sympathizers. This minority support tarnished its reputation.

Believing that Hitler did not menace American security, the movement sought to keep the country out of the war by building up the defenses of the Western Hemisphere. "American democracy," the committee's announcement of principles said, "can be preserved only by keeping out of the European war."[24] It opposed any aid to Britain, such as the destroyer deal, that might involve the country in war.

The Third Term Campaign

Public opinion, as reflected in the polls of the autumn of 1940, showed paradoxical support for the widely differing objectives of both the Committee to Defend America by Aiding the Allies and the America First Committee. An overwhelming majority of Americans questioned by the poll takers favored aid to Britain and opposition to Hitler, and at the same time opposed entry into the war.[25]

This confused state of public sentiment formed the background of the presidential election. Republican "internationalists" outmaneuvered the "isolationists" in their party by securing the nomination of Wendell Willkie of Indiana for the Presidency and by winning the adoption of a platform calling for prompt aid to the victims of aggression. Willkie was a likeable political novice, a colorful figure, and a former Democrat who favored aid to Britain and had supported the President's foreign policy.

Roosevelt defied the two-term tradition in accepting the nomination of his party, and in foreign affairs, of course, stood on his record of aid to Britain. Since both candidates opposed the Axis, for awhile it looked as if isolationism had been removed as an issue in the campaign. "Whatever happens in the election," *The Economist* of London pointed out, "the foreign policy of the United States in the remainder of 1940 and for four more years will be based on assistance to Great Britain." Both parties and both candidates, nonetheless, catered to the desire to stay out of the war.

As the campaign progressed, fear of the war seemed to become a dominant issue. In the last weeks before the election, Old Guard politicians persuaded Willkie he had to take advantage of the antiwar sentiment if he expected to win. Willkie, therefore, questioned the sincerity of the President's statements that he wanted to keep the country out of war and isolationist Republicans dubbed Roosevelt a warmonger. Willkie's attacks appeared to be bringing results, so the President abandoned his campaign of aloofness and lashed back. "I have said this before, but I shall say it again and again and again," Roosevelt told the people. "Your boys are not going to be sent into any foreign wars."[26]

This categorical statement undoubtedly seemed assurance enough to most voters of the President's intentions. Later, however, critics were to use the statement as evidence that the President had tried to deceive the people. In any event,

Roosevelt won another victory, though with a majority considerably less than that of 1936. Whether or not Roosevelt's re-election was, as many considered it, a mandate for more aid to Britain and China, the administration interpreted it as such.

During the election campaign, it had already become clear that Britain would need drastically increased aid from the United States if she were to survive. She had no more funds for continued cash payment for American supplies. Churchill explained his country's plight in detail to Roosevelt. Britain, he said, would need enormous amounts of arms, ships, planes, and other goods, and he asked the President to make them available to her through a "decisive act of non-belligerency."[27]

With the election behind him, Roosevelt had made plans for more assistance to the British, but found that he had exhausted the stopgap devices for aiding them under the existing laws. The time had come, his advisers told him, to go to Congress and the people for legislation that would give the British the all-out aid he had promised.

Seeking some way, as he put it, of removing the "silly, foolish, old dollar sign," Roosevelt hit upon the novel idea of lending goods instead of dollars. As he saw it, his plan would get around Britain's financial crisis, avoid the problem of more uncollectable war debts, and replace the dollar sign, he said, with a "gentlemen's obligation to repay in kind." The President explained the idea with the analogy of the garden hose. If my neighbor's home caught fire, he said, I would not demand payment beforehand for use of my hose. "If he can take my garden hose and connect it up with his hydrant, I may help him put out his fire."[28] The neighbor would return the hose later. So it would be with the loan of supplies to Britain.

In a fireside chat Roosevelt frankly told the people that the United States "must be the great arsenal of democracy," and asked them, in effect, to go beyond aid to Britain short of war by committing themselves to increased assistance even at the risk of war.[29]

The Lend-Lease Law

A few days later the President sent his annual message to Congress and again emphasized that the fate of the nation was linked to the European war. He asked for authority and funds to manufacture war equipment of all kinds for opponents of the "aggressor nations" to be paid for at the end of the war in goods and services. The United States, he declared, must help make secure a world where "four essential freedoms"—of speech, of worship, from want, and from fear—would prevail.[30]

Four days later Roosevelt's plan, drafted in the Treasury Department and known as the Lend-Lease bill, was introduced simultaneously to both houses of Congress. Two months of heated debate followed. The America First Committee mobilized its forces to defeat the bill. In Congress most of the opposition came from isolationist Republicans and a few conservative Democrats. Senator Robert A. Taft, a Republican from Ohio, summarized the essence of the opposition argument in a few words. The bill, he said, would "give the President power to carry on a kind of undeclared war all over the world, in which America would do everything except actually put soldiers in the front-line trenches where the fighting is."[31]

Despite the intense opposition, the bill, with a few amendments, passed in the House by a vote of 260 to 165 and in the Senate by a vote of 60 to 31. It passed primarily as a party measure, for Republicans voted heavily against it. The President signed Lend-Lease into law on March 11, 1941.

Under the deceptive title, "An Act to Promote the Defense of the United States," Lend-Lease authorized the President to sell, lease, or lend, under such terms as he thought proper, arms, munitions, food, and other defense articles to any country whose defense he deemed vital to the defense of the United States. It forbade the Navy to convoy vessels carrying Lend-Lease equipment. By removing the isolationist restrictions on the President's actions, Lend-Lease added another bond to the unwritten alliance with Britain.[32]

During February and March, while Congress had been debating, British and American Chiefs of Staff had been supporting the unwritten alliance with secret conferences in Washington. They adopted a joint report, the "ABC-1 Staff Agreement," outlining common military strategy against the Axis that would make Lend-Lease most effective, and agreed upon a plan of joint or coordinated military operations if and when the United States entered the war. If Japan joined her allies in the war, the British and Americans agreed nonetheless to continue to regard Germany as the principal enemy and to devote their main effort to her defeat.

Just after the Washington staff conferences ended the American Chief of Naval Operations wrote to his fleet commanders. "The question as to our entry into the war," he said, "now seems to be *when*, and not *whether*."[33] The admiral was premature. Neither the President nor his State Department had yet gone that far, but foreign policy had completed another decisive change. Although not yet fighting, the United States had taken measures that placed it unofficially at war with the Axis powers.

Before the Lend-Lease program could get started, misfortune again overtook the British and brought the question of American aid to another crisis. Late in October, 1940, Mussolini's poorly prepared army had invaded Greece in a campaign that turned into an ignominious defeat for the Italians. In Africa, Italian troops suffered equally disastrous defeats at the hands of the British. Hitler intervened in the spring of 1941 to aid his faltering ally. In less than three weeks of *blitz* warfare in April, Nazi troops conquered Yugoslavia and Greece, forcing the British to evacuate without equipment the small forces they had sent to Greece. In North Africa, British forces fell back before the slashing attack of the brilliant German tank commander, Erwin Rommel.

The Battle of the Atlantic

At the same time, Hitler stepped up his assault on British shipping. In March, he extended the combat area of his submarines and surface raiders to include Iceland and the coastal waters of Greenland. To stop the flow of American supplies to Britain, he flung part of his air force into the battle of the Atlantic and sent his U-boats out in swarms called "wolf packs." These new tactics took a staggering toll of British shipping.

To help the British withstand the new assaults, Roosevelt, primarily through his powers as Commander-in-Chief of the Armed Forces, took a number of steps that gradually brought the United States into the battle of the Atlantic. In March, 1941, he authorized naval yards to repair British ships; transferred ten Coast Guard cutters to the British to help them in antisubmarine operations; and seized thirty Axis and thirty-five Danish ships interned in American ports.

In answer to Hitler's extension of the Atlantic war zone, the President pushed the neutrality zone, proclaimed at Panama in 1939, far out into the Atlantic on April 10 to include Greenland within the Western Hemisphere. He ordered naval patrols to comb the Atlantic for, but not to attack, Nazi submarines and raiders from the American coastlines to 25° of west longitude and to broadcast the position of the U-boats to British ships and planes. On that same day the destroyer u.s.s. *Niblack*, while on reconnaissance in waters near Iceland, dropped depth bombs on a U-boat and touched off the first known clash between American and Axis naval vessels.

On that day, too, Roosevelt took two more steps to relieve the British shipping crisis. The Department of State announced an agreement, disavowed by the captive government at Copenhagen, with the Danish Minister in Washington placing Greenland temporarily under American control and allowing the United States to build bases there. The President also issued a proclamation declaring the Red Sea no longer a combat zone forbidden to American ships. This made possible the shipment of goods in American ships directly to the hard-pressed British forces in Egypt.

Those measures were not enough. By mid-April, it became clear that the United States could not serve effectively as an "arsenal of democracy" if the goods it produced never reached the British. The next step in overcoming the U-boat menace was to convoy ships carrying Lend-Lease equipment. "I realized from the first," a leading isolationist, was reported as saying, "after the Lend-Lease bill was passed, that the next step would be that the warmongers in this country would cry for convoys, and everyone recognizes the fact that convoys mean war." [34] Roosevelt's strategy of presenting Lend-Lease as a means of assuring a British victory without American intervention had backfired.

Although convinced that the battle of the Atlantic was crucial and that more had to be done to protect the North Atlantic shipping lanes, Roosevelt did not resort to convoy escorts. He called his antisubmarine ships "patrols."

In May, the President ordered three battleships, an aircraft carrier, and supporting vessels, from Pearl Harbor to join the Atlantic patrols. On May 21, a German submarine sank the American freighter *Robin Moor* in the middle of the South Atlantic, leaving the survivors in open lifeboats. This was the first torpedoing of an American ship, an act that apparently violated Hitler's orders not to attack American ships, for the *Führer* was anxious to avoid incidents with the United States. Within a few days, nonetheless, his chief naval commander announced that vessels carrying Lend-Lease equipment were subject to attack under international law, and that German forces would attack ships escorting them.

Immediately thereafter, Roosevelt broadcast another of his fireside chats. He told the people of the Navy's activities in the North Atlantic, explained that a German victory there would imperil the security of the United States itself, and that even though Britain's navy had blocked a Germany victory, U-boats were sinking ships twice as fast as the combined British and American shipyards could replace them. The only way to meet the Nazi peril, he warned, was to increase the nation's shipbuilding program and to help in cutting the losses at sea. "Our patrols," he added, "are helping now to insure delivery of the needed supplies to Britain. All additional measures necessary to deliver the goods will be taken." [35] He closed by proclaiming an unlimited national emergency.

Roosevelt's next step was an executive order of June 14 freezing German and Italian economic assets in the United States, followed two days later by a notice to the two Axis powers that they were to close their consulates, tourist agencies, and information bureaus in the United States. Germany and Italy retaliated immediately by closing American consulates in their jurisdiction. That same month British and American military and naval authorities began regular consultation and planning in Washington and London.

Friction with Japan

As an answer to the Tripartite Alliance, meanwhile, some of the President's advisers had urged him to take strong measures against Japan also, particularly a full oil embargo. Anxious to avoid a war in the Far East that would jeopardize aid to England, Roosevelt had resisted most of the pressures, but had cautiously hardened policy against the Japanese.

Early in October, 1940, the Department of State had shown its concern over increasing friction with Japan by warning Americans in the Far East to leave unless compelled to remain because of urgent business. The stronger American policy also stiffened British resistance. In July, despite American disapproval, the British had yielded to Japanese demands and had closed the Burma Road, the main overland supply route to Chiang's China, but now they reopened it. At the same time Chiang Kai-shek had pleaded for more assistance and an alliance with the United States and Britain to counterbalance the Tripartite Pact. Roosevelt would not commit himself to such an entanglement, but after his re-election had promised more aid and had adopted a bolder course against Japan.

The American government placed more and more restrictions on exports going to Japan. It cut off machine tools, chemicals, and various raw materials essential to war production. In applying the economic sanctions piecemeal, the government hoped to produce a cumulative effect that would deter further Japanese expansion but that would not provoke immediate retaliation.

"This was," Cordell Hull explained, "the policy of slowing Japan up, so to speak, as much as we could by fighting a rear guard diplomatic action, without doing it so stringently as to drive her to get her supplies by making an attack on the Netherlands [East Indies]."

The United States also increased its aid to Chiang Kai-shek, ultimately promising him Lend-Lease equipment, encouraged the Dutch to resist Japanese demands on their Southwest Pacific possessions, reinforced the Philippines, fortified Guam, and coordinated plans with the British and Dutch for the defense of the East Indies and Malaya against a Japanese attack. An American diplomat in Tokyo bluntly told the Japanese in February, 1941, that the United States did not want war, but if their forces moved south, attacked Singapore for example, war might come. In March the American Navy sent several cruisers and a number of destroyers to Australia and New Zealand, a visit symbolizing Anglo-American solidarity in the Pacific.

Japan's response to the new American policy was mixed. Certain of her leaders, through unofficial channels, sought an understanding with the hope of averting war. Others, particularly militarists, wished to take advantage of Hitler's victories by strengthening Axis ties and moving southward. Before embarking on a program of expansion to the south, they wanted to neutralize the threat of a huge Soviet army hovering on the borders of Manchukuo and China and to make Japan's international position as strong as possible in case of a showdown with the United States.

Foreign Minister Yosuke Matsuoka, therefore, visited Berlin, obtained a promise of support from Hitler in case of war with the United States, and then journeyed to Moscow. There, on April 13, he signed a five-year neutrality pact with the Soviets. It pledged each country to respect the other's territory and to remain neutral if the other were attacked by outside powers. On paper, at least, it gave Japan security in the north if her advance to the south brought war with the United States and Britain.

In Washington in March, as if to counterbalance Matsuoka's diplomacy, Japan's new Ambassador, Admiral Kichisaburo Nomura, began informal conversations with Secretary Hull directed toward some kind of an understanding that would patch up relations between their countries.[36] The repetitious talks, held in Hull's apartment over a period of several months, grew out of Japan's desire to end the American sanctions, and from the American objective of separating Japan from the Axis.

Six proposals, three by the Japanese dated April 9, May 12, and June 15, and three by the Americans of May 16, May 31, and June 21, were the significant products of the talks. Three major points of conflict stood out: interpretation of the Tripartite Pact, how to settle the China "incident," and the nature of Japan's economic activities and expansion in China and the Southwest Pacific.

The United States urged Japan to nullify the Axis alliance; the Japanese refused. The Japanese wanted the United States to stop its aid to Chiang Kai-shek and to leave them to deal with China without outside interference. Americans demanded that Japan evacuate China, respect her territorial integrity, and recognize the principle of the Open Door. In the Southwest Pacific the United States insisted on specific Japanese pledges against territorial expansion of any kind. Japan refused such pledges but insisted that her planned expansion in that area was economic, not military.

In addition to seeking an end to sanctions, the Japanese wanted the United States not to acquire new bases in the Southwest Pacific. Citing Japan's recent expansion in that area, particularly in Indochina and Siam, the United States refused to make such a promise. Each side distrusted the moves of the other in the Southwest Pacific.[37]

By the middle of June, it was clear, the United States was determined to convert Japan to policies of peace, and Japan still insisted on a free hand in Asia. The United States wanted a sweeping agreement based on principles, and Japan sought any kind of an agreement that would end the sanctions and preserve her gains in Asia. The conversations between Hull and Nomura had brought no agreement and no retreat by either side. They were stalemated.

Russian–German Front

Hitler, who had never given up his idea of conquering what the Nazis called "living space" in the East, had in the meanwhile completed plans for invading Russia. His accommodation with the Soviets had begun to deteriorate soon after the fall of France. Distrusting each other, the Germans and the Russians had disagreed over the division of spoils in Europe and the Middle East, over who should dominate Finland, Bulgaria, Rumania, and other countries where their interests clashed. To eliminate the Soviet Union as an obstacle to his planned domination of eastern Europe, Hitler sent his war machine into Russia over a front two thousand miles wide on June 22, 1941.

In addition to making a dramatic change in the character of the war, the invasion of Russia opened a new chapter in American diplomacy. It relieved the United States of the fear that the Germans would soon overwhelm the British in North Africa and dispelled the danger of an immediate invasion of England. It also freed Japan from any lingering apprehension over a Russian attack while she expanded southward and hence left the United States as the only major opponent of Japanese policy.

The American government had known of Hitler's invasion plans for many months and had warned the Russians about them. Roosevelt had also promised Churchill he would offer Stalin assistance once the Germans marched eastward. Yet at the time of Hitler's attack, American relations with Russia were strained, and opinion toward the Soviets was hostile. Many Americans were pleased to see the rival totalitarian countries trying to destroy each other and were opposed to any kind of aid for Russia. "It's a case of dog eat dog," one of the President's isolationist critics remarked. "Stalin is as bloody-handed as Hitler. I don't think we should help either one."[38] Yet, most Americans preferred to see Stalin rather than Hitler win.

Roosevelt, therefore, moved cautiously in extending help to the Russians. A short time earlier the government had frozen Soviet funds in the United States amounting to about $40 million. The President freed them on June 24. Two days later he announced that he would not invoke the Neutrality Act against the Soviet Union because the Russo-German war did not imperil the United States. He also declared his readiness to assist the Russians but pointed out that aid could be effective only if the war were a long one. Most Americans and the President's own military advisers were convinced that the Russians would collapse before the Nazi juggernaut within three months or less.

Roosevelt, nonetheless, was determined to honor his promise to Churchill by offering the Soviets whatever assistance he could as quickly as possible. Since Americans were torn between their loathing for Hitler and their hatred of Communism, few of them made strong protests when the President announced that he would help the Soviet Union. Most Americans could justify assistance to Stalin by reasoning that they were not contributing to a Communist victory but instead were helping to prolong the Nazi-Soviet fighting. Their aid would buy time for the United States and Britain to build stronger defenses against Hitler.

Roosevelt, moreover, used the breathing spell brought by the Russian war to build defenses and strengthen the North Atlantic supply route. Foremost among various pressing defense needs was that of keeping the recently enlarged Army intact. Under the Selective Service Act of 1940 the terms of service of the 900,000 men drafted in the autumn of that year were soon to expire. Early in July, 1941, therefore, the President gave the War Department permission to ask Congress to extend the term of service for draftees and to remove the provisions of the draft law prohibiting selectees from serving outside the Western Hemisphere.

The War Department's request spurred Congress into heated controversy, pitting some administration supporters as well as isolationists against any change in the draft law. The widely publicized remarks of two prominent British field generals contributed to the determination of the opposition. "We certainly are going to need American manpower," one of them said, "just as we did in the last war." [39] The administration's leading military spokesman tried to assure Congress that there was no plan for a new expeditionary force, arguing that the needs of national security alone required an extension of the draft.

After a long debate, the Senate added six months to a draftee's term of service, making a total obligation of eighteen months. In the House the opposition to the extension was firm and bitter. When the bill finally came to a vote on August 12 it passed with 203 for and 202 against. Only one vote kept the Army from dissolution in a time of national emergency.

Shortly after the beginning of the debate on the draft law, the President dramatically extended America's commitment in the North Atlantic. Following an agreement with Churchill and the Prime Minister of Iceland, he sent about four thousand Marines to join British forces in the occupation of Iceland.

This move pushed the defense zone farther out into the Atlantic and made the United States virtually a cobelligerent of the British in the battle of the Atlantic. Naval patrols could now convoy American and Icelandic shipping as far as Iceland and had orders to destroy hostile forces which threatened it. The next logical step was to convert the "patrols" into convoy escorts protecting British shipping.

The Atlantic Charter

Roosevelt, who had been corresponding with Churchill for over a year, had long wanted to meet the Prime Minister. "I have just got to see Churchill myself," he told a cabinet officer, "in order to explain things to him." [40] Hitler's Russian offensive finally gave both statesmen the short respite needed for their first meeting at Placentia Bay, Newfoundland, aboard the cruiser *Augusta* on August 9.

During the four days of secret conferences, the two statesmen arranged for the American Navy to escort British as well as American ships in the convoys of the North Atlantic, a system that went into operation later in the month. This was one of the few definite commitments Roosevelt made. Churchill urged the President to join him in warning Japan that if she struck at Malaya or the Netherlands East Indies, war would follow. Roosevelt refused, because he could not promise to use the armed forces without approval from Congress. He did not, moreover, wish to divert any strength from the struggle against Hitler.

Although more concerned with the immediate problems of winning the war than with postwar political objectives, Roosevelt and Churchill issued as a press release a vague joint declaration calling "for a better future world," and known as the Atlantic Charter. The eight principles of this document, which was merely a by-product and yet the most publicized result of the conference, were: 1. Neither country sought territorial aggrandizement; 2. They desired no territorial changes that did not agree with the wishes of the people concerned; 3. They recognized the right of all peoples to choose their own form of government; 4. Without impairing existing obligations, they favored access to the trade and raw materials of the world to all nations; 5. They wished collaboration between all nations to secure improved labor standards, economic advancement, and social security; 6. They sought a peace that would secure all peoples freedom from fear and want; 7. All should have freedom to travel the seas; 8. They wanted a peace based on an abandonment of the use of force and on disarmament, pending the establishment of a permanent system of general security.

More significant than the Atlantic Charter's principles was the fact that it announced the common purpose behind the unwritten Anglo-American alliance, a particularly bold step for Roosevelt to take while the United States was not yet a belligerent. Isolationists, aware of its implied significance, greeted the news of the Placentia conference with a flurry of protest. "President Roosevelt is retracing, one by one," the New York *Journal-American* said, "all of the steps toward war taken by President Woodrow Wilson—steps which the American people later and in the light of calm reflection and sober judgment overwhelmingly stamped as mistakes."[41] Roosevelt countered with assurances that he had made no new commitments, and that he believed a shooting war more likely to come in the Pacific than in the Atlantic.

Before the news stories on the Atlantic Charter had faded, an incident in the Middle East cast a shadow across its principles. On August 25, after presenting Iran with an ultimatum she rejected, Britain and Russia invaded and occupied that strategically helpless country. The Shah immediately appealed to Roosevelt to take "steps to put an end to these acts of aggression."[42]

The invasion itself had placed the United States in the predicament of trying to uphold the recently enunciated principles of the Atlantic Charter and at the same time of attempting to avoid any action that would obstruct Britain's and Russia's fight against Hitler. The American government, therefore, did nothing. With a twist of bitterness, the Iranian Minister in Washington told Hull that he was disappointed in the failure of the United States "to carry out its preachments of the eight principles underlying peaceful and free nations. . . ."[43]

The Undeclared War

Despite their growing determination to stand by Britain, most Americans still hoped to stay out of the shooting war. Public opinion polls at the end of September showed that 75 to 80 per cent of those who expressed themselves were opposed to direct participation in the war. These readings on the available barometers of public opinion placed Roosevelt in a dilemma. His military advisers all agreed that Germany could not be defeated without American military intervention. Yet, if he wanted to bring his people into the fight, as Churchill believed he did, he was unable to see how he could do it without dividing the country. Until a slim pretext presented itself, Roosevelt even groped for a way of telling the people of his decision to extend the protection of convoy escorts to British ships.

A destroyer, the U.S.S. *Greer*, en route to Iceland on the night of September 4, had trailed a German submarine for several hours, broadcasting its position to British planes. When the harassed Nazis fired two torpedoes that missed, the *Greer* dropped depth bombs on them. Even before he had all the facts, the President seized upon the incident to justify his new convoy policy. The U-boat attack, he announced over a world-wide radio hookup on September 11, was "piracy, legally and morally." Since the time for "active defense" had come, he said, "our patrolling vessels and planes will protect all merchant ships—not only American ships but ships of any flag—engaged in commerce in our defensive waters."[44] He then gave the Navy orders to shoot on sight all German and Italian ships of war in the American patrol zone.

The President thus finally resolved the convoy issue by declaring a shooting war against the naval forces of the European Axis powers. "So far as the Atlantic is concerned," the Chief of Naval Operations told a subordinate several days later, "we are all but, if not actually in it."[45] Regardless of point of view, few could deny that the President's new policy was the logical outcome of Lend-Lease and the unofficial war against the Axis.

Isolationists, nonetheless, charged the President with deceiving the people and with conspiring to drive them into war. Roosevelt's defenders denied this charge. They pointed out that available evidence on public opinion at the time indicated that most Americans, though not a vast majority of them, favored the President's policy.

Soviet funds in the United States, meanwhile, were almost exhausted. To keep supplies rolling to the Russians, the American government gave them a credit of $100 million in September to be repaid in the indefinite future with shipments of manganese, platinum, and other raw materials. The President and his advisers

602 A HISTORY OF AMERICAN FOREIGN POLICY

realized that this was a stopgap measure. Lend-Lease was the answer to Russia's lack of funds, and the core of the program of large-scale aid Roosevelt had in mind to buttress her resistance, but popular distrust of the Soviet Union was so strong that the President advanced his aid program slowly and indirectly.

Later that month, special American and British missions went to Moscow to appraise Russian needs. As a result, the United States agreed to send about one billion dollars in supplies, including tanks, planes, and guns, to Russia over a period of nine months. A month later Roosevelt declared the Soviet Union eligible for Lend-Lease aid.[46]

Roosevelt's next step, one he had considered for many months, was revision of the neutrality act. Since the United States was no longer neutral and the law stood in the way of untrammeled aid to Britain, he considered repeal or revision urgent. He asked Congress for a revision on October 9 to permit the arming of merchant ships and indirectly to abolish the war zones so that American ships could go to belligerent ports. These revisions, he said, would "carry out the true intent of the Lend-Lease Act by making it possible for the United States to help deliver the articles to those who are in a position effectively to use them."[47]

While Congress was debating the revision, a German submarine torpedoed the destroyer u.s.s. *Kearny* on the night of October 16–17 about four hundred miles south of Iceland, in a naval action that took eleven American lives. In a speech ten days later the President exploited the incident, announcing that "the shooting has started. And history has recorded who fired the first shot."[48]

Four days later the destroyer u.s.s. *Reuben James*, while on convoy duty about six hundred miles west of Iceland, became the first American warship to be destroyed in the war. Hit by a German torpedo, she went down with the loss of 115 lives. The President's fighting words had stirred the country. Yet neither incident produced a popular clamor for war. Isolationists, however, were alarmed. "You cannot," one of them said, "shoot your way a little bit into a war any more than you can go a little bit over Niagara Falls."[49]

Hitler, deeply enmeshed in the Russian campaign, still would not unleash an all-out submarine campaign against the United States. He gave orders to his submarine commanders, in fact, to avoid incidents that might provoke the United States into more drastic action. They were to fire only in self-defense.

Despite the increased tempo of the sea war, when the question of revising the neutrality law came to a vote in Congress in November, it passed by a slim majority. Congress, it was clear, still opposed active intervention. It had, nonetheless, voted to allow merchant ships to arm and sail to belligerent ports, a policy that would lead to more armed clashes with Axis U-boats. Without a formal declaration, the United States had at last expanded the shooting war by directly entering the battle of the North Atlantic.

Sanctions Against Japan

Hitler's attack on Russia, meanwhile, had disrupted Hull's talks with Nomura, but more important it had convinced Japan's militarists, led by Foreign Minister Matsuoka, that the golden moment for massive expansion to the south had come. To gain their southern objectives, Japan's leading civil and military figures, in an Imperial Conference of July 2, had decided they were willing to risk war with the United States, the only power at that time capable of stopping them.

In the previous December American cryptographers had cracked Japan's secret diplomatic code and were regularly deciphering messages from Tokyo's Foreign Office. Roosevelt and a few of his close advisers, therefore, were able to follow some of the internal workings of Japanese policy. Fearing an attack on Russia, as Matsuoka desired, the President warned Prime Minister Fumimaro Konoye on July 4 that Japanese aggression would endanger peace in the Pacific. Konoye replied with professions of peace and a denial of intentions to attack the Soviets.

Konoye, trapped by his hunger for imperial spoils, fear of the United States, and the knowledge that he could not go too far in denying the wishes of the militarists, led an allegedly moderate faction in the government that hoped to achieve some of Japan's objectives without war. Since Matsuoka stood in the way of such a policy, Konoye eased him out of the cabinet in the middle of July. The reshuffled cabinet did not, however, offer any basic change in Japanese policy, at least that was what the intercepted messages from "Magic," the broken Japanese code, seemed to indicate.

Two days before Matsuoka's departure, the Japanese demanded that Vichy France allow them to occupy southern Indochina. The State Department told Nomura that Japan's ultimatum impressed the American government as being the first move in a program of large-scale expansion in the South Seas. It could not, therefore, see any reason to continue the Washington conversations.

Alarmed, Nomura asked to see the President. Hinting at the possibility of an oil embargo, Roosevelt warned that expansion into the Dutch East Indies would mean war with Britain and the Netherlands, and probably with the United States as well. He also offered a compromise to dispel Japanese fears of encirclement. If Japan withdrew from Indochina, he said, he would attempt to neutralize France's colony in the Swiss pattern. Nothing came of the neutralization proposal, and Vichy yielded to the Japanese demands.

Since Japan now threatened the Netherlands East Indies, Malaya, and the Philippines, Roosevelt retaliated with stringent economic sanctions, the most drastic move he was to take against the Japanese. On July 26, he froze all Japanese funds in the United States, then closed the Panama Canal to Japan and mustered the Philippine military forces into service with the American Army. Britain, her dominions, and the Netherlands East Indies also cut off all trade with Japan. These sanctions, virtually a world-wide embargo, meant that Japan could no longer obtain essential supplies for her war machine from the Western powers. The sanctions also presented Japan with the grim alternatives of consummating her expansion and conquering the supplies she needed, courting economic ruin, or surrendering to American terms.

Although shocked, the Japanese refused to surrender. They froze American, British, and Dutch funds within their control and went ahead with the occupation of all of Indochina.

Public opinion polls in the United States indicated that the economic sanctions were popular. Most of those questioned expressed a willingness to risk war to keep Japan from growing stronger. Nomura reported home that the American people backed their government's firm policy and seemed more concerned with relations with Japan than with Germany.

Japan's militarists wanted to answer the American challenge with war, but Konoye and certain naval leaders foresaw only defeat in a long naval war and sought to avoid it. Instead of retreating, however, Konoye's cabinet decided to try to revive the Washington conversations, hoping to find some way of preserving most of Japan's territorial gains and still keep the peace with the United States.

The new Foreign Minister sent Nomura fresh proposals on August 5. They promised that Japan would not send troops anywhere but to Indochina and would evacuate that French colony after settling the China "incident." In return, Japan asked for access to raw materials in the Southwest Pacific, American assistance in negotiations with Chiang Kai-shek, and recognition of her special position in Indochina even after she withdrew. Apparently realizing that the proposals would be unacceptable to the United States, Prince Konoye immediately followed them with an idea of his own, a meeting between Roosevelt and himself somewhere in the Pacific, what he called a Leaders' Conference. Hull turned down Nomura's proposals, but the answer to Konoye's idea had to await the President's return from Placentia.

Roosevelt returned to Washington on Sunday, August 17, and saw Nomura that afternoon. Before taking up the requests for a resumption of the Washington conversations and the meeting with Konoye, the President delivered a watered-down version of a warning he and Churchill had agreed upon at Placentia. If Japan made any more aggressive moves toward neighboring countries, he said, the United States would immediately take steps to safeguard its security and the rights of its citizens. Then he added, if Japan were willing to embrace a program of peace in the Pacific to which his government was committed, he would resume the conversations that were interrupted in July. Before taking up the talks again or considering a conference with Konoye, he said, he wanted a clear statement on Japan's plans and attitudes.

Roosevelt received Konoye's reply on August 28 from Admiral Nomura. Japan, the Prime Minister said, did not intend to use force against any neighboring nation. She accepted the American principles as a sound basis for peace. Roosevelt received the message cordially and indicated that he was looking forward to meeting Konoye.

Intercepted messages at the same time revealed that Japan meant to reduce Chiang to impotency before withdrawing from Indochina. Hull and others, therefore, opposed the Leaders' Conference. Since he regarded the problem of China as pivotal in the relations with Japan, the Secretary of State insisted that the United States must know the specific terms to be offered to Chiang in advance of the proposed Pacific conference. Roosevelt accepted his Secretary's reasoning and told Nomura on September 3 that he would be pleased to meet with the Prime Minister but first must have advance commitments on China.

Roosevelt's critics have argued that the President's reply doomed the conference and whatever chances there were for peace with Japan. Roosevelt and his advisers, these critics have said, rejected Konoye's offer in order to goad Japan into an attack. The evidence does not support the thesis that the President sought war. On the contrary, he and his advisers still considered Hitler the main enemy and wanted to keep the peace in the Pacific, but not at the cost of sacrificing China and the British and Dutch possessions there. At this point they still believed a firm policy would deter the Japanese. "Magic's" messages, moreover, indicated that Japan had no serious intention of drawing back, and was preparing to resume her southern advance.[50]

Japan's Decision

Three days after Roosevelt had rejected the proposed meeting, Japan's highest leaders met in another Imperial Conference in Tokyo. They agreed on minimum demands in negotiations with the United States and if those were not met, they would resort to war to avoid economic strangulation, but first they would try every possible diplomatic means to gain acceptance of their demands. The Imperial Conference ended with the decision that preparations for war must follow if Japan's demands were not met by early October.

The next few weeks brought the United States and Japan no nearer to an agreement than they had been before the Imperial Conference. The October deadline came, and Japan's economic situation became almost desperate. Her vital oil supplies were dwindling and hardly one of her basic industries operated without scrimping, saving, or curtailing production to conserve some raw material. At his home, on October 12, Konoye conferred with his cabinet. He suggested accepting the American terms in principle, though not in essence, but the Minister of War, General Hideki Tojo, would not agree. The army's morale would break, he said, if the troops after four years of sacrifice withdrew from China under American pressure. Japan must fight while the time was favorable.

Unable to overcome the army's resistance, Konoye resigned. On October 17 Emperor Hirohito appointed a new cabinet with the militant Tojo as Prime Minister. Only Tojo, it seemed, could hope to control the war faction in the army. In ordering Tojo to form a government, the emperor told him to continue the conversations in Washington and to make one last effort at compromise.

Leaders on both sides of the Pacific made warlike statements in the interim. "We are satisfied in our own minds," Secretary of the Navy Frank Knox said, "that the Japanese have no intention of abandoning their expansion plans. If they pursue that course, a collision is inevitable." Tojo himself announced that his country's policies were "immutable and irrevocable" and that there would be no retreat. "If a hundred million people merge into one iron solidarity to go forward," he said, "nothing can stop us."[51]

The Washington conversations, which Hull described as "going around and around the same circle," had no chance of success. The Japanese were eager for an agreement but only if they could have it without sacrificing their plans for expansion, especially gains in China. The Americans were equally anxious for peace in the Pacific so they could concentrate on Hitler, but not at the sacrifice of Chiang Kai-shek and fundamental principles. As the negotiations approached their last round, the Japanese worked against a deadline and sought a quick settlement whereas the Americans sparred for time, hoping to forestall action for as long as possible.

In a meeting of October 23, the leading members of Tojo's cabinet agreed to continue the Washington conversations with a deadline of only three weeks. At the same time they would rush ahead with plans for military action. On November 3, Japan's Chief of Naval Operations finally accepted the plan for an attack on Pearl Harbor. Two days later, operation orders went out saying that war with the Netherlands, the United States, and England was inevitable and that preparations were to be completed by early December.[52] In two more days the date for the attack was tentatively set for December 8, Japanese time.

Unaware of these conditions, Nomura began the last round of his conversations with Hull on November 7, at which time he presented the first part, or Plan A, of Japan's final proposal for a diplomatic agreement. It called for a general settlement, but offered nothing new except the principle of nondiscrimination in trade in China and throughout the Pacific, which Japan would accept if it were adopted in the rest of the world.[53] If this proposal failed, then Plan B was to be tried as the last resort before war. Hull rejected Nomura's offer.

A week later, in an effort to give a sense of urgency to the talks, Tojo sent an experienced diplomat as a special emissary, Saburo Kurusu, to aid Nomura in his informal negotiations. Kurusu the "trouble shooter," with no new concessions or even new instructions, arrived in Washington on November 17, and three days later he and Nomura presented Plan B, what the Japanese called an ultimatum but what was in most particulars the offer of a limited temporary agreement.[54] It sought to free Japan from the pressure of the American embargo and, for a while at least, to set at rest American fears of Japanese expansion to the south. Through intercepted messages Hull knew it had a time limit, and if not accepted the alternative was war. Hence he viewed it as an ultimatum. The main obstacle to an understanding, however, was the fifth point which required the United States to stop its aid to Chiang's China.

Nonetheless, the Japanese thought that Plan B might lead to a later settlement of larger issues, and their Foreign Minister was so hopeful that it would be accepted that he induced the government to push back the deadline for war from November 25 to the 29th. "After that," he warned his ambassadors, in a telegram that American naval cryptographers intercepted, "things are automatically going to happen."[55]

The Americans now knew without doubt that probably only some kind of a stopgap agreement could avoid war. In response to Japan's *modus vivendi* they prepared one of their own, as well as the outline of a proposed general settlement known as the Ten Point plan. The American *modus vivendi*, calling for a truce of ninety days, went a long way toward the Japanese position. It even offered to endorse an armistice between China and Japan.

The Chinese, supported in principle by the British, violently opposed the American *modus vivendi*. So agitated was Chiang Kai-shek by what he felt was appeasement of Japan at China's expense that he said Chinese resistance would collapse if the United States went ahead with the truce agreement. Hull, therefore, dropped the *modus vivendi* and the idea of a truce.

Hull's Ten Point Plan

When Hull met with Nomura and Kurusu on November 26, he rejected their *modus vivendi* and presented the Ten Point program calling for a long-range settlement. Although the Ten Point note reaffirmed principles Hull had stressed in the past, in several particulars it went beyond any previous American statement in the long Washington conversations. Japan, it said, had to evacuate all of China and Indochina, withdraw her support from the puppet regime in Nanking, and virtually disavow the Tripartite Pact.

Hull's note technically was not, as Tojo dubbed it, an ultimatum.[56] It was, nonetheless, an uncompromising statement that met Japan's minimum demands with America's maximum terms. For the Japanese it ended all basis for future discussions, though it was not the brutal demand they said it was.

Within the next few days Army and Navy commanders in the Pacific received warnings that Japan might strike at Guam and the Philippines. The message to Admiral Husband E. Kimmel, Commander of the Pacific fleet at Pearl Harbor, read: "This dispatch is to be considered a war warning."[57]

In Tokyo preparations for war became firm. At 6:00 a.m. on November 26, Japanese time, a carrier task force left the Kurile Islands to attack the naval base at Pearl Harbor. The army in Indochina stood poised to strike at Malaya. Hull's Ten Point note had confirmed the Japanese decision for war.

The emperor and his Privy Council on December 1 approved the war plans. Two days later the Japanese government formally asked Germany and Italy to join the imminent war against the United States and to agree not to conclude a separate peace.

Through "Magic" the American government was aware of Japan's main steps for war almost as soon as they were taken. The President, Hull, and the top military planners knew that Japan planned a surprise attack but not where. None of them anticipated a strike at Pearl Harbor. They assumed that bastion was too strong and that Japan would not dare a direct assault on American soil. So intense was their concern with the problem of how to meet an attack in Southeast Asia that they overlooked warnings about Pearl Harbor.

Some critics have said that the President invited an attack on Pearl Harbor in order to bring the United States into the European war via the back door of the Pacific. There is no sound evidence to support this thesis.[58] The President and his cabinet had agreed that if Japan attacked the British and the Dutch in the Pacific, the United States must fight, but up until the last minute Roosevelt refused to give the British and the Dutch assurances that he would intervene.

As news of Japanese troop and naval movements came into Washington, Roosevelt sent a last minute appeal to Japan's emperor on December 6 warning him that the people of the Southwest Pacific could not "sit either indefinitely or permanently on a keg of dynamite," and asking him to take action to avert war.[59] The next morning the Japanese Foreign Minister told the American Ambassador in Tokyo that negotiations had been broken off. That was the emperor's answer to the President's message.

That same afternoon the Japanese reply, a long one, to Hull's Ten Point note began coming over the wires. Navy cryptographers decoded it as it came in and by 9:30 p.m. the President and the Secretary of State knew what it meant. "This means war," the President said.[60] The full message was in Roosevelt's hands by 10:00 a.m. the next morning. It rejected Hull's terms, saying an agreement was impossible through further negotiations.

Nomura and Kurusu were to have delivered the note to Hull at 1:00 p.m., but the Japanese decoders were slower than the Americans. The two ambassadors asked for a postponement of their appointment and did not see Hull until 2:20 p.m.

THE ATTACK ON PEARL HARBOR, DECEMBER 7, 1941

By that time the first reports of the attack on Pearl Harbor had reached the President and his advisers.

The Pearl Harbor Attack

The Japanese carrier task force from the Kuriles had approached Hawaii undetected from the northwest. In complete surprise at 7:55 a.m. on Sunday, December 7, 1941, the first wave of Japanese planes bombed the fleet anchored in Pearl Harbor. With virtually no opposition, the Japanese either sank or disabled every battleship, destroyed practically every plane on the island of Oahu, and killed over 2400 service men. As the last of the attacking planes winged their way back to their carriers at about 9:45 a.m., they left behind them smoking shambles that had been the greatest concentration of American power in the Pacific.

Hull received the Japanese emissaries while the bombs were still falling. Hot with anger, he denounced the message they brought, which he had already seen, as "crowded with infamous falsehoods and distortions." [61] Not knowing of the Pearl Harbor attack, the envoys were dumbfounded. Hull nodded toward the door, and they left without another word.

Later that afternoon, and in the evening, news reached Washington that Japan was attacking on a wide front simultaneously in the Philippines, Siam, Malaya, and elsewhere, and that she had officially declared war on the United States and Britain. The next day the President went before a joint session of Congress and asked it to declare that since the Pearl Harbor attack "a state of war has existed between the United States and the Japanese Empire." [62] In less than an hour, with only one dissenting vote in the House, Congress passed the war resolution. The President signed it that afternoon.

At noon on December 8, the Japanese officially asked the German government to join the war against the United States. Pleased that Japan had taken the plunge, Hitler, who had revised his policy of trying to prevent American intervention, quickly acted.[63] Germany and Italy declared war on the United States on December 11. The same afternoon Congress unanimously declared war on them. "The long known and the long expected," the President told Congress, "has thus taken place." [64]

Staggered by the Japanese attack, the American people did not know of the diplomatic circumstances and the desperate negotiations that preceded it. They regarded the blow as an act of treachery. Since Roosevelt did not himself initiate the final move from undeclared to official war, isolationists ended their opposition to his foreign policy.

→ "In my own mind," Senator Arthur H. Vandenberg, a leading isolationist, wrote several years later, "my convictions regarding international cooperation and collective security for peace took firm form on the afternoon of the Pearl Harbor attack. That day ended isolationism for any realist." [65]

The Pearl Harbor attack, made possible by perplexing strategic errors, was a psychological blunder. Although the Japanese succeeded in their objective of crippling the American fleet, their surprise hit-and-run strike united the American people behind the President's foreign policy as nothing had up to that time. Until the bombs fell at Pearl Harbor, most Americans still hoped to avoid an all-out war, but when it came, they turned grimly to the task of defeating the enemy.[66]

NOTES

1. Sept. 3, 1939, in Samuel I. Rosenman, comp., *The Public Papers and Addresses of Franklin D. Roosevelt* (13 vols., New York, 1938–50), VIII, 463.

2. This seemed to be the case even before war began. See, for instance, the results of the public opinion poll of May 27, 1938, in Hadley Cantril, ed., *Public Opinion, 1935–1946* (Princeton, 1951), p. 1061. Propaganda, moreover, apparently did not change public sentiment. See John W. Osborne, "Highlights of British and German Propaganda in the United States, 1939–1941," *Journal of Rutgers University Library*, XXVI (Dec. 1960), 14–23.

3. *The Memoirs of Cordell Hull* (2 vols., New York, 1948), I, 684.

4. See Robert A. Divine, *The Illusion of Neutrality* (Chicago, 1962), pp. 331–333. John C. Donovan, in "Congressional Isolationists and the Roosevelt Foreign Policy," *World Politics*, III (April 1951), 306, suggests that the law was a decision against isolationism.

5. Roosevelt to Lincoln MacVeagh, Dec. 1, 1939, in Elliott Roosevelt, ed., *The Roosevelt*

Letters: Being the Personal Correspondence of Franklin Delano Roosevelt (3 vols., London, 1949–52), III, 290.

6. For a detailed history of America's part in the Finnish struggle against Russia, based on State Department files, see Andrew J. Schwartz, *America and the Russo-Finnish War* (Washington, 1960). Robert Sobel, in *The Origins of Interventionism: The United States and the Russo-Finnish War* (New York, 1960), sees the American reaction to the winter war as marking a turning point in the United States from isolationism to interventionism. For a similar idea dealt with less emphatically, see Max Jakobson, *The Diplomacy of the Winter War: An Account of the Russo-Finnish War, 1939–1940* (Cambridge, Mass., 1961), pp. 190–197.

7. Quoted in William L. Langer and S. Everett Gleason, *The Challenge to Isolation, 1937–1940* (New York, 1952), p. 513.

8. June 10, 1940 in Rosenman, comp., *Papers of Franklin D. Roosevelt*, IX, 264.

9. U.S. Department of State, *Peace and War: United States Foreign Policy, 1931–1941* (Washington, 1942), p. 75.

10. See the pertinent surveys in Cantril, ed., *Public Opinion*, pp. 970–71, 1159–60.

11. Telegram, June 10, 1940, quoted in Walter Johnson, *The Battle Against Isolation* (Chicago, 1944), p. 82.

12. May 16, 1940, in Rosenman, comp., *Papers of Franklin D. Roosevelt*, IX, 198.

13. For details, see James Phinney Baxter III, *Scientists Against Time* (Boston, 1947), pp. 419–447 and Richard D. Hewlett and Oscar E. Anderson, Jr., *The New World, 1939–1946*, Vol. I of *A History of the United States Atomic Energy Commission* (University Park, Pa., 1962), pp. 65, 115, 119–120.

14. Quoted in Langer and Gleason, *Challenge to Isolation*, p. 682.

15. John W. Masland, in "Commercial Influences upon American Far Eastern Policy, 1937–1941," *Pacific Historical Review*, XI (Oct. 1942), 281–299, points out that economic considerations did not shape American Far Eastern policy. Business interests, in fact, were opposed to strong measures against Japan because of injury to a satisfactory trade. Roland N. Stromberg, in "American Business and the Approach of War, 1935–1941," *Journal of Economic History*, XIII (Winter 1953), 58–78, suggests that in the general drift toward unneutrality and war American business interests did not wield decisive or even independent influence.

16. Sept. 26, 1940, quoted in William L. Langer and S. Everett Gleason, *The Undeclared War, 1940–1941* (New York, 1953), p. 21.

17. For details, see John Huizenga, "Yosuke Matsuoka and the Japanese-German Alliance," in Gordon A. Craig and Felix Gilbert, eds., *The Diplomats, 1919–1939* (Princeton, 1953), pp. 615–648.

18. See, for example, Joseph C. Grew's diary entry of Nov. 1, 1940, in his *Ten Years in Japan* (New York, 1944), p. 349.

19. Aug. 6, 1940, quoted in Langer and Gleason, *Challenge to Isolation*, p. 757.

20. Sept. 3, 1940, in Rosenman, comp., *Papers of Franklin D. Roosevelt*, IX, 391.

21. Sept. 4, 1940, quoted in Charles C. Tansill, *Back Door to War* (Chicago, 1952), p. 599. The New York *Daily News* pointed out that "The United States has one foot in the war and the other on a banana peel." Sept. 26, 1940, quoted in Langer and Gleason, *Challenge to Isolation*, p. 772.

22. Winston Churchill, *The Second World War* (6 vols., Boston, 1948–53), *Their Finest Hour* (Boston, 1949), p. 404.

23. It had no influence in the South, however. See Wayne S. Cole, "America First and the South, 1940–1941," *Journal of Southern History*, XXII (Feb. 1956), 36–47.

24. Quoted in Wayne S. Cole, *America First: The Battle Against Intervention, 1940–1941* (Madison, Wis., 1953), p. 15.

25. See, for instance, the poll of Sept. 26, 1940, in which 83% of those questioned opposed entry into the war, in Cantril, *Public Opinion*, pp. 971–972. For aid to Britain, see pp. 1060–61.

26. Boston, Oct. 30, 1940, quoted in Robert E. Sherwood, *Roosevelt and Hopkins: An Intimate History* (New York, 1948), p. 191.

27. The text of Churchill's letter, dated Dec. 8, 1940, is in Churchill, *Their Finest Hour*, pp. 558–567.

28. Dec. 17, 1940, in Rosenman, comp., *Papers of Franklin D. Roosevelt*, IX, 607–608.

29. Dec. 29, 1940, *ibid.*, IX, 643.

30. Jan. 8, 1941, *ibid.*, IX, 663–678.

31. Quoted in Charles A. Beard, *President Roosevelt and the Coming of the War, 1941* (New Haven, 1948), pp. 67–68.

32. For details, see Edward R. Stettinius, Jr., *Lend-Lease: Weapon for Victory* (New York, 1944).

33. Admiral Harold R. Stark quoted in Herbert Feis, *The Road to Pearl Harbor* (Princeton, 1950), p. 171.

34. *Christian Science Monitor*, April 2, 1941, quoted in Langer and Gleason, *Undeclared War*, p. 443.

35. May 27, 1941, in Rosenman, comp., *Papers of Franklin D. Roosevelt*, X, 190.

36. For a fine analysis of the conversations from the Japanese side, in which the author points out that Nomura, a man lacking political and diplomatic experience, failed to report adequately to his own government and probably contributed to the misunderstanding between the two governments, see Robert C. Butow, "The Hull-Nomura Conversations: A Fundamental Misconception," *The American Historical Review*, LXV (July 1960), 822–836.

37. In a memorandum of April 16, 1941, Hull summarized the American position as consisting of four basic points. They are given in Paul W. Schroeder, *The Axis Alliance and Japanese-American Relations, 1941* (Ithaca, N.Y., 1958), p. 37.

38. Senator Bennett C. Clark of Missouri, quoted in Langer and Gleason, *Undeclared War*, p. 542. See also the comments in Raymond H. Dawson, *The Decision to Aid Russia, 1941: Foreign Policy and Domestic Politics* (Chapel Hill, N.C., 1959), pp. 102–104.

39. Archibald P. Wavell, quoted in Langer and Gleason, *Undeclared War*, p. 571.

40. Feb. 17, 1941, Morgenthau Diaries, *ibid.*, p. 663.

41. Aug. 17, 1941, *ibid.*, p. 690. The story of the Atlantic Charter is told by Sumner Welles in *Where Are We Heading?* (New York, 1946), pp. 6–18.

42. Quoted in Langer and Gleason, *Undeclared War*, p. 806.

43. *Ibid.*, p. 807.

44. Rosenman, comp., *Papers of Franklin D. Roosevelt*, X, 385, 390–391.

45. Husband E. Kimmel, Sept. 22, 1941, quoted in Langer and Gleason, *Undeclared War*, p. 747.

46. The most detailed study of the subject, Dawson, *Decision to Aid Russia, 1941*, concludes that military necessity was the primary motive behind Roosevelt's decision.

47. Rosenman, comp., *Papers of Franklin D. Roosevelt*, X, 410.

48. *Ibid.*, p. 48.

49. C. Wayland Brooks, Nov. 7, 1941, quoted in Langer and Gleason, *Undeclared War*, p. 757. See also the comments recorded in Beard, *Roosevelt and the War*, Chap. VI.

50. Actually, Japan's military leaders had made the decision to expand hostilities sometime between Aug. 16 and Sept. 5, 1941. See Robert J. C. Butow, *Tojo and the Coming of the War* (Princeton, 1961), p. 225.

51. Tojo and Knox are quoted in *The New York Times*, Oct. 27, 30, 1941, in Langer and Gleason, *Undeclared War*, p. 837. Butow, in *Tojo*, p. 314, points out that Tojo did not become Premier to lead Japan into war, but was willing, unlike Konoye, to lead the nation into war to carry out national policy.

52. Details are in Feis, *Road to Pearl Harbor*, p. 296.

53. The text is in *Foreign Relations, Japan*, II, 709–710.

54. *Ibid.*, pp. 755–756. Immanuel C. Y. Hsu, in "Kurusu's Mission to the United States and the Abortive *Modus Vivendi*," *Journal of Modern History*, XXIV (Sept. 1952), 301–307, argues that Kurusu was sent not to cover up Japan's military preparations for a surprise attack but to seek some last minute means of avoiding war. For a different view, see Joseph W. Ballantine, "Mukden to Pearl Harbor: The Foreign Policies of Japan," *Foreign Affairs*, XXVII (July 1949), 651–664. Feis, in *Road to Pearl Harbor*, p. 297, points out that Kurusu knew of the Japanese program and schedule of action, but probably not of the Pearl Harbor plans.

55. Shigenori Togo to Nomura, Nov. 22, 1941, quoted in Feis, *Road to Pearl Harbor*, p. 313.

56. Norman Hill, in "Was There an Ultimatum before Pearl Harbor?" *American Journal of International Law*, XLII (April 1948), 355–367, concludes that neither Japan's Plan B nor Hull's note were *bona fide* ultimatums. Butow, in *Tojo*, pp. 339, 343, points out that the Japanese looked upon the Hull note an as ultimatum, one they could not possibly accept.

57. Nov. 27, 1941, quoted in Feis, *Road to Pearl Harbor*, p. 324.

58. On this point, see the penetrating analysis by Richard N. Current, "How Stimson Meant to 'Maneuver' the Japanese," *Mississippi Valley Historical Review*, XL (June 1953), 67–74. See also the bibliographical interpretive articles by Louis Morton, "Pearl Harbor in Perspective," *United States Naval Institute Proceedings*, LXXXI (April 1955), 460–468, Robert H. Ferrell, "Pearl Harbor and the Revisionists," *The Historian*, XVII (Spring 1955), 215–233, and Herbert Feis, "War Came at Pearl Harbor: Suspicions Considered," *Yale Review*, XLV (March 1956), 378–390.

59. Rosenman, comp., *Papers of Franklin D. Roosevelt*, X, 513.

60. Quoted in Feis, *Road to Pearl Harbor*, p. 339.

61. *Memoirs of Cordell Hull*, II, 1096. For details on the Japanese planning for the attack, see Robert E. Ward, "The Inside Story of the Pearl Harbor Plan," *United States Naval Institute Proceedings*, LXXVII (Dec. 1951), 1270–83. The best account of Japan's problems in delivering the war message is in Butow, *Tojo*, pp. 376–384. International law requires advance notice of war but does not specify how long in advance. The Japanese had planned an advance notice of only a few minutes, but were snarled in transmission difficulties.

62. Rosenman, comp., *Papers of Franklin D. Roosevelt*, X, 515.

63. Hans L. Trefousse, "Failure of German Intelligence in the United States, 1935–1945," *Mississippi Valley Historical Review*, XLII (June 1955), 97.

64. Rosenman, comp., *Papers of Franklin D. Roosevelt*, X, 532.

65. Arthur H. Vandenberg, Jr., ed., *The Private Papers of Senator Vandenberg* (Boston, 1952), p. 1.

66. Roberta Wohlstetter, in *Pearl Harbor: Warning and Decision* (Stanford, Calif., 1962), explains why Americans were surprised and offers a full scholarly analysis of the events leading to the Pearl Harbor attack.

Chapter Twenty-Four

POLITICS OF
THE GRAND COALITION

UNLIKE its detached participation in the First World War as an "associated power," the United States in the Second became the leader in the military decisions and in the politics of the war. It signed no formal treaty of alliance, yet Roosevelt forged a grand alliance with Churchill's England and drew Stalin's Russia into it. These three men, leaders of the world's greatest wartime coalition, agreed fundamentally on one purpose—the destruction of their Axis enemies. They led their peoples in a common struggle without prior agreement on political objectives.

As in the first war against Germany, the United States fought without seeking territorial gains. Its objectives were primarily the destruction of Hitlerism and a security system that would prevent future wars. Its two major allies were more specific. Russia had territorial desires in Europe and Asia, and Britain was determined to preserve her predominant position in the Mediterranean. Although America's major interests were in the Pacific, she agreed to subordinate the war there to that in Europe.

In their war strategy America's leaders placed military objectives ahead of political aims, wishing to defer discussion of political issues until after defeat of the Axis powers, but were unsuccessful. They could not fight as part of a coalition without becoming enmeshed in the politics of coalition warfare. Even basic military planning involved political decisions that affected the course of diplomacy during and after the war.[1]

The Grand Coalition

Immediately after Pearl Harbor, Churchill crossed the Atlantic to discuss war strategy directly with Roosevelt. Churchill's visit marked the beginning of a personal diplomacy between himself and Roosevelt, and later with Stalin, that characterized the politics of the war. The Prime Minister feared that the shock of the Japanese attack might cause Americans to divert most of their resources to the war in the Pacific. "We are conscious of a serious danger that the United States might pursue the war against Japan in the Pacific," he wrote, "and leave us to fight Germany and Italy in Europe, Africa, and in the Middle East."[2]

Churchill's fears were justified. Many Americans considered Japan the main enemy and agreed with military commanders in the Pacific that her defeat should have a higher priority than the war against Hitler.

In a series of conferences with Roosevelt and other American leaders in December and January, 1941–1942, known by the code name of ARCADIA, Churchill preserved the principle of concentrating the primary war effort in Europe. Germany had to be the main foe, the two leaders agreed, because she controlled manpower and technological resources superior to Japan's and hence was the more dangerous enemy. They decided to defer aid to the Chinese, pour resources into Europe and Russia, and ultimately to launch the first offensives against Italy and Germany.

Roosevelt and his advisers did not, however, intend entirely to neglect China and the Pacific war. They agreed on a holding operation in the Pacific with the intention of teaming up ultimately with the Chinese to defeat Japan.

At the White House on New Year's Day, 1942, Roosevelt and Churchill, Ambassador Maxim Litvinov for the Soviet Union, and the representatives of twenty-three other nations at war with the Axis powers, brought the grand coalition into formal existence by signing the Declaration of the United Nations. It bound all signatory governments in an alliance against the Axis that pledged them to uphold the principles of the Atlantic Charter and not to make a separate peace. With this executive agreement, never submitted to the Senate, Roosevelt defied the long tradition of nonentanglement.

Before the ink had dried, Roosevelt and Churchill had to deal with Russia's territorial ambitions in Europe, ambitions that placed endless strain on the grand coalition. Although the Russians had accepted the Atlantic Charter, placing them on record as desiring no new territory, they had done so with important qualifications. From the beginning they made it clear that they intended to keep as their own the three Baltic states, the eastern part of Poland, a segment of Finland, and portions of Rumania that they had absorbed before Hitler struck. Moreover, they

FIGHTING A GLOBAL WAR, 1942–1943

insisted that their allies recognize their control over those territories as legitimate, something Churchill and Roosevelt would not do.

Stalin had presented the first version of his territorial demands to the British Foreign Secretary, Anthony Eden, in December before the signing of the United Nations Declaration. The Kremlin sought payment in advance for Russia's role in the alliance, asking for a definition of what she would get at the end of the war, and a settlement of certain European political and territorial questions.

A few months later, Russia's Commissar for Foreign Affairs, Vyacheslav Molotov, visited London and asked the British to endorse the Soviet demands in a treaty of alliance. Supported by the United States, the British resisted. Roosevelt even appealed directly to Stalin to put aside the territorial issue. Resenting what they called "American interference," the Russians finally signed a twenty-year treaty of alliance with Britain in May that contained no reference to territorial matters, but did not abandon their territorial claims. Even when suffering severe military reversals, the Soviets pressed the claims upon their allies.

Military operations proved another source of friction between Russia and her Anglo-American allies. In the spring and summer of 1942, the Red armies faced the main might of Hitler's forces and suffered appalling losses. To stave off defeat and cut their casualties, the Russians urged the United States and Britain to create a second fighting front in Europe that would force Hitler to divide his armies.

With this objective, Molotov came to the United States late in May. If immediate help were not forthcoming, he told Roosevelt, Hitler might shatter the Russian lines and the United States and Britain would then have to bear the full brunt of the war. Molotov did not present his request as a threat but more as an effort to show the Western powers that it was in their own interests to relieve the immediate pressure on Russia.

Although impressed, Roosevelt could do nothing more than promise a cross-channel invasion sometime in 1942. The Western Allies could not offer immediate action because they were short of shipping. Molotov, therefore, returned to Moscow with only a promise, while German armies drove deeper into Russia.

Several problems paralleled the insistent demands for a second front. The Soviets dismissed as virtually inconsequential the fact that the Western Allies were confronting at least forty-four German divisions in Africa and other theaters of war. The Russians also turned aside American requests to consider cooperation against Japan in a future second or third front on the mainland of Asia. Stalin, apparently, looked upon the American efforts as an attempt to incite Japan to attack Siberia.

Roosevelt and his advisers, nonetheless, believed that they and the British must launch some kind of offensive in Europe, probably at the northern coast of France, in 1942 to avert disaster on the eastern front. This conviction brought the President into conflict with Churchill.

The Prime Minister and his military advisers were convinced that the first combined British and American military offensive should be a landing in North Africa. Churchill pictured Hitler's Europe as a crocodile with the Mediterranean as its "soft underbelly." While Russia was striking at the hard snout, he explained, British and American forces would deliver a vital thrust at the underbelly. American military planners, however, considered the North African operation wasteful and dangerous.[3]

Aware that the Americans were determined to try some kind of landing in Europe in 1942 to relieve the pressure on the Soviets, Churchill decided in June to go to Washington to argue his case with Roosevelt and the American military leaders. He was determined not to go through with a European invasion, no matter how limited, with only the resources then available.

Roosevelt, Churchill, and their chiefs of staff conversed at Hyde Park, Roosevelt's home in New York, and in Washington for a week. While they talked the British position in North Africa crumbled and it looked as if German and Italian forces would sweep through Egypt to the Suez Canal. The new crisis diverted American attention from Europe to Africa and gave force to Churchill's arguments for a North African expedition. Roosevelt quickly sent aid to Egypt and after the crisis had passed decided to settle the issue of a second front.

Unable to bend the British toward a cross-channel invasion and convinced that the Western Allies must begin offensive operations somewhere in the fall, Roosevelt acquiesced in a North African operation, given the code name TORCH. To Churchill fell the unpleasant task of explaining to Stalin why there would be no invasion of Europe in 1942. In August he flew to Moscow and offered the North African expedition as the substitute for the cross-channel attack that Roosevelt had vaguely promised. Stalin considered it an inadequate substitute but accepted it because he had no other choice.

Spain and France

One reason why Roosevelt and his advisers had at first opposed a North African offensive was their distrust of the Spanish *Caudillo*, Francisco Franco. In any operation inside the Straits of Gibraltar, menaced by Spanish shore batteries, they feared that the Spaniards, or German troops streaming through Spain from the north, might cut off Allied forces and turn the offensive into a disaster. Across the straits, athwart the contemplated invasion route in Spanish Morocco, were about 100,000 Spanish troops who could also deal the Allied forces decisive blows, particularly if supported by Germans.

Although Franco had not joined the war by the side of Hitler, he still maintained a "nonbelligerency" favorable to the Axis and even sent "volunteers," the "Blue

Division," to fight with the Nazis in Russia. To keep Franco on the fence, at least until the Allies had gained complete control of the Mediterranean, Roosevelt had sent a prominent Catholic layman to Madrid as Ambassador, the historian from Columbia University, Carlton J. H. Hayes. Roosevelt also bought up strategic materials in Spain such as wolfram, cork, and mercury at high prices to keep them from going to Germany, a policy called "preclusive" buying. To keep Franco from openly joining the Axis, he allowed him to purchase carefully rationed supplies from the United States, particularly oil.

Liberals attacked Roosevelt's policy toward Franco as "appeasement" of a fascist dictator at a time when the American people were waging a crusade to crush fascism. The President nonetheless persisted but, before the African invasion, sent large forces to watch the Spanish troops in Morocco and, if necessary, to invade that colony. He also told Franco that "the United States will take no action of any sort which would in any way violate Spanish territory."[4]

Roosevelt's Spanish diplomacy paid off. As the British and American expedition built up for the TORCH operation, the Spanish guns remained silent, and Franco did not open his northern frontier to German troops.

Relations with the French presented a more complicated problem. Prior to the North African expedition neither Britain nor Russia had maintained diplomatic relations with Marshal Pétain's government at Vichy, but the United States did. In January, 1941, Roosevelt had sent a prominent naval officer, Admiral William D. Leahy, to Vichy France as Ambassador in order to counteract Hitler's influence, to prevent the French from surrendering their fleet and North African bases to the Axis, and to use unoccupied France as a source of information on Axis activities.

In an effort to bring the French in North Africa into the war against the Axis, Roosevelt had also agreed in March to supply them with goods, such as sugar, cotton, and coal, to be consumed in the area. The French, in turn, had allowed American officials to come to North Africa to supervise and control the shipments. This arrangement, known as the Murphy-Weygand Agreement, was concluded by an American diplomat, Robert D. Murphy, and the supreme authority of the Vichy regime in North Africa, General Maxime Weygand.

The British, on the other hand, supported what was in effect a French government in exile, the Free French National Committee headed by General Charles de Gaulle. Finding de Gaulle haughty and difficult, and not wishing to alienate Pétain, Roosevelt and Hull refused to recognize the Free French movement as a government in exile. Yet the President gave the Free French forces in the colonies they controlled, such as New Caledonia, Lend-Lease equipment.

In North Africa, American control officers gathered information and made secret agreements with French leaders for assistance during the scheduled Anglo-American invasion. In an effort to forestall resistance, Americans also made arrangements for General Henri H. Giraud, a distinguished French army officer who had twice escaped from German captivity, to land with them in the hope that he could command the loyalty of all French forces in North Africa.

Finally, on November 8, 1942, the British and American invaders struck at three places, at Oran and Algiers in Algeria on the Mediterranean coast, and at Casablanca on the Atlantic coast of French Morocco. Neither the Spaniards nor the Germans interfered, though the Allied forces had taken risks in a choppy sea at Casablanca in order to establish a supply line outside the Mediterranean that the Spaniards could not cut. The preparations with the French, however, had been inadequate. Neither the secret arrangements of the American agents nor the prestige of Giraud had won over all the French forces. The invaders met military resistance everywhere, but especially on the Moroccan coast.

By coincidence, Admiral Jean François Darlan, the tainted commander of all of Vichy's armed forces, who had a record of collaboration with the Nazis, was in Algiers. To end French resistance, General Dwight D. Eisenhower, commander of the combined Allied forces, made an agreement with Darlan two days after the initial landings. The admiral would order the French forces to cease fire against the Allies and to resist the Germans in Tunisia, and the United States would recognize him as the French political authority in North Africa. On the next day, after he heard that German troops were occupying all of France, Darlan, whose legal authority the French officers recognized, issued the order, and resistance in North Africa stopped.

Liberals in the United States and Britain denounced the deal with Darlan, but Eisenhower defended it as militarily expedient. The unsavory collaboration ended when Darlan fell before an assassin's bullet on Christmas Eve.[5]

Later, American authorities recognized Giraud as civil and military chief of the French forces fighting with the Allies and rebuffed the efforts of de Gaulle's Free French to gain control over them. Roosevelt, moreover, resisted any centralizing of French authority without knowing what the French people themselves wanted. De Gaulle, proud and determined to restore France to a position of power, construed American policy as being opposed to a strong France and as favoring a breakup of the French empire.

Like de Gaulle, Churchill was determined to keep his own empire intact, and hence could sympathize with de Gaulle's views. He continued to support the Free French, favoring de Gaulle's concept of a unified French authority that could represent and command French interests all over the world.

In June, 1943, Giraud and de Gaulle as co-chairmen, combined their forces in a new French Committee of National Liberation, "the central French power." Roosevelt and Churchill accepted this committee and its claims. In November, de Gaulle's followers eased Giraud out of the committee and de Gaulle took over full control. Eight months later the leader of the Free French visited the United States where Roosevelt and Hull found him more agreeable than they had expected.

Finally, in October, 1944, after the Allies had invaded France and captured Paris, the United States, Britain, and Russia recognized de Gaulle's administration as the Provisional Government of France. Thus, under de Gaulle, France ultimately won formal readmission as a member of the wartime coalition.

Unconditional Surrender

Meanwhile, in North Africa, British and American armies had crushed most Axis resistance, and Roosevelt, Churchill, and their advisers had gathered at Casablanca on January 14, 1943, for another high level conference. The Americans accepted a British plan calling for the invasion of Sicily as the next combined Allied offensive, but a controversial political decision made the Casablanca conference memorable. At the close of the meeting Roosevelt announced a policy of "unconditional surrender" toward the Axis enemies. "It does not mean the destruction of the population of Germany, Italy, or Japan," he told a press conference, "but it does mean the destruction of the philosophies in those countries which are based on conquest and the subjugation of other people." [6]

The President's critics and others later condemned the formula of "unconditional surrender" as ill-advised, as springing from sheer impulse, and as one of the greatest mistakes of the war. [7] It stiffened Axis resistance, they argued, particularly that of Germany; it left no room for political maneuver in dealing with the enemy, and had the unfortunate effect of prolonging the war.

Roosevelt had had that idea in his head for some time and had discussed it with his military advisers and Churchill beforehand. All had approved. His policy was not, therefore, the result of impulse. Unconditional surrender, moreover, did not rigidly determine either the terms to be imposed on the enemy or the political conduct of the war. It allowed the Allied leaders to offer terms to an enemy considering surrender, and hence did not force that enemy to fight on without recourse. [8]

The ghost of Woodrow Wilson and the dead peace of 1919 helped shape the formula of "unconditional surrender." Roosevelt sought to avoid any misunderstanding, as with the Fourteen Points, over surrender terms; in addition, he sought to strengthen the will of the Allies to fight on to victory, and to thwart Nazi efforts to split the grand coalition. [9]

Plans for Postwar Collective Security

A month later Britain's Foreign Secretary, Anthony Eden, visited Washington to seek cooperation in postwar planning. He and the American planners agreed to cultivate Russia's friendship and to try to win her cooperation in a new system of collective security. Roosevelt, in fact, advanced the idea of a world-wide security organization that would place the power over important decisions in the hands of the United States, Britain, Russia, and China.

Secretary Hull had already been making plans for American leadership in a new security system through an Advisory Commission on Postwar Foreign Policy which he had established in 1942. Although public opinion seemed favorable, he and Roosevelt had proceeded slowly, trying to avoid the pitfalls that had confronted Wilson. They carefully cultivated congressional support, among Republicans as well as Democrats. In September, 1943, the high command of the Republican party met at Mackinac Island, Michigan, and unanimously adopted a declaration known as the Mackinac Charter that announced Republican support for participation in a postwar international organization. Even isolationists such as Governor John W. Bricker and Senator Robert A. Taft of Ohio gave, though reluctantly, support to the concept of collective security at that time.

Responding to the mood of the times and to administration leadership, the House of Representatives, by a lopsided vote of 360 to 29 on September 21, adopted a resolution introduced by J. William Fulbright of Arkansas promoting support for an international agency to maintain peace, with the United States as a member. On November 5, with a vote of 85 to 5, the Senate approved a resolution advanced by Tom Connally of Texas calling on the United States to join and support an international organization "with power to prevent aggression and to preserve the peace of the world." The Fulbright-Connally resolutions assured congressional support for American leadership in organizing the postwar world and uprooted the remnants of prewar isolationism.

Roosevelt, meanwhile, had been continuing his high-level diplomacy. Churchill and his advisers had arrived in the United States on May 11, for two weeks of conferences given the code name TRIDENT. Overcoming the resistance of the American Chiefs of Staff, who wished to halt operations in the Mediterranean after the capture of Sicily, the Prime Minister persuaded Roosevelt to make Italy the next objective. This meant postponing the cross-channel invasion at least until the spring of 1944, a decision that angered the Russians.

Within a few months after the TRIDENT conference, the American and British armies overran Sicily and forced the first break in the Axis ranks. Italy's king overthrew Mussolini on July 25 and formed a new government under Marshal Pietro Badoglio, which soon sent word that it wished to negotiate a surrender.

Delighted with the news of Mussolini's downfall, Roosevelt immediately sent Churchill a message proposing a consultation. He hoped, he said, to obtain an Italian arrangement "as close as possible to unconditional surrender." [10] Americans looked upon the king and Badoglio as still representing some of the worst elements of the Fascist regime and disliked dealing with them, but Churchill, with broad military and political objectives in mind for the Mediterranean area, was willing to do so to gain his ends without delay. "Now Mussolini is gone," he told Roosevelt, "I would deal with any non-Fascist Italian government which can deliver the goods."[11]

With these divergent views in mind, Roosevelt and Churchill met again, this time in Quebec in August, 1943, in a conference called QUADRANT. They reconciled their differences and agreed to negotiate with Badoglio's government, but insisted on "unconditional surrender," terms the Italians accepted in a preliminary armistice signed at Cassibile, Sicily, on September 3. The surrender, as made clear in additional terms signed on September 29, was also conditional in that Roosevelt and Churchill promised to treat the Italians humanely and to reward what help they might give in the war against Germany. On October 13, Roosevelt, Churchill, and Stalin accepted Italy, though much of its territory was held by the Germans, as a cobelligerent.

At Quebec, Roosevelt and Churchill also agreed to launch a massive cross-channel invasion, operation OVERLORD, by May 1, 1944. For the first time, moreover, they gave major consideration to the war in the Pacific, agreeing to increase aid to Chiang Kai-shek and to step up an offensive against Japan.

Roosevelt had long wanted to confer with Stalin and after the Italian surrender urged a meeting of the Big Three to discuss world-wide strategy. Since Stalin insisted that he could not leave the eastern battle front where he personally commanded the Red armies, Churchill, Roosevelt, and Stalin agreed to an immediate meeting of the Big Three foreign ministers in Moscow. Although frail in health and fearful of flying, seventy-two-year-old Cordell Hull made the arduous air journey there for the Conference of Foreign Ministers held that October.

The discussion of military affairs, mainly Anglo-American preparations for the second front in France, absorbed a great deal of time, but the most notable agreement at Moscow was the Declaration of the Four Nations on General Security, signed on October 30, 1943, by the American, British, Russian, and Chinese representatives. Molotov at first had balked at allowing China to become one of the original sponsors, but gave in at the urging of Hull. Although vague in most of its principles, the Moscow Declaration contained two important specific commitments. The signatories pledged themselves to cooperate in matters pertaining to surrender and to fight until their enemies surrendered unconditionally. This was the first time the Soviets formally endorsed that policy. Secondly, the four powers agreed to establish "a general international organization" for the maintenance of "peace and security," the first international commitment for a postwar system of collective security.

Before Hull departed, Stalin told him that after the defeat of Germany the Soviet Union would join the war against Japan. The Moscow Conference thus ended on a note of good will and gave the impression that Russia would cooperate with her Western Allies in the postwar era. No longer, Hull told Congress meeting in joint session after his return, would there "be need for spheres of influence, for alliances, for balance of power. . . ."[12]

Pleased with the results, Roosevelt looked forward eagerly to meeting Stalin, believing that he could thaw the old Bolshevik and create a friendship with him that might lead to mutual trust between Russia and the West. "I tell you," he had written to Churchill earlier, "that I think I can personally handle Stalin better than either your Foreign Office or my State Department."[13] When Stalin stubbornly refused to travel far from his homeland, the President reluctantly agreed to go to distant Teheran in Iran for a meeting with him and Churchill.

Cairo and Teheran

Roosevelt had also long felt the need for a conference with Chiang Kai-shek to discuss China's place in global strategy. He had therefore invited Chiang to Cairo to meet with himself and Churchill before the Big Three conferred at Teheran. From November 23 to 27 the three statesmen discussed offensive operations in Burma and other military and supply matters relating to China, but their most important agreement, stemming from American initiative, was the Cairo Declaration announced on December 1, after the Russians had approved.

This momentous statement, designed to bolster China's sagging morale and stiffen her will to fight, pledged the Allies to strip Japan of all her continental and island possessions except her home islands. It meant the dissolution of the Japanese empire with the choicest portions, Manchuria, Formosa, and the Pescadores, to go to China, and ultimate independence for Korea.[14] A basic assumption behind the Cairo decision, essentially an American assumption, was that China would become unified and strong enough to assume the responsibilities of a great power and to administer her vast domains properly.

From Cairo the President flew to Teheran where the Big Three met each day and evening from November 28 to December 2. Most of their decisions dealt with military matters and the political problems connected with them. Roosevelt and Churchill assured Stalin that the cross-channel invasion he so ardently desired would take place in May or soon after. Stalin again promised he would take Russia into the war against Japan after Germany's defeat. "We shall," he said, "be able by our common front to beat Japan."[15]

The Big Three deliberated over the future of Germany, apparently at this time favoring dismemberment. They also discussed the nature of the postwar system of collective security, and in keeping with an earlier proposal made by Hull, signed a Declaration on Iran, promising to maintain that occupied country's independence.

Roosevelt left the meeting feeling that there would be fruitful cooperation with

Russia in the years to come. The closing words of the Declaration of Teheran reflected his optimism. "We came here with hope and determination," it read. "We leave here, friends in fact, in spirit, and in purpose." [16] After visiting American troops in the area of the Persian Gulf, the President returned to Cairo for more talks with Churchill and with the President of Turkey, who at this time resisted efforts to bring his country into the war against Hitler.

The Fourth-Term Election

Six months later, in the morning light of June 6, 1944, American and British armies attacked the beaches of Normandy and later spread through France and Belgium. The long-planned OVERLORD operation was a success and Stalin was delighted. "The history of war has never witnessed so grandiose an operation," he told the American Ambassador in Moscow. "Napoleon himself never attempted it. Hitler had envisaged it and was a fool for never having tried it." [17] In the east, the Russians exploded a massive new offensive and rolled through Poland and the Balkan states, ultimately forcing Germany's lesser allies, Finland, Rumania, Hungary, and Bulgaria out of the war.

While their soldiers were smashing Hitler's European fortress, Americans at home prepared for another wartime presidential election. The Republicans held their convention first, a few weeks after the invasion of France began. For President, they nominated Governor Thomas E. Dewey of New York, a vigorous young politician who favored international cooperation, and Governor John W. Bricker of Ohio, an isolationist, for Vice-President.

Even though the party leaders would have preferred a more conservative candidate, the Democrats, meeting in July, responded to the popular will and renominated Roosevelt. For the vice-presidential spot they chose a compromise candidate, Senator Harry S. Truman of Missouri. Their platform pledged continued vigorous international leadership in the postwar era.

Since both parties and both candidates promised to support participation in the world affairs, foreign policy, unlike the campaign of 1920, was not a basic issue. Yet some Republicans attacked Roosevelt's conduct of foreign affairs, and at the close of the campaign the President lashed back, reminding the voters that Dewey and the Republicans were tainted with isolationism. "The power which this Nation has attained—the political, the economic, the military, and above all the moral power—has brought to us the responsibility, and with it the opportunity, for leadership in the community of Nations," he said in one of his speeches. "In our own best interest, and in the name of peace and humanity, this Nation cannot, must not, and will not shirk that responsibility." [18]

The Allies, remembering 1920 and uncertain as to what to expect from Dewey, wanted Roosevelt to win, and Churchill predicted that he would. If wrong, Churchill told a colleague, "I will underwrite the British National Debt and subscribe to the Chicago *Tribune*." [19] The Prime Minister was not wrong. Roosevelt won re-election to an unprecedented fourth term. Europeans and Americans saw in the victory a commitment by both parties to support American leadership in world affairs, a leadership Americans had rejected twenty-four years earlier.

Postwar Planning and the German Question

During the campaign the administration had gone ahead with plans for leadership in the postwar world. In July it had sponsored the United Nations Monetary and Financial Conference which met at Bretton Woods, a resort in the mountains of New Hampshire. Representatives of forty-four nations agreed upon a plan for an international Monetary Fund designed to promote stability in international currencies and to encourage the expansion of world trade. They also decided to establish an International Bank for Reconstruction and Development that would help finance the rebuilding of devastated areas and would facilitate the flow of capital into foreign trade and into countries needing it for productive purposes. Although merely a beginning, the Bretton Woods Conference contrasted sharply with the economic nationalism of the 1920's and early 1930's.

A month later American initiative brought together American, British, Russian, and Chinese representatives at Dumbarton Oaks, an estate outside Washington, to discuss the structure and political composition of the postwar system of collective security. Before the delegates disbanded on October 7, they had agreed on a tentative charter for a new permanent international organization, the United Nations. They were, however, unable to concur on a voting formula in the Security Council, the body with jurisdiction over matters of war and peace.

Still bitter over their expulsion from the League of Nations in December, 1939, the Soviets insisted on a veto the great nations could use without exception, a power technically broader than the United States was willing to concede. Since Stalin would not budge, even after a direct appeal from Roosevelt, the President decided to try to settle the veto question at the next meeting of the Big Three.

In September, while the Dumbarton Oaks Conference was still in session, Churchill, Roosevelt, and their military staffs, at the insistence of the Prime Minister, met in a second conference in Quebec. They gave primary attention to the war on the mainland of Asia and adopted a vast program for the defeat of Japan. Since the collapse of Germany seemed imminent, they also agreed to a strategic program for the end of the war in Europe that would leave their forces in occupation of the heart of Germany, but their planning revealed confusion on the future treatment of Germany, the most noteworthy feature of the second Quebec conference.

"It is of the utmost importance," Roosevelt had told Secretaries Hull and

Stimson a few weeks earlier, "that every person in Germany should realize that this time Germany is a defeated nation, collectively and individually, [and this fact] must be so impressed upon them that they will hesitate to start any new war." [20]

In this state of mind, a few days before the conference, despite the objections of Hull and Stimson, the President approved a proposal prepared in the Treasury Department and advanced by Secretary of the Treasury Henry Morgenthau, Jr. The Morgenthau Plan suggested giving parts of Germany to Poland, Russia, Denmark, and France, dividing what was left into two independent states, stripping those states of heavy industry, and reducing the standard of living of their people to a subsistence level. At Quebec, the President and Morgenthau, whom Roosevelt had invited, persuaded Churchill to assent to the Morgenthau Plan. Both leaders initialed an agreement on September 16 saying they planned to convert "Germany into a country primarily agricultural and pastoral in its character." [21]

Within six weeks Roosevelt regretted his action and dropped the drastic Morgenthau Plan, saying he had no intention of turning Germany into an agrarian state. "Henry Morgenthau pulled a boner," he told Stimson, and added that he himself had evidently initialed the Quebec agreement without much thought. [22] The Nazis, however, made useful propaganda of the plan, telling their people it revealed the true meaning of "unconditional surrender." One of their influential newspapers warned that it would mean "the destruction of German industry to such an extent that fifty per cent of the German population would be faced with starvation" and urged unconditional resistance. [23]

Deeply concerned over Russian policy in eastern and central Europe, Churchill urged another Big Three meeting to follow immediately after the second Quebec conference. Since Stalin still would not move far from Russia and Roosevelt would not make a distant journey during his re-election campaign, Churchill, who considered another talk with the Communist leader urgent, flew to Moscow in October. For more than a week he and Stalin conferred on the future boundaries of a reconstituted Poland, agreed to divide the Balkan states into Russian and British areas of responsibility, and discussed plans for the Soviet entry into the war against Japan.

Up to this time the Western Allies had assumed that Russia would join the war in the Pacific, as the United States had gone to war against Hitler, by reserving whatever claims she had against the Japanese until after the final victory. But Stalin, for the first time, said he wanted a precise understanding beforehand as to what Russia would obtain from the defeat of Japan.

"There is in this global war," Roosevelt had written to Stalin before the Moscow talks, "literally no question, either military or political, in which the United States is not interested." [24] W. Averell Harriman, the American Ambassador in Moscow, therefore, represented him in the talks. The President also said he could not be bound by any important decisions made at Moscow and that he regarded the talks merely as preliminary to the Big Three meeting he desired after the American election.

Within a few months, some of the political settlements discussed at Moscow began to dismay the Western Allies. As the hour of final victory over Hitler approached, moreover, dissension threatened to split the grand alliance. British and American statesmen quarreled over a new Italian government and over British intervention in Greece. Greater danger to the stability of the wartime coalition lurked in Russia's political measures in eastern and central Europe, particularly in Poland—areas her armies had overrun.

The Yalta Conference

In December Roosevelt reluctantly consented to meet Stalin and Churchill at Yalta, a resort in Russian Crimea, after his inauguration in January. The President also decided to go by ship to Malta and arranged to have his military staff and new Secretary of State, Edward R. Stettinius, Jr., precede him there to confer with the British before the Big Three met.

Churchill was delighted that the President would stop on soil where the British flag flew, expressing his enthusiasm in this rhyme:

> No more let us falter!
> From Malta to Yalta!
> Let nobody alter!

He also suggested the symbolic code name of ARGONAUT for the Yalta Conference, a suggestion that pleased Roosevelt. "You and I," the President told the Prime Minister, "are direct descendants." [25]

In a serious mood, Churchill wrote to Roosevelt with foreboding: "What are your ideas of the length of our stay at Yalta? This may well be a fateful Conference, coming at a moment when the Great Allies are so divided and the shadow of the war lengthens out before us. At the present time I think the end of this war may well prove to be more disappointing than was the last." [26] Roosevelt replied that he thought they should stay at Yalta no more than five or six days.

The President and his party arrived at Malta on February 2, 1945, where the military staffs had reports of their conference ready. Late that night Roosevelt, Churchill, and their parties flew the fourteen hundred miles to Crimea. The conferences with Stalin, the most controversial and momentous of the entire war, began on February 4 and ended on February 11. In addition to military matters, the Yalta talks encompassed four main topics: the Far East, the governments of Poland and the eastern European countries, the future of Germany, and the United Nations Organization.

In their discussions of the war in the Far East, Roosevelt and Stalin began where

Churchill had left off during his visit to Moscow in the previous October. Believing it would take as long as eighteen months after Germany's defeat to crush Japan, with perhaps a million casualties, the American military heads urged Russia's entry into the war in the Pacific "at as early a date as possible."[27] The Soviets promised to join the war about three months after Germany's defeat. Having little faith in the Chinese armies, and being opposed to the use of large American ground forces in China and Manchuria, the President and his military advisers were pleased with the Soviet promise.

Six weeks earlier, Stalin had divulged to Ambassador Harriman his price for fighting Japan. Now he presented his terms to Roosevelt, and the President accepted most of his desires. Almost immediately the Soviets drew up their terms in written form, in a paper entitled "Draft of Marshal Stalin's Political Conditions for Russia's Entry in the War against Japan." Based on the Soviet demands, the final agreement approved the transfer of Japan's Kurile Islands to the Soviet Union, recognized Russia's control of Outer Mongolia, and acquiesced in Russia's recovery of the territory she had lost at the end of the Russo-Japanese War. This last commitment gave the Soviets the southern half of Sakhalin Island, internationalized the port of Dairen while safeguarding Russia's "pre-eminent interest" there, restored the Russian lease on Port Arthur as a naval base, and sanctioned joint Soviet-Chinese operation of the Chinese Eastern and the South Manchurian railroads.

In return, Stalin said he would recognize Chinese sovereignty over Manchuria and make a treaty of friendship and alliance with Chiang Kai-shek's Nationalist government. Churchill, in the closing hours of the conference, signed the agreement without demur. Independently of the written understanding, Roosevelt and Stalin subscribed to a four-power international trusteeship for Korea. Primarily to preserve Soviet military security, the Big Three blanketed the Far Eastern agreement with secrecy.

When the details did become public in February, 1946, it appeared that Roosevelt had made his country responsible for what the Soviets had exacted as their price for entering the war. By that time, moreover, it had become clear that Russian participation in the Japanese war had not been needed, and hence the President's critics denounced the Yalta accord as a sellout of Chiang Kai-shek.

In contrast to his willingness to sponsor territorial adjustments in the Far East, Roosevelt tried to avoid responsibility in dealing with Poland and the countries of eastern Europe. Even though it became the subject of more controversy than any other issue at Yalta, coming up at practically every meeting of the Big Three, the Polish question did not, as some had feared, disrupt the conference. Yet it symbolized a conflict between two concepts of security, the Soviet and the Western.

Although Roosevelt and Churchill at first resisted, they finally agreed to changes in Poland's eastern frontier, accepting the so-called Curzon Line as the new Poland's eastern boundary. That decision allowed Russia to keep a large slice of territory formerly controlled by the Poles. Stalin would not take less, saying he would rather continue the war, even though it would cost more Russian blood, than compromise. As compensation for their loss, the Poles were to receive chunks of eastern Germany, territory containing some twelve million Germans. While agreeing vaguely to what seemed at the time a practical solution, Roosevelt and Churchill refused definite approval of Poland's new western frontiers.

Who would control the new Poland? That was the next question the Big Three had to decide. The United States and Britain recognized and sponsored a Polish government in exile in London that the Soviets would not tolerate. Stalin and his advisers insisted that the Western democracies should recognize a provisional government established by a Polish Communist Committee of National Liberation with its capital at Lublin, sponsored, controlled, and recognized by the Soviets. Roosevelt and Churchill refused.

In a compromise declaration on Poland, published as part of the conference report, the Big Three agreed that the Lublin government should be reorganized on a broad democratic basis to include Polish leaders at home and abroad, and that it should hold free elections, based on universal suffrage and the secret ballot, at an early date to determine the future government. Since the Soviets would not allow international supervision, Roosevelt insisted that the American and British Ambassadors in Warsaw should have the responsibility of determining whether or not the Communists carried out their pledge of unfettered elections. In "The Declaration on Liberated Europe," drafted by Americans, the Big Three announced some vague principles and pledged themselves to assist the peoples of the smaller countries of eastern Europe to establish, through free elections, democratic governments.

In dealing with the main enemy, Germany, the Big Three quickly agreed on the instrument of unconditional surrender, discussed punishment of Nazi leaders as war criminals, and control of the country after surrender. Although they decided in principle to divide Germany into several separate states, they acted in fact on the premise of a single German state reduced in size by cessions to Russia and Poland, with the northern part of East Prussia, including Konigsberg, to go to Russia and the southern half to Poland.[28] Roosevelt and Churchill would not concur in a definite cession of other German territory, east of the Western Neisse and Oder Rivers, to Poland as compensation for the former Polish provinces in the east that Russia was annexing.

The Americans asked for no reparations except to retain German assets in the United States. The British wanted some German equipment and products to repair war damage, but the Russians insisted on large reparations, a total of twenty billion dollars in equipment and goods, of which they would receive half. Roosevelt and Churchill would not accept any fixed sum but assented to the Russian proposal as a basis of discussion within a Reparations Commission with head-quarters in Moscow. The accord also included a Russian suggestion for the "use of German labor," some two or three million Germans to be used for reconstruction work in Russia for ten years.

Earlier the Big Three had decided to divide Germany into three zones to be occupied by their troops.[29] Roosevelt and Churchill wanted to give France a zone of occupation but Stalin would not agree until the end of the conference, and only after he had received assurance it would be within the British and American areas. In addition, Stalin accepted France as a member of an Allied Control Council. The Big Three also decided to eliminate all German industry that could be used for military production. These agreements on Germany were the most crucial European decisions taken at Yalta.

In discussing the United Nations Organization with Stalin, Roosevelt quickly brought up the main source of disagreement at Dumbarton Oaks, the voting rules in the Security Council. Surprisingly, the Russians accepted the American formula, agreeing that the veto power would not apply in "procedural matters," essentially a minor concession. They also agreed that in certain disputes before the Security Council for settlement, a member of that body who was a party to the dispute should abstain from voting.

The Soviets at Dumbarton Oaks had asked for membership in the new inter-national organization of all sixteen of the constituent republics of the Union of Soviet Socialist Republics. At Yalta they withdrew that demand and settled for individual membership for two of their republics, the Ukraine and White Russia, thus obtaining three votes in the organization's General Assembly. In return, Stalin and Churchill said that the United States, if it so desired, might also have three votes.

Stalin made another concession that seemed important at the time. He accepted Roosevelt's suggestion that all nations at war with Germany by March 1, 1945, might become original members of the United Nations Organization. This allowed a number of Latin-American nations to enter the war, join the organiza-tion, and hence strengthen the position of the United States in the General Assembly.

Before returning home from Crimea, Roosevelt kept a date at Suez with the kings of Ethiopia, Egypt, and Saudi Arabia. There the President brought up one of the most controversial questions in the international politics of the Middle East, the status of the Jews in Palestine. He asked King Ibn Saud of Arabia, as spokesman for the Arab world, to admit more Jews into Palestine. "No," Ibn Saud answered grimly, indicating that the Arabs would fight any further Jewish immigration.[30] Although shocked by this stand, Roosevelt said he would take no action which might prove hostile to the Arab people.

As Roosevelt, frail and weary, headed home, he and his party were nonetheless in an exultant mood, believing that the eight days at Yalta had laid the foundations for a firm peace.[31] Communiqués summarizing some of the agreements preceded them, giving the American people the same optimistic impression. In reporting on the Crimea Conference to a joint session of Congress, the President asked the legislators and the people to support the decisions reached at Yalta, saying that without such support "the meeting will not have produced lasting results."[32]

Controversy over Yalta

Not long after Roosevelt's return, disillusionment with the diplomacy of Yalta began to set in. Stalin, it became clear, did not intend to honor his pledges as Americans had thought he would. The Soviets began systematically despoiling the areas of Germany that their armies controlled and showed themselves dedicated to a policy of converting the states of eastern Europe, including Poland, into Communist satellites. The Red armies, not the promises of Yalta, became the arbiters of politics in eastern Europe.

Americans had a deep-rooted prejudice against secret diplomacy, and Roosevelt buried some of the basic decisions of Yalta in secret White House files. Later as the secret accords became public—those on the Far East, on the dismemberment of Germany, on reparations, and on voting in the United Nations Organization— disillusion turned into bitter criticism. Critics charged that the Yalta agreements cynically violated the Atlantic Charter, appeased Stalin's greed, betrayed the peoples of Poland and eastern Europe, and paved the way for Communism in China.

Defenders of the President argued that Russia had also made concessions at Yalta, and important ones. They insisted that Roosevelt gave away nothing the Russians would not have seized anyway and may even have placed restraints on Stalin's appetite. Red armies, they pointed out, held eastern and central Europe, and the Western Allies did not have the power to drive them out. Even if the United States had been willing to try by force to save eastern and central Europe, from Communism, the war-weary American people would not have countenanced a new war to do so, nor even the maintenance of large armies in eastern Europe to keep the Soviets out. In the Far East the United States could not have prevented the Russians from going to war against Japan when they considered it to their advantage to do so. Yalta, these defenders have concluded, received a bad reputation not because of Roosevelt's concessions but because the Soviets failed to keep their pledges.

Regardless of point of view, the following facts seem clear: At the time the diplomacy of Yalta seemed practical; later events made some of the American concessions appear unwise. Careful analysts of Yalta's diplomacy have pointed out that the concessions were not an abject surrender. They reflected the great strength of Russia in Europe and her potential power in Asia. Yalta foreshadowed a new balance of power in the world with the Soviet Union a decisive weight in that balance.[33]

"The Conference in the Crimea," Roosevelt had said in a mood of optimism, "was a turning point—I hope in our history and therefore in the history of the world."[34] He never saw what kind of a turning point it really was. On April 12, 1945, while in Warm Springs, Georgia, he died suddenly of a massive cerebral hemorrhage. At the end of that same month his major antagonist, Adolf Hitler, committed suicide in besieged Berlin. A week later, in the early morning hours of May 7, in Rheims, France, Hitler's successor government signed an unconditional surrender for all fronts. Hostilities ceased at midnight May 8.

The San Francisco Conference

At Yalta the Big Three had agreed to call a conference, the United Nations Conference on International Organization, to frame a constitution, known as the charter, for a new league for postwar security. Since Roosevelt had been eager to have the conference in the United States, the others had agreed. Deciding on San Francisco as the place, they had set April 25, 1945, as the opening date. The governments of the United States, Russia, Britain, and China sponsored the gathering and sent invitations to forty-six governments who were at war with the Axis powers.

The selection of San Francisco, washed by the waters of the Pacific, reflected the change in international politics that had been taking place since the peace-making of the First World War. The center of world diplomacy had shifted to the United States, Asia had gained a new importance, and Europe had lost its pre-eminence in world politics.

Determined to avoid political troubles such as had bedeviled Wilson twenty-five years earlier, Roosevelt had carefully selected a bipartisan delegation to speak for the United States. Headed by the new Secretary of State, Edward R. Stettinius, Jr., the delegation included leaders from both houses of Congress, important Republicans as well as Democrats. The leading politicians were Tom Connally of Texas, chairman of the Senate Committee on Foreign Relations, and Senator Arthur H. Vandenberg of Michigan, a prominent Republican member of that committee. Both had previously committed themselves to the idea of American leadership in the new international organization.

Wishing to continue the grand alliance into the postwar era and to make it the permanent basis for the new collective security, Roosevelt was convinced that the Allies should draft the charter at a time of maximum cooperation, while the smell of gunpowder and death still filled the air in Europe and Asia. Unlike

Wilson, he thought it wise to separate the drafting of the charter from the peace-making. Unlike the Paris Conference of 1919, therefore, the San Francisco Conference had only one function—to give life to the United Nations Organization.

Roosevelt's death did not shatter the plans he had made. The new President, Harry S. Truman, on the same evening he took the oath of office, announced that he would not postpone the San Francisco Conference and would retain the delegation Roosevelt had named. A few days later he instructed that delegation "to write a document that would pass the u.s. Senate and that would not arouse such opposition as confronted Woodrow Wilson." [35]

At the same time other problems, basically Western disagreement with Russia over the government of the new Poland, threatened to disrupt the conference before it opened. By refusing to send his Foreign Minister to San Francisco, moreover, Stalin showed a lack of interest in the United Nations Organization. Truman finally persuaded him to place Molotov at the head of the Soviet delegation, thus preserving the appearance of continued Big Three collaboration.

Publicly, the San Francisco Conference opened with a colorful fanfare of massed flags and on the crest of glowing publicity. Peoples everywhere looked to the assembled delegates to bring forth a new system of collective security that would insure the long peace they all desired. Nowhere was the evangelic fervor in support of the United Nations idea greater than in the United States. Two weeks after the conference had convened, the war in Europe ended. The joy of victory gave additional support to the popular optimism surrounding the delegates.

Yet the diplomacy of the conference itself began inauspiciously, "with Russian clouds in every sky," Senator Vandenberg wrote. [36] For two months the American and Russian delegates argued. At one time, during the most serious crisis, they reached an impasse over voting procedure in the Security Council.

The Russians demanded the right to veto even the discussion of a dispute while the Americans and British insisted that such a broad veto would strangle freedom of discussion in the Security Council. It means, Vandenberg said, "that the Russians can raise Hell all over the world" and "stop the new League from even inquiring into it." [37] To break the deadlock, Truman appealed to Stalin to carry out the Yalta formula on voting procedure. Stalin then accepted the American view that discussion of a dispute was a matter of agenda to be decided by a simple majority vote.

As agreed at Yalta, the United States and Britain sponsored the Ukraine and White Russia and the conference approved their admission into the United Nations Organization, but on that same day the Latin-American delegates tried to bring Argentina, who had belatedly declared war on the Axis powers, into the conference. Arguing that Argentina had aided the Axis through most of the war, the Soviets opposed her admittance. Since the United States wanted to preserve Western Hemisphere solidarity, it supported the desire of the Latin-American representatives. Despite the bitter opposition of the Soviets, Argentina, through the massed votes of the small powers, gained membership.

Another problem that confronted the men of San Francisco was the distribution of power within the United Nations Organization. Convinced that the responsibility for keeping the peace would fall directly on them, the great powers in the Dumbarton Oaks proposals and at Yalta had given themselves a permanent position of predominance. Since they had included France as one of the dominant nations, the great powers constituted a Big Five composed of the United States, Russia, Britain, France, and China. The small powers challenged the supremacy of the Big Five and sought changes within the charter that would give them greater place and influence.

Even though they differed on other matters, the Big Five presented a virtually solid front against the attacks of the small powers. They insisted that great power unity and responsibility were prerequisites for a successful world organization and would not compromise on anything that would detract from their supremacy. Since the United Nations could function successfully only if the great powers were members, the small states could not dislodge the Big Five from the predominant position they had created for themselves.

Russia, moreover, refused to allow any increase of power among the small nations. She feared that any authority the small powers acquired would go to the West, since they most likely would vote with the United States and Britain. Before the conference convened, in fact, the Soviets had made it clear that they must have protection against an extension of authority to the small powers who might isolate them. If they could not have such protection, the Russians indicated, they would not support the new system of collective security.

Crisis over Regionalism

Another crisis grew out of the desires of some countries for a broad recognition of "regional arrangements" in the charter. The Dumbarton Oaks proposals had made room for regional agencies in the United Nations and had said that the Security Council should encourage the settlement of local disputes through such agencies, but many countries considered this recognition inadequate. The United States and the Latin-American countries wished to safeguard the Western Hemisphere from outside interference through their own regional agreements; some European countries wanted to retain their right to make mutual security treaties; and some countries wished to create an alternative form of security in case the Security Council was crippled by the veto. The Russians and some State Department officials opposed regional security pacts, arguing that such arrangements would undermine the effectiveness of the United Nations.

The American delegation finally proposed a plan that became Article 52 of the charter. It said that regional agencies for "the maintenance of international peace and security as are appropriate for regional action" were compatible with the charter, provided their activities were consistent with the purposes and principles of the United Nations. Article 51, moreover, recognized the right of collective self-defense, giving regional agencies the right to use force if necessary, but regional organizations, according to Article 53, could not initiate the use of force without authorization from the Security Council. This was the solution that harmonized regionalism with the idea of universal collective security.

As signed by fifty nations on June 26, 1945, the charter of the United Nations represented a solid victory for the great powers. They would have it no other way. Yet they had made some concessions to the small powers, particularly in giving the General Assembly more power than the Dumbarton Oaks proposals had allowed. In the Assembly the small nations won an untrammeled freedom of debate.

Since it embodied most of the American proposals, represented American ideas, and contained few major contributions from the Soviets, the charter was essentially an American document. Except for its most striking feature that was never carried out—the building of an international armed force to be made available to the Security Council for instant use—the United Nations was virtually a revamped League of Nations.

The Structure of the United Nations

The central body, consisting of all members, was the General Assembly. Conceived as a forum of small nations, it functioned as a diplomatic conference, though some people mistakenly considered it a legislative body. In the General Assembly each member had one vote, could have as many as five delegates, and could participate in debate and discussion. The members could discuss any question within the scope of the charter or relating to any of the organs of the United Nations. They could also send recommendations to the members or to the Security Council on any question, but could not make recommendations on any dispute being considered by the Council unless it requested them. That was the limit of the General Assembly's power. It could not make decisions that were legally binding on its members nor could it enforce its decisions.

A more powerful body was the Security Council, the castle of the great powers. There the Big Five reigned as permanent members aided by six other members elected by the General Assembly for two-year terms. The Council could function continuously and had the power to make decisions binding on all members of the United Nations. The rigid predominance of the Big Five rested on the practical fact that they had the greatest resources, and regardless of any mechanical structure of international organization they would have the decisive responsibility in matters of peace and war.

"The Council of the United Nations," Roosevelt had said, "must have the power to act quickly and decisively to keep the peace by force, if necessary."[38] It had that power. It was the enforcement agency of the new system of collective security, but its enforcement power was based on the principle of unanimity. That, too, was a practical principal. Regardless of world opinion, it could not carry out any decision to use force against the opposition of one or more of the great powers.

Except for "procedural" matters, the Security Council could settle any question through an affirmative vote of seven members including all of the Big Five. This gave any one of the Big Five a veto over all substantive matters, including proposals to amend the charter. The small powers had tried to curb the veto power but had failed. Then they had attempted to remove the veto over amendments to the charter. Again the big powers resisted. Their supremacy under the charter, the Big Five said, would mean nothing if they could not veto amendments. Through amendments, they pointed out, the small powers with votes out of proportion to their population and strength could take away the special status of the big powers.

To deal with lesser but still important matters of international concern, the charter created four other organs. The Economic and Social Council, which operated under the General Assembly, dealt with problems that were not strictly political. It coordinated the work of various "specialized" agencies of the United Nations.

The Trusteeship Council supervised nonstrategic areas, former colonies of countries defeated in the two world wars, under the authority of the General Assembly. Since the American Army and Navy had captured, with great sacrifice, islands in the Pacific that Japan had held under a League mandate—the Carolines, the Marshalls, and the Marianas—they wanted the United States to annex them. Those islands, the military explained, lay athwart the approaches to the Philippines and Guam and in unfriendly hands could threaten communications with Australia and New Zealand. "The State Department," Senator Vandenberg said, "is afraid this will set a bad example to the other great powers." Pointing out that the United States had foresworn territorial gains in its war objectives, had a tradition of opposition to colonialism, and had itself sponsored the trusteeship idea, the Department of State opposed annexation.

As a result, the American delegation proposed a compromise that created a special kind of trusteeship arrangement. Under Article 82 of the charter, any area in a trust territory could be declared a "strategic area." In the case of "strategic areas" the Trusteeship Council functioned under the authority of the Security Council, where the United States could use its veto to prevent any interference in the administration of the Pacific islands it held under a United Nations trust. This compromise assured American military control and at the same time recognized the principle of responsibility to the United Nations for a trust territory.

The other two organs of the United Nations presented no critical problems for the United States. The Secretariat, consisting of the Secretary General and his staff, was responsible for routine tasks of administration. As the principal judicial organ of the United Nations, the International Court of Justice had two kinds of responsibility. It decided cases members brought before it and gave advisory opinions on legal questions. Dozens of other specialized agencies, such as the Food and Agricultural Organization and the United Nations Educational, Scientific and Cultural Organization (UNESCO), were allied or subsidiary to the United Nations.

Acceptance of the United Nations

Since the chief purpose of the United Nations was collective security, meaning to some the prevention of war, many Americans looked to the new organization to inaugurate an era of peace. Some did not realize that it was not a world government and that collective security did not represent much more than an ideal. The United Nations was an association of sovereign nations that had developed out of the wartime alliance. It had no authority to keep peace other than what the great powers would allow it. As before, the politics of power still prevailed in international affairs.

The President wasted no time. He sent the completed charter to the Senate on July 2 to be voted on as a treaty. Popular support and the administration's coddling of the Senate speeded deliberations. The Senate Committee on Foreign Relations held public hearings, but unlike Senator Lodge in 1919, chairman Tom Connally did not use them to delay action. The great majority of witnesses urged approval of the charter, though a few denounced it. One witness said he represented the United Nations of Earth Associates. When pressed, he admitted he was the only member. He spoke his piece, for as one senator remarked, "I knew of no law which prevents a man from associating with himself." [39]

After only five days of hearings, the committee voted 20 to 1 to recommend favorable action without an amendment or reservation. Hiram Johnson, the old "irreconcilable," sent the single dissenting vote from his sick bed.

After six days of formal debate, the Senate approved the charter on July 28 by the landslide vote of 89 to 2, an action that reflected public sentiment. The newspapers, the radio commentators, and others overwhelmingly wanted the United States to take a leading part in the new system of collective security. Public opinion polls showed that among those questioned, sentiment in favor of the charter was twenty to one. In keeping with this sentiment, the United States was the first nation to join the new organization.

In embracing the United Nations, the American people showed an optimism

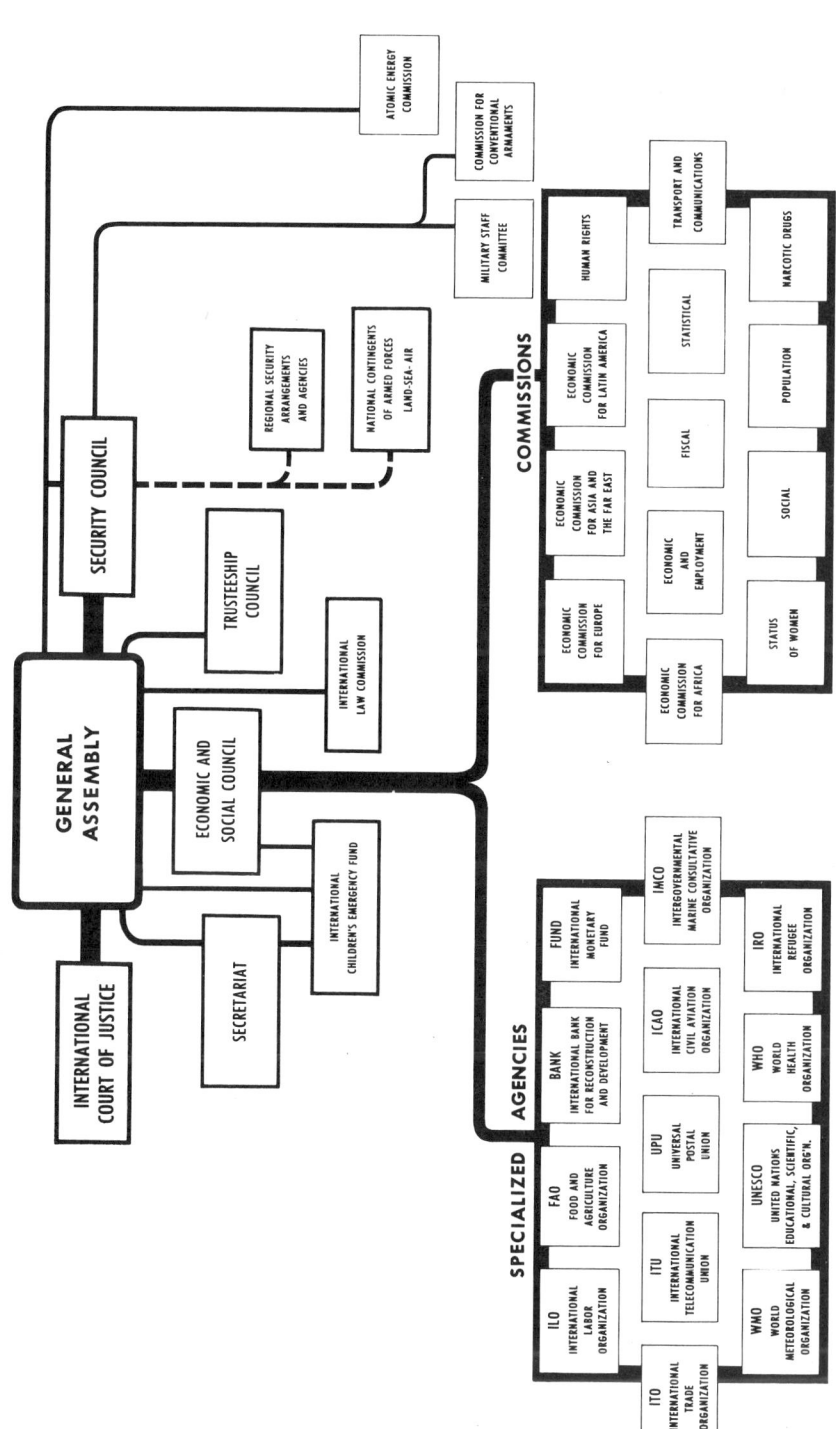

UNITED NATIONS, 1946

that grew out of the impending victory over the Axis powers. They believed that the grand coalition would maintain itself within the United Nations and that the great powers, especially Russia and the United States, would work together with a minimum of friction. They took for granted a will for peace among the Grand Allies, a will that would prevail all over the world once the "aggressor" nations lost their strength.

Within the year a pollster asked some Americans what they thought of the United Nations. One response, although naïve, appeared to express the view of many. "The idea is fine," the random American said. "I'm all for it. I'd like to see wars abolished from the face of the earth, and that's what the u.n. will stand for."[40] Many Americans held similarly exaggerated views of the power of the United Nations.

China—Neglected Ally

While Allies were writing the charter, one of the Big Five, China, was reeling from exhaustion and internal strife. Instead of aiding China to overcome her troubles, which were old ones, the war of the grand coalition had aggravated them. When China had signed the Declaration of the United Nations in January, 1942, and joined the grand alliance, she had already become weary of fighting alone for four and a half years. Japan controlled most of her coastal areas, her richest and most industrialized provinces, and had driven Chiang Kai-shek's National government inland to the fugitive capital of Chungking.

As soon as the United States had become their active ally, the Chinese had assumed that theirs would no longer be a neglected and almost isolated battle front. They had expected massive aid in supplies, guns, planes, and manpower. Such aid never came. With the expansion of the war, in fact, China's plight became worse. Japan's victories in the Pacific, her conquest of Southeast Asia, particularly her cutting of the Burma Road, China's main supply route to the outside world, virtually isolated China from her allies.

Roosevelt had never intended neglecting China. He was himself pro-Chinese, wanted to keep her fighting in the war, and was anxious to win the friendship of her people. He had these objectives in mind in almost every military and political decision he made. Too, he often feared that without Allied support, Chiang, as he sometimes threatened to do, would make a separate peace with Japan.

As soon as the United States began discussions of world-wide strategy with the British and the Russians, the question came up: How important was China as a battle front? Churchill and Stalin considered her of minor importance, whereas Roosevelt and his advisers believed the maintenance of the front in China to be an essential part of Allied strategy. After all, American reluctance to abandon China had led to the breakdown of negotiations with Japan and had been basic in the question of war and peace in the Pacific.

When the British and Russians stubbornly refused to divert scarce men and resources to the war in China, the United States had subordinated its own desires in the interest of harmony and world-wide strategy. Roosevelt thought that the subordination would be temporary and that after the defeat of Germany the United States and its allies would fight in China to expel the Japanese.

America's chief military officer in China, General Joseph W. Stilwell, known as "Vinegar Joe" because of his tart tongue, explained Allied strategy with a bitter humor. "Peanut and I are on a raft," he wrote, "with one sandwich between us, and the rescue ship is heading away from the scene. They are too busy elsewhere for small fry like us, so we can go right ahead developing our characters and working on that shoestring I had presented to me."[41] Stilwell privately referred to Chiang Kai-shek as a "peanut dictator."

Within the United States there was considerable sympathy for China. Most Americans and members of Congress showed more concern for the war in the Pacific than for the conflict in Europe. When Roosevelt spoke to Congress in December, 1941, and paid tribute to the country's British, Russian, and Chinese allies, the loudest applause was reserved for the Chinese.

America's broad policy toward China, within the limits imposed by the strategy of giving first priority to the war in Europe, reflected the sympathy of the American people. That policy had two objectives. The first was to aid China as much as possible so that she would continue to fight the Japanese. The second was to raise a strong, democratic, and unified China to the status of a great power so she could replace Japan as the dominant force in Asia and stabilize the Far East in the postwar era.

A logical corollary to raising China's prestige was to free her from the taint of inequality that for a century had marked her relations with the United States. Even before the United States had entered the war, Japanese propaganda had pictured China as a tool of the Western democracies, alleged friends who would once more victimize her as they had done in the past. Pleading for equal status with the other anti-Axis powers, Chiang Kai-shek asked Roosevelt to remove the stigma of inferiority imposed upon his people.

In October, 1942, the United States offered to negotiate a treaty that would at last give China complete control of her own affairs. A few months later, on January 11, 1943, Secretary of State Hull signed a treaty relinquishing America's rights of extraterritoriality and other unilateral privileges in China. This treaty, ending the inequalities that had contributed to the bitter anti-American agitation in the China of the 1920's, received unanimous approval in the Senate. The British signed a similar treaty with the Chinese on the same day. The Chinese press hailed these pacts as ending a hundred years of humiliation.

In October, Roosevelt made another striking effort to express good will toward China. He urged Congress to "correct a historic mistake and silence the distorted Japanese propaganda" by repealing the exclusion laws barring Chinese from the United States.[42] Although old prejudices had not disappeared, Congress responded to the pressures of war by passing a bill, which became law on December 7, ending Chinese exclusion. The government set the annual quota of Chinese at 105, thus treating them, in principle at least, in the same way it did European immigrants.

The Chinese were delighted. Sun Fo, son of Sun Yat-sen, said that the new law has "reaffirmed our faith in American fair play and American friendship."[43] Although it had acted belatedly, the United States had at last erased the inconsistency of discriminating against an ally it sought to build into a major power.

Although the United States could not offer much direct aid to Chiang because of precarious supply lines and because China was at the end of the line in priorities, it did its best between 1941 and 1945 to show good faith and to keep China fighting. In February, 1942, Roosevelt sent General Stilwell to Chungking to take command of American forces in China, to serve as Chiang's Chief of Staff, and to supervise American aid. Slowly the United States built up a supply route by air over the towering "Hump" of the Himalaya Mountains from India into China. That same month it granted Chiang a political loan of a half billion dollars without security, without prearranged terms, and without means of repayment.

Yet the supplies Chiang received formed a mere trickle. He resented the fact, moreover, that he had no part in the major decisions of his allies affecting the fate of China. He felt slighted when Roosevelt and Churchill met at Casablanca without inviting him. In February, 1943, Madame Chiang Kai-shek, while on a tour of the United States, spoke to a joint session of Congress urging greater support for China. Despite her persuasiveness and the popular acclaim she received, Roosevelt clung to his policy of "Germany first." She also pleaded for the inclusion of China in top level talks on postwar policy.

In August, China asked to be included in the summit conferences at Quebec. For various reasons, including distrust of Chiang's ability to guard the secrecy of military plans, Roosevelt and Churchill refused China an equal place in the conduct of the war. In this respect they treated her as a minor ally. A few months later, however, at Cairo, they gave China the high place the Chiangs had sought. The Declaration of Cairo implied that the heads of state had accepted China as a great power. At least it gave her the chance to become one.

Later, at the Dumbarton Oaks talks, the United States insisted that China should have a permanent seat on the Security Council. The other Allies objected, but finally acquiesced.

China's Internal Problems

While China's international position reached its peak, internal conditions reduced her value as an ally. Economic and social problems, particularly a runaway inflation, made the people sullen and dissatisfied. The Nationalist government became increasingly conservative, and even reactionary, unwilling to take military risks. Chiang's main concern seemed to be to survive the war. An Allied military victory, which appeared certain in 1944, would do him no good if his government collapsed. To the north he knew there were Communists waiting to expand their power and destroy him. All during the war, in fact, he had faced two enemies, the Japanese in the east and the Communists in the north.

In 1937 Chiang's Nationalists and the Chinese Communists had come to an understanding on a united front against the Japanese. Gradually the truce had broken down. Although both fought the Japanese, the Nationalists and Communists did not cooperate. Each claimed the other was sabotaging the war effort. Each said the other was more concerned with building up political power for a postwar internal struggle than in fighting the Japanese.

As tension mounted in 1944 between the Nationalists and the Communists, Roosevelt began exerting increasing pressure on Chiang to overcome the country's economic problems and create a truly united front against the Japanese, who were beginning a new offensive against American air bases in China. Although Roosevelt continued to recognize the Nationalist government as the only legal one, some of his advisers were impressed with the growing power of the Communist regime. They believed that the Allies could not ignore the military power of the Communists in plans for carrying the war to the Chinese mainland.

Concerned about the Japanese offensive and fearing that China might collapse, Roosevelt sent Vice-President Henry A. Wallace on a special mission to Chungking in June, 1944. Wallace urged Chiang to stop fighting the Communists, seek a settlement, and unite with them to resist the Japanese. "Please do not press," Chiang said; "please understand that the Communists are not good for the war effort against Japan." [44]

In August Roosevelt sent General Patrick J. Hurley to Chungking as his personal representative to press essentially the same objectives. On his way, Hurley stopped at Moscow for talks with Stalin. Whether truthfully or not, Stalin assured him that he was not interested in the Chinese Communists, "margarine" or synthetic Communists he had called them several times. He indignantly denied that his government was responsible for the internal divisions in China. Hurley received the impression that the Soviets would not aid the Chinese Communists.

Chiang resisted American pressure for unification with the Communists, insisting that they were bent on dominating all of China. Unification could come, he said, only if the Communists submitted their military forces to his command, something they were unwilling to do. Relations between Chungking and Washington deteriorated. American reporters who had visited the Communist capital of Yenan wrote glowing accounts of Communist efficiency, in striking contrast to stories of Nationalist corruption and incompetence. Their reports, and similar ones by American officials in China, had the effect of weakening American faith in Chiang's ability to govern China.

Those reports and the Japanese offensive contributed to a crisis in Chinese-American relations. In mid-September, 1944, Roosevelt sent Chiang a stiff note telling him that the whole situation in China faced disaster unless he placed Stilwell in command of all military forces, including the Communist. Chiang refused to give a foreigner command of the Chinese armies. All efforts, including Hurley's, to bring about cooperation with the Communists now broke down. The Generalissimo insisted that the irascible and tactless Stilwell, a man he had always detested, must go. Rather than risk an open break with Chiang, Roosevelt recalled Stilwell in October.

General Albert C. Wedemeyer, a man with more tact, replaced "Vinegar Joe" as commander of the American forces in China and as Chiang's Chief of Staff. In December Roosevelt made Hurley Ambassador to Chungking. Both Hurley and Wedemeyer tried to work with Chiang and to create a program of American aid that would strengthen the Nationalists.

At Yalta Roosevelt had obtained a permanent seat on the Security Council for China and won Stalin's support for Chiang's Nationalist government. Fearing security leaks in Chungking, Roosevelt told Chiang nothing of the Far Eastern agreements and of Russia's plans to enter the war against Japan. Chiang was not informed of the secret concessions at Yalta until June, 1945.

Differences between Ambassador Hurley and the Foreign Service experts in China, however, added new snarls to American policy. Hurley urged continued support of Chiang Kai-shek while striving for an accord between the Nationalists and the Communists. The Foreign Service experts, considering Chiang's regime hopelessly corrupt and tyrannical, wanted the United States to deal with all factions to expedite the fight against Japan. The experts attacked what they considered a "blank-check" support of Chiang.

Roosevelt had backed Hurley and had continued to support only Chiang; he had tried to avoid large-scale civil war by bringing the Nationalists and the Communists together in some kind of a coalition government. In the middle of March, 1945, he appealed to the Generalissimo to include members of the Communist Party in the Chinese delegation to the San Francisco Conference. Chiang agreed and several Communists went to San Francisco and worked under the direction of the Nationalist government.

Central Europe

President Truman, meanwhile, prepared himself to carry out Roosevelt's wartime agreements. At Truman's first press conference, held just five days after he became President, a reporter asked if he would be willing to meet Churchill and Stalin. "I should be very happy to meet them," the new President replied, "and General Chiang Kai-shek also. And General de Gaulle; if he wants to see me I will be glad to see him. I would like to meet all of the Allied heads of governments." [45]

A few weeks later, disturbed by the mounting friction with Russia, Churchill told Truman, "It seems to me that matters can hardly be carried further by correspondence, and that as soon as possible there should be a meeting of the three heads of Governments."[46] Believing that in her naked grab for control of eastern and central Europe, Russia had become "a mortal danger" to the West, he urged Truman to order General Eisenhower to push his American and British armies as far east as possible. He also suggested holding the positions in central Europe until Stalin honored the pledges he had made at Yalta.

Advance American units had penetrated east to the suburbs of Berlin and into the western portions of Czechoslovakia late in April, but later withdrew. Since Berlin and Prague were in the zone the Russians would occupy, Eisenhower refused to send his troops toward those cities, arguing that the military disadvantages outweighed the political advantages in trying to take them. To the disappointment of Churchill, Truman supported him.[47]

Truman, nonetheless, had become deeply disturbed over the difficulties with the Soviets in Europe and the Far East. Late in May, therefore, he sent Harry L. Hopkins, his personal adviser, on a special mission to Moscow to get to the root of Soviet animosity. If all went well, Hopkins would make arrangements for a meeting between Truman, Stalin, and Churchill.

Hopkins arrived at Moscow on May 25, and conferred with Stalin until June 7. The Russian and the American both had grievances to air. Stalin showed particular anger over Truman's order of a few weeks earlier that had abruptly terminated Lend-Lease shipments. Hopkins expressed special concern over Soviet actions in Poland shutting out the Western Allies.

After pressing the Russians to set a date for their entry into the Japanese war, Hopkins reported that Stalin "repeated his statement made at Yalta that the Russian people must have a good reason for going to war and that depended on China's willingness to agree to the proposals made at Yalta."[48] Stalin also reiterated that he would do all he could to promote a stable and unified China under Chiang Kai-shek and said that he agreed with America's Open Door policy. Before leaving, Hopkins completed arrangements for a new Big Three meeting at Potsdam, outside Berlin, to discuss outstanding problems.

The Potsdam Conference

Churchill suggested TERMINAL as the code name for the Potsdam Conference, the last meeting of the leaders of the grand alliance, and Truman agreed. Before the conference ended on August 2, a general election swept Churchill from power, and the head of the new Labour government, Clement Attlee, replaced him as Prime Minister and as one of the Big Three.

As the conference opened on July 17, 1945, Truman received news that on the previous day, on a tower above the sands of New Mexico, the world's first atomic bomb had been detonated. Truman and Churchill agreed that now "we should not need the Russians" in the war against Japan. The President did not tell Stalin about the dreadful new weapon until July 24. The old dictator showed little interest and asked no questions. Unknown to Americans, Russian intelligence apparently had already uncovered the secret of Los Alamos.[49]

Instead of optimism bred of victory, an uneasiness clouded the atmosphere at Potsdam. The three allies, whose greatest need was unity, bickered over various issues, such as reparations from Italy and Germany and the Yalta agreements on eastern and central Europe.

In dealing with Germany, their main problem, the Big Three agreed to disarm, demilitarize, and denazify her, and to try her Nazi leaders as war criminals. Since she no longer had a central government, they decided for awhile at least to govern her through an Allied Control Council, composed of the military commanders from the four occupied zones. Although Germany was reduced in size and divided into zones of military occupation, the Big Three decided to treat her as a single economic unit and to try to build democracy there, but without attempting to define it. On the reparations question they accepted a compromise worked out by Truman's new Secretary of State, James F. Byrnes. Each occupying power would take reparations from its own zone, and the Western Allies, since they controlled the industrial areas, would transfer ten per cent of the capital equipment in their zones to Russia for additional reparations without strings attached and another fifteen per cent in exchange for food, coal, and other raw materials.

The Polish question again defied settlement. Although slightly reorganized to include a few non-Communists and now recognized by the Western Allies, the Polish government set up by the Soviets still had not held free elections. The Western Allies refused to recognize the new Poland's western frontier, on the Western Neisse and Oder Rivers, as permanent. The Potsdam Agreement, signed by Truman, Stalin, and Attlee, declared that final delimitation of Poland's western boundary would have to await the peace settlement. Germany's eastern provinces, meantime, would remain under Poland's control. This meant the expulsion of millions of Germans who became refugees in the occupied zones, primarily the Western ones.

Other troublesome issues, such as Russia's demand for control of Italy's North African colony of Tripolitania and for virtual control of the Dardanelles, could not be settled, so the Big Three left them for future discussion. They also agreed to establish a Council of Foreign Ministers, representing the Big Three and France, to prepare peace treaties for Italy, Hungary, Bulgaria, Rumania, and Finland.

Truman had brought an ultimatum with him containing peace terms for Japan. It said the Allies would occupy Japan, reduce her sovereignty to her home islands, and disarm her, but would eventually allow her to participate in world trade and would not enslave her people or destroy her as a nation. In conclusion it called on

SECRETARY OF STATE JAMES F. BYRNES AND PRESIDENT TRUMAN
EN ROUTE TO THE POTSDAM CONFERENCE

the Japanese to surrender unconditionally or face "prompt and utter destruction."[50] Since Russia was still at peace with Japan, Stalin did not become a party
to it, but Chiang Kai-shek joined Truman and Attlee in sponsoring the ultimatum
which was made public on July 26, as the Potsdam Declaration.

In Japan, meanwhile, a peace party had been working to bring the war to an
end as quickly as possible. Its efforts gained strength as American naval and
amphibious forces won victory after victory in the Pacific, and planes and warships
pounded the Japanese home islands. Tojo had fallen from power in July, 1944,
and a new government, containing a few leaders who desired peace, had taken
over. In April, 1945, after the Americans had invaded Okinawa, the emperor
appointed Admiral Kantaro Suzuki Premier, with intimations that he wanted the
admiral to end the war.

The Japanese army, determined to fight on regardless of consequences,
threatened to revolt if the government sued for peace. Nonetheless, a representative
of the Suzuki cabinet began secret discussions in June with the Soviet Ambassador
in Japan, Jacob A. Malik, seeking Russian mediation in the war. Malik was noncommittal. In the following month, before Molotov would leave for Potsdam,
the Japanese Ambassador in Moscow made direct overtures for peace. At Potsdam
Stalin told Truman of the overtures and explained that he did not give a definite
reply because the Japanese had not offered to surrender unconditionally.

When Truman issued the Potsdam Declaration, therefore, the Japanese were
ready to surrender but hesitated in accepting the ultimatum because it did not
offer to preserve the emperor, the one prerequisite they had included in all their

peace efforts. As a result, the Suzuki cabinet informed the Japanese people on July 28 that it was taking the position of *mokusatsu*, a colloquial phrase capable of two meanings. The government wished to "withhold comment" on the Potsdam ultimatum, but Japanese newspapers interpreted the term as saying that the declaration was of "no great value" and hence would be "ignored."[51]

The Atomic Bomb

Taking the Suzuki statement as a contemptuous rejection, Truman and his advisers decided to use atomic bombs against Japan, hoping their use would save American lives by making a direct invasion of the Japanese homeland unnecessary.[52] On August 6 a lone bomber circled Hiroshima and dropped an atomic bomb, the first to be used on human beings. It leveled 4.4 square miles of the city and killed some eighty thousand people. The President announced that if the Japanese "do not now accept our terms, they may expect a rain of ruin from the air, the like of which has never been seen on this earth."[53] Still the Japanese army leaders opposed a surrender.

Two days later, without waiting as he said he would for China to agree to his Far Eastern rewards for entering the war, Stalin declared war on Japan and sent his armies into Manchuria, where they met meager resistance. On the following day, August 9, another atomic bomb exploded over Nagasaki, leveling that city.

Although their country was now exposed to destruction on all sides, Japan's leaders in hurried conferences failed to reach an agreement on accepting the Potsdam Declaration. The emperor acted. "I swallow my own tears and give my sanction,"[54] he said. On the following day the cabinet unanimously supported the emperor's decision and informed the United States through the Swiss government that it accepted the Potsdam terms with the condition that the status of the emperor would not be changed.

Secretary of State Byrnes replied on the following day that the emperor must be subject to the Supreme Commander of the Allied Powers. Dissatisfied with the reply, the military chiefs in Tokyo balked, but the emperor again intervened and on August 14 the Suzuki government formally accepted the Allied terms, terms that were slightly short of unconditional surrender.

In Moscow, on that same day, Stalin gained China's agreement to his price for entering the war against Japan. Chiang Kai-shek's Foreign Minister and Molotov signed a Treaty of Friendship and Alliance and eight other related documents.[55] Those agreements validated the Far Eastern concessions Stalin had exacted at Yalta and pledged the Soviets to support only Chiang's Nationalist government. The terms of the agreements were not announced until twelve days later. The United States hoped the treaty would eliminate any causes of friction between China and Russia and help to stabilize the Far East in the postwar era.

THE GERMAN SURRENDER AT RHEIMS, MAY 7, 1945

THE JAPANESE SURRENDER ON
THE "MISSOURI," SEPTEMBER 2, 1945

Back in Tokyo the emperor prepared an Imperial Rescript ordering all his armed forces to cease hostilities. The government, after fending off attacks by army fanatics, sent representatives to General Douglas MacArthur, designated Supreme Commander for the Allied Powers, at Manila to arrange for the formal surrender ceremony, which took place on September 2, 1945, in Tokyo Bay on the battleship *Missouri*. The grand alliance had mastered the world and the Second World War was over.

NOTES

1. For a provocative analysis, see William L. Langer, "Political Problems of a Coalition," *Foreign Affairs*, XXVI (Oct. 1947), 73–89. For the problems of command in a coalition, see Forrest C. Pogue, *The Supreme Command* (Washington, 1954).

2. Winston Churchill, *The Grand Alliance* (Boston, 1950), p. 641.

3. For interpretive analyses of this strategic problem, see John F. McCloy, "The Great Military Decisions," *Foreign Affairs*, XXVI (Oct. 1947), 52–72; Trumbull Higgins, *Winston Churchill and the Second Front, 1940–1943* (New York, 1957); Samuel E. Morison, *Strategy and Compromise* (Boston, 1958); and Leo J. Meyer, "The Decision to Invade North Africa (TORCH)," in Kent Roberts Greenfield, ed., *Command Decisions* (New York, 1959), pp. 129–153.

4. Hayes to Franco, Nov. 2, 1942, quoted in Herbert Feis, *The Spanish Story* (New York, 1948), p. 183. The full text is in Carlton J. H. Hayes, *Wartime Mission in Spain, 1942–1945* (New York, 1945), pp. 87–88.

5. For a detailed analysis of policy toward the Vichy regime, one favorable to Hull and Roosevelt, see William L. Langer, *Our Vichy Gamble* (New York, 1947). For critical commentaries on the policy toward Vichy, see Ellen Hammer, "Hindsight on Vichy," *Political Science Quarterly*, LXI (June 1946), 175–188 and Louis Gottschalk, "Our Vichy Fumble," *Journal of Modern History*, XX (March 1948), 47–56. See also Paul Farmer, *Vichy: Political Dilemma* (New York, 1955).

6. Jan. 24, 1943, in Samuel I. Rosenman, comp., *The Public Papers of Franklin D. Roosevelt* (13 vols., New York, 1938–50), XII, 39.

7. Hanson W. Baldwin stresses this view in *Great Mistakes of the War* (New York, 1950) and "Churchill Was Right," *Atlantic Monthly*, CXCIV (July 1954), 23–32. Similarly, Anne Armstrong, in *Unconditional Surrender: The Impact of the Casablanca Policy upon World War II* (New Brunswick, N.J., 1961), argues that unconditional surrender prolonged the war.

8. For details on this interpretation, see Paul Kecskemeti, *Strategic Surrender: The Politics of Victory and Defeat* (Stanford, Calif., 1958).

9. John L. Chase's analysis, "Unconditional Surrender Reconsidered," *Political Science Quarterly*, LXX (June 1955), 270–271, makes this point.

10. Quoted in Herbert Feis, *Churchill, Roosevelt, Stalin* (Princeton, 1957), p. 156.

11. *Ibid.*, p. 157.

12. Nov. 18, 1943, *The Memoirs of Cordell Hull* (2 vols., New York, 1948), II, 1314.

13. March 18, 1942, quoted in Winston Churchill, *The Hinge of Fate* (Boston, 1950), p. 201.

14. The declaration is in Rosenman, comp., *Papers of Franklin D. Roosevelt*, XII, 531.

15. Quoted in Robert E. Sherwood, *Roosevelt and Hopkins* (New York, 1948), p. 779.

16. Dec. 1, 1943, in Rosenman, comp., *Papers of Franklin D. Roosevelt*, XII, 533.

17. Quoted in Feis, *Churchill, Roosevelt, Stalin*, p. 310.

18. New York, Oct. 21, 1944, in Rosenman, comp., *Papers of Franklin D. Roosevelt*, XIII, 349.

19. Quoted in Sherwood, *Roosevelt and Hopkins*, p. 830.

20. Aug. 26, 1944, quoted in *Memoirs of Cordell Hull*, II, 1603.

21. Quoted in Feis, *Churchill, Roosevelt, Stalin*, p. 370. A photographic copy of a summary of the Morgenthau Plan, which Roosevelt took with him to Quebec, is in Henry Morgenthau, Jr., *Germany Is Our Problem* (New York, 1945).

22. Quoted in Elting E. Morison, *Turmoil and Tradition: A Study of the Life and Times of Henry L. Stimson* (Boston, 1960), p. 609.

23. *Völkischer Beobachter*, quoted in Chester Wilmot, *The Struggle for Europe* (New York, 1952), p. 550. A detailed scholarly analysis of the Morgenthau Plan and its abandonment is in John L. Snell, *Wartime Origins of the East-West Dilemma Over Germany* (New Orleans, 1959), pp. 64–126.

24. Quoted in Sherwood, *Roosevelt and Hopkins*, p. 834.

25. The rhyme and the Roosevelt quotation are in Winston Churchill, *Triumph and Tragedy* (Boston, 1953), pp. 338–339.

26. Jan. 8, 1945, *ibid.*, p. 341.

27. Memo of the Joint Chiefs of Staff of Jan. 22, 1945, quoted in Feis, *Churchill, Stalin, Roosevelt*, p. 503. See also John L. Snell, ed., *The Meaning of Yalta* (Baton Rouge, La., 1956), pp. 198–203 and Ernest R. May, "The United States, the Soviet Union, and the Far Eastern War, 1941–1945," *Pacific Historical Review*, XXIV (May 1955), 153–174, which stresses that military reasons governed the American desire to bring Russia into the Far Eastern war.

28. For details, see Philip E. Moseley, "Dismemberment of Germany: The Allied Negotiations from Yalta to Potsdam," *Foreign Affairs*, XXVIII (April 1950), 487–498 and Snell, *Dilemma over Germany*, pp. 141–144, who points out that the question of partition was in effect postponed.

29. Details are in Philip E. Moseley, "The Occupation of Germany: New Light on How the Zones Were Drawn," *Foreign Affairs*, XXVIII (July 1950), 580–604.

30. Sherwood, *Roosevelt and Hopkins*, p. 872.

31. For an analysis dealing with Roosevelt's physical appearance at this time, see Herman E. Bateman, "Observations on President Roosevelt's Health during World War II," *Mississippi Valley Historical Review*, XLIII (June 1956), 82–102.

32. March 1, 1945, in Rosenman, comp., *Papers of Franklin D. Roosevelt*, XIII, 570.

33. Much of the commentary on Yalta is summarized in Snell, ed., *Meaning of Yalta*. Louis Morton, in "The Military Background of the Yalta Agreements," *The Reporter*, XII (April 7, 1955), 19–21, points out that Russia's entrance into the Far Eastern war had at least as much effect on Japan's decision to surrender as had the atomic bomb, and hence the Yalta decision was justified. See also Raymond J. Sontag, "Reflections on the Yalta Papers," *Foreign Affairs*, XXXIII (July 1955), 615–623; Rudolph A. Winnacker, "Yalta—Another Munich?" *Virginia Quarterly Review*, XXIV (Autumn 1948), 521–537; and G. F. Hudson, "The Lesson of Yalta," *Commentary*, XVII (April 1954), 373–380, a criticism of Yalta's diplomacy.

34. March 1, 1945, in Rosenman, comp., *Papers of Franklin D. Roosevelt*, XIII, 585.

35. Harry S. Truman, *Memoirs* (2 vols., Garden City, N.Y., 1955), I, 46.

36. April 25, 1945, in Arthur H. Vandenberg, Jr., ed., *The Private Papers of Senator Vandenberg* (Boston, 1952), p. 176.

37. May 20, 1945, *ibid.*, p. 196.

38. Oct. 21, 1944, Rosenman, comp., *Papers of Franklin D. Roosevelt*, XIII, 350.

39. Alben Barkley, quoted in Thomas J. Connally, *My Name is Tom Connally* (New York, 1954), p. 285.

40. Quoted in Leonard S. Cottrell, Jr. and Sylvia Eberhart, *American Opinion on World Affairs in the Atomic Age* (Princeton, 1948), p. 40.

41. To Mrs. Stilwell, in Theodore H. White, ed., *The Stilwell Papers* (New York, 1948), pp. 171–172.

42. Oct. 11, 1943, in Rosenman, comp., *Papers of Franklin D. Roosevelt*, XII, 428.

43. Quoted in Fred W. Riggs, *Pressures on Congress: A Study of the Repeal of Chinese Exclusion* (New York, 1950), p. 160.

44. Quoted in Herbert Feis, *The China Tangle* (Princeton, 1953), p. 149.

45. April 17, 1945, Truman, *Memoirs*, I, 49.

46. May 7, 1945, quoted in Herbert Feis, *Between War and Peace: The Potsdam Conference* (Princeton, 1960), p. 82.

47. Forrest C. Pogue, in "The Decision To Halt at the Elbe," in Greenfield, ed., *Command Decisions*, pp. 374–387, points out that Eisenhower halted his troops short of Berlin and Prague for military reasons only and that militarily his decision was the proper one. See also Feis, *Between War and Peace*, pp. 18–20, 74–77.

48. Quoted in Sherwood, *Roosevelt and Hopkins*, p. 902.

49. See Feis' surmise in *Between War and Peace*, p. 178, and his *Japan Subdued: The Atomic Bomb and the End of the War in the Pacific* (Princeton, 1961), p. 90.

50. The text of the Potsdam Declaration of July 26, 1945, is printed in Truman, *Memoirs*, I, 390–392.

51. For an analysis and detailed discussion of *mokusatsu*, see Robert J. C. Butow, *Japan's Decision to Surrender* (Stanford, Calif., 1954), pp. 142–149. Samuel E. Morison, in "Why Japan Surrendered," *Atlantic Monthly*, CCVI (Oct. 1960), 44, points out that if Suzuki's cabinet had accepted the Potsdam Declaration as a basis for peace, the atomic bomb would not have been dropped in Japan.

52. For the debates on this fateful decision, see Feis, *Japan Subdued*, pp. 37, 178–187; Henry L. Stimson, "Decision to Use The Atomic Bomb," *Harper's Magazine*, CXCIV (Feb. 1947), 97–107; Louis Morton, "The Decision to Use the Atomic Bomb," in Greenfield, ed., *Command Decisions*, pp. 388–410; Richard G. Hewlett and Oscar E. Anderson, Jr., *The New World, 1939–1946*, Vol. I of *A History of the United States Atomic Energy Commission* (University Park, Pa., 1962), pp. 347–407; and two popular accounts, Michael Amrine, *The Great Decision: The Secret History of the Atomic Bomb* (New York, 1959) and Fletcher Knebel and Charles W. Bailey III, *No High Ground* (New York, 1960).

53. Truman, *Memoirs*, I, 422.

54. Quoted in Butow, *Japan's Decision to Surrender*, p. 176.

55. The text of the agreements is in U.S. Department of State, *United States Relations with China: With Special Reference to the Period 1944–1949* (Washington, 1949), pp. 585–596. The Russians, in viewing the Far Eastern war, claimed that the intervention of the Red army forced the Japanese to capitulate. John A. White, "As the Russians Saw Our China Policy," *Pacific Historical Review*, XXVI (May 1957), 156.

Chapter Twenty-Five

INTO THE COLD WAR

N<small>EVER</small> before had any nation attained such immense power as had the United States at the end of the Second World War. It had a magnificent battle-tested army, a navy more powerful than all of the other fleets of the world combined, the greatest air force the world had yet seen, strategic bases scattered over the globe, and in the atomic bomb it held the secret of a weapon capable of such vast destruction that no one had a defense against it. America's industrial capacity and production of wealth was so far ahead of the rest of the world as to make all other nations, even her two major allies, Great Britain and Russia, seem like poor cousins.

Even though Americans were not fully aware of the responsibilities that went with their power, they did not wish to return to the isolation so many had sought after the First World War.[1] Seemingly, their predominant position had given them an almost unassailable security. Yet for them, the immediate postwar years were years of acute international tension. The source of that tension, Americans were convinced, was the Soviet Union.

Despite the efforts of American statesmen to preserve the wartime alliance with the Soviet Union, even at the cost of assenting to distasteful claims in Europe and Asia, distrust between the Soviets and the Western Allies made the tension almost inevitable. American leaders had always been hostile to the Communist dictatorship which had achieved, by the end of the war, a power second only to that of the United States. The Soviets were equally, if not more, distrustful of the United States and the West. During and after the war they sought to protect their frontiers by extending them, by maintaining their wartime military might, and by treating the United States as a potential enemy rather than as an ally.

Just as Americans were dismayed by Russia's arbitrary and at times brutal policies in central and eastern Europe, Russians were alarmed by the efforts of

Americans to confine the secret of the atom bomb to themselves. During the war, even though the Soviets had accepted them ungraciously, the Western Allies had transmitted other scientific secrets, such as those of radar and penicillin, to Russia. The "ultimate weapon" was a different matter; the United States would not assist the Soviets in arming themselves with atomic weapons. That attitude, coupled with the memory of prewar American hostility toward them, confirmed their view that they must regard the United States as an enemy after the war. Whether rightly or wrongly, the Soviets believed that they themselves were the rivals of a powerful people who would, if they could, destroy their regime.

Only the task of overcoming a common peril had kept American and Soviet discord beneath the surface of diplomacy. The wartime cordiality, despite Franklin D. Roosevelt's hope that it would blossom into a lasting accommodation, had never been more than a temporary accord. It was a mistake therefore to think, as did many Americans, that without cause the Soviets after the war inaugurated a new policy of deliberate hostility. Basic Soviet policy had not changed. The mutual distrust of the prewar era merely continued into the postwar years, but became acute because of the tremendous increase in power of both the United States and the Soviet Union.

Germany

Nowhere was tension more acute than in Germany. As agreed at Yalta and Potsdam, the Big Three had divided Germany into four zones occupied by American, Russian, British, and French troops. They had also split Berlin, located 110 miles within the Soviet zone, into four sectors. In each major zone, supreme authority rested with the Allied military commander. The four military commanders formed the Allied Control Council, the administrative organ responsible for matters affecting Germany as a whole. Since the Council could act only if its decisions were unanimous, each of the occupying powers had a veto over policy affecting the whole of Germany.

From the beginning of their occupation the Allies had agreed on one fundamental objective. They wanted to render Germany so impotent that she would never again be able to threaten them. All embarked on a program of rooting out Naziism, of dismantling industries that could produce armaments, and of reducing the production of all German capital goods, such as steel, to a level that could not support a war machine.

These and other measures were designed to keep Germany's living standard on a level not to exceed the average standards of other European countries. To insure the production of food and supplies for the occupying forces and for the German people, to preserve a balanced economy throughout Germany, and to reduce the need for imports, the Allies had agreed that the several zones would exchange essential commodities.

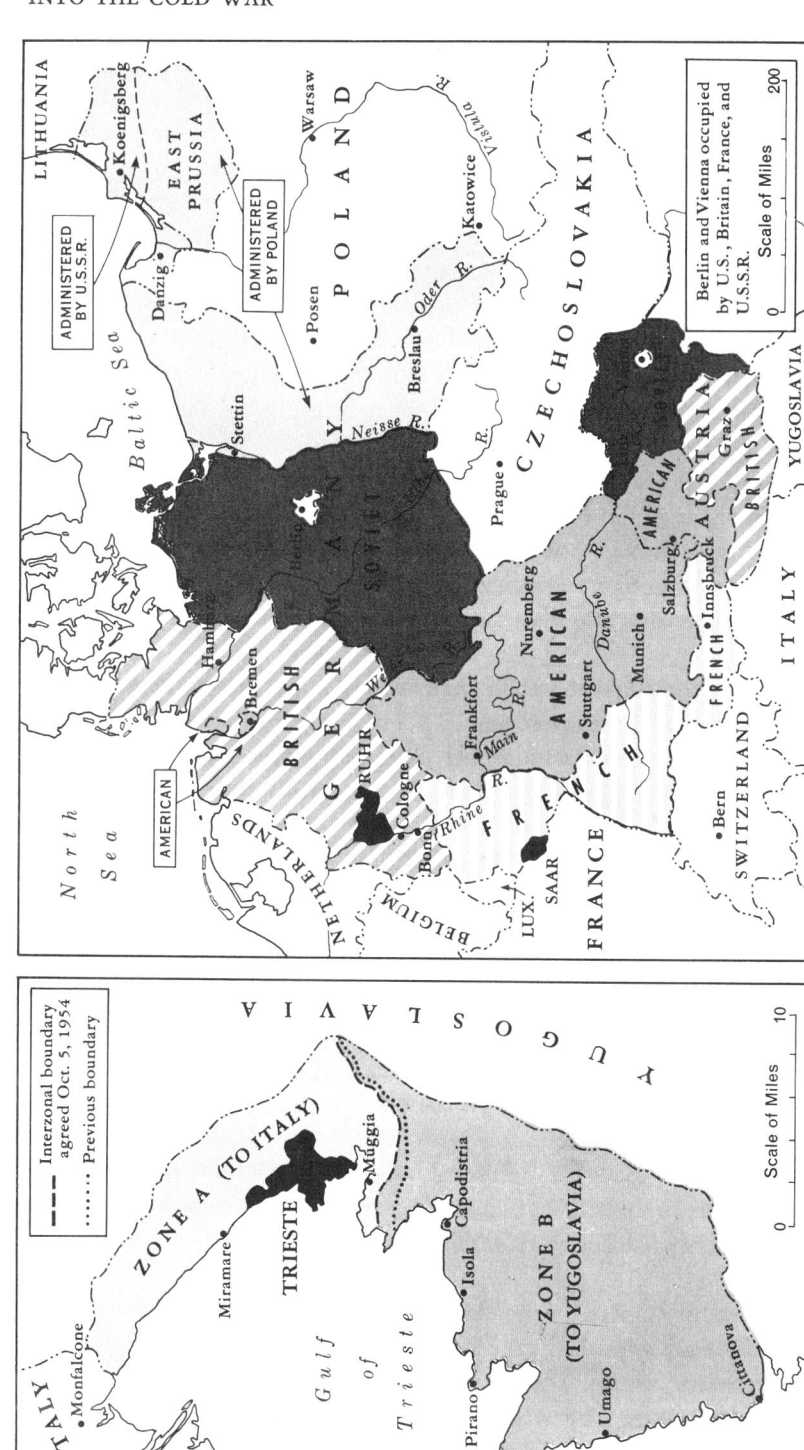

ALLIED OCCUPATION OF EUROPE: GERMANY, AUSTRIA, TRIESTE

One part of the cooperative postwar Allied policy, that of punishing Nazis for various categories of "war crimes," culminated in the Nuremberg trials that ran from November, 1945, to October, 1946. The International Military Tribunal that conducted the trials tried twenty-two high Nazi officials and convicted nineteen, meting out prison terms to seven and death sentences to the others.

Although the tribunal observed many of the established procedures of law and justice, some Americans criticized the trials as violating the traditions of Anglo-American jurisprudence.[2] In particular they disliked the *ex post facto* nature of the punishment, that is the punishment of men for deeds that were not, according to accepted law, crimes when committed. Critics also pointed out that the trials established the principle, under the guise of the judicial process, that the victors in a war could put to death the leaders of defeated nations.

Defenders of the trials said that the Nuremberg precedents would force the leaders of nations to observe moral and humanitarian principles in their conduct, would imbed those principles into international practice, and would contribute to future peace by deterring "aggression." By defining international crimes, some scholars added, the trials also placed a limitation on the absolute sovereignty of states.

The United States sought to punish Germany but not to destroy her. American statesmen had envisaged the severe unified policy as the first step toward building a new democratic Germany who would ultimately take her place in the community of nations. France, who had three times suffered from the crushing invasions of German armies, had announced that since she had not been represented at Potsdam, she was not bound by the Potsdam decisions. Seeking to separate the Saar, the Ruhr, and the Rhineland from Germany, she opposed any policy that carried the risk of reviving German power. Through her representative on the Allied Control Council, she appeared at first the main obstacle to a unified Allied policy.

Actually, the Potsdam arrangements for a unified control of Germany broke down because of Russia, not France. Instead of cooperating within the Control Council in treating Germany as a single economic unit, as they had agreed to do, the Russians governed their zone as an area completely independent of the other zones. They appeared to regard their zonal boundary as if it were an international frontier. They removed factories, industrial equipment, and crops and transported Germans to Russia for labor there without regard for the economy of Germany as a whole.

Since the rest of Germany depended on foodstuffs raised in Russia's eastern zone, the Western powers had expected the Soviets to supply their zones with food. The Russians refused. The people of the western zones, therefore, had to depend on food from the United States or starve. In addition, the Russians insisted on taking ten billion dollars in reparations out of current German production, arguing that Roosevelt had agreed to that amount at Yalta. The United States and Britain opposed the demand, saying that so great a sum could be extracted only if they themselves financed the Germans.

While the Soviets and the United States were deadlocked in their policy, the German standard of living fell dangerously low, well below that anticipated by the Western Allies. The American taxpayer, moreover, carried most of the cost of keeping the western zones going. In May, 1946, therefore, the American military commander in Germany suspended the dismantling of plants in the American zone for reparations to Russia. The British and French did the same in their zones.

So that the Germans would pay their own way, the United States now promoted a policy of industrial recovery. In July, Secretary of State James F. Byrnes offered to merge the American zone economically with any other zone. "We cannot continue to administer Germany in four airtight compartments," he said; it would lead to "economic paralysis."[3] Russia and France declined, but the British accepted.

Three months earlier, in an effort to overcome Russian and French fears of a unified Germany, Byrnes had offered them a four-power treaty guaranteeing German disarmament for twenty-five years. "Such a treaty," he had previously told Stalin, "will give all European states assurance that the United States would not return to a policy of isolation."[4] The Russians, however, had argued that the Allies were already pledged to disarm Germany. Since they and the French desired stronger guarantees, mainly a mutual defense pact, they refused Byrnes' treaty.

Five months later, in a speech in Stuttgart, Byrnes summarized America's new policy. He suggested uniting Germany not only economically but also politically on a federal pattern with a central government. The purpose of the occupation, he declared, was not "a prolonged alien dictatorship" but to build a political democracy.[5] The final decision on Germany's eastern frontier, the Oder-Neisse boundary, he said, should be made at a peace conference and not unilaterally by Poland or Russia. He then renewed his earlier offer of a security treaty to Russia and France, this time extending the time period to forty years, but again they refused.

Byrnes' speech implied that the United States now looked upon Germany as a prize to be won and kept out of Russian hands. Britain, in accord with the American policy, went ahead and fused her zone with the American zone, a fusion that formally went into effect on January 1, 1947. This step marked the beginning of a division of Germany into two hostile areas, one Western and the other Communist, each completely separated from the other.

In March the new Secretary of State, George C. Marshall, renewed the offer of a security treaty against German rearmament. This time France supported the proposal, but the Russians again turned it down. Rather than commit the United States to a control of Germany for forty years, the Soviets now wanted the

Americans to withdraw from Europe. The Soviets continued to refuse to merge their zone economically with the others unless the Western powers gave them a share in the control of the Ruhr and recognized their claim for ten billion dollars in reparations.

The United States and Britain, therefore, went ahead with their bizonal merger and set new levels of production for German industry in the combined zones. The Soviets formally protested the new industrial arrangements as violating the Potsdam agreements, a charge the United States and Britain did not deny. They pointed out, however, that the Soviets themselves had already violated the Potsdam program by refusing to treat Germany as an economic unit. By the end of the summer of 1947 the Potsdam arrangements on Germany were defunct.

Austria

Although a less important problem than Germany, Austria also became a sore spot in the relations between the Soviet Union and the United States. In 1943, the Allies had agreed to treat her not as a former enemy but as a liberated state and to restore her independence. At Potsdam the Big Three had decided to exempt Austria from payment of reparations but had assigned certain German assets in the country to Russia. Even though the Allies called Austria a "liberated" nation, they divided her into four occupied zones as they had Germany, cut Vienna into four compartments, and governed her through a Control Council. Unlike Germany, however, the occupying powers treated Austria as a unit and allowed her an elected central government subject to their military control.

American policy toward Austria sought the elimination of Naziism, Pan-Germanism, militarism, and the establishment of a democratic government under Austrian control as soon as possible. The United States, like Britain and France, favored generous terms for the Austrians. Pointing out that the Austrians, as soldiers of Hitler's Germany, had fought against them and had caused damage in Russia, the Soviets wished to punish them. They insisted on snatching a large share of Austria's oil, industry, and other equipment as "German assets" to equal the reparations they sought. Since the Russians held the largest zone containing most of the industry and the best agricultural land, and the American zone held little more than scenery, the Austrians found their food and goods going to the Soviets and their own people on the verge of starvation in the first years of the occupation. The Austrians survived only on relief supplies sent primarily from the United States.

If only to reduce the cost of supporting the Austrians, Secretary of State Byrnes in February, 1946, sought a treaty between the Allies and Austria that would re-establish her independence and fix her frontiers. The Russians refused. By keeping their troops in Austria they had an excuse for continuing their occupation of

Rumania and Hungary, claiming they had to keep their lines of communication to Austria intact. The Soviets had nothing to gain in a settlement with Austria and profited from the existing occupation. Although the United States would gain from a truly independent Austria, her case was not important enough to warrant strong measures against the Soviets. For a decade after liberation, therefore, the fate of that little republic remained uncertain. The forces of the four great powers—"four elephants in a canoe," Austria's president called them—still occupied the country.

The Dilemma of Poland

Like Austria, Poland in the immediate postwar years remained a source of big power controversy. Stalin and Molotov blocked American and British attempts to send observers into Poland and to bring anti-Communist Poles into effective positions in the government there. The elections Stalin had promised for early 1945 were not held until January, 1947, and were so controlled by Communists as to shatter all pretense that they were "free and unfettered."

Even more disturbing to Americans was Communist action on Poland's western frontier. "The western frontier question was open," Stalin had told President Truman at Potsdam, "and the Soviet Union was not bound."[6] Just fifteen weeks later, however, on August 16, 1945, the Soviet Union signed a treaty with Poland's Communist-controlled government recognizing the Oder-Neisse line as Poland's western boundary. As agreed at Potsdam, the Poles continued to expel the inhabitants of the German provinces they had taken over, just as Hitler had moved masses of people all over Europe. Ultimately the Poles, in one of mankind's great forced mass movements, uprooted some nine million Germans.

By the middle of 1946 the Poles, supported by the Russians, made it clear that they regarded the Potsdam boundary as permanent. To hold that boundary Poland was dependent on Russia, for the Germans could not forget their lost provinces, *terra irredenta*, that a revived Germany might try to reclaim. The United States would not recognize the *de facto* Oder-Neisse boundary as final but could not change it without resorting to force, a last resort which the American people could not be expected to accept. Poland had become a Russian satellite beyond the reach of American foreign policy.

Five Peace Treaties

As with Austria, the United States sought a quick and effective peace settlement with Italy, Hungary, Rumania, Bulgaria, and Finland, the five European states who had fought on the side of Germany. It wished to re-establish them as independent nations with democratic governments. The Soviets, particularly in the states of eastern Europe, wanted governments along Communist lines that they could control. This became the basic issue in the peacemaking, a frustrating task that exacerbated the differences between the Soviets and Americans.

In the summer of 1945, the United States and Russia had agreed that the great powers should draft the peace treaties and that there should be no large peace conference as in 1919. At Potsdam the Big Three had created a Council of Foreign Ministers composed of the foreign ministers of the five great powers, but Stalin insisted that in drafting the peace treaties the Council should be composed of governments who had signed the armistice terms with the former enemy states. Thus, the Big Three would draft the treaties with the Balkan states; France and the Big Three the Italian treaty; and since the United States had not gone to war against the Finns, Russia and Britain the treaty with Finland.

Holding its first meeting in London in September, 1945, the Council of Foreign Ministers approached its initial task, the drafting of the five peace treaties, with the view that it would be easier to handle than the thorny problems of Germany. That view proved an illusion. Molotov again demanded a Soviet trusteeship over Tripolitania or some other Italian colony in the Mediterranean and insisted on a hundred million dollars as a reparation from Italy. The Western Allies said the impoverished Italians could not pay such a large sum unless it came from the United States and Britain. The Americans and the British also resisted the Soviet challenge to their dominance in the Mediterranean.

In the case of the Balkan countries, Molotov said, all the peace treaties had to do was to confirm the armistice terms. Secretary of State Byrnes replied that the United States would not sign treaties with puppet regimes there, established in violation of the Yalta Declaration on Liberated Europe. Pointing out that the United States had not consulted Russia fully in the arrangements for the control of Japan, Molotov countered with the charge that the Western Allies were insisting on the right to interfere in the political settlement of eastern Europe while excluding the Soviet Union from the political arrangements of the Far East.

After more wrangling, the conference ended in failure. All the London Conference had done was to expose more openly than before the deep differences between the Soviets and the Western Allies. The grand alliance was breaking up.

In an effort to end the impasse of London, Secretary Byrnes suggested a special meeting of the Big Three ministers in Moscow that took place in December. By agreeing to recognize the Rumanian and Bulgarian satellite governments and by proposing an Allied Control Council for Japan, Byrnes made concessions to the Soviets. In return, the Russians accepted the program for a peace conference to be held in Paris not later than May 1, 1946.

Critics called the Moscow Conference an "eastern Munich," and President Truman considered the Moscow agreements "unreal" successes. He scolded Byrnes, saying, "I'm tired of babying the Soviets." [7] Nonetheless, the Moscow agreements once again set the peacemaking in motion.

The Iron Curtain

Ten weeks later, in a speech at Fulton, Missouri, with Truman at his side, Winston Churchill called for a tough policy against the Soviets, one backed by an Anglo-American alliance. "From Stettin in the Baltic to Trieste in the Adriatic," he said, "an iron curtain has descended across the Continent."[8] All those living behind it were controlled from Moscow.

Stalin replied bitterly, calling the speech a dangerous act and Churchill a war-monger, and intemperately compared him to Hitler. The Soviets, apparently, took the speech as new evidence of Anglo-American hostility and of a new hardening in the division between the Communist and Western worlds. Although Americans quickly grasped the phrase "iron curtain" and added it to their vocabulary on foreign affairs, many of them criticized the Fulton speech as charting a course that would wreck the United Nations and provoke war with the Soviet Union.

Deputies of the foreign ministers, meantime, were unable to complete their assigned work on drafts of the peace treaties in time for a peace conference by the deadline of May 1. To speed up the work of the deputies, Secretary Byrnes suggested a second conference of the Council of Foreign Ministers. The first session, held in Paris in April and May, 1946, accomplished little except to free Italy of most military controls. The weary ministers returned the peace treaties to the deputies, called a "recess," and agreed to meet again a month later. The second session met in June and July, arranged a compromise on reparations from Italy that gave the Soviets most of what they wanted, finally worked out an agreement on drafts for the peace treaties, and decided to hold the peace conference on July 29.

Twenty-one nations, the Big Five plus sixteen of the smaller Allies who had fought in the European war, sent delegates to the peace conference that met at the Luxembourg Palace in Paris. Few of the powers were satisfied with the treaties, but the small states could do little to change them because the conference could only recommend. The power of final decision rested with the foreign ministers of the Big Four. After passing a total of ninety-four recommendations, the conference adjourned on October 15 and gave the recommendations to the Council of Foreign Ministers which held its third session in New York in November and December.

At the meetings in the Waldorf-Astoria Hotel, Secretary Byrnes took the position that the treaties would be completed at this session of the Council or would not be consummated at all. After some hard bargaining, the Soviets made some concessions, accepted the main proposals adopted at the peace conference, and the ministers announced that the treaties were ready for signature. The five peace treaties were signed on February 10, 1947, that with Italy in Paris and the others in Moscow.

Four of the treaties, those with Russia's smaller neighbors, confirmed the armistice terms the Soviets had dictated, including the cession of small amounts of territory and the payment of reparations to Russia. By signing those treaties, except that with Finland, the United States recognized Soviet control of southeastern Europe, a retreat from its position that Stalin must fulfill his Yalta pledges. American military weakness and strategic disadvantage in eastern Europe relative to the Soviet Union made a firmer course almost impossible.

Confronted with insistent demands by the people and Congress to bring the boys back home immediately after the war, the American government from August, 1945, to the middle of 1946 had cut back the Army from eight to less than two million men. What remained was an army composed of untrained personnel, replacements for wartime draftees, scattered over Europe and the Far East. The Air Force had suffered a similar reduction in effectiveness. The Soviets, on the other hand, had maintained a large part of their wartime army. In 1946, they had an estimated six million men under arms and could easily have overrun all of Europe.

Italy's Peace Terms

Italy's treaty had presented a special problem. Britain and the United States had recognized the Italians as "cobelligerents" and had said they would treat them kindly in the peace settlement, if the Italians earned their way by fighting the Germans. The Western Allies had officially recognized that the Italians had earned their way and tried to modify the armistice terms, but Stalin and Molotov insisted that Italy should receive no consideration not accorded to Hungary, Rumania, and Bulgaria. The peacemakers, therefore, treated Italy as an enemy state meriting punishment.

The peace treaty stripped Italy of all her colonies and of her fleet, transferred some minor Italian territory to France and a larger piece to Yugoslavia, reduced her armed forces to token size, and gave the Soviets the hundred million dollars in reparations they desired. Italians were dismayed by the peace treaty, which they considered unnecessarily harsh. More than anything else they resented the loss of territory with Italian population to Yugoslavia, particularly the fate of Trieste, a city over eighty per cent Italian.

Trieste had become a prize in the struggle between the Soviets and the Western Allies. Communist Yugoslavia, with Russia's support, tried to annex it. The Western powers wanted it to remain Italian. The peace treaty made it and some surrounding land a "free territory" under the Security Council of the United Nations, a compromise that satisfied no one. That area remained a sore spot until October, 1954, when Italy and Yugoslavia divided it between themselves.

Behind the leadership of Senators Vandenberg and Connally, who had taken

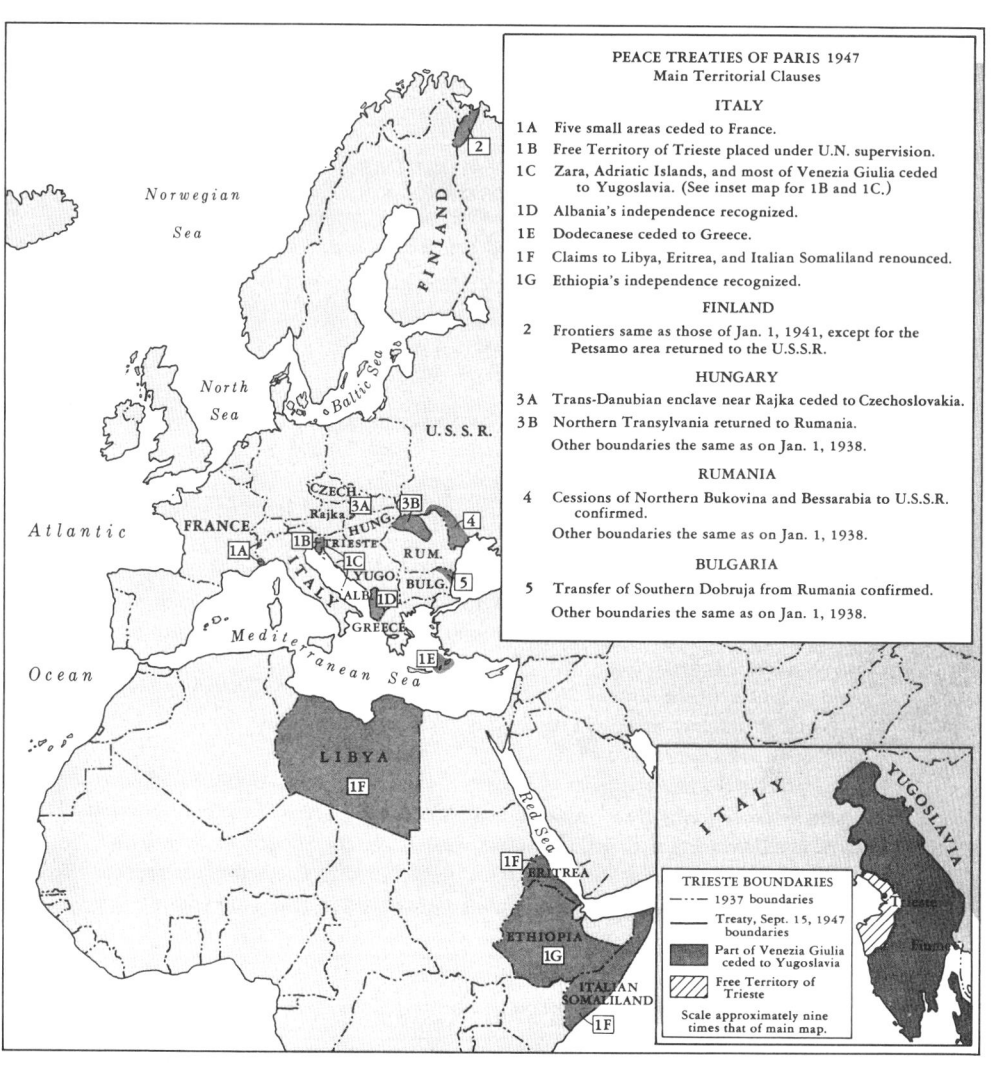

PEACE TREATIES OF PARIS 1947
Main Territorial Clauses

ITALY
1 A Five small areas ceded to France.

1 B Free Territory of Trieste placed under U.N. supervision.

1 C Zara, Adriatic Islands, and most of Venezia Giulia ceded to Yugoslavia. (See inset map for 1B and 1C.)

1 D Albania's independence recognized.

1 E Dodecanese ceded to Greece.

1 F Claims to Libya, Eritrea, and Italian Somaliland renounced.

1 G Ethiopia's independence recognized.

FINLAND
2 Frontiers same as those of Jan. 1, 1941, except for the Petsamo area returned to the U.S.S.R.

HUNGARY
3 A Trans-Danubian enclave near Rajka ceded to Czechoslovakia.

3 B Northern Transylvania returned to Rumania.

Other boundaries the same as on Jan. 1, 1938.

RUMANIA
4 Cessions of Northern Bukovina and Bessarabia to U.S.S.R. confirmed.

Other boundaries the same as on Jan. 1, 1938.

BULGARIA
5 Transfer of Southern Dobruja from Rumania confirmed.

Other boundaries the same as on Jan. 1, 1938.

TRIESTE BOUNDARIES
- - - - - 1937 boundaries
——— Treaty, Sept. 15, 1947 boundaries

Part of Venezia Giulia ceded to Yugoslavia

Free Territory of Trieste

Scale approximately nine times that of main map.

THE PEACE TREATIES OF PARIS, 1947

part in the peacemaking, the Senate Committee on Foreign Relations unanimously endorsed the four peace treaties signed by the United States. The Senate consented to the Italian treaty on June 5, 1947, by a vote of 79 to 10, and approved the Balkan treaties by a voice vote.[9]

Disillusion and the United Nations

Another area of conflict with the Soviets was the United Nations. Like the poet Alfred Tennyson, many Americans had hoped for a time when

> The war-drum throbb'd no longer,
> And the battle-flags were furl'd
> In the Parliament of man, the
> Federation of the world.[10]

Congress had unanimously passed a joint resolution inviting the world organization to establish its permanent headquarters in the United States. The United Nations did so, ultimately selecting New York City as its seat. For Americans as for the rest of the world, this was evidence that the United States had abandoned its traditional isolation and placed its faith in the new collective security.

As the grand alliance broke up and the United Nations became a forum for the bitter political quarrels between the Soviet Union and the Western powers, however, Americans began to lose their faith in the United Nations as an instrument of peace and collective security. Almost continuously, beginning with the first annual session of the General Assembly held in London early in 1946, the Soviets showed themselves unwilling to modify their own desires for the sake of co-operation with their wartime allies.

Central to the idea of collective security in the United Nations was the enforcement of peace through an "international police force." None of the great powers envisaged replacing national armies and navies, but they hoped to have armed forces from each nation made available to the Security Council when needed. The United States wished to contribute specialized forces in keeping with the size and capabilities of each power. It and Britain, for example, would supply air and naval contingents, while Russia, with her large pool of manpower, would contribute most of the land forces.

The Soviets balked, insisting on the "principle of equality," whereby each nation would make available the same number of land, air, and sea forces. Since the Western powers and the Soviet Union could not overcome their disagreement, the United Nations never established its security force.

In the General Assembly, the Soviet Union and its friends, Poland and Yugoslavia, soon found themselves a lonely minority. This position, among other reasons, led the Soviets to rely heavily on their veto power in the Security Council.

The Western powers had assumed that the Big Five would not use their right of veto except in rare circumstances, and then only as a last resort to protect their vital interests when threatened by a hostile majority. To the dismay of the West, the Russians employed the veto to block any action they did not like.

When the Western powers refused to admit Soviet satellites, such as Albania, Hungary, and Rumania, into the United Nations, the Soviets used their veto to prevent the admission of states such as Ireland, Italy, and Portugal. In 1946, for example, they wielded the veto nine times to obstruct action by the Security Council. Americans were angered by what they called an abuse of the veto power.

Atomic Controls

What shocked Americans most was Russia's refusal to bring armaments, particularly the manufacture of atomic weapons, under a tight international control. Most Americans did not want to share atomic secrets with any country. In November, 1945, nonetheless, President Truman and Prime Ministers Clement Attlee and Mackenzie King, leaders of the other two countries who had co-operated in the development of the atomic bomb, issued a joint declaration calling for international control over atomic energy. They offered to share information for peacetime uses of atomic energy and suggested a United Nations commission to establish proper controls.

At the Moscow meeting of the Big Three foreign ministers in December, the Russians accepted the substance of the joint American, British, and Canadian proposals, and in January the General Assembly voted unanimously to create the United Nations Atomic Energy Commission. At the first meeting of that commission, on June 14, Bernard M. Baruch, the American member, offered a plan that would place all control over atomic energy activities in an International Atomic Development Authority. Once the international authority established its control, the United States would stop manufacturing atomic bombs and destroy its stockpiles, and atomic weapons would be outlawed.

To make certain that no nation, principally the Soviet Union, would construct atomic facilities in secret, the Authority would have unprecedented powers of inspection within national territories. "There must be," Baruch said, "no veto to protect those who violate their solemn agreements not to develop or use atomic energy for destructive purposes." [11]

Whether or not they liked the Baruch Plan, most Americans considered it truly magnanimous, an offer to surrender a vast power they alone possessed. Since the United States would retain its knowledge of how to make atomic bombs and would most likely control the international atomic authority, the Russians saw the proposal as a hostile one. It would, they believed, tie their hands in atomic matters and allow the United States to retain its terrible monopoly before their own scientists could capture the secret of the atom. They rejected the American plan and offered one of their own that simply outlawed atomic weapons without effective international control, required the United States to destroy its monopoly immediately, and subjected questions of atomic energy to the veto in the Security Council. Since the Russians would not accept the Baruch Plan and the United States rejected theirs, a stalemate resulted.

That stalemate worked to Russia's advantage. On September 23, 1949, the White House summoned reporters to a momentous news conference. "We have evidence," the President announced, "that within recent weeks an atomic explosion occurred in the u.s.s.r." [12] The American monopoly was no more. In Chicago a Nobel Prize winner and leader in atomic research, Harold C. Urey, was stunned. "There is only one thing worse than one nation having the atomic bomb—," he told newspapermen, "that's two nations having it." [13] Equally important, America's loss of the nuclear monopoly foreshadowed a shift in the world balance of power, a shift that would aid Soviet diplomacy and constrain American action.

Iran

Another area of conflict with the Soviets was the Middle East, a part of the world of small concern to the United States before the war but of critical importance in the postwar years. At the Teheran Conference the Big Three had agreed to withdraw their troops from Iran six months after the end of the war, a promise the Soviets were reluctant to keep. Through a local organization subject to Communist control, the Tudeh party, they supported a movement for autonomy for Azerbaijan, Iran's northernmost province. Concerned about the spread of Soviet influence there, Truman at Potsdam brought up the Iranian question. "So as to rid the United States of any worries," Stalin assured the President, "we promise you that no action will be taken by us against Iran." [14]

In November, 1945, however, a revolt supported by Soviet arms and troops broke out in Azerbaijan. The Communists, it appeared, were going to detach that province from the rest of the country. Since protests to Moscow accomplished nothing, at the first sessions of the United Nations Security Council in London in January, 1946, the Iranians formally accused the Soviet Union of interfering in the internal affairs of their country and asked the Council to investigate. The Russians violently denied the charges. Finally, the Council referred the matter to direct negotiation between the Soviets and the Iranians.

During the negotiations, the Russians demanded the right to keep troops in Iran indefinitely, the formation of a joint Russian-Iranian oil company in which they would hold 51 per cent of the shares, and autonomy for Azerbaijan. The Iranians refused the demands and with American support reopened their complaint with the Security Council. Meanwhile, the deadline for the withdrawal of Russian troops, March 2, passed, and the Russians instead of withdrawing pushed more troops, tanks, and heavy combat equipment into Iran. That small country, it seemed, was destined to become another Soviet satellite.

Alarmed, the United States three days later bluntly protested the retention of Soviet troops in Iran. Russia's demands, it appeared to the President and his advisers, threatened the security of Turkey, then under Soviet pressure, would remove the Iranian oil fields from British and hence Western control, and flouted the principles of the United Nations charter by trampling the rights of a small defenseless nation.

Confronted by American firmness and a hostile world opinion, the Soviets did not go through with their *coup*. As a result of separate negotiations with the Iranians, supported by the United States, the Soviets withdrew their forces in May. Seemingly, the Security Council had successfully met the first major challenge to its authority, and the United States had emerged as the champion of the charter's principles. Actually, in its agreement with Iran, the Soviet Union got most of what it wanted—autonomy for Azerbaijan and the proposed Russian-Iranian oil company. After the Iranian question disappeared from the front pages, Iran began to slip behind the iron curtain.

Later, in December, 1946, the Iranian government, strengthened by American aid, crushed the autonomy of Azerbaijan. The Soviets did not interfere. By that time the American people realized, as Truman had earlier told them, that "the Near and Middle East might become an area of intense rivalry between outside powers," a rivalry that might lead to war.[15]

Turkey

Russia's pressure on Iran was part of a larger thrust into the Middle East. The Soviets also sought control of Turkey and Greece and hence of the eastern Mediterranean.

For two centuries the Russians had tried to gain a foothold in the Turkish Straits on the Black Sea. Although they had no troops in Turkey, the Soviets at the close of the Second World War revived this old policy of the Tsars. At Potsdam the Big Three had agreed to a revision of the Montreux Convention of 1936, an international agreement controlling the use of the straits, so as to give the Soviet Union more favorable terms. Although not a signatory to the Montreux Convention, the United States said it would be a party to any new system of control.

In March, 1945, the Soviets announced that they would abandon a twenty-year-old treaty of friendship and neutrality with the Turks, and in June told the Turks they could have a new treaty, but for a stiff price. Arguing that the Turkish provinces of Kars and Ardahan were historically Russian, the Soviets said they should be ceded to them. The Soviets asked the Turks to replace the Montreux

Convention with an agreement between themselves, to eliminate British influence in Turkey, and to lease them strategic bases in the straits for the purpose of "joint defense."

When Turkey rejected the proposals, the Communist press unleashed a violent anti-Turkish campaign. The Turks defied the threats and strengthened their already mobilized army. Then, on August 7, the Soviets presented formal notes to Turkey, Britain, and the United States, making a second bid for the straits. The United States backed up the Turks, sent a naval task force to the Mediterranean, and took the position that Turkey's independence was at stake. In a note of August 19, it told the Soviets that any threat or attack against the straits would be a matter for action by the Security Council.

That note went to the Soviets at approximately the same time the United States was sending an ultimatum to Marshal Tito (Josip Broz), Communist dictator of Yugoslavia. Within a space of ten days Yugoslav fighter planes had shot down two American transport planes, killing the soldiers in the second plane. The ultimatum demanded that the Yugoslavs release the survivors from the first plane within 48 hours. Tito complied and agreed to pay an indemnity to the families of the dead soldiers. The tension then eased. The strong stand against Yugoslavia and the concurrent firm note to the Soviet Union indicated a toughening of American policy.

When the Soviets renewed their demands on Turkey in October, the United States and Britain, who had a mutual assistance treaty with Turkey and military rights there, encouraged the Turks to hold fast. The President and his advisers believed that if the Soviets gained control over Turkey, Greece would be the next victim. With the fall of Greece and Turkey, Britain might lose her grip in the Mediterranean, and the Soviets would be masters of the Middle East.

Greece

Events in Greece appeared to confirm the American estimate.[16] Greece's postwar difficulties had begun in 1944 when the Germans pulled out. Greek Communists attempted to gain control of the government, and in December civil war erupted. With the aid of British troops the conservative government drove the rebels from Athens and signed a truce with them in January, 1945. Stalin, who had agreed that Greece was a British sphere of influence, did not at that time aid the rebels. Ultimately a restored monarchy took over Greece.

In 1946, as the grand alliance was breaking up and after Greece's northern neighbors were firmly under Communist control, the Soviet attitude toward the Greek Communists changed. Yugoslavia and Bulgaria demanded pieces of Greek territory and the Soviet and satellite press denounced Greece's "monarchofascist" government. In August, Greek Communist guerrillas, trained, armed, and supported in Yugoslavia, Albania, and Bulgaria, began raiding northern Greece in force.

Impoverished by years of war, Greece could not cope with the new depredations. She needed the help of British troops who had remained in the country. Beset by a financial crisis of its own, the British government in February, 1947, decided it could no longer afford the burden of supporting Greece. It withdrew half of its troops and planned to withdraw the other half soon.

On the morning of February 24, the British Ambassador in Washington called on Secretary of State George C. Marshall. He formally delivered two notes, one on Greece and one on Turkey. Economic necessity, one note explained, was forcing Britain to relinquish her financial and military commitments in Greece no later than April 1. The other note said the British could no longer provide the Turks with the aid necessary to withstand Communist pressure. The British hoped the United States would assume the burden they had borne in those two countries.

Greece's fall appeared certain unless the United States acted to prevent it. Greece now became the critical link in the security of the eastern Mediterranean.

The Greeks, feeling abandoned, were in a panic. Several times they had appealed to Washington for financial and military aid beyond the immediate relief it had been supplying. So chaotic were Greek finances that the American government realized that the Greeks could not repay a loan and that they would probably waste whatever money and arms they received. If American aid were to be effective, the President's advisers concluded, it would have to be accompanied by an unprecedented intervention in Greece's internal affairs.

The Truman Doctrine

The State Department decided that intervention was the only alternative to Soviet control, and the President agreed. He discussed the crisis with congressional leaders of both parties who went along with the idea that he should explain it to the people and ask Congress for authority to intervene. "Mr. President, if that's what you want, there's only one way to get it," Senator Vandenberg remarked. "That is to make a personal appearance before Congress and scare hell out of the country."[17]

At the suggestion of the State Department, the Greek government formally appealed for assistance on March 3. With the way now clear for large-scale aid, the State Department prepared the President's speech. At 1 p.m. on March 12, Truman strode into the Chamber of the House of Representatives where Congress was assembled in joint session.

"I believe," the President said, "that it must be the policy of the United States to support free peoples who are resisting attempted subjugation by armed minorities or by outside pressures."[18] This, in essence, was what became known as the Truman Doctrine. He justified the policy in terms of national security. To support his doctrine, the President asked Congress for four hundred million dollars for assistance to Greece and Turkey and for authority to send civilian and military personnel there to supervise the use of American aid.

Even though the Truman Doctrine committed the United States to interventions and entanglements in distant lands hitherto alien to American ideas on foreign policy, it won widespread popular support. "The epoch of isolation and occasional intervention is ended," *The New York Times* said. "It is being replaced by an epoch of American responsibility."[19]

There were plenty of critics too, but they fell mainly into three groups. There were those who attacked the Truman program as "aid to reactionary governments," as an effort to "bail out the British Empire," and as a unilateral "bypassing of the United Nations." The last were the most effective critics. "The United Nations died today," an Illinois congressman told reporters after the President's speech.[20] "The administration," Senator Vandenberg wrote later, "made a colossal blunder in ignoring the U.N."[21] Vandenberg helped overcome some of the criticism by adding an amendment to the bill for aid to Greece and Turkey that said American assistance would cease whenever the United Nations took action making it unnecessary.

The Senate Committee on Foreign Relations held public hearings for a week and then approved the bill unanimously. After two weeks of debate the Senate passed it by a vote of 67 to 23. The House debated the bill two days and voted 287 to 107 for approval. The President signed it into law on May 22, saying it was "helping to further aims and purposes identical with those of the United Nations."[22] He thus attempted to answer Andrei A. Gromyko, the Russian representative on the Security Council, who had charged that the Truman Doctrine was inconsistent with the principles of the United Nations charter.

Two days before Truman had announced his doctrine, the Council of Foreign Ministers had begun another session in Moscow. The Truman speech dispelled any faint hopes of accomplishment. The main question before the ministers was the future of Germany, but on that as on every other important item on the agenda there was a deadlock. That conference showed that the Soviets and the Western Allies could not reconcile their objectives for Germany or for the rest of the world. Marking the final breakup of the grand alliance, the conference ended on April 24, 1947, with nothing decided except that the ministers would meet again in London in November.

The Cold War

The Truman Doctrine and the failure of the Moscow Conference heralded a new departure in American foreign policy. Instead of relying on the United Nations for security, the United States turned to a system of defensive alliances of

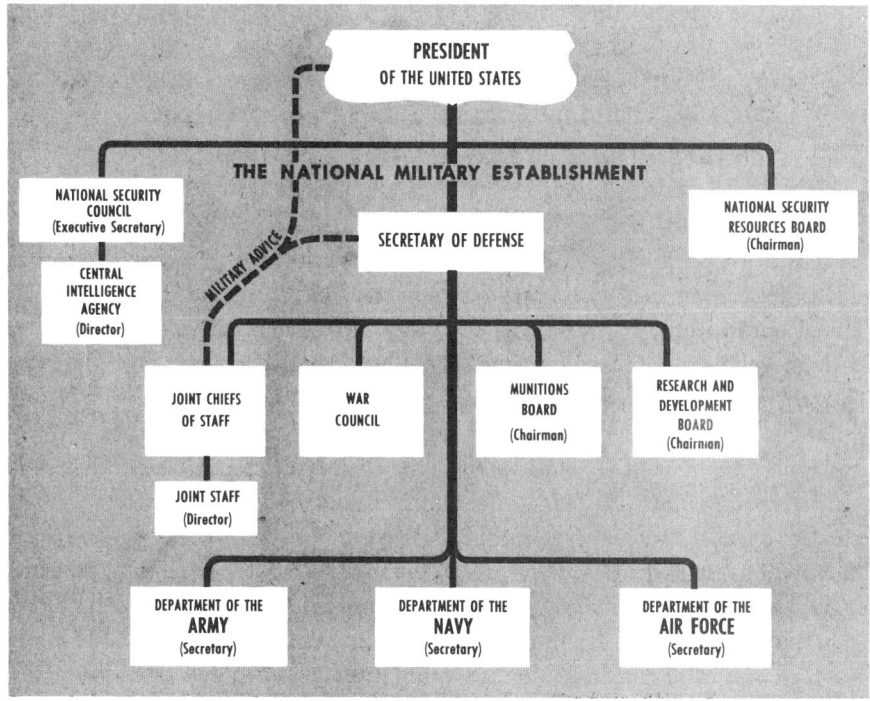

ORGANIZATION FOR NATIONAL SECURITY, 1947

the traditional kind, though in theory it did this within the framework of the United Nations. This was the beginning of what became known as the "cold war," a term made popular by the widely read journalist, Walter Lippmann.[23]

The cold war, a non-shooting political conflict between the Soviet Union and its satellites on one side and the United States and its friends on the other, assumed a bipolar international system. It also had an ideological base, an assumption that the rivals had irreconcilable philosophies and political systems. Whether or not this was a valid assessment of world politics, it formed a basis for American diplomatic strategy for the remainder of the Truman era, a policy known as "containment."

George F. Kennan, a Foreign Service Officer with a deep knowledge of Russia, publicly presented the policy of containment for the first time in an unsigned article in *Foreign Affairs*. Outward "toughness" and single sporadic efforts to counteract Soviet policy, he said, were not enough. The main element of any policy, he suggested "must be that of a long-term, patient but firm and vigilant containment of Russian expansive tendencies." The United States, he wrote, must apply counterforce "at a series of constantly shifting geographical and political points, corresponding to the shifts and maneuvers of Soviet policy."[24]

Ironically, Kennan had objected to the Truman message as being too broad. Yet containment, closely associated with his name, became the policy employed in carrying out the Truman Doctrine.

UNRRA

The economic ills of Greece and Turkey, the President and his advisers realized, were part of a much larger European problem and of Britain's desperate financial plight. During the war the United States, primarily through Lend-Lease aid, had poured out its immense wealth not only to arm its Allies but to clothe and feed them as well. A prominent wartime slogan had been "Food will win the war." Toward the end of the war it changed to "Food will win the peace."

Anticipating the hunger and misery that would and did follow in the wake of retreating German and Japanese armies, the United States had taken the lead in organizing the United Nations Relief and Rehabilitation Administration, usually referred to as UNRRA. Forty-eight nations ultimately joined this emergency organization established in November, 1943, to bring food, clothing, shelter, medical supplies, and other necessities to the war-stricken in Europe and the Far East. It also aided in restoring crippled agricultural and industrial production in war-torn areas and helped to care for millions of homeless and unwanted "displaced persons."

UNRRA went into operation in April, 1945, and from the beginning the United States was its leader and main financial backer. The United States paid 72 per cent of the operating expenses, and 90 per cent of the food and supplies UNRRA distributed came from American farms and factories. The headquarters were in Washington and the organization's three directors-general were all Americans. Although UNRRA functioned as an international organization, its life blood was American. Altogether the United States contributed almost three billion dollars to UNRRA. Total American assistance to the distressed peoples of Europe, including the UNRRA contributions, loans, grants, and gifts through private organizations such as the Red Cross, between the end of the war and the spring of 1947 amounted to more than eleven billion dollars.

As tension with Russia grew, UNRRA became unpopular in the United States. To many Americans it became obvious that food was not winning the peace. They believed that recipient governments, particularly those in Communist eastern Europe, were using food as a weapon, giving it to political supporters and withholding it from others. In 1946, therefore, the United States decided to withdraw, and UNRRA was doomed. Without American funds it could not survive.

The political conflict with the Soviets thus helped make a casualty of American aid to the needy through international channels. "I should say," Secretary of State Byrnes explained, "that it is our position that whatever the United States does in the way of relief should be done by the United States unilaterally. We want to give as the United States and not as a member of an international organization." [25] The United States made its last payments to UNRRA in 1947, at about the time

INTO THE COLD WAR   673

Congress passed the aid bill for Greece and Turkey and when Europeans, despite American postwar generosity, were still cold and hungry, and their economies were still stagnant.

Great Britain, America's major ally, posed a special problem. She had been a main contributor to UNRRA, not a recipient of its aid, but she, her colonies, and her dominions had received two-thirds of all Lend-Lease aid. Without that assistance her wartime economy could not have survived.

The British Loan of 1946

Britain had long imported more than she exported. During the war her imports had risen higher than ever, and her means of paying for them—her exports, her foreign investments, and her shipping—had declined. Her trade deficits had tripled. Lend-Lease had helped fill the gap. To pay for imports, therefore, the British had to reconstruct their economy and double or triple their exports. Before they could do so they had to cover the deficits in the immediate postwar years of reconstruction. Only American dollars could help them do that.

British statesmen had hoped that the United States would gradually taper off Lend-Lease and then replace it with a loan to keep their economy from floundering. One week after Japan's surrender, however, Truman had abruptly terminated Lend-Lease, a flow of supplies that had amounted to a total of forty-eight and one-half billion dollars.

Shocked, the British sent a special economic mission to the United States in September, 1945, to seek a gift, a grant-in-aid, or an interest-free loan. Since the Truman administration believed that Congress, for political reasons, would not approve, it rejected those requests.

After three months of negotiation, the two nations announced a loan agreement, actually three separate conventions, on December 6. One dealt with commercial policy, one settled the question of Lend-Lease payments so as to eliminate possible new antagonisms over war debts such as had followed the First World War, and the third set up the terms of the loan.

In summary, the United States granted a total line of credit of $4.4 billion dollars to be repaid in fifty equal annual installments with an interest rate of two per cent. Since the agreement included a five-year period of grace before the interests payments would begin, the rate of interest was in fact reduced to 1.63 per cent. In return, in the interest of freeing international trade, the British agreed to ease certain commercial and currency restrictions in their empire trading area.

The British had hoped for more money and for more generous terms. "I shall never so long as I live," Lord Keynes, one of the negotiators, told the House of Lords, "cease to regret that this is not an interest-free loan." [26] The Americans met the British objections by pointing out that they were granting loans to other needy nations at a usual and higher interest rate of two and three-eighths per cent. An additional loan from Canada of one and a quarter billion dollars helped Britain meet her minimum desires.

Congress debated the British loan for seven months before acting. The Truman administration defended it as a contribution to world recovery and hence to the nation's self-interest. Undersecretary of State Dean Acheson pointed out that the loan was "not a reward for an ally, however gallant and enduring. It is not a pension, gift, or handout of any description whatever," he said. "It is an investment in the future." [27] World economic recovery depended on that of Britain.

Although the administration itself did not use the argument, many of the loan's supporters pointed out the need to strengthen Britain as an ally against Russia. This reasoning proved to be the most effective of all in gaining congressional support. The Senate passed the loan bill in May and the House on July 13, 1946. Two days later Truman signed it. Rising prices, meanwhile, had reduced the value of the loan by about twenty-three per cent since its date of negotiation.

The Marshall Plan

The American and Canadian loans proved to be insufficient. British imports continued to soar above exports, and the loan funds dwindled away without making Britain self-supporting. Coal and power shortages in the cruel winter of 1946–47, moreover, forced British factories to shut down and curtail production. That winter also brought increased food shortages and the specter of famine throughout Europe. The recovery of Europe stalled and Communism, profiting from misery and poverty, made sweeping gains, particularly in Italy and France.

"What is Europe now?" Winston Churchill said. "It is a rubble-heap, a charnel house, a breeding ground of pestilence and hate." [28] With the British loan disappearing and UNRRA gone, American statesmen even during the Greek and Turkish crisis realized that only a broad program of economic aid for Europe as a whole could prevent the possible disintegration of Western Europe and the triumph of Communism.

While Congress was still debating the Truman Doctrine, State Department planners, assisted by representatives from the War and Navy Departments, had begun investigations of the emergency and long-range needs of certain European countries. The Truman Doctrine, they realized, emphasized military assistance and hence was unpopular in liberal circles. What the people of Europe needed was food, fuel, raw materials, and machinery that would bring an economic recovery which would itself help to check the growth of Communism.

Secretary of State Marshall agreed with this analysis. When he returned from the Moscow Conference of Foreign Ministers late in April, 1947, he asked George Kennan, chief of the State Department's Policy Planning Staff, to study the problem of Europe's revival.

Other thinkers outside the government were also concerned with the problem. "To prevent the crisis which will otherwise engulf Europe and spread chaos throughout the world," Walter Lippmann had written, "the measures will have to be very large—in Europe no less than an economic union, and over here no less than the equivalent to a revival of Lend-Lease." [29] He suggested an innovation in American aid. Why not, he said, contribute assistance to Europe as a whole or to a large part of it instead of to individual countries? Why not, he pointed out, ask the European countries to get together, agree on a common recovery program, and present it to the United States? Lippmann's idea had an impact on the State Department planners.

The new approach to European recovery also appealed to Truman, who decided to embody it in a speech he was scheduled to give in Mississippi's delta country. Since he could not leave Washington, he sent Undersecretary of State Dean Acheson to the little cotton town of Cleveland, Mississippi. There, on May 8, Acheson expressed the idea that the plight of the European countries was one problem. Public discussion of the Truman Doctrine, he said, had overemphasized its military aspects. He stressed Europe's economic needs and explained the basic features of what was to become the European Recovery Program. [30] Although Acheson's speech aroused some public comment on a "different approach" to the problem of European reconstruction, it did not make much of a splash.

At the same time Undersecretary of State for Economic Affairs William L. Clayton urged Marshall and other State Department planners to attempt to reconstruct Europe's economy along European lines rather than by individual countries. [31] On May 23, Kennan's Policy Planning Staff presented the result of its study to Secretary Marshall. It also stressed the idea of massive aid to Europe as a whole. Marshall took that idea expounded by his subordinates, shaped it with his own thinking, and made it the theme of a commencement address at Harvard University on June 5.

"It is logical that the United States should do whatever it is able to do to assist in the return of normal economic health in the world, without which there can be no political stability and no assured peace," Marshall said. "Our policy is directed not against any country or doctrine but against hunger, poverty, desperation, and chaos." The key to his offer was the suggestion that the Europeans themselves should take the initiative in drafting a joint recovery program that the United States could support. [32]

Almost immediately Britain's Minister for Foreign Affairs, Ernest Bevin, "grabbed the Marshall offer with both hands." [33] Together with France's Minister for Foreign Affairs, Georges Bidault, he took the initiative in organizing Europe's response. At a press conference a week after his Harvard speech, Secretary Marshall said his offer was open to all European countries, including Russia, who were willing to cooperate. The Moscow newspaper *Pravda*, nonetheless, attacked the Marshall program as a disguised Truman Doctrine that would apply pressure on

SECRETARY OF STATE
GEORGE C. MARSHALL AT
HARVARD UNIVERSITY WHERE
HE PROPOSED THE MARSHALL
PLAN ON JUNE 5, 1947

Europe through dollar aid. The United States, it said, could not seriously want Soviet participation.

Yet a few days later the Soviet Foreign Minister, Vyacheslav Molotov, accepted an invitation to meet with Bevin and Bidault to discuss the American suggestion. The three ministers met in Paris on June 27. Fearing that the Marshall proposal would bring American control of Europe, Molotov advanced conditions unacceptable to the Western powers.

The three-power conference thus broke up in failure, and Russia withdrew from participation in the Marshall program. Her withdrawal simplified the position of the Truman administration, for the Marshall Plan, as it came to be called, would have encountered difficulty in Congress if the Soviets had had a part in it. The Marshall Plan, although an unprecedented act of national generosity, now became a part of the containment policy.

Two days after the three-power conference had closed, Britain and France sent invitations to all European countries, including the Soviet satellites but not Spain, to a general Marshall Plan conference. Fourteen Western European countries accepted. For a while it looked as if Poland and Czechoslovakia might attend, but when Russia exerted pressure they, like all the other countries behind the iron curtain, rejected the invitation. Thus the Marshall Plan had the effect of widening the gulf between the Communist and the Western worlds.

With sixteen countries present, the Marshall Plan conference opened in Paris in July, and quickly set up a Committee of European Economic Cooperation to gather information on Europe's requirements. The committee report, presented to Secretary Marshall in September, called for a four-year program of recovery supported by $22.4 billion in American aid.

West Germany's economic revival, the United States was convinced, was essential to the success of the Marshall Plan. The Marshall Plan countries agreed, and included Western Germany in the plan for European recovery.

To counter the Marshall Plan, at this time, the Soviets consolidated the nations of eastern Europe through a series of political and economic treaties with them and between them. Through a number of strikes in France and Italy, inspired by Communists, they also attempted to prevent those countries from accepting Marshall aid. In September Communist leaders from nine European countries met in Poland to map strategy to wreck the Marshall Plan. They established the Communist Information Bureau, or Cominform (a successor to the Comintern that had been dissolved in 1943), with headquarters in Belgrade.

During this period of increasing tension between the Soviet bloc and the Western nations, the Council of Foreign Ministers met again in London in November and December. Although the future of Germany again proved an insoluble issue, the larger conflict between the Soviets and the United States over the Marshall Plan doomed the conference to failure.

Four days after the end of the London Conference, Truman presented the European Recovery Program, or Marshall Plan, to Congress. He asked for $17 billion, five billion less than in the original European request. The Marshall Plan immediately ran into rough weather. More than ninety witnesses testified in the hearings held by the Senate Foreign Relations Committee. Opponents attacked the plan as being too expensive, saying Uncle Sam had played Santa Claus long enough. Former Vice-President Henry Wallace denounced the whole idea as a "Martial Plan" that would breed a war. Senator Robert Taft referred to it disparagingly as "a European TVA."[34]

Despite the opposition from the right and left wings of American politics, the Marshall Plan had considerable popular support. Farm, labor, and industrial groups went on record as favoring it, and editorial opinion throughout the country supported it. Outside pressures also worked in favor of the plan. In February, 1948, Communists in Czechoslovakia, in a naked lunge for power, overthrew the democratic government there and installed one firmly attached to the Soviets. Italy had an election coming up on April 18, and the Communists there appeared to have at least an even chance of winning. These developments heightened congressional fears of a growing Communist tide that Marshall aid might help to stem.

The Senate passed the aid bill on March 20 by a vote of 69 to 17, but the House did not approve until the last day in March by a vote of 329 to 74. The President signed the Economic Cooperation Act, or Marshall Plan legislation, on April 3, just in time to have a favorable effect on the Italian elections.

To administer the flow of Marshall aid, the United States established a special governmental agency, the Economic Cooperation Administration, with headquarters in Washington. To carry out the program in Europe, the Marshall Plan

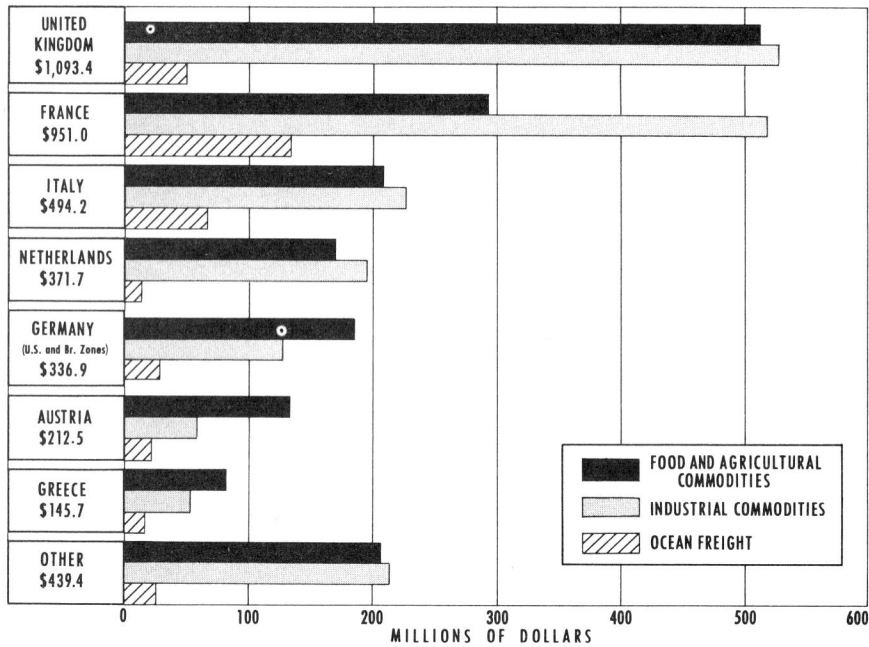

MARSHALL PLAN AID, 1948

European Recovery Program—American funds as allocated according to country and commodity group.

countries created an Organization for European Economic Cooperation. Although Congress gave the Europeans less than they had desired, in the four years following adoption of the European Recovery Program it appropriated some $13.2 billion. This aid helped the European countries stabilize their economies and raise their production well above prewar figures.

Throughout Western Europe, but especially in Italy and France, Communists lost voting strength and hence political power. The Marshall Plan thus reached most of its original objectives. Economically and politically it acted as a dike against Communism in Western Europe. The Marshall Plan was a success, but its success added new tensions to America's relations with the Soviet Union.

Western Union

Even before the Marshall Plan had gone into effect, the United States had begun efforts to weld Europe into a military and political coalition against the Soviets. After the failure of the London Conference of Foreign Ministers in December, 1947, Britain's Foreign Minister, Ernest Bevin, had publicly launched the idea of "Western Union." "I believe the time is ripe," he told Parliament, "for a consolidation of Western Europe."[35] As a beginning he had suggested an alliance

	MEN	DIVISIONS	TANKS
COMBAT STRENGTH OF THE FOUR MAJOR POWERS, 1948 *These figures represent the approximate forces available for combat on short notice.*			
U.S.S.R.	4,000,000	100	15,000
UNITED STATES	645,000	12	1,500
GREAT BRITAIN	530,000	10	1,000
FRANCE	430,000	7	500

between Britain, France, Belgium, the Netherlands, and Luxembourg. The existing Treaty of Dunkirk between Britain and France, signed in March, 1947, and directed against Germany, he said, could serve as a nucleus. Later, he added, the alliance could be enlarged to include "other historic members of European civilization."

From the start, Bevin's idea had received strong American support. His proposal became the Brussels Pact, a fifty-year treaty of alliance, signed on March 17, 1948, that also called for economic, social, and cultural collaboration. As a regional alliance, the Brussels Pact meant little without American support. It had no effective military force at its disposal, but American and Canadian observers were closely associated with it. On the day it was signed, Truman told Congress it was "a notable step in the direction of unity in Europe" and would receive American support "by appropriate means."[36]

The next step toward Western Union, the inclusion of Western Germany, touched off the most dangerous European crisis of the immediate postwar era. In February, Britain, France, and the United States had agreed to coordinate the economic policies of their zones in Germany and to include those zones in the European Recovery Program. Several months later, on June 7, those three countries plus the Netherlands, Belgium, and Luxembourg agreed to establish a West German government, which would exercise sovereignty over domestic affairs and have a limited control over foreign relations. It could not, however, rearm, and the Allied military occupation would continue "until the peace of Europe is secured."

The Berlin Airlift

Despite Soviet protests, the Western powers went ahead with their German program and on June 18 announced a reform of currency in Western Germany. They had hoped to arrange a four-power control of currency in Berlin, but the

Soviets would not agree and went ahead with their own German currency reform. When the Western powers introduced their new currency in their sectors of Berlin, the Soviets retaliated with a tight land blockade of the city.

In their sectors the three Western powers were responsible for about 2,500,000 Berliners. Since Berlin was deep in the Russian zone, the Soviets could easily deny access to the city by road, rail, and canal. If the Western powers were unable to feed the people in their sectors, the Soviets reasoned, they would have to evacuate the city.

The Soviet blockade had, in fact, begun gradually. In March the Soviets had walked out of the Allied Control Council for Germany and on April 1, had imposed annoying rail and road restrictions on Allied traffic to Berlin. In the middle of June they had marched out of the Kommandatura, the Allied governing body for Berlin, announcing that the four-power administration of Berlin no longer existed. They argued that the Western powers had destroyed the four-power control of Germany and hence had no further business in Berlin.

The Western sectors of Berlin had food stocks sufficient only for thirty-six days and coal for forty-five. President Truman and his advisers decided that a retreat from Berlin might wreck Allied plans for Western Germany. To remain there, the United States had to make a show of strength supported by Britain and France. Truman rejected the idea of forcing an entrance into Berlin with armed convoys. The Soviets might shoot and a third world war would follow. Instead, he decided on an airlift, a continuous shuttle service into West Berlin by American and British planes.

"Operation Vittles," as the Americans called the airlift, flew food, clothing, various raw materials, and medicine into the Western sectors of Berlin. Soviet planes occasionally threatened the Allied transports but never attacked them. By the spring of 1949 the Allies were flying in an average of 8000 tons of supplies per day. In return for a Western agreement to hold another meeting of the Council of Foreign Ministers in Paris on May 23, the Soviets lifted the Berlin blockade on May 12, 1949. The airlift, a decisive American and Allied victory in the cold war, ended in September.[37]

Meeting for four weeks in Paris, the Council of Foreign Ministers produced no new agreement on Germany. It merely confirmed the *modus vivendi* that had ended the Berlin blockade. At the same time it also confirmed the relaxation of tension following the end of the blockade.

The airlift's success drew the people of Western Germany closer to the United States and helped win their support for a West German state, even though it would postpone reunification of the whole of Germany, something practically every German desired. On May 23, 1949, after organizing state governments and adopting a constitution, the West Germans officially proclaimed the German Federal Republic with its capital at Bonn.

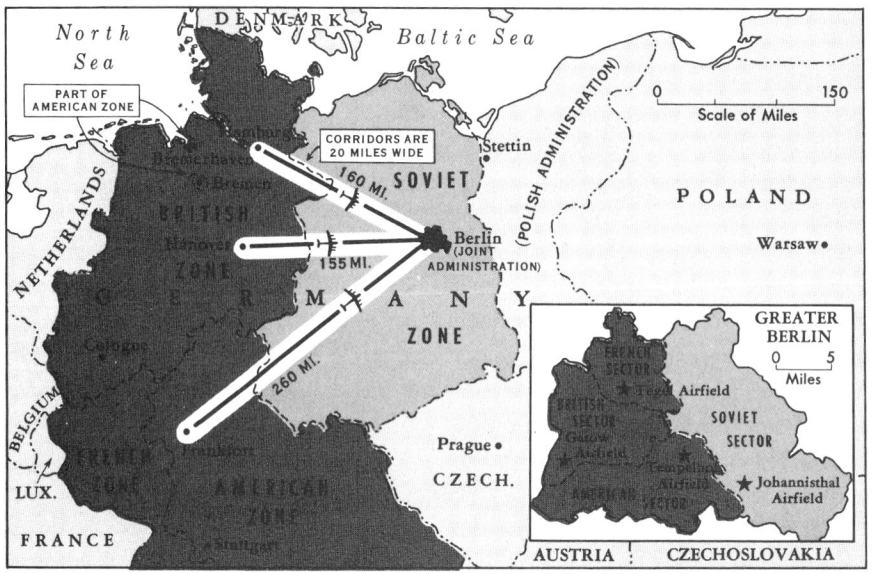

AIRLIFT CORRIDORS TO BERLIN, 1947-1948

Russia protested its establishment and in retaliation proclaimed a new government for the Russian zone of Germany, the "German Democratic Republic," in October. Two Germanies had come into existence, one anchored in the Soviet bloc and the other tied to Western Union and in the American orbit.

At the beginning of the Berlin airlift, Marshal Tito of Yugoslavia had broken with the Soviet Union and the Cominform and thus contributed to another American gain in the cold war. The break had become public in June, 1948, and had widened as time went on. Ultimately, Tito withdrew support from the Greek Communists, leaving the American-trained Greek national army to crush the guerrillas. By October, 1949, therefore, the Greek civil war was over and the Truman Doctrine was a success.

The Vandenberg Resolution

Soviet resistance to the Marshall Plan and the warlike Berlin blockade, meanwhile, had increased the desire of the Western Europeans for closer military ties with the United States. The Truman administration, although working closely with the Brussels Pact powers, had at first feared that Congress would not accept a European military alliance that would obligate the United States to fight. Senator Vandenberg, in cooperation with the Department of State, provided a way out of the dilemma.

Vandenberg introduced a resolution advocating the negotiation of "regional and other collective arrangements for individual and collective self-defense" in accordance with provisions of the United Nations charter.[38] The Senate had approved the resolution on June 11, 1948, with only four dissenting votes. In other words, Congress had agreed in advance, with some conditions, to support entrance into military alliances, a revolutionary procedure in the history of American foreign policy.

The Vandenberg resolution had cleared the way for strengthening the policy of containment with a system of military alliances. Since its author was a Republican of national stature and it had received overwhelming bipartisan support, it also helped eliminate the cold war as a major issue in the presidential campaign of 1948 that followed it. The platforms of both the Republican and Democratic parties showed only slight differences in their foreign policy planks. Both supported foreign aid and "regional arrangements." Until the last week of the campaign neither Thomas E. Dewey, the Republican candidate, nor Harry Truman, the Democratic choice, abandoned the idea of a bipartisan foreign policy. At times Dewey did talk a bit about foreign affairs, saying on one occasion that in his first campaign for the Presidency he had founded the bipartisan approach which had made possible the Marshall Plan.

Truman's former Secretary of Commerce, Henry A. Wallace, a liberal idealist who ran on the ticket of the Progressive party and who was endorsed by Communists, attempted in vain to make foreign policy a basic issue. In his "fight for peace," he denounced the Truman Doctrine, the Marshall Plan, and other features of Truman's foreign policy.[39] Public opinion polls and all other weathervanes pointed to a clear victory for Dewey. Despite the odds and the fact that Wallace bit into the Democratic vote in several key states, Truman won. His amazing victory brought new strength to his foreign policy.

The Point Four Program

With the election victory and the Vandenberg resolution behind him, Truman stepped up negotiations already in progress with the signers of the Brussels Pact and with Canada for a regional defense arrangement covering the North Atlantic area. In his inaugural address he explained the purpose of the proposed North Atlantic treaty. "If we can make it sufficiently clear, in advance," he said, "that any armed attack affecting our national security would be met with overwhelming force, the armed attack might never occur."[40]

The President also listed three other important points in foreign policy. Two, support of the United Nations and the Marshall Plan, were familiar to Americans, but the fourth was fresh and startling, a proposal for world-wide technical assistance to poor and backward countries to aid in their economic development. "We must embark on a bold new program," the President said, "for making the benefits of our scientific advances and industrial progress available for the improvement and growth of underdeveloped areas." Newspapers quickly dubbed the proposal "Point Four."

The Point Four program, as intended, filled a gap in foreign policy. Many nations, notably the countries of Latin America, the Middle East, and the Far East, who had recently emerged from colonial status, had no place in the main stream of American foreign relations. The people of those so-called "underdeveloped" countries, producers of raw materials for the industrialized nations, wished to escape crushing poverty and desired progress as much as did the more advanced Europeans. If they did not receive the help they sought from the United States, they might, it seemed clear, turn to Communism.

Point Four, as the President advanced it, was not merely an anti-Communist measure. Nor was it a lending or a giveaway program. It was a plan for self-help promoted by American skill and a limited number of dollars. Yet it was also considered by some as an antidote to Communism, a world-wide expansion of the containment policy.

Most Americans liked the Point Four idea, but the Russians called it "imperialism," domestic critics labeled it "globaloney," and Congress hesitated in adopting it, disliking the indefinite duration and the cost of the "bold new program." Fearing that it would be an entering wedge for future big expenditures, Senator Robert Taft said it would spread the taxpayer's money "around the world in places where there is no particular demand for it."[41]

After persistent urging by the President, Congress finally appropriated $35.4 million for the program in June, 1950, a modest sum when compared to other foreign aid projects, and ten million less than the minimum requested. By the end of the following year the United States had concluded Point Four agreements, under the supervision of a Technical Cooperation Administration within the Department of State, with thirty-three countries. In 1953 Congress expanded its appropriation for the program to $155.6 million.

Despite its modest support, the technical assistance program, through a band of devoted individuals, fought malaria in Peru, typhus in Iran, and famine in India. Its "shirt-sleeve diplomats" helped build a hydroelectric plant in Mexico, irrigation systems in Jordan, and brought hope of an improved living standard to peoples in Egypt, Haiti, and elsewhere. Yet the "bold new program" remained small, operating on the fringes of American foreign policy.

Russia, meantime, as another counterweight to the Marshall Plan, had launched an assistance program of her own. Representatives from six of the Soviet satellite states, after a meeting in Moscow, had joined the Russians in forming a Council for Mutual Economic Assistance. The Soviet bloc announced its new program on January 25, 1949, just five days after Harry Truman had made his Point Four proposal. Members of the Communist Council promised each other technical assistance, food, raw materials, and machinery. They declared their plan open to other European states who shared its principles and who sought "broad economic cooperation."

The North Atlantic Treaty

At the same time, the Soviets, through the Cominform, were sponsoring a "peace offensive" and were using it to counteract the negotiation of the North Atlantic Treaty. On April 1 they sent official protests to the sponsoring governments denouncing the treaty as hostile to the Soviet Union, as incompatible with obligations under the United Nations charter, and as contributing "to the whipping-up of war hysteria." [42] The United States denied any aggressive designs in adhering to the treaty, and on April 4, 1949, in Washington the foreign ministers of twelve nations, Belgium, Canada, Denmark, France, Great Britain, Iceland, Italy, Luxembourg, the Netherlands, Norway, Portugal, and the United States, formally signed the North Atlantic Treaty.

The treaty's key paragraph appeared in Article 5. It stated that an armed attack against one or more of the signatories "in Europe or North America shall be considered an attack against them all." [43] In case of an attack, it added, each country, as recognized by Article 51 of the United Nations charter, will assist the party under attack with "such action it deems necessary, including the use of armed force." By not pledging the signatories to automatic action in case of an attack, this provision did not deprive Congress of its constitutional power to declare war. On the surface the loophole committed the United States to nothing definite, yet when viewed in the full context of the treaty the American commitment was a strong one.

To carry out its purposes, the treaty provided for a council representing all the signatories and a defense committee to recommend appropriate military measures. The alliance would remain in force indefinitely, but at the end of ten years any party to it could request a review of the treaty, and at the end of twenty years any signatory could withdraw.

Truman sent the treaty to the Senate on April 12. Sixteen days of public hearings followed. The chief witness against the treaty was Henry Wallace. "It will," he shouted, "make Russia into a wild and cornered beast." Since the treaty had been carefully negotiated with advice and assistance by leading members of the Senate, the Committee on Foreign Relations unanimously recommended approval without reservations or crippling interpretations.

Nonetheless, twelve days of sharp debate on the Senate floor covered every aspect of the treaty. The most intense criticism centered on Article 5. Critics denounced the treaty as an "old-fashioned military alliance," which basically it was.[44] Senator Taft, who considered the alliance a magnet that would draw the country into war, emerged as its leading opponent. A number of senators introduced reservations prohibiting the stationing of American troops in Europe and denying any obligation to furnish arms, including atomic bombs, to the signatories. All reservations met defeat.

Finally, on July 21, the Senate voted approval by a margin of 82 to 13. Four days later the President ratified it. On August 25, 1949, after a sufficient number of signatories had ratified it, the North Atlantic Treaty officially went into effect.

Some called the North Atlantic Treaty a regional agreement as provided for by the United Nations charter. Since it included Italy, North Africa, and ultimately Greece and Turkey in the North Atlantic region, the treaty stretched the term beyond its true meaning. Others who contended that the treaty fitted the United Nations concept of collective security ignored the fact that the United States had turned to it because, among other reasons, the United Nations had not become an effective instrument of collective security. The North Atlantic Treaty, essentially an alliance of collective self-defense, was a substitute for a broad collective security.

Whatever its strengths and weaknesses, the North Atlantic Treaty was the first formal military alliance with any part of Europe that the United States had committed itself to since the French alliance of 1778. Few could deny the fact that it was an "entangling alliance" in the traditional sense of the term.[45]

NORTH ATLANTIC TREATY, 1949

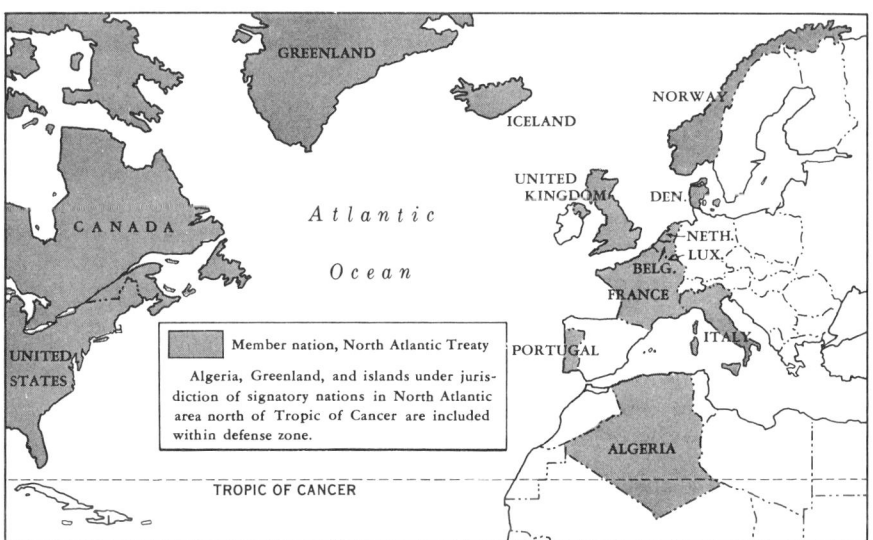

NOTES

1. This attitude is reflected in various public opinion polls taken in 1945. A poll of March 20, for instance, had 90% of those questioned giving approval to American membership in a postwar international organization. See Hadley Cantril, ed., *Public Opinion, 1935–1946* (Princeton, 1951), pp. 908–914.

2. In "The Nuremberg Trials and One World," in George L. Anderson, ed., *Issues and Conflicts: Studies in Twentieth Century American Diplomacy* (Lawrence, Kans., 1959), Eugene Davidson points out that the United States was not only the host nation at Nuremberg but also the most zealous in praising the trials (p. 234). He also suggests that Nuremberg was mainly a product of American thinking (p. 250). For details see Peter Calvocoressi, *Nuremberg: The Facts, the Law, and the Consequences* (London, 1947); August von Knieriem, *The Nuremberg Trials* (Chicago, 1959); and Robert K. Woetzel, *The Nuremberg Trials in International Law* (London, 1960).

3. July 11, 1946, quoted in John C. Campbell, *The United States in World Affairs, 1945–1947* (New York, 1947), pp. 190–191.

4. Dec. 24, 1945, in James F. Byrnes, *Speaking Frankly* (New York, 1947), p. 171.

5. Sept. 6, 1946, *ibid.*, p. 190.

6. Cited in Harry S. Truman, *Memoirs* (2 vols., Garden City, N.Y., 1955), I, 367.

7. Letter of Jan. 5, 1946, *ibid.*, I, 552.

8. March 5, 1946, quoted in William H. McNeill, *America, Britain, and Russia: Their Cooperation and Conflict, 1941–1946* (London, 1953), p. 657. For a critical analysis of the speech, see Denna F. Fleming, *The Cold War and Its Origins, 1917–1960* (2 vols., Garden City, N.Y., 1961), I, 348–357.

9. Details of negotiation and the texts of the five peace treaties are in Amelia Leiss and Raymond Dennett, eds., *European Peace Treaties after World War II* (Boston, 1954).

10. From "Locksley Hall" in Alfred Tennyson, *The Poetical Works of Tennyson*, selected by John Gawsworth (London, 1951), p. 89.

11. Quoted in Joseph P. Murray, *From Yalta to Disarmament: Cold War Debate* (New York, 1961), p. 74. For details on the Baruch Plan, see Richard G. Hewlett and Oscar E. Anderson, Jr., *The New World, 1939–1946*, Vol. I of *A History of the United States Atomic Energy Commission* (University Park, Pa., 1962), pp. 531–619. See also Robert Gilpin, *American Scientists and Nuclear Weapons Policy* (Princeton, 1962), pp. 52–63.

12. Truman, *Memoirs*, II, 307.

13. Quoted in Eric F. Goldman, *The Crucial Decade—And After: America, 1945–1960* (New York, 1961), p. 100.

14. July 23, 1945, quoted in Herbert Feis, *Between War and Peace: The Potsdam Conference* (Princeton, 1960), p. 304.

15. April 11, 1946, quoted in William Reitzel, Morton A. Kaplan, and Constance G. Coblenz, *United States Foreign Policy 1945–1955* (Washington, 1956), p. 210.

16. For a brief introduction to the historical background of the problem, see Leften S. Stavrianos, "The United States and Greece: The Truman Doctrine in Historical Perspective," in Dwight E. Lee and George E. McReynolds, eds., *Essays in Honor of George Hubbard Blakeslee* (Worcester, Mass., 1949), pp. 36–59.

17. Quoted in Goldman, *Crucial Decade*, p. 59.

18. The text of the speech is in Louis W. Koenig, ed., *The Truman Administration: Its Principles and Practice* (New York, 1956), pp. 296–301.

19. March 12, 1947, quoted in Joseph M. Jones, *The Fifteen Weeks* (New York, 1955), p. 173.

20. Thomas L. Owens, *ibid.*, p. 180.

21. Arthur H. Vandenberg, Jr., ed., *The Private Papers of Senator Vandenberg* (Boston, 1952), p. 21. For unfavorable reactions to the Doctrine, see Fleming, *Cold War and Its Origins*, pp. 445–456.

22. Quoted in Jones, *Fifteen Weeks*, p. 198.

23. See, for instance, Walter Lippmann, *The Cold War: A Study in U.S. Foreign Policy* (New York, 1947). Walt W. Rostow, in *The United States in the World Arena* (New York, 1960), p. 141, holds that the cold war had roots in the nineteenth century and in fact began early in 1943 when the Soviets held back the Nazis at Stalingrad.

24. [George F. Kennan], "The Sources of Soviet Conduct," *Foreign Affairs*, XXV (July 1947), pp. 575, 576.

25. Nov. 13, 1945, quoted in Campbell, *U.S. in World Affairs, 1945–1947*, p. 335.

26. Dec. 18, 1945, quoted in Richard N. Gardner, *Sterling-Dollar Diplomacy: Anglo-American Cooperation in the Reconstruction of Multilateral Trade* (Oxford, 1956), p. 227.

27. "The Credit to Britain, the Key to Expanded Trade," *Department of State Bulletin*, XIV (Feb. 3, 1946), 186.

28. May 14, 1947, quoted in Goldman, *Crucial Decade*, p. 66.

29. April 5, 1947, quoted in Jones, *Fifteen Weeks*, p. 229.

30. For the text of Acheson's speech, see *ibid.*, pp. 274–281. See also, Alexander DeConde, "George Catlett Marshall, 1947–1949," in Norman A. Graebner, ed., *An Uncertain Tradition: American Secretaries of State in the Twentieth Century* (New York, 1961), p. 253.

31. For Clayton's contribution to the Marshall Plan, see Ellen Clayton Garwood, *Will Clayton: A Short Biography* (Austin, Texas, 1958). Pertinent documents are reproduced on pp. 115–128.

32. The text of Marshall's speech is in Jones, *Fifteen Weeks*, pp. 281–284. For additional details on the shaping of the Marshall Plan, see William C. Mallalieu, "The Origin of the Marshall Plan: A Study in Policy Formation and National Leadership," *Political Science Quarterly*, LXXIII (Dec. 1958), 481–504.

33. Quoted in Jones, *Fifteen Weeks*, p. 30.

34. Quoted in John C. Campbell, *The United States in World Affairs, 1947–1948* (New York, 1948), p. 486. Taft was one of the most influential critics of foreign policy. For his ideas, see John P. Armstrong's article, "The Enigma of Senator Taft and American Foreign Policy," *Review of Politics*, XVII (April 1955), 206–231.

35. Jan. 22, 1948, quoted in Andrew and Frances Boyd, *Western Union: A Study of the Trend Toward European Unity* (Washington, 1949), p. 123.

36. Truman, *Memoirs*, II, 242.

37. John L. Snell, in *Wartime Origins of the East-West Dilemma Over Germany* (New Orleans, 1959), p. 237, points out that the Soviets blockaded West Berlin to disrupt creation of a republic in West Germany and failed. For popular accounts of the airlift, see Max Charles, *Berlin Blockade* (London, 1959) and Robert Rodrigo, *Berlin Airlift* (London, 1960).

38. Vandenberg, *Private Papers*, p. 407.

39. For a detailed history of the "fight for peace," see Karl M. Schmidt, *Henry A. Wallace: Quixotic Crusade, 1948* (Syracuse, N.Y., 1948). Communist support of Wallace is analyzed on pp. 14–15.

40. The text of the inaugural of Jan. 20, 1949, is in Koenig, ed., *The Truman Administration*, pp. 274–279.

41. Quoted in Jonathan B. Bingham, *Shirt-Sleeve Diplomacy: Point 4 in Action*

(New York, 1954), p. 13. For historical precedents for the Point Four idea, see Merle Curti and Kendall Birr, *Prelude to Point Four: American Technical Assistance Missions Overseas, 1838–1938* (Madison, Wis., 1954).

42. Quoted in Kenneth Ingram, *History of the Cold War* (London, 1955), p. 129.

43. The text of the treaty is in John C. Campbell, *The United States in World Affairs, 1948–1949* (New York, 1949), pp. 587–591.

44. Lawrence S. Kaplan, in "NATO and the the Language of Isolationism," *The South Atlantic Quarterly*, XVI (Spring 1958), 204–215, points out, however, that the treaty's supporters carefully presented it to Congress as being different in spirit and structure from the usual military alliance. See also his analysis of the literature dealing with the alliance, "NATO and Its Commentators: The First Five Years," *International Organization*, VIII (Nov. 1954), 447–467.

45. This theme is stressed in Robert E. Osgood, *NATO: The Entangling Alliance* (Chicago, 1962).

Chapter Twenty-Six

CHINA, JAPAN, AND THE KOREAN WAR

WHILE the United States was building containment in Europe, events in eastern Asia were shaping into the most startling and far-reaching political development in the immediate postwar era—the triumph of Communism in China.

The sudden end of the war against Japan had intensified the rivalry between the Kuomintang and the Chinese Communists and had caught Chiang Kai-shek unable to take over from the Japanese and the United States unprepared to offer immediate assistance. Like Franklin D. Roosevelt, President Truman followed a policy of working for a unified China while supporting only Chiang's Nationalist regime. American planners had envisaged a gradual return of Nationalist forces to the areas held by the Japanese, but two factors made that plan impossible: the impotence of the Kuomintang regime and the distribution of Communist forces in China.

With an army of about a half million men and even larger guerrilla forces, the Communists had controlled the countryside of north China and strong points in other areas. Some of the local governors and military chieftains who were not Communists, moreover, were hostile to the Kuomintang. The Japanese, with more than a million soldiers in China proper and almost as many in Manchuria, had controlled the big cities, the railroad centers, and the main ports. Chiang's forces had held only the southwest corner of China.

As soon as the Japanese had asked for peace, the Nationalists and the Communists began a race for control of the Japanese areas, the richest and most important parts of China. Without American assistance, Chiang and his advisers realized, they could not win that race. If, for example, the Japanese were told to lay down their arms and march to the coast for evacuation, the Communists would probably take over the entire country. Chiang, therefore, appealed for American military assistance in taking over the Japanese areas.

The United States agreed to help, but without troops on the Chinese mainland and with transport facilities tied up elsewhere, the Americans could not move quickly. Therefore, the United States ordered the Japanese to hold their positions, in effect to ward off the Communists, until it could transport Nationalist troops into the interior and land Marines on the coast to guard the seaports.

Such action seemed imperative, for the Communists, without waiting for the official Japanese surrender, had started taking over as much of China as they could. On August 10, 1945, Chu Teh, the commanding general of the Communist forces, had ordered Communist army units to advance against the Japanese at all points. He also ordered the Japanese to lay down their arms and surrender to the Communist officials under the threat of destruction. Denouncing this as "an abrupt and illegal action," Chiang forbade Chu Teh to take independent action against the Japanese.[1]

Five days later Chu Teh sent identical notes to the American, British, and Soviet governments demanding the right to accept the surrender of the Japanese. He also asked the United States to cease Lend-Lease aid to Chiang's government and to refuse to help him if civil war broke out in China. The American government answered that the Big Three had agreed that Chiang Kai-shek, as Allied Commander in Chief in China, should receive the surrender of Japanese forces and that it hoped the Communists would cooperate with him.

Civil War in China

On August 16, Patrick J. Hurley, the American Ambassador in China, had induced Chiang to invite Mao Tse-tung, the Communist leader, to Chungking for talks that might lead to cooperation between the rival regimes. After some hesitation, Mao accepted the invitation and flew to Chungking with Hurley. Mao stayed in Chungking all through September and into October arguing the Communist cause. Nothing came of the talks except a vague agreement that the Nationalists and the Communists would submit their differences to a future Political Consultative Council. Both leaders vowed that they wanted national unity.

While the talks were in progress, American transport planes moved three Nationalist armies to key cities in eastern and northern China. About fifty thousand American Marines took possession of ports and airfields at Tsingtao, Tientsin, Peiping, and Chinwangtao. With American help, therefore, the Nationalists were able to take control of Nanking, Shanghai, and the area south of the Yangtze. They secured the surrender of the majority of the Japanese troops in those regions and thus forestalled a Communist seizure.

In north China the story was different. There Communist troops swarmed through the countryside, blocking roads and cutting railroad communications, and might have captured the big cities if the Japanese had not held on according to American orders. Despite Japanese resistance, however, the Communists were able to seize substantial stocks of Japanese arms, ammunition, and supplies, and in October began infiltrating Manchuria, where the Soviets were in control and had already accepted the surrender of Japanese troops. Fighting broke out between Nationalists and Chinese Communists in north China as soon as Americans brought Chiang's troops there to take over from the Japanese. The Soviets, despite their pledges to support and assist only the Nationalists, cooperated with the Chinese Communists, allowing them to take weapons surrendered by the Japanese in Manchuria and to gain the upper hand in large areas of that province.

Frustrated by Soviet and Communist opposition, Chiang pleaded for more American assistance. Truman promised aid to maintain internal peace and security but, he said, "it should be clearly understood that military assistance furnished by the United States would not be diverted for use in fratricidal warfare or to support undemocratic administration." [2] Ironically, fratricidal strife had already begun, and Chiang's one-party regime could not be called democratic.

More military assistance to Chiang, American leaders realized, would probably lead to irregular warfare between their Marines and the Communists. As it was, the Communists carefully avoided clashes with American troops but complained bitterly about the American aid that made possible Nationalist control of large parts of China.

While refusing to cooperate with Chiang in efforts to strike directly at the Communists, the United States nonetheless continued Lend-Lease aid to him after it had stopped giving it to other allies. It also maintained a military mission in China to help him in training his troops.

Yet by the middle of November, three months after Japan's surrender, China appeared to be falling apart. The Soviets were placing obstacles in the way of Nationalist efforts to take control of Manchuria, the Chinese Communists were entrenched there and in north China, and even in areas where the Nationalists had full control there was trouble. Too many of Chiang's appointees were incompetent, untrustworthy, or corrupt. His government not only failed to gain support of the Chinese masses but also aroused resentment among them.

Americans were alarmed. Roosevelt's dream of a friendly and unified China among the great powers was vanishing. American policymakers had hoped that unity would come under Chiang and that then they could withdraw the Marines. If they pulled the troops out of China and abruptly ended direct support of Chiang, however, the entire American effort in China would collapse. The Communists, it seemed certain, would either divide the country or control it.

An American official who returned home from China at this time summed up the situation. "The Kuomintang must have our support to be able to cope with the situation," he said. "If the Russians, however, decide to give active support to the Chinese Communists, then we are in a real mess." [3]

Ambassador Hurley, who had returned to Washington in October, for example, had become convinced that his secret reports to the State Department were being passed on to the Communists. He talked over the Chinese situation with the President and the Secretary of State and then, on November 27, without consulting them, publicly resigned. Resenting what he construed to be an indifference to the fate of Chiang's regime, he blasted American policy in China. Hurley's blast focused the people's attention on China and led the government to explain its China policy to them.

First, Truman went to the telephone and called General George C. Marshall, just recently retired as Chief of Staff. "General," the President said, "I want you to go to China for me." [4] Marshall immediately accepted the assignment, going to China as the President's special emissary with the personal rank of ambassador. Marshall's instructions held no new departure in policy, but behind them now lurked the fear that if China did not become strong the Soviets would retain control of Manchuria and gain a dominant influence in north China.

On December 15, the day Marshall left for China, the President issued a statement, titled "U.S. POLICY TOWARD CHINA," explaining the general's mission. He reiterated the two main objectives—to aid in achieving "a strong, united and democratic China" while recognizing only the Nationalist regime, "the only legal government in China," and to help it in extending its sovereignty over Manchuria.[5] Marshall would try to effect a truce in the civil war, Truman said, and would attempt to bring all political elements together in a representative national regime. But, he announced, the United States would not intervene in China's internal strife.

At the Council of Foreign Ministers meeting in Moscow, as Marshall began his mission, the Soviets appeared to accept American policy as enunciated by the President. They again agreed to withdraw their troops from Manchuria and to support a broadly democratic and unified China under the leadership of Chiang's Nationalists.

For a short time after Marshall's arrival in China, it appeared that he would succeed in his mission. He brought the Communists and the Kuomintang together and on January 10, 1946, persuaded them to agree to an armistice. On that day Chiang Kai-shek also proclaimed a series of political and economic reforms that seemed to promise a democratic beginning. In February the rivals seemingly overcame their main point of contention; they agreed to merge their troops into a new national army. In March, Marshall returned to the United States for a visit.

The Russians, in this interval, evacuated all of Manchuria except Dairen and

Port Arthur. Before pulling out they removed factories and stripped others of their equipment. When the United States protested, the Russians cited the conqueror's privilege, saying they had merely removed Japanese "war booty."

In the wake of the Russian withdrawal, the Nationalists and the Chinese Communists ignored Marshall's truce and scrambled to gain the upper hand. Heavy fighting broke out and Manchuria became the main theater of a civil war. Since American planes and ships had brought the Nationalists to Manchuria and they were fighting with American weapons, the Communists denounced American intervention. Only the stopping of American aid to Chiang and the evacuation of American troops, Mao Tse-tung said, would bring peace to China.

Marshall hurried back to China in April and tried to quench the spreading civil war. Anti-American propaganda, much of it planted by the Communists and some by the Nationalists, made his efforts painful. To aid Marshall in his thankless task, the President, in July, appointed John Leighton Stuart Ambassador to China. Stuart, the President of Yenching University in Peiping, had been born in China and spoke Chinese fluently. Both men found their efforts to bring peace to be hopeless. In September, Marshall reported home that "Dr. Stuart and I are stymied." [6]

The United States continued to send assistance to Chiang. In July Congress had passed a law calling for the transfer of over two hundred naval vessels to the Nationalists to help them build a navy. This aid to Chiang and a request for more set off a bitter debate in Congress. Conservatives said it was not enough and demanded more help for Chiang. Liberals denounced "our shameful military intervention against the forces of Chinese democracy." [7]

At the end of the year the President called Marshall home to become Secretary of State. In reviewing the failure of his mission, the general deplored the Communist propaganda designed "to arouse a bitter hatred of Americans" among the Chinese people. He also said, however, that the efforts to arrive at a peaceful settlement "have been frustrated time and again by extremist elements of both sides." [8]

At the same time, the United States began withdrawing its troops from China, though leaving several thousand for guard duty and for aid in training Nationalist forces. This withdrawal did not end the China crisis in American foreign policy, for, as Senator Vandenberg announced prophetically, "there will never be a minute when China's destiny is not of acute concern to the United States and to a healthy world." [9]

The struggle in China now burgeoned into one of the great civil wars of modern times involving millions of fighting men on both sides and affecting nearly a quarter of the world's population. At first the Nationalists, who had the advantage in troops and equipment, appeared to have the upper hand. They profited, moreover, from American aid, over a billion dollars of it from the time of the Japanese surrender until the end of 1946, most of it military Lend-Lease.

Early in 1947, prominent Republicans, the influential Luce publications that included *Time* and *Life* magazines, and the Scripps-Howard newspapers, urged stronger support for Chiang Kai-shek. In June, Ambassador Stuart reported that the Nationalist victories were deceptive and that Chiang faced disaster in Manchuria.

Bending somewhat to the Republican pressure, the President a month later sent General Albert C. Wedemeyer to China to survey conditions there and to make recommendations for future policy. Returning to Washington in September, the general submitted an inconclusive report, not published until 1949, confirming the dire position of the Nationalists.[10] Although he saw no hope for a Nationalist victory, he advised, among other things, increased economic and military aid for Chiang. Believing the report inadequate, impractical, and a source of embarrassment to the American and Chinese governments, Marshall urged its suppression. Truman agreed.

Having committed itself to a major effort to contain the Soviets in Europe, moreover, the Truman administration was reluctant to launch a program of massive assistance for Nationalist China. Such aid, its leaders felt, would probably make little difference in the civil war and would weaken the European program.

Since they had not committed themselves to bipartisanism in Far Eastern affairs, Republicans now vigorously attacked the administration's policy toward China, which they considered politically vulnerable. In November, Governor Thomas E. Dewey of New York denounced the administration's China policy as bankrupt, saying the United States needed a strong policy in Asia as well as in Europe. If the Communists took China, he warned, all of Asia would fall into hostile hands. He and others urged the extension of the Truman Doctrine to China to save her from Communism.

Despite the attacks, the administration persisted in a policy of watchful waiting, coupled with limited assistance to Chiang to help ward off economic collapse. The strategy of containment suited Europe, administration supporters argued, but not China. After all, China's territory was about forty-five times that of Greece and her population eighty-five times as large. Many billions of dollars and millions of American troops would have been necessary in an intervention on the Greek pattern. Success, moreover, seemed unlikely.

Already the leading role the United States had played in Chinese affairs had made Americans offensive to Chinese national pride; even those Chinese who profited from American aid were hostile. In addition, the war-weary, tax-weary American people, administration defenders added, would not support massive intervention. Therefore, Truman's advisers concluded, the government had no choice but to remain aloof.

Critics of administration policy nonetheless persisted in demanding vigorous intervention. During the debate over the Marshall Plan, the administration partially gave in and asked for funds for China. In the Foreign Assistance Act of May, 1948, Congress appropriated $338 million for economic aid and $125 million for military assistance to China for one year. This new aid, essentially a Republican commitment to the Nationalist side in the civil war, did not reach Chiang in time to do him any good.

The Communist Triumph

The Communists vastly enlarged their armies, conquered Manchuria, and pushed on into China proper. Suffering from astronomical inflation, widespread corruption, and poor leadership, the demoralized Nationalists slowly fell back. During the two and one-half years from January, 1946, to August, 1948, for example, prices in Nationalist China doubled sixty-seven times. In January, 1949, the Communists took Peiping, Nanking in April, Shanghai in May, and then swept southward for more victories.

Americans were astounded. Their influence in China, dominant at the end of the Second World War, had dwindled to zero. Few could deny that the Communist victory, accompanied by an open hatred of Americans, was a defeat for the United States. "In any event," Vandenberg wrote, "our China policy has been a tragic failure and, now that the chips are down, I can't help saying so."[11]

Others said the same thing; some implied that American treachery had lost China to the Communists. The "crime," critics charged, began when F.D.R. "sold China down the river" at Yalta. So intense did the charges and countercharges become that the Department of State issued a "White Paper" in August, 1949, really a book with some 400 pages of history and 600 pages of documents, telling the story of American relations with China since 1844. In a letter of transmittal, Secretary of State Dean Acheson defended the administration's policy.

The ominous result of the Chinese civil war, he said, was beyond American control. "Nothing that this country did or could have done within the reasonable limits of its capabilities could have changed that result; nothing that was left undone by this country has contributed to it," he claimed. "It was the product of internal Chinese forces, forces which this country tried to influence but could not."[12]

Many Americans agreed, but a group of Republican senators did not. In a memorandum they condemned the White Paper as "a 1,054-page whitewash of wishful, do-nothing policy which has succeeded only in placing Asia in danger of Soviet conquest."[13]

In Peking, whose name had been changed from Peiping, the Communists proclaimed the "People's Republic of China" on October 1. By the end of the

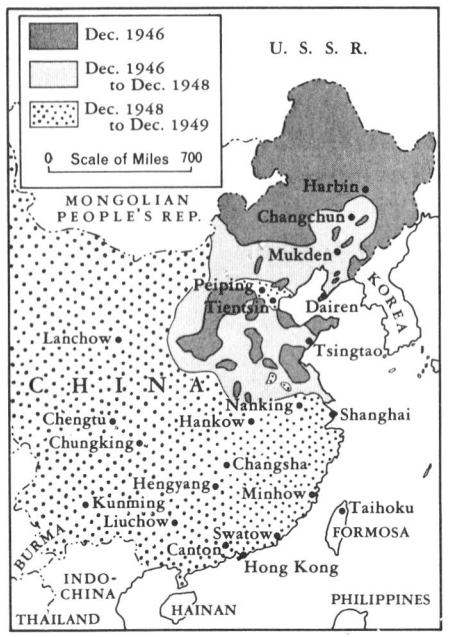

ADVANCE OF THE
CHINESE COMMUNISTS

year their armies controlled all of China except Tibet. Chiang abandoned the mainland in December and fled to the island of Formosa, or Taiwan. All that remained of his forces on the continent were a few scattered remnants who fought a pitiful guerrilla war.

Ironically, as Chiang's power practically vanished, the problem of policy toward China created a deeper division between Democrats and Republicans. Two main questions exacerbated the bruising political battle. Should the United States recognize "Red China?" Should it aid Chiang Kai-shek in defending Taiwan against the Communists?

Immediately after Mao Tse-tung had proclaimed his "People's Republic," the Soviet Union and its satellites extended it recognition. By the beginning of 1950 some twenty-five nations, including Britain, had done so. Supported by the Soviets, Mao's regime not only sought international recognition but also tried to gain China's permanent seat in the Security Council of the United Nations, a post still in the hands of the refugee Nationalist government.

Shocked by the Communist mistreatment of American consular officials in China, the American people felt a revulsion for Mao Tse-tung's regime. Reflecting this sentiment, particularly the political pressures by critics of its China policy, the government refused to recognize the Red Chinese government and blocked its efforts to break into the United Nations.

At the same time, even though Chiang's warships were trying to enforce an annoying blockade on Red ports, the Chinese Communists appeared eager to attack, or in their phrase, to "liberate" Formosa. Certain Republicans in Congress, including a group often called the "China bloc," demanded continued support for Chiang's regime on Formosa, including naval assistance, to keep the Reds out.

To the consternation of those Republicans, the President took a differing position. "The United States government will not pursue a course which will lead to involvement in the civil conflict in China," he announced. "Similarly, the United States government will not provide military aid or advice to Chinese forces on Formosa," but, he added, it would continue economic aid to Chiang, as long as Congress voted it.[14]

Republican critics considered this statement a virtual abandonment of Chiang, an effort to squirm out of an uncomfortable entanglement, and the prelude to recognition of Red China. Yet a week later, in retaliation for the brutal treatment of Americans there, the United States recalled all official personnel in China and thus severed its last official link with the Communist regime.

American hostility toward the Chinese Communists mounted when Mao visited Moscow in February, 1950, and signed a thirty-year treaty of friendship, alliance, and mutual assistance with the Soviet Union. Mao had now definitely committed his country to an anti-American policy. As he had written several months earlier, henceforth China's foreign policy would be based on "alliance with the u.s.s.r., with the countries of the new democracy in Europe, and alliance with the proletariat and masses of the people in all other countries."[15]

Even though most Americans did not accept the charge of the "China bloc" and others that traitorous Communists or sympathizers in the government had shaped Far Eastern policy for the benefit of foreign Communists, they realized that in Asia the policy of containment, though never applied as in Europe, had failed. The most populous people on earth, about 500 million, had become allies of Russia. The Soviet Union, with its cluster of satellites, was no longer a Communist oasis in a hostile world. Communist influence was ascendant in Asia; the Moscow-Peking Axis had added new weight to the shift in the balance of power toward the Communist world. Without much choice, therefore, the United States turned to its recent foe, Japan, as the fulcrum of its Far Eastern policy.

The Occupation of Japan

The idea of reviving Japan as an important power marked a reversal in American thinking, for at first, policy toward postwar Japan turned on the idea of reducing her to a second-rate state while building up China. The immediate objectives of postwar policy were to uproot and destroy what remained of Japanese military and economic power. In the process the United States hoped to reform and educate the Japanese people so that Japan would become a democratic and peaceful nation.

Unlike that of Germany, the occupation of Japan was almost wholly American. The harsh frustrations in the early months of the German occupation had created a determination in American policymakers to avoid similar experiences in Japan. "I was determined that the Japanese occupation would not follow in the footsteps of our German experience," Truman wrote. "I did not want divided control or separate zones. I did not want to give the Russians any opportunity to behave as they had in Germany and Austria." [16]

General Douglas MacArthur became the instrument of American and hence of Allied policy in Japan under the title of Supreme Commander for the Allied Powers, or scap in Army jargon. Few men have fitted their roles as well as did the majestic MacArthur. He set himself up as a proconsul, the benevolent but almost absolute master of eighty million people. His aloofness, his sonorous phrases, his austerity, his capacity for hard work, his insistence on strict obedience and unswerving loyalty from his subordinates, and his impatience with criticism, were all qualities that the Japanese admired and accepted.

To the Japanese, MacArthur became the personification of American power. They regarded him as the source of occupation policy, the Yankee shogun. Even though he ruled as a foreign conqueror, the people treated him with unlimited respect. Even MacArthur's daily automobile trips, from his home in the former American Embassy in Tokyo to his office in the Daiichi Building across the moat from the emperor's palace, had a sense of the dramatic. Each day as he stepped from his car at his headquarters he drew crowds of awed Japanese.

As soon as MacArthur and his soldiers had set foot in Japan they began carrying out the Potsdam terms of surrender. In the first few months of the occupation MacArthur issued sweeping directives ordering, among other things, the arrest and trial of Japanese leaders whom the Allies considered war criminals, the dissolution of militaristic societies and the arrest of their leaders, and changes in Japanese social institutions. Ultimately, in the major war crimes trials held in Tokyo beginning in 1946, a number of Japan's highest wartime leaders were convicted of crimes against peace and humanity. Some were imprisoned; a few were hanged. Men still debate the legality and importance of those trials.

The occupation forces also tried to revamp Japan's education system and hence to tutor the Japanese into accepting the imposed changes as logical developments. With remarkable efficiency the conquerors also plunged immediately into the task of disarming and demobilizing millions of Japanese soldiers. Within two years the United States swept Asia and the Pacific islands clean of the Japanese, bringing back to the home islands some 6 million soldiers and civilians. In accordance with Allied policy, the United States stripped Japan of her conquered territories and limited her sovereignty to her home islands. All this and more the Japanese accepted with an amazing tractability.

The Allies, too, accepted the American program, but objected to MacArthur's highhanded manner in carrying it out and the fact that the United States did as it pleased. The Russians were particularly resentful. Although the Allies recognized that the United States had conquered Japan practically unaided and hence was entitled to the main voice in deciding policy there, they did not like being shut out almost completely.

To outsiders, moreover, American policy seemed grossly inconsistent. While Americans objected bitterly to Russia's free hand in eastern Europe, they exercised a freer one in Japan. The smaller Allies, such as Australia, muttered about international cooperation "always preached and not always practiced." [17]

At the first meeting of the Council of Foreign Ministers in London in September, 1945, for instance, Molotov protested American policy in Japan. In October, Stalin himself told the American Ambassador that the Soviet government could not accept responsibility for MacArthur's actions since it was neither consulted nor informed about them. "The Soviet Union," the old Bolshevik said, "was being treated like an American satellite in the Pacific—a role it could not accept." It would, he added, be better for Russia not to be represented in Japan than to remain there "like a piece of furniture." [18] The Soviets desired another system of four-power control and occupation wherein they could exercise a veto over policy, the precise program the United States was determined to block.

Although the United States stood firm in its determination to retain the ultimate power in Japan, at the Moscow meeting of the Council of Foreign Ministers in December, 1945, it agreed to include the Allies in the policymaking. Eleven powers, finally thirteen, who had fought against Japan formed a Far Eastern Commission that sat in Washington and in theory became the supreme policy-making body for Japan. In practice it was not. The United States continued to send independent directives to MacArthur, and he continued to interpret them in his own way.

In addition, representatives of the United States, the British Commonwealth, Russia, and China formed an Allied Council in Tokyo, an advisory body that MacArthur was supposed to consult on matters of policy. He seldom did so and it degenerated into a debating society. From beginning to end MacArthur remained subject only to orders from the President of the United States and at times even resented control from Washington, arguing that policy for Japan should be made in Tokyo.

The Moscow Agreement also included arrangements for broadening the occupation forces. China could not spare troops, and the Russians refused an invitation to participate. Britain, Australia, and New Zealand sent troop contingents which remained until 1947, but their share in the occupation was small. Japan's control, with little outside restraint, remained an American responsibility.

Policy Transformations in Japan

MacArthur, meantime, went ahead with a program of political reform. Russia, China, Australia, and some of the other Allies wanted to treat the emperor as a war criminal and get rid of him, but the United States took a different view. It kept him in office but forced him, in an imperial rescript of New Year's Day, 1946, to renounce the theory of his own divinity. Japan's new constitution, written in part at least by Americans, reduced him to a constitutional figurehead, "the symbol of the State and of the unity of the people, deriving his position from the will of the people with whom resides sovereign power." [19] This was indeed a revolutionary doctrine for the Japanese.

Another unusual provision said that "the Japanese people forever renounce war as a sovereign right of the nation." Other parts of the constitution granted comprehensive rights in matters of police, freedom of the press, education, representation, and elections. By offering the Japanese liberties they had never before enjoyed, the new constitution marked a high point in the American program of political reform.

The most sensitive barometer of the American attitude toward conquered Japan was the economic program. From 1945 to 1947 the Allies had intended this program, as well as other parts of the occupation policy, to be punitive but not Carthaginian. Briefly, the United States sought to reduce Japan's economy to the level of the years 1930–1934, before she had completed her major conquests. By eliminating munitions plants and the aircraft industry, and by reducing such industries as steel, shipbuilding, and synthetic oil, the United States attempted to uproot the economic base of her military power. Everything above the permitted economic level might be used as reparations for war damage suffered at the hands of the Japanese by the Allies.

The wrecked state of the Japanese economy made the American program almost impossible. What Americans had found in Japan was a destitute population whose morale had apparently been shattered by war and defeat. Forty per cent of the nation's densely packed urban areas had been destroyed. Flames from American fire bombs had swept through flimsy wooden houses as they would through an open prairie. Even if the occupation had not shut down plants, the Japanese would not have been able to support themselves. In 1946, industrial production sank to less than one-third of what it had been in 1930 and to one-seventh of the total in 1937. Japan's primary means of support became an inadequate agricultural system.

The United States, therefore, had the task of keeping the Japanese from starving.

In addition to the costs of the occupation, the American Treasury at first paid some $200 million per year, and more later, to support the Japanese. MacArthur, besides importing foodstuffs, encouraged the Japanese to build up their peacetime industries and thus made the first change in American policy.

Despite protests from Allies, such as Australia and the Philippines, the United States directed its revised economic policies toward the objective of making Japan pay her own way and even assisted her with interim aid. As in Germany, the American authorities sought to relieve the taxpayer of part of his heavy burden in supporting conquered peoples.

After completing most of his political reforms, General MacArthur announced that the prolonged occupation was impeding economic recovery and advanced the idea of a prompt peace treaty that would leave Japan to her own resources. In July, 1947, the United States approached the powers of the Far Eastern Commission with the suggestion of holding a preliminary conference to discuss peace terms for Japan. Russia and China objected.

The Soviets desired a treaty drafted by the Big Four or the Big Five that would give them the power of veto. Aware that Russia would veto any treaty that would align Japan with the Western powers, the United States sought a broad peace conference where the decisions would be made by a friendly two-thirds majority. Since it could not at this time avoid the Soviet veto, the United States put aside the peace treaty and continued the occupation.

By the end of 1948 another phase of American policy began to emerge, and in the following year, with the Communist victory in China, it became clear. The United States would help Japan regain her prewar industrial supremacy in Asia with the idea of making her a future "bastion against Communism" there. The cold war had thus forced a complete reversal of policy toward Japan.

Since Japan was still weak and had no armed forces, she could contribute little to the containment program, but at this point American policy did not intend to use Japan against Russia. It merely wanted to keep the Soviets out. In March, 1949, MacArthur announced that "we never intended to use Japan as an ally. All we want her to do is to remain neutral." [20] Nonetheless, American planners concluded that the Japanese islands had become essential to defense in the Far East, particularly as bases in the event of war.

This new policy of building up Japan as an Asian bulwark against Communism now took on a military significance and heightened the tension with the Soviet Union and Communist China. It was, the Soviets argued, more evidence of the "aggressive" aims of American foreign policy. Russia's and Communist China's concern over the future of Japan was clear in their alliance, which they directed specifically against "the rebirth of Japanese imperialism" and "any other state which should unite in any form with Japan in acts of aggression." [21]

American policymakers, despite the antiwar provisions of the Japanese constitution, had also begun to think of encouraging the Japanese to rearm. In addition, they considered the idea of a peace treaty without the Soviets or China, if their postwar allies would go along. Thus, as the cold war erupted into a hot war in Korea in the summer of 1950, Japan had changed from a conquered enemy to an informal ally of the United States.

Background of Relations with Korea

Before discussing the war in Korea, it is useful to pause for a look into the background of events leading to that conflict.

An ancient land located at the crossroads of Asian empires, Korea had a long history of invasions. Like Japan, she had tried to isolate herself from the rest of the world. For over two hundred years, beginning in the early part of the seventeenth century, she had fended off virtually all contact with the outside world. The first Western nation to break into Korea's seclusion was the United States. With Chinese assistance, Commodore Robert W. Shufeldt of the American Navy signed a commercial treaty with the Korean kingdom in May, 1882. It provided for the exchange of diplomatic and consular officers and gave the United States trading rights and other privileges in Korea.

In the next two decades, as China and Japan sought to gain control of the kingdom, Americans were favored in the Korean court. In 1895, Japan, after defeating China in a short war, gained ascendancy and formally annexed Korea in 1910. Korea remained a colony until 1942 when she became an integral part of Japan. Except for some business and missionary activity, American influence in Korea in the Japanese era disappeared.

During that era, a Korean underground movement and exiles abroad kept alive a yearning for independence. In March, 1919, Korean nationalists fomented an unsuccessful uprising against the Japanese and fled to China where they set up a Korean Provisional Government with Syngman Rhee as the first president.

After 1920, Koreans living in Russia organized a Korean Communist Party and received Soviet political and military training. In later years, notably after 1935, a militant group of Communists was active in northeastern Korea.

Soon after the United States went to war against Japan, Korean nationalists again began agitating for an independent Korea. The Korean Provisional Government, still alive in China, sought American recognition but failed to receive it. The first formal American commitment came in November, 1943, at the Cairo conference. There, Roosevelt, Churchill, and Chiang Kai-shek declared that they were "mindful of the enslavement of the people of Korea" and were "determined that in due course Korea shall become free and independent."[22]

At Yalta, Roosevelt and Stalin discussed the idea of a four-power trusteeship to prepare Korea for independence. The Potsdam Declaration reaffirmed the Cairo pledge, and on going to war against Japan, the Soviets announced their adherence to the Potsdam Declaration, thus publicly committing themselves to the principle of an independent Korea.

Several days later Russian troops entered northeastern Korea. At the suggestion of the United States, the Soviets agreed to accept the surrender of Japanese troops north of the 38th parallel, while the Japanese south of that line would surrender to American forces. American troops did not enter southern Korea until September 8, 1945, almost a month after the Russians had set foot in Korea.

The decision on the 38th parallel was military, a temporary line to facilitate the surrender of the Japanese. The line corresponded to no geographical, economic, or social division in the Korean peninsula. If there had been no division along the 38th parallel, the Soviets probably could have overrun most of the country before the Americans arrived.[23] Since the line limited the area of Communist control, it favored the United States.

Almost as soon as American and Russian troops began facing each other across the 38th parallel, the line took on a political significance. The Americans ruled their zone through a military government, and the Russians ran theirs through local Korean "people's committees." As postwar tension mounted between the Soviet Union and the United States, the two zones increasingly functioned as separate entities and the 38th parallel became almost an international frontier.

Bitter over the division of their country and eager for independence, the Koreans grew restless. At the Moscow meeting of the Council of Foreign Ministers in December, 1945, therefore, the Soviets and the United States agreed to sponsor a "provisional Korean democratic government" and after a period of four-power trusteeship to re-establish Korea as an independent state. When the Koreans learned of the Moscow agreement, they held mass demonstrations in the streets of Seoul, their capital city, angrily denouncing the trusteeship plan. They demanded immediate independence and unification.

For almost two years after the Moscow agreement, American and Russian negotiators vainly sought to find a formula that would unify Korea and assure its independence. They failed because the United States would not agree to any settlement that might bring the whole peninsula under Communist control, and the Soviets would not accept a unified Korea that would be linked to the United States. As the cold war hardened the hostility between the Soviet Union and the United States, many Koreans came to feel that their legitimate aspirations were suffering because of the rivalry between the occupying powers.

The Division of Korea

In an effort to break the diplomatic stalemate, Secretary of State Marshall referred the question of Korea's independence to the General Assembly of the United Nations in September, 1947. The Russians objected, offering a substitute plan that would remove all foreign troops from Korea by the beginning of the next year. Thus, they said, the Koreans would be able to form their own government. Fearing that an abrupt withdrawal of their troops would leave the South Koreans at the mercy of the well-armed North, the Americans rejected the Soviet plan.

Despite the Soviet opposition, the General Assembly voted to take up the Korean question on terms suggested by the United States. It created a United Nations Temporary Commission on Korea to supervise elections for a Korean national assembly. The United Nations recommended that once the Koreans had established a national government, they should make their own arrangements for the withdrawal of Russian and American troops.

The Russians and the North Koreans boycotted the United Nations Commission. In May, 1948, therefore, the commission went ahead with elections in the American zone only, saying in its final report that they "were a valid expression of the free will of the electorate of that part of Korea."[24]

The newly elected national assembly adopted a constitution, elected Syngman Rhee, now seventy-three years old, as the first president of the Republic of Korea, and on August 15 the new government was formally inaugurated. On that same day the Russians held elections in North Korea, and then the North Koreans established their own "Democratic People's Republic of Korea." Two Korean governments had now come into existence, each claiming to represent all of Korea and each backed by a rival great power. A month later the Soviets announced that in response to an appeal from the North Korean government they would withdraw all their troops by the end of December. They did so.

Early in December the General Assembly of the United Nations, as suggested by the United States, recommended withdrawal of the occupying forces and replaced the temporary commission on Korea with a permanent one. It also called on member states to cooperate with the new commission in bringing about "the complete independence and unity of Korea," and recognized the South Korean government as the only lawful regime in Korea.

The United States and thirty other countries also recognized only the South Korean government, but the Soviet Union and other Communist nations recognized only the North Korean government. When the South Koreans sought admission to the United Nations, a Soviet veto blocked the application.

In accordance with the General Assembly's recommendation, the United States withdrew its troops from South Korea by June, 1949. Five hundred men and officers remained as an advisory group to help train a constabulary.

During the next year, the 38th parallel became a line of uncontrolled tension as North and South Koreans raided the border and exchanged fire. Both sides threatened to unify the country by force, and the United Nations Commission on Korea warned that "barbarous civil war" might engulf the peninsula.

The United States supported the efforts of the watchdog United Nations Commission to bring peace and unity to Korea but did not offer the South Koreans protection. Speaking before the National Press Club in Washington, Secretary of State Dean Acheson gave the impression that the United States would not defend the South Koreans. The American "defensive perimeter" in the Far East, he explained, extended in a great arc that included the Aleutian Islands, Japan, the Ryukyus, and the Philippines. If an attack occurred outside that arc, in Korea perhaps, he suggested that "the initial reliance must be on the people attacked to resist it and then upon the commitments of the entire civilized world under the Charter of the United Nations. . . ."[25]

In the following months the United States appeared more concerned with South Korea's weak economy, plagued by a zooming inflation, than with any threat of an attack from the north. In February, 1950, President Truman signed a bill alloting a total of $110 million for South Korea's economic rehabilitation. In addition, the United States gave the South Koreans military assistance. When the American troops withdrew, they left behind millions of dollars in military equipment, such as rifles and ammunition. Since Rhee had threatened to invade North Korea, the United States withheld tanks, planes, and heavy guns that might be used in offensive operations. The Russians had supplied the North Koreans with tanks and heavy artillery.

The North Korean Invasion

In the early morning hours of Sunday, June 25, 1950, North Korean forces, supported by Russian-made tanks, struck across the 38th parallel in a surprise attack that shattered the uneasy peace of the cold war. South Korean troops, lightly armed, broke under the impact of armor and fire and began a disorganized retreat southward. The North Koreans claimed that the South Koreans had attacked first and that they were merely counterattacking, but the United Nations Commission on Korea pointed out that the northern Communists had launched a "well-planned, concerted, and full-scale invasion of South Korea."

As soon as Secretary of State Acheson received news of the attack he telephoned the President who was vacationing in Independence, Missouri. Truman agreed to call the Security Council of the United Nations into emergency session. When the Council met that Sunday afternoon at Lake Success, the Soviet delegate was not present. He had been boycotting the Council since January because it had refused to replace Nationalist China's representative with one from Red China, and did not return until August 1.

Without fear of a Russian veto, therefore, the Security Council, by a vote of nine to zero, passed a resolution, proposed by the United States, declaring the North Korean attack "a breach of the peace." The Council called for the immediate cessation of hostilities, the withdrawal of North Korean forces to the 38th parallel, and asked all members of the United Nations not to aid the North Koreans.[26]

Truman rushed back to Washington and that evening held emergency meetings with his advisers. The next day the South Koreans sent him a desperate appeal for "effective and timely aid." That evening, in his capacity as Commander-in-Chief, he took a decisive step. He ordered General MacArthur to use American naval and air forces to attack North Korean military targets south of the 38th parallel. He also ordered the Seventh Fleet to prevent any Communist assault on Formosa and to keep the Nationalists from attacking the Chinese mainland. By the last order he hoped to prevent reprisals from the Chinese Communists and thus to keep the Korean War from spreading.

On the following day, the President justified his action as being in support of the Security Council's resolution that the Korean Communists had defied. "The attack upon Korea," he said, "makes it plain beyond all doubt that Communism has passed beyond the use of subversion to conquer independent nations and will now use armed invasion and war." [27]

Seeking a clear-cut endorsement for its action, the United States asked the Security Council to impose stringent sanctions against the North Koreans. The Communist action, the American delegate told the Council that afternoon, was "an attack upon the United Nations itself." [28] After some debate the Council passed an American resolution by a vote of seven to one, urging members of the United Nations to "furnish such assistance to the Republic of Korea as may be necessary to repel the armed attack and to restore international peace and security in the area." [29]

Within a week, after MacArthur reported that only American ground forces could stop the Communist advance, Truman sent troops into action, permitted American planes to bomb targets in North Korea, and ordered a naval blockade of the Korean coast. At the suggestion of the United States, the Security Council passed a resolution on July 7 recommending a unified command under the United States and authorizing the use of the blue flag of the United Nations in Korea. The President named MacArthur the United Nations commander. [30]

In a few months the American combat forces in Korea grew into an army of more than 210,000 men. Ultimately sixteen other nations sent armed units to Korea, but their contribution, partly because Britain and France had commitments elsewhere, was meager. The United States and South Korea contributed over 90 per cent of the ground forces and the United States alone supplied over 93 per cent of the air forces and more than 85 per cent of the naval forces. Even though the banner of the United Nations flew over the battle fronts, the Korean War was essentially an American war.

At first the American people, and even Republican critics of the administration's Far Eastern policy, overwhelmingly supported Truman's prompt action. They approved the intervention, seeing it as a necessary effort to save a small country from Communist aggression and to show allies, or potential ones, that the United States would help defend them. "The White House gang is today enormously popular, incredibly popular," the normally critical Chicago *Tribune* admitted. [31]

Later, as the war budget mounted and the casualties multiplied, critics denounced the President for allegedly usurping Congress' power to declare war and for involving the country in a perilous fight outside the national interest.

The first American troops to reach Korea were raw, young recruits fresh from occupation duty in Japan. They, too, fell back before the well-organized foe. Finally, early in August, the United Nations forces established a strong defensive perimeter around the port of Pusan at the southeastern tip of Korea. A month later, on September 15, in a brilliantly conceived maneuver, MacArthur launched an amphibious attack on Inchon, near the western end of the 38th parallel, which caught the North Koreans by surprise. The American troops cut swiftly across the peninsula, trapping most of the North Koreans who surrendered by the thousands. Others fled beyond the 38th parallel with United Nations forces in hot pursuit.

As September turned into October, the Chinese Communists watched the American advance to the 38th parallel with hostile anxiety. Chou En-lai, Red China's Foreign Minister, denounced the United States as "the most dangerous enemy of the People's Republic of China." The Chinese people, he warned two weeks later, will not "supinely tolerate seeing their neighbors being savagely invaded by the imperialists." [32] China, he and other Communists indicated, would defend North Korea.

Shortly after the American intervention began, Secretary Acheson had said that it was "solely for the purpose of restoring the Republic of Korea to its status prior to the invasion from the north and of re-establishing the peace broken by that aggression." [33] By October Acheson's view and American policy changed. The President and the United Nations allowed MacArthur, who believed the Chinese would not intervene, to push on beyond the 38th parallel. In effect, the United States had decided to unify Korea through military action.

MacArthur's troops advanced north to the banks of the Yalu River which separated Korea from China's Manchuria. Late in November MacArthur launched his "final" offensive, and there was talk of "the boys being home for Christmas." "The war," the general told newspapermen, "very definitely is coming to an end shortly." [34]

Red China Intervenes

Chinese troops, "volunteers," the Communists called them, had already entered Korea. The big attack came on November 26. With flares lighting the night and bugle blasts piercing the cold air, hordes of Chinese slammed into the center of the over-extended United Nations lines. Two days later, as outnumbered American and associated troops were falling back in a bloody retreat over frozen ground, MacArthur announced that he faced "an entirely new war." His command, he told his superiors a few days later, was "facing the entire Chinese nation in an undeclared war." [35]

GENERAL MACARTHUR ADDRESSING CONGRESS, APRIL 19, 1951

Victory, MacArthur now maintained, would not be possible unless he could blockade China, bomb targets in China, and use Chinese Nationalist troops in Korea and for diversionary attacks on the China coast. The President, his advisers, and the Joint Chiefs of Staff all opposed the course MacArthur suggested, fearing that it would lead to a third world war, precisely what their containment policy was designed to prevent. "If we began to attack Communist China," Truman wrote, "we had to anticipate Russian intervention." [36] The men in the White House could not forget that Russia and China were allies and that the Chinese Communists had not bluffed in their previous warnings.

America's allies and other members of the United Nations also opposed any action that might enlarge the Korean War. The United Nations tried to arrange a cease-fire but the Chinese, confident of victory, rejected the offer. They demanded that all foreign troops leave Korea, a condition unacceptable to the United States. On February 1, 1951, the General Assembly of the United Nations declared Communist China guilty of aggression. By the end of the month, reinforced American troops stopped the Chinese offensive below the 38th parallel, deep in South Korea. MacArthur's generals then regrouped their forces and in April drove the Communists back across the 38th parallel.

MacArthur, meanwhile, brought his disagreement with the administration into the open by publicly criticizing its foreign policy. On March 24, as Truman was seeking arrangements for a cease-fire, the general issued a statement threatening Red China with an attack and offered to meet the enemy commander in the field to realize the political objectives of the United Nations in Korea. A week and a half later the Republican leader in the House of Representatives released a letter from MacArthur contradicting the government's policy of limited war in Korea. "There is," the general said, "no substitute for victory." [37]

The President could stand no more. MacArthur, Truman and his advisers concluded, was guilty of insubordination to his Commander-in-Chief. Of deeper significance were the constitutional issues. The general had challenged the principle of civilian supremacy in government and the President's authority to direct foreign policy. At a special news conference at 1:00 a.m., April 11, Truman announced that because MacArthur could not support government and United Nations policies, he had relieved the general of his commands.

Most Americans were astonished; many were angry. Outraged Republicans denounced the President; some muttered that he should be impeached. Public opinion polls showed that 69 per cent of those questioned opposed the firing and only 29 per cent approved.

When MacArthur returned to the United States, television viewers saw the same drama in city after city—San Francisco, Chicago, New York, and elsewhere. Crowds filled the streets, pushed, fought, or just waited for a glimpse of the man in the famous cap with the tarnished gold braid. Most dramatic of all was MacArthur's appearance before Congress. With an oratorical skill seldom witnessed on Capitol Hill, he gave his own version of the policy difficulties with the administration. "War's very object is victory, not prolonged indecision," he said in getting to the root of his view. [38] So moved was one Republican congressman that he remarked, "We saw a great hunk of God in the flesh, and we heard the voice of God." [39]

Several weeks later, in a congressional inquiry into MacArthur's dismissal and the conduct of the Korean War, the administration answered the general's criticisms and his desire to "go it alone" if America's allies would not support the kind of Asian policy he advocated. General Omar N. Bradley, chairman of the Joint Chiefs of Staff, and Secretary Acheson summed up the administration's case. Russia, not Red China, Bradley said, was the main enemy. MacArthur's strategy, he pointed out, "would involve us in the wrong war, at the wrong place, at the wrong time, and with the wrong enemy." [40] Acheson pointed out that MacArthur's policy involved the risk of a big war with China and Russia "in return for measures whose effectiveness in bringing the conflict to an early conclusion are judged doubtful by our responsible military authorities." [41]

Truce Talks

Late in June, before the MacArthur furor had died and while the Chinese and American armies were stalemated in the hills above the 38th parallel, Jacob A. Malik, the Soviet representative to the United Nations, indicated that the Chinese and North Koreans were willing to discuss an armistice. The President and his advisers accepted the overture and truce talks began on July 10, 1951, at Kaesong on the Communist side of the battle line. Since neither side trusted the other, the talks progressed slowly.

In August the Communists abruptly broke off the negotiations, charging that the United Nations had violated the neutrality zone around Kaesong. In October they agreed to resume the talks, this time at Panmunjom, a site midway between the battle lines. By the end of the year the negotiators had reached agreement on most issues but had deadlocked on the question of the exchange of prisoners.

Many of the prisoners in United Nations camps said they would not return to their Communist homelands, fearing death or injury there. The United States, supported by most of the members of the United Nations, refused to force those prisoners to return. The Communist negotiators insisted that all Chinese and North Korean prisoners must be repatriated. In October, 1952, the United States suspended the discussions. The war, now a "grim, face-saving slugging match," continued in the Korean hills, but the battle line remained substantially unchanged.

The endless fighting and the truce marathon had made the frustrating Korean conflict one of the most unpopular of American wars.[42] In their campaign for the Presidency in 1952, the Republicans made it a central issue. In their platform the foreign policy plank came first. That statement, written by John Foster Dulles, attacked "the negative, futile and immoral policy of 'containment.'" "Liberation" of peoples under Communist domination became the Republican theme. "With foresight," the platform said, "the Korean war would never have happened."[43]

Adlai E. Stevenson, the Democratic candidate, went along with Truman's and Acheson's foreign policy, but General Dwight D. Eisenhower, the Republican candidate, in the final days of the campaign appeared to accept the MacArthur approach to the Korean puzzle. He promised, if elected, to bring the Korean War to an early and honorable end. "That job requires a personal trip to Korea. I shall make that trip. I shall go to Korea."[44]

Eisenhower won the election by a landslide. In December he went to Korea for a three-day visit. A month later, as the Korean War completed its thirtieth month, he became President.

Soon after his inauguration, President Eisenhower "unleashed" Chiang Kai-shek. The Seventh Fleet, he told Congress, would no longer "be employed to shield Communist China." Critics feared that Chiang would attack the mainland and drag the United States into a war with Red China, but the Generalissimo was too weak to act effectively and nothing happened.

Eisenhower's announcement appeared to be the main move in the new "positive" Far Eastern policy the Republicans had promised. Nevertheless, the stalemate in Korea continued and the Eisenhower policy seemed as cautious as Truman's. Yet the new Secretary of State, John Foster Dulles, and the President had decided upon Eisenhower's return trip from Korea to try for a truce and if that effort failed, to fight for victory with tactical atomic bombs if necessary. Dulles thought that this decision, relayed to Red China through India's Prime Minister, broke the deadlock in the truce negotiations.[45] In any event, the truce talks were resumed in April, 1953, and on July 27 the negotiators signed an armistice. Hours later the sixteen nations who had fought with the United States signed a declaration saying they would offer prompt and united resistance to a renewed attack. At 10 p.m. that night, the guns in the hills of Korea fell silent for the first time in three years and thirty-two days.

The Armistice

The armistice did not settle the Korean question. It merely said that fighting would stop at the battle line, which would be demilitarized and which for most of the distance ran slightly north of the 38th parallel. The armistice also called for the exchange of prisoners under complicated terms and for a peace or political

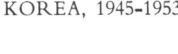

KOREA, 1945–1953

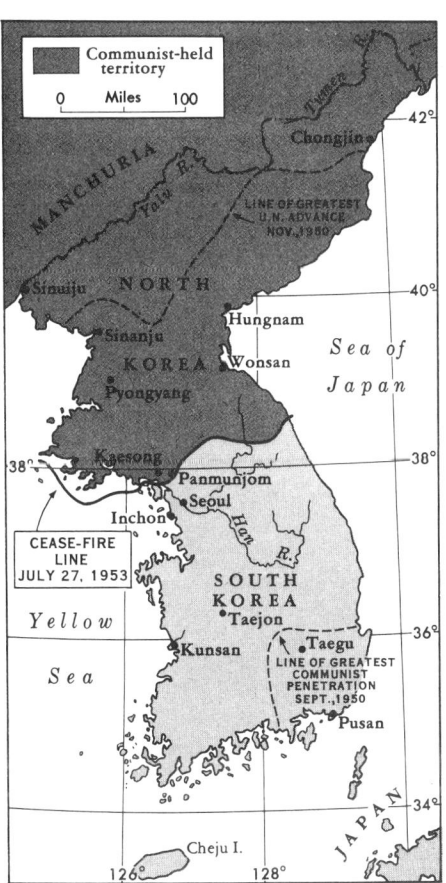

conference to settle the Korean problem. The conference was held later in the spring of 1954, in Geneva, Switzerland, but failed to settle anything.

Syngman Rhee had rebelled against the armistice and had almost wrecked it by releasing 27,000 North Korean prisoners so as to prevent their repatriation. Secretary of State Dulles had placated him by promising South Korea long-term economic aid and a mutual security pact. In August Congress voted an initial sum of $200 million for Korean aid. At the same time, Dulles visited Korea, negotiated the promised mutual defense treaty with Rhee, and signed it on October 1, in Washington. Dulles told the Senate Foreign Relations Committee that he hoped the pact would "disabuse the Communists of any ideas of launching another aggression in Korea."[46] Even though the treaty itself had the usual loophole requiring implementation through "constitutional processes," meaning through Congress, the Senate on January 26, 1954, gave its approval by a vote of 81 to 6, only with the stipulation that the United States would not support any South Korean effort to unite the peninsula by force.

The Koreans suffered most from the war, being left with vast casualties and a devastated land. America's cost was high, too. Estimates placed Americans killed at 23,000, the wounded at 105,785, and the cost to the United States alone at over $18 billion.

America's main enemies, Russia and Red China, emerged from the war more powerful than ever, and the Moscow-Peking axis gained strength. Korea remained divided. Yet for the first time, no matter how feeble the united effort, an international organization had attempted to use force on a large scale and the United States had served notice on the Communist bloc that it was willing to meet armed aggression with military force.[47] The United States could, moreover, take some satisfaction from the stalemate. The new boundary favored South Korea; the war had succeeded in "containing" Communism in Korea; and the limited conflict had not become a third world war.

NOTES

1. Quoted in Herbert Feis, *The China Tangle* (Princeton, 1953), p. 357.

2. *Ibid.*, p. 372.

3. John J. McCloy, Assistant Secretary of War, *ibid.*, p. 389.

4. Harry S. Truman, *Memoirs* (2 vols., Garden City, N.Y., 1955), II, 66.

5. See *ibid.*, II, 68, 69.

6. *Ibid.*, II, 86. Oliver E. Clubb, in "Manchuria in the Balance, 1945-1946," *Pacific Historical Review*, XXVI (Nov. 1957),

377-380, analyzes the source of conflict and places it in Manchuria.

7. Quoted in John C. Campbell, *The United States in World Affairs, 1945-1947* (New York, 1947), p. 291.

8. Marshall's statement of Jan. 7, 1947, is in John K. Fairbank, *The United States and China* (Cambridge, Mass., 1948), pp. 343-349. A revised edition was published in 1958.

9. Diary entry of Jan. 11, 1947, in Arthur H. Vandenberg, Jr., ed., *The Private Papers of Senator Vandenberg* (Boston, 1952), p. 522.

10. The parts of the Report to the President, Sept. 19, 1947, dealing with China were published in U.S. Department of State, *United States Relations with China: With Special Reference to the Period 1944–1949* (Washington, 1949), pp. 764–814. Parts I–V are also in Albert C. Wedemeyer, *Wedemeyer Reports* (New York, 1958), pp. 461–479.

11. Vandenberg, *Private Papers*, p. 534.

12. July 30, 1949, in U.S. Department of State, *United States Relations with China*, p. xvi.

13. Aug. 21, 1949, quoted in H. Bradford Westerfield, *Foreign Policy and Party Politics: Pearl Harbor to Korea* (New Haven, 1955), p. 356.

14. Jan. 5, 1950, *ibid.*, p. 364.

15. *Pravda*, July 6, 1949, quoted in Richard P. Stebbins, *The United States in World Affairs, 1949* (New York, 1950), p. 54.

16. Truman, *Memoirs*, I, 432.

17. Herbert V. Evatt, quoted in Campbell, *U.S. in World Affairs, 1945–1947*, p. 261.

18. Quoted in Feis, *China Tangle*, p. 393.

19. The text of the constitution is in Edwin O. Reischauer, *The United States and Japan*, rev. ed. (Cambridge, Mass., 1957), pp. 349–362. For the American contributions to the "MacArthur Constitution" see Robert E. Ward, "The Origins of the Present Japanese Constitution," *American Political Science Review*, L (Dec. 1956), 980–1010.

20. Quoted in the *The New York Times*, March 2, 1949, in John C. Campbell, *The United States in World Affairs, 1948–1949* (New York, 1949), p. 303.

21. Quoted in Richard P. Stebbins, *The United States in World Affairs, 1950* (New York, 1951), p. 181.

22. Quoted in Leland M. Goodrich, *Korea: A Study of United States Policy in the United Nations* (New York, 1956), p. 214, where the Cairo Declaration is reproduced.

23. This is emphasized by Arthur L. Grey, Jr., in "Thirty-Eighth Parallel," *Foreign Affairs*, XXIX (April 1951), 482–487.

24. Quoted in Carl Berger, *The Korean Knot: A Military-Political History* (Philadelphia, 1957), p. 87.

25. "Crisis in Asia—An Examination of U.S. Policy," Jan. 12, 1950, *Department of State Bulletin*, XXII (Jan. 23, 1950), 116. Acheson merely expressed publicly the views held by the Joint Chiefs of Staff. In 1947, when headed by Dwight D. Eisenhower, they had written off South Korea as a military liability. See John W. Spanier, *The Truman-MacArthur Controversy and the Korean War* (Cambridge, Mass., 1959), pp. 16–21.

26. Goodrich, *Korea*, pp. 104–106.

27. Truman, *Memoirs*, II, 339.

28. Warren Austin, quoted in Goodrich, *Korea*, p. 112.

29. For the resolution, see *ibid.*, p. 222.

30. For an analysis of the reaction of American policymakers to the crisis in the first ten days of the North Korean invasion, see Alexander L. George, "American Policymaking and the North Korean Aggression," *World Politics*, VII (Jan. 1955), 209–232.

31. Quoted in Eric F. Goldman, *The Crucial Decade—And After: America, 1945–1960* (New York, 1961), p. 172.

32. Chou's first statement of Oct. 1, 1950, is quoted in Spanier, *Truman-MacArthur Controversy*, p. 86; the second, of Oct. 16, is quoted in Allen S. Whiting, *China Crosses the Yalu: The Decision to Enter the Korean War* (New York, 1960), p. 108.

33. "Review of U.N. and U.S. Action to Restore Peace," June 29, 1950, *Department of State Bulletin*, XXIII (July 10, 1950), 46.

34. Quoted in Goldman, *Crucial Decade*, p. 178.

35. To Joint Chiefs of Staff, Dec. 3, 1950, in Truman, *Memoirs*, II, 392. For a detailed analysis of the Chinese intervention and its

military impact, see Roy E. Appleman, *South to the Naktong, North to the Yalu* (*June–November, 1950*) (Washington, 1961) and Robert Leckie, *Conflict: The History of the Korean War, 1950–1953* (New York, 1962), pp. 154–228.

36. Truman, *Memoirs*, II, 382. For an analysis of MacArthur's proposals and the ensuing debate, see John Norman, "MacArthur's Blockade Proposals against Red China," *Pacific Historical Review*, XXVI (May 1957), 161–174.

37. To Joseph W. Martin, Jr., March 20, 1951. The text of the letter is in Trumbull Higgins, *Korea and the Fall of MacArthur: A Précis in Limited War* (New York, 1960), pp. 113–114.

38. The main text of the speech, April 19, 1951, is in Richard H. Rovere and Arthur M. Schlesinger, Jr., *The General and the President: And the Future of American Foreign Policy* (New York, 1951), pp. 269–275.

39. Dewey Short, quoted in Spanier, *Truman-MacArthur Controversy*, p. 220.

40. Bradley's opening statement before the Senate committees, May 15, 1951, is printed in Rovere and Schlesinger, *General and President*, pp. 282–287.

41. June 1, 1951, quoted in McGeorge Bundy, ed., *The Pattern of Responsibility* (Boston, 1952), p. 280.

42. Even though the United States never formally declared war and Truman referred

to the Korean conflict as a "police action," it was a war and the courts have said it was. See Maurer Maurer, "The Korean Conflict Was a War," *Military Affairs*, XXIV (Fall 1960), 137–145.

43. The quotations are from John R. Beal, *John Foster Dulles: A Biography* (New York, 1957), p. 131; a revised edition was published in 1959. See also Norman A. Graebner, *The New Isolationism: A Study in Politics and Foreign Policy Since 1950* (New York, 1956), p. 96.

44. Detroit, Oct. 24, 1952, quoted in Sherman Adams, *Firsthand Report: The Story of the Eisenhower Administration* (New York, 1961), pp. 42–44.

45. This point is made in Beal, *Dulles*, pp. 181–184 and Robert J. Donovan, *Eisenhower: The Inside Story* (New York, 1956), pp. 118–119.

46. Jan. 13, 1954, quoted in Berger, *Korean Knot*, p. 178.

47. This interpretation is stressed in Arnold Wolfers, "Collective Security and the War in Korea," *Yale Review*, XLIII (Summer 1954), 481–496, which also points out that the result was not a victory for collective security. For a brief analysis of the Korean conflict as an experiment in limited warfare, see Martin Lichterman, "Korea: Problems in Limited War," in Gordon B. Turner and Richard D. Challener, eds., *National Security in the Nuclear Age* (New York, 1960), pp. 31–56.

Chapter Twenty-Seven

FERMENT IN
THE AMERICAS

UNLIKE Europe and Asia, Latin America had been a negligible factor in the diplomacy of the Second World War. To the United States, however, the republics to the south, although outside the main stream of world politics, had been of special concern as sources of valuable raw materials and as non-fighting allies in the defense of the Western Hemisphere.

Immediately after the attack on Pearl Harbor, most of the Latin-American republics showed their appreciation for the Good Neighbor policy. Within a few days nine of them, all in the Caribbean region where American influence was especially strong, declared war on the three Axis powers. Three other Latin governments broke off relations with the Axis. With those countries the United States quickly concluded Lend-Lease agreements. The remaining republics of the Americas refused to regard the United States as a belligerent and granted it special favors.

Two days after Pearl Harbor, the United States called together the Third Conference of Ministers of Foreign Affairs of the American Republics, which met in Rio de Janeiro in January, 1942, to discuss cooperative action against the Axis. The United States delegation tried to persuade all the republics to sign a joint declaration pledging themselves to break off relations with the Axis powers. As anticipated, Argentina, supported by Chile, refused to accept such a resolution. Secretary of State Hull opposed any concession, feeling that "the Argentines must accept this situation or go their own way," but Sumner Welles, the head of the American delegation, agreed to a compromise in order to preserve unanimity.[1]

As finally accepted, the resolution merely recommended the rupture of diplomatic relations with the Axis, with each country to decide for itself. Before the meeting closed, all the republics which had not already done so, except Argentina and Chile, broke with the Axis, and Chile did so a year later. The conference also approved an economic boycott against the Axis, with reservations by Argentina and Chile, and several resolutions aimed at curbing subversive activities in the Americas. In addition, it created an Inter-American Joint Defense Board to study and recommend measures for hemispheric defense.

Although the United States did not win a complete victory at Rio, the Latin-American states showed a greater unity in support of their northern neighbor than they had in the First World War. During the second conflict, most of the Latin republics collaborated with the United States by supplying it with air bases and strategic materials. The United States gave them the protection of its armed might, financial aid, and manufactured goods. It sent them over a half billion dollars in Lend-Lease supplies, more than two-thirds going to Brazil, who received special consideration because she was the only active belligerent in South America. She sent an expeditionary force to Italy, made available air bases in Natal that the Allies used in their "air ferry" that transported men and goods to Africa, and joined in the Allied campaign against German U-boats. Mexico, the only other active Latin-American belligerent, toward the end of the war sent some air force units to the Far East.[2]

Difficulties with Argentina

Argentina, who resented the hegemony of the United States, was the main obstacle to unity against the Axis in the Western Hemisphere. The war had upset her plans to make herself the leading power of South America, by drawing the Latin-American states closer to the United States and thus virtually isolating her.

During most of the war Argentina followed a policy of neutrality. Many of her leaders expressed open admiration for Fascism, particularly for Franco's Spain, and allowed Nazi agents considerable freedom within their country. The other Latin-American countries and the United States condemned her failure to break with the Axis powers, and in August, 1943, Secretary of State Hull expressed American displeasure by abruptly rejecting an Argentine request for arms to balance Brazil's growing armaments.

Hull wanted to go further in cracking down on Argentina by imposing economic sanctions against her, but the British would not cooperate. Sanctions would have cut them off from Argentine beef which could be replaced only by pork from the United States. "We like the Argentine brand of Fascism as little as does Mr. Cordell Hull," the *Manchester Guardian* explained, "but we also prefer Argentine beef to American pork."[3] Developments within Argentina added to her mounting friction with the United States, even though her anti-democratic government partially yielded to American pressure in January, 1944, by breaking relations with Germany and Japan. A month later a group of nationalistic army officers, called *Grupo de Oficiales Unidos*, or the "Colonels' Clique," tightened its grip on the government by installing General Edelmiro J. Farrell, actually a puppet, as acting president. The real power had fallen into the hands of Colonel Juan D. Perón who became vice-president in July.

The "Colonels' Clique" launched a program of sweeping social reforms, crushed civil liberties, and reorganized the state along fascist lines. Refusing to recognize the Farrell regime, the United States also persuaded other American republics to withhold recognition. Several months later Argentine assets in the United States were frozen.

In October the Argentine government asked for a meeting of foreign ministers to discuss its problem. Although opposed to such a meeting, the United States yielded to the pressure of other American republics and agreed to a face-saving compromise in the form of a special conference to strengthen arrangements for collective security in the Americas. That gathering, called the Inter-American Conference on Problems of War and Peace, which assembled in February, 1945, in the castle of Chapultepec near Mexico City, excluded Argentina but discussed the Argentine situation. Despite the resentment of the United States against the Argentines, the delegates invited Argentina to declare war against the Axis and resolved that if she subscribed to principles embodied in a temporary compact, called the Act of Chapultepec, she would be eligible for membership in the United Nations.

That act, adopted on March 6, although not a treaty, broadened the Monroe Doctrine into a defense arrangement and was the most significant accomplishment of the conference. It announced the principle that an attack on one American state would be considered an aggression against all, and contained a provision calling for a defense treaty to be negotiated at the end of the war. The delegates also agreed to reorganize the inter-American system with some form of written constitution and to revise the existing inter-American peace instruments so that they would fit into the new structure.

Grasping the chance to break out of her isolation, Argentina declared war on Germany and Japan on March 27 and adhered to the Act of Chapultepec. Her government then won recognition from the United States and support for admittance to the United Nations. At San Francisco, therefore, all of the American republics became original members of the United Nations. Under the leadership of the United States, they gained a place for regional arrangements in the charter and thus made possible, within the scope of the charter, the kind of security system envisaged at Chapultepec.

For a while it seemed that Argentina and the United States had overcome their basic differences and that hemispheric unity would prevail in the postwar era, but American statesmen disliked Argentina's military dictatorship, considering it a threat to peace in the Americas. In November, 1945, Uruguay accused Argentina of preparing "aggression" against her neighbors and asked for an inter-American consultation to consider the problem. The United States supported the Uruguayan proposal, but the other American republics did not.

In an effort to force the military dictatorship from power, the American Ambassador in Buenos Aires, Spruille Braden, had intervened in Argentina's internal politics. A short time later he returned to Washington to become Assistant Secretary of State in charge of Latin-American affairs. Perón, sure of his hold on the masses, had in the interval authorized national elections and ran for president as the candidate of his own party.

Early in January, 1946, Braden said in a radio broadcast that the United States did not intend "to stand idly by while the Nazi-Fascist ideology against which we fought a war endeavors to entrench itself in this hemisphere." [4] In the following month, just two weeks before the Argentine elections, the Department of State issued a pamphlet known as the Argentine Blue Book. It accused the Argentine militarists of cooperating with the Nazis during the war and of failing to carry out their obligations under the Act of Chapultepec. The price of American friendship, it implied, was the defeat of Perón. [5]

Resenting American interference and seeing the election as a choice between "Braden or Perón," the Argentines went to the polls on February 24 and made Perón legal president. The United States suffered a severe diplomatic defeat, one that had unpleasant repercussions throughout Latin America. [6]

During the next year, relations with Argentina became so tense as to endanger hemispheric solidarity. No other regime, other than those of the Communist countries, received such a bad press in the United States as did Perón's. Most Latin-American countries disliked Perón's blustering dictatorship but feared American intervention even more.

Not wishing to bring the split with the Latin-American republics into the open, the Truman administration postponed calling the conference that would give permanent form to the arrangements of Chapultepec. In the meantime, the deadlock with Perón threatened to destroy what remained of the Good Neighbor policy. Faced with mounting criticism in Latin America and at home, the President and Secretary of State Marshall finally decided to try to refurbish the Good Neighbor policy and to end the feud with Perón, particularly after the dictator had cracked down on former Nazi agents in Argentina.

In March, 1947, Truman visited Mexico City, the first President to make a state visit there, spoke of inter-American good will, and reaffirmed the devotion of the United States to the principle of nonintervention in the affairs of its neighbors. That trip helped to arrest declining American prestige in Latin America. On June 3 the President announced that Argentina had fulfilled her inter-American commitments and the United States was ready to call a special conference to carry out the Chapultepec proposals.

The Rio Pact—1947

Delegates from the United States and from nineteen of the Latin republics then met from August 15 to September 2 at Petrópolis, just outside Rio de Janeiro. That meeting, called the Inter-American Conference for the Maintenance of Continental Peace and Security, drew up a permanent defensive military alliance named the Inter-American Treaty of Reciprocal Assistance but usually known as the Rio Pact.

That treaty, signed on September 2, gave legal sanction to the principle that the republics would consider an attack against any one of them an attack against all. When two-thirds of the signatories voted to do so, each state would assist in meeting the attack, but no member would be required to use its armed forces without its consent. In addition, the treaty created a security zone defining the area of commitment. "A gigantic, irregular ellipse, a great oval, encompassing North, Central, and South America and the surrounding seas and contiguous lands," is what Senator Vandenberg called the zone.[7]

The Rio Pact, the most far-reaching agreement the nations of the Americas had yet signed and the first regional defense arrangement under Article 51 of the United Nations charter, became the model for other regional collective security arrangements, notably the North Atlantic Alliance. Secretary Marshall was the head of the United States delegation, but Truman attested to the importance of the occasion by flying to Rio to address the delegates at the close of the conference.

The Senate acted speedily on the Rio Pact. The Foreign Relations Committee held hearings on the pact for only four days, and on December 8 the Senate approved the treaty without amendment by the overwhelming vote of 72 to 1.

The Organization of American States

With the framing of the Rio Pact one-half of the Chapultepec program was completed. The other half became a reality within the next year when the Ninth International Conference of American States, meeting in Bogotá in April, created the Charter of the Organization of American States, often known as the Bogotá Charter. Together with the American Treaty of Pacific Settlement, also signed at this time and usually called the Pact of Bogotá, the new charter completed and gave constitutional status to the new Pan-American system. The Organization of American States, the new name for the inter-American system, had a Secretariat, situated in Washington; a permanent executive body named the Council; a "supreme organ" called the Inter-American Conference; and the Meeting of Consultation of Ministers of Foreign Affairs designed to consider urgent problems.

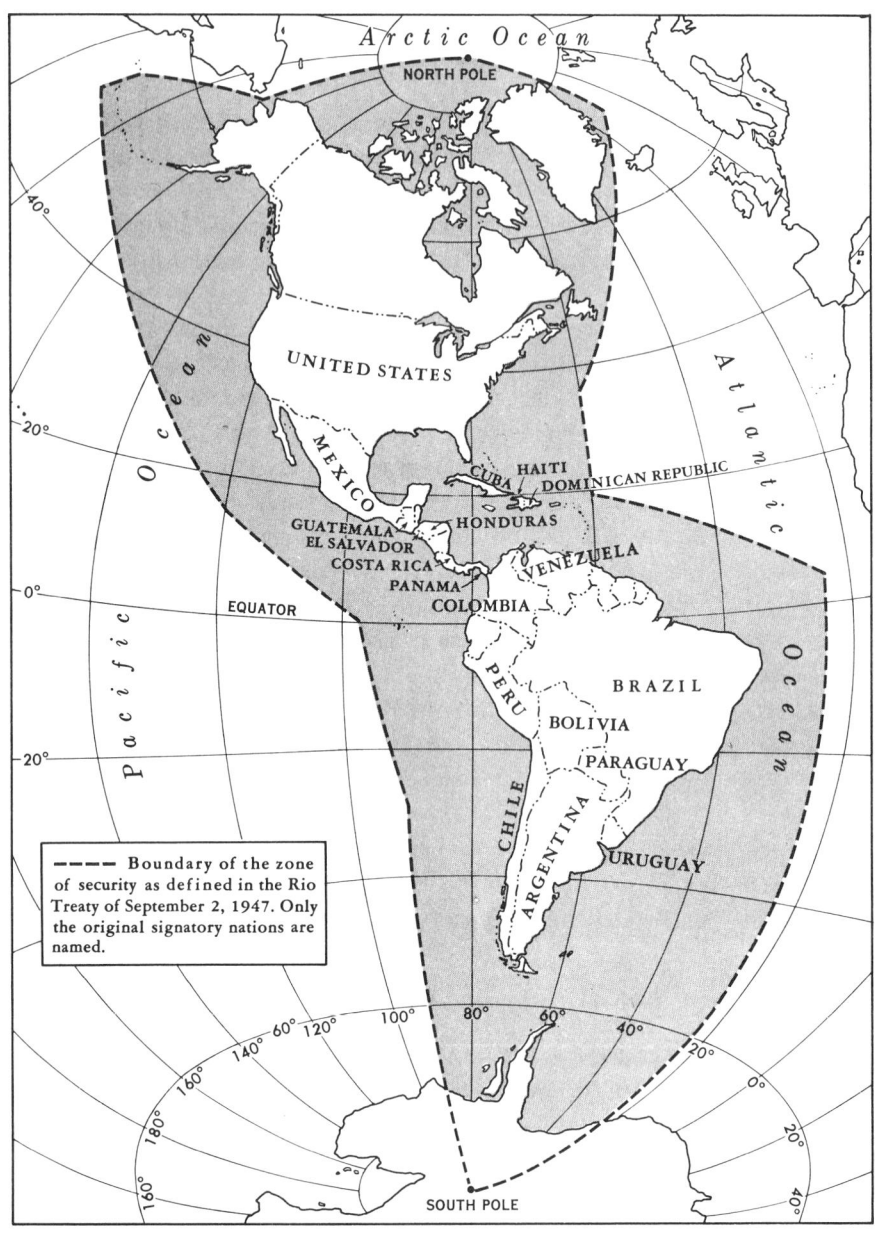

INTER-AMERICAN SECURITY ZONE, 1947

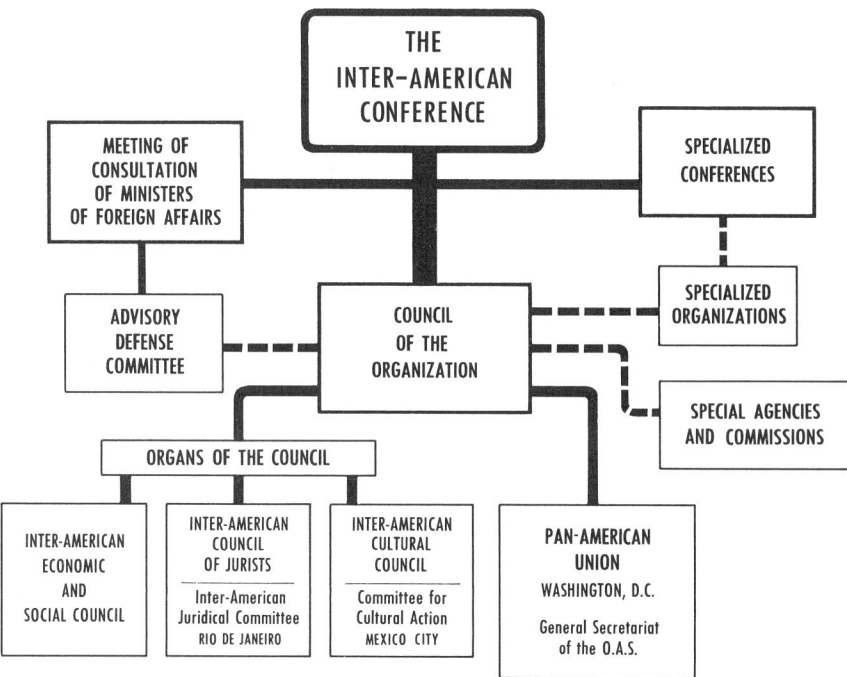

ORGANIZATION OF AMERICAN STATES

At the heart of the regional organization were the charter provisions for the maintenance of peace and security among its members, the most important of which was the now established principle that an attack against one member was an aggression against all. The charter also contained procedures for the settling of disputes between organization members before they were referred to the Security Council of the United Nations. What particularly appealed to the Latin Americans was the fact that no member had the power of veto. Each state had one vote and most decisions were to be made by a two-thirds vote, though in some instances only a simple majority was necessary.

The Charter of the Organization of American States went into force in December, 1951, after two-thirds, or fourteen, of the members had ratified it. The United States, whose Senate approved adherence on August 28, 1950, was the thirteenth state to ratify.

Seemingly the treaties framed at Rio de Janeiro and Bogotá had brought the Good Neighbor policy to institutional maturity. They may have done that, but in other ways the Good Neighbor policy had declined. During the war the United States, eager to increase the flow of strategic raw materials from Latin America, had aided its southern neighbors in rapid economic development. After the war, when the United States was concerned mainly with the problems of Europe and Asia, it seemed to the Latin Americans that their northern neighbor now paid little attention to their economic growth.

Wartime plans of the Latin Americans for industrialization, moreover, had misfired. Many of the southern republics had squandered a large part of their foreign exchange on luxuries instead of purchasing the capital goods they needed. The result was severe economic dislocation throughout Latin America. The economic problems and a burgeoning nationalism in turn led to a political unrest unequaled since the depression years.

When the Latin peoples demanded social improvements and material progress their governments could not or would not provide, the Latin-American politicians, as they had done in the past, turned on the United States as a scapegoat for their troubles. They denounced the American government for neglecting them. At the same time they attacked the American private investor in their countries for exploiting them, and American big business for taking advantage of them. through controls over the prices of their raw materials.

A more important reason for the decline of the Good Neighbor policy probably lay in the orientation of American foreign policy in the five years after the war. In the 1930's the Good Neighbor policy had been almost an obsession with many Americans, and the government may have "oversold" it to its own people and to the Latin Americans. After 1945 the United States assumed unprecedented world-wide commitments and devoted most of its attention to the areas of crisis. Latin America, as in the past, gave birth to no crises that threatened the peace of the world.

Latin Americans were disappointed over postwar American foreign policy. They had liked the courtship of the Good Neighbor era and reacted with shock to what they considered postwar neglect. To many of them, the era of the Good Neighbor now appeared merely an interlude of good will in a history of normally distant, and at times hostile, relations with the United States.

Canada and the Americas

At Mexico City in 1945, at Rio de Janeiro in 1947, and at Bogotá in 1948, the Latin republics had expressed hope that Canada would join the inter-American system. Senator Vandenberg, as a member of the American delegation at Rio, had even suggested placing a special provision in the Rio Pact for her adherence. Since all present understood that the terminology "American states" included Canada and that she could adhere if she so desired, they decided that the special provision was unnecessary. When the Bogotá Charter created the Organization of American States, the signatories understood that the term "states" covered membership for Canada if she wished to join. Canada preferred to remain aloof from the new, as well as from the old inter-American system, but at the same time had been drawing closer to the United States.[8]

At no time had the cooperation between the United States and Canada been more complete than during their co-belligerency in the Second World War. In keeping with the principles of the Hyde Park Declaration of 1941, they had meshed their war efforts through various boards such as the Joint Economic Committees and the Joint War Production Committee. Many of the joint committees were specialized and temporary and had operated outside the normal channels of diplomacy. Yet they had come into existence only through the agreements of the political leaders of both countries.

Behind the economic and military cooperation, as in American maintenance of the Alaska Highway running through Canada, lay the fact that both countries shared the same international political objectives. They wished to defend North America and use their combined economic power to the fullest so that they could serve as arsenals for the coalition of United Nations. Canada, though far less powerful than the United States, during the war had grown into a major industrial power, the fourth largest among the United Nations. She was about the only important ally who did not ask for or receive Lend-Lease assistance.

After the war the United States and Canada continued their cooperation, but not without some friction, in economic, military, and scientific matters. In November, 1946, Canada suggested a modification of the Rush–Bagot Agreement of 1817 so that either party could station naval vessels on the Great Lakes for purposes of training. The United States agreed, pointing out that it was the spirit of the agreement rather than its specific prohibitions that guided American policy.

Fear of Russia, coupled with technological advances in long-range bombers, nuclear weapons, and guided missiles, meanwhile gave the arctic regions of Canada a strategic importance they had not previously held. This concern over the Arctic, what some military men called "the undefended roof of North America," emphasized the need for a common defense system and for joint bases and weather stations in the far north. Canada alone was incapable of financing and manning a defense system in so vast a region.

At the urging of the United States, Canadian officials early in 1947 discussed plans for defense of the hitherto neglected northland. One result was the Declaration on Defense announced on February 12 from Washington and Ottawa. The two English-speaking countries agreed to collaborate "for peacetime joint security purposes" by continuing indefinitely the Permanent Joint Board on Defense of 1941. This cooperation included standardization of arms and equipment as well as reciprocal use of military, naval, and air facilities in each country. Since the agreement rested on no contractual obligation, on neither treaty nor executive agreement, each country could at any time end the collaboration.

Despite the efforts to safeguard Canada's sovereignty, some Canadians feared American pressure and power. "We have the highest respect for the United States," a member of Canada's Parliament declared the next day, "but we were a long time getting rid of control by Downing Street and I do not want to see

Washington substituted for Downing Street. Let us see that we do not have United States control of our country."9

President Truman helped overcome some of Canada's uneasiness when he visited Ottawa in June, 1947, the first state visit to Canada by any President. "Canada and the United States," he said, "have reached the point where we no longer think of each other as 'foreign' countries. We think of each other as friends, as peaceful and cooperative neighbors on a spacious and fruitful continent." 10

In December of that year, Canadians and Americans learned that their economic ties were also becoming stronger. American investments in Canada at that time amounted to $4,446,000,000, a total four times as great as that invested in any other country. By the late 1950's more than a quarter of Canada's total industrial investment was controlled by Americans, and 90 per cent of her imports of capital goods came from the United States.11 As never before, moreover, American and Canadian statesmen were cooperating in world affairs, particularly in such matters as the control of atomic energy and the defense of the North Atlantic area.

In any nuclear war between the United States and the Soviet Union, Canadians realized, their country would be directly in the line of fire of long-range bombers and guided missiles. In 1950, therefore, the two North American countries began work on a joint radar network, the "Pinetree Chain," stretching across Canada just north of the American border. A year later, on March 27, they signed a "Civil Defense Mutual Aid Agreement," envisaging coordination in civil defense activities in time of war "as if there were no border." In October, 1953, they carried their cooperation a step further by agreeing on a second joint radar network some five hundred miles north of the Pinetree Chain, called the "Mid-Canada Line."

In November, 1953, President Eisenhower visited Ottawa, and he and Prime Minister Louis S. St. Laurent issued a joint communiqué stressing the "importance of effective methods for joint defense, especially in the light of evidence of increasing technical capability of direct attack on both countries by weapons of great destructive power." 12 Two years later, in May, 1955, the United States and Canada showed continuing awareness of their interdependence by making an executive agreement for the construction of a third radar warning line near Canada's northern limits.

Canada had financed the Mid-Canada Line but the new northern network, called the Distant Early Warning system but usually known as the DEW line, was financed, constructed, and operated by the United States with Canadian cooperation. The DEW line was completed in August, 1957, at an estimated cost of $500 million. Canada had become a main line of defense against any direct Soviet attack on the United States, or as her Secretary for External Affairs said, "the ham in a sandwich."

President Eisenhower, with Secretary of State Dulles, visited Ottawa again in July, 1958, primarily to overcome some Canadian concern over American foreign and economic policies. In his talks, the President stressed Canada's vital role in continental defense. To assure "civil decision and guidance" in their countries' cooperative defense efforts, he and Prime Minister John G. Diefenbaker announced that they had agreed to establish a joint committee of cabinet rank to be known as the Canadian-United States Committee on Joint Defense. Seldom, in time of peace, had two independent nations cooperated so closely in the sensitive areas of defense and foreign policy.

The St. Lawrence Seaway

Another project in Canadian-American cooperation, an old and troublesome one, came to fruition on April 25, 1959, with the opening of the St. Lawrence Seaway.[13] On that day, for the first time, large ocean-going vessels began passage through the 185 miles of newly completed deep-water canals and locks leading from the Gulf of St. Lawrence through the St. Lawrence River to the inland ports of the Great Lakes.

For over half a century, many Americans and Canadians had dreamed of opening the heart of the North American continent to ships traveling directly from the Atlantic. Every President since the First World War had supported the idea of the St. Lawrence Seaway, but until 1954 the project had always run into insurmountable opposition in Congress. Powerful special interests, primarily eastern railroads, east coast seaports that feared a diversion of their traffic to lake ports, the coal industry, and power companies, fought the seaway and related electrical power projects.

After the Senate had defeated the St. Lawrence Seaway Treaty in March, 1934, the waterway project was neglected for a number of years. Finally, in 1940, Franklin D. Roosevelt revived it. Trying to circumvent the congressional opponents, he made an executive agreement with Canada in March, 1941, calling for the completion of the St. Lawrence Seaway and related power projects. The Second World War delayed further action. After the war, the 1941 agreement aroused considerable controversy in Congress but no legislation to implement it.

In an effort to spur Congress into action, the government stressed the defense advantages of the seaway project. In February, 1949, Secretary of Defense James Forrestal reported that the deep-water seaway would open the shipbuilding and repair facilities of the Great Lakes to large cargo vessels, give the United States easy access to the abundant iron ore deposits of the Quebec-Labrador region, provide inexpensive additional electric power to the northeastern United States and eastern Canada, and in time of emergency would relieve the strain on existing means of transportation. Yet, even endorsement by the American-Canadian Permanent Joint Board on Defense in 1951 failed to overcome congressional opposition.

Having waited ten years for Americans to make up their minds about executing the seaway agreement, Canadians grew impatient and decided to go ahead on their own with an all-Canadian seaway. In 1951 they created a St. Lawrence Seaway Authority to construct and operate the new waterway facilities. Electric power commissions in the state of New York and the province of Ontario made plans to build power plants along the seaway and applied to their central governments for licenses to do so.

Faced with Canada's determination to proceed independently, Congress finally yielded to President Eisenhower's importunities. It passed the Wiley-Dondero Seaway Act, approved in May, 1954, establishing a St. Lawrence Seaway Development Corporation to construct the American portion of the waterway and to cooperate with the Canadians in controlling and operating the seaway. An important factor in winning congressional support, in addition to Canada's challenge, had been the fact that the Second World War had depleted ore reserves in the Lake Superior region and had made Midwestern steel mills increasingly dependent on the iron ore of the Quebec-Labrador area.[14]

Canadians were disappointed with the offer of cooperation. They felt that the United States was unwilling to assume an equitable share of the seaway's total cost. Since they were anxious to avoid further delay in completing the related power projects, for which American cooperation was essential, they accepted the terms. Negotiations on construction responsibilities began in Ottawa in July, 1954, and in the following month the two countries exchanged notes in an agreement that assured immediate beginning of the seaway construction.

Despite the difficulties engendered by twenty-two years of delay, the completion

ST. LAWRENCE SEAWAY

of the St. Lawrence Seaway in 1959 on the basis of full partnership added another bond to a unique relationship. Canadian-American relations in the seaway project, as in others, was something of a model in regional international relations.

Even though Canada's foreign policy was closely identified with that of the United States, she insisted on the right to determine her own course in world affairs. Like other parts of the postwar world, she too had experienced a quickened nationalism. She expressed it in various ways, as in January, 1959, when the Royal Canadian Air Force began taking over control of the DEW line stations from the United States. Canadians, who were often critical of American foreign policy, were particularly anxious to dispel any impression that they were wholly dependent on the United States.

President John F. Kennedy recognized this desire of Canadians for their own foreign policy. In a two-day state visit to Ottawa in May, 1961, his first presidential trip outside the borders of the United States, he asked Canada to become a partner in containing Communism and helping underdeveloped countries. In particular he urged Canadians to look southward. "I believe," he said, "that all the free members of the Organization of American States would be both heartened and strengthened by any increase in your hemispheric role. . . ." And, he asked, "Can we not now become partners in inter-American affairs?"[15] It appeared that Canada might heed his plea, for in the previous year her foreign minister had visited Latin America and had indicated that Canada was considering participation in the Organization of American States. Prime Minister Diefenbaker, moreover, assured Kennedy of Canada's increasing interest in inter-American affairs.

Anti-Communism and the Americas

The Latin-American countries, meantime, showed less sympathy for the anti-Communist focus of American foreign policy than did Canada. While the main emphasis of the United States in its Latin-American policy after 1947 was to prevent the Communist movement from gaining a foothold in the Americas, the Latin Americans were concerned primarily with their economic ills, believing the Communist threat a remote one. The best way for the United States to combat Communism, they argued, was to aid their countries in achieving economic and social stability. Nonetheless, they followed American leadership in adopting a number of resolutions condemning international Communism.

At the Ninth Inter-American Conference at Bogotá in April, 1948, a meeting disrupted for a week by violent riots that Secretary of State Marshall said were part of a Communist pattern, the American states, after some resistance, adopted the first of their anti-Communist resolutions. The Bogotá resolution declared that "the political activity of international Communism or any other totalitarian doctrine" was incompatible with the concept of American freedom.[16]

Not satisfied with the vague Bogotá resolution that offered no means of combating Communism, the United States late in 1950 called a meeting of American foreign ministers to consider defense measures against Communist subversion. Nothing politically significant came out of the Fourth Meeting of Consultation of the American Ministers of Foreign Affairs held in Washington in March and April, 1951, except another indefinite resolution known as the Declaration of Washington. It called for adequate internal measures by the American republics and cooperation between them to counter "the aggressive activities of international communism." [17]

The Eisenhower administration, aware of the rising tide of anti-Americanism south of the Rio Grande and implying that the Truman administration had neglected Latin America, promised more than a program of anti-Communism for its Latin-American policy.[18] In June, 1953, a few months after taking office, the President sent his brother, Dr. Milton Eisenhower, to South America as his personal representative to survey economic and social conditions there and to strengthen Latin-American relations. In his report, dated November 18, Milton Eisenhower pointed out that economic cooperation was the key to better relations with the Latin republics. "Everything else," he said, "no matter how important, must take a secondary place, at least in the absence of war." [19] Before the President could act on his brother's recommendations, his administration had to deal with Communist activity in Guatemala.

Through Colonel Jacobo Arbenz Guzmán, who had become president in 1951, local Communists had gained control of key posts in Guatemala's government. American policymakers, occupied with crises in Europe and Asia, had paid little attention to the growth of Communism in the small Central-American republic. In August, the Department of State quarreled with Arbenz over his expropriation of lands belonging to the United Fruit Company, an American corporation. A month later the Assistant Secretary of State for Inter-American Affairs publicly charged Guatemala with "openly playing the Communist game."

The American government never questioned Guatemala's right to expropriate the disputed property; it merely sought adequate payment, which Arbenz would not offer. After Arbenz, in February, 1954, refused to bring the dispute before the Court of Arbitration at The Hague as provided for in the fruit company's contract, American officials became convinced that Communists, in part at least, had inspired the attack on the fruit company. Guatemalans, who had some legitimate grievances against the company, believed that the charges of Communism were camouflage for Yankee economic imperialism.

Unwilling to endure a Communist regime in the Western Hemisphere, especially near the Panama Canal, the United States decided to bring the issue of Communism in Guatemala before the Organization of American States for multilateral action to eliminate it. If the United States acted alone, the State Department realized, the

Latins could accuse it of violating pledges against intervention in the internal affairs of a sister republic.

At the Tenth Inter-American Conference which met in Caracas in March, 1954, the United States offered a general anti-Communist resolution. Although it did not mention Guatemala, the resolution could serve as a means of measuring Guatemala's conduct. "What we need to do," Secretary of State Dulles said, "is to identify the peril; to develop the will to meet it unitedly if ever united action should be required. . . ."[20]

The Latin Americans were not truly united behind the resolution. Many of them had gone to Caracas to discuss their economic problems but supported the resolution because they knew that only those who opposed Communism would receive the economic aid that all desired. The resolution passed, therefore, by a vote of 17 to 1. Only Guatemala voted against it. Costa Rica, who had refused to attend the conference, cast no ballot, and two important states, Argentina and Mexico, abstained. Even though the vote was a questionable triumph for the United States and the delegates showed considerable sympathy for Guatemala, Secretary Dulles was satisfied.

In its final form the resolution, called the "Declaration of Solidarity. . .against International Communist Intervention," condemned international Communism as a threat to the peace and security of the Americas. It called for consultation, according to existing treaties, to consider appropriate action in case any American state fell under Communist control and for the exchange of information on Communists and their activities.

The Guatemala Affair

Two months later relations with Guatemala reached a stage of crisis. On May 17, the State Department announced that a shipment of 1900 tons of Communist arms, originating in Czechoslovakia, had arrived in Guatemala. "By this arms shipment," Dulles announced several days later, "a government in which Communist influence is very strong has come into a position to dominate militarily the Central American area." And, he added, "the extension of Communist colonialism to this hemisphere would, in the words of the Caracas resolution, endanger the peace of this hemisphere."[21]

The United States unsuccessfully sought permission from its North Atlantic allies to search their merchant ships suspected of carrying arms to Guatemala. It also promptly began airlifting arms to Nicaragua and Honduras, with whom it had hastily signed mutual security treaties. Under the Caracas resolution, it made arrangements for an emergency conference of American foreign ministers in July, but events in Guatemala came to a head before the ministers could meet.

Colonel Carlos Castillo Armas, an exiled Guatemalan army officer, in the early morning hours of June 18, led a makeshift army of a few hundred men from Honduras into Guatemala to overthrow Arbenz. Within two weeks Arbenz' government collapsed and Castillo Armas assumed power. The United States recognized the Castillo Armas government on July 13. To alleviate the conditions that gave rise to Communism, it extended Guatemala considerable economic aid.

Although the Guatemalan revolution eliminated a Communist government in Central America, the Latin-American reaction to it tarnished the reputation of the United States as a champion of collective security. Contending that the invasion had been backed by foreigners, meaning essentially Americans, the Arbenz government had appealed to the Security Council of the United Nations for aid. To keep the Soviets from supporting Arbenz and from gaining a voice in the affairs of the Western Hemisphere, the United States blocked action by the Security Council.

Even close friends were disturbed by American policy. They felt that in denying a small nation the right to be heard in the Security Council, the United States had set a dangerous precedent. In Britain, former Prime Minister Clement Attlee expressed dismay, saying that "one cannot take one line on aggression in Asia and another line in Central America."[22]

Since the United States had openly sympathized with Castillo Armas, many Latin Americans believed he was a puppet of the State Department and that the United States had intervened in Guatemala's internal affairs. Even some Americans admitted that John E. Peurifoy, their Ambassador in Guatemala, had engineered the revolution.[23] Others, including Peurifoy himself, denied this, pointing out that Arbenz fell because the army would not fight for him. The Guatemalans themselves, Dulles argued, had rid their country of Communism. Later, the overthrow of Arbenz was attributed to the work of the Central Intelligence Agency.

Gusts of anti-Yankeeism had already swept through the Latin-American countries. Intellectuals and students denounced what they called a revival of "big stick" diplomacy, noisy demonstrators in a number of cities paraded before American embassies, some publicly burned the stars and stripes, and others hanged President Eisenhower in effigy. Sensitive nationalists, in the Middle East and North Africa as well as in Latin America, were convinced that the United States had behaved as an "imperialist" power. The Guatemalan affair had given new life to Yankeephobia in Latin America, and it seemed apparent that the United States needed more than a policy of anti-Communism to overcome it.[24]

The Nixon Episode

President Eisenhower attempted to improve hemisphere relations by reviving the ideas of the Good Neighbor policy. He asked the Latin Americans to join "the United States in common dedication to the Policy of the Good Partner." He

VICE-PRESIDENT NIXON IN SOUTH AMERICA, 1958

Student rioters in Caracas, Venezuela, in the act of kicking Nixon's car.

supported this policy with personal diplomacy.[25] To become better acquainted with Canada's prime minister and Mexico's president, for example, and to talk about common problems in a relaxed atmosphere, he informally entertained them at White Sulphur Springs, West Virginia, in March, 1956. In July he visited Panama for a meeting, in commemoration of the first Pan-American gathering there in 1826, with sixteen of the twenty Latin-American chiefs of state. In his formal remarks, Eisenhower again stressed the inter-American partnership.

To enhance the partnership and represent the United States at the inauguration of Argentina's first constitutionally elected president since the downfall of Perón in September, 1955, Vice-President Richard M. Nixon and his wife began a highly publicized good will tour of eight South American countries in April, 1958. Suddenly Latin America's Yankeephobia exploded. From his first stop at Montevideo to his last at Caracas, Nixon encountered increasing torrents of abuse. Angry students spit on him, swore at him, pelted him with eggs, and stoned him. At Caracas a mob attacked his limousine and forced him to terminate his trip and return to Washington.

Angered by Nixon's ordeal, Eisenhower immediately rushed a thousand

Marines to bases in the Caribbean and asked the Venezuelan government if it was "willing and able" to protect the Vice-President. On his return home, Nixon told reporters that the nation's Latin-American policy must be upgraded to a "top priority position."

Yet, Secretary of State Dulles maintained more than once that Latin America had not been truly neglected. Despite the heavy demands of Europe and Asia on its resources, the United States had spent more non-military dollars on Latin America than on any other part of the world. In recent years, his figures showed, the Latin republics had received more assistance for economic development than at any time in the past. "I suppose," he said, "we devote as much time and thought to the problems of the Americas as we do to the problems of any other region in the world." [26]

Early in June, 1958, a few weeks after Nixon's return home, the president of Brazil sent Eisenhower a letter deploring Nixon's mistreatment and suggesting immediate measures to repair inter-American relations because "before world public opinion the ideal of Pan-American unity has suffered serious impairment." Eisenhower agreed, and his administration quickly expressed a more intense interest in Latin-American problems. In July he sent his brother Milton on a three-week tour of Central America, and in August Secretary Dulles made a special trip to Rio de Janeiro to discuss plans for a conference of American foreign ministers.

Those ministers met in Washington in September where they agreed to create an Inter-American Development Bank which would provide credits and other assistance to all the American countries who became members. Latin Americans had been urging the establishment of such an institution for over a half century, but the United States had opposed it. When the United States accepted membership, therefore, it marked a striking reversal in economic foreign policy and at the same time contributed to the most concrete achievement in inter-American economic affairs in the postwar era. The bank came into existence in December, 1959.

New steps in the direction of economic and social development for Latin America were taken in September, 1960, at Bogotá where economic experts, popularly known as the "Committee of Twenty-One," met to discuss a broader aid program to be financed by the United States. This program grew out of a proposal announced by President Eisenhower in July. Congress later authorized an initial sum of $500 million for it. This proposal, embodied in what was called the Act of Bogotá, had been stimulated by events in Cuba.

The Cuban Revolution

Even though Communists, as some Americans believed, may have been in part responsible for the attacks on Nixon, a burning nationalism mixed with a yearning for social justice that expressed itself in anti-Yankeeism appeared to be the basic cause. That same yearning reached a climax in Cuba on January 1, 1959, when a five-year-old revolutionary movement headed by Fidel Castro, a bearded young lawyer of twenty-nine, overthrew the tyrannical dictatorship of Fulgencio Batista.

The United States promptly recognized the new government, but within two years American feelings toward Castro changed from sympathy, to patience, to exasperation, and then to anger. It soon became clear that he intended to carry out a far-reaching social revolution, one directed against the past of domestic and foreign exploitation. In particular he struck out against the United States as a symbol of past oppression and evinced a determination to free Cuba of its economic dependence on the United States. In addition to resenting Castro's expropriation of American property in Cuba on the basis of inadequate compensation, many Americans were alarmed by his tirades against the United States and by evidence that Communists were becoming increasingly active in his government. They were also shocked by his summary "war crimes" trials and firing squads that killed hundreds of former Batista henchmen and by his denial of civil liberties to his people. To many Latin Americans, however, Castro became a symbol of protest against the past of right-wing dictatorship, injustices, and low living standards.

Castro's drift toward the Communist bloc became especially alarming in February, 1960, when Soviet Deputy Premier Anastas I. Mikoyan visited Cuba. He signed an economic pact with Castro in which the Soviet Union agreed to purchase Cuban sugar at a price lower than that being paid by the United States and extended $100 million in credit at $2\frac{1}{2}$ per cent interest. American policymakers now feared that Cuba would become a fountainhead of Communism in the Americas and that Castro would export his revolution to other parts of Latin America. Now, for the first time since the Second World War, Latin-American affairs became of foremost concern to United States foreign policy.

Toward the end of February this new concern led Eisenhower to make a nine-day tour of Argentina, Brazil, Chile, and Uruguay, where he attempted to counteract the old feeling that the United States had been neglecting Latin America while courting other parts of the world. In striking contrast to Nixon's receptions almost two years earlier, he was greeted enthusiastically everywhere he went. His visit did not, however, contribute to better relations with Castro's Cuba.

In June the Department of State reversed its policy of patience by asking Congress to approve an embargo against Cuban sugar, which the President imposed in the following month. Castro countered this action by charging, before the Security Council of the United Nations, that the United States was guilty of "economic aggression" and by expropriating most of the remaining American property in Cuba. Soviet Prime Minister Nikita S. Khrushchev stepped into the quarrel by threatening to rain rockets on the United States if it intervened in Cuba, a threat received with jubilation by Cubans but with deep concern by other Latin Americans. Later Khrushchev said the rocket threat was merely symbolic, but he had made clear his view that the Monroe Doctrine was finished. "We consider that the Monroe Doctrine," he warned, "has outlived its time, has outlived itself, has died, so to say, a natural death."[27] The State Department retorted that the doctrine was still as valid as on the day of its proclamation.

It was at this time, to prevent the spread of *Fidelismo*, that Eisenhower announced his program of $500 million in aid for Latin America. Latin critics said it was poorly timed, giving the appearance of a bribe for support against Castro. Some Americans agreed, among them Mike Mansfield, the assistant Democratic leader in the Senate, who said bluntly that it "looks like a callous attempt to purchase favor in Latin America."[28]

As a result of the Soviet missile-rattling, the foreign ministers of the Organization of American States met in August, 1960, in San José, Costa Rica, for their seventh consultation, to take up the question of outside threats to the hemisphere. The United States urged the delegates to condemn Russian and Chinese Communist inroads in the Americas and to force Castro to renounce the protection of Soviet missiles. Instead of adopting a strong anti-Castro resolution, however, the delegates unenthusiastically voted for a watered-down statement, called the Declaration of San José, which vaguely condemned intervention, or the threat of it, in the Americas by an extra-continental power.[29]

Castro then established diplomatic relations with Red China and announced acceptance of Soviet protection. In Russia, Foreign Minister Gromyko claimed that the Soviet Union had the same right of intervention in the Americas as had the United States in Europe and Asia. With Soviet support, Castro had thus defied the whole idea of hemispheric security, as espoused by the United States and embodied in the inter-American system. He had, in effect, brought Cuba directly into the cold war and contributed to making Latin America a new weight in the world balance of power politics.

To advance his program of making Cuba completely independent of the United States, Castro now turned to barter deals with Communist countries, accepted Communist arms and technicians, and appeared to be taking Cuba into the Communist bloc. The United States now feared that Castro would use his Soviet arms to bolster *Fidelista* regimes in neighboring countries and in October imposed an embargo on all exports to Cuba except foodstuffs and medical supplies.

Already Castro's Cuba had become a main issue in the presidential campaign between Richard M. Nixon and John F. Kennedy. Vice-President Nixon, the Republican candidate, presented himself as the man best qualified to handle foreign affairs in perilous times. Kennedy questioned that claim, particularly by criticizing the Republicans for having followed a short-sighted policy toward Cuba, in fact, toward all of Latin America. He said Cuba had become a "Communist satellite" and that the Republicans had failed to associate the United States with the aspirations of the masses there and elsewhere in the Americas, and had dissipated the good will built up by Roosevelt's Good Neighbor policy.

THE EMBRACE: FIDEL CASTRO AND
NIKITA S. KHRUSHCHEV
IN NEW YORK, 1960

When Kennedy won the election, though by an extremely narrow popular vote, many Latin Americans were delighted, for they expected him to revive the Good Neighbor policy, particularly through increased economic and technical aid. His advisers, moreover, indicated that he intended to give Latin America high priority in his foreign policy.

Early in January another crisis in Cuba stressed anew the importance of Latin-American affairs. Castro demanded that the American Embassy in Havana, that normally had a staff of 130, cut its personnel to eleven. The President felt that he could not disregard this affront to American prestige. "There is" he said, "a limit to what the United States in self-respect can endure. That limit has now been reached."[30] Thus, with less than two weeks to go before Kennedy took office, Eisenhower broke off diplomatic relations with Cuba.

When Kennedy entered the White House he made no immediate effort to change the status of relations with Cuba but did try to carry out his campaign promise of devoting more effort to Latin-American relations. On March 13 he held a reception for Latin-American diplomats where he launched what he called an "alliance for progress," a vast aid program designed to transform the sixties into a decade of progress for the Americas. On the following day he asked Congress to appropriate the $500 million for the Inter-American Fund for Social Progress that had been authorized under Eisenhower. The *alianza para el progreso*, an obvious effort to recapture the magic of Roosevelt's Good Neighbor policy, was received with favor in Latin America and became the name of Kennedy's hemisphere policy.

In April, Kennedy took his first decisive step in Latin-American policy by issuing a White Paper of thirty-six pages that denounced the Castro regime as a threat to

FLORIDA

Gulf of Mexico

Miami

BAHAMA ISLANDS

① EXILES GATHERED AFTER FLEEING FROM CUBA

Atlantic Ocean

Havana

C U B A

④ Bay of Pigs

EXILE INVASION CRUSHED BY CASTRO

Guantanamo Bay

DOMINICAN REPUBLIC

PUERTO RICO

Vieques I.

⑤ DEFEATED INVADERS TAKEN TO U.S. BASE

M E X I C O

BRITISH HONDURAS

JAMAICA

HAITI

Caribbean Sea

GUATEMALA

HONDURAS

Puerto Cabezas

EL SALVADOR

NICARAGUA

③ EXILES TOOK OFF FOR INVASION

② U.S. TRAINED REBELS FOR ATTACK ON CASTRO

COSTA RICA

Panama Canal

Pacific Ocean

PANAMA

VENEZUELA

COLOMBIA

THE ATTACK ON CASTRO'S CUBA

peace in the Americas and called on it to break its ties to the Communist bloc.[31] Cuba's foreign minister then accused the United States of preparing an army of some four to five thousand Cuban exiles for an invasion of Cuba. A week of intense sabotage and guerrilla warfare in Cuba followed. When questioned about the invasion rumors, Kennedy ruled out "under any conditions, an intervention in Cuba by United States armed force," but indicated support for a revolutionary council of Cuban exiles that was in fact planning an invasion.[32]

Just before dawn on April 17, 1961, some 1200 anti-Castro Cubans were put ashore at the "Bay of Pigs" on the southern coast of central Cuba. Expected internal uprisings against Castro did not materialize, and within seventy-two hours his militia succeeded in capturing or wiping out the invaders.

Although the government at first denied it, various sources soon made it clear that the exile volunteers had been trained by American military specialists, transported in American ships, and armed with American weapons. The Central Intelligence Agency, in fact, had managed the entire invasion program.[33] As a result, American prestige suffered a major decline and Communist propaganda gained an impressive victory. Castro, who charged the United States with "aggression" before the United Nations and said that it had waged an undeclared war against him, emerged from the fiasco with new strength.

There were turbulent anti-American demonstrations not only in the Communist countries, where they were expected, but also in friendly nations in Latin America and Europe. "Everyone knows," the *Manchester Guardian* said for instance, "that sort of invasion by proxy with which the u.s. has now been charged is morally indistinguishable from open aggression." [34]

In the face of these developments Kennedy took full responsibility for American involvement, which had begun under Eisenhower, and sought to rally bipartisan support behind his Cuban policy. As Walter Lippmann pointed out, however, this could not erase his appalling lack of judgment in this venture.

Later in the month when Castro offered to negotiate his differences with the United States, Secretary of State Dean Rusk replied that "Communism in this hemisphere is not negotiable." [35] On May 1 Castro proclaimed Cuba a socialist state and took other measures to tighten his left-wing dictatorship. Then, while Americans debated the moral implications of the Cuban adventure, Kennedy turned his attention to shoring up his Alliance for Progress through economic aid.

On August 5, 1961, at a fashionable resort in Uruguay, called Punte del Este, finance ministers and economic experts from all the American republics met for their first conference on the Alliance for Progress. Twelve days later all the republics except Cuba signed the Act of Punte del Este which became the charter for the Alliance. It offered Latin America a minimum of $20 billion for economic development spread over a decade. More than half would come from the United States and the remainder was to be supplied by international agencies, Western Europe, and private capital. For Latin America this was aid on an unprecedented scale in its struggle against poverty, disease, illiteracy, population growth, and lack of capital. [36]

In December, Kennedy himself attempted to give the Alliance an extra push by flying to Venezuela and Colombia. This was the first visit to those countries by a President in office. At Caracas he said that the American nations must be "more than good neighbors—we must be partners in a hemisphere whose history has shaped us."

At the same time, the Kennedy administration sought to use the Alliance to contain Castro's Cuban revolution. Early in December, Castro had dispelled any doubts concerning the nature of his revolutionary regime. He announced publicly that he was a "Marxist-Leninist," claimed that he had been one from the start of his revolution, and said that he intended to re-shape Cuba into a Communistic state.

To deal with Castro's regime, which a State Department White Paper now called "a bridgehead of Sino-Soviet imperialism within the inner defenses of the Western Hemisphere," the United States exerted pressure on the Latin republics which led to a conference of foreign ministers of the Organization of American States in January, 1962, at Punte del Este. The United States sought sanctions against Castro by all the republics, severance of diplomatic relations with Cuba, an embargo on trade, and suspension of Cuba from the Organization of American

States. Many of the republics participated reluctantly, and the leading Latin states opposed the United States plan. From the outset, therefore, Secretary of State Dean Rusk, the head of the United States delegation, was forced to retreat from the original program and seek a compromise.

In the resolution that emerged from Rusk's negotiations, the key provision called for Cuba's expulsion from the Organization of American States, a measure considerably short of a diplomatic quarantine. Yet Argentina, Brazil, Chile, Bolivia, Ecuador, and Mexico abstained. They represented more than three-quarters of Latin America's population and two-thirds of its area. Although the United States gained broader support on other provisions, such as twenty votes for the provision that labeled Castro's regime, as a Marxist-Leninist government, "incompatible" with the inter-American system, the conference produced an open split between the United States and the largest Latin nations over the issue of expelling the Cubans. Those nations took the position that there was no legal way of excluding a state from the inter-American system.

Some diplomats and members of Congress considered the conference ill-conceived because the United States was forced to reduce its demands and still failed to prevent the embarrassment of a breach with the large republics. Nonetheless, early in February the Kennedy administration pressed forward with its action against Castro by declaring an embargo on trade with Cuba. The effect appeared to be mainly psychological because virtually all trade with Cuba had been cut off and Castro had already committed his nation's economy to the Communist bloc. The Latin-American policy of the Kennedy administration, it seemed, needed more than slogans, anti-Communism, and the economic attractions of the Alliance for Progress to gain the full support of the Latin republics.

To gain support from Mexico, which had not accepted United States policy toward Fidel Castro, the President and Mrs. Kennedy went to Mexico City on a state visit late in June, 1962, where they were greeted by crowds of about 1,000,000 people, an unprecedented outpouring for Mexico. During the visit President Kennedy helped heal an old sore by reaching an accord with President López Mateos of Mexico on a division of water from the Colorado River for use by their peoples. This visit also reduced some of the friction between the two countries that had been generated by differing attitudes toward Castro's Cuba.

A New Concern for Latin America

Even before the announcement of the Alliance for Progress, many Latin Americans acknowledged that the United States had been giving them extensive economic aid, but added that it had not been enough and had been politically misguided. They argued that since the days of the Good Neighbor policy the United States had not comprehended their true desires and needs. Instead of encouraging the growth of democracy, they would insist, it had often supported reactionary dictators. In 1954, for instance, it had bestowed medals on the dictators of Peru and Venezuela. As the State Department pointed out, however, when it took a strong hand against tyrants it was accused of intervention in the internal affairs of weak neighbors. The record shows, furthermore, that the United States has also eagerly supported the more democratic governments, as in Costa Rica, Mexico, and Uruguay, and has had good relations with them. Yet in 1958, Richard Nixon and Milton Eisenhower saw enough truth in what critics said to suggest "that we have an *abrazo*," or warm embrace, for democratic leaders and a formal handshake for dictators.

After 1955 about half a dozen right-wing dictators fell from power in Latin America. One result of this was a release of resentment against the United States that had in part at least been suppressed by the dictators who sought to curry favor with Washington. The Latins were outspokenly critical, for instance, of the continuing racial violence in the United States, such as seen in the anti-Negro demonstrations in Little Rock, Arkansas, in 1957, and the brutal beating of "Freedom Riders" who defied segregation in Alabama in the spring of 1961. Ironically, criticism was particularly strong in friendly Mexico, which saw a parallel in the status of Mexicans and Negroes in the United States, and in Brazil, which contained a large Negro population of her own.[37]

The difficulties of dealing with Latin-American sensibilities can be seen in the response of the Kennedy administration to military coups in Argentina and Peru and the counter-response by some Latin Americans. After hesitating for some weeks, Arturo Frondizi, the president of Argentina, acted in accordance with the resolution of Punte del Este to sever diplomatic relations with Castro's Cuba. This move led many followers of exiled Juan D. Perón, who were allowed to present candidates of their own for the first time since 1955, to vote against Frondizi's party in the elections for congress and state governments held in March, 1962. Peronists accused Frondizi of selling out to the Yankees. The election results, in any case, were disastrous for the government.

Alarmed by the victories of the Peronists and the weakness of the government, the army stepped in. It nullified the elections, forced Frondizi out of office, and installed its own president, José Maria Guido. Since the Alliance for Progress was based on the idea of economic reform through democratic processes, this coup was a blow to the United States policy. Nonetheless, Kennedy reluctantly recognized Guido's government and extended it economic aid.

In July, perhaps stimulated by what had occurred in Argentina, the armed forces in Peru nullified elections recently held for the presidency and took over the government in another coup. The army acted to prevent an old enemy, Dr. Víctor Raúl Haya de la Torre and his American Popular Revolutionary Alliance, from gaining a prominent place in the government as a result of election victories. In this instance Kennedy, who said that the cause of the Alliance for Progress "has suffered a serious setback," quickly suspended diplomatic relations with Peru and halted economic aid to that country under the Alliance. In this instance the United States openly expressed its distaste for a right-wing regime and attempted to act as a tough defender of democracy.

Regardless of intention, Kennedy's policy stirred controversy in Latin America. Critics argued that it violated the tradition of nonintervention in the internal affairs of the Latin republics. Critics also pointed out that the United States was inconsistent. It followed one policy toward Argentina and another toward Peru.

Finally, in August, the United States recognized the military regime in Peru and resumed economic aid. In principle the United States continued adherence to the policy of encouraging democracy in Latin America. "We do not," a State Department spokesman announced, "look with favor upon military coups against constitutional democratic regimes." [38] In theory, it was said, American policy was on the side of the angels. Nonetheless, that policy had to recognize the practicalities of Latin-American politics. These practicalities indicated that the entrenched few in Latin America would not easily surrender their privileges, and that the masses, despite their yearning for social justice, could not benefit as they should from the Alliance for Progress without deeply rooted political reform.

Regardless of the seemingly inherent paradoxes in Latin American attitudes toward the United States and the difficulties of strengthening democratic institutions and aiding the people there, it seemed clear that the United States would have to show more concern for the feelings of the Latin-American peoples than in the past. Thoughtful men pointed out that the civilization and political ideals of Latin Americans, despite their shortcomings, were certainly closer to those of the United States, and indeed of the Western world as a whole, than were those of the Arabs, Asians, and Africans. In 1962, moreover, Latin America seemed destined for a more important part in world affairs, and hence in the calculations of United States policy, than it had in the past.

NOTES

1. The quotation is from *The Memoirs of Cordell Hull* (2 vols., New York, 1948), II, 1144.

2. During the war, on April 20, 1943, Franklin D. Roosevelt visited President Manuel Avila Camacho in Monterrey, the first President to enter Mexico officially and the second to meet a Mexican president face to face. See Howard F. Cline, *The United States and Mexico* (Cambridge, Mass., 1953), pp. 271–272.

3. Quoted in Arthur P. Whitaker, *The United States and Argentina* (Cambridge, Mass., 1954), p. 130.

4. Jan. 5, 1946, quoted in John C. Campbell, *The United States in World Affairs, 1945–1947* (New York, 1946), p. 220.

5. U.S. Dept. of State, *Consultation among the American Republics with respect to the Argentine Situation, February 13, 1946* (Washington, Inter-American Series 48, 1946).

6. Oscar E. Smith, Jr., *Yankee Diplomacy: U.S. Intervention in Argentina* (Dallas, Tex., 1953), pp. 162–164 and Donald M. Dozer, *Are We Good Neighbors?* (Gainesville, Fla., 1959), pp. 216–220, summarize the Latin-American reactions.

7. Dec. 8, 1947, in Arthur H. Vandenberg, Jr., ed., *The Private Papers of Senator Vandenberg* (Boston, 1952), p. 368.

8. For an analysis of Canada's attitude toward the inter-American system, see Frederic H. Soward and A. M. Macauley, *Canada and the Pan-American System* (Toronto, 1948) and Eugene H. Miller, "Canada, the United States and Latin America," in Dwight E. Lee and George E. McReynolds, eds., *Essays in Honor of George Hubbard Blakeslee* (Worcester, Mass., 1949), pp. 83–103.

9. M. J. Coldwell, Feb. 13, 1947, quoted in Frederic H. Soward, *Canada in World Affairs: From Normandy to Paris, 1944–1946* (Toronto, 1950), p. 277.

10. June 11, 1947, *Department of State Bulletin*, XVI (June 22, 1947), p. 1210.

11. John J. Deutsch, "Recent American Influence in Canada," in Hugh G. J. Aitken, et al., *The American Economic Impact on Canada* (Durham, N.C., 1959), pp. 46–47. Aitken pointed out that while Canada's dependence on the outside world as a whole was decreasing, its dependence on the United States was increasing, in "The Changing Structure of the Canadian Economy," *ibid.*, p. 9. See also Hugh G. J. Aitken, *American Capital and Canadian Resources* (Cambridge, Mass., 1961).

12. Nov. 14, 1953, quoted in Richard P. Stebbins, *The United States in World Affairs, 1953* (New York, 1955), p. 419.

13. The formal opening took place on June 26 in ceremonies attended by President Eisenhower and Queen Elizabeth II. See William R. Willoughby, *The St. Lawrence Waterway: A Study in Politics and Diplomacy* (Madison, Wis., 1961), pp. 169–170.

14. For other important reasons, see *ibid.*, pp. 258–260 and in Carleton Mabee, *The Seaway Story* (New York, 1961), pp. 167–168.

15. The text of this speech to Canada's Parliament, May 17, 1961, is in *The New York Times*, May 18, 1961, p. 12.

16. Quoted in John C. Campbell, *The United States in World Affairs, 1948–1949* (New York, 1949), p. 358. The Argentine delegate, Foreign Minister Juan Atilio Bramuglia, criticized the resolution. "Communism is not stopped by passing resolutions," he said, "but by improving the living conditions of our peoples who have been exploited by privileged classes." *La Prensa* (Buenos Aires), April 5, 1948, quoted in Smith, *Yankee Diplomacy*, p. 172.

17. The text of the act is in *Department of State Bulletin*, XXIV (April 16, 1951), 606.

18. Critics, such as Simon G. Hanson in "The End of the Good Neighbor Policy," *Inter-American Economic Affairs*, VII (Autumn 1953), 3–49, say that the Good Neighbor policy declined more under Eisenhower than under Truman.

19. Quoted in Stebbins, *U.S. in World Affairs, 1953*, p. 344.

20. Quoted in John R. Beal, *John Foster Dulles* (New York, 1957), p. 233.

21. May 25, 1954, *ibid.*, pp. 234–235.

22. July 14, 1954, quoted in Philip B. Taylor, Jr., "The Guatemalan Affair: A Critique of United States Foreign Policy," *American Political Science Review*, L (Sept. 1956), 804.

23. Taylor, *ibid.*, p. 797, concludes that the United States had an important part in the uprising, and John Gillin and K. H. Silver, in "Ambiguities in Guatemala," *Foreign Affairs*, XXXIV (April 1956), 469–482, say that except in the United States the regime of Castillo Armas was considered a puppet of the Department of State.

24. See the analysis in J. Lloyd Mecham, *The United States and Inter-American Security, 1889–1960* (Austin, Tex., 1961), pp. 451–453. Frederick B. Pike, in "Guatemala, the United States, and Communism in the Americas," *Review of Politics*, XVII (April 1955), 261, says that even though the United States acted injudiciously in Guatemala, its reawakened interest in its Latin-American responsibilities may have outweighed the ill effects. For an analysis of writings on the Guatemalan revolution, see Julio Adolfo Rey, "Revolution and Liberation: A Review of Recent Literature on the Guatemalan Situation," *Hispanic American Historical Review*, XXXVIII (Feb. 1958), 239–255.

25. The President directed his remarks to a meeting of Inter-American Financial Ministers in Brazil in 1954 and is quoted in Dozer, *Are We Good Neighbors?* p. 369. His Latin-American policy is assessed on pp. 389–391.

26. May 20, 1958, quoted in Richard P. Stebbins, *The United States in World Affairs, 1958* (New York, 1959), p. 351. Louis J. Halle, in "Why We Are Losing Latin America," *Harper's Magazine*, CCX (April 1955), 50, points out that the more the United States has done for Latin America in the postwar years, the more it was blamed for the inadequacy of its efforts. Aid extended to Latin America in the postwar decade is summarized in J. Fred Rippy, *Globe and Hemisphere: Latin America's Place in the Postwar Foreign Relations of the United States* (Chicago, 1958), pp. 81–95. Richard M. Nixon describes his ordeal in *Six Crises* (Garden City, N.Y., 1962), pp. 183–234.

27. *The New York Times*, July 13, 1960, 1: 4.

28. Quoted in Ronald Hilton, ed., *Hispanic American Report*, XIII (Sept. 1960), 489.

29. The seventh meeting of consultation was held Aug. 22–29, and was preceded by the sixth meeting, Aug. 16–21, which condemned the Dominican Republic for aggres-

sive acts against Venezuela. As a result, the United States broke off diplomatic relations with the Dominican Republic. For details, see Richard P. Stebbins, *The United States in World Affairs, 1960* (New York, 1961), pp. 308–315.

30. Quoted in *The New York Times*, Jan. 8, 1961, IV, 1: 1.

31. U.S. Department of State, *Cuba* (Washington, Inter-American Series 66, 1960).

32. Quoted in *The New York Times*, April 16, 1961, IV, 2: 1.

33. Details on the invasion and its planning are in Stuart Novins, "The Invasion That Could Not Succeed," *The Reporter*, XXIV (May 11, 1961), 19–23, Charles L. Markmann and Mark Sherwin, *John F. Kennedy: A Sense of Purpose* (New York, 1961), pp. 163–179, and Karl E. Meyer and Tad Szulc, *The Cuban Invasion: The Chronicle of a Disaster* (New York, 1962).

34. Quoted in *The New York Times*, April 23, 1961, IV, 1: 5. Herbert L. Matthews, in *The Cuban Story* (New York, 1961), p. 267, points out that the United States violated the Bogotá Charter.

35. Quoted in *The New York Times*, April 30, 1960, IV, 1: 6.

36. The title for the gathering was "The Inter-American Economic and Social Conference." For details, see Richard P. Stebbins, *The United States in World Affairs, 1961* (New York, 1962), pp. 326–332. Earlier, Congress had appropriated the $500 million for the Inter-American Fund for Social Progress, p. 321.

37. See Dozer, *Are We Good Neighbors?* p. 405, and Matthews, *Cuban Story*, p. 113. For an analysis critical of United States policy, see Frank Tannenbaum, "The United States and Latin America," *Political Science Quarterly*, LXXVI (June 1961), 161–180.

38. *The New York Times*, Aug. 19, 1962, IV, 2E: 6.

Chapter Twenty-Eight

THE MIDDLE EAST IN AMERICAN POLICY

Aᴄᴄᴏʀᴅɪɴɢ to American usage, the term Middle East embraces the meeting place of three continents, of Europe, Asia, and Africa, and in extent ranges from Istanbul to Teheran and from Kabul to Cairo.[1] When the Second World War began, Great Britain and France were dominant in this region, a colonial area sprinkled with a few independent states such as Turkey and Iraq, a region of secondary importance in international politics. Like the peoples of postwar Latin America, those of the Middle East experienced a quickened nationalism, but one that was anti-European and invariably fused with anticolonialism.

To Americans, prior to the war the Middle East, or the Arab world, was remote and of little interest. Some missionaries were scattered through the area and Protestants supported several educational institutions there. The United States had virtually no political or strategic concern in the Middle East. The most important American interest in the Arab states was economic and dated back to the discovery of extensive oil fields in Persia, now called Iran, shortly before the First World War. But American oil companies did not gain solid footholds in the region until 1928 when the Standard Oil Company of California obtained a concession from the Sheikdom of Bahrain and 1934 when the Arabian-American Oil Company was formed to exploit deposits in Saudi Arabia. Productive operations, however, did not begin until the late 1930's.

The Second World War brought great change to the Middle East and to American policy toward the Arab states. American troops were stationed in Morocco, Algeria, Tunisia, Iran, and Egypt. After the war the troops left, but the Middle East, stretching across the periphery of the Soviet bloc, became strategically

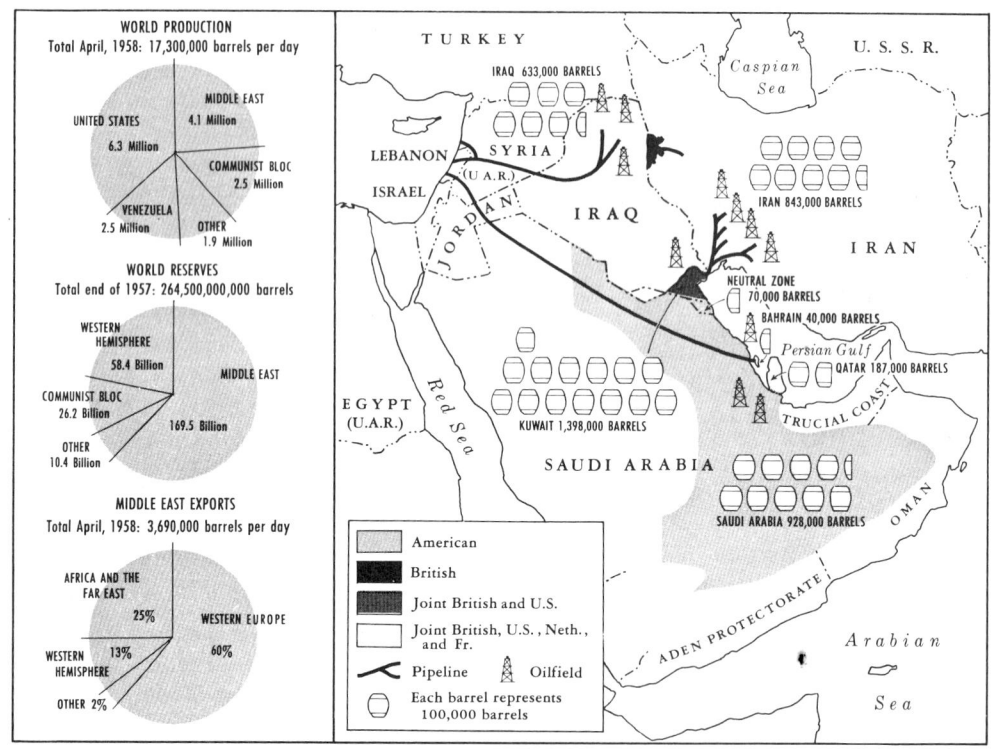

WORLD PRODUCTION
Total April, 1958: 17,300,000 barrels per day

UNITED STATES
6.3 Million

MIDDLE EAST
4.1 Million

COMMUNIST BLOC
2.5 Million

VENEZUELA
2.5 Million

OTHER
1.9 Million

WORLD RESERVES
Total end of 1957: 264,500,000,000 barrels

WESTERN
HEMISPHERE
58.4 Billion

COMMUNIST BLOC
26.2 Billion

OTHER
10.4 Billion

MIDDLE EAST
169.5 Billion

MIDDLE EAST EXPORTS
Total April, 1958: 3,690,000 barrels per day

AFRICA AND THE
FAR EAST
25%

WESTERN
HEMISPHERE
13%

WESTERN EUROPE
60%

OTHER 2%

American
British
Joint British and U.S.
Joint British, U.S., Neth., and Fr.
Pipeline   Oilfield
Each barrel represents 100,000 barrels

TURKEY
IRAQ 633,000 BARRELS
LEBANON
SYRIA
(U.A.R.)
ISRAEL
JORDAN
IRAQ
IRAN 843,000 BARRELS
IRAN
NEUTRAL ZONE 70,000 BARRELS
BAHRAIN 40,000 BARRELS
QATAR 187,000 BARRELS
Persian Gulf
TRUCIAL COAST
EGYPT (U.A.R.)
Red Sea
KUWAIT 1,398,000 BARRELS
SAUDI ARABIA
SAUDI ARABIA 928,000 BARRELS
OMAN
ADEN PROTECTORATE
Caspian Sea
U. S. S. R.
Arabian Sea

MIDDLE EAST OIL PRODUCTION, 1958

important in the policy of containment. Iran and Turkey were the first states in which the United States attempted to block Soviet penetration.

Oil, as well as strategic geography, then made the Middle East of vital concern to American foreign policy. The war had created a prodigious drain on American petroleum reserves, causing strategists to look to the oil fields of the Middle East as a source for the future. Those fields were incredibly rich, containing, according to an estimate in 1948, 60 per cent of the proved oil reserves in the world.

Most of the world's known oil reserves outside the Americas, in fact, were concentrated in what has been called the Islamic belt, a broad stretch of earth and water covering not only the Middle East but also the deposits in the Caucasus and Indonesia. These were all lands occupied by Moslem peoples. For the sake of oil, therefore, American relations with the Arab world and with Moslems everywhere gained a new importance. Moreover, the American reaction to the nationalist aspirations of the Moslem peoples, many of whom had recently won independence or were seeking it from European nations, influenced the Arabs of the Middle East in their attitude toward the United States.[2]

The Palestine Question

Aside from the questions of oil and strategic containment of Communism, the fate of Palestine aroused the greatest American interest in the Middle East. That problem, involving a clash between Arab and Jewish nationalisms, grew out of irreconcilable promises the British had made to both peoples in trying to win their support during the First World War. To the Arabs, in 1916, they had given a vague pledge of independence. To the Jews they had said in the Balfour Declaration of November, 1917, that they favored "the establishment in Palestine of a national home for the Jewish people" and that they would do their best to achieve that objective without, however, violating the rights of Arabs already living in Palestine.[3] A year later President Wilson guardedly endorsed the Balfour Declaration.[4]

The British promises thus had appealed to a new Arab nationalism, one kindled by Wilson's idea of national self-determination. They also gave new life to an old dream of the Jews of returning to Palestine as the land from which they had been exiled, an idea known as Zionism.

After the war, Britain obtained a League of Nations mandate over Palestine that committed her to putting the Balfour Declaration into effect. Jews in the United States, at the same time, attempted to gain the support of the government for a Jewish homeland in Palestine. The State Department resisted all action that would indicate official approval of Zionism, but in September, 1922, Congress passed a joint resolution in favor of the Balfour Declaration. Two years later the United States signed a treaty with Britain assenting to the mandate and indirectly to the Balfour Declaration. Technically, that treaty formed the basis of American relations with Palestine for almost a quarter of a century.

The Palestine Arabs feared Zionism, considering it a threat to the land they considered their own by right of long and continued occupation. They regarded any share in sovereignty by the Jews as a violation of British promises. The Zionists, on the other hand, interpreted the promised homeland in Palestine as meaning a Jewish state. In the 1920's the force of Zionism waned. The Arabs, therefore, did not object to a limited Jewish immigration to Palestine.

Hitler's rise gave new life to Zionism. Fleeing murder and persecution by the Nazis in Germany, Jews by the thousands streamed into Palestine in the 1930's. Alarmed by the influx that seemingly would create a Jewish majority and believing that British policy favored the Jews, the Palestine Arabs called a general strike in 1936, fought the British, and attacked Jewish settlements.[5] The Arab Rebellion did not die until 1939. To conciliate the angry Arab world, the British issued a White Paper in May, 1939, severely curtailing Jewish immigration into Palestine.

Stunned, the Jews turned against the British. In 1942 the World Zionist Organization adopted a program calling for a Jewish state, a Jewish army, and unlimited immigration into Palestine. Zionist groups in Palestine, following the Arab example, then started a campaign of terror against the British and the Arabs. The violence against the British was designed to compel them to ease the immigration laws, which were in fact being flouted by an increasingly heavy illegal influx of Jews from Hitler's Europe. During this wartime period, the center of the world Zionist movement shifted from London to New York and gained most of its support from American Jews.

Since it sought to cultivate the good will of the Arab world and did not wish to impair relations with Britain, the American government followed a policy of nonintervention in Palestine's affairs. "I may say," Secretary of State Cordell Hull announced, "that Palestine is a British responsibility."[6]

A large body of American public opinion, however, most of it probably motivated by humanitarian concern for the plight of persecuted Jews who had nowhere to turn and some apparently by a political concern for Jewish votes in metropolitan centers, openly sympathized with the Zionist cause. Congress reflected this sympathy. In 1944 resolutions were introduced in both houses calling on the government to intervene in Palestine to help achieve a Jewish state. The party platforms of both the Democrats and the Republicans of that year, moreover, contained planks supporting the Zionist program. President Roosevelt, too, promised to support "a free and democratic Jewish commonwealth" in Palestine.[7]

A seemingly united Arab world, shortly after, announced its hostility to Zionism and hence to the American position. In Cairo in March, 1945, seven Arab states, Egypt, Syria, Lebanon, Transjordan, Iraq, Saudi Arabia, and Yemen, formed a loose organization called the Arab League. Although they were divided on many matters, all members of the League pledged resistance to Jews in Palestine.

President Truman openly supported the Zionist cause. He said later that the fate of the Jews was "a matter of deep personal concern" with him, but critics argued that his concern stemmed more from a desire to win Jewish political support.[8] In any event, in August, 1945, he wrote to Prime Minister Clement Attlee of Britain suggesting the admission of 100,000 Jewish refugees into Palestine. Alarmed Arabs protested, saying the proposal violated Roosevelt's promise to Ibn Saud not to intervene in Palestine without the consent of the Arabs.

Weakened by the war, Britain meanwhile was no longer able to police the Middle East unaided. She had, moreover, become more concerned over relations with the United States than with the Palestine quarrel between Jews and Arabs. She therefore welcomed Truman's intervention as an opportunity to induce the United States to accept a share of responsibility in the Middle East.

Attlee said, nonetheless, that conditions in Palestine made it impossible to accept Truman's proposal. His government then suggested the formation of an Anglo-American Committee of Inquiry to consider the whole Jewish problem. The United States accepted the suggestion; the committee held extensive hearings, and in April, 1946, submitted its final report.

That report suggested that Palestine should be neither an Arab nor a Jewish state and recommended the admission of 100,000 Jews into Palestine as Truman had proposed. The President immediately expressed satisfaction with the portion calling for renewed Jewish immigration. His statement irked the British who wanted the United States to support the whole report, parts of which ran counter to the Zionist program. They were also disappointed in the failure of the United States to accept part of the military and financial responsibilities in Palestine, their basic reason for suggesting the Anglo-American Committee.

Truman's military and political advisers opposed such involvement, arguing that American troops in Palestine would turn the Arab world against the United States. They did not wish to lose access to the oil of the Middle East or to drive the Arabs into the arms of the Soviets. Since Truman would not support the whole program of the Anglo-American Committee, the plan collapsed and the result was a split between the United States and Britain over Palestine.

In October, 1946, preceding the congressional elections of that year, Truman repeated his suggestion that 100,000 Jews be admitted into Palestine. Not to be outdone, Governor Dewey of New York, a few days later, urged that several hundreds of thousands of Jews be admitted.[9]

The Creation of Israel

In February, 1947, looking for a way out of the Palestine dilemma, the British finally turned the problem over to the United Nations which set up a special committee to investigate it. On the basis of the committee's report and as a result of considerable American and Jewish pressure behind the scenes, the General Assembly in November recommended the partitioning of Palestine into three parts, an Arab state, a Jewish state, and the city of Jerusalem, which would be placed under an international trusteeship. All would be tied together in an economic union.

Since the partition plan would give them the independent state they wanted, the Jews accepted the proposal. The Arabs were bitter against the United States for supporting partition, and resisted, starting guerrilla warfare against the Jews in Palestine. Caught in the middle of the Arab and Jewish warfare, the British announced in December that in the following May they would end their mandate.

Alarmed by the chaos in Palestine but unwilling to supply troops to help control the area, the United States suddenly reversed its policy in March. Since the partition plan could not be carried out peacefully, the American delegate told the Security Council, the United States now favored a temporary United Nations trusteeship over Palestine. That plan failed. Arab-Jewish hostilities, meantime, spread throughout Palestine.

At six p.m. Washington time, May 14, 1948, when Britain formally terminated her mandate and pulled the last of her troops from Palestine, the Jews proclaimed the independent state of Israel. Eleven minutes later Truman announced that he had granted Israel *de facto* recognition.

Shortly after, troops from the Arab League states entered Palestine and full-scale war followed. The war was short and terrible. The outnumbered Jews not only defended themselves but also routed the Arab armies. Half the Arab population of Palestine, almost a million people, fled its homes and sought refuge in miserable camps in neighboring Arab states.

The United States did not take sides in the war or directly in the efforts to stop it. Few could deny, however, that financial support from American Zionists and President Truman's policy—one opposed by specialists in the State Department and by military strategists—had been among the decisive factors in the creation of Israel.[10] In the presidential campaign of 1948, moreover, both parties promised support for an independent Israel, and after the election, on January 31, 1949, Truman extended it *de jure* recognition.

After several failures in attempting to mediate the war in Palestine, the United Nations, by July, 1949, worked out armistice agreements between Israel and the Arab states. A distinguished American Negro, Dr. Ralph J. Bunche, employed by the United Nations, had a key role in the truce arrangements.

Israel and the Arab states remained only nominally at peace. Although the formal hostilities had stopped, there were constant raids and reprisals across the truce line. The Arabs, bitter in their defeat, nursed a rankling resentment not only against Israel but also against the United States for championing the Zionist cause.

The humiliated Arab states refused to recognize Israel's existence, tried to strangle her with an economic blockade, mainly by closing the Suez Canal to Israeli shipping, and some of them threatened to annihilate Israel in a second war. Although it tried, the United Nations was unable to bring true peace to the Middle East; it could not stop the border raids. Both sides, the Arabs and the Jews, whenever they felt it was to their advantage to do so, flouted the United Nations.

The United States and its Western Allies, therefore, did not rely solely on the United Nations to keep the peace in the Middle East. As a result of American initiative, Britain, France, and the United States attempted to guarantee the armistice settlement. In a Tripartite Declaration in May, 1950, they announced that if either the Arabs or the Israelis tried to violate the armistice lines in Palestine, they would take immediate action, "both within and outside the United Nations, to prevent such a violation."[11] The three powers also deplored the armaments race in the Middle East and promised to maintain a balance in supplying arms to Israel and the Arab states as a means of protecting the peace.

The Honest Broker in Iran

Even though the Tripartite Declaration may have slowed down the armaments race in the Middle East, it did not ease the tensions. In May, 1951, Iran added to those tensions by nationalizing the Anglo-Iranian Oil Company, a British concern that had a concession to develop the oil fields in southern Iran. The British demanded that the Iranian government abide by its contracted obligations to the oil company and also pay for the confiscated holdings. When Iran's Prime Minister, an emotional old nationalist named Mohammed Mossadegh, refused, the British retaliated by withdrawing all technical personnel from Iran and imposing a financial and commercial embargo on the country. Production at Abadan, the largest oil refinery in the world, was reduced to a trickle and the Iranians were unable to market what oil they did produce.

Throughout the quarrel, the United States outwardly tried to play the part of an honest broker. It regarded the crisis as another incident in the cold war and hence sought a settlement that would not weaken the Western position in Iran in favor of Russia. Americans made it clear that they would not support a policy of force and persuaded the British to accept the principle of nationalization. To appease Iranian nationalism, moreover, the United States continued limited Point Four assistance and military aid to Mossadegh's government, but after June, 1953, refused any further financial assistance.

Britain's blockade, assisted apparently by the cutting off of American aid, finally made Mossadegh's position economically untenable. In August, 1953, a military coup, supported by the Shah, overthrew him. Rumors insisted that the Central Intelligence Agency had a hand in Mossadegh's downfall.[12] In any event, the United States quickly supported the new government and helped work out a settlement of the crisis acceptable to the British and the Iranians. Iran, through the National Oil Company, retained ownership of the oil fields, but under the terms of an agreement reached in October, 1954, an international consortium of eight oil companies would produce and market the oil.

Under pressure from their government, five American companies joined the consortium, gaining about 40 per cent of the shares. The British, through the Anglo-Iranian Oil Company, renamed British Petroleum, and through Royal Dutch Shell, gained over 50 per cent of the shares. Since the Shah looked to the American government as the main support for his shaky regime, the United States, as a result of the crisis, replaced Britain as Iran's protector, and added to its involvement in the politics of the Middle East.

Middle Eastern Defense

Several months after the Iranian crisis began, the United States and its Western Allies attempted to strengthen their military position throughout the Arab world. They worked out a plan for a Middle Eastern collective defense organization to protect that region against Soviet attack. Egypt held the leadership of the Arab League, and on her soil, at the Suez Canal, Britain still controlled a great military base that military men considered indispensable to the defense of the Middle East. In October, 1951, therefore, the Western powers asked Egypt to join the plan. If Egypt accepted, the Western Allies believed, the other Arab states would do the same. Egypt's government, however, immediately rejected the offer and unilaterally denounced the Anglo-Egyptian treaty of 1936 that allowed the British to maintain troops in the Suez Canal zone.

Egypt then began a violent campaign to oust the British from the military base at Suez. Arab nationalism, in conflict with British imperial interests, again upset the stability and defense of the Middle East. Taking the stand that it could not condone the unilateral repudiation of treaties, the United States this time promptly backed the British. It thus found itself once more in the position of defending a colonial power and incurred increased Egyptian hostility.

The continuing crisis over Suez and domestic problems in July, 1952, touched off a bloodless revolution in Egypt, led by a group of junior army officers, that ended the corrupt regime of King Farouk. Ultimately, a young colonel, Gamal Abdel Nasser, emerged as Egypt's strong man. The new regime transformed Egypt into a republic, launched a program of economic and land reform, and adopted a foreign policy that reflected Egypt's aroused nationalism.

In October, 1954, Nasser concluded an agreement with England that called for the evacuation of British troops from the great base at Suez. To most Egyptians this was a successful culmination to the long struggle to rid their land of foreign troops, and Nasser received most of the acclaim from Arab nationalists for winning that diplomatic victory over Western "imperialists."

Taking the view that the British evacuation would appease Arab nationalism and might lead to future Egyptian cooperation with the Western powers, the United States had urged both sides to make the agreement. The British resented the pressure and charged the United States with major responsibility for the loss of the key base at Suez and the weakening of the Western position in the Middle East. Americans argued that the British made the decision on their own.

Nonetheless, both Britain and the United States hoped that Nasser would now join a new alliance system that Secretary of State John Foster Dulles was shaping along the "northern tier," that is, among those states of the Middle East closest to the Soviet Union. The central treaty was an alliance of February, 1955, between

Turkey and Iraq. By October of that year, three other powers, Britain, Pakistan and Iran, adhered to it. Since the treaty was signed at Baghdad and that city became the headquarters of a formal body set up by the signatories, called the Middle East Treaty Organization, the alliance became known as the Baghdad Pact.[13]

Nasser would have nothing to do with the alliance. In his view it broke up the solidarity of the Arab League, since it included Iraq, and threatened Egypt's leadership in the Middle East. The Soviets, too, denounced the Baghdad Pact as adding to the tensions in the Middle East.

Although the United States sponsored the Baghdad Pact, offered members military aid, and sent observers to meetings held by the regional organization, it did not join. The United States did not wish to increase Nasser's antagonism, alienate Israel, who was hostile to the pact, or attract further ill will from the anticolonial powers of Asia and Africa who also opposed the alliance.

Before the Baghdad Pact had been completed, Nasser had accepted American economic aid. He had also sought arms, but the United States had refused to give them on his terms. In February, 1955, Israeli troops carried out a large-scale raid on Gaza, a strip of land on their border controlled by Egyptian forces. That raid exposed Nasser's military weakness and convinced him of the immediate need to build up Egypt's fighting strength. As a result he turned to the Soviets, and in September announced that he would exchange cotton for a large quantity of arms from Communist Czechoslovakia.

Despite the fact that Nasser's Communist arms would upset the rationing imposed by the Tripartite Declaration of 1950, the United States did not meet Israel's demands for military equipment to counterbalance the growth of Egyptian armaments. Instead, it decided to try to preserve some of its diminishing influence in Egypt and to prevent further Soviet penetration into the Middle East.

As part of his reform program, Nasser wished to build a huge dam and hydro-electric power station on the Nile River at Aswan, some 800 miles south of Cairo. The proposed high dam would be one of the largest in the world and through irrigation would increase Egypt's arable lands by one-third. Since Egypt lacked the resources to finance so vast a project, estimated to cost $1.3 billion, Nasser sought outside assistance. In December, 1955, the United States said it would help finance the dam, offering an initial grant of $56 million. Britain also offered $14 million.

Nasser then delayed his acceptance and dickered with the Soviets, apparently seeking better terms. He also increased trade with the nations of the Soviet bloc, mortgaging his cotton crop, Egypt's main export, to them. In May, 1956, as if contemptuous of American good will, he withdrew recognition from Chiang Kai-shek and established diplomatic relations with Communist China. Egypt, it seemed clear, would not be able to hold up her end in financing the Aswan Dam and was determined to follow an anti-Western policy.

Under pressure from Congress and others who opposed the Aswan project, Secretary of State Dulles suddenly reversed himself in July by withdrawing his initial offer to help finance the Aswan Dam. Britain did the same. In a press conference months later, Dulles said that Egypt had forced the issue to which there was only one proper response. "That issue was," he explained, "do nations which play both sides get better treatment than nations which are stalwart and work with us?"

The Suez Crisis

Humiliated, Nasser took the "great refusal" as an effort to topple him. A week later he struck back by nationalizing the Universal Suez Canal Company, owned mainly by British and French stockholders, and announced that Egyptians henceforth would run the canal.[14] He promised to compensate the stockholders and announced that he would build the Aswan Dam from canal profits. Since he acted in the sacred name of nationalism and in defiance of "imperialists," Nasser won overwhelming acclaim from the Arab peoples and other anticolonial nations.

On Britain and France Nasser's act had a shattering impact, not so much the nationalization itself as the fact that an international waterway vital to their economies was now at the mercy of a man they distrusted. Britain's Prime Minister, Anthony Eden, said England would fight if necessary to protect her access to Middle Eastern oil and labeled Nasser's deed "an act of plunder." The French National Assembly adopted a resolution calling Nasser "a permanent menace to peace."[15]

THE CHALLENGE: NASSER'S
SEIZURE OF THE SUEZ CANAL

The United States opposed the use of force or even stringent economic measures against Nasser, though it did freeze Egyptian assets under its control. Seeking a solution by negotiation, Dulles suggested a Suez Canal Users' Association, a vague international body that would control canal shipping. As proposed by Dulles, the association was unacceptable to all parties immediately concerned. Disgusted by what seemed indefinite talk and no action, the British and French concluded that they would have to impose a solution on Egypt.[16]

Israel, meanwhile, had watched Nasser's rearmament with alarm. For eight years her people had lived under siege, and in 1956 the Arabs had stepped up their raids into Israel, using suicide squadrons, or *fedayeen*, that had penetrated even to Tel Aviv, the nation's capital. Israel decided to attack. On October 29, 1956, Israel's army knifed into Egypt with the objective of wiping out the *fedayeen* bases and overthrowing Nasser.

On the following day Britain and France, without informing the United States, sent ultimatums to Israel and Egypt ordering them to keep their armies ten miles from the Suez Canal. Their troops, the British and French said, would occupy the canal zone and would use force if resisted.

There was evidence of military coordination, some charged collusion, between Israel, France, and Britain. The French, for example, sent the Israelis arms and aided them with aircraft and naval units.[17] What had first appeared to be another Middle Eastern quarrel thus turned into a Western assault on Egypt.

In a lightning campaign the Israelis overran the Sinai Peninsula and routed the Egyptians. As expected, Egypt rejected the Anglo-French ultimatum. British and French planes bombed Egyptian airfields and other targets for four days and then landed troops who occupied Port Said and the western end of the Suez Canal. Egypt blocked the canal with sunken hulks, and Arabs blew up pumping stations on the pipelines in Syria that brought oil from Iraq to the Mediterranean. Western Europe, as a result, was forced to resort to oil rationing.

Americans, then involved in the last days of a presidential campaign and frustrated by their helplessness as Russia brutally crushed a rebellion in Hungary, were shocked by the attack on Egypt. The United States, on October 30, immediately placed a resolution before the Security Council of the United Nations calling on Israel and Egypt to stop fighting and on Israel to withdraw her forces from Egypt. Britain and France vetoed it and a similar resolution offered by Russia. The Suez case then went to the General Assembly under a "Uniting for Peace" resolution of 1950, designed originally to circumvent Russia's use of the veto in the Security Council.

Many Americans feared war. President Eisenhower, on the following day, spoke over radio and television about the crisis and assured the nation he would keep the peace. "There can be no peace without law," he said. "And there can be no law if we were to invoke one code of international conduct for those who oppose us and another for our friends."[18] The United States thus joined Russia in condemning the British and French attack.

The next day, under American leadership, the General Assembly took up the Suez case. On November 2 it passed a resolution introduced by Secretary Dulles calling for an immediate cease-fire and the withdrawal of foreign troops from Egypt. Only France, Britain, Israel, Australia, and New Zealand voted against the resolution. In the next few days the General Assembly voted a number of other resolutions favoring Egypt.

At the same time Russia threatened to use arms, even guided missiles, against the British, French, and Israelis and announced that she would send "volunteers" to assist Egypt. On November 5 she suggested joint action with the United States to end the "aggression," a proposal Eisenhower promptly rejected as "unthinkable." The United States, he said, would use force to prevent Soviet interference.

Faced by hostile world opinion, by Soviet threats, and by the opposition of their major ally, the British and French gulped their pride, stifled their resentment, and agreed to withdraw from Egypt. Israel was left with no choice. She, too, had to agree to pull out her troops.

In the United States the presidential campaign was almost overshadowed by the crises abroad. In foreign affairs the Republicans, headed by Eisenhower who sought a second term, emphasized peace. The Suez war undercut the claim that peace was a result of Dulles' diplomacy, and briefly appeared to injure Eisenhower's chance for re-election. Adlai Stevenson, heading the Democratic ticket for the second time, attacked the administration's foreign policy as being irresponsible and damaging to relations with Britain and France. After the Suez war began, the Democrats stepped up that line of attack.

Despite the Democratic charges and the fact that the Middle Eastern war damaged the Republican peace claims, Eisenhower probably profited politically from the Suez crisis. Since Eisenhower himself had often made clear his obviously sincere desire for peace, many voters apparently considered it wise in time of international crises to retain a President experienced in military matters and world affairs. Domestic problems and Eisenhower's personal appeal to the voters, moreover, outweighed foreign policy issues. He won the election overwhelmingly, by a greater margin than in 1952.

In the last days of the campaign, Vice-President Nixon explained how American foreign policy gained from the Suez crisis. "For the first time in history," he said, "we had shown independence of Anglo-French policies toward Asia and Africa which seemed to us to reflect the colonial tradition. That declaration of independence has had an electrifying effect throughout the world."[19]

Although exaggerated for political purposes, what Nixon said was essentially true. The American stand in the Suez crisis won new respect for the United States in the Arab world and among the other anticolonial nations of Asia and Africa. It also plunged relations with Britain and France to their lowest point since the Second World War, and almost wrecked the North Atlantic Treaty. [20]

The cease-fire in Egypt, that went into effect on November 6, at the same time removed the threat of war with Russia. A United Nations Emergency Force went into Egypt and supervised the troop withdrawals. By Christmas the British and French had pulled out the last of their forces. Israel retreated slowly but by March, 1957, partly as a result of "friendly persuasion" by the United States, finally withdrew her forces behind the old armistice lines, and a tenuous peace returned to the Middle East.

For Britain and France the Suez invasion proved a fiasco, showing that they no longer had the strength to play independently the part of great powers. The invasion achieved none of the objectives they sought and forced the resignation of Prime Minister Eden in January, 1957. British and French prestige nearly vanished throughout the Middle East.[21]

Despite the miserable showing of his army against Israel, Nasser emerged from the crisis stronger than ever, a hero of Arab nationalism. The Soviets, because of their support of Egypt and Arab nationalism and their denunciations of Western colonialism, gained new stature in the Middle East. [22]

The Eisenhower Doctrine

During and after the Suez crisis, Russia exploited her newly acquired prestige, moving into the Middle East with enhanced influence. She replaced the guns, tanks, and planes Egypt had lost to Israel and sent arms to Syria. To counter the stepped-up Soviet penetration, to salvage what remained of Western influence in the Arab world, and to fill the power vacuum created by the British and French retreat, the United States pondered emergency measures. American policymakers took a first step in November, 1956, when they assured the northern tier members of the Baghdad Pact that a threat to their territorial integrity and political independence "would be viewed by the United States with the utmost gravity." [23]

Those states were not satisfied. They wanted a stronger commitment to the defense of the Middle East and urged the United States to join the Baghdad Pact as a means of expressing that commitment. Since a formal adherence would further antagonize Egypt and other Arab states, the United States said no. Instead, the Eisenhower administration decided to issue a unilateral warning to the world that the United States would defend the whole Middle East against Soviet attack. In a special message of January 5, 1957, the President presented the declaration of policy, which became known as the "Eisenhower Doctrine," to Congress and asked the legislators to support it with a joint resolution.

Congress did not respond as quickly as the administration desired. Hearings in both houses brought forth severe criticism not only of the Eisenhower Doctrine but also of the administration's entire Middle Eastern policy. Critics called Dulles' policy reckless and pointed out that the greatest danger in the Middle East was not "overt armed aggression" but Communist subversion, a danger the Eisenhower Doctrine seemingly ignored. Russia, they argued, had increased her influence in the Arab states through well-timed political moves during the Palestine and Suez crises and not through military means.

Dulles vigorously defended the doctrine, saying the United States could not protect the Middle East against Communist political penetration through defense treaties without becoming involved in local disputes not connected with Communist action. Since the Soviets had the means of striking and might use force, he argued, he wanted to deter any attack by removing the danger of a Soviet miscalculation as to the American commitment in the Middle East.

After two months of debate, Congress slightly modified and finally approved the Eisenhower Doctrine. The vote in the Senate was 72 to 19 and in the House, 350 to 60. The President signed the joint resolution into law on March 9. The United States, the doctrine read, "regards as vital to the national interest and world peace the preservation of the independence and integrity of the nations of the Middle East." When the President decided the need for it, the doctrine authorized him to use the armed forces to assist any Middle Eastern nation who requested help in resisting "armed attack from any country controlled by international communism."[24] It also offered those countries economic and military assistance and authorized the President to spend initially, without restriction, $200 million already appropriated for such aid.

The United States thus assumed almost entire responsibility for Western defense of the Middle East, a defense of strategic territory and of resources, mainly oil, essential to Western Europe. No power—friend, potential enemy, or "neutralist" Arab state—could now assume that the United States would not fight for the Middle East. In this sense, the Eisenhower Doctrine was a dramatic turn in foreign policy. Yet, in a broader context, it was another link in a world-wide chain of regional treaties and alliances the United States was constructing in an effort to contain Communist expansion.

Turkey, Pakistan, Iran, and Iraq, the northern tier states of the Baghdad Pact, embraced the Eisenhower Doctrine, but among the other Arab nations only Lebanon formally welcomed it. Even those Arab states friendly to the United States would not publicly align themselves on the American side against the Soviet Union. The Soviets denounced the doctrine as a threat to Arab independence and charged that the United States wished to replace the imperial influence of Britain and France in the Middle East.

Israel officially approved the doctrine. The United States noted that approval but would not promise Israel assistance, fearing that aid to Israel would jeopardize relations with the Arab world. Egypt and Syria attacked the Eisenhower Doctrine as vehemently as they had the Baghdad Pact but were at this time unique among the Arab states in their close ties to the Soviet Union.

Jordan, Syria, Iraq, and Lebanon

As the Eisenhower Doctrine went into effect, the small Arab kingdom of Jordan became the center of the next Middle Eastern crisis. Before the Suez invasion that state had depended on an annual subsidy from Britain for its existence. In March, 1957, under pressure from Egypt and his own Arab nationalists, the king terminated his alliance with England and gave up the subsidy. Egypt, Syria, and Saudi Arabia promised to assume Jordan's economic burden. In April internal disturbances, apparently fomented by Egypt and Syria, threatened to destroy the monarchy.

President Eisenhower announced that Jordan's independence was of vital interest to the United States and sent special units of the Sixth Fleet to the eastern Mediterranean. Jordan's young king declared martial law, crushed the opposition, withdrew from an alliance with Egypt and Syria, and turned to the United States for the financial aid Egypt and Syria had failed to provide. That same month the United States offered him $10 million and in June another $20 million and thus took up Britain's old task of keeping Jordan afloat.

As the Jordan crisis eased, the focus of tension in the Middle East shifted to Syria, the Arab country with the most active Communist Party. Her leaders received a large consignment of Soviet arms and with them several hundred Russian instructors and technicians to train the Syrian army in the use of the weapons. The Syrians denied that acceptance of the arms and the technicians implied Soviet domination of their country. Their policy in the cold war, they insisted, was one of "positive neutralism."

Yet Syria's government was hostile to the United States, particularly after August, 1957, when left-wing officers took over the control of the army and gained power in the government. In August the government accused three officials of the American Embassy of plotting to overthrow it and forced them to leave the country. The United States retaliated by expelling the Syrian Ambassador in Washington, and in September offered immediate air delivery of arms to Syria's neighbors. Huge American air transports arrived in Jordan, for example, with weapons and military vehicles.

Turkey, Syria's northern neighbor, at the same time expressed alarm over the growth of Soviet influence in Syria and took precautionary measures to protect her border. Syria's Foreign Minister then charged the United States with trying to dominate his country and complained to the United Nations that the massing of

Turkish troops along the Syrian border was a threat to peace. Russia's Nikita S. Khrushchev, at the same time, accused Secretary of State Dulles of fomenting a war by inciting Turkey to attack Syria. He warned Turkey that Russia would use force to protect her interests in the Middle East. On October 10, Dulles announced that the United States would honor its obligations under the North Atlantic Treaty and the Eisenhower Doctrine by going to Turkey's defense in case she were attacked.

Four days later, Egypt added to the tension by landing troops at Latakia, Syria, under her joint defense agreement with Syria. Three days later, Dulles bluntly told reporters that a Soviet attack on Turkey would bring American retaliation against Russian territory. Although the Turkish-Syrian quarrel remained unsettled, the Syrian crisis eased after Khrushchev, at a reception at the Turkish Embassy in Moscow on October 28, remarked that "there would be no war."

Syria's leaders, many of whom desired federation with Egypt, welcomed the arrival of Egyptian troops as a sign of solidarity between the two countries. Several months later, in February, 1958, Egypt and Syria went beyond federation by merging themselves into a single state called the United Arab Republic with Nasser as president. A month later Yemen federated itself with the new republic in a close union called the United Arab States, a union open to other Arab nations who might wish to join.[25] The only political group in Syria that had opposed the union with Egypt was the Communist Party, but Nasser, as soon as he assumed power there, outlawed the Communists. His new regime received prompt American recognition.

Since the creation of the United Arab Republic weighted the balance of power in the Middle East in favor of Nasser, two weeks later the kings of Jordan and Iraq tried to redress the balance by signing a treaty that bound their countries together in a federation they called Arab Union, a move endorsed by the United States. Two rival blocs thus came into existence, each claiming to represent Arab nationalism and the ideal of Arab unity.

That rivalry kept the attention of American statesmen riveted on the Middle East and touched off another crisis. Syria's union with Egypt upset the delicate balance in Lebanon between Christians and Moslems who formed almost equal halves of the population. Like the Syrians, the Moslems and other nationalists in Lebanon desired closer ties with Egypt, wanted their government to disentangle itself from the commitments to the West, primarily the United States, and favored a policy of "positive neutralism" as proclaimed by Nasser.

In May, 1958, civil war broke out in Lebanon. Moslems, spurred on by Nasser's nationalist propaganda, feared that President Camille Chamoun, a Maronite Christian, would seek a second term in defiance of the constitution and perpetuate his friendly policy toward the United States. Chamoun's government immediately accused the United Arab Republic of instigating and aiding the rebellion and formally complained to the Security Council that Nasser was interfering in Lebanon's internal affairs and endangering the peace of the Middle East. In June the United Nations sent observers to Lebanon but did not find evidence to substantiate Chamoun's charge of "massive intervention" by Nasser and did not stop the fighting.

At the same time Nasser had loosed a torrent of propaganda against Iraq's pro-Western government. Suddenly, on July 14, a group of army officers in Baghdad overthrew the government, murdering the king, the crown prince, and the prime minister, and announced the founding of the Republic of Iraq. The new regime, headed by Brigadier General Abdel Karim Kassim, quickly dissolved the Union with Jordan and made a defensive alliance with the United Arab Republic.

The swift success of the Iraqi revolution shocked the United States who had looked upon Iraq as the main Arab bulwark in the Baghdad Pact. Although Kassim's regime did not immediately denounce the pact, it was clear that as far as Iraq was concerned the alliance was dead. Dulles' northern tier was thus left with a gaping hole. Nonetheless, on August 2, after Russia had done so, the United States recognized Kassim's government.

Intervention in Lebanon

Frightened by the developments in neighboring Iraq, Lebanon's Chamoun meantime had sent an urgent plea for help to President Eisenhower, saying his country could not survive both domestic rebellion and "indirect aggression." Eisenhower responded quickly. On July 15, the day following the Iraqi revolution, he rushed 5000 Marines to Beirut, Lebanon's chief port, to defend that country's independence. "I have concluded that, given the developments in Iraq," he told Congress, "the measures thus far taken by the United Nations Security Council are not sufficient to preserve the independence and integrity of Lebanon."[26]

Ultimately, 14,000 American soldiers and Marines occupied strategic areas in Lebanon, but with orders not to shoot unless shot at. Three days after the initial American landings, British paratroops, protected by American jet fighters, swarmed into Amman, Jordan's capital, to bolster the sagging monarchy. Britain had responded to a plea for protection from Jordan's king.

To the United Arab Republic the American intervention was "another Suez," and to the Russians it was an "open act of aggression." When the United States, on the day of the initial landings, asked the Security Council to establish an international military force to preserve Lebanon's independence, the Soviet delegate vetoed the American resolution. Ominously, the Soviet press announced that on July 18 military maneuvers would begin near the Turkish and Iranian frontiers.

Khrushchev warned Eisenhower that the Soviet Union "cannot remain indifferent to what is happening in the Middle East, next to its borders" and demanded

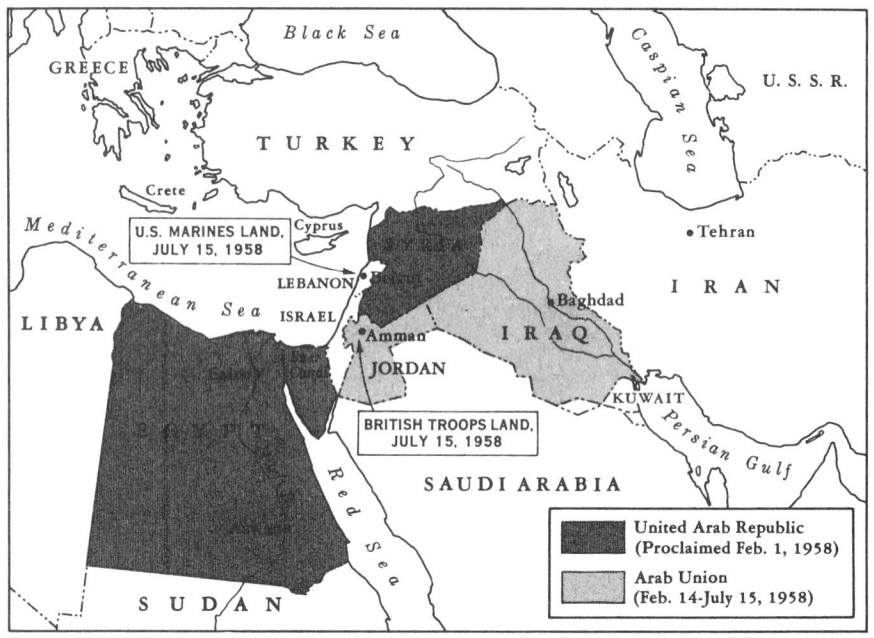

INTERVENTION IN THE MIDDLE EAST, 1958

an immediate five-power summit conference, composed of Russian, American, British, French, and Indian heads of government, to deal with the crisis.[27] Three days later the President agreed to an immediate summit conference, but only within the framework of the Security Council. Within a few days the situation in Lebanon itself eased a bit after Fuad Chehab, a general acceptable to both sides in the civil war, won election to the presidency.

Dulles, at this time, flew to London for a ministerial meeting of the members of the Baghdad Pact. He promised increased military aid to Turkey, Pakistan, and Iran and on July 28, 1958, signed a declaration of collective security committing the United States to cooperate with the nations of the Baghdad Pact for their defense. Through executive action, the United States thus finally assumed the obligations of the Baghdad alliance.

Early in August, after returning from a secret conference in Peking with Mao Tse-tung, Khrushchev rejected the five-power conference he had previously urged, presumably because Mao had objected to China's exclusion. Instead, Khrushchev suggested a special meeting of the General Assembly to consider the Middle Eastern situation.

Accordingly, the Security Council summoned the General Assembly into emergency session, and Eisenhower opened the meeting on August 13 with a speech offering a six-point program for peace in the Middle East. Among other things, he suggested that a United Nations force protect Lebanon and Jordan and presented a regional economic plan that would be controlled by the Arab states, "avoid a new arms-race spiral in the area," and enable the Arab peoples to raise their living standards.[28] As they had declared many times before, the United States and Britain at the same time pledged themselves to withdraw their troops from Lebanon and Jordan as soon as the General Assembly voted action that would maintain peace in the Middle East.

After some involved American and Russian political maneuvering, the Arab League states themselves drafted a compromise resolution calling on the Secretary General of the United Nations to make practical arrangements that would facilitate the early withdrawal of American and British troops from Lebanon and Jordan. The Arab countries promised not to interfere in the internal affairs of neighboring states. The General Assembly unanimously adopted the resolution and then adjourned.

Lebanon's new president, General Chehab, took office in September and won a promise of American support for his government. After a trip to the Middle East at the end of the month the Secretary General recommended that United Nations observation teams be stationed in Lebanon and Jordan to prevent infiltration and smuggling of arms into those countries.

The United States had been withdrawing troops steadily, and by the end of October both British and American troops were entirely evacuated from Lebanon and Jordan. Meanwhile, alien infiltration into those countries ceased. America's first armed intervention in the Arab world, and with it the Middle Eastern crisis that had started in May, thus came to an end. There is little doubt that the general reaction to the intervention, particularly in the Middle East, Asia, and Africa, was unfavorable, but by showing that the United States was willing to use force in the Middle East it may have given pause to aggressive plans in Cairo and Moscow.

New Alliances

Although Lebanon and Jordan retained their independence, the American intervention did not stop Communist political and economic penetration into the Middle East. The Soviet Union delivered planes, tanks, and other arms to Iraq. It aided the United Arab Republic with the construction of airports and industrial plants, and in December signed an agreement in Cairo to finance the first stage of the high dam at Aswan with interest on the huge loan at 2.5 per cent annually, a rate lower than that usually charged by the United States. Soviet technicians would plan and supervise the construction, using only Russian equipment.[29]

To counter the spread of Soviet influence southward and to fulfill its pledge to the Baghdad Pact nations, the United States signed separate bilateral defense agreements with Turkey, Pakistan, and Iran in March, 1959. Those treaties committed the United States to taking "such appropriate action, including the use of armed forces, as may be agreed upon" in the event of attacks against the other signatories.[30]

The United States, more firmly than before, thus allied itself with what remained of the northern tier nations without formally joining the Baghdad Pact. The Soviet Union denounced the alliances, particularly the Iranian treaty. Iran, in fact, had signed despite violent threats from the Soviets. American policymakers hoped that with the new alliance Iran would be less likely to follow the example of Iraq.

In Iraq, meantime, Kassim's government drew closer to the Soviet Union. In February Kassim had said that Iraq was "out of all foreign alliances" and that the Baghdad Pact had been reduced "to less than a shadow." Several weeks later pro-Nasser rebels tried to overthrow him. With the support of local Communists, Kassim crushed the uprising within twenty-four hours. Nasser then split with Kassim, denounced "communist domination" of Iraq, and softened his attacks against the West.

Late in March Kassim officially withdrew Iraq from the Baghdad Pact, and in August the alliance's name was officially changed to the Central Treaty Organization, or CENTO, a name that stressed its place in the world-wide security system that American statesmen had constructed. CENTO had a position between the North Atlantic Treaty Organization in the west and another security organization in southeast Asia. New headquarters were established in Ankara.

This change reflected the fact that Russian influence in the Middle East was stronger than ever. Before the end of the year, however, Kassim showed dissatisfaction with Communist pressures and in the following year embarked on a policy of independence for Iraq, one that committed him to neither the Soviet Union nor the United States.[31] Thus as the sixties began, the United States was more deeply involved in the Middle East than ever before in its history, but its influence had receded from what it had been in the preceding decade. Most Arab states had repudiated pro-Western policies.

Middle Eastern Dilemma

In 1962, the Middle East remained the source of one of the perplexing problems of American foreign policy. In the first place, the United States had committed itself to two conflicting objectives. It sought to win the friendship of the Arabs so that they would not turn to Russia, and at the same time it supported Israel. So deep was Arab hostility to Israel that it appeared virtually impossible to achieve the first objective without abandoning the second. Arab nationalists considered Israel practically a creature of the United States. The impact of their hostility toward Israel on American foreign policy can be seen in the case of the *Cleopatra*.

For years Nasser had refused Israel the use of the Suez Canal, but in 1959 he tightened his restrictions by excluding American ships bearing Israeli goods from the canal and by blacklisting those which touched Israeli ports. In retaliation the

Seafarers International Union threw a picket line around the Egyptian freighter *Cleopatra* when she arrived in New York in April, 1960. Longshoremen respected the picket line and refused to unload the ship. Nasser charged that Israel was behind the move, and then Arab unions throughout the Middle East began to boycott American ships.

Finally the State Department persuaded the Seafarers to call off the pickets by promising to try to remove Arab restrictions against American seamen in Middle Eastern ports. The Senate, despite State Department opposition, then passed an amendment to a foreign aid bill giving the President discretionary authority to refuse aid to the United Arab Republic until Nasser opened Suez to Israel. Although the President ignored the amendment, it irritated the Arabs. The issue also influenced domestic politics, for 1960 was an election year. The chairman of the Senate Foreign Relations Committee charged that the picketing represented an effort to shape foreign policy for the benefit of minority groups in the United States, meaning that it and the amendment were designed to attract Zionist votes.

The second part of the dilemma in American Middle Eastern policy was imbedded in Arab anticolonialism. If the United States, as did Russia, openly sided with the Arabs in their struggle for national independence, it would run the risk of splitting the North Atlantic alliance, for Britain and France still held on to scraps of their Arab empires. Arab nationalists, on the other hand, could not forget that in a long civil war in Algeria the French had killed Moslems with American weapons.

Even though the United States had not openly backed the British and French colonial policies, Arab nationalists believed that without American diplomatic, military, and financial support, British and French colonialism would have collapsed sooner than it did. To many Arabs, therefore, the United States was an imperial power who had made possible a prolonged survival of Western colonialism.

American policymakers were aware of the Arab attitude and hence were particularly pleased when one of the most embarrassing of the anticolonial struggles, that of the Algerians against the French, came to end on June 3, 1962, when President Charles de Gaulle of France proclaimed Algeria's independence. Freedom came after 132 years of French rule, seven years and eight months of rebellion, and six months of murderous terrorism by die-hard European colonialists against Moslems. The United States quickly recognized Algeria's independence.

Until the end of the Algerian conflict, American commitments to Europe and support of Arab nationalism had been virtually irreconcilable. This was so because America's main foreign policy, the containment of the Soviet Union, centered in Europe. Her oldest and most loyal allies, Britain and France, were essential to that policy. The United States could not logically preserve their interests in Europe and at the same time help destroy them in the Middle East.

The weak and frequently unreliable countries of the Middle East were also important in stemming Communist expansion, but less so than Britain and France. Those Arab states created a great din in the 1950's, often out of proportion to their weight in the balance of world politics. Nonetheless, this did not obscure the basic dilemma of American policy in the Middle East, that of trying to bring the Arab world into a policy of containing Communism while retaining close ties to Israel and Western Europe.

NOTES

1. The Geographer of the State Department, G. Etzel Pearcy, points out that there is no clear-cut definition of the Middle East. *Department of State Bulletin*, XL (March 23, 1959), 407–416.

2. For the influence of American education in the Middle East, see N. Marbury Efimenco, "American Impact on Middle East Leadership," *Political Science Quarterly*, LXIX (June 1954), 202–218.

3. The text of the declaration is in Carol A. Fisher and Fred Krinsky, *Middle East in Crisis: A Historical and Documentary Review* (Syracuse, N.Y., 1959), p. 83. For a detailed history of the declaration, see Leonard Stein, *The Balfour Declaration* (New York, 1961).

4. Selig Adler, in "The Palestine Question in the Wilson Era," *Jewish Social Studies*, X, (Oct. 1948), 314, believes that Wilson's endorsement was "a landmark in the story of the relations between the United States and the Zionist movement."

5. From 1922, the beginning of the mandate, to 1936, Jews and Arabs had both increased in population, but the Jewish growth had been at a faster rate. During this period Jewish population had risen from 13 to 30 per cent of Palestine's total. See Harry B. Ellis, *Israel and the Middle East* (New York, 1957), p. 102.

6. Jan. 18, 1944, quoted in Frank E. Manuel, *The Realities of American-Palestine Relations* (Washington, 1949), p. 310.

7. *Ibid.*, p. 312.

8. Harry S. Truman, *Memoirs* (2 vols., Garden City, N.Y., 1955), II, 132. See also,

Robert H. Ferrell, "United States Policy in the Middle East," in Stephen D. Kertesz, ed., *American Diplomacy in a New Era* (Notre Dame, Ind., 1961), pp. 280–281.

9. Tables showing Arab and Jewish population figures from 1922 to 1944 and beyond are in George Lenczowski, *The Middle East in World Affairs*, 2nd ed. (Ithaca, 1956), p. 547.

10. Evidence of opposition within the administration to Truman's policy may be found in Walter Millis and E. S. Duffield, eds., *The Forrestal Diaries* (New York, 1951). Forrestal's concern over the effect of political pressure on Middle Eastern policy is evident in pp. 309, 322, 341–348, 359–365. Kermit Roosevelt, in "The Partition of Palestine: A Lesson in Pressure Politics," *Middle East Journal*, II (Jan. 1948), 1-16, stresses the influence of domestic politics on policy toward Palestine. For a summary of Jewish influence on this policy, see Milton Plesur, "The Relations Between the United States and Palestine," *Judaism: A Quarterly Journal of Jewish Life and Thought*, III (Fall 1954), 469–479.

11. The text is in Fisher and Krinsky, *Middle East in Crisis*, p. 126.

12. Harry H. Ransom, *Central Intelligence and National Security* (Cambridge, Mass., 1958), p. 88 and Robert Engler, *The Politics of Oil: A Study of Private Power and Democratic Directions* (New York, 1961), pp. 205–208.

13. This was sometimes called the Middle East Defense Organization, or MEDO, as well as METO. For details, see Halford L.

Hoskins, "Some Aspects of the Security Problem in the Middle East," *American Political Science Review*, XLVII (March 1953), 188–198. The treaty is printed in Jacob C. Hurewitz, ed., *Diplomacy in the Near and Middle East: A Documentary Record* (2 vols., Princeton, 1956), II, 390–391.

14. M. A. Fitzsimons, in "The Suez Crisis and the Containment Policy," *Review of Politics*, XIX (Oct. 1957), 440, points out that even though the seizure had been in preparation for nearly two years, Nasser's action was hasty.

15. Anthony Eden's quotation is from his speech of Aug. 8, 1956, and is in *Full Circle: The Memoirs of Anthony Eden* (Boston, 1960), p. 495. The French quotation is in Richard P. Stebbins, *The United States in World Affairs, 1956* (New York, 1957), p. 259.

16. Anthony Eden asserts that Dulles' actions left no alternative but force, *Full Circle*, p. 540. These memoirs contain a detailed account of the entire Suez affair.

17. See Lionel Gelber, *America in Britain's Place: The Leadership of the West and Anglo-American Unity* (New York, 1961), pp. 240–241.

18. The speech is in Fisher and Krinsky, *Middle East in Crisis*, pp. 167–170.

19. Nov. 2, 1956, quoted in Stebbins, *U.S. in World Affairs, 1956*, p. 327.

20. A few days after the election Eden called Eisenhower by phone and asked to see the President so that the Anglo-American breach might be healed, but was refused. Details are in Sherman Adams, *Firsthand Report: The Story of the Eisenhower Administration* (New York, 1961), pp. 259–260.

21. Albert H. Hourani, in "The Decline of the West in the Middle East," *International Affairs*, XXIX (Part I, Jan. 1953), 22–42 and (Part II, April 1953), 156–183, explains why

British and American influence had been falling even before the Suez affair.

22. For an analysis that stresses the Soviet gain, see Richard H. Nolte, "Year of Decision in the Middle East," *Yale Review*, XLVI (Winter 1957), 228–244.

23. Nov. 29, 1956, quoted in Stebbins *U.S. in World Affairs, 1956*, p. 384.

24. The text is in Fisher and Krinsky, *Middle East in Crisis*, pp. 175–176.

25. The United Arab Republic was dissolved in September, 1961, by a coup of Syrian army officers and in December was followed by the break-up of Egypt's federation with Yemen. See Richard P. Stebbins, *The United States in World Affairs, 1961* (New York, 1962), 186–187, 190.

26. The text of the message is in the *Department of State Bulletin*, XXXIX (Aug. 4, 1958), 182–183. Sherman Adams points out, in *Firsthand Report*, p. 293, that the sending of the Marines was an unhappy and frustrating experience for Eisenhower.

27. Khrushchev's letter of July 19 is in the *Department of State Bulletin*, XXXIX (Aug. 11, 1958), 231–233.

28. For the speech, see *ibid.* (Sept. 1, 1958), 337–342.

29. Construction on the first stage of the dam began on Jan. 9, 1960, *The New York Times*, Jan. 10, 1960, IV, 2: 3. The Russians also agreed to finance the second stage of the dam. Richard P. Stebbins, *The United States in World Affairs, 1960* (New York, 1961), p. 220.

30. The text of the treaty with Turkey, March 4, 1959, is in the *Department of State Bulletin*, XL (March 23, 1959), 417–418.

31. Iraqi Communists met this rebuff by restraining themselves and cooperating with Kassim anyway. John C. Campbell, *Defense of the Middle East: Problems of American Policy*, rev. ed. (New York, 1960), p. 152.

Chapter Twenty-Nine

EUROPEAN SECURITY

WHILE the United States tried to accommodate its foreign policy to rival nationalisms in the Middle East and elsewhere, in Europe it attempted to overcome old nationalist fears and urged a supranational unity. The political union of Western Europe had become a major aim of American foreign policy. The Marshall Plan, with its emphasis on Europe as a whole and on integration across national boundaries, had given the movement toward unification a strong stimulus.

In May, 1949, with "Western Union," or the five powers of the Brussels Pact as a nucleus, ten nations of Western Europe had signed a treaty creating a "Council of Europe." Since it had no legislative or military powers, that council served mainly as a forum for the discussion of the European idea. Americans, nonetheless, were pleased with this first postwar European institution. It was, Secretary of State Dean Acheson said, "a welcome step forward toward the political integration of the free nations of Europe."[1]

The Building of NATO

At about the same time, as we have seen, the United States through the North Atlantic Treaty had taken the lead in shaping the military integration of Western Europe. In the middle of September, 1949, the foreign ministers of the twelve treaty powers held their first meeting in Washington and set up the administrative machinery for the North Atlantic Treaty Organization, or NATO.

At this time NATO did not aspire to build a European army that would match the strength of Soviet ground forces. It sought instead to create a defense force that would "deter" the Russians from attacking by showing them that an assault

EUROPE'S ALIGNMENTS, 1949

on Western Europe would be costly and dangerous, or that might at least hold the Soviets back until American air power could strike. Since the European Allies could not afford to arm themselves, they formally asked for American military assistance.

Considerable debate in both houses of Congress followed the President's request for authority to supply military aid. Finally, on September 28, five days after President Truman had announced that Russia had exploded an atomic bomb, Congress passed the Mutual Defense Assistance Act. Truman approved it on October 6. That act authorized nearly $1.5 billion for foreign military aid, $1 billion of it for the North Atlantic countries. Before the President could make the major funds available, the act required European Allies to agree on "an integrated defense of the North Atlantic area."

The Mutual Defense Assistance Act marked a shift in policy from economic to comprehensive long-range military aid for Europe. In support of NATO, this act in effect replaced the European Recovery Program. Since the United States alone set the terms of the assistance, Americans became the leading influence in the military unity of Western Europe. American foreign policy, based on the idea of an identity of interest between the United States and Western Europe, had thus achieved at least a part of its objective. It had forged Western Europe into a coalition against Communism, one that might form the basis for a broader unification.

Within a few months the European Allies fulfilled the American conditions. In Washington, on January 27, 1950, therefore, the United States signed bilateral aid agreements with eight of its Allies, and by April 1 the first consignments of American airplanes and weapons were arriving in Europe. The rearmament of Western Europe had begun.

Through Marshall Plan aid, moreover, the countries of Western Europe, had become stronger by spring than at any time since the end of the Second World War. Statistics compiled by the Economic Cooperation Administration showed that industrial production of the eighteen countries participating in the Marshall Plan in the first quarter of 1950 had climbed to 138 per cent of its 1938 level. Yet Western Europe needed more economic unification if it were to stand on its own feet. The movement toward European unity, however, made little progress. Great Britain, who cherished her ties to the world-wide Commonwealth and her special relationship to the United States, was unwilling to transfer any national sovereignty, economic or political, to a supranational community as envisaged by the Council of Europe.

Another obstacle to European unity was the German question. Believing that without Germany Western Europe could have no defense in depth, the United States wanted to bring West Germany into Europe's defense arrangements. Haunted by memories of three German invasions in seventy years, the French, however, resisted all efforts to rearm the Germans. They also feared that West

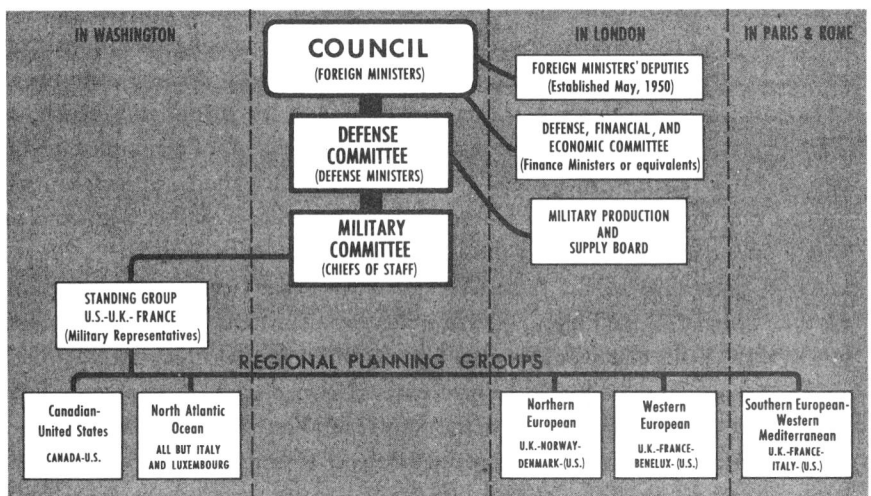

NATO, 1950

Germany's revived steel industry might some day make weapons for a rearmed Germany. France's Foreign Minister, Robert Schuman, therefore advanced a bold scheme in May, 1950, calling for a supranational organization for the control of coal and steel, Europe's basic industries. Americans were enthusiastic, and Secretary Acheson called the proposal "a major contribution toward the resolution of the pressing political and economic problems of Europe."[2]

Since the Schuman Plan would keep their economy free from restrictions the wartime Allies might otherwise impose, the Germans were willing to surrender some of their national sovereignty and join. Britain refused to do so. The states of "Little Europe," Belgium, France, Italy, Luxembourg, the Netherlands, and West Germany, therefore, went ahead with a supranational community of their own. Their foreign ministers signed a treaty creating the European Community for Coal and Steel in April, 1951. In September, 1952, they established a formal organization for the merger of their coal and steel industries within a common control and customs union. It abolished tariffs and quotas in coal and steel throughout "Little Europe." Since the community for steel and coal was the first truly supranational organization in postwar Europe, the United States hoped that it would become the basis for a political confederation.

The announcement of the Schuman Plan did not deflect American foreign policy from its aim of trying to bring West Germany into Western Europe's defense forces. The Communist assault on South Korea produced a cold fear among the governments of Western Europe, who trembled at the thought that the Red army might march west. They desperately sought an immediate increase in their military strength.

In an effort to overcome the anxieties of the Allies, President Truman agreed to send additional troops to Europe, but with the aim of making them a part of a balanced defense force that would include Germans. This peacetime commitment of troops to Europe, Secretary Acheson explained to the British and French, was "absolutely unprecedented in our history." He even called it "a complete revolution in American foreign policy."[3] Yet for the French the basic problem now became one of finding a way to use German manpower within a scheme that would offer a guarantee against the revival of German militarism.[4]

As an alternative to the American desire to create German army divisions, France's Premier, René Pleven, offered a plan for a European Defense Community in October, 1950, that would merge German units into an integrated European army. In this way there would be no separate German army and no general staff. German troops would contribute to the defense of Western Europe, but only under the supranational control of the European Defense Community. Impatient to get a large unified defense force started, the United States accepted the French plan. Negotiations between the North Atlantic Allies and West Germany followed.

At the same time, the United States accelerated plans to transform NATO into a larger and more effective military system. In December, Truman appointed General Dwight D. Eisenhower Supreme Commander for the Allied Powers in Europe. Eisenhower immediately began selection of an international staff and in April, 1951, established his command, known as the Supreme Headquarters for the Allied Powers in Europe, or SHAPE, near Paris.

In his State of the Union message, Truman emphasized that the developments in Europe were a foremost concern of American foreign policy. "The heart of our common defense effort," he said, "is the North Atlantic community. The defense of Europe is the basis for the defense of the whole free world—ourselves included."[5]

To carry out that commitment, the Truman administration combined economic and military aid in its request for appropriations and curtailed economic aid not directly related to military purposes. Since the Marshall Plan had attained its objectives, Congress could not understand why the President continued to ask for huge appropriations for European economic assistance. In the Mutual Security Act of October, 1951, therefore, it reduced economic aid for Europe by some $600 million below the amount requested and required those who received assistance to fulfill their military obligations and contribute to their own defense and to "the defensive strength of the free world." The President appointed W. Averell Harriman, his foreign policy coordinator, Director for Mutual Security. This agency replaced the Economic Cooperation Administration, created originally to administer Marshall Plan aid.

Even though Western Europe had "recovered," it was incapable of meeting the minimum requirements of the accelerated rearmament program without American assistance. Hence the President and his advisers felt compelled to continue economic aid, even though it had been originally designed as a short-term program to help Europe become self-supporting. That situation, moreover, convinced them that European unity was as urgent as ever.

The European Defense Community

If the nations of Western Europe merged their economies and created a unified market, American planners argued, they would encourage large-scale production and build a strong Europe. If the Allies replaced their national armies with a European defense force and a common military budget, they would not only provide a safe means for rearming Germany but would also advance toward the economic and political unification of Western Europe. The defense of Europe and the common interest of the European peoples, it was maintained, called for a Western European political union. In the interest of reducing the burden on the taxpayer, of increasing European productivity, and of building a strong European defense system, the concept of European unity in 1952, particularly through the European Defense Community, now became a basic part of American foreign policy.

At the ninth meeting of the North Atlantic Council in Lisbon in February, 1952, the delegates endorsed the European Defense Community, formally welcomed Greece and Turkey into the alliance, and worked out a schedule for European rearmament. The heart of the Lisbon program was the decision to rearm Germany within the European Defense Community, a community the United States assumed would soon come into existence.

Three months later, at Bonn on May 26, the foreign ministers of France, Britain, the United States, and West Germany signed a "peace contract," the "Convention on Relations between the Three Powers and the Federal Republic of Germany." It recognized West Germany as a partner in the community of Europe and for all practical purposes ended the occupation and restored German sovereignty. It was the first official American tie to a supranational European union.

On the following day in Paris, the foreign ministers of Belgium, France, Italy, Luxembourg, the Netherlands, and West Germany signed a fifty-year treaty creating the European Defense Community. At the same time, among other agreements, the fourteen foreign ministers of the North Atlantic nations signed a protocol to the North Atlantic Treaty linking it to the European Defense Community. That protocol, through the North Atlantic Treaty, committed the United States to go to the defense of the European Defense Community if attacked. The protocol also constituted the second official tie between the United States and the European community.

President Truman submitted the Bonn convention and the North Atlantic protocol to the Senate in June. They were approved a month later by votes of

77 to 5 and 72 to 5, respectively, but none of the Bonn or Paris agreements would take effect until all the signatories had ratified them.

Within a few months the European Defense Community ran into snags, and the rearmament program began to falter. The goals of the Lisbon schedule became politically and economically unattainable. The taxpayers of the Western Allies, including those of the United States, would not accept the sacrifices necessary to match the huge forces of the Soviet Union and its satellites. France, moreover, who had advanced the idea of the European Defense Community primarily as an alternative to a national German army, became increasingly alarmed by West Germany's remarkable economic resurgence that presaged a revival of military power. Most Frenchmen, despite the fear of Soviet Russia, still believed that the safety of their country required German disarmament. They expressed increasing opposition to the European Defense Community.

The "New Look" in Defense Policy

When Eisenhower became President in 1953, he continued to support Western European unity as a foremost objective of foreign policy, but his administration launched what came to be called a "new look" in military policy. "Our problem," the new President said in February, "is to achieve military strength within the limits of endurable strain upon our economy."[6]

The Eisenhower administration replaced the Truman program—calling for a fast increase in European rearmament—with one to meet defense needs over the "long pull," or a period of ten to twenty years. It was essentially a military "stretch out" that reduced the pace and scale of rearmament in the interests of economy. Under the slogan of "substituting machines for men," it emphasized the use of nuclear weapons to fill the gaps in manpower.[7] The new look, administration supporters argued, would offer more defense for less money, or as some said, "more bang for the buck."

Since the new look appeared to commit the United States to the idea of nuclear warfare as basic defense policy, it alarmed Europeans. To rely upon the "deterrent" and "retaliatory" capacity of the American Air Force seemed recklessly dangerous to them. They realized that in any atomic war with Russia, Western Europe would be the most likely target and that Western European civilization as they knew it might disappear in a radioactive wasteland.

This fear, plus the relaxation of tension with the Soviet Union after the death of Stalin in March, led many Europeans to talk about "peaceful coexistence" alongside the Soviets. In France it encouraged those who wished to avoid the rearming of Germany. If nuclear weapons were to be substituted for manpower, they reasoned, why rearm the Germans?

Like the French, the British also hoped for some kind of agreement with the Soviet Union that might relax cold war tensions. Winston Churchill once more

Britain's Prime Minister, in speeches before the House of Commons in April and May, suggested a Big Four meeting on the highest level. He even proposed a security pact, similar to the Locarno treaty of 1925, for Western Europe. "I do not believe," he said, "that the immense problem of reconciling the security of Russia with the freedom and safety of Western Europe is insoluble." [8] The French were enthusiastic and their National Assembly passed a resolution calling for a meeting of the Big Four.

The United States gave a cold response to the suggestions of a high-level Big Four meeting, saying it would open discussions with the Soviet Union only after the Russians offered tangible evidence that such a gathering would produce results. Nonetheless, it agreed to a Big Three meeting of American, British, and French leaders. Before the conference could take place, Churchill suffered a stroke. The Big Three foreign ministers, therefore, met in Washington in July, 1953. As a result of that meeting, they invited the Soviets to a conference of Big Four foreign ministers to attempt to solve the problem of German unification and the Austrian peace treaty, an invitation the three Allies later repeated. The Russians, as they had earlier, insisted on broader discussions that would include Red China, a proposal the United States would not accept.

In the following month the Soviets announced they had mastered the production of the hydrogen bomb. This weapon, vastly more destructive than the atomic bomb, had been tested by the United States in 1951 and 1952. The ominous Soviet development increased the desire of Europeans for some kind of settlement of cold war issues. Europeans were deeply disappointed by American unwillingness to negotiate with a country now capable of making weapons of unmeasured destructiveness.

Finally, in response to the widespread desire for negotiations with the new Soviet leaders, the long postponed meeting between Eisenhower, Churchill, and Premier Joseph Laniel of France took place in December in Bermuda. There the three heads of government agreed to final arrangements for a four-power conference of foreign ministers in Berlin, as proposed by the Soviets in November.

From Bermuda President Eisenhower flew directly to New York where, in a televised speech before the General Assembly of the United Nations, he made a dramatic proposal known as the "Atoms-for-Peace" plan. The United States, he said, would be willing, in accordance with any specific plan to be worked out with interested states, including Russia, to make atomic material available for peaceful and industrial uses through an international agency. Such a plan would have to be accompanied by the control of atomic weapons.

At first the Soviets expressed interest in the idea but then turned away from it. Congress, moreover, would not at this time authorize atomic contributions to an international pool. It limited the President to making bilateral agreements on atomic research with individual nations.

Three years later, in October, 1956, at the conclusion of an international conference in New York, seventy nations, including Russia and other Communist countries, signed the Statute of an International Atomic Energy Agency. Under pressure from the State Department, a reluctant Senate mustered a 67 to 19 vote of approval for the statute in the following June, but with the proviso that the United States could withdraw from the new international organization if the Senate did not approve later amendments to the statute. The President ratified the agreement and in July the agency went into existence. Thus, Eisenhower finally saw part of his plan for the sharing of atomic energy for peaceful uses become a reality.

Eisenhower, meanwhile, had committed himself to the support of the European Defense Community, and he and his advisers expressed impatience with French indecision concerning it. Several days after his New York speech, the twelfth session of the North Atlantic Council opened in Paris. There, Secretary of State Dulles said that without the European Defense Community he doubted that continental Europe could be made a place of safety. If France did not approve, he warned, "that would compel an agonizing reappraisal of basic United States policy."[9] This statement suggested that the United States might rearm West Germany on its own or pull out of Europe and rely on its own nuclear power for defense. Either was a distasteful alternative to its allies.

Dulles then interrupted his pressure on France to attend the four-power conference in Berlin in January and February, 1954, the first meeting of Big Four foreign ministers in five years. The Western ministers suggested German unification on terms unacceptable to the Soviets. The Russians, who had consistently fought West German rearmament and the European Defense Community, offered a security treaty in their place, one that would have prevented a unified Germany from entering the defense system of Western Europe. Since the conference produced no agreement on either the German or Austrian questions, it ended in deadlock.

Nor could American diplomacy save the European Defense Community. Despite Dulles' tough policy, in August the French National Assembly defeated the European Defense Community treaty. The President called it a "major setback" to American foreign policy.[10] "It looked," Dulles said a few weeks later, "as though the whole North Atlantic treaty structure, its whole system, might be undermined and even swept away by political indecisions and uncertainties."[11]

Western European Union

Although the cause of European union had suffered a major blow, Western European defense had not. Almost immediately, in a nine-power conference in London in September and October that included the United States, British statesmen devised a substitute for the defunct European Defense Community. They suggested enlarging the five-power "Western Union" treaty of 1948, or Brussels Pact, to include Germany and Italy. The whole structure would be known as "Western European Union." To placate the French fear of German rearmament, the British abandoned their traditional policy of not committing troops to the continent. They pledged themselves, with three qualifications, to maintain four divisions and a tactical air force across the channel as long as the majority of the Brussels powers desired. Dulles promised that after Western European Union was established he would recommend to the President that the United States continue to contribute its "fair share" of troops to Europe's defense. The West German Chancellor, Dr. Konrad Adenauer, also promised that Germany would not manufacture certain arms, such as atomic weapons and guided missiles.

A few weeks later, on October 23, the foreign ministers of the North Atlantic Allies and West Germany met in Paris and signed the treaty for Western European Union and related documents. Among those agreements, a protocol to the Bonn convention of 1952 formally restored West German sovereignty by ending the American, British, and French occupation, a convention allowed the Allies to station troops in West Germany with German consent rather than by right of conquest, and a special protocol to the North Atlantic Treaty called for West Germany's admission to the alliance. Pleased by the results, Dulles called the Paris agreements "a near miracle." [12]

The new arrangements, based on national armies and a system of interrelated alliances of which the North Atlantic Treaty formed the core, eliminated the supranational features of the European Defense Community. That was as close to union, in matters of defense, as Western Europe was willing to go at that time. In March, 1955, France ratified the Paris agreements. They went into effect in May after the other signatories, including the United States, had ratified them. Thus, ten years after her defeat, Germany had her occupation formally terminated and, as an ally of her former enemies, began to rearm.

Russia, meantime, had done her best to block the treaty of Western European Union and German rearmament. She denounced the Paris agreements as an obstacle to any understanding over cold war issues, threatened Germany with permanent partition, and demanded another four-power conference on Germany. In May, 1955, after the Paris agreements had gone into effect, she abrogated her wartime nonaggression treaties with Britain and France. A week later, as a counter-move to Western European Union and the North Atlantic Treaty, she signed an alliance with her European satellites known as the "Warsaw Pact."

At the same time, the Soviets made a conciliatory gesture by agreeing to a treaty for Austria. Russia's price for the Austrian State Treaty, signed by the foreign ministers of the Big Four in Vienna on May 15, was a related memorandum pledging Austria to "perpetual neutrality" and not to join any alliances, meaning the North Atlantic Treaty. In December, the United States formally recognized Austria's neutrality, and once again Austria became a sovereign nation.

Foreign Economic Policy

Meanwhile, in August, 1953, the President had reorganized the foreign aid program by placing the Mutual Security Agency and the Technical Cooperation, or "Point Four," program under a new agency called the Foreign Operations Administration. In May, 1955, he replaced the Foreign Operations Administration with the International Cooperation Administration which functioned as a semi-autonomous unit within the Department of State. This administrative change appeared to give foreign economic aid a permanent place in American foreign policy. "It is," President Eisenhower said, "emphatic recognition of the principle that the security and welfare of the United States are directly related to the economic and social advancement of all peoples who share our concern for the freedom, dignity, and well-being of the individual." [13]

Foreign aid, moreover, had become another front in the cold war. Since underdeveloped countries were struggling for economic and social improvement, the Soviet Union in 1954 began a foreign aid program of its own to gain influence among them. Prior to 1954 the Soviets had not attempted to establish trade with the less developed countries, but after that date they promoted it through trade agreements, trade missions, and trade fairs. "We are," Secretary Dulles said in January, 1956, "in a contest in the field of economic development of underdeveloped countries which is bitterly competitive." [14]

Despite strong opposition within his own party, Eisenhower encouraged expanded trade. He urged lower tariffs and consistently promoted the Trade Agreements Program, which Congress continued on a temporary basis. In January, 1954, a bipartisan Commission on Foreign Economic Policy headed by Clarence B. Randall, a steel industrialist, recommended that the government curtail grants and gifts and replace them with lower tariffs so that friendly countries could sell goods on the American market on an expanded scale. The President urged Congress to adopt the Randall recommendations, saying they reflected "the plain truth that if we wish to sell abroad we must buy abroad." [15]

At the same time the United States also attempted to lower tariff barriers through the General Agreement on Tariffs and Trade, or GATT, signed originally in Geneva in the fall of 1947 by twenty-three countries. That agreement called for freer world trade and lower tariffs on a multilateral basis. [16] The most effective means of reducing American restrictions, however, remained the Trade Agreements Act which Congress extended in August, 1958, for four years, the eleventh extension of the President's authority to revise tariff rates.

Although some manufacturers grumbled about competition from cheap foreign goods, substantial elements in both the Republican and Democratic parties opposed

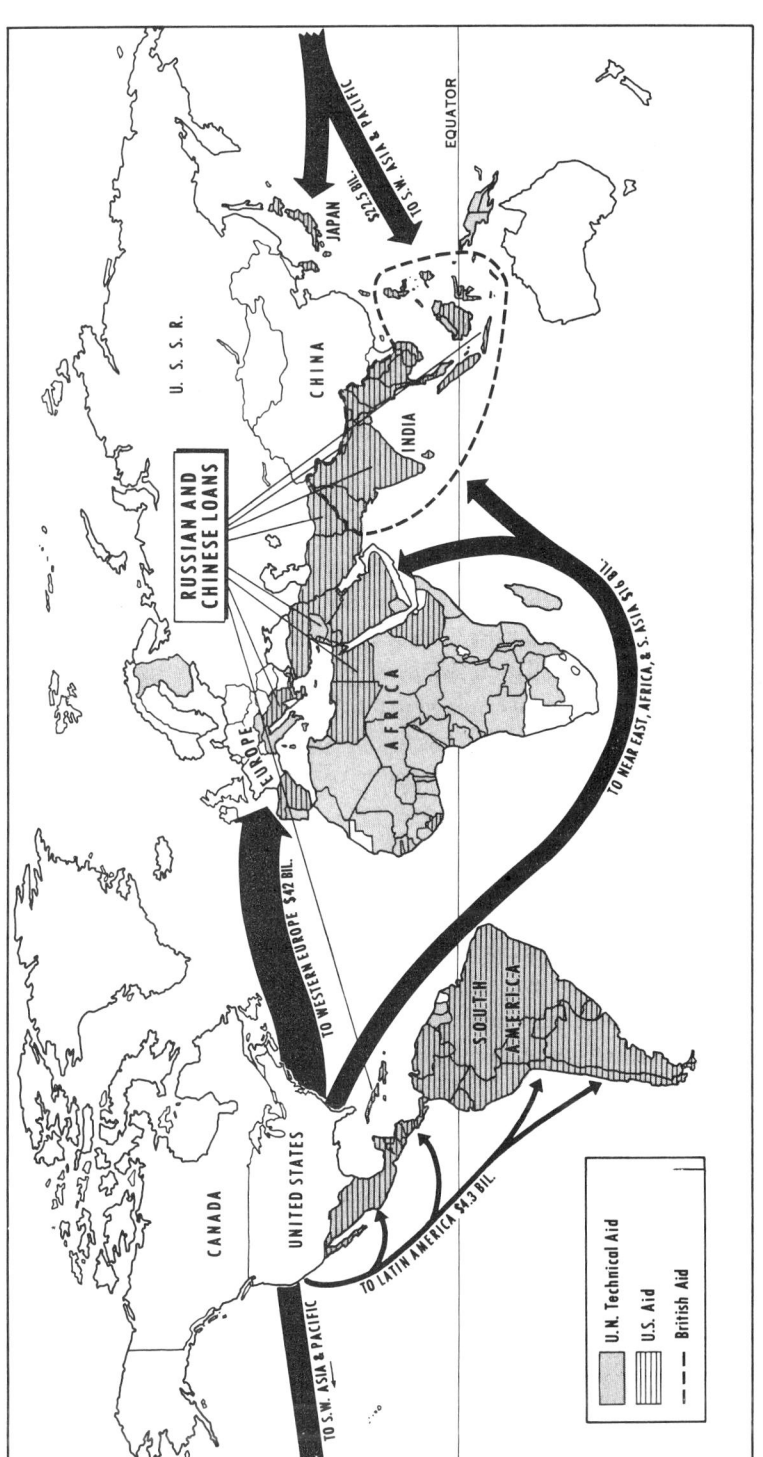

THE FLOW OF UNITED STATES ECONOMIC AND MILITARY AID, 1946-1960

the principle of a high protective tariff. The United States had, perhaps reluctantly, committed itself to the support of world trade.

Conservatives in the President's own party challenged not only the reciprocal trade agreements program but also the President's power over foreign policy, particularly over the making of treaties. Resenting executive agreements, such as those made at Yalta, Senator John W. Bricker of Ohio sponsored an amendment to the Constitution that would have given Congress the power to regulate all executive agreements with foreign countries, in addition to its power over treaties. The Bricker amendment cut across party lines and gained vociferous support from isolationists, states righters, the American Medical Association, Daughters of the American Revolution, and other conservative groups, and aroused considerable emotion in Congress.

As the showdown approached, the President, who had at one time shown sympathy for the amendment, and Secretary Dulles expressed strong opposition to it. "The President," Eisenhower said, "must not be deprived of his historic position as the spokesman for the nation in its relations with other countries." [17] In a lighter mood, he quipped that the Constitution was being demolished "brick by brick by Bricker."[18] Basically, isolationists sought to shackle the President's power at a time when international crises were moving with an awesome swiftness, and he needed more flexibility and not less in the conduct of foreign policy. Yet, when the Senate voted on a modified version of the Bricker amendment in February, 1954, it was defeated by only one vote. Even William F. Knowland, the Republican leader in the Senate, voted for it.[19]

During the debate over the Bricker amendment, the United States concluded several executive agreements with Spain, agreements, ironically, that conservatives supported and liberals opposed. After the Second World War, as a sign of disapproval of Franco's fascist regime, many members of the United Nations, including the United States, had tried to ostracize Spain by withdrawing their ambassadors from Madrid. Later, as the United States tried to build Europe's defenses against Russia, American military men wanted Spain to have a part in those defenses. They looked upon the Iberian Peninsula, protected by the rugged Pyrenees Mountains, as a defensible bridgehead in case the Red army overran Western Europe, and hence sought naval and air bases there.

The American *rapprochement* began in 1950 when Congress authorized the extension of $62.5 million in loans to Spain and President Truman announced that he was appointing an ambassador to fill the Madrid post that had been vacant since 1945. Finally, in September, 1953, the United States signed three agreements with Spain, known collectively as the Pact of Madrid, that made available $226 million in economic and military aid, already appropriated by Congress. In return, the Spaniards allowed the United States to build and use naval and air bases in their country.[20] Those bases were completed in 1958, and indirectly Spain became a part of Western Europe's defense system.

European Unity and the Common Market

Western Europe itself, spurred on by its helplessness during the Suez fiasco and a crisis in Hungary, had by this time moved closer than ever toward a supranational union. "For each of our countries," French Premier Guy Mollet had said in February, 1957, "Europe offers the only opportunity for real independence. Beside those colossi, which the Soviet Union and the United States are, what European country can claim to make its own views prevail?" He hoped for a united Europe that would become an independent world force.

A month later, on March 25 at the Conservatori Palace in Rome, the six states of "Little Europe," France, West Germany, Italy, the Netherlands, Belgium, and Luxembourg, signed two treaties binding their peoples, some 160 million of them, to the European Economic Community, or Common Market, and the European Atomic Energy Community, or Euratom. The Common Market sought to achieve economic union within twelve to fifteen years by eliminating tariffs, equalizing taxes, and removing other national restrictions among members. Then, as if they were units in a single nation, all members would establish a common tariff against outsiders.[21] Euratom would establish a common development of atomic energy for peacetime purposes. Some hoped that these plans would also lead to political union, perhaps to a United States of Europe, and make another war within Western Europe practically impossible.

On January 1, 1959, the Common Market was formally established, and exactly one year later the six members began lowering their tariffs and trade quotas. Although the United States pledged cooperation with the Common Market and supported the political motive behind it, Britain opposed it. She could not reconcile membership in it with her economic ties to the Commonwealth, wished to retain her special relationship to the United States, and did not want to integrate herself with Europe in an arrangement that would require her to surrender some of her national sovereignty. Yet Britain was so dependent on trade that she could not afford to be shut out of the Common Market. To prevent that, she suggested enlarging the market to a free-trade area of thirteen nations which would abolish trade barriers, except in agricultural products, among themselves without building a common external tariff.

Britain, in other words, wished to gain the benefits of the Common Market without endangering her other connections. France and Italy objected, saying she could not have all the advantages without sharing all of the obligations. Britain met this rejection by forming the Free Trade Association in November, 1959, with Sweden, Switzerland, Austria, Norway, Denmark, and Portugal. They became known as the Outer Seven, and the members of the Common Market, as the Inner Six. The Outer Seven agreed to reduce their tariffs to keep pace with the

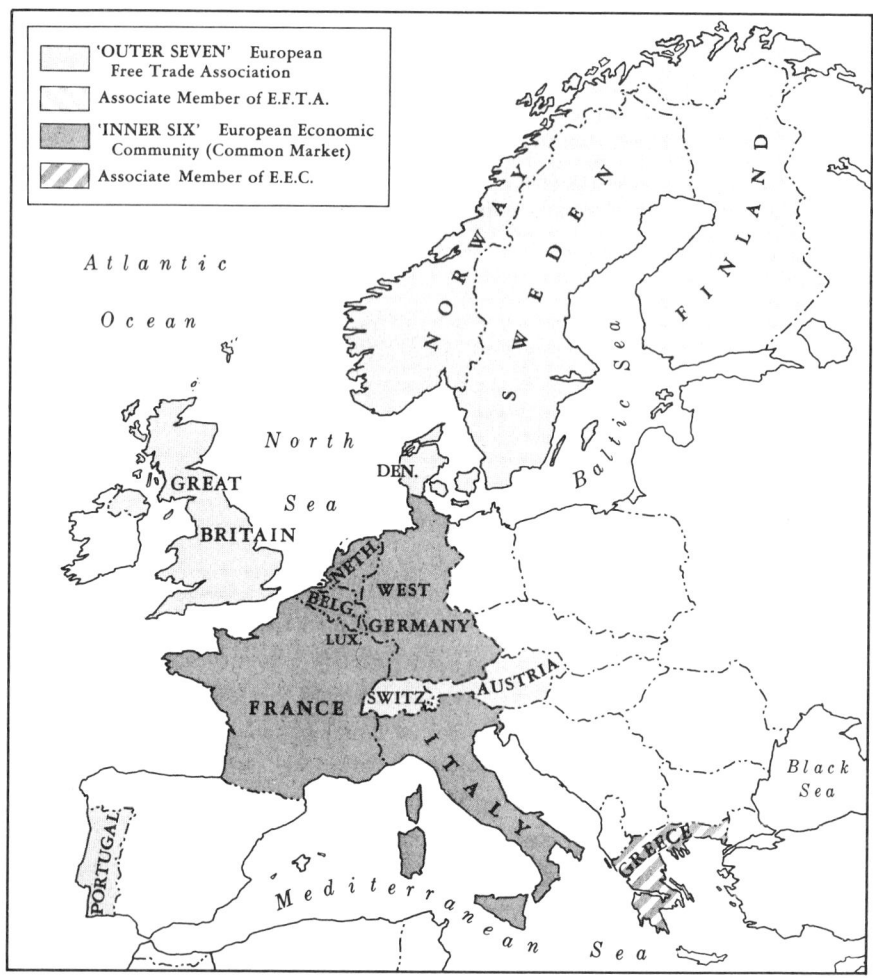

THE COMMON MARKET IN EUROPE, 1961

Inner Six. Basically, they arranged to have free trade with each other while retaining their own tariffs against the outside world. Theirs was essentially an economic arrangement without political motive. Their objective was not to split Western Europe, but to unite it in a single free-trading system without an external tariff.

Yet the result was a split, an economic conflict between the two groups that threatened the unity of NATO. In an effort to end the rivalry, the United States intervened by bringing the two bodies together in 1960 in a special economic committee, and in the following year helped establish the Organization for Economic Cooperation and Development, composed at first of eighteen European nations, the United States, and Canada. Thus, for the first time, the United States directly associated itself with Europe's trade policies and involved itself in Europe's internal economic affairs.[22]

The Soviet Union denounced these steps toward European unity as heightening the danger of war by placing the Western Europeans in bondage to the United States. Despite the difficulties, the United States hailed the Common Market as a significant development, perhaps the decisive one, in strengthening Europe. It preferred that body to the Outer Seven because it promised to go further toward genuine European unity.

The representatives of the Common Market met regularly to discuss economic and political matters, and in 1960 and 1961 the Market enjoyed an economic boom while Britain did not. From 1959 through 1961 the exports of the Market had increased by thirty per cent, while Britain had registered only a modest gain of twelve per cent. As the Market's strength grew, coupled with a faster lowering of economic barriers than originally agreed upon, Britain's economy suffered in the competition. In October, 1961, in a move welcomed by the United States, Britain therefore applied for membership in the European Economic Community.

Britain's negotiations with the Six proved long and complicated. Reports circulated that President Charles de Gaulle of France was cool to Britain's entry into the Common Market because Britain would counterbalance French leadership in that body. The difficulties between Britain and the Six alarmed Kennedy, for his own design for a new foreign trade program was based on the assumption of British membership in the European Economic Community. The United States wanted Britain in to assure a mutually profitable trade with an expanded European market, to bring greater strength to European democracy through stable British political institutions and practices, and to have another particularly close friend at the court of the new Europe. In effect, the United States wished France to surrender her ambition to become the paramount force in a united Western Europe and Britain to give up some of her emotional ties to her Commonwealth.

On July 4, 1962, in a speech in Philadelphia, Kennedy reiterated American policy toward European unity by saying that the United States did not regard a strong and united Europe as a rival, but as a partner. Then he declared that "the United States will be ready for a declaration of interdependence, that we will be prepared to discuss with a United Europe the ways and means of forming a concrete Atlantic partnership. . . ." This partnership, of course, included Britain in a key position.

Despite Kennedy's grand design for an Atlantic partnership, Britain's negotiations with the Common Market entered their twelfth month without the end in sight. The crux of the matter, a spokeman of the British Foreign Office explained late in August, 1962, was that Britain wanted to change some of the rules of the game before playing, and France and West Germany were willing to allow fewer changes than she desired.

The Dollar Crisis

During this period another development, growing primarily out of economic conditions in Western Europe, had brought American foreign economic policy to a turning point. For the first time in the postwar era, dollars were flowing out of the United States faster than they were coming in. They were going for military aid, payments for imports, private investments abroad, and spending by tourists. Thus, where previously its European Allies had been short of dollars and their books had shown a "dollar gap," the United States now had a "dollar gap" of its own.[23] The problem was compounded by the fact that foreign holders could, and did, convert their dollars into gold and cause a serious drain on that metal in the United States. In the 1950's the United States lost about $20 billion in gold and in a rise of net short-term liabilities in dollars. The deficit was especially striking in 1958, 1959, and 1960, when the total loss exceeded by far that of the preceding eight years.

This gold drain led the United States to exert pressure on the West Europeans to end their discriminatory restrictions against American exports, which could no longer be justified on the basis of adverse balance of payments. A number of countries did. The United States also urged the Allies, particularly booming West Germany, to assume part of the foreign aid burden and a greater share of defense costs, which they did.

The United States Wishes to Compete

The prosperity of the Common Market, economists pointed out, had contributed to the dollar crisis. By the winter of 1961, even skeptics no longer questioned the fact that the Common Market had become an impressive economic unit. It had outstripped the Free Trade Association, which was breaking up, and was the fastest growing market in the world. Its rate of economic growth, for example, was twice that of the United States. All this forced the United States to consider means of meeting this new and formidable competition. Some, such as former Secretary of State Christian A. Herter, argued that the United States could hold its major export markets only by associating itself with the Common Market.

This approach did not appeal to the Kennedy administration because it would mean repudiation of the traditional most-favored-nation principle and might suggest to the rest of the world that the rich industrial nations of the West were ganging up on the poor ones. Moreover, the United States could not shut itself off from other important markets and allies, such as in Latin America and Japan. Nonetheless, the Kennedy administration decided that basic trade policy, embodied in the Reciprocal Trade Agreement Act of 1934, was incapable of meeting the challenge of the Common Market. A bold new program was required.

Early in December the President told a news conference that the United States must maintain "the power to negotiate with the Common Market to protect our export industry." In his message on the State of the Union in January, 1962, he asked Congress for a general liberalization of trade which would allow the United States to cut tariffs across the board in exchange for equivalent cuts by the Common Market, a procedure not permitted by the law of 1934.

Several days later the Six of the Common Market reached agreement on agricultural policy, essentially for free trade within the Market on farm products. This was the critical stage in the growth of the European Economic Community, a forward move toward political as well as economic unity.

Two days later, on January 16, the United States signed an agreement with the Common Market, one that had been delayed during the farm discussions, which called for tariff reductions up to twenty per cent, the maximum allowed by American law, on a large number of industrial items. The President followed this on January 25 with the first basically new trade program in twenty-eight years. He asked Congress for a trade expansion act designed to meet the swift growth of the Common Market. Some action seemed imperative, for if all the nations seeking to enter the European Economic Community, such as Britain and Denmark, did so, the Common Market would have a population of some 270 million with a single external tariff and an economy about equal to that of the United States.

Kennedy's program sought to eliminate or reduce tariffs from eighty to fifty per cent on broad groups of products in negotiations with the Common Market. To American workers and firms who suffered injury through the increased

UNITED STATES PAYMENTS AND GOLD SUPPLY

U. S. PAYMENTS BALANCE (BILLIONS OF DOLLARS)

PAYMENTS BY U.S.

PAYMENTS TO U.S.

Deficit

1953 '54 '55 '56 '57 '58 '59 1st Q. 2nd Q. 1960

COMPONENTS OF BALANCE (1959) (BILLIONS OF DOLLARS)

Foreign investments here $0.6 BIL.
Unrecorded transactions $0.8 BIL.
Repayment of Gov't. loans $1.0 BIL.
Services
Exports → $16.2 BIL.

Remittances & Pensions $0.7 BIL.
Private investment → $2.3 BIL.
$2.9 BIL.
Gov't. aid → $8.2 BIL.
Services
Imports → $15.3 BIL.

$7.2 BIL.

TOTAL RECEIPTS $25.8 BIL.

TOTAL PAYMENTS $29.4 BIL.

competition, he would offer federal aid in re-training and federal subsidies. As expected, there was immediate opposition from protectionist groups. One thing was clear: American policy had helped to create the European economic giant, and that giant in turn had compelled the United States to consider a revolutionary change in its economic foreign policy.

In May, 1962, the President devoted a major speech to his Trade Expansion Bill, stressing that "we must either trade or fade." That there was some substance to the slogan became clear shortly after, when the Six of the Common Market showed that they could act as one on a trade issue. In March, Kennedy had increased tariffs on glass and carpets, saying publicly that these imports had imperiled American industries. Privately he explained his move as being designed to win protectionist support for his Trade Expansion Bill. Regardless, on June 4 the Common Market retaliated with a higher common external tariff on some American textiles, effective August 1.

Late in June, the House of Representatives by a vote of 298 to 125 passed the Trade Expansion Bill. The traditional alignments on tariff issues broke down on this bill. Formerly, protectionist business groups in the North and on the West Coast had supported the bill, and some of the new industrialists from the historically free trade South had opposed it.

At the same time Kennedy's foreign aid bill received bipartisan support in Congress. At first Congress tried to cut off aid to Communist Yugoslavia and Poland, and placed other restrictions on the President's power to conduct the aid program. Finally, in response to administration pleas, most restrictions were eliminated. In July, Congress authorized the expenditure of more than $4.6 billion in foreign aid. The next step was actual appropriation of the funds.

The Spirit of Geneva

Previous to the rise of the Common Market and after the establishment of Western European Union in 1955, pressure from Britain, France, Russia, and his own people had led President Eisenhower to participate in a Big Four meeting, the first of what were now called "summit" meetings. In July, 1955, Eisenhower, Prime Minister Anthony Eden of Britain, Premier Edgar Faure of France, Premier Nikolai A. Bulganin of Russia, and the head of Russia's Communist Party, Nikita S. Khrushchev, met at Geneva and discussed three main problems: disarmament, the reunification of Germany, and increased contacts between the Communist nations and those of the West.

On none of those problems did the conference produce agreement. Eisenhower, speaking spontaneously and to the surprise of every one, including those in his own delegation, made the most startling proposal of the conference. He suggested that Russia and the United States give each other "blueprints" of their military establishments and that each allow the other to take aerial photographs of its territory. This plan, he said, would guard against surprise attack and relax tension. Nothing came of this "open skies" proposal because the Russians later rejected it.[24]

The most memorable development of the conference was an intangible thaw in the cold war that some called the "spirit of Geneva." Smiling and amiable, Bulganin and Khrushchev stressed "peaceful coexistence" and "the relaxation of of world tensions." In particular, Eisenhower's warm personality made an impact on the delegates. At one point he said "the United States will never take part in an aggressive war" with such sincerity that Bulganin replied simply, "We believe that statement."[25] The Geneva Conference left people all over the world with the optimistic impression that Russia and the United States would settle their differences without a nuclear war.

After the close of the meeting, the heads of state turned over their agenda to their foreign ministers who met again in Geneva in October and November. That conference also ended without accomplishment. Like the leaves on the trees, the summer "spirit of Geneva" withered with the autumn.

Revolt in the Soviet Bloc

Within the year, the Suez crisis and a revolt in Hungary shattered the rosy illusions about the "relaxation of tensions." Discontent within the Soviet bloc burst violently to the surface in 1956, but the first crack in the Iron Curtain had come in 1948 when Marshal Tito of Yugoslavia had broken with Stalin. Although Tito remained a staunch Communist and followed a policy of neutralism in the cold war, the United States sent him over $1 billion in military and economic aid to keep Yugoslavia independent of Russian control. The American policy appeared to bring results, particularly in August, 1954, when Yugoslavia signed a twenty-year alliance, known as the Balkan Pact, with Turkey and Greece, members of the North Atlantic Treaty.

The next crack in the Soviet bloc came after Stalin's successors had begun to relax some of his harsh controls over the captive countries of Eastern Europe. In June, 1953, the workers of East Berlin rioted against the Soviets and the revolt spread to other East German cities, but Soviet tanks and troops crushed the unarmed street fighters. Even though Dulles and Eisenhower had from the beginning of their administration pledged themselves to a policy of "liberation" of the peoples behind the Iron Curtain, the United States could do nothing to help the East Germans except to express sympathy and to commend their "heroic resistance."

Bulganin and Khrushchev nonetheless continued their softened policy toward the satellite countries and also attempted to conciliate Tito and bring "deviationist"

Yugoslavia back into the Soviet family circle. In May, 1955, they made a highly publicized visit to Yugoslavia and apologized for expelling Tito from the Communist family eight years earlier. A year later Tito visited Moscow and signed a joint declaration with the Soviets saying that Communist countries could choose their own paths to "socialism." This expression of harmony so alarmed Americans that Congress considered shutting off aid to Tito, but the policymakers regarded an independent, though Communist, Yugoslavia as too valuable an asset in the cold war to be abandoned. Eisenhower continued to give her limited aid.

The successful independence of Tito's Yugoslavia and the doctrine of "separate roads to socialism" encouraged other peoples of Eastern Europe to hope that they too might be able to remove Moscow's yoke. They were also stimulated by a secret speech made by Khrushchev in February, 1956, in which he attacked Stalin's brutal rule and the "cult of personality" associated with it, but did not renounce the principles underlying Stalin's policies. News of the speech leaked, and early in June the State Department released an apparently authentic text. Almost immediately some of the people in the satellite countries who had writhed helplessly under Stalinism began reappraising their relationship to the Soviet Union.

In Poland, in June, the workers in the industrial city of Poznan rioted against their Communist bosses and attacked Communist Party and police headquarters. In September the rioters received open and apparently fair trials, and under Wladyslaw Gomulka, a leader who insisted on a measure of autonomy within the Communist orbit, Poland won an unprecedented internal freedom for a satellite country. Poland did not repudiate Soviet friendship, for Gomulka stressed moderation and demanded only a limited national independence.

Hungary, moved by the same yearnings, did not stop half-way. In Budapest, on October 23, students began a national anti-Communist revolution. As the revolt spread, the Hungarians demanded not only freedom within the Communist camp but freedom from Communism as well. In November, they denounced the Warsaw Pact and appealed to the United Nations to help them defend their neutrality. That effort to escape from the Soviet bloc brought a massive invasion of Russian tanks and artillery. In one of the most heart-rending and unequal struggles in the twentieth century, young Hungarians, almost with bare hands, futilely fought the Soviet tanks block by block in battered Budapest. The Russians brutally crushed the rebellion and clamped a loyal Communist regime on Hungary.

Shocked and frustrated, Americans could do nothing to help the Hungarian "freedom fighters." Eisenhower, "in the name of humanity and in the cause of peace," pleaded with Bulganin to withdraw Soviet troops and accept Hungary's right to self-government, but Bulganin replied that Hungary's affairs were none of America's business.[26] Americans thought otherwise, but their leaders would not intervene at the risk of touching off a third world war.

Hungarians were bitterly disappointed. They had hoped for aid from the West in their fight for liberation. Critics, at home and abroad, accused the Eisenhower administration of recklessly inciting captive peoples to revolt only to face helpless slaughter. The President replied that the policy of "liberation" had never urged "any kind of armed revolt that could bring about disaster to our friends."[27] Yet American foreign policy suffered. Few could distinguish the difference between encouraging "peaceful liberation" and inciting rebellion.[28]

Russian foreign policy suffered a severe setback. Even "neutralists" could see that the Soviet system rested on force and tyranny.

NATO and the Threat of Soviet Technology

The Hungarian revolt and the general ferment in Eastern Europe had exposed the weakness of the Warsaw Pact and had shown that Russia could not rely on her satellites. At the same time, however, the Suez crisis had shaken the North Atlantic alliance to its roots. To mend that alliance and to restore cordial relations with the United States became the major objective of British and French statesmen at the beginning of 1957.

The *rapprochement* began with the visits to Washington of the British and French ministers of defense in January and February of that year. In March Britain's new Prime Minister, Harold Macmillan, conferred for two days with President Eisenhower in Bermuda. There the two leaders stressed the importance of European unity and the need to continue tests of nuclear weapons. In their official communiqué they announced a "missile agreement" whereby the United States would supply British forces with intermediate-range missiles.

Russia denounced the agreement and in the weeks following the Bermuda conference warned at least eight of the North Atlantic countries that they risked retaliation if they permitted missile bases on their soil. In particular, she threatened to turn West Germany into "one big cemetery" if the Germans accepted American missiles.

In its first years the North Atlantic alliance had been built on the assumption of deterring or meeting a massive Soviet land attack supported by air power, but now the danger appeared to be a long-range nuclear attack. Many Europeans doubted that the North Atlantic alliance could shield them against such an attack. They were alarmed, moreover, by American reliance on long-range nuclear weapons as a "deterrent." They feared that in case of a Russian invasion the United States might abandon Central Europe and fall back on Britain, Spain, or other remote bases to launch counterattacks.

Europe's fears increased when Britain announced a new defense policy similar to the American "new look." In a Defense White Paper released in April, 1957, she said she would reduce her armed forces on the continent in the interest of economy. In view of the new scientific advances in warfare, the British announced, the overwhelming need was "to prevent war rather than to prepare for it."[29] Henceforth, they would rely on the threat of retaliation with nuclear weapons for their defense.

Several months later, on October 4, the North Atlantic alliance suffered another jolt when Russia sent the world's first earth satellite, known as Sputnik I, whirling into outer space. That accomplishment, achieved before the United States had perfected its missiles, upset the balance of scientific power in the cold war and shook Europe's confidence in the pre-eminence of American technological and military might. The North Atlantic shield seemed less sturdy than ever. At the same time the Russians announced that they had successfully tested a "super-long distance intercontinental ballistic rocket" and on November 3 they launched Sputnik II, six times heavier than the first. Few could now doubt Russia's clear superiority in missile technology. Even Secretary Dulles said two days later that Russia had overcome the "preponderance of power" the United States had enjoyed a decade earlier.

A few weeks after the launching of Sputnik I, Macmillan visited the United States and conferred with Eisenhower. The two leaders issued a "Declaration of Common Purpose," saying that "the concept of national self-sufficiency is now out of date" and urged European unity.[30] The Macmillan mission helped restore the Anglo-American partnership to something of its old intimacy. Next, the North Atlantic alliance needed buttressing.

So urgent did the need seem that Eisenhower, despite the fact that he suffered a slight stroke on November 25, went to Paris for a "summit" meeting of the North Atlantic Council. There the United States urged the Western European Allies to accept missiles with nuclear warheads, as Britain had done at Bermuda, to keep NATO's strength intact. The United States, it seemed, wanted to use European bases and intermediate-range missiles to neutralize Russia's long-range missiles.

American statesmen won only partial acceptance of their program. Following their triumph in outer space, the Soviets adopted a tough and seemingly reckless policy of threats, "ballistic blackmail," some called it, against the North Atlantic Allies. America's European Allies, in fear of provoking the Russians, therefore showed considerable reluctance in agreeing to accept missiles. Instead, they urged a new negotiation with the Soviets for controlled disarmament. In the resulting compromise, the United States offered missiles to the Allies who could accept or reject them on an individual basis, and agreed to attempt to negotiate with the Russians. The Allies also agreed on the need to coordinate their manufacture of weapons and to pool their scientific and research programs.

The Berlin Crisis—1958

On November 10, 1958, Khrushchev suddenly announced that the Soviet Union had decided "to renounce the remnants of the occupation regime in Berlin."[31] In subsequent notes to the United States, Britain, and France on November 27, he demanded that they withdraw their occupation forces of some 10,000 men from West Berlin, declare it a demilitarized "free city," and negotiate directly with the East German government on terms of access to the city. He was willing to discuss the status of Berlin, but in any event, he said, if the Western powers did not make an agreement with the East Germans within six months the Soviet Union would give the "German Democratic Republic" control of the Western military supply routes to the city.

In January, 1959, Khrushchev suggested separate peace treaties for West and East Germany. If the Allies did not agree, he said later, Russia would make her own peace treaty with East Germany. Taken together, the Soviet demands sought to force the Western powers to leave Berlin, to recognize the East German government, to abandon their goal of a reunified Germany, and to accept the *status quo* in Eastern Europe favorable to the Soviet Union.

"We are most solemnly committed to hold West Berlin," Secretary Dulles said in his initial reaction to the first Communist demands, "if need be by military force."[32] Khrushchev responded that if the United States attacked the East Germans, Russia would retaliate. Both sides subsequently made it clear that the use of force would mean war.

Since the United States and its Allies did not recognize the East German regime, they had no agreement with it on their right of access to West Berlin. That right rested on four-power agreements concluded at the end of the Second World War that Khrushchev had renounced. Thus the Soviet moves endangered the Western supply routes to West Berlin and held the threat of a new blockade.

The United States denounced Russia's abrogation of her four-power commitment as violating pledges to support a unified Germany with Berlin as the capital. It opposed separate peace treaties because they would tend to insure the permanent partition of Germany. Only a free and united Germany, it insisted, could sign a peace treaty.

In arming West Germany, the Russians argued, the United States had violated its pledges of never again permitting Germany to become a military power. The separate peace treaties the Soviets had drafted called for a neutralized Germany, allowing that divided nation only enough arms to maintain internal security. If the United States accepted the Soviet demands, therefore, West Germany would have to withdraw from the North Atlantic Treaty and the defense structure of Western Europe would be in jeopardy.

Thus the Berlin question had expanded into a crisis that penetrated to the core of cold war issues in Europe. To counter the Russian moves, therefore, the United States and its Allies tried to formulate a strategy linking the Berlin question, German unification, and European security.

Seeking some basis for a negotiated settlement, Prime Minister Harold Macmillan took the initiative and finally persuaded President Eisenhower to agree to a summit meeting. Eisenhower insisted on two conditions, however: the meeting must be preceded by a conference of the Big Four foreign ministers that would prepare a basis for agreement, and the Soviets must withdraw their six-month ultimatum. The Russians denied that their Berlin demand was an ultimatum and Khrushchev said that even though he thought it better if "the heads of government, the heavyweights," would attack the issues at stake directly, he would accept a preliminary meeting of the foreign ministers.

At the same time the Berlin question caused a rift among the North Atlantic Allies. The British were willing to negotiate a new status for Berlin and recognize the East German government if the Soviets would guarantee the Western rights of access to the city. Chancellor Adenauer and President Charles de Gaulle of France, who had formed close political ties, on the other hand, opposed any yielding on Berlin unless the Soviets made a major concession on German unification.

Through American initiative the European Allies patched their quarrel, and before the foreign ministers met in Geneva in May, 1959, the Western powers had agreed on compromise tactics. They sought a step-by-step plan for German unification, with free elections coming last instead of first as the United States had always insisted in the past; proposed the limitation of armaments in a gradually expanded area of Central Europe, in addition to other measures for European security; and demanded guarantees for their freedom of access to West Berlin, with the maintenance of the *status quo* there until the city became the capital of a unified Germany.

The Russians, on the other hand, wanted to separate the problems of Berlin and a German peace treaty from the questions of German unification and European security. At the conference, the Western powers and the Soviets failed to close the gap between their views. On May 27, the date of Krushchev's Berlin deadline, the four foreign ministers interrupted their meeting to fly to Washington for former Secretary of State Dulles' funeral. Dulles had died of cancer three days before. When Secretary of State Christian A. Herter and the other ministers returned to Geneva, a stalemate awaited them. The conference broke up in August with the Soviet Foreign Minister stating that the West could continue its occupation for eighteen months while definitive arrangements were being worked out.

At the Vienna meeting in June, 1961, Khrushchev revived the Berlin crisis by repeating his demands of 1958 and setting a new deadline of six months for a settlement on the status of the city. President Kennedy, who called this the most "somber" aspect of his meeting with the Soviet premier, asserted that the United States and its Allies would take "any risk" in defending their rights in Berlin. In a television broadcast late in July, he told the nation that the United States must build its capacity to resist, but that he would also welcome negotiations with the Soviets. "We do not want to fight," he said, "but we have fought before."

With the support of Congress, the President augmented the military budget with more than three billion dollars, expanded the authorized strength of the armed forces, and called reservists to active duty. Khrushchev increased his military spending and built up the Red army.

At the same time, Soviet belligerence sent a flow of East Germans into West Berlin that became a flood of more than 2000 per day early in August. Finally, to stop this record flight from Communist rule, the Communists at 2:00 a.m. on August 13 began sealing off the border between East and West Berlin. They started with barbed wire and ended with a concrete block wall, *Die Mauer*, the Germans called it, twenty-eight miles long. The flow of refugees from the East first receded to a trickle and then practically stopped.

Khrushchev pressed for negotiations on Soviet terms, and Kennedy agreed to preliminary talks on the foreign minister level. In September, however, he rejected a plea from leaders of neutralist nations for a summit conference with Khrushchev on the Berlin question. Like Eisenhower before him, Kennedy said the United States would not negotiate with the Soviet Union under "ultimata or threats."

A month later, on October 17, in a speech before the twenty-second congress of the Soviet Communist Party, Khrushchev withdrew the six-month deadline he had fixed for a settlement, but insisted that the Western Allies must negotiate and did not alter his terms for an agreement. Neither side had retreated and the Berlin crisis continued, but the heat had been taken off. With the Communist wall still standing, now a frustrating symbol of a divided Germany, the American Ambassador in Moscow in the early months of 1962 held probing talks with the Soviets on the Berlin issue.

The wall itself became the backdrop to violence and death as refugees attempted to crash through it or scale it and East German police fired on them. In some instances, as the shots sprayed into West Berlin, West German police returned the fire, and there was always danger of war through accident or miscalculation. In an effort to overcome the crisis, the United States in April, 1962, suggested a plan to its Allies that would have placed an international authority of thirteen nations in control of the Western access routes to Berlin. Since the Soviets showed no interest in the plan, it was shelved.

In August, as incidents increased and tension mounted, the Russians closed the office of their Commandant in East Berlin and turned over his duties to an East German Communist. This was another move to force the West to deal with the

East Germans. On August 24, the United States, Britain, and France sent formal notes to Moscow repeating a suggestion they had made in June for four-power discussions to ease the tension in Berlin. The Soviets publicly rejected such consultations, but when the United States repeated the suggestion three days later the Soviets privately expressed interest.

The Quest for Disarmament

During this period of fruitless wrangling over the Berlin question, relations with Russia regarding disarmament were as strained as at any time in the postwar era. As Americans had expected, the road to negotiation with the Russians over disarmament proved rocky. The Soviet leaders persistently demanded a summit conference to deal with European problems and disarmament. "You say you do not want to attack us. We do not want to attack you," Khrushchev remarked in urging a summit meeting. "Why don't we then get together and put that on paper?" [33]

The United States wanted more than paper promises. Remembering the deceptive "spirit of Geneva" of 1955, the President and his advisers were reluctant to go to the summit merely to satisfy Soviet propaganda. But, Eisenhower said, he would go if a conference of Big Four foreign ministers prepared the way beforehand and thus assured positive results.

In February, 1958, Poland's Foreign Minister, Adam Rapacki, advanced a plan, supported by the Soviets, calling for a zone in Central Europe to be kept free of nuclear weapons. The United States rejected the Rapacki Plan. Dulles pointed out that the zone, comprising Poland, Czechoslovakia, and the two Germanies, "would perpetuate the basic cause of tension in Europe by accepting the continuation of the division of Germany." [34] In view of Russia's large military forces and long-range weapons, Dulles and Eisenhower both said, such a small nuclear-free zone would add nothing to the security of Western Europe. [35]

In dismay, men of all nations watched the vast race in nuclear weapons and missiles. Many of them, including the leaders of "neutralist" nations such as Jawaharlal Nehru of India, were also alarmed by the testing of nuclear weapons by the United States, Russia, and Britain. Those men were convinced that the radioactive fallout from the tests endangered all mankind and must be stopped before it did irreparable harm.

Seemingly in response to the world-wide desire, the Soviet Union after completing a series of test explosions announced in March, 1958, that it was suspending further testing of nuclear weapons. It asked the United States and Britain to join the suspension and suggested an international agreement banning future tests.

Although Secretary Dulles called the suspension a "gimmick" and propaganda, the Soviet action was popular and placed the United States on the defensive.

Several weeks later, therefore, the United States and Britain suggested that their scientists join Soviet scientists in ascertaining whether or not nuclear tests could be detected. The Soviets accepted, and in July and August technicians from both sides of the Iron Curtain conferred in Geneva. They agreed in principle that tests could be discovered through a world-wide system of detection stations.

Early in May the United States, through the United Nations, had advanced a plan of its own calling for an international inspection zone in the arctic to guard against a "massive surprise attack" by either Russians or Americans. The Soviets vetoed it. They objected because the Soviet territory subject to inspection would be larger than the American. Basically, since the Russians feared an attack from Central Europe most and the United States dreaded an arctic attack, the Soviet and American plans were irreconcilable.

On August 22, President Eisenhower announced that the United States would suspend its testing of nuclear weapons for one year if the Soviets continued their ban and would agree to negotiate an agreement on the effective control of future tests. The Soviets agreed to negotiate but late in September resumed testing with the most concentrated series of nuclear explosions held anywhere up to that time. Nonetheless, the United States said it would carry out its promise as of October 31, when negotiations with the Russians would begin, but warned the Soviets it would resume testing if they did not stop theirs.

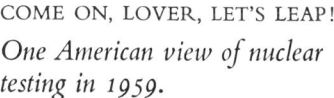

COME ON, LOVER, LET'S LEAP!
One American view of nuclear testing in 1959.

The three-power conference on the "Discontinuance of Nuclear Weapons Tests" opened as scheduled in Geneva. Americans hoped it would produce a political agreement on the control of nuclear testing that would lead to broader agreements on general disarmament. After three years of interrupted negotiation and 353 fruitless sessions, the conference brought about agreement on minor matters but no final understanding. As far as the United States was concerned, the crucial issue was the Soviet demand, in various guises, for the right of veto over inspection teams which would investigate suspected violations of any ban, a right it would not allow. The United States and Britain, the other conference member, furnished evidence that underground tests could be concealed. They insisted that all "seismic events," therefore, must be investigated. The Soviets argued that the West wished to use free inspection of suspected explosions as a subterfuge for espionage.[36]

Despite the lack of progress in the nuclear test negotiations, the Big Four foreign ministers decided in September, 1959, to establish a Disarmament Commission, supported by the United Nations and representing ten nations, to study general disarmament, actually to negotiate a means of limiting armaments under an effective system of international control. So pressing did the United States consider the disarmament question that it agreed, as it had refused to do in the past, to parity for the Soviet bloc with the Western nations. The commission, therefore, was composed of five members from the West—United States, Britain, France, Italy, and Canada—and five from the East—Russia, Bulgaria, Czechoslovakia, Poland, and Rumania. Negotiations began in March, 1960, in Geneva and broke down in June when the Communist bloc delegates accused the Westerners of bad faith and walked out.

Those talks revealed no basic change in the positions of the Soviet Union and the United States. The Soviets desired general and total disarmament within a few years, but advanced no system of effective control. As a first step they demanded the dismantling of all foreign military bases, meaning that they wished the United States to withdraw from Europe and other strategic areas. The United States urged gradual step-by-step disarmament, with each step dependent on successful completion of the preceding one. General disarmament agreements would come only when this process was well-advanced. The United States stressed measures that would prevent a surprise attack and narrow the danger of a missile war.

Later in 1960, the Russians added new obstacles to the renewal of negotiations by insisting that the ten-nation group must be enlarged with five members from the neutralist states. In effect, they wanted acceptance of the *troika* principle, which called for an executive composed of three representatives, one each from the West, the Soviet bloc, and the neutralist group, to supervise any test-ban agreement. Since this body would require unanimous agreement before it could act, the Soviets would have a veto over any inspection for violation of the ban.

The Spirit of Camp David

In July, 1959, Vice-President Nixon visited the Soviet Union to open an American exhibition in Moscow as a good will gesture and to reciprocate a recent visit by First Deputy Premier Frol R. Kozlov who opened a Soviet exhibition in New York. The outstanding feature of Nixon's trip was his impromptu television debate with Khrushchev in the kitchen of the so-called typical American home at the Moscow exhibit. More important, Nixon left Moscow convinced that Khrushchev held serious misconceptions about the United States and might profit from a firsthand view of American conditions.

At the same time, even though the Foreign Ministers' Conference of the summer of 1959 had produced no basis for a summit meeting and the Soviets had not removed the menace from their demand on Berlin, the President felt that the Berlin crisis was so pressing that it needed discussion on the highest level. In July, therefore, he invited Khrushchev to visit the United States and expressed willing-

THE SPIRIT OF CAMP DAVID, SEPTEMBER, 1959

ness to travel to the Soviet Union in return. To avoid the appearance of a retreat before Soviet pressure, the administration insisted that Khrushchev's visit would not be a trip to the summit, that Eisenhower did not intend to negotiate with him, and that the only purpose of the invitation was "to melt a little of the ice" of the cold war.[37]

This reversal in Eisenhower's policy required explanations to startled European Allies, particularly to de Gaulle and Adenauer. De Gaulle, who earlier in the year had become the powerful president of France's Fifth Republic, was determined to enhance France's international status by making her an independent nuclear power and by obtaining a larger role for her in NATO's councils. He demanded, in fact, that the United States, Britain, and France form a directorate within NATO that would give France equal status with Britain in shaping the global policies of the Western Allies. When he failed to gain the increased influence he desired, de Gaulle refused to permit the United States to establish NATO missile bases on French soil, as Britain and Italy had, or to stockpile nuclear weapons there. This, of course, struck at Allied unity.[38]

To attempt to reinforce this unity and to discuss France's concerns, Eisenhower visited Europe late in August and September. He went to West Germany where he talked with Adenauer, then to Paris where he met with de Gaulle and also conferred with Italy's Premier, Antonio Segni. Eisenhower assured his Allies that Khrushchev's visit marked no break in the basic continuity of American policy in Europe, but he did not succeed in overcoming the difficulties with France.

Khrushchev arrived in the United States on September 15, less than forty-eight hours after Russia's second planetary rocket, Lunik II, had scored a direct hit on the moon. Basking in the glow of this scientific triumph, he insisted that capitalism and Communism could peacefully coexist. Three days later he addressed the General Assembly of the United Nations in New York where he unwrapped a sensational plan for universal and total disarmament in four years. It gained approval in other parts of the world, but in the United States it was looked upon as an old Soviet idea in new clothes, basically a propaganda gesture.

Propaganda was also the key word in Khrushchev's spectacular pilgrimage from Washington to New York, Los Angeles, San Francisco, Des Moines, and Pittsburgh, and then the return for final talks with the President at Camp David, Maryland. There he waived a time limit for negotiations on Berlin. This cleared the way for a summit meeting of the Big Four that the Soviet leader desired. In explaining the agreement, the President said that "we now can negotiate . . . without an axe hanging over our heads."[39] Since the Eisenhower-Khrushchev agreement pushed the idea of war over Berlin into the background of cold war issues, the Russians spoke of the "Spirit of Camp David," but neither side had retreated on fundamental issues.

В З Л Е Т...   **...И ПОСАДКА.**

Рис. Ю. Черепанова.

TAKE OFF ... AND LANDING

A Soviet view of the U-2 episode by Yu. Cherepanov, published in "Pravda," May 9, 1960.

The U-2 Fiasco

President de Gaulle had persuaded the Allies to postpone the Big Four summit meeting until the spring of 1960. To fix the date for that conference and to decide on a joint Western policy, Eisenhower again traveled to Europe in December. This time he visited three other NATO countries, Italy, Turkey, and Greece, and held a Western summit meeting in Paris with Macmillan, de Gaulle, and Adenauer. They decided on Paris as the place for meeting Khrushchev and ultimately May 16 as the date. As further preparation, de Gaulle visited the United States in April, where he made a coast-to-coast tour.

Before the summit meeting could take place, the careful preparations were shattered by a new crisis. On May 1, over Sverdlovsk, some 1300 miles within the Soviet Union, a high-flying American plane, called the U-2, was brought down. The administration reacted to this news, announced by Khrushchev on May 5, by saying that a weather plane was missing and may have strayed into Russia. The State Department denied any deliberate attempt to violate Soviet borders.

Then Khrushchev sprang his trap. He called the American version of the flight a lie, said that the pilot, Francis G. Powers, was alive and had confessed to espionage,

THE ALBATROSS

The impact of the U-2 episode on the summit conference, 1960.

and that photographic equipment on the plane had been recovered with exposed shots of Soviet military installations. Secretary of State Herter then compounded the blunders by admitting that American planes had been flying into Russia for several years and implied that they would continue to do so. Khrushchev countered with a warning that foreign bases used by the United States for spying missions would be showered with rockets, a threat later supported by a military order to Soviet missile installations.[40] President Eisenhower, in an action unprecedented in espionage cases, finally assumed personal responsibility for the spy flights and left for the Paris summit.

At Paris, Khrushchev destroyed the summit meeting in three hours. He demanded that the United States call off all flights over Russia, apologize for past "aggressions," and punish those responsible for them. Furious over Khrushchev's harsh language, Eisenhower said the U-2 flights had been suspended and would not be resumed, but rejected the other terms which would, in effect, have caused him to punish himself. Khrushchev then suggested that the summit meeting be postponed for six to eight months and culminated his attack on the President by withdrawing his invitation for the visit to Russia, scheduled for June.

Few could deny that the Soviet Union had initially won a great propaganda victory, for the borders of a sovereign state had been illegally violated. Any government, certainly the American one, would have been furious under similar circumstances. Yet Khrushchev dissipated his advantage by his personal abuse of Eisenhower. Thus the U-2 episode and the Paris summit marked another crisis, one that saw the relative calm of Camp David turned into a storm.[41]

The Election of 1960

In September, 1960, Khrushchev visited the Fifteenth General Assembly of the United Nations in New York, one distinguished by the attendance of more than a score of heads of state and government. He denounced the United States, gave off-the-cuff interviews to reporters from the balcony of the Russian embassy, thumped his desk at the United Nations when he was displeased, and at one time even removed his shoe to bang the desk.

These antics filled the headlines in the midst of a presidential campaign that had foreign policy as its focal point. Both Nixon and Kennedy campaigned on the issue of who could best stand up to the tough, thumping Khrushchev. The campaign also stressed such points as whether or not the United States had lost prestige abroad during the Eisenhower years and whether or not there was a "missile gap." Critics of the administration said that the Soviet lead in intercontinental ballistic missiles neutralized America's long-range bombers capable of delivering nuclear bombs. Republicans denied that there was a gap between Soviet and American nuclear potential.

Kennedy won the election and inherited whatever gap there was. His eloquent inaugural address, devoted almost entirely to foreign affairs, underscored the perilous international situation. His most quoted words, "Let us never negotiate out of fear. But let us never fear to negotiate," indicated that he would seek to alleviate cold war tensions at the conference table.[42]

On April 12, 1961, before the new President could negotiate with the Russians, he was dramatically reminded of their massive lead in missile boosters. On that day the Soviets made a spectacular space accomplishment; they launched the first man into space and retrieved him unharmed. Flight Major Yuri A. Gagarin, the twenty-seven-year-old son of a peasant, circled the earth in 108 minutes. Khrushchev left no doubt that it was another Soviet cold war victory. In congratulating the young cosmonaut, he said, "Let the capitalist countries try to catch up with our country."[43]

The United States tried. On May 5 it hurled Navy Commander Alan B. Shepard to an altitude of 115 miles in fifteen minutes and recovered him unharmed, but on August 7 the Soviets sent a man orbiting the earth seventeen times in 25.3 hours and recovered him. Finally, on February 20, 1962, a Lieutenant Colonel of the Marine Corps, John H. Glenn, Jr., circled the earth three times in 4.9 hours and returned. His flight gave Americans a psychological lift and renewed confidence in their ability to compete in the space race.

The Vienna Meeting

In the interim, so powerful did the Soviet position seem and so pressing its probing of Western defenses that Secretary of State Dean Rusk told a meeting of NATO foreign ministers at Oslo in May, 1961, that there were no longer any peripheral areas in the cold war and that the North Atlantic Allies must accept world-wide responsibilities. The Allies agreed. This, however, was not enough. Kennedy decided that he must talk to Khrushchev, even though he had previously opposed a summit meeting, to try to stem a sharp, even dangerous, deterioration in relations with the Soviets. He made arrangements to see the Russian after a visit with de Gaulle in Paris early in June.

In his three days with the French president, Kennedy took a partial step toward meeting de Gaulle's desire for a greater role in the Western alliance. He assured de Gaulle of closer consultation in the future on issues concerning the Allies. The French president, in turn, seemingly went out of his way to play down differences with the United States.

KHRUSHCHEV AND KENNEDY: VIENNA, 1961

From Paris, Kennedy flew directly to Vienna to confront Khrushchev. Like Eisenhower before him, he stressed that this was not a formal summit conference and that he would not negotiate. Yet the President and the Soviet dictator discussed, in blunt conversations covering two days, all of the major issues of the cold war. Khrushchev gave no ground on the *troika* issue or nuclear testing itself. He indicated little interest in an agreement forbidding nuclear tests unless it were part of a larger one on general disarmament. He suggested, in fact, that the two Geneva negotiations be merged. No agreement was reached, though Khrushchev said he was pleased with the talks as forming a good beginning toward an improvement in relations with the United States.

From Vienna, Kennedy flew to London where he talked with Macmillan and brought him up to date on the latest in relations with the Soviets. Like de Gaulle, Macmillan reaffirmed Allied unity and said that the West must withstand Soviet pressure on Berlin. Thus Kennedy's first trip to the summit brought no change to the positions already established in the cold war.

There was concern, in the United States and elsewhere, that without some formal agreement prohibiting testing at least, the production of nuclear weapons would spread to other nations and would shortly be beyond control. France had exploded a nuclear device in the Sahara in February, 1960, and later had tested others. Communist China, it was feared, was destined to become the next nuclear power.

France's entrance into what was called the nuclear club was not greeted happily by the United States. By law the United States could share nuclear secrets only with Britain among its Allies. To cut costs in their nuclear effort, the French, too, desired American assistance and could not understand America's refusal to aid one ally while helping the other. President de Gaulle, therefore, was determined to develop an independent nuclear deterrent of his own. He worked out a close relationship with West Germany to counterbalance the Anglo-American bloc in the Western alliance, and advanced the idea of a European "Third Force" in world politics, led by France and West Germany. This new force, armed with atomic weapons, would stand between what he called the "Anglo-Saxons" and Russia. Military autonomy, de Gaulle insisted, was the prerequisite to political autonomy, and of course, to French diplomatic equality with the United States and Britain in world councils.

Americans argued that France's desire for an independent nuclear force could only lead to the proliferation of nuclear weapons among many nations.[44] Furthermore, as Secretary of Defense Robert S. McNamara warned in June, 1962, independent nuclear forces such as France was building would be too small to be effective deterrents, and if used against Russia would be tantamount to suicide. Since de Gaulle could not be swayed by such reasoning, the United States switched to the idea of placing the French nuclear force under some form of Allied control.

This, it was thought, might help prevent the start of a nuclear war the United States would have to finish.

This new policy struck many Europeans, particularly the French and Germans, as illogical. Under this plan, it was pointed out, the United States would have everything its own way; it would have a veto over Europe's nuclear force but would be free to use its own nuclear power without the restriction of a European veto.

France's nuclear capability, her efforts to maintain an independent foreign policy, and American resistance to such desires shook the North Atlantic alliance. France's attitude, shared in part at least, by West Germany was another indication that Europe was no longer completely dependent on the United States, economically or militarily. That attitude, nonetheless, added new danger to the nuclear arms race.

The Spiraling Nuclear Arms Race

On September 1, 1961, Russia broke the informal moratorium on nuclear tests with an explosion over central Asia. President Kennedy denounced the Soviet action as "atomic blackmail," and the peoples of the world reacted as if they had suffered a sudden chill. Before completing their series of tests in November, the Soviets set off some fifty explosions totaling 120 megatons, thereby increasing radioactive contamination of the atmosphere by half. This two-month series, moreover, included the explosion of a 58-megaton bomb over the arctic, a bomb 3000 times as powerful as that which destroyed Hiroshima in 1945. This was the most awesome explosion ever set off by man.

The Soviet tests led to the suspension of the Geneva test-ban talks on September 8. They were renewed in November through American and British initiative and as a result of the pressure of world opinion. Nonetheless, the talks quickly collapsed because, as charged by the United States, Russia refused all proposals for effective international control. At one point the Russians even turned down what they themselves had previously proposed. They refused an American and British offer to merge the test-ban negotiations with those at a new general disarmament conference of eighteen nations—five Western, five from the Communist bloc, and eight from the neutral group—which was sponsored by the General Assembly of the United Nations and scheduled to meet in Geneva on March 14, 1962.[45]

President Kennedy was deeply concerned over the failure of the test-ban talks. Their collapse, he told a news conference, "represented the biggest disappointment of my first year in office." The Soviet tests, moreover, had placed him under immediate pressure to resume American testing, which he did at first with a few underground explosions in Nevada in September, 1961.

Tensions in the cold war fluctuated for the remainder of the year, but in February, 1962, a thaw appeared when the Soviets exchanged U-2 pilot, Francis G.

Powers, who was convicted of espionage and imprisoned in Russia, for a Soviet spy who had been imprisoned in the United States since 1957. Despite this seeming thaw, Kennedy resisted pressure from Khrushchev for another meeting at the summit, particularly a summit meeting of eighteen nations at the Geneva disarmament conference in March. The President demanded progress at a lower level, primarily in a conference of foreign ministers, before he would again participate in a summit meeting.

Then, in a television broadcast to the nation on March 2, 1962, Kennedy announced that the Soviet tests of September, 1961, had threatened American security and that the United States therefore would resume nuclear tests in the air in April unless the Soviets signed a "firm agreement" prohibiting tests. Negotiations concerning the agreement, he said, could be held at the general disarmament conference in Geneva.

The Soviets backed down from their demand for a summit meeting and the disarmament conference at Geneva opened on schedule, with the foreign ministers of the major powers in attendance, but with only seventeen nations participating. France boycotted the gathering on the ground that the Soviet Union interpreted Western eagerness to negotiate as weakness. The Soviets did discuss the banning of nuclear tests, but the conference itself made no progress. Khrushchev again rejected Western proposals for international inspection and control of armaments, repeating that Russia would not allow "unhindered espionage" over her territory. He insisted on the Soviet version of total disarmament and also announced that Russia would match all nuclear explosions by the West.

After a last appeal to the Soviets for an agreement to end the spiraling nuclear arms race, the United States resumed nuclear testing in the atmosphere on April 25, 1962, in the vicinity of Britain's Christmas Island. This was the first of some thirty tests.

Since the negotiators at Geneva accomplished nothing, they took a month's vacation beginning on June 15. Early in August the United States scaled down its demands for international control over any test-ban agreement, but did not abandon all controls. New evidence indicated that many more underground nuclear explosions could be detected and distinguished than had previously been considered possible. Nonetheless, Russia rejected the American proposal.

On August 5, Khrushchev carried out his earlier threat by resuming tests with a 30-megaton explosion in the arctic. Three weeks later the United States and Britain offered the Soviet Union a choice between a total test-ban treaty with international inspection and an uninspected limited ban while negotiations continued. The Soviets rejected the proposals.

At the same time, the race in missile technology lent a new sense of urgency to plans for control of armaments. On May 24, 1962, the United States had launched its third astronaut, who completed three orbits around the earth. This feat was eclipsed by the Soviets on August 11 and 12 when they sent two cosmonauts into almost identical orbits. One cosmonaut circled the earth 64 times and the other completed 48 orbits. This accomplishment, the most impressive yet in outer space, not only sent Russian scientific prestige soaring but also confirmed Soviet superiority in the space race. Clearly, Soviet missile scientists had mastered the technology of delivering nuclear weapons over vast spaces with deadly accuracy.

The arms race, in its various manifestations, had thus picked up speed with immeasurable danger to mankind. In the year following Russia's breaking of the moratorium on nuclear tests, the Soviet Union and the United States had unchained much more nuclear power in test explosions than in any of the preceding sixteen years of the atomic age. In Geneva the disarmament conference had deadlocked on the same issues as its predecessors, but the nuclear powers continued to discuss the test-ban problem. As for the nuclear arms race, after seventeen years of proposing and arguing various forms of disarmament the United States and the Soviet Union had gotten no further than to agree that the limitation of armaments was desirable. By almost any standard, this is a dismal record of negotiation.[46]

NOTES

1. Quoted in Richard P. Stebbins, *The United States in World Affairs, 1949* (New York, 1950), p. 111.

2. May 19, 1950, quoted in Richard P. Stebbins, *The United States in World Affairs, 1950* (New York, 1951), p. 143.

3. Acheson to Truman, Sept. 15, 1950, in Harry S. Truman, *Memoirs* (2 vols., Garden City, N.Y., 1955), II, 254. It was Acheson who at this time, despite French and Belgian objections, persuaded NATO to rearm the Germans. See Roger Hilsman, "NATO: The Developing Strategic Context," in Klaus Knorr, ed., *NATO and American Security* (Princeton, 1959), p. 18.

4. For an analysis of the German view, see Gordon A. Craig, "Germany and NATO: The Rearmament Debate, 1950–1958," *ibid.*, pp. 236–259.

5. Jan. 8, 1951, *Congressional Record*, 82nd Congress, 1 sess., p. 99.

6. Quoted in Norman A. Graebner, *The New Isolationism: A Study in Politics and Foreign Policy Since 1950* (New York, 1956), p. 131.

7. The slogans are quoted in Walter Millis, *Arms and Men: A Study in American Military History* (New York, 1956), pp. 338–340.

8. May 11, 1953, quoted in Richard P. Stebbins, *The United States in World Affairs, 1953* (New York, 1955), pp. 133–134.

9. Dec. 14, 1953, quoted in Robert E. Osgood, *NATO: The Entangling Alliance* (Chicago, 1962), p. 95. "Agonizing reappraisal" became one of the grandiloquent phrases of the 1950's. See Roscoe Drummond and Gaston Coblentz, *Duel at the Brink: John Foster Dulles' Command of American Power* (New York, 1960), p. 85. Churchill called the phrase "most formidable."

10. Quoted in Robert J. Donovan, *Eisenhower: The Inside Story* (New York, 1956), p. 309.

11. Oct. 25, 1954, quoted in Richard P. Stebbins, *The United States in World Affairs, 1954* (New York, 1956), p. 150.

12. Oct. 28, 1954, *ibid.*, p. 163.

13. Eisenhower to Dulles, April 15, 1955, *Department of State Bulletin*, XXXII (May 2, 1955), 716.

14. Jan. 11, 1956, quoted in Richard P. Stebbins, *The United States in World Affairs, 1956* (New York, 1957), p. 259. In analyzing the American and Soviet aid programs, Lucian W. Pye, in "Soviet and American Styles in Foreign Aid," *Orbis*, IV (Summer 1960), 159–173, points out that the outstanding characteristic of Soviet aid is its emphasis on the political goal.

15. Quoted in Stebbins, *U.S. in World Affairs, 1954*, p. 79. For Clarence B. Randall's own ideas, see his *A Foreign Economic Policy for the United States* (Chicago, 1954).

16. Ultimately every major trading nation outside the Communist bloc associated itself with GATT. For more details, see Raymond Vernon, *America's Foreign Trade Policy and the GATT* (Princeton, 1957).

17. To William F. Knowland, Jan. 25, 1954, in Donovan, *Eisenhower*, p. 239. Eisenhower's efforts to reach a compromise with Bricker are explained in Sherman Adams, *Firsthand Report: The Story of the Eisenhower Administration* (New York, 1961), pp. 104–110.

18. Quoted in Donovan, *Eisenhower*, p. 241.

19. Isolationists brought out another version of the amendment in 1956. See Selig Adler, *The Isolationist Impulse* (New York, 1957), pp. 451–452.

20. Arthur P. Whitaker, *Spain and Defense of the West: Ally and Liability* (New York, 1961), pp. 44–48. Objectives of U.S. policy toward Spain are summarized on pp. 82–83.

21. For a brief history of efforts at economic integration that preceded the Common Market, see Leopold Kohr, "The History of the Common Market," *The Journal of Economic History*, XX (Sept. 1960), 441–454. For an analysis of the movement toward European unity, 1950–1960, which stresses partnership with the United States, see Jean Monnet, "Economic Integration: New Forms of Partnership," in Carnegie Endowment for International Peace, *Perspectives on Peace, 1910–1960* (New York, 1960), pp. 97–106.

22. For a detailed analysis, see Miriam Camps, "Britain, the Six and American Policy," *Foreign Affairs*, XXXIX (Oct. 1960), 112–122. Emile Benoit, in *Europe at Sixes and Sevens: The Common Market, The Free Trade Association, and the United States* (New York, 1961), p. 84, points out that the F.T.A. had been deliberately constructed to avoid any tie-in with the political unification of Europe. The OECD was formally launched on Sept. 30, 1961. See Richard P. Stebbins, *The United States in World Affairs, 1961* (New York, 1962), p. 151.

23. The balance of payments problem and gold drain is analyzed in Benoit, *Europe at Sixes and Sevens*, pp. 123–137. For an analysis of the dollar crisis by a group of experts, see Seymour E. Harris, ed., *The Dollar in Crisis* (New York, 1962).

24. For details, see Joseph P. Morray, *From Yalta to Disarmament: Cold War Debate* (New York, 1961), pp. 231–247.

25. The quotations are in Hollis W. Barber, *The United States in World Affairs, 1955* (New York, 1957), p. 64.

26. Nov. 4, 1956, quoted in Richard P. Stebbins, *U.S. in World Affairs, 1956*, p. 348.

27. Nov. 14, 1956, *ibid.*, p. 306. In his analysis of American policy toward Hungary, Denna F. Fleming, in *The Cold War and Its Origins, 1917–1960* (2 vols., Garden City, N.Y., 1961), II, 806–814, blames the "liberation" campaign for part of the tragedy.

28. In *A History of the Cold War* (New York, 1961), p. 135, John A. Lukacs suggests that by their actions Dulles and Eisenhower showed they considered Suez more important than Eastern Europe. World attention was so overwhelmingly on the Suez crisis that what was happening in Hungary was not made

clear and its full significance not understood. See Wilbur Schramm, ed., *One Day in the World's Press: Fourteen Great Newspapers on a Day of Crisis, November 2, 1956* (Stanford, Calif., 1959), p. 138.

29. Quoted in Richard P. Stebbins, *The United States in World Affairs, 1957* (New York, 1958), p. 95.

30. The text is in *Department of State Bulletin*, XXXVII (Nov. 11, 1957), 739–741.

31. Quoted in Edgar McInnis, Richard Hiscocks, and Robert Spencer, *The Shaping of Postwar Germany* (New York, 1960), p. 142.

32. News conference of Nov. 7, 1958, *Department of State Bulletin*, XXXIX (Nov. 24, 1958), 813. The first demand that the Westerners get out of Berlin had been made by the East Germans on October 27.

33. Jan. 27, 1958, *The New York Times*, Jan. 28, 1958, 1: 7.

34. For Rapacki's note and memorandum of July 17, 1958, see *ibid.*, Feb. 18, 1958, 6: 3–6. Rapacki first presented his plan to the UN in October, 1957; see Osgood, *NATO*, p. 309n.

35. In a provocative series of lectures, George F. Kennan, in *Russia, the Atom and the West* (New York, 1958), p. 61, advanced the idea of disengagement, similar to Rapacki's, calling for the withdrawal of American, British, and Russian armed forces from the heart of Europe.

36. The Soviet position, based on resistance to outside control, is summarized in Joseph L. Nogee, *Soviet Policy towards International Control of Atomic Energy* (Notre Dame, Ind., 1961), pp. 201–227. For a detailed analysis of the work of the experts at Geneva, see Robert Gilpin, *American Scientists and Nuclear Weapons Policy* (Princeton, 1962), pp. 186 *ff.*

37. The quotation belongs to Eisenhower and is in Richard P. Stebbins, *The United States in World Affairs, 1959* (New York, 1960), p. 30.

38. For relations with de Gaulle's republic, see Edgar S. Furniss, *France: Troubled Ally* (New York, 1960), pp. 474-492.

39. Oct. 28, 1959, quoted in Stebbins, *U.S. in World Affairs, 1959*, p. 164.

40. Richard P. Stebbins, *The United States in World Affairs, 1960* (New York, 1961), p. 90. For Herter's statement, see Fleming, *Cold War Origins*, II, 1004. For a popular analysis, see David Wise and Thomas B. Ross, *The U-2 Affair* (New York, 1962).

41. Eisenhower believed that Khrushchev had planned to wreck the summit conference and withdraw the invitation before the U-2 was brought down, for the Soviets had known of the high altitude flights at the time of the Camp David meeting and had not made an issue of them. See Adams, *Firsthand Report*, p. 455.

42. The text of the inaugural address, Jan. 20, 1961, is in *Vital Speeches*, XXVII (Feb. 1, 1961), 226–227.

43. *The New York Times,* April 16, 1961, IV, 1: 3.

44. For an analysis of the problem of "nuclear diffusion," see Osgood, *NATO*, pp. 212–274.

45. For background details, see Stebbins, *U.S. in World Affairs, 1961*, pp. 109–110.

46 Fifteen years of this record are summarized in Bernhard G. Bechhoefer, *Postwar Negotiations for Arms Control* (Washington, 1961).

Chapter Thirty

EMERGENCE OF AFRO-ASIAN NATIONALISM

Aᴌᴛʜᴏᴜɢʜ American foreign policy concerned itself mainly with the Soviet Union and related problems in the years after the Second World War, a unique feature of that era was the nationalist awakening of the Asian and African peoples. When the war began, large parts of the world were still under the political or economic control of European peoples, notably most of Africa, Southeast Asia, and sections of the Middle East. The war broke the grip of the Europeans on their colonies and destroyed white prestige. In Asia and the islands of the Pacific, the Japanese had evicted the whites, including Americans, had presented themselves as a kindred people, and had trumpeted the slogan of "Asia for Asians." That slogan had far greater appeal to the colonials than anything the Europeans had offered.

After their defeat, the Japanese left behind them tough nationalist movements which made it virtually impossible for the European colonial powers in Asia to regain their old dominance.[1] Those movements shared a double aspiration. They sought to destroy almost every form of white control and to achieve political independence. In part, the civil war in China and the Korean struggle for independence and unity reflected this anti-imperialist nationalism.

When the Europeans tried to reassert their former control, the result was more than a decade of unprecedented upheaval. Almost everywhere they met a fierce resistance, a deep yearning for self-determination that revolutionized the relations between white and colored peoples. This yearning has been described as the revolution of rising expectations.[2]

Unlike its European Allies, the United States sympathized with the nationalist yearnings of the colonials. Viewing the triumph of colored nationalism as inevitable, Americans urged the Europeans not to fight the nationalist movements but to meet them gracefully. The alternative, Americans pointed out, was unrest and violence that would threaten peace throughout the world.

In the early postwar years, as a result, it seemed as though the United States would become a champion of anticolonialism.[3] "I had always been opposed to colonialism," Harry Truman wrote. "I still believed in Woodrow Wilson's philosophy of 'self-determination.'"[4] Relations with the Philippines demonstrated America's sympathy for Asian nationalism, relations which many Americans believed should serve as an example for the colonial powers of Europe.

Independence for the Philippines

When the Japanese conquered the Philippines, they granted those islands a nominal independence and organized a puppet government there. The top leaders of the Philippine Commonwealth fled to the United States and formed a government-in-exile. During the war the United States treated this government as a partner, virtually as that of an independent people. To stiffen Filipino resistance to the Japanese, President Roosevelt several times promised full independence as soon as the Japanese were defeated. "I give the Filipino people my word," he said in 1943, "that the Republic of the Philippines will be established the moment the power of our Japanese enemies is destroyed."[5] By a joint resolution, approved in June, 1944, Congress reaffirmed the pledge and authorized the President to proclaim independence prior to July 4, 1946, the date set by the Tydings-McDuffie Act.

Although President Truman did not act as promptly as Roosevelt had promised the United States would, he went ahead with plans for Philippine independence. Before proclaiming it, he waited for a series of laws defining the relations between the new republic and the United States.

One of these, the Bell Act, or Philippine Trade Act of April, 1946, set the terms for commercial relations with the infant nation and tied it to the American economy. That law called for free trade for eight years followed by a gradually rising tariff over twenty years, after which the United States would charge full duties on Filipino goods. It also required the Filipinos to give Americans equality with their own people in business and in the exploitation of Philippine resources. Since this last provision gave Americans rights that Filipinos did not enjoy in the United States and placed Americans in a special status above other foreigners, Filipinos denounced it as evidence of an American desire to dominate their economy. Later, the American privileges were cut down.

Another law, the Philippine Rehabilitation Act, appropriated $400 million as compensation to property owners for war damage, approved the transfer of $100 million in surplus property to the Philippines, and allocated $120 million for restoration of public services and property there.

After Truman had signed the necessary laws, including the Filipino Naturalization Bill that placed Filipinos on an immigration quota and permitted them to become naturalized American citizens, the Commonwealth became the fully independent Republic of the Philippines on July 4, 1946. A treaty of general relations completed the formalities. Under its terms the United States surrendered all control over the islands except the use of such bases as it, by agreement with the Philippines, might deem necessary to retain for their mutual protection.[6]

Many Filipinos resented some of the conditions of their independence, yet they had gained a great deal. They had finally achieved their long-sought goal of freedom and had retained the good will of the United States. For the United States, Philippine independence was a landmark in both colonial and foreign policy. It fulfilled an old pledge, satisfied Filipino nationalism, ended the half century of controversy over "imperialism," and set an example throughout Asia for the peaceful transition of a colony to a self-governing nation.

Since most Filipino leaders agreed that their country would need protection, they accepted American terms for bases on their islands. Under the Philippines Military Assistance Act passed by Congress in 1946, the United States assumed responsibility for training the Philippine armed forces. A year later the United States concluded a treaty that gave it 99-year leases on fifteen army bases and naval "operating areas" in the Philippines. In addition, the United States assumed responsibility for defense of the islands in case of an outside attack. This agreement linked the Philippines to the American security system in the Pacific.

Despite the relatively smooth transition to independence, the new republic from its inception had to deal with an armed revolt in central Luzon, its main island. Leaders of the old Filipino ruling class, mostly conservative landlords and merchants, dominated the new government. Many of them had collaborated with the Japanese occupiers. During the war, militant peasants and radicals, with some Communist leadership, had formed the Hukbalahap or "People's Anti-Japanese Army." After the war, they resented the return to power of the old ruling class and fought the new government in the name of social justice, demanding a social and economic revolution.

With the aid of American arms, the Philippine government tried to suppress the Hukbalahap. That aid stimulated anti-Americanism among the Huks, as they came to be called. In February, 1947, their leader claimed that without American support the conservative government would have fallen. Later, as the cold war increased in intensity and Communist leadership among the Huks became more pronounced, the United States expressed deep concern over the rebellion and the social conditions in the archipelago.

In 1950 an American economic survey committee, headed by Daniel W. Bell, a Washington banker and former Treasury official, made a study of domestic affairs in the Philippines. Its report criticized the government for inefficiency and corruption, and recommended an overhaul of the nation's economy and a five-year program of economic development supported by American aid. Despite the censure, many prominent Filipinos accepted most of the report's conclusions.

In 1954 a popular and vigorous leader, Ramón Magsaysay, began eliminating the corruption, hit hard at the Huks, and brought their rebellion under control.[7] In September, 1955, Magsaysay's government signed an executive agreement in Washington that revised the earlier trade terms in favor of greater economic independence for the Philippine Republic, an agreement that appeased Filipino nationalism. Thus, as a relatively democratic and stable government took root, the Philippines became a major asset in America's Far Eastern policy.

The Japanese Peace Settlement

At the same time the United States had gone ahead with its policy of drawing Japan into its security system in the Pacific, a policy of deep concern to the Filipinos who feared the power of a revived Japan. In the middle of June, 1950, John Foster Dulles, as a consultant to the State Department, visited Tokyo to discuss the basis of a Japanese peace treaty with General Douglas MacArthur and other military leaders. During the discussions the Korean War broke out, strengthening the determination of the American government to make an early peace settlement with Japan without allowing the Russians an opportunity to veto it.

Seven months later President Truman appointed Dulles his special representative with the rank of ambassador and with responsibility for negotiating the Japanese peace treaty. Dulles immediately began negotiations with America's allies and other powers interested in the peace settlement. He assured the Philippines, Australia, and New Zealand that a sovereign Japan would not be a threat to them, and to gain their consent to the peace settlement, he offered them defense treaties. In March he circulated a working draft of the peace treaty among the interested powers.

In June, Dulles went to London and Paris to work out some unresolved problems, ultimately gaining Britain's support as a joint sponsor of the peace treaty. As expected, the Soviet Union objected, saying it opposed Japanese rearmament, wanted no American troops or bases to remain on Japanese soil, and insisted that Red China be consulted. Since the Russian demands contravened American objectives, the United States disregarded them.

After Dulles had completed his negotiations, the President invited fifty-five nations, excluding Nationalist and Red China, to a conference in San Francisco "for conclusion and signature of a Treaty of Peace with Japan on the terms of that

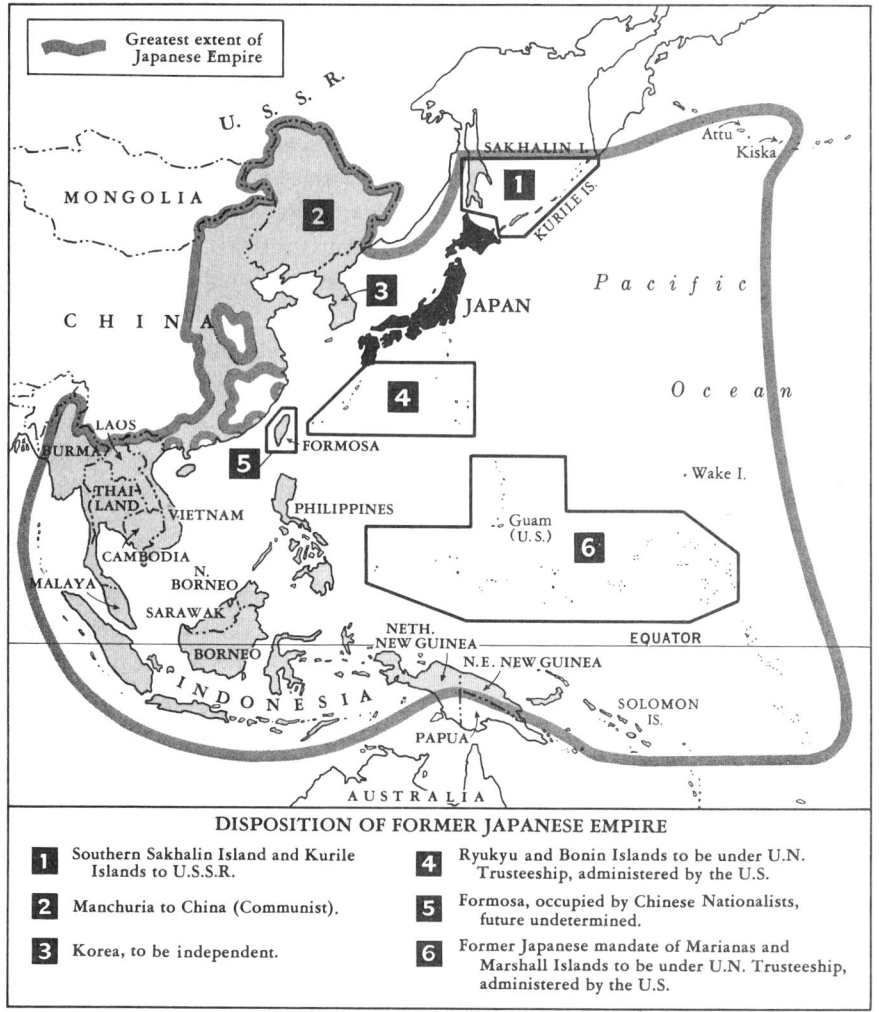

U. S. S. R.

MONGOLIA

SAKHALIN I.

1

Attu
Kiska

2

KURILE IS.

JAPAN

Pacific

3

C H I N A

Ocean

4

LAOS
BURMA

5

FORMOSA

Wake I.

THAI-
LAND
VIETNAM

PHILIPPINES

Guam
(U.S.)

6

CAMBODIA

MALAYA

N.
BORNEO

SARAWAK

BORNEO

NETH.
NEW GUINEA

EQUATOR

N.E. NEW GUINEA

I N D O N E S I A

SOLOMON
IS.

PAPUA

A U S T R A L I A

DISPOSITION OF FORMER JAPANESE EMPIRE

1 Southern Sakhalin Island and Kurile Islands to U.S.S.R.

2 Manchuria to China (Communist).

3 Korea, to be independent.

4 Ryukyu and Bonin Islands to be under U.N. Trusteeship, administered by the U.S.

5 Formosa, occupied by Chinese Nationalists, future undetermined.

6 Former Japanese mandate of Marianas and Marshall Islands to be under U.N. Trusteeship, administered by the U.S.

THE JAPANESE PEACE SETTLEMENT, 1951

text."[8] That invitation emphasized a significant feature of the peace settlement: it was the result of private diplomatic negotiations, not of a public peace conference. Hence, members of the conference could not reopen negotiations on the terms of the treaty.

Fifty-two nations accepted. Despite their objections, the Soviet Union and two of its satellites unexpectedly accepted, primarily with the intent of forcing changes in the treaty.

Shortly before the conference convened, the United States concluded the promised defense treaties with three of its wartime Allies in the Pacific. In Washington on August 30, 1951, it signed a pact with the Philippine Republic calling for consultation if the territory of either party in the Pacific were threatened. In case of an attack, each country would come to the aid of the other "in accordance with its constitutional processes."[9] The mutual defense treaty, though of indefinite duration, could be terminated by either party after one year's notice.

Two days later in San Francisco, the United States signed a similar commitment with Australia and New Zealand, a tripartite defense treaty known as the ANZUS pact. It provided for a council of foreign ministers who could meet and consult at any time and thus bound the United States to another regional arrangement.

Although on paper the security treaties appeared weak, they did constitute a guarantee of American protection and did ally three of the important countries of the Pacific with the United States. There should be no doubt in any quarter, Dulles later told the Senate Foreign Relations Committee, that an attack upon Australia, New Zealand, or the Philippines would, in fact, involve the United States.

President Truman opened the Japanese peace conference on the evening of September 4 in San Francisco's Opera House. Through television, millions of Americans watched Secretary of State Dean Acheson, who presided, parry the efforts of the Communist delegations to block the treaty. Dulles spoke and described the treaty as "a peace of justice, not of vengeance" and "a peace of reconciliation."[10] Four days later the representatives of forty-nine nations signed the treaty. Russia, Poland, and Czechoslovakia abstained.

In accordance with the surrender terms of 1945 and the various Allied wartime conferences, the treaty reduced Japan's sovereignty to her home islands. Japan renounced all claim to the Kurile Islands and southern Sakhalin, which Russia kept. Although Japan did not renounce her sovereignty over the Bonin and Ryukyu island groups, she agreed to American control over them.

The reparations provisions were mild. They obligated Japan to negotiate agreements with the Allied powers who desired reparations, such as the Philippines, and who had suffered from Japanese conquest and occupation. The treaty did not, however, specify the amount to be paid to any nation and said that payments would be in services by the Japanese people. It placed no important restrictions on the future economic development of Japan and no limitations on war industries or armaments. By recognizing Japan's right to self-defense, the Allies consented to rearmament.

To allay American and Canadian fears of unrestricted Japanese fishing off North America, Japan agreed to negotiate agreements on the limitation of fishing on the high seas. The treaty also called for an end to Japan's occupation not later than ninety days after the pact went into effect, except for troops which would remain under special agreements.

By most standards, the treaty was moderate. Japan's prime minister recognized this. "The Japanese Delegation," he said, "gladly accepts this fair and generous treaty."[11] He was, nevertheless, concerned about several points. His people, he explained, were unhappy about the loss of the Ryukyus and Bonins, the Kuriles and southern Sakhalin.

On the same day the peace treaty was signed, the United States and Japan also concluded a security treaty permitting American troops to remain in Japan to defend her against outside attack and to suppress internal disturbances, such as a Communist uprising. That pact said that Japan "will itself increasingly assume responsibility for its own defense against direct and indirect aggression." [12] In essence, the United States would defend Japan until she herself assumed that responsibility.

In February, 1952, before the Senate acted on the peace treaty, the United States and Japan signed an "administrative agreement," commonly called a status of forces agreement, that conferred special privileges on the members of American forces and their families stationed in Japan. Since those privileges evoked resentment among the Japanese people, they were later amended.

The peace treaty and related agreements, based on the idea of close relations with Japan, strengthened the American position in the Pacific and constituted a diplomatic defeat for Russia and Red China. The agreements were, therefore, popular in the United States. The Senate voted down all proposed reservations to the peace treaty except one introduced by the Committee on Foreign Relations. The reservation said that the treaty did not diminish Allied and Japanese rights to southern Sakhalin and the Kuriles and did not imply recognition of the Yalta agreements on Japan that favored the Soviet Union.

On March 20, 1952, the Senate approved the peace treaty by a vote of 66 to 10, the Japanese security treaty by 58 to 9, and the other two security treaties by a voice vote. The peace treaty went into effect on April 28, thus officially ending the Second World War in the Pacific and returning sovereignty to Japan.

Several days later the United States, Japan, and Canada signed a North Pacific Fisheries Convention for the conservation of fish off the American and Canadian coasts and permitting the Japanese to fish in those waters under certain conditions. A month later, on June 30, President Truman proclaimed the heavily criticized McCarran-Walter Immigration and Nationality Act, passed three days earlier over his veto. It placed Japanese immigrants, like those of other Asian nations, on a small annual quota and thus eliminated a specific racial discrimination that had been one of the long-standing grievances of the Japanese people against the United States.

In April of the following year, the United States concluded a commercial treaty with Japan, replacing the old commercial treaty of 1911. In November, Vice-President Richard M. Nixon visited Japan and urged an increase in her armed forces. The United States, he said, had made "an honest mistake" in insisting in 1946 that the Japanese disarm.[13] Nonetheless, the Japanese rearmed slowly. In March, 1954, they signed a Mutual Defense Assistance Agreement with the

United States that obligated them to rebuild their armed forces and provided for American military and economic assistance.

As Japan's defense force grew, the United States withdrew its troops. Finally, in February, 1958, the American Army announced withdrawal of the last of its ground combat troops.

Anti-Americanism in Japan

All did not run smoothly in these years, however, for several incidents revealed a widespread but not necessarily deep anti-Americanism in Japan. When the United States conducted a nuclear test explosion in the Marshall Islands in March, 1954, the crew of the Japanese fishing boat, the *Lucky Dragon*, suffered from radioactive fallout. One man subsequently died. Although the United States expressed regret and paid two million dollars to the Japanese government as a token of good will, to be distributed to those who suffered injury, there was resentment in Japan against American carelessness in the use of the frightful nuclear test bombs.[14]

Another source of difficulty was the status of forces agreement of 1952, one similar to others that the United States had concluded in the postwar years with countries where its armed forces were stationed. Those agreements made American servicemen accused of committing crimes while off duty liable to trial in the host country according to its laws. Since the host country usually waived jurisdiction, few American servicemen were locked in foreign jails. Nonetheless, isolationists, patriotic groups, and various extreme nationalists objected to the whole principle of the agreements, and there were recurrent demands in Congress that they be repudiated, or at least drastically revised.

This agitation was brought to a head in 1957 by a number of sensational cases in which servicemen killed foreign civilians. The most prominent was that of William S. Girard, a soldier who killed a Japanese woman while she was hunting scrap metal on a firing range near Tokyo. As called for in the status of forces agreement with Japan, the United States turned Girard over to the Japanese government for prosecution. Later, while under pressure from opinion at home, it tried to gain jurisdiction. This effort ignited popular feeling in Japan against the United States, an anti-Americanism fanned by Socialists and nationalists.

Since the good faith of the United States and the integrity of its pledges had now been placed in question, the Secretaries of State and Defense stepped into the case. They decided that Girard should after all be tried in Japan. In July the Supreme Court upheld this decision, saying that under the status of forces agreement there was no basis for contesting Japanese jurisdiction.

The court's action helped the Eisenhower administration fight a congressional resolution calling for withdrawal of all status of forces agreements. So determined were the opponents of the agreements that in a special White House meeting William F. Knowland, the Republican leader in the Senate, exploded. In a scene complete with his fist pounding on a table, he insisted that American boys should not be turned over to foreigners for trial.[15]

Eisenhower warned that repudiation of the agreements would jeopardize American security, alienate allies, and give comfort to enemies. "I can think of no recent legislative proposal," he said, "which would so threaten the essential security of the United States."[16] The only alternative to the agreements, he implied, would be to bring American troops home and revert to a prewar isolationism.

Girard was tried by a Japanese court. In November, 1957, it sentenced him to three years imprisonment and immediately suspended the sentence. This decision seemed to satisfy the Japanese sense of justice and gave no ground for a strong reaction in the United States.

The settlement of the Girard case did not remove the basic cause of Japanese anti-Americanism, which was the security treaty of 1951. Since the treaty allowed the United States a free hand in deploying its forces in and around Japan, many Japanese, particularly ultra-nationalists, neutralists, and Communists, wished to get rid of it. Some considered it humiliating and demanded an equal partnership with the United States. In 1958, therefore, Secretary of State Dulles began negotiations for a revision. Finally, on January 19, 1960, in a White House ceremony, Premier Nobusuke Kishi and President Eisenhower signed a new Mutual Security Treaty.

Unlike the old pact, which merely called for consultation in case of an attack and which many Japanese felt did not commit the United States strongly enough to the defense of Japan, the new one pledged each signatory to treat an armed attack against the other as dangerous to its own peace and to act to meet the common danger. This alliance allowed the United States to base military forces in Japan for ten years, but also pledged it to consult with the Japanese on their deployment. This was spelled out in an exchange of clarifying notes and in a communiqué issued after the signing in which Eisenhower declared that "The United States Government has no intention of acting . . . contrary to the wishes of the Japanese Government."[17] The White House also announced that the President would visit Japan in June and that he had invited Crown Prince Akihito to come to the United States.

Kishi considered the treaty a distinct gain for Japan. "This is the first time since the war that the Japanese people have been able to exercise their free will in determining Japan's foreign policy orientation," he explained. "This point can't be stressed too much."[18] Many of his countrymen did not agree.

Neutralists, Socialists, Communists, and others viewed the alliance as leading Japan to entrapment in the cold war. Some denounced it because it failed to return the Ryukyus, Okinawa, and the Bonins—islands occupied by Americans—to

Japan, and others because it gave Japan no right of veto over the deployment of guided missiles and nuclear weapons within her borders. After the U-2 crisis, some warned that the pact might invite Soviet and Red Chinese retaliation against Japan for American actions over which she had no control. Still others were upset by privileges for Americans embodied in the lengthy status of forces agreement linked to the treaty.

The chief opposition party, the Socialist Party, tried to kill the treaty with violent student demonstrations. This turmoil did not prevent ratification, which came in May, so the left-wing demonstrators demanded that Kishi cancel Eisenhower's visit. Leftists feared that the visit would strengthen the position of the unpopular Kishi and assure full approval of the treaty. A few days before the President was to arrive, some 12,000 students in Tokyo stormed the Diet in the most violent riot of that spring, some of them carrying signs that read "We Dislike Ike." Secretary of State Christian Herter said that Eisenhower would not cancel the trip because of the mob actions, especially since a postponement would deal a serious blow to Kishi's prestige and encourage the opponents of the security treaty.

Nonetheless, on June 17, two days before Eisenhower's scheduled arrival, Kishi asked him to postpone the visit, admitting that he could not guarantee the President's safety. Eisenhower received the humiliating news while he was on a nine-day good will trip to Asia. The cancellation seriously damaged American prestige throughout Asia, and bolstered Asian neutralism. Almost everywhere it was accepted as another cold war victory for Communism.[19]

The security treaty itself did not become a victim, for the emperor signed it on June 21, and on the following day the American Senate approved it by a vote of 90 to 2. Ratifications were exchanged hours later in Tokyo.

That treaty led to Kishi's fall. His successor, Hayato Ikeda, took office on the promise of new elections in which the treaty would be the chief issue. In October, at a joint election meeting in Tokyo, before a nation-wide television audience, a seventeen-year-old youth murdered the Socialist leader and opponent of the treaty, Inejiro Asanuma, with a foot-long samurai sword. That brutal deed raised new doubts about the future of the alliance, particularly since neutralist sentiment in Japan was rising. Those fears were quieted by the November elections which gave Ikeda a new mandate and hence indicated at least a qualified acceptance of the alliance. Japan, therefore, remained an ally, the most important strategic link in the American security system in the Pacific.

India and Pakistan

The most important of the new Asian nations, the Republic of India, had refused an invitation to the San Francisco peace conference and had not signed the Japanese treaty. By imposing American control over the Ryukyus and the Bonins and by allowing American troops to remain in Japan, Indians argued, that treaty was incompatible with Japanese independence. India's position reflected her distaste for American foreign policy, her sensitiveness to any infringements on Asian independence, and her desire to be a champion of Asian nationalism.

Strained relations with India was one of the anomalies of postwar American foreign policy. Before the Second World War, when Indian nationalists sought independence from Britain, American relations with India had been remote and indirect. During the war, in cooperation with the British, the United States had exchanged diplomatic representatives with India and after Pearl Harbor had stationed troops on her soil.

In those war years Americans sympathized with India's nationalist aspirations. In 1942, for example, President Roosevelt sent Winston Churchill a cable suggesting temporary dominion status for India so that her people would cooperate in fighting the Axis. Yet he did not press the issue of self-government because he did not wish to antagonize Britain.

Indians admired Roosevelt and saw in him a champion of the oppressed, but Americans as a whole, they felt, were objectionably race-conscious. Many Indians even believed that the United States had dropped the atomic bomb on the Japanese rather than on the Germans because of racial animus. After the war the United States erased some of its internal racial discrimination against Indians, as it had against other Asians. In June, 1946, Congress passed the India Immigration and Naturalization Bill, signed into law on July 2 by President Truman, allowing Indians in the United States to become American citizens.

When India finally achieved independence in August, 1947, she did so as two separate countries within the British Commonwealth of Nations. The larger Hindu state became the Republic of India and the smaller one, the Moslem nation of Pakistan. The relations of those two new nations with the United States followed different paths. Pakistan in time aligned herself closely with American foreign policy, whereas India chose an independent course in world affairs.

India avoided alliances with either the Communist bloc or the United States and hence took a "neutralist" position in the cold war. Her main interest in foreign policy, her leaders declared in December, 1948, was "in the freedom of nations and peoples of Asia and Africa, who have suffered under various forms of colonialism for many generations." [20]

India's leaders, notably Prime Minister Jawaharlal Nehru, disliked the intense emphasis of American foreign policy on the cold war. The emergence of Asia to a prominent position in world affairs, he thought, was more important. The United States, Indians felt, was interested primarily in buying allies. Even though impressed by the American record in the Philippines, many of them came to believe that the United States had replaced Britain as the leading exponent of imperialism in Asia. This mistaken idea stemmed in part from America's general support of her European Allies, which, Indians concluded, also implied American backing of British and French rule in Asia and Africa. As the cold war became critical, Americans, on the other hand, became dissatisfied with Indian neutralism, considering it too friendly to the Soviets and Red China and unrealistic in a world of power politics.

Despite their philosophical and policy differences with India, American leaders considered her important to their Far Eastern policy. Since India's economic and military power were not great nor necessarily decisive in the cold war, the United States did not fear it or seek to use it. Americans sought India's friendship because of her vast population and moral leadership among the anticolonial peoples of Asia.

To help India create and maintain a stable democratic government, the United States offered her various kinds of economic assistance. Late in 1950 it concluded a Point Four agreement with her calling for technical assistance to the value of $1.2 million in agriculture, river valley development, and transportation. To help avert a famine in 1951, it loaned her $190 million for wheat. In comparison to sums expended elsewhere, the money the United States spent on India was small. In three years ending in 1954, the total amounted to slightly more than one dollar for each of India's 360 million people. Yet those dollars represented three-quarters of all foreign aid India had received up to that time.

In the decade 1951 to 1961, the United States extended $3,900,600,000 in grants and loans to India. Among the tangible results of this aid were the irrigation of millions of acres of farm land, the electrification of wide areas, and help in the virtual elimination of malaria as a major killer in India.

No serious clash marred relations with India, but a number of minor ones did. To the displeasure of American policymakers, India cultivated close relations with Communist China and supported her efforts to displace Nationalist China in the United Nations. During the Korean War, India remained aloof from the fighting, opposed the American advance into North Korea, and warned that it might provoke Red China. Indians considered American nuclear test explosions dangerous and warlike, and persistently denounced them. They expressed opposition to virtually all phases of American Far Eastern policy.

One of India's rankling specific grievances against the United States arose out of her feud with Pakistan over who should control the northern frontier province of Kashmir. Indians believed that the United States favored the Pakistanis and viewed American efforts to mediate the conflict as meddling in their affairs.

When the United States decided to give military assistance to Pakistan in 1953, that decision seemed to confirm American favoritism and aroused anti-American sentiment in India. To Americans the move seemed logical, for Pakistan's willingness to stand with the United States against Communism contrasted sharply with India's policy of nonalignment. President Eisenhower sent Nehru a personal letter assuring him that the proposed aid to Pakistan was "not directed in any way

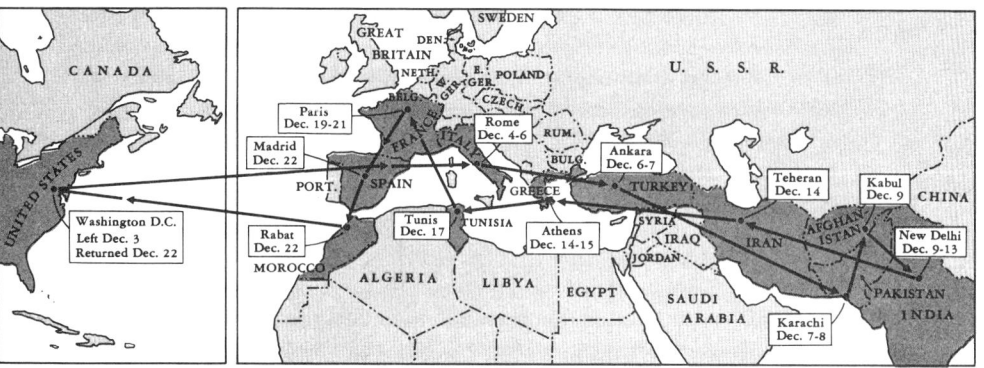

EISENHOWER'S ELEVEN-NATION GOOD-WILL TRIP, DECEMBER, 1959

against India" and did not "in any way affect the friendship we feel for India."[21] To placate the disturbed Indians, he offered them military equipment on the same terms offered to Pakistan, but Nehru refused the arms.

Several months later, in May, 1954, the United States and Pakistan signed a mutual defense treaty and completed arrangements for shipping military equipment to the Pakistanis. Pakistan's Foreign Minister stressed that the accord did not establish a military alliance or obligate Pakistan to provide bases for American forces. India, nonetheless, resented the arming of her rival, for it seemed obvious that Pakistan intended to use its arms as leverage in the bargaining over Kashmir.

American relations with India remained friendly but cool. They appeared to warm a bit in 1959 when Communist China ruthlessly crushed a rebellion in neighboring Tibet, claimed and invaded borderlands India considered hers, and killed Indians in border clashes. Despite the fact that Nehru gave political asylum to Tibet's Dalai Lama and condemned Chinese "aggression," and despite the widespread sympathy among his people for the Tibetans and their resentment against Red China, he refused to abandon his neutralist position for closer ties to the United States.

The bellicosity of the Chinese, nonetheless, did lead to some improvement in America's relations with India, an improvement highlighted by President Eisenhower's visit there and to ten other countries of Asia and Europe in December. He received enthusiastic receptions everywhere, but especially in neutralist India.

Relations with India dropped to a low point in December, 1961, as a result of a dispute over Goa and other enclaves on India's coast held by Portugal since 1510. Despite pleas to Nehru from President Kennedy and Acting Secretary General U Thant of the United Nations to solve the dispute by peaceful means, Indian troops invaded and seized the enclaves. Since India had repeatedly professed devotion to the principle of nonviolence in international affairs, the United States and its Western Allies were shocked by her use of force. The Soviet bloc and the Afro-Asians, however, hailed it as another victory over colonialism.

When the Western Allies proposed a resolution in the Security Council deploring India's use of force and calling for a cease-fire and negotiations, it was vetoed by the Soviet Union and opposed by the three Afro-Asian members of the Council. The United States took the position that there should not be a double standard of behavior in the United Nations, one for the Afro-Asians and another for the Western colonial powers. Indians reacted by accusing the United States of supporting colonialism and failing to understand their point of view. In the case of Goa, India's representative at the United Nations said, Portugal was the "aggressor" because "colonialism is permanent aggression."

The Kennedy administration, to the chagrin of Portugal, appeared to have protested the Goa invasion merely for the record, for it was careful not to press India too hard. This difference with Asia's leading neutralist country soon blew over and Jacqueline Kennedy, the President's wife, continued with plans for a semi-official visit to India and Pakistan. Her good-will mission, in March, 1962, implied more than a usual concern for political relations with India.

Disapproval of the discrepancy in India's professions of peaceful neutrality and her belligerent conduct toward Goa and Pakistan did not pass away so quickly in Congress. In May, the Senate Committee on Foreign Relations gave expression to this resentment by recommending a slash of $200 million, or a cut of 25 per cent, from the President's request for economic and military aid to India. Kennedy was able to get the amount restored, but congressional resentment flared up again in June when Russia offered to sell India some MIG-12 supersonic jet planes, and a factory to produce them. India wanted the jets, saying she needed them to match American F-104 supersonic jets given to Pakistan. The United States feared that the purchase of the Soviet jets would forge a link between India and Russia to America's disadvantage. Nonetheless, Prime Minister Nehru had several times spoken of the recently improved relations with the United States, a recognition of the Kennedy administration's obvious efforts to woo India.

Indonesia

Another source of Indian resentment was American policy toward Indonesia, formerly the Netherlands East Indies, in her struggle for independence from the Dutch. Indians thought that the United States gave unwarranted moral support to Dutch colonialism. During the periodic fighting between the Dutch and Indonesian nationalists, from the end of Indonesia's Japanese occupation late in 1945 to independence in 1949, the United States found itself in the dilemma of attempting to reconcile its support of anticolonialism and Asian self-determination with its efforts to remain on good terms with the Netherlands, a country important to the containment policy in Europe.

Finally the United States placed pressure on the Dutch to make important concessions to Indonesians. Primarily through the work of the American representative on a United Nations Committee of Good Offices, Dutch and Indonesians met aboard the American warship u.s.s. *Renville* in January, 1948, and signed a truce and an agreement that led to the independence of the United States of Indonesia.

Although at first friendly to the United States, the Indonesians resented the fact that the Dutch had fought against them with American Lend-Lease arms and felt that the United States had not done enough for their cause. The Dutch, on the other hand were convinced that the United States had done too much for the Indonesians. Even though they gave in to American pressure, the Dutch believed that the United States had intervened unjustifiably in their "internal" affairs.

Like India, with whom she cooperated closely, the new Indonesian republic followed an anticolonial and neutralist policy that seemed to many Americans implicitly anti-American. Indonesia, again like India, disliked America's Far Eastern policy and her intense preoccupation with the cold war. Indonesians even refused military and economic aid from the United States, fearing it would invite American dictation of their foreign policy. "Indonesia," one of her leaders wrote in 1953, "plays no favorite between the two opposed blocs and follows its own path through various international problems." 22

When Indonesia won her independence, the Netherlands retained West New Guinea, called West Irian by the Indonesians, which the Indonesians claimed as part of their domain. The Dutch, backed at first by Australia, refused to give up the territory. The United States, wishing to alienate neither the Indonesians nor its Dutch ally, for years supported neither side.

As the years passed, the quarrel became increasingly heated and even dangerous. The Indonesians threatened repeatedly to take West New Guinea by force. Finally, in March, 1962, when the Indonesians began landing commando forces on the large island and war seemed close, the United States stepped into the dispute as mediator. Although American policymakers did not fully trust President Sukarno of Indonesia, the United States abandoned its neutrality in the conflict and advised the Dutch to give up their colony to Indonesia. Through this partiality, the United States apparently hoped to counteract Soviet influence over Sukarno.

A former American Ambassador, Ellsworth D. Bunker, acting as mediator, worked out the plan for turning over West New Guinea to the Indonesians, with the United Nations acting as a broker in the transaction. The pact embodying the Bunker plan was signed on August 15, 1962, at the United Nations' headquarters in New York. Even though this agreement ended thirteen years of acrimonious argument and may have averted war, America's Dutch allies were unhappy. They contended that the failure of the United States to support their position had forced them to abandon the native peoples of New Guinea to the Indonesians. The Dutch also charged that American support of Indonesia in effect sanctioned the use of force in acquiring territory and hence violated the United Nations charter. It remained to be seen if American policy had stopped or even deflected what some feared was Indonesia's drift into the Communist orbit.

Civil War in Indochina

A more critical manifestation of anti-American nationalism, used by Communists, developed in France's former colony of Indochina. As in other areas conquered by Japan, nationalists in Indochina opposed the return of European rule. Americans sympathized with their desire. President Roosevelt had favored an international trusteeship for Indochina, and President Truman had favored some form of self-government there.

Before the French had returned, a nationalist political organization, called Viet Minh, had founded the Democratic Republic of Vietnam, comprising the three Indochinese states of Tonkin, Annam, and Cochin China. In March, 1946, the French agreed to a limited autonomy for Vietnam, but controversy arose over carrying out the agreement and in December the Viet Minh, led by Ho Chi Minh, an able Communist trained in Russia, attacked the French in Hanoi. That attack marked the beginning of seven and one-half years of intense warfare.

At first the United States remained aloof from the conflict and tried to deal impartially with both sides. It refused to support the French, even though the battle went against them.

The French had re-established their dominant position in two other Indochinese provinces, Cambodia and Laos, but had been unable to attract solid native support in Vietnam. Finally, in June, 1949, the French created the State of Vietnam with a former emperor of Annam, Bao Dai, as its head. Even though the French gave Bao Dai considerable independence, he did not win popular support. The Vietnamese considered him a French puppet.

When the Chinese Communists reached Indochina's frontier at the beginning of 1950 and apparently began supplying Ho Chi Minh with arms, the war in Indochina took on a new significance for American foreign policy. Backed by the Chinese, the Viet Minh rebels expanded their operations and drove the French from several important strongholds. American policymakers now became convinced that the hard-pressed French were fighting not merely a colonial war but also international Communism in Indochina. Since the war was draining France of resources and fighting men, American leaders felt that they had to help her in Indochina if she were to be an effective ally in Europe. The strategy of containment, they concluded, should apply to Indochina as elsewhere.

In May, the United States recognized Bao Dai's government and agreed to give the French in Indochina economic and military aid. Taking note of critics who disliked any support of colonialism, Secretary of State Acheson said American aid should contribute to security and the development of "genuine nationalism" in Indochina. In June, after the outbreak of the Korean War, the President announced he would step up aid to the French and would send a military mission to Indochina to work closely with French forces. The war in Indochina now became part of the larger struggle against Communism, with the United States bearing the major burden in Korea, and France the main share in Indochina.

As American arms began reaching Indochina, Ho Chi Minh denounced the United States, accusing it of having aided the French from the beginning of the war. "Thus we have now one principal opponent—the French bandits—" he said, "and one more opponent—the American interventionists. . . ." Referring to the recognition of his regime by Russia, Red China, and the Soviet satellites, he pointed out, "we are definitely on the democratic side and belong to the anti-imperialist bloc of 800 million people." [23]

Even with huge quantities of American war equipment, the French forces were unable to subdue the tough Viet Minh fighters. When the Eisenhower administration came to power in January, 1953, it increased aid to the French, taking the view ultimately that if the Communists triumphed in Indochina, all the states of Southeast Asia, like a row of dominoes, would fall to them.[24] The President said that peace in Korea must not mean that Communist armies would be released for action in Indochina. In April, Secretary of State Dulles announced "that a new order of priority and urgency has been given to the Far East." The United States and its Allies, he said, were facing "a single hostile front" there.[25]

In its determination to keep Indochina from falling to the Communists, the United States took on the burden of financing most of the cost of the war there. By 1954 it was contributing almost eighty per cent to the total of all French military expenditures in Indochina. From the time American military aid began in 1950 until 1954, American assistance amounted to $500 million annually.

Nonetheless, in the spring of 1954 the war took a disastrous turn for the French and touched off a crisis in American foreign policy. The Viet Minh trapped some twenty-thousand French and loyal Vietnamese troops in a remote fortress in northern Vietnam called Dien Bien Phu. In desperation the French finally appealed for American intervention, primarily a massive air strike from carriers to relieve besieged Dien Bien Phu.

The President, Secretary of State Dulles, and the Chief of Staff, had already discussed the Indochina crisis and had decided on "united action," meaning armed intervention under certain conditions. If Congress consented and Britain joined the move, the United States, they apparently agreed, would fight in defense of Indochina.[26] The President, however, had ruled out an air strike or unilateral intervention.

On April 10, Secretary Dulles flew to London where he failed to gain British support for united action.[27] A few days later Vice-President Nixon spoke to a group of newspaper editors in Washington on the crisis. "If, to avoid further Communist expansion in Asia and Indochina we must take the risk now by putting our boys in," he said, "I think the Executive has to take the politically unpopular decision and do it."[28]

Public reaction to the Vice-President's idea was so hostile that the administration abandoned its plan. Several days after Nixon's speech, Dulles announced that it was "unlikely" that the United States would send troops to Indochina. No American boys, he reiterated in a television broadcast, would be sent to Indochina or elsewhere in Asia without the consent of Congress. Dien Bien Phu fell on May 7, 1954, after fifty-five days of siege.

Many had feared that Indochina would become another Korea, or worse, the beginning of another world war. If the United States and its Allies sent troops, Red China, it appeared, would send fighters swarming into Vietnam. India, Indonesia, and other Asian countries, moreover, stood solidly against American policy. They looked upon the war in Indochina as basically a part of Asia's struggle to throw off the yoke of white imperialism. To them Communism appeared an incidental issue.

The Geneva Conference on Asia

Several days earlier, on April 26, the five strongest powers to emerge from the Second World War—the United States, Russia, Britain, France, and Red China—had met together for the first time, with a number of the lesser states, at the Geneva Conference on Korea and Indochina. Dulles participated in the discussions over Korea, and after they failed, withdrew, leaving France and Britain to deal with the Communist powers on the issue of Indochina. If Dulles had taken part in the negotiations over Indochina, in what critics feared would be an Asian "Munich," he would have alienated the "Asia Firsters" of his own party, something he was not prepared to do.

The settlement on Indochina, consisting of three cease-fire agreements, signed on June 21, recognized the independence of the kingdoms of Laos and Cambodia and divided Vietnam at the 17th parallel. The land to the north of that line, the "Democratic Republic of Vietnam," went to Ho Chi Minh's regime and the territory to the south, the State of Vietnam, remained under the control of Bao Dai's government. The Geneva agreement was a triumph for the Viet Minh and a setback for American prestige. Yet it denied the Communist-supported nationalists the whole peninsula which they might have conquered, and for a while at least it brought peace to Southeast Asia.

Later, Eisenhower expressed distaste for the results of the diplomacy at Geneva

INDOCHINA AFTER THE
ARMISTICE OF 1954

Map labels: CHINA · Dien Bien Phu · Hanoi · Haiphong · Gulf of Tonkin · HAINAN · LAOS · NORTH VIETNAM · Vientiane · Hue · THAILAND · SOUTH VIETNAM · CAMBODIA · Phnom Penh · Gulf of Siam · Saigon · South China Sea · Communist areas

but said the United States, who had not joined in the settlement, accepted it and would make the best of a bad bargain. Undersecretary of State Walter Bedell Smith felt that "Munich" was "a damned poor term" for the Geneva truce. The terms, he said, were the best obtainable because "diplomacy has rarely been able to gain at the conference table what cannot be gained or held on the battlefield."[29]

After the armistice, to the surprise of many, the State of Vietnam overcame internal strife, resisted Communist penetration, and with American military and economic aid, amounting to $150 million annually, gained strength. In 1955 a strongman, Ngo Dinh Diem, overthrew Bao Dai and established the Republic of Vietnam, which the United States quickly recognized. Diem justified his dictatorial regime by saying that the Communist threat required it.

SEATO and "Deterrence"

Secretary of State Dulles, meanwhile, had gone ahead with his plan for united action to block further Communist gains in Asia, a plan that had failed to bring results during the crisis over Dien Bien Phu. At Manila, on September 6, 1954, he met with the representatives of Britain, France, Australia, New Zealand, the Philippines, Thailand, and Pakistan. Although invited, India, Burma, Ceylon, and Indonesia declined to attend the conference, preferring to follow their common policy of noninvolvement in the cold war. Only three Asian nations, therefore, participated.

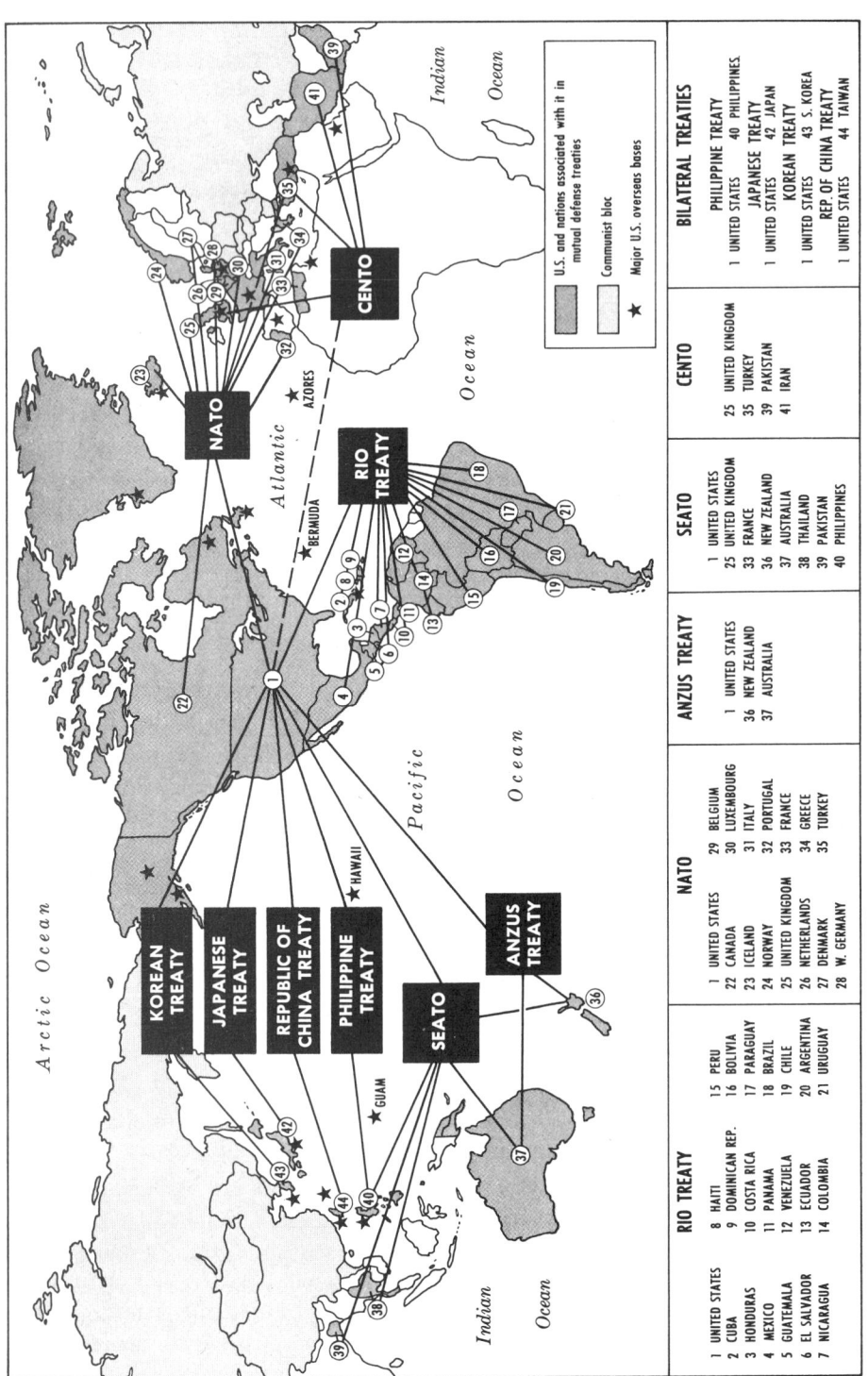

UNITED STATES ALLIANCES, 1947-1961

RIO TREATY

1 UNITED STATES	8 HAITI	15 PERU
2 CUBA	9 DOMINICAN REP.	16 BOLIVIA
3 HONDURAS	10 COSTA RICA	17 PARAGUAY
4 MEXICO	11 PANAMA	18 BRAZIL
5 GUATEMALA	12 VENEZUELA	19 CHILE
6 EL SALVADOR	13 ECUADOR	20 ARGENTINA
7 NICARAGUA	14 COLOMBIA	21 URUGUAY

NATO

1 UNITED STATES	22 CANADA	29 BELGIUM
	23 ICELAND	30 LUXEMBOURG
	24 NORWAY	31 ITALY
	25 UNITED KINGDOM	32 PORTUGAL
	26 NETHERLANDS	33 FRANCE
	27 DENMARK	34 GREECE
	28 W. GERMANY	35 TURKEY

ANZUS TREATY

| 1 UNITED STATES |
| 36 NEW ZEALAND |
| 37 AUSTRALIA |

SEATO

| 1 UNITED STATES |
| 25 UNITED KINGDOM |
| 33 FRANCE |
| 36 NEW ZEALAND |
| 37 AUSTRALIA |
| 38 THAILAND |
| 39 PAKISTAN |
| 40 PHILIPPINES |

CENTO

| 25 UNITED KINGDOM |
| 35 TURKEY |
| 39 PAKISTAN |
| 41 IRAN |

BILATERAL TREATIES

PHILIPPINE TREATY
1 UNITED STATES   40 PHILIPPINES

JAPANESE TREATY
1 UNITED STATES   42 JAPAN

KOREAN TREATY
1 UNITED STATES   43 S. KOREA

REP. OF CHINA TREATY
1 UNITED STATES   44 TAIWAN

Legend:
☐ U.S. and nations associated with it in mutual defense treaties
☐ Communist bloc
★ Major U.S. overseas bases

KOREAN TREATY
JAPANESE TREATY
REPUBLIC OF CHINA TREATY
PHILIPPINE TREATY
SEATO
ANZUS TREATY
NATO
CENTO
RIO TREATY

Two days later, the delegates signed a vague alliance called the Southeast Asia Collective Defense Treaty or the "Manila Pact." Following the pattern of the Philippine and ANZUS treaties, it said that each signatory would recognize an attack on any one of them as endangering its own peace and safety. Each party agreed to meet the common danger according to its constitutional process.

If threats to independence developed from internal, meaning Communist, subversion, the signatories agreed to consult immediately through a council that formed another regional arrangement, the Southeast Asia Treaty Organization or SEATO. Ultimately, the organization established headquarters and a secretariat at Bangkok, the capital of Thailand. The treaty also called for economic cooperation and technical aid among the members. Since the Geneva armistice prevented South Vietnam, Laos, and Cambodia from joining an alliance, the Manila Pact extended protection to those countries through a separate protocol.

To overcome criticism that the new organization would perpetuate colonialism, the eight powers signed a Pacific Charter. It announced their determination to "uphold the principle of equal rights and self-determination of peoples" and to promote Asian self-government.[30] In a special reservation the United States explained that it would act only in case of a Communist attack but would consult its partners on all other dangers.

Without India, Burma, Ceylon, and Indonesia, critics pointed out, the treaty included less than half the countries and less than a quarter of the people in Asia it had originally intended to defend. SEATO, unlike NATO, moreover, did not rely on contributions from its members to a common armed force. It depended for its effectiveness mainly on the striking power of the American Navy and Air Force armed with atomic weapons. In this respect it fitted the "new look" in American defense and foreign policy. The threat of American retaliation, it was hoped, would prevent Communist attacks. "The deterrent power we thus create," Dulles explained, "can protect many as effectively as it protects one."[31]

The Manila Pact, approved by the Senate on February 1, 1955, by a vote of 82 to 1, thus left the United States with considerable freedom of action. Fundamentally, the United States could act in support of the treaty when and how it deemed necessary.

To Asian neutrals a limited military agreement and a policy based on deterring Communist expansion had no appeal. They wanted a positive commitment to anti-colonialism, but such a forthright position would have created a new dilemma for American policy by alienating some of America's most important European allies.

The Laos Dilemma

The Geneva agreement of 1954 had stipulated that Laos and Cambodia were to be neutral, a status that proved difficult for Laos to maintain. With its independence that kingdom had inherited a large body of resistance fighters, called the Pathet

Lao movement, which had fought the Japanese and later the French. The Pathet Lao movement, which received most of its support from Communist North Vietnam, refused to integrate its forces with those of the government. This led to years of civil turmoil, an instability that proved particularly perplexing to American policymakers.

At first, from 1954 to 1958, the United States supported a neutralist government that tried and failed to reach an accord with the Pathet Lao. In 1959 and 1960 the United States backed conservative regimes that fought the Pathet Lao, giving them massive aid that amounted to more than $40 million annually, more than ninety per cent of which went to the anti-Communist army. In this period the Soviets stepped in with massive aid of their own; they airlifted guns and other military equipment directly to the Pathet Lao. This led to a situation in which the anti-Communist troops, supplied and trained by the United States, held the main towns, and the pro-Communist Pathet Lao controlled the jungles and the strategic northern plains and appeared capable of conquering the entire kingdom if it were not stopped by a superior outside force.

These developments confronted the United States with a dilemma from which no satisfactory escape seemed possible. American policy had no substantial support among the people of Laos. The Pathet Lao had presented itself to them as a nationalist movement and its propaganda insisted that Americans were responsible for the slaughter of Laotians by their own countrymen. Regardless of the hollowness of the charge, it did appear to the people that the United States was opposing national self-determination. This, in effect, ruled out direct American intervention. Intervention according to the SEATO guarantee was also unacceptable to the policymakers, for it might trigger counteraction by Red China, as in Korea, and enlarge the struggle. Furthermore, neither Britain, nor France, nor the American people appeared willing to support direct military intervention and risk another Korea.

By January, 1961, as John F. Kennedy took office, it was clear that the Soviet Union had established itself in Southeast Asia and that the line of containment on the Indochina peninsula drawn in 1954 had been breached. Kennedy tried to seal the breach through diplomacy. He abandoned Eisenhower's policy of aiding pro-Western regimes in carrying out anti-Communist crusades, and supported a British plan calling for a cease-fire in Laos supervised by an international commission. In a dramatic televised news conference in March, in which he pointed out that Communist control of Laos would jeopardize the West's entire strategic position in Southeast Asia, he defined America's objective as being "a neutral and independent Laos, tied to no outside power."[32] He suggested that after a cease-fire had been verified, a conference of interested nations could work out a political settlement and provide guarantees for the strife-ridden kingdom. Linked to this overture was a warning to Moscow that the United States was determined to prevent

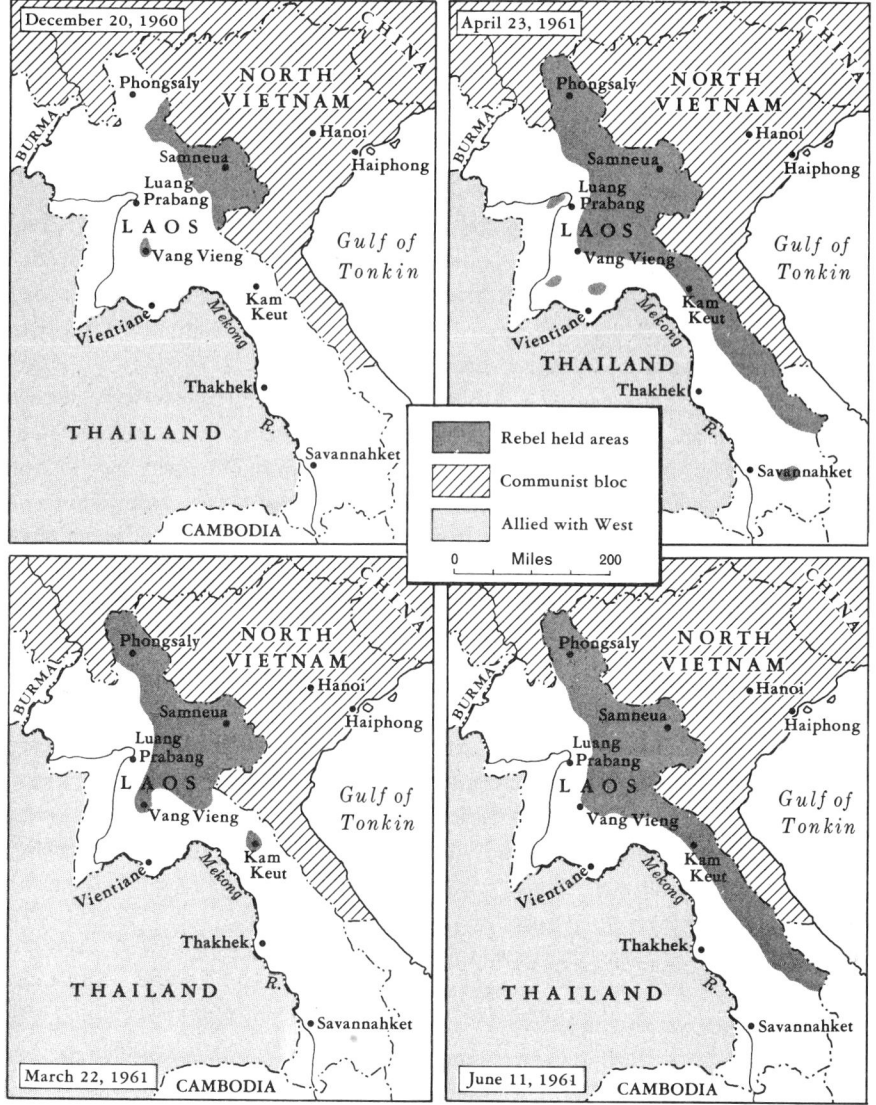

LAOS: COMMUNIST GAINS, DECEMBER, 1960 – JUNE, 1961

Communist absorption of Laos. Kennedy implied that if a cease-fire did not come, the United States might intervene.

The Russians accepted Kennedy's overture by suggesting a conference of fourteen nations to resolve the Laotian crisis, but delayed any agreement on a cease-fire until the Pathet Lao had gained control of about half of Laos. Kennedy, the United States, and SEATO, as a result, all suffered a loss of prestige by failing to prevent the Communist seizure. Nonetheless, the fourteen-nation conference finally convened in Geneva in May. It soon became stalemated and the Pathet Lao, moreover, violated the truce arrangements.

Kennedy brought up the Laotian stalemate with Khrushchev in Vienna in June. Both endorsed the idea of a neutral and independent Laos. This was, the President reported, "the one area which afforded some immediate prospect of accord." [33]

It soon became apparent that a neutral regime in Laos could be dominated from within by Communists. American policy, therefore, no longer tried to place the line of containment in Laos. Instead it sought to use Laos as a buffer against the Communist drive southward and draw a new defense line in South Vietnam, but there, too, the Western position had become precarious.

The Viet Cong, or Vietnamese Communists, fanning out from bases in southern Laos and Cambodia in October, 1961, mounted attacks against population centers in South Vietnam in an effort to overthrow the regime of President Ngo Dinh Diem. American policymakers agreed that in order to stop Communist infiltration, Diem's government, virtually a family dictatorship opposed to social and economic reform, had to win popular support and needed extensive military assistance. The United States stepped up its flow of weapons to South Vietnam and in December issued a White Paper attacking Communist tactics and defending its military aid.

By the summer of 1962 the American military mission in South Vietnam, used mainly to advise and train Diem's army, had swollen to 8000 men. American naval vessels patrolled the coast of South Vietnam, and American servicemen flew the South Vietnamese into battle in helicopters and sometimes accompanied them in combat. The Americans had orders to fire only if fired upon, yet Americans were being killed, wounded, and captured by the Viet Cong. However, considering the extent of the American involvement, which was getting deeper, the casualty rate was low.

In Laos, meanwhile, the shaky cease-fire of May, 1961, had collapsed. On May 7, 1962, the Pathet Lao struck at a government stronghold in the north and routed the rightist forces which fled into neighboring Thailand. The Pathet Lao now held about two-thirds of Laos and apparently could take over the remainder of the kingdom with ease.

President Kennedy reacted to the new crisis with a show of strength. He ordered units of the Seventh Fleet into the waters of Southeast Asia, and on May 17 began landing the first of 5000 combat troops in Thailand. The American action, requested by Thailand in line with obligations under SEATO, was designed to shore up Thailand's defenses along the Laotian border and preserve what remained of containment in Southeast Asia. Kennedy also wished to place pressure on Russia and Communist China through the implied threat of intervention, to halt the fighting in Laos, and to resume negotiations.

Whether in response to the American threat or for reasons of their own, the Pathet Lao stopped its offensive, and in June the three Laotian factions—pro-Western, neutralist, and Communist—agreed on a coalition government that would neutralize the country. In Geneva, on July 23, 1962, the foreign ministers of the fourteen-nation commission, representing Western, Communist, and Asian neutralist countries, signed agreements guaranteeing the independence and neutrality of Laos. An international control commission was to supervise Laotian neutrality. Thus, after more than two years of civil strife, Laos, in theory at least, was taken out of the cold war.

Cambodia, too, wished to escape the tension and battles of the cold war. Late in August Cambodia's chief of state asked to have the fourteen-nation guarantee of Laos extended to his country. Russia and Red China quickly approved, but the United States, Britain, and the other nations involved took time to study the request.

The Crises in Formosa Strait

While Dulles was fashioning the SEATO alliance, a new crisis had developed in Formosa Strait, one that seemingly put the policy of deterrence to a test. Early in August, 1954, Red China's Prime Minister, Chou En-lai, had said his government would "liberate" Formosa from Nationalist control. "Any invasion of Formosa," President Eisenhower replied, "would have to run over the Seventh Fleet." [34]

The Chinese Communists did not attempt to invade Formosa but threatened a string of small islands, including the Tachen, Matsu, and Quemoy groups, stretching some 350 miles along the China coast and held tenaciously by Chiang Kai-shek's Nationalists. A few days before the Manila conference began, the Reds started a heavy bombardment of the two Quemoys, located about five miles outside the port of Amoy. The shelling from the big coastal guns became so intense that invasion seemed imminent.

On his way home from Manila, Dulles therefore stopped at Taipei, the capital of Formosa. After talks with Chiang, he agreed to an alliance with the Nationalist regime. In Washington on December 2, the United States and the Republic of China, Chiang's government, signed a Mutual Defense Treaty similar to the Manila Pact. Each country, the treaty stated, would recognize an attack on the other's territories in the West Pacific as dangerous to its own peace and safety, and to meet the danger, each would act according to its constitutional process.

The treaty did not define the extent of Chiang's domain but declared that the word "territories," in respect to Nationalist China, meant "Taiwan and the Pescadores." In supplementary notes dated December 10, the signatories said the United States, by joint agreement, could act in the offshore islands but was not bound to do so. No one knew, therefore, whether or not the Eisenhower administration would defend the offshore islands. Many Americans and American Allies feared that war would follow if the Communists invaded the islands.

A fear that the alliance might drag the United States into war also stemmed from Chiang's avowed objective of reconquering the Chinese mainland. The United

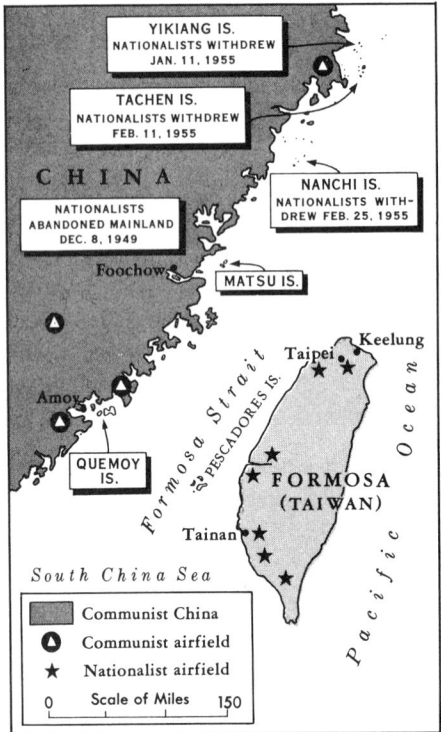

THE FORMOSA STRAIT:
CRISIS OF 1955

States did not wish to commit itself to a war, one in which it would do most of the fighting, solely to serve Chiang's interests. Yet it did not wish to deny his claim to the mainland. To have done so would have been an admission that the Communists were China's true masters and, hence, the logical incumbents of China's seat in the United Nations, an admission American policymakers would not make.

The supplementary notes got around this difficulty by pledging Chiang not to use force, except in self-defense, without American consent. That agreement once again placed Chiang on a leash.

The Communists denounced the Formosa alliance, continued the heavy shelling, and on January 18, 1955, invaded the island of Yikiang, eight miles north of the Tachens. Eisenhower and Dulles immediately made it clear that they did not consider that island and the exposed Tachens essential to the defense of Formosa, some two hundred miles away. Nonetheless, the new Communist challenge added to the crisis atmosphere in Washington.

Five days later Eisenhower asked Congress for clear authority to deal with any emergency that might arise in Formosa Strait. Although the President already had this authority, he and Dulles wanted the Communists to know that retaliation would be supported by Congress if they attempted to invade Quemoy and

Matsu. Congress immediately responded with a joint resolution authorizing the President to use the armed forces to protect Formosa and the Pescadores and "such related positions and territories of that area now in friendly hands. . . ." [35]

The House approved the Formosa Resolution on January 25 by a vote of 409 to 3, and the Senate three days later by a margin of 85 to 3. Eisenhower signed it on the following day. To allay fear that Chiang or some excited American military officer in the area might trigger a war, the President announced that he alone would decide on when and how to use the authority Congress had voted him.

In February, under American pressure and with American assistance, Chiang reluctantly evacuated the Tachens and some other small islands. The Communists then took them over. In April, at an Asian-African conference at Bandung, Indonesia, Chou En-Lai suggested direct discussions with the United States to ease the tension in the Far East. The United States agreed and the first crisis over Formosa Strait passed, a crisis, Dulles said indirectly, that had brought the United States to the "brink of war." [36] The talks with the Chinese Communists at Geneva brought no settlement. Nonetheless, the question of the offshore islands remained dormant for over three years.

Suddenly, in August, 1958, the Chinese Reds renewed their massive shelling of Quemoy, practically cutting the island off from the outside world, and another crisis over Formosa Strait burst into the headlines. American warships, with orders to shoot back against any attack, convoyed Nationalist supply ships to within three miles of the guns trained on Quemoy and Matsu.

This time the Eisenhower administration said it would repel any Communist attack and announced that the protection of Quemoy and Matsu, primarily because Chiang had committed about one-third of his troops to those islands, had become "increasingly related to the defense of Taiwan." Khrushchev, in several letters to Eisenhower in September, then warned that he would support his Chinese ally if the United States became involved in any attack on the Chinese mainland.

Many Americans became alarmed. Why, they asked, should the government risk a nuclear war over some remote and indefensible islands? Chiang, they charged, had purposely committed a third of his troops to the vulnerable islands with the hope of drawing the United States into his own war aimed at the re-conquest of the mainland. The chorus of criticism, swelled by voices from America's European Allies, became so loud that Dulles made a major switch in policy.

Chiang, Dulles said, had been "rather foolish" in placing a large garrison on Quemoy. If the Communists would establish an informal, or *de facto*, cease-fire, he announced that he would recommend a reduction in the Nationalist garrison. The United States, he added, had "no commitment of any kind" to aid the Nationalists in regaining the mainland.[37] This was the first time the United States had said publicly that it would not support a war of reconquest. It thus assured the Communists that they did not have to fear a Nationalist invasion. In exchange, the Chinese Reds eased their pressure on Quemoy, though, ironically, they reserved the right to shell the islands on alternate days of the week.

In October, Dulles visited Formosa and persuaded a reluctant Chiang to thin out his troops on Quemoy and to announce that his Nationalists would not use force to win the mainland. A month earlier American and Chinese Communist Ambassadors in Warsaw had resumed conversations that had been held previously in Geneva on the fate of Americans imprisoned in China. Now they took up the question of Formosa and the lesser islands, and while they talked, the second crisis of Formosa Strait passed.

Two years later, the place of Quemoy and Matsu in American strategy became the source of the bitterest dispute of the presidential campaign. In his second television debate with Richard Nixon in October, 1960, John F. Kennedy said that American defense in the Pacific should not be based on those islands but on Formosa itself. Nixon denounced this as "woolly thinking" and insisted that the United States should not surrender one inch of territory inside the "area of freedom." Kennedy called Nixon's attitude trigger-happy. Regardless of the subsequent backing and filling on this issue, it was clear that Nixon favored holding the islands and that Kennedy did not wish to have American policy anchored to them.

When Kennedy became President he did nothing to change the Eisenhower policy toward the islands. In June, 1962, in fact, when the Chinese Communists again built up their military forces opposite Quemoy and Matsu and another crisis appeared imminent, Kennedy gave special emphasis to his policy on Formosa Strait. That policy, he said, remains just what it has been since 1955.

Africa

Linked to the nationalist ferment in Asia in the postwar era was a young nationalism in Africa, the continent where colonialism and white rule over masses of colored peoples had been more complete than in Asia. Not until the Second World War had weakened the grip of Europeans over their colonies did Africans launch a broad movement to eliminate every vestige of colonialism, political or economic, and every other form of white dominance from their continent. The African revolt against the whites, because the peoples of Africa were generally less civilized and less politically conscious than those of Asia, embraced anticolonialism to a greater degree than it did nationalism.

Until the postwar awakening, the United States had not paid much attention to Africa, a continent remote from the centers of civilization and of minor importance in international politics. Africa had seldom been the center of crises involving American interests. Except for troops belonging to rival European powers, it had not contained military forces that threatened the security or the position of the United States in world affairs.

After the United States had tangled with the Barbary States in the late 18th and early 19th centuries, its interest in Africa derived mainly from the slave trade. Liberia, the one area on the African continent of special concern to Americans, grew out of efforts of the American Colonization Society in 1821 to find a place to settle freed Negro slaves. In 1847 Liberia proclaimed herself an independent republic and drew up a constitution based on that of the United States, but did not receive American recognition until 1862, after the southern states had seceded from the Union.

The United States had taken no part in the European scramble for African colonies in the 19th century, but in 1884, in the interest of trade, it became the first major power to recognize and negotiate a treaty of friendship and commerce with the International Association of the Congo. In November of that year, American delegates participated in the Berlin Conference that called for free trade in the Congo Basin and recognized the Congo association as a sovereign state, a territory that became known as the Congo Free State, the personal domain of Leopold II, King of the Belgians.[38]

Later American interest in Africa, except for the Algeciras Conference of 1906, came mainly through missionary activity there, primarily Protestant. In the 1930's American missionary work in Africa expanded and within three decades the number of missionaries increased fourfold.

After the Second World War, but primarily in the 1950's, Americans showed a new interest in Africa, primarily in Negro Africa, or what the French called *L'Afrique noire*, in contrast to Mediterranean Africa of the north, a region tied to the culture of the Middle East and largely Moslem. Articles, books, especially John Gunther's *Inside Africa*, and a spate of motion pictures all focused attention on the continent's problems and its place in the world. Demands for independence in France's North African possessions of Morocco, Tunisia, and Algeria, racial tensions in South Africa, and especially the atrocities of the Mau Mau, a secret native society in Kenya dedicated to driving the white "intruder" from the land, made all of Africa's turmoil a part of American thinking. So important did the continent of Africa become that in 1958 the Department of State finally established a special Bureau of African Affairs headed by an Assistant Secretary of State.

Since many Africans made it clear that they were unwilling captives of white colonialism and looked to the United States for encouragement in their quest for self-government, their desire for freedom posed a dilemma for policymakers. Americans sympathized with the African desire and in some ways encouraged it. Yet their British, and particularly their French, allies, who were bearing the brunt of the onslaught of African anticolonialism and nationalism, resented American pressure that urged concessions to the Africans.

In October, 1953, therefore, the United States announced a middle-of-the-road policy toward colonialism in Africa, saying it would determine its position on specific colonial issues as they arose. Africans, who had looked upon the United States, itself a former colonial area, as a symbol of success in the anticolonial struggle, thus could not forget that America's main Allies were the very powers from whom they had sought and were seeking independence. In its neutrality on the issues of colonialism the United States puzzled and disappointed many Africans.[39]

The Soviets and the Red Chinese, who wished to eliminate Western influence from Africa, endorsed African anticolonialism as strongly as they did Asian nationalism. With considerable success the Soviets cultivated the good will of newly independent African and Asian countries by their bold support and by promising the new nations assistance in political and economic development.

Africa and Asia's dislike of America's neutral stand on colonialism and the appeal of the Communist position stood out at the Asian-African Conference in April, 1955, in the mountain resort city of Bandung, Indonesia. Twenty-nine Asian and African states, most of whom had won independence in the past decade, sent delegates to this meeting that President Sukarno of Indonesia described as "the first international conference of colored peoples in the history of mankind!"[40] What gave those peoples a feeling of solidarity was their common struggle against European imperialism and later a belief in a common destiny.

The United States took a detached view of the conference, believing it would be anticolonial and anti-American, which in part it was. America also had her advocates, mainly the Filipino and Pakistani delegates, who defended their alliances with the United States and praised its program of economic assistance in Asia.

After some controversy over the definition of colonialism, the Bandung delegates, representing about 65 per cent of the world's population, adopted the principle that "colonialism in all its manifestations is an evil which should speedily be brought to an end."[41] They also condemned racial discrimination and segregation, particularly in the Union of South Africa, thus stressing that racialism was an important source of tension with the whites.

More violent attacks on colonialism and the Western powers took place at the end of December, 1957, in Cairo at the Asian-African Peoples Solidarity Conference, a meeting dominated by the Soviet delegation. Nearly 500 delegates from more than forty Asian and African countries, representing "peoples" rather than governments, heard a Soviet delegate promise to support independence movements and offer economic aid to all Asians and Africans.

In 1958, Accra, the capital of Ghana, played host to two international meetings that reflected Africa's growing nationalism. In April, eight countries sent representatives to a conference of independent African states, and in December delegates from twenty-five countries took part in the All-African Peoples Conference. The first one announced as its message to the world: "Hands off Africa! Africa must be free," [42] and the second was planned as the final assault on imperialism and colonialism. Those conferences thus marked a high point in African anticolonialism.

The Congo Tragedy

Among the delegates to the second conference was a young man from the Belgian Congo, Patrice Lumumba, the leader of a new political organization known as the *Mouvement National Congolais*. He returned to Leopoldville to tell 7000 excited residents that the conference had called for immediate independence for all of Africa and that he endorsed that decision for the Congo. From that moment on, events moved with startling and tragic swiftness in Belgium's colony, a land in the heart of Africa as big as all of Western Europe, but with only thirteen and a half million people.

In the following month, January, 1959, there was a riot in Leopoldville in which the police killed many Africans, and which stirred panic among the whites. Frightened by the specter of a racial revolution, Belgium then promised independence which was proclaimed on June 30, 1960. It was immediately followed by a breakdown in law and order in which the Congolese army turned on its white officers and on Belgian settlers. The government of Lumumba, who had become Prime Minister, was unable to control the army and other dissident elements. Belgian forces intervened, and partly as a result of the intervention, it seemed, secessionist movements sprang up. Lumumba appealed to the United Nations for assistance, which was voted in the middle of July along with a call for Belgian withdrawal from the Congo. At the same time Khrushchev brought the cold war to Africa by threatening intervention in the Congo. The United States then stepped in with a warning that it would do whatever was necessary to keep Soviet troops out.

When the United Nations troops arrived, Lumumba demanded that they suppress those who were challenging his authority. Secretary General Dag Hammarskjold insisted that the mandate of the United Nations called only for the restoration of law and order, not for intervention in the Congo's internal disputes. Yet the Soviets encouraged Lumumba's demands, posed as supporters of Congolese nationalism against foreign interference, and themselves intervened unilaterally by supplying Lumumba with a hundred trucks and fifteen air transports complete with crews and maintenance personnel. They succeeded in generating antagonism between Lumumba's government and the West.

The United States, in contrast to Russia, tried officially to follow a policy of neutrality and noninvolvement in the specific issues troubling the Congo. For this policy the United Nations seemed the ideal instrument, for the United States

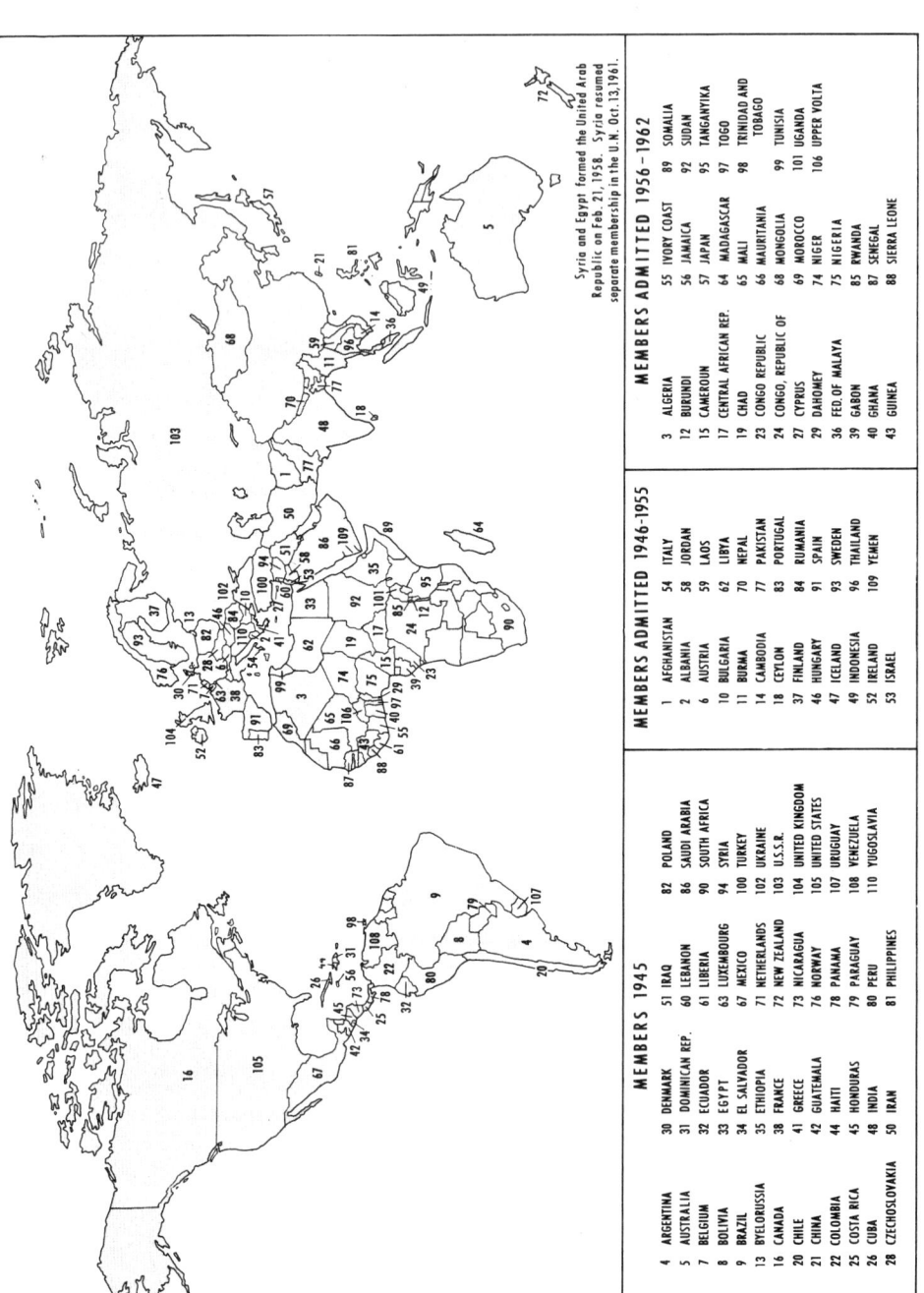

MEMBERS 1945

4	ARGENTINA	30	DENMARK	51	IRAQ	82	POLAND
5	AUSTRALIA	31	DOMINICAN REP.	60	LEBANON	86	SAUDI ARABIA
7	BELGIUM	32	ECUADOR	61	LIBERIA	90	SOUTH AFRICA
8	BOLIVIA	33	EGYPT	63	LUXEMBOURG	94	SYRIA
9	BRAZIL	34	EL SALVADOR	67	MEXICO	100	TURKEY
13	BYELORUSSIA	35	ETHIOPIA	71	NETHERLANDS	102	UKRAINE
16	CANADA	38	FRANCE	72	NEW ZEALAND	103	U.S.S.R.
20	CHILE	41	GREECE	73	NICARAGUA	104	UNITED KINGDOM
21	CHINA	42	GUATEMALA	76	NORWAY	105	UNITED STATES
22	COLOMBIA	44	HAITI	78	PANAMA	107	URUGUAY
25	COSTA RICA	45	HONDURAS	79	PARAGUAY	108	VENEZUELA
26	CUBA	48	INDIA	80	PERU	110	YUGOSLAVIA
28	CZECHOSLOVAKIA	50	IRAN	81	PHILIPPINES		

MEMBERS ADMITTED 1946-1955

1	AFGHANISTAN	54	ITALY
2	ALBANIA	58	JORDAN
6	AUSTRIA	59	LAOS
10	BULGARIA	62	LIBYA
11	BURMA	70	NEPAL
14	CAMBODIA	77	PAKISTAN
18	CEYLON	83	PORTUGAL
37	FINLAND	84	RUMANIA
46	HUNGARY	91	SPAIN
47	ICELAND	93	SWEDEN
49	INDONESIA	96	THAILAND
52	IRELAND	109	YEMEN
53	ISRAEL		

MEMBERS ADMITTED 1956-1962

3	ALGERIA	55	IVORY COAST	89	SOMALIA
12	BURUNDI	56	JAMAICA	92	SUDAN
15	CAMEROUN	57	JAPAN	95	TANGANYIKA
17	CENTRAL AFRICAN REP.	64	MADAGASCAR	97	TOGO
19	CHAD	65	MALI	98	TRINIDAD AND TOBAGO
23	CONGO REPUBLIC	66	MAURITANIA	99	TUNISIA
24	CONGO, REPUBLIC OF	68	MONGOLIA	101	UGANDA
27	CYPRUS	69	MOROCCO	106	UPPER VOLTA
29	DAHOMEY	74	NIGER		
36	FED. OF MALAYA	75	NIGERIA		
39	GABON	85	RWANDA		
40	GHANA	87	SENEGAL		
43	GUINEA	88	SIERRA LEONE		

Syria and Egypt formed the United Arab Republic on Feb. 21, 1958. Syria resumed separate membership in the U.N. Oct. 13, 1961.

THE GROWTH IN MEMBERSHIP OF THE UNITED NATIONS, 1945–1962

wanted it and not the Soviet Union to fill the vacuum created by the abrupt ending of Belgian rule. The United States refused to send its own troops, but contributed $5 million in cash to the United Nations for use in the Congo, as well as most of the airlift that brought the United Nations forces to the Congo, and its Air Force helped deploy these troops.

This did not please Lumumba, who charged that the United Nations was aiding his enemies. When he visited the United States in July and August, he asked for American help in throwing out the Belgians and crushing the secessionists, but received no commitment. Thus, the Congo tangle revealed that the United States could no longer play a secondary, or even indirect, part in African affairs. Africa's leaders demanded that it exert itself economically, morally, and politically in helping them to solve their problems.

The tide of Soviet influence receded as quickly as it had risen. In September, Joseph Kasavubu, the Congo's president, declared Lumumba deposed, and Colonel Joseph Mobutu, the twenty-nine-year-old chief of staff of the army, forced Soviet and other Communist personnel to leave the country. In November, Mobutu arrested Lumumba. The Soviets then accused Hammarskjold of treason to the Congolese people and of siding with a coalition of Western powers in the Congo.

The worst crisis came in February, 1961, when internal enemies brutally murdered Lumumba, an act that shocked world opinion. For a while it appeared that the Congo might be plunged into unrestrained tribal warfare, or into a civil war in which the Soviets actively supported Lumumba's successors. The war did not ensue, but the unrest continued.

In one sense the Congo situation caught the United States in what had by now become a familiar dilemma, one that seemingly required it to choose between loyalty to a European ally linked to a dying colonialism and friendship for a new and unstable African nation. The situation was complicated, moreover, by Russia's efforts to exploit the Congo difficulties to her own advantage and by the fact that Belgium had a poor colonial record. Yet the United States could not take a strong stand against its NATO ally, particularly when there was no convincing evidence available of Belgian double-dealing in the Congo.

The impact of the Congo tragedy on American policy and the importance of independent Africa in the cold war was also evident in the fifteenth session of the General Assembly of the United Nations that convened in New York in September, 1960. At that session seventeen new nations, all but one of them African and all former colonial territories, were admitted to the United Nations. The agenda was crammed, as never before, with African items. There was considerable substance to the observation that 1960 was the African year in the United Nations. The admittance of the new states completed the process whereby the Afro-Asian nations transformed the nature of the membership. The United Nations was no longer predominantly an association of the victors of the Second World War, for the African bloc, with twenty-six members, was now the largest in the world organization. Furthermore, an even larger Afro-Asian bloc had become a fact of international relations.

The Afro-Asians and the United Nations

The fifteenth session began in an atmosphere of crisis because of events in the Congo. The Communist bloc and the West competed for the favor of the Afro-Asian powers. Khrushchev himself attended as the chief Soviet delegate, with the aim of widening Soviet influence and gaining supporters among the uncommitted Afro-Asians, especially among the newly admitted African states. Moreover, he persuaded heads of governments from all over the world, but mostly from Communist bloc or neutralist states, to attend. Never before in modern history had so many world leaders a chance to see and talk to each other in one brief period.

President Eisenhower could not allow this Soviet wooing of the Afro-Asians on his own doorstep to go unchallenged. On September 22 he addressed the General Assembly and presented a five-point program for Africa, which was in effect the first authoritative statement of American policy applicable to the whole of that continent.[43] That policy stressed multilateral action through the United Nations.

On the following day Khrushchev delivered his address, a third of which was devoted to attacks on Western colonialism. In a bid for the favor of the Afro-Asians, he called for the abolition of colonialism everywhere. He also demanded Hammarskjold's removal from office for allegedly pursuing the policy of the colonialists in the Congo. In fact, he suggested that the post of Secretary General be abolished and replaced with a collective executive of three men representing Western, socialist, and neutralist countries, another application of the *troika* principle.

To many Americans the *troika* proposal appeared nothing more than an effort to cripple the United Nations, and the anti-imperialist Communist slogans seemed like efforts to revive dead or dying issues. Most Africans and Asians were now masters of their own houses and no longer held the place of servant in their relations with Europeans. Moreover, it was said, they and the whites needed each other; logically they should be economic partners. Yet it was clear that the Afro-Asians could still be stirred by those old slogans.

In the winter of 1960, the General Assembly approved an Afro-Asian resolution calling on members to take "immediate steps" toward independence for their dependent territories. In April, 1961, it passed another Afro-Asian resolution which asked Portugal to introduce reforms in her African colony of Angola. The debate on it brought a shift in American policy. Instead of remaining neutral and abstaining on such prickly colonial issues, as had Eisenhower, the Kennedy administration voted for the resolution. It did the same on a similar one in June.

THE EMERGENCE OF AFRICA, 1950–1962

There was no question that this shift gained applause from the Afro-Asians, but it hurt an old ally and put a strain on NATO, for Britain and France, as well as Portugal, resented it. One thing was clear; Kennedy had committed himself to a policy of improving relations with the Afro-Asians.

This policy encountered new difficulties in the strife-ridden Congo. In July, 1961, Cyrille Adoula, a moderate, was elected premier, and the United States increasingly supported his efforts to unify his country, particularly against the opposition of Moise Tshombe, president of Katanga, a province rich in copper and other minerals, which had seceded from the Congo eleven days after independence. In September, when a United Nations force attempted to carry out a resolution of the Security Council which directed that force to strip the Katanga army of its white mercenaries, the United Nations found itself virtually at war with Katanga.

Dag Hammarskjold tried to arrange a cease-fire and while flying to Northern Rhodesia to talk with Tshombe was killed in a plane crash. Hammarskjold's death plunged the United Nations into another crisis, for the Soviets attempted to take advantage of it to advance their *troika* plan for the Secretariat. To block such a move, the United States threatened to use its veto for the first time. The Russians then retreated and agreed, as did the Americans, upon U Thant of Burma as Acting Secretary General to fill the remaining time in Hammarskjold's term. U Thant took over on November 3.

Shortly after, on November 11, mutinous Congolese troops brutally butchered thirteen noncombatant Italian airmen of the United Nations force. The massacre shocked the world and led many to conclude that only the United Nations could prevent civil war, curb atrocities, and keep the cold war out of central Africa. Two weeks later, therefore, the Security Council again authorized the use of force to rid Katanga of its foreign mercenaries. The United States supported this Afro-Asian resolution, though it preferred a broader one directed against left-wing dissidents as well.

Early in December, a United Nations offensive against Katangese forces led to an open break between the United States and its British, French, Belgian, and Portuguese allies over policy in the Congo. The United States gave considerable financial and logistical support to the United Nations force, and its European Allies protested. Even within the United States, particularly among conservatives, there was strong sentiment in favor of Tshombe, who was considered staunchly anti-Communist, and against the United Nations, which was now regarded as being under the influence of the Afro-Asian bloc. Nonetheless, the Kennedy administration persisted in its policy because it viewed a united Congo, aided by the United Nations, as offering the best hope of thwarting Communist penetration of central Africa. Finally, the United Nations offensive forced Tshombe to agree to end Katanga's secession, seemingly strengthened Adoula, and led to suppression of left-wing dissidents also.

Despite its successful offensive, the United Nations failed to bring stability to the Congo. Like a cancer that refuses to be excised, the Katanga secession persisted. Tshombe stalled in carrying out his promise and by June, 1962, talks between him and Adoula to unify the Congo had broken down. Desperately in need of Katanga's mining revenues, the central government was on the verge of bankruptcy.

Ironically, the financing of the Congo operation had also brought the United Nations face to face with the possibility of bankruptcy. Many countries, but mainly Russia and France, refused to pay their share for the support of the United Nations forces in the Congo. To aid the United Nations and to continue the Congo operation, the Kennedy administration wished to loan the world organization, through the purchase of special bonds, $100 million. This loan was endangered by congressional hostility towards the United Nations because of the neutralism of the now influential Afro-Asians, a neutralism which appeared to favor the Soviet Union in many issues. Critics such as the Democratic senator from Washington, Henry M. Jackson, argued that American policy should not rely heavily on the United Nations, particularly in situations such as that in the Congo.

Nonetheless, the Kennedy administration continued to support U Thant's efforts to unify the Congo. In July, 1962, the Department of State denounced Tshombe's "intransigence." In the following month, when U Thant prepared to ask the Security Council of the United Nations to allow the use of sanctions against Katanga, the American government stood behind his plan without reservation. Friendship for the Africans and determination to keep the cold war out of Africa thus remained a basic part of American policy.

The Factor of Race

Another new element in American policy was the Peace Corps, a program that initially aroused more public enthusiasm than any other proposed by Kennedy. The Peace Corps idea, that of sending skilled young men and women to underdeveloped countries to help the people help themselves, grew out of the presidential campaign of 1960 and was revealed to the public at a whistle stop at the University of Michigan where student response was overwhelmingly favorable. As finally established by executive order in March, 1961, and on a permanent basis by Congress in September, the corps became a semiautonomous agency within the State Department. It required those who served to do so without pay and to accept the standard of living of those they served.[44] The plan drew a particularly warm reception from the Afro-Asian nations, the main hosts to the corps.

The members of the Peace Corps learned more quickly than most Americans, perhaps, that emerging Africa had made race a more vital issue in American foreign policy than ever before. One American in every ten claimed descent from Africa, and the treatment American Negroes received at home had considerable effect on the attitude of Africans toward the United States. "It should be understood," a prominent young African nationalist warned, "that we feel a special kinship with American Negroes, and that we see our struggles as closely related."[45] Racial discrimination alienated both Africans and Asians, and had become as much a problem of foreign policy as it was an internal one.

"We cannot talk equality to the peoples of Africa and Asia," Vice-President Nixon had reported after a tour of seven independent African countries, "and practice inequality in the United States."[46] It could hardly be questioned that the impact of discrimination against the Negro, in the North as well as the South, was harming American policy in Africa. In September, 1960, for instance, Khrushchev spoke of moving the seat of the United Nations out of New York, apparently as a means of drawing attention to the discrimination there against Asian and African delegates. In the national capital itself, the diplomats and their staffs from the new nations quickly encountered white bigotry and Jim Crow attitudes that barred them from restaurants and desirable housing. So acute did the problem become in 1961 that the State Department's chief of protocol, Angier Biddle Duke, assigned a special staff to aid the Africans in their quest for housing and schools for their children.[47]

Africans and Asians, many of whom had looked to the United States as a beacon of freedom, expected it to live up to its political ideals. Yet in 1962, it appeared that they had still to be convinced that the American concern for freedom embraced the colored man as well as the white.[48]

NOTES

1. See George McT. Kahin, "The Postwar Revolutions in Southeast Asia," *The Antioch Review*, XI (June 1951), 204–222.

2. For details, see Chester Bowles, *Africa's Challenge to America* (Berkeley, Calif., 1956), pp. 41–42.

3. Although the ideology of the United States was basically anticolonialist, its postwar record on the colonial question was inconsistent. At times it sided with the colonial powers, as with France in opposition to Algerian nationalists, and at other times it supported the anticolonial cause. See Robert C. Good, "The United States and the Colonial Debate," in Arnold Wolfers, ed., *Alliance Policy in the Cold War* (Baltimore, 1959), pp. 224–270. See also Philip W. Bell, "Colonialism as a Problem in American Foreign Policy," *World Politics*, V (Oct. 1952), 86–109 and Matthew J. Kust, "The Great Dilemma of American Foreign Policy," *Virginia Quarterly Review*, XXXIV (Spring 1958), 224–239.

4. Harry S. Truman, *Memoirs* (2 vols., Garden City, N.Y., 1955), I, 275. Roosevelt, as President, had also consistently been an anticolonialist. See Foster Rhea Dulles and Gerald E. Ridinger, "The Anti-Colonial

Policies of Franklin D. Roosevelt," *Political Science Quarterly*, LXX (March 1955), 1–18.

5. Aug. 12, 1943, in Samuel I. Rosenman, comp., *The Public Papers of Franklin D. Roosevelt* (13 vols., New York, 1938–1950), XII, 349.

6. Summarized in Garel A. Grunder and William E. Livezey, *The Philippines and the United States* (Norman, Okla., 1951), pp. 171–172.

7. The story of the Hukbalahap and its suppression is in Alvin H. Scaff, *The Philippine Answer to Communism* (Stanford, Calif., 1955).

8. The invitation is in the *Department of State Bulletin*, XXV (July 30, 1951), 186–187.

9. John Foster Dulles, "Security in the Pacific," *Foreign Affairs*, XXX (Jan. 1952), 181.

10. Dulles' statement is in the *Department of State Bulletin*, XXV (Sept. 17, 1951), 452–459.

11. Shigeru Yoshida, Sept. 7, 1951, quoted in Richard P. Stebbins, *The United States in World Affairs, 1951* (New York, 1952), p. 196. For additional details on the Japanese

reaction, see Shigeru Yoshida, *The Yoshida Memoirs: The Story of Japan in Crisis* (Boston, 1962), pp. 254-275.

12. Bernard C. Cohen, *The Political Process and Foreign Policy: The Making of the Japanese Peace Settlement* (Princeton, 1957), p. 20.

13. Richard P. Stebbins, *The United States in World Affairs, 1953* (New York, 1955), pp. 260-261.

14. For the story of the twenty-three crew members of the tuna trawler, see Ralph E. Lapp, *The Voyage of the Lucky Dragon* (New York, 1958).

15. July 9, 1957, quoted in Sherman Adams, *Firsthand Report: The Story of the Eisenhower Administration* (New York, 1961), p. 410.

16. *Ibid.*, p. 411.

17. *Department of State Bulletin*, XLII (Feb. 8, 1960), 180. The text of the treaty and related documents are on pp. 184-201.

18. Quoted in Dan Kurzman, *Kishi and Japan: The Search for the Sun* (New York, 1960), p. 326.

19. In an excellent analysis of the Japanese riots and opposition to the security treaty, "The Broken Dialogue with Japan," *Foreign Affairs*, XXXIX (Oct. 1960), 11-26, Edwin O. Reischauer points out that there was, ironically, no general anti-American feeling among the Japanese people.

20. A resolution of the Indian National Congress, quoted in Lawrence K. Rosinger, *India and the United States: Political and Economic Relations* (New York, 1950), p. 34.

21. Feb. 24, 1954, quoted in Richard P. Stebbins, *The United States in World Affairs, 1954* (New York, 1956), p. 325. For relations with Pakistan, see Norman D. Palmer, "The United States and Pakistan," *Current History*, XXXIV (March 1958), 141-147.

22. Vice-President Mohammed Hatta, quoted in Russell H. Fifield, *The Diplomacy*

of *Southeast Asia, 1945-1958* (New York, 1958), p. 110. For an analysis critical of American policy in Indonesia, see Denna F. Fleming, *The Cold War and Its Origins, 1917-1960* (2 vols., New York, 1960), II, 662-667.

23. Viet Nam News Agency, Aug. 17, 1950, quoted in Ellen J. Hammer, *The Struggle for Indochina* (Stanford, Calif., 1954), p. 251.

24. Eisenhower used the analogy of the falling dominoes in a news conference of April 17, 1954. For details, see Robert J. Donovan, *Eisenhower: The Inside Story* (New York, 1956), p. 261.

25. Address of April 18, 1953, *Department of State Bulletin*, XXVIII (April 27, 1953), 605.

26. For details on a secret conference of Dulles and congressional leaders on the question of intervention, see Chalmers M. Roberts, "The Day We Didn't Go to War," *The Reporter*, XI (Sept. 14, 1954), 31-35. The day was April 3, 1954.

27. See *Full Circle: The Memoirs of Anthony Eden* (Boston, 1960), pp. 106-119.

28. April 16, 1954, quoted in Norman A. Graebner, *The New Isolationism: A Study in Politics and Foreign Policy Since 1950* (New York, 1956), p. 164.

29. July 23, 1954, quoted in Stebbins, *U.S. in World Affairs, 1954*, p. 255.

30. The texts of the charter, treaty, and protocol are in *Department of State Bulletin*, XXXI (Sept. 20, 1954), 393-396.

31. Sept. 15, 1954, quoted in Stebbins, *U.S. in World Affairs, 1954*, p. 261. For a detailed appraisal of the American commitment to SEATO, see Myron Weiner, "United States Policy in South and Southeast Asia," in Stephen D. Kertesz, ed., *American Diplomacy in a New Era* (Notre Dame, Ind., 1961), pp. 178-181.

32. March 23, 1961, *Department of State Bulletin*, XLIV (April 17, 1961), 543.

33. Address to the nation of June 6 in *The New York Times*, June 7, 1961, 16–17.

34. Press conference of Aug. 17, 1954, quoted in Donovan, *Eisenhower*, p. 300.

35. Quoted in Hollis W. Barber, *The United States in World Affairs, 1955* (New York, 1957), p. 94. Eisenhower's reasons for seeking the resolution are explained in Adams, *Firsthand Report*, pp. 129–130.

36. See James Shepley, "How Dulles Averted War," *Life*, XL (Jan. 16, 1956), 70–72, 77–78. Sherman Adams, Eisenhower's close adviser, doubted that the President had been led as close to the brink as Dulles claimed in this article. See Adams, *Firsthand Report*, p. 118.

37. News conference of Sept. 30, 1960, in *Department of State Bulletin*, XXXIX (Oct. 20, 1958), 599. Critical analyses of American policy in the Formosa crises are in Fleming, *Cold War Origins*, II, 707–736, 930–939.

38. For American financial interest in the Congo, see Robert Wuliger, "The Congo Tragedy: The Americans' Early Role," *The Nation*, CLXXVII (Dec. 26, 1953), 568–569. The rise of American interest in Negro Africa is summarized in J. Gus Liebnow, "United States Policy in Africa South of the Sahara," in Kertesz, ed., *American Diplomacy in a New Era*, pp. 236–269.

39. Robert C. Good, in "The United States and the Colonial Debate," in Wolfers, ed., *Alliance Policy*, p. 263, suggests that American policy on colonialism was based on what would best promote the collective defense of the non-Communist world, that this was the decisive question asked as each controversial case arose. See also Hans. J. Morgenthau, "United States Policy toward Africa," in Calvin W. Stillman, ed., *Africa in the Modern World* (Chicago, 1955), pp. 317–325.

40. The opening address, quoted in Richard Wright, *The Color Curtain: A Report on the Bandung Conference* (Cleveland, 1956), p. 136.

41. From the final communiqué in George McT. Kahin, *The Asian-African Conference* (Ithaca, New York, 1956), p. 81.

42. Dr. Kwame Nkrumah, quoted in Richard P. Stebbins, *The United States in World Affairs, 1958* (New York, 1959), p. 261.

43. Richard P. Stebbins, *The United States in World Affairs, 1960* (New York, 1961), p. 195.

44. The Executive order of March 1, 1961, and a message to Congress recommending a permanent Peace Corps are in *Department of State Bulletin*, XLIV (March 20, 1961), 400–403. For details on the corps, see Maurice L. Albertson *et al.*, *New Frontiers for American Youth: Perspective on the Peace Corps* (Washington, 1961).

45. Tom Mboya, "Key Questions for Awakening Africa," *The New York Times Magazine* (June 28, 1959), p. 39. James Reston, in *The New York Times*, Feb. 17, 1961, pointed out that "we are beginning to see a confluence of the world struggle for freedom in Black Africa and the struggle for equal rights in the Negro communities of America."

46. Nixon's report of April 7, 1957, is in *Department of State Bulletin*, XXXVI (April 22, 1957), 635–640. This point is also stressed in Robert S. Browne, *Race Relations in International Affairs* (Washington, 1961). Browne, himself a Negro, visited forty countries, mostly Asian and African, and in each one the question of the Negro in America came up for discussion, pp. 28–29.

47. For other details, see Richard P. Stebbins, *The United States in World Affairs, 1961* (New York, 1962), pp. 248–249.

48. According to Rupert Emerson, in "American Policy in Africa," *Foreign Affairs*, XL (Jan. 1962), 305, "So long as men's lives are prejudiced by the color of their skins the American standing in Africa will rest on shaky foundations."

Chapter Thirty-One

GLOBALISM
IN CRISIS

In the 1960's America's global commitments involved her in crises and conflicts whose demands exceeded her resources. Defenders of government policy said the United States must fight Communism and help its friends wherever needed. They warned against the revival of an ostrichlike isolationism. Critics argued that the United States, even with its immense wealth, could not afford to assume the burdens of the world's policeman. Its foreign policy should still follow the principle of enlightened self-interest, committing resources to battle only where the effort would serve the nation's interest and had a chance of succeeding. Nowhere did these attitudes stand out in sharper contrast than in debates over intervention in Vietnam. There Americans were fighting the longest, most divisive war in their history. That conflict, in the last half of the decade, affected all aspects of foreign policy and corroded much of American life.

Cuba: The Missile Crisis

Before the Vietnam War came to dominate the conduct of American foreign policy the most frightening crisis of the decade took place not in Asia but in neighboring Cuba. After the Bay of Pigs fiasco the United States tightened its economic sanctions against Cuba. Fidel Castro turned to the Soviet Union for aid and protection, and the Soviets supplied him with modern fighter planes and anti-aircraft missiles. They also sent him offensive weapons, mainly jet planes capable of delivering nuclear bombs and ballistic missiles that could take nuclear warheads.

Late in August, 1962, photographs taken by U-2 reconnaissance flights over Cuba showed missile sites under construction. Worried more about developments in Berlin and Southeast Asia than in Cuba, President Kennedy assumed that the new installations were defensive and saw no threat in them. Yet throughout September the government remained alert, increasing the U-2 surveillance. It also continued efforts to isolate Cuba, gaining support from the foreign ministers of the Americas who at the invitation of the State Department met informally in Washington on October 2–3 and urged special measures for tightening control over strategic shipments going to Castro.

On October 15 the President viewed new photographs from a U-2 flight showing a launching pad and other installations for medium-range nuclear missiles in a field near San Cristóbal. Kennedy and his advisers interpreted the work of Soviet technicians, who were readying other sites, as a challenge to the Monroe Doctrine and an effort to change the balance of power between the Soviet bloc and the West. Ruling out an air strike to destroy the missile sites, an attack that would kill thousands of civilians and undermine America's moral position in the world, the President decided, as a first step, to blockade Cuba. This would prevent entry of further offensive weapons; then he would force removal of the missiles already there.

On the evening of October 22, 1962, Kennedy addressed the American people via television telling them he had "unmistakable evidence" that the Soviets were building missile sites in Cuba to strike against American cities. He announced his blockade. So that the Soviet leaders would not miscalculate his intentions, he gave them a clear warning, saying he would "regard any nuclear missile launched from Cuba against any nation in the Western Hemisphere as an attack by the Soviet Union on the United States requiring a full retaliatory response upon the Soviet Union." America's armed forces then went on a war alert.

Meeting in emergency session on the following day, the Council of the Organization of American States voted unanimously to support Kennedy's actions. The blockade, euphemistically called a "quarantine" because international law does not permit a blockade in time of peace, went into effect on October 24.[1] If the Soviet ships resisted orders to stop and be searched, American naval commanders were authorized to fire on them. U Thant, Secretary General of the United Nations, proposed a suspension of both the Soviet arms shipments and the American quarantine to permit time for negotiation. Khrushchev, who said he was determined to avoid "reckless decisions," accepted this suggestion at once, but Kennedy refused because it ignored the missiles already in Cuba. The President did make clear his desire not to fire on Soviet ships and also his determination to enforce the quarantine.

A fearful and tense world waited to see if the two great powers would collide. Fortunately reason prevailed. A number of Russian ships bound for Cuba reversed course and others never challenged the blockade. Seeing that a nuclear war would benefit no one, least of all his own country, Khrushchev apparently was willing to back down, but a mutually acceptable solution had to be found to end the confrontation.[2]

STRATEGIC FACTORS IN CUBAN CRISIS

The Soviets quickly came up with a plan for peace. Aleksander Fomin, a counselor in the Soviet embassy, told John Scali, a correspondent for the American Broadcasting Company, that the Soviet Union would remove the missiles from Cuba under inspection of the United Nations if the United States would lift the blockade and promise publicly not to invade Cuba. Scali transmitted the proposal to the Department of State. Then two letters from Khrushchev arrived that confused Washington. One, dated October 26, confirmed the proposal made through Scali; the second, on the following day, asked the United States to take its missiles from Turkey in exchange for removal of Soviet missiles from Cuba. Kennedy ignored the latter proposal and replied to the first one, promising to lift the quarantine and "give assurances against an invasion of Cuba." At 9 a.m. Sunday, October 28, the President received word that Khrushchev had accepted his terms. The "eyeball to eyeball" confrontation was over; the world had not been blown up as a result of its first thermonuclear crisis.

Tension continued for weeks, mainly because Castro angrily refused to permit the United Nations to verify the Russian withdrawal. Nonetheless the Soviets dismantled their bases, crated their missiles and jet bombers, and pulled them and most of their troops out of Cuba. The United States verified the withdrawal through aerial surveillance and lifted the quarantine on November 20. Since ground inspection of the sites was never made, the United States withheld its formal promise not to invade Cuba. The Kennedy–Khrushchev agreement was never fully honored, but its substance was, and that was the crucial factor in preserving peace.

Most observers concluded that the Soviet Union had suffered a diplomatic defeat and that American prestige had risen everywhere, but prestige amounted to nothing in comparison to the stakes—the fate of mankind. As Khrushchev later explained, "We were very close—very, very close—to a thermonuclear war."[3] Kennedy himself never claimed a great victory, and he ordered his policy advisers not to do so. "He respected Khrushchev for properly determining what was in his own country's interest and what was in the interest of mankind," Robert F. Kennedy recalled of his brother.[4] Victory belonged to all the statesmen who had looked into the furnace of nuclear war and had had the wisdom to pull back.

After the passing of the missile crisis the United States continued efforts to destroy Castro, but through economic and political means, not military measures. It tried to block all trade between nations of the West and Cuba. In July, 1964, after the Organization of American States had substantiated charges that Castro was smuggling arms into Venezuela, the United States persuaded that organization to impose economic sanctions on Cuba and to bar all members from official relations with Havana. Despite this support for the United States many Latin Americans sympathized with Castro's efforts to export revolution. They and some liberals within the United States questioned the value of high sounding programs such as the Alliance for Progress which seemed less concerned about finding cures for Latin American ills than in stemming Communism. This exaggerated fear of Communism and of *Fidelismo* led to an unpopular intervention in the Dominican Republic.

The Dominican Intervention

The roots of the trouble were embedded in the thirty-year regime of Rafael Leonidas Trujillo, a vicious dictator. He was assassinated in May, 1961, and later his family, which attempted to perpetuate his tyranny, was expelled from the

Dominican Republic. In December, 1962, the Dominicans elected Juan Bosch, a liberal intellectual, president. Seven months later a military *coup* overthrew him, its leaders charging him with being too lenient toward Communists. Dismayed by the reestablishment of a dictatorship, the Kennedy administration cut off economic aid to the republic. When Lyndon B. Johnson became President he resumed some assistance, assuming it would benefit the United States to have stability there even though he preferred a democratic regime.

Yet stability eluded the Dominicans. Drought, widespread unemployment, strikes, sabotage, and underground resistance to the rulers kept the country in turmoil. Then on April 24, 1965, a group of young army officers favorable to Bosch attempted a *coup* and failed, plunging the country into civil war. American policymakers suspected that the rebel movement was being infiltrated by disciplined Communists, but Washington at first refused requests for intervention. Fearing that the rebels were about to triumph, the American ambassador, W. Tapley Bennett, on the afternoon of April 28 urged the immediate landing of troops, an "armed intervention," as requested by the conservative regime. Within a few hours President Johnson decided to send in the marines. That evening, after notifying Congress, he addressed the nation in a televised broadcast explaining that he was rushing troops to the Dominican Republic to protect the lives of Americans there. Within a few weeks, as the civil war continued, the American invaders, who set up a neutral zone between the warring Dominicans, numbered more than twenty thousand.

Since the intervention violated commitments to the Organization of American States and the United Nations, and seemed a repudiation of nonintervention policies going back thirty years, it angered Latin Americans and aroused the wrath of many liberals in the United States. Critics quickly pointed out that Johnson had notified neither Congress nor the Organization of American States before deciding to intervene. He did not, moreover, immediately reveal his real motive: to prevent the Dominican Republic from becoming another Cuba. He explained his fear on television on May 2. "The revolutionary movement took a tragic turn," the President asserted. "Communist leaders, many of them trained in Cuba...joined the revolution. They took increasing control." "We don't expect to sit here on our rocking chairs with our hands folded and let the Communists set up any government in the Western Hemisphere," he said emphatically on the following day.[5] Yet neither he nor the Department of State offered convincing evidence of such Communist control. Regardless of how he justified his hasty invasion, Johnson could not stem the new wave of anti-Americanism that swept over Latin America. He had, obviously, departed from the principles of the Good Neighbor Policy and the Alliance for Progress, and he had resurrected the "big stick" tactics of the past.

Embarrassed, the President then tried to repair the damage as best he could with the help of the Organization of American States. He persuaded that body to set up an Inter-American Peace Force to police the Dominican Republic. Five Latin American nations, as well as the United States, contributed troops. Placed under the command of a Brazilian general, this force took over responsibility from the Americans on May 24. This arrangement converted the military venture into a multilateral occupation less offensive to Latin Americans than the original American intervention. It also saved face for Johnson, permitting him to remove most American troops without appearing to bow to pressure and without having to admit he had made a mistake.[6]

Even though civil strife subsided, the Dominican Republic remained a place of tension for about a year when new national elections were held. To everyone's surprise the voters in June, 1966, chose Joacquín Balaguer, a right-of-center politician of the Trujillo era, for president. Then the Inter-American Peace Force, amid demonstrations of "Yankees go home," began withdrawing, officially ending the intervention in September.

On the surface Johnson appeared to have won his objectives: protection of American lives, the halting of violence, the prevention of an alleged Communist *coup*, and the establishment of a democratically chosen government. Despite this fortuitous ending, his high-handed use of force seriously damaged the Alliance for Progress and intensified distrust and hostility toward the United States throughout Latin America. The cost of the intervention, more than $150 million, far exceeded the value of aid the United States had been giving to the Dominicans.

Panama: Canal Rights and Riots

Johnson handled a concurrent crisis in Panama with greater circumspection. Panamanians had long resented their protectorate relationship to the United States, especially in the Canal Zone with its privileges for Americans and discriminations against their own people. They also desired a larger share of the canal's earnings, even though in treaties signed in March, 1936, and August, 1955, the United States alleviated some of Panama's grievances and raised its annual payment of rent for the canal to $1.93 million. Basically the Panamanians wanted to abrogate the original Hay-Bunau-Varilla Treaty of 1903, and thereby terminate the perpetual right of control over the Canal Zone by the United States.

In November, 1959, Panamanian nationalists had vented their feelings by attempting a symbolic occupation of the Canal Zone. When demonstrators carrying Panamanian flags were repelled by American soldiers, both sides suffered injuries. Mobs then attacked the embassy and other American property, and Panama asked the right to display its flag over the Canal Zone. Congress expressed opposition, but as a conciliatory gesture President Eisenhower in September, 1960, ordered Panama's flag flown in a park in the Canal Zone as evidence of its "titular sovereignty." In 1961 the Panamanians demanded a "total revision" of the canal treaties. President Kennedy held back, mainly because of opposition in Congress where security of the canal was a touchy issue and because he wished to reach a decision on a new sea-level canal, then under study, before negotiating. The old canal was too narrow, too congested, and too vulnerable to sabotage. American officials did extend Eisenhower's agreement by permitting Panama's flag to fly at all points in the Canal Zone where civilian authorities displayed the Stars and Stripes. To avoid difficulties with chauvinistic resident Americans, or "Zonians," the authorities decided in December, 1963, not to fly flags at all in the schools in the zone.

When American students returned to Balboa High School after their Christmas vacation they ignored the request of the Canal Zone governor. On January 7, 1964, they raised the American flag at the school. Two days later Panamanian high school students marched into the zone and ran up their own flag. These incidents set off four days of anti-American riots, leading at times to guerrilla fighting between Panamanians and American troops. Before the violence ended twenty-one Panamanians and four American soldiers died, more than $2 million in property was destroyed, and Panama broke off diplomatic relations with the United States, charging it with "unjustifiable aggression" before the Security Council of the United Nations.

Then the Inter-American Peace Committee of the Organization of American States stepped in with good offices. On January 15 Panama agreed to resume diplomatic relations, assuming that in the future the United States would consent to revision of the treaty of 1903, a symbol of "Yankee imperialism." Johnson went ahead with negotiations, which moved slowly. On December 18 he broke the stalemate by announcing a major decision, that the United States planned to build a new sea-level canal either in Central America or Columbia and would negotiate a new canal treaty with Panama.[7]

Finally, in June, 1967, after negotiating more than two years, the presidents of the two countries announced agreement on the abrogation of the treaty of 1903 and its replacement with three new treaties. These would recognize Panama's sovereignty over the canal area, give her greater control over it than in the old agreement, and provide for joint defense of the canal. They would also permit the building of a new sea-level waterway or the improvement of the existing canal, and would grant rights for American military forces and installations in the Canal Zone. Even though they provided for eventual Panamanian operation of the canal, the terms, which perpetuated special privileges for Zonians, did not satisfy the nationalists. In September, 1970, Panama's government rejected the three treaties.[8] Having anticipated the rejection, American policy-makers financed a study on the feasibility of building a second canal beyond Panama's borders.

Anti-Americanism in the Americas

In the late sixties strain and discord characterized the relations of the United States with many of the Latin American republics; almost everywhere anti-Americanism in one form or another could be found. As in the past the Latins complained of neglect and of insufficient economic help. The American government argued, on the other hand, that they should do more than they had for themselves, mainly through social and political reforms. Policymakers in Washington wanted the republics to spend less on armaments and more on projects which could generate their own capital. Reflecting this attitude, Congress in 1967 cut funds for the Alliance for Progress. By the end of the decade the Alliance as an effective instrument of policy was dead.

Within the United States planners believed that important reforms could come through a revision of the charter of the Organization of American States and the creation of a Latin American common market similar to the one in Europe. In February, 1967, the foreign ministers of the Americas adopted a protocol amendment to the OAS charter that would make important structural changes and give the organization enhanced authority in social and economic matters. But this amendment could not overcome a basic Latin criticism of the Organization of American States, that it was not truly independent of United States policy, a criticism made sharper by the acquiescence of the OAS in the intervention in the Dominican Republic. In April at a meeting of presidents from the nations of the Americas in Punta del Este, Uruguay, President Johnson persuaded the leaders there to plan for a Latin American common market within fifteen years. Secretary of State Dean Rusk hailed the agreement as one of the most important since the independence of Latin America. But plans for the common market quickly bogged down.

Anti-Americanism also expressed itself through the old idea that United States corporations in Latin America were instruments for carrying out Washington's foreign policy. This attitude could be seen in a long dispute in Peru between the government and the International Petroleum Company, a subsidiary of Standard Oil of New Jersey. In October, 1968, the ruling military *junta* in Lima expropriated all assets of International Petroleum without payment, alleging that the company owed $690 million in back taxes. This led to a crisis with the United States complicated also by a "fishermen's war." Peru and Ecuador tried to enforce control of a maritime fishing zone extending two hundred miles offshore. American fishing vessels from California followed schools of bluefin tuna to twenty to sixty miles off the coast. Peruvian and Ecuadorian naval vessels then "arrested" the American ships, forcing them to pay fines. After some heated diplomatic exchanges, with the United States threatening to retaliate by cutting off aid to Peru, President Richard M. Nixon in August, 1969, sent a special envoy to Lima who managed to patch the quarrel.

Despite such conciliatory actions Nixon was not popular in Latin America, largely because he gave that part of the world a secondary place in his foreign policy and also because he wished to replace government loans there with private capital. The Latins disliked the idea of paying higher interest for private loans.

Aware of Latin dissatisfactions, Nixon in May, 1969, sent Governor Nelson A. Rockefeller of New York on a fact finding mission to twenty Latin American nations. Anti-American violence, similar to that encountered by Nixon himself in 1958, marred all four of Rockefeller's visits. The governments of Peru, Chile, and Venezuela even asked him to stay away; his mere presence seemed to act as a catalyst for violence, leading critics to ask if his trips were necessary or even desirable. His exhaustive report, made public by the White House in November, recommended changes in the inter-American system, and most important, it urged preferential trade treatment for Latin American products coming to the United States. But his mission and report did little to alleviate anti-Americanism in the Americas. Nixon, moreover, did not accept the thrust of Rockefeller's recommendations.

Canadians, too, went through a period of mild anti-Americanism, summed up in their phrase, "The United States is our best friend—whether we like it or not." In January, 1963, American policymakers publicly reproved the Canadians for not living up to defense responsibilities with NATO, causing an uproar in Ottawa. Prime Minister John G. Diefenbaker then called for new elections and made a political issue of American interference in Canada's internal affairs, but it was not enough to save his government which fell in April.

The new Liberal prime minister, Lester B. Pearson, immediately tried to repair relations with the United States. In January, 1964, after meeting the objections of his countrymen to the original version of 1961, he concluded a revised treaty for the joint development of the power resources of the Columbia River.[9] He ran into difficulty, however, over American policy in Vietnam, which many Canadians opposed. In April, 1965, when President Johnson took offense at Pearson's criticism of the Vietnam War, the prime minister insisted on the right of Canadian officials to express themselves openly on American foreign policy.

Pearson's successor, Pierre Elliott Trudeau, also emphasized Canada's independence from American hegemony while remaining a friend and ally, a position he made clear to President Nixon in March, 1969, when he visited Washington. Independence also came out in Trudeau's support of Canada's claim to ownership of the Arctic archipelago. Americans challenged that claim because they wished free passage of the channels between the islands, especially as a route for transporting Alaskan oil by ice-breaking tankers. Trudeau maintained that Canada would exercise full sovereign control over all the waters between the islands, "no matter what they say in the United States."[10] The State Department refused to recognize any exercise of coastal jurisdiction over "our vessels in the high seas." So two of the world's friendliest neighbors were facing a confrontation over the status of the Arctic seas.

Continuing Tension in the Middle East

In the Middle East Arab nationalism and hostility between neighbors kept the area in ferment. As before, Egypt's Gamal Abdel Nasser and the reaction to him stimulated much of the unrest. He denounced Saudi Arabia and Yemen's feudal regimes, urging the Arab masses to liberate their countries from backwardness. When in September, 1962, pro-Nasser revolutionaries overthrew the monarchy in Yemen, proclaiming a republic and triggering a civil war, he rushed troops to aid the new government. Saudi Arabia backed the monarchists. While recognizing the republican regime, the United States took a neutral stand and worked to prevent the war from spreading beyond Yemen's borders.[11]

At the same time violence became a way of life along Israel's borders. Arab commandos raided Israel from Syria, Jordan, and Egypt. When the Soviets started supplying Egypt and Syria with modern weapons Israeli leaders asked the United States for an alliance, or guarantee of Israel's independence. President Kennedy refused, but he said in May, 1963, the United States would oppose aggression anywhere in the Middle East. In August when Israel complained, for the first time, to the United Nations against Syria for attacking her the United States and Britain asked for condemnation of Syria, but the Soviet Union vetoed the proposal.

In the following year, Nasser devoted more attention to Israel. He and other Arab leaders created a new Palestine Liberation Organization and a Palestine army to wrench Palestine from Israel. In 1965 a Palestine underground terrorist group, *Al Fatah* (conquest), began raiding Israel from Syria and Jordan; Israelis retaliated with punitive raids into Jordan. The Syrians encouraged *Al Fatah* and called on all Arab revolutionaries to join the crusade against Israel. The Soviets supported this bellicosity and spoke of Syria as a neighbor who merited help. In 1966 Israel again asked the Security Council of the United Nations to stop stepped-up attacks from Syria, and again the Soviets vetoed such action. Israel retaliated with a massive attack on Jordan in November.

This reprisal did not halt Arab raids either from Syria or Jordan. So the Israelis escalated their own attacks. In April, 1967, Israeli jet planes struck across the border to smash Syrian artillery, destroy six Syrian jets, and pursue others to the edge of Damascus, sixty miles away. Now both sides were moving toward full-scale war. The final push came not from Syria, but from her ally Egypt.

The Six Day War

Claiming that Israel was mobilizing huge forces on Syria's border, Nasser promised the Syrians help if attacked, placed Egyptian forces on a war footing, and ordered them northward toward Israel. On May 18 he formally asked for with-drawal of the peacekeeping United Nations Emergency Force of thirty-four hun-dred men that for ten years had patrolled the armistice line between Egypt and Israel. They were stationed on Egyptian soil from the Sinai border to Sharm el-Sheikh, a camp overlooking the Strait of Tiran, the narrow entrance to the Gulf of Aqaba. U Thant, the Secretary General of the United Nations, ordered the troops withdrawn, and Egyptians took over.

On May 22 Nasser closed the Strait of Tiran to Israeli shipping, saying "the Aqaba Gulf constitutes Egyptian territorial waters."[12] This action involved the United States, for Israel had withdrawn from Sharm el-Sheikh after the Sinai War of 1956 only under pressure from President Eisenhower, who also had promised to uphold Israel's right to use the gulf freely. On that basis in the preceding decade Israel had built up the port of Elath at the head of the gulf for importing oil and as her only outlet to the south. Israel's prime minister called the closing an act of aggression against his country. President Johnson, saying the United States con-siders the Gulf of Aqaba "an international waterway," on the following day condemned the Egyptian blockade as illegal and "disastrous to the cause of peace." He then appealed to Egypt to permit free passage of the strait and to Israel to hold back any reprisal; he promised to work out an international guarantee of free passage. Nasser rejected the appeal, asserting "Israel today is the United States." Israelis were disappointed; Premier Levi Eshkol later said, "Johnson promised great things," but came across with nothing concrete.[13] So Johnson's appeals had no effect.

Other Arab nations rushed to Nasser's support; Egypt, Syria, and Jordan massed troops on Israel's borders. As they did so, but before they could move in, Israel, which had held back her forces only because of American pressure, struck. On the morning of June 5, 1967, her planes caught most of the Egyptian air force on the ground and destroyed it, and her army raced across the Sinai Peninsula. Johnson and Soviet Premier Aleksei N. Kosygin quickly assured each other that their countries would not plunge into the war. The United States called for a truce, but to no effect. On June 6, with the Arab forces going down to defeat, the Security Council of the United Nations adopted a Soviet proposal for a cease-fire. Accusing the United States of using war planes to aid Israel, Nasser broke off diplomatic relations with Washington.

Within the week Israelis expelled Egyptian troops from the Sinai Peninsula, including Sharm el-Sheikh, and drove them back to the western side of the Suez Canal. Israelis conquered the west bank of Jordan, took over all of Jerusalem, and occupied the high ground along the Syrian border, the Golan Heights. They also captured or destroyed an estimated $1 billion in Russian military equipment. By June 10 all belligerents had accepted the United Nations demand for a cease-fire and the war was over.

No True Peace

Despite Israel's sweeping victory, a peace settlement eluded her. The United Nations condemned the war, demanding that the Israelis evacuate the lands they conquered. The Israelis refused, saying they would discuss the issue only in direct peace negotiations with their Arab enemies. Even though beaten and humiliated, the Arab states demanded withdrawal as a condition for talking peace. The Soviet Union backed the Arab position. While the United States insisted on the principle of preserving the territorial integrity of all Middle Eastern nations, it would not join the Russians in pressuring Israel to surrender her gains without Arab guarantees recognizing her freedom to exist. American policymakers pointed out that the restoration of the *status quo ante bellum* would bring no real peace; in fact, it would solve nothing.

Johnson, however, refused to recognize Israel's annexation of old Jerusalem. What he desired was a negotiated settlement that would preserve Israel as a nation, return conquered lands to the Arabs, and create machinery for keeping the peace. Yet Johnson and other Americans found Israel's victory more acceptable than an Arab triumph would have been; the war stimulated a widespread pro-Israeli feeling in the United States. This attitude, coupled with a commitment to keep Israel from being sacrificed to Arab nationalism, again brought the United States into confrontation with the Soviet Union.

Virtually before the guns were cold the Soviets rushed new arms to Egypt, Syria, and Iraq. This time, to make sure they would be used properly, the Russians also sent technicians and military advisers. In 1968 and 1969 the Soviet battle fleet frequently penetrated the Mediterranean and usually could be seen in Arab ports. Ironically, the Arab defeat enhanced rather than diminished Soviet penetration in the Middle East. American policymakers now had to recognize that the Soviet Union had gained a dominant position in the area.

Bitter Arab nationalists were turning more and more to socialist revolutionary doctrines as the hope of the future. In this attitude they had the support, at least ideologically, of much of the Afro-Asian world. The Afro-Asian leaders, as did Arabs and Soviet propagandists, considered Israel the instrument of American imperialism, just as the Israelis believed that Soviet backing of the Arabs threatened their survival. In 1969 the Arab states, particularly Egypt and Syria, and various Arab commando organizations, raided Israel's borders and daily shelled her fortifications along the Suez Canal. Israel struck back with daily air raids on Egyptian positions. The cease-fire no longer had meaning. As for the American policy of theoretical impartiality, it was discredited throughout the Arab world; Arabs were convinced that without support from the United States Israel would be no threat. As a result, a main ingredient of revolutionary Arab nationalism became a bitter anti-Americanism. Yet American policymakers had to do something about the

Middle East because the Arab-Israeli conflict could trap the United States in a war with the Soviet Union that neither wanted. So both powers sought means of resolving the rivalry.[14]

Their search brought results early in August, 1970, when Arabs and Israelis accepted a peace proposal that Secretary of State William P. Rogers had advanced in June, and that the Soviets supported. According to this plan both sides renewed the broken cease-fire for three months while United Nations' representatives tried to mediate the conflict. Before the new truce took effect the Arab states acknowledged Israel's right to exist and Israel accepted the resolution of the Security Council of November, 1967, calling for withdrawal of her troops from occupied territories. Rogers' plan did not assure peace, but for the first time since the end of the Six-Day War it silenced the guns and bombs along the Suez Canal and opened a dialogue for peace. The truce did not last long. Arab guerrillas refused to accept it; both sides, but mainly Egypt, violated it; civil war broke out in Jordan in September, bringing the threat of American and Israeli intervention; and American peacemaking suffered in the cross-fire.

Resolving the Congo Dilemma

Throughout the sixties black Africa, too, continued to experience turmoil and political instability, but its troubles, unlike those in the Middle East, did not threaten the peace of the world. In the winter of 1962 the most serious problem, as far as the United States was concerned, remained Moise Tshombe's refusal to end Katanga's secession from the Republic of the Congo.

President Kennedy and the United Nations force in the Congo tried to avoid another clash, but failed. On Christmas Eve at Elisabethville the Katangese shot down a United Nations' helicopter, and three days later they fired on Indian and Ethiopian troops in the United Nations force. The U.N. troops then launched an all-out drive against the secessionists, forcing Tshombe in mid-January to offer to end the rebellion in exchange for a general amnesty. Kennedy supported this move, believing that a policy of conciliation toward the dissidents would help unify the Congo. The plan worked. Tshombe went into exile and the Katanga secession crisis ended, but strife persisted elsewhere.

In 1963 a group of exiled Congolese, supported by Chinese Communists, organized a Committee for National Liberation. Exploiting tribal grievances, the committee launched a revolt against the central government. The United States helped the government with a military aid mission, planes, and arms, but the revolutionary movement gained momentum. In June, 1964, as the last contingent of the United Nations force withdrew from the country and as the rebels took over more and more territory, Tshombe returned. In the following month he was named premier. Unable to end the rebellion with the Congo's own army, he hired white mercenaries who managed to turn back the rebels. The United States supplied him with some planes and helped in other ways.

Other African states which had banded together in 1963 as the Organization of African Unity, disliked Tshombe, particularly his use of mercenaries and dependence on outside help. In September, 1964, it sent a special delegation to Washington to ask President Johnson to cut off military assistance to Tshombe's regime. American policymakers refused to do this without consulting the Congo government.

Then in November, as government forces closed in on Stanleyville, the rebels herded several hundred whites, including some sixty Americans, together as hostages. To help rescue the hostages the United States flew about four hundred Belgian paratroopers into Stanleyville. Just as they arrived rebel troops massacred over thirty of the hostages. Most African states, as well as Russia and Red China, denounced the rescue operation as "flagrant aggression" in the Congo's affairs, as evidence of lingering colonialism, and as an effort to prop up Tshombe's unpopular regime.[15] Early in 1965 the revolt petered out and later in the year Tshombe was dismissed. The Congo in the next few years experienced a stability it had not known since the departure of the Belgians.

South Africa, Southern Rhodesia, and Nigeria

Events in the Congo were matched by political violence in other newly independent African states. In South Africa, Rhodesia, and Portugal's colonies of Angola and Mozambique these developments strengthened the resolve of the ruling white regimes to hang on and resist the demands of African nationalists for independence or political power. American policymakers repeatedly said they shared the aspirations of the African nationalists but would not give them the material support they demanded. The United States stood behind numerous resolutions in the United Nations calling for an end to the segregation of non-whites in South Africa, called *apartheid*, but it would not go along with sanctions and use of force against the South African whites as the blacks desired. American officials would not act because South Africa was the source of important strategic materials; she contained sizable American investments; she sided with the United States in the cold war, making available port facilities to the American Navy; and she would probably thereby be subjected to racial violence on a scale hitherto not witnessed.

A similar problem persisted in Southern Rhodesia where a white establishment of 200 thousand ruled a population of 3.7 million blacks who were allowed no political privileges. In November, 1965, Prime Minister Ian Douglas Smith, a segregationist, unilaterally proclaimed Southern Rhodesia's independence from Britain, and in March, 1970, the white minority made Rhodesia a republic. The London government had insisted that an independent Rhodesia should also guarantee political rights for the black majority. Britain therefore declared the proclamation illegal. The United Nations and others condemned Smith's action, refused to recognize Rhodesia's government, and called for economic sanctions against it, which the United Nations invoked in December, 1966. The United States supported these measures, but they failed because South Africa and Portugal supplied the Rhodesians with oil and other critical boycotted materials.[16]

Another problem of concern to American statesmen was a civil war that broke out in Nigeria, the most populous of African states, and one of the richest, in May, 1967. Ibo tribesmen of the eastern region, resenting the ruling regime which was composed mainly of Hausa tribesmen, proclaimed a republic called Biafra and tried to secede. Europeans quickly took sides in the conflict. The Russians, British, and others aided the government forces; France, mainly, supplied the rebels with limited arms. The United States recognized the federal regime as Nigeria's legitimate government and embargoed the sale of arms to both sides; otherwise it tried to remain aloof from the struggle. But it incurred the wrath of the central government because American humanitarian organizations, and a pro-Biafra lobby, exerted pressure on the White House to pierce its blockade with planes carrying food and medical supplies for starving Biafrans. In January, 1970, after more than thirty months of fighting and a toll of two million deaths, Biafra capitulated. Hard feelings between Nigeria and the United States lingered for awhile, but basically the American hands-off policy toward the conflict had justified itself.[17]

Elsewhere in Africa the American policy of restraint toward the white-ruled regions was also under fire. Angry African nationalists, and black Americans at home, too, denounced such moderation as merely a tolerance for *apartheid* and for white exploitation of black majorities. In February, 1970, Secretary of State Rogers went on a goodwill tour of Africa, the first American official of his rank to do so, to show the country's interest in that continent. He assured his hosts that the United States, even though unwilling to sanction force to attain it, sympathized with the principle of black equality; America stood opposed to white minority rule.

Restiveness in Europe

In Western Europe, too, at a time of bursting prosperity and confident strength, many were openly restive under American leadership against the Soviet bloc. Although France under Charles de Gaulle took the lead in the reaction against unquestioning dependence on the United States, other Europeans shared his attitude. They showed a willingness to use the competitive power of the Common Market, if necessary, against the United States. That power persuaded Congress in September, 1962, to adopt overwhelmingly the Trade Expansion Act President Kennedy had been championing. Kennedy believed that the act would strengthen ties with a more powerful Europe. Yet agreement on international tariff reductions did not materialize until May, 1967, after extended negotiations under the auspices of the GATT, the General Agreement on Tariffs and Trade. Kennedy and his advisers also looked forward to Britain's entry into the Common Market and to greater cooperation from the Europeans in matters of defense. Both aspirations ran afoul of de Gaulle's desire for a Western European policy of independence from the United States.

At this time Britain found herself financially unable to maintain a usable, independent nuclear strike force. De Gaulle suggested that she and France work together to produce ballistic missiles and create the basis for an effective European nuclear armament. Since the United States possessed about 97 percent of the West's nuclear weapons and at the time it alone had the means of using them effectively, President Kennedy felt that a separate European nuclear program would merely duplicate what was already available for Europe's defense through NATO and thereby squander precious resources. What the Europeans should do instead, he felt, was to supply more ground forces for their own defense. They had never contributed enough troops to NATO so that it could reach its projected strength of thirty ready divisions.

This problem on the nature of Western Europe's defense status came to a head in December, 1962, when Britain's Harold Macmillan conferred with Kennedy at Nassau. There the two leaders signed an agreement whereby Britain would turn over her nuclear arms to a NATO force commanded in the final analysis by Americans. In return the United States offered Britain Polaris missiles without nuclear warheads. Only if Britain's "supreme national interests" were at stake, the agreement said, could she use nuclear arms unilaterally. Later, Kennedy offered the same terms to de Gaulle who turned them down.[18]

De Gaulle was annoyed by the Nassau talks, since acceptance of the pact meant British rejection of his plan for a European nuclear force and showed British insistence upon retaining a special relationship with the United States beyond that of other allies. America, he said, would probably not fight for Europe in a crisis if in doing so she exposed her own cities to destruction. So Europe must have her own nuclear force. England, he felt, was not willing to become sufficiently European to support this view or to belong to the Common Market. So in January, 1963, despite American pressure on her behalf, he vetoed Britain's bid to enter the European Economic Community, suggesting that if admitted she would act as a Trojan horse for the United States. The other members, seeing logic in his views, went along.

In June, 1963, Kennedy traveled to several European cities to counteract America's declining influence among NATO allies. The President stopped first in West Berlin where, in response to a tumultuous welcome, he said that in the sense of resisting Communist pressure, he too was a Berliner ("*Ich bin ein Berliner*") and that the United States would stand by the beleaguered city. In Frankfurt, as though to answer doubts raised by de Gaulle, he stressed that the United States "will risk its cities to defend yours because we need your freedom to protect ours."[19] He also conferred with statesmen in Italy and England, discussing with them a plan for a "multilateral force" (MLF) that had grown out of the Nassau talks. The force would be composed of allied ships carrying nuclear missiles and manned by international crews. These allies were cool to the idea, but in France, where Kennedy had not stopped because he had no invitation, opposition was outspokenly strong.

Since the United States would retain a veto over the use of the missiles de Gaulle considered the project American, not European, and another example of Americans treating their allies as dependents rather than true partners. The Russians reacted to the "multilateral force" with alarm, claiming it would place the finger of West Germans on the "nuclear trigger." Britain and Italy too saw danger of an enhanced German power in the plan, so Kennedy's successor, Lyndon B. Johnson, who at first was determined to go ahead regardless of the opposition, in 1965 dropped it.[20]

Since the United States refused to share nuclear secrets with France and consistently tried to bar her from the nuclear club, Frenchmen were resentful. They went ahead on their own to build a nuclear capability, or *force de frappe*. American policymakers considered this and de Gaulle's insistence on an independent policy for France as anti-American, whereas the French viewed American nuclear policy and other actions as anti-French. De Gaulle insisted that he was not anti-American, and that he considered the United States a true friend. He merely wanted a France and a Europe free of American hegemony. The United States, he explained, was so powerful that regardless of good intentions it could not help trying to dominate the affairs of other nations. They had to resist. Other Europeans were also concerned with the proliferation of American business investment in Europe, fearing the Americanization of their countries.

Regardless of where the blame lay, relations between France and the United States suffered from a widening rift. In January, 1964, to the dismay of American strategists, de Gaulle recognized Red China; in April he withdrew French naval forces from NATO commands; and in 1965 he pressured the Common Market into slowing down the movement toward political unity. In March, 1966, he announced removal of French troops from NATO's command, and he asked the allies to pull out their forces and installations from France by April 1, 1967, which they did. Washington protested, arguing that these actions weakened NATO. De Gaulle said the integrated military structure in NATO had served its purpose; it was no longer needed. France, he insisted, stood second to none in loyalty to the alliance itself and in a crisis would "fight beside her allies." In May and December, 1967, he again opposed British attempts to enter the Common Market, implying that Britain was still subservient to the United States.

Most Europeans were showing a lack of confidence in the quality of American leadership, but the French, particularly de Gaulle, were the most outspoken. De Gaulle gave up France's presidency in April, 1969, at a time when relations with the United States were beginning to improve. His successor, Georges Pompidou, later in the year visited the United States and tried to accelerate the rapprochement, but he did not reverse the basic policies de Gaulle had set.[21]

A New Immigration Policy

In the sixties the United States erased an old source of European anti-Americanism. It completed changes in its immigration policy that eliminated discriminations that had long rankled Asians such as the Japanese as well as southern Europeans such as Italians and Greeks. The process began in 1947 when Congress started studying the old laws and their operation. Three years later it produced a voluminous report that became the basis of the McCarran-Walter Act. Since the measure retained the national origins formula with its built-in ethnic prejudices, Jews, Italians, and others opposed it, and President Truman in June, 1952, vetoed it, saying it discriminated against important cold war allies. But Congress overrode the veto and in December the Immigration and Nationality Act of 1952 became law. Its most important positive feature, as it affected foreign policy, was its elimination of race in the case of Asians as a barrier to admittance. For others, it perpetuated old discriminations. As the President's Commission on Immigration and Naturalization reported in the following year, the law "applies discriminations against human beings on account of national origin, race, creed and color," working against our foreign policy in friendly countries such as Italy.[22]

Four presidents—Truman, Eisenhower, Kennedy, and Johnson—urged Congress to revise the McCarran-Walter Act so as to remove its prejudicial features. Opposition did not begin to give way until July, 1963, when Kennedy called for a new immigration law that would reflect "in every detail the principle of equality and human dignity to which our Nation subscribes." Johnson took up where Kennedy left off, pushing for change. In September, 1965, Congress passed the Immigration and Nationality Amendments of 1965.

The new law, over a period of three years, eliminated the national origins formula. At the end of June, 1968, it abolished the quota system. The new formula allowed each independent country outside the Western Hemisphere to send up to twenty thousand immigrants into the United States each year according to categories defined to suit American needs. Unused visas became available to qualified immigrants from any country on a first come, first served basis. At last American immigration policy fitted the credo of equality of opportunity. Critics of American foreign policy could no longer cite it as part of a pattern of hypocrisy that opposed discrimination abroad while giving it official sanction at home.

Soviet-American Détente

Early in the decade, after the Cuban missile crisis, there came a pause in the tension between Russians and Americans, leading to a *détente*. In June, 1963, as a result of the missile confrontation, Kennedy and Khrushchev agreed to an emergency phone and teletype, or "hot line," connection between Washington and Moscow. It provided a means of instant communication between the heads of the two powers when one or the other feared miscalculation in a crisis. The line began operating in August.

Kennedy also tried to take advantage of the thaw in the cold war to check the nuclear arms race. He had created an Arms Control and Disarmament Agency for just that purpose. In April and June, 1963, he appealed to Khrushchev to take up negotiations for a treaty barring the spread of nuclear weapons. The President also announced that the United States would not conduct any further nuclear tests in the atmosphere "so long as other states do not do so." In July Khrushchev responded favorably. His feud with Chinese Communist leaders made him accommodating and facilitated negotiations in Moscow for the test ban agreement. Soviet, American, and British diplomats swiftly completed the Limited Nuclear Test Ban Treaty which was signed on August 5, 1963. The signatories promised not to conduct nuclear tests in the atmosphere, in outer space, or under water, and not to abet tests by others. Underground testing was permitted and it continued. France and Red China refused to sign, but more than a hundred other countries did.

Even though the treaty itself did not stop the nuclear arms race, many considered it a first step in that direction. It reduced radioactive fallout and made the perfecting of nuclear weapons more difficult than in the past. It was, Kennedy pointed out, "the first concrete result of 18 years of effort by the United States to impose limits on the nuclear arms race."[23] People everywhere were pleased; Americans, according to opinion polls, overwhelmingly favored the test ban. The Senate approved the treaty in September, and it went into effect on October 10, after ratification by the three original signers.[24]

At this time Soviet efforts to buy grain from Canada and the United States, because of shortages at home, became a major issue in Russian-American relations. Cold war warriors opposed the sale to Russia as "trading with the enemy," but Kennedy, emphasizing the need for flexibility in foreign economic policy, in October authorized the sale of $250 million in surplus wheat and wheat flour to the Soviet Union and Eastern European countries. Congressional efforts to block the sale and bickering over price held up the deal for months. The hope of some that it would, within the context of the *détente*, lead to a general expansion of trade with the Soviets, disappeared.

Yet, as part of the *détente* the Soviet Union and the United States wished to enlarge their economic and cultural contacts. One step in this direction would be the reestablishment of consular relations broken off in 1948. So on June 1, 1964, American and Soviet negotiators in Moscow signed a consular convention, the first bilateral agreement between the two governments, promoting commercial and cultural relations and providing for the protection of tourists and other travelers. The agreement infuriated anti-Communist patriots such as J. Edgar Hoover, Director of the Federal Bureau of Investigation, who considered Russian embassies and consulates "focal points" for espionage and subversion. For nearly three years fear of this opposition kept the Johnson administration from submitting the agreement to the Senate and risking rejection. The convention finally reached the Senate where supporters in March, 1967, mustered the necessary two-thirds majority for approval. To the administration the treaty was especially important as a symbol of the *détente*.

Nuclear Nonproliferation

Since several nations already had, and others soon would have, the capability of making nuclear weapons, Johnson, like Kennedy, wanted to go beyond the Test Ban Treaty with an agreement that would place significant restraints on their manufacture. Soviet leaders dismissed some of Johnson's ideas on disarmament, such as a "verified freeze" on missiles and bombers that carried nuclear weapons, as propaganda, but they were willing, at least, to explore for a basis of agreement. On October 15, 1964, Khrushchev fell from power and was succeeded by two colorless Communist party functionaries, Aleksei N. Kosygin and Leonid I. Brezhnev. On the following day Communist China announced that she had exploded her first atomic device. Now, more than ever, American leaders felt that something had to be done to block the proliferation of nuclear arms. The new Soviet rulers, as they failed to patch the quarrel with Red China, came to share this view.

In 1965 the British drafted a nonproliferation treaty which the American delegate presented to the United Nations Disarmament Committee in Geneva, but the Russians rejected it, and for two years nonproliferation made no progress. In January, 1967, more than sixty members of the United Nations signed an agreement banning nuclear weapons in outer space. The United States approved it in April and Russia in May. Then in June, 1967, Premier Kosygin visited the United States to attend a special emergency session of the United Nations General Assembly dealing with the Arab-Israeli war. During his stay he conferred with Johnson in an improvised summit meeting in the town of Glassboro, set amid the chicken farms and apple orchards of New Jersey, where they disagreed on issues affecting the Middle East and Vietnam but agreed on nonproliferation. "I want friendship with the American people...," Kosygin shouted to curious onlookers, "we want nothing but peace with the American people." [25]

In August the United States and the Soviet Union submitted separate but identical drafts of a treaty banning the spread of nuclear weapons or weapons technology to the Disarmament Committee in Geneva. In June, 1968, the United Nations approved the Nonproliferation Treaty which provided for a limited system of international inspection of the facilities of nonnuclear nations but not those of the nuclear powers. For this and other reasons potential nuclear states such as India, Italy, Japan, and West Germany held out against it, but on July 1 the United States, the Soviet Union, Britain, and fifty-six nonnuclear powers signed the treaty. Since Red China and France rejected it and since it placed no restraints on the continued development of nuclear arms by the powers already possessing them, the agreement did not stop the arms race. But, supporters argued, it would keep other countries from entering it. Johnson hailed it in exaggerated rhetoric as "the most important international agreement in the field of disarmament since the nuclear age began."[26]

Two other developments refueled the arms race and added new complexities to the efforts of those who wished to end it. The Soviets went ahead with the building of a network of antiballistic missiles (ABM) designed to destroy offensive missiles while keeping their own intact. American military leaders feared that if the United States did not deploy a similar system to protect its missiles its nuclear arsenal would lose its effectiveness as a deterrent. Critics argued that new weapons would quickly make the ABM system obsolete. The multiple independently targeted reentry vehicles (MIRV) being developed could saturate a defensive screen. Each of these missiles could recock and reaim itself in space and fire from three to a dozen warheads at as many targets at one time. Why, opponents asked, spend $40 billion to start an ABM system? They urged either better offensive missiles or effective arms limitation as the answer to the Soviet system.

Nixon and his military advisers disagreed, insisting that a missile defense system was essential to national safety. In August, 1969, Congress approved the President's ABM program by narrow votes. The Soviets then went ahead with tests of another multiwarhead system, space bombs.

The American and Soviet maneuvering over weapons demonstrated the uncertainties in the building of defenses against a rapidly changing military technology that had become virtually a Frankenstein monster. Each side in the arms race was chained to a cycle of building bigger, better, and more expensive weapons because the other side did so. So, after years of false starts, American and Soviet leaders in October, 1969, decided to discuss directly the costly race that was bringing security to no one. In November in Helsinki representatives of the United States and Russia began strategic arms limitation talks, usually referred to by the acronym SALT; the five weeks of secret preliminary discussions were the first formal negotiations between the two nations alone on the subject of halting their nuclear competition. Full-scale talks followed from April to August, 1970, in

VIENNESE WALL FLOWER

Vienna. While aside from optimism nothing tangible emerged from SALT, at least the giant rivals were together exploring the idea of arms limitation and reduction.

The arms competition had its parallel in the space rivalry, but in space the United States won a dramatic victory; it overtook the Soviets in the race to the moon and in most aspects of manned space flights. In 1969 America landed two manned space vehicles on the moon, completing the program started by Kennedy in 1961 to get there ahead of the Soviets. The first moon mission, Apollo 11, placed astronauts Neil A. Armstrong and Edwin Aldrin, Jr., on the lunar surface on July 20; Apollo 12 landed two men on the moon on November 19. These achievements, witnessed on worldwide television, sent American prestige soaring. Some Americans proposed more ambitious space projects, such as a mission to Mars, but critics questioned the cost and value of such a venture. Giving up the race to place a man on the moon, the Soviets now concentrated on unmanned probes and on large-scale earth orbital projects; these had a clearly discernible strategic value in the arms race.

Soviet Intervention in Czechoslovakia

As far as American leaders were concerned no event did more to set back the *détente* and reactivate the arms race than Russian intervention in Czechoslovakia in 1968. In the postwar era no country in the Soviet bloc of central Europe had been more faithful to Moscow than Czechoslovakia. In the late sixties economic troubles stimulated unrest and a desire for greater freedom in political and economic life than Communist rulers had allowed. Early in 1968 Alexander Dubcek, a colorless but loyal party man, took over as head of the Czech Communist party and became the nation's leader. While proclaiming devotion to the Soviet Union and Communism, he permitted his people, in a "spring of freedom" to reform their government, regain some lost liberties, and work toward the creation of "a new model of socialist democracy."

These developments alarmed the Soviet leaders who feared a counterrevolution that would pull Czechoslovakia out of the Warsaw Pact, wrench her from their control, and spread a desire for civil liberties in other satellite countries. Such disaffection would not only shatter the already split Communist world, it would also endanger Russia's defenses on her western frontier. So on August 20, 1968, after warning Dubcek of the risks he was running, the Soviets, as well as token Polish, East German, Bulgarian, and Hungarian troops brought together under the terms of the Warsaw Pact, invaded Czechoslovakia. Overpowered, the Czechs did not resist. Capitulating to demands to end the liberalization program, Dubcek and other leaders agreed to a treaty legalizing the Soviet occupation.

President Johnson immediately appeared on nationwide television to denounce the invasion and demand withdrawal of the Soviets and their allies. "It is a sad commentary on the Communist mind," he said, "that a sign of liberty is deemed a fundamental threat to the security of the Soviet system." But, as in the case of Hungary in 1956, the United States could not do much to help the Czechs. Secretary of State Dean Rusk announced that the government planned no "retaliatory actions or sanctions" against Russia, in effect acknowledging what was long known, that the Communist countries of Eastern Europe were beyond the reach of American power.[27] Moreover, restraint by men who themselves had not hesitated to use force in the Dominican Republic and Vietnam seemed logical.

While perhaps saving the Warsaw Pact the invasion of Czechoslovakia solidified the rival Atlantic Alliance. Once again Europeans were reminded that when concerned about vital interests the Soviets could be as brutal as ever. "They [Europeans], wouldn't accept Kosygin's word now," an American observer said, "if it were tattooed with Bible pictures."[28] What caused continuing concern was the insistence of Russian leaders that Moscow had the right to invade any Communist country. The NATO countries therefore reappraised their alliance, concluding that they still needed the United States and its ready nuclear arsenal. In the United States the Soviet intervention for a while endangered the Nonproliferation Treaty and gave new strength to the advocates of the antiballistic missile system.

Soviet activity in the Mediterranean also created concern among NATO countries, particularly in Italy; it made the alliance seem as valuable as ever. With the use of facilities at Mers El Kebir, Algeria, and other Arab ports, the Russians built a powerful fleet in the Mediterranean, one that challenged the supremacy of the American Sixth Fleet with headquarters at Naples. If the Soviet navy gained control of that sea it could eliminate American missile submarines operating there and isolate friendly countries such as Italy and Israel.

Nonetheless many American officials were losing their old intense interest in Europe as such, particularly in her political and economic integration, feeling that de Gaulle had killed European unity and that other Europeans had not opposed him. Aware of this feeling and of European unrest, Richard M. Nixon in March, 1969, soon after becoming President, visited his NATO allies to assure them he would not neglect Europe and would listen to their views on international affairs.

Late in October, 1969, after the Czech crisis had cooled, the Warsaw Pact countries renewed an earlier proposal to NATO for an all-European security conference. The United States opposed such a meeting, from which it would be excluded, warning its allies not to let down their guard for an "illusory *détente*." But in August, 1970, Department of State officials hailed the conclusion of a nonaggression treaty between West Germany and the Soviet Union pledging both nations to renounce the use of force in settling disputes and to accept current boundaries as inviolable. It was, a spokesman said, "a first real step forward toward a relaxation of tension in Europe" that could lead to the long delayed security conference.

The Quicksands of Asia

Even during the period of *détente* in Europe the United States found itself unable to come to terms with Communism and nationalism in Asia. There policymakers seemed to step into quicksand. The more they threshed around seeking solutions to the problems of war, poverty, and nationalism, the deeper and more helplessly the United States itself sank in its involvement with long lasting conflicts.

For Americans the central concern was the hostility and growing power of Communist China. The effect of this power on neighboring countries friendly to the United States could be seen in a border conflict between China and India. In October, 1962, after several months of clashes, Chinese troops launched mass attacks across India's frontier, inflicting six thousand casualties and pushing back Indian forces everywhere. India, for the first time, appealed directly to the United States for military aid, but aside from emergency shipments of arms the latter could do little to help. Fortunately the conflict did not expand. In November, for reasons not clear, China unilaterally declared a cease-fire along the entire frontier and by the end of the year withdrew her troops from the Indian territory they had penetrated.

Pakistanis deeply resented the military aid of their American ally to India, their most feared enemy.[29] Believing that the American arms India received would be used against them, Pakistani leaders turned to Communist China for support. In 1965 when Pakistan and India fought a small war over the old issue of Kashmir, both sides used American arms contrary to military assistance agreements with the United States. Red China supported Pakistan and demanded India's evacuation of fortifications on their common frontier in the area of Sikkim. Although the United States reportedly told China that it would come to India's defense if China attacked, Johnson actually wanted to avoid involvement in a second Asian war, especially against China. He cut off military aid to both India and Pakistan, was relieved when the Chinese did not carry out their threat, and was pleased when the belligerents in September accepted a truce under the auspices of the United Nations.

To American statesmen these actions against India made Red China seem more dangerous then ever. They realized that even her quarrel with the Soviet Union, that began after Stalin's death, was based in part on anti-Americanism.[30] The Chinese disliked the Soviet-American *détente*, wanted it to end, and urged the men of the Kremlin to pursue an aggressive policy against the "imperialist" United States, one that should risk nuclear war if necessary. The Russians resisted these tactics and several times tried to heal the rift, but failed. All during the sixties Communist China remained unbending in her hostility toward Russia and more hostile toward the United States.

Creeping Involvement in Vietnam

This continuing menace of Red China coupled with increased Communist activity in Southeast Asia made officials in Washington jittery. Some of them, especially the members of the East Asian establishment within the Department of State, felt that the fate of the entire region would hinge on the outcome of the struggle in South Vietnam between the Viet Cong, who had organized a shadowy political coalition called the National Liberation Front, and the regime of Ngo Dinh Diem.[31] Seeing China as the real enemy there, they urged the President to increase aid to Diem, which Kennedy did, but he was embarrassed by Diem's oppressive tactics against his political opponents, especially Buddhists. Only with changes in policy designed "to win popular support," Kennedy believed, could the government defeat the Viet Cong. "In the final analysis," he said in September, 1963, "it is their war. They are the ones who have to win it or lose it. We can help them; but they have to win it, the people of Vietnam, against the Communists." [32]

Early in November Diem and his brother were murdered in a military *coup*. Diem's overthrow did not bring the liberalization that Kennedy desired. What followed were a succession of corrupt military dictatorships which did little to earn the people's support against the Viet Cong. Within three weeks of Diem's fall Kennedy was assassinated in Dallas, Texas. Johnson, a man far more experienced in the rough politics of Texas and the cloakroom tactics of Capitol Hill in Washington than in the intricacies of international relations in Asia, became President and immediately put his mark on policy in Vietnam.[33] He and his advisers ruled out negotiations for a settlement based on Vietnam's reunification and neutralization in accord with the Geneva Agreement of 1954. Such a settlement would, they believed, amount to a surrender to the North Vietnamese Communists headed by Ho Chi Minh in Hanoi. "I am not going to lose Vietnam," Johnson reportedly said a few days after taking office. "I am not going to be the President who saw Southeast Asia go the way China went." [34] But he did not come out for full-scale involvement by the United States. He hoped to strengthen the government in Saigon so that it could fight on its own.

The Tonkin Gulf Retaliation

These hopes proved illusory. An incident in the Gulf of Tonkin, where the American Navy maintained patrols to report on ships suspected of moving men and supplies from North Vietnam to the Viet Cong, became the basis for changing the nature of America's involvement. Both the Red Chinese and the North Vietnamese resented the American warships in their home waters, and they charged that American ships and planes had struck at settlements in North Vietnam. On August 2, 1964, in apparent retaliation, three North Vietnamese torpedo boats attacked an American destroyer thirty miles from the coast but caused no damage.

The President immediately doubled the patrols in the Gulf of Tonkin and ordered the Navy to destroy future attackers. Two days later, according to administration sources, "an undetermined number of North Vietnamese PT boats" attacked again, with American ships firing back and sinking two of the boats, but details are hazy. Investigation later raised doubts about whether or not the attack occurred. Hanoi, while admitting the first clash, denied any attack on August 4, calling the American account a fabrication.[35] The President and his advisers reacted swiftly. Within hours Johnson ordered American bombers to blast coastal bases and an oil installation in North Vietnam. Appearing on television shortly before midnight, he explained his action as a reply to "repeated acts of violence against the armed forces of the United States."

On the following day the President asked Congress to support what he had already done and what he would do in the future against "aggression," saying "the United States intends no rashness, and seeks no wider war." On August 7, in a crisis atmosphere with little debate and virtually no opposition, Congress committed itself as Johnson requested. The Gulf of Tonkin resolution it approved also asserted that the security of Southeast Asia was "vital" to the "national interest" and authorized the President "to take all steps necessary, including the use of armed force" to help any state in the area which sought assistance "in defense of its freedom." It was, Johnson said later in private, "like grandma's nightshirt— it covered everything." [36]

Later that month Johnson won the Democratic nomination for President by acclamation. A month earlier the Republicans had nominated Barry M. Goldwater, a senator from Arizona who had long been the favorite of the right wing of the party. Goldwater attacked Johnson's conduct of foreign policy, belligerently called for a policy of action not merely words against Communism, spoke of "carrying the war to North Vietnam" and of dropping "a low yield atomic bomb on Chinese supply lines in North Vietnam." The campaign made foreign policy a central issue and aroused concern throughout the world. To many Goldwater gave the impression of being a "trigger happy" man who would not hesitate to plunge the nation, even the world, into a nuclear holocaust. Johnson, in contrast, tried to convey the image of a prudent man who desired peace. As for Vietnam, he told the voters, "We don't want our American boys to do the fighting for Asian boys. We don't want to ... get tied down in a land war in Asia." [37] Johnson won by a landslide. Most analysts concluded that fear of a recklessly escalated war in Vietnam caused Americans to shun Goldwater; they preferred Johnson and peace.

Escalation

Even though the small-scale intervention, some sixteen thousand American troops when Kennedy died, in South Vietnam was not going well Johnson continued the caution of his campaign after the election. Fearing Chinese or Russian intervention and an adverse reaction from his own people, he turned aside military advice to expand the American commitment. He even held out against the air power advocates who urged the bombing of transportation centers in North Vietnam on the theory that this would deprive the Viet Cong of essential help, causing them to collapse.

Johnson's attitude changed early in 1965, and clearly in February after the Viet Cong infiltrated and attacked the American Special Forces camp at Pleiku in central South Vietnam, killing eight and wounding over a hundred men. Claiming that the assault had been directed from Hanoi, he immediately ordered bombing attacks on camps in North Vietnam. In March he announced another fateful decision, the sending of more than four thousand troops to South Vietnam. American ground forces, for the first time, now went into battle in large numbers against the Viet Cong. What started as a fight between Vietnamese was becoming an American war against the Viet Cong and North Vietnamese. Like the Spanish civil war of the thirties, it involved other powers. Communist China and Russia supplied the Viet Cong and North Vietnamese with arms. Australia, New Zealand, the Philippines, Thailand, and South Korea, all countries geographically concerned with containing China, supported the American intervention, but only the Koreans gave more than token aid. The American forces became South Vietnam's backbone.

Many at home and abroad were puzzled by why Johnson had expanded the war. So in a major speech at the Johns Hopkins University on April 7, 1965, he explained the intervention as a defense of South Vietnam's independence that he was determined to uphold. For the first time he also said he would welcome "unconditional discussions" for peace. In addition he offered a billion-dollar program for the economic development of Southeast Asia, including North Vietnam. North Vietnam's premier responded on the following day with a four-point program for peace talks. It demanded withdrawal of the United States from Vietnam, neutralization of the country following removal of foreign troops and bases, acceptance of the National Liberation Front's program as the basis for settling South Vietnam's internal affairs, and the peaceful reunification of Vietnam by the Vietnamese people in both zones without outside interference. Johnson rejected these terms. Since Ho Chi Minh would not bargain on any other basis, no chance for peace existed.

The President then tried to do two things at once, to press for a negotiated settlement while expanding the war in search of a military victory. His generals told him that, unlike the French who lacked carrier-based planes, swarms of helicopters, or superbly equipped troops, the United States could stop the help from the north and overwhelm ill-clad guerrillas who moved supplies on bicycles and the backs of old women. All this was logical enough, but the enemy did not respect the odds. It regarded the fight as a struggle for the survival of the Vietnamese people, a sacred war.

Slowly but steadily Johnson escalated the war, saturating North Vietnam with bombings that extended to the outskirts of Hanoi and Haiphong. These cities became virtual thickets of antiaircraft guns and missiles. The American ground forces climbed to 380,000 men by December, 1966, and to 450,000 by the following December, with no end in sight. Despite American claims of crippling blows against the Viet Cong, the latter and the North Vietnamese also escalated, matching the

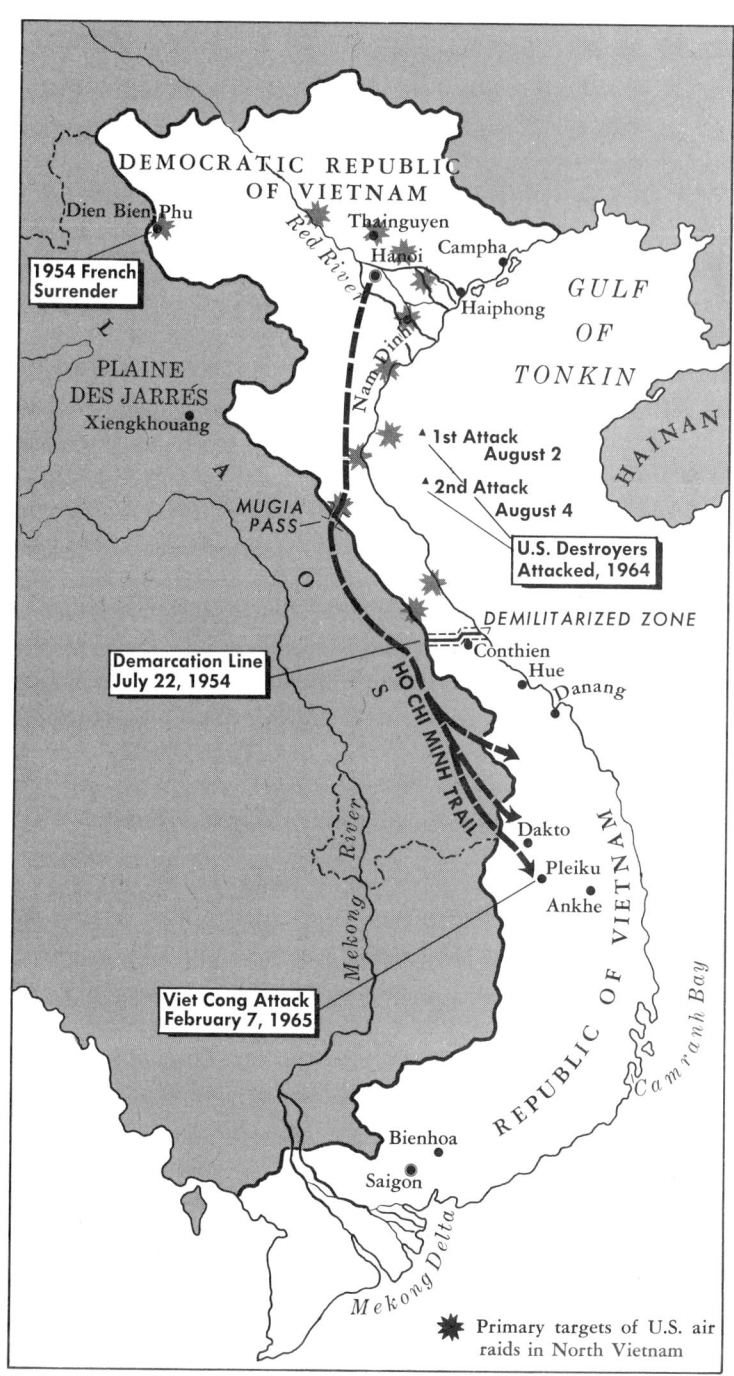

UNITED STATES INVOLVEMENT IN VIETNAM

growth of American forces and growing stronger. In 1967 the National Liberation Front claimed half or more of South Vietnam's countryside. The Chinese Communists offered to send in "volunteers" if the Viet Cong wanted them. No one, therefore, could discount the possibility that escalation would bring Chinese intervention and perhaps another world war.

The quest for peace proved just as frustrating as the escalation. In May and December, 1965, Johnson ordered pauses in the bombing of North Vietnam, hoping they would stimulate peace talks, but nothing happened. At a meeting in Manila in October, 1966, with leaders of the countries who supported the Vietnam intervention he came out with another of a number of peace offers. He promised to withdraw American forces from South Vietnam within six months of a withdrawal of North Vietnamese troops. Rejecting this and all other American proposals, Ho Chi Minh insisted that only the four-point program of the National Liberation Front could serve as the basis for peace talks. In his State of the Union message in January, 1967, Johnson expressed determination to continue bombing and exerting military pressure until Hanoi talked peace.

As the tempo of combat increased, so did American casualties. From 1961 through 1967 nearly 16,000 Americans were killed and almost 100,000 were wounded. Casualties for 1967 exceeded those of the previous six years. In September, 1967, in San Antonio, Texas, the President offered to stop the bombings if Hanoi would come to the peace table and not take advantage of the cessation. In December North Vietnam's foreign minister said that after the United States ended the bombings and other acts of war against his country there would be peace talks. For the first time peace appeared to have faint hope.

Hawks and Doves

As Johnson escalated the war his critics escalated their opposition until the Vietnam conflict became the most bitterly attacked and most unpopular war in the nation's history. It also became the most emotional issue in American life. Criticism in volume began in 1965, spearheaded by professors, students, and intellectuals on the nation's college campuses. They attacked the arguments of Secretary of State Dean Rusk and other administration hawks that China was the real enemy, that the United States had to defend a small helpless country against Communist aggression. To do less would amount to an Asian "Munich." Knowledgeable critics called the analogy dubious and a distortion of history.

Wherever Johnson, Rusk, and other administration leaders went, young people demonstrated, heckling them, calling them "murderers." Finally, the President would make no public appearances except under heavy guard. When he and his generals would claim that the enemy was on the run and then push more troops into South Vietnam many Americans began talking about a "credibility gap" in the government. Some considered Johnson devious, claiming that he was enlarging the war almost by stealth. They questioned his integrity and that of the government he led, saying he had created a "crisis of confidence."

As the government curtailed domestic programs against poverty, grappled with a painful inflation, published mounting lists of casualties, and as more and more public figures spoke out against the war, disaffection spread beyond the militant doves to all parts of American life. Opinion throughout the world, even in the friendliest of allied countries, denounced Johnson and was unfavorable to the United States. Some saw in another war against an Asian people a kind of crypto-racism, one that made acceptable the slaughter of brown-skinned civilians with guns, bombs, and napalm.

J. William Fulbright, chairman of the Senate Committee on Foreign Relations, emerged as the chief congressional critic of the war policy. In 1966 he held televised hearings on the conflict that placed the views of hawks and doves in the context of a debate. By the beginning of 1967, according to polls, Johnson's handling of the war had lost the approval of the majority of Americans; a poll in November suggested that only 23 percent of the people had confidence in his conduct of it. A month earlier dissent had taken the form of scattered antiwar demonstrations across the nation. On October 21 an organization of young people, called the National Mobilization Committee to End the War in Vietnam, brought together thousands who protested outside the Pentagon in Washington.

Doves, especially intellectuals, did more than just demonstrate. They tried with every legitimate means at their disposal—through books, articles, pleas in newspapers, speeches, and teach-ins—to change the war policy.[38] To dramatize their protest distinguished authors and artists publicly refused invitations to the White House. Other doves condemned the war as illegal because Congress had not declared it; as immoral and barbaric because a big nation was killing the civilians of a small one; and as unjust because the United States had assumed the role of aggressor in a civil war in violation of the principle of national self-determination.

The government rejected their reasoning and questioned their wisdom. The hawks insisted that the war was legal, that Congress, according to Under Secretary of State Nicholas de B. Katzenbach, had voted a "functional equivalent" to a declaration of war with the Gulf of Tonkin resolution.[39] Moreover, as Johnson himself claimed, the President as Commander-in-Chief had the authority to send troops wherever he wished. Since civilians always get hurt in modern wars, hawks argued, the war in Vietnam was no more immoral than any other. It was not, they said, a true civil war; the North Vietnamese were outsiders and aggressors. National self-interest demanded the containment of Communism, they claimed in old cold war terms, to keep other small Asian nations from falling like dominoes before Communist wars of national liberation. If the United States did not fight for South Vietnam it would lose the trust of other allies. Then there was the matter of human ego and national pride. Mistakenly believing that the United States had never lost a war, Johnson insisted that he would not be the first President to do so by accepting defeat in Vietnam.

Johnson's Retreat

Regardless of the merits and flaws of the controversy, by the end of 1967 most Americans were tired of the war and wanted it to end. But it did not slacken. On January 30, 1968, during the Vietnamese Lunar New Year holiday period called *Tet*, the Viet Cong launched well-coordinated surprise attacks across the length and breadth of South Vietnam. They struck inside American defense lines against thirty key cities and towns, including Saigon where twenty Viet Cong seized the American embassy compound building. This *Tet* offensive convinced many supporters of the war that reports of progress were false and that peace could not come through military means; criticism of Johnson's war policy rose.

These events also affected the political situation. Those who desired peace were frustrated because the leading Republicans were hawks and the doves in the Democratic party would not challenge Johnson, who seemed certain to run for reelection. So regardless of whether Johnson or a Republican won, the war policy appeared certain to continue into the next presidential term. Because of this in November, 1967, an articulate Democratic senator from Minnesota, Eugene J. McCarthy, decided to take up the antiwar cause and oppose Johnson. He quickly attracted the support of students, intellectuals, and other doves who announced in newspaper advertisements that "at last we have a Democrat against the war in Vietnam who dares to challenge Lyndon Johnson!"[40] To everyone's surprise in the New Hampshire Democratic presidential primary on March 12, 1968, where the party machinery, conducting a campaign for write-in votes, was all on Johnson's side, McCarthy polled 42.4 percent of the vote and gained twenty of the delegates. Five days later Senator Robert F. Kennedy of New York who had been opposing the war for about a year, also entered the Democratic race as a dove.

Despite the mounting opposition and the shock of New Hampshire, until this time Johnson had not deviated from his policy of seeking victory while pressing for peace, and he had built up the American forces in Vietnam to more than a half million men. As in the past General William C. Westmoreland, the American commander in Vietnam who had expressed dismay at "unpatriotic acts" by doves and called the *Tet* offensive the Viet Cong's "last gasp," predicted victory but asked for 200,000 more men to clinch it. Now Johnson hesitated, and on March 31 he publicly changed his position. In a dramatic television broadcast he said, "I am taking the first step to deescalate the conflict," mainly by ending the bombing of North Vietnam except for a narrow southern sector and by sending Westmoreland only 13,500 troops as reinforcements. The President hoped these concessions would persuade North Vietnam to discuss peace. Then he announced he would not run for another term.

Johnson gave up the presidential race not because he considered his war policies wrong but because his party was on the verge of explosion and he felt he might lose the renomination, or if he got it, lose the election in November. He also believed that his badly divided nation needed a unity that he obviously could not bring about. One part of his desire was realized. In May, 1968, the North Vietnamese agreed to meet in Paris with American negotiators for "formal talks" about the possibility of peace. At the conference table the North Vietnamese demanded that all bombing and acts of war against their country end before meaningful discussions could begin. The Americans said no, not until North Vietnamese troops and supplies stopped filtering into South Vietnam. So the Paris talks failed to get off the ground at that time.

All the while the expense of the war was zooming. It had cost $7 billion in 1966, but by the middle of 1968 it was costing American taxpayers more than $30 billion a year. The price in human lives was more depressing; American deaths exceeded 25,000 and wounded 100,000.* The war had steadily expanded until it had become the longest, and except for the Second World War, the costliest in the nation's history.[41]

Indonesia, Korea, and Japan

Even though Vietnam dominated American thinking on foreign policy other lesser events in Asia also influenced that policy. In the mid-sixties relations with Indonesia sank to a point so low that Americans assumed she would become a hostile state closely aligned with Red China. In January, 1965, President Sukarno, who had fomented a widely criticized guerrilla war in Malaysia, angrily withdrew Indonesia from the United Nations and encouraged harassment of American property and anti-American demonstrations. In February he set the tone for anti-Americanism by telling university students, "To hell with U.S. aid." Later he forced Peace Corps members out of the country. To all of this the Johnson administration reacted cautiously.

In October, 1965, an attempted *coup* by pro-Chinese military officers and young Communists backfired. Army officers accused the rebels of trying to take over the country and turn it into a Communist state. This charge and the uprising itself unleashed a wave of anti-Communist and anti-Chinese sentiment which Sukarno tried unsuccessfully to restrain. In a frenzy of racial and nationalist wrath the people slaughtered thousands upon thousands of Communists and Chinese, and even those merely suspected of Communist leanings. Rivers ran red with the blood of massacre victims.

* By July, 1970, deaths exceeded 50,000 and wounded 250,000.

The massacres destroyed the Indonesia Communist party, the third largest in the world. In 1966 the generals pushed Sukarno out of power and placed a professional soldier, Suharto, in control of the country. General Suharto, who officially became president in 1968, outlawed the Communist party, abandoned Sukarno's pro-Chinese foreign policy, and made friendly overtures to the United States. Without American intervention the largest and most important country in Southeast Asia had rejected Communism. As friendliness toward the United States increased, private American investment in Indonesia underwent a spectacular growth.

Involvement in Vietnam and fear of provoking another conflict with Communist China also led to caution in a confrontation with North Korea. On January 23, 1968, North Korean patrol boats fired on the American naval intelligence ship *Pueblo*. The Communist sailors seized the ship and imprisoned the eighty-three members of its crew for allegedly penetrating their territorial waters on a spying mission. Americans called the action high-handed and illegal, insisting that the ship had been captured in international waters. Angry nationalists demanded strong measures, such as the bombing of North Korean ports and military installations, to rescue the ship and men, or at least to avenge national honor. This time Johnson, unlike his reaction in the Tonkin Gulf crisis, withheld force and tried to gain release of the ship and crew through negotiations.

After eleven months of haggling representatives of the American government, in a bizarre diplomatic exchange in December, 1968, signed an apology for violating North Korean waters; the Communists then freed the men but not the ship. The American government actually repudiated the apology beforehand saying its negotiator had signed the document of "confession" to all the crimes charged merely as a means of freeing the prisoners. The North Koreans apparently accepted the confession for purposes of propaganda. Commander Lloyd M. Bucher, captain of the *Pueblo* who surrendered the ship without a fight, and his crew went through a highly publicized court-martial that recounted their suffering, the brutality of their captors, and the inadequacies of naval intelligence activities. The American government emerged from the affair with tarnished honor, but at least it did not plunge the country into another war merely to avenge insult when no discernible vital interests were at stake. The Nixon administration followed a similar policy in April, 1969, despite demands of hawks for retaliation against "fourth-rate countries," when North Koreans shot down an American reconnaissance plane over the Sea of Japan. "The weak can be rash," Secretary of State William P. Rogers explained, "the powerful must be more restrained."

The *Pueblo* episode and the Vietnam War caused uneasiness in Japan because American bases there and on Okinawa were staging areas for operations against North Vietnam and would also be used in any renewed conflict in Korea. Students, nationalists, and others were becoming increasingly critical of American policy in

Asia; many demonstrated against visits of American nuclear submarines to Japan and in protest of America's continued occupation of the Bonin and Ryukyu Islands. Eager to wipe away the last vestiges of defeat and to win acceptance from the United States as an equal, Japan wanted to regain control of these islands, particularly Okinawa, the home of about a million Japanese. In June, 1968, the United States returned the Bonins to Japanese rule and in November, 1969, President Nixon, after three days of negotiation, promised Prime Minister Eisaku Sato that the United States would return Okinawa by 1972. The United States in exchange gained more flexibility in the use of its forces based in Japan proper than in the past.

Like others, the Japanese criticized American intervention in Vietnam; they disliked seeing whites again warring on Asians. Yet the government remained firm in its friendship with the United States. Red China's growing nuclear capability confirmed the view of Japanese leaders that they needed the protection of their Mutual Security Treaty with the United States, which was subject to review in 1970. So in his visit to Washington in November, 1969, Sato agreed formally with Nixon to maintain the treaty indefinitely. This alliance remained important because Japan, now a prosperous and technically advanced country of 100 million people, had again risen to become the most powerful, or second most, nation in Asia. In August, 1970, the American government revealed that Japan had now become responsible for her own defense.[42]

Vietnam as the Political Issue

The intervention in Vietnam meanwhile remained the nation's basic political issue. When Johnson quit the race three men sought the Democratic nomination. His Vice-President, Hubert H. Humphrey, who had entered immediately, gained the backing of the party organization, but for a price—loyalty to Johnson's war policy. Kennedy and McCarthy both attacked that policy, keeping it constantly before the electorate. Just as Kennedy's campaign was gaining momentum with a victory in the California primary on June 6 a young Arab nationalist murdered him in Los Angeles. The leading Republican candidate, Richard M. Nixon, was a hawk of long standing on the Vietnam War, but also an experienced politician who swayed with the winds of change. He saw that Johnson's hard line on Vietnam had made his presidency untenable, so Nixon softened what had been a harsh prowar attitude. His well-oiled campaign swept aside all opposition, bringing him the Republican nomination in August, 1968, in Miami on the first ballot.

Later that month the Democrats met in Chicago in a convention hall ringed by a seven-foot fence topped by barbed wire. The Vietnam issue virtually tore their party apart. McCarthy's followers demanded that the party go on record as opposed

to the war, that it call for the end of all bombing in North Vietnam without conditions, and that it support negotiations for a phased withdrawal of all foreign troops.
Since the Humphrey-Johnson forces controlled the convention and opposed
termination of the bombing without North Vietnamese concessions, the peace
plank was defeated. This setback embittered thousands of young people who had
converged on Chicago to plead, demonstrate, and battle for McCarthy and peace.
They sang folk songs, taunted the police and National Guardsmen on riot duty
with obscenities, hurled rocks, waved Viet Cong flags, and denounced Johnson.
Enraged police retaliated with canisters of tear gas and club-swinging assaults on
the heads and bodies of demonstrators. Hundreds, including bystanders and
newspapermen, were hurt and arrested.

These wild scenes, giving the impression of a convention under siege, filled the
world's television screens; they resurrected old feelings among Europeans and others
that Americans were an unnecessarily brutal people.[43] The turmoil had no effect on
the outcome of the nomination; Humphrey won it on the first ballot. The South
fielded a segregationist party headed by two extreme hawks, George C. Wallace
and General Curtis E. LeMay who favored using "anything we could dream up,
including nuclear weapons," to end the war in Vietnam.

The results of the Democratic convention caused greater disaffection than ever
before among the young, the intellectuals, and the doves in general. Since all the
candidates were hawks, the doves as voters had no way of expressing themselves
on what they considered the overriding issue of the election—the Vietnam intervention. The platforms of both parties called vaguely for peace, but without breaking away from Johnson's policy. Nixon hedged on Vietnam, saying he had a plan
for ending the war, but committed himself to nothing concrete.[44] On October 31,
1968, less than a week before the voting, Johnson gave Humphrey a boost with the
doves. He announced that on the next day he would stop all bombing of North
Vietnam and would maintain the moratorium if it led to fruitful discussions at
Paris. This concession did not help Humphrey enough; Nixon won the election,
but by the narrowest of margins. Even in the congressional races the effect of the
Vietnam issue was not clear; no pattern of dove or hawk victories was discernible.[45]
But in Paris the stalemate was broken. In the middle of January, 1969, the
delegates from Vietnam agreed to begin talking about substantive issues.

Nixon and the War

When Nixon took office he modified Johnson's policy without changing it and
without revealing the "peace plan" he had promised. He tried to deescalate the
war and defuse the doves. In July and August, 1969, he visited six Asian countries
and at Guam announced what his advisers called the Nixon Doctrine, which said

Nixon Doctrine

essentially that the United States would aid its Asian allies, but not with troops. They must defend themselves. This concept fitted another announcement, that he would "Vietnamize" the war, meaning that he would turn over more and more of the fighting to the South Vietnamese and in that way eventually pull most American soldiers out of South Vietnam.[46] In August he promised to withdraw twenty-five thousand troops and in September sixty thousand more.

Despite these promises Congress in late September erupted with discontent over his Vietnam policy. Critics denounced the slow pace of withdrawals and the policy of "Vietnamization," calling it a "semantic hoax." The French, Eisenhower, Kennedy, and Johnson had all espoused similar policies. None worked because the South Vietnamese army, even after years of training and equipping by Americans, failed to fight effectively against the Viet Cong, and this was why the United States had intervened on a large-scale in the first place.

The President denounced his critics as defeatists and accused them of undermining his plan to end the war. He declared on September 26 that mounting antiwar protests would have no effect on him or his policies. To doves his position seemed rigid and callous. People across the nation protested the war and staged a "Vietnam Moratorium" on October 15, 1969. On November 15, 250,000 people participated in a forty-hour "March Against Death" from Arlington National Cemetery to the White House. At the same time counterdemonstrators were urging support for Nixon, and Vice-President Spiro T. Agnew denounced the antiwar activities, saying they had been "encouraged by an effete corps of impudent snobs who characterize themselves as intellectuals." Opinion on the war had become polarized. A short time later the nation's conscience was touched by the allegations that an American infantry unit in the previous March had massacred some five hundred civilians, men, women, and children in the Vietnamese village of My Lai. Everyone was shocked by the atrocities. Critics argued that they were the fruits of a war that was brutalizing and dehumanizing American youth.

During these months of agitation at home the President was becoming increasingly upset by intelligence reports of stepped-up Communist activity in Cambodia. South and North Vietnam's neighbors, Cambodia, Laos, and Thailand, had for years been threatened by Communist guerrillas. Thailand's government welcomed help in fighting them, allowing Americans to build huge military installations within its borders. Many of the air raids on North Vietnam began on Thai airfields. While many Thais resented the American presence in their country, the government remained a firm anti-Communist ally.

Laos, with its Pathet Lao, teemed with guerrilla activity. Even though the Geneva agreement of 1962 forbade outside powers from sending military forces into Laos the North Vietnamese did. One of their main routes for supplying and reinforcing troops in South Vietnam was the Ho Chi Minh trail which ran through Laos. Americans secretly bombed the trail and gave combat support to government troops who fought the Pathet Lao and North Vietnamese, thereby also violating Laotian neutrality. Doves in the United States denounced the secret war in northern Laos that by 1970 everybody knew was being fought.[47]

For years Cambodia had been trying to balance herself between the belligerents so as not to be drawn into the Vietnam War, but she had allowed the North Vietnamese to build and equip a dozen or so bases on her soil for troops fighting in South Vietnam. For years American generals had wanted to attack those sanctuaries, but President Johnson had refused permission, fearing an enlarged war. Nonetheless, sometimes American troops chased Viet Cong into Cambodia. This led the government in 1965 to sever diplomatic relations with Washington for violations of neutrality.

Nixon unhappily went along with Johnson's policy and tolerated the sanctuary until a change of government in Cambodia in March, 1970. The new regime asked the North Vietnamese to reduce their troops in Cambodia, but Hanoi refused. In mid-April the North Vietnamese and Cambodian Communists started attacking government forces in large numbers. Nixon and his advisers then decided they had to do something, for if they acquiesced in a Communist absorption of Cambodia and Laos their rationale for fighting in Vietnam would collapse. Moreover, the enemy in Cambodia offered a seemingly easy target for an effective military campaign that would enhance the United States' bargaining position with Communists in Paris and elsewhere.[48]

On April 30, in a nationwide television speech that he himself wrote, the President told the American people that their troops were invading Cambodia to disperse the enemy massing in sanctuaries to attack South Vietnam. He implied that they would capture "the headquarters for the entire Communist military operation in South Vietnam." The troops, about sixteen thousand of them, he said, would be out in six to eight weeks, and no American soldier would penetrate more than twenty-one miles. This intervention would not enlarge the Vietnam War, he explained, but actually shorten it by saving American lives.

The Cambodian invasion virtually tore American society apart. Protests and riots exploded on college campuses across the nation. At Kent State University in Ohio National Guardsmen called in to control protests there on May 4 killed four unarmed students with point-blank rifle fire, causing a new wave of revulsion against the administration's war policy. The foreign reaction was overwhelmingly negative. Old and new critics, moderates as well as militants, agreed that now the conflict had become "Mr. Nixon's War," and that it was "no longer a Vietnam war but an Indochina war."

In Congress, which Nixon had not consulted before launching his invasion, doves, moderates, and even some hawks were furious. They launched a campaign to place restraints on the President's war-making powers. The proposal that gained the most support was an amendment to a military sales bill sponsored by senators

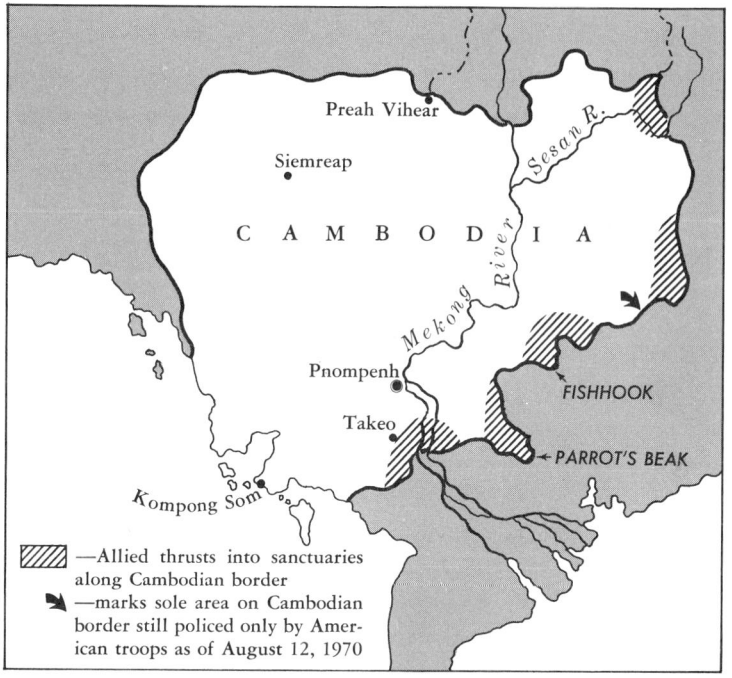

UNITED STATES AND CAMBODIA

Frank Church of Idaho and John Sherman Cooper of Kentucky. The Church-Cooper amendment called for limiting military activity in Cambodia after July 1, Nixon's deadline for withdrawing troops, unless Congress approved such activity. Nixon opposed any such law, claiming it would unwisely curtail the President's constitutional power as Commander-in-Chief.

In June, 1970, the Senate repealed the Gulf of Tonkin resolution and early in July passed a modified Church-Cooper amendment by a vote of 58 to 38. For the first time in the nation's history that body tried to place restraints on the President in time of war, mainly by its control of purse strings. The House refused to go along, but the effort was not a failure. It represented a rebuff to the President and made him cautious about taking moves that would broaden the war without congressional approval.

But the President did not change his basic war policy. He defended his Cambodian venture, telling his fellow Americans in June that it was "the most successful operation of this long and very difficult war." In effect he also praised the old domino theory and asked for support virtually as a matter of patriotism. Public opinion polls indicated that many Americans—wealthy, poor, white collar and blue collar—responded approvingly, but not the young, the intellectuals, the blacks, and the doves. The nation was deeply divided. Polls taken in September 1970 suggested deep dissatisfaction with the war; a majority of those polled favored withdrawal from Vietnam within a year, but the Senate rejected a plan calling for that kind of withdrawal.[49]

On the evening of October 7, less than a month before congressional elections, the President appeared on nationwide television with a five-point peace proposal. He called for a standstill cease-fire throughout Indochina, an enlarged peace conference designed to break the stalemate in Paris and that would include Russia and Communist China, withdrawal of American troops on a fixed timetable, a political settlement, and release of prisoners of war by both sides. Essentially it repeated earlier offers, but the first two points were new. Since Nixon spoke without the belligerent rhetoric he had sometimes used in the past and appeared genuinely concerned about peace rather than in arousing nationalistic fervor, the proposal received widespread support. Even doves and Senate critics responded favorably. Nonetheless the North Vietnamese and the Viet Cong, who had several weeks earlier come up with a "peace initiative" of their own unacceptable to American policymakers, rejected the Nixon proposal; they still wanted unilateral American withdrawal.

The President followed his offer with announcements of accelerated troop withdrawals from Vietnam. On October 15 he pulled out another 50,000, leaving some 380,000 troops in South Vietnam, or about 160,000 less than the peak figure

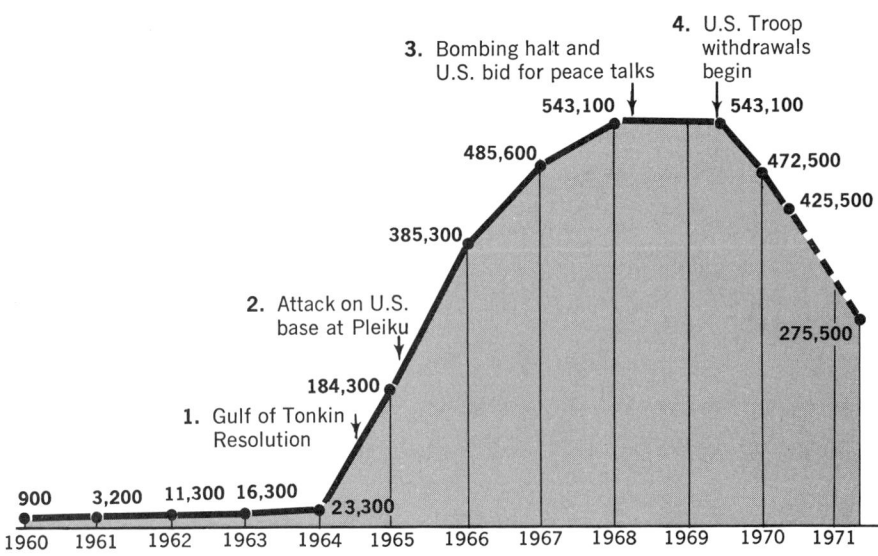

UNITED STATES TROOP WITHDRAWALS

under Johnson. Caualties, too were declining.* He promised further withdrawals and also reductions in draft calls. All this and the peace proposal disarmed many of Nixon's critics and, as polls showed, regained some of the good will in dealing with the war that he had had before the Cambodian invasion. He could not, however, ignore the continuing concern, at home and abroad, over the blood-letting. Even America's South Vietnamese allies were not happy; anti-American-ism could be felt everywhere in their country, especially in the streets of Saigon.

NOTES

1. See Quincy Wright, "The Cuban Quarantine," *American Journal of International Law*, LVII (July, 1963), 546–565. For defenders of the quarantine see Leonard C. Meeker, "Defensive Quarantine and the Law," *ibid.*, 515–524; Carl Q. Christol and Charles R. Davis, "Maritime Quarantine: The Naval Interdiction of Offensive Weapons and Associated Matériel to Cuba, 1962," *ibid.*, 525–545; and comments on the legality of the quarantine by Charles G. Fenwick, Brunson MacChesney, and Myres S. Mc-Dougal, *ibid.*, 588–604.

2. For an interesting study of the probable Soviet reasoning, see Arnold L. Horelick, "The Cuban Missile Crisis: An Analysis of Soviet Calculations and Behavior," *World Politics*, XVI (April, 1964), 363–389.

3. Quoted in Richard P. Stebbins, *The United States in World Affairs, 1962* (New York, 1963), p. 2.

4. Robert F. Kennedy, *Thirteen Days: A Memoir of the Cuban Missile Crisis* (New York, 1969), p. 128.

5. Quoted in Richard P. Stebbins, *The United States in World Affairs, 1965* (New York, 1966), p. 87. See also Johnson's comments on not letting "Castro take that island," in John B. Martin, *Overtaken by Events: The Dominican Crisis from the Fall of Trujillo to the Civil War* (Garden City, N.Y., 1966), p. 661.

6. For a critical analysis of issues raised by the intervention, see Charles G. Fenwick, "The Dominican Republic: Intervention or Collective Self-Defense," *American Journal of International Law*, LX (Jan. 1966), 65–67, who defends the action, and R. T. Bohan, "The Dominican Case: Unilateral Intervention," *ibid.*, (Oct., 1966), 809–812, which is critical.

7. For details on the flag crisis, see Sheldon B. Liss, *The Canal: Aspects of United States Panamanian Relations* (Notre Dame, Ind., 1967), pp. 117–166.

8. See Mercer D. Tate and Edward H. Allen, "The Proposed New Treaties for the Panama Canal," *International Affairs*, XLV (April, 1969), 269–278. *New York Times*, Sept. 3, 1970.

9. For details see Gerald M. Craig, *The United States and Canada* (Cambridge, Mass., 1968), pp. 319–322.

10. *New York Times*, April 26, 1970; E3:7.

11. For details on the war in Yemen and American policy, see John S. Badeau, *The American Approach to the Arab World* (New York, 1968), pp. 123–151.

12. Quoted in Richard P. Stebbins, *The United States in World Affairs, 1967* (New York, 1968), p. 96.

13. Nasser is quoted in Theodore Draper, *Israel and World Politics: Roots of the Third*

* For the week of October 18–24 there were fewer than fifty American deaths for the fourth consecu-tive week.

Arab-Israeli War (New York, 1968), p 112, and Johnson's statement is printed on pp. 263–64. Eshkol is quoted in Stebbins, *United States in World Affairs, 1967*, p. 97.

14. For a summary of the Nixon administration's policy toward the rivalry see Joseph J. Sisco, "The United States and the Arab-Israeli Dispute," *Annals of the American Academy of Political and Social Science*, CCCLXXXIV (July, 1969), 66–72.

15. For the effect of the airdrop on the American image in Africa, see Waldemar A. Neilsen, *The Great Powers and Africa* (New York, 1970), pp. 308–309.

16. For details see the Department of State's special background paper, "Southern Rhodesia and the United Nations: The U.S. Position," *Department of State Bulletin*, LVI (March 6, 1967), 366–377.

17. Later that year it was revealed that elsewhere in Africa the United States had not followed a hands-off policy. In 1960 it had agreed to support Ethiopia against any threats to her territorial integrity. See the *New York Times*, Oct. 19, 1970, 1:5, 24:4.

18. For an analysis of the Nassau conference and its effect on France, see Robert Kleiman, *Atlantic Crisis: American Diplomacy Confronts a Resurgent Europe* (New York, 1964), pp. 47–61.

19. Quoted in Richard P. Stebbins, *The United States in World Affairs, 1963* (New York, 1964), p. 116.

20. For an analysis of the contradictions in MLF policy see William B. Bader, *The United States and the Spread of Nuclear Weapons* (New York, 1968), pp. 45–49, and Henry A. Kissinger, *The Troubled Partnership: A Reappraisal of the Atlantic Alliance* (New York, 1965), pp. 127–159.

21. For a critical appraisal of de Gaulle's relationship to the United States by a prominent American policymaker, see George W. Ball, *The Discipline of Power: Essentials of a*

Modern World Structure (Boston, 1968), pp. 118–148.

22. The pros and cons of the 1952 legislation are summarized in Robert A. Divine, *American Immigration Policy, 1924–1952* (New Haven, Conn., 1957) and Marion T. Bennett, *American Immigration Policies: A History* (Washington, 1963).

23. Stebbins, *United States in World Affairs, 1963*, p. 26.

24. For an analysis of the Test Ban negotiations see Seyom Brown, *The Faces of Power: Constancy and Change in United States Foreign Policy from Truman to Johnson* (New York, 1968), pp. 267–293.

25. Quoted in the *New York Times*, June 25, 1967, El:2.

26. *Ibid.*, June 16, 1968.

27. Walter Clemens, Jr., in "Czechoslovakia and U.S. Policy: All or Nothing at All," *War/Peace Report*, X (Jan., 1970), 14–19, argues that American leaders, who expected the Soviet invasion, could have done more than they did to forestall it.

28. *New York Times*, November 17, 1968, 3E:3.

29. For an analysis of Pakistani hostility see John Hohenberg, *Between Two Worlds: Policy, Press, and Public Opinion in Asian-American Relations* (New York, 1967), pp. 365–367. In India American esteem rose, *ibid.*, pp. 360–361.

30. For elaboration on this point, see Donald S. Zagoria, *Vietnam Triangle: Moscow, Peking, Hanoi* (New York, 1967), pp. 21–24.

31. For a critical analysis of the China attitude of the policymakers see James C. Thomson, Jr., "How Could Vietnam Happen? An Autopsy," *Atlantic*, CCXXI (April, 1968), 47–48, 53.

32. Quoted in Roger Hilsman, *To Move a Nation: The Politics of Foreign Policy in the Administration of John F. Kennedy* (New York, 1967), p. 578.

33. For an analysis of Johnson's inexperience in foreign affairs, see Rowland Evans and Robert Novak, *Lyndon B. Johnson: The Exercise of Power* (New York, 1966), pp. 391–393, and Philip Geyelin, *Lyndon B. Johnson and the World* (New York, 1966), pp. 15–17.

34. Quoted in Tom Wicker, *JFK and LBJ: The Influence of Personality Upon Politics* (New York, 1968), p. 205.

35. For a detailed analysis see the *New York Times*, August 27, 1967, 6E:3–4.

36. Louis Heren, *No Hail, No Farewell* (New York, 1970), p. 51.

37. Quoted in Arthur M. Schlesinger, Jr., *The Bitter Heritage: Vietnam and American Democracy, 1941–1968* (Boston, 1967), p. 29.

38. For an intellectual's criticism of the war policy, see the essays by Noam Chomsky, *American Power and the New Mandarins* (New York, 1967). The book is dedicated "To the brave young men who refuse to serve in a criminal war." See also the analysis by Irving Kristol, "American Intellectuals and Foreign Policy," *Foreign Affairs*, XLV (July, 1967), 594–609.

39. For the debate on the legality of the war, see the anthology edited by Richard A. Falk, *The Vietnam War and International Law* (Princeton, N.J., 1968).

40. Full page advertisement, *New York Times*, Jan. 14, 1968, E5.

41. For an economic analysis see James L. Clayton, "Vietnam: The 200-year Mort-

gage," *The Nation*, CCVIII (May 26, 1970), 661–63.

42. *New York Times*, Aug. 24, 1970, 1, 12.

43. For details, see Daniel Walker and others, *Right in Conflict* (New York, 1968), the report to the National Commission on the Causes and Prevention of Violence.

44. See Jules Witcover, *The Resurrection of Richard Nixon* (New York, 1970), pp. 371–72.

45. This fits the earlier analysis by Sidney Verba, *et al.*, "Public Opinion and the War in Vietnam," *American Political Science Review*, LXI (June, 1967), 317–333.

46. Nixon's adviser on foreign policy, Henry A. Kissinger, had urged such a policy, saying "We should continue to strengthen the Vietnamese army to permit a gradual withdrawal of some American forces", in *American Foreign Policy: Three Essays* (New York, 1969), p. 134.

47. For a critical analysis of the "secret American war" in Laos and of other presidential Asian ventures, see Stuart Symington, "Congress' Right to Know," *New York Times Magazine* (August 9, 1970), pp. 7, 62–65.

48. The decisions and reasoning leading to the Cambodian invasion are analyzed in an article by Hedrick Smith and others in *New York Times*, June 30, 1970, 1, 14.

42. A Gallup Poll summarized in *ibid.*, September 27, 1970, p. 16:1.

IN CONCLUSION

I am afeard there are few die well that die in a battle; for how can they charitably dispose of any thing, when blood is their argument?

SHAKESPEARE *Henry V*[1]

Since the days of the founding fathers, American foreign policy, whatever its shortcomings or virtues, has sought to protect national security. Despite extensive changes in American and world society that objective has remained constant, but the concept of national self-interest has changed. In the fifties and sixties the concept became so broad that the problems of peoples everywhere also became the concerns of Americans. The American people heard time and again that their foreign policy could and did affect the destiny of mankind. They were importuned constantly not to retreat into isolationism, to accept the burdens of international responsibility. These included a globe girdling system of alliances and efforts to manipulate events almost everywhere outside the Communist countries. In contrast to isolationism this use of power amounted to a kind of globalism never before witnessed in any nation's foreign policy.[1]

The American political experience offered no guide for the use of power in such huge dimensions. The past showed a proud tradition and a record in foreign policy of unparalleled success, but old principles and shibboleths such as freedom of the seas, isolationism, nonentanglement, the Monroe Doctrine, and the Open Door do not fit the new context of American diplomacy. They are, as historians fondly remind us, part of a past that Americans cannot escape, should understand, and frequently do use. Yet that past cannot offer and does not offer a model for future policy, for since 1945 a distinctive quality of American foreign policy has been its frustrating lack of continuity with much of the past.[2]

Another assumption of the past, at least since 1898, that the present has made obsolete is that of omnipotence, that the United States has an immense potential for war that can be mobilized after diplomacy has failed. A scientific and technological revolution has changed the whole concept of war and the conduct of foreign policy. Within minutes new weapons can now produce more death and destruction anywhere on the globe than have all the wars of the past.[3] The "hot line" between Moscow and Washington symbolizes the change that technology has brought to foreign policy. During the Cuban missile crisis the emergency communications between Kennedy and Khrushchev took several hours for transmission through diplomatic channels. The intercontinental missiles being readied for war could span the distance in minutes. For crises of the future policymakers saw the need for a system of communication where words could travel faster than missiles.

Since war is now predicated on new dimensions of time and force our foreign policy has lost its former margin of safety. Americans now know that the experience of fighting great wars against major opponents thousands of miles from their shores is a luxury of the past. If another world war were to come new weapons would bring it instantly to America's doorstep. A frightful insecurity has replaced the old, comforting feeling of the era of isolation. Now radar constantly scans the skies for hostile objects and aircraft, and planes and submarines equipped with nuclear weapons patrol the skies and seas twenty-four hours a day ready for instant, surprise destruction.[4] For Americans one of the great ironies of this nuclear age is that with their vast power has come the deepest insecurity in their history.

This dilemma of insecurity amidst power has caused some Americans to seek solace in the idea that the unlimited destructiveness of new weapons has made war virtually unthinkable, or at least has restrained those men who might plunge into conflict on a grand scale. The new weapons, they argue, have deprived diplomacy of its ultimate sanction—war. This nuclear stalemate, often called a balance of terror, has supposedly removed the possibility of another great general war.[5] If this is so, then diplomacy is indeed undergoing revolutionary change, for war has always been the ultimate resort of sovereign states when they could resolve their conflicts in no other way.

Man has long recognized that war is a frightful waste of human life, but that knowledge has not stopped wars. Conflict has been so much a part of the human experience, so much one of man's truly critical problems, that peace has always been unstable, perhaps nothing more than an interlude between wars. In recent years psychologists, biologists, and others have turned to the study of war as part of the general human experience. They have sought to find out if man is by nature violent, aggressive, and warlike. One of the best known of these scholars, Konrad Lorenz, the German founder of ethology, or the study of animal behavior, argues that war is a derailment of the normal instinct of men and animals. Collective aggression, he feels, is the major danger to modern civilization.[6] Anthony Storr, a British psychotherapist, suggests that aggression in man is as necessary as sexual expression, that man is by nature aggressive, and hence warlike. He believes, therefore, "that if stability in world affairs is ever to be achieved, the psychological point of view deserves equal consideration with the political, economic and other aspects."[7]

What has attracted scientists and scholars such as these to the study of aggression and has made war an almost unthinkable alternative to peace is the growth of man's destructive power to such a magnitude as to threaten to erase civilization as we know it.[8] Yet there is no assurance the the balance of terror between nuclear powers has removed the possibility of large-scale war from the practice of diplomacy.[9] The arms race continues, motivated by fear that one rival or another will upset the balance. Men have long been known, as in the dropping of atomic bombs on Japan, to use weapons of mass destruction in the quest for a "lasting peace." It could happen again, as it almost did in the "eyeball to eyeball" nuclear confrontation of October, 1962. There are no certainties in international politics. President Kennedy recognized this and pointed it out to the American people. "We have," he said during a crisis over Berlin, a "sober responsibility to recognize the possibilities of nuclear war in the missile age."[10]

While mankind trembles before the unknown dangers of multiwarhead missiles and constantly orbiting space bombs, world statesmen still reckon on the possibility of war, still bargain in the language and diplomacy of force, and generals still plan for a big war. They also still fight lesser but terribly brutal wars, as in Korea, Vietnam, and the Middle East, always aware that any of these conflicts can escalate into a worldwide nuclear armageddon.

These attitudes point to another of the great ironies of our time. Now, when war is most intolerable and hazardous, militarism and trial by battle have achieved an ascendancy in American life that they have never before known. Never before has the conduct of American foreign policy been so dependent on the military establishment and on military theory, and never before have armaments and wars consumed so much of the national wealth. The bulk of taxes go for the payment of arms and to those who use them, and much of the economy is dependent on the production of armaments.[11]

This dependence on the military establishment reflects one of man's weaknesses, his seeming inability to avoid war. Too often war has come because diplomacy failed, because statesmen blundered, because they placed pride, passion, prestige, or greed ahead of reason. No man or group of men should gamble with the destiny of mankind because of his or their own limitations, nor should they view power politics as a game. Civilization cannot afford many mistakes in big power diplomacy.[12] [Today foreign policy has become more than a means of serving the national self-interest at someone else's expense; it has become a means of survival, for others as well as for Americans.]

How can American foreign policy provide some assurance of survival in this world of untamed nuclear forces, a world of incredibly swift scientific achievement, a world where old ideas and methods are outmoded so fast that ordinary men are bewildered? The foreign policy establishment cannot on its own assure survival, but it could do more than it has in seeking out the social and political wisdom available to it throughout the nation. The establishment itself could become less remote and more representative of all Americans, particularly of the young and minorities, than it has been and is. Leaders could seek to channel international rivalry into nonviolent conflicts. Americans could themselves gain a sense of security if they could assure others of their dedication to peace. They could gain more respect and be less the objects of fear if they would overcome their attitudes of moral superiority towards others, shed their national arrogance, show a willingness to live side by side with peoples of different cultures, values, skins, and ideologies. Some of this Americans could do at home. Bigotry and racism at home form barriers to trust abroad. If there is no trust, no understanding across national boundaries, then there will be, as there has always been between strangers, tension, explosive hate, and disaster.

Social progress at home aids relations with other nations, for the foreign policy of virtually any government is an extension of its domestic policy. Most thoughtful Americans now realize that their country, despite its great power, cannot alone secure its survival[13] and still less the survival of its ideals without friends; the United States, no matter how much it tries, cannot remake the world in its own image. Nor can it intervene with impunity everywhere, even in the cause of justice. Such interventions have always aroused resentment; such resentment against the United States is today worldwide. It underscores a point made by critics and friends alike, that the United States cannot act the role of the world's policeman.[14]

Americans should see foreign policy as a central concern, but in balance with domestic policies of social justice. Their leaders should understand the past and anticipate the future, and be flexible enough to change with new trends. They should not misuse the past, petulantly denounce those who differ with them, or condemn as cowardly appeasers those who seek peace. Real peace, not a peace secured at the price of enslavement, can be won only with all elements of American society working for it; peace must be loved. Peace, like love, can be gained only gradually through a foreign policy that balances frustration, humanism, and patience. A long peace, the major problem of our time, means staying at the peace table, or some diplomatic equivalent of it, permanently. Such a peace is worth the sacrifice of patience. That is why we have diplomacy.

NOTES

1. For a left-wing critique of this globalism, equating it with imperialism, see Robert Wolf, "American Imperialism and the Peace Movement," *Studies on the Left*, VI (May-June 1966), 28–43. See also Robert E. Osgood and others, *America and the World: From the Truman Doctrine to Vietnam* (Baltimore, 1970), pp. 1–24, which analyzes global policy and its critics.

2. This theme is elaborated in Henry A. Kissinger, *The Necessity for Choice: Prospects of American Foreign Policy* (New York, 1961), pp. 175–180. He points out that "our historical experience is very much at variance with the world in which we live." For a discussion of "The Larger Implications of the Changed World Power Structure" by another policymaker, see George W. Ball, *The Discipline of*

Power (Boston, 1968), pp. 15–28. For a discussion of "America and World Revolution," see Edmund Stillman and William Pfaff, *Power and Impotence: The Failure of America's Foreign Policy* (New York, 1966), pp. 220–225.

3. See Herman Kahn, *On Thermonuclear War*, 2nd ed. (Princeton, 1961), particularly pp. 145–149; Walt W. Rostow, *The Stages of Economic Growth* (Cambridge, Eng., 1960), p. 124; Bernard Brodie, *Strategy in the Missile Age* (Princeton, 1959), p. 402; Henry A. Kissinger, *Nuclear Weapons and Foreign Policy* (New York, 1957); and Zbigniew Brzezinski, *Between Two Ages: America's Role in the Technetronic Age* (New York, 1970), particularly pp. 3–62.

4. In the United States the power to unleash this instant death rests solely with the President. As James Reston points out, "No sovereign in history ever had such power or responsibility." See his *The Artillery of the Press: Its Influence on American Foreign Policy* (New York, 1966), p. 47.

5. This is, for example, a theme in Louis J. Halle, *The Cold War As History* (London, 1967); see in particular p. 418.

6. See Lorenz's *On Aggression*, trans. by Marjorie Kerr Wilson (New York, 1966). He defines aggression as "the fighting instinct in beast and man which is directed *against* members of the same species," p. ix.

7. Anthony Storr, *Human Aggression* (New York, 1968), pp. xiv–xv.

8. See Hans J. Morgenthau, *The Purpose of American Politics* (New York, 1960), p. 170.

9. For an early analysis of the precariousness of the thermonuclear balance, see Albert Wohlstetter, "The Delicate Balance of Terror," *Foreign Affairs*, XXXVII (Jan. 1959), 211–234.

10. *New York Times*, July 30, 1961. E1:1.

11. In his "farewell address" of Jan. 17, 1961, President Eisenhower warned that the size and economic ramifications of the military establishment posed a danger to democracy. The address is in the *Department of State Bulletin*, XLIV (Feb. 6, 1961). 179–182. Since that time the military-industrial complex has grown considerably. For a wide-ranging discussion of "the militarization of American foreign policy and domestic life," see Erwin Knoll and Judith N. McFadden, eds., *American Militarism 1970: A Dialogue on the Distortion of Our National Priorities and the Need to Reassert Control over the Defense Establishment* (New York, 1969).

12. Erich Fromm, *May Man Prevail? An Inquiry into the Facts and Fictions of Foreign Policy* (Garden City, New York, 1961), p. 204, criticizes the game theory approach to international politics. In a game, unlike war, a player is not threatened by extinction if he loses.

13. See Harvey Wheeler, *Democracy in a Revolutionary Era: The Political Order Today* (Santa Barbara, Calif., 1970) p. 190.

14. For discussions of global interventionism and leftist isolationism, see Ronald Steel, *Pax Americana* (New York, 1968), especially pp. 336, 354, and Henry M. Pachter's essay "Collective Security, Interventionism, and the Left," in *A Dissenter's Guide to Foreign Policy*, ed. by Irving Howe (New York, 1968), pp. 109–130.

Appendix A

THE PRESIDENTS
AND THEIR SECRETARIES OF STATE

President	Political Party	Secretary of State	Dates of Service
Continental Congress		John Jay	Dec. 21, 1784–
George Washington	Fed.	John Jay	Mar. 22, 1790
		Thomas Jefferson	Mar. 22, 1790– Dec. 31, 1793
		Edmund Randolph	Jan. 2, 1794– Aug. 20, 1795
		Timothy Pickering	Dec. 10, 1795–
John Adams	Fed.	Timothy Pickering	May 12, 1800
		John Marshall	June 6, 1800– Feb. 4, 1801
Thomas Jefferson	Rep.	James Madison	May 2, 1801– Mar. 3, 1809
James Madison	Rep.	Robert Smith	Mar. 6, 1809– Apr. 1, 1811
		James Monroe	Apr. 6, 1811– Sept. 30, 1814 Mar. 1, 1815– Mar. 3, 1817
James Monroe	Rep.	John Quincy Adams	Sept. 22, 1817– Mar. 3, 1825
John Quincy Adams	Rep.	Henry Clay	Mar. 7, 1825– Mar. 3, 1829
Andrew Jackson	Dem.	Martin Van Buren	Mar. 28, 1829– May 23, 1831
		Edward Livingston	May 24, 1831– May 29, 1833
		Louis McLane	May 29, 1833– June 30, 1834
		John Forsyth	July 1, 1834–
Martin Van Buren	Dem.	John Forsyth	Mar. 3, 1841

895

President	Political Party	Secretary of State	Dates of Service
William Henry Harrison	Whig	Daniel Webster	Mar. 6, 1841–
John Tyler	Whig	Daniel Webster	May 8, 1843
		Abel P. Upshur	July 24, 1843–
			Feb. 28, 1844
		John C. Calhoun	Apr. 1, 1844–
James Knox Polk	Dem.	John C. Calhoun	Mar. 10, 1845
		James Buchanan	Mar. 10, 1845–
			Mar. 7, 1849
Zachary Taylor	Whig	John M. Clayton	Mar. 8, 1849–
			July 22, 1850
Millard Fillmore	Whig	Daniel Webster	July 23, 1850–
			Oct. 24, 1852
		Edward Everett	Nov. 6, 1852–
			Mar. 3, 1853
Franklin Pierce	Dem.	William L. Marcy	Mar. 8, 1853–
			Mar. 6, 1857
James Buchanan	Dem.	Lewis Cass	Mar. 6, 1857–
			Dec. 14, 1860
		Jeremiah Black	Dec. 17, 1860–
			Mar. 5, 1861
Abraham Lincoln	Rep.	William H. Seward	Mar. 6, 1861–
Andrew Johnson	Rep.	William H. Seward	Mar. 4, 1869
Ulysses Simpson Grant	Rep.	Elihu B. Washburne	Mar. 5, 1869–
			Mar. 16, 1869
		Hamilton Fish	Mar. 17, 1869–
			Mar. 12, 1877
Rutherford Birchard Hayes	Rep.	William M. Evarts	Mar. 12, 1877–
			Mar. 7, 1881
James Abram Garfield	Rep.	James G. Blaine	Mar. 7, 1881–
Chester Alan Arthur	Rep.	James G. Blaine	Dec. 19, 1881
		Frederick T. Freylinghuysen	Dec. 19, 1881–
			Mar. 6, 1885
Grover Cleveland	Dem.	Thomas F. Bayard	Mar. 7, 1885–
			Mar. 6, 1889
Benjamin Harrison	Rep.	James G. Blaine	Mar. 7, 1889–
			June 4, 1892
		John W. Foster	June 29, 1892–
			Feb. 23, 1893
Grover Cleveland	Dem.	Walter G. Gresham	Mar. 7, 1893–
			May 28, 1895
		Richard Olney	June 10, 1895–
			Mar. 5, 1897

President	Political Party	Secretary of State	Dates of Service
William McKinley	Rep.	John Sherman	Mar. 6, 1897–Apr. 27, 1898
		William R. Day	Apr. 28, 1898–Sept. 16, 1898
		John Hay	Sept. 30, 1898–
Theodore Roosevelt	Rep.	John Hay	July 1, 1905
		Elihu Root	July 19, 1905–Jan. 27, 1909
		Robert Bacon	Jan. 27, 1909–Mar. 5, 1909
William Howard Taft	Rep.	Philander C. Knox	Mar. 6, 1909–Mar. 5, 1913
Woodrow Wilson	Dem.	William Jennings Bryan	Mar. 5, 1913–June 9, 1915
		Robert Lansing	June 24, 1915–Feb. 13, 1920
		Bainbridge Colby	Mar. 23, 1920–Mar. 4, 1921
Warren Gamaliel Harding	Rep.	Charles E. Hughes	Mar. 5, 1921–
Calvin Coolidge	Rep.	Charles E. Hughes	Mar. 4, 1925
		Frank B. Kellogg	Mar. 5, 1925–Mar. 28, 1929
Herbert Clark Hoover	Rep.	Henry L. Stimson	Mar. 28, 1929–Mar. 4, 1933
Franklin Delano Roosevelt	Dem.	Cordell Hull	Mar. 4, 1933–Nov. 21, 1944
		Edward R. Stettinius	Dec. 1, 1944–
Harry S. Truman	Dem.	Edward R. Stettinius	June 27, 1945
		James F. Byrnes	July 3, 1945–Jan. 21, 1947
		George C. Marshall	Jan. 21, 1947–Jan. 20, 1949
		Dean Acheson	Jan. 21, 1949–Jan. 20, 1953
Dwight David Eisenhower	Rep.	John F. Dulles	Jan. 21, 1953–Apr. 15, 1959
		Christian A. Herter	Apr. 22, 1959–Jan. 20, 1961
John Fitzgerald Kennedy	Dem.	Dean Rusk	Jan. 21, 1961–
Lyndon B. Johnson	Dem.	Dean Rusk	Jan. 20, 1969
Richard M. Nixon	Rep.	William P. Rogers	Jan. 21, 1969–

Appendix B

EXTRACTS FROM THE CONSTITUTION
CONCERNING FOREIGN RELATIONS

ARTICLE I

SECTION 8. *The Congress shall have Power . . .*
To regulate Commerce with Foreign Nations . . .
To . . . regulate the Value . . . of foreign Coin . . .
To define and punish Piracies and Felonies committed on the high Seas, and Offences against the Law of Nations;
To declare War, grant Letters of Marque and Reprisal, and make Rules concerning Captures on Land and Water;

SECTION 9.
No Title of Nobility shall be granted by the United States: And no Person holding any Office of Profit or Trust under them, shall, without the Consent of the Congress, accept of any present, Emolument, Office, or Title, of any kind whatever, from any King, Prince, or foreign State.

ARTICLE II

SECTION 2. *He [the President]*
shall have Power, by and with the Advice and Consent of the Senate, to make Treaties, provided two thirds of the Senators present concur; and he shall nominate, and by and with the Advice and Consent of the Senate, shall appoint Ambassadors, other public Ministers and Consuls, . . . and all other Officers of the United States, whose Appointments are not herein otherwise provided for, and which shall be established by Law: but the Congress may by Law vest the Appointment of such inferior Officers, as they think proper, in the President alone, . . . or in the Heads of Departments.
The President shall have Power to fill up all Vacancies that may happen during the Recess of the Senate, by granting Commissions which shall expire at the End of their next Session.

SECTION 3. *. . . he shall receive Ambassadors and other public Ministers . . . and shall Commission all the Officers of the United States.*

SECTION 4. *The President, Vice-President and all Civil Officers of the United States, shall be removed from Office on Impeachment for, and on Conviction of, Treason, Bribery, or other high Crimes and Misdemeanors.*

ARTICLE III

SECTION 2. *The judicial Power shall extend to all Cases, in Law and Equity, arising under this Constitution, the Laws of the United States, and Treaties made, or which shall be made, under their Authority;—to all Cases affecting Ambassadors, other public Ministers and Consuls;—to all Cases of admiralty and maritime Jurisdiction. . . .*

In all Cases affecting Ambassadors, other public Ministers and Consuls, . . . the supreme Court shall have original Jurisdiction. In all the other Cases before mentioned, the supreme Court shall have appellate Jurisdiction, both as to Law and Fact, with such Exceptions, and under such Regulations as the Congress shall make.

SECTION 3. *Treason against the United States, shall consist only in levying War against them, or in adhering to their Enemies, giving them Aid and Comfort. No Person shall be convicted of Treason unless on the Testimony of two Witnesses to the same overt Act, or on Confession in open Court.*

ARTICLE VI

This Constitution . . . and all Treaties made, or which shall be made, under the Authority of the United States, shall be the supreme Law of the Land; and the Judges in every State shall be bound thereby, any Thing in the Constitution or Laws of any State to the Contrary notwithstanding.

AMENDMENT XI

The Judicial power of the United States shall not be construed to extend to any suit in law or equity, commenced or prosecuted against one of the United States by Citizens of another State, or by Citizens or Subjects of any Foreign State.

Appendix C

TREATY MAKING IN THE UNITED STATES

I. What is a treaty?

  A. A contract between two or more states.

    1. A convention is the same thing, though agreements of primary importance, as in the making of peace, are always called treaties.

    2. To be valid the contract must be between sovereign states.

    3. Moreover, it must be the expression of an agreement.

    4. Not until ratified is a treaty valid in modern practice.

  B. In case of war between the contracting parties, their treaties are suspended, if not terminated.

  C. Treaties cannot be unilaterally abrogated unless the contract so stipulates.

  D. There is no supranational court or agency by which a treaty can be enforced; a treaty derives its obligation from the plighted faith of the signatories.

II. There are five steps to treaty making in the United States.

  A. *Preliminary negotiation and signature:* function of the Executive.

  B. *Action of the Senate:* "advice and consent."

    1. Two-thirds vote of those present is necessary for approval.

    2. The Senate may attach amendments or reservations; amendments require the consent of the other party, reservations do not.

  C. *Ratification:* act of the President.

    1. The President signs an instrument of ratification which is attested by the Secretary of State and is attached to the treaty.

    2. The great seal of the United States is then impressed upon the document.

  D. *Exchange of Ratifications.*

    1. The United States keeps one copy of the treaty and delivers another, which bears the evidence of ratification, to the other government.

    2. A plenipotentiary delivers the ratified treaty and receives a ratified copy with seal from the other government.

    3. The treaty becomes binding upon the signatories upon exchange of ratifications, although it frequently takes effect retroactively from the time of signature.

E. *Proclamation:* act of the President.
   1. By proclamation the President gives notice to the people of the treaty's terms and of its ratification.
   2. The treaty takes effect as the law of the land (according to the Constitution) at the time of its proclamation.

III. The primary work of American treaty making is in the *negotiation* and *action* of the Senate.
   A. With each step the binding effect of a treaty is increased.
      1. Signature binds the negotiating governments.
      2. Ratification and exchange of ratifications commits the states.
      3. Proclamation obligates the people to observe the terms.
   B. There are no explicit constitutional limitations on the treaty making power of the Federal government.

IV. Executive agreements are not treaties.
   A. An executive agreement is an arrangement between the President and the executive head of another country.
      1. It does not require approval by the Senate. This is the basic distinction between a treaty and an executive agreement.
      2. It may be formally negotiated and signed.
      3. It may be consummated merely through an exchange of notes whereby the two governments explain the terms of the understanding to each other.
      4. When supported by congressional approval, it possesses the force of law and is enforceable in the courts.
      5. Like a treaty, it constitutes a binding international agreement.
      6. Unlike a treaty, it may not bind the state. It may bind only the President who makes it.
   B. A *modus vivendi* is a temporary agreement usually negotiated to serve until permanent arrangements can be made in the form of a treaty.

Appendix D

CLASSIFICATION OF DIPLOMATS

I. Diplomatic agents are divided into three classes:

    A. Ambassadors, legates, or nuncios;

    B. Envoys, ministers, and others who, like those in the first class, are accredited to the sovereigns of the countries to which they are sent;

    C. *Chargés d'affaires*, who are accredited to ministers for foreign affairs of the governments to which they are sent.

II. Diplomatic Precedence.

    A. Diplomatic agents on extraordinary missions do not, on that account, have any superiority in rank.

    B. Diplomatic agents take precedence in their respective classes according to the date of the official notification of their arrival.

    C. In respect to precedence, ministers resident form an intermediate class between ministers of the second class and *chargés d'affaires*.

III. The diplomatic representatives of the United States are of the first, second, intermediate, and third classes.

    A. The following three grades are accredited by the President and their nominations are approved by the Senate:

        1. Ambassadors extraordinary and plenipotentiary;

        2. Envoys extraordinary and plenipotentiary, and special commissioners, when styled as having the rank of envoy extraordinary and minister plenipotentiary;

        3. Ministers resident.

    B. *Chargés d'affaires* are commissioned by the President as such and are accredited by the Secretary of State.

    C. In the absence of the chief of mission, the first secretary of the mission acts *ex officio* as *chargé d'affaires ad interim* and needs no special letter of credence. When the first secretary or second secretary is absent, the Secretary of State may designate any competent person to act *ad interim*, but that person is specifically accredited with a letter to the minister for foreign affairs.

Appendix E

ORGANIZATION OF THE DEPARTMENT OF STATE

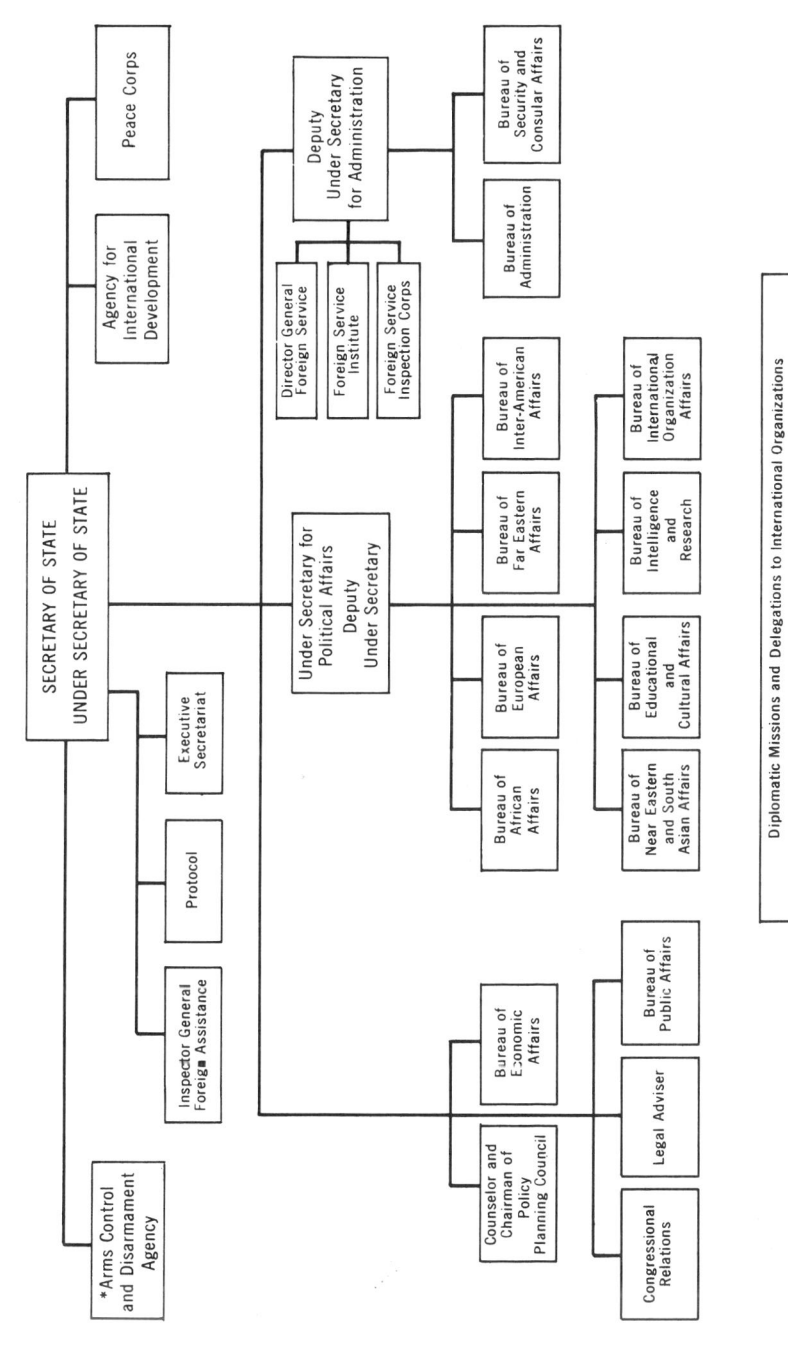

Diplomatic Missions and Delegations to International Organizations

*A Separate Agency with the Director Reporting Directly to the Secretary and Serving as
Principal Adviser to the Secretary and the President on Arms Control and Disarmament

Appendix F

BASIC ORGANIZATION OF A DIPLOMATIC MISSION

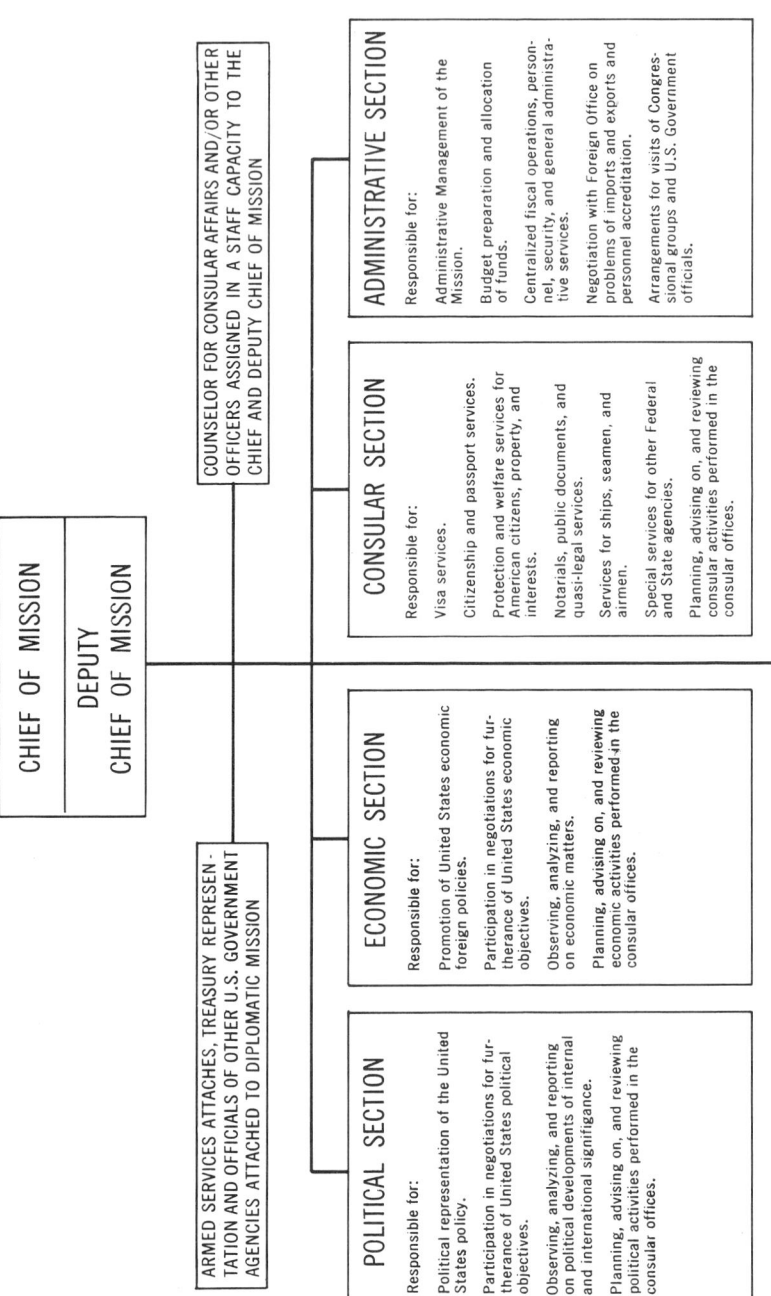

CHIEF OF MISSION

DEPUTY CHIEF OF MISSION

ARMED SERVICES ATTACHES, TREASURY REPRESENTATION AND OFFICIALS OF OTHER U.S. GOVERNMENT AGENCIES ATTACHED TO DIPLOMATIC MISSION

COUNSELOR FOR CONSULAR AFFAIRS AND/OR OTHER OFFICERS ASSIGNED IN A STAFF CAPACITY TO THE CHIEF AND DEPUTY CHIEF OF MISSION

POLITICAL SECTION

Responsible for:

Political representation of the United States policy.

Participation in negotiations for furtherance of United States political objectives.

Observing, analyzing, and reporting on political developments of internal and international signifigance.

Planning, advising on, and reviewing political activities performed in the consular offices.

ECONOMIC SECTION

Responsible for:

Promotion of United States economic foreign policies.

Participation in negotiations for furtherance of United States economic objectives.

Observing, analyzing, and reporting on economic matters.

Planning, advising on, and reviewing economic activities performed in the consular offices.

CONSULAR SECTION

Responsible for:

Visa services.

Citizenship and passport services.

Protection and welfare services for American citizens, property, and interests.

Notarials, public documents, and quasi-legal services.

Services for ships, seamen, and airmen.

Special services for other Federal and State agencies.

Planning, advising on, and reviewing consular activities performed in the consular offices.

ADMINISTRATIVE SECTION

Responsible for:

Administrative Management of the Mission.

Budget preparation and allocation of funds.

Centralized fiscal operations, personnel, security, and general administrative services.

Negotiation with Foreign Office on problems of imports and exports and personnel accreditation.

Arrangements for visits of Congressional groups and U.S. Government officials.

CONSULAR OFFICES

Supplementary Readings

For those who wish to pursue their studies in depth, the indispensable guide is Samuel F. Bemis and Grace G. Griffin, *Guide to the Diplomatic History of the United States 1775–1921* (Washington, 1935). The best bibliography for American history as a whole, but which also contains numerous references to the most important diplomatic studies, is Oscar Handlin *et al.*, eds., *Harvard Guide to American History* (Cambridge, Mass., 1954). These books should be supplemented with three volumes published under the title *Foreign Affairs Bibliography*. The first, covering the period 1919–1932, was edited by William F. Langer and Hamilton F. Armstrong (New York, 1933); the second was edited by Robert G. Woolbert and covers the years 1932–1942 (New York, 1945); and the third includes the years 1942–1952 and was edited by Henry L. Roberts (New York, 1955). One may keep abreast of new publications dealing with American foreign policy and international relations through the bibliographies in each issue of *Foreign Affairs: An American Quarterly Review*.

Most valuable among the published documentary collections is Department of State, *Papers Relating to the Foreign Relations of the United States*, volumes published each year which contain broad selections from American diplomatic dispatches and instructions. They have been published since 1862. Prior to this time, diplomatic documents were printed in collections such as U.S. Congress, *American State Papers, Documents, Legislative and Executive of the Congress of the United States* (38 vols., Washington, 1832–61). The first six volumes deal specifically with foreign relations. David Hunter Miller, ed., *Treaties and Other International Acts of the United States of America* (8 vols., Washington, 1931–48) is the best compilation of treaties for the years 1778 to 1863 and is valuable for the full explanatory notes on many of the negotiations leading to the treaties. Useful supplements are: William M. Malloy, ed., *Treaties, Conventions, International Acts, Protocols and Agreements between the United States of America and Other Powers, 1776–1937* (4 vols., Washington, 1910–38); U.S. treaties etc., *United States Treaties and Other International Agreements* (Washington, 1950–), annual volumes which systematically bring together all American international agreements; and U.S. Dept. of State, *American Foreign Policy: Current Documents* (Washington, 1956–), an annual one-volume selective collection of the principal addresses, statements, reports, diplomatic notes, and treaties made in a given calendar year. The outstanding analysis of international law as it pertains to American diplomacy is John Bassett Moore, *A Digest of International Law* (8 vols., Washington, 1906). It is supplemented by Green H. Hackworth, *Digest of International Law* (8 vols., Washington, 1940–44).

The only detailed multivolume study that deals specifically with the history of American diplomacy, but unevenly because of its many authors, is Samuel F. Bemis, ed., *The American Secretaries of State and Their Diplomacy* (10 vols., New York, 1927–29). It is, in effect, brought up to date by Norman A. Graebner, ed., *An Uncertain Tradition: American Secretaries of State in the Twentieth Century* (New York, 1961). An important series that touches on American foreign policy in most parts of the world, though most volumes concentrate on the foreign country under consideration, is the *American Foreign Policy Library* published by Harvard University Press under various editors, including Sumner Welles, Donald C. McKay, and Crane Brinton. Well worth the serious student's attention are the interpretive and bibliographical pamphlets published by the Service Center for Teachers of History of the American Historical Association. Two of them, Alexander DeConde, *New Interpretations in American Foreign Policy*, rev. ed. (Washington, 1961) and Ernest R. May, *American Intervention: 1917–1941* (Washington, 1960) deal directly with American diplomatic history.

Familiarity with geography and maps is important for the student of American foreign policy. The following are useful and available in most college or university libraries: Charles O. Paullin, *Atlas of the Historical Geography of the United States* (Washington, 1932); James T. Adams, *Atlas of American History* (New York, 1943); Clifford O. Lord and E. H. Lord, *Historical Atlas of the United States* (New York, 1944); R. R. Palmer, *Atlas of World History* (Chicago, 1951); and Andrew Boyd, *An Atlas of World Affairs*, 4th rev. ed. (New York, 1959). Useful one-volume chronologies are Richard B. Morris, ed., *Encyclopedia of American History*, rev. ed. (New York, 1961) and William L. Langer, *An Encyclopedia of World History*, rev. ed. (Boston, 1948). By far the best biographical cyclopedia for American statesmen is Allen Johnson and Dumas Malone, eds., *Dictionary of American Biography* (20 vols. and 2 supplements or 11 vols., New York, 1928–).

For studies on special subjects, with emphasis on works not previously cited in the notes, see the bibliographies arranged by chapters and topics within chapters.

CHAPTER ONE

In addition to the works cited in the notes, the following offer more material on the topics discussed in this chapter. Stephen D. Kertesz and M. A. Fitzsimons, eds., *Diplomacy in a Changing World* (Notre Dame, Ind., 1959) is a symposium that deals with various aspects of diplomacy, as does Kertesz, ed., *American Diplomacy in a New Era* (Notre Dame, 1961). Gabriel Almond, *The American People and Foreign Policy* (New York, 1950), treats foreign policy broadly, using all the techniques of social science in analyzing it. Thomas A. Bailey, *The Man in the Street: The Impact of American Public Opinion on Foreign Policy* (New York, 1948) is a spicy analysis of public opinion and pressure groups that criticizes the ignorance of the public. Percy E. Corbett, *Law in Diplomacy* (Princeton, 1959), avoids the technical jargon of international law in a readable effort to measure the influence of legal notions on foreign policy. Morton Gordon and Kenneth Vines, eds., *Theory and Practice of American Foreign Policy* (New York, 1955) is a useful collection of readings. Marshall Knappen, *An Introduction to American Foreign Policy* (New York, 1956), stresses the factors that influence the formulation of foreign policy.

Two books, James L. McCamy, *The Administration of American Foreign Affairs* (New York, 1950) and Arthur W. McMahon, *Administration in Foreign Affairs* (University, Ala., 1953), explain how foreign policy is made and carried out from the viewpoint of an administrator. Roy C. Macridis, ed., *Foreign Policy in World Politics* (Englewood Cliffs, N.J., 1958) contains two essays which summarize recent theory and practice in the United States. Walter Millis, *Arms and Men: A Study in American Military History* (New York, 1956), reviews military history in its broad political, economic, and social context. See also William R. Kintner *et al.*, *Forging a New Sword: A Study of the Department of Defense* (New York, 1958) and Paul Y. Hammond, *Organizing for Defense: The American Military Establishment in the Twentieth Century* (Princeton, 1961). Elmer Plischke, *Conduct of American Diplomacy* (New York, 1950), offers a convenient summary of the principles, procedures, and governmental machinery involved in the conduct of foreign relations. Richard C. Snyder and Edgar S. Furniss, Jr., *American Foreign Policy: Formulation, Principles, and Programs* (New York, 1954), attempt to relate theory and practice and stress techniques such as decision-making. See also H. Field Haviland, Jr., *et al.*, *The Formulation and Administration of United States Foreign Policy* (Washington, 1960); James N. Rosenau, ed., *International Politics and Foreign Policy: A Reader in Research and Theory* (New York, 1961); and Rosenau, *Public Opinion and Foreign Policy* (New York, 1961).

Two books by Graham H. Stuart offer basic details on organization and procedure in the State Department and the Overseas Establishment: *The Department of State: A History of Its Organization, Procedure, and Personnel* (New York, 1949) and *American Diplomatic and Consular Practice*, 2nd ed. (New York, 1952). See also Robert E. Elder, *The Policy Machine: The Department of State and American Foreign Policy* (Syracuse, N.Y., 1960), which analyzes policymaking in the State Department; Don K. Price, ed., *The Secretary of State* (Englewood Cliffs, N.J., 1960), which deals with the same problem but concentrates on the Secretaryship; and Warren P. Ilchman, *Professional Diplomacy in the United States, 1779–1939: A Study in Administrative History* (Chicago, 1961).

CHAPTER TWO

The basic monograph for the diplomacy of this period is Samuel F. Bemis, *The Diplomacy of the American Revolution* (New York, 1935). Bemis has also edited *The American Secretaries of State and Their Diplomacy* (10 vols., New York, 1927–29), in which the historical introduction and the essay on Robert R. Livingston gives background material for this period. No one should overlook Felix Gilbert's excellent book, *To the Farewell Address: Ideas of Early American Foreign Policy* (Princeton, 1961), which is particularly valuable for its analysis of ideas from Europe and their impact on American foreign policy. Arthur B. Darling's early chapters in *Our Rising Empire, 1763–1803* (New Haven, 1940) offer a sound general treatment, as does Lawrence H. Gipson, *The Triumphant Empire: Thunder-Clouds Gather in the West, 1763–1766* (New York, 1961), which is vol. X of *The British Empire before the American Revolution* (10 vols., New York, 1958–1960).

For French diplomacy, see Edward S. Corwin, *French Policy and the American Alliance of 1778* (Princeton, 1916); John J. Meng, *The Comte de Vergennes: European Phases of His Diplomacy* (Washington, 1932); Henri Doniol, *Histoire de la participation de la France à l'établissement des États-Unis d'Amérique* (5 vols., Paris, 1886–92, and supplementary vol., 1899), a collection of documents from the archives of the French Foreign Office.

For British policy, see Vincent T. Harlow, *The Founding of the Second British Empire, 1763–1793* (London, 1952), which examines the peace negotiations from the viewpoint of imperial objectives; Clarence W. Alvord, *The Mississippi Valley in British Politics* (2 vols., Cleveland, 1917); Bernhard Knollenberg, *Origin of the American Revolution* (New York, 1960); and Isabel de Madariaga, *Britain, Russia, and the Armed Neutrality of 1780: Sir James Harris's Mission to St. Petersburg During the American Revolution* (New Haven, 1962), a detailed history of European aspects of the diplomacy of the revolutionary years.

Other readable general studies based upon sound scholarship that provide background material are: John C. Miller, *Origins of the American Revolution* (Boston, 1943); Edmund S. Morgan, *The Birth of the Republic, 1763–89* (Chicago, 1956); Verner W. Crane, *Benjamin Franklin and a Rising People* (Boston, 1954); Arthur H. Buffinton, *The Second Hundred Years War, 1689–1815* (New York, 1929); and George Dangerfield, *Chancellor Robert R. Livingston of New York, 1746–1813* (New York, 1960). See also the works cited in the notes.

CHAPTER THREE

Merrill Jensen, *The New Nation: A History of the United States during the Confederation, 1781–1789* (New York, 1950), offers the fullest treatment of the Confederation period. He devotes considerable space to foreign relations. His thesis states that this was not "the critical period" that earlier historians have said it was. Although marked by a Federalist bias, the most useful books on the Federalist period are Nathan Schachner, *The Founding Fathers* (New York, 1954) and John C. Miller, *The Federalist Era, 1789–1801* (New York, 1960). Two other important studies that deal with both domestic and foreign affairs in this period are Manning J. Dauer, *The Adams Federalists* (Baltimore, 1953) and Joseph Charles, *The Origins of the American Party System* (Williamsburg, Va., 1956). Both offer provocative interpretations on the influence of domestic politics and quarrels on foreign policy in the Federalist era.

In Arthur B. Darling, *Our Rising Empire, 1763–1803* (New Haven, 1940) may be found a sound, detailed history of diplomatic relations, the only one covering the whole period. On relations with Great Britain, three monographs stand out: Samuel F. Bemis, *Jay's Treaty: A Study in Commerce and Diplomacy* (New York, 1923); Alfred L. Burt, *The United States, Great Britain and British North America from the Revolution to the Establishment of Peace after the War of 1812* (New Haven, 1940); and Bradford Perkins, *The First Rapprochement: England and the United States, 1795–1805* (Philadelphia, 1955).

Relations with France are dealt with in Charles D. Hazen, *Contemporary American Opinion of the French Revolution* (Baltimore, 1897); Beverly W. Bond, *The Monroe Mission to France, 1794–1796* (Baltimore, 1907); Gardner W. Allen, *Our Naval War with France* (Boston, 1909), which deals more with naval warfare than with diplomacy; Alexander DeConde, *Entangling Alliance: Politics And Diplomacy under George Washington* (Durham, N.C., 1958), which covers political as well as diplomatic influences in relations with France; Stuart G. Brown, ed., *The Autobiography of James Monroe* (Syracuse, N.Y., 1959), which emphasizes Monroe's diplomatic career; Louis M. Sears, *George Washington and the French Revolution* (Detroit,

1960); and Felix Gilbert, *To the Farewell Address: Ideas of Early American Foreign Policy* (Princeton, 1961).

Three scholarly monographs, two of which offer differing interpretations, deal with Spanish relations: Samuel F. Bemis, *Pinckney's Treaty* (Baltimore, 1926); Arthur P.Whitaker, *The Spanish-American Frontier, 1783-1795* (Boston, 1927); and his *The Mississippi Question, 1795-1803* (New York, 1934). Noteworthy special studies are: Charles M. Thomas, *American Neutrality in 1793: A Study in Cabinet Government* (New York, 1931); Vernon G. Setser, *The Commercial Reciprocity Policy of the United States, 1774-1829* (Philadelphia, 1937); Frederick B. Tolles, *George Logan of Philadelphia* (New York, 1953); Marshall Smelser, *The Congress Founds the Navy, 1787-1798* (Notre Dame, Ind., 1959); and Arthur A. Richmond, "Napoleon and the Armed Neutrality of 1800: A Diplomatic Challenge to British Sea Power," *Journal of the Royal United Service Institution*, CIV, No. 614 (May 1959), 186-194.

Biographies of the founding fathers, of which a number of good ones are easily available, offer excellent supplementary reading, as do articles in the scholarly journals. See also citations included in the notes.

CHAPTER FOUR

Although superseded in some particulars, Henry Adams, *History of the United States of America during the Administrations of Jefferson and Madison* (9 vols., New York, 1889-1909) is still the classic work of this period. Its first four volumes deal with Jefferson's diplomacy and are well worth reading just for pleasure. Irving Brant, *James Madison: Secretary of State, 1800-1809* (Indianapolis, 1953) is based on exhaustive research and uncovers flaws in Adams' history.

The following all offer special insights on the Louisiana question: Arthur P. Whitaker, *The Mississippi Question, 1795-1803* (New York, 1934); Alfred L. Burt, *The United States, Great Britain, and British North America* (New Haven, 1940); Arthur B. Darling, *Our Rising Empire, 1763-1803* (New Haven, 1940); Charles C. Tansill, *The United States and Santo Domingo, 1798-1873* (Baltimore, 1938); Rayford W. Logan, *The Diplomatic Relations of the United States with Haiti, 1776-1891* (Chapel Hill, N.C., 1941); Bradford Perkins, *The First Rapprochement* (Philadelphia, 1955); and George Dangerfield, *Chancellor Robert R. Livingston of New York, 1746-1813* (New York, 1960).

For the Barbary warfare and diplomacy, the basic study is Ray W. Irwin, *The Diplomatic Relations of the United States with the Barbary Powers, 1776-1816* (Chapel Hill, N.C., 1931). See also Gardner W. Allen, *Our Navy and the Barbary Corsairs* (Boston, 1905) and Louis B. Wright and Julia H. McLeod, *The First Americans in North Africa: William Eaton's Struggle for a Vigorous Policy against the Barbary Pirates, 1799-1805* (Princeton, 1945).

For maritime and other problems, see Louis M. Sears, *Jefferson and the Embargo* (Durham, N.C., 1927), the basic study on the embargo; Robert G. Albion and Jennie B. Pope, *Sea Lanes in Wartime: The American Experience, 1775-1942* (New York, 1942); Eli F. Heckscher, *The Continental System: An Economic Interpretation* (Oxford, 1922); James F. Zimmerman, *Impressment of American Seamen* (New York, 1925); and I-Mien Tsiang, *The Question of Expatriation in America Prior to 1907* (Baltimore, 1942). Other useful works are cited in the notes.

CHAPTER FIVE

The second half of Henry Adams, *History of the United States of America during the Administrations of Jefferson and Madison* (9 vols., New York, 1889–1909) remains the most readable account of the diplomacy and politics of the War of 1812. In some respects its scholarship is superseded by Bradford Perkins, *Prologue to War: England and the United States, 1805–1812* (Berkeley, Calif., 1961), which emphasizes the development of British policy, and Reginald Horsman, *The Causes of the War of 1812* (Philadelphia, 1962). Irving Brant, in *James Madison: The President, 1809–1812* (Indianapolis, 1956), is much kinder than Adams or Perkins toward Madison's statesmanship. Brant's study corrects some errors in Adams. Julius W. Pratt, in *Expansionists of 1812* (New York, 1925), advances the hotly disputed thesis on the war hawks and western expansionists. His views are sharply challenged by Alfred L. Burt, in *The United States, Great Britain, and British North America* (New Haven, 1940), who insists that the old thesis of maritime rights, as advanced by Adams, is the correct interpretation of the war's causes. A fine survey of the war's diplomacy is Samuel F. Bemis, *John Quincy Adams and the Foundations of American Foreign Policy* (New York, 1949). While still useful, Frank A. Updyke, *The Diplomacy of the War of 1812* (Baltimore, 1915), has been largely superseded by Fred L. Engelman, *The Peace of Christmas Eve* (New York, 1962).

For readable general accounts of the war, see Glenn Tucker, *Poltroons and Patriots: A Popular Account of the War of 1812* (2 vols., Indianapolis, 1954), which leans heavily on the Pratt thesis, and Albert Z. Carr, *The Coming of War: An Account of the Remarkable Events Leading to the War of 1812* (Garden City, N.Y., 1960). Alfred J. Mahan's account, *Sea Power in Its Relations to the War of 1812* (Boston, 1905), has not yet been superseded. Alec R. Gilpin, *The War of 1812 in the Old Northwest* (East Lansing, Mich., 1958) is a useful specialized study. In addition to those cited in the notes, another important study for the diplomacy of this period is: Raymond Walters, Jr., *Albert Gallatin: Jeffersonian Financier and Diplomat* (New York, 1957), a scholarly study; but Henry Adams, *The Life of Albert Gallatin* (Philadelphia, 1879) is still valuable, particularly for the large number of documents it reproduces. See also Bernard Mayo, *Henry Clay: Spokesman of the New West* (Boston, 1937); Morton Borden, *The Federalism of James A. Bayard* (New York, 1955); and Francois Crouzet, *L'Economie Britannique et le Blocus Continental, 1806–1813* (2 vols., Paris, 1958).

CHAPTER SIX

The most thorough and scholarly study of the diplomacy of the entire period is Samuel F. Bemis, *John Quincy Adams and the Foundations of American Diplomacy* (New York, 1949).

The best and most readable work on the complicated Florida revolutions is Rembert W. Patrick, *Florida Fiasco: Rampant Rebels on the Georgia–Florida Border, 1810–1815* (Athens, Ga., 1954). Superseded but still useful is Herbert B. Fuller, *The Purchase of Florida: Its History and Diplomacy* (Cleveland, 1906). The pertinent volumes in Henry Adams' *History* still offer a vivid and fairly sound account of the early Florida diplomacy.

The best and most readable account of the Monroe Doctrine is Dexter Perkins, *A History of the Monroe Doctrine*, 2nd ed. (Boston, 1955). More detailed is his *The Monroe Doctrine, 1823–1826* (Cambridge, Mass., 1927). George Dangerfield, in *The Era of Good Feelings* (New York, 1952), offers a skillful and well-written synthesis of American diplomacy and politics against the background of European diplomacy. The outstanding account of the Florida treaty in its broad context is Philip C. Brooks, *Diplomacy and the Borderlands: The Adams-Onís Treaty of 1819* (Berkeley, Calif., 1939). For the European diplomacy of the Monroe Doctrine, see Edward H. Tatum, *The United States and Europe, 1815–1823* (Berkeley, Calif., 1936). The leading account of the diplomacy of recognition during the Latin-American revolutions is Arthur P. Whitaker, *The United States and the Independence of Latin America, 1800–1830* (Baltimore, 1941). See also Charles C. Griffin, *The United States and the Disruption of the Spanish Empire, 1810–1822* (New York, 1937); J. Fred Rippy, *Rivalry of the United States and Great Britain over Latin America, 1808–1830* (Baltimore, 1929); William S. Robertson, *France and Latin-American Independence* (Baltimore, 1939); Myrtle A. Cline, *American Attitude toward the Greek War of Independence, 1821–1828* (Atlanta, Ga., 1930); Benjamin P. Thomas, *Russo-American Relations, 1815–1867* (Baltimore, 1930); Charles A. Manning, *Russian Influence on Early America* (New York, 1953); and references cited in the notes.

CHAPTER SEVEN

The basic monograph on the West Indian trade question is Frank L. Benns, *The American Struggle for the British West India Carrying-Trade, 1815–1830* (Bloomington, Ind., 1923). For the claims question, the fullest treatment is in Richard A. McLemore, *Franco-American Diplomatic Relations, 1816–1836* (Baton Rouge, 1941). On the issues of the slave trade and search at sea, the most useful volume is Hugh G. Soulsby, *The Right of Search and the Slave Trade in Anglo-American Relations, 1814–1862* (Baltimore, 1933).

The best single volume on the issues of Canadian-American frontier is Albert B. Corey, *The Crisis of 1830–1842 in Canadian-American Relations* (New Haven, 1941). See also Samuel F. Bemis, *John Quincy Adams and the Foundations of American Foreign Policy* (New York, 1949); Oliver P. Chitwood, *John Tyler: Champion of the Old South* (New York, 1939); Claude M. Fuess, *Daniel Webster and the Rise of National Conservatism* (New York, 1955), a brief, readable account; Wilbur D. Jones, *Lord Aberdeen and the Americas* (Athens, Ga., 1958); and Raymond Walters, Jr., *Albert Gallatin: Jeffersonian Financier and Diplomat* (New York, 1957).

For the most intensive scholarly work on the Oregon question, see the articles by Frederick Merk cited in the footnotes and also his *Albert Gallatin and the Oregon Problem* (Cambridge, Mass., 1950). Another stimulating study of this question is in Norman A. Graebner, *Empire on the Pacific: A Study of American Continental Expansion* (New York, 1955). See also Edwin E. Rich, *Hudson's Bay Company: 1670–1870* (3 vols., New York, 1961); vol. III, 657–734, deals with the Oregon rivalry. Melvin C. Jacobs, *Winning Oregon: A Study of an Expansionist Movement* (Caldwell, Idaho, 1938); Walter Sage, "The Oregon Treaty of 1846," *Canadian Historical Review*, XXVII (Dec. 1946), 349–367; and Jesse S. Reeves, *American Diplomacy under Tyler and Polk* (Baltimore, 1907)—all provide pertinent material.

The basic volume on Manifest Destiny, a pioneer study in the influence of ideas on foreign policy, is Albert K. Weinberg, *Manifest Destiny: A Study of Nationalist Expansionism in American History* (Baltimore, 1935). For a readable general account of this period, one that covers domestic affairs as well as diplomacy, see Glyndon G. Van Deusen, *The Jacksonian Era, 1828–1848* (New York, 1959).

CHAPTER EIGHT

Although inadequate in its interpretations, Justin H. Smith, *The War with Mexico* (2 vols., New York, 1919) is still the best and most thorough scholarly study of the diplomacy of this period. See also Smith's *The Annexation of Texas* (New York, 1911), the basic study of its subject. George L. Rives, *The United States and Mexico, 1821–1848* (2 vols., New York, 1913) and Jesse S. Reeves, *American Diplomacy under Tyler and Polk* (Baltimore, 1907) are still useful. See also Eugene C. Barker, *Mexico and Texas, 1821–1835* (Dallas, 1928). William C. Binkley, *The Texas Revolution* (Baton Rouge, 1952) is a small, carefully reasoned book that combines ripe scholarship with readability. Norman A. Graebner, *Empire on the Pacific* (New York, 1955), rejects Manifest Destiny as the basic cause for expansion and provides provocative insights on the diplomacy of California and Texas.

For the Mexican point of view and the background in Mexico, see José Fernando Ramírez, *Mexico during the War with the United States*, Walter V. Scholes, ed. and Elliott B. Scherr, trans. (Columbia, Mo., 1950) and Ramón Alcaraz, *The Other Side: or Notes for the History of the War between Mexico and the United States*, Albert C. Ramsay, trans. and ed. (New York, 1850).

The best short popular account is Otis A. Singletary, *The Mexican War* (Chicago, 1960). Two other readable popular histories are Alfred H. Bill, *Rehearsal for Conflict* (New York, 1947) and Robert S. Henry, *The Story of the Mexican War* (Indianapolis, 1950). See also Glyndon G. Van Deusen, *The Jacksonian Era, 1828–1848* (New York, 1959).

The following specialized studies or biographies all offer background material or cast light on particular problems: Ephraim D. Adams, *British Interests and Activities in Texas, 1838–1846* (Baltimore, 1910); Eugene C. Barker, *The Life of Stephen F. Austin* (Nashville, 1925); Henry Blumenthal, *A Reappraisal of Franco-American Relations, 1830–1871* (Chapel Hill, N.C., 1959), containing material on French interest in Texas and California; Wilfrid H. Callcott, *Santa Anna* (Norman, Okla., 1936); Robert G. Cleland, *From Wilderness to Empire: A History of California, 1542–1900* (New York, 1947); Ilerena Friend, *Sam Houston: The Great Designer* (Austin, Texas, 1954); John D. P. Fuller, *The Movement for the Acquisition of All Mexico, 1846–1848* (Baltimore, 1936); Marquis James, *The Raven: A Biography of Sam Houston* (Indianapolis, 1937); Eugene I. McCormac, *James K. Polk: A Political Biography* (Berkeley, Calif., 1922); Allan Nevins, *Frémont: The West's Greatest Adventurer* (2 vols., New York, 1928); Joseph W. Schmitz, *Texan Statecraft, 1836–1845* (San Antonio, Tex., 1941); and Stanley Siegel, *A Political History of the Texas Republic, 1836–1845* (Austin, Tex., 1956). See also the notes in this chapter and the supplementary readings in the preceding one.

CHAPTER NINE

The best study of the diplomatic rivalry over Central-American transit routes is Mary W. Williams, *Anglo-American Diplomacy, 1815–1915* (Washington, 1916). See also Ira D. Travis, *The History of the Clayton-Bulwer Treaty* (Ann Arbor, Mich., 1900); Richard W. Van Alstyne, ed., "Anglo-American Relations, 1853–1857," *The American Historical Review*, XLII (April

1937), 491–500; and Lawrence Greene, *The Filibuster: The Career of William Walker* (Indianapolis, 1937). For Mexican relations, consult Paul N. Garber, *The Gadsden Treaty* (Philadelphia, 1923); Agustín Cue Cánovas, *El Tratado McLane-Ocampo: Juárez, los Estados Unidos y Europa,* 2nd ed. (Mexico City, 1959); Dexter Perkins, *The Monroe Doctrine, 1826–1867* (Baltimore, 1933); and Ollinger Crenshaw, "The Knights of the Golden Circle: The Career of George Bickley," *The American Historical Review,* XLVII (Oct. 1941), 23–50, which deals with George W. L. Bickley who sought to lead a filibustering expedition into Mexico and annex it for slavery.

The most thorough treatment of the political union movement in Canada is in Donald F. Warner, *The Idea of Continental Union: Agitation for the Annexation of Canada to the United States, 1849–1893* (Lexington, Ky., 1960). See also Charles C. Tansill, *The Canadian Reciprocity Treaty of 1854* (Baltimore, 1922) and Donald C. Masters, *The Reciprocity Treaty of 1854* (London, 1937).

For the problems of "Young America," Europe, and Cuba, see John G. Gazley, *American Opinion of German Unification, 1848–1871* (New York, 1926); John W. Oliver, "Louis Kossuth's Appeal to the Middle West—1852," *Mississippi Valley Historical Review,* XIV (March 1928), 481–495; John F. H. Claiborne, *Life and Correspondence of John A. Quitman* (2 vols., New York, 1860); Robert G. Caldwell, *The López Expeditions to Cuba, 1848–1851* (Princeton, 1915); Herminio Portell Vilá, *Narciso López y su Época* (La Habana, Cuba, 1930); and C. Stanley Urban, "The Africanization of Cuba Scare, 1853–1855," *Hispanic American Historical Review,* XXXVII (Feb. 1957), 29–45.

The most detailed treatment of early relations with China is Earl Swisher, *China's Management of the American Barbarians: A Study of Sino-American Relations, 1841–1861, with Documents* (New Haven, 1953). See also Eldon Griffin, *Clippers and Consuls: American Consular and Commercial Relations with Eastern Asia, 1845–1860* (Ann Arbor, Mich., 1938); Frederick W. Williams, *Anson Burlingame and the First Chinese Mission to Foreign Powers* (New York, 1912); John W. Foster, *American Diplomacy in the Orient* (Boston, 1903); Foster Rhea Dulles, *The Old China Trade* (Boston, 1930); Lawrence H. Battistini, *The United States and Asia* (New York, 1955) and his *The Rise of American Influence in Asia* (East Lansing, Mich., 1960); Maurice Collis, *Foreign Mud: Being an Account of the Opium Imbroglio at Canton in the 1830's and the Anglo-Chinese War that Followed* (New York, 1947); and Paul H. Clyde, ed., *United States Policy Toward China: Diplomatic and Public Documents, 1838–1939* (Durham, N.C., 1940), a useful collection of source materials.

For relations with Japan, see Lawrence H. Battistini, *Japan and America: From Earliest Times to the Present* (New York, 1954); Inazo Nitobe, *The Intercourse between the United States and Japan: An Historical Sketch* (Baltimore, 1891); Allan B. Cole, ed., *With Perry in Japan: The Diary of Edward Yorke McCauley* (Princeton, 1942); Henry F. Graff, *Bluejackets with Perry in Japan* (New York, 1952); Arthur Walworth, *Black Ships off Japan: The Story of Commodore Perry's Expedition* (New York, 1946); Chitoshi Yanaga, *Japan Since Perry* (New York, 1949), valuable for the Japanese internal background; Hikomatsu Kamikawa, ed., *Japan-American Relations in the Meiji-Taisho Era,* Kimura Michiko, trans. (Tokyo, 1958); and Mario E. Cosenza, *The Complete Journal of Townsend Harris,* 2nd ed. (Rutland, Vt., 1959). See also the notes.

CHAPTER TEN

Despite the tremendous amount of attention historians have given to the Civil War, there is no satisfactory scholarly synthesis that brings together Union and Confederate foreign policy and diplomacy. The two outstanding studies that deal with special areas of that diplomacy are Ephraim D. Adams, *Great Britain and the American Civil War* (2 vols., London, 1925) and Frank L. Owsley, *King Cotton Diplomacy: Foreign Relations of the Confederate States of America*, 2nd ed., rev. by Harriet C. Owsley (Chicago, 1959). For Union diplomacy, the best account is Jay Monaghan's readable book, *Diplomat in Carpet Slippers: Abraham Lincoln Deals with Foreign Affairs* (Indianapolis, 1945). Another readable volume is Donaldson Jordan and Edwin J. Pratt, *Europe and the American Civil War* (Boston, 1931), which deals with opinion abroad. Karl Marx and Frederick Engels, *The Civil War in the United States* (New York, 1937) is a compilation of newspaper articles and letters useful for a European view of American Civil War diplomacy, and A. R. Tyrner-Tyrnauer, *Lincoln and the Emperors* (New York, 1962) is a popular synthesis which makes limited use of documents in the Austrian State Archives.

In addition to those listed in the notes, the following specialized works may be consulted with profit: Henry Adams, "Why Did Not England Recognize the Confederacy?" *Massachusetts Historical Society Proceedings*, LXVI (1936–41), 204–222, which stresses that the strength of Northern armies basically prevented recognition; Thomas L. Harris, *The Trent Affair* (Indianapolis, 1896); Carlton Savage, *Policy of the United States toward Maritime Commerce in War* (Washington, 1934); Frank L. Owsley, "America and the Freedom of the Seas, 1861–1865," in Avery Craven, ed., *Essays in Honor of William E. Dodd* (Chicago, 1935); Norman A. Graebner, "Northern Diplomacy and European Neutrality," in David Donald, ed., *Why the North Won the Civil War* (Baton Rouge, 1960), pp. 49–75; William O. Henderson, *The Lancashire Cotton Famine, 1861–1865* (Manchester, England, 1934); Margaret A. Clapp, *Forgotten First Citizen: John Bigelow* (Boston, 1947), the American Consul in Paris; Charles F. Adams, Jr., *Charles Francis Adams* (Boston, 1900); Robert D. Meade, *Judah P. Benjamin: Confederate Statesman* (New York, 1943), the outstanding Secretary of State of the Confederacy; Frank A. Golder, "The Russian Fleet and the Civil War," *The American Historical Review*, XX (July 1915), 801–812, the pioneer study, based on Russian archival sources, which exposed the true purpose of the fleet visits; Thomas A. Bailey, "The Russian Fleet Myth Re-examined," *Mississippi Valley Historical Review*, XXXVIII (June 1951), 81–90, which analyzes whether or not Americans were deceived by the fleet visits; Bailey, *America Faces Russia: Russian-American Relations from Early Times to Our Day* (Ithaca, N.Y., 1950); and James G. Randall, *Lincoln, the President* (4 vols., New York, 1945–55). The fourth volume of this foremost scholarly biography, in which there is much on foreign relations, was completed by Richard N. Current. In addition, see the notes.

CHAPTER ELEVEN

The notes refer to most of the important studies covering the subjects in this chapter. In addition, for the French and Spanish interventions in Santo Domingo and Mexico, the following are useful: Harford M. Hyde, *Mexican Empire: The History of Maximilian and Carlota of Mexico* (London, 1946); Dexter Perkins, *The Monroe Doctrine, 1826–1867* (Baltimore, 1933) and *The Monroe Doctrine, 1867–1907* (Baltimore, 1937); J. Fred Rippy, *The*

United States and Mexico (New York, 1926); James M. Callahan, *American Foreign Policy in Mexican Relations* (New York, 1932); Warren R. West, *Contemporary French Opinion of the American Civil War* (Baltimore, 1924); John G. Gazley, *American Opinion of German Unification, 1848–1871* (New York, 1926); and Otto zu Stolberg-Wernigerode, *Germany and the United States of America during the Era of Bismarck* (Reading, Pa., 1937). The best and most thorough treatment of the Mexican affair is still Egon C. Corti's *Maximilian and Charlotte of Mexico*, trans. from the German (2 vols., New York, 1928).

For expansionism under Seward, see Ludwell L. Montague, *Haiti and the United States, 1714–1938* (Durham, N.C., 1940); Rayford W. Logan, *The Diplomatic Relations of the United States with Haiti, 1776–1891* (Chapel Hill, N.C., 1941); and Roy F. Nichols, *Advance Agents of American Destiny* (Philadelphia, 1956).

For expansion in the Pacific, see Foster Rhea Dulles, *America in the Pacific* (Boston, 1932) and his *The Road to Teheran* (Princeton, 1944); Charles C. Tansill, *The Purchase of the Danish West Indies* (Baltimore, 1932); Victor J. Farrar, *The Annexation of Russian America to the United States* (Washington, 1937), the most thorough treatment of the subject; Thomas A. Bailey, *America Faces Russia* (Ithaca, N.Y., 1950); and Benjamin P. Thomas, *Russo-American Relations, 1815–1867* (Baltimore, 1930).

For Canadian relations, see Florence E. Gibson, *The Attitudes of the New York Irish toward State and National Affairs, 1848–1892* (New York, 1951), useful for the Fenian movement; James M. Callahan, *American Foreign Policy in Canadian Relations* (New York, 1937); Robin W. Winks, *Canada and the United States: The Civil War Years* (Baltimore, 1960), the latest and most thorough analysis of the subject; Frederick W. Howay, Walter N. Sage, and Henry F. Angus, *British Columbia and the United States* (Toronto, 1942), valuable for annexationist agitation in the Northwest, confederation, and the San Juan boundary controversy; Hugh L. Keenleyside and Gerald S. Brown, *Canada and the United States*, rev. ed. (New York, 1952), a readable survey that is especially useful because of its historical treatment of broad topics; Rising L. Morrow, "The Negotiation of the Anglo-American Treaty of 1870," *The American Historical Review*, XXXIX (July 1934), 663–681, dealing with the naturalization problem; Hunter Miller, *San Juan Archipelago: Study of the Joint Occupation of San Juan Islands* (Bellows Falls, Vt., 1943); Brainerd Dyer, *The Public Career of William M. Evarts* (Berkeley, Calif., 1933) and Chester L. Barrows, *William M. Evarts: Lawyer, Diplomat, Statesman* (Chapel Hill, N.C., 1941), useful for the *Alabama* claims; Charles Francis Adams, *Lee at Appomattox and Other Papers* (Boston, 1902), especially the section on "The Treaty of Washington: Before and After"; and French E. Chadwick, *The Relations of the United States with Spain: Diplomacy* (New York, 1909), valuable for the *Virginius* affair. The most thorough and scholarly treatment of relations with Canada in this period is Lester B. Shippee, *Canadian-American Relations, 1849–1874* (New Haven, 1939), and the best source on the diplomacy of the Grant and Fish era is Allan Nevins, *Hamilton Fish: The Inner History of the Grant Administration*, rev. ed. (2 vols., New York, 1957).

CHAPTER TWELVE

For the general background of the foreign policy of this period, the most useful studies are Alice F. Tyler, *The Foreign Policy of James G. Blaine* (Minneapolis, 1927); Charles C. Tansill, *The Foreign Policy of Thomas F. Bayard, 1885–1897* (New York, 1940), detailed and based upon extensive use of manuscript sources; Edward Younger, *John A. Kasson: Politics And Diplomacy from Lincoln to McKinley* (Iowa City, 1955), a balanced account of politics as well as diplomacy; William M. Armstrong, *E. L. Godkin and American Foreign Policy, 1865–1900* (New York, 1957); Brainerd Dyer, *The Public Career of William M. Evarts* (Berkeley, Calif., 1933); George F. Howe, *Chester A. Arthur: A Quarter Century of Machine Politics* (New York, 1934); David S. Muzzey, *James G. Blaine: A Political Idol of Other Days* (New York, 1935); and Albert T. Volwiler, *The Correspondence between Benjamin Harrison and James G. Blaine, 1882–1893* (Philadelphia, 1940).

Details on canal diplomacy and Latin-American policy may be found in Gerstle Mack, *The Land Divided: A History of the Panama Canal and Other Isthmian Canal Projects* (New York, 1944), a lively, well-written account; Miles P. DuVal, Jr., *Cadiz to Cathay: The Story of the Long Diplomatic Struggle for the Panama Canal*, 2nd ed. (Stanford, Calif., 1947); Dexter Perkins, *The Monroe Doctrine, 1867–1907* (Baltimore, 1937); E. Taylor Parks, *Colombia and the United States, 1765–1934* (Durham, N.C., 1935); Herbert Millington, *American Diplomacy and the War of the Pacific* (New York, 1948); Harold Lindsell, *The Chilean-American Controversy of 1891–1892* (New York, 1943), an abridged doctoral dissertation; William R. Sherman, *The Diplomatic and Commercial Relations of the United States and Chile, 1820–1914* (Boston, 1926); and Henry C. Evans, Jr., *Chile and Its Relations with the United States* (Durham, N.C., 1927).

The best historical treatment of relations with China over immigration is still Mary R. Coolidge, *Chinese Immigration* (New York, 1909); for the situation in California it is Elmer C. Sandmeyer, *The Anti-Chinese Movement in California* (Urbana, Ill., 1939). See also R. D. McKenzie, *Oriental Exclusion* (New York, 1927); Roy L. Garis, *Immigration Restriction* (New York, 1927); and Rose Hum Lee, *The Chinese in the United States of America* (Hong Kong, 1960).

For the pork controversy and relations with Germany, see Jeannette Keim, *Forty Years of German-American Political Relations* (Philadelphia, 1919); Clara E. Schieber, *The Transformation of American Sentiment toward Germany, 1870–1914* (Boston, 1923); Alfred Vagts, *Deutschland und die Vereinigten Staaten in der Weltpolitik* (2 vols., New York, 1935); and Otto zu Stolberg-Wernigerode, *Germany and the United States of America during the Era of Bismarck*, trans. from the German (Reading, Pa., 1937).

For information on the Sackville-West episode, see Florence E. Gibson, *The Attitudes of the New York Irish toward State and National Affairs, 1848–1892* (New York, 1892).

For accounts of the fisheries and seal problems, see Charles C. Tansill, *Canadian-American Relations, 1875–1911* (New Haven, 1943); John W. Foster, *Diplomatic Memoirs* (2 vols., New York, 1919); and John B. Brebner, *North Atlantic Triangle: The Interplay of Canada, the United States, and Great Britain* (New Haven, 1945). See also the references in the notes.

CHAPTER THIRTEEN

The best treatment of the New Manifest Destiny is in Julius W. Pratt, *Expansionists of 1898* (Baltimore, 1936). See also his essay, "The Ideology of American Expansion," in Avery Craven, ed., *Essays in Honor of William E. Dodd* (Chicago, 1935), pp. 335–353; his *America's Colonial Experiment* (New York, 1950); Albert K. Weinberg, *Manifest Destiny* (Baltimore, 1935); Hans Kohn, *American Nationalism: An Interpretative Essay* (New York, 1957); Harold and Margaret Sprout, *The Rise of American Naval Power, 1776–1918* (Princeton, 1939); Merle Curti, *Peace or War: The American Struggle, 1636–1936* (New York, 1936), useful for anti-imperialist sentiment; and Earle M. Winslow, *The Pattern of Imperialism: A Study in the Theories of Power* (New York, 1948), an excellent analysis of imperialism from the point of view of theory.

For three readable surveys of events in this period, see Foster Rhea Dulles, *America in the Pacific* (Boston, 1932), his *Imperial Years* (New York, 1956), and Ernest R. May, *Imperial Democracy* (New York, 1961). See also Alfred L. P. Dennis, *Adventures in American Diplomacy, 1876–1906* (New York, 1928).

For Samoa, the most useful and detailed account of American diplomacy is George H. Ryden, *The Foreign Policy of the United States in Relation to Samoa* (New Haven, 1933). It should be supplemented with Sylvia Masterman, *The Origins of International Rivalry in Samoa, 1845–1884* (Stanford, Calif., 1934) and Jean I. Brookes, *International Rivalry in the Pacific Islands, 1800–1875* (Berkeley, Calif., 1941), which supply the international context; and Alfred Vagts, *Deutschland und die Vereinigten Staaten in der Weltpolitik* (2 vols., New York, 1935), which fills in from German sources. See also Alice F. Tyler, *The Foreign Policy of James G. Blaine* (Minneapolis, 1927) and Otto zu Stolberg-Wernigerode, *Germany and the United States of America during the Era of Bismarck* (Reading, Pa., 1937).

The best scholarly treatment of early expansion into Hawaii is Harold W. Bradley, *The American Frontier in Hawaii: The Pioneers, 1789–1843* (Stanford, Calif., 1942), and for the later period it is Sylvester K. Stevens, *American Expansion in Hawaii, 1842–1898* (Harrisburg, Pa., 1945). For the diplomacy of the revolution and annexation, see William A. Russ, Jr., *The Hawaiian Revolution (1893–1894)*, (Selingsgrove, Pa., 1959) and his *The Hawaiian Republic (1894–1898)*, (Selingsgrove, Pa., 1961). Ralph S. Kuykendall, in *The Hawaiian Kingdom, 1778–1854* (Honolulu, 1938) and *The Hawaiian Kingdom, 1842–1898* (Honolulu, 1953) has written the best scholarly general history. See also Theodore Morgan, *Hawaii: A Century of Economic Change, 1778–1876* (Cambridge, Mass., 1948) and John W. Foster, *Diplomatic Memoirs* (2 vols., New York, 1919).

For the Venezuelan affair, see Dexter Perkins, *The Monroe Doctrine, 1867–1907* (Baltimore, 1937) and Allan Nevins, *Henry White—Thirty Years of American Diplomacy* (New York, 1930).

For general studies and biographies that touch on the subjects of this chapter, see George R. Dulebohn, *Principles of Foreign Policy under the Cleveland Administrations* (Philadelphia, 1941); Doris A. Graber, *Crisis Diplomacy: A History of U.S. Intervention Policies* (Washington, 1959); Lionel M. Gelber, *The Rise of Anglo-American Friendship* (London, 1938); Allan Nevins, *Grover Cleveland: A Study in Courage* (New York, 1932); Henry James, *Richard Olney and His Public Service* (Boston, 1923); and Tyler Dennett, *John Hay: From Poetry to Politics* (New York, 1938). See also the pertinent essays in Bemis, *Secretaries of State* and the references in the notes.

CHAPTER FOURTEEN

The most readable and thought-provoking treatment of the war and its diplomacy is still Walter Millis, *The Martial Spirit: A Study of Our War with Spain* (New York, 1931), but it should be balanced by Ernest R. May, *Imperial Democracy: The Emergence of America as a Great Power* (New York, 1961), a scholarly analysis based on a wide variety of sources that is more sympathetic to McKinley. Margaret Leech's *In The Days of McKinley* (New York, 1959) is scholarly and careful and tells the story from the administration's side. It does not, therefore, pay attention to the newspaper war and the Spanish end. Still important and valuable, particularly for the long quotations from the documents which they contain, are the volumes by French E. Chadwick, *The Relations of the United States with Spain: Diplomacy* (New York, 1909) and his *The Relations of the United States with Spain: The Spanish-American War* (2 vols., New York, 1911). See also Julius W. Pratt, *Expansionists of 1898* (Baltimore, 1936); Orestes Ferrara, *The Last Spanish War: Revelations in "Diplomacy,"* trans. from the Spanish (New York, 1937), particularly valuable for the background of European diplomacy, as is Alfred Vagts, *Deutschland und die Vereinigten Staaten in der Weltpolitik* (2 vols., New York, 1935); Horace E. Flack, *Spanish-American Diplomatic Relations Preceding the War of 1898* (Baltimore, 1906); and Elbert J. Benton, *International Law and Diplomacy of the Spanish-American War* (Baltimore, 1908).

A collection of documents translated from the Spanish, which reveal the Spanish attitude toward the war and the defeatism of the naval leaders, is in Pascual Cervera, ed., *The Spanish-American War* (Washington, 1899).

For public opinion and the newspapers, see Marcus H. Wilkerson, *Public Opinion and the Spanish-American War: A Study in War Propaganda* (Baton Rouge, 1932) and Jacob E. Wisan, *The Cuban Crisis as Reflected in the New York Press, 1895-1898* (New York, 1934). For the Anglo-American *rapprochement*, see Bertha A. Reuter, *Anglo-American Relations during the Spanish-American War* (New York, 1924); Lionel M. Gelber, *The Rise of Anglo-American Friendship* (London, 1938); and Richard H. Heindel, *The American Impact on Great Britain, 1898-1914: A Study of the United States in World History* (Philadelphia, 1940).

Useful biographies are Charles S. Olcott, *The Life of William McKinley* (2 vols., Boston, 1916); William C. Spielman, *William McKinley: Stalwart Republican* (New York, 1954); Henry F. Pringle, *Theodore Roosevelt* (New York, 1931), containing a colorful account of T.R.'s war exploits; and Tyler Dennett, *John Hay: From Poetry to Politics* (New York, 1938).

Pertinent specialized accounts are in Alfred L. P. Dennis, *Adventures in American Diplomacy, 1896-1906* (New York, 1928); Merle E. Curti, *Peace or War: The American Struggle, 1636-1936* (New York, 1936); Julius W. Pratt, *America's Colonial Experiment* (New York, 1950); Earl S. Pomeroy, *Pacific Outpost: American Strategy in Guam and Micronesia* (Stanford, Calif., 1951); and William R. Braisted, *The United States Navy in the Pacific, 1897-1909* (Austin, Texas, 1958). See also the references cited in the notes.

CHAPTER FIFTEEN

For most phases of Theodore Roosevelt's diplomacy, the most scholarly and detailed treatment is in Howard K. Beale, *Theodore Roosevelt and the Rise of America to World Power* (Baltimore, 1956). Readable general treatments of the period may be found in Foster Rhea Dulles, *America's Rise to World Power, 1898-1954* (New York, 1954) and George E. Mowry, *The Era of Theodore Roosevelt, 1900-1912* (New York, 1958). For emphasis on the ideas of foreign policy, see Robert E. Osgood, *Ideals and Self-Interest in America's Foreign Relations: The Great Transformation of the Twentieth Century* (Chicago, 1953).

For the Open Door policy, see Tyler Dennett, *Americans in Eastern Asia* (New York, 1922); George F. Kennan, *American Diplomacy, 1900-1950* (Chicago, 1951); Charles S. Campbell,

Jr., *Special Business Interests and the Open Door Policy* (New Haven, 1951); and Paul A. Varg, *Open Door Diplomat: The Life of W. W. Rockhill* (Urbana, Ill., 1952). The interpretations in the latter three studies supersede Dennett. See also, William A. Williams, *The Tragedy of American Diplomacy* (Cleveland, 1959); Stephen C. Y. Pan, *American Diplomacy Concerning Manchuria* (Providence, R.I., 1938); Foster Rhea Dulles, *China and America* (Princeton, 1946); Lawrence H. Battistini, *The United States and Asia* (New York, 1955); and Paul A. Varg, *Missionaries, Chinese, and Diplomats* (Princeton, 1958).

The best source on the San Francisco school crisis and the fleet cruise is Thomas A. Bailey, *Theodore Roosevelt and the Japanese-American Crises* (Stanford, Calif., 1934); see also Payson J. Treat, *Diplomatic Relations between the United States and Japan, 1895–1905* (Stanford, Calif., 1938); Outten J. Clinard, *Japan's Influence on American Naval Power, 1897–1917* (Berkeley, Calif., 1947); and William R. Braisted, *The United States Navy in the Pacific, 1897–1909* (Austin, Texas, 1958).

For relations with Russia in this period, consult Edward H. Zabriskie, *American-Russian Rivalry in the Far East, 1895–1914* (Philadelphia, 1946); Pauline Tompkins, *American-Russian Relations in the Far East* (New York, 1949); Thomas A. Bailey, *America Faces Russia* (Ithaca, N.Y., 1950); and William A. Williams, *American-Russian Relations, 1781–1917* (New York, 1952).

The best general treatment of Latin-American relations is in Samuel F. Bemis, *The La'in American Policy of the United States* (New York, 1943). See also Wilfrid H. Callcott, *The Caribbean Policy of the United States: 1890–1920* (Baltimore, 1942); J. Fred Rippy, *The Caribbean Danger Zone* (New York, 1940); Rippy, *Latin America in World Politics*, 3rd ed. (New York, 1938); Dana G. Munro, *The United States and the Caribbean Area* (Boston, 1934); and David A. Lockmiller, *Magoon in Cuba: A History of the Second Intervention, 1906–1909* (Chapel Hill, N.C., 1938).

The best study of the diplomacy of the Panama Canal is Dwight C. Miner, *The Fight for the Panama Route* (New York, 1940). See also Gerstle Mack, *The Land Divided* (New York, 1944); Howard C. Hill, *Roosevelt and the Caribbean* (Chicago, 1927); E. Taylor Parks, *Colombia and the United States, 1765–1934* (Durham, N.C., 1935); and William D. McCain, *The United States and the Republic of Panama* (Durham, N.C., 1937).

Valuable special studies are: Charles C. Tansill, *The Purchase of the Danish West Indies* (Baltimore, 1932); Allan Nevins, *Henry White: Thirty Years of American Diplomacy* (New York, 1930); Richard W. Leopold, *Elihu Root and the Conservative Tradition* (Boston, 1954); and Tyler Dennett, *John Hay: From Poetry to Politics* (New York, 1938), a prize-winning biography. See also the pertinent reference in the notes.

CHAPTER SIXTEEN

The best general survey of Anglo-American problems is Harry C. Allen, *Great Britain and the United States: A History of Anglo-American Relations, 1783–1952* (New York, 1955). The best scholarly monograph, based on hitherto unexploited sources, of the *rapprochement* is Charles S. Campbell, Jr., *Anglo-American Understanding, 1898–1903* (Baltimore, 1957). See also Lionel M. Gelber, *The Rise of Anglo-American Friendship* (London, 1938) and Alexander E. Campbell, *Great Britain and the United States, 1895–1903* (London, 1960).

For the Moroccan crisis from the American viewpoint, the best account is in Howard K.

Beale, *Theodore Roosevelt and the Rise of America to World Power* (Baltimore, 1956). For the European view, see Eugene N. Anderson, *The First Moroccan Crisis, 1904–1906* (Chicago, 1930). Good accounts are also in Alfred Vagts, *Deutschland und die Vereinigten Staaten in der Weltpolitik* (2 vols., New York, 1935); Alfred L. P. Dennis, *Adventures in American Diplomacy, 1896–1906* (New York, 1928); and Allan Nevins, *Henry White: Thirty Years of American Diplomacy* (New York, 1930).

Details on the peace movement and the Hague conferences may be found in Calvin D. Davis, *The United States and the First Hague Conference* (Ithaca, N.Y., 1962); Merle E. Curti, *Peace or War: The American Struggle, 1636–1936* (New York, 1936); Merze Tate, *The Disarmament Illusion: The Movement for a Limitation of Armaments to 1907* (New York, 1942); Frederick W. Holls, *The Peace Conference at The Hague, and Its Bearings on International Law and Policy* (New York, 1900); and James B. Scott, *The Hague Peace Conferences of 1899 and 1907* (2 vols., Baltimore, 1909). The fullest treatment of its subject is John H. Ferguson, *American Diplomacy and the Boer War* (Philadelphia, 1939). For Canadian reciprocity, see L. Ethan Ellis, *Reciprocity of 1911* (New Haven, 1939).

For Dollar Diplomacy in Asia, the most thorough scholarly study is Charles Vevier, *The United States and China, 1906–1913: A Study of Finance and Diplomacy* (New Brunswick, N.J., 1955). See also Scott Nearing and Joseph Freeman, *Dollar Diplomacy: A Study in American Imperialism* (New York, 1925), a broad analysis along Marxian lines; Benjamin A. Williams, *Economic Foreign Policy of the United States* (New York, 1929); John G. Reid, *The Manchu Abdication and the Powers, 1908–1912* (Berkeley, Calif., 1935); Stephen C. Y. Pan, *American Diplomacy Concerning Manchuria* (Providence, R.I., 1938); Edward H. Zabriskie, *American-Russian Rivalry in the Far East, 1895–1914* (Philadelphia, 1946); and Pauline Tompkins, *American-Russian Relations in the Far East* (New York, 1949).

The fullest treatment of Wilsonian diplomacy in Asia is Roy W. Curry, *Woodrow Wilson and Far Eastern Policy: 1913–1921* (New York, 1957). An excellent scholarly study, though narrower in scope, is Russell H. Fifield, *Woodrow Wilson and the Far East: The Diplomacy of the Shantung Question* (New York, 1952). For a short interpretive treatment, see Harold M. Vinacke, "Woodrow Wilson's Far Eastern Policy," in Edward H. Buehrig, ed., *Wilson's Foreign Policy in Perspective* (Bloomington, Ind., 1957), pp. 61–104.

Useful biographical studies are Herbert Croly, *Willard Straight* (New York, 1924); Tyler Dennett, *John Hay: From Poetry to Politics* (New York, 1938); and Richard W. Leopold, *Elihu Root and the Conservative Tradition* (Boston, 1954). See also the references in the notes and pertinent titles cited in the previous chapter.

CHAPTER SEVENTEEN

The best general surveys of Caribbean diplomacy in this period are Wilfrid H. Callcott, *The Caribbean Policy of the United States: 1890–1920* (Baltimore, 1942) and Samuel F. Bemis, *The Latin American Policy of the United States* (New York, 1943). Still useful are Dana G. Munro, *The United States and the Caribbean Area* (Boston, 1934) and Chester L. Jones, *The Caribbean Since 1900* (New York, 1936).

For analyses of American policies in a pattern of intervention, see Doris A. Graber, *Crisis Diplomacy: A History of U.S. Intervention Policies and Practices* (Washington, 1959) and Scott Nearing and Joseph Freeman, *Dollar Diplomacy* (New York, 1925).

The outstanding survey of Wilson's policy, based on fresh sources, is Arthur S. Link, *Woodrow Wilson and the Progressive Era, 1910–1917* (New York, 1954). The first three volumes of Link's biography of Wilson offer greater detail and more documentation. Still useful is Harley Notter, *The Origins of the Foreign Policy of Woodrow Wilson* (Baltimore, 1937).

For the Caribbean, the following special studies are valuable: Carl Kelsey, *The American Intervention in Haiti and the Dominican Republic* (Philadelphia, 1922); Isaac J. Cox, *Nicaragua and the United States, 1909–1927* (Boston, 1927); Arthur C. Millspaugh, *Haiti under American Control, 1915–1930* (Boston, 1931); Charles C. Tansill, *The Purchase of the Danish West Indies* (Baltimore, 1932); Ludwell L. Montague, *Haiti and the United States, 1714–1938* (Durham, N.C., 1940); and Dexter Perkins, *The United States and the Caribbean* (Cambridge, Mass., 1947).

For relations with Mexico from the American point of view, the best account is in Howard F. Cline, *The United States and Mexico* (Cambridge, Mass., 1953); from the Mexican side, it is Isidro Fabela, *Historia Diplomática de la Revolución Mexicana, 1912–1917* (2 vols., Mexico City, 1958–59), written by an eye witness and participant in the events described. For a time Fabela was in charge of the Mexican Foreign Office in the Carranza era.

The following may be consulted with profit: Charles W. Hackett, *The Mexican Revolution and the United States, 1910–1926* (Boston, 1926); J. Fred Rippy, *The United States and Mexico* (New York, 1926); James M. Callahan, *American Foreign Policy in Mexican Relations* (New York, 1932); George M. Stephenson, *John Lind of Minnesota* (Minneapolis, 1935); and Charles C. Cumberland, *Mexican Revolution: Genesis under Madero* (Austin, Texas, 1952). See also the references in the notes and in the previous chapter.

CHAPTER EIGHTEEN

Three recent books have added new depth to our knowledge of America's entry into the First World War. The first, Arthur S. Link, *Wilson: The Struggle for Neutrality, 1914–1915* (Princeton, 1960), covers only a year and a half, but is based on broad scholarship and an intimate knowledge of the sources. Karl E. Birnbaum, *Peace Moves and U-Boat Warfare: A Study of Imperial Germany's Policy towards the United States, April 18, 1916–January 9, 1917* (Stockholm, 1958) is even narrower in scope, focusing on German policy toward the United States, but is based on hitherto unexploited German sources. Although the title is deceptive, Ernest R. May, *The World War and American Isolationism, 1914–1917* (Cambridge, Mass., 1958) also casts light on German policy and presents a balanced account of American diplomacy. Like Link's book, it is favorably disposed toward Wilson and, like the earlier studies by Charles Seymour, stresses the submarine issue as a main cause for war. The scholarship of Seymour's books, *Woodrow Wilson and the World War* (New York, 1921), *American Diplomacy during the World War* (Baltimore, 1934), and *American Neutrality: 1914–1917* (New Haven, 1935), is still considered sound and his interpretation generally accepted by historians. The two outstanding books that are hostile to Wilson's diplomacy and to American intervention are Walter Millis, *Road to War, 1914–1917* (Boston, 1935) and Charles C. Tansill, *America Goes to War* (Boston, 1938).

Among the other volumes dealing with American neutrality, the following are especially rewarding: Harley Notter, *The Origins of the Foreign Policy of Woodrow Wilson* (Baltimore,

1937); Alice M. Morrissey, *The American Defense of Neutral Rights, 1914–1917* (Cambridge, Mass., 1939); Kent Forster, *The Failures of Peace: The Search for a Negotiated Peace during the First World War* (Philadelphia, 1941); Dexter Perkins, *America and Two Wars* (Boston, 1944); Armin Rappaport, *The British Press and Wilsonian Neutrality* (Stanford, Calif., 1951), valuable for its emphasis on British opinion; Edward H. Buehrig, *Woodrow Wilson and the Balance of Power* (Bloomington, Ind., 1955), important for its analysis of the beginnings of collective security; Arthur S. Link, *Wilson the Diplomatist* (Baltimore, 1957); Daniel M. Smith, *Robert Lansing and American Neutrality, 1914–1917* (Berkeley, Calif., 1958); and Jean-Baptiste Duroselle, *De Wilson à Roosevelt: politique extérieure des États-Unis, 1913–1945* (Paris, 1960).

For the role of propaganda, see James D. Squires, *British Propaganda at Home and in the United States from 1914 to 1917* (Cambridge, Mass., 1935); Horace C. Peterson, *Propaganda for War: The Campaign against American Neutrality, 1914–1917* (Norman, Okla., 1939); and Horace C. Peterson and Gilbert C. Fite, *Opponents of War, 1917–1918* (Madison, Wis., 1957), which deals with nationalistic intolerance and those affected by it.

See also the following specialized studies which concentrate on groups or geographical areas: Carl Wittke, *German-Americans and the World War* (Columbus, Ohio, 1936); Clifton J. Child, *The German-Americans in Politics, 1914–1917* (Madison, Wis., 1939); John C. Crighton, *Missouri and the World War, 1914–1917* (Columbia, Mo., 1947); Cedric Cummins, *Indiana Public Opinion and the World War, 1914–1917* (Indianapolis, 1945); and Edwin Costrell, *How Maine Viewed the War, 1914–1917* (Orono, Maine, 1940). See also Alex M. Arnett, *Claude Kitchin and the Wilson War Policies* (Boston, 1937); Robert G. Albion and Jennie B. Pope, *Sea Lanes in Wartime: The American Experience* (New York, 1942); George F. Kennan, *American Diplomacy, 1900–1950* (Chicago, 1951); and Arthur Willert, *The Road to Safety: A Study in Anglo-American Relations* (London, 1952).

In addition to the multivolume biography of Wilson by Arthur S. Link, the following biographical studies offer valuable insights: Merlo J. Pusey, *Charles Evans Hughes* (2 vols., New York, 1951), a prize-winning study; Alexander L. and Juliette L. George, *Woodrow Wilson and Colonel House: A Personality Study* (New York, 1956), written by psychologists using historical materials; and Arthur Walworth, *Woodrow Wilson* (2 vols., New York, 1958), another prize winner.

The following bibliographical essays will aid anyone who wishes to pursue the subject further: Bernadotte E. Schmitt, "American Neutrality, 1914–1917," *Journal of Modern History*, VIII (June 1936), 200–211, and his "With How Little Wisdom . . . ," *The American Historical Review*, LXXVI (Jan. 1961), 299–322; Richard W. Leopold, "The Problem of American Intervention, 1917: An Historical Retrospect," *World Politics*, II (April 1950), 405–425; Ernest R. May, *American Intervention: 1917 and 1941* (Washington, 1960); and for Wilson literature, Richard L. Watson, Jr., "Woodrow Wilson and His Interpreters, 1947–1957," *Mississippi Valley Historical Review*, XLIV (Sept. 1957), 207–236. See also the citations in the notes.

CHAPTER NINETEEN

The literature on the diplomacy of the war, the peace conference, and the League is voluminous, but the two most readable scholarly volumes dealing with this period are

Thomas A. Bailey, *Woodrow Wilson and the Lost Peace* (New York, 1944) and *Woodrow Wilson and the Great Betrayal* (New York, 1945), brought together in one volume in 1947 as *Wilson and the Peacemakers*. Bailey blames Wilson's stubbornness, in part at least, for the failure of the League, whereas Denna F. Fleming, in *The United States and the League of Nations, 1918-1920* (New York, 1932), places responsibility on the Senate, mainly on Henry Cabot Lodge. A more detailed account is Ray S. Baker, *Woodrow Wilson and World Settlement* (3 vols., Garden City, N.Y., 1923-27). An able analysis which reflects the Keynes view of the peace settlement is Paul Birdsall, *Versailles Twenty Years After* (New York, 1941). Another is Harold Nicolson, *Peacemaking, 1919* (New York, 1939). For a detailed study, see Harold W. V. Temperley, *A History of the Peace Conference of Paris* (6 vols., London, 1920-24).

For wartime diplomacy, the following special studies and memoirs are useful: Arthur Willert, *The Road to Safety: A Study in Anglo-American Relations* (London, 1952); Thomas A. Bailey, *The Policy of the United States toward the Neutrals, 1917-1918* (Baltimore, 1942); Robert Lansing, *War Memoirs of Robert Lansing* (Indianapolis, 1935); Josephus Daniels, *The Wilson Era: Years of War and After, 1917-1921* (Chapel Hill, N.C., 1946); George F. Kennan, *American Diplomacy, 1900-1950* (Chicago, 1951); and Lawrence W. Martin, *Peace without Victory: Woodrow Wilson and the British Liberals* (New Haven, 1958), which deals mainly with war aims and the one theme of a similarity of interest between the ideas of Wilson and the British radicals.

For special phases of the peace negotiations and the League, the following studies and memoirs are important: D. Hunter Miller, *The Drafting of the Covenant* (2 vols., New York, 1928); Bernard Baruch, *The Making of the Reparations and Economic Sections of the Treaty* (New York, 1920); Robert Lansing, *The Peace Negotiations* (Boston, 1921); Edward M. House and Charles Seymour, *What Really Happened at Paris* (New York, 1921); W. Stull Holt, *Treaties Defeated by the Senate* (Baltimore, 1933); George B. Noble, *Policies and Opinions at Paris, 1919* (New York, 1935); James T. Shotwell, *At the Paris Peace Conference* (New York, 1937); René Albrecht-Carrié, *Italy at the Peace Conference* (New York, 1938); Georges Clemenceau, *Grandeur and Misery of Victory* (New York, 1930); David Lloyd George, *Memoirs of the Peace Conference* (2 vols., New Haven, 1939); Ruhl J. Bartlett, *The League to Enforce Peace* (Chapel Hill, N.C., 1944); Stephen Bonsal, *Unfinished Business* (Garden City, N.Y., 1944) and his *Suitors and Suppliants* (Englewood Cliffs, N.J., 1946); Rayford W. Logan, *The Senate and the Versailles Mandate System* (Washington, 1945); Louis L. Gerson, *Woodrow Wilson and the Re-Birth of Poland, 1914-1920* (New Haven, 1953); Claudius O. Johnson, *Borah of Idaho* (New York, 1936); Marian C. McKenna, *Borah* (Ann Arbor, Mich., 1961); Herbert Hoover, *America's First Crusade* (New York, 1942) and his *Ordeal of Woodrow Wilson* (New York, 1958); and Charles C. Tansill, *America and the Fight for Irish Freedom, 1866-1922* (New York, 1957), which devotes considerable space to Wilson's feud with certain Irish-American leaders.

For relations with Russia and Far Eastern issues, see George F. Kennan, *Russia and the West under Lenin and Stalin* (Boston, 1961); Leonid I. Strakhovsky, *The Origins of American Intervention in North Russia, 1918* (Princeton, 1937), his *Intervention at Archangel* (Princeton, 1944), and his *American Opinion About Russia, 1917-1920* (Toronto, 1961); William A. Williams, *American-Russian Relations, 1781-1947* (New York, 1952); Betty M. Unterberger, *America's Siberian Expedition, 1918-1920* (Durham, N.C., 1956); Russell H. Fifield, *Woodrow Wilson and the Far East: The Diplomacy of the Shantung Question* (New York, 1952); and Roy

W. Curry, *Woodrow Wilson and Far Eastern Policy, 1913–1921* (New York, 1957). Important titles are also cited in the notes and in the previous chapter.

CHAPTER TWENTY

For general or broad treatments of this period, see Denna F. Fleming, *The United States and World Organization, 1920–1933* (New York, 1938); Allan Nevins, *The United States in a Chaotic World, 1918–1933* (New Haven, 1950); Selig Adler, *The Isolationist Impulse* (New York, 1957); and two studies that stress domestic history and offer a sound background, but also include some data on foreign affairs: Arthur M. Schlesinger, Jr., *The Crisis of the Old Order, 1919–1933* (Boston, 1957) and John D. Hicks, *Republican Ascendancy, 1921–1933* (New York, 1960).

Relations with Japan are dealt with in Hector D. Bywater, *Seapower in the Pacific: A Study of the American-Japanese Naval Problem* (New York, 1921); Eleanor Tupper and George E. McReynolds, *Japan in American Public Opinion* (New York, 1957); Alfred W. Griswold, *The Far Eastern Policy of the United States* (New York, 1938); John A. White, *The Siberian Intervention* (Princeton, 1950); Russell H. Fifield, *Woodrow Wilson and the Far East* (New York, 1952); Clarence A. Manning, *The Siberian Fiasco* (New York, 1952); Roy W. Curry, *Woodrow Wilson and Far Eastern Policy, 1913–1921* (New York, 1957); and James W. Morley, *The Japanese Thrust into Siberia* (New York, 1957), which approaches the problem from the Japanese side and through the use of Japanese sources.

For disarmament, naval rivalry, and the Washington Conference, see C. Leonard Hoag, *Preface to Preparedness: The Washington Disarmament Conference and Public Opinion* (Washington, 1921); Raymond L. Buell, *The Washington Conference* (New York, 1922); Yamato Ichihashi, *The Washington Conference and After* (Stanford, Calif., 1928); Benjamin H. Williams, *The United States and Disarmament* (New York, 1931); John W. Wheeler-Bennett, *Disarmament and Security since Locarno: 1925–1931* (London, 1932); George T. Davis, *A Navy Second to None: The Development of Modern American Naval Policy* (New York, 1940); Harold and Margaret Sprout, *Toward a New Order of Sea Power: American Naval Policy and the World Scene, 1918–1922* (Princeton, 1940), the outstanding study of the Washington Conference from the point of view of naval influence on foreign policy; Armin Rappaport, *The Navy League of the United States* (Detroit, 1962); Merze Tate, *The United States and Armaments* (Cambridge, Mass., 1948), the best treatment of disarmament and foreign policy; and John C. Vinson, *The Parchment Peace* (Athens, Ga., 1955), the fullest scholarly assessment of the Senate's influence on the Washington treaties.

The best book on the Kellogg Pact is Robert H. Ferrell, *Peace in Their Time: The Origins of the Kellogg-Briand Pact* (New Haven, 1952). For specialized studies of the pact, the peace movement, and League diplomacy, see David Hunter Miller, *The Geneva Protocol* (New York, 1925) and his *The Peace Pact of Paris* (New York, 1928); James T. Shotwell, *War as an Instrument of National Policy* (New York, 1929); Manly O. Hudson, *The Permanent Court of International Justice and the Question of American Participation* (New York, 1934); John W. Wheeler-Bennett, *The Pipe Dream of Peace* (New York, 1935); Merle E. Curti, *Peace or War: The American Struggle, 1636–1936* (New York, 1936); John E. Stoner, *S. O. Levinson and the Pact of Paris* (New York, 1943); Francis P. Walters, *A History of the League of Nations*

(2 vols., London, 1952); and John C. Vinson, *William E. Borah and the Outlawry of War* (Athens, Ga., 1957).

Important biographical studies and memoirs are: Claudius O. Johnson, *Borah of Idaho* (New York, 1936); David Bryn-Jones, *Frank B. Kellogg* (New York, 1937); Philip C. Jessup, *Elihu Root* (2 vols., New York, 1938); Henry L. Stimson and McGeorge Bundy, *On Active Service in Peace and War* (New York, 1948); *The Memoirs of Herbert Hoover* (3 vols., New York, 1951–52); *Elihu Root and the Conservative Tradition* (Boston, 1954); Richard N. Current, *Secretary Stimson: A Study in Statecraft* (New Brunswick, N.J., 1954); Dexter Perkins, *Charles Evans Hughes and American Democratic Statesmanship* (Boston, 1956); and Marian C. McKenna, *Borah* (Ann Arbor, Mich., 1961). See also the works cited in the notes and pertinent titles in the previous chapter.

CHAPTER TWENTY-ONE

Many of the outstanding studies pertinent to this chapter are cited in the notes and a few in the previous chapter. The best general diplomatic history for its period is Robert H. Ferrell, *American Diplomacy in the Great Depression: Hoover-Stimson Foreign Policy, 1929–1933* (New Haven, 1957). Two books by Allan Nevins give a brief, readable view of the diplomacy of the entire period: *The United States in a Chaotic World, 1918–1933* (New Haven, 1950) and *The New Deal in World Affairs* (New Haven, 1950).

For Far Eastern policy, although outmoded in some points by later scholarship, Alfred W. Griswold's *The Far Eastern Policy of the United States* (New York, 1938) is still worth careful reading. See also Russell M. Cooper, *American Consultation in World Affairs for the Preservation of Peace* (New York, 1934); Westel W. Willoughby, *The Sino-Japanese Controversy* (Baltimore, 1935); Henry L. Stimson, *The Far Eastern Crisis: Recollections and Observations* (New York, 1936); William C. Johnstone, *The United States and Japan's New Order* (New York, 1941); Thomas A. Bisson, *America's Far Eastern Policy* (New York, 1945); Foster Rhea Dulles, *China and America* (Princeton, 1946); Robert Langer, *Seizure of Territory: The Stimson Doctrine and Related Principles in Legal Theory and Diplomatic Practice* (Princeton, 1947); Sara R. Smith, *The Manchurian Crisis, 1931–1932: A Tragedy in International Relations* (New York, 1948); James W. Christopher, *Conflict in the Far East: American Diplomacy in China from 1928–1933* (Leiden, Netherlands, 1950); Reginald Bassett, *Democracy and Foreign Policy, A Case History: The Sino-Japanese Dispute, 1931–1933* (New York, 1952); Joseph C. Grew, *Turbulent Era: A Diplomatic Record of Forty Years*, Walter Johnson, ed. (2 vols., Boston, 1952); Yale C. Maxon, *Control of Japanese Foreign Policy: A Study of Civil-Military Rivalry, 1930–1945* (Berkeley, Calif., 1957); and Paul A. Varg, *Missionaries, Chinese, and Diplomats* (Princeton, 1958). For relations with Russia, see George S. Moyer, *Attitude of the United States towards the Recognition of Soviet Russia* (Philadelphia, 1926); Meno Lovenstein, *American Opinion of Soviet Russia* (Washington, 1941); and Thomas A. Bailey, *America Faces Russia* (Ithaca, N.Y., 1950).

There is need for a new scholarly survey of relations with Latin America. Until one is written, Samuel F. Bemis, *The Latin American Policy of the United States* (New York, 1943), although superseded in a number of areas by new scholarship and interpretations, stands as the major book on its subject. Another useful survey is Dexter Perkins, *A History of the*

Monroe Doctrine, 2nd ed.(Boston, 1955). Notable for its broad sweep and balanced judgments is Arthur P. Whitaker, *The Western Hemisphere Idea* (Ithaca, N.Y., 1954). See also, J. Fred Rippy, *The Caribbean Danger Zone* (New York, 1940); Dexter Perkins, *The United States and the Caribbean* (Cambridge, Mass., 1947); and Arthur P. Whitaker, *The United States and South America: The Northern Republics* (Cambridge, Mass., 1948). The fullest treatment of its subject is Alexander DeConde, *Herbert Hoover's Latin American Policy* (Stanford, Calif., 1951). See also Henry L. Stimson, *American Policy in Nicaragua* (New York, 1927). Roosevelt's Good Neighbor policy receives penetrating treatment in Donald M. Dozer, *Are We Good Neighbors? Three Decades of Inter-American Relations, 1930–1960* (Gainesville, Fla., 1959) and in Bryce Wood, *The Making of the Good Neighbor Policy* (New York, 1961). Edward O. Guerrant, *Roosevelt's Good Neighbor Policy* (Albuquerque, N.M., 1950) offers an able survey, as does Robert F. Smith, *The United States and Cuba: Business and Diplomacy, 1917–1960* (New York, 1960). E. David Cronon, in his delightful *Josephus Daniels in Mexico* (Madison, Wis., 1960), maintains that Daniels' accomplishment "was the high-water mark of Good Neighbor diplomacy." See also, Howard F. Cline, *The United States and Mexico* (Cambridge, Mass., 1953); Wendell C. Gordon, *The Expropriation of Foreign-Owned Property in Mexico* (Washington, 1941); Sumner Welles, *The Time for Decision* (New York, 1944), important for the Good Neighbor policy; and Stetson Conn and Byron Fairchild, *The Western Hemisphere: The Framework of Hemisphere Defense* (Washington, 1960).

For relations with Canada, see Edgar W. McInnis, *The Unguarded Frontier* (New York, 1942); John B. Brebner, *North Atlantic Triangle* (New Haven, 1945); and Hugh L. Keenleyside and Gerald S. Brown, *Canada and the United States*, rev. ed. (New York, 1952), the best general survey.

Important biographical studies and memoirs are: David Bryn-Jones, *Frank B. Kellogg* (New York, 1937); Harold Nicolson, *Dwight Morrow* (New York, 1935); Merlo J. Pusey, *Charles Evans Hughes* (2 vols., New York, 1951); Dexter Perkins, *Charles Evans Hughes and American Democratic Statesmanship* (Boston, 1956); Charles G. Dawes, *Journal as Ambassador to Great Britain* (New York, 1939); Josephus Daniels, *Shirt-Sleeve Diplomat* (Chapel Hill, N.C., 1947); Henry L. Stimson and McGeorge Bundy, *On Active Service in Peace and War* (New York, 1948); Richard N. Current, *Secretary Stimson* (New Brunswick, N.J., 1954), highly critical of Stimson and his diplomacy; Elting E. Morison, *Turmoil and Tradition: A Study of the Life and Times of Henry L. Stimson* (Boston, 1960), a full and sympathetic treatment; *The Memoirs of Herbert Hoover* (3 vols., New York, 1951–52); Frank Freidel, *Franklin D. Roosevelt* (3 vols., Boston, 1952–); *The Memoirs of Cordell Hull* (2 vols., New York, 1948); James M. Burns, *Roosevelt: The Lion and the Fox* (New York, 1956); and Nancy H. Hooker, ed., *The Moffat Papers: Selections from the Diplomatic Journals of Jay Pierrepont Moffat* (Cambridge, Mass., 1956).

CHAPTER TWENTY-TWO

Important works pertinent to topics in this chapter are cited in the notes and in the previous chapter. For the general impact of immigration policy and racism on American life and foreign relations as well, the best book is John Higham's *Strangers in the Land: Patterns of American Nativism, 1860–1925* (New Brunswick, N.J., 1955). See also Robert A. Divine, *American Immigration Policy, 1924–1952* (New Haven, 1957). The only general study on nationalism, a suggestive introductory essay more than an effort to probe the subject deeply, is Hans Kohn, *American Nationalism: An Interpretive Essay* (New York, 1957).

On economics and foreign policy, the fullest and best balanced treatment is Raymond F. Mikesell, *United States Economic Policy and International Relations* (New York, 1952). Old, but still useful is Benjamin H. Williams, *Economic Foreign Policy of the United States* (New York, 1929). See also Herbert Feis, *The Diplomacy of the Dollar: First Era, 1919–1932* (Baltimore, 1950); Harold G. Moulton and Leo Pasvolsky, *War Debts and World Prosperity* (New York, 1932), the best book on its subject; Cleona Lewis, *America's Stake in International Investments* (Washington, 1938); John W. Wheeler-Bennett, *The Wreck of Reparations* (New York, 1933), which deals with the Lausanne Agreement; Paul Einzig, *World Finance, 1914–1935* (New York, 1935); Charles G. Dawes, *A Journal of Reparations* (London, 1939); Bascom N. Timmons, *Portrait of an American: Charles G. Dawes* (New York, 1953); and Peter B. Kenan, *Giant Among Nations: Problems in United States Foreign Economic Policy* (New York, 1960), a number of clearly written lectures on selected topics.

For the tariff problem, see Percy W. Bidwell, *Tariff Policy of the United States: A Study of Recent Experience* (New York, 1933); Joseph M. Jones, Jr., *Tariff Retaliation: Repercussions of the Hawley-Smoot Bill* (Philadelphia, 1934); Grace Beckett, *The Reciprocal Trade Agreements Program* (New York, 1941); and Joe R. Wilkinson, *Politics and Trade Policy* (Washington, 1960), an analysis of the political process as it operated relative to the Reciprocal Trade Agreements Program, 1934–1958.

The most important work on isolationism is Selig Adler's *The Isolationist Impulse* (New York, 1957). A group of essays touching on the theme of isolationism is Alexander DeConde, ed., *Isolation and Security* (Durham, N.C., 1957); the subject is also covered in Robert E. Osgood, *Ideals and Self-Interest in America's Foreign Relations* (Chicago, 1953) and William A. Williams, *The Tragedy of American Diplomacy* (New York, 1952). See also Claudius O. Johnson, *Borah of Idaho* (New York, 1936) and Marian C. McKenna, *Borah* (Ann Arbor, Mich., 1961).

For the Hoover period and the transition to the era of Roosevelt, see Elting E. Morison, *Turmoil and Tradition: A Study of the Life and Times of Henry L. Stimson* (Boston, 1960); Walter Johnson, *1600 Pennsylvania Avenue: Presidents and the People, 1929–1959* (Boston, 1960); Harris G. Warren, *Herbert Hoover and the Great Depression* (New York, 1959); Arthur M. Schlesinger, Jr., *The Age of Roosevelt* (3 vols., Boston, 1957–); Robert H. Ferrell, *American Diplomacy in the Great Depression* (New Haven, 1957); Richard N. Current, *Secretary Stimson* (New Brunswick, N.J., 1954); *The Memoirs of Herbert Hoover* (3 vols., New York, 1951–52); and Henry L. Stimson and McGeorge Bundy, *On Active Service in Peace and War* (New York, 1948).

The outstanding scholarly work on the diplomacy leading to the Second World War is William L. Langer and S. Everett Gleason, *The Challenge to Isolation, 1937–1940* (New York, 1952), which is generally favorable to Roosevelt's policies. Donald F. Drummond, *The Passing of American Neutrality, 1937–1941* (Ann Arbor, Mich., 1955) covers the same ground in briefer compass, is also favorable to Roosevelt, and is valuable for its analysis of isolationism. Charles A. Beard, *American Foreign Policy in the Making, 1932–1940* (New Haven, 1946), is critical of Roosevelt and is in turn criticized by Basil Rauch, *Roosevelt: From Munich to Pearl Harbor* (New York, 1950), who lauds Roosevelt's policies. Also critical of Roosevelt are Charles C. Tansill, *Back Door to War: The Roosevelt Foreign Policy, 1933–1941*

(Chicago, 1952) and the essays in Harry E. Barnes, ed., *Perpetual War for Perpetual Peace: A Critical Examination of the Foreign Policy of Franklin D. Roosevelt* (Caldwell, Idaho, 1953).

For analyses of the neutrality legislation, see Charles G. Fenwick, *American Neutrality: Trial and Failure* (New York, 1940); Edwin Borchard and William P. Lage, *Neutrality for the United States*, 2nd ed. (New Haven, 1940); and Robert A. Divine, *The Illusion of Neutrality* (Chicago, 1962), the best scholarly account.

For their special topics, see the following: Claude G. Bowers, *My Mission to Spain* (New York, 1954), the American Ambassador to Spain during its civil war; Jay F. Taylor, *The United States and the Spanish Civil War* (New York, 1956), which examines the American reaction to the conflict; Dante A. Puzzo, *Spain and the Great Powers, 1936–1941* (New York, 1962); Williard D. Range, *Franklin D. Roosevelt's World Order* (Athens, Ga., 1959); Wilfred Funk, ed., *Roosevelt's Foreign Policy, 1933–1941* (New York, 1941); Sumner Welles, *The Time for Decision* (New York, 1944); Edgar E. Robinson, *The Roosevelt Leadership, 1933–1945* (Philadelphia, 1955), a critical study; and James M. Burns, *Roosevelt: The Lion and the Fox* (New York, 1956), an outstanding short biography.

CHAPTER TWENTY-THREE

The literature on the topic of the coming of the war has been treated controversially. Even though William L. Langer and S. Everett Gleason have been accused of trying to present Roosevelt's foreign policy in its most favorable light, they have written the best balanced scholarly study of the diplomacy leading to war, *The Challenge to Isolation, 1937–1940* (New York, 1952) and *The Undeclared War, 1940–1941* (New York, 1953). A shorter history that reflects a similar interpretation is Donald F. Drummond, *The Passing of American Neutrality* (Ann Arbor, Mich., 1955). Another indispensable study favorable to Roosevelt but not uncritical is Robert E. Sherwood, *Roosevelt and Hopkins: An Intimate History* (New York, 1948). Winston Churchill, *The Second World War* (6 vols., Boston, 1948–53) is already something of a classic and another basic source for the period.

The best accounts of relations with Japan at this time are Herbert Feis, *The Road to Pearl Harbor: The Coming of the War between the United States and Japan* (Princeton, 1950) and Robert J. C. Butow, *Tojo and the Coming of the War* (Princeton, 1961). See also Walter Millis, *This is Pearl! The United States and Japan—1941* (New York, 1947); Forrest Davis and Ernest K. Lindley, *How War Came: An American White Paper; from the Fall of France to Pearl Harbor* (New York, 1942); and Basil Rauch's strongly pro-Roosevelt study *Roosevelt: From Munich to Pearl Harbor* (New York, 1950).

There are a number of revisionist, or anti-Roosevelt books, some of which bitterly accuse him of conspiring to bring on the war. Of these, although filled with harsh adjectives, the most substantial is Charles C. Tansill, *Back Door to War: The Roosevelt Foreign Policy, 1933–1941* (Chicago, 1952). Other volumes in the same category are Charles A. Beard, *American Foreign Policy in the Making, 1932–1940* (New Haven, 1946) and *President Roosevelt and the Coming of the War, 1941* (New Haven, 1948); George E. Morgenstern, *Pearl Harbor: The Story of the Secret War* (New York, 1947); Frederic R. Sanborn, *Design for War: A Study of Secret Power Politics, 1937–1941* (New York, 1951); Harry E. Barnes, ed., *Perpetual War for*

Perpetual Peace (Caldwell, Idaho, 1953); Robert A. Theobald, *The Final Secret of Pearl Harbor* (New York, 1954); William H. Chamberlin, *America's Second Crusade* (Chicago, 1950); and Husband E. Kimmel, *Admiral Kimmel's Story* (Chicago, 1955).

Other pertinent studies are: Jean-Baptiste Duroselle, *De Wilson à Roosevelt: Politique Extérieure des États-Unis, 1913–1945* (Paris, 1960); William W. Kaufmann, "Two American Ambassadors: Bullitt and Kennedy," in Gordon Craig and Felix Gilbert, eds., *The Diplomats, 1919–1939* (Princeton, 1953), pp. 649–681; Harold Lavine and James Wechsler, *War Propaganda and the United States* (New Haven, 1940); Robert E. Osgood, *Ideals and Self-Interest in America's Foreign Relations* (Chicago, 1953); Maurice Matloff and Edwin M. Snell, *Strategic Planning for Coalition Warfare, 1941–1942* (Washington, 1953); Samuel E. Morison, *The Rising Sun in the Pacific, 1931–April 1942* (Boston, 1948), a naval history; Toskikazu Kase, *Journey to the "Missouri"* (New Haven, 1950), a Japanese account; Walter Lord, *Day of Infamy* (New York, 1957) a journalistic account of the Pearl Harbor attack; Hans L. Trefousse, ed., *What Happened at Pearl Harbor* (New York, 1958); Paul W. Schroeder, *The Axis Alliance and Japanese-American Relations, 1941* (Ithaca, N.Y., 1958), a detailed analysis critical of American diplomacy; Hans L. Trefousse, *Germany and American Neutrality, 1939–1941* (New York, 1951), a basic account; and Wayne S. Cole, "American Entry into World War II: A Historiographical Appraisal," *Mississippi Valley Historical Review*, XLIII (March 1957), 595–617, an excellent bibliographical survey. See also the pertinent titles cited in the previous chapter and in the notes of this one.

CHAPTER TWENTY-FOUR

Four books by Herbert Feis offer the fullest scholarly treatment of the diplomacy of the war. They are: *The China Tangle: The American Effort in China from Pearl Harbor to the Marshall Mission* (Princeton, 1953); *Churchill, Roosevelt, Stalin: The War They Waged and the Peace They Sought* (Princeton, 1957); *Between War and Peace: The Potsdam Conference* (Princeton, 1960); and *Japan Subdued: The Atomic Bomb and the End of the War in the Pacific* (Princeton, 1961). Indispensable sources for the period are three beautifully written memoirs and histories: Robert E. Sherwood, *Roosevelt and Hopkins* (New York, 1948); Winston Churchill, *The Second World War* (6 vols., Boston, 1948–53); and Charles de Gaulle, *War Memoirs* (3 vols., New York, 1955–60). An excellent general history of the period is William H. McNeil, *America, Britain, and Russia: Their Cooperation and Conflict, 1941–1946* (London, 1953), vol. III of the *Survey of International Affairs, 1939–1946* edited by Arnold Toynbee.

For the diplomacy of relations with the Soviet Union, eastern and central Europe, and the Yalta Conference, see John R. Deane, *The Strange Alliance: The Story of Our Efforts at Wartime Cooperation with Russia* (New York, 1947); Vera M. Deane, *The United States and Russia* (Cambridge, Mass., 1948); Thomas A. Bailey, *America Faces Russia* (Ithaca, N.Y., 1950); William A. Williams, *American-Russian Relations, 1781–1947* (New York, 1952); William H. Standley and A. A. Ageton, *Admiral Ambassador to Russia* (Chicago, 1955); Harold P. Stern, *The Struggle for Poland* (Washington, 1953); John A. Lukacs, *The Great Powers and Eastern Europe* (New York, 1953); Stephen Kertész, ed., *The Fate of East Central Europe* (Notre Dame, Ind., 1956); Edward J. Rozek, *Allied Wartime Diplomacy: A Pattern in Poland* (New York, 1958); Edward R. Stettinius, Jr., *Roosevelt and the Russians: The Yalta*

Conference (Garden City, N.Y., 1947); *Foreign Relations of the United States: Diplomatic Papers: The Conferences at Malta and Yalta, 1945* (Washington, 1955); and John L. Snell, ed., *The Meaning of Yalta: Big Three Diplomacy and the New Balance of Power* (Baton Rouge, 1956), a careful study based on the preceding Yalta Papers.

The best book on the problem of Germany is John L. Snell's, *Wartime Origins of the East-West Dilemma Over Germany* (New Orleans, 1959). See also Wolfgang Wagner, *The Genesis of the Oder-Niesse Line: A Study in the Diplomatic Negotiations During World War II* (Stuttgart, Germany, 1957); Benjamin U. Ratchford and William D. Ross, *Berlin Reparations Assignment* (Chapel Hill, N.C., 1947); and Lucius D. Clay, *Decision in Germany* (Garden City, N.Y., 1950).

For Spain, Italy, and the Mediterranean, see Carlton J. H. Hayes, *The United States and Spain: An Interpretation* (New York, 1951) and Raymond DeBelot, *The Struggle for the Mediterranean, 1939–1945* (Princeton, 1951), a study in naval history.

The best book on the surrender of Japan is Robert C. Butow, *Japan's Decision to Surrender* (Stanford, Calif., 1954). Other important studies dealing with Far Eastern problems are: Toshikazu Kase, *Journey to the "Missouri"* (New Haven, 1950); Lawrence K. Rosinger, *China's Wartime Politics, 1937–1944* (Princeton, 1944); Theodore White and Annalee Jacoby, *Thunder Out of China* (New York, 1946); Charles T. Romanus and Riley Sunderland, *Stilwell's Mission to China* (Washington, 1952) and their *Stilwell's Command Problems* (Washington, 1956); and Albert C. Wedemeyer, *Wedemeyer Reports* (New York, 1958).

For special studies of wartime politics and diplomacy, see William L. Neumann, *Making the Peace: The Diplomacy of the Wartime Conferences* (Washington, 1950); Redvers Opie *et al., The Search for Peace Settlements* (Washington, 1951); Bradford H. Westerfield, *Foreign Policy and Party Politics: Pearl Harbor to Korea* (New Haven, 1955); Roland Young, *Congressional Politics in the Second World War* (New York, 1956); Elmer Plischke, *Summit Diplomacy: Personal Diplomacy of the President of the United States* (College Park, Md., 1958); Arthur Kemp, "Summit Conferences during World War II as Instruments of American Diplomacy," in George L. Anderson, ed., *Issues and Conflicts* (Lawrence, Kan., 1959), pp. 256–283. The outstanding scholarly historical study of American policy toward the United Nations is Ruth B. Russell and Jeanne E. Muther, *A History of the United Nations Charter: The Role of the United States, 1940–1945* (Washington, 1958), and for the theoretical basis of the U.N., it is Inis Claude, *Swords into Ploughshares: The Problems and Progress of International Organization*, 2nd ed. (New York, 1959).

Other important memoirs and special studies are: James F. Byrnes, *Speaking Frankly* (New York, 1947) and his *All in One Lifetime* (New York, 1958); Dwight D. Eisenhower, *Crusade in Europe* (Garden City, N.Y., 1948); William D. Leahy, *I Was There: The Personal Story of the Chief of Staff to Presidents Roosevelt and Truman* (New York, 1950); Sumner Welles, *Seven Decisions that Shaped History* (New York, 1951); Ernest J. King and Walter M. Whitehill, *Fleet Admiral King* (New York, 1952); Arthur Bryant, *The Turn of the Tide, 1939–1943* (London, 1957) and his *Triumph in the West, 1943–1946* (Garden City, N.Y., 1959), both based on the diaries of Britain's Field Marshal Lord Alanbrooke; and Elting E. Morison, *Turmoil and Tradition* (Boston, 1960). See also the notes and the references in the preceding chapters.

CHAPTER TWENTY-FIVE

Several interpretive histories analyze America's part in the onset of the cold war. They are Walt W. Rostow, *The United States in the World Arena: An Essay in Recent History* (New York, 1960), particularly Book Three, which interprets foreign policy in this period in terms of a "national style"; John W. Spanier, *American Foreign Policy Since World War II*, rev. ed. (New York, 1962), a short lively account; John A. Lukacs, *A History of the Cold War* (New York, 1960), which stresses Russian-American relations in Europe with some reference to the Far East; and Denna F. Fleming, *The Cold War and Its Origins, 1917-1960* (2 vols., New York, 1961), which castigates American policy. William Reitzel, Morton A. Kaplan, and Constance G. Coblenz, *United States Foreign Policy, 1945-1955* (Washington, 1956) offers emphasis on factual details as do the volumes published by the Council on Foreign Relations, *The United States in World Affairs*, covering the years 1945-1949. For the cold war in a world-wide setting, see Hugh Seton-Watson, *Neither War Nor Peace: The Struggle for Power in the Postwar World* (London, 1960).

For Europe's problems, see Theodore White, *Fire in the Ashes: Europe in Mid-Century* (New York, 1953) and Vera Micheles Dean, *Europe and the United States* (New York, 1950), two well-written popular accounts. See also Thomas A. Bailey, *America Faces Russia* (Ithaca, N.Y., 1950) and Ellis M. Zacharias, *Behind Closed Doors: The Secret History of the Cold War* (New York, 1950).

There is a considerable literature on American policy in and toward postwar Germany. The two best accounts of the occupation are Eugene Davidson, *The Death and Life of Germany: An Account of the American Occupation* (New York, 1959) and Harold Zink, *The United States in Germany, 1944-1955* (New York, 1957). See also Michael Balfour and John Mair, *Four-Power Control in Germany and Austria, 1945-46* (London, 1956); Manuel Gottlieb, *The German Peace Settlement and the Berlin Crisis* (New York, 1960); Edgar McInnis, Richard Hiscocks, and Robert Spencer, *The Shaping of Postwar Germany* (New York, 1960); Frank Howley, *Berlin Command* (New York, 1950); Lucius D. Clay, *Decision in Germany* (Garden City, N.Y., 1950); and Walter Phillips Davison, *The Berlin Blockade: A Study in Cold War Politics* (Princeton, 1958), the best scholarly account.

For east central Europe and Poland, see Stephen Kertesz, ed., *The Fate of East Central Europe: Hopes and Failures of American Foreign Policy* (Notre Dame, Ind., 1956); and Arthur Bliss Lane, *I Saw Poland Betrayed: An American Ambassador Reports to the American People* (Indianapolis, 1948). For Italy, see H. Stuart Hughes, *The United States and Italy* (Cambridge, Mass., 1953).

The best history of the origins of the Truman Doctrine, written by one who took part in shaping that policy, is Joseph M. Jones, *The Fifteen Weeks* (New York, 1955). See also William H. McNeill, *Greece: American Aid in Action, 1947-1956* (New York, 1957). For details on the satellite peace treaties, see Redvers Opie and others, *The Search for Peace Settlements* (Washington, 1951); for UNRRA, see George Woodbridge and others, *UNRRA: The History of the United Nations Relief and Rehabilitation Administration* (3 vols., New York, 1950). The best history of the Marshall Plan is Harry B. Price, *The Marshall Plan and Its Meaning* (Ithaca, N.Y., 1955). William C. Mallalieu, *British Reconstruction and American*

Policy, 1945–1955 (New York, 1956) stresses Britain's role in the development of the Marshall Plan. For Point Four and economic assistance programs, see William A. Brown and Redvers Opie, *American Foreign Assistance* (Washington, 1953) and Eugene Staley, *The Future of Underdeveloped Countries: The Political Implications of Economic Development* (New York, 1954).

Most of the literature on the North Atlantic Treaty stresses military affairs and strategy. The following volumes do also, but in addition they contain perceptive analyses of considerable value to the student of diplomatic history: Robert E. Osgood, *NATO: The Entangling Alliance* (Chicago, 1962), the best scholarly account; Klaus Knorr, ed., *NATO and American Security* (Princeton, 1959); Arnold Wolfers, ed., *Alliance Policy in the Cold War* (Baltimore, 1959); Ben T. Moore, *NATO and the Future of Europe* (New York, 1958); Arthur C. Turner, *Bulwark of the West: Implications and Problems of NATO* (Toronto, 1953); and Halford L. Hoskins, *The Atlantic Pact* (Washington, 1949).

Harry S. Truman, *Memoirs* (2 vols., Garden City, N.Y., 1955) contain the most important personal source materials yet published for this period. Other important memoirs and diaries are: James F. Byrnes, *All in One Lifetime* (New York, 1958), which does not supplant the detailed information in his *Speaking Frankly* (New York, 1947); Walter Millis and E. S. Duffield, eds., *The Forrestal Diaries* (New York, 1951); and Walter Bedell Smith, *My Three Years in Moscow* (Philadelphia, 1950). Other pertinent titles are cited in the notes and in the preceding chapter.

CHAPTER TWENTY-SIX

Two small books, Kenneth S. Latourette, *The American Record in the Far East, 1945–1951* (New York, 1952) and Harold M. Vinacke, *The United States and the Far East, 1945–1951* (Stanford, Calif., 1952), offer general histories of American Far Eastern policy in this period. For a broad analysis of Far Eastern policy with emphasis on military and strategic considerations, see Walt W. Rostow, *The United States in the World Arena* (New York, 1960). H. Bradford Westerfield, *Foreign Policy and Party Politics: Pearl Harbor to Korea* (New Haven, 1955) and Norman Graebner, *The New Isolationism* (New York, 1956) stress the influence of domestic political strife in the shaping of foreign policy in the postwar years.

For policy toward China until the Marshall mission, the best book is Herbert Feis, *The China Tangle* (Princeton, 1953). For the later period, see A. Doak Barnett, *Communist China: Challenge to American Policy* (New York, 1960). An excellent general study, with emphasis on Chinese internal developments and their influence on American policy, is John K. Fairbank, *The United States and China*, rev. ed. (Cambridge, Mass., 1958).

The outstanding survey of relations with Japan is Edwin O. Reischauer, *The United States and Japan*, rev. ed. (Cambridge, Mass., 1957). For the occupation years, with emphasis on the Japanese, the best account is that by a Tokyo editor, Kazuo Kawai, *Japan's American Interlude* (Chicago, 1960). Other useful volumes that deal with the same subject are: Edwin M. Martin, *The Allied Occupation of Japan* (Stanford, Calif., 1948); Robert A. Fearey, *The Occupation of Japan: Second Phase, 1948–50* (New York, 1950); Baron E. J. Lewe Van Aduard, *Japan: From Surrender to Peace* (New York, 1954); and Harry E. Wildes, *Typhoon in Tokyo: The Occupation and Its Aftermath* (New York, 1954).

George McCune, *Korea Today* (Cambridge, Mass., 1950), offers historical background and a good analysis of the American and Russian occupations. Edward G. Meade, in *American Military Government in Korea* (New York, 1951), stresses the American side of the occupation. The best scholarly study of the Korean War and its repercussions at home is John W. Spanier, *The Truman-MacArthur Controversy and the Korean War* (Cambridge, Mass., 1959). For a brilliant case study of the military impact of the Chinese intervention, see S. L. A. Marshall, *The River and the Gauntlet: Defeat of the Eighth Army by the Chinese Communist Forces, November, 1950, in the Battle of the Chongchon River, Korea* (New York, 1953). Other volumes that deal with the Korean War are: Robert Oliver, *Why War Came to Korea* (New York, 1950) and his *Verdict in Korea* (State College, Pa., 1952), both of them critical of administration policy; Guy Wint, *What Happened in Korea* (London, 1954); Charles T. Joy, *How Communists Negotiate* (New York, 1955); Robert E. Osgood, *Limited War* (Chicago, 1957), stressing the influence of military policy on diplomacy; and William H. Vatcher, *Panmunjom: The Story of the Korean Armistice Negotiations* (New York, 1958).

Useful memoirs and biographies are: Robert Payne, *The Marshall Story* (New York, 1951); John Leighton Stuart, *Fifty Years in China* (New York, 1954); Courtney Whitney, *MacArthur: His Rendezvous with History* (New York, 1956); Don Lohbeck, *Patrick J. Hurley* (Chicago, 1956); and Roscoe Drummond and Gaston Coblentz, *Duel at the Brink: John Foster Dulles' Command of American Power* (New York, 1960). Some of the most important sources are cited in the notes and in the previous chapter.

CHAPTER TWENTY-SEVEN

There is no scholarly history of Latin-American relations comparable to Samuel F. Bemis, *The Latin American Policy of the United States* (New York, 1943) for the war and postwar years. Donald M. Dozer, *Are We Good Neighbors? Three Decades of Inter-American Relations, 1930-1960* (Gainesville, Fla., 1959) is valuable mainly for the Latin-American reaction to United States policy. Thomas W. Palmer, Jr., *Search for a Latin American Policy* (Gainesville, Fla., 1957) is a well-written critical analysis of why Latin America was neglected in the immediate postwar years, but is based on a limited use of sources and is selective in emphasis. J. Fred Rippy, *Globe and Hemisphere: Latin America's Place in the Postwar Foreign Relations of the United States* (Chicago, 1958) also offers selected critical emphasis, mainly on economic relations. Dexter Perkins, *The United States and Latin America* (Baton Rouge, 1961) consists of lectures on a broad theme. The lectures in Charles G. Fenwick, *The Inter-American Regional System* (New York, 1949), however, deal with a narrower topic and are documented. For an analysis critical of the conduct of inter-American relations from 1945 to 1961, see William Manger, *Pan America in Crisis: The Future of the OAS* (Washington, 1961). The first year of the Kennedy program is appraised in John C. Drier, ed., *The Alliance for Progress* (Baltimore, 1962).

For special topics, such as the Good Neighbor policy, see Lawrence Duggan, *The Americas: The Search for Hemisphere Security* (New York, 1949) and Isidro Fabela, *Buena y Mala Vecindad* (Mexico City, 1958), which is critical of United States policy, particularly in the Guatemalan affair. Wladimir S. Woytinsky, *The United States and Latin America's Economy* (New York, 1958) is a pamphlet which contains personal observation, historical data, and statistics. The best sources for relations with Argentina are: Arthur P. Whitaker,

The United States and Argentina (Cambridge, Mass., 1954) and Oscar E. Smith, Jr., *Yankee Diplomacy: U.S. Intervention in Argentina* (Dallas, Tex., 1953). For the internal factors in the Guatemalan affair, the best book is Ronald M. Schneider, *Communism in Guatemala, 1944–1954* (New York, 1958). See also Daniel James, *Red Design for the Americas: Guatemalan Interlude* (New York, 1954). For Cuban relations, including the first year of the Castro revolution, see Robert F. Smith, *The United States and Cuba: Business and Diplomacy, 1917–1960* (New York, 1960). For the invasion and its preparation, see Theodore Draper, *Cuba and U.S. Policy*, a pamphlet issued as a special supplement to the *New Leader*, XLIV (June 5, 1961) and Draper, *Castro's Revolution: Myths and Realities* (New York, 1962).

The following stress Latin-American problems, but all have reference or pertinence to United States policy: Robert J. Alexander, *Communism in Latin America* (New Brunswick, N.J., 1957); Edwin Lieuwen, *Arms and Politics in Latin America* (New York, 1960), which is critical of military aid to the Latin countries; Charles O. Porter and Robert J. Alexander, *The Struggle for Democracy in Latin America* (New York, 1961); Richard N. Adams, *et al.*, *Social Change in Latin America: Its Implications for United States Policy* (New York, 1961); and Robert N. Burr, ed., "Latin America's Nationalistic Revolutions," in *The Annals of the American Academy of Political and Social Science*, CCCXXXIV (March 1961), a group of essays by various scholars. For relations with Canada, see Irving Brecher and S. S. Reisman, *Canada-United States Economic Relations* (Ottawa, 1957); Edgar W. McInnis, *The Atlantic Triangle and the Cold War* (Toronto, 1959); James M. Minifie, *Peacemaker or Powder-Monkey: Canada's Role in a Revolutionary World* (Toronto, 1960), which is critical of American policy; and W. L. Morton, *The Canadian Identity* (Madison, Wis., 1961), perceptive essays which contain much on Canadian-American relations. Excellent summaries of Canadian and Latin-American relations may be found in the postwar volumes of the *United States in World Affairs* published for the Council on Foreign Relations. See also the notes in this chapter and pertinent references in preceding chapters.

CHAPTER TWENTY-EIGHT

There is no comprehensive scholarly history of American diplomacy in the Middle East. The best study is John C. Campbell, *Defense of the Middle East: Problems of American Policy*, rev. ed. (New York, 1960). The first part of the book offers a fine history of American policy since the Second World War, and the second deals with the problems the Middle East poses for that policy. William C. Spielman, *The United States in the Middle East: A Study of American Foreign Policy* (New York, 1959) is so brief that it offers little more than an outline. For an Asian analysis, see Mohammed Shafi Agwani, *The United States and the Arab World, 1945–1952* (Aligarh, India, 1955). Ephraim A. Speiser, *The United States and the Near East*, rev. ed. (Cambridge, Mass., 1950) and Lewis V. Thomas and Richard N. Frye, *The United States and Turkey and Iran* (Cambridge, Mass., 1951) are excellent surveys with emphasis on American policy. See also Jacob C. Hurewitz, *Middle East Dilemmas: The Background of United States Policy* (New York, 1953); Raymond F. Mikesell and Hollis B. Chenery, *Arabian Oil: America's Stake in the Middle East* (Chapel Hill, N.C., 1949); and Halford L. Hoskins, *Middle East Oil in United States Foreign Policy* (Washington, 1950).

Although the following do not deal directly with American policy in the Middle East, they all touch upon it: George Kirk, *The Middle East, 1945–1950* (London, 1954);

Richard N. Frye, ed., *The Near East and the Great Powers* (Cambridge, Mass., 1951); Halford L. Hoskins, *The Middle East: Problem Area in World Politics* (New York, 1954); Benjamin Shwadran, *The Middle East, Oil, and the Great Powers, 1959,* 2nd ed. (New York, 1955); Walter Z. Laqueur, *The Soviet Union and the Middle East* (New York, 1959); and Ivar Spector, *The Soviet Union and the Muslim World, 1917–1958* (Seattle, Wash., 1959).

The best history of America's involvement with the Palestine issue is Frank E. Manuel, *The Realities of American-Palestine Relations* (Washington, 1949). For a scholarly study of the Zionist movement, see Ben Halpern, *The Idea of the Jewish State* (Cambridge, Mass., 1961). See also Jacob C. Hurewitz, *The Struggle for Palestine* (New York, 1950); William R. Polk, David M. Stamler, and Edmund Asfour, *Backdrop to Tragedy: The Struggle for Palestine* (Boston, 1957); and Jon Kimche and David Kimche, *A Clash of Destinies: The Arab-Jewish War and the Founding of the State of Israel* (New York, 1960). The following deal with the Suez crisis: Arthur G. Mezerik, *Suez Canal: Nationalization, Invasion, International Action* (New York, 1956); Michael Foot and Mervyn Jones, *Guilty Men, 1957: Suez and Cyprus* (New York, 1957); and Guy Wint and Peter Calvocoressi, *Middle East Crisis* (New York, 1957). For Dulles' role, see Roscoe Drummond and Gaston Coblentz, *Duel at the Brink: John Foster Dulles' Command of American Power* (New York, 1960), and for Eisenhower's, Sherman Adams, *Firsthand Report: The Story of the Eisenhower Administration* (New York, 1961). William E. Warne, *Mission for Peace: Point 4 in Iran* (Indianapolis, 1956) is explained by its title. See also the note references in this chapter and pertinent titles cited in previous chapters.

CHAPTER TWENTY-NINE

Although there is a considerable literature covering the diplomacy of this recent period, most of it is ephemeral. There are already several good accounts of the cold war, based mainly on newspaper sources and printed governmental material. The most useful interpretative surveys, aside from the annual volumes put out by the Council on Foreign Relations on *The United States in World Affairs,* are John A. Lukacs, *A History of the Cold War* (New York, 1960) and Denna F. Fleming, *The Cold War and Its Origins, 1917–1960* (2 vols., New York, 1960). Still valuable is Kenneth Graham, *History of the Cold War* (London, 1955). John W. Spanier, *American Foreign Policy Since World War II,* rev. ed. (New York, 1962) is readable, but selective and brief. Walt W. Rostow, *The United States in the World Arena* (New York, 1960) is full and provocative, but heavy on jargon. William Reitzel, Morton A. Kaplan, and Constance G. Coblenz, *United States Foreign Policy, 1945–1955* (Washington, 1956) and Norman A. Graebner, *The New Isolationism: A Study in Politics and Foreign Policy Since 1950* (New York, 1956) bring perspective to contemporary foreign policy. Walter Johnson, *1600 Pennsylvania Avenue: Presidents and the People, 1929–1959* (Boston, 1960) devotes considerable attention to foreign policy. Edmund Stillman and William Pfaff, *The New Politics: America and the End of the Postwar World* (New York, 1961) is a journalistic account, and Hugh Seton-Watson's *Neither War nor Peace* (London, 1960) offers a world background.

The best studies of NATO, Europe, and American policy are Ben J. Moore, *NATO and the Future of Europe* (New York, 1958) and Robert E. Osgood, *NATO: The Entangling Alliance* (Chicago, 1962). See also Arnold Wolfers, ed., *Alliance Policy in the Cold War*

(Baltimore, 1959), a book of analytical essays; Gordon A. Craig, *NATO and the New German Army* (Princeton, 1955), a pamphlet; Maurice E. Bathurst and J. L. Simpson, *Germany and the North Atlantic Community: A Legal Survey* (London, 1956); Mary M. Ball, *NATO and the European Union Movement* (London, 1959); F. S. C. Northrop, *European Union and United States Foreign Policy* (New York, 1954); and H. Field Haviland, Jr., ed., *The United States and the Western Community* (Haverford, Pa., 1957). The following do not stress American foreign policy, but they offer valuable background material for that policy in Europe: Arnold J. Zurcher, *The Struggle to Unite Europe, 1940–1958* (New York, 1958); Ernst B. Haas, *The Uniting of Europe: Political, Social, and Economic Forces, 1950–1957* (Stanford, Calif., 1958); Arthur H. Robertson, *European Institutions: Cooperation, Integration, Unification* (New York, 1959); Henry L. Mason, *The European Coal and Steel Community: Experiment in Supranationalism* (The Hague, 1955); Louis Lister, *Europe's Coal and Steel Community: An Experiment in Economic Union* (New York, 1960); and Jean F. Deniau, *The Common Market* (New York, 1960). Harry C. Allen, *The Anglo-American Predicament: The British Commonwealth and European Unity* (New York, 1960) is a plea for a federal Atlantic Union, and Emile Benoit, *Europe at Sixes and Sevens: The Common Market, The Free Trade Association, and the United States* (New York, 1961) is the best study of its subject.

For relations with Spain, see Herbert L. Matthews, *The Yoke and the Arrows: A Report on Spain*, rev. ed. (New York, 1961), a competent journalistic account, and Arthur P. Whitaker, *Spain, and Defense of the West: Ally and Liability* (New York, 1961). On the Berlin issue, see Hans Speier, *Divided Berlin: The Anatomy of Soviet Political Blackmail* (New York, 1961) and John Mander, *Berlin: Hostage for the West* (Baltimore, 1961).

Regarding armaments, nuclear weapons and foreign policy, and disarmament, there is a large literature, but the most influential book of its decade on nuclear policy is Henry A. Kissinger, *Nuclear Weapons and Foreign Policy* (New York, 1957). See also Thomas E. Murray, *Nuclear Policy for War and Peace* (Cleveland, 1960), in which a former member of the Atomic Energy Commission calls for a more democratic control of the atom; Hanson W. Baldwin, *The Great Arms Race: A Comparison of U.S. and Soviet Power Today* (New York, 1958); Richard J. Barnet, *Who Wants Disarmament?* (Boston, 1960); and Arthur J. Hadley, *The Nation's Safety and Arms Control* (New York, 1961). The following three books deal with military strategy and its relation to foreign policy and analyze the "new look," deterrence, and massive retaliation; all are critical of deterrence as a basic policy. See Bernard Brodie, *Strategy in the Missile Age* (Princeton, 1959); Maxwell D. Taylor, *The Uncertain Trumpet* (New York, 1959); and B. H. Liddell Hart, *Deterrent or Defense: A Fresh Look at the West's Military Position* (New York, 1960).

For special topics, see Henry L. Roberts, *Russia and America: Dangers and Prospects* (New York, 1956); Isaac Deutscher, *The Great Contest: Russia and the West* (New York, 1960), brilliant lectures that analyze Russia since the death of Stalin and the state of world diplomacy; Thomas K. Finletter, *Foreign Policy: The Next Phase, the 1960's* (New York, 1960); Gordon B. Turner and Richard D. Challener, eds., *National Security in the Nuclear Age* (New York, 1960); Hans J. Morgenthau, *The Purpose of American Politics* (New York, 1960); John R. Beal, *John Foster Dulles* (New York, 1959); *Full Circle: The Memoirs of Anthony Eden* (Boston, 1960); Robert T. Holt and Robert W. van de Velde, *Strategic Psychological Operations and American Foreign Policy* (Chicago, 1960), which includes a case study of American propaganda and pressure during the Italian elections of 1948; George Liska, *The New State-*

craft: Foreign Aid in American Foreign Policy (Chicago, 1960); Frederick L. Schuman, *The Cold War: Retrospect and Prospect* (Baton Rouge, La., 1962); Joseph Kraft, *The Grand Design: From Common Market to Atlantic Partnership* (New York, 1962); and Walter Lippmann, *Western Unity and the Common Market* (Boston, 1962), a collection of newspaper essays. See also the works cited in the notes of this chapter and the pertinent ones in preceding chapters.

CHAPTER THIRTY

There is as yet no substantial scholarly literature on American foreign policy in Southeast Asia and Africa. The annual volumes by the Council on Foreign Relations on *The United States in World Affairs* carry excellent summaries of relations with those parts of the world.

Although its focus is not on American foreign policy as such, the best book on the diplomacy of Southeast Asia, which includes material on American policy, is Russell H. Fifield, *The Diplomacy of Southeast Asia: 1945–1958* (New York, 1958). See also Norman W. Brown, *The United States and India and Pakistan* (Cambridge, Mass., 1955). Inadequate, but still the only useful volume on its subject, is Walter Goldschmidt, ed., *The United States and Africa* (New York, 1958), made up of the background papers prepared for the American Assembly at Columbia University in May, 1958. The latest broad study is Max F. Millikan and Donald L. M. Blackmer, *The Emerging Nations: Their Growth and United States Policy* (Boston, 1961).

For general background, see Eugene Staley, *The Future of Underdeveloped Countries* (New York, 1954); Robert Strausz-Hupé *et al.*, eds., *American-Asian Tensions* (New York, 1956); Strausz-Hupé and Harry W. Hazard, eds., *The Idea of Colonialism* (New York, 1958); Amry Vandenbosch and Richard A. Butwell, *Southeast Asia among the World Powers* (Lexington, Ky., 1957); Gabriel A. Almond and James S. Coleman, eds., *The Politics of Developing Areas* (Princeton, 1960); Lincoln P. Bloomfield, *The United Nations and U.S. Foreign Policy* (Boston, 1960), containing one chapter on underdeveloped countries and another on colonialism and American policy; Rupert Emerson, *From Empire to Nation: The Rise to Self-Assertion of Asian and African Peoples* (Cambridge, Mass., 1960), stressing the rise of non-European nationalism as the consequence of the imperial spread of European civilization; and John B. Oakes, *The Edge of Freedom* (New York, 1961), a newspaperman's report on neutralism with considerable emphasis on sub-saharan Africa.

For specific problems or areas, see Robert A. Smith, *Philippine Freedom: 1946–1958* (New York, 1958); Bernard C. Cohen, *The Political Process and Foreign Policy: The Making of the Japanese Settlement* (Princeton, 1957), the best on its subject; and Edwin O. Reischauer, *The United States and Japan*, rev. ed. (Cambridge, Mass., 1957). There is no scholarly history of relations with India, but the following interpretive accounts are useful: Lawrence K. Rosinger, *India and the United States: Political and Economic Relations* (New York, 1950); Phillips Talbot and S. L. Poplai, *India and America: A Study of their Relations* (New York, 1958); Barbara Ward, *India and the West* (New York, 1961); and Selig Harrison, ed., *India and the United States* (New York, 1961), a summary of views expressed at a conference on relations with India held in Washington in 1957. For Indonesia, see George McT. Kahin, *Nationalism and Revolution in Indonesia* (Ithaca, N.Y., 1952).

Background on the problems of the Indochina peninsula may be found in Ellen J. Hammer, *The Struggle for Indochina* (Stanford, Calif., 1954); Bernard Newman, *Report on Indochina*

(New York, 1954); Allan B. Cole, ed., *Conflict in Indochina and International Repercussions: A Documentary History* (New York, 1956); Donald Lancaster, *The Emancipation of French Indochina* (London, 1961), a thorough account written by a member of the staff of the British Legation in Saigon from 1950–1954; and Bernard B. Fall, *Street without Joy: Indochina at War, 1946–1954* (Harrisburg, Pa., 1961). On relations with China, see John K. Fairbank, *The United States and China*, rev. ed. (Cambridge, Mass., 1958); Doak A. Barnett, *Communist China: Challenge to American Policy* (New York, 1960); and Sheldon Appleton, *The Eternal Triangle: Communist China, the United States, and the United Nations* (East Lansing, Mich., 1961).

Raymond W. Bixler, *The Foreign Policy of the United States in Liberia* (New York, 1957) is the only history of American relations with an independent African state. For background data on emerging Africa, see Gwendolen Carter, *Independence for Africa* (New York, 1960); James Cameron, *The African Revolution* (London, 1961); Colin Legum, *Congo Disaster* (Baltimore, 1961); Alan P. Merriam, *Congo: Background of Conflict* (Evanston, Ill., 1961), which contains a day-by-day summary of the turmoil following independence; and George W. Shepherd, Jr., *The Politics of African Nationalism: Challenge to American Policy* (New York, 1962).

For general accounts, biographies, and analyses of American policy, see Chester Bowles, *Ambassador's Report* (New York, 1954) and his *The New Dimensions of Peace* (New York, 1955), an analysis by the former Ambassador to India which stresses the relevance of the American revolutionary tradition to America's standing in the colonial world; Hugh Seton-Watson, *Neither War Nor Peace: The Struggle for Power in the Postwar World* (London, 1960); Walt W. Rostow, *The United States in the World Arena* (New York, 1960); John W. Spanier, *American Foreign Policy Since World War II*, rev. ed. (New York, 1962); A. Merriman Smith, *A President's Odyssey* (New York, 1960), an account of Eisenhower's good will trips abroad, as to India; and two popular studies of Dulles' diplomacy, Roscoe Drummond and Gaston Coblentz, *Duel at the Brink: John Foster Dulles' Command of American Power* (New York, 1960) and Dean C. and David Heller, *John Foster Dulles: Soldier for Peace* (New York, 1960). See also the notes in this chapter and pertinent titles cited in the previous chapters.

IN CONCLUSION

Concern over the race in missiles and nuclear weapons has given rise to an extensive literature on arms control. In addition to those cited in the notes and elsewhere, see the following titles: *Daedalus*, Journal of the American Academy of Arts and Sciences (Fall, 1960), published as a special issue, and vol. LXXXIX of the *Proceedings* of the Academy; this issue was devoted entirely to "Arms Control." An expansion of the *Daedalus* volume is Donald G. Brennan, ed., *Arms Control, Disarmament, and National Security* (New York, 1961). Thomas C. Schelling and Morton Halperin, *Strategy and Arms Control* (New York, 1961) analyzes arms control with special emphasis on military policy. Louis Henkin, ed., *Arms Control: Issues for the Public* (Englewood Cliffs, N.J., 1961) is a readable summary prepared for the Nineteenth American Assembly. See also Nathan Glazer, "The Peace Movement—1961," *Commentary*, XXXI (April 1961), 288–296, which analyzes SANE (National Committee for a Sane Nuclear Policy); John C. Bennett, ed., *Nuclear Weapons and the Conflict of Conscience* (New York, 1962); and Dexter Perkins, *America's Quest for Peace* (Bloomington, Ind., 1962).

Supplementary Readings, Second Edition

This bibliographical addendum is selective because the number of books and articles dealing with American foreign policy and its history has grown tremendously and space limitations do not permit a comprehensive listing. For the same reasons, even though there is an increasing foreign literature on the subject, this addendum lists mainly works in English and does not include textbooks, anthologies, and collections of documents. For broader coverage the student can go to the pertinent bibliographical guides, or to the fine bibliographies in Thomas A. Bailey, *A Diplomatic History of the American People* (8th ed., New York, 1968) and Richard W. Leopold, *The Growth of American Foreign Policy* (New York, 1962). For periodical literature since 1955 see *Historical Abstracts* and *America and Life* published by the American Bibliographical Center, Santa Barbara, Calif. About a fifth of the annotated entries deal with foreign relations. See also Eric H. Boehm, ed., *Bibliographies on International Relations and World Affairs: An Annotated Directory* (Santa Barbara, 1965), which covers recent foreign journals as well as American, and the specialized work by David F. Trask, Michael C. Meyer, and Roger R. Trask, comps., *A Bibliography of United States-Latin American Relations Since 1810: A Selected List of Eleven Thousand Published References* (Lincoln, Nebr., 1968). U.S. Department of State, Office of External Research, *Foreign Affairs Research: A Directory of Governmental Resources* (Washington, 1969) lists resources within the government related to foreign affairs. In 1963 Robert H. Ferrell took over as editor and expanded the series, *The American Secretaries of State and Their Diplomacy*, so far to eighteen volumes. Robert A. Divine has edited two series of brief interpretive books in American diplomatic history under the general titles *America in Crisis* and *America and the World*. The *American Diplomatic History Series* edited by Armin Rappaport is more ambitious and more thorough in coverage; so far four volumes have been published.

CHAPTER ONE

Interpretations of American foreign policy are numerous. Three that are particularly stimulating and based on solid scholarship are Paul Seabury, *Power, Freedom and Diplomacy: The Foreign Policy of the United States of America* (New York, 1963); Donald Brandon, *American Foreign Policy: Beyond Utopianism and Realism* (New York, 1966); and Arthur A. Ekirch, Jr., *Ideas, Ideals, and American Diplomacy: A History of Their Growth and Interaction*

(New York, 1966). See also David F. Long, *The Outward View: An Illustrated History of United States Foreign Relations* (Chicago, 1963) and Francis L. Lowenheim, *The Historian and the Diplomat: The Role of History and Historians in American Foreign Policy* (New York, 1967).

For the machinery of foreign policy and diplomacy see Kurt London, *The Making of Foreign Policy: East and West* (Phil., 1967); Burton M. Sapin, *The Making of United States Foreign Policy* (Washington, 1966); H. Bradford Westerfield, *The Instruments of America's Foreign Policy* (New York, 1963); Lawrence I. Radway, *The Liberal Democracy in World Affairs: Foreign Policy and National Defense* (Glenview, Ill., 1969); John E. Harr, *The Professional Diplomat* (Princeton, 1969); John R. Wood and Jean Serres, *Diplomatic Ceremonial and Protocol: Principles, Procedures and Practices* (New York, 1970); Smith Simpson, *Anatomy of the State Department* (Boston, 1967); Norman L. Hill, *Mr. Secretary of State* (New York, 1963); and Ronald J. Stupak, *The Shaping of Foreign Policy: the Role of the Secretary of State as Seen by Dean Acheson* (New York, 1969). Former Foreign Service Officer and State Department officials give their views on the subject in Ellis Briggs, *Farewell to Foggy Bottom* (New York, 1964) and *Anatomy of Diplomacy: The Origin and Execution of American Foreign Policy* (New York, 1968); Henry S. Villard, *Affairs at State* (New York, 1965); Lawrence E. Gelfand, ed., *A Diplomat Looks Back: Lewis Einstein* (New Haven, 1968); and Charles Frankel, *High on Foggy Bottom: An Outsider's Inside View of the Government* (New York, 1969).

For the role of the President, see Sidney Warren, *The President as World Leader* (Phil., 1964); Edgar E. Robinson, Alexander De Conde, Raymond G. O'Connor, and Martin B. Travis, Jr., *Powers of the President in Foreign Affairs: 1945–1965* (San Francisco, 1966); Leroy N. Rieselbach, *The Roots of Isolationism: Congressional Voting and Presidential Leadership in Foreign Policy* (Indianapolis, 1966); and Manfred Landecker, *The President and Public Opinion: Leadership in Foreign Affairs* (Washington, 1968). Hugh G. Gallagher, *Advise and Obstruct: The Role of the United States Senate in Foreign Policy Decisions* (New York, 1969), a critical view. For analysis of public opinion and the press in relation to foreign policy there are: Ernest R. May, "An American Tradition in Foreign Policy: The Role of Public Opinion," in *Theory and Practice in American Politics*, ed. by William H. Nelson and Francis L. Loeweheim (Chicago, 1964), pp. 101–122; Elmer E. Cornwell, Jr., *Presidential Leadership of Public Opinion* (Bloomington, Ind., 1965); Lloyd A. Free and Hadley Cantril, *The Political Beliefs of Americans: A Study of Public Opinion* (New Brunswick, N.J., 1967); Lee Benson, "An Approach to the Scientific Study of Past Public Opinion," *Public Opinion Quarterly*, XXX (Winter, 1967–68), 522–567; Bernard C. Cohen, *The Press and Foreign Policy* (Princeton, 1963), and James Reston, *The Artillery of the Press: Its Influence on American Foreign Policy* (New York, 1967).

The military influence is discussed in Donald A. Wells, *The War Myth* (New York, 1968); Thomas C. Schelling, *Arms and Influence* (New Haven, Conn., 1966); George Thayer, *The War Business: The International Trade in Armaments* (New York, 1969); Merlo J. Pusey, *The Way We Go to War* (Boston, 1969); Bruce M. Russett, *What Price Vigilance: The Burdens of National Defense* (New Haven, 1970); Richard A. Yudkin, "American Armed Strength and Its Influence," *Annals of the American Academy of Political and Social Science*, CCCLXXXIV (July, 1969), 1–13; and Paul Findlay, "Does American Foreign Policy Entail Frequent Wars?", *ibid.*, pp. 45–52. On intelligence activities new studies are: Washington Platt, *National Character in Action: Intelligence Factors in Foreign Relations* (New Brunswick, N.J., 1961); David Wise and Thomas B. Ross, *The Invisible Government* (New York, 1964) and *The Espionage Establishment* (New York, 1967); and Harry H. Ransom, *The Intelligence Establishment* (Cambridge, Mass., 1970), a revision of his *Central Intelligence*...

For other topics pertinent to this chapter see Robert Blum, ed., *Cultural Affairs and Foreign Relations* (Englewood Cliffs, N.J., 1963); "Minority Groups and Foreign Policy," *Political Science Quarterly*, LXXXIV (June 1959), 161–175; Thomas A. Bailey, *The Art of Diplomacy: The American Experience* (New York, 1968) and *Essays Diplomatic and Undiplomatic of Thomas A. Bailey*, ed. by Alexander De Conde and Armin Rappaport (New York, 1969); Joseph C. McKenna, *Diplomatic Protest in Foreign Policy: Analysis and Case Studies* (Chicago, 1962); Harvey Magdoff, *The Age of Imperialism: The Economics of U.S. Foreign Policy* (New York, 1969), a Marxist analysis; Merle E. Curti, *American Philanthropy Abroad* (New Brunswick, N.J., 1963); Ronald Radosh, *American Labor and United States Foreign Policy* (New York, 1969); Samuel E. Morison, Frederick Merk, and Frank Freidel, *Dissent in Three American Wars* (Cambridge, Mass., 1970); and two books by Peter Brock, *Pacifism in the United States: From the Colonial Era to the First World War* (Princeton, 1968) and *Radical Pacifism in Antebellum America* (Princeton, 1968).

CHAPTER TWO

Max Savelle, *The Origins of American Diplomacy: The International History of Angloamerica, 1492–1763* (New York, 1967) is the fullest treatment of the diplomacy of the colonial era, and the only narrative history of the subject. See also Savelle, "The International Approach to Early Anglo-American History, 1492–1763," in Ray A. Billington, ed., *The Reinterpretation of Early American History: Essays in Honor of John Edwin Pomfret* (San Marino, Calif., 1966); Robert L. Gold, *Borderland Empires in Transition: The Triple Nation Transfer of Florida* (Carbondale, Ill., 1969) and Norman E. Saul, "The Beginnings of American-Russian Trade, 1763–1766," *William and Mary Quarterly*, 3rd Ser., XXVI (Oct., 1969). Richard W. Van Alstyne, *Empire and Independence: The International History of the American Revolution* (New York, 1965) and *Genesis of American Nationalism* (Waltham, Mass., 1970) stress the British and European background. Richard B. Morris, *The Peacemakers: The Great Powers and American Independence* (New York, 1965) is the fullest treatment of the subject, the basic work. See also Morris's *The American Revolution Reconsidered* (New York, 1967) and *John Jay, the Nation and the Court* (Boston, 1967); Oliver P. Chitwood, *Richard Henry Lee: Statesman of the Revolution* (Morgantown, W. Virginia, 1967); Herbert E. Klingelhofer, ed., "Matthew Ridley's Diary During the Peace Negotiations of 1782," *William and Mary Quarterly*, 3rd. Ser., XX (Jan., 1963), 95–133; William C. Stinchcombe, *The American Revolution and the French Alliance* (Syracuse, N.Y., 1969); Ralph L. Ketcham, "France and American Politics, 1763–1793," *Political Science Quarterly*, LXXVIII (June, 1963), 198–223; and Hildor A. Barton, "Sweden and the War of American Independence," *William and Mary Quarterly*, 3rd. Ser., XXIII (July, 1966), 408–430. John R. Alden, *A History of the American Revolution* (New York, 1969) and Piers Mackesy, *The War for America, 1775–1783* (London, 1964) are fine brief accounts that place the struggle in broad settings. For Franklin's diplomacy, see Claude Anne Lopez, *Mon Cher Papa: Franklin and the Ladies of Paris* (New

Haven, 1966); Roger Burlingame, *Benjamin Franklin: Envoy Extraordinary* (New York, 1967); and the second edition (1969) of Stourzh's study.

CHAPTER THREE

Paul A. Varg, *Foreign Policies of the Founding Fathers* (East Lansing, Mich., 1963) gives a broad analysis of the foreign policy of the period. Alexander De Conde, *The Quasi-War: The Politics and Diplomacy of the Undeclared War with France, 1797–1801* (New York, 1966) is the fullest account of the conflict. Other specialized studies are: Jerald A. Combs, *The Jay Treaty: Political Battleground of the Founding Fathers* (Berkeley, Calif., 1970) a stimulating analysis; Charles Ritcheson, *Aftermath of Revolution: British Policy Toward the United States, 1783–1795* (Dallas, 1969); Alfred W. Crosby, Jr., *America, Russia Hemp, and Napoleon: American Trade with Russia and the Baltic, 1783–1812* (Columbus, Ohio, 1965); H. G. Barnby, *The Prisoners of Algiers: An Account of the Forgotten American-Algerian War, 1785–1797* (New York, 1966); Lawrence S. Kaplan, *Jefferson and France: An Essay on Politics and Political Ideas* (New Haven, Conn., 1967); Helene Looze, *Alexander Hamilton and the British Orientation of American Foreign Policy, 1793–1803* (The Hague, 1969); Gilbert L. Lycan, *Alexander Hamilton and American Foreign Policy: A Design for Greatness* (Norman, Okla., 1970); Julian P. Boyd, *Number 7: Alexander Hamilton's Secret Attempts to Control American Foreign Policy* (Princeton, N.J., 1964), a critical account; Joanne L. Neel, *Phineas Bond: A Study in Anglo-American Relations, 1786–1812* (Phil., 1968); Jack L. Cross, *London Mission: The First Critical Years* (East Lansing, Mich., 1968) deals with Thomas Pinckney; Marvin Zahniser, *Charles Cotesworth Pinckney: Founding Father* (Chapel Hill, N.C., 1967), the first scholarly study of this important secondary figure; Robert Ernst, *Rufus King: American Federalist* (Chapel Hill, N.C., 1968); Gerard H. Clarfield, *Timothy Pickering and American Diplomacy, 1795–1800* (Columbia, Missouri, 1969); and Page Smith, *John Adams* (2 vols., New York, 1962), a fine biography that contains considerable data on foreign policy.

Important articles are Harry Ammon, "The Genet Mission and the Devopment of American Political Parties," *Journal of American History*, LII (March, 1966), 725–741; Arthur A. Markowitz, "Washington's Farewell and the Historians: A Critical Review," *Pennsylvania Magazine of History and Biography*, XCIV (April, 1970), 173–191; Lawrence S. Kaplan, "Jefferson's Foreign Policy and Napoleon's Ideologies," *William and Mary Quarterly*, 3rd Ser., XIX (July 1962), 344–359; Merrill D. Peterson, "Thomas Jefferson and Commercial Policy, 1783–1793," *ibid* (Oct., 1965), 584–610; Marvin R. Zahniser, "The First Pinckney Mission to France [1795]" *South Carolina Historical Magazine*, LXVI (Oct., 1965), 205–217; George G. Shackelford, "William Short: Diplomat in Revolutionary France, 1785–1793," *Proceedings of the American Philosophical Society*, CII (Dec. 15, 1958), 596–612; Stephen G. Kurtz, "The French Mission of 1799–1800: Concluding Chapter in the Statecraft of John Adams," *Political Science Quarterly*, LXXX (Dec. 1965), 543–557; Raymond Young, "Pinckney's Treaty—A New Perspective," *Hispanic American Historical Review*, XLIII (Nov., 1963), 526–535, Gerard H. Clarfield, "Victory in the West: A Study of the Role of Timothy Pickering in the Successful Consummation of Pinckey's Treaty," *Essex Institute Historical Collection*, CI (Oct., 1965), 333–353; James A Carr, "John Adams and the Barbary Problem:

The Myth and the Record," *American Neptune*, XXVI (Oct., 1966), 231–257; James W. Gould, "The Origins of the Senate Committee on Foreign Relations," *Western Political Quarterly*, XII (Sept., 1959), 670–682; and Robert W. Sellen, "The American Museum, 1787–1792, as a Forum for Ideas of American Foreign Policy," *Pennsylvania Magazine of History and Biography*, XCII (April, 1969), 179–187.

CHAPTER FOUR

Titles cited for the previous and following chapters are also pertinent to this one. Dumas Malone, *Jefferson the President: First Term, 1801–1805* (Boston, 1970), gives the fullest scholarly coverage to Jefferson in these years; for a brief analysis see Malone, "Presidential Leadership and National Unity: The Jeffersonian Example," *Journal of Southern History*, XXXV (Feb., 1969), 3–17. See also Merrill D. Peterson, "Henry Adams on Jefferson the President," *Virginia Quarterly Review*, XXXIX (Spring, 1963), 187–201; and Julia H. McLeod, "Jefferson and the Navy: A Defense," *Huntington Library Quarterly*, VIII (Nov.-Aug., 1944–45), 153–184. For problems in the Mediterranean world, see Milton Cantor, "Joel Barlow's Mission to Algiers," *The Historian*, XXV (Feb., 1963), 172–194; James Woodress, *A Yankee's Odyssey: The Life of Joel Barlow* (Phil., 1958); Raymond W. Bixler, *The Open Door on the Old Barbary Coast* (New York, 1959); David H. Finnie, *Pioneers East: The Early American Experience in the Middle East* (Cambridge, Mass., 1967); and James A. Field, Jr., *America and the Mediterranean World, 1776–1886* (Princeton, N.J., 1969), which sheds new light on a neglected area of American activity.

CHAPTER FIVE

The War of 1812 continues to attract considerable scholarly attention. The most solid account of the war's diplomacy is in Bradford Perkins, *Castlereagh and Adams: England and the United States, 1812–1823* (Berkeley, Calif., 1964). Roger H. Brown, *The Republic in Peril: 1812* (New York, 1964) attacks previous interpretations of causation while presenting a nationalistic analysis. Other brief accounts are: Harry L. Coles, *The War of 1812* (Chicago, 1965); J. Mackay Hitsman, *The Incredible War of 1812* (Toronto, 1965); a Canadian view Patrick C. T. White, *A Nation on Trial: America and the War of 1812* (New York, 1965); Reginald Horsman, *The War of 1812* (New York, 1969), based on recent scholarship and archival sources; and Victor A. Sapio, *Pennsylvania and the War of 1812* (Lexington, Ken., 1970), stresses political causation.

Important essays are: Philip P. Mason, ed., *After Tippecanoe: Some Aspects of the War of 1812* (East Lansing, Mich., 1963), a collection of six essays; Roger H. Brown and Reginald Horsman, "The War Hawks of the War of 1812," *Indiana Magazine of History*, LX (June, 1964), 119–158, two essays that disagree on whether or not there were war hawks. Alexander DeConde and Norman K. Risjord offer critical commentaries. See also William R. Barlow, "Ohio's Congressman and the War of 1812," *Ohio History*, LXXII (July, 1963), 175–194; Leland R. Johnson, "The Suspense Was Hell: The Senate Vote for War in 1812," *ibid.*, LXV

(Dec., 1969) 247–267; Irving Brant, "Madison and the War of 1812," *Virginia Magazine of History and Biography*, LXXIV (Jan., 1966), 51–67; Richard Glover, "The French Fleet, 1807–1814: Britain's Problem and Madison's Opportunity," *Journal of Modern History*, XXXIX (Sept., 1967), 233–252; and two essays by Lawrence S. Kaplan, "France and Madison's Decision for War, 1812," *Mississippi Valley Historical Review*, L (March, 1964), 652–671; "France and the War of 1812," *Journal of American History*, LVII (June, 1970), 36–47.

CHAPTER SIX

On the Florida question, see Clifford L. Egan, "United States, France, and West Florida, 1803–1807," *Florida Historical Quarterly*, XLVII (Jan. 1969), 227–252; and Maury Baker, "The Spanish War Scare of 1816," *Mid-America*, XLV (April, 1963), 67–78. New works on the Latin American question are: Harold F. Peterson, *Argentina and the United States, 1810–1960* (New York, 1964) and Edward B. Billingssey, *In Defense of Neutral Rights: The United States Navy and the Wars of Independence in Chile and Peru* (Chapel Hill, N.C., 1967). For the Monroe Doctrine see Irby C. Nicholas, Jr., "The Russian Ukase, and the Monroe Doctrine: A Re-evaluation," *Pacific Historical Review*, XXXVI (Feb., 1967), 13–26. See also two general accounts, George Dangerfield, *The Awakening of American Nationalism, 1815–1828* (New York, 1965) and William H. Goetzmann, *When the Eagle Screamed: The Romantic Horizon in American Diplomacy, 1800–1860* (New York, 1966), and the pertinent titles for the previous chapter.

CHAPTER SEVEN

For the controversy with France, see René Rémond, *Les États-Unis devant l'opinion Française, 1815–1852* (2 vols., Paris, 1962) and Henry Blumenthal, *France and the United States: Their Diplomatic Relations, 1789–1914* (Chapel Hill, N.C., 1970). Three books by Frederick Merk deal with Manifest Destiny, expansionism, and relations with Britain: *Manifest Destiny and Mission in American History* (New York, 1963); *The Monroe Doctrine and American Expansionism, 1843–1849* (New York, 1966); and *The Oregon Question: Essays in Anglo-American Diplomacy* (Cambridge, Mass., 1967). See also Oscar A. Kinchen, *The Rise and Fall of the Patriot Hunters* (New York, 1956); Thomas LeDuc, "The Webster-Ashburton Treaty and the Minnesota Iron Ranges," *Journal of American History*, LI (Dec., 1964), 476–481; Richard S. Cramer, "British Magazines and the Oregon Question," *Pacific Historical Review*, XXXII (Nov., 1963), 369–382; James O. McCabe, "Arbitration and the Oregon Question," *Canadian Historical Review*, XLI (Dec., 1960), 308–327; and Kenneth Bourne, *Britain and the Balance of Power in North America, 1815–1908* (Berkeley, 1967).

Other works pertinent to this period are: William E. B. DuBois, *The Suppression of the African Slave Trade to the United States of America, 1638–1870* (New York, 1896); Peter Duignan and Clarence Clendenen, *The United States and the African Slave Trade, 1619–1862* (Stanford, Calif., 1963); Harris J. Booras, *Hellenic Independence and America's Contribution to the Cause* (Rutland, Vt., 1936); and Stephen A. Larrabee, *Hellas Observed: The American Experience of Greece, 1775–1865* (New York, 1957).

CHAPTER EIGHT

An important bibliographical article is Peter T. Harstad and Richard W. Resh, "The Causes of the Mexican War: A Note on Changing Interpretations," *Arizona and the West*, VI (Winter, 1964), 289–302. Charles Sellers, *James K. Polk: Continentalist, 1843–1846* (Princeton, 1966), an excellent study containing the results of the latest scholarship; Charles L. Dufour, *The Mexican War: A Compact History, 1846–1848* (New York, 1968); Thomas E. Cotner and Carlos E. Castañeda, eds., *Essays in Mexican History* (Austin, Tex., 1958), the essays by J. C. McElhannon, F. A. Knapp, Jr., and C. C. Hutchinson, are pertinent; Glenn W. Price, *Origins of the War with Mexico: The Polk-Stockton Intrigue* (Austin, Tex., 1967); Joseph M. Nance, *After San Jacinto: The Texas-Mexican Frontier, 1836–1841* (Austin, Texas, 1963) and *Attack and Counterattack: The Texas-Mexican Frontier, 1842* (Austin, Texas, 1964); George W. Smith and Charles Judah, eds., *Chronicles of the Gringos: The U.S. Army in the Mexican War, 1846–1848: Accounts of Eyewitnesses and Combatants* (Albuquerque, 1968); John A. Hawgood, "The Pattern of Yankee Infiltration in Mexican Alta California, 1821–1846," *Pacific Historical Review*, XXVII (1958), 27–37; and Charles A. Lofgren, "Force and Diplomacy, 1846–1848: The View from Washington," *Military Affairs*, XXXI (Summer, 1967), 57–64. See also titles listed for the previous chapter.

CHAPTER NINE

For Central American issues see Thomas L. Karnes, *The Failure of Union: Central America, 1824–1860* (Chapel Hill, N.C., 1961); Albert H. Carr, *The World and William Walker* (New York, 1963); Mario Rodríguez, *A Palmerstonian Diplomat in Central America: Frederick Chatfield, Esq.* (Tucson, Ariz., 1964) and Rodríguez, "The 'Prometheus' and the Clayton Bulwer Treaty," *Journal of Modern History*, XXXVI (Sept., 1964), 260–278. On expansion see Walter G. Sharrow, "William Henry Seward and the Basis for American Empire, 1850–1860," *Pacific Historical Review*, XXXVI (Aug., 1967), 325–342. For Canadian relations see Alvin C. Gluck Jr., *Minnesota and the Manifest Destiny of the Canadian Northwest: A Study in Canadian-American Relations* (Toronto, 1965) and Irene W. D. Hecht, "Israel D. Andrews and the Reciprocity Treaty of 1854: A Reappraisal," *Canadian Historical Review*, XLIV (Dec., 1963), 313–329. For the reaction to European uprisings see Howard R. Marraro, *American Opinion on the Unification of Italy, 1846–1861* (New York, 1932) and Marraro, ed., *Diplomatic Relations Between the United States and the Kingdom of the Two Sicilies, 1816–1861* (2 vols, New York, 1951). For Cuba there is Philip S. Foner, *A History of Cuba and Its Relations with the United States* (2 vols., New York, 1962–63) and Lester D. Langley, *The Cuban Policy of the United States: A Brief History* (New York, 1968).

On Chinese relations there are John K. Fairbank, *Trade and Diplomacy on the China Coast* (Cambridge, Mass., 1953); Fairbank, ed., *The Chinese World Order: Traditional China's Foreign Relations* (Cambridge, Mass., 1968); George H. Danton, *The Cultural Contacts of the United States and China: The Earliest Sino-American Culture Contacts, 1784–1844* (New York, 1931); Te-kong Tong, *United States Diplomacy in China, 1844–1860* (Seattle, 1964); Christopher Hibbert, *The Dragon Wakes: China and the West, 1793–1911* (London, 1970), Kwang-Ching Liu, *Americans and Chinese: A Historical Essay and a Bibliography* (Cambridge, Mass.,

1963); Liu, *Anglo-American Steamship Rivalry in China, 1862–1874* (Cambridge, Mass., 1962); Jacques M. Downs, "American Merchants and the China Opium Trade, 1800–1840," *Business History Review*, XLIII (Winter, 1968), 418–442; and Arnold H. Taylor, "Opium and the Open Door," *South Atlantic Quarterly*, LXIX (Winter, 1970), 79–95. New works on relations with Japan are: Richard J. Chang, *From Prejudice to Tolerance: A Study of the Japanese Image of the West, 1826–1864* (Tokyo, 1970); Foster R. Dulles, *Yankees and Samurai: America's Role in the Emergence of Japan, 1791–1900* (New York, 1965); Matthew C. Perry, *The Japan Expedition 1852–1854: The Personal Journal of Commodore Matthew C. Perry*, ed. by Roger Pineau (Washington, D.C., 1969); Samuel E. Morison, *"Old Bruin": Commodore Matthew C. Perry* (Boston, 1967); and Oliver Statler, *Shimoda Story* (New York, 1969), the story of Townsend Harris in Japan. Broad studies are: Robert S. Schwantes, *Japanese and Americans: A Century of Cultural Relations* (New York, 1955); William L. Neumann, *America Encounters Japan: From Perry to MacArthur* (Baltimore, 1963); and Richard O'Connor, *Pacific Destiny, An Informal History of the U.S. in the Far East: 1776–1968* (Boston, 1969).

CHAPTER TEN

Important new books are: Philip Van Doren Stern, *When the Guns Roared: World Aspects of the American Civil War* (Garden City, N.Y., 1965); Harold Hyman, ed., *Heard Round the World: The Impact Abroad of the Civil War* (New York, 1969), a collection of essays; Stuart L. Bernath, *Squall Across the Atlantic: American Civil War Prize Cases and Diplomacy* (Berkeley, 1970), the fullest scholarly account of the subject; Frank J. Merli, *Great Britain and the Confederate Navy* (Bloomington, Ind., 1970); Glyndon G. Van Deusen, *William Henry Seward* (New York, 1967), the foremost scholarly biography; Charles P. Cullop, *Confederate Propaganda in Europe, 1861–1865* (Miami, 1969); John H. Franklin, *The Emancipation Proclamation* (Garden City, N.Y., 1963); Serge Govronsky, *The French Liberal Opposition and the American Civil War* (New York, 1968); Lynn M. Case and Warren F. Spencer, *The United States and France: Civil War Diplomacy* (Phil., 1970); a full scholarly account, Mary P. Trauth, *Italo-American Diplomatic Relations, 1861–1882: The Mission of George Perkins Marsh, First American Minister to the Kingdom of Italy* (Washington, D.C., 1958); and Raimondo Luraghi, *Storia della guerra civile americana* (Twin, 1966), which places the conflict in the broad stream of European revolutionary upheaval.

For useful periodical literature see Amos Khasigian, "Economic Factors and British Neutrality, 1861–1865," *Historian* XXV (Aug., 1963), 451–465; John Kutolowski, "The Effect of the Polish Insurrection of 1863 on American Civil War Diplomacy," *ibid.*, XXVII (Aug., 1965), 560–577; Robert H. Jones, "Anglo-American Relations, 1861–1865, Reconsidered," *Mid America*, XLV (Jan., 1963), 36–49; Jones, "Long Live the King," *Agricultural History* (July, 1963), 166–169; Joseph M. Hernon, Jr., "British Sympathies in the American Civil War: A Reconsideration," *Journal of Southern History*, XXXIII (Aug., 1967), 356–367; Patrick Sowle, "A Reappraisal of Seward's Memorandum of April 1, 1861, to Lincoln," *ibid.* (May, 1967), 234–239; Henry Blumenthal, "Confederate Diplomacy: Popular Notions and International Realities," *ibid.*, XXXII (May, 1966), 151–171; Stuart L. Bernath, "Squall Across the Atlantic: The *Peterhoff* Episode," *ibid.*, XXXIV (Aug., 1968), 382–401; Bernath, "British Neutrality and the Civil War Prize Cases," *Civil War History*, XV (Dec., 1969),

320–331; Eugene A. Brady, "A Reconsideration of the Lancashire 'Cotton Famine'," *Agricultural History*, XXXVII (July, 1963), 156–162; John B. Heffernan, "The Blockade of the Southern Confederacy, 1861–1865," *Smithsonian Journal of History*, II (Winter, 1967–68), 23–44; and Richard A. Heckman, "British Press Reaction to the Emancipation Proclamation," *Lincoln Herald*, LXXI (Winter, 1969).

CHAPTER ELEVEN

Two major works, both of which stress economic interpretation and offer revisions of traditional scholarship, cover the general problem of expansion in the post-Civil War era: Walter La Feber, *The New Empire: An Interpretation of American Expansionism, 1860–1898* (Ithaca, N.Y., 1963) and William A. Williams, *The Roots of the Modern American Empire: A Study of the Growth and Shaping of Social Consciousness in a Marketplace Society* (New York, 1969). See also Robert L. Beisner, "Thirty Years Before Manila: E. L. Godkin, Carl Schurz, and Anti-Imperialism in the Gilded Age," *Historian*, XXX (Aug., 1968), 561–577. For Mexico and the Caribbean see, Edward J. Berbusse, "The Origins of the McLane-Ocampo Treaty of 1859," *The Americas*, XIV (Jan., 1958), 223–245; Carl H. Bock, *Prelude to Tragedy: The Negotiation and Breakdown of the Tripartite Convention of London, October 31, 1861* (Phil., 1966); and Clifford L. Egan, "The Monroe Doctrine and Santo Domingo in Spanish-American Diplomacy, 1861–1865," *Lincoln Herald*, LXXI (Summer, 1969), 55–66. On Alaska see, Hector Chevigny, *Russian America: The Great Alaskan Venture, 1741–1867* (New York, 1965); Archie W. Shiels, *The Purchase of Alaska* (College, Alaska, 1967), documents with commentary; and Ian C. Jackson, "The Stikine Territory Lease and Its Relevance to the Alaska Purchase," *Pacific Historial Review*, XXXVI (Aug., 1967), 289–306. New literature on the Fenians is: Brian Jenkins, *Fenians and Anglo-American Relations during Reconstruction* (Ithaca, N.Y., 1969); Mabel G. Walker, *The Fenian Movement* (Colorado Springs, 1969); Thomas N. Brown, *Irish-American Nationalism 1870–1890* (Phil., 1966); Arthur H. De Rosier, Jr., "Importance in Failure: The Fenian Raids of 1866–1871," *Southern Quarterly*, III (April, 1965), 181–197; and Hereward Senior, "Quebec and the Fenians," *Canadian Historical Review*, XLVIII (March, 1967), 26–44. See also D. G. Creighton, "The United States and Canadian Confederation," *ibid.*, XXXIX (Sept., 1958). 209–222; Maureen M. Robson, "The *Alabama* Claims and the Anglo-American Reconciliation, 1865–71," *ibid.*, XLII (March, 1961), 1–22; Arthur H. De Rosier, "The Settlement of the San Juan Controversy," *Southern Quarterly*, IV (Oct., 1965), 74–88; James O. McCabe, *The San Juan Water Boundary Question* (Toronto, 1965); Sydney F. Wise and Robert C. Brown, *Canada Views the United States: Nineteenth-Century Political Attitudes* (Seattle, 1967); and Marlene J. Mayo, "A Catechism of Western Diplomacy: The Japanese and Hamilton Fish, 1872," *Journal of Asian Studies*, XXVI (May, 1967), 389–410. See also pertinent titles listed for previous chapters.

CHAPTER TWELVE

David M. Pletcher, *The Awkward Years: American Foreign Relations under Garfield and Arthur* (Columbia, Missouri, 1962), is the best scholarly study of its subject. See also Harry J. Sievers: *Benjamin Harrison, Hoosier President* (Indianapolis, 1968); Allan Spetter, "Harrison and Blaine: Foreign Policy, 1889–1893," *Indiana Magazine of, History* LXV (Sept., 1969), 215–227; two articles by Milton Plesur, "Across the Wide Pacific," *Pacific Historical Review*, XXVII (Feb., 1959), 73–80 and "America Looking Outward: The Years from Hayes to Harrison," *Historian*, XXII (May, 1960), 280–295; Mary P. Chapman, "The Mission of Lansing Bond Mizner to Central America," *ibid.*, XIX (Aug., 1957), 385–401; Jackson Crowell, "The United States and a Central American Canal, 1869–1877," *Hispanic American Historical Review*, XLIX (Feb., 1969), 27–52; and Frederick B. Pike, *Chile and the United States, 1880–1962* (Notre Dame, Ind., 1963). Stuart C. Miller, *The Unwelcome Stranger: The American Image of the Chinese, 1785–1882* (Berkeley, 1969) is a fine treatment of Chinese exclusion. On German problems, see Bingham Duncan, "Protectionism and Pork: White-law Reid as Diplomat, 1889–1891," *Agricultural History*, XXXIII (Oct., 1959), 190–195 and G. A. Dobbert, "German-Americans Between New and Old Fatherland, 1870–1914," *American Quarterly*, XIX (Winter, 1967), 663–680.

For relations with Britain, Canada, Italy and other problems, see: Robert C. Brown, *Canada's National Policy, 1883–1900: A Study in Canadian-American Relations* (Princeton, 1964); John A. S. Grenville and George B. Young, *Politics, Strategy, and American Diplomacy: Studies in Foreign Policy, 1873–1917* (New Haven, 1966), a group of perceptive essays on different but related problems; Charles L. Campbell, Jr., "The Bering Sea Settlements of 1892," *Pacific Historical Review*, XXXII (Nov., 1963), 347–367; Campbell, "American Tariff Interests and the Northeastern Fisheries, 1883–1888," *Canadian Historical Review*, XLV (Sept., 1964), 212–228; James Bryce, "Legal and Constitutional Aspects of the Lynching at New Orleans," *The New Review*, IV (May, 1891), 384–397, a perceptive contemporary analysis; Morton Rothstein, "The American West and Foreign Markets, 1850–1900," in D. M. Ellis, ed., *The Frontier in American Development: Essays in Honor of Paul Wallace Gates* (Ithaca, N.Y., 1969), and Daniel Cosío Villegas, *The United States versus Porfirio Diaz*, trans. by Nettie Lee Benson (Lincoln, Nebr. 1963). See also the bibliographical entries for previous chapters.

CHAPTER THIRTEEN

For a provocative new interpretation of the new manifest destiny, see Ernest R. May, *American Imperialism: A Speculative Essay* (New York, 1968). Paul S. Holbo, "Perspectives on American Foreign Policy, 1890–1916: Expansion and World Power," *Social Studies*, LVIII (1967), 246–256, is a useful bibliographical survey. See also Foster R. Dulles, *Prelude to World Power: American Diplomatic History*, 1860–1900 (New York, 1965); Dorothea R. Muller, "Josiah Strong and American Nationalism: A Re-evaluation," *Journal of American History*, LIII (Dec., 1966), 487–503; and Paul S. Holbo, "Economics, Emotion, and Expansion: An Emerging Foreign Policy," in H. Wayne Morgan, ed., *The Gilded Age* (2nd ed., Syracuse, N.Y., 1970), pp. 199–221. On Samoa there are: Ernest S. Dodge, *New England and the South Seas* (Cambridge, Mass., 1965) and Edwin P. Hoyt, *The Typhoon that Stopped a War* (New York, 1967). Merze Tate has added a new depth to the literature on Hawaii's diplomacy with a series of scholarly articles and two books that bring together her important findings: *The United States and the Hawaiian Kindgom: A Political History* (New Haven, Conn., 1965) and *Hawaii: Reciprocity or Annexation* (East Lansing, Mich., 1968). See also Ralph S.

Kuykendall, *The Hawaiian Kingdom, 1874–1893: The Kalakua Dynasty* (Honolulu, 1967). Joseph J. Mathews, "Informal Diplomacy in the Venezuela Crisis of 1896," *Mississippi Valley Historical Review*, L (Sept., 1963), 195–212 and John A. S. Grenville, *Lord Salisbury and Foreign Policy: The Close of the Nineteenth Century* (London, 1964) are fresh accounts of aspects of the Venezuela crisis. The citations for other chapters also contain references pertinent to this one.

CHAPTER FOURTEEN

Works cited for other chapters, such as those by La Feber and Grenville, are also important for this one. Significant new books not previously cited are: H. Wayne Morgan, *William McKinley and His America* (Syracuse, 1963); Morgan, *America's Road to Empire: The War with Spain and Overseas Expansion* (New York, 1965); Morgan, ed., *Making Peace with Spain: The Diary of Whitelaw Reid, September–December, 1898* (Austin, Tex., 1965); W. A. Swanberg, *Citizen Hearst: A Biography of William Randolph Hearst* (New York, 1961); Jack Cameron, *A Leap to Arms: The Cuban Campaign of 1898* (Phil., 1970); R. G. Neale, *Great Britain and United States Expansion: 1898–1900* (East Lansing, Mich., 1966); Robert L. Beisner, *Twelve Against Empire: The Anti-Imperialists, 1898–1900* (New York, 1968), deals with intellectual and emotional sources of selected anti-imperialists; E. Berkeley Tompkins, *Anti-Imperialism in the United States: The Great Debate, 1890–1920* (Phil., 1970); Henry F. Graff, ed., *American Imperialism and the Philippine Insurrection* (Boston, 1969); and Bonifacio S. Salamanca, *The Filipino Reaction to American Rule, 1901–1913* (Hamden, Conn., 1968).

There is a considerable periodical literature on the war and related topics, of which the following are representative articles: Nancy L. O'Connor, "The Spanish-American War: A Re-evaluation of Its Causes," *Science and Society*, XXII (Spring, 1958), 129–143, which challenges the Pratt thesis on the businessman; Walter La Feber, "That 'Splendid Little War' in Historical Perspective," *Texas Quarterly*, XI (Winter, 1968), 89–98; John A. S. Grenville, "American Naval Preparations for War with Spain, 1896–1898," *Journal of American Studies*, II (April, 1968), 33–47; Paul S. Holbo, "Presidential Leadership in Foreign Affairs: William McKinley and the Turpie-Foraker Amendment," *American Historical Review*, LXII (July, 1967), 1321–1335; Holbo, "The Convergence of Minds and the Cuban Bond 'Conspiracy' of 1898," *Journal of American History*, LV (June, 1968), 54–72; H. Wayne Morgan, "The De Lome Letter: A New Appraisal," *Historian*, XXVI (Nov., 1963), 36–49; Lejeune Cummins, "The Formulation of the Platt Amendment," *The Americas*, XXIII (1967), 370–389; James H. Hitchman, "The Platt Amendment Revisited: A Bibliographical Survey," *ibid.*, pp. 343–369; Gilmore N. Ray, "Mexico and the Spanish-American War," *Hispanic-American Historical Review*, XLIII (Nov., 1963), 511–525; Christopher Lasch, "The Anti-Imperialists, the Philippines, and the Inequality of Man," *Journal of Southern History*, XXIV (Aug., 1958), 319–331; John W. Rollins, "The Anti-Imperialists, and Twentieth Century American Foreign Policy," *Studies on the Left*, III (No. 1, 1962), 9–25; Richard E. Welch, Jr., "Senator George Frisbie Hoar and the Defeat of Anti-Imperialism, 1898–1900," *Historian*, XXVI (May, 1964), 362–380; E. Berkeley Tompkins, "Scylla and Charybdis: The Anti-Imperialist Dilemma in the Election of 1900," *Pacific Historical Review*, XXXVI (May, 1967), 143–161; Tompkins, "The Old Guard: A Study of the Anti-Imperialist Leadership," *Historian*, XXX (May, 1968), 366–388; and Philip W. Kennedy, "The Racial Overtones of Imperialism as a Campaign Issue, 1900," *Mid-America*, XLVIII (July, 1966), 196–205.

CHAPTER FIFTEEN

A solid study touching on most important problems for the period is Bradford Perkins, *The Great Rapprochement: England and the United States, 1895–1914* (New York, 1968). On China and the Open Door see Stuart C. Miller, *American Ideas of a Special Relationship with China, 1784–1900* (Cambridge, Mass., 1968); Thomas McCormick, "Insular Imperialism and the Open Door: The China Market and the Spanish-American War," *Pacific Historical Review*, XXXII (May, 1963), 155–169; McCormick, *China Market: America's Quest for Informal Empire, 1893–1901* (Chicago, 1967); Paul A. Varg, "The Myth of the China Market, 1890–1914," *American Historical Review*, LXXIII (Feb., 1968), 742–758; Varg, *The Making of a Myth: The United States and China, 1897–1912* (East Lansing, Mich., 1968); Edmund S. Wehrle, *Britain, China, and the Antimissionary Riots, 1891–1900* (Minneapolis, 1966); Marilyn B. Young, "American Expansion, 1870–1900: The Far East," in Barton J. Bernstein, ed., *Towards a New Past: Dissenting Essays in American History* (New York, 1968), pp. 176–201; and Young, *The Rhetoric of Empire: American China Policy, 1895–1901* (Cambridge, Mass., 1969).

New studies dealing with Japanese relations are: John A. White, *The Diplomacy of the Russo-Japanese War* (Princeton, N.J., 1964); Raymond A. Esthus, *Theodore Roosevelt and Japan* (Seattle, 1966); Charles E. Neu, *An Uncertain Friendship: Theodore Roosevelt and Japan, 1906–1909* (Cambridge, Mass., 1967); Eugene P. Trani, *The Treaty of Portsmouth: An Adventure in American Diplomacy* (Lexington, Ken., 1969); Roger Daniels, *The Politics of Prejudice: The Anti-Japanese Movement in California and the Struggle for Japanese Exclusion* (Berkeley, 1962); Robert A. Hart, *The Great White Fleet: Its Voyage Around the World, 1907–1909* (Boston, 1965), and two articles; Charles E. Neu, "Theodore Roosevelt and American Involvement in the Far East, 1901–1909," *Pacific Historical Review*, XXXV (Nov., 1966), 433–449 and Edward B. Parsons, "Roosevelt's Containment of the Russo-Japanese War," *ibid.*, XXXVII (Feb., 1969), 21–44. See also Jongsuk Chay, "The Taft-Katsura Memorandum Reconsidered," *Pacific Historical Review*, XXXVI (Aug., 1968), 321–326; David H. Burton, *Theodore Roosevelt: Confident Imperialist* (Phil., 1968); and Raymond A. Esthus, *Theodore Roosevelt and the International Rivalries* (Waltham, Mass., 1970).

For Latin American problems, see David F. Healy, *The United States in Cuba, 1898–1902* (Madison, Wis., 1963); Allan R. Millet, *The Politics of Intervention: The Military Occupation of Cuba, 1906–1909* (Columbus, Ohio, 1968); Robert F. Smith, "Cuba: Laboratory for Dollar Diplomacy, 1898–1917," *Historian*, XXVIII (Aug., 1966), 586–609; Charles D. Ameringer, "Philippe Banau-Varilla: New Light on the Panama Canal Treaty," *Hispanic-American Historical Review*, XLVI (Feb., 1966), 28–52; Ameringer, "The Panama Canal Lobby of Philippe Banau-Varilla and William N. Cromwell," *American Historical Review*, LXVIII (Jan., 1963), 346–363; E. Bradford Burns, *The Unwritten Alliance: Rio Branco and Brazilian-American Relations* (New York, 1966); Paul S. Holbo, "Perilous Obscurity: Public Diplomacy and the Press in the Venezuela Crisis, 1902–1903," *Historian*, XXXII (May,

1970), 428–448; Paolo E. Coletta, "William Jennings Bryan and the United States-Colombia Impasse, 1903–1921," *Hispanic-American Historical Review*, XLVIII (Nov., 1967), 486–501; and A. L. Tibawi, *American Interests in Syria, 1800–1901: A Study of Educational, Literary and Religious Work* (Oxford, 1966). Titles for the preceding chapter are also useful for this one.

CHAPTER SIXTEEN

A new survey is Julius Pratt, *Challenge and Rejection: The United States and World Leadership, 1900–1921* (New York, 1967). On the Moroccan issue see Anthony F. Eastman, "The Algeciras Conference," *Southern Quarterly*, VII (Jan. 1969), 185–205 and George W. Collins, "The Lure of Morocco: A Sidelight on United States Economic and Foreign Policy, 1904–1912," *North Dakota Quarterly*, XXXVII (Autumn, 1969), 25–42. Other works touching on subjects within this chapter are: John P. Campbell, "Taft, Roosevelt, and the Arbitration Treaties of 1911," *Journal of American History*, LIII (Sept., 1966), 279–298; Robert R. Wilson, *et al., Canada-United States Treaty Relations* (Durham, N.C., 1963), a collection of essays covering various subjects; Alvin C. Gluek, "The Passamaquoddy Bay Treaty, 1910: A Diplomatic Sideshow in Canadian-American Relations," *Canadian Historical Review*, XLVII (March, 1966), 1–21; Alan J. Ward, "America and the Irish Problem, 1899–1921," *Irish Historical Studies* (March, 1968); Ward, *Ireland and Anglo-American Relations, 1899–1921* (London, 1969); Paolo E. Coletta, "Bryan, Anti-Imperialism, and Missionary Diplomacy," *Nebraska History*, XLIV (Sept., 1963), 167–187; Barton J. Bernstein and Franklin A. Leib, "Progressive Republican Senators and American Imperialism, 1898–1916: A Reappraisal," *Mid-America*, L (July, 1968), 163–205; John M. Cooper, Jr., "Progressivism and American Foreign Policy: A Reconsideration," *ibid.*, LI (Oct. 1969), 260–277; William S. Coker, "The Panama Canal Tolls Controversy: A Different Perspective," *Journal of American History*, LV (Dec., 1968), 555–564; and Dana G. Munro, *Intervention and Dollar Diplomacy in the Caribbean, 1900–1921* (Princeton, 1964).

For Asian policy see Dorothy Borg, ed., *Historians and American Far Eastern Policy* (New York, 1966); Kwang-Ching Liu, ed., *American Missionaries in China: Papers from Harvard Seminars* (Cambridge, Mass., 1966); Madeleine S. Chi, *China Diplomacy* (Cambridge, Mass., 1969); Chi, *The Chinese Question During the First World War* (Cambridge, Mass., 1969); Spencer C. Olin, Jr., "European Immigrant and Oriental Alien: Acceptance and Rejection by the California Legislature of 1913," *Pacific Historical Review*, XXXIV (Aug., 1966), 305–315; Poalo E. Coletta, "'The Most Thankless Task' Bryan and the California Alien Land Legislation," *Pacific Historical Review*, XXXVI (May, 1967), 163–187; Jerry Israel, "'For God, for China and for Yale'—The Open Door in Action," *American Historical Review*, LXXV (Feb., 1970), 796–807; and William R. Braisted, *The United States Navy in the Pacific, 1909–1922* (Austin, Tex., 1970). Other important studies are: John De Novo, "A Railroad for Turkey: The Chester Project, 1908–1913," *Business History Review*, XXXIII (Autmn, 1959), 300–329; De Novo, *American Interests and Policies in the Middle East, 1900–1939* (Minneapolis, 1963); and Naomi W. Cohen, "The Abrogation of the Russo-American Treaty of 1832," *Jewish Social Studies*, XXV (1963), 3–41. Material cited for previous chapters is frequently applicable to this one also.

CHAPTER SEVENTEEN

Noteworthy new books are: Paolo E. Coletta, *William Jennings Bryan* (3 vols., Lincoln, Nebraska, 1964–1969); David E. Cronon, ed., *The Cabinet Diaries of Josephus Daniels, 1913–1921* (Lincoln, Nebr., 1963); Peter A. R. Calvert, *The Mexican Revolution, 1910–1914: The Diplomacy of Anglo-American Conflict* (Cambridge, Eng., 1968); Kenneth J. Grieb, *The United States and Huerta* (Lincoln, Nebraska, 1969); and Herbert M. Mason, Jr., *The Great Pursuit* (New York, 1970), deals with Pershing's punitive expedition into Mexico.

The significant periodical literature includes: Paolo E. Coletta, "Secretary of State William Jennings Bryan and 'Deserving Democrats,'" *Mid-America*, XLVIII (April, 1966), 75–98; six articles by George W. Baker, "Ideals and Realities in the Wilson Administration's Relations with Honduras," *The Americas*, XXI (July, 1964), 3–19; "Woodrow Wilson's Use of the Nonrecognition Policy in Costa Rica," *The Americas*, XXII (July, 1965), 3–21; "The Woodrow Wilson Administration and Guatemalan Relations," *Historian*, XXVII (Feb., 1965), 155–169; "The Woodrow Wilson Administration and El Salvadorean Relations, 1913–1921," *Social Studies*, LVI (March, 1965), 97–103; "The Wilson Administration and Cuba, 1913–1921," *Mid-America*, XLVI (Jan., 1964), 48–63; and "Robert Lansing and the Purchase of the Danish West Indies," *Social Studies*, LVII (Feb., 1966), 64–71; Guy R. Donnell, "The United States Military Government at Veracruz, Mexico," in Thomas E. Cotner and Carlos E. Castañeda, eds., *Essays in Mexican History* (Austin, Tex., 1958), pp. 229–247; Walter V. and Marie V. Scholes, "Wilson, Grey, Huerta," *Pacific Historical Review*, XXXVII (May, 1968), 151–162; Peter A. R. Calvert, "The Murray Contract: An Episode in International Finance and Diplomacy," *ibid.*, XXXV (May, 1966), 203–244; Kenneth J. Grieb, "The Role of the Mexican Revolution in Contemporary American Policy," *Midwest Quarterly*, X (Winter, 1969), 113–129; and Daniel M. Smith, "Bainbridge Colby and the Good Neighbor Policy, 1902–1921," *Mississippi Valley Historical Review*, L (June, 1963), 56–78. See also overlapping material cited for previous chapters.

CHAPTER EIGHTEEN

An important new bibliographical essay is Daniel M. Smith, "National Interest and American Intervention, 1917: An Historiographical Appraisal," *Journal of American History*, LII (June, 1965), 5–24. An older essay Paul Birdsall, "Neutrality and Economic Pressures, 1914–1917," *Science Society*, III (Spring, 1939), 217–228, is one of the best revisionist pieces. Noteworthy new books are: Fritz Fischer, *Germany's Aims in the First World War* (New York, 1967), important for the background of American policy; Denna F. Fleming, *The Origins and Legacies of World War I* (Garden City, N.Y., 1968); W. B. Fowler, *British-American Relations, 1917–1918: The Role of Sir William Wiseman* (Princeton, N.J., 1969); two new volumes in Arthur S. Link's biography of Wilson: *Wilson: Confusions and Crises, 1915–1916* (Princeton, 1964) and *Wilson: Campaigns for Progressivism and Peace, 1916–1917* (Princeton, 1965); Daniel M. Smith, *The Great Departure: The United States and World War I, 1914–1920* (New York, 1965); N. Gordon Levin, Jr., *Woodrow Wilson and World Politics: America's Response to War and Revolution* (New York, 1968); Seward W. Livermore, *Politics in Ad-*

journed: Woodrow Wilson and the War Congress, 1916–1918 (Middletown, Conn., 1966); John M. Cooper, *The Vanity of Power: American Isolationism and World War I, 1914–1917* (Westport, Conn., 1969); Gaddis Smith, *Britain's Clandestine Submarines, 1914–1915* (New Haven, 1964); Sondra R. Herman, *Eleven Against War: Studies in American Internationalist Thought, 1898–1921* (Stanford, Calif., 1969); Warren I. Cohen, *The American Revisionists: The Lessons of Intervention in World War I* (Chicago, 1967); and Gregory Ross, *Walter Hines Page: Ambassador to the Court of St. James* (Lexington, Ken., 1970).

Especially useful in the extensive periodical literature are: Felice A. Bonadio, "The Failure of German Propaganda in the United States, 1914–17," *Mid-America*, XLI (Jan., 1959), 40–57; Walter I. Trattner, "Progressivism and World War I: A Reappraisal," *ibid.*, XLIV (July, 1962), 131–145; Dean R. Esslinger, "American, German and Irish Attitudes Toward Neutrality, 1914–1917: A Study of Catholic Minorities," *Catholic Historical Review*, LIII (July, 1967), 194–216; Edward Cuddy, "Irish-American Propagandists and American Neutrality, 1914–1917," *Mid-America*, XLIX (Oct., 1967), 252–275; William M. Leary, Jr., "Woodrow Wilson, Irish Americans, and the Election of 1916," *Journal of American History*, LIV (June, 1967), 57–72; Richard Lowitt, "The Armed-Ship Bill Controversy: A Legislative View," *Mid-America*, XLVI (Jan., 1964), 38–47; Gerald H. Davies, "The *Ancona* Affair: A Case of Preventive Diplomacy," *Journal of Modern History*, XXXVIII (Sept., 1966), 267–277; and Gregory Ross, "A New Look at the Case of the *Dacia*," *Journal of American History*, LV (Sept., 1968), 292–296.

CHAPTER NINETEEN

Worthwhile new books are: Edward M. Coffman, *The War to End All Wars: The American Military Experience in World War I* (New York, 1968); Charles Gilbert, *American Financing of World War I* (Westport, Conn., 1970); Joan M. Jensen, *The Price of Vigilance* (Chicago, 1968), deals with anti-espionage activities in the First World War; Lawrence E. Gelfand, *The Inquiry: American Preparations for Peace, 1917–1919* (New Haven, Conn., 1963); Christopher Lasch, *The American Liberals and the Russian Revolution* (New York, 1962); John M. Thompson, *Russia, Bolshevism, and the Versailles Peace* (Princeton, N.J., 1966); Charles Seymour, *Letters from the Paris Peace Conference*, ed. by Harold B. Whiteman, Jr. (New Haven, 1965); Arno J. Mayer, *Politics and Diplomacy of Peacemaking: Containment and Counterrevolution at Versailles, 1918–1919* (New York, 1967); Ivo J. Lederer, *Yugoslavia at the Peace Conference: A Study in Frontier-Making* (New Haven, 1963); Ralph A. Stone, *The Irreconcilables: The Fight Against the League of Nations* (Lexington, Ken., 1970); Joseph P. O'Grady, ed., *The Immigrants' Influence on Wilson's Peace Policies* (Lexington, Ken., 1967); Louis L. Gerson, *The Hyphenate in Recent American Politics and Diplomacy* (Lawrence, Kans., 1964); two studies by Warren F. Kuehl, *Hamilton Holt* (Gainesville, Fla., 1960) and *Seeking World Order: The United States and International Organization to 1920* (Nashville, Tenn., 1969); Daniel M. Smith, *Aftermath of War: Bainbridge Colby and Wilsonian Diplomacy, 1920–1921* (Phil., 1970); Harry N. Howard, *The King-Crane Commission: An American Inquiry in the Middle East* (Beirut, 1963); and Laurence Evans, *United States Policy and the Partition of Turkey, 1914–1924* (Baltimore, 1965). The following biographical studies touch on important diplomatic issues: Gene Smith, *When the Cheering Stopped: The Last Years of Woodrow Wilson* (New York, 1964); Lawrence W. Levine, *Defender of the Faith: William Jennings Bryan, the Last Decade, 1915–1925* (New York, 1965); Beatrice Farnsworth, *William C. Bullitt and the Soviet Union* (Bloomington, Ind., 1967); *Thomas Woodrow Wilson, Twenty-eighth President of the United States: A Psychological Study* (Boston, 1967), a study written in the thirties and refuted by Arthur S. Link, "The Case for Woodrow Wilson," *Harper's Magazine*, CCXXXIV (April, 1967), 85–93.

In the large periodical literature the following essays are among those worthy of note: Edwin A. Weinstein, "Woodrow Wilson's Neurological Illness," *Journal of American History*, LVII (Sept., 1970), 324–351; David Burner, "The Breakup of the Wilson Coalition of 1916," *Mid-America*, XLV (Jan., 1963), 18–35; Christopher Lasch, "American Intervention in Siberia: A Reinterpretation," *Political Science Quarterly*, LXXVII (June, 1962), 205–223; William A. Williams, "American Intervention in Russia, 1917–1920," *Studies on the Left*, III (Fall, 1963), 24–48; Keith L. Nelson, "What Colonel House Overlooked in the Armistice," *Mid-America*, LI (April, 1969), 75–91; John B. Posey, "David Hunter Miller as an Informal Diplomat: The Fiume Question at the Paris Peace Conference, 1919," *Southern Quarterly*, V (April, 1967), 251–272; Dragan R. Živojinović, "The Vatican, Woodrow Wilson, and the Dissolution of the Hapsburg Monarchy, 1914–1918," *Eastern European Quarterly*, III (March, 1969), 31–70; Leon E. Booth, "Anglo-American Pro-League Groups Lead Wilson, 1915–18," *Mid-America*, LI (April, 1969), 92–107; John H. Flannagan, Jr., "The Disillusionment of a Progressive: U.S. Senator David I. Walsh and the League of Nations Issue, 1918–1920," *New England Quarterly*, XLI (Dec., 1968), 483–504; John B. Duff, "The Versailles Treaty and the Irish-Americans," *Journal of American History*, LV (Dec., 1968), 582–598; Kent G. Redmond, "Henry L. Stimson and the Question of League Membership," *Historian*, XXV (Feb., 1963), 200–212; Kurt Wimer, "Woodrow Wilson Tries Conciliation: An Effort That Failed," *ibid.*, XXV (Aug., 1963), 419–438; Wimer, "Senator Hitchcock and the League of Nations," *Nebraska History*, XLIV (Sept., 1963), 189–204; and Richard L. Merritt, "Woodrow Wilson and the 'Great and Solemn Referendum,' 1920," *Review of Politics*, XXVII (Jan., 1965), 78–104. See also the additional readings for the previous chapter.

CHAPTER TWENTY

Two new surveys are: Selig Adler, *The Uncertain Giant, 1921–1941: American Foreign Policy Between Wars* (New York, 1965) and L. Ethan Ellis, *Republican Foreign Policy, 1921–1933* (New Brunswick, 1968). Other titles of value are: Roland N. Stromberg, *Collective Security and American Foreign Policy: From the League of Nations to NATO* (New York, 1963); Raymond B. Fosdick, *Letters on the League of Nations from the Files of Raymond B. Fosdick* (Princeton, 1966); Betty Glad, *Charles Evan Hughes and the Illusions of Innocence: A Study in American Diplomacy* (Urbana, Ill., 1966); Joseph Brandes, *Herbert Hoover and Economic Diplomacy: Department of Commerce Policy, 1921–1928* (Pittsburgh, 1962); Robert J. Maddox, *William E. Borah and American Foreign Policy* (Baton Rouge, La., 1969); Robert H. Ferrell, *Frank B. Kellogg; Henry L. Stimson* (New York, 1963); Gerald E. Wheeler, *Prelude to Pearl*

Harbor: The United States Navy and the Far East, 1921–1931 (Columbia, Mo., 1963); Akira Iriye, *After Imperialism: The Search for a New Order in the Far East, 1921–1931* (Cambridge, Mass., 1965); Iriye, *Across the Pacific: An Inner History of American-East Asian Relations* (New York, 1967), a sweeping interpretive study; Arnold H. Taylor, *American Diplomacy and the Narcotics Traffic, 1900–1939* (Durham, N.C., 1969); and Albert N. Tarulis, *American-Baltic Relations, 1918–1922: The Struggle over Recognition* (Washington, 1965). Two new biographical studies that contain insights on foreign policy are: Robert K. Murray, *The Harding Era* (Minneapolis, 1969) and Donald R. McCoy, *Calvin Coolidge: The Quiet President* (New York, 1967).

Important new essays are: Robert F. Smith, "American Foreign Relations, 1920–1924," in Barton J. Bernstein, ed., *Towards a New Past: Dissenting Essays in American History* (New York, 1968), pp. 202–262; Kurt and Sarah Wimer, "The Harding Administration, the League of Nations, and the Separate Peace Treaty," *Review of Politics*, XXIX (Jan., 1967), 13–24; Richard D. Burns, "Inspection of the Mandates, 1919–1941," *Pacific Historical Review*, XXXVII (Nov., 1968), 445–462; Ernest Andrade, "The United States Navy and the Washington Conference," *Historian* XXI (May, 1969), 345–363; Merze Tate and Fidele Foy, "More Light on the Abrogation of the Anglo-Japanese Alliance," *Political Science Quarterly*, LXXIV (Dec., 1959), 532–554; M. G. Fry, "The North Atlantic Triangle and the Abrogation of the Anglo-Japanese Alliance," *Journal of Modern History*, XXXIX (March, 1967), 46–64; and Richard D. Burns, "International Arms Inspection Policies Between World Wars, 1919–1934," *Historian*, XXXI (Aug., 1969), 583–603. See also the new notes for the preceding chapter.

CHAPTER TWENTY-ONE

Important new studies on Asian relations are: Dorothy Borg, *The United States and the Far Eastern Crisis of 1933–1938* (Cambridge, Mass., 1964); Russell D. Buhite, *Nelson J. Johnson and American Policy Toward China, 1925–1941* (East Lansing, Mich., 1968); James C. Thomson, Jr., *While China Faced West: American Reformers in Nationalist China, 1928–1937* (Cambridge, Mass., 1969); John Carter Vincent: *The Extraterritorial System in China: Final Phase* (Cambridge, Mass., 1970); Takehiko Yoshihashi, *Conspiracy at Mukden: The Rise of the Japanese Military* (New Haven, 1963); Sadako N. Ogata, *Defiance in Manchuria: The Making of Japanese Foreign Policy, 1931–1932* (Berkeley, 1964); James B. Crowley, *Japan's Quest for Autonomy: National Security and Foreign Policy, 1930–1938* (Princeton, 1966); Armin Rappaport, *Henry L. Stimson and Japan, 1931–1933* (Chicago, 1963); Thaddeus V. Tuleja, *Statesmen and Admirals* (New York, 1963); and Theodore Friend, *Between Two Empires: The Ordeal of the Philippines, 1929–1946* (New Haven, 1965). On relations with Russia see: Peter G. Filene, *Americans and the Soviet Experiment, 1917–1933: American Attitudes toward Russia from the February Revolution until Diplomatic Recognition* (Cambridge, Mass., 1967); Donald G. Bishop, *The Roosevelt-Litvinov Agreements: The American View* (Syracuse, 1965); Paul W. Blackstock, *The Secret Road to World War II: Soviet versus Western Intelligence, 1921–1939* (Chicago, 1969); and Edward Bennett, *Recognition of Russia: An American Foreign Policy Dilemma* (Waltham, Mass., 1969).

For relations with Latin America there are: Gordon Connell-Smith, *The Inter-American System* (London, 1966); Bryce Wood, *The United States and Latin American Wars, 1932–1942* (New York, 1966); Elizabeth M. Rice, *The Diplomatic Relations between the United States and Mexico as Affected by the Struggle for Religious Liberty in Mexico, 1925–1929* (Washington, 1959); James C. Carey, *Peru and the United States, 1900–1962* (Notre Dame, 1964); William Kammen, *A Search for Stability: United States Diplomacy Toward Nicaragua, 1925–1933* (Notre Dame, 1968); and Alton Frye, *Nazi Germany and the American Hemisphere, 1933–1941* (New Haven, 1967). See also Richard N. Kottman, *Reciprocity and the North Atlantic Triangle, 1932–1938* (Ithaca, N.Y., 1968).

Noteworthy periodical literature is: Russell D. Buhite, "Nelson Johnson and American Policy toward China, 1925–1928," *Pacific Historical Review*, XXXV (Nov., 1966), 451–465; Kell F. Mitchell, Jr., "Diplomacy and Prejudice: The Morris-Shidehara Negotiations, 1920–1921," *ibid.*, XXXIX (Feb., 1970), 85–104; Gerald E. Wheeler, "Republican Philippine Policy, 1921–1933," *ibid.*, XXVII (Nov., 1959), 377–390; Claude E. Fike, "Aspects of the New American Recognition Policy toward Russia following World War I," *Southern Quarterly*, IV (Oct., 1965), 1–16; Robert E. Bowers, "Hull, Russian Subversion in Cuba, and Recognition of the U.S.S.R." *Journal of American History*, LIII (Dec., 1966), 542–554; Arthur P. Whitaker, "The U.S. in Latin America to 1933: An Overview," *Current History,* LVI (June, 1969), 321–326; D. B. Cooper, "The Withdrawal of the United States from Haiti 1928–1934," *Journal of Inter-American Studies*, V (1963), 83–101; Dana G. Munro, "The American Withdrawal from Haiti, 1929–1934," *Hispanic-American Historical Review*, XLIX (Feb., 1969), 1–26; Robert H. Ferrell, "Repudiation of a Repudiation," *Journal of American History*, LI (March, 1965), 669–673, deals with the J. Reuben Clark Memorandum; Lester D. Langley, "Negotiating New Treaties with Panama, 1936," *Hispanic-American Historical Review*, XLVII (May, 1968), 220–223; Herbert S. Klein, "American Oil Companies in Latin America: The Bolivian Experience," *Inter-American Economic Affairs*, XVIII (Autumn, 1964), 47–72; Richard N. Kottman, "The Canadian-American Trade Agreement of 1935," *Journal of American History*, LII (Sept., 1965), 275–296; and Paul M. Holsinger, "The '*I'm Alone*' Controversy: A Study in Inter-American Diplomacy, 1929–1935," *Mid-America*, L (Oct., 1968), 305–313.

CHAPTER TWENTY-TWO

Noteworthy new studies dealing with economic policy are: Herbert Feis, *1933: Characters in Crisis* (Boston, 1966), which deals with the World Economic Conference, Lloyd C. Gardner, *Economic Aspects of New Deal Diplomacy* (Madison, Wis., 1964), and Carl P. Parrini, *Heir to Empire: United States Economic Diplomacy, 1916–1923* (Pittsburgh, 1969). On aspects of isolationism see Manfred Jonas, *Isolationism in America, 1935–1941* (Ithaca, N.Y., 1966); John E. Wiltz, *In Search of Peace: The Senate Munitions Inquiry, 1934–36* (Baton Rouge, La., 1963); Wiltz, *From Isolation to War, 1931–1941* (New York, 1968); Wayne S. Cole, *Senator Gerald P. Nye and American Foreign Relations* (Minneapolis, 1962); Julius W. Pratt, *Cordell Hull* (2 vols., New York, 1964); and Charles C. Alexander, *Nationalism in American Thought, 1930–1945* (Chicago, 1969). For the Ethiopian and Spanish wars see Brice Harris, Jr., *The United States and the Italo-Ethiopian Crisis* (Stanford, Calif., 1964); George W. Baer, *The*

Coming of the Italian-Ethiopian War (Cambridge, Mass., 1967); Angelo De Boca, *Ethiopian War, 1935–1941*, trans. by P. D. Cummins (Chicago, 1969); Allen Guttman, *The Wound in the Heart: America and the Spanish Civil War* (New York, 1962); and Richard P. Traina, *American Diplomacy and the Spanish Civil War* (Bloomington, Ind., 1968). On German relations see James V. Compton, *The Swastika and the Eagle: Hitler, the United States and the Origins of World War II* (Boston, 1967); and Arnold, A. Offner, *American Appeasement: United States Foreign Policy and Germany, 1933–1938* (Cambridge, Mass., 1969). For Asian relations there are: Johanna M. Meskill, *Hitler and Japan: The Hollow Alliance* (New York, 1966); Manny J. Koginos, *The Penay Incident: Prelude to War* (Lafayette, Ind., 1967); and Hamilton D. Perry, *The Panay Incident: Prelude to Pearl Harbor* (New York, 1969). Important biographical studies and memoirs are: James M. Burns, *Roosevelt: The Soldier of Fortune* (New York, 1970); John M. Blum, *From the Morgenthau Diaries: Years of Crisis, 1928–1938* (Boston, 1959), *Years of Urgency, 1938–1941* (Boston, 1965); *The Memoirs of Anthony Eden: Facing the Dictators* (Boston, 1962); Fred L. Israel, *Nevada's Key Pittman* (Lincoln, Nebr., 1963); Robert Dallek, *Democrat and Diplomat: The Life of William E. Dodd* (New York, 1968); George F. Kennan, *Memoirs, 1925–1950* (Boston, 1967); and Kennan, *From Prague to Munich: Diplomatic Papers, 1938–1940* (Princeton, 1968). See also Keith Eubank, *The Origins of World War II* (New York, 1969).

Illuminating periodical literature is: Elliot A. Rosen, "Intranationalism *vs.* Internationalism: The Interregnum Struggle of the Sanctity of the New Deal," *Political Science Quarterly*, LXXXI (July, 1966), 274–297; Arthur W. Schatz, "The Anglo-American Trade Agreement and Cordell Hull's Search for Peace, 1936–1938," *Journal of American History*, LVII (June, 1970), 85–103; John C. Vinson, "War Debts and Peace Legislation: The Johnson Act of 1934," *Mid-America*, L (July, 1968), 206–222; Richard D. Burns and W. Addams Dixon, "Foreign Policy and the 'Democratic Myth': The Debate on the Ludlow Amendment." *Mid-America*, XLVII (Oct., 1965), 288–306; Walter R. Griffin, "Louis Ludlow and the War Referendum Crusade, 1935–1941," *Indiana Magazine of History*, LXIV (Dec., 1968), 267–288; Travis B. Jacobs, "Roosevelt's 'Quarantine Speech,'" *Historian*, XXIV (Aug., 1962), 483–502, argues that newspaper and public opinion supported Roosevelt's stand; Robert A. Friedlander, "New Light on the Anglo-American Reaction to the Ethiopian War, 1935–1936," *Mid-America*, XLV (April, 1963), 115–125; four essays by John P. Diggins, "Flirtation with Fascism: American Pragmatic Liberals and Mussolini's Italy," *American Historical Review*, LXXI (Jan., 1966), 487–506; "Mussolini and America: Hero Worship, Charisma, and the 'Vulgar Talent,'" *Historian* (Aug., 1966), 559–585; "American Catholics and Italian Fascism," *Journal of Contemporary History*, II (Oct., 1967), 51–58; and "The Italo-American Anti-Fascist Opposition," *Journal of American History*, LIV (Dec., 1967), 579–598; J. David Valaik, "Catholics, Neutrality, and the Spanish Embargo, 1937–1939," *ibid.*, LIV (June, 1967), 73–85; Robert Dallek, "Beyond Tradition: The Diplomatic Careers of William E. Dodd and George S. Messersmith, 1933–1938," *South Atlantic Quarterly*, LXVI (Spring, 1967), 233–244; Joachim Remak, "'Friends of the New Germany': The Bund and German-American Relations," *Journal of Modern History*, XXXIX (March, 1957), 38–41; Gerhard L. Weinberg, "Hitler's Image of the United States," *American Historical Review*, LXIX (July, 1964), 1006–1021; Warren F. Kimball, "Dieckhoff and America: A German's View of German-American Relations, 1937–1941," *Historian*, XXVII (Feb., 1965), 218–243; Les K.

Alder and Thomas G. Paterson, "Red Fascism: The Merger of Nazi Germany and Soviet Russia in the American Image of Totalitarianism, 1930's–1950's," *American Historical Review*, LXXV (April, 1970), 1046–1064; Bernard Sternsher, "The Stimson Doctrine: F.D.R. versus Moley and Tugwell," *Pacific Historical Review*, XXXI (Aug., 1962), 281–289; and James B. Crowley, "A Reconsideration of the Marco Polo Bridge Incident," *Journal of Asian Studies*, XXII (May, 1963), 227–229. The readings for the previous chapters are frequently pertinent to this one.

CHAPTER TWENTY-THREE

Among the recent noteworthy books are: Lawrence Lafore, *The End of Glory: An Interpretation of the Origins of World War II* (Phil., 1970); J. R. Fehrenbach, *F.D.R.'s Undeclared War, 1939–1941* (New York, 1967); A. A. Hoehling, *America's Road to War, 1939–1941* (New York, 1970); Robert A. Divine, *The Reluctant Belligerent: American Entry into World War II* (New York, 1965); Mark L. Chadwin, *The Hawks of World War II* (Chapel Hill, N.C., 1968); David S. Wyman, *Paper Walls: America and the Refugee Crisis, 1938–1941* and Arthur D. Morris, *While Six Million Died: A Chronicle of American Apathy* (New York, 1968) deal with Nazi persecution of Jews, and American policy toward Jewish refugees; Saul Friedlander, *Prelude to Downfall: Hitler and the United States, 1939–1941* (New York, 1967); Theodore A. Wilson, *The First Summit: Roosevelt and Churchill at Placentia Bay, 1941* (Boston, 1969); Douglas G. Anglin, *The St. Pierre and Miquelon Affair of 1941: A Study in Diplomacy of the North Atlantic Quadrangle* (Toronto, 1966); Philip Goodhart, *Fifty Ships that Saved the World: The Foundation of the Anglo-American Alliance* (New York, 1965); Herbert S. Parmet and Marie B. Hecht, *Never Again: A President Runs for a Third Term* (New York, 1968), story of Roosevelt against Willkie, 1940; Warren F. Kimball, *The Most Unsordid Act: Lend-Lease, 1939–1941* (Baltimore, 1969); Robert H. Jones, *The Roads to Russia: United States Lend-Lease to the Soviet Union* (Norman, Okla., 1969); Charles A. Lindbergh, *The Wartime Journals of Charles A. Lindbergh* (New York, 1970); Fred L. Israel, ed., *The War Diary of Breckinridge Long: Selections from the Years 1939–1944* (Lincoln, Nebr., 1966); Nobutaka Ike, ed., *Japans Decision for War: Records of the 1941 Policy Conferences* (Stanford, Calif., 1967); Paul S. Burtness and Warren U. Ober, eds., *The Puzzle of Pearl Harbor* (Evanston, Ill., 1962); a collection of documents; Adrienne D. Hytier, *Two Years of French Foreign Policy: Vichy, 1940–1942* (Geneva, 1958); Ladislas Farago, *The Broken Seal: The Story of "Operation Magic" and the Pearl Harbor Disaster* (New York, 1967); Leonard Baker, *Roosevelt and Pearl Harbor* (New York, 1970); Gerald D. Nash, *United States Oil Policy, 1890–1964: Business and Government in Twentieth Century America* (Pittsburgh, 1968). Two biographical studies: Richard J. Whalen, *The Founding Father: The Story of Joseph P. Kennedy* (New York, 1964), for his role as ambassador to Britain, and Waldo H. Henrichs, Jr., *American Ambassador: Joseph C. Grew and the Development of the American Diplomatic Tradition* (Boston, 1966); and a valuable collection of documents, Edgar B. Nixon, ed., *Franklin D. Roosevelt and Foreign Affairs* (3 vols., Cambridge, Mass., 1969).

For scholarly periodical literature see, Ernest R. May, "Nazi Germany and the United States: A Review Essay," *Journal of Modern History*, XLI (June, 1969), 207–214; Julius W.

Pratt, "The Ordeal of Cordell Hull," *Review of Politics*, XXVIII (Jan., 1966), 76–98; William M. Tuttle, Jr., "Aid-to-the-Allies Short-of-War versus American Intervention, 1940: A Reappraisal of William Allen White's Leadership," *Journal of American History*, LVI (March, 1970), 840–858; Raymond A. Esthus, "President Roosevelt's Commitment to Britain to Intervene in a Pacific War," *Mississippi Valley Historical Review*, L (June, 1963), 28–38; James H. Herzog, "Influence of the United States Navy in the Embargo of Oil to Japan, 1940–1941," *Pacific Historical Review*, XXXV (Aug., 1966), 317–328; John H. Boyle, "The Drought-Walsh Mission to Japan," *ibid.*, XXXIV (May, 1965), 141–161; and Richard W. Steele, "Preparing the Public for War: Efforts to Establish a National Propaganda Agency, 1940–41," *American Historical Review*, LXXV (Oct., 1970), 1640–1653. See also citations for previous chapters.

CHAPTER TWENTY-FOUR

Important general studies are: Robert A. Divine, *Roosevelt and World War II* (Baltimore, 1969); Divine, *Second Chance: The Triumph of Internationalism in America during World War II* (New York, 1967); Gaddis Smith, *American Diplomacy during the Second World War, 1941–1945* (New York, 1965); Willard Range, *Franklin D. Roosevelt's World Order* (Athens, Ga., 1959); Nicholas Halasz, *Roosevelt through Foreign Eyes* (Princeton, 1961); Gabriel Kolko, *The Politics of War: The World and United States Foreign Policy, 1943–1945* (New York, 1969), a scholarly revisionist critique of American policy; Lloyd C. Gardner, *Architects of Illusion: Men and Ideas in American Foreign Policy, 1941–1949* (Chicago, 1970); William L. Neumann, *After Victory: Churchill, Roosevelt, Stalin and the Making of the Peace* (New York, 1967); and Paul Dukes, *The Emergence of the Super-Powers: A Short Comparative History of the U.S.A. and U.S.S.R.* (London, 1970). For the Mediterranean area see Norman Kogan, *Italy and the Allies* (Cambridge, Mass., 1956), the only book on its subject, and a good one; Herbert Feis, *The Spanish Story: Franco and the Nations at War* (New York, 1948); and Milton Viorst, *Hostile Allies: F.D.R. and Charles de Gaulle* (New York, 1965).

Other significant specialized studies are: Kent R. Greenfield, *American Strategy in World War II: A Reconsideration* (Baltimore, 1963), deals with military history; Keith Eubank, *The Summit Conferences 1919–1960* (Norman, Okla., 1966); Diane S. Clemens, *Yalta* (New York, 1970), the fullest, deepest, analysis; Stephen E. Ambrose, *Eisenhower and Berlin, 1945: The Decision to Halt at the Elbe* (New York, 1967); Allen Dulles, *The Secret Surrender* (New York, 1966), recounts the maneuvering for Axis surrender in northern Italy; Anthony Kubek, *How the Far East Was Lost: American Policy and the Creation of Communist China, 1941–1949* (Chicago, 1963); Tang Tsou, *America's Failure in China, 1941–1950* (Chicago, 1963); George E. Taylor, *The Philippines and the United States: Problems of Partnership* (New York, 1964); Herbert Feis, *The Atomic Bomb and the End of World War II* (Princeton, 1966), a new version of *Japan Subdued*; Robert C. Batchelder, *The Irreversible Decision, 1939–1950* (Boston, 1962), deals with the building and use of atomic bombs; Martin F. Herz, *Beginnings of the Cold War* (Bloomington, Ind., 1966); Gar Alperovitz, *Atomic Diplomacy: Hiroshima and Potsdam: The Use of the Atomic Bomb and the American Confrontation with Soviet Power* (New York, 1965); Lansing Lamont, *Day of Trinity* (New York, 1965); Len Giovannetti and

Fred Freed, *The Decision to Drop the Bomb* (New York, 1965); Lawrence S. Wittner, *Rebels Against War: The American Peace Movement, 1941–1960* (New York, 1969); Davis R. B. Ross, *Preparing for Ulysses: Politics and Veterans During World War II* (New York, 1969); and Richard L. Walker and George Curry, *E. R. Stettinius, Jr.; James F. Byrnes* (New York, 1965). Noteworthy personal papers and memoirs are: Alfred D. Chandler, Jr., ed., *The Papers of Dwight David Eisenhower: The War Years* (5 vols., Baltimore, 1970); John M. Blum, *From the Morgenthau Diaries: Years of War, 1941–1945* (Boston, 1967); Robert Murphy, *Diplomat Among Warriors* (Garden City, N.Y., 1964); Lord Moran, *Churchill: Taken from the Diaries of Lord Moran* (Boston, 1966); and Harold Macmillan, *The Blast of War, 1939–1945* (New York, 1968). See also Daniel R. Beaver, ed., *Some Pathways in Twentieth Century History: Essays in Honor of Reginald Charles McGrane* (Detroit, 1969) for several essays on foreign policy.

In the periodical literature see: Richard M. Leighton, "Overlord Revisited: An Interpretation of American Strategy in the European War, 1942–1944," *American Historical Review*, LXVIII (July, 1963); John P. Diggins, "The American Writers, Fascism, and the Liberation of Italy," *American Quarterly*, XVIII (Winter, 1966), 599–614; Robert H. McNeal, "Roosevelt through Stalin's Spectacles," *International Journal*, XVIII (1963), 194–206; Donald R. McCoy, "Republican Opposition during Wartime, 1941–1945," *Mid-America*, XLIX (July, 1967), 174–189; Athan Theoharis, "James F. Byrnes: Unwitting Yalta Myth-Maker," *Political Science Quarterly*, LXXXI (Dec., 1966), 581–592; John P. Glennon, "'This Time Germany Is a Defeated Nation': The Doctrine of Unconditional Surrender and Some Unsuccessful Attempts to Alter It, 1943–1944," in Gerald N. Grob., ed., *Statesmen and Statecraft of the Modern West: Essays in Honor of Dwight E. Lee and H. Donaldson Jordan* (Barre, Mass., 1967), pp. 109–151; Walter L. Dorn, "The Debate over American Occupation Policy in Germany in 1944–1945," *Political Science Quarterly*, LXXII (Dec., 1957), 481–501; Donald G. Gillin, "China and the Foreigner, 1911 to 1950," *South Atlantic Quarterly*, LXVIII (Spring, 1969), 208–219; Russell D. Buhite, "Patrick J. Hurley and the Yalta Far Eastern Agreement," *Pacific Historical Review*, XXXVII (Aug., 1968), 343–353; Herbert A. Fine, "The Liquidation of World War II in Thailand," *Pacific Historical Review*, XXXV (Aug., 1966), 347–349; George C. Herring, Jr., "Lend-Lease to Russia and the Origins of the Cold War, 1944–1945," *Journal of American History*, LVI (June, 1969), 93–114; Thomas G. Paterson, "The Abortive American Loan to Russia and the Origins of the Cold War, 1943–1946," *ibid.* (June, 1969), 70–92; and Stephen G. Xydis, "America, Britain and the U.S.S.R. in the Greek Arena, 1944–1947," *Political Science Quarterly*, LXXVIII (Dec., 1963), 581–596. Readings for preceding chapters also contain items useful for this one.

CHAPTER TWENTY-FIVE

There is now a considerable scholarly and polemical literature on the origins of the cold war, its causes, and who was basically responsible for launching it. Most of the polemics come from "revisionist" and New Left historians who attack the writings of "traditionalists" or "liberal" scholars. Essentially the conventional view blames the Soviets for initiating the cold war; the revisionist approach places the onus on American leaders. Important revisionist studies by Alperovitz, Gardner, Kolko, and others are cited in the preceding chapters.

Norman Graebner, "Cold War Origins and the Continuing Debate: A Review of Recent Literature," *Journal of Conflict Resolution*, XIII (March, 1969), 123–132 is a perceptive bibliographical analysis. An excellent critique of cold war scholarship, particularly of revisionism, is Charles S. Maier, "Revisionism and Beyond: Considerations on the Origins of the Cold War," *Perspectives in American History*, IV (Cambridge, Mass., 1970), 313–347. Noteworthy books are: Frederick L. Schuman, *The Cold War: Retrospect and Prospect* (Baton Rouge, La., 1962), revisionist; Desmond Donelly, *Struggle for the World: The Cold War, 1917–1965* (New York, 1965), revisionist; David Horowitz, *The Free World Colossus* (New York, 1965); Martin F. Herz, *Beginnings of the Cold War* (Bloomington, Ind., 1966); Dexter Perkins, *The Diplomacy of a New Age: Major Issues in U.S. Policy Since 1945* (Bloomington, Ind., 1967), conventional; Walter La Feber, *America, Russia, and the Cold War, 1945–1966* (New York, 1967); Louis J. Halle, *The Cold War as History* (London, 1967); Paul Seabury, *The Rise and Decline of the Cold War* (New York, 1967); André Fontaine, *History of the Cold War*, trans. by D. D. Paige and Renaud Bruce (2 vols., New York, 1968–69), by a French journalist; Paul Y. Hammond, *The Cold War Years: American Foreign Policy Since 1945* (New York, 1969), a brief survey; Gar Alperovitz, *Cold War Essays* (New York, 1970); Lloyd C. Gardner, Arthur M. Schlesinger, Jr., and Hans Morgenthau, *The Origins of the Cold War* (Waltham, Mass., 1970); Robert E. Osgood, *et al.*, *America and the World: From the Truman Doctrine to Vietnam* (Baltimore, 1970); Herbert Feis, *From Trust to Terror: The Onset of the Cold War, 1945–1950* (New York, 1970); and Thomas G. Paterson, ed., *Cold War Critics: Alternatives to American Foreign Policy in the Truman Period* (Chicago, 1970). For interpretive periodical literature see Staughton Lynd, "How the Cold War Began," *Commentary*, XXX (Nov., 1960), 379–389; Arthur Schlesinger, Jr., "Origins of the Cold War," *Foreign Affairs*, XLV (Oct., 1967), 22–52; William A. Williams, "The Cold War Revisionists," *Nation*, CCV (Nov. 13, 1967), a rebuttal to Schlesinger; Christopher Lasch, "The Cold War: Revisited and Re-Visioned," *New York Times Magazine* (Jan. 14, 1968), 26ff; and Joseph R. Starobin, "Origins of the Cold War: The Communist Dimension," *Foreign Affairs*, XLVII (July, 1969), 681–696. Other works that touch on cold war problems are: Cabell Phillips, *The Truman Presidency: The History of a Triumphant Succession* (New York, 1966); Barton J. Bernstein and Allen J. Matusow, eds., *The Truman Administration: A Documentary History* (New York, 1966); Robert H. Ferrell, *George C. Marshall* (New York, 1966); Barton J. Bernstein, ed., *Politics and Policies of the Truman Administration* (Chicago, 1970), contains several essays on foreign policy; David S. McLellan and John W. Reuss, "Foreign and Military Policies," in Richard S. Kirkendall, ed., *The Truman Period as a Research Field* (Columbia, Mo., 1967), pp. 15–85; Herbert Druks, *Harry S. Truman and the Russians, 1945–1953* (New York, 1966); Joseph L. Lieberman, *The Scorpion and the Tarantula: The Struggle to Control Atomic Weapons, 1945–1949* (Boston, 1970); and Anatol Rapoport, *The United States and the Soviet Union: Perceptions of Soviet-American Relations Since World War II* (New York, 1970).

For the German problem there are: John Gimbel, *A German Community under American Occupation: Marburg, 1945–1952* (Stanford, Calif., 1961); Gimbel, *The American Occupation of Germany: Politics and the Military, 1945–1949* (Stanford, Calif., 1968); Eugene Davidson, *The Trial of the Germans: An Account of the Twenty-Two Defendants Before the International Military Tribunal at Nuremberg* (New York, 1966); William J. Bosch, *Judgment on Nuremberg: American Attitudes toward the Major German War-Crime Trials* (Chapel Hill, N.C., 1970); and

William M. Franklin, "Zonal Boundaries and Access to Berlin," *World Politics*, XVI (Oct., 1963), 1–31. On Italian peacemaking and cold war policy, see F. Lee Benns, "The Two Paris Peace Conferences of the Twentieth Century," in Dwight E. Lee and George E. McReynolds, eds., *Essays in History and International Relations*... (Worcester, Mass., 1949), pp. 153–170; Jean-Baptiste Duroselle, *Le conflit de Trieste, 1943–1954* (Brussels, 1966); and Massimo Bonanni, ed., *La politica estera della republica italiana* (3 vols., Milan, 1967), containing essays by various scholars. Works on other topics in this chapter are: Lincoln P. Bloomfield, *The United Nations and U.S. Foreign Policy* (Boston, 1960); Francis Duncan, "Atomic Energy and Anglo-American Relations, 1946–1954," *Orbis*, XII (Winter, 1969), 1188–1203; Lawrence A. Kaplan, "The United States and the Origins of NATO, 1946–1949," *Review of Politics*, XXXI (April, 1969), 210–222; John J. McCloy, *The Atlantic Alliance: Its Origin and Future* (New York, 1969); Carl N. Degler, "The Great Revolution in American Foreign Policy," *Virginia Quarterly Review*, XXXVIII (Summer, 1962), 380–399, the story of the Marshall Plan; and Harold L. Hitchens, "Influences on the Congressional Decision to Pass the Marshall Plan," *Western Political Quarterly*, XXI (March, 1968), 51–68. Important memoirs or accounts by participants are: Dean Acheson, *Present at the Creation: My Years in the State Department* (New York, 1969); Charles E. Bohlen, *The Transformation of American Foreign Policy* (New York, 1969); and Harold Macmillan, *Tides of Fortune, 1945–1955* (New York, 1969). The readings for previous chapters also contain material relevant to this one.

CHAPTER TWENTY-SIX

On China, her revolution, and American relations see the works by Kubek and Tang Tsou cited for chapter twenty-four, and Arthur N. Young, *China and the Helping Hand, 1937–1945* (Cambridge, Mass., 1963); John F. Melby, *The Mandate of Heaven: Record of a Civil War: China, 1945–1949* (Toronto, 1968); John R. Beal, *Marshall in China* (New York, 1970); Joseph C. Keeley, *The China Lobby Man: The Story of Alfred Kohlberg* (New Rochelle, N.Y., 1969). Two studies on how Americans perceive China are: Harold R. Isaacs, *Scratches on Our Minds: The American Image of China and India* (New York, 1958) and Archibald T. Steele, *The American People and China* (New York, 1966). On the occupation of Japan see Shigeru Yoshida, *The Yoshida Memoirs: The Story of Japan in Crisis* (Boston, 1962), by a former premier of the era, and Herbert Feis, *Contest over Japan* (New York, 1967).

New studies on the Korean War are: Martin Lichterman, *To the Yalu and Back* (Montgomery, Ala., 1963); David Rees, *Korea: The Limited War* (New York, 1964); Douglas MacArthur, *Reminiscences* (New York, 1964); Richard H. Rovere and Arthur Schlesinger, Jr., *The MacArthur Controversy and American Foreign Policy* (New York, 1965), a revision of their 1951 book; Soon Sung Cho, *Korea in World Politics, 1940–1950: An Evaluation of American Responsibility* (Berkeley, Calif., 1967); Matthew B. Ridgway, *The Korean War* (Garden City, N.Y., 1967); Ronald J. Caridi, *The Korean War and American Politics: The Republican Party as a Case Study* (Phil., 1968); Glenn D. Paige, *The Korean Decision, June 24–30, 1950* (New York, 1968); J. Lawton Collins, *War in Peacetime: The History and Lessons of Korea* (New York, 1969); Morton H. Halperin, "The Limiting Process in the Korean War," *Political Science Quarterly*, LXXVIII (March, 1963), 13–39; David S. McLellan, "Dean

Acheson and the Korean War," *Political Science Quarterly*, LXXXIII (March, 1968), 16–39; Ronald J. Caridi, "The G.O.P. and the Korean War," *Pacific Historical Review*, XXXVII (Nov., 1968), 423–443; and Charles A. Lofgren, "Mr. Truman's War: A Debate and Its Aftermath," *Review of Politics*, XXXI (April, 1969), 223–241. Two studies that show the influence of domestic politics and fear of communism on foreign policy are: Earl Latham, *The Communist Controversy in Washington: From New Deal to McCarthy* (Cambridge, Mass., 1966) and Robert Griffith, *The Politics of Fear: Joseph R. McCarthy and the Senate* (Lexington, Ken., 1970).

CHAPTER TWENTY-SEVEN

Edwin Lieuwen, *U.S. Policy in Latin America: Short History* (New York, 1965) is a new survey. Ann Van Wynen Thomas and A. J. Thomas, Jr., *The Organization of American States* (Dallas, Tex., 1963) analyzes the regional organization; and Dexter Perkins, *The United States and the Caribbean* (rev. ed., Cambridge, Mass., 1966), is an older work brought up to date. The following are commentaries, usually on the contemporary situation: William Benton, *The Voice of Latin America* (rev. ed., New York, 1965); Adolph A. Berle, *Latin America: Diplomacy and Reality* (New York, 1962); Salvador de Madariaga, *Latin America between the Eagle and the Bear* (New York, 1962); Philip A. Ray, *South Wind Red: Our Hemispheric Crisis* (Chicago, 1962); Milton S. Eisenhower, *The Wine is Bitter: The United States and Latin America* (New York, 1963); and Lincoln Gordon, *A New Deal for Latin America: The Alliance for Progress* (Cambridge, Mass., 1963). See also Ernest R. May, "The Alliance for Progress in Historical Perspective," *Foreign Affairs*, XLI (July, 1963), 757–774 and Francis J. Michael, "The United States and the Act of Chapultepec," *Southwestern Social Science Quarterly*, XLL (1964), 249–257. Two books that show how relations between countries are affected by basically nonpolitical controversies are: Norris Hundley, *Dividing the Waters: A Century of Controversy between the United States and Mexico* (Berkely, Calif., 1966), deals with the Rio Grande boundary, and Manuel A. Machado, Jr., *Aftosa: A Historical Survey of Foot-and-Mouth Disease and Inter-American Relations* (New York, 1969), stresses relations with Argentina. For Canadian relations, see John S. Dickey, ed., *The United States and Canada* (Englewood Cliffs, N.J., 1964). On relations with Cuba see Ruby H. Phillips, *Cuba: Island of Paradox* (New York, 1959); C. Wright Mills, *Listen Yankee!* (New York, 1960); Leo Huberman and P. M. Sweezy, *Cuba: Anatomy of a Revolution* (New York, 1960); William A. Williams, *The United States, Cuba, and Castro* (New York, 1962); James Daniel, *Cuba: The First Soviet Satellite in the Americas* (New York, 1961); and Earl E. T. Smith, *The Fourth Floor: An Account of the Castro Communist Revolution* (New York, 1962), by a former ambassador to Cuba.

CHAPTER TWENTY-EIGHT

The most comprehensive book on Zionism is the new edition of Ben Halpern, *The Idea of the Jewish State* (2nd ed., Cambridge, Mass., 1969). See also Richard P. Stevens, *American Zionism and U.S. Foreign Policy* (New York, 1962); Nadav Safran, *The United States and*

Israel (Cambridge, Mass., 1963); Alfred M. Lilienthal, *The Other Side of the Coin* (New York, 1965), anti-Zionist; James G. McDonald, *My Mission in Israel: 1948-1951* (New York, 1951); Herbert Feis, *The Birth of Israel: The Tousled Diplomatic Bed* (New York, 1969); and Ian J. Bickerton, "President Truman's Recognition of Israel," *American Jewish Historical Quarterly*, LVIII (Dec., 1968), 173-239. For the Suez crisis there are: Kenneth Love, *Suez: The Twice Fought War* (New York, 1969); Anthony Nutting, *No End of Lesson: The Story of Suez* (New York, 1967); Herman Finer, *Dulles over Suez: The Theory and Practice of His Diplomacy* (Chicago, 1964); Carey B. Joynt, "John Foster Dulles and the Suez Crisis," in Gerald N. Grob, ed., *Statesmen and Statecraft of the Modern West* (Barre, Mass., 1967); Leon D. Epstein, *British Politics in the Suez Crisis* (Urbana, Ill., 1964); Richard E. Neustadt, *Alliance Politics* (New York, 1970); J. E. Dougherty, "The Aswan Decision in Perspective," *Political Science Quarterly*, LXXXIV (1959), 21-45; and O. M. Smolansky, "Moscow and the Suez Crisis, 1956: A Reappraisal," *Political Science Quarterly*, LXXX (Dec., 1965), 581-605. See also Leila M. T. Meo, *Lebanon: Improbable Nation, A Study in Political Development* (Bloomington, Ind., 1965) and Charles F. Gallagher, *The United States and North Africa: Morocco, Algeria and Tunisia* (Cambridge, Mass., 1963).

Important memoirs and biographical studies are: Dwight D. Eisenhower, *The White House Years* (2 vols., Garden City, N.Y., 1963-1965); Arthur Larson, *Eisenhower, The President Nobody Knew* (New York, 1968); David B. Capitanchik, *The Eisenhower Presidency and American Foreign Policy* (London, 1969); Eleanor Lansing Dulles, *John Foster Dulles: The Last Year* (New York, 1963); Andrew H. Berding, *Dulles on Diplomacy* (Princeton, N.J., 1965); Louis L. Gerson, *John Foster Dulles* (New York, 1967); and Lewis L. Strauss, *Men and Decisions* (New York, 1962).

CHAPTER TWENTY-NINE

Readings for preceding chapters are often applicable to this one. Among the new studies touching on policy toward Europe, see Arnold Wolfers, *Discord and Collaboration: Essays on International Politics* (Baltimore, 1962); Kenneth W. Thompson, *American Diplomacy and Emergent Patterns* (New York, 1962), critical essays; Ronald Steel, *The End of Alliance: America and the Future of Europe* (New York, 1964); Stephen D. Kertesz, *The Quest for Peace Through Diplomacy* (Englewood Cliffs, N.J., 1967); Harold B. Van Cleveland, *The Atlantic Idea and Its European Rivals* (New York, 1966); Miriam Camps, *European Unification in the Sixties* (New York, 1966); Merry and Serge Bromberger, *Jean Monnet and the United States of Europe*, trans. by Elaine P. Halperin (New York, 1969); William H. Clark, *The Politics of the Common Market* (Englewood Cliffs, N.J., 1967); and Werner Feld, *The European Common Market and the World* (Englewood Cliffs, N.J., 1967). On the German question see Jean E. Smith, *The Defense of Berlin* (Baltimore, 1963) and John W. Keller, *Germany, the Wall and Berlin: Internal Politics During an International Crisis* (New York, 1968). On military influences in the foreign policy of this period see William W. Kaufmann, *The McNamara Strategy* (New York, 1964); Bernard Brodie, *Escalation and the Nuclear Option* (Princeton, 1966); and Klaus Knorr, *On the Uses of Military Power in the Nuclear Age* (Princeton, 1966). For the influence of espionage, see Allen Dulles, *The Craft of Intelligence* (New York, 1963);

Dan J. Moore and Martha Waller, *Cloak and Cipher* (Indianapolis, 1962); and Christopher Felix, *A Short Course in the Secret War* (New York, 1963). On other relevant topics, including the United Nations, arms reduction, economics, and neutralism, see Clark M. Eichelberger, *U.N.: The First Twenty Years* (New York, 1965); Ernest W. Lefever, ed., *Arms and Arms Control: A Symposium* (New York, 1962); John W. Spanier and Joseph L. Nogee, *The Politics of Disarmament: A Study in Soviet-American Gamesmanship* (New York, 1962); Gordon L. Weill and Ian Davidson, *The Gold War: The Story of the World's Monetary Crisis* (New York, 1970); Paul H. Douglas, *America in the Market Place: Trade, Tariffs, and the Balance of Payments* (New York, 1966); Cecil V. M. Crab, Jr., *The Elephants and the Grass: A Study of Nonalignment* (New York, 1965); Robert L. Rothstein, *Alliances and Small Powers* (New York, 1968); Robert C. Carey, *The Peace Corps* (New York, 1970); Walter Johnson and Francis J. Colligan, *The Fulbright Program: A History* (Chicago, 1965); and Harry Schwartz, *Tsars, Mandarins and Commissars* (New York, 1964).

For relations with individual countries see the expanded version of H. Stuart Hughes, *The United States and Italy* (rev. ed., Cambridge, Mass., 1965); Crane Brinton, *The Americans and the French* (Cambridge, Mass., 1968); Herbert G. Nicholas, *Britain and the U.S.A.* (London, 1963); Bruce M. Russett, *Community and Contention: Britain and America in the Twentieth Century* (Cambridge, Mass., 1963); and Arthur C. Turner, *The Unique Partnership: Britain and the United States* (New York, 1970). Two books that deal with domestic sectional influences are: Charles O. Lerche, *The Uncertain South: Its Changing Patterns of Politics in Foreign Policy* (Chicago, 1964) and Alfred O. Hero, Jr., *The Southerner and World Affairs* (Baton Rouge, La., 1965). See also G. Bernard Noble, *Christian A. Herter* (New York, 1970). Useful in the periodical literature are: Elmer Plishcke, "Eisenhower's 'Correspondence Diplomacy' with the Kremlin—Case Study in Summit Diplomatics," *Journal of Politics*, XXX (1968), 137–159; Julius W. Pratt, "De Gaulle and the United States: How the Rift Began," *The History Teacher*, I (1968), 5–15; and Jacob Canter, "Our Cultural 'Exports': A View of the United States Exchange Program," *The American Academy of Political and Social Science*, CCCLXXIII (July, 1969), 85–95.

CHAPTER THIRTY

Useful general studies on Asian policy are: Charles Wolf, *Foreign Aid: Theory and Practice in Southern Asia* (Princeton, 1960); Claude A. Buss, *The Arc of Crisis* (New York, 1961); Oliver E. Clubb, *The United States and the Sino-Soviet Bloc in Southeast Asia* (Washington, 1962); and Russell H. Fifield, *Southest Asia in United States Policy* (New York, 1963). For relations with the Philippines, see Milton W. Meyer, *A Diplomatic History of the Philippine Republic* (Honolulu, 1965) and Sung Yong Kim, *United States-Philippine Relations, 1946–1956* (Washington, 1968). On Japanese matters there are: Frederick S. Dunn, *Peace-Making and the Settlement with Japan* (Princeton, 1963); George R. Packard III, *Protest in Tokyo: The Security Treaty Crisis of 1960* (Princeton, 1966); James Carcy, *Japan Today: Reluctant Ally* (New York, 1962); Edward O. Reischauer, *The United States and Japan* (3rd ed., Cambridge, Mass., 1965); and Herbert Passin, ed., *The United States and Japan* (Englewood Cliffs, N.J., 1966). See also Joseph G. Starke, *The ANZUS Treaty Alliance* (Melbourne, 1965). For India and Pakistan see Norman W. Brown, *The United States and India and Pakistan* (rev. ed., Cambridge, Mass., 1963); Barbara Ward, *India and the West* (rev. ed., New York, 1964); Norman D. Palmer, *South Asia and United States Policy* (Boston, 1966); and Guy A. Hope, *America and Swaraj: The U.S. Role in Indian Independence* (Washington, D.C., 1968). For Indochina see John J. McAllister, Jr., *Vietnam: The Origins of Revolution* (New York, 1969); Jean Lacouture, *Vietnam: Between Two Truces*, trans. from the French by Konrad Kellen and Joel Carmichael (New York, 1966); Melvin Gurtov, *The First Vietnam Crisis: Chinese Communist Strategy and United States Involvement, 1953–1954* (New York, 1967); King C. Chen, *Vietnam and China, 1938–1954* (Princeton, 1969); Phillipe Devillers and Jean Lacouture, *End of a War: Indochina 1954*, trans. by Alexander Lieven and Adam Roberts (New York, 1969); and Robert F. Randle, *Geneva 1954: The Settlement of the Indochinese War* (Princeton, 1969).

On Communist China and Taiwan, see Harold C. Hinton, *Communist China in World Politics* (Boston, 1966); Oliver E. Clubb, "Formosa and the Offshore Islands in American Policy, 1950–1955," *Political Science Quarterly*, LXXIV (1959), 517–531; and Michael A. Guhin, "The United States and the Chinese People's Republic: The Non-Recognition Policy Reviewed," *International Affairs*, XLV (Jan., 1969), 44–63. See also James W. Gould, *The United States and Malaysia* (Cambridge, Mass., 1969). For Africa see M. N. Hennessy, *The Congo: A Brief History and Appraisal* (London, 1961); Smith Hempstone, *Rebels, Mercenaries, and Dividends: The Katanga Story* (New York, 1962); Vernon McKay, *Africa in World Politics* (New York, 1963); and David W. Wainhouse, *Remnants of Empire: The United Nations and the End of Colonialism* (New York, 1964). See pertinent titles listed for previous chapters.

CHAPTER THIRTY-ONE

The fullest scholarly account of foreign policy in the Kennedy years is Roger Hilsman, *To Move A Nation: The Politics of Foreign Policy in the Administration of John F. Kennedy* (Garden City, New York, 1967). Arthur M. Schlesinger, Jr., *A Thousand Days: John F. Kennedy in the White House* (Boston, 1965) is a prize-winning biography with considerable insight on foreign policy. See also Theodore C. Sorenson, *Kennedy* (New York, 1965) and John K. Galbraith, *Ambassador's Journal: A Personal Account of the Kennedy Years* (Boston, 1969). At the time of writing there were yet no comparable studies for Presidents Johnson and Nixon, but for the Johnson years see: Philip Geylin, *Lyndon B. Johnson and the World* (New York, 1966); Rowland Edwards and Robert Novak, *Lyndon B. Johnson: The Exercise of Power* (New York, 1966); Edward Weintal and Charles Bartlett, *Facing the Brink: An Intimate Study of Crisis Diplomacy* (New York, 1967); Eric F. Goldman, *The Tragedy of Lyndon Johnson* (New York, 1969); Henry F. Graff, *The Tuesday Cabinet: Deliberation on Peace and War under Lyndon B. Johnson* (New York, 1970); Lady Bird Johnson, *A White House Diary* (New York, 1970); George Christian, *The President Steps Down* (New York, 1970); and George Reedy, *The Twilight of the Presidency* (New York, 1970).

For relations with Latin America in general there are J. Warren Nystrom and Nathan A. Haverstock, *The Alliance for Progress: Key to Latin America's Development* (Princeton, 1966); Robert N. Burr, *Our Troubled Hemisphere: Perspectives on United States-Latin American*

Relations (Washington, 1967); William D. Rogers, *The Twilight Struggle: The Alliance for Progress and the Politics of Development in Latin America* (New York, 1967); Jarome Levinson and Juan da Onis, *The Alliance that Lost Its Way: A Critical Report on the Alliance for Progress* (Chicago, 1970); George C. Lodge, *Engines of Change: United States Interests and Revolution in Latin America* (New York, 1969); and Margaret M. Ball, *The OAS in Transition* (Durham, 1969). For the Cuban situation see James Daniel and John G. Hubbard, *Strike in the West: The Complete Story of the Cuban Crisis* (New York, 1963); David L. Larson, ed., *The "Cuban Crisis" of 1962: Selected Documents and Chronology* (Boston, 1963); Theodore Draper, *Castroism: Theory and Practice* (New York, 1965); Elie Abel, *The Missile Crisis* (Phil., 1966); Roberta Wohlstetter, "Cuba and Pearl Harbor: Hindsight and Foresight," *Foreign Affairs*, XLIII (July, 1965), 691–707; Albert and Roberta Wohlstetter, "Controlling the Risks in Cuba," *Adelphi Papers* (April, 1965); John Plank, ed., *Cuba and the United States: Long Range Perspectives* (Washington, 1967); Jerome Slater, *The OAS and United States Foreign Policy* (Columbus, Ohio, 1967); and Paul D. Bethel, *The Losers* (New York, 1969). On the Dominican and Panama crisis, see Dan Kurzman, *Santo Domingo: Revolt of the Damned* (New York, 1965); Tad Szulc, *Dominican Diary* (New York, 1965); Theodore Draper, *The Dominican Revolt: A Case Study in American Policy* (New York, 1968); Jerome Slater, *Intervention and Negotiation: The United States and the Dominican Revolution* (New York, 1970); and Jules Dubois, *Danger over Panama* (Indianapolis, 1964).

Useful studies for policy toward the Middle East are: Bernard Lewis, *The Middle East and the West* (Bloomington, Ind., 1964); Malcolm Kerr, *The Arab Cold War, 1958–1964: A Study in Ideology in Politics* (New York, 1967); Walter Z. Lacquer, *The Road to Jerusalem: The Origins of the Arab-Israel Conflict, 1967* (New York, 1967); Hisham Sarabi, *Palestine and Israel: The Lethal Dilemma* (New York, 1969); William R. Polk, *The United States and the Arab World* (rev. ed., Cambridge, Mass., 1969); Arthur S. Lall, *The U.N. and the Middle East Crisis* (New York, 1970); and Nadav Safran, *From War to War: The Arab Israeli Confrontation, 1948–1967* (New York, 1970). For Africa see Vernon McKay, ed., *African Diplomacy: Studies in the Determinants of Foreign Policy* (New York, 1966); Rupert Emerson, *Africa and United States Policy* (Englewood Cliffs, N.J., 1967); Ernest W. Lefever, *Uncertain Mandate: Politics of the U.N. Congo Operation* (Baltimore, 1967); William G. Baker, *The United States and Africa in the United Nations* (Geneva, 1968); and Richard Butwell, ed., *Foreign Policy and the Developing Nations* (Lexington, Ken., 1969).

For relations with Europe and the Atlantic community, see Karl H. Cerny and Henry W. Briefs, eds., *NATO in Quest of Cohesion* (New York, 1965); Stanley W. Smith, *NATO in Transition: The Future of the Atlantic Alliance* (New York, 1965); Stanley W. Smith and Darell M. Whitt, *Detente Diplomacy and European Security in the 1970's* (New York, 1970); Stanley Hoffman, *Gulliver's Troubles, Or the Setting of American Foreign Policy* (New York, 1968); Lawrence B. Krause, *European Economic Integration and the United States* (Washington, 1968); Edward Heath, *Old World, New Horizons: Britain, Europe, and the Atlantic Alliance* (Cambridge, Mass., 1970); Omer de Raeymaeker and Albert H. Bowman, eds., *American Foreign Policy in Europe: A Colloquium on the American Presence in Belgium, the Federal Republic of Germany, France, Italy, March 29–30, 1968* (Louvain, Belgium, 1969); John Newhouse, *De Gaulle and the Anglo-Saxons* (New York, 1970); Amaury de Riencourt, *The American Empire* (New York, 1968); and Herbert I. Schiller, *Mass Communications and American Empire* (New

York, 1969). For economic policy, immigration, and the United Nations see Herbert Feis, *Foreign Aid and Foreign Policy* (New York, 1964); Kenneth W. Dam, *The GATT: Law and International Economic Organization* (Chicago, 1970); Abba P. Schwartz, *The Open Society* (New York, 1968), deals with events leading to the immigration law of 1965; and Ruth B. Russell, *The United Nations and United States Security Policy* (Washington, 1968). For arms control, see Arthur H. Dean, *Test Ban and Disarmament: The Path of Negotiation* (New York, 1966); Harold K. Jacobson and Eric Stein, *Diplomats, Scientists and Politicians: The United States and the Nuclear Test Ban Negotiations* (Ann Arbor, Mich., 1966); James H. McBride, *The Test Ban Treaty: Military, Technological, and Political Implications* (Chicago, 1967); Stephen D. Kertesz, ed., *Nuclear Non-Proliferation in a World of Nuclear Powers* (Notre Dame, Ind., 1967); William B. Bader, *The United States and the Spread of Nuclear Weapons* (New York, 1968); David W. Wainhouse and others, *Arms Control Agreements: Designs for Verification and Organization* (Baltimore, 1968); and Chalmers M. Roberts, *The Nuclear Years: The Arms Race and Arms Control, 1945-1970* (New York, 1970). For Soviet policy see Adam B. Ulam, *Expansion and Coexistence: The History of Soviet Foreign Policy, 1917-1967* (New York, 1968) and Harry Schwartz, *Prague's 200 Days: The Struggle for Democracy in Czechoslovakia* (New York, 1969). See also George S. McGovern, "Are Our Military Alliances Meaningful?" *Annals of the American Academy of Political and Social Science*, CCCLXXXIV (July, 1969), 14-20. This entire issue of the *Annals*, devoted to "America's Changing Role as a World Leader," is pertinent.

On policy toward Asia see Morton Halperin, *China and the Bomb* (New York, 1965); Akira Iriye, ed., *U.S. Policy Toward China: Testimony Taken from the Senate Foreign Relations Committee Hearings—1966* (Boston, 1966); Edwin O. Reischauer, *Beyond Vietnam: The United States and Asia* (New York, 1967); Robert E. Osgood, George R. Packard III, and John H. Badley, *Japan and the United States in Asia* (Baltimore, 1968); Denna F. Fleming, *America's Role in Asia* (New York, 1969); Ishwer C. Ojha, *Chinese Foreign Policy in an Age of Transition: The Diplomacy of Cultural Despair* (Boston, 1969); Yuan-li Wu, *As Peking Sees Us: "People's War" in the United States and Communist China's America Policy* (Stanford, Calif., 1969); Robert Shaplen, *Time Out of Hand: Revolution and Reaction in Southeast Asia* (New York, 1969); and Lawrence Olson, *Japan in Postwar Asia* (New York, 1970). Two books deal with the *Pueblo* incident: Trevor Armbrister, *A Matter of Accountability: The True Story of the Pueblo Affair* (New York, 1970) and Lloyd M. Bucher, *Bucher: My Story* (New York, 1970). Stanley A. de Smith, *Microstates and Micronesia: Problems of America's Pacific Islands and Other Minute Territories* (New York, 1969) deals with American territories in the Pacific. On the decline of the Peace Corps, see Marshall Windmiller, *The Peace Corps and Pax Americana* (Washington, 1970).

The literature on the Vietnam War is extensive. The following titles offer a good sampling of scholarly works, journalistic analyses, and polemical writings. See Dennis Warner, *The Last Confucian* (New York, 1963), deals with Ngo Dinh Diem; Malcolm W. Browne, *The New Face of War* (Indianapolis, 1965); David Halberstam, *The Making of a Quagmire* (New York, 1965); Richard N. Goodwin, *Triumph and Tragedy: Reflections on Vietnam* (New York, 1966); Robert Shaplen, *The Lost Revolution: Twenty Years of Neglected Opportunities in Vietnam...* (New York, 1965), and the updated version *The Road from War: Vietnam 1965-1970* (New York, 1970); Bernard Fall, *The Two Vietnams: A Political and Military Analysis*

(2nd rev. ed., New York, 1967); John R. Boettinger, ed., *Vietnam and American Foreign Policy* Boston, 1968); Dennis J. Duncanson, *Government and Revolution in Vietnam* (New York, 1968); Richard Harris, *America and East Asia: A New Thirty Years War?* (London, 1968); H. Field Haviland, Jr., and others, *Vietnam After the War: Peacekeeping and Rehabilitation* (Washington, 1968); David Kraslow and Stuart H. Loory, *The Secret Search for Peace in Vietnam* (New York, 1968); Richard Rovere, *Waist Deep in the Big Muddy: Personal Reflections on 1968* (Boston, 1968), deals with Vietnam and the election of 1968; Richard M. Pfeffer, ed., *No More Vietnams?: The War and the Future of American Foreign Policy* (New York, 1968); Howard Zinn, *Vietnam: The Logic of Withdrawal* (Boston, 1967); George McT. Kahin and John W. Lewis, *The United States in Vietnam* (rev. ed., New York, 1969), one of the best volumes on the subject; Henry Brandon, *Anatomy of Error: The Inside Story of the Asian War on the Potomac, 1954–1969* (Boston, 1969); Joseph C. Goulden, *Truth is the First Casualty: The Gulf of Tonkin Affair—Illusion and Reality* (Chicago, 1969); Gabriel Kolko, *The Roots of American Foreign Policy: An Analysis of Power and Purpose* (Boston, 1969); Eugene V. Rostow, *Law, Power, and the Pursuit of Peace* (Lincoln, Nebr., 1969), a defense of Johnson's Vietnam policy; Robert Thompson, *No Exit from Vietnam* (New York, 1969); Samuel Lubell, *The Hidden Crisis in American Politics* (New York, 1970), contains a discussion on the domestic reaction to the war; and Naom Chomsky, *At War with Asia: Essays on Indochina* (New York, 1970). See also the notes for this chapter and pertinent materials cited earlier.

IN CONCLUSION

Erwin Unger, "The 'New Left' and American History: Some Recent Trends in United States Historiography," *American Historical Review*, LXXII (July, 1967), 1237–63, and Arthur Schlesinger Jr., "Nationalism and History," *Journal of Negro History*, LIV (Jan., 1969), 19–31, are important essays with observations on the writing of recent diplomatic history. Books that deal with human behavior and the nature of violence are: Robert Ardrey, *The Territorial Imperative: A Personal Inquiry into the Animal Origins of Property and Nations* (New York, 1966); M. F. Ashley, Motagu, ed., *Man and Aggression* (New York, 1968); Robert Bigelow, *The Dawn Warriors: Man's Evolution Toward Peace* (Boston, 1969); and Hannah Arendt, *On Violence* (New York, 1970). For contemporary critiques of foreign policy see J. William Fulbright, *Old Myths and New Realities* (New York, 1964) and his *The Arrogance of Power* (New York, 1966); Cleveland Harlan, *The Obligations of Power: American Diplomacy in Search for Peace* (New York, 1966); Hans J. Morgenthau, *A New Foreign Policy for the United States* (New York, 1969); and Theodore H. Von Laue, *The Global City: Freedom, Power, and Necessity in the Age of World Revolutions* (Phil., 1970). On the "military-industrial complex" see Fred J. Cook, *The Warfare State* (New York, 1962); Ralph E. Lapp, *The Weapons Culture* (New York, 1968); John S. Baumgartner, *The Lonely Warriors: Case for the Military Industrial Complex* (Los Angeles, 1970); James G. Donovan, *Militarism U.S.A.* (New York, 1970); Sidney Lens, *The Military Industrial Complex* (Phil., 1970); Seymour Melman, *Pentagon Capitalism: The Political Economy of War* (New York, 1970); and William Proxmire, *Report from Wasteland: America's Military-Industrial Complex* (New York, 1970).

Index

Picture Sources